# TELEVISION DRAMA
# SERIES PROGRAMMING:
## A Comprehensive Chronicle,

## 1959-1975

by

## Larry James Gianakos

## The Scarecrow Press, Inc.
## Metuchen, N.J. & London
## 1978

Library of Congress Cataloging in Publication Data

Gianakos, Larry James.
  Television drama series programming.

  Includes index.
  1.  Television programs--United States.
I.  Title.
PN1992.3.U5G5      791.45'7'0202      78-650
ISBN 0-8108-1116-2

To

My mother and my father;
my sister Patricia and especially my sister Irene

# CONTENTS

# PREFACE

The principal purpose of this volume is to allow the librarian to grasp television drama series programming as it has progressed over the fifteen-year period beginning with the fall of 1959. It is hoped that the enumeration of series episodes in sequence will aid the reader in finding that particular drama which has somehow made a lasting impression upon the memory.

To compose the chronicle of programming, three basic television sources were researched for the years included: TV Guide (the Cleveland edition); CUE, and the New York Times (on microfilm) television section for the listings. In addition, James Robert Parish's Actors' Television Credits: 1950-1972 (Metuchen, N.J.: The Scarecrow Press, 1973) was consulted. However, even the combination of these essential sources could not provide all the episode information. The most important reference, therefore, was my own viewing of these series over the past several years for episode titles, casts, writers and technical credits. Since much of programming is syndicated, the older series also could be viewed for their credits. The reader may be assured that where there are missing titles and/or cast credits every means available to the author to recover them had been exhausted.

There were, of course, a number of title conflicts among the sources. In these cases, the reader is advised that the obvious correct title--that which appears on the screen--is most often the one recorded here. I have been as meticulous as possible when placing the episodes in sequence. In the event of a preemption or a postponement, the episode in question is numbered for the date of its actual telecast, even if it were filmed prior to the episode which would take its place in number.

I selected for special review those series which, my memory permitting, I feel to have a certain social or cultural significance. Despite the plethora of programs, network television--the profit motive overriding--is inherently repetitive. Programs derive from tried formulas, making possible a core series, a socially significant one.

My years of research on this volume have led me to the following conclusions:

First, that you are what you are in large part because American television has made you so, even if you have never watched it a single day (that being most unlikely). There is no escaping its influence; to withstand the banalities of much of the programming is not to be immune to them, or to be unaffected by those who are influenced by them. The medium has permeated; it is an unretractable part of us all.

Second, that the artistic spirit in the medium, to the time of the conclusion of this chronicle, has steadily declined. As an art form the medium reached its pinnacle, of course, in the days of live drama. However, it is necessary to distinguish between being creative with original drama and being creative with series television, where the writer is given several characters and must adhere to a certain direction. For series television--the chronicle commencing just about the time the live dramas were a dying breed --the creative climax was attained, significantly enough, during the John Kennedy era. As proof of this I would ask the reader to consider the episode title. But would you judge a book by its cover? As the cover should provide a surface beauty at least, so too should one be impressed by the literary inspiration of writers of this period--quotes of Swinburne, Hodgson, Webster, Carroll, Arnold, Spenser, Milne, Shakespeare and the Bible. With Bartlett's in hand, go through them and you will feel the decline. Particularly in recent years, when much in the way of network programming is bereft of artistry, it became increasingly difficult to write of a series but a single line.

Last, if the medium has radically declined as an art form,

we must share in the cause of it.  The medium is geared to certain segments of the population where there is profit; but to the greater number, composing those segments.  And the greater number, I have come to believe, are a mirror reflection of what is desirable for viewing by those empowered to create today's programming.

As was the case with my predecessor, Mr. James Robert Parish for his Actors' Television Credits, so too do I recommend as supplementary material for this volume (in addition to the aforementioned Parish work) the following:

TV Guide

Broadcast Information Bureau--TV Series Source Book (New York City, Semi Annual Updates)

The Emmy Awards:  A Pictorial History (Crown, 1971)

How Sweet It Was (Shorecrest, 1966)

A Pictorial History of Television (Chilton/Bonanza, 1959)

as well as:

CUE

The New York Times television section

For subsequent editions, at which time I hope to include the drama programming of the medium for the years previous to the start of this chronicle, I should appreciate additional information on material in this volume.

Larry James Gianakos
1786 Dodge Drive N.W.
Warren, Ohio   44485

March 28, 1977

## ACKNOWLEDGMENTS

I am first of all indebted to Mr. James Robert Parish for permitting me to utilize his Actors' Television Credits, 1950-1972.

Two library staffs expended many hours of their time:

    The Warren Public Library Reference Staff--consummate librarians Mr. Jerome Stephens, Mrs. Lois Stephens, Mrs. Louise Kjera, Miss Kathleen Unks, Miss Becky D. Peters, assistant Mrs. Diane Thomas; assistant library director Mr. Larry Rees, director Mrs. Shirley Sippola;

    The Akron Public Library Fine Arts Staff; Mr. John Rebenack, library director.

Miss Debbie Diehl

Mr. Mark Dorn and the Department of Popular Culture of Bowling Green State University

And, for their encouragement, Miss Myrna Jean Warren and Mrs. Vivian Pemberton.

# ABOUT THIS VOLUME

## Omissions of Dramatic Programming

The central purpose of the volume being a chronicle of epi-sodes, certain dramatic programming had to be selectively omitted if a continuity was to be maintained.  A number of westerns--Gun-smoke, Lancer, Have Gun--Will Travel among them--frequently appeared untitled in the source material and, not having been able to view them from the television screen, I was at a loss to find a way to properly list them.  It is hoped that subsequent editions will rectify the matter.


## Format

In both Sections I and II, the series progress from year to year, with seasons commencing with a Saturday and progressing through Friday.  Certain syndicated programming corresponds to the format prescribed above.

In Section II, not every series appears with an introductory review.  For the most part, these are anthology series.

# SECTION I

Days and Times for Network Prime Time Programming,
fall, 1959-spring, 1975

|       | ABC | NBC | CBS |
|-------|-----|-----|-----|
| **Saturday** | | | |
| 7:30 | The Dick Clark Show (9/12) | Bonanza†* (9/12) | Perry Mason* (10/3) |
| 8:00 | John Gunther's High Road† (9/12) | Bonanza†* | Perry Mason* (10/3) |
| 8:30 | Leave It to Beaver | The Man and the Challenge†* (9/12) | Wanted: Dead or Alive (9/26) |
| 9:00 | The Lawrence Welk Show | The Deputy†* (9/12) | Mr. Lucky† (10/24 |
| 9:30 | The Lawrence Welk Show | Five Fingers†* (10/3) | Have Gun--Will Travel |
| 10:00 | Jubilee, U.S.A. | Five Fingers†* | Gunsmoke (9/19) |
| 10:30 | Local/Sea Hunt | It Could Be You | Markham (9/19) |
| **Sunday** | | | |
| 7:00 | Colt .45 (9/20) | Riverboat†* (9/13) | Lassie |
| 7:30 | Maverick* (9/13) | Riverboat†* | Dennis the Menace† (10/4) |
| 8:00 | Maverick* | Sunday Showcase†* (9/20) | Ed Sullivan |
| 8:30 | Lawman* (10/4) | Sunday Showcase†* | Ed Sullivan |
| 9:00 | The Rebel†* (10/4) | The Dinah Shore Chevy Show (10/4) | General Electric Theatre* (9/20) |
| 9:30 | The Alaskans†* (10/4) | The Dinah Shore Chevy Show | Alfred Hitchcock Presents* (9/27) |
| 10:00 | The Alaskans†* | The Loretta Young Show* (9/20) | The George Gobel Show† (9/20); alternating with The Jack Benny Program (9/27) |
| 10:30 | Dick Clark's World of Talent (9/27) | Local | What's My Line? |
| **Monday** | | | |
| 7:30 | Cheyenne* (9/21) | Richard Diamond (10/5) | Name That Tune |
| 8:00 | Cheyenne* | Love and Marriage† (9/21) | The Texan (9/14) |
| 8:30 | Bourbon Street Beat†* (10/5) | Tales of Wells Fargo* (9/7) | Father Knows Best (10/5) |
| 9:00 | Bourbon Street Beat†* | Peter Gunn* (9/21) | The Danny Thomas Show (10/5) |

*Indicates that the drama is included with this volume.
†Indicates that the series--whatever the type--was a new entry in the season.

| | ABC | NBC | CBS |
|---|---|---|---|
| 9:30 | Adventures in Para-<br>dise†* (10/5) | The Alcoa Theatre*<br>(9/21); alternating<br>with The Goodyear<br>Theatre* (9/14) | The Ann Sothern Show<br>(10/5) |
| 10:00 | Adventures in Para-<br>dise†* | The Steve Allen Show<br>(9/28) | Hennesey† (9/28) |
| 10:30 | Man with a Camera<br>(10/19) | The Steve Allen Show | The June Allyson<br>Show†* (9/28) |

**Tuesday**

| | | | |
|---|---|---|---|
| 7:30 | Sugarfoot* (9/15)/<br>Bronco* (9/22) | Laramie†* (9/15) | Grand Jury |
| 8:00 | Sugarfoot*/Bronco* | Laramie†* | The Dennis O'Keefe<br>Show† (9/22) |
| 8:30 | Wyatt Earp (9/8) | Fibber McGee and<br>Molly† (9/15) | The Many Loves of<br>Dobie Gillis† (9/29) |
| 9:00 | Rifleman* (9/29) | The Arthur Murray<br>Party (9/29) | Tightrope!†* (9/8) |
| 9:30 | Philip Marlowe†*<br>(10/6) | Ford Startime†* (10/<br>6) | The Red Skelton Show<br>(9/29) |
| 10:00 | Alcoa Presents*<br>(9/15) | Ford Startime†* | The Garry Moore Show<br>(9/29) |
| 10:30 | Keep Talking (9/29) | State Trooper (10/13) | The Garry Moore Show<br>(9/29) |

**Wednesday**

| | | | |
|---|---|---|---|
| 7:30 | Local | Wagon Train* (10/7) | The Lineup* (9/30) |
| 8:00 | Charley Weaver's<br>Hobby Lobby† (9/30) | Wagon Train* | The Lineup* |
| 8:30 | Ozzie and Harriet<br>(10/7) | The Price Is Right | Men into Space† (9/30) |
| 9:00 | Hawaiian Eye†* (10/7) | Perry Como Show<br>(9/30) | The Millionaire (9/30) |
| 9:30 | Hawaiian Eye†* | Perry Como Show | I've Got a Secret |
| 10:00 | Wednesday Night<br>Fights | This Is Your Life<br>(9/30) | Armstrong Circle The-<br>atre* (9/30)/United<br>States Steel Hour*<br>(9/9) |
| 10:30 | Wednesday Night<br>Fights | Wichita Town†* (9/30) | Armstrong Circle The-<br>atre*/United States<br>Steel Hour* |

**Thursday**

| | | | |
|---|---|---|---|
| 7:30 | Gail Storm<br>(10/1) | The Law of the<br>Plainsman†* (10/1) | To Tell the Truth |
| 8:00 | Donna Reed Show<br>(10/1) | Bat Masterson* (10/1) | Betty Hutton Show†<br>(10/1) |
| 8:30 | The Real McCoys<br>(10/1) | Johnny Staccato†*<br>(9/10) | Johnny Ringo†* (10/1) |
| 9:00 | Pat Boone Show<br>(10/1) | Bachelor Father (10/1) | Zane Grey Theatre†*<br>(10/1) |
| 9:30 | The Untouchables†*<br>(10/15) | Tennessee Ernie Ford<br>Show (10/1) | Playhouse 90* (10/1) |
| 10:00 | The Untouchables†* | Groucho Marx Show<br>(10/1) | Playhouse 90* |
| 10:30 | Local/Take a Good<br>Look | Lawless Years (10/1) | Playhouse 90* |

| | ABC | NBC | CBS |
|---|---|---|---|
| **Friday** | | | |
| 7:30 | Walt Disney Presents* (10/2) | People Are Funny | Rawhide* (10/2) |
| 8:00 | Walt Disney Presents* | Troubleshooters†* (9/11) | Rawhide* |
| 8:30 | Man from Black Hawk†* (10/9) | Art Carney Dramas† (10/2)/Specials | Hotel de Paree†* (10/2) |
| 9:00 | 77 Sunset Strip* (9/18) | Art Carney Dramas†/Specials | Lucy-Desi Comedy (9/25)/Desilu Playhouse* (10/2) |
| 9:30 | 77 Sunset Strip* | M Squad (9/18) | Lucy-Desi Comedy Hour/Desilu Playhouse* |
| 10:00 | The Detectives†* (10/6) | Bell Telephone Hour (10/9) | The Twilight Zone†* (10/2) |
| 10:30 | Black Saddle (10/2) | Bell Telephone Hour | Person to Person (10/2) |

## 1959-1960 MIDSEASON

| | ABC | NBC | CBS |
|---|---|---|---|
| **Saturday** | | | |
| 7:30 | The Dick Clark Show | Bonanza | Perry Mason |
| 8:00 | John Gunther's High Road | Bonanza | Perry Mason |
| 8:30 | Leave It to Beaver | The Man and the Challenge | Wanted: Dead or Alive |
| 9:00 | The Lawrence Welk Show | The Deputy | Mr. Lucky |
| 9:30 | The Lawrence Welk Show | World Wide 60† (1/30/60) | Have Gun--Will Travel |
| 10:00 | How to Marry a Millionaire (2/13/60) | World Wide 60† | Gunsmoke |
| 10:30 | Jubilee, U.S.A. | Man from Interpol†* (1/30/60) | Local |
| **Sunday** | | | |
| 7:00 | You Asked for It (9-27-59) | Overland Trail†* (2/7/60) | Lassie |
| 7:30 | Maverick | Overland Trail†* | Dennis the Menace |
| 8:00 | Maverick | Sunday Showcase | Ed Sullivan |
| 8:30 | Lawman | Sunday Showcase | Ed Sullivan |
| 9:00 | The Rebel | The Dinah Shore Chevy Show | General Electric Theatre |
| 9:30 | The Alaskans | The Dinah Shore Chevy Show | Alfred Hitchcock Presents |
| 10:00 | The Alaskans | The Loretta Young Show | George Gobel Show; alternating with The Jack Benny Program |
| 10:30 | Dick Clark's World of Talent | Local | What's My Line? |
| **Monday** | | | |
| 7:30 | Cheyenne | Riverboat | Kate Smith Show† (1/25/60) |

| | ABC | NBC | CBS |
|---|---|---|---|
| 8:00 | Cheyenne | Riverboat | The Texan |
| 8:30 | Bourbon Street Beat | Tales of Wells Fargo | Father Knows Best |
| 9:00 | Bourbon Street Beat | Peter Gunn | The Danny Thomas Show |
| 9:30 | Adventures in Paradise | The Alcoa Theatre; alternating with The Goodyear Theatre | Ann Sothern Show |
| 10:00 | Adventures in Paradise | The Steve Allen Show | Hennesey |
| 10:30 | Man with a Camera | The Steve Allen Show | The June Allyson Show |

**Tuesday**

| | | | |
|---|---|---|---|
| 7:30 | Sugarfoot/Bronco | Laramie | Grand Jury |
| 8:00 | Sugarfoot/Bronco | Laramie | The Dennis O'Keefe Show |
| 8:30 | Wyatt Earp | Ford Startime | The Many Loves of Dobie Gillis |
| 9:00 | The Rifleman | Ford Startime | Tightrope! |
| 9:30 | Philip Marlowe | Arthur Murray Party | The Red Skelton Show |
| 10:00 | Alcoa Presents | M Squad | The Garry Moore Show |
| 10:30 | Keep Talking | Local | The Garry Moore Show |

**Wednesday**

| | | | |
|---|---|---|---|
| 7:30 | Local | Wagon Train | Be Our Guests† (1/27/60) |
| 8:00 | Charley Weaver's Hobby Lobby | Wagon Train | Be Our Guests† |
| 8:30 | Ozzie and Harriet | The Price Is Right | Men into Space |
| 9:00 | Hawaiian Eye | Perry Como Show | The Millionaire |
| 9:30 | Hawaiian Eye | Perry Como Show | I've Got a Secret |
| 10:00 | Wednesday Night Fights | This Is Your Life | Armstrong Circle Theatre/United States Steel Hour |
| 10:30 | Wednesday Night Fights | Wichita Town | Armstrong Circle Theatre/United States Steel Hour |

**Thursday**

| | | | |
|---|---|---|---|
| 7:30 | The Gale Storm Show | The Law of the Plainsman | To Tell the Truth |
| 8:00 | The Donna Reed Show | Bat Masterson | The Betty Hutton Show |
| 8:30 | The Real McCoys | Johnny Staccato | Johnny Ringo |
| 9:00 | The Pat Boone Show | Bachelor Father | Zane Grey Theatre |
| 9:30 | The Untouchables | Tennessee Ernie Ford Show | Markham |
| 10:00 | The Untouchables | Groucho Marx Show | The Revlon Revue† (1/28/60) |
| 10:30 | The Ernie Kovacs Show† (12/24/59) | Lawless Years | The Revlon Revue† |

**Friday**

| | | | |
|---|---|---|---|
| 7:30 | Walt Disney Presents | People Are Funny | Rawhide |

|  | ABC | NBC | CBS |
|---|---|---|---|
| 8:00 | Walt Disney Presents | Troubleshooters | Rawhide |
| 8:30 | Man from Black Hawk | Art Carney Dramas/Specials | Hotel de Paree |
| 9:00 | 77 Sunset Strip | Art Carney Dramas/Specials | Lucy-Desi Comedy Hour/Desilu Playhouse |
| 9:30 | 77 Sunset Strip | Masquerade Party† (1/29/60) | Lucy-Desi Comedy Hour/Desilu Playhouse |
| 10:00 | The Detectives | Bell Telephone Hour | The Twilight Zone |
| 10:30 | The Detectives | Bell Telephone Hour | Person to Person |

## Summer Drama Series, 1960

Dow Hour of Great Mysteries†* (Thursday, 3/31/60, NBC)
Mystery Show†* (Sunday, 5/29/60, 9:00-10:00 NBC)
Tate†* (Wednesday, 6/8/60, 9:30-10:00 NBC)
Moment of Fear†* (Thursday, 7/1/60, 10:00-11:00 NBC)
The Wrangler†* (Thursday, 8/4/60, 9:30-10:00 NBC)

## 1960-1961 SEASON

Saturday

|  | ABC | NBC | CBS |
|---|---|---|---|
| 7:30 | The Roaring Twenties†* (10/15) | Bonanza* (9/10) | Perry Mason* (9/17) |
| 8:00 | The Roaring Twenties†* | Bonanza* | Perry Mason* |
| 8:30 | Leave It to Beaver (9/30) | The Tall Man†* (9/10) | Checkmate†* (9/17) |
| 9:00 | The Lawrence Welk Show | The Deputy†* (10/1) | Checkmate†* |
| 9:30 | The Lawrence Welk Show | Campaign and the Candidates/The Nation's Future† (11/12) | Have Gun--Will Travel (9/10) |
| 10:00 | Fight of the Week | Campaign and the Candidates/The Nation's Future† | Gunsmoke (9/17) |
| 10:30 | Fight of the Week | Local/Man from Interpol* | Local |

Sunday

|  | ABC | NBC | CBS |
|---|---|---|---|
| 7:00 | Walt Disney Presents* (starts at 6:30, 10/16) | Shirley Temple Theatre†* (9/18) | Lassie |
| 7:30 | Maverick* (9/18) | Shirley Temple Theatre†* (9/18) | Dennis the Menace |
| 8:00 | Maverick* | National Velvet† (9/18) | Ed Sullivan Show (10/2) |
| 8:30 | Lawman* (9/18) | The Tab Hunter Show† (9/18) | Ed Sullivan Show |
| 9:00 | The Rebel* (9/18) | The Dinah Shore Show (10/9) | General Electric Theatre* (9/18) |

| | ABC | NBC | CBS |
|---|---|---|---|
| 9:30 | The Islanders†* (10/2) | The Dinah Shore Show | Jack Benny Program (10/9) |
| 10:00 | The Islanders †* | Loretta Young Show* (9/18) | Candid Camera (10/2) |
| 10:30 | The Walter Winchell Show† (10/2) | This Is Your Life (9/25) | What's My Line |

### Monday

| | | | |
|---|---|---|---|
| 7:30 | Cheyenne* (9/26) | Riverboat* (9/19) | To Tell the Truth (10/3) |
| 8:00 | Cheyenne* | Riverboat* | Pete and Gladys† (9/19) |
| 8:30 | Surfside 6†* (10/3) | Tales of Wells Fargo* (10/3) | Bringing Up Buddy† (10/3) |
| 9:00 | Surfside 6†* | Klondike†* (10/10) | Danny Thomas Show (10/3) |
| 9:30 | Adventures in Paradise* (10/3) | Dante's Inferno†* (10/3) | Andy Griffith Show† (10/3) |
| 10:00 | Adventures in Paradise* | Barbara Stanwyck Theatre†* (9/19) | Hennesey (10/3) |
| 10:30 | Peter Gunn* (10/3) | Jackpot Bowling† (9/19) | Face the Nation |

### Tuesday

| | | | |
|---|---|---|---|
| 7:30 | Bugs Bunny Show† (10/11) | Laramie* (9/20) | Exclusive (9/20) |
| 8:00 | The Rifleman* (9/27) | Laramie* | CBS Reports (10/4) |
| 8:30 | Wyatt Earp* (9/27) | Alfred Hitchcock* (9/27) | Dobie Gillis Show (9/27) |
| 9:00 | Stagecoach West†* (10/4) | Thriller†* (9/13) | The Tom Ewell Show† (9/27) |
| 9:30 | Stagecoach West†* | Thriller†* | Red Skelton Show (9/27) |
| 10:00 | Alcoa Presents* (9/27) | Dow Hour of Great Mysteries* (9/20)/Specials | Garry Moore Show (9/27) |
| 10:30 | Local/Rescue 8 | Dow Hour of Great Mysteries*/Specials | Garry Moore Show |

### Wednesday

| | | | |
|---|---|---|---|
| 7:30 | Hong Kong†* (9/28) | Wagon Train* (9/28) | Aquanauts†* (9/14) |
| 8:00 | Hong Kong†* | Wagon Train* | Aquanauts†* |
| 8:30 | Ozzie and Harriet (9/28) | The Price Is Right (10/5) | Wanted: Dead or Alive* (9/21) |
| 9:00 | Hawaiian Eye* (9/14) | Perry Como Show (10/5) | My Sister Eileen† (10/5) |
| 9:30 | Hawaiian Eye* | Perry Como Show | I've Got a Secret |
| 10:00 | The Naked City†* (10/12) | Peter Loves Mary† (10/12) | Armstrong Circle Theatre* (10/12)/ United States Steel Hour* (9/21) |
| 10:30 | The Naked City†* | Johnny Midnight | Armstrong Circle Theatre/United States Steel Hour |

|  | ABC | NBC | CBS |
|---|---|---|---|

**Thursday**

| | ABC | NBC | CBS |
|---|---|---|---|
| 7:30 | Guestward Ho!† | The Outlaws†* (9/29) | The Witness†* (9/29) |
| 8:00 | Donna Reed Show (9/15) | The Outlaws†* | The Witness†* |
| 8:30 | The Real McCoys (9/29) | Bat Masterson* (9/29) | Zane Grey Theatre* (10/6) |
| 9:00 | My Three Sons† (9/29) | Bachelor Father (9/15) | Angel† (10/6) |
| 9:30 | The Untouchables* (10/13) | The Tennessee Ernie Ford Show (9/22) | Ann Sothern Show (10/6) |
| 10:00 | The Untouchables* | The Groucho Show (9/22) | Person to Person (9/29) |
| 10:30 | Ernie Kovacs (10/6) | Lawless Years (9/29) | The June Allyson Show* (9/29) |

**Friday**

| | ABC | NBC | CBS |
|---|---|---|---|
| 7:30 | Matty's Funnies† (9/30) | Dan Raven†* (9/23) | Rawhide* (9/30) |
| 8:00 | Harrigan and Son† (10/7) | Dan Ravens†* | Rawhide* |
| 8:30 | The Flintstones† (9/30) | The Westerner†* (9/30) | Route 66†* (10/7) |
| 9:00 | 77 Sunset Strip* (9/16) | Bell Telephone Hour (9/30) | Route 66†* |
| 9:30 | 77 Sunset Strip* | Bell Telephone Hour | Mr. Garlund† (10/7) |
| 10:00 | The Detectives* (9/16) | Michael Shayne†* (9/30) | The Twilight Zone* (9/30) |
| 10:30 | The Law and Mr. Jones†* (10/7) | Michael Shayne†* | Eyewitness to History† (9/30) |

## 1960-1961 MIDSEASON

**Saturday**

| | ABC | NBC | CBS |
|---|---|---|---|
| 7:30 | The Roaring Twenties | Bonanza | Perry Mason |
| 8:00 | The Roaring Twenties | Bonanza | Perry Mason |
| 8:30 | Leave It to Beaver | The Tall Man | Checkmate |
| 9:00 | Lawrence Welk Show | The Deputy | Checkmate |
| 9:30 | Lawrence Welk Show | The Nation's Future | Have Gun--Will Travel |
| 10:00 | Fight of the Week | The Nation's Future | Gunsmoke |
| 10:30 | Fight of the Week | Local | Local |

**Sunday**

| | ABC | NBC | CBS |
|---|---|---|---|
| 7:00 | Walt Disney Presents (starts at 6:30) | Shirley Temple Theatre | Lassie |
| 7:30 | Maverick | Shirley Temple Theatre | Dennis the Menace |
| 8:00 | Maverick | National Velvet | Ed Sullivan |
| 8:30 | The Lawman | The Tab Hunter Show | Ed Sullivan |
| 9:00 | The Rebel | Dinah Shore Show | General Electric Theatre |

| | ABC | NBC | CBS |
|---|---|---|---|
| 9:30 | The Islanders | Dinah Shore Show | The Jack Benny Program |
| 10:00 | The Islanders | Loretta Young Show | Candid Camera |
| 10:30 | Walter Winchell Show | This Is Your Life | What's My Line? |

**Monday**

| | | | |
|---|---|---|---|
| 7:30 | Cheyenne | The Americans †* (1/23/61) | To Tell the Truth |
| 8:00 | Cheyenne | The Americans †* | Pete and Gladys |
| 8:30 | Surfside 6 | Tales of Wells Fargo | Bringing Up Buddy |
| 9:00 | Surfside 6 | Acapulco†* (2/27/61) | The Danny Thomas Show |
| 9:30 | Adventures in Paradise | Dante's Inferno | Andy Griffith Show |
| 10:00 | Adventures in Paradise | Barbara Stanwyck Theatre | Hennesey |
| 10:30 | Peter Gunn | Jackpot Bowling | Face the Nation |

**Tuesday**

| | | | |
|---|---|---|---|
| 7:30 | Bugs Bunny Show | Laramie | Exclusive |
| 8:00 | The Rifleman | Laramie | CBS Reports |
| 8:30 | Wyatt Earp | Alfred Hitchcock | The Dobie Gillis Show |
| 9:00 | Stagecoach West | Thriller | The Tom Ewell Show |
| 9:30 | Stagecoach West | Thriller | The Red Skelton Show |
| 10:00 | Alcoa Presents | Dow Hour of Great Mysteries/Specials | The Garry Moore Show |
| 10:30 | Local/Rescue 8 | Dow Hour of Great Mysteries/Specials | The Garry Moore Show |

**Wednesday**

| | | | |
|---|---|---|---|
| 7:30 | Hong Kong | Wagon Train | Malibu Run†* (3/1/61) |
| 8:00 | Hong Kong | Wagon Train | Malibu Run†* |
| 8:30 | Ozzie and Harriet | The Price Is Right | Wanted: Dead or Alive |
| 9:00 | Hawaiian Eye | Perry Como Show | My Sister Eileen |
| 9:30 | Hawaiian Eye | Perry Como Show | I've Got a Secret |
| 10:00 | The Naked City | Peter Loves Mary | Armstrong Circle Theatre/United States Steel Hour |
| 10:30 | The Naked City | Local/Johnny Midnight | Armstrong Circle Theatre/United States Steel Hour |

**Thursday**

| | | | |
|---|---|---|---|
| 7:30 | Guestward Ho! | The Outlaws | The Ann Sothern Show |
| 8:00 | The Donna Reed Show | The Outlaws | Angel |
| 8:30 | The Real McCoys | Bat Masterson | Zane Grey Theatre |
| 9:00 | My Three Sons | Bachelor Father | The Gunslinger†* (2/9/61) |
| 9:30 | The Untouchables | The Tennessee Ernie Ford Show | The Gunslinger†* |
| 10:00 | The Untouchables | The Groucho Show | Person to Person |
| 10:30 | Ernie Kovacs Show | Lawless Years | The June Allyson Show |

|  | ABC | NBC | CBS |
|---|---|---|---|
| **Friday** | | | |
| 7:30 | Matty's Funnies | Happy† (1/13/61) | Rawhide |
| 8:00 | Harrigan and Son | One Happy Family† (1/13/61) | Rawhide |
| 8:30 | The Flintstones | Yes, Yes Nanette† (1/6/61) | Route 66 |
| 9:00 | 77 Sunset Strip | Bell Telephone Hour | Route 66 |
| 9:30 | 77 Sunset Strip | Bell Telephone Hour | You're in the Picture† (1/20/61) |
| 10:00 | The Detectives | Michael Shayne | The Twilight Zone |
| 10:30 | The Law and Mr. Jones | Michael Shayne | Eyewitness to History |

## Summer Drama Series, 1961

'Way Out†* (Friday, 3/31/61, 9:30-10:00 CBS)
The Asphalt Jungle†* (Sunday, 4/2/61, 9:30-10:30 ABC)
The Danger Man†* (Wednesday, 4/5/61, 8:30-9:00 CBS)
Whispering Smith†* (Monday, 5/8/61, 9:00-9:30 NBC)
Kraft Mystery Theatre†* (Wednesday, 6/14/61, 9:00-10:00 NBC)
Great Ghost Tales†* (Thursday, 7/6/61, 9:30-10:00 NBC)

## 1961-1962 SEASON

|  | ABC | NBC | CBS |
|---|---|---|---|
| **Saturday** | | | |
| 7:30 | The Roaring Twen-ties* (10/7) | Tales of Wells Fargo* (9/30) | Perry Mason* (9/30) |
| 8:00 | The Roaring Twen-ties* | Tales of Wells Fargo* | Perry Mason* |
| 8:30 | Leave It to Beaver (9/30) | The Tall Man* (9/16) | The Defenders†* (9/16) |
| 9:00 | Lawrence Welk Show | Saturday Night Movie† (9/23) | The Defenders†* |
| 9:30 | Lawrence Welk Show | Saturday Night Movie† | Have Gun--Will Travel (9/16) |
| 10:00 | Fight of the Week | Saturday Night Movie† | Gunsmoke (9/30) |
| 10:30 | Make That Spare | Saturday Night Movie | Gunsmoke |
| **Sunday** | | | |
| 7:00 | Maverick* (starts at 6:30, 9/24) | Bullwinkle Show† (9/24) | Lassie (9/10) |
| 7:30 | Follow the Sun†* (9/17) | Walt Disney* (9/24) | Dennis the Menace (10/1) |
| 8:00 | Follow the Sun†* | Walt Disney* | The Ed Sullivan Show |
| 8:30 | The Lawman* (9/17) | Car 54, Where Are You?† (9/17) | The Ed Sullivan Show |
| 9:00 | Bus Stop†* (10/1) | Bonanza* (9/24) | General Electric Theatre* (9/24) |
| 9:30 | Bus Stop†* | Bonanza* | The Jack Benny Show (10/8) |
| 10:00 | Adventures in Para-dise* (10/1) | Dupont Show of the Week†* (9/17) | Candid Camera (10/1) |

|  | ABC | NBC | CBS |
|---|---|---|---|
| 10:30 | Adventures in Paradise* | Dupont Show of the Week†* | What's My Line? (10/8) |

**Monday**

|  | ABC | NBC | CBS |
|---|---|---|---|
| 7:30 | Cheyenne* (9/25) | Local/Everglades | To Tell the Truth |
| 8:00 | Cheyenne* | National Velvet (9/18) | Pete and Gladys (9/18) |
| 8:30 | The Rifleman* (10/2) | The Price is Right | A Window on Main (10/2) |
| 9:00 | Surfside 6* (9/18) | 87th Precinct†* (9/25) | Danny Thomas Show (10/2) |
| 9:30 | Surfside 6* | 87th Precinct†* | Andy Griffith Show (10/2) |
| 10:00 | Ben Casey†* (10/2) | Thriller* (9/18) | Hennesey (9/25) |
| 10:30 | Ben Casey†* | Thriller* | I've Got a Secret (9/25) |

**Tuesday**

|  | ABC | NBC | CBS |
|---|---|---|---|
| 7:30 | Bugs Bunny Show | Laramie* (9/26) | Marshal Dillon |
| 8:00 | Bachelor Father (10/3) | Laramie* (9/26) | The Dick Van Dyke (10/3) |
| 8:30 | Calvin and the Colonel† (10/3) | Alfred Hitchcock* (10/10) | Dobie Gillis Show (10/10) |
| 9:00 | The New Breed†* (10/3) | Dick Powell Theatre†* (9/26) | Red Skelton Show (9/26) |
| 9:30 | The New Breed†* | Dick Powell Theatre†* | Ichabod and Me† (9/26) |
| 10:00 | Alcoa Premiere†* (10/10) | Cain's Hundred†* (9/19) | Garry Moore Show (9/26) |
| 10:30 | Alcoa Premiere†* | Cain's Hundred†* | Garry Moore Show |

**Wednesday**

|  | ABC | NBC | CBS |
|---|---|---|---|
| 7:30 | The Steve Allen Show† (9/27) | Wagon Train* (9/27) | Alvin and the Chipmunks Show† (10/4) |
| 8:00 | The Steve Allen Show† | Wagon Train* | Father Knows Best |
| 8:30 | Top Cat† (9/27) | The Joey Bishop Show† (9/20) | Checkmate* (10/4) |
| 9:00 | Hawaiian Eye* (9/27) | Perry Como Show (10/4) | Checkmate* |
| 9:30 | Hawaiian Eye* | Perry Como Show | Mrs. G. Goes to College† (10/4) |
| 10:00 | The Naked City* (9/27) | The Bob Newhart Show† (10/11) | Armstrong Circle Theatre* (10/11)/United States Steel Hour* (10/4) |
| 10:30 | The Naked City* | David Brinkley's Journal† (10/11) | Armstrong Circle Theatre*/United States Steel Hour* |

**Thursday**

|  | ABC | NBC | CBS |
|---|---|---|---|
| 7:30 | Ozzie and Harriet (9/28) | The Outlaws* (9/28) | Frontier Circus†* (10/5) |
| 8:00 | Donna Reed Show (9/28) | The Outlaws* | Frontier Circus†* |
| 8:30 | The Real McCoys (9/28) | Dr. Kildare†* (9/28) | Bob Cummings Show† (10/5) |

| | ABC | NBC | CBS |
|---|---|---|---|
| 9:00 | My Three Sons (9/28) | Dr. Kildare†* | The Investigators†* (10/5) |
| 9:30 | Margie† (10/12) | Hazel† (9/28) | The Investigators†* |
| 10:00 | The Untouchables* (10/12) | Mitch Miller (9/28) | CBS Reports (10/5) |
| 10:30 | The Untouchables* | Mitch Miller | CBS Reports |

**Friday**

| | | | |
|---|---|---|---|
| 7:30 | Straightaway†* (10/6) | International Show-time† (9/15) | Rawhide* (9/29) |
| 8:00 | The Hathaways† (10/6) | International Show-time† | Rawhide* |
| 8:30 | The Flintstones (9/15) | The Detectives* (9/29) | Route 66* (9/22) |
| 9:00 | 77 Sunset Strip* (9/22) | The Detectives* | Route 66* |
| 9:30 | 77 Sunset Strip* | Bell Telephone Hour / Dinah Shore Show (10/6) | Father of the Bride† (9/29) |
| 10:00 | Target! The Corruptors†* (9/29) | Bell Telephone Hour / Dinah Shore Show | The Twilight Zone* (9/29) |
| 10:30 | Target! The Corruptors†* | Frank McGee's Here and Now† (9/29) | Eyewitness to History (9/29) |

## 1961-1962 MIDSEASON

**Saturday**

| | | | |
|---|---|---|---|
| 7:30 | Calvin & the Colonel | Tales of Wells Fargo | Perry Mason |
| 8:00 | Room for One More† (2/17/62) | Tales of Wells Fargo | Perry Mason |
| 8:30 | Leave It to Beaver | The Tall Man | The Defenders |
| 9:00 | Lawrence Welk Show | Saturday Night Movie | The Defenders |
| 9:30 | Lawrence Welk Show | Saturday Night Movie | Have Gun--Will Travel |
| 10:00 | Fight of the Week | Saturday Night Movie | Gunsmoke |
| 10:30 | Make That Spare | Saturday Night Movie | Gunsmoke |

**Sunday**

| | | | |
|---|---|---|---|
| 7:00 | Maverick (from 6:30) | Bullwinkle Show | Lassie |
| 7:30 | Follow the Sun | Walt Disney | Dennis the Menace |
| 8:00 | Follow the Sun | Walt Disney | Ed Sullivan Show |
| 8:30 | The Lawman | Car 54, Where Are You? | Ed Sullivan Show |
| 9:00 | Bus Stop | Bonanza | General Electric Theatre |
| 9:30 | Bus Stop | Bonanza | The Jack Benny Show |
| 10:00 | Adventures in Paradise | Dupont Show of the Week | Candid Camera |
| 10:30 | Adventures in Paradise | Dupont Show of the Week | What's My Line? |

**Monday**

| | | | |
|---|---|---|---|
| 7:30 | Cheyenne | Local/Everglades | To Tell the Truth |

|       | ABC | NBC | CBS |
|-------|-----|-----|-----|
| 8:00  | Cheyenne | National Velvet | Pete and Gladys |
| 8:30  | The Rifleman | The Price Is Right | A Window on Main Street |
| 9:00  | Surfside 6 | 87th Precinct | The Danny Thomas Show |
| 9:30  | Surfside 6 | 87th Precinct | Andy Griffith Show |
| 10:00 | Ben Casey | Thriller | Hennesey |
| 10:30 | Ben Casey | Thriller | I've Got a Secret |

**Tuesday**

|       | ABC | NBC | CBS |
|-------|-----|-----|-----|
| 7:30  | Bugs Bunny | Laramie | Marshal Dillon |
| 8:00  | Bachelor Father | Laramie | Dick Van Dyke Show |
| 8:30  | The New Breed | Alfred Hitchcock | Dobie Gillis Show |
| 9:00  | The New Breed | Dick Powell Theatre | Red Skelton Show |
| 9:30  | Yours For a Song (3/6) | Dick Powell Theatre | Ichabod and Me |
| 10:00 | Alcoa Premiere | Cain's Hundred | Garry Moore Show |
| 10:30 | Alcoa Premiere | Cain's Hundred | Garry Moore Show |

**Wednesday**

|       | ABC | NBC | CBS |
|-------|-----|-----|-----|
| 7:30  | Steve Allen Show | Wagon Train | Alvin & the Chipmunks Show |
| 8:00  | Steve Allen Show | Wagon Train | A Window on Main Street (3/7) |
| 8:30  | Top Cat | Joey Bishop Show | Checkmate |
| 9:00  | Hawaiian Eye | Perry Como Show | Checkmate |
| 9:30  | Hawaiian Eye | Perry Como Show | Dick Van Dyke Show |
| 10:00 | The Naked City | Bob Newhart Show | Armstrong Circle Theatre/United States Steel Hour |
| 10:30 | The Naked City | David Brinkley's Journal | Armstrong Circle Theatre/United States Steel Hour |

**Thursday**

|       | ABC | NBC | CBS |
|-------|-----|-----|-----|
| 7:30  | Ozzie and Harriet | The Outlaws | Oh, Those Bells! (3/8) |
| 8:00  | The Donna Reed Show | The Outlaws | Frontier Circus |
| 8:30  | The Real McCoys | Dr. Kildare | Frontier Circus |
| 9:00  | My Three Sons | Dr. Kildare | Tell It to Groucho |
| 9:30  | Margie | Hazel | The Gertrude Berg Show |
| 10:00 | The Untouchables | Mitch Miller | CBS Reports |
| 10:30 | The Untouchables | Mitch Miller | CBS Reports |

**Friday**

|       | ABC | NBC | CBS |
|-------|-----|-----|-----|
| 7:30  | Local | International Show-time | Rawhide |
| 8:00  | The Hathaways | International Show-time | Rawhide |
| 8:30  | The Flintstones | The Detectives | Route 66 |
| 9:00  | 77 Sunset Strip | The Detectives | Route 66 |
| 9:30  | 77 Sunset Strip | Bell Telephone Hour / Dinah Shore Show | Father of the Bride |
| 10:00 | Target! The Corruptors | Bell Telephone Hour / Dinah Shore Show | The Twilight Zone |
| 10:30 | Target! The Corruptors | Frank McGee's Here and Now | Eyewitness to History |

1962-1963 SEASON

| | ABC | NBC | CBS |
|---|---|---|---|
| **Saturday** | | | |
| 7:30 | Roy Rogers/Dale Evans Variety Show† (9/29) | Sam Benedict†* (9/15) | The Jackie Gleason Show† (9/29) |
| 8:00 | Roy Rogers/Dale Evans Variety Show† | Sam Benedict†* | The Jackie Gleason Show† |
| 8:30 | Mr. Smith Goes to Washington† (9/29) | Joey Bishop Show (9/15) | The Defenders* (9/15) |
| 9:00 | Lawrence Welk Show | Saturday Night Movie | The Defenders* |
| 9:30 | Lawrence Welk Show | Saturday Night Movie | Have Gun--Will Travel (9/15) |
| 10:00 | Fight of the Week | Saturday Night Movie | Gunsmoke (9/15) |
| 10:30 | Saturday Sports Final | Saturday Night Movie | Gunsmoke |
| **Sunday** | | | |
| 7:00 | Father Knows Best | Ensign O'Toole† (9/23) | Lassie |
| 7:30 | The Jetsons† (9/23) | Walt Disney* (9/16) | Dennis the Menace |
| 8:00 | Hollywood Special Movie | Walt Disney | The Ed Sullivan Show |
| 8:30 | Hollywood Special Movie | Car 54, Where Are You? (9/16) | The Ed Sullivan Show |
| 9:00 | Hollywood Special Movie | Bonanza* (9/23) | The Real McCoys (9/30) |
| 9:30 | Hollywood Special Movie | Bonanza* | General Electric True†* (9/30) |
| 10:00 | Voice of Firestone† (9/30) | Dupont Show of the Week* (9/16) | Candid Camera |
| 10:30 | Howard K. Smith-- News and Comment | Dupont Show of the Week* | What's My Line? |
| **Monday** | | | |
| 7:30 | Cheyenne* (9/24) | It's a Man's World†* (9/17) | To Tell the Truth (9/24) |
| 8:00 | Cheyenne* | It's a Man's World†* | I've Got a Secret (9/24) |
| 8:30 | The Rifleman* (10/1) | Saints and Sinners†* (9/17) | The Lucy Show† (10/1) |
| 9:00 | Stoney Burke†* (10/1) | Saints and Sinners†* | Danny Thomas Show (10/1) |
| 9:30 | Stoney Burke†* | The Price Is Right | Andy Griffith Show (10/1) |
| 10:00 | Ben Casey* (10/1) | David Brinkley's Journal (10/1) | The New Loretta Young Show† (9/24) |
| 10:30 | Ben Casey* | Local | Stump the Stars† (9/17) |
| **Tuesday** | | | |
| 7:30 | Combat!†* (10/2) | Laramie* (9/25) | Marshal Dillon |
| 8:00 | Combat!†* | Laramie* | The Lloyd Bridges Show†* (9/11) |

| | ABC | NBC | CBS |
|---|---|---|---|
| 8:30 | Hawaiian Eye* (10/2) | Empire†* (9/25) | Red Skelton Hour (9/25) |
| 9:00 | Hawaiian Eye* | Empire†* | Red Skelton Hour |
| 9:30 | The Untouchables* (9/25) | Dick Powell Theatre* (9/25) | Jack Benny Show (9/25) |
| 10:00 | The Untouchables* | Dick Powell Theatre* | Garry Moore Show (9/25) |
| 10:30 | Bell & Howell Close-Up! | Chet Huntley Reporting† (10/2) | Garry Moore Show |

**Wednesday**

| | ABC | NBC | CBS |
|---|---|---|---|
| 7:30 | Wagon Train* (9/19) | Virginian†* (9/19) | CBS Reports |
| 8:00 | Wagon Train* | Virginian†* | CBS Reports |
| 8:30 | Going My Way† (10/3) | Virginian†* | Dobie Gillis Show (9/26) |
| 9:00 | Going My Way† | Perry Como's Kraft Music Hall (10/3) | Beverly Hillbillies† (9/26) |
| 9:30 | Our Man Higgins† (10/3) | Perry Como's Kraft Music Hall | The Dick Van Dyke Show (9/26) |
| 10:00 | The Naked City* (9/19) | Eleventh Hour†* (10/3) | Armstrong Circle Theatre* (9/26)/ United States Steel Hour* (10/3) |
| 10:30 | The Naked City* | Eleventh Hour†* | Armstrong Circle Theatre*/United States Steel Hour* |

**Thursday**

| | ABC | NBC | CBS |
|---|---|---|---|
| 7:30 | Ozzie and Harriet (9/27) | Wide Country†* (9/20) | Mister Ed (9/27) |
| 8:00 | The Donna Reed Show (9/20) | Wide Country†* | Perry Mason* (9/27) |
| 8:30 | Leave It to Beaver (9/20) | Dr. Kildare* (9/27) | Perry Mason* |
| 9:00 | My Three Sons (9/20) | Dr. Kildare* | The Nurses†* (9/27) |
| 9:30 | McHale's Navy† (10/11) | Hazel (9/20) | The Nurses†* |
| 10:00 | Alcoa Premiere* (10/4) | Andy Williams Show† (9/27) | Alfred Hitchcock Hour* (9/20) |
| 10:30 | Alcoa Premiere* | Andy Williams Show† | Alfred Hitchcock Hour* |

**Friday**

| | ABC | NBC | CBS |
|---|---|---|---|
| 7:30 | Gallant Men†* (10/5) | International Showtime (9/21) | Rawhide* (9/21) |
| 8:00 | Gallant Men†* | International Showtime | Rawhide* |
| 8:30 | The Flintstones | Mitch Miller (9/21) | Route 66* (9/21) |
| 9:00 | I'm Dickens--He's Fenster† (9/28) | Mitch Miller | Route 66* |
| 9:30 | 77 Sunset Strip* (10/12) | Don't Call Me Charlie!† (9/21) | Fair Exchange† (9/21) |
| 10:00 | 77 Sunset Strip* | Jack Paar Show† (9/21) | Fair Exchange† |
| 10:30 | Local/Third Man | Jack Paar Show† | Eyewitness to History |

1962-1963 MIDSEASON

| | ABC | NBC | CBS |
|---|---|---|---|
| **Saturday** | | | |
| 7:30 | Gallant Men | Sam Benedict | The Jackie Gleason Show |
| 8:00 | Gallant Men | Sam Benedict | The Jackie Gleason Show |
| 8:30 | Hootennany† | The Joey Bishop Show | The Defenders |
| 9:00 | Lawrence Welk Show | Saturday Night Movie | The Defenders |
| 9:30 | Lawrence Welk Show | Saturday Night Movie | Have Gun--Will Travel |
| 10:00 | Fight of the Week | Saturday Night Movie | Gunsmoke |
| 10:30 | Saturday Sports Final | Saturday Night Movie | Gunsmoke |
| **Sunday** | | | |
| 7:00 | Father Knows Best | Ensign O'Toole | Lassie |
| 7:30 | The Jetsons | Walt Disney | Dennis the Menace |
| 8:00 | Jane Wyman Presents | Walt Disney | The Ed Sullivan Show |
| 8:30 | Movie | Car 54, Where Are You? | The Ed Sullivan Show |
| 9:00 | Movie | Bonanza | The Real McCoys |
| 9:30 | Movie | Bonanza | General Electric True |
| 10:00 | Movie | Dupont Show of the Week | Candid Camera |
| 10:30 | News Specials | Dupont Show of the Week | What's My Line? |
| **Monday** | | | |
| 7:30 | The Dakotas†* (1/7/63) | Monday Night Movie† (2/4/63) | To Tell the Truth |
| 8:00 | The Dakotas†* | Monday Night Movie† | I've Got a Secret |
| 8:30 | The Rifleman | Monday Night Movie† | The Lucy Show |
| 9:00 | Stoney Burke | Monday Night Movie† | The Danny Thomas Show |
| 9:30 | Stoney Burke | Art Linkletter† (2/4/63) | Andy Griffith Show |
| 10:00 | Ben Casey | David Brinkley's Journal | Password (3/18/63) |
| 10:30 | Ben Casey | Local | Stump the Stars |
| **Tuesday** | | | |
| 7:30 | Combat! | Laramie | Marshal Dillon |
| 8:00 | Combat! | Laramie | Lloyd Bridges Show |
| 8:30 | Hawaiian Eye | Empire | Red Skelton Hour |
| 9:00 | Hawaiian Eye | Empire | Red Skelton Hour |
| 9:30 | The Untouchables | Dick Powell Theatre | The Jack Benny Show |
| 10:00 | The Untouchables | Dick Powell Theatre | Garry Moore Show |
| 10:30 | Local | Chet Huntley Reporting | Garry Moore Show |
| **Wednesday** | | | |
| 7:30 | Wagon Train | Virginian | CBS Reports |
| 8:00 | Wagon Train | Virginian | CBS Reports |
| 8:30 | Going My Way | Virginian | Dobie Gillis Show |
| 9:00 | Going My Way | Perry Como's Kraft Music Hall | Beverly Hillbillies |

|  | ABC | NBC | CBS |
|---|---|---|---|
| 9:30 | Our Man Higgins | Perry Como's Kraft Music Hall | The Dick Van Dyke Show |
| 10:00 | The Naked City | Eleventh Hour | Armstrong Circle Theatre/Reckoning† |
| 10:30 | The Naked City | Eleventh Hour | Armstrong Circle Theatre/Reckoning† |

### Thursday
| 7:30 | Ozzie and Harriet | Wide Country | Fair Exchange |
|---|---|---|---|
| 8:00 | The Donna Reed Show | Wide Country | Perry Mason |
| 8:30 | Leave It to Beaver | Dr. Kildare | Perry Mason |
| 9:00 | My Three Sons | Dr. Kildare | Twilight Zone* (1/3/63) |
| 9:30 | McHale's Navy | Hazel | Twilight Zone* |
| 10:00 | Alcoa Premiere/ Premiere | Andy Williams Show | The Nurses |
| 10:30 | Alcoa Premiere/ Premiere | Andy Williams Show | The Nurses |

### Friday
| 7:30 | Cheyenne | International Show-time | Rawhide |
|---|---|---|---|
| 8:00 | Cheyenne | International Show-time | Rawhide |
| 8:30 | The Flintstones | Mitch Miller | Route 66 |
| 9:00 | I'm Dickens--He's Fenster | Mitch Miller | Route 66 |
| 9:30 | 77 Sunset Strip | The Price Is Right | Alfred Hitchcock Hour |
| 10:00 | 77 Sunset Strip | The Jack Paar Show | Alfred Hitchcock Hour |
| 10:30 | Local | The Jack Paar Show | Portrait† |

### 1963-1964 SEASON

### Saturday
| 7:30 | Hootenanny (9/21) | The Lieutenant†* (9/21) | The Jackie Gleason Show (9/28) |
|---|---|---|---|
| 8:00 | Hootenanny | The Lieutenant†* | The Jackie Gleason Show |
| 8:30 | Lawrence Welk Show | The Joey Bishop Show (9/14) | New Phil Silvers Show† (9/28) |
| 9:00 | Lawrence Welk Show | Saturday Night Movie | The Defenders* (9/28) |
| 9:30 | The Jerry Lewis Show† (9/21) | Saturday Night Movie | The Defenders* |
| 10:00 | The Jerry Lewis Show† | Saturday Night Movie | Gunsmoke (9/28) |
| 10:30 | The Jerry Lewis Show† | Saturday Night Movie | Gunsmoke |

### Sunday
| 7:00 | Local | The Bill Dana Show† (9/22) | Lassie |
|---|---|---|---|
| 7:30 | Travels of Jaimie McPheeters†* (9/15) | Disney's World* (9/29) | My Favorite Martian† (9/29) |

|       | ABC | NBC | CBS |
|-------|-----|-----|-----|
| 8:00  | Travels of Jaimie McPheeters†* | Disney's World* | Ed Sullivan Show (9/29) |
| 8:30  | Arrest and Trial†* (9/15) | Grindl† (9/15) | Ed Sullivan Show |
| 9:00  | Arrest and Trial†* | Bonanza* (9/22) | Judy Garland Show† (9/29) |
| 9:30  | Arrest and Trial†* | Bonanza* | Judy Garland Show† |
| 10:00 | 100 Grand† (9/15) | Dupont Show of the Week* (9/15) | Candid Camera |
| 10:30 | ABC News Specials† (9/15) | Dupont Show of the Week* | What's My Line? |

### Monday

|       | ABC | NBC | CBS |
|-------|-----|-----|-----|
| 7:30  | The Outer Limits†* (9/16) | Monday Night Movie | To Tell the Truth (9/9) |
| 8:00  | The Outer Limits†* | Monday Night Movie | I've Got a Secret (9/9) |
| 8:30  | Wagon Train* (9/16) | Monday Night Movie | The Lucy Show (9/30) |
| 9:00  | Wagon Train* | Monday Night Movie | Danny Thomas Show (9/30) |
| 9:30  | Wagon Train* | Hollywood and the Stars† (9/16) | Andy Griffith Show (9/30) |
| 10:00 | The Breaking Point†* (9/16) | Sing Along with Mitch | East Side/West Side†* (9/30) |
| 10:30 | The Breaking Point†* | Sing Along with Mitch | East Side/West Side†* |

### Tuesday

|       | ABC | NBC | CBS |
|-------|-----|-----|-----|
| 7:30  | Combat!* (9/17) | Mr. Novak†* (9/24) | Marshal Dillon |
| 8:00  | Combat!* | Mr. Novak†* | Red Skelton Hour (9/24) |
| 8:30  | McHale's Navy (9/17) | Redigo†* (9/24) | Red Skelton Hour |
| 9:00  | Greatest Show on Earth†* (9/17) | Richard Boone Show†* (9/24) | Petticoat Junction† (9/24) |
| 9:30  | Greatest Show on Earth†* | Richard Boone Show†* | Jack Benny Show (9/24) |
| 10:00 | The Fugitive†* (9/17) | Andy Williams Show/Bell Telephone Hour/NBC News Specials | Garry Moore Show (9/24) |
| 10:30 | The Fugitive†* | Andy Williams Show/Bell Telephone Hour/NBC News Specials | Garry Moore Show |

### Wednesday

|       | ABC | NBC | CBS |
|-------|-----|-----|-----|
| 7:30  | Ozzie and Harriet (9/18) | Virginian* (9/18) | CBS Reports/Chronicle (9/25) |
| 8:00  | Patty Duke Show† (9/18) | Virginian* | CBS Reports/Chronicle |
| 8:30  | The Price Is Right (9/18) | Virginian* | Glynis† (9/25) |
| 9:00  | Ben Casey* (9/18) | Espionage†* (10/2) | Beverly Hillbillies (9/25) |
| 9:30  | Ben Casey* | Espionage†* | Dick Van Dyke Show (9/25) |
| 10:00 | Channing†* (9/18) | Eleventh Hour* (10/2) | Danny Kaye Show† (9/25) |

|  | ABC | NBC | CBS |
|---|---|---|---|
| 10:30 | Channing†* | Eleventh Hour* | Danny Kaye Show† |

**Thursday**

|  | ABC | NBC | CBS |
|---|---|---|---|
| 7:30 | The Flintstones (9/19) | Temple Houston†* (9/19) | Password |
| 8:00 | Donna Reed Show (9/19) | Temple Houston†* | Rawhide* (9/26) |
| 8:30 | My Three Sons (9/19) | Dr. Kildare* (9/26) | Rawhide* |
| 9:00 | Jimmy Dean Show† (9/19) | Dr. Kildare* | Perry Mason* (9/26) |
| 9:30 | Jimmy Dean Show† | Hazel (9/19) | Perry Mason* |
| 10:00 | Sid Caesar/Here's Edie† (9/19) | Kraft Suspense Theatre†* (10/10)/ Perry Como's Music Hall | The Nurses* (9/26) |
| 10:30 | Local | Kraft Suspense Theatre†*/Perry Como's Music Hall | The Nurses* |

**Friday**

|  | ABC | NBC | CBS |
|---|---|---|---|
| 7:30 | 77 Sunset Strip* (9/20) | International Show-time (9/20) | Great Adventure†* (9/27) |
| 8:00 | 77 Sunset Strip* | International Show-time | Great Adventure†* |
| 8:30 | Burke's Law†* (9/20) | Bob Hope Chrysler Theatre†* (10/4)/ Bob Hope Comedies | Route 66* (9/27) |
| 9:00 | Burke's Law†* | Bob Hope Chrysler Theatre†*/Bob Hope Comedies | Route 66* |
| 9:30 | The Farmer's Daughter† (9/20) | Harry's Girls† (9/13) | Twilight Zone* (9/27) |
| 10:00 | Fight of the Week | The Jack Paar Show | Alfred Hitchcock Hour* (9/27) |
| 10:30 | Fight of the Week | The Jack Paar Show | Alfred Hitchcock Hour* |

## 1963-1964 MIDSEASON

**Saturday**

|  | ABC | NBC | CBS |
|---|---|---|---|
| 7:30 | Hootenanny | The Lieutenant | The Jackie Gleason Show |
| 8:00 | Hootenanny | The Lieutenant | The Jackie Gleason Show |
| 8:30 | Lawrence Welk Show | The Joey Bishop Show | The Defenders |
| 9:00 | Lawrence Welk Show | Saturday Night Movie | The Defenders |
| 9:30 | The Hollywood Palace† (1/4/64) | Saturday Night Movie | New Phil Silvers Show |
| 10:00 | The Hollywood Palace† | Saturday Night Movie | Gunsmoke |
| 10:30 | Local | Saturday Night Movie | Gunsmoke |

**Sunday**

|  | ABC | NBC | CBS |
|---|---|---|---|
| 7:00 | Local | The Bill Dana Show | Lassie |

| | ABC | NBC | CBS |
|---|---|---|---|
| 7:30 | Travels of Jaimie McPheeters | Disney's World | My Favorite Martian |
| 8:00 | Travels of Jaimie McPheeters | Disney's World | The Ed Sullivan Show |
| 8:30 | Arrest and Trial | Grindl | The Ed Sullivan Show |
| 9:00 | Arrest and Trial | Bonanza | Judy Garland Show |
| 9:30 | Arrest and Trial | Bonanza | Judy Garland Show |
| 10:00 | Local/News Specials | Dupont Show of the Week | Candid Camera |
| 10:30 | Local/News Specials | Dupont Show of the Week | What's My Line? |

Monday

| | | | |
|---|---|---|---|
| 7:30 | The Outer Limits | Monday Night Movie | To Tell the Truth |
| 8:00 | The Outer Limits | Monday Night Movie | I've Got a Secret |
| 8:30 | Wagon Train | Monday Night Movie | The Lucy Show |
| 9:00 | Wagon Train | Monday Night Movie | The Danny Thomas Show |
| 9:30 | Wagon Train | Hollywood and the Stars | The Andy Griffith Show |
| 10:00 | The Breaking Point | Mitch Miller | East Side/West Side |
| 10:30 | The Breaking Point | Mitch Miller | East Side/West Side |

Tuesday

| | | | |
|---|---|---|---|
| 7:30 | Combat! | Mr. Novak | Marshal Dillon |
| 8:00 | Combat! | Mr. Novak | Red Skelton Show |
| 8:30 | McHale's Navy | You Don't Say† (1/14/64) | Red Skelton Show |
| 9:00 | Greatest Show on Earth | Richard Boone Show | Petticoat Junction |
| 9:30 | Greatest Show on Earth | Richard Boone Show | The Jack Benny Show |
| 10:00 | The Fugitive | Andy Williams Show/ Bell Telephone Hour/NBC News Specials | The Garry Moore Show |
| 10:30 | The Fugitive | Andy Williams Show/ Bell Telephone Hour/NBC News Specials | The Garry Moore Show |

Wednesday

| | | | |
|---|---|---|---|
| 7:30 | Ozzie and Harriet | Virginian | CBS Reports/Chronicle |
| 8:00 | The Patty Duke Show | Virginian | CBS Reports/Chronicle |
| 8:30 | The Farmer's Daughter | Virginian | Tell It to the Camera†/ Suspense†* (3/25/64) |
| 9:00 | Ben Casey | Espionage | Beverly Hillbillies |
| 9:30 | Ben Casey | Espionage | Dick Van Dyke Show |
| 10:00 | Channing | Eleventh Hour | The Danny Kaye Show |
| 10:30 | Channing | Eleventh Hour | The Danny Kaye Show |

Thursday

| | | | |
|---|---|---|---|
| 7:30 | The Flintstones | Temple Houston | Password |
| 8:00 | The Donna Reed Show | Temple Houston | Rawhide |

| | ABC | NBC | CBS |
|---|---|---|---|
| 8:30 | My Three Sons | Dr. Kildare | Rawhide |
| 9:00 | The Jimmy Dean Show | Dr. Kildare | Perry Mason |
| 9:30 | The Jimmy Dean Show | Hazel | Perry Mason |
| 10:00 | Sid Caesar/Here's Edie | Kraft Suspense Theatre/Perry Como's Music Hall | The Nurses |
| 10:30 | Local/ABC News Reports | Kraft Suspense Theatre/Perry Como's Music Hall | The Nurses |

**Friday**

| | | | |
|---|---|---|---|
| 7:30 | Destry†* (2/14/64) | International Show-time | Great Adventure |
| 8:00 | Destry†* | International Show-time | Great Adventure |
| 8:30 | Burke's Law | Bob Hope Chrysler Theatre/Bob Hope Comedies | Route 66 |
| 9:00 | Burke's Law | Bob Hope Chrysler Theatre/Bob Hope Comedies | Route 66 |
| 9:30 | The Price is Right | Harry's Girls | The Twilight Zone |
| 10:00 | Fight of the Week | The Jack Paar Show | Alfred Hitchcock Hour |
| 10:30 | Make That Spare | The Jack Paar Show | Alfred Hitchcock Hour |

### 1964-1965 SEASON

**Saturday**

| | | | |
|---|---|---|---|
| 7:30 | The Outer Limits* (9/19) | Flipper† (9/19) | Jackie Gleason Show (9/26) |
| 8:00 | The Outer Limits* | Mr. Magoo† (9/19) | Jackie Gleason Show |
| 8:30 | Lawrence Welk Show (9/19) | Kentucky Jones† (9/19) | Gilligan's Island† (9/26) |
| 9:00 | Lawrence Welk Show | Saturday Night Movie (10/3) | Mr. Broadway†* (9/26) |
| 9:30 | Hollywood Palace (9/19) | Saturday Night Movie | Mr. Broadway†* |
| 10:00 | Hollywood Palace | Saturday Night Movie | Gunsmoke (9/26) |
| 10:30 | Local | Saturday Night Movie | Gunsmoke |

**Sunday**

| | | | |
|---|---|---|---|
| 7:00 | Local | Local/Profiles in Courage†* (starts at 6:30, 11/8) | Lassie |
| 7:30 | Wagon Train* (9/20) | Disney's World* (9/20) | My Favorite Martian (9/27) |
| 8:00 | Wagon Train* | Disney's World* | The Ed Sullivan Show (9/27) |
| 8:30 | Broadside† (9/20) | Bill Dana Show (9/20) | The Ed Sullivan Show |
| 9:00 | Sunday Night Movie† (9/20) | Bonanza* (9/20) | My Living Doll† (9/27) |

| | ABC | NBC | CBS |
|---|---|---|---|
| 9:30 | Sunday Night Movie† | Bonanza* | The Joey Bishop Show (9/27) |
| 10:00 | Sunday Night Movie† | The Rogues†* (9/13) | Candid Camera |
| 10:30 | Sunday Night Movie† | The Rogues†* | What's My Line? |

**Monday**

| | ABC | NBC | CBS |
|---|---|---|---|
| 7:30 | Voyage to the Bottom of the Sea†* (9/14) | 90 Bristol Court† (10/5) | To Tell the Truth |
| 8:00 | Voyage to the Bottom of the Sea†* | 90 Bristol Court† | I've Got a Secret |
| 8:30 | No Time for Sergeants† (9/14) | 90 Bristol Court† | Andy Griffith Show (9/21) |
| 9:00 | Wendy and Me† (9/14) | Andy Williams Show (10/5) | The Lucy Show (9/21) |
| 9:30 | Bing Crosby Show† (9/14) | Andy Williams Show | Many Happy Returns† (9/21) |
| 10:00 | Ben Casey* (9/14) | Alfred Hitchcock Hour* (10/5) | Slattery's People†* (9/21) |
| 10:30 | Ben Casey* | Alfred Hitchcock Hour* | Slattery's People†* |

**Tuesday**

| | ABC | NBC | CBS |
|---|---|---|---|
| 7:30 | Combat!* (9/15) | Mr. Novak* (9/22) | Local |
| 8:00 | Combat!* | Mr. Novak* | World War I†* (9/22) |
| 8:30 | McHale's Navy (9/15) | The Man from U.N.C.L.E.†* (9/22) | Red Skelton Hour (9/22) |
| 9:00 | The Tycoon† (9/15) | The Man from U.N.C.L.E.†* | Red Skelton Hour |
| 9:30 | Peyton Place† (9/15) | That Was the Week That Was† (9/22) | Petticoat Junction (9/22) |
| 10:00 | The Fugitive* (9/15) | Bell Telephone Hour (10/6)/NBC News Specials (9/15) | The Nurses* (9/22) |
| 10:30 | The Fugitive* | Bell Telephone Hour/ NBC News Specials | The Nurses* |

**Wednesday**

| | ABC | NBC | CBS |
|---|---|---|---|
| 7:30 | Ozzie and Harriet (9/16) | The Virginian* (9/13) | CBS Reports/CBS News Specials |
| 8:00 | Patty Duke Show (9/16) | The Virginian* | CBS Reports/CBS News Specials |
| 8:30 | Shindig† (9/16) | The Virginian* | Beverly Hillbillies (9/23) |
| 9:00 | Mickey† (9/16) | Wednesday Night Movie† (9/16) | Dick Van Dyke Show (9/23) |
| 9:30 | Burke's Law* (9/16) | Wednesday Night Movie† | Cara Williams Show† (9/23) |
| 10:00 | Burke's Law* | Wednesday Night Movie† | Danny Kaye Show (9/23) |
| 10:30 | ABC Close-Up (9/16) | Wednesday Night Movie† | Danny Kaye Show |

**Thursday**

| | ABC | NBC | CBS |
|---|---|---|---|
| 7:30 | The Flintstones (9/17) | Daniel Boone†* (9/24) | The Munsters† (9/24) |
| 8:00 | The Donna Reed Show (9/17) | Daniel Boone†* | Perry Mason* (9/24) |

|  | ABC | NBC | CBS |
|---|---|---|---|
| 8:30 | My Three Sons (9/17) | Dr. Kildare* (9/24) | Perry Mason* |
| 9:00 | Bewitched† (9/17) | Dr. Kildare* | Password (9/24) |
| 9:30 | Peyton Place† (9/17) | Hazel (9/17) | The Baileys of Balboa† (9/24) |
| 10:00 | Jimmy Dean Show (9/17) | Kraft Suspense Theatre*(10/1)/ Perry Como's Music Hall (10/29) | The Defenders* (9/24) |
| 10:30 | Jimmy Dean Show | Kraft Suspense Theatre/Perry Como's Music Hall | The Defenders* |

Friday

| 7:30 | Jonny Quest† (9/18) | International Show-time | Rawhide* (9/25) |
|---|---|---|---|
| 8:00 | The Farmer's Daughter (9/18) | International Show-time | Rawhide* |
| 8:30 | The Addams Family† (9/18) | Bob Hope Chrysler Theatre* (10/2)/ Bob Hope Comedies (9/25) | The Entertainers† (9/25) |
| 9:00 | Valentine's Day† (9/18) | Bob Hope Chrysler Theatre*/ Bob Hope Comedies | The Entertainers† |
| 9:30 | 12 O'Clock High†* (9/18) | Jack Benny Show (9/25) | Gomer Pyle, U.S.M.C.† (9/25) |
| 10:00 | 12 O'Clock High†* | Jack Paar Show (9/25) | The Reporter†* (9/25) |
| 10:30 | Local | Jack Paar Show | The Reporter†* |

## 1964-1965 MIDSEASON

Saturday

| 7:30 | The King Family† (1/23/65) | Flipper | The Jackie Gleason Show |
|---|---|---|---|
| 8:00 | The King Family† | Kentucky Jones | The Jackie Gleason Show |
| 8:30 | Lawrence Welk Show | Mr. Magoo | Gilligan's Island |
| 9:00 | Lawrence Welk Show | Saturday Night Movie | The Entertainers |
| 9:30 | Hollywood Palace | Saturday Night Movie | The Entertainers |
| 10:00 | Hollywood Palace | Saturday Night Movie | Gunsmoke |
| 10:30 | Local | Saturday Night Movie | Gunsmoke |

Sunday

| 7:00 | Local | Local | Lassie |
|---|---|---|---|
| 7:30 | Wagon Train | Disney's World | My Favorite Martian |
| 8:00 | Wagon Train | Disney's World | The Ed Sullivan Show |
| 8:30 | Broadside | Branded†* (1/24/65) | The Ed Sullivan Show |
| 9:00 | Sunday Night Movie | Bonanza | For the People†* (1/31/65) |
| 9:30 | Sunday Night Movie | Bonanza | For the People†* |
| 10:00 | Sunday Night Movie | The Rogues | Candid Camera |
| 10:30 | Sunday Night Movie | The Rogues | What's My Line? |

| | ABC | NBC | CBS |
|---|---|---|---|
| **Monday** | | | |
| 7:30 | Voyage to the Bottom of the Sea | Karen | To Tell the Truth |
| 8:00 | Voyage to the Bottom of the Sea | The Man from U.N.C.L.E. | I've Got a Secret |
| 8:30 | No Time for Sergeants | The Man from U.N.C.L.E. | The Andy Griffith Show |
| 9:00 | Wendy and Me | Andy Williams Show | The Lucy Show |
| 9:30 | Bing Crosby Show | Andy Williams Show | Many Happy Returns |
| 10:00 | Ben Casey | Alfred Hitchcock Hour | CBS Reports |
| 10:30 | Ben Casey | Alfred Hitchcock Hour | CBS Reports |
| | | | |
| **Tuesday** | | | |
| 7:30 | Combat! | Mr. Novak | Local |
| 8:00 | Combat! | Mr. Novak | Joey Bishop Show |
| 8:30 | McHale's Navy | Hullabaloo† (1/12/65) | Red Skelton Hour |
| 9:00 | The Tycoon | Hullabaloo† | Red Skelton Hour |
| 9:30 | Peyton Place | That Was the Week That Was | Petticoat Junction |
| 10:00 | The Fugitive | Bell Telephone Hour / NBC News Specials | Doctors and Nurses |
| 10:30 | The Fugitive | Bell Telephone Hour / NBC News Specials | Doctors and Nurses |
| | | | |
| **Wednesday** | | | |
| 7:30 | Ozzie and Harriet | The Virginian | Mr. Ed |
| 8:00 | Patty Duke Show | The Virginian | My Living Doll |
| 8:30 | Shindig | The Virginian | Beverly Hillbillies |
| 9:00 | Shindig | Wednesday Night Movie | Dick Van Dyke Show |
| 9:30 | Burke's Law | Wednesday Night Movie | Cara Williams Show |
| 10:00 | Burke's Law | Wednesday Night Movie | Danny Kaye Show |
| 10:30 | ABC Close-Up | Wednesday Night Movie | Danny Kaye Show |
| | | | |
| **Thursday** | | | |
| 7:30 | Jonny Quest | Daniel Boone | The Munsters |
| 8:00 | Donna Reed Show | Daniel Boone | Perry Mason |
| 8:30 | My Three Sons | Dr. Kildare | Perry Mason |
| 9:00 | Bewitched | Dr. Kildare | On Broadway Tonight† |
| 9:30 | Peyton Place | Hazel | On Broadway Tonight† |
| 10:00 | Jimmy Dean Show | Kraft Suspense Theatre / Perry Como's Music Hall | The Defenders |
| 10:30 | Jimmy Dean Show | Kraft Suspense Theatre / Perry Como's Music Hall | The Defenders |

|  | ABC | NBC | CBS |
|---|---|---|---|

**Friday**

|  | ABC | NBC | CBS |
|---|---|---|---|
| 7:30 | The Flintstones | International Show-time | Rawhide |
| 8:00 | Farmer's Daughter | International Show-time | Rawhide |
| 8:30 | The Addams Family | Bob Hope Chrysler Theatre/Bob Hope Comedies | Password |
| 9:00 | Valentine's Day | Bob Hope Chrysler Theatre/Bob Hope Comedies | Baileys of Balboa |
| 9:30 | F. D. R. † (1/8/65) | Jack Benny Show | Gomer Pyle, U. S. M. C. |
| 10:00 | 12 O'Clock High | Jack Paar Show | Slattery's People |
| 10:30 | 12 O'Clock High | Jack Paar Show | Slattery's People |

Summer Drama Series, 1965

    Secret Agent†* (Saturday, 4/3/65, 9:00-10:00 CBS)

### 1965-1966 SEASON

**Saturday**

|  | ABC | NBC | CBS |
|---|---|---|---|
| 7:30 | Shindig (9/18) | Flipper (9/18) | Jackie Gleason Show (9/18) |
| 8:00 | The King Family (9/18) | I Dream of Jeannie† (9/18) | Jackie Gleason Show |
| 8:30 | Lawrence Welk Show (9/18) | Get Smart!† (9/18) | Trials of O'Brien†* (9/18) |
| 9:00 | Lawrence Welk Show | Saturday Night Movie (9/18) | Trials of O'Brien†* |
| 9:30 | Hollywood Palace (9/18) | Saturday Night Movie | The Loner†* (9/18) |
| 10:00 | Hollywood Palace | Saturday Night Movie | Gunsmoke (9/18) |
| 10:30 | ABC Scope (9/18) | Saturday Night Movie | Gunsmoke |

**Sunday**

|  | ABC | NBC | CBS |
|---|---|---|---|
| 7:30 | Voyage to the Bottom of the Sea* (starts at 7:00, 9/19) | Disney's World* (9/19) | My Favorite Martian (9/12) |
| 8:00 | The F. B. I. †* (9/19) | Disney's World* | Ed Sullivan Show (9/12) |
| 8:30 | The F. B. I. †* | Branded* (9/12) | Ed Sullivan Show |
| 9:00 | Sunday Night Movie | Bonanza* (9/12) | Perry Mason* (9/12) |
| 9:30 | Sunday Night Movie | Bonanza* | Perry Mason* |
| 10:00 | Sunday Night Movie | Wackiest Ship in the Army†* (9/19) | Candid Camera (9/12) |
| 10:30 | Sunday Night Movie | Wackiest Ship in the Army†* | What's My Line? (9/12) |

**Monday**

|  | ABC | NBC | CBS |
|---|---|---|---|
| 7:30 | 12 O'Clock High* (9/13) | Hullabaloo (9/13) | To Tell the Truth |
| 8:00 | 12 O'Clock High* | John Forsythe Show† (9/13) | I've Got a Secret |

|  | ABC | NBC | CBS |
|---|---|---|---|
| 8:30 | Legend of Jesse James†* (9/13) | Dr. Kildare* (9/13) | Lucille Ball (9/13) |
| 9:00 | Man Called Shenandoah†* (9/13) | Andy Williams Show (9/13) | Andy Griffith Show (9/13) |
| 9:30 | The Farmer's Daughter (9/13) | Andy Williams Show | Hazel (9/13) |
| 10:00 | Ben Casey* (9/13) | Run for Your Life†* (9/13) | Local/Steve Lawrence† (9/13) |
| 10:30 | Ben Casey* | Run for Your Life†* | Local/Steve Lawrence† |

Tuesday

|  | ABC | NBC | CBS |
|---|---|---|---|
| 7:30 | Combat!* (9/14) | My Mother, the Car† (9/14) | Rawhide* (9/14) |
| 8:00 | Combat!* | Please Don't Eat the Daisies† (9/14) | Rawhide* |
| 8:30 | McHale's Navy (9/14) | Dr. Kildare* (9/14) | Red Skelton Hour (9/14) |
| 9:00 | F Troop† (9/14) | Tuesday Night Movie† (9/14) | Red Skelton Hour |
| 9:30 | Peyton Place | Tuesday Night Movie† | Petticoat Junction (9/14) |
| 10:00 | The Fugitive* (9/14) | Tuesday Night Movie† | CBS Reports |
| 10:30 | The Fugitive* | Tuesday Night Movie† | CBS Reports |

Wednesday

|  | ABC | NBC | CBS |
|---|---|---|---|
| 7:30 | Ozzie and Harriet (9/15) | Virginian* (9/15) | Lost in Space†* (9/15) |
| 8:00 | Patty Duke Show (9/15) | Virginian* | Lost in Space†* |
| 8:30 | Gidget† (9/15) | Virginian* | Beverly Hillbillies (9/15) |
| 9:00 | Big Valley†* (9/15) | Bob Hope Chrysler Presents* (9/15) | Green Acres† (9/15) |
| 9:30 | Big Valley†* | Bob Hope Chrysler Presents* | Dick Van Dyke Show (9/15) |
| 10:00 | Amos Burke, Secret Agent†* (9/15) | I Spy†* (9/15) | Danny Kaye Show (9/15) |
| 10:30 | Amos Burke, Secret Agent†* | I Spy†* | Danny Kaye Show |

Thursday

|  | ABC | NBC | CBS |
|---|---|---|---|
| 7:30 | Shindig (9/16) | Daniel Boone* (9/16) | The Munsters (9/16) |
| 8:00 | Donna Reed Show (9/16) | Daniel Boone* | Gilligan's Island (9/16) |
| 8:30 | O. K. Crackerby!† (9/16) | Laredo†* (9/16) | My Three Sons (9/16) |
| 9:00 | Bewitched (9/16) | Laredo†* | Thursday Night Movie (9/16) |
| 9:30 | Peyton Place | Mona McClusky† (9/16) | Thursday Night Movie |
| 10:00 | The Long, Hot Summer†* (9/16) | Dean Martin Show† (9/16) | Thursday Night Movie |
| 10:30 | The Long, Hot Summer†* | Dean Martin Show† | Thursday Night Movie |

| | ABC | NBC | CBS |
|---|---|---|---|

**Friday**

| | ABC | NBC | CBS |
|---|---|---|---|
| 7:30 | The Flintstones (9/17) | Camp Runamuck† (9/17) | The Wild, Wild West†* (9/17) |
| 8:00 | Tammy† (9/17) | Hank† (9/17) | The Wild, Wild West†* |
| 8:30 | Addams Family (9/17) | Convoy†* (9/17) | Hogan's Heroes† (9/17) |
| 9:00 | Honey West†* (9/17) | Convoy† | Gomer Pyle, U.S.M.C. (9/17) |
| 9:30 | Peyton Place | Mr. Roberts†* (9/17) | Smothers Brothers Show† (9/17) |
| 10:00 | Jimmy Dean Show (9/17) | The Man from U.N.C.L.E.* (9/17) | Slattery's People* (9/17) |
| 10:30 | Jimmy Dean Show | The Man from U.N.C.L.E.* | Slattery's People* |

## 1965-1966 MIDSEASON

**Saturday**

| | ABC | NBC | CBS |
|---|---|---|---|
| 7:30 | Ozzie and Harriet | Flipper | The Jackie Gleason Show |
| 8:00 | Donna Reed Show | I Dream of Jeannie | The Jackie Gleason Show |
| 8:30 | Lawrence Welk Show | Get Smart! | Secret Agent* (12/4/65) |
| 9:00 | Lawrence Welk Show | Saturday Night Movie | Secret Agent* |
| 9:30 | Hollywood Palace | Saturday Night Movie | The Loner |
| 10:00 | Hollywood Palace | Saturday Night Movie | Gunsmoke |
| 10:30 | ABC Close Up | Saturday Night Movie | Gunsmoke |

**Sunday**

| | ABC | NBC | CBS |
|---|---|---|---|
| 7:30 | Voyage to the Bottom of the Sea (starts at 7:00) | Disney's World | My Favorite Martian |
| 8:00 | The F.B.I. | Disney's World | The Ed Sullivan Show |
| 8:30 | The F.B.I. | Branded | The Ed Sullivan Show |
| 9:00 | Sunday Night Movie | Bonanza | Perry Mason |
| 9:30 | Sunday Night Movie | Bonanza | Perry Mason |
| 10:00 | Sunday Night Movie | Wackiest Ship in the Army | Candid Camera |
| 10:30 | Sunday Night Movie | Wackiest Ship in the Army | What's My Line? |

**Monday**

| | ABC | NBC | CBS |
|---|---|---|---|
| 7:30 | 12 O'Clock High | Hullabaloo | To Tell the Truth |
| 8:00 | 12 O'Clock High | John Forsythe Show | I've Got a Secret |
| 8:30 | Legend of Jesse James | Dr. Kildare | Lucille Ball |
| 9:00 | A Man Called Shenandoah | Andy Williams Show | Andy Griffith Show |
| 9:30 | Peyton Place | Andy Williams Show | Hazel |
| 10:00 | Ben Casey | Run for Your Life | Art Linkletter's Hollywood Talent Scouts† (12/20/65) |

| ABC | NBC | CBS |
|-----|-----|-----|
| 10:30 Ben Casey | Run for Your Life | Art Linkletter's Holly-wood Talent Scouts† |

Tuesday

| | ABC | NBC | CBS |
|-----|-----|-----|-----|
| 7:30 | Combat! | My Mother, the Car | Daktari† (1/11/66) |
| 8:00 | Combat! | Please Don't Eat the Daisies | Daktari† |
| 8:30 | McHale's Navy | Dr. Kildare | Red Skelton Hour |
| 9:00 | F Troop | Tuesday Night Movie | Red Skelton Hour |
| 9:30 | Peyton Place | Tuesday Night Movie | Petticoat Junction |
| 10:00 | The Fugitive | Tuesday Night Movie | CBS Reports |
| 10:30 | The Fugitive | Tuesday Night Movie | CBS Reports |

Wednesday

| | ABC | NBC | CBS |
|-----|-----|-----|-----|
| 7:30 | Batman†* (1/12/66) | Virginian | Lost in Space |
| 8:00 | Patty Duke Show | Virginian | Lost in Space |
| 8:30 | Blue Light†* (1/12/66) | Virginian | Beverly Hillbillies |
| 9:00 | Big Valley | Bob Hope Chrysler Presents | Green Acres |
| 9:30 | Big Valley | Bob Hope Chrysler Presents | Dick Van Dyke Show |
| 10:00 | The Long, Hot Summer | I Spy | Danny Kaye Show |
| 10:30 | The Long, Hot Summer | I Spy | Danny Kaye Show |

Thursday

| | ABC | NBC | CBS |
|-----|-----|-----|-----|
| 7:30 | Batman†* (1/13/66) | Daniel Boone | The Munsters |
| 8:00 | Gidget | Daniel Boone | Gilligan's Island |
| 8:30 | The Double Life of Henry Phyfe† (1/13/66) | Laredo | My Three Sons |
| 9:00 | Bewitched | Laredo | Thursday Night Movie |
| 9:30 | Peyton Place | Mona McClusky | Thursday Night Movie |
| 10:00 | The Baron†* (1/20/66) | Dean Martin Show | Thursday Night Movie |
| 10:30 | The Baron | Dean Martin Show | Thursday Night Movie |

Friday

| | ABC | NBC | CBS |
|-----|-----|-----|-----|
| 7:30 | The Flintstones | Camp Runamuck | The Wild, Wild West |
| 8:00 | Tammy | Hank | The Wild, Wild West |
| 8:30 | Addams Family | Sammy Davis Jr. Show† (1/7/66) | Hogan's Heroes |
| 9:00 | Honey West | Sammy Davis Jr. Show† | Gomer Pyle, U.S.M.C. |
| 9:30 | Farmer's Daughter | Mr. Roberts | Smothers Brothers Show |
| 10:00 | Jimmy Dean Show | The Man from U.N.C.L.E. | Trials of O'Brien |
| 10:30 | Jimmy Dean Show | The Man from U.N.C.L.E. | Trials of O'Brien |

Summer Drama Series, 1966

> The Avengers†* (Monday, 3/28/66, 10:00-11:00 ABC)
> Court Martial†* (Friday, 4/8/66, 10:00-11:00 ABC)
> Preview Tonight†* (Sunday, 8/14/66, 8:00-9:00 ABC)

### 1966-1967 SEASON

| | ABC | NBC | CBS |
|---|---|---|---|
| **Saturday** | | | |
| 7:30 | Shane†* (9/10) | Flipper (9/17) | Jackie Gleason Show (9/17) |
| 8:00 | Shane†* | Please Don't Eat the Daisies (9/17) | Jackie Gleason Show |
| 8:30 | Lawrence Welk Show | Get Smart! (9/17) | Pistols 'n' Petticoats† (9/17) |
| 9:00 | Lawrence Welk Show | Saturday Night Movie | Mission: Impossible†* (9/17) |
| 9:30 | Hollywood Palace (9/17) | Saturday Night Movie | Mission: Impossible†* |
| 10:00 | Hollywood Palace | Saturday Night Movie | Gunsmoke (9/17) |
| 10:30 | Local/ABC Scope | Saturday Night Movie | Gunsmoke |
| **Sunday** | | | |
| 7:30 | Voyage to the Bottom of the Sea* (starts at 7:00, 9/18) | Disney's World* (9/11) | It's About Time† (9/11) |
| 8:00 | The F.B.I.* (9/18) | Disney's World* | Ed Sullivan Show (9/11) |
| 8:30 | The F.B.I.* | Hey Landlord!† (9/11) | Ed Sullivan Show |
| 9:00 | Sunday Night Movie (9/18) | Bonanza* (9/11) | Garry Moore Show (9/11) |
| 9:30 | Sunday Night Movie | Bonanza* | Garry Moore Show |
| 10:00 | Sunday Night Movie | Andy Williams Show (9/11) | Candid Camera |
| 10:30 | Sunday Night Movie | Andy Williams Show | What's My Line? |
| **Monday** | | | |
| 7:30 | The Iron Horse†* (9/12) | The Monkees† (9/12) | Gilligan's Island (9/12) |
| 8:00 | The Iron Horse†* | I Dream of Jeannie (9/12) | Run, Buddy, Run† (9/12) |
| 8:30 | The Rat Patrol†* (9/12) | Roger Miller Show† (9/12) | Lucille Ball (9/12) |
| 9:00 | The Felony Squad†* (9/12) | The Road West†* (9/12) | Andy Griffith Show (9/12) |
| 9:30 | Peyton Place | The Road West†* | Family Affair† (9/12) |
| 10:00 | Big Valley* (9/12) | Run for Your Life (9/12) | Jean Arthur Show† (9/12) |
| 10:30 | Big Valley* | Run for Your Life* | I've Got a Secret |
| **Tuesday** | | | |
| 7:30 | Combat!* (9/13) | The Girl from U.N.C.L.E.†* (9/13) | Daktari (9/13) |

| | ABC | NBC | CBS |
|---|---|---|---|
| 8:00 | Combat!* | The Girl from U. N. C. L. E. †* | Daktari |
| 8:30 | The Rounders† (9/13) | Occasional Wife† (9/13) | Red Skelton Hour (9/13) |
| 9:00 | Pruitts of Southampton† (9/13) | Tuesday Night Movie (9/13) | Red Skelton Hour |
| 9:30 | Love on a Rooftop† (9/13) | Tuesday Night Movie | Petticoat Junction (9/13) |
| 10:00 | The Fugitive* (9/13) | Tuesday Night Movie | CBS Reports (9/13) |
| 10:30 | The Fugitive* | Tuesday Night Movie | CBS Reports |

Wednesday

| | | | |
|---|---|---|---|
| 7:30 | Batman* (9/7) | Virginian* (9/14) | Lost in Space* (9/21) |
| 8:00 | The Monroes†* (9/7) | Virginian* | Lost in Space* |
| 8:30 | The Monroes†* | Virginian* | Beverly Hillbillies (9/14) |
| 9:00 | The Man Who Never Was†* (9/7) | Bob Hope Chrysler Theatre* (9/14) | Green Acres (9/14) |
| 9:30 | Peyton Place | Bob Hope Chrysler Theatre* | Gomer Pyle, U. S. M. C. (9/14) |
| 10:00 | ABC Stage '67†* (9/14) | I Spy* (9/14) | Danny Kaye Show (9/14) |
| 10:30 | ABC Stage '67†* | I Spy* | Danny Kaye Show |

Thursday

| | | | |
|---|---|---|---|
| 7:30 | Batman* (9/8) | Daniel Boone* (9/15) | Jericho†* (9/15) |
| 8:00 | F Troop (9/8) | Daniel Boone* | Jericho†* |
| 8:30 | Tammy Grimes Show (9/8)/ Dating Game | Star Trek†* (9/8) | My Three Sons (9/15) |
| 9:00 | Bewitched (9/15) | Star Trek†* | Thursday Night Movie (9/15) |
| 9:30 | That Girl† (9/8) | The Hero† (9/8) | Thursday Night Movie |
| 10:00 | Hawk†* (9/8) | Dean Martin Show (9/15) | Thursday Night Movie |
| 10:30 | Hawk†* | Dean Martin Show | Thursday Night Movie |

Friday

| | | | |
|---|---|---|---|
| 7:30 | The Green Hornet†* (9/9) | Tarzan†* (9/8; in this time slot 9/16) | The Wild, Wild West* (9/16) |
| 8:00 | The Time Tunnel†* (9/9) | Tarzan†* | The Wild, Wild West* |
| 8:30 | The Time Tunnel†* | The Man from U. N. C. L. E. * (9/16) | Hogan's Heroes (9/16) |
| 9:00 | The Milton Berle Show† (9/9) | The Man from U. N. C. L. E. * | Friday Night Movie† (9/16) |
| 9:30 | The Milton Berle Show† | T. H. E. Cat†* (9/16) | Friday Night Movie† |
| 10:00 | 12 O'Clock High* (9/9) | Laredo* (9/16) | Friday Night Movie† |
| 10:30 | 12 O'Clock High* | Laredo* | Friday Night Movie† |

1966-1967 MIDSEASON

| | ABC | NBC | CBS |
|---|---|---|---|

**Saturday**

| | ABC | NBC | CBS |
|---|---|---|---|
| 7:30 | The Dating Game | Flipper | The Jackie Gleason Show |
| 8:00 | Newlywed Game† (1/7/67) | Please Don't Eat the Daisies | The Jackie Gleason Show |
| 8:30 | Lawrence Welk Show | Get Smart! | Mission: Impossible |
| 9:00 | Lawrence Welk Show | Saturday Night Movie | Mission: Impossible |
| 9:30 | Hollywood Palace | Saturday Night Movie | Pistols 'n' Petticoats |
| 10:00 | Hollywood Palace | Saturday Night Movie | Gunsmoke |
| 10:30 | Local/ABC Scope | Saturday Night Movie | Gunsmoke |

**Sunday**

| | ABC | NBC | CBS |
|---|---|---|---|
| 7:30 | Voyage to the Bottom of the Sea (starts at 7:00) | Disney's World | It's About Time |
| 8:00 | The F.B.I. | Disney's World | Ed Sullivan Show |
| 8:30 | The F.B.I. | Hey Landlord! | Ed Sullivan Show |
| 9:00 | Sunday Night Movie | Bonanza | Smothers Brothers Comedy Hour† (2/5/67) |
| 9:30 | Sunday Night Movie | Bonanza | Smothers Brothers Comedy Hour† |
| 10:00 | Sunday Night Movie | Andy Williams Show | Candid Camera |
| 10:30 | Sunday Night Movie | Andy Williams Show | What's My Line? |

**Monday**

| | ABC | NBC | CBS |
|---|---|---|---|
| 7:30 | The Iron Horse | The Monkees | Gilligan's Island |
| 8:00 | The Iron Horse | I Dream of Jeannie | Mr. Terrific† (1/9/67) |
| 8:30 | The Rat Patrol | Captain Nice† (1/9/67) | Lucille Ball |
| 9:00 | The Felony Squad | The Road West | Andy Griffith Show |
| 9:30 | Peyton Place | The Road West | Family Affair |
| 10:00 | The Big Valley | Run for Your Life | Local |
| 10:30 | The Big Valley | Run for Your Life | Local |

**Tuesday**

| | ABC | NBC | CBS |
|---|---|---|---|
| 7:30 | Combat! | The Girl from U.N.C.L.E. | Daktari |
| 8:00 | Combat! | The Girl from U.N.C.L.E. | Daktari |
| 8:30 | The Invaders†* (1/10/67) | Occasional Wife | Red Skelton Hour |
| 9:00 | The Invaders†* | Tuesday Night Movie | Red Skelton Hour |
| 9:30 | Peyton Place | Tuesday Night Movie | Petticoat Junction |
| 10:00 | The Fugitive | Tuesday Night Movie | CBS Reports |
| 10:30 | The Fugitive | Tuesday Night Movie | CBS Reports |

**Wednesday**

| | ABC | NBC | CBS |
|---|---|---|---|
| 7:30 | Batman | Virginian | Lost in Space |
| 8:00 | The Monroes | Virginian | Lost in Space |
| 8:30 | The Monroes | Virginian | Beverly Hillbillies |

| | ABC | NBC | CBS |
|---|---|---|---|
| 9:00 | Wednesday Night Movie† | Bob Hope Chrysler Theatre | Green Acres |
| 9:30 | Wednesday Night Movie† | Bob Hope Chrysler Theatre | Gomer Pyle, U. S. M. C. |
| 10:00 | Wednesday Night Movie† | I Spy | Danny Kaye Show |
| 10:30 | Wednesday Night Movie† | I Spy | Danny Kaye Show |

Thursday

| | ABC | NBC | CBS |
|---|---|---|---|
| 7:30 | Batman | Daniel Boone | The Coliseum† (1/26/67) |
| 8:00 | F Troop | Daniel Boone | The Coliseum† |
| 8:30 | Bewitched | Star Trek | My Three Sons |
| 9:00 | That Girl | Star Trek | Thursday Night Movie |
| 9:30 | Love on a Rooftop | Dragnet† (1/12/67) | Thursday Night Movie |
| 10:00 | ABC Stage '67 | Dean Martin Show | Thursday Night Movie |
| 10:30 | ABC Stage '67 | Dean Martin Show | Thursday Night Movie |

Friday

| | ABC | NBC | CBS |
|---|---|---|---|
| 7:30 | The Green Hornet | Tarzan | The Wild, Wild West |
| 8:00 | The Time Tunnel | Tarzan | The Wild, Wild West |
| 8:30 | The Time Tunnel | The Man from U. N. C. L. E. | Hogan's Heroes |
| 9:00 | Rango† (1/13/67) | The Man from U. N. C. L. E. | Friday Night Movie |
| 9:30 | Pruitts of Southampton | T. H. E. Cat | Friday Night Movie |
| 10:00 | The Avengers†* (1/20/67) | Laredo | Friday Night Movie |
| 10:30 | The Avengers†* | Laredo | Friday Night Movie |

Summer Drama Series, 1967

The Saint†* (Friday, 5/21/67, 10:00-11:00 NBC)
Coronet Blue†* (Monday, 5/29/67, 10:00-11:00 CBS)


1967-1968 SEASON


Saturday

| | ABC | NBC | CBS |
|---|---|---|---|
| 7:30 | The Dating Game (9/16) | Maya†* (9/16) | Jackie Gleason Show (9/9) |
| 8:00 | Newlywed Game (9/16) | Maya†* | Jackie Gleason Show |
| 8:30 | Lawrence Welk (9/16) | Get Smart! (9/16) | My Three Sons (9/9) |
| 9:00 | Lawrence Welk | Saturday Night Movie (9/16) | Hogan's Heroes (9/9) |
| 9:30 | The Iron Horse* (9/16) | Saturday Night Movie | Petticoat Junction |
| 10:00 | The Iron Horse* | Saturday Night Movie | Mannix†* (9/16) |
| 10:30 | Local | Saturday Night Movie | Mannix†* |

|  | ABC | NBC | CBS |
|---|---|---|---|
| **Sunday** | | | |
| 7:30 | Voyage to the Bottom of the Sea* (starts at 7:00, 9/17) | Disney's World* (9/10) | Gentle Ben† (9/10) |
| 8:00 | The F. B. I. * (9/17) | Disney's World* | Ed Sullivan Show (9/10) |
| 8:30 | The F. B. I. * | The Mothers-in-Law† (9/10) | Ed Sullivan Show |
| 9:00 | Sunday Night Movie | Bonanza* (9/17) | Smothers Brothers Comedy Hour (9/10) |
| 9:30 | Sunday Night Movie | Bonanza* | Smothers Brothers Comedy Hour |
| 10:00 | Sunday Night Movie | The High Chaparral†* (9/10) | Mission: Impossible* (9/10) |
| 10:30 | Sunday Night Movie | The High Chaparral†* | Mission: Impossible* |
| **Monday** | | | |
| 7:30 | Cowboy in Africa†* (9/11) | The Monkees (9/11) | Gunsmoke (9/11) |
| 8:00 | Cowboy in Africa†* | The Man from U. N. C. L. E. * (9/11) | Gunsmoke |
| 8:30 | The Rat Patrol* (9/11) | The Man from U. N. C. L. E. * | Lucille Ball (9/11) |
| 9:00 | The Felony Squad* (9/11) | The Danny Thomas Show† (9/11) | Andy Griffith Show (9/11) |
| 9:30 | Peyton Place | The Danny Thomas Show† | Family Affair (9/11) |
| 10:00 | The Big Valley* (9/11) | I Spy* (9/11) | Carol Burnett Show† (9/11) |
| 10:30 | The Big Valley* | I Spy* | Carol Burnett Show† |
| **Tuesday** | | | |
| 7:30 | Garrison's Gorillas†* (9/5) | I Dream of Jeannie (9/12) | Daktari (9/5) |
| 8:00 | Garrison's Gorillas†* | Jerry Lewis Show† (9/12) | Daktari |
| 8:30 | The Invaders* (9/5) | Jerry Lewis Show† | Red Skelton Hour (9/5) |
| 9:00 | The Invaders* | Tuesday Night Movie (9/12) | Red Skelton Hour |
| 9:30 | N. Y. P. D. †* (9/5) | Tuesday Night Movie | Good Morning World† (9/5) |
| 10:00 | Hollywood Palace (9/5) | Tuesday Night Movie | CBS Reports (9/5) |
| 10:30 | Hollywood Palace | Tuesday Night Movie | CBS Reports |
| **Wednesday** | | | |
| 7:30 | Custer†* (9/6) | Virginian* (9/13) | Lost in Space* (9/6) |
| 8:00 | Custer†* | Virginian* | Lost in Space* |
| 8:30 | The Second Hundred Years† (9/6) | Virginian* | Beverly Hillbillies (9/6) |
| 9:00 | Wednesday Night Movie (9/6) | Kraft Music Hall† (9/13) | Green Acres (9/6) |

| | ABC | NBC | CBS |
|---|---|---|---|
| 9:30 | Wednesday Night Movie | Kraft Music Hall† | He & She† (9/6) |
| 10:00 | Wednesday Night Movie | Run for Your Life* (9/13) | Dundee & the Culhane†* (9/6) |
| 10:30 | Wednesday Night Movie | Run for Your Life* | Dundee & the Culhane†* |

Thursday

| | | | |
|---|---|---|---|
| 7:30 | Batman* (9/14) | Daniel Boone* (9/14) | Cimarron Strip†* (9/7) |
| 8:00 | The Flying Nun† (9/7) | Daniel Boone* | Cimarron Strip†* |
| 8:30 | Bewitched (9/7) | Ironside†* (9/14) | Cimarron Strip†* |
| 9:00 | That Girl (9/7) | Ironside†* | Thursday Night Movie (9/7) |
| 9:30 | Peyton Place | Dragnet (9/14) | Thursday Night Movie |
| 10:00 | Good Company† (9/7) | Dean Martin Show (9/14) | Thursday Night Movie |
| 10:30 | Local | Dean Martin Show | Thursday Night Movie |

Friday

| | | | |
|---|---|---|---|
| 7:30 | Off to See the Wizard†* (9/8) | Tarzan* (9/15) | The Wild, Wild West* (9/8) |
| 8:00 | Off to See the Wizard†* | Tarzan* | The Wild, Wild West* |
| 8:30 | Hondo†* (9/8) | Star Trek* (9/15) | Gomer Pyle, U.S.M.C. (9/8) |
| 9:00 | Hondo †* | Star Trek* | Friday Night Movie (9/8) |
| 9:30 | Guns of Will Sonnett†* (9/8) | Accidental Family† (9/15) | Friday Night Movie |
| 10:00 | Judd, for the Defense†* (9/8) | Bell Telephone Hour† (9/15) | Friday Night Movie |
| 10:30 | Judd, for the Defense†* | Bell Telephone Hour† | Friday Night Movie |

## 1967-1968 MIDSEASON

Saturday

| | | | |
|---|---|---|---|
| 7:30 | The Dating Game | The Saint* (2/17/68) | Jackie Gleason Show |
| 8:00 | Newlywed Game | The Saint* | Jackie Gleason Show |
| 8:30 | Lawrence Welk Show | Get Smart! | My Three Sons |
| 9:00 | Lawrence Welk Show | Saturday Night Movie | Hogan's Heroes |
| 9:30 | Hollywood Palace | Saturday Night Movie | Petticoat Junction |
| 10:00 | Hollywood Palace | Saturday Night Movie | Mannix |
| 10:30 | Local | Saturday Night Movie | Mannix |

Sunday

| | | | |
|---|---|---|---|
| 7:30 | Voyage to the Bottom of the Sea (starts at 7:00) | Disney's World | Gentle Ben |
| 8:00 | The F.B.I. | Disney's World | Ed Sullivan Show |
| 8:30 | The F.B.I. | The Mothers-in-Law | Ed Sullivan Show |
| 9:00 | Sunday Night Movie | Bonanza | Smothers Brothers Comedy Hour |

|  | ABC | NBC | CBS |
|---|---|---|---|
| 9:30 | Sunday Night Movie | Bonanza | Smothers Brothers Comedy Hour |
| 10:00 | Sunday Night Movie | High Chaparral | Mission: Impossible |
| 10:30 | Sunday Night Movie | High Chaparral | Mission: Impossible |

**Monday**

| 7:30 | Cowboy in Africa | The Monkees | Gunsmoke |
|---|---|---|---|
| 8:00 | Cowboy in Africa | Rowan and Martin's Laugh-In† (1/22/68) | Gunsmoke |
| 8:30 | The Rat Patrol | Laugh-In† | Lucille Ball |
| 9:00 | The Felony Squad | Danny Thomas Show | Andy Griffith Show |
| 9:30 | Peyton Place | Danny Thomas Show | Family Affair |
| 10:00 | Big Valley | I Spy | Carol Burnett Show |
| 10:30 | Big Valley | I Spy | Carol Burnett Show |

**Tuesday**

| 7:30 | Garrison's Gorillas | I Dream of Jeannie | Daktari |
|---|---|---|---|
| 8:00 | Garrison's Gorillas | Jerry Lewis Show | Daktari |
| 8:30 | It Takes a Thief†* (1/9/68) | Jerry Lewis Show | Red Skelton Hour |
| 9:00 | It Takes a Thief†* | Tuesday Night Movie | Red Skelton Hour |
| 9:30 | N.Y.P.D. | Tuesday Night Movie | Good Morning World |
| 10:00 | The Invaders | Tuesday Night Movie | CBS Reports |
| 10:30 | The Invaders | Tuesday Night Movie | CBS Reports |

**Wednesday**

| 7:30 | The Avengers* (1/10/68) | Virginian | Lost in Space |
|---|---|---|---|
| 8:00 | The Avengers* | Virginian | Lost in Space |
| 8:30 | Second Hundred Years | Virginian | Beverly Hillbillies |
| 9:00 | Wednesday Night Movie | Kraft Music Hall | Green Acres |
| 9:30 | Wednesday Night Movie | Kraft Music Hall | He & She |
| 10:00 | Wednesday Night Movie | Run for Your Life | Jonathan Winters Show (12/27/67) |
| 10:30 | Wednesday Night Movie | Run for Your Life | Jonathan Winters Show |

**Thursday**

| 7:30 | Batman | Daniel Boone | Cimarron Strip |
|---|---|---|---|
| 8:00 | The Flying Nun | Daniel Boone | Cimarron Strip |
| 8:30 | Bewitched | Ironside | Cimarron Strip |
| 9:00 | That Girl | Ironside | Thursday Night Movie |
| 9:30 | Peyton Place | Dragnet | Thursday Night Movie |
| 10:00 | Local | Dean Martin Show | Thursday Night Movie |
| 10:30 | Local | Dean Martin Show | Thursday Night Movie |

**Friday**

| 7:30 | Off to See the Wizard | Tarzan | The Wild, Wild West |
|---|---|---|---|
| 8:00 | Off to See the Wizard | Tarzan | The Wild, Wild West |

|       | ABC | NBC | CBS |
|-------|-----|-----|-----|
| 8:30  | Operation: Entertainment† (1/5/68) | Star Trek | Gomer Pyle, U.S.M.C. |
| 9:00  | Operation: Entertainment† | Star Trek | Friday Night Movie |
| 9:30  | Guns of Will Sonnett | Hollywood Squares† (1/12/68) | Friday Night Movie |
| 10:00 | Judd, for the Defense | Bell Telephone Hour | Friday Night Movie |
| 10:30 | Judd, for the Defense | Bell Telephone Hour | Friday Night Movie |

Summer Drama Series, 1968

> Man in a Suitcase†* (Friday, 5/3/68, 8:30-9:30 ABC)
> The Prisoner†* (Saturday, 6/1/68, 7:30-8:30 CBS)
> The Champions†* (Monday, 6/10/68, 8:00-9:00 NBC)

1968-1969 SEASON

Saturday

|       | ABC | NBC | CBS |
|-------|-----|-----|-----|
| 7:30  | Dating Game (9/21) | Adam-12† (9/21) | The Jackie Gleason Show (9/28) |
| 8:00  | Newlywed Game (9/21) | Get Smart! (9/21) | The Jackie Gleason Show |
| 8:30  | Lawrence Welk Show (9/21) | The Ghost and Mrs. Muir† (9/21) | My Three Sons (9/28) |
| 9:00  | Lawrence Welk | Saturday Night Movie (9/21) | Hogan's Heroes (9/28) |
| 9:30  | Hollywood Palace (9/28) | Saturday Night Movie | Petticoat Junction (9/28) |
| 10:00 | Hollywood Palace | Saturday Night Movie | Mannix* (9/28) |
| 10:30 | Local | Saturday Night Movie | Mannix* |

Sunday

|       | ABC | NBC | CBS |
|-------|-----|-----|-----|
| 7:00  | Land of the Giants†* (9/22) | Huckleberry Finn† (9/15) | Lassie (9/29) |
| 7:30  | Land of the Giants†* | Walt Disney* (9/15) | Gentle Ben (9/29) |
| 8:00  | The F.B.I.* (9/22) | Walt Disney* | Ed Sullivan Show (9/29) |
| 8:30  | The F.B.I.* | Mothers-in-Law (9/15) | Ed Sullivan Show |
| 9:00  | Sunday Night Movie (9/22) | Bonanza* (9/15) | Smothers Brothers Comedy Hour (9/29) |
| 9:30  | Sunday Night Movie | Bonanza* | Smothers Brothers Comedy Hour |
| 10:00 | Sunday Night Movie | Phyllis Diller Show† (9/15) | Mission: Impossible* (9/29) |
| 10:30 | Sunday Night Movie | Phyllis Diller Show† | Mission: Impossible* |

Monday

|       | ABC | NBC | CBS |
|-------|-----|-----|-----|
| 7:30  | The Avengers* (9/23) | I Dream of Jeannie (9/16) | Gunsmoke (9/23) |

|  | ABC | NBC | CBS |
|---|---|---|---|
| 8:00 | The Avengers* | Rowan and Martin's Laugh-In (9/16) | Gunsmoke |
| 8:30 | Peyton Place | Rowan and Martin's Laugh-In | Here's Lucy† (9/23) |
| 9:00 | The Outcasts†* (9/23) | Monday Night Movie† (9/16) | Mayberry R.F.D. † (9/23) |
| 9:30 | The Outcasts†* | Monday Night Movie† | Family Affair (9/23) |
| 10:00 | Big Valley* (9/23) | Monday Night Movie† | Carol Burnett Show (9/23) |
| 10:30 | Big Valley* | Monday Night Movie† | Carol Burnett Show |

**Tuesday**

|  | ABC | NBC | CBS |
|---|---|---|---|
| 7:30 | The Mod Squad†* (9/24) | Jerry Lewis Show (9/17) | Lancer† (9/24) |
| 8:00 | The Mod Squad†* | Jerry Lewis Show | Lancer† |
| 8:30 | It Takes a Thief* (9/24) | Julia† (9/17) | Red Skelton Hour (9/24) |
| 9:00 | It Takes a Thief* | Tuesday Night Movie (9/17) | Red Skelton Hour |
| 9:30 | N.Y.P.D.* (10/1) | Tuesday Night Movie | Doris Day Show† (9/24) |
| 10:00 | That's Life† (9/24) | Tuesday Night Movie | News Hour/60 Minutes† (9/24) |
| 10:30 | That's Life† | Tuesday Night Movie | News Hour/60 Minutes† |

**Wednesday**

|  | ABC | NBC | CBS |
|---|---|---|---|
| 7:30 | Here Come the Brides† (9/25) | Virginian* (9/18) | Daktari (9/25) |
| 8:00 | Here Come the Brides† | Virginian* | Daktari |
| 8:30 | Peyton Place | Virginian* | Good Guys† (9/25) |
| 9:00 | Wednesday Night Movie (9/25) | Music Hall (10/2) | Beverly Hillbillies (9/25) |
| 9:30 | Wednesday Night Movie | Music Hall | Green Acres (9/25) |
| 10:00 | Wednesday Night Movie | Outsider†* (9/18) | Jonathan Winters Show (9/25) |
| 10:30 | Wednesday Night Movie | Outsider†* | Jonathan Winters Show |

**Thursday**

|  | ABC | NBC | CBS |
|---|---|---|---|
| 7:30 | The Ugliest Girl in Town† (9/26) | Daniel Boone* (9/19) | Blondie† (9/26) |
| 8:00 | Flying Nun (9/26) | Daniel Boone* | Hawaii Five-O†* (9/26) |
| 8:30 | Bewitched (9/26) | Ironside* (9/19) | Hawaii Five-O†* |
| 9:00 | That Girl (9/26) | Ironside* | Thursday Night Movie (9/26) |
| 9:30 | Journey to the Unknown†* (9/26) | Dragnet (9/19) | Thursday Night Movie |
| 10:00 | Journey to the Unknown†* | Dean Martin Show (9/19) | Thursday Night Movie |
| 10:30 | Local | Dean Martin Show | Thursday Night Movie |

**Friday**

|  | ABC | NBC | CBS |
|---|---|---|---|
| 7:30 | Operation: Entertainment (9/27) | High Chaparral* (9/20) | The Wild, Wild West* (9/27) |

|  | ABC | NBC | CBS |
|---|---|---|---|
| 8:00 | Operation: Entertainment | High Chaparral* | The Wild, Wild West* |
| 8:30 | Felony Squad* (9/27) | The Name of the Game†* (9/20) | Gomer Pyle, U.S.M.C. (9/27) |
| 9:00 | Don Rickles Show† (9/27) | The Name of the Game†* | Friday Night Movie (9/27) |
| 9:30 | Guns of Will Sonnett* (9/27) | The Name of the Game†* | Friday Night Movie |
| 10:00 | Judd, for the Defense* (9/27) | Star Trek* (9/20) | Friday Night Movie |
| 10:30 | Judd, for the Defense* | Star Trek* | Friday Night Movie |

## 1968-1969 MIDSEASON

### Saturday
| | | | |
|---|---|---|---|
| 7:30 | Dating Game | Adam-12 | The Jackie Gleason Show |
| 8:00 | Newlywed Game | Get Smart! | The Jackie Gleason Show |
| 8:30 | Lawrence Welk Show | The Ghost and Mrs. Muir | My Three Sons |
| 9:00 | Lawrence Welk Show | Saturday Night Movie | Hogan's Heroes |
| 9:30 | Hollywood Palace | Saturday Night Movie | Petticoat Junction |
| 10:00 | Hollywood Palace | Saturday Night Movie | Mannix |
| 10:30 | Local | Saturday Night Movie | Mannix |

### Sunday
| | | | |
|---|---|---|---|
| 7:00 | Land of the Giants | Huckleberry Finn | Lassie |
| 7:30 | Land of the Giants | Walt Disney | Gentle Ben |
| 8:00 | The F.B.I. | Walt Disney | Ed Sullivan Show |
| 8:30 | The F.B.I. | Mothers-In-Law | Ed Sullivan Show |
| 9:00 | Sunday Night Movie | Bonanza | Smothers Brothers Comedy Hour |
| 9:30 | Sunday Night Movie | Bonanza | Smothers Brothers Comedy Hour |
| 10:00 | Sunday Night Movie | My Friend Tony†* (1/5/69) | Mission: Impossible |
| 10:30 | Sunday Night Movie | My Friend Tony†* | Mission: Impossible |

### Monday
| | | | |
|---|---|---|---|
| 7:30 | The Avengers | I Dream of Jeannie | Gunsmoke |
| 8:00 | The Avengers | Rowan and Martin's Laugh-In | Gunsmoke |
| 8:30 | Peyton Place | Rowan and Martin's Laugh-In | Here's Lucy |
| 9:00 | The Outcasts | Monday Night Movie | Mayberry R.F.D. |
| 9:30 | The Outcasts | Monday Night Movie | Family Affair |
| 10:00 | Big Valley | Monday Night Movie | Carol Burnett Show |
| 10:30 | Big Valley | Monday Night Movie | Carol Burnett Show |

### Tuesday
| | | | |
|---|---|---|---|
| 7:30 | The Mod Squad | Jerry Lewis Show | Lancer |
| 8:00 | The Mod Squad | Jerry Lewis Show | Lancer |

| | ABC | NBC | CBS |
|---|---|---|---|
| 8:30 | It Takes a Thief | Julia | Red Skelton Hour |
| 9:00 | It Takes a Thief | Tuesday Night Movie | Red Skelton Hour |
| 9:30 | N.Y.P.D. | Tuesday Night Movie | Doris Day Show |
| 10:00 | That's Life | Tuesday Night Movie | News Hour/60 Minutes |
| 10:30 | That's Life | Tuesday Night Movie | News Hour/60 Minutes |

Wednesday

| | | | |
|---|---|---|---|
| 7:30 | Here Come the Brides | Virginian | Glen Campbell Show† (1/22/69) |
| 8:00 | Here Come the Brides | Virginian | Glen Campbell Show† |
| 8:30 | Turn-On† (2/5/69) | Virginian | Good Guys |
| 9:00 | Wednesday Night Movie | Music Hall | Beverly Hillbillies |
| 9:30 | Wednesday Night Movie | Music Hall | Green Acres |
| 10:00 | Wednesday Night Movie | The Outsider | Hawaii Five-O |
| 10:30 | Wednesday Night Movie | The Outsider | Hawaii Five-O |

Thursday

| | | | |
|---|---|---|---|
| 7:30 | Flying Nun | Daniel Boone | The Queen and I† (1/16/69) |
| 8:00 | That Girl | Daniel Boone | Jonathan Winters |
| 8:30 | Bewitched | Ironside | Jonathan Winters |
| 9:00 | What's It All About World?† (2/6/69) | Ironside | Thursday Night Movie |
| 9:30 | What's It All About World?† | Dragnet | Thursday Night Movie |
| 10:00 | Local | Dean Martin Show | Thursday Night Movie |
| 10:30 | Local | Dean Martin Show | Thursday Night Movie |

Friday

| | | | |
|---|---|---|---|
| 7:30 | Tom Jones† (2/7/69) | High Chaparral | The Wild, Wild West |
| 8:00 | Tom Jones† | High Chaparral | The Wild, Wild West |
| 8:30 | Generation Gap† (2/7/69) | The Name of the Game | Gomer Pyle, U.S.M.C. |
| 9:00 | Let's Make a Deal† (2/7/69) | The Name of the Game | Friday Night Movie |
| 9:30 | Guns of Will Sonnett | The Name of the Game | Friday Night Movie |
| 10:00 | Judd, for the Defense | Star Trek | Friday Night Movie |
| 10:30 | Judd, for the Defense | Star Trek | Friday Night Movie |

1969-1970 SEASON

Saturday

| | | | |
|---|---|---|---|
| 7:30 | The Dating Game (9/13) | Andy Williams Show† (9/20) | Jackie Gleason Show (10/4) |

|  | ABC | NBC | CBS |
|---|---|---|---|
| 8:00 | Newlywed Game (9/13) | Andy Williams Show† | Jackie Gleason Show |
| 8:30 | Lawrence Welk Show (9/13) | Adam-12 (9/20) | My Three Sons (10/4) |
| 9:00 | Lawrence Welk Show | Saturday Night Movie (9/20) | Green Acres (10/4) |
| 9:30 | Hollywood Palace (9/20) | Saturday Night Movie | Petticoat Junction (10/4) |
| 10:00 | Hollywood Palace | Saturday Night Movie | Mannix* (9/27) |
| 10:30 | Local | Saturday Night Movie | Mannix* |

### Sunday

|  | ABC | NBC | CBS |
|---|---|---|---|
| 7:00 | Land of the Giants* (9/21) | Wild Kingdom (9/14) | Lassie |
| 7:30 | Land of the Giants* | Walt Disney* (9/14) | To Rome with Love† (9/28) |
| 8:00 | The F.B.I.* (9/14) | Walt Disney* | The Ed Sullivan Show (9/28) |
| 8:30 | The F.B.I.* | Bill Cosby Show† (9/14) | The Ed Sullivan Show |
| 9:00 | Sunday Night Movie (9/14) | Bonanza* (9/14) | The Leslie Uggams Show (9/28) |
| 9:30 | Sunday Night Movie | Bonanza* | The Leslie Uggams Show |
| 10:00 | Sunday Night Movie | The Bold Ones†* (9/14) | Mission: Impossible (9/28) |
| 10:30 | Sunday Night Movie | The Bold Ones†* | Mission: Impossible |

### Monday

|  | ABC | NBC | CBS |
|---|---|---|---|
| 7:30 | The Music Scene† (45 minutes, 9/22) | My World and Welcome to It† (9/15) | Gunsmoke (9/29) |
| 8:00 | The Music Scene†/ The New People†* (starts at 8:15, 9/22) | Rowan and Martin's Laugh-In (9/15) | Gunsmoke |
| 8:30 | The New People†* | Rowan and Martin's Laugh-In | Here's Lucy (9/29) |
| 9:00 | The Survivors†* (9/29) | Monday Night Movie (9/15) | Mayberry R.F.D. (9/29) |
| 9:30 | The Survivors†* | Monday Night Movie | Doris Day Show (9/29) |
| 10:00 | Love, American Style† (9/29) | Monday Night Movie | Carol Burnett Show (9/22) |
| 10:30 | Love, American Style† | Monday Night Movie | Carol Burnett Show |

### Tuesday

|  | ABC | NBC | CBS |
|---|---|---|---|
| 7:30 | The Mod Squad* (9/23) | I Dream of Jeannie (9/16) | Lancer (9/23) |
| 8:00 | The Mod Squad* | Debbie Reynolds Show† (9/16) | Lancer |
| 8:30 | Movie of the Week† (9/23) | Julia (9/16) | Red Skelton Hour (9/23) |
| 9:00 | Movie of the Week† | Tuesday Night Movie (9/16)/First Tuesday† | Red Skelton Hour |

| | ABC | NBC | CBS |
|---|---|---|---|
| 9:30 | Movie of the Week† | Tuesday Night Movie / First Tuesday† | The Governor and J.J. † (9/23) |
| 10:00 | Marcus Welby, M.D. †* (9/23) | Tuesday Night Movie / First Tuesday† | News Hour /60 Minutes (9/23) |
| 10:30 | Marcus Welby, M.D. †* | Tuesday Night Movie / First Tuesday† | News Hour /60 Minutes |

**Wednesday**

| | ABC | NBC | CBS |
|---|---|---|---|
| 7:30 | Flying Nun (9/17) | Virginian* (9/17) | Glen Campbell Show (9/24) |
| 8:00 | Courtship of Eddie's Father† (9/17) | Virginian* | Glen Campbell Show |
| 8:30 | Room 222† (9/17) | Virginian* | Beverly Hillbillies (9/24) |
| 9:00 | Wednesday Night Movie (9/24) | Music Hall (9/17) | Medical Center†* (9/24) |
| 9:30 | Wednesday Night Movie | Music Hall | Medical Center†* |
| 10:00 | Wednesday Night Movie | Then Came Bronson†* (9/17) | Hawaii Five-O* (9/24) |
| 10:30 | Wednesday Night Movie | Then Came Bronson†* | Hawaii Five-O* |

**Thursday**

| | ABC | NBC | CBS |
|---|---|---|---|
| 7:30 | Ghost and Mrs. Muir (9/18) | Daniel Boone* (9/18) | Family Affair (9/25) |
| 8:00 | That Girl (9/18) | Daniel Boone* | Jim Nabors Show† (9/25) |
| 8:30 | Bewitched (9/18) | Ironside* (9/18) | Jim Nabors Show† |
| 9:00 | Tom Jones (9/25) | Ironside* | Thursday Night Movie (9/25) |
| 9:30 | Tom Jones | Dragnet (9/18) | Thursday Night Movie |
| 10:00 | It Takes a Thief* (9/25) | Dean Martin Show (9/18) | Thursday Night Movie |
| 10:30 | It Takes a Thief* | Dean Martin Show | Thursday Night Movie |

**Friday**

| | ABC | NBC | CBS |
|---|---|---|---|
| 7:30 | Let's Make a Deal (9/26) | High Chaparral* (9/19) | Get Smart! (9/26) |
| 8:00 | The Brady Bunch† (9/26) | High Chaparral* | Good Guys (9/26) |
| 8:30 | Mr. Deeds Goes to Town† (9/26) | The Name of the Game* (9/19) | Hogan's Heroes (9/26) |
| 9:00 | Here Come the Brides (9/26) | The Name of the Game* | Friday Night Movie (9/26) |
| 9:30 | Here Come the Brides | The Name of the Game* | Friday Night Movie |
| 10:00 | Jimmy Durante Presents the Lennon Sisters Hour† (9/26) | Bracken's World†* (9/19) | Friday Night Movie |
| 10:30 | Jimmy Durante Presents the Lennon Sisters Hour† | Bracken's World†* | Friday Night Movie |

1969-1970 MIDSEASON

| | ABC | NBC | CBS |
|---|---|---|---|
| **Saturday** | | | |
| 7:30 | Let's Make a Deal | Andy Williams Show | Jackie Gleason Show |
| 8:00 | Newlywed Game | Andy Williams Show | Jackie Gleason Show |
| 8:30 | Lawrence Welk Show | Adam-12 | My Three Sons |
| 9:00 | Lawrence Welk Show | Saturday Night Movie | Green Acres |
| 9:30 | Lennon Sisters Show | Saturday Night Movie | Petticoat Junction |
| 10:00 | Lennon Sisters Show | Saturday Night Movie | Mannix |
| 10:30 | Local | Saturday Night Movie | Mannix |
| **Sunday** | | | |
| 7:00 | Land of the Giants | Wild Kingdom | Lassie |
| 7:30 | Land of the Giants | Walt Disney | To Rome with Love |
| 8:00 | The F.B.I. | Walt Disney | The Ed Sullivan Show |
| 8:30 | The F.B.I. | Bill Cosby Show | The Ed Sullivan Show |
| 9:00 | Sunday Night Movie | Bonanza | Glen Campbell Show |
| 9:30 | Sunday Night Movie | Bonanza | Glen Campbell Show |
| 10:00 | Sunday Night Movie | The Bold Ones | Mission: Impossible |
| 10:30 | Sunday Night Movie | The Bold Ones | Mission: Impossible |
| **Monday** | | | |
| 7:30 | It Takes a Thief | My World and Welcome to It | Gunsmoke |
| 8:00 | It Takes a Thief | Laugh-In | Gunsmoke |
| 8:30 | Movie† (1/19/70) | Laugh-In | Here's Lucy |
| 9:00 | Movie† | Monday Night Movie | Mayberry R.F.D. |
| 9:30 | Movie† | Monday Night Movie | Dorris Day Show |
| 10:00 | Movie† | Monday Night Movie | Carol Burnett Show |
| 10:30 | Local/Now† (3/23/70) | Monday Night Movie | Carol Burnett Show |
| **Tuesday** | | | |
| 7:30 | The Mod Squad | I Dream of Jeannie | Lancer |
| 8:00 | The Mod Squad | Debbie Reynolds Show | Lancer |
| 8:30 | Movie of the Week | Julia | Red Skelton Hour |
| 9:00 | Movie of the Week | Tuesday Night Movie/First Tuesday | Red Skelton Hour |
| 9:30 | Movie of the Week | Tuesday Night Movie/First Tuesday | Governor and J.J. |
| 10:00 | Marcus Welby, M.D. | Tuesday Night Movie/First Tuesday | News Hour/60 Minutes |
| 10:30 | Marcus Welby, M.D. | Tuesday Night Movie/First Tuesday | News Hour/60 Minutes |
| **Wednesday** | | | |
| 7:30 | Nanny and the Professor† (1/21/70) | Virginian | Hee Haw† (12/17/69) |
| 8:00 | Courtship of Eddie's Father | Virginian | Hee Haw† |
| 8:30 | Room 222 | Virginian | Beverly Hillbillies |
| 9:00 | Johnny Cash Show† (1/21/70) | Music Hall | Medical Center |
| 9:30 | Johnny Cash Show† | Music Hall | Medical Center |

|  | ABC | NBC | CBS |
|---|---|---|---|
| 10:00 | Englebert Humper-dinck† (1/21/70) | Then Came Bronson | Hawaii Five-O |
| 10:30 | Englebert Humper-dinck† | Then Came Bronson | Hawaii Five-O |

**Thursday**

| 7:30 | Pat Paulsen Show† (1/22/70) | Daniel Boone | Family Affair |
|---|---|---|---|
| 8:00 | That Girl | Daniel Boone | Jim Nabors Show |
| 8:30 | Bewitched | Ironside | Jim Nabors Show |
| 9:00 | Tom Jones | Ironside | Thursday Night Movie |
| 9:30 | Tom Jones | Dragnet | Thursday Night Movie |
| 10:00 | Paris 7000†* (1/22/70) | Dean Martin Show | Thursday Night Movie |
| 10:30 | Paris 7000†* | Dean Martin Show | Thursday Night Movie |

**Friday**

| 7:30 | Flying Nun | High Chaparral | Get Smart! |
|---|---|---|---|
| 8:00 | Brady Bunch | High Chaparral | Tim Conway Show† (1/30/70) |
| 8:30 | Ghost and Mrs. Muir | Name of the Game | Hogan's Heroes |
| 9:00 | Here Come the Brides | Name of the Game | Friday Night Movie |
| 9:30 | Here Come the Brides | Name of the Game | Friday Night Movie |
| 10:00 | Love, American Style | Bracken's World | Friday Night Movie |
| 10:30 | Love, American Style | Bracken's World | Friday Night Movie |

## 1970-1971 SEASON

**Saturday**

| 7:30 | Let's Make a Deal (9/19) | Andy Williams Show (9/19) | Mission: Impossible* (9/19) |
|---|---|---|---|
| 8:00 | Newlywed Game (9/19) | Andy Williams Show | Mission: Impossible* |
| 8:30 | Lawrence Welk Show (9/19) | Adam-12 (9/19) | My Three Sons (9/19) |
| 9:00 | Lawrence Welk Show | Saturday Night Movie (9/26) | Arnie† (9/19) |
| 9:30 | The Most Deadly Game†* (10/10) | Saturday Night Movie | Mary Tyler Moore† (9/19) |
| 10:00 | The Most Deadly Game†* | Saturday Night Movie | Mannix* (9/19) |
| 10:30 | Local | Saturday Night Movie | Mannix* |

**Sunday**

| 7:00 | The Young Rebels†* (9/20) | Wild Kingdom (9/20) | Lassie (9/20) |
|---|---|---|---|
| 7:30 | The Young Rebels†* | Walt Disney* (9/13) | Hogan's Heroes (9/20) |
| 8:00 | The F.B.I.* (9/20) | Walt Disney* | Ed Sullivan Show (9/20) |

|  | ABC | NBC | CBS |
|---|---|---|---|
| 8:30 | The F.B.I.* | Bill Cosby Show (9/13) | Ed Sullivan Show |
| 9:00 | Sunday Night Movie (9/20) | Bonanza* (9/13) | Glen Campbell Show (9/20) |
| 9:30 | Sunday Night Movie | Bonanza* | Glen Campbell Show |
| 10:00 | Sunday Night Movie | The Bold Ones* (9/13) | Tim Conway Comedy Hour† (9/20) |
| 10:30 | Sunday Night Movie | The Bold Ones* | Tim Conway Comedy Hour† |

Monday

| | ABC | NBC | CBS |
|---|---|---|---|
| 7:30 | The Young Lawyers†* (9/21) | Red Skelton Show (9/14) | Gunsmoke (9/14) |
| 8:00 | The Young Lawyers†* | Laugh-In (9/14) | Gunsmoke |
| 8:30 | Silent Force†* (9/21) | Laugh-In | Here's Lucy (9/14) |
| 9:00 | NFL Monday Night Football† (9/21)/ Monday Night Movie (12/14) | Monday Night Movie (9/21) | Mayberry R.F.D. (9/14) |
| 9:30 | NFL Monday Night Football/ Monday Night Movie | Monday Night Movie | Doris Day Show (9/14) |
| 10:00 | NFL Monday Night Football/ Monday Night Movie | Monday Night Movie | Carol Burnett Show (9/14) |
| 10:30 | NFL Monday Night Football/Monday Night Movie | Monday Night Movie | Carol Burnett Show |

Tuesday

| | ABC | NBC | CBS |
|---|---|---|---|
| 7:30 | The Mod Squad* (9/22) | Don Knotts Show† (9/15) | Beverly Hillbillies (9/15) |
| 8:00 | The Mod Squad* | Don Knotts Show† | Green Acres (9/15) |
| 8:30 | Movie of the Week (9/22) | Julia (9/15) | Hee Haw (9/15) |
| 9:00 | Movie of the Week | Tuesday Night Movie (9/22)/ First Tuesday | Hee Haw |
| 9:30 | Movie of the Week | Tuesday Night Movie/ First Tuesday | To Rome with Love (9/15) |
| 10:00 | Marcus Welby, M.D.* (9/22) | Tuesday Night Movie/ First Tuesday | News Hour/60 Minutes (9/15) |
| 10:30 | Marcus Welby, M.D.* | Tuesday Night Movie/ First Tuesday | News Hour/60 Minutes |

Wednesday

| | ABC | NBC | CBS |
|---|---|---|---|
| 7:30 | Courtship of Eddie's Father (9/23) | Men from Shiloh* (9/16) | Storefront Lawyers†* (9/16) |
| 8:00 | Make Room for Granddaddy† (9/23) | Men from Shiloh* | Storefront Lawyers†* |
| 8:30 | Room 222 (9/23) | Men from Shiloh* | Governor and J.J. (9/23) |
| 9:00 | Johnny Cash Show (9/23) | Music Hall (9/16) | Medical Center* (9/16) |

|  | ABC | NBC | CBS |
|---|---|---|---|
| 9:30 | Johnny Cash Show | Music Hall | Medical Center* |
| 10:00 | Dan August†* (9/23) | Four-in-One†* (9/16) | Hawaii Five-O* (9/16) |
| 10:30 | Dan August†* | Four-in-One†* | Hawaii Five-O* |

**Thursday**

|  | ABC | NBC | CBS |
|---|---|---|---|
| 7:30 | Matt Lincoln†* (9/24) | Flip Wilson Show† (9/17) | Family Affair (9/17) |
| 8:00 | Matt Lincoln†* | Flip Wilson Show† | Jim Nabors Show (9/17) |
| 8:30 | Bewitched (9/24) | Ironside* (9/17) | Jim Nabors Show |
| 9:00 | Barefoot in the Park† (9/24) | Ironside* | Thursday Night Movie (9/17) |
| 9:30 | The Odd Couple† (9/24) | Nancy† (9/17) | Thursday Night Movie |
| 10:00 | The Immortal†* (9/24) | Dean Martin Show (9/17) | Thursday Night Movie |
| 10:30 | The Immortal†* | Dean Martin Show | Thursday Night Movie |

**Friday**

|  | ABC | NBC | CBS |
|---|---|---|---|
| 7:30 | Brady Bunch (9/25) | High Chaparral* (9/18) | The Interns†* (9/18) |
| 8:00 | Nanny and the Professor (9/25) | High Chaparral* | The Interns†* |
| 8:30 | Partridge Family† (9/25) | Name of the Game* (9/18) | Headmaster† (9/18) |
| 9:00 | That Girl (9/25) | Name of the Game* | Friday Night Movie (9/18) |
| 9:30 | Love, American Style (9/25) | Name of the Game* | Friday Night Movie |
| 10:00 | Tom Jones (9/25) | Bracken's World* (9/18) | Friday Night Movie |
| 10:30 | Tom Jones | Bracken's World* | Friday Night Movie |

## 1970-1971 MIDSEASON

**Saturday**

|  | ABC | NBC | CBS |
|---|---|---|---|
| 7:30 | Lawrence Welk Show | Andy Williams Show | Mission: Impossible |
| 8:00 | Lawrence Welk Show | Andy Williams Show | Mission: Impossible |
| 8:30 | Pearl Bailey Show† (1/23/71) | Adam-12 | My Three Sons |
| 9:00 | Pearl Bailey Show† | Saturday Night Movie | Arnie |
| 9:30 | Local | Saturday Night Movie | Mary Tyler Moore |
| 10:00 | Local | Saturday Night Movie | Mannix |
| 10:30 | Local | Saturday Night Movie | Mannix |

**Sunday**

|  | ABC | NBC | CBS |
|---|---|---|---|
| 7:30 | Local | Walt Disney | Hogan's Heroes |
| 8:00 | The F. B. I. | Walt Disney | Ed Sullivan Show |
| 8:30 | The F. B. I. | Bill Cosby Show | Ed Sullivan Show |
| 9:00 | Sunday Night Movie | Bonanza | Glen Campbell Show |
| 9:30 | Sunday Night Movie | Bonanza | Glen Campbell Show |
| 10:00 | Sunday Night Movie | The Bold Ones | The Jackie Gleason Show |

| | ABC | NBC | CBS |
|---|---|---|---|
| 10:30 | Sunday Night Movie | The Bold Ones | The Jackie Gleason Show |

**Monday**

| | ABC | NBC | CBS |
|---|---|---|---|
| 7:30 | Let's Make a Deal | Red Skelton Show | Gunsmoke |
| 8:00 | Newlywed Game | Laugh-In | Gunsmoke |
| 8:30 | Reel Game† | Laugh-In | Here's Lucy |
| 9:00 | Monday Night Movie | Monday Night Movie | Mayberry R.F.D. |
| 9:30 | Monday Night Movie | Monday Night Movie | Doris Day Show |
| 10:00 | Monday Night Movie | Monday Night Movie | Carol Burnett Show |
| 10:30 | Monday Night Movie | Monday Night Movie | Carol Burnett Show |

**Tuesday**

| | ABC | NBC | CBS |
|---|---|---|---|
| 7:30 | The Mod Squad | Julia | Beverly Hillbillies |
| 8:00 | The Mod Squad | Don Knotts Show | Green Acres |
| 8:30 | Movie of the Week | Don Knotts Show | Hee Haw |
| 9:00 | Movie of the Week | Tuesday Night Movie | Hee Haw |
| 9:30 | Movie of the Week | Tuesday Night Movie | All in the Family† (1/12/71) |
| 10:00 | Marcus Welby, M.D. | Tuesday Night Movie | News Hour/60 Minutes |
| 10:30 | Marcus Welby, M.D. | Tuesday Night Movie | News Hour/60 Minutes |

**Wednesday**

| | ABC | NBC | CBS |
|---|---|---|---|
| 7:30 | Courtship of Eddie's Father | Men from Shiloh | Storefront Lawyers |
| 8:00 | Room 222 | Men from Shiloh | Storefront Lawyers |
| 8:30 | Smith Family† (1/20/71) | Men from Shiloh | To Rome with Love |
| 9:00 | Johnny Cash Show | Music Hall | Medical Center |
| 9:30 | Johnny Cash Show | Music Hall | Medical Center |
| 10:00 | Young Lawyers | Four-in-One | Hawaii Five-O |
| 10:30 | Young Lawyers | Four-in-One | Hawaii Five-O |

**Thursday**

| | ABC | NBC | CBS |
|---|---|---|---|
| 7:30 | Alias Smith and Jones† (1/21/71) | Flip Wilson Show | Family Affair |
| 8:00 | Alias Smith and Jones† | Flip Wilson Show | Jim Nabors Show |
| 8:30 | Bewitched | Ironside | Jim Nabors Show |
| 9:00 | Make Room for Granddaddy | Ironside | Thursday Night Movie |
| 9:30 | Dan August | Adam-12 | Thursday Night Movie |
| 10:00 | Dan August | Dean Martin Show | Thursday Night Movie |
| 10:30 | Local | Dean Martin Show | Thursday Night Movie |

**Friday**

| | ABC | NBC | CBS |
|---|---|---|---|
| 7:30 | Brady Bunch | High Chaparral | The Interns |
| 8:00 | Nanny and the Professor | High Chaparral | The Interns |
| 8:30 | Partridge Family | Name of the Game | Andy Griffith |
| 9:00 | That Girl | Name of the Game | Friday Night Movie |
| 9:30 | Odd Couple | Name of the Game | Friday Night Movie |
| 10:00 | Love, American Style | Strange Report†* (1/8/71) | Friday Night Movie |
| 10:30 | Love, American Style | Strange Report†* | Friday Night Movie |

Summer Drama Series, 1971

The Six Wives of Henry VIII†* (Sunday, 8/1/71, 9:30-11:00 CBS)

1971-1972 SEASON

| | ABC | NBC | CBS |
|---|---|---|---|
| **Saturday** | | | |
| 8:00 | Getting Together† (9/18) | The Partners† (9/18) | All in the Family (9/18) |
| 8:30 | Movie of the Week-end† (9/18) | The Good Life† (9/18) | Funny Face† (9/18) |
| 9:00 | Movie of the Week-end† | Saturday Night Movie (9/18) | Dick Van Dyke Show† (9/18) |
| 9:30 | Movie of the Week-end† | Saturday Night Movie | Mary Tyler Moore (9/18) |
| 10:00 | The Persuaders†* (9/18) | Saturday Night Movie | Mission: Impossible* (9/18) |
| 10:30 | The Persuaders†* | Saturday Night Movie | Mission: Impossible* |
| **Sunday** | | | |
| 7:30 | Local | Walt Disney* (9/19) | Sunday Night Movie† (9/19) |
| 8:00 | The F.B.I.* (9/12) | Walt Disney* | Sunday Night Movie† |
| 8:30 | The F.B.I.* | Jimmy Stewart Show† (9/19) | Sunday Night Movie† |
| 9:00 | Sunday Night Movie (9/12) | Bonanza* (9/19) | Sunday Night Movie† |
| 9:30 | Sunday Night Movie | Bonanza* | Cade's County† (9/19) |
| 10:00 | Sunday Night Movie | Bold Ones* (9/19) | Cade's County† |
| 10:30 | Sunday Night Movie | Bold Ones* | Local |
| **Monday** | | | |
| 8:00 | Nanny and the Pro-fessor (9/13) | Laugh-In (9/13) | Gunsmoke (9/13) |
| 8:30 | Local | Laugh-In | Gunsmoke |
| 9:00 | NFL Football (9/20)/Monday Night Movie (1/24/72) | Monday Night Movie (9/20) | Here's Lucy (9/13) |
| 9:30 | NFL Football/Monday Night Movie | Monday Night Movie | Doris Day Show (9/13) |
| 10:00 | NFL Football/Monday Night Movie | Monday Night Movie | My Three Sons (9/13) |
| 10:30 | NFL Football/Monday Night Movie | Monday Night Movie | Arnie (9/13) |
| **Tuesday** | | | |
| 7:30 | The Mod Squad* (9/14) | Ironside* (9/21) | Glen Campbell Show (9/14) |
| 8:00 | The Mod Squad* | Ironside* | Glen Campbell Show |
| 8:30 | Movie of the Week (9/14) | Sarge†* (9/21) | Hawaii Five-O* (9/14) |
| 9:00 | Movie of the Week | Sarge†* | Hawaii Five-O* |
| 9:30 | Movie of the Week | The Funny Side† (9/14) | Cannon†* (9/14) |

| ABC | NBC | CBS |
|---|---|---|
| 10:00 Marcus Welby, M.D.* (9/14) | The Funny Side† | Cannon†* |
| 10:30 Marcus Welby, M.D.* | Local | Local |

**Wednesday**

| | ABC | NBC | CBS |
|---|---|---|---|
| 8:00 | Bewitched (9/15) | Adam-12 (9/15) | Carol Burnett Show (9/15) |
| 8:30 | Courtship of Eddie's Father (9/15) | NBC Mystery Movie†* (9/15) | Carol Burnett Show |
| 9:00 | Smith Family (9/15) | NBC Mystery Movie†* | Medical Center* (9/15) |
| 9:30 | Shirley's World† (9/15) | NBC Mystery Movie†* | Medical Center* |
| 10:00 | The Man and the City†* (9/15) | Night Gallery* (9/15) | Mannix* (9/15) |
| 10:30 | The Man and the City†* | Night Gallery* | Mannix* |

**Thursday**

| | ABC | NBC | CBS |
|---|---|---|---|
| 8:00 | Alias Smith and Jones (9/16) | The Flip Wilson Show (9/16) | Bearcats!† (9/16) |
| 8:30 | Alias Smith and Jones | The Flip Wilson Show | Bearcats!† |
| 9:00 | Longstreet†* (9/16) | Nichols† (9/16) | Thursday Night Movie (9/16) |
| 9:30 | Longstreet†* | Nichols† | Thursday Night Movie |
| 10:00 | Owen Marshall, Counselor at Law†* (9/16) | Dean Martin Show (9/16) | Thursday Night Movie |
| 10:30 | Owen Marshall, Counselor at Law†* | Dean Martin Show | Thursday Night Movie |

**Friday**

| | ABC | NBC | CBS |
|---|---|---|---|
| 8:00 | The Brady Bunch (9/17) | The D. A.†* (9/17) | The Chicago Teddy Bears† (9/17) |
| 8:30 | Partridge Family (9/17) | NBC World Premiere Movie (9/17)/ Chronolog | O'Hara, United States Treasury† (9/17) |
| 9:00 | Room 222 (9/17) | NBC World Premiere Movie/Chronolog | O'Hara, United States Treasury† |
| 9:30 | The Odd Couple (9/17) | NBC World Premiere Movie/Chronolog | Friday Night Movie (9/17) |
| 10:00 | Love, American Style (9/17) | NBC World Premiere Movie/Chronolog | Friday Night Movie |
| 10:30 | Love, American Style | Local | Friday Night Movie |

**1971-1972 MIDSEASON**

**Saturday**

| | ABC | NBC | CBS |
|---|---|---|---|
| 8:00 | Bewitched | Emergency!† (1/22/72) | All in the Family |
| 8:30 | Movie of the Weekend | Emergency!† | Mary Tyler Moore |

|  | ABC | NBC | CBS |
|---|---|---|---|
| 9:00 | Movie of the Week-end | Saturday Night Movie | Dick Van Dyke Show |
| 9:30 | Movie of the Week-end | Saturday Night Movie | Arnie |
| 10:00 | The Sixth Sense†* (1/15/72) | Saturday Night Movie | Mission: Impossible |
| 10:30 | The Sixth Sense†* | Saturday Night Movie | Mission: Impossible |

Sunday

| 7:30 | Local | Walt Disney | Sunday Night Movie |
|---|---|---|---|
| 8:00 | The F.B.I. | Walt Disney | Sunday Night Movie |
| 8:30 | The F.B.I. | Jimmy Stewart Show | Sunday Night Movie |
| 9:00 | Sunday Night Movie | Bonanza | Sunday Night Movie |
| 9:30 | Sunday Night Movie | Bonanza | Cade's County |
| 10:00 | Sunday Night Movie | The Bold Ones | Cade's County |
| 10:30 | Sunday Night Movie | The Bold Ones | Local |

Monday

| 8:00 | Specials/Monday Night Sports† | Laugh-In | Gunsmoke |
|---|---|---|---|
| 8:30 | Specials/Monday Night Sports† | Laugh-In | Gunsmoke |
| 9:00 | Monday Night Movie | Monday Night Movie | Here's Lucy |
| 9:30 | Monday Night Movie | Monday Night Movie | Doris Day Show |
| 10:00 | Monday Night Movie | Monday Night Movie | Sonny & Cher† (12/27/71) |
| 10:30 | Monday Night Movie | Monday Night Movie | Sonny & Cher† |

Tuesday

| 7:30 | The Mod Squad | Search for the Nile†* (1/25/72) | Glen Campbell Show |
|---|---|---|---|
| 8:00 | The Mod Squad | Search for the Nile†* | Glen Campbell Show |
| 8:30 | Movie of the Week | Specials | Hawaii Five-O |
| 9:00 | Movie of the Week | Specials | Hawaii Five-O |
| 9:30 | Movie of the Week | Nichols | Cannon |
| 10:00 | Marcus Welby, M.D. | Nichols | Cannon |
| 10:30 | Marcus Welby, M.D. | Local | Local |

Wednesday

| 8:00 | Courtship of Eddie's Father | Adam-12 | Carol Burnett Show |
|---|---|---|---|
| 8:30 | ABC Comedy Hour† (1/12/72) | NBC Mystery Movie | Carol Burnett Show |
| 9:00 | ABC Comedy Hour† | NBC Mystery Movie | Medical Center |
| 9:30 | Persuaders | NBC Mystery Movie | Medical Center |
| 10:00 | Persuaders | Night Gallery | Mannix |
| 10:30 | Local | Night Gallery | Mannix |

Thursday

| 8:00 | Alias Smith and Jones | The Flip Wilson Show | Me and the Chimp† |
|---|---|---|---|
| 8:30 | Alias Smith and Jones | The Flip Wilson Show | My Three Sons |
| 9:00 | Longstreet | Ironside | Thursday Night Movie |
| 9:30 | Longstreet | Ironside | Thursday Night Movie |
| 10:00 | Owen Marshall | Dean Martin Show | Thursday Night Movie |
| 10:30 | Owen Marshall | Dean Martin Show | Thursday Night Movie |

|        | ABC | NBC | CBS |
|--------|-----|-----|-----|

**Friday**

|        | ABC | NBC | CBS |
|--------|-----|-----|-----|
| 8:00  | Brady Bunch | Sanford and Son† (1/14/72) | O'Hara, U.S. Treasury |
| 8:30  | Partridge Family | Friday Night Movie | O'Hara, U.S. Treasury |
| 9:00  | Room 222 | Friday Night Movie | Friday Night Movie |
| 9:30  | The Odd Couple | Friday Night Movie | Friday Night Movie |
| 10:00 | Love, American Style | Friday Night Movie | Friday Night Movie |
| 10:30 | Love, American Style | Local | Friday Night Movie |

## 1972-1973 SEASON

**Saturday**

|        | ABC | NBC | CBS |
|--------|-----|-----|-----|
| 8:00  | Alias Smith and Jones (9/23)/ Kung Fu†* (10/14) | Emergency! (9/16) | All in the Family (9/16) |
| 8:30  | Alias Smith and Jones/Kung Fu†* | Emergency! | Bridget Loves Bernie† (9/16) |
| 9:00  | Streets of San Francisco†* (9/16) | Saturday Night Movie (9/16) | Mary Tyler Moore (9/16) |
| 9:30  | Streets of San Francisco†* | Saturday Night Movie | Bob Newhart Show† (9/16) |
| 10:00 | Sixth Sense* (9/16) | Saturday Night Movie | Mission: Impossible* (9/16) |
| 10:30 | Sixth Sense* | Saturday Night Movie | Mission: Impossible* |

**Sunday**

|        | ABC | NBC | CBS |
|--------|-----|-----|-----|
| 7:30  | Local | Walt Disney* (9/17) | Anna and the King† (9/17) |
| 8:00  | The F.B.I.* (9/17) | Walt Disney* | M.A.S.H.† (9/17) |
| 8:30  | The F.B.I.* | NBC Sunday Mystery Movie* (9/17) | Sandy Duncan Show (9/17) |
| 9:00  | Sunday Night Movie (9/17) | NBC Mystery Movie* | Dick Van Dyke Show (9/17) |
| 9:30  | Sunday Night Movie | NBC Mystery Movie* | Mannix* (9/17) |
| 10:00 | Sunday Night Movie | Night Gallery* (9/24) | Mannix* |
| 10:30 | Sunday Night Movie | Local | Local |

**Monday**

|        | ABC | NBC | CBS |
|--------|-----|-----|-----|
| 8:00  | The Rookies†* (9/11) | Laugh-In (9/11) | Gunsmoke (9/11) |
| 8:30  | The Rookies†* | Laugh-In | Gunsmoke |
| 9:00  | NFL Football (9/25)/Monday Night Movie | Monday Night Movie (9/11) | Here's Lucy (9/11) |
| 9:30  | NFL Football/Monday Night Movie | Monday Night Movie | Doris Day Show (9/11) |
| 10:00 | NFL Football/Monday Night Movie | Monday Night Movie | Bill Cosby Show† (9/11) |
| 10:30 | NFL Football/Monday Night Movie | Monday Night Movie | Bill Cosby Show† |

| | ABC | NBC | CBS |
|---|---|---|---|
| **Tuesday** | | | |
| 8:00 | Temperature's Rising† (9/12) | Bonanza* (9/12) | Maude† (9/12) |
| 8:30 | Movie of the Week (9/12) | Bonanza* | Hawaii Five-O* (9/12) |
| 9:00 | Movie of the Week | The Bold Ones* (9/19) | Hawaii Five-O* |
| 9:30 | Movie of the Week | The Bold Ones* | Tuesday Night Movie (9/12) |
| 10:00 | Marcus Welby, M.D.* (9/12) | NBC Reports/ America/First Tuesday (9/19) | Tuesday Night Movie |
| 10:30 | Marcus Welby, M.D.* | NBC Reports/ America/First Tuesday | Tuesday Night Movie |
| | | | |
| **Wednesday** | | | |
| 8:00 | Paul Lynde Show† (9/13) | Adam-12 (9/13) | Carol Burnett Show (9/13) |
| 8:30 | Movie of the Week (9/13) | NBC Wednesday Mystery Movie†* (9/13) | Carol Burnett Show |
| 9:00 | Movie of the Week | NBC Wednesday Mystery Movie†* | Medical Center* (9/13) |
| 9:30 | Movie of the Week | NBC Wednesday Mystery Movie†* | Medical Center* |
| 10:00 | Julie Andrews Hour† (9/13) | Search†* (9/13) | Cannon* (9/13) |
| 10:30 | Julie Andrews Hour† | Search†* | Cannon* |
| | | | |
| **Thursday** | | | |
| 8:00 | Mod Squad* (9/14) | Flip Wilson Show (9/14) | The Waltons†* (9/14) |
| 8:30 | Mod Squad* | Flip Wilson Show | The Waltons†* |
| 9:00 | The Men†* (9/21) | Ironside* (9/14) | Thursday Night Movie (9/14) |
| 9:30 | The Men†* | Ironside* | Thursday Night Movie |
| 10:00 | Owen Marshall, Counselor at Law* (9/14) | Dean Martin Show (9/14) | Thursday Night Movie |
| 10:30 | Owen Marshall, Counselor at Law* | Dean Martin Show | Thursday Night Movie |
| | | | |
| **Friday** | | | |
| 8:00 | Brady Bunch (9/22) | Sanford and Son (9/15) | Sonny & Cher (9/15) |
| 8:30 | Partridge Family (9/15) | Little People† (9/15) | Sonny & Cher |
| 9:00 | Room 222 (9/15) | Ghost Story†* (9/15) | Friday Night Movie (9/15) |
| 9:30 | The Odd Couple (9/15) | Ghost Story†* | Friday Night Movie |
| 10:00 | Love, American Style | Banyon†* (9/15) | Friday Night Movie |
| 10:30 | Love, American Style | Banyon†* | Friday Night Movie |

1972-1973 MIDSEASON

| | ABC | NBC | CBS |
|---|---|---|---|
| **Saturday** | | | |
| 8:00 | Here We Go Again† (1/20/73) | Emergency! | All in the Family |
| 8:30 | A Touch of Grace† (1/20/73) | Emergency! | Bridget Loves Bernie |
| 9:00 | Julie Andrews Show | Saturday Night Movie | Mary Tyler Moore Show |
| 9:30 | Julie Andrews Show | Saturday Night Movie | Bob Newhart Show |
| 10:00 | The Men | Saturday Night Movie | Carol Burnett Show |
| 10:30 | The Men | Saturday Night Movie | Carol Burnett Show |
| **Sunday** | | | |
| 7:30 | Local | Walt Disney | Dick Van Dyke Show |
| 8:00 | The F.B.I. | Walt Disney | M*A*S*H |
| 8:30 | The F.B.I. | NBC Mystery Movie | Mannix |
| 9:00 | Sunday Night Movie | NBC Mystery Movie | Mannix |
| 9:30 | Sunday Night Movie | NBC Mystery Movie | Barnaby Jones†* (1/28/73) |
| 10:00 | Sunday Night Movie | NBC Mystery Movie/ Local | Barnaby Jones†* |
| 10:30 | Sunday Night Movie | Local | Local |
| **Monday** | | | |
| 8:00 | The Rookies | Laugh-In | Gunsmoke |
| 8:30 | The Rookies | Laugh-In | Gunsmoke |
| 9:00 | Monday Night Movie | Monday Night Movie | Here's Lucy |
| 9:30 | Monday Night Movie | Monday Night Movie | Doris Day Show |
| 10:00 | Monday Night Movie | Monday Night Movie | Bill Cosby Show |
| 10:30 | Monday Night Movie | Monday Night Movie | Bill Cosby Show |
| **Tuesday** | | | |
| 8:00 | Temperature's Rising | Tuesday Night Movie† (1/30/73) | Maude |
| 8:30 | Movie of the Week | Tuesday Night Movie† | Hawaii Five-O |
| 9:00 | Movie of the Week | Tuesday Night Movie† | Hawaii Five-O |
| 9:30 | Movie of the Week | Tuesday Night Movie† | Tuesday Night Movie |
| 10:00 | Marcus Welby, M.D. | NBC Reports | Tuesday Night Movie |
| 10:30 | Marcus Welby, M.D. | NBC Reports | Tuesday Night Movie |
| **Wednesday** | | | |
| 8:00 | Paul Lynde Show | Adam-12 | Sonny & Cher |
| 8:30 | Movie of the Week | NBC Mystery Movie | Sonny & Cher |
| 9:00 | Movie of the Week | NBC Mystery Movie | Medical Center |
| 9:30 | Movie of the Week | NBC Mystery Movie | Medical Center |
| 10:00 | Owen Marshall, Counselor at Law | Search | Cannon |
| 10:30 | Owen Marshall, Counselor at Law | Search | Cannon |
| **Thursday** | | | |
| 8:00 | Mod Squad | Flip Wilson Show | The Waltons |
| 8:30 | Mod Squad | Flip Wilson Show | The Waltons |
| 9:00 | Kung Fu | Ironside | Thursday Night Movie |

| | | ABC | NBC | CBS |
|---|---|---|---|---|
| | 9:30 | Kung Fu | Ironside | Thursday Night Movie |
| | 10:00 | Streets of San Fran-cisco | Dean Martin Show | Thursday Night Movie |
| | 10:30 | Streets of San Fran-cisco | Dean Martin Show | Thursday Night Movie |

Friday

| 8:00 | Brady Bunch | Sanford and Son | Mission: Impossible |
|---|---|---|---|
| 8:30 | Partridge Family | Little People | Mission: Impossible |
| 9:00 | Room 222 | Circle of Fear | Friday Night Movie |
| 9:30 | The Odd Couple | Circle of Fear | Friday Night Movie |
| 10:00 | Love, American Style | Bobby Darin Show† (1/19/73) | Friday Night Movie |
| 10:30 | Love, American Style | Bobby Darin Show† | Friday Night Movie |

## 1973-1974 SEASON

Saturday

| 8:00 | Partridge Family (9/15) | Emergency! (9/22) | All in the Family (9/15) |
|---|---|---|---|
| 8:30 | ABC Suspense Movie† (9/15)/ Six Million Dollar Man†* (10/20) | Emergency! | M*A*S*H (9/15) |
| 9:00 | ABC Suspense Movie†/Six Mil-lion Dollar Man†* | Saturday Night Movie (9/15) | Mary Tyler Moore (9/15) |
| 9:30 | ABC Suspense Movie†/Six Mil-lion Dollar Man†* | Saturday Night Movie | Bob Newhart Show (9/15) |
| 10:00 | Griff†* (9/29) | Saturday Night Movie | Carol Burnett Show (9/15) |
| 10:30 | Griff†* | Saturday Night Movie | Carol Burnett Show |

Sunday

| 7:30 | The F.B.I.* (9/16) | Walt Disney* (9/16) | New Perry Mason†* (9/16) |
|---|---|---|---|
| 8:00 | The F.B.I.* | Walt Disney* | New Perry Mason†* |
| 8:30 | Sunday Night Movie (9/16) | NBC Mystery Movie* (9/23) | Mannix* (9/16) |
| 9:00 | Sunday Night Movie | NBC Mystery Movie* | Mannix* |
| 9:30 | Sunday Night Movie | NBC Mystery Movie* | Barnaby Jones* (9/16) |
| 10:00 | Sunday Night Movie | NBC Mystery Movie* | Barnaby Jones* |
| 10:30 | Local | Local | Local |

Monday

| 8:00 | Rookies* (9/10) | Lotsa Luck!† (9/10) | Gunsmoke (9/10) |
|---|---|---|---|
| 8:30 | Rookies* | Diana† (9/10) | Gunsmoke |
| 9:00 | NFL Football (9/24)/Monday Night Movie | Monday Night Movie (9/10) | Here's Lucy (9/16) |
| 9:30 | NFL Football/Mon-day Night Movie | Monday Night Movie | Dick Van Dyke Show (9/10) |

|  | ABC | NBC | CBS |
|---|---|---|---|
| 10:00 | NFL Football/Monday Night Movie | Monday Night Movie | Medical Center* (9/10) |
| 10:30 | NFL Football/Monday Night Movie | Monday Night Movie | Medical Center* |

**Tuesday**

|  | ABC | NBC | CBS |
|---|---|---|---|
| 8:00 | Temperature's Rising (9/18) | Chase†* (9/11) | Maude (9/11) |
| 8:30 | Movie of the Week (9/11) | Chase†* | Hawaii Five-O* (9/11) |
| 9:00 | Movie of the Week | The Magician†* (10/2) | Hawaii Five-O* |
| 9:30 | Movie of the Week | The Magician†* | Tuesday Night Movie (9/11)/Hawkins†* (10/2)/Shaft†* (10/9) |
| 10:00 | Marcus Welby, M.D.* (9/11) | Police Story†* (10/2) | Tuesday Night Movie/Hawkins†*/Shaft†* |
| 10:30 | Marcus Welby, M.D.* | Police Story†* | Tuesday Night Movie/Hawkins†*/Shaft†* |

**Wednesday**

|  | ABC | NBC | CBS |
|---|---|---|---|
| 8:00 | Bob & Carol & Ted & Alice† (9/26) | Adam-12 (9/12) | Sonny & Cher (9/12) |
| 8:30 | Movie of the Week (9/12) | NBC Mystery Movie* (10/3) | Sonny & Cher |
| 9:00 | Movie of the Week | NBC Mystery Movie* | Cannon* (9/12) |
| 9:30 | Movie of the Week | NBC Mystery Movie* | Cannon* |
| 10:00 | Owen Marshall* (9/12)/Doc Elliott†* (10/10) | Love Story†* (10/3) | Kojak†* (10/24) |
| 10:30 | Owen Marshall*/Doc Elliott†* | Love Story†* | Kojak†* |

**Thursday**

|  | ABC | NBC | CBS |
|---|---|---|---|
| 8:00 | Toma†* (10/4) | Flip Wilson Show (9/20) | The Waltons* (9/13) |
| 8:30 | Toma†* | Flip Wilson Show | The Waltons* |
| 9:00 | Kung Fu* (9/27) | Ironside* (9/13) | Thursday Night Movie (9/13) |
| 9:30 | Kung Fu* | Ironside* | Thursday Night Movie |
| 10:00 | Streets of San Francisco* (9/13) | NBC Follies† (9/13) | Thursday Night Movie |
| 10:30 | Streets of San Francisco* | NBC Follies† | Thursday Night Movie |

**Friday**

|  | ABC | NBC | CBS |
|---|---|---|---|
| 8:00 | Brady Bunch (9/14) | Sanford and Son (9/14) | Calucci's Department† (9/14) |
| 8:30 | The Odd Couple (9/14) | Girl with Something Extra† (9/14) | Roll Out!† (10/5) |
| 9:00 | Room 222 (9/14) | Needles and Pins† (9/21) | Friday Night Movie (9/14) |
| 9:30 | Adam's Rib† (9/14) | Brian Keith Show (9/21) | Friday Night Movie |

|  | ABC | NBC | CBS |
|---|---|---|---|
| 10:00 | Love, American Style (9/14) | Dean Martin Show (9/14) | Friday Night Movie |
| 10:30 | Love, American Style | Dean Martin Show | Friday Night Movie |

## 1973-1974 MIDSEASON

### Saturday

|  | ABC | NBC | CBS |
|---|---|---|---|
| 8:00 | Partridge Family | Emergency! | All in the Family |
| 8:30 | Suspense Movie / Six Million Dollar Man | Emergency! | M*A*S*H |
| 9:00 | Suspense Movie / Six Million Dollar Man | Saturday Night Movie | Mary Tyler Moore |
| 9:30 | Suspense Movie / Six Million Dollar Man | Saturday Night Movie | Bob Newhart Show |
| 10:00 | Owen Marshall | Saturday Night Movie | Carol Burnett Show |
| 10:30 | Owen Marshall | Saturday Night Movie | Carol Burnett Show |

### Sunday

|  | ABC | NBC | CBS |
|---|---|---|---|
| 7:30 | The F. B. I. | Walt Disney | Apple's Way†* (2/10/74) |
| 8:00 | The F. B. I. | Walt Disney | Apple's Way†* |
| 8:30 | Sunday Night Movie | NBC Mystery Movie | Mannix |
| 9:00 | Sunday Night Movie | NBC Mystery Movie | Mannix |
| 9:30 | Sunday Night Movie | NBC Mystery Movie | Barnaby Jones |
| 10:00 | Sunday Night Movie | NBC Mystery Movie | Barnaby Jones |
| 10:30 | Local | Local | Local |

### Monday

|  | ABC | NBC | CBS |
|---|---|---|---|
| 8:00 | Rookies | Magician | Gunsmoke |
| 8:30 | Rookies | Magician | Gunsmoke |
| 9:00 | Monday Night Movie | Monday Night Movie | Here's Lucy |
| 9:30 | Monday Night Movie | Monday Night Movie | Dick Van Dyke Show |
| 10:00 | Monday Night Movie | Monday Night Movie | Medical Center |
| 10:30 | Monday Night Movie | Monday Night Movie | Medical Center |

### Tuesday

|  | ABC | NBC | CBS |
|---|---|---|---|
| 8:00 | Happy Days† (1/15/74) | Adam-12 | Maude |
| 8:30 | Movie of the Week | NBC Mystery Movie | Hawaii Five-O |
| 9:00 | Movie of the Week | NBC Mystery Movie | Hawaii Five-O |
| 9:30 | Movie of the Week | NBC Mystery Movie | Tuesday Night Movie / Hawkins /Shaft |
| 10:00 | Marcus Welby | Police Story | Tuesday Night Movie / Hawkins /Shaft |
| 10:30 | Marcus Welby | Police Story | Tuesday Night Movie / Hawkins /Shaft |

### Wednesday

|  | ABC | NBC | CBS |
|---|---|---|---|
| 8:00 | The Cowboys† (1/16/74) | Chase | Sonny & Cher |

|  | ABC | NBC | CBS |
|---|---|---|---|
| 8:30 | Movie of the Week | Chase | Sonny & Cher |
| 9:00 | Movie of the Week | Wednesday Night Movie | Cannon |
| 9:30 | Movie of the Week | Wednesday Night Movie | Cannon |
| 10:00 | Doc Elliott | Wednesday Night Movie | Kojak |
| 10:30 | Doc Elliott | Wednesday Night Movie | Kojak |

**Thursday**

|  | ABC | NBC | CBS |
|---|---|---|---|
| 8:00 | Chopper One† (1/17/74) | Specials | The Waltons |
| 8:30 | Firehouse† (1/17/74) | Specials | The Waltons |
| 9:00 | Kung Fu | Ironside | Thursday Night Movie |
| 9:30 | Kung Fu | Ironside | Thursday Night Movie |
| 10:00 | Streets of San Francisco | Music Country, U.S.A. † (1/17/74) | Thursday Night Movie |
| 10:30 | Streets of San Francisco | Music Country, U.S.A. † | Thursday Night Movie |

**Friday**

|  | ABC | NBC | CBS |
|---|---|---|---|
| 8:00 | Brady Bunch | Sanford and Son | Dirty Sally† (1/11/74) |
| 8:30 | Six Million Dollar Man | Lotsa Luck! | Good Times† (2/8/74) |
| 9:00 | Six Million Dollar Man | Girl with Something Extra | Friday Night Movie |
| 9:30 | Six Million Dollar Man | Brian Keith Show | Friday Night Movie |
| 10:00 | Toma | Dean Martin Show | Friday Night Movie |
| 10:30 | Toma | Dean Martin Show | Friday Night Movie |

## 1974-1975 SEASON

**Saturday**

|  | ABC | NBC | CBS |
|---|---|---|---|
| 8:00 | The New Land†* (9/14) | Emergency! (9/14) | All in the Family (9/14) |
| 8:30 | The New Land†* | Emergency! | Friends and Lovers† (9/14) |
| 9:00 | Kung Fu* (9/14) | Saturday Night Movie (9/14) | Mary Tyler Moore (9/14) |
| 9:30 | Kung Fu* | Saturday Night Movie | Bob Newhart Show (9/14) |
| 10:00 | Nakia†* (9/21) | Saturday Night Movie | Carol Burnett Show (9/14) |
| 10:30 | Nakia†* | Saturday Night Movie | Carol Burnett Show |

**Sunday**

|  | ABC | NBC | CBS |
|---|---|---|---|
| 7:30 | Local | Walt Disney* (9/15) | Apple's Way* (9/15) |
| 8:00 | Sonny Comedy Revue (9/22) | Walt Disney* | Apple's Way* |
| 8:30 | Sonny Comedy Revue | NBC Mystery Movie* (9/15) | Kojak* (9/15) |

|  | ABC | NBC | CBS |
|---|---|---|---|
| 9:00 | Sunday Night Movie (9/22) | NBC Mystery Movie* | Kojak* |
| 9:30 | Sunday Night Movie | NBC Mystery Movie* | Mannix* (9/15) |
| 10:00 | Sunday Night Movie | NBC Mystery Movie* | Mannix* |
| 10:30 | Sunday Night Movie | Local | Local |

**Monday**

|  | ABC | NBC | CBS |
|---|---|---|---|
| 8:00 | Rookies* (9/9) | Born Free†* (9/9) | Gunsmoke (9/9) |
| 8:30 | Rookies* | Born Free†* | Gunsmoke |
| 9:00 | NFL Football/Monday Night Movie | Monday Night Movie (9/9) | Maude (9/9) |
| 9:30 | NFL Football/Monday Night Movie | Monday Night Movie | Rhoda† (9/9) |
| 10:00 | NFL Football/Monday Night Movie | Monday Night Movie | Medical Center* (9/9) |
| 10:30 | NFL Football/Monday Night Movie | Monday Night Movie | Medical Center* |

**Tuesday**

|  | ABC | NBC | CBS |
|---|---|---|---|
| 8:00 | Happy Days (9/10) | Adam-12 (9/10) | Good Times (9/10) |
| 8:30 | Movie of the Week (9/10) | Tuesday Night Movie (9/10) | M*A*S*H (9/10) |
| 9:00 | Movie of the Week | Tuesday Night Movie | Hawaii Five-O* (9/10) |
| 9:30 | Movie of the Week | Tuesday Night Movie | Hawaii Five-O* |
| 10:00 | Marcus Welby* (9/10) | Police Story* (9/10) | Barnaby Jones* (9/10) |
| 10:30 | Marcus Welby* | Police Story* | Barnaby Jones* |

**Wednesday**

|  | ABC | NBC | CBS |
|---|---|---|---|
| 8:00 | That's My Mama† (9/4) | Little House on the Prairie†* (9/11) | Sons and Daughters†* (9/11) |
| 8:30 | Movie of the Week (9/11) | Little House on the Prairie†* | Sons and Daughters†* |
| 9:00 | Movie of the Week | Lucas Tanner†* (9/11) | Cannon* (9/11) |
| 9:30 | Movie of the Week | Lucas Tanner†* | Cannon* |
| 10:00 | Get Christie Love!†* (9/11) | Petrocelli†* (9/11) | Manhunters†* (9/11) |
| 10:30 | Get Christie Love!†* | Petrocelli†* | Manhunters†* |

**Thursday**

|  | ABC | NBC | CBS |
|---|---|---|---|
| 8:00 | Odd Couple (9/12) | Sierra† (9/12) | The Waltons* (9/12) |
| 8:30 | Paper Moon† (9/12) | Sierra† | The Waltons* |
| 9:00 | Streets of San Francisco* (9/12) | Ironside* (9/12) | Thursday Night Movie (9/19) |
| 9:30 | Streets of San Francisco* | Ironside* | Thursday Night Movie |
| 10:00 | Harry O†* (9/12) | Movin' On†* (9/12) | Thursday Night Movie |
| 10:30 | Harry O†* | Movin' On†* | Thursday Night Movie |

**Friday**

|  | ABC | NBC | CBS |
|---|---|---|---|
| 8:00 | Kodiak† (9/13) | Sanford and Son (9/13) | Planet of the Apes†* (9/13) |
| 8:30 | Six Million Dollar Man* (9/13) | Chico and the Man† (9/13) | Planet of the Apes†* |

| | ABC | NBC | CBS |
|---|---|---|---|
| 9:00 | Six Million Dollar Man* | Rockford Files†* (9/13) | Friday Night Movie (9/13) |
| 9:30 | Texas Wheelers† (9/13) | Rockford Files†* | Friday Night Movie |
| 10:00 | Night Stalker†* (9/13) | Police Woman†* (9/13) | Friday Night Movie |
| 10:30 | Night Stalker†* | Police Woman†* | Friday Night Movie |

## 1974-1975 MIDSEASON

### Saturday

| | ABC | NBC | CBS |
|---|---|---|---|
| 8:00 | Kung Fu | Emergency! | All in the Family |
| 8:30 | Kung Fu | Emergency! | The Jeffersons† (1/18/75) |
| 9:00 | Saturday Night Movie | Saturday Night Movie | Mary Tyler Moore |
| 9:30 | Saturday Night Movie | Saturday Night Movie | Bob Newhart Show |
| 10:00 | Saturday Night Movie | Saturday Night Movie | Carol Burnett Show |
| 10:30 | Saturday Night Movie | Saturday Night Movie | Carol Burnett Show |

### Sunday

| | ABC | NBC | CBS |
|---|---|---|---|
| 7:30 | Six Million Dollar Man | Walt Disney | Cher† (2/16/75) |
| 8:00 | Six Million Dollar Man | Walt Disney | Cher† |
| 8:30 | Sunday Night Movie | NBC Mystery Movie | Kojak |
| 9:00 | Sunday Night Movie | NBC Mystery Movie | Kojak |
| 9:30 | Sunday Night Movie | NBC Mystery Movie | Mannix |
| 10:00 | Sunday Night Movie | NBC Mystery Movie | Mannix |
| 10:30 | Local | Local | Local |

### Monday

| | ABC | NBC | CBS |
|---|---|---|---|
| 8:00 | The Rookies | Smothers Brothers† (1/20/75) | Gunsmoke |
| 8:30 | The Rookies | Smothers Brothers† | Gunsmoke |
| 9:00 | Monday Night Movie | Monday Night Movie | Maude |
| 9:30 | Monday Night Movie | Monday Night Movie | Rhoda |
| 10:00 | Monday Night Movie | Monday Night Movie | Medical Center |
| 10:30 | Monday Night Movie | Monday Night Movie | Medical Center |

### Tuesday

| | ABC | NBC | CBS |
|---|---|---|---|
| 8:00 | Happy Days | Adam-12 | Good Times |
| 8:30 | Movie of the Week | Tuesday Night Movie | M*A*S*H |
| 9:00 | Movie of the Week | Tuesday Night Movie | Hawaii Five-O |
| 9:30 | Movie of the Week | Tuesday Night Movie | Hawaii Five-O |
| 10:00 | Marcus Welby | Police Story | Barnaby Jones |
| 10:30 | Marcus Welby | Police Story | Barnaby Jones |

### Wednesday

| | ABC | NBC | CBS |
|---|---|---|---|
| 8:00 | That's My Mama | Little House on the Prairie | Tony Orlando and Dawn† (1/15/75) |

| | ABC | NBC | CBS |
|---|---|---|---|
| 8:30 | Movie of the Week | Little House on the Prairie | Tony Orlando and Dawn† |
| 9:00 | Movie of the Week | Lucas Tanner | Cannon |
| 9:30 | Movie of the Week | Lucas Tanner | Cannon |
| 10:00 | Get Christie Love! | Petrocelli | Manhunter |
| 10:30 | Get Christie Love! | Petrocelli | Manhunter |

Thursday

| | ABC | NBC | CBS |
|---|---|---|---|
| 8:00 | Barney Miller† (1/23/75) | Mac Davis† (1/16/75) | The Waltons |
| 8:30 | Karen† (1/30/75) | Mac Davis† | The Waltons |
| 9:00 | Streets of San Francisco | Archer†* (1/30/75) | Thursday Night Movie |
| 9:30 | Streets of San Francisco | Archer†* | Thursday Night Movie |
| 10:00 | Harry O | Movin' On | Thursday Night Movie |
| 10:30 | Harry O | Movin' On | Thursday Night Movie |

Friday

| | ABC | NBC | CBS |
|---|---|---|---|
| 8:00 | Night Stalker | Sanford and Son | Khan!† (2/7/75) |
| 8:30 | Night Stalker | Chico and the Man | Khan!† |
| 9:00 | Hot L Baltimore† (1/24/75) | Rockford Files | Friday Night Movie |
| 9:30 | Odd Couple | Rockford Files | Friday Night Movie |
| 10:00 | Baretta†* (1/17/75) | Police Woman | Friday Night Movie |
| 10:30 | Baretta†* | Police Woman | Friday Night Movie |

Summer Drama Series, 1975

Caribe†* (Monday, 2/17/75, 10:00-11:00 ABC)
The Law†* (Wednesday, 3/19/75, NBC)

# SECTION II

Television Drama Series Programming:
A Comprehensive Chronicle, 1959-1975

## SERIES COMMENCING PREVIOUS
## TO 1959

Note: This section contains those series beginning
prior to the 1959-1960 television season, but continuing through that season. Series are arranged in
chronological order, from the date of the first episode
chronicled--not necessarily their first episode.


## ALFRED HITCHCOCK PRESENTS

The master of suspense kept us enthralled for ten years with
these for the most part original dramas, the most distinguished
being those which Hitchcock himself directed. His knack for drawing fascinating characterizations from featured performers uplifts
such episodes as "Lamb to the Slaughter" (with the often-used theme
of the wife who, unyielding to requests for divorce, murders her
spouse) starring Barbara Bel Geddes, and "Arthur" with Laurence
Harvey.

An abundance of superior teleplays included the Cornell
Woolrich tale "Post Mortem," the three-part whodunit "I Killed the
Count" (the variation being that there are an excess of suspects),
Ray Bradbury's study of a fanatic puppeteer with "And So Died
Riabouchinska," a re-telling of the Lizzie Borden case in "The Old-
er Sister," the Ellery Queen mystery "Fog Closing In," John Col-
lier's "De Mortuis," and the Ambrose Bierce classic "An Occur-
rence at Owl Creek Bridge."

Beginning 1962, the dramas expanded to a full hour. Among
the best of these were John Collier's masterful adaptation of the
H. G. Wells story of a boy's satanic possession in "The Magic
Shop," James Bridges' adaptation of a Francis Didelot novel "The
Star Juror," Robert Bloch's "A Home Away from Home," and W. W.
Jacobs' classic "The Monkey's Paw." A stylish use of the camera
is the hallmark of two shockers: "Don't Look Behind You," in which
a maniacal Jeffrey Hunter stalks Vera Miles on a university campus,
and "An Unlocked Window," wherein the terrified are a group of
nurses (among them Dana Wynter) caring for an invalid.

The Regulars: Alfred Hitchcock, host.

The Episodes:

1. "Revenge" (10-2-55) Ralph Meeker, Vera Miles
2. "Premonition" (10-9-55) John Forsythe, Warren Stevens, George Macready, Cloris Leachman
3. "Triggers in Leash" (10-16-55) Gene Barry, Darren McGavin, Ellen Corby
4. "Don't Come Back Alive" (10-23-55) Sidney Blackmer
5. "Into Thin Air" (10-30-55) Patricia Hitchcock, Alan Napier, Mary Forbes, Geoffrey Tune, Gerry Gaylor
6. "Salvage" (11-6-55) Gene Barry, Donald Cook, Nancy Gates
7. "Breakdown" (11-13-55) Joseph Cotten, Raymond Bailey
8. "Our Cook's Treasure" (11-20-55) Beulah Bondi, Janet Ward, Everett Sloane
9. "The Long Shot" (11-27-55) John Williams, Peter Lawford, Gertrude Hoffman
10. "The Case of Mr. Pelham" (12-4-55) Tom Ewell
11. "Guilty Witness" (12-11-55) Judith Evelyn, Joe Mantell, Robert F. Simon, Kathleen Maguire
12. "Santa Claus and the 10th Avenue Kid" (12-18-55) Barry Fitzgerald
13. "The Cheney Vase" (12-25-55) Patricia Collinge, Carolyn Jones, Darren McGavin, George Macready
14. "A Bullet for Baldwin" (1-1-56) Sebastian Cabot, John Qualen
15. "The Big Switch" (1-8-56) George Mathews
16. "You Got to Have Luck" (1-15-56) John Cassavetes, Marisa Pavan
17. "The Older Sister" (1-22-56) Joan Lorring, Polly Rowles, Patricia Hitchcock, Carmen Mathews
18. "Shopping for Death" (1-29-56) Michael Ansara, Robert H. Harris, Jo Van Fleet, Mike Ross, John Qualen
19. "The Derelicts" (2-5-56) Robert Newton, Johnny Silver, Philip Reed, Peggy Knudsen
20. "And So Died Riabouchinska" (2-12-56) Claude Rains, Charles Bronson, Bill Haade, Lowell Gilmore, Charles Cantor, Claire Carleton
21. "Safe Conduct" (2-19-56) Jacques Bergerac, Claire Trevor, Werner Klemperer
22. "Place of Shadows" (2-26-56) Everett Sloane, Mark Damon
23. "Back for Christmas" (3-4-56) John Williams, Isobel Elsom
24. "The Perfect Murder" (3-11-56) Philip Coolidge, Hurd Hatfield, Mildred Natwick
25. "There Was an Old Woman" (3-18-56) Estelle Winwood, Norma Crane, Charles Bronson
26. "Whodunit" (3-25-56) John Williams
27. "Help Wanted" (4-1-56) Lorne Greene, John Qualen
28. "Portrait of Jocelyn" (4-8-56) John Baragrey, Nancy Gates, Philip Abbott
29. "The Orderly World of Mr. Appleby" (4-15-56) Robert H. Harris, Michael Ansara
30. "Never Again" (4-22-56) Phyllis Thaxter, Warren Stevens, Louise Albritton
31. "The Gentleman from America" (4-29-56) Biff McGuire

32. "The Baby-Sitter" (5-6-56) Thelma Ritter, Carmen Mathews, Michael Ansara
33. "The Belfry" (5-13-56) Patricia Hitchcock, Dabbs Greer, Jack Mullaney, Horst Ehrhardt
34. "The Hidden Thing" (5-20-56) Robert H. Harris, Judith Ames, Biff McGuire
35. "The Legacy" (5-27-56) Jacques Bergerac, Alan Hewitt, Enid Markey, Leora Dana
36. "Mink" (6-3-56) Ruth Hussey, Vinton Hayworth
37. "The Decoy" (6-10-56) Robert Horton, Cara Williams, Harry Lewis, David Orrick, Mary Jean Yamaji, Eileen Harley
38. "The Creeper" (6-17-56) Dick Foran, Constance Ford, Steve Brodie
39. "Momentum" (6-24-56) Joanne Woodward, Skip Homeier

Second Season

40. "Wet Saturday" (9-30-56) Sir Cedric Hardwicke
41. "Fog Closing In" (10-7-56) Phyllis Thaxter, George Grizzard, Paul Langton
42. "De Mortuis" (10-14-56) Cara Williams, Robert Emhardt
43. "Kill with Kindness" (10-21-56) Hume Cronyn, Carmen Mathews, James Gleason
44. "None Are So Blind" (10-28-56) Mildred Dunnock, Hurd Hatfield
45. "Toby" (11-4-56) Robert H. Harris, Jessica Tandy
46. "Alibi Me" (11-11-56) Lee Philips
47. "Conversation Over a Corpse" (11-18-56) Ray Collins, Carmen Mathews, Dorothy Stickney, Ted Stanhope
48. "Crack of Doom" (11-25-56) Robert Horton
49. "Jonathan" (12-2-56) Corey Allen, Douglas Kennedy
50. "A Better Bargain" (12-9-56) Robert Middleton, Henry Silva
51. "The Rose Garden" (12-16-56) Patricia Collinge, John Williams, Evelyn Varden, Ralph Peters
52. "Mr. Blanchard's Secret" (12-23-56) Mary Scott, Dayton Lummis, Meg Mundy, Robert Horn
53. "John Brown's Body" (12-30-56) Leora Dana, Russell Collins, Hugh Marlowe
54. "Crackpot" (1-6-57) Biff McGuire, Robert Emhardt, Michael Fox, Mary Scott
55. "Nightmare in 4-D" (1-13-57) Barbara Baxley, Henry Jones
56. "My Brother Richard" (1-20-57) Inger Stevens, Royal Dano, Harry Townes, Ray Teal, Bobby Ellis
57. "Manacled" (1-27-57) Gary Merrill, William Redfield
58. "Bottle of Wine" (2-3-57) Robert Horton, Herbert Marshall
59. "Malice Domestic" (2-10-57) Ralph Meeker, Phyllis Thaxter, Vinton Hayworth, Ralph Clanton
60. "Number 22" (2-17-57) Rip Torn, Russell Collins, James Nolan
61. "The End of Indian Summer" (2-24-57) Gladys Cooper, Steve Forrest, James Gleason, Kathleen Maguire, Philip Coolidge
62. "One for the Road" (3-3-57) John Baragrey, Georgann Johnson, Louise Platt

63. "The Cream of the Jest" (3-10-57) Claude Rains, James
    Gregory, Paul Picerni
64. "I Killed the Count" [Part I] (3-17-57) John Williams,
    Charles Davis, John Hoyt, Alan Napier, Charles Cooper,
    Rosemary Harris
65. "I Killed the Count" [Part II] (3-24-57) as above
66. "I Killed the Count" [Part III] (3-31-57) as above
67. "One More Mile to Go" (4-7-57) David Wayne
68. "Vicious Circle" (4-14-57) George Macready, Dick York
69. "The Three Dreams of Mr. Findlater" (4-21-57) Barbara
    Baxley, Isobel Elsom, John Williams, Arthur Gould-Porter,
    Walter Kingsford
70. "The Night the World Ended" (4-28-57) Russell Collins,
    Edith Barrett
71. "The Hands of Mr. Ottermole" (5-5-57) Theodore Bikel
72. "A Man Greatly Beloved" (5-12-57) Sir Cedric Hardwicke,
    Hugh Marlowe, Evelyn Rudie
73. "Martha Mason, Movie Star" (5-19-57) Judith Evelyn,
    Robert Emhardt
74. "The West Warlock Time Capsule" (5-26-57) Henry Jones,
    Mildred Dunnock
75. "Father and Son" (6-2-57) Edmund Gwenn, Frederic Wor-
    lock
76. "The Indestructible Mr. Weems" (6-9-57) Russell Collins
77. "A Little Sleep" (6-16-57) Vic Morrow, Barbara Cook
78. "The Dangerous People" (6-23-57) Robert H. Harris, Al-
    bert Salmi, Harry Tyler, Ken Clark, David Armstrong

Third Season

79. "The Glass Eye" (10-6-57) William Shatner, Tom Conway,
    Rosemary Harris, Jessica Tandy
80. "The Mail Order Prophet" (10-13-57) Jack Klugman, E. G.
    Marshall, Judson Pratt
81. "The Perfect Crime" (10-20-57) Vincent Price, James
    Gregory, Mark Dana, Marianne Stewart, Gavin Gordon
82. "Heart of Gold" (10-27-57) Mildred Dunnock, Nehemiah
    Persoff, Darryl Hickman, Edward Binns, Cheryl Callaway
83. "The Silent Witness" (11-3-57) Dolores Hart, Don Taylor
84. "Reward to Finder" (11-10-57) Oscar Homolka, Ann Hunter,
    Jo Van Fleet, Claude Akins
85. "Enough Rope for Two" (11-17-57) Jean Hagen, Steven Hill,
    Steve Brodie
86. "The Last Request" (11-24-57) Harry Guardino, Hugh Mar-
    lowe, Cara Williams
87. "The Young One" (12-1-57) Vince Edwards, Carol Lynley
88. "The Diplomatic Corpse" (12-8-57) Peter Lorre, George
    Peppard
89. "The Deadly" (12-15-57) Craig Stevens, Phyllis Thaxter
90. "Miss Paisley's Cat" (12-22-57) Dorothy Stickney, Harry
    Tyler
91. "Night of the Execution" (12-29-57) Pat Hingle
92. "The Percentage" (1-5-58) Carmen Mathews, Alex Nicol

93. "Together" (1-12-58) Joseph Cotten, Christine White
94. "Sylvia" (1-19-58) John McIntire, Ann Todd, Philip Reed
95. "The Motive" (1-26-58) Carl Betz, Skip Homeier, Carmen Phillips, William Redfield
96. "Miss Bracegirdle Does Her Duty" (2-2-58) Mildred Natwick, Tita Purdom, Gavin Muri
97. "The Equalizer" (2-9-58) Leif Erickson, Martin Balsam, Norma Crane
98. "On the Nose" (2-16-58) David Opatoshu, Karl Swenson, Jan Sterling
99. "Guest for Breakfast" (2-23-58) Scott McKay, Richard Sheppard, Joan Tetzel
100. "Return of the Hero" (3-2-58) Jacques Bergerac, Susan Kohner
101. "The Right Kind of House" (3-9-58) Jeanette Nolan
102. "Foghorn" (3-16-58) Michael Rennie, Barbara Bel Geddes, Bartlett Robinson
103. "Flight to the East" (3-23-58) Gary Merrill, Anthony George, Konstantin Shayne, Mel Welles, Patricia Colts
104. "Bull in a China Shop" (3-30-58) Dennis Morgan, Estelle Winwood, Elizabeth Patterson, Ellen Corby, Ida Moore
105. "The Disappearing Trick" (4-6-58) Robert Horton, Betsy Von Furstenberg
106. "Lamb to the Slaughter" (4-13-58) Barbara Bel Geddes, Allan Lane
107. "Fatal Figures" (4-20-58) John McGiver, Vivian Nathan, Ward Wood, Nesdon Booth
108. "Death Sentence" (4-27-58) James Best
109. "Festive Season" (5-4-58) Carmen Mathews, Richard Waring, Edmon Ryan
110. "Listen, Listen..." (5-11-58) Edgar Stehli, Adam Williams
111. "Post Mortem" (5-18-58) Steve Forrest, Joanna Moore
112. "The Crocodile Case" (5-25-58) Denholm Elliott, Hazel Court, Arthur Gould-Porter
113. "A Dip in the Pool" (6-1-58) Fay Wray, Keenan Wynn
114. "The Safe Place" (6-8-58) Robert H. Harris, Joanne Linville, Philip Pine, Wendell Holmes, Jerry Paris, Robert Carnes
115. "The Canary Sedan" (6-15-58) Jessica Tandy, Murray Matheson, Gavin Muir
116. "Impromptu Murder" (6-22-58) Hume Cronyn, Valerie Cossart, David Frankham, Doris Lloyd, Robert Douglas
117. "Little White Frock" (6-29-58) Julie Adams, Herbert Marshall, Tom Helmore, Bartlett Robinson, Jacqueline Mayo, Roy Dean

## Fourth Season

118. "Poison" (10-5-58) Wendell Corey
119. "Don't Interrupt" (10-12-58) Chill Wills, Peter Lazer, Cloris Leachman
120. "The Jokester" (10-19-58) Albert Salmi
121. "The Crooked Road" (10-26-58) Patricia Breslin, Richard

Kiley

122. "Two Million Dollar Defense" (11-2-58) Leslie Nielsen, Barry Sullivan, Lori March

123. "Design for Loving" (11-9-58) Barbara Baxley, Norman Lloyd, Marian Seldes

124. "Man with a Problem" (11-16-58) Gary Merrill, Mark Richman, Elizabeth Montgomery

125. "Safety for the Witness" (11-23-58) Art Carney, James Westerfield, Robert Bray

126. "Murder Me Twice" (12-1-58) Phyllis Thaxter, Tom Helmore, King Calder, Herbert Anderson, Robert Carson, Alan Marshall, Liz Carr

127. "Tea Time" (12-14-58) Marsha Hunt, Margaret Leighton

128. "And the Desert Shall Blossom" (12-21-58) Ben Johnson

129. "Mrs. Herman and Mrs. Fenimore" (12-28-58) Mary Astor, Doro Merande, Russell Collins

130. "Six People, No Music" (1-4-59) John McGiver, Peggy Cass, Howard Smith

131. "The Morning After" (1-11-59) Robert Alda, Dorothy Provine, Jeanette Nolan

132. "A Personal Matter" (1-18-59) Wayne Morris, Frank Silvera, Joe Maross

133. "Out There--Darkness" (1-25-59) Bette Davis, James Congdon, Frank Albertson

134. "Total Loss" (2-1-59) Ralph Meeker, Nancy Olson

135. "The Last Dark Step" (2-8-59) Robert Horton, Joyce Meadows, Fay Spain, David Carlile, Herb Ellis

136. "The Morning of the Bride" (2-15-59) Barbara Bel Geddes, Don Dubbins

137. "The Diamond Necklace" (2-22-59) Claude Rains, Betsy Von Furstenberg

138. "Relative Value" (3-1-59) Torin Thatcher, Tom Conway, Frederic Worlock, Denholm Elliott

139. "The Right Price" (3-8-59) Eddie Foy Jr.

140. "I'll Take Care of You" (3-15-59) Ralph Meeker, Russell Collins, Elizabeth Fraser

141. "The Avon Emeralds" (3-22-59) Roger Moore, Alan Napier, Hazel Court, Gertrude Flynn

142. "Kind Waitress" (3-29-59) Olive Deering

143. "Cheap Is Cheap" (4-5-59) Dennis Day

144. "The Waxwork" (4-12-59) Barry Nelson, Everett Sloane

145. "The Impossible Dream" (4-19-59) Mary Astor, Franchot Tone, Carmen Mathews, Irene Windust

146. "Banquo's Chair" (5-3-59) Reginald Gardiner, John Williams

147. "A Night with the Boys" (5-10-59) John Smith, Joyce Meadows, Sam Buffington

148. "Your Witness" (5-17-59) Brian Keith, Gordon Wynn

149. "Human Interest Story" (5-24-59) Arthur Hill, Steve McQueen

150. "The Dusty Drawer" (5-31-59) Dick York, Philip Coolidge, Wilton Graff

151. "A True Account" (6-7-59) Jocelyn Brando, Kent Smith,

Jane Greer
152. "Touche" (6-14-59) Paul Douglas, Dody Heath
153. "Invitation to an Accident" (6-21-59) Gary Merrill

## Fifth Season

154. "Arthur" (9-27-59) Laurence Harvey
155. "The Crystal Trench" (10-4-59) James Donald, Patricia
    Owens, Harold Dyrenforth
156. "Appointment at Eleven" (10-11-59) Sean McClory, Clint
    Kimbrough, Clu Gulager, Norma Crane, Amy Douglass,
    Michael J. Pollard
157. "Coyote Noon" (10-18-59) Macdonald Carey, Collin Wilcox
158. "No Pain" (10-25-59) Brian Keith, Joanna Moore, Yale
    Wexler
159. "Anniversary Gift" (11-1-59) Barbara Baxley, Harry Mor-
    gan, Michael J. Pollard
160. "Dry Run" (11-8-59) Robert Vaughn, Walter Matthau
161. "The Blessington Method" (11-15-59) Henry Jones, Dick
    York, Elizabeth Patterson
162. "Dead Weight" (11-22-59) Julie Adams, Joseph Cotten
163. "Special Delivery" (11-29-59) Michael Burns, Beatrice
    Straight, Cece Whitney, Steve Dunne, Frank Maxwell,
    Peter Lazer
164. "Road Hog" (12-6-59) Raymond Massey, Roscoe Ates,
    Robert Emhardt
165. "Specialty of the House" (12-13-59) Robert Morley
166. "An Occurrence at Owl Creek Bridge" (12-20-59) James
    Coburn, Ronald Howard, Juano Hernandez
167. "Graduation Class" (12-27-59) Gigi Perreau, Jocelyn
    Brando, Wendy Hiller, Robert H. Harris
168. "The Ikon of Elijah" (1-10-60) Oscar Homolka, Sam Jaffe
169. "The Cure" (1-24-60) Mark Richman, Nehemiah Persoff,
    Cara Williams
170. "Backward, Turn Backward" (1-31-60) Tom Tully, Phyllis
    Love, Alan Baxter
171. "Not the Running Type" (2-7-60) Paul Hartman
172. "The Day of the Bullet" (2-14-60) Biff Elliott, Dennis
    Patrick, John Craven, Barry Gordon, Glenn Walken
173. "Hitchhike" (2-21-60) John McIntire, Suzanne Pleshette,
    Robert Morse
174. "Across the Threshold" (2-28-60) Barbara Baxley, George
    Grizzard, Patricia Collinge
175. "Craig's Will" (3-6-60) Dick Van Dyke, Stella Stevens,
    Stephen Roberts, Paul Stewart, Harry Tyler
176. "Man from the South" (3-13-60) Peter Lorre, Neile Adams,
    Steve McQueen
177. "Mme. Mystery" (3-27-60) Audrey Totter, Joby Baker,
    Harp McGuire
178. "The Little Man Who Was There" (4-3-60) Arch Johnson,
    Norman Lloyd, R. G. Armstrong
179. "Mother, May I Go Out to Swim?" (4-10-60) William
    Shatner, Jessie Royce Landis, Gia Scala, Robert Carson

180. "The Cuckoo Clock" (4-17-60) Beatrice Straight
181. "Forty Detectives Later" (4-24-60) James Franciscus
182. "The Hero" (5-1-60) Oscar Homolka, Eric Portman
183. "Insomnia" (5-8-60) Dennis Weaver
184. "I Can Take Care of Myself" (5-15-60) Myron McCormick, Frankie Darro
185. "One Grave Too Many" (5-22-60) Jeremy Slate, Neile Adams
186. "Party Line" (5-29-60) Judy Canova
187. "Cell 227" (6-5-60) Brian Keith
188. "The Schartz-Metterklume Method" (6-12-60) Hermione Gingold, Elspeth March
189. "Letter of Credit" (6-19-60) Bob Sweeney, Cyril Delevanti, Robert Bray
190. "Escape to Sonoita" (6-26-60) Burt Reynolds, James Bell, Murray Hamilton

Sixth Season

191. "Mrs. Bixby and Colonel's Cat" (9-27-60) Audrey Meadows, Les Tremayne
192. "The Doubtful Doctor" (10-4-60) Dick York, Gena Rowlands, John Zaremba, Michael Burns
193. "Very Moral Theft" (10-11-60) Betty Field, Walter Matthau
194. "The Contest for Aaron Gold" (10-18-60) Barry Gordon, Sydney Pollack, Frank Maxwell, William Thourlby
195. "The Five Forty-Eight" (10-25-60) Zachary Scott, Phyllis Thaxter, Irene Windust
196. "Pen Pal" (11-1-60) Clu Gulager, Katherine Squire
197. "Outlaw in Town" (11-15-60) Constance Ford, Ricardo Montalban
198. "Oh, Youth and Beauty" (11-22-60) Patricia Breslin, David Lewis, Gary Merrill
199. "The Money" (11-29-60) Robert Loggia, Doris Dowling
200. "Sybilla" (12-6-60) Barbara Bel Geddes, Alexander Scourby
201. "The Man with Two Faces" (12-13-60) Steve Dunne, Bethel Leslie, Spring Byington
202. "The Baby Blue Expression" (12-20-60) Sarah Marshall, Peter Walker, Liz Carr, Leonard Weinrib, Richard Gaines, Chet Stratton, Edith Angold
203. "The Man Who Found the Money" (12-27-60) Arthur Hill, Rod Cameron, R. G. Armstrong
204. "The Changing Heart" (1-3-61) Abraham Sofaer, Anne Helm, Robert Sampson, Nicholas Pryor
205. "Summer Shade" (1-10-61) Julie Adams, James Franciscus, Susan Gordon, Charity Grace
206. "A Crime for Mothers" (1-24-61) Claire Trevor, Biff Elliott, Patricia Smith, Robert Sampson
207. "The Last Escape" (1-31-61) Keenan Wynn, Jan Sterling
208. "The Greatest Monster of Them All" (2-14-61) Richard Hale, Robert H. Harris, Sam Jaffe, William Redfield
209. "The Landlady" (2-21-61) Dean Stockwell, Patricia Collinge

210. "The Throwback" (2-28-61) Murray Matheson, Scott Mar-
     lowe, Joyce Meadows, John Indrisano
211. "The Kiss-Off" (3-7-61) Rip Torn, Mary Mundy, Bert
     Freed
212. "The Horse Player" (3-14-61) Claude Rains, Ed Gardner
213. "Incident in a Small Jail" (3-21-61) Richard Jaeckel, John
     Fiedler, Ron Nicholas
214. "A Woman's Help" (3-28-61) Scott McKay, Geraldine Fitz-
     gerald, Antoinette Bower
215. "Museum Piece" (4-4-61) Myron McCormick, Larry Gates,
     Bert Convy, Edward C. Platt
216. "Coming, Mama" (4-11-61) Don DeFore, Eileen Heckart
217. "Deathmate" (4-18-61) Gia Scala, Lee Philips
218. "Gratitude" (4-25-61) Peter Falk, Paul Hartman, Edmund
     Hashim, John Dennis
219. "A Pearl Necklace" (5-2-61) Hazel Court, Jack Cassidy,
     Ernest Truex
220. "You Can't Trust a Man" (5-9-61) Polly Bergen, Joe
     Maross
221. "The Gloating Place" (5-16-61) Susan Harrison, Marta
     Kristen, Henry Brandt
222. "Self-Defense" (5-23-61) George Nader, Audrey Totter
223. "A Secret Life" (5-30-61) Patricia Donahue, Ronald How-
     ard, Addison Richards
224. "Servant Problem" (6-6-61) Joan Hackett, Jo Van Fleet,
     John Emery
225. "Coming Home" (6-13-61) Crahan Denton, Susan Silo,
     Jeanette Nolan
226. "Final Arrangements" (6-20-61) Martin Balsam, Slim
     Pickens, Vivian Nathan
227. "Make My Death Bed" (6-27-61) Diana Van Der Vlis
228. "Ambition" (7-4-61) Leslie Nielsen

Seventh Season

229. "The Hat Box" (10-10-61) Billy Gray, Paul Ford
230. "Bang, You're Dead" (10-17-61) Billy Mumy, Biff Elliott,
     Steve Dunne, Lucy Prentiss
231. "Maria" (10-24-61) Nita Talbot, Norman Lloyd
232. "Cop for a Day" (10-31-61) Walter Matthau, Glenn Cannon
233. "Beta Delta Gamma" (11-14-61) Burt Brinckerhoff
234. "You Can't Be a Little Girl All Your Life" (11-21-61)
     Carolyn Kearney, Dick York, Ted De Corsia
235. "The Old Pro" (11-28-61) Richard Conte, Sarah Shane
236. "I Spy" (12-5-61) Kay Walsh, Eric Barker, Cecil Parker,
     William Kendall
237. "Services Rendered" (12-12-61) Hugh Marlowe, Steve Dunne
238. "The Right Kind of Medicine" (12-19-61) Robert Redford,
     Joby Baker, Russell Collins
239. "A Jury of Her Peers" (12-26-61) Ann Harding, June
     Walker
240. "The Silk Petticoat" (1-2-62) Michael Rennie, Antoinette
     Bower

241. "Bad Actor" (1-9-62) Robert Duvall, Charles Robinson,
     Carole Eastman
242. "The Door Without a Key" (1-16-62) Claude Rains, Billy
     Mumy, John Larch, Robert Carson
243. "The Case of M. J. H. " (1-23-62) Barbara Baxley, Robert
     Loggia
244. "The Faith of Aaron Menefee" (1-30-62) Andrew Prine,
     Robert Armstrong, Sidney Blackmer, Maggie Pierce,
     Olan Soule
245. "The Woman Who Wanted to Live" (2-6-62) Lola Albright,
     Charles Bronson
246. "Strange Miracle" (2-13-62) David Opatoshu, Miriam Colon,
     Eduardo Ciannelli
247. "The Test" (2-20-62) Brian Keith, Eduardo Ciannelli
248. "Burglar Proof" (2-27-62) Robert Webber, Paul Hartman
249. "The Big Score" (3-6-62) Evans Evans, Philip Reed,
     Rafael Campos
250. "Profit Sharing Plan" (3-13-62) Henry Jones, Ruth Storey,
     Rebecca Sand
251. "Apex" (3-20-62) Patricia Breslin, Mark Miller, Vivienne
     Segal, George Kane
252. "The Last Remains" (3-27-62) Ed Gardner, John Fiedler
253. "Ten O'Clock Tiger" (4-3-62) Frankie Darro, Robert
     Keith
254. "Act of Faith" (4-10-62) George Grizzard, Dennis King
255. "The Kerry Blues" (4-17-62) Carmen Mathews, Gene Evans
256. "The Matched Pearl" (4-24-62) John Ireland, Ernest Truex
257. "What Frightened You, Fred?" (5-1-62) Edward Asner,
     Adam Williams, R. G. Armstrong
258. "Most Likely to Succeed" (5-8-62) Joanna Moore, Howard
     Morris, Jack Carter
259. "Victim Four" (5-15-62) Peggy Ann Garner, John Lupton,
     Paul Comi
260. "The Opportunity" (5-22-62) Richard Long, Coleen Gray
261. "The Twelve Hour Caper" (5-29-62) Dick York, Sarah
     Marshall
262. "The Children of Alda Nuova" (6-5-62) Jack Carson
263. "First Class Honeymoon" (6-12-62) Robert Webber, Jeremy
     Slate
264. "The Big Kick" (6-19-62) Anne Helm, Wayne Rogers,
     Brian Hutton
265. "Where Beauty Lies" (6-26-62) George Nader, Cloris
     Leachman

[Hereafter titled THE ALFRED HITCHCOCK HOUR]

1. "A Piece of the Action" (9-20-62) Gig Young, Martha Hyer,
   Robert Redford
2. "Don't Look Behind You" (9-27-62) Vera Miles, Jeffrey
   Hunter, Alf Kjellin
3. "Night of the Owl" (10-4-62) Brian Keith, Patricia Breslin
4. "I Saw the Whole Thing" (10-11-62) John Forsythe, Kent
   Smith, John Zaremba, Rusty Lane

5. "Captive Audience" (10-18-62) James Mason, Angie Dickinson, Roland Winters
6. "Final Vow" (10-25-62) Carol Lynley, Clu Gulager, Isobel Elsom
7. "Annabel" (11-1-62) Susan Oliver, Dean Stockwell, Kathleen Nolan, Henry Brandt
8. "House Guest" (11-8-62) Macdonald Carey, Peggy McCay, Robert Sterling
9. "The Black Curtain" (11-15-62) Richard Basehart, Lee Philips, Lola Albright, Harold J. Stone
10. "Day of Reckoning" (11-22-62) Louis Hayward, Claude Akins, Barry Sullivan, Katherine Bard, Hugh Marlowe, K. T. Stevens
11. "Ride the Nightmare" (11-29-62) Gena Rowlands, Hugh O'Brian
12. "Hangover" (12-6-62) Jayne Mansfield, Tony Randall, June Levant
13. "Bonfire" (12-13-62) Peter Falk, Patricia Collinge, Dina Merrill
14. "The Tender Poisoner" (12-20-62) Howard Duff, Dan Dailey, Jan Sterling
15. "The Thirty-First of February" (1-4-63) William Conrad, Elizabeth Allen, David Wayne
16. "What Really Happened" (1-11-63) Gladys Cooper, Anne Francis, Ruth Roman
17. "Forecast: Low Clouds and Coastal Fog" (1-18-63) Dan O'Herlihy, Inger Stevens, Chris Robinson, Richard Jaeckel
18. "A Tangled Web" (1-25-63) Barry Morse, Robert Redford, Zohra Lampert, Gertrude Flynn
19. "To Catch a Butterfly" (2-1-63) Bradford Dillman, Diana Hyland, Mickey Sholdar
20. "The Paragon" (2-8-63) Joan Fontaine, Gary Merrill
21. "I'll Be the Judge, I'll Be the Jury" (2-15-63) Peter Graves, Albert Salmi
22. "Diagnosis: Danger" (3-1-63) Charles McGraw, Michael Parks
23. "The Lonely Hours" (3-8-63) Nancy Kelly, Juanita Moore, Gena Rowlands
24. "The Star Juror" (3-15-63) Dean Jagger, Will Hutchins, Betty Field, Crahan Denton, Katherine Squire, Cathie Merchant
25. "The Long Silence" (3-22-63) Michael Rennie, Phyllis Thaxter, Natalie Trundy
26. "An Out for Oscar" (4-5-63) Linda Christian, Henry Silva, Larry Storch
27. "Death and the Joyful Woman" (4-12-63) Laraine Day, Gilbert Roland
28. "Last Seen Wearing Blue Jeans" (4-19-63) Michael Wilding, Randy Boone, Anne Lee
29. "The Dark Pool" (5-3-63) Lois Nettleton, Anthony George, Madlyn Rhue
30. "Dear Uncle George" (5-10-63) Gene Barry, John Larkin, Patricia Donahue, Lou Jacobi, Dabney Coleman

31. "Run for Doom" (5-17-63) Scott Brady, John Gavin, Diana Dors
32. "Death of a Cop" (5-24-63) Victor Jory, Peter Brown, Richard Jaeckel, Lawrence Tierney

Second Season

33. "A Home Away from Home" (9-27-63) Ray Milland, Claire Griswold, Virginia Gregg
34. "A Nice Touch" (10-4-63) Anne Baxter, George Segal, Harry Townes, Charlene Holt
35. "Terror in Northfield" (10-11-63) Dick York, Jacqueline Scott, R. G. Armstrong
36. "You'll Be the Death of Me" (10-18-63) Robert Loggia, Pilar Seurat, Carmen Phillips, Kathleen Freeman
37. "Blood Bargain" (10-25-63) Anne Francis, Richard Long, Richard Kiley
38. "Nothing Ever Happens in Linvale" (11-8-63) Fess Parker, Gary Merrill, Phyllis Thaxter
39. "Starring the Defense" (11-15-63) Richard Basehart, Teno Pollick, Russell Collins, S. John Launer
40. "Body in the Barn" (11-22-63) Lillian Gish, Peter Lind Hayes, Maggie McNamara
41. "The Dividing Wall" (12-6-63) James Gregory, Chris Robinson, Katherine Ross, Norman Fell
42. "Goodbye, George" (12-13-63) Robert Culp, Patricia Barry, Stubby Kaye, Elliott Reid
43. "How to Get Rid of Your Wife" (12-20-63) Bob Newhart, Jane Withers, Joyce Jameson
44. "Three Wives Too Many" (1-3-64) Dan Duryea, Teresa Wright, Jean Hale
45. "The Magic Shop" (1-10-64) John Megna, David Opatoshu, Leslie Nielsen, Peggy McCay, Tony Grainger
46. "The Cadaver" (1-17-64) Michael Parks, Ruth McDevitt, Joby Baker, Rafer Johnson, Brooke Hayward
47. "Beyond the Sea of Death" (1-24-64) Mildred Dunnock, Jeremy Slate, Diana Hyland, Abraham Sofaer
48. "Night Caller" (1-31-64) Felicia Farr, Bruce Dern
49. "The Evil of Adelaide Winters" (2-7-64) Kim Hunter, John Larkin, Gene Lyons
50. "The Jar" (2-14-64) Collin Wilcox, Pat Buttram
51. "Final Escape" (2-21-64) Edd Byrnes, Stephen McNally, Robert Keith
52. "Murder Case" (3-6-64) Gena Rowlands, John Cassavetes, Murray Matheson
53. "Anyone for Murder?" (3-13-64) Patricia Breslin, Barry Nelson, Richard X. Slattery
54. "Beast in View" (3-20-64) Joan Hackett, Kevin McCarthy, Kathy Nolan
55. "Behind the Locked Door" (3-27-64) James MacArthur, Gloria Swanson, Whit Bissell, Lynn Loring
56. "A Matter of Murder" (4-3-64) Darren McGavin, Patricia Crowley, Telly Savalas, Patrick McVey

57. "The Gentleman Caller" (4-10-64) Roddy McDowall, Juanita Moore, Diane Sayer, Ruth McDevitt
58. "The Ordeal of Mrs. Snow" (4-17-64) Patricia Collinge, Jessica Walter, Lorna Richmond, Don Chastain
59. "Ten Minutes from Now" (5-1-64) Donnelly Rhodes, Lou Jacobi, Lonny Chapman, Lou Adams
60. "The Sign of Satan" (5-8-64) Christopher Lee, Gia Scala, Adam Roarke, Gilbert Green
61. "Who Needs an Enemy?" (5-15-64) Steven Hill, Joanna Moore
62. "Bed of Roses" (5-22-64) Patrick O'Neal, Kathie Browne
63. "Second Verdict" (5-29-64) Frank Gorshin, Martin Landau
64. "Isabel" (6-5-64) Bradford Dillman, Barbara Barrie

Third Season

65. "The Return of Verge Likens" (10-5-64) Peter Fonda, Robert Emhardt
66. "Change of Address" (10-12-64) Victor Jory, Arthur Kennedy, Phyllis Thaxter, Tisha Sterling, Royal Dano
67. "Water's Edge" (10-19-64) John Cassavetes, Ann Sothern
68. "The Life and Work of Juan Diaz" (10-26-64) Alejandro Rey, Frank Silvera, Pina Pillicer
69. "See the Monkey Dance" (11-9-64) Efrem Zimbalist Jr., Roddy McDowall, Patricia Medina
70. "Lonely Place" (11-16-64) Bruce Dern, Pat Buttram, Teresa Wright
71. "The McGregor Affair" (11-23-64) Elsa Lanchester, Andrew Prine, Michael Pate
72. "Misadventure" (12-7-64) Barry Nelson, Lola Albright, George Kennedy
73. "Triumph" (12-14-64) Ed Begley, Jeanette Nolan, Than Wyenn
74. "Memo from Purgatory" (12-21-64) James Caan, Tony Musante, Mark Slade, Lynn Loring, Walter Koenig
75. "Consider Her Ways" (12-28-64) Leif Erickson, Barbara Barrie, Robert H. Harris
76. "The Crimson Witness" (1-4-65) Martha Hyer, Peter Lawford, Joanna Moore, Julie London
77. "Where the Woodbine Twineth" (1-11-65) Margaret Leighton, Carl Benton Reid, Juanita Moore
78. "The Final Performance" (1-18-65) Franchot Tone, Roger Perry, Sharon Farrell
79. "Thanatos Place Hotel" (2-1-65) Angie Dickinson, Steven Hill, Barry Atwater
80. "One of the Family" (2-8-65) Kathryn Hays, Lilia Scala, Jeremy Slate
81. "An Unlocked Window" (2-15-65) John Kerr, Dana Wynter, E. J. Andre, Louise Latham
82. "The Trap" (2-22-65) Anne Francis, Robert Strauss, Donnelly Rhodes
83. "Wally the Beard" (3-1-65) Larry Blyden, Kathie Browne, Berkeley Harris

84. "Death Scene" (3-8-65) Vera Miles, John Carradine, James Farentino, Buck Taylor
85. "The Photographer and the Undertaker" (3-15-65) Jack Cassidy, Harry Townes, Alfred Ryder
86. "Thou Still Unravished Bride" (3-22-65) Sally Kellerman, David Carradine, Ron Randall, Michael Pate
87. "Completely Foolproof" (3-29-65) Geoffrey Horne, J. D. Cannon, Patricia Barry
88. "Power of Attorney" (4-5-65) Fay Bainter, Geraldine Fitzgerald, Richard Johnson
89. "The World's Oldest Motive" (4-12-65) Robert Loggia, Henry Jones, Linda Lawson, Kathleen Freeman
90. "The Monkey's Paw--A Retelling" (4-19-65) Collin Wilcox, Leif Erickson, Lee Majors, Jane Wyatt, Zolya Talma
91. "The Second Wife" (4-26-65) June Lockhart, John Anderson
92. "Night Fever" (5-3-65) Colleen Dewhurst
93. "Off Season" (5-10-65) John Gavin, Indus Arthur, Tom Drake, Dody Heath, Richard Jaeckel, William O'Connell

GENERAL ELECTRIC THEATRE

The Regulars: Ronald Reagan, host.

The Episodes (chronicled from fall of 1955):

1. "Tryout" (10-2-55) Ann Harding, Gene Nelson
2. "Bounty Court Martial" (10-9-55) Raymond Massey, Francis L. Sullivan
3. "Lash of Fear" (10-16-55) Keenan Wynn, John Payne, Nancy Gates
4. "Outpost of Home" (10-23-55) Ralph Bellamy
5. "Shadow on the Heart" (10-30-55) John Ericson, Kathryn Grayson
6. "Winner by Decision" (11-6-55) Harry Belafonte, Ethel Waters
7. "Farewell to Kennedy" (11-13-55) Alan Ladd
8. "Prosper's Old Mother" (11-20-55) Ethel Barrymore, Charles Bronson
9. "From the Top" (11-27-55) Lisa Kirk
10. "Feathertop" (12-4-55) Natalie Wood
11. "The Seeds of Hate" (12-11-55) Charlton Heston
12. "Let It Rain" (12-18-55) Cloris Leachman
13. "Portrait of a Ballerina" (1-1-56) Lili Darvas, Steven Geray, Joyce Vanderveen
14. "Estaban's Legacy" (1-8-56) Ricardo Montalban, Movita
15. "The Ballad of Mender McClure" (1-15-56) Thomas Mitchell, Vincent Price
16. "The Muse and Mr. Parkinson" (1-22-56) Edward Everett Horton
17. "In Summer Promise" (1-29-56) Joan Fontaine, Betsy Palmer, Scott Marlowe, Sally Fraser, Philip Ober

18. "The Song Caruso Sang" (2-5-56) Anna Maria Alberghetti
19. "Prologue to Glory" (2-12-56) John Ireland, Joanne Wood-
     ward, Marjorie Rambeau
20. "The Honest Man" (2-19-56) Jack Benny, Zsa Zsa Gabor,
     Jack La Rue, Mary Lawrence, Barbara Lawrence
21. "Try to Remember" (2-26-56) Angie Dickinson, Kim Hunter,
     Ronald Reagan, Barry Kelley
22. "A Letter from the Queen" (3-4-56) Polly Bergen, Paul
     Muni
23. "Steinmetz" (3-11-56) Franchot Tone
24. "The Night Goes On" (3-18-56) George Macready, Rosalind
     Russell, Carmen Matthews
25. "Reflected Glory" (3-25-56) Ethel Merman
26. "Easter Gift" (4-1-56) MacDonald Carey
27. "That's the Man" (4-15-56) Nancy Davis, Ray Milland
28. "The Lord's Dollar" (4-22-56) Ronald Reagan
29. "H. M. S. Marlborough" (4-29-56) Joseph Cotten
30. "The Shunning" (5-6-56) Joan Lorring
31. "The Hat with the Roses" (5-20-56) Gisele MacKenzie
32. "The Golden Key" (5-27-56) Joe E. Brown
33. "O'Hoolihan and the Leprechaun" (6-3-56) Anne Jackson,
     E. G. Marshall, Roddy McDowall
34. "Exits and Entrances" (6-10-56) Charlie Applewhite
35. "Alien Angel" (6-17-56) Patty McCormack
36. "Emergency Call" (6-24-56) Claire Trevor
37. "Man with a Vengeance" (7-1-56) Walter Matthau, Dennis
     King

## Fifth Season

38. "The Glorious Gift of Molly Malloy" (9-23-56) Greer Garson
39. "Professor Beware" (9-30-56) Ronald Reagan
40. "The Pot of Gold" (10-7-56) Hume Cronyn, Jessica Tandy
41. "The Enemies" (10-14-56) Joseph Cotten
42. "The Invitation" (10-21-56) Kathryn Grayson, Larry Pennell
43. "The Second Stranger" (10-28-56) Burl Ives
44. "The Rider on the Pale Horse" (11-4-56) Gower Champion,
     Marge Champion
45. "The Charlatan" (11-11-56) George Sanders
46. "The Road that Led Afar" (11-25-56) Dan Duryea, Piper
     Laurie, Beverly Washburn
47. "The Orphans" (12-2-56) Kim Hunter, Ronald Reagan
48. "The Breach" (12-9-56) Betty Field, Marion Seldes, Bob
     Burton
49. "The Chess Game" (12-16-56) Ronald Colman
50. "A Child Is Born" (12-23-56) Nadine Conner, Robert Mid-
     dleton
51. "The Shadow Outside" (12-30-56) Terry Moore
52. "Never Turn Back" (1-6-57) Ray Milland
53. "The Earring" (1-13-57) Greer Garson
54. "Lady of the House" (1-20-57) Myrna Loy
55. "The Doctors of Pawnee Kill" (1-27-57) Kevin McCarthy,
     Lee Marvin, Margaret Hayes

56. "No Skin Off Me" (2-3-57) Ronald Reagan
57. "The Town with a Past" (2-10-57) James Stewart, Beulah Bondi
58. "The Big Shooter" (2-17-57) Eva Gabor, Art Linkletter
59. "Flight from Tormendero" (2-24-57) Helmut Dantine, Donna Reed, George Macready
60. "The Fenton Touch" (3-3-57) Jack Benny
61. "With Malice Towards One" (3-10-57) John Baragrey, Bette Davis
62. "The Victorian Chaise Lounge" (3-17-57) Joan Fontaine
63. "Too Good with a Gun" (3-24-57) Robert Cummings, Michael Landon
64. "Bargain Bride" (4-7-57) Eva Bartok, Ronald Reagan
65. "Cab Driver" (4-14-57) Imogene Coca, Keenan Wynn
66. "Bitter Choice" (4-21-57) Anne Baxter, Vince Edwards
67. "I Will Not Die" (4-28-57) Jacques Bergerac, Merle Oberon
68. "Angel of Wrath" (5-5-57) Ray Milland
69. "A Question of Survival" (5-12-57) Kevin McCarthy, Ronald Reagan
70. "The Man Who Inherited Everything" (5-19-57) George Sanders, Carolyn Jones
71. "A New Girl in His Life" (5-26-57) John Forsythe

Sixth Season

72. "The Questioning Note" (10-6-57) James Mason
73. "Father and Son Night" (10-13-57) Ronald Reagan, Bobby Clark
74. "Thousand Dollar Gun" (10-20-57) John Agar, George Montgomery
75. "Mr. Kensington's Finest Hour" (10-27-57) Phyllis Avery, Richard Eyer
76. "Mischief at Bandy Leg" (11-3-57) Gower Champion, Marge Champion
77. "Cornada" (11-10-57) Tony Curtis
78. "Love Came Late" (11-17-57) Melvyn Douglas, Myrna Loy
79. "The Iron Horse" (11-24-57) Vincent Price, Fay Wray, Sterling Hayden
80. "Imp on a Cobweb Leash" (12-1-57) Fred Astaire
81. "Eyes of a Stranger" (12-8-57) Tallulah Bankhead, Richard Denning
82. "The Trail to Christmas" (12-15-57) Richard Eyer, John McIntire, James Stewart
83. "The Young Years" (12-22-57) Margaret O'Brien, Rod Taylor, Dorothy Stickney
84. "Kid at the Stick" (1-5-58) Tim Hovey, Art Linkletter
85. "Letters from Cairo" (1-12-58) Richard Denning, Ann Todd
86. "Time to Go Now" (1-19-58) Pat Crowley
87. "Silent Ambush" (1-26-58) Phyllis Avery, Alan Ladd, Elisha Cook
88. "All I Survey" (2-2-58) Lee Marvin, Don Taylor
89. "Incident" (2-9-58) Audie Murphy
90. "Last Town Car" [Part I] (2-16-58) Claudette Colbert, Kent

Smith
91. "Last Town Car" [Part II] (2-23-58) as above.
92. "New York Knight" (3-2-58) Charles Laughton
93. "Angel in the Air" (3-9-58) Vincent Price, Janice Rule
94. "The Coward of Ft. Bennett" (3-16-58) Neville Brand,
John Dall, Ronald Reagan
95. "Strange Witness" (3-23-58) Joan Crawford, Tom Tryon,
John McIntire
96. "The Unfamiliar" (3-30-58) Peggy Ann Garner, Burgess
Meredith
97. "No Hiding Place" (4-6-58) David Opatoshu, Geraldine
Page, Ronald Reagan
98. "The Cold Touch" (4-13-58) Bette Davis, Leif Erickson,
Forrest Tucker
99. "God Is My Judge" (4-20-58) Nina Foch, Gary Merrill,
Dean Stockwell
100. "Stopover" (4-27-58) Anne Baxter, Beverly Washburn
101. "Ah There, Beau Brummel" (5-4-58) Hume Cronyn, Eva
Gabor
102. "Bold Loser" (5-11-58) Guy Madison
103. "The Young and the Scared" (5-18-58) Jack Klugman,
Carol Lynley, James MacArthur

Seventh Season
104. "Blaze of Glory" (9-21-58) Lou Costello
105. "One Is a Wanderer" (9-28-58) Fred MacMurray
106. "Auf Wiederschen" (10-5-58) Sammy Davis Jr.
107. "The Castaway" (10-12-58) Ronald Reagan
108. "The World's Greatest Quarterback" (10-19-58) Ernie Kovacs, Audrey Totter, Ronnie Burns
109. "At Miss Minner's" (10-26-58) Joan Fontaine, John Newland
110. "Battle for a Soul" (11-2-58) Ray Milland
111. "A Question of Romance" (11-9-58) Betsy Drake, John
Kerr, Harold (Pee Wee) Reese
112. "The Falling Angel" (11-16-58) Edie Adams, Louis Jourdan
113. "A Turkey for the President" (11-23-58) Ward Bond, Nancy
Davis, Ronald Reagan
114. "The Last Rodeo" (12-7-58) Robert Horton, Nancy Olson
115. "The Girl with the Flaxen Hair" (12-14-58) Ray Bolger,
Gena Rowlands
116. "The Odd Ball" (12-28-58) Leon Ames, Art Linkletter
117. "And One Was Loyal" (1-4-59) Joan Crawford
118. "Man on a Bicycle" (1-11-59) Fred Astaire, Roxane Berard
119. "The Stone" (1-18-59) John Baragrey, Tony Curtis, Rita
Moreno
120. "Bill Bailey, Won't You Please Come Home" (1-25-59)
Dan Dailey, Patricia Barry, Barry Sullivan
121. "No Man Can Tame Me" (2-1-59) Gisele MacKenzie, John
Raitt, Eddie Foy Jr.
122. "The Last Lesson" (2-8-59) Charles Laughton, Patricia
Medina
123. "I Was a Blood Hound" (2-15-59) Ernie Kovacs

124. "The Family Man" (2-22-59) Lon Chaney Jr., Dean Stockwell, Albert Salmi
125. "Deed of Mercy" (3-1-59) Carol Lynley, Ronald Reagan, Agnes Moorehead
126. "The Incredible Jewel Robbery" (3-8-59) Chico Marx, Harpo Marx
127. "Train for Tecumseh" (3-15-59) John Cassavetes, Pauline Myers, Janice Rule
128. "The Lady's Choice" (3-22-59) William Bishop, Don De Fore, Joan Caulfield
129. "Beyond the Mountains" (3-29-59) Danny Zaldivar
130. "The Flying Wife" (4-5-59) Janet Gaynor, Bill Williams
131. "Caesar and Cleopatra" (4-12-59) Maurice Evans, Piper Laurie
132. "Robbie and His Mary" (4-19-59) Pippa Scott, Dan O'Herlihy
133. "Nora" (5-3-59) Vera Miles, Leslie Nielsen
134. "Nobody's Child" (5-10-59) Sheilah Graham, Ronald Reagan, Evelyn Rudie, Diane Brewster
135. "The Indian Giver" (5-17-59) Jackie Coogan, Boris Karloff, Carmen Matthews

Eighth Season

136. "Miracle at the Opera" (9-20-59) Ed Wynn, Sig Ruman
137. "The Last Reunion" (9-27-59) Lee Marvin, Kevin Hagen
138. "Hitler's Secret" (10-4-59) Raymond Massey, Everett Sloane
139. "Night Club" (10-11-59) Amanda Blake, Barbara Hale, June Lockhart, Rosemary De Camp, Glenda Farrell
140. "The Tallest Marine" (10-18-59) Red Buttons, John Lupton
141. "The Day of the Hanging" (10-25-59) Tom Ewell, Joan Leslie, Noah Beery Jr.
142. "Disaster" (11-1-59) Tab Hunter, Jo Van Fleet
143. "Signs of Love" (11-8-59) Pat Carroll, Ronald Reagan, Paula Raymond
144. "Survival" (11-15-59) Jose Ferrer, Martin Landau
145. "The Last Dance" (11-22-59) Mary Astor, Carol Lynley
146. "Platinum on the Rocks" (11-29-59) George Burns
147. "Absalom, My Son" (12-6-59) Burl Ives, Patricia Medina
148. "The House of Truth" (12-13-59) Phyllis Thaxter, Ronald Reagan
149. "Mr. O'Malley" (12-20-59) Bert Lahr, Ronny Howard
150. "Silhouette" (12-27-59) Ray Bolger, Vanessa Brown
151. "Sarah's Laughter" (1-3-60) Thelma Ritter
152. "R.S.V.P." (1-10-60) Virginia Grey
153. "Lear vs. the Committeeman" (1-17-60) Lee J. Cobb, Sylvia Sidney
154. "They Like Me Fine" (1-24-60) George Gobel
155. "Early to Die" (2-7-60) Kim Hunter, Rod Taylor
156. "The Patsy" (2-21-60) Sammy Davis Jr.
157. "The Story of Judith" (2-28-60) Joan Fontaine
158. "The Book of Silence" (3-6-60) Ruth Roman, Rod Steiger

159. "So Deadly, So Evil" (3-13-60) Peggy Lee
160. "Do Not Disturb" (3-20-60) David Wayne, Scott Davey, Peggy Knudsen, Gil Rogers
161. "The Web of Guilt" (3-27-60) Arthur Kennedy
162. "Mystery of Malibu" (4-10-60) Dan Duryea, Audrey Totter
163. "Aftermath" (4-17-60) Fess Parker
164. "Adam's Apple" (4-24-60) Leon Ames
165. "The Ugly Duckling" (5-1-60) Richard Haydn, Oscar Homolka
166. "Don't You Remember?" (5-8-60) Lee Marvin, Simone Signoret
167. "At Your Service" (5-22-60) Van Johnson, Jan Sterling
168. "Hot Footage" (5-29-60) Richard Greene, Robert Strauss

Ninth Season

169. "The Man Who Thought for Himself" (9-18-60) Steve Allen, Laurin Chapin, Jayne Meadows
170. "Journal of Hope" (9-25-60) Jeanne Crain, Leslie Nielsen
171. "Good-By My Love" (10-16-60) Anne Baxter, Nestor Pevis, Chet Stratton
172. "The Camel's Foot" (10-23-60) Vera Miles, Connie Gilchrist
173. "A Graduation Dress" (10-30-60) Buddy Ebsen, Hugh O'Brian, Ellen Corby, Stella Stevens
174. "The Playoff" (11-20-60) Dana Andrews, Nancy Davis, Regis Toomey, Ryan O'Neal
175. "Journey to a Wedding" (11-27-60) Gene Tierney, Jim Davis, Alice Backes, Dennis Ruse, Malcolm Atterbury
176. "Learn to Say Good-By" (12-4-60) Michael Burns, Coleen Gray, Frank Wilcox, Ronald Reagan, Claire Carleton
177. "Strictly Solo" (12-11-60) Sally Forrest, John Austin, Tony Randall, Vaughn Taylor, Barbara Ruick
178. "The Money Driver" (12-18-60) Jocelyn Brando, Mickey Rooney, Teddy Rooney
179. "The Other Wise Man" (12-25-60) Harry Townes, Abraham Sofaer, Francis X. Bushman
180. "Don't Let It Throw You" (1-1-61) Gloria Graham, Dick Shawn
181. "Memory in White" (1-8-61) Charles Bronson, Bert Freed, Sammy Davis Jr.
182. "The Devil You Say" (1-22-61) Sid Caesar, Patricia Barry, Ronald Reagan
183. "The Drop-Out" (1-29-61) Billy Gray, Ray Montgomery, Carmen Matthews, Russ Conway, Walter Baldwin, Edward G. Robinson
184. "A Little White Lye" (2-5-61) Dorothy Malone, Michael Pate, John Gabriel, Pitt Herbert, Dorothy Newmann
185. "The Legend That Walks Like a Man" (2-12-61) Ernest Borgnine, Zsa Zsa Gabor, William Schallert
186. "A Possibility of Oil" (2-19-61) Brad Dexter, Joan Fontaine, Josephine Hutchinson, Jane Withers, Joseph Wiseman, Chubby Johnson

187. "Image of a Doctor" (2-26-61) Ida Lupino, Simon Oakland,
     Robert Lansing, Rita Brooking
188. "Open House" (3-5-61) Elisha Cook, Robert Strauss, Paul
     Ford, Gertrude Flynn, Florence MacMichael
189. "The Small Elephants" (3-12-61) Barbara Nichols, Cliff
     Robertson, Jonathan Harris, George Sanders
190. "Love Is a Lion's Roar" (3-19-61) Fifi D'Orsay, Jack
     Weston, James Franciscus, Suzanne Pleshette, Mariellen
     Smith
191. "Labor of Love" (3-26-61) David Brian, Jane Wyatt, Terry
     Burnham, Dorothy Ann Collier
192. "The Red Balloon" (4-2-61) Pascal Lamorisse, Sabine
     Lamorisse
193. "Sis Bowls 'Em Over" (4-9-61) Billy Gray, Raymond Bail-
     ey, Audrey Meadows, Jack Cassidy
194. "The Joke's On Me" (4-16-61) Bud Abbott, Lee Marvin,
     Mala Powers
195. "My Darling Judge" (4-23-61) Fred Clark, Audrey Totter,
     Melinda Plowman, Anne Whitfield
196. "Louise and the Horseless Buggy" (4-30-61) Eddie Albert,
     Alice Backes, Michael Burns, Alan Hale

Tenth Season

197. "The Iron Silence" (9-24-61) Carol Lawrence
198. "Cat in the Cradle" (10-1-61) Lola Albright, John Saxon,
     Elsa Lanchester
199. "A Musket for Jessica" (10-8-61) Dick York, Piper Laurie
200. "The $200 Parley" (10-15-61) Bob Crane, Glynis Johns,
     Shelley Berman
201. "The Wishbook" (10-22-61) Ricky Nelson, Roberta Shore
202. "The Great Alberti" (11-5-61) Stella Stevens, Charles
     McGraw, Cornel Wilde
203. "Star Witness" (11-12-61) Lloyd Bridges, Barbara Stanwyck
204. "A Voice on the Phone" (11-19-61) Nick Adams, Elinor
     Donahue
205. "Money and the Minister" (11-26-61) Nancy Davis, Jaye P.
     Morgan, Fay Wray, Gary Merrill, Ronald Reagan
206. "We're Holding Your Son" (12-3-61) Scott Brady, William
     Bendix, Barbara Parkins, Catherine McLeod
207. "Call to Danger" (12-10-61) Larry Blyden, Lloyd Nolan
208. "Tippy-Top" (12-17-61) Red Buttons, Ronny Howard
209. "A Friendly Tribe" (12-31-61) George Gobel, Barbara
     Parkins
210. "The Wall Between" (1-7-62) Stephen Boyd, Gloria Talbot,
     Ronald Reagan, Everett Sloane
211. "The Hold-Out" (1-14-62) Fred Clark, Dennis Hopper,
     Groucho Marx, Dorothy Green, Brook Hayward
212. "The Little Hours" (1-21-62) John Payne
213. "Go Fight City Hall" (1-28-62) Irene Dunne, Allyn Joslyn
214. "Shadow of a Hero" (2-4-62) Arlene Whelan, Ronald Rea-
     gan, David Janssen
215. "Badge of Honor" (2-11-62) Art Linkletter

216. "The Free Wheelers" (2-18-62) Jacques Bergerac, Patricia Barry, Tommy Noonan
217. "Ten Days in the Sun" (3-4-62) Ed Wynn, Andy Devine, Jerry Paris
218. "A Very Special Girl" (3-11-62) Barbara Rush, Miriam Hopkins
219. "My Dark Days" [Part I] (3-18-62) Jeanne Crain, Ronald Reagan
220. "My Dark Days" [Part II] (3-25-62) as above.
221. "Hercule Poirot" (4-1-62) Nina Foch, Martin Gabel, James Callahan
222. "The Roman Kind" (4-8-62) Gene Barry, Diane Brewster
223. "The Bar Mitzvah of Major Orlovsky" (4-15-62) Ernest Borgnine, Theodore Bikel, Cloris Leachman
224. "The Troubled Heart" (4-22-62) Geraldine Brooks, Earl Holliman, Parley Baer
225. "Mister Doc" (4-29-62) Dean Jagger, Billy Hughes
226. "The Unstoppable Gray Fox" (5-6-62) Lee J. Cobb
227. "Acres and Pains" (5-13-62) Anne Jackson, Walter Matthau
228. "Somebody Please Help Me" (5-20-62) Dorothy Malone
229. "First Hundred Years" (5-27-62) Nick Adams


THE ARMSTRONG CIRCLE THEATRE/THE UNITED STATES STEEL HOUR (rotating with The Twentieth Century-Fox Hour, Playwrights '56, and Kaiser Aluminum Hour)

The Episodes:

1. Playwrights '56: "The Day the Trains Stopped Running" (1-3-56) Joseph Sweeney
2. The United States Steel Hour: "Bring Me a Dream" (1-4-56) John Cassavetes, George Grizzard, Steve McQueen, Lois Smith
3. The Armstrong Circle Theatre: "Ward Three: 4 P.M. to Midnight" [by Phil Reisman Jr.] (1-10-56) Mary Pickett, Patricia Collinge
4. The Twentieth Century Fox Hour: "Yacht on the High Sea" (1-11-56) Nina Foch, Gary Merrill
5. Playwrights '56: "Lost" [by Arnold Schulman] (1-17-56) Steven Hill, Sally Gracie, Kerwin Mathews
6. The United States Steel Hour: "The Great Adventure" (1-18-56) Hume Cronyn, Jessica Tandy, Richard Long
7. The Armstrong Circle Theatre: "Nightmare in Red" [a documentary on how Communism came to Russia] (1-24-56)
8. The Twentieth Century Fox Hour: "One Life" (1-25-56) Nina Foch, Dane Clark, Audrey Totter, William Hopper
9. Playwrights '56: "This Business of Murder" (1-31-56) E. G. Marshall, Warren Stevens, Henry Jones, Thomas Gomez
10. The United States Steel Hour: "A Fair Shake" (2-1-56) John Kerr, Cliff Robertson

11. The Armstrong Circle Theatre: "The Third Ear" (2-7-56) Mark Richman, Joe Mantell, Russell Collins, Jack Klugman

12. The Twentieth Century Fox Hour: "Crack-Up" (2-8-56) Bette Davis, Gary Merrill

13. Playwrights '56: "Return to Cassino" (2-14-56) John Forsythe, Dina Merrill, Kurt Kasznar

14. The United States Steel Hour: "Command" (2-15-56) Cameron Mitchell, Biff McGuire

15. The Armstrong Circle Theatre: "Terror at My Heels" (2-21-56) Darren McGavin

16. The Twentieth Century Fox Hour: "In Times Like These" [adapted from MacKinlay Kantor's novel] (2-22-56) Macdonald Carey, Fay Wray

17. Playwrights '56: "Flight" [by Horton Foote] (2-28-56) Kim Stanley, Ruth Hussey, Albert Dekker

18. The United States Steel Hour: "Moments of Courage" (2-29-56) Macdonald Carey, Kim Hunter, Don Murray, Paul Stevens

19. The Armstrong Circle Theatre: "Man in Shadow" (3-6-56) Leora Dana, Harry Townes

20. The Twentieth Century Fox Hour: 'Deception" (3-7-56) Linda Darnell, Trevor Howard

21. Playwrights '56: "Adam and Evening" (3-13-56) Nehemiah Persoff, Estelle Winwood, Lori March

22. The United States Steel Hour: "The Candidate" (3-14-56) Ralph Bellamy

23. The Armstrong Circle Theatre: "Five Who Shook the World" (3-20-56) Philip Abbott

24. The Twentieth Century Fox Hour: "Laura" [repeat of episode of 10/19/55] (3-21-56) George Sanders, Dana Wynter, Robert Stack

25. Playwrights '56: "The Undiscovered Country" [by J. P. Miller] (3-27-56) Cyril Ritchard, Nina Foch, J. Pat O'Malley

26. The United States Steel Hour: "Thirty Year Man" (3-28-56) Pat O'Brien, Jocelyn Brando

27. The Armstrong Circle Theatre: "A Baby Named X" (4-3-56) Kathleen Maguire, Anne Seymour, Frank Overton, Bibi Osterwald

28. The Twentieth Century Fox Hour: "Gun in His Hand" (4-4-56) Debra Paget, Charles Drake

29. Playwrights '56: "You and Me--and the Gatepost!" (4-10-56) Arlene Francis, Mary Astor, John Emery

30. The United States Steel Hour: "Funny Heart" (4-11-56) Imogene Coca, Jack Klugman, Wally Cox, Robert Culp

31. The Armstrong Circle Theatre: "The Case of Colonel Patroy" (4-17-56) Michael Gorrin, Sanford Masner

32. The Twentieth Century Fox Hour: "Mr. Belvedere" (4-18-56) Reginald Gardiner, ZaSu Pitts, Eddie Bracken, Margaret Hayes

33. Playwrights '56: "The Center of the Maze" (4-24-56) Ann Harding, Dina Merrill

34. The United States Steel Hour: "Noon on Doomsday" [by Rod Serling] (4-25-56) Everett Sloane, Jack Warden, Lois Smith, Philip Abbott, Albert Salmi
35. The Armstrong Circle Theatre: "Seventy-three Seconds into Space" (5-1-56) Patrick McVey, James Daly, Biff McGuire
36. The Twentieth Century Fox Hour: "Broken Arrow" (5-2-56) Ricardo Montalban, John Lupton, Rita Moreno
37. Playwrights '56: "You Sometimes Get Rich" (5-8-56) Larry Blyden, Georgiann Johnson
38. The United States Steel Hour: "Honest in the Rain" (5-9-56) Ethel Merman
39. The Armstrong Circle Theatre: "Devil at the Door" [by Alvin Yudkoff] (5-15-56) Ruth White, John Kellogg
40. The Twentieth Century Fox Hour: "Overnight Haul" (5-16-56) Richard Conte, Lizabeth Scott, Richard Eyer
41. Playwrights '56: "Keyhole" (5-22-56) Lee Grant, E. G. Marshall, Henry McNaughton, John Sutton
42. The United States Steel Hour: "The Old Lady Shows Her Medals" [adapted by Robert Anderson from the James M. Barrie play] (5-23-56) Gracie Fields, Jackie Cooper, Alfred Lunt, Biff McGuire, Cathleen Nesbitt
43. The Armstrong Circle Theatre: "The Second Family" [by Art Wallace] (5-29-56) Loretta Leversee, Larry Gates, Harry Townes
44. The Twentieth Century Fox Hour: "The Empty Room" [adapted from the book by Charles Morgan] (5-30-56) Jeffrey Hunter, Virginia Field, Audrey Dalton, Patrick Knowles
45. Playwrights '56: "Nick and Lettie" (6-5-56) Nancy Walker, Norman Feld
46. The United States Steel Hour: "The Boarding House" [based on James Joyce's short story, The Dubliners] (6-6-56) Evelyn Varden, Lisa Daniels, Jerome Kilty
47. The Armstrong Circle Theatre: "H. R. 8438: The Story of a Lost Boy" (6-12-56) Maureen Stapleton, Luis Van Rooten, Voytek Dolinski
48. The Twentieth Century Fox Hour: "The Heffeman Family" [adapted by Dorothy Cooper from the play Chicken Every Sunday] (6-13-56) Paul Douglas, Alexis Smith
49. Playwrights '56: "Honor" [by Gore Vidal] (6-19-56) Ralph Bellamy, Dick York, Katherine Squire
50. The United States Steel Hour: "Moments of Courage" [repeat of episode of 2/29/56] (6-20-56)
51. The Armstrong Circle Theatre: "Five Who Shook the World" [repeat of episode of 3/20/56] (6-26-56)
52. The Twentieth Century Fox Hour: "The Ox Bow Incident" [repeat of episode of 11/2/55] (6-27-56) Robert Wagner, Cameron Mitchell, Raymond Burr, Wallace Ford, E. G. Marshall, Hope Emerson
53. The Kaiser Aluminum Hour: "The Army Game" (7-3-56) Paul Newman, George Grizzard, Edward Andrews, Patrick McVey
54. The United States Steel Hour: "Operation Three R's" (7-4-

56) Robert Culp, Sallie Brophy, Frank Milan, Gerald Price

55. The Armstrong Circle Theatre: "Man in Shadow" [repeat of episode of 3/6/56] (7-10-56)

56. The Twentieth Century Fox Hour: "The Late Christopher Bean" [repeat of episode of 11/30/55] (7-11-56) Thelma Ritter, Gene Lockhart

57. The Kaiser Aluminum Hour: "Man on a White Horse" (7-17-56) Andrew Duggan, James Barton, Barton MacLane

58. The United States Steel Hour: "The Partners" (7-18-56) Mark Richman, Luther Adler, Virginia Vincent

59. The Armstrong Circle Theatre: "A Baby Named X" [repeat of episode of 4/3/56] (7-24-56)

60. The Twentieth Century Fox Hour: "Deception" [repeat of episode of 3/7/56] (7-25-56) Linda Darnell, Trevor Howard

61. The Kaiser Aluminum Hour: "Roar of the Lion" (7-31-56) Nancy Kelly, Bert Freed, Ann Shoemaker

62. The United States Steel Hour: "Stopover at Sublimity" (8-1-56) Lisa Daniels, John Napier, Efrem Zimbalist Jr.

63. The Armstrong Circle Theatre: "Ward Three: 4 P.M. to Midnight" [repeat of episode of 1/10/56] (8-7-56)

64. The Twentieth Century Fox Hour: "Crack-Up" [repeat of episode of 2/8/56] (8-8-56)

65. The Kaiser Aluminum Hour: "A Fragile Affair" [adapted from Ferenc Molnar's Delicate Story] (8-28-56) Eli Wallach, Gaby Rodgers

66. The United States Steel Hour: "The Five Fathers of Pepi" [adapted by Ira and Jane Avery] (8-29-56) Paul Newman, Phyllis Hill, Ben Astar

67. The Armstrong Circle Theatre: "Lost: $2,000,000" [a documentary drama of Hurricane Diane and its effect on the town of Winsten, Conn.] (9-4-56)

68. The Twentieth Century Fox Hour: "Man on the Ledge" [repeat of episode of 12/28/55] (9-5-56) William Gargan, Cameron Mitchell, Vera Miles, James Bell, Sylvia Sidney

69. The Kaiser Aluminum Hour: "Antigone" [adapted by Lewis Galantiere from the Jean Anouilh play of the Sophocles classic] (9-11-56) Mildred Natwick, Claude Rains, Alexander Scourby, Marisa Pavan

70. The United States Steel Hour: "We Must Kill Toni" [adapted by Leslie Duncan from the play by Ian Stuart Black] (9-12-56) Norman Lloyd, Fritz Weaver, Lisa Daniels

71. The Armstrong Circle Theatre: "The Second Family" [repeat of episode of 5/29/56] (9-18-56)

72. The Twentieth Century Fox Hour: "Overnight Haul" [repeat of episode of 5/16/56] (9-19-56)

73. The Kaiser Aluminum Hour: "Mr. Finchley Versus the Bomb" [by Rod Serling] (9-25-56) Henry Hull, Roland Winters

74. The United States Steel Hour: "Bang the Drum Slowly" [adapted by Arnold Schulman from the book by Mark Harris] (9-26-56) Paul Newman, Georgann Johnson

75. The Armstrong Circle Theatre: "The Bystander" [adapted by Art Wallace] (10-2-56) William Prince, Peggy McKay,

Gerald Sarracini

76. The Twentieth Century Fox Hour: "Child of the Regiment"
(10-3-56) Teresa Wright, Robert Preston, Everett Sloane
77. The Kaiser Aluminum Hour: "Carnival" [by Jerry deBoni]
(10-9-56) Natalie Wood, Dennis Hopper
78. The United States Steel Hour: "Sauce for the Goose" (10-10-
56) Bob Emmett, Gig Young, Gypsy Rose Lee, Leora
Dana
79. The Armstrong Circle Theatre: "SOS from the Andrea Doria"
[by George Lefferts] (10-16-56) Kent Smith, Bibi Osterwald, Val Avery; narrated by John Cameron Swayze
80. The Twentieth Century Fox Hour: "Stranger in the Night"
(10-17-56) Elsa Lanchester, Joan Fontaine, Michael Wilding, Tom Conway
81. The Kaiser Aluminum Hour: "Angels' Ransom" [adapted by
Evan Hunter from the novel by David Dodge] (10-23-56)
Hume Cronyn, Robert Sterling, Geraldine Brooks, Paul
Langton
82. The United States Steel Hour: "Wetback Run" (10-24-56)
Rip Torn, David Opatoshu, Joe De Santis
83. The Armstrong Circle Theatre: "Flareup" [by Sheldon Stark]
(10-30-56) Biff McGuire, Lorne Greene, Alexander Scourby
84. The Twentieth Century Fox Hour: "The Money Maker" (10-
31-56) Spring Byington, Terry Moore, Robert Sterling
85. The United States Steel Hour: "Survival" (11-7-56) Franchot
Tone, Albert Salmi, Arnold Moss
86. The Armstrong Circle Theatre: "Flight Number 307 from
Budapest" [by Harold Gast] (11-13-56) Jacqueline Scott,
Gerald Sarracini
87. The Twentieth Century Fox Hour: "Smoke Jumpers" (11-14-
56) Dan Duryea, Dean Jagger, Richard Jaeckel, Joan
Leslie
88. The Kaiser Aluminum Hour: "The Rag Jungle" [by Steven
Gethers] (11-20-56) Paul Newman
89. The United States Steel Hour: "Tom Sawyer" [a musical version by Frank Luther] (11-21-56) Jimmy Boyd, John
Sharpe, Bennye Gatteys, Ross Bampton, Clarence Cooper
90. The Twentieth Century Fox Hour: "The Last Patriarch"
(11-28-56) Walter Slezak, John Cassavetes, Vince Edwards, Virginia Leigh
91. The Kaiser Aluminum Hour: "Cracker Money" [by Steven
Gethers] (12-4-56) Glenda Farrell, Louis Jean Heydt
92. The United States Steel Hour: "Hunted" [by Mort Wishengrad]
(12-5-56) Ann Sheridan, Theodore Bikel
93. The Armstrong Circle Theatre: "Search, Seizure, and Arrest" (12-11-56) Robert Pastene
94. The Twentieth Century Fox Hour: "Men Against Speed" [by
John Robinson] (12-12-56) Farley Granger, Regis
Toomey, Rick Jason, Mona Freeman
95. The Kaiser Aluminum Hour: "Gwyneth" [adapted by Elliott
Baker from the story by Michael Gareth Llewelyn] (12-18-
56) Roddy McDowall, Joanne Linville, Rex Thompson,

John Laurie

96. The United States Steel Hour: "The Old Lady Shows Her Medals" [repeat of episode of 5/23/56] (12-19-56)

97. The Armstrong Circle Theatre: "Operation Deepfreeze: Crash of the Otter" [by Irve Tunick] (12-25-56) Philip Abbott

98. The Twentieth Century Fox Hour: "Operation Cicero" [by Ben Feiner Jr.] (12-26-56) Ricardo Montalban, Maria Riva, Peter Lorre

99. The Kaiser Aluminum Hour: "Members in Good Standing" [by Dick Berg] (1-1-57) Forrest Tucker, Nancy Coleman

100. The United States Steel Hour: "The Human Pattern" [by Irving H. Cooper] (1-2-57) Thelma Ritter, Frank McHugh, Michael Higgins, Lori March

101. The Armstrong Circle Theatre: "Divorcees Anonymous" [by Vance Bourjally] (1-8-57) June Dayton, Bibi Osterwald

102. The Twentieth Century Fox Hour: "End of a Gun" (1-9-57) Lyle Bettger, Marilyn Erskine, John Barrymore Jr.

103. The Kaiser Aluminum Hour: "A Real Fine Cutting Edge" [by Robert Dozier] (1-15-57) Dick York, Jack Wharton

104. The United States Steel Hour: "To Die Alone" [by Bob and Wanda Duncan] (1-16-57) Burl Ives, Jane Pickens

105. The Armstrong Circle Theatre: "Freedom Fighters of Hungary" [by Art Wallace] (1-22-57) Eva Soreny, Gerald Sarracini, Jon Cypher

106. The Twentieth Century Fox Hour: "False Witness" (1-23-57) Fred MacMurray, Lisa Golm, Natalie Norwick, Joe Mantell

107. The Kaiser Aluminum Hour: "Throw Me a Rope" [by Fielder Cook from the play by Franklin Barton] (1-29-57) Franchot Tone

108. The United States Steel Hour: "They Never Forget" [adapted by Norman Brooks from the play by Don Gregory] (1-30-57) Viveca Lindfors, Lloyd Bridges

109. The Armstrong Circle Theatre: "Error in Judgment: The Case of Prisoner #16688" (2-5-57) Biff McGuire, Patricia Smith

110. The Twentieth Century Fox Hour: "Young Man from Kentucky" (2-6-57) Tom Tryon, Ann Harding, Marshall Thompson

111. The Kaiser Aluminum Hour: "So Short a Season" [by Gene Roddenberry] (2-12-57) Albert Salmi, Rip Torn

112. The United States Steel Hour: "Inspired Alibi" (2-13-57) Shelley Winters, Pat Hingle

113. The Armstrong Circle Theatre: "The Trial of Poznan" (2-19-57) Peter Cookson, Hurd Hatfield, Bert Freed

114. The Twentieth Century Fox Hour: "Man of the Law" [adapted by David Lang from the story by Frank Fenton and Joseph Petracca] (2-20-57) Wendell Corey, Marsha Hunt, Ron Randell, Johnny Washbrook

115. The Kaiser Aluminum Hour: "Whereabouts Unknown" [by Sumner Locke Elliott] (2-26-57) Macdonald Carey, Kim

Hunter, Jan Sterling
116. The United States Steel Hour: "Shadow of Evil" (2-27-57)
Jack Cassidy, Shirley Jones, Lee Marvin
117. The Twentieth Century Fox Hour: "City in Flames" [adapted
by Kitty Buhler] (3-6-57) Anne Jeffreys, Kevin McCarthy, Roland Winters, Jeff Morrow, Lurene Tuttle
118. The Kaiser Aluminum Hour: "The Story of a Crime" (3-12-
57) Richard Kiley, Larry Gates, June Lockhart, Barbara
Baxley
119. The United States Steel Hour: "The Bottle Imp" (3-13-57)
Farley Granger, Susan Oliver
120. The Armstrong Circle Theatre: "Four Homes for Danny"
(3-19-57) Raymond Duke, Joe Maross, Peggy McCay
121. The Twentieth Century Fox Hour: "The Man Who Couldn't
Wait" [by Leo Liberman] (3-20-57) Arthur Franz,
Charles Bickford, Jay C. Flippen, Josephine Hutchinson
122. The Kaiser Aluminum Hour: "Hollywood Award Winner"
(3-26-57) Ralph Bellamy, Lee Philips
123. The United States Steel Hour: "Hidden Fury" [by George
Bellak] (3-27-57) James Gregory
124. The Armstrong Circle Theatre: "Arson--File #732" (4-2-57)
John Kellogg, Carl Low, Barbara Waide
125. The Twentieth Century Fox Hour: "The Still Trumpet" (4-3-
57) Dale Robertson, Victor Jory, Carol Ohmart
126. The Kaiser Aluminum Hour: "Murder in the House" (4-9-
57) Oscar Homolka, Gerald Sarracini, Joan Tetzel
127. The United States Steel Hour: "The Hill Wife" [by Alfred
Brenner] (4-10-57) Geraldine Page, Albert Salmi,
Melvyn Douglas, narrator
128. The Armstrong Circle Theatre: "Slow Assassination: Peron
vs. La Prensa" [by Irve Tunick] (4-16-57) Kent Smith
129. The Twentieth Century Fox Hour: "The Men in Her Life"
(4-17-57) Phyllis Kirk, Kendall Scott, Malcolm Broderick, Ann Doran
130. The Kaiser Aluminum Hour: "A Man's Game" [a musical
comedy by David Swift] (4-23-57) Nanette Fabray, Gene
Nelson, Paul Ford, Lew Parker, Leo Durocher
131. The United States Steel Hour: "A Matter of Pride" [adapted
by Frank Gilroy from the story by John Langdon] (4-24-
57) Burt Brinckerhoff, Pat Hingle, Philip Abbott
132. The Armstrong Circle Theatre: "Night Court" [by Art Wal-
lace] (4-30-57) David White, June Dayton, Wesley Lau,
Dennis Patrick
133. The Twentieth Century Fox Hour: "Deep Water" (5-1-57)
Ralph Meeker, James Whitmore, Richard Arlen
134. The Kaiser Aluminum Hour: "The Man Who Vanished" [by
Art Wallace] (5-7-57) Bruce Gordon
135. The United States Steel Hour: "A Drum Is a Woman" [a
jazz fantasy composed and narrated by Duke Ellington]
(5-8-57) Joya Sherrill, Margaret Tynes, Ozzie Bailey
136. The Armstrong Circle Theatre: "Day of Disaster: Riker's
Island" [by George Lefferts] (5-14-57)
137. The Twentieth Century Fox Hour: "The Great American

Hoax" [by Paddy Chayefsky] (5-15-57) Ed Wynn, Jesse White, Walter Abel, Kathleen Crowley, Conrad Nagel

138. The Kaiser Aluminum Hour: "The Deadly Silence" [by Irving Gaynor Neiman] (5-21-57) Ben Astar, Lili Darvas, Harry Guardino, William Shatner

139. The United States Steel Hour: "Shadow in the Sky" [by S. S. Schweitzer] (5-22-57) Richard Kiley, Peter Cookson, Bonita Granville

140. The Armstrong Circle Theatre: "Three Cents Worth of Fear" [by Harold Gast] (5-28-57) Frank Albertson, Hugh Reilly, Lois Wheeler, James Broderick, Ann Flood

141. The Twentieth Century Fox Hour: "Threat to a Happy Ending" (5-29-57) William Bendix, Gene Barry, Lori Nelson

142. The Kaiser Aluminum Hour: "Article Number 94: Homicide" [by Phil Reisman Jr.] (6-4-57) Jacqueline Scott, Sally Kemp, Janice Morris

143. The United States Steel Hour: "The Little Bullfighter" [by Juarez Roberts] (6-5-57) Nehemiah Persoff, Rip Torn, Olga Bellin, Kiko Oscard

144. The Armstrong Circle Theatre: "The Counterfeiters" (6-11-57) Jerome Cowan, Jerome Kilty

145. The Twentieth Century Fox Hour: "The Marriage Broker" (6-12-57) William Bishop, Glenda Farrell, Kipp Hamilton, Harry Morgan, Jesse White

146. The Kaiser Aluminum Hour: "A Passion for Revenge" [by Leslie Slote] (6-18-57) Alexander Scourby, Joanne Le-Compte, Frank Sutton

147. The United States Steel Hour: "Upbeat" (6-19-57) Patti Page, Biff McGuire, Jon Cypher

148. The Armstrong Circle Theatre: "The Hunted" (6-25-57) Eva Soreny, Robert Goodier, Cic Linder, Sandor Szabo

149. The Twentieth Century Fox Hour: "End of a Gun" [repeat of episode of 1/9/57] (6-26-57)

150. The United States Steel Hour: "Sideshow" [by Shelby Gordon] (7-3-57) Lisa Daniels, Abe Simon, Read Morgan

151. The Twentieth Century Fox Hour: "Operation Cicero" [repeat of episode of 12/26/56] (7-20-57)

152. The United States Steel Hour: "Victim" [by James Edward] (7-17-57) Dean Stockwell, Walter Matthau

153. The Twentieth Century Fox Hour: "False Witness" [repeat of episode of 1/23/57] (7-24-57)

154. The United States Steel Hour: "The Change in Chester" [by Arthur Hailey] (7-31-57) John McGiver, Tom Poston, Alan Hewitt, Marcel Hillaire, Barbara Hall

155. The Twentieth Century Fox Hour: "Man of the Law" [repeat of episode of 2/20/57] (8-7-57)

156. The United States Steel Hour: "A Loud Laugh" (8-14-57) June Lockhart

157. The Twentieth Century Fox Hour: "The Men in Her Life" [repeat of episode of 4/17/57] (8-21-57)

158. The United States Steel Hour: "Up Above the World So High" [by Mort Thaw] (8-28-57) Jack Warden, Carmen

Matthews, Dennis Kohler

159. The Twentieth Century Fox Hour: "The Great American Hoax" [repeat of episode of 5/15/57] (9-4-57)

160. The United States Steel Hour: "Windfall" [by Bob and Wanda Duncan] (9-11-57) Ed Begley, Burt Brinckerhoff, Andrew Duggan

161. The Twentieth Century Fox Hour: "Threat to a Happy Ending" [repeat of episode of 5/29/57] (9-18-57)

162. The United States Steel Hour: "Haunted Harbor" [by Henry Misrock] (9-25-57) Joseph Campanella, Burgess Meredith, Gaby Rodgers

163. The Armstrong Circle Theatre: "Buried Two Thousand Years: The Dead Sea Scrolls" [by Irve Tunick] (10-2-57) with Dr. Elagar Sukenik

164. The United States Steel Hour: "Who's Earnest?" [a musical adapted by Anne Croswell and Lee Pockriss from the Oscar Wilde story] (10-9-57) Edward Mulhare, Dorothy Collins

165. The Armstrong Circle Theatre: "Crisis on Longier Island" [by Roger Hirson] (10-16-57) Kent Smith, Frances Reid

166. The United States Steel Hour: "Crisis in Corona" [by Elliott Baker] (10-23-57) Elliott Nugent, Charles Ruggles, John McGovern, Betty Lou Kelm

167. The Armstrong Circle Theatre: "Assignment: Junkies' Alley" [by Mel Goldberg] (10-30-57) Monica Lovett, Addison Powell

168. The United States Steel Hour: "The Locked Door" [by Gertrude Schweitzer] (11-6-57) Ralph Bellamy, June Lockhart, Brandon de Wilde

169. The Armstrong Circle Theatre: "John Doe #154" [adapted by Abram Ginnes] (11-13-57) John Napier, William Prince

170. The United States Steel Hour: "The Adventures of Huckleberry Finn" [a musical version with music and lyrics by Frank Luther; Lee Pockriss and Anne Croswell adapted] (11-20-57) Jack Carson, Jimmy Boyd, Basil Rathbone, Earle Hyman, Florence Henderson, Karlen Wolfe

171. The Armstrong Circle Theatre: "Have Jacket, Will Travel" [by Vance Bourjally] (11-27-57) Patty Duke

172. The United States Steel Hour: "You Can't Win" [by Robert Emmet] (12-4-57) Bert Lahr, Margaret Hamilton

173. The Armstrong Circle Theatre: "Thief of Diamonds" [by Alvin Yudkoff] (12-11-57) Carol Bruce

174. The United States Steel Hour: "Little Charlie Don't Want a Saddle" [by Juarez Roberts] (12-18-57) June Lockhart, John Beal

175. The Armstrong Circle Theatre: "The Shepherd of Paris" [adapted by Michael Dyne from the book by Boris Simon] (12-25-57) Martin Brooks

176. The United States Steel Hour: "The Charmer" [by Douglas Taylor] (1-1-58) Gypsy Rose Lee, Rip Torn

177. The Armstrong Circle Theatre: "The Complex Mummy Complex" [by Abram Ginnes] (1-8-58) Lois Nettleton, James

Broderick, Julia Meade
178. The United States Steel Hour: "The Bromley Touch" [adapted by Kay Arthur from the story by Edward Newhouse] (1-15-58) Biff McGuire, Cameron Mitchell, Leora Dana
179. The Armstrong Circle Theatre: "U.F.O.: The Enigma of the Skies" [by Irve Tunick] (1-22-58) narrated by Douglas Edwards
180. The United States Steel Hour: "Never Know the End" [by Irving Gaynor Neiman] (1-29-58) Larry Blyden, Andy Griffith, Nehemiah Persoff, Patricia Beroit
181. The Armstrong Circle Theatre: "The New Class" [adapted by Alvin Boretz from The New Class: The Book Heard 'Round the World] (2-5-58) Peter Falk, Fritz Weaver, Vera Fusek
182. The United States Steel Hour: "The Reward" [adapted by Mort Thaw from the story by Laura Z. Hobson] (2-12-58) Patty Duke, Nancy Coleman, Cathleen Nesbitt, Hugh Reilly
183. The Armstrong Circle Theatre: "Have Jacket, Will Travel" [repeat of episode of 11/27/57] (2-19-58)
184. The United States Steel Hour: "Walk with a Stranger" [by H. N. Blauss] (2-26-58) Ed Begley, William Shatner
185. The Armstrong Circle Theatre: "Thirty Days to Reconsider" [by Roger Hirson] (3-5-58) Lin McCarthy
186. The United States Steel Hour: "Give Me My Son" [adapted by Abby Mann from the story by Ann Wormsar and Jess Oppenheimer] (3-12-58) Richard Kiley, Betsy Palmer, Lori March, Alexander Scourby
187. The Armstrong Circle Theatre: "The Meanest Crime in the World" [by Jerome Coopersmith] (3-19-58) William Prince, Nancy Wickwire
188. The United States Steel Hour: "Top Secret Mission" [by Irving Gaynor Neiman from the book by Madeleine Duke] (3-26-58) Beatrice Straight
189. The Armstrong Circle Theatre: "The Twisted Thief" [by Alvin Boretz] (4-2-58)
190. The United States Steel Hour: "The Beaver Patrol" [by John Vlahos] (4-9-58) Walter Slezak
191. The Armstrong Circle Theatre: "The Vanished" [based on the novel I Was a Slave in Russia by John Noble] (4-16-58)
192. The United States Steel Hour: "The Public Prosecutor" [by Theodore Apstein from the play by Fritz Hock Walders] (4-23-58) John Baragrey, Dolores Del Rio
193. The United States Steel Hour: "A Man in Hiding" [by Leonard Moran] (5-7-58) William Shatner
194. The Armstrong Circle Theatre: "Accused of Murder" [by Art Wallace] (5-14-58) Tom Carlin, Lois Nettleton
195. The United States Steel Hour: "Hour of the Rat" [adapted by Arthur Hailey from the play by John Manchip White] (5-21-58) Dan Duryea
196. The United States Steel Hour: "A Family Alliance" [adapted by Kay Arthur from the story by Dorothy Canfield] (6-

4-58)  Florence Henderson, Robert Haynes, Bill Hayes

197. The Armstrong Circle Theatre: "Kidnap Story: Hold for Release" [adapted by John Campbell Bruce from an article by Leonard Moskovitz] (6-11-58)

198. The United States Steel Hour: "The Littlest Enemy" [adapted by Lois Jacoby from the play by Nigel Kneale] (6-18-58) Lili Darvas, Miko Oscard, Frank Conroy, Mary Astor

199. The Armstrong Circle Theatre: "Twelve Cases of Murder" [by Irve Tunick] (6-25-58) Simon Oakland, William Post, Norman Rose; narrated by Douglas Edwards

200. The United States Steel Hour: "The Hidden River" [adapted by Theodore Apstein from the Broadway play by Ruth and Augustus Goetz from the novel by Storm Jameson] (7-2-58) Farley Granger, Richard Kiley

201. The Armstrong Circle Theatre: "The Complex Mummy Complex" [repeat of episode of 1/8/58] (7-9-58)

202. The United States Steel Hour: "Flint and Fire" [adapted by Robert Van Scoyk from the story by Dorothy Canfield] (7-16-58) Robert Culp, Una Merkel

203. The Armstrong Circle Theatre: "Thirty Days to Reconsider" [repeat of episode of 3/5/58] (7-23-58) Lin McCarthy, Joan Copeland

204. The United States Steel Hour: "The Climate of Marriage" [by Helen Cotton] (7-30-58) James Daly, Leora Dana, Larry Hagman, Betsy Palmer

205. The Armstrong Circle Theatre: "The Trusted Thief" [repeat of episode of 4/2/58] (8-6-58)

206. The United States Steel Hour: "Old Marshals Never Die" [adapted by John Vlahos from the story by John H. Holland] (8-13-58) William Shatner, Kevin Coughlin, Cameron Prud'homme

207. The Armstrong Circle Theatre: "Twelve Cases of Murder" [repeat of episode of 6/25/58] (8-20-58)

208. The United States Steel Hour: "Be My Guest" [by John Whedon] (8-27-58) Elliott Nugent, Joanna Moore, Augusta Dabney

209. The Armstrong Circle Theatre: "Kidnap Story: Hold for Release" [repeat of episode of 6/11/58] (9-3-58)

210. The United States Steel Hour: "The Wound Within" [by Henry Denker] (9-10-58) Farley Granger, Frank Conroy, Mary Sinclair

211. The Armstrong Circle Theatre: "Buried Two Thousand Years: The Dead Sea Scrolls" (9-17-58)

212. The United States Steel Hour: "Death Minus One" [by Arthur Hailey] (9-24-58) Alexander Scourby, Meg Murphy, Beverly Lunsford

213. The Armstrong Circle Theatre: "The Case for Room 310" [by Alvin Boretz] (10-1-58) Robert Drivas; Douglas Edwards narrates

214. The United States Steel Hour: "Mid-Summer" [adapted by Arthur Heinemann from the play by Vina Delmar] (10-8-58) Barbara Bel Geddes, Jackie Cooper

215. The United States Steel Hour: "Secret in the Family"

[adapted by Louis Pelletier from the novel by Helen Hull]
(10-22-58) Faye Emerson, Edward Andrews

216. The Armstrong Circle Theatre: "The House of Flying Objects" [by Irve Tunick] (10-29-58) narrated by Douglas Edwards

217. The United States Steel Hour: "Second Chance" [by Steven Gethers] (11-5-58) Melvyn Douglas, Nancy Olson, Meg Mundy

218. The Armstrong Circle Theatre: "Money for Sale" [by David Davidson] (11-12-58) Fred Scollay

219. The United States Steel Hour: "This Day in Fear" [adapted by Arthur Heinemann from the play by Eric Paice and Malcolm A. Hulke] (11-19-58) Geraldine Brooks, Barry Sullivan

220. The Armstrong Circle Theatre: "SSN-571: The Nautilus" [by Jerome Coopersmith] (11-26-58) James Mitchell; narrated by Douglas Edwards

221. The United States Steel Hour: "The Enemies" [adapted by Robert Van Scoyk from the story by Stephen Vincent Benet] (12-3-58) Ed Begley, Betsy Palmer, Arthur Hill, Bramwell Fletcher

222. The Armstrong Circle Theatre: "The Invisible Mark" (12-10-58) narrated by Douglas Edwards

223. The United States Steel Hour: "One Red Rose for Christmas" [adapted by Leonard Moran from the novelette by Paul Horgan] (12-17-58) Helen Hayes, Patty Duke, Joseph Sweeney, Ruth McDevitt, Ruth White

224. The United States Steel Hour: "Goodbye ... But It Doesn't Go Away" [by Rafael Hayes] (12-31-58) Jeff Donnell, Inga Swenson, George Voskovec, Jack Carson, June Lockhart, Geraldine Brooks, Neville Brand

225. The Armstrong Circle Theatre: "And Bring Home a Baby" (1-7-59) Philip Abbott; narrated by Douglas Edwards

226. The United States Steel Hour: "Dangerous Interlude" (1-14-59) Viveca Lindfors, Torin Thatcher

227. The Armstrong Circle Theatre: "The Man with a Thousand Names" (1-21-59) Larry Gates, Milton Selzer, Joseph Campanella

228. The Armstrong Circle Theatre: "Miracle at Spring Hill" [by Art Wallace] (2-4-59) Nancy Marchand, Michael Constantine, Frank Martin

229. The United States Steel Hour: "Family Happiness" [adapted from the Leo Tolstoy novel] (2-11-59) Gloria Vanderbilt, Patty Duke, Jean Pierre Aumont

230. The Armstrong Circle Theatre: "House of Cards" (2-18-59) David White, Simon Oakland, Kathleen Maguire; Dr. George B. Stevenson, guest

231. The United States Steel Hour: "Trap for a Stranger" (2-25-59) George C. Scott, Dick Van Dyke, Teresa Wright

232. The Armstrong Circle Theatre: "The White Collar Bandit" (3-4-59) Douglas Edwards, host

233. The United States Steel Hour: "The Square Egghead" [by Louis Pelletier] (3-11-59) Tom Ewell, Robert Lansing,

June Lockhart

234. The United States Steel Hour: "Night of Betrayal" (3-25-59) Melville Cooper, Roddy McDowall, Victor Jory, Carol Lawrence

235. The Armstrong Circle Theatre: "The Innocent Killer" [by Mel Goldberg] (4-1-59) Scott McKay; Douglas Edwards narrates

236. The United States Steel Hour: "Trouble-in-Law" (4-8-59) Betsy Von Furstenberg, John McGiver, Gertrude Berg

237. The Armstrong Circle Theatre: "Trail of Diamonds" [by Harold Gast] (4-15-59) Frederick O'Neal; Douglas Edwards narrates

238. The United States Steel Hour: "Little Tin God" [by Joe Palmer Jr.] (4-22-59) Jeff Donnell, Richard Boone, Gene Hackman

239. The Armstrong Circle Theatre: "Sound of Violence: The Juke Box Racket" [by Art Wallace] (4-29-59) Vincent Gardenia, Frank Sutton, Val Avery; Senator John McClellan of Arkansas

240. The United States Steel Hour: "The Wayward Widow" [adapted by Michael Dyne from the Thomas Hardy novel] (5-6-59) Richard Greene, Betsy Palmer

241. The Armstrong Circle Theatre: "Thunder Over Berlin" [by Roger Hirson] (5-13-59) Douglas Edwards narrates

242. The United States Steel Hour: "Call It a Day" (5-20-59) Faye Emerson, Edward Andrews, Zina Bethune

243. The Armstrong Circle Theatre: "Prescription: Hypnosis" [by Jerome Coopersmith] (5-27-59) Douglas Edwards narrates

244. The United States Steel Hour: "Whisper of Evil" (6-3-59) John Beal, Nina Foch, Chester Morris

245. The Armstrong Circle Theatre: "The Monkey Ride" (6-10-59) Val Avery, Susan Oliver, Conrad Janis; Douglas Edwards narrates

246. The United States Steel Hour: "No Leave for the Captain" (6-17-59) Geraldine Brooks, Maurice Evans, Diana Van Der Vlis, Nicolas Costas

247. The Armstrong Circle Theatre: "The Zone of Silence" [by Roger O. Hirson] (6-24-59) Patty Duke

248. The United States Steel Hour: "Apple of His Eye" (7-1-59) Eddie Albert, Carol Lawrence, Frank McHugh

249. The Armstrong Circle Theatre: "Sound of Violence: The Juke Box Racket" [repeat of episode of 4/29/59] (7-8-59)

250. The United States Steel Hour: "The Pink Burrow" (7-15-59) June Havoc, Jane Withers, Edward Andrews

251. The Armstrong Circle Theatre: "House of Cards" [repeat of episode of 2/18/59] (7-22-59)

252. The United States Steel Hour: "We Wish on the Moon" [by Sumner Locke Elliott] (7-29-59) Peggy Ann Garner, Biff McGuire, Erin O'Brien, William Gaxton

253. The Armstrong Circle Theatre: "Prescription: Hypnosis" [repeat of episode of 5/27/59] (8-5-59)

254. The United States Steel Hour: "Seed of Guilt" [by Barbara Chain] (8-12-59) Patty Duke, Lois Nettleton, Gloria Vanderbilt, Peggy Wood, Herbert Nelson
255. The Armstrong Circle Theatre: "SSN-571: The Nautilus" [repeat of episode of 11/26/58] (8-19-59)
256. The United States Steel Hour: "A Taste of Champagne" [adapted by Robert Van Scoyk from the story by Allan Seager] (8-26-59) Hans Conried, Monique Van Vooren, Scott McKay
257. The Armstrong Circle Theatre: "The White Collar Bandit" [repeat of episode of 3/4/59] (9-2-59)
258. The United States Steel Hour: "The Case of Julia Walton" [adapted by Harold Gast from a screenplay by Jay Ingram] (9-9-59) Robert Lansing, Nina Foch, Jeffrey Lynn, Peter Lazer, Alan Baxter
259. The United States Steel Hour: "The Hours Before Dawn" (9-23-59) Colleen Dewhurst, Mark Richman, Teresa Wright
260. The Armstrong Circle Theatre: "The Zone of Silence" [repeat of episode of 6/24/59] (9-30-59)
261. The United States Steel Hour: "Rachel's Summer" [adapted by Ron Sproat from the story by Charles Jackson] (10-7-59) Patty McCormack, Martha Scott
262. The Armstrong Circle Theatre: "The Jailbreak" [by Irve Tunick] (10-14-59) Robert Duvall, John McQuade; Douglas Edwards narrates
263. The United States Steel Hour Special: "Holiday on Wheels" (10-21-59) Sid Caesar, Audrey Meadows, Tony Randall, Giselle MacKenzie
264. The Armstrong Circle Theatre: "35 Rue Du Marche" [by Harold Gast] (10-28-59) Telly Savalas
265. The United States Steel Hour: "Big Doc's Girl" [adapted by Leonard Moran from the story by Mary Medearis] (11-4-59) Robert Lansing, Margaret O'Brien, Gene Hackman
266. The United States Steel Hour: "The Lost Autumn" [adapted by Arthur Heinemann from the novel by Herbert Gutterson] (11-18-59) Pat Hingle, House Jameson, Alexis Smith
267. The Armstrong Circle Theatre: "Security Risk" [by Jerome Coopersmith] (11-25-59) Larry Gates; Douglas Edwards narrates
268. The United States Steel Hour Special: "Marriage--Handle with Care" (12-2-59) with Sid Caesar, Jose Ferrer, Connie Francis, Marge and Gower Champion
269. The Armstrong Circle Theatre: "Operation Moonshine" [by Art Wallace] (12-9-59) William Smithers; Douglas Edwards narrates
270. The United States Steel Hour: "One Red Rose for Christmas" [repeat of episode of 12/17/58] (12-16-59)
271. The Armstrong Circle Theatre: "The Boy on Page One" [by Jerome Coopersmith] (12-23-59) Nancy Wickwire, Jay Barney, Bibi Osterwald
272. The United States Steel Hour: "Act of Terror" [by Thomas

Weitzner] (12-30-59) George Grizzard, Nancy Berg,
Mark Richman, Frank Conroy
273. The United States Steel Hour: "Queen of the Orange Bowl"
[adapted by Robert Van Scoyk from the play by Roger
Squire] (1-13-60) Johnny Carson, Glenda Farrell, Anne
Francis, Frank McHugh
274. The Armstrong Circle Theatre: "Full Disclosure" [by Harold
Gast] (1-20-60) Martin E. Brooks, Lawrence Hugo,
Don Briggs, Joseph Leon; Douglas Edwards narrates
275. The United States Steel Hour: "You Can't Have Everything"
[adapted by James Yaffee from the play by Jack Pulman]
(1-27-60) Piper Laurie, Donald Moffat, Florence Reed
276. The Armstrong Circle Theatre: "Ghost Bomber: Lady Be
Good" [by Roger O. Hirson] (2-3-60) Douglas Edwards
narrates, George Segal, Conrad Fawks
277. The United States Steel Hour Special: "The American Cowboy" (2-10-60) with Fred MacMurray, Wally Cox,
Carol Burnett, Hans Conried, Edie Adams
278. The Armstrong Circle Theatre: "Iron City Justice" (2-17-
60)
279. The United States Steel Hour: "The Women of Hadley" [see
episode of 3/9/60] (2-24-60) Mary Astor, Rita Gam,
Mona Freeman, Richard Kiley, Sir Cedric Hardwicke
280. The Armstrong Circle Theatre: "Raid in Beatnik Village"
[by Abram S. Ginnes] (3-2-60) Conrad Janis; Douglas
Edwards narrates
281. The United States Steel Hour: "Revolt in Hadley" [adapted
by Eric Barnouw from the novel by Roger Eddy] (3-9-
60) Mary Astor, Rita Gam, Mona Freeman, Richard
Kiley, Sir Cedric Hardwicke
282. The Armstrong Circle Theatre: "The Desperate Season"
(3-16-60)
283. The United States Steel Hour: "The Charlie and Kid" (3-23-
60) Richard Boone
284. The Armstrong Circle Theatre: "Trial by Fury" (3-30-60)
285. The United States Steel Hour: "How to Make a Killing" (4-
6-60) Robert Loggia, Claude Dauphin, Eva Gabor
286. The Armstrong Circle Theatre: "The Numbers Racket" (4-
13-60)
287. The United States Steel Hour: "The Girl Who Knew Too
Much" (4-20-60) Mona Freeman, Arthur Hill
288. The Armstrong Circle Theatre: "Dishonor System" (4-27-
60) Frank Aletter
289. The United States Steel Hour: "The Girl in the Golden
Bathtub" (5-4-60) Johnny Carson, Jessie Royce Landis
290. The Armstrong Circle Theatre: "Separate Parents" [by
Alvin Boretz] (5-11-60) Nancy Wickwire; Douglas Edwards, host
291. The Armstrong Circle Theatre: "Positive Identification"
(5-25-60) Robert Duvall
292. The United States Steel Hour: "Game of Hearts" (6-1-60)
Jeff Donnell, Arthur Hill, Betsy Palmer
293. The Armstrong Circle Theatre: "Illegal Entry" [by Art

Wallace] (6-8-60) Staats Cotsworth, Fred Scollay;
Douglas Edwards, host

294. The United States Steel Hour: "The Imposter" (6-15-60)
Jean Pierre Aumont, Ann Sheridan

295. The Armstrong Circle Theatre: "The Prison Professor"
(6-22-60) Simon Oakland, Robert Gerringer

296. The United States Steel Hour: "The Great Gold Mountain"
(6-29-60) Ed Begley, Robert Lansing, Polly Bergen

297. The Armstrong Circle Theatre: "Full Disclosure" [repeat
of episode of 1/20/60] (7-6-60)

298. The United States Steel Hour: "Shadow of a Pale Horse"
(7-20-60) Carroll O'Connor, Dan Duryea, Frank Lovejoy

299. The Armstrong Circle Theatre: "Raid in Beatnik Village"
[repeat of episode of 3/2/60] (8-3-60)

300. The United States Steel Hour: "The Case of the Missing
Wife" (8-10-60) Red Buttons, Nancy Wickwire, John
Colicos, Gaby Rogers, Eric Berry

301. The Armstrong Circle Theatre: "Operation Moonshine" [re-
peat of episode of 12/9/59] (8-17-60)

302. The United States Steel Hour: "Bride of the Fox" (8-24-60)
Ina Balin, Gene Hackman, Richard Kiley

303. The Armstrong Circle Theatre: "Security Risk" [repeat of epi
sode of 11/25/59] (8-31-60)

304. The United States Steel Hour: "When in Rome" (9-7-60)
Arlene Francis

305. The Armstrong Circle Theatre: "Dishonor System" [repeat
of episode of 4/27/60] (9-14-60)

306. The United States Steel Hour: "The Man Who Knew Tomorrow" (9-21-60) Cliff Robertson, Paul Lee, Jeanne
Crain

307. The Armstrong Circle Theatre: "Ghost Bomber: Lady Be
Good" [repeat of episode of 2/3/60] (9-28-60)

308. The United States Steel Hour: "The Revolt of Judge Lloyd"
(10-5-60) Claire Trevor, Jeff Morrow

309. The Armstrong Circle Theatre: "Engineer of Death: The
Eichmann Story" [by Dale Wasserman] (10-12-60) Carroll O'Connor; Douglas Edwards narrates

310. The United States Steel Hour: "A Time to Decide" (11-2-
60) Nina Foch, Barry Nelson, Cathleen Nesbitt

311. The Armstrong Circle Theatre: "The Antique Swindle" (11-
9-60) Harry Townes, Joan Copeland, Robert Gerri

312. The Armstrong Circle Theatre: "The Hidden World" (11-23-
60) Peter Von Zerneck, Suzanne Storrs; Douglas Edwards narrates

313. The United States Steel Hour: "The Yum Yum Girl" (11-30-
60) Robert Sterling, Anne Francis

314. The Armstrong Circle Theatre: "A Memory of a Murder"
[by Harold Gast] (12-7-60) Harry Millard; Douglas Edwards narrates

315. The United States Steel Hour: "Shame the Devil" (12-14-60)
Betsy Palmer, Conrad Janis, Vincent Price, J. D. Cannon

316. The Armstrong Circle Theatre: "The Immortal Piano" (12-
21-60) Douglas Edwards narrates

317. The United States Steel Hour: "Operation Northstar" (12-28-60) Mona Freeman, J. D. Cannon, Barry Sullivan
318. The Armstrong Circle Theatre: "Black Market Babies" (1-4-61) Barbara Barrie, Paul Sparer, Olive Deering
319. The United States Steel Hour: "The Mating Machine" (1-11-61) Geraldine Brooks, George Grizzard, Diana Lynn, John Ericson
320. The Armstrong Circle Theatre: "Medicine Man" (1-18-61) Carroll O'Connor, Addison Powell, Philip Bosco
321. The United States Steel Hour: "The Devil Makes Sunday" (1-25-61) Dane Clark, Martyn Green, Brooke Hayward, Frank Conroy
322. The Armstrong Circle Theatre: "The Zone of Silence" [repeat of episode of 6/24/59] (2-1-61)
323. The United States Steel Hour: "The Big Splash" (2-8-61) Elizabeth Ashley, Keir Dullea, Michael Tolan, Jack Carson, Arlene Francis
324. The Armstrong Circle Theatre: "The Spy Next Door" (2-15-61) Wesley Addy, Max Slater, Lori March, Bill Daniels, Carl Low
325. The United States Steel Hour: "The Two Worlds of Charlie Gordon" (2-22-61) Cliff Robertson, Mona Freeman, Gerald S. O'Loughlin, Maxwell Shaw, Joanna Roos
326. The Armstrong Circle Theatre: "The Fortune Tellers" (3-1-61) Rose Gregorio, Val Avery, Carmen Matthews, Louise Latham
327. The United States Steel Hour: "Private Eye, Private Eye" (3-8-61) Ernie Kovacs, Edie Adams, Pat Carroll, Hans Conried
328. The Armstrong Circle Theatre: "Minerva's Children" (3-15-61) Douglas Edwards narrates
329. The United States Steel Hour: "Welcome Home" (3-22-61) Shirley Booth, Elizabeth Wilson, Henderson Forsythe, Flora Campbell
330. The Armstrong Circle Theatre: "The Crime Without a Country" [by Max Ehrlich] (3-29-61) Dort Clark, Frank Daley, Jamie Zakkai
331. The United States Steel Hour: "The Oddball" (4-5-61) Hans Conried, Faye Emerson, Beverly Lunsford, John Garson
332. The Armstrong Circle Theatre: "Engineer of Death: The Eichmann Story" [repeat of episode of 10/12/60] (4-12-61)
333. The United States Steel Hour: "The Shame of Paula Marsten" (4-19-61) Anne Baxter, Mark Richman, Gene Raymond
334. The Armstrong Circle Theatre: "Briefing from Room 103" (4-26-61) Michael Tolan, John Balzac; Douglas Edwards narrates
335. The United States Steel Hour: "Summer Rhapsody" (5-3-61) Glenda Farrell, Clinton Kimbrough, Tom Tully, Abigail Kellogg
336. The Armstrong Circle Theatre: "Moment of Panic" (5-10-61) Kevin McCarthy, Frank Marth, Rosemary Murphy, Lou Frizzelli
337. The United States Steel Hour: "The Lionardi Code" (5-17-

61) Sally Ann Howes, Barry Morse, Tim O'Connor, Chris Wiggins

338. The Armstrong Circle Theatre: "Days of Confusion: The Story of College Admissions" [by Harold Gast] (5-24-61) Lori Nelson, Ronnie Welch, Robert Gerring; Douglas Edwards, host

339. The United States Steel Hour: "Famous" [adapted from the story by Stephen Vincent Benet] (5-31-61) Eddie Albert, Lola Albright, Dolores Gray, Zina Bethune, Louise Albritton, Malcolm Broderick

340. The Armstrong Circle Theatre: "Parole Granted" (6-7-61) Philip Abbott, Fred J. Scollay, Michael Constantine

341. The United States Steel Hour: "Trial Without Jury" [by Elliott Baker] (6-14-61) Richard Kiley, Paul Stevens, Mary Fickett

342. The Armstrong Circle Theatre: "The Dedicated American: The Story of Dr. Gordon Seagrave" (6-21-61) Walter Cronkite narrates

343. The United States Steel Hour: "The Haven" [by Tad Mosel] (6-28-61) Shirley Booth, Gene Raymond, Joseph Sweeney, Truman Smith

344. The Armstrong Circle Theatre: "The Spy Next Door" [repeat of episode of 2/15/61] (7-5-61)

345. The United States Steel Hour: "Watching Out for Dulle" [from the novel by David Westheimer] (7-12-61) Larry Blyden, Shari Lewis

346. The Armstrong Circle Theatre: "A Memory of a Murder" [repeat of episode of 12/7/60] (7-19-61)

347. The United States Steel Hour: 'Double Edged Sword" (7-26-61) Cathleen Nesbitt, Leo G. Carroll, Sarah Marshall

348. The Armstrong Circle Theatre: "Black Market Babies" [repeat of episode of 1/4/61] (8-2-61)

349. The United States Steel Hour: "The Golden Thirty" (8-9-61) Keir Dullea, Henny Youngman

350. The Armstrong Circle Theatre: "The Crime Without a Country" [repeat of episode of 3/29/61] (8-16-61)

351. The United States Steel Hour: "Woman Across the Hall" [by Robert Wallsten] (8-23-61) Glenda Farrell, Ruth Ford, Alan Bunce

352. The Armstrong Circle Theatre: "Moment of Panic" [repeat of episode of 5/10/61] (8-30-61)

353. The United States Steel Hour: 'Delayed Honeymoon" [adapted by Robert Van Scoyk from the story by Peter Taylor] (9-6-61)

354. The Armstrong Circle Theatre: 'Days of Confusion: The Story of College Admissions" [repeat of episode of 5/24/61] (9-13-61)

355. The United States Steel Hour: "Street of Love" [adapted by Harold Gast from the story by Max Ehrlich] (9-20-61) Doug McClure, Millie Perkins

356. The United States Steel Hour: "Brandenberg Gate" [by John Vlahos] (10-4-61) Gene Hackman, Dina Merrill,

Richard Kiley
357. The Armstrong Circle Theatre: "Legend of Murder--The
Untold Story of Lizzie Borden" [by Don Mankiewicz]
(10-11-61) Claire Blackburn, Paul McGrath
358. The United States Steel Hour: "Bury Me Twice" (10-18-61)
Leo G. Carroll, Phyllis Thaxter, Dan O'Herlihy
359. The Armstrong Circle Theatre: "A Chapter on Tyranny:
Dateline Berlin" [by Jerome Ross] (10-25-61) Ron
Cochran narrates
360. The United States Steel Hour: "Little Lost Sheep" (11-1-
61) Rochelle Oliver, Jane Wyatt, Garrick Hagon, Hans
Conried
361. The Armstrong Circle Theatre: "The Thief of Charity"
(11-8-61) Frank Aletter, Vince O'Brien; Ron Cochran
narrates
362. The United States Steel Hour: "Man on the Mountain Top"
(11-15-61) Cliff Robertson, Paul McGrath, Salome Jens
363. The Armstrong Circle Theatre: "Track of an Unknown:
The Story of North American Air Defense" [by Jerome
Coopersmith] (11-22-61) Michael Higgens, Alexander
Scourby
364. The United States Steel Hour: "Tangle of Truth" (11-29-61)
Jeff Donnell, Darryl Hickman, Macdonald Carey
365. The Armstrong Circle Theatre: "Spin a Crooked Record"
(12-6-61) Edmond Ryan, William Smithers, Mindy Carson; Ron Cochran narrates
366. The United States Steel Hour: "My Wife's Best Friend"
(12-13-61) Larry Blyden, Joanna Moore, Doris Dalton
367. The Armstrong Circle Theatre: "The Battle of Hearts"
(12-20-61) Arthur Hill, Lydia Bruce, Luke Halpin
368. The United States Steel Hour: "The Bitter Sex" (12-27-61)
Lloyd Bochner, Barry Morse, Mona Freeman
369. The Armstrong Circle Theatre: "Window on the West" (1-
3-62) Ron Cochran narrates
370. The United States Steel Hour: "Far from the Shade Tree"
(1-10-62) Keir Dullea, Jack Carson, Gene Hackman,
Anita Louise
371. The Armstrong Circle Theatre: "Securities for Suckers"
[by Harold Gast] (1-17-62) Fred Clark, Howard Caine,
Mark Dawson; Ron Cochran narrates
372. The United States Steel Hour: "The Big Laugh" (1-24-62)
Arthur Hill, Teresa Wright, Murray Hamilton, Michael Sivy
373. The Armstrong Circle Theatre: "Runaway Road: Story of
a Missing Person" (1-31-62) Kevin Coughlin, Aina
Niemala
374. The United States Steel Hour: "A Nightmare at Bleak Hill"
(2-7-62) Douglas Fairbanks Jr., Leora Dana, Donald
Madden
375. The Armstrong Circle Theatre: "The Perfect Accident"
(2-21-62) Shepperd Strudwick, Robert Horton, Alan
Bruce, Nancy Wickwire, Carolyn Groves
376. The Armstrong Circle Theatre: "Assignment--Teenage
Junkies" (2-28-62) Patrick McVey, Joseph Leon, Don

Morgan, James Dimitri, Dabney Coleman

377. The United States Steel Hour: "Who Is This Woman?" (3-7-62) Gloria De Haven, Donald Davis, Arthur Hill

378. The Armstrong Circle Theatre: "The Man Who Refused to Die" (3-14-62) Alexander Scourby, Carl Low

379. The United States Steel Hour: "Two Black Kings" (3-21-62) Kevin McCarthy, James Broderick, Eva Gabor

380. The Armstrong Circle Theatre: "Merchants of Evil" (3-28-62) Carlos Montalban, Tim O'Connor, Peter Von Zerneck

381. The United States Steel Hour: "The Loves of Claire Ambler" (4-4-62) Nancy Carroll, Maurice Evans, Janice Rule

382. The Armstrong Circle Theatre: "Patterns of Hope: A Story of Cancer Control" (4-11-62)

383. The United States Steel Hour: "The Go-Between" (4-18-62) Keefe Brasselle, Barbara Cook

384. The Armstrong Circle Theatre: "Black Bird of Space: The Story of the X-15" (4-25-62)

385. The United States Steel Hour: "A Man for Oona" (5-2-62) Tallulah Bankhead, Nancy Carroll

386. The Armstrong Circle Theatre: "Anatomy of Betrayal--Dateline Cuba" (5-9-62)

387. The United States Steel Hour: "The Other Woman" (5-16-62) Jeanne Crain, Hugh Reilly, Lloyd Bochner

388. The Armstrong Circle Theatre: "The Secret Crime" (5-23-62) Gene Raymond, Barbara Baxley

389. The Armstrong Circle Theatre: "Journey to Oblivion" [by Don M. Mankiewicz] (6-6-62) Kevin McCarthy, Alexander Scourby, Olive Deering

390. The United States Steel Hour: "You Can't Escape" (6-13-62) Shirley Knight, Simon Oakland, Mark Richman, Michael Tolan, Alice Ghostley

391. The United States Steel Hour: "Scene of the Crime" (6-27-62) Patricia Collinge, Bette White, Harry Townes

392. The Armstrong Circle Theatre: "A Chapter on Tyranny: Dateline Berlin" [repeat of episode of 10/25/61] (7-4-62)

393. The United States Steel Hour: "The Night of the Fourth" (7-11-62) Barry Sullivan, Zia Mohyeddin, Nan Martin

394. The Armstrong Circle Theatre: "Assignment--Teenage Junkies" [repeat of episode of 2/28/62] (7-18-62)

395. The United States Steel Hour: "Honor in Love" (7-25-62) John Kerr, Carol Lawrence, Eli Mintz

396. The Armstrong Circle Theatre: "The Battle of Hearts" [repeat of episode of 12/20/61] (8-1-62)

397. The United States Steel Hour: "Male Call" (8-8-62) Larry Blyden, Godfrey Cambridge, Fred Clark, Zohra Lampert

398. The Armstrong Circle Theatre: "The Man Who Refused to Die" [repeat of episode of 3/14/62] (8-15-62)

399. The United States Steel Hour: "Murder on the Agenda" [adapted by Joe Palmer from the play by Eyvon Evans] (8-22-62) Ralph Meeker, James Daly, Mona Freeman, Harry Guardino

400. The Armstrong Circle Theatre: "Merchants of Evil" [repeat

of episode of 3/28/62] (8-29-62)

401. The United States Steel Hour: "Dry Rain" (9-5-62) John
Kerr, Johnny Desmond
402. The United States Steel Hour: "The Inner Panic" (9-12-62)
Martin Sheen, Tommy Sands, Glenda Farrell, Simon Oakland, Cynthia Pepper
403. The Armstrong Circle Theatre: "The Cross and the Dragon"
(9-26-62) James Daly
404. The United States Steel Hour: "The White Lie" (10-3-62)
David Wayne, Neva Patterson
405. The Armstrong Circle Theatre: "Smash Up" (10-10-62)
Lonny Chapman, Alfred Hinckley
406. The United States Steel Hour: "Wanted: Someone Innocent"
(10-17-62) Kim Hunter, Diana Hyland, Robert Lansing
407. The Armstrong Circle Theatre: "The Friendly Thieves"
(10-24-62) George Segal, Stuart Erwin, Richard Himbler
408. The United States Steel Hour: "A Break in the Weather"
(10-31-62) Eddie Albert
409. The Armstrong Circle Theatre: "Tunnel to Freedom" [by
Leon Tokatyan] (11-7-62) Conrad Nagel, Herman Rudin
410. The United States Steel Hour: "Marriage Marks the Spot"
(11-14-62) Darren McGavin, Pippa Scott, Julius La
Rosa, John McGiver, Walter Greaza
411. The Armstrong Circle Theatre: "A City Betrayed" (11-21-
62) Patrick McVey, Carl Low, Ramon Bieri
412. The United States Steel Hour: "Farewell to Innocence"
(11-28-62) John Beal, Jeff Donnell, Vicki Cummings,
Thomas Chalmers
413. The Armstrong Circle Theatre: "The Assassin" (12-5-62)
Jon Berger, Olga Pellin, Carl Low
414. The United States Steel Hour: "Big Day for a Scrambler"
(12-12-62) James Whitmore, Peter Palmer, Priscilla
Gillette
415. The Armstrong Circle Theatre: "Escape to Nowhere" (12-
19-62) James Broderick
416. The United States Steel Hour: "The Duchess and the Mugs"
(12-26-62) Patty Duke, Eugenie Leontovich
417. The Armstrong Circle Theatre: "Invitation to Treason" (1-
2-63) Clifford David
418. The United States Steel Hour: "The Young Avengers" (1-9-
63) Elizabeth Ashley, Keir Dullea
419. The Armstrong Circle Theatre: "The Journey of Poh Lin"
(1-16-63) Irene Sen, Zia Mohyeddin
420. The United States Steel Hour: "Fair Young Ghost" (1-23-
63) Shirley Knight, Robert Lansing, Cathleen Nesbitt
421. The Armstrong Circle Theatre: "The Counterfeit League"
(1-30-63) Bruce Gordon
422. The United States Steel Hour: "The Troubled Heart" (2-6-
63) John Colicos
423. The Armstrong Circle Theatre: "Ordeal by Fire" (2-13-63)
Leo Leyden
424. The United States Steel Hour: "Night Run to the West" (2-
20-63) Martin Sheen, Ralph Meeker, Colleen Dewhurst

425.  The Armstrong Circle Theatre: "Project--Pied Piper" (2-27-63)  Philip Abbott
426.  The United States Steel Hour: "Moment of Rage" (3-6-63)  Glenda Farrell, Charles Aidman, Kathryn Hays
427.  The Armstrong Circle Theatre: "Five Kilos of Junk" (3-13-63)  Rudy Bond
428.  The United States Steel Hour: "The Secrets of Stella Crozier" (3-20-63)  Elinor Donahue
429.  The Armstrong Circle Theatre: "The Health Fraud" (3-27-63)  Murray Hamilton
430.  The United States Steel Hour: "Mission of Fear" (4-3-63)  Piper Laurie
431.  The Armstrong Circle Theatre: "The Embezzler" (4-10-63)  Gene Saks
432.  The United States Steel Hour: "The Soldier Ran Away" (4-17-63)  Martin Sheen
433.  The Armstrong Circle Theatre: "A Square Mile of Hope" (4-24-63)  Sam Groom, Audra Lindley
434.  The United States Steel Hour: "The Many Ways of Heaven" (5-1-63)  Dan Duryea, Cathleen Nesbitt, Casey Peters, Nancy Wickwire, Abby Lewis, Robert Burr, Lee Peters, Jonathan Carter
435.  The Armstrong Circle Theatre: "The Aggressor Force" (5-8-63)  Martin Sheen, Tim O'Connor
436.  The United States Steel Hour: "Don't Shake the Family Tree" (5-15-63)  Fred Gwynne, Orson Bean, Frank McHugh, Jim Backus, Fran Sharon, Ethel Griffies
437.  The Armstrong Circle Theatre: "Swindler in Paradise" (5-22-63)  William Redfield, Carl Low, Alfred Hinckley
438.  The United States Steel Hour: "A Taste of Champagne" (5-29-63)  Hans Conried, Monique Van Vooren
439.  The Armstrong Circle Theatre: "Secret Document" (6-5-63)  Barry Newman, Alexander Scourby
440.  The United States Steel Hour: "The Old Lady Shows Her Medals" (6-12-63)  Alfred Lunt, Lynn Fontanne, Donald Madden
441.  The Armstrong Circle Theatre: "Operation Moonshine" [repeat of episode of 12/9/59] (6-19-63)
442.  Reckoning: "Ticket to Tahiti" [repeat of "Studio One" episode of 6/2/58] (6-26-63)  Franchot Tone, Kim Hunter, James MacArthur, Olive Sturgess
443.  The Armstrong Circle Theatre: "The Spy Next Door" [repeat of episode of 2/15/61] (7-3-63)
444.  Reckoning: "Shadow of Genius" [repeat of "Studio One" episode of 3/31/58] (7-10-63)  Boris Karloff, Eva La Gallienne
445.  The Armstrong Circle Theatre: "Sound of Violence--The Juke Box Racket" [repeat of episode of 4/29/59] (7-17-63)
446.  Reckoning: "The Enemy Within" [repeat of "Studio One" episode of 4/7/58] (7-24-63)  Dane Clark, Don DeFore, Dick York, Noah Beery Jr.
447.  The Armstrong Circle Theatre: "Assignment--Teenage Junkies" [repeat of episode of 2/28/62] (7-31-63)

448. The Armstrong Circle Theatre: "The Journey of Poh Lin"
     [repeat of episode of 1/16/63] (8-14-63)
449. Reckoning: "Tongues of Angels" [repeat of "Studio One" epi-
     sode of 3/17/58] (8-21-63)
450. The Armstrong Circle Theatre: "Escape to Nowhere" [re-
     peat of episode of 12/19/62] (8-28-63)
451. Reckoning: "On the Take" [repeat of "Climax!" episode of
     4/3/58] (9-4-63) Paul Douglas, Katherine Bard, Nehe-
     miah Persoff


WALT DISNEY PRESENTS (initially titled DISNEYLAND)

      The celebrated animator entered series television in 1954
as the host of a series of children's stories, nature documentaries,
feature films, drama series and, of course, animated features.
The best remembered episodes of the first season, which is not
chronicled below, were the three "Davy Crockett" adventures, featuring Fess Parker as the hero and Buddy Ebsen as his friend
George Russell. They were: "Davy Crockett, Indian Fighter"
(telecast December 15, 1954), "Davy Crockett Goes to Congress"
(telecast January 26, 1955), and "Davy Crockett at the Alamo"
(telecast February 23, 1955). Two sequels followed: "Davy
Crockett and the Keelboat Race" (telecast November 16, 1955) and
"Davy Crockett and the River Pirates" (telecast December 14, 1955).

The Regulars: Walt Disney, host (died December 15, 1966)

The Episodes (chronicled from the second season, January of 1956):

1.  "When Knighthood Was in Flower" [1953 feature film; Part I]
    (1-4-56) Richard Todd, Glynis Johns
2.  "When Knighthood Was in Flower" [Part II] (1-11-56) as
    above
3.  "A Tribute to Joel Chandler Harris" (1-18-56)
4.  "Davy Crockett's Keelboat Race" [repeat of episode of 11/
    16/55] (1-25-56)
5.  "A Day in the Life of Donald Duck" [animated feature, with
    Jimmie Dodd and Roy Williams] (2-1-56)
6.  "Survival in Nature" [nature documentary] (2-8-56)
7.  "Our Unsung Villains" [narrated by Hans Conried] (2-15-56)
8.  "Davy Crockett and the River Pirates" [repeat of episode of
    12/14/55] (2-22-56)
9.  "A Trip Through Adventureland--Water Birds" [nature study]
    (2-29-56)
10. "On Vacation" [animated feature with "Jiminy Cricket"] (3-
    7-56)
11. "Stormy, the Thoroughbred" [a documentary drama] (3-14-56)
12. "The Goofy Sports Story" [animated feature] (3-21-56)
13. "A Tribute to Joel Chandler Harris" [repeat of episode of
    1/18/56] (3-28-56)
14. "Where Do the Stories Come From?" [study of the origins

of cartoons]   (4-4-56)
15. "The Story of the Silly Symphony" [animated feature]   (4-11-56)
16. "Adventureland--People and Places"   (4-18-56)
17. "The Story of the Animated Drawing"   (4-25-56)
18. "A Trip Through Adventureland--Water Birds" [repeat of episode of 2/29/56]   (5-2-56)
19. "A Day in the Life of Donald Duck" [repeat of episode of 2/1/56]   (5-9-56)
20. "Survival in Nature" [repeat of episode of 2/8/56]   (5-16-56)
21. "The Goofy Sports Story" [repeat of episode of 3/21/56]   (5-23-56)
22. "Behind the Scenes with Fess Parker" [the filming of The Great Locomotive Chase]   (5-30-56)
23. "Where Do the Stories Come From?" [repeat of episode of 4/4/56]   (6-6-56)
24. "Man and the Moon"   (6-13-56)
25. "Behind True-Life Cameras, Olympic Elk"   (6-20-56)

Third Season

26. "Antarctica--Past and Present" [documentary narrated by Winston Hibler]   (9-12-56)
27. "The Great Cat Family" [historical tribute]   (9-19-56)
28. "Searching for Nature's Mysteries" [nature study]   (9-26-56)
29. "Rob Roy, the Highland Rogue" [1953 feature film; Part I]   (10-3-56)   Richard Todd, Glynis Johns
30. "Rob Roy, the Highland Rogue" [Part II]   (10-10-56)   as above
31. "Fantasyland--The Goofy Cavalcade of Sports" [animated feature]   (10-17-56)
32. "Behind the Cameras in Lapland--The Alaskan Eskimo" [documentary]   (10-24-56)
33. "The Plausible Impossible"   (10-31-56)
34. "Life in Samoa and the Story of Holland and Her Dykes" [documentary]   (11-7-56)
35. "Along the Oregon Trail" [feature film]   (11-14-56)   Fess Parker, Jeff York, Kathleen Crowley
36. "At Home with Donald Duck" [animated feature]   (11-21-56)
37. "Treasure Island" [1950 feature film; Part I]   (11-28-56)   Robert Newton, Bobby Driscoll, Walter Fitzgerald, Basil Sydney
38. "Treasure Island" [Part II]   (12-5-56)   as above
39. "Pluto's Day" [animated feature]   (12-12-56)
40. "A Present for Donald" [a tribute to Latin America]   (12-19-56)
41. "Searching for Nature's Mysteries" [repeat of episode of 9/26/56]   (12-26-56)
42. "So Dear to My Heart" [1949 feature film]   (1-2-57)   Bobby Driscoll, Burl Ives, Luana Patten, Beulah Bondi
43. "Alice in Wonderland" [1951 film]   (1-9-57)
44. "Your Host, Donald Duck" [animated feature]   (1-16-57)
45. "Our Friend, the Atom" [adapted from the book by Dr. Heinz Haber]   (1-23-57)

46. "All About Magic" [with Hans Conried] (1-30-57)
47. "The Goofy Cavalcade of Sports" [repeat of episode of 10/17/56] (2-6-57)
48. "Tricks of the Trade" [discussion of animation] (2-13-57)
49. "Along the Oregon Trail" [repeat of episode of 11/14/56] (2-20-57)
50. "The Crisler Story--Prowlers of the Everglades" [nature study] (2-27-57)
51. "Man in Flight" [aviation documentary] (3-6-57)
52. "The Great Cat Family" [repeat of episode of 9/19/56] (3-13-57)
53. "The Adventure Story" [animated feature] (3-20-57)
54. 'Donald's Award" [animated feature] (3-27-57)
55. 'Disneyland; The Park--Pecos Bill" (4-3-57)
56. "People of the Desert" [documentary] (4-10-57)
57. "More About Silly Symphonies" [animated feature] (4-17-57)
58. 'Our Friend, the Atom" [repeat of episode of 1/23/57] (4-24-57)
59. "The Yellowstone Country--Bear Country" [nature study] (5-1-57)
60. "At Home with Donald Duck" [animated feature] (5-8-57)
61. "Antarctica--Past and Present" [repeat of episode of 9/12/56] (5-15-57)
62. "The Plausible Impossible" [repeat of episode of 10/31/56] (5-22-57)
63. "The Liberty Story" [animated feature] (5-29-57)
64. "Antarctica--Operation Deep Freeze" [documentary] (6-5-57)
65. "All About Magic" [repeat of 1/30/57] (6-12-57)
66. "Fauna in the Arctic and the Everglades" [nature documentary] (6-19-57)

Fourth Season

67. "Adventure in Wildwood Heart" (9-25-57)
68. "The Saga of Andy Burnett" [feature film; Part I] (10-2-57) Jerome Courtland, Jeff York
69. "The Saga of Andy Burnett" [Part II] (10-9-57) as above
70. "The Saga of Andy Burnett: Andy's Love Affair" [Part III] (10-16-57) as above
71. 'Duck for Hire" [animated feature] (10-23-57)
72. "The Legend of Sleepy Hollow" [1948 animated feature narrated by Bing Crosby] (10-30-57)
73. "Adventures in Fantasy" [animated feature] (11-6-57)
74. "To the South Pole for Science" [nature study] (11-13-57)
75. "The Best Dog-goned Dog in the World" [narrated by Dorothy McGuire] (11-20-57)
76. "How to Relax" [animated feature with "Goofy"] (11-27-57)
77. "Mars and Beyond" [cartoon satire] (12-4-57)
78. "The Horse of the West" [nature study narrated by Rex Allen] (12-11-57)
79. "Adventure in Wildwood Heart" [repeat of episode of 9/25/57] (12-18-57)
80. 'Dumbo" [1941 animated feature film] (12-25-57)

81. "Faraway Places--High, Hot and Wet" [nature study] (1-1-58)
82. "Saludos Amigos" [1943 feature film with "José Carioca," "Donald Duck" and "Goofy"] a) "Lake Titicaca"; b) "Pedro"; c) "Aquarela do Brasil"; d) "El Gaucho Goofy" (1-8-58)
83. "Donald's Weekend" [animated feature] (1-15-58)
84. "The Littlest Outlaw" [1955 feature film; Part I] (1-22-58) Andres Velasquez, Joseph Calleia
85. "The Littlest Outlaw" [Part II] (1-29-58) as above
86. "The Saga of Andy Burnett" [Part I; repeat of episode of 10/2/57] (2-5-58)
87. "The Saga of Andy Burnett" [Part II; repeat of episode of 10/9/57] (2-12-58)
88. "The Saga of Andy Burnett" [Part III; repeat of episode of 10/16/57] (2-19-58)
89. "The Saga of Andy Burnett: The Land of Enemies" [Part IV] (2-26-58) Jerome Courtland, Jeff York, Andrew Duggan
90. "The Saga of Andy Burnett: White Man's Medicine" [Part V] (3-5-58) as above
91. "The Saga of Andy Burnett" [Part VI] (3-12-58) as above
92. "Magic and Music" [with Hans Conried] (3-19-58)
93. "The Best Dog-goned Dog in the World" [repeat of episode of 11/20/57] (3-26-58)
94. "Man in Flight" (4-2-58)
95. "Adventure in the Magic Kingdom" (4-9-58)
96. "Four Tales on the Mouse" [animated feature with "Mickey Mouse"] (4-16-58)
97. "To the South Pole for Science" [repeat of episode of 11/13/57] (4-23-58)
98. "An Adventure in Art" (4-30-58)
99. "Stormy, the Thoroughbred" [repeat of episode of 3/14/56] (5-7-58)
100. "Magic Highway, U.S.A." [a history of the American road] (5-14-58)

Fifth Season

101. "Elfego Baca: The Nine Lives of Elfego Baca" [Part I] (10-3-58) Robert Loggia
102. "The Pigeon That Worked a Miracle" [nature study] (10-10-58)
103. "Elfego Baca: Four Down and Five Lives to Go" [Part II] (10-17-58) Robert Loggia
104. "Rusty and the Falcon" [feature film] (10-24-58) Rudy Lee
105. "Texas John Slaughter: Texas John Slaughter, Lawman" [Part I] (10-31-58) Tom Tryon
106. "His Majesty, the King of Beasts" [nature study] (11-7-58)
107. "Texas John Slaughter: Ambush at Laredo" [Part II] (11-14-58) Tom Tryon
108. "Boston Tea Party" [feature film] (11-21-58) Richard Beymer, Hal Stalmaster
109. "Elfego Baca: Lawman or Gunman?" [Part III] (11-28-58)

Robert Loggia, Ramon Novarro, James Dunn
110. "Elfego Baca: Law and Order, Inc. " [Part IV] (12-12-58)
as above
111. "From All of Us to All of You" [Christmas program] (12-19-58)
112. "Texas John Slaughter: Killers from Kansas" [Part III]
(1-9-59) Tom Tryon, Beverly Garland, Harry Carey Jr.
113. "Niok" [study of the elephant] (1-16-59)
114. "Texas John Slaughter: Showdown at Sandoval" [Part IV]
(1-23-59) Tom Tryon, Dan Duryea
115. "The Peter Tchaikovsky Story" [feature film] (1-30-59)
Grant Williams
116. "Elfego Baca: Elfego Baca, Attorney at Law" [Part V] (2-6-59) Robert Loggia, James Dunn
117. "Duck Flies the Coop" [animated feature film with "Donald
Duck"] (2-13-59)
118. "Elfego Baca: The Griswold Murder" [Part VI] (2-20-59)
Robert Loggia, Patric Knowles, James Dunn
119. "The Adventures of Chip 'n' Dale" [animated feature film]
(2-27-59)
120. "Texas John Slaughter: The Man from Bitter Creek" [Part
V] (3-6-59) Tom Tryon, Stephen McNally, Bill Williams
121. "Highway to Trouble" [animated feature film with Donald
Duck] (3-13-59)
122. "Texas John Slaughter: The Slaughter Trail" [Part VI] (3-20-59)
123. "Toot, Whistle, Plunk, and Boom" [1953 animated short sub-
ject] (3-27-59)
124. "The Wetback Hound" [1957 nature study] (4-24-59)
125. "I Captured the King of the Leprechauns" [feature film] (5-29-59) Pat O'Brien
126. "The Story of the Silly Symphony" [animated feature] (6-5-59)

Sixth Season

127. "Man in Space" [feature film] (9-18-59)
128. "Tomorrow the Moon" [feature film] (9-25-59)
129. "Moochie of the Little League: A Diamond Is a Boy's Best
Friend" [Part I] (10-2-59) Kevin Corcoran, Reginald
Owen, Stuart Erwin
130. "Moochie of the Little League: Wrong Way Moochie" [Part
II] (10-9-59) as above
131. "Killers of the High Country" [documentary of hunters and
mountain lions] (10-16-59)
132. "The Swamp Fox: The Birth of the Swamp Fox" [Part I]
(10-23-59) Leslie Nielsen, Dick Foran
133. "The Swamp Fox: Brother Against Brother" [Part II] (10-30-59) as above
134. "Perilous Assignment" [with Gaston Rebuffat] (11-6-59)
135. "Elfego Baca: Move Along, Mustangers" [Part I] (11-13-59)
Robert Loggia, Brian Keith, Beverly Garland
136. "Elfego Baca: Mustang Man, Mustang Maid" [Part II] (11-

20-59) as above
137. "A Storm Called Maria" [feature film] (11-27-59)
138. "Texas John Slaughter: The Robber Stallion" [Part I] (12-4-59) Tom Tryon, Darryl Hickman, Barton MacLane
139. "Texas John Slaughter: Wild Horse Revenge" [Part II] (12-11-59) as above
140. "Texas John Slaughter: Range War at Tombstone" [Part III] (12-18-59)
141. "Alice in Wonderland" [repeat of episode of 11/3/54 and 1/9/57] (12-25-59)
142. "The Swamp Fox: Tory Vengeance" [Part III] (1-1-60) Leslie Nielsen, Sherry Jackson, Henry Daniell, Dick Foran
143. "The Swamp Fox: Day of Reckoning" [Part IV] (1-8-60) as above
144. "The Swamp Fox: Redcoat Strategy" [Part V] (1-15-60) as above
145. "The Swamp Fox: A Case of Treason" [Part VI] (1-22-60) as above
146. "Wild Burro of the West" [documentary feature] (1-29-60)
147. "Two Happy Amigos" [animated feature with 'Donald Duck" and "John Carioca"] (2-5-60)
148. "Texas John Slaughter: Desperado from Tombstone" [Part I] (2-12-60) Tom Tryon
149. "Texas John Slaughter: Apache Friendship" [Part II] (2-19-60) as above
150. "Texas John Slaughter: Kentucky Gunslick" [Part III] (2-26-60) as above
151. "Texas John Slaughter: Geronimo's Revenge" [Part IV] (3-4-60) as above
152. "This Is Your Life, Donald Duck" [animated feature hosted by "Jiminy Cricket"] (3-11-60)
153. "Elfego Baca: Friendly Enemies at Law" [Part I] (3-18-60) Robert Loggia, John Kerr
154. "Elfego Baca: Gus Tomlin Is Dead" [Part II] (3-25-60) as above
155. "The Mad Hermit of Chimney Butte" [animated feature film with 'Donald Duck"] (4-1-60)
156. "The Goofy Success Story" [animated feature film] (4-8-60)

Seventh Season

157. "Rapids Ahead and Bear Country" [nature documentary; Part I] (10-16-60)
158. "Rapids Ahead and Bear Country" [Part II] (10-23-60)
159. "Zorro: El Bandito" [Part I] (10-30-60) Guy Williams, Gilbert Roland, Rita Moreno
160. "Zorro: Adios El Cuchillo" [Part II] (11-6-60) as above
161. "Donald's Silver Anniversary" [animated feature with 'Donald Duck"] (11-13-60)
162. "Moochie of Pop Warner Football: The Pee Wees Versus City Hall" [Part I] (11-20-60) Kevin Corcoran, Dennis Joel

163. "Moochie of Pop Warner Football: From Ticonderoga to Disneyland" [Part II] (11-27-60) as above
164. "Daniel Boone: The Warrior's Path" [Part I] (12-4-60) Dewey Martin, Mala Powers, Terry Thompson, Richard Banke
165. "Daniel Boone: And Chase the Buffalo" [Part II] (12-11-60) as above
166. a) "Escape to Paradise" [feature film] Dorothy McGuire, James MacArthur, Janet Munro, John Mills; b) "Water Birds" [nature study] (12-18-60)
167. "From All of Us to All of You" [Christmas program] (12-25-60)
168. "Zorro: The Postponed Wedding" (1-1-61) Guy Williams, Annette Funicello
169. "The Swamp Fox: A Woman's Courage" [Part I] (1-8-61) Leslie Nielsen
170. "The Swamp Fox: Horses for Greene" [Part II] (1-15-61) as above
171. "A Salute to Father" [animated feature with "Goofy"] (1-22-61)
172. "Texas John Slaughter: The End of the Trail" [Part I] (1-29-61) Tom Tryon
173. "Texas John Slaughter: A Holster Full of Law" [Part II] (2-5-61) as above
174. "Ambush at Wagon Gap" [Part I] (2-19-61) Fess Parker, Kathleen Crowley
175. "White Man's Medicine" [Part II] (2-26-61) as above
176. "The Coyote's Lament" [nature study] (3-5-61)
177. "Daniel Boone: The Wilderness Road" [Part I] (3-12-61) Dewey Martin, Mala Powers, Terry Thompson, Richard Banke, Kevin Corcoran
178. "Daniel Boone: Promised Land" [Part II] (3-19-61) as above
179. "Man in Flight" [repeat of episode of 4/2/58] (3-28-61)
180. "Zorro: Auld Acquaintance" (4-2-61) Guy Williams, Ricardo Montalban, Suzanne Lloyd
181. "Texas John Slaughter: A Trip to Tucson" [Part I] (4-16-61) Tom Tryon, Ralph Meeker
182. "Texas John Slaughter: Frank Clell Is in Town" [Part II] (4-23-61) as above
183. "Flash, the Teenage Otter" [nature study] (4-30-61)
184. "Andrew's Raiders: The Secret Mission" [Part I] (5-7-61) Fess Parker, Jeffrey Hunter
185. "Andrew's Raiders: Escape to Nowhere" [Part II] (5-14-61) as above
186. "Wonders of the Water Worlds" [nature study] (5-21-61)
187. "Disneyland '61" [a visit to the park of Olympic Elk] (5-28-61)

Eighth Season [hereafter titled WALT DISNEY'S WONDERFUL WORLD OF COLOR]

188. "Mathmagic Land" (9-24-61)

189. "The Horsemasters" [feature film; Part I] (10-1-61) Donald
       Pleasance
190. "The Horsemasters" [Part II] (10-8-61) as above
191. "Chico, the Misunderstood Coyote" [nature study] (10-15-61)
192. "The Hunting Instinct" [animated feature with "Donald Duck,"
       "Goofy," "Mickey Mouse" and "Professor Ludwig Von
       Drake"] (10-22-61)
193. "Inside Donald Duck" [animated feature] (11-5-61)
194. "The Light in the Forest" [1958 feature film; Part I] (11-
       12-61) James MacArthur, Fess Parker, Jessica Tandy,
       Joanne Dru, Wendell Corey
195. "The Light in the Forest" [Part II] (11-19-61) as above
196. "Holliday for Hen-Pecked Husbands" [animated feature with
       "Goofy"] (11-26-61)
197. "A Fire Called Jeremiah" [nature study] (12-3-61)
198. "Kids Is Kids" [animated feature with "Professor Ludwig Von
       Drake"] (12-10-61)
199. "Backstage Party" [a studio tour] (12-17-61)
200. "The Great Cat Family" [repeat of episode of 9/19/56] (12-
       24-61)
201. "The Goofy Cavalcade of Sports" [repeat of episode of 10/
       17/56] (12-31-61)
202. "Hans Brinker and the Silver Skates" [feature film; Part I]
       (1-7-62) Ronny Zeander, Carin Roseby
203. "Hans Brinker and the Silver Skates" [Part II] (1-14-62)
       as above
204. "Sancho, the Homing Steer" [nature study, with Bill Shurley,
       Part I] (1-21-62)
205. "Sancho, the Homing Steer: The Perils of a Homesick
       Steer" [Part II] (1-28-62)
206. "Fantasy on Skis" (2-4-62)
207. "Comanche" [1958 feature film; Part I] (2-18-62) Sal Mineo,
       Philip Carey
208. "Comanche" [Part II] (2-25-62) as above
209. "Carnival Time" [animated feature with "Donald Duck" and
       "Joe Carioca"] (3-4-62)
210. "The Prince and the Pauper" [feature film; Part I] (3-11-
       62) Guy Williams, Sean Scully, Laurence Naismith
211. "The Prince and the Pauper" [Part II] (3-18-62) as above
212. "The Prince and the Pauper" [Part III] (3-25-62) as above
213. "Spy in the Sky" [feature film] (4-1-62) Brian Keith, Ed-
       mond O'Brien
214. "Von Drake in Spain" [animated feature] (4-8-62)
215. "Disneyland After Dark" (4-15-62)
216. "The Pigeon That Worked a Miracle" [repeat of episode of
       10/10/58] (4-22-62)
217. "Treasure Island" [Part I; repeat of episode of 11/28/56 and
       12/5/56] (4-29-62)
218. "Treasure Island" [Part II] (5-6-62)

Ninth Season

219. "Cavalcade of Song" [musical program] (9-16-62)

220. "The Golden Horseshoe Revue" [feature film]  (9-23-62)
      Ed Wynn, Annette Funicello, Gene Sheldon, Betty Taylor
221. "Escapade in Florence" [feature film; Part I]  (9-30-62)
      Annette Funicello, Tommy Kirk
222. "Escapade in Florence" [Part II]  (10-7-62)  as above
223. "The Silver Fox and Sam Davenport" [nature study, with
      Gordon L. Perry]  (10-14-62)
224. "Why Man Is His Own Worst Enemy" [animated feature with
      "Donald Duck" "Ludwig Von Drake" and "Foxy Loxy"]
      (10-21-62)
225. "Sammy, the Way-Out Seal" [feature film; Part I]  (10-28-
      62)  Robert Culp, Patricia Barry, Jack Carson
226. "Sammy, the Way-Out Seal" [Part II]  (11-4-62)  as above
227. "His Majesty, the King of Beasts" [repeat of episode of
      11/7/58]  (11-11-62)
228. "The Magnificent Rebel" [feature film; Part I]  (11-18-62)
      Karl Boehm, Giulia Rubini, Ivan Desny, Peter Arens
229. "The Magnificent Rebel" [Part II]  (11-25-62)  as above
230. "The Mooncussers" [feature film; Part I]  (12-2-62)  Oscar
      Homolka, Kevin Corcoran
231. "The Mooncussers" [Part II]  (12-9-62)  as above
232. "Hurricane Hannah" [nature study]  (12-16-62)
233. "Holiday Time at Disneyland"  (12-23-62)
234. "Adventures in Fantasy" [repeat of episode of 11/6/57]
      (12-30-62)
235. "Three Tall Tales" [animated feature with "Professor Lud-
      wig Von Drake"] a) "Casey at the Bat"; b) "Windwagon
      Smith"; c) "Paul Bunyon"  (1-6-63)
236. "Little Dog Lost" [nature drama with Dennis Yanglin]  (1-13-63)
237. "Johnny Shiloh" [feature film; Part I]  (1-20-63)  Kevin Cor-
      coran, Brian Keith, Darryl Hickman
238. "Johnny Shiloh" [Part II]  (1-27-63)  as above
239. "Greta, the Misfit Greyhound" [nature study]  (2-3-63)
240. "Inside Outer Space" [animated feature with "Professor Lud-
      wig Von Drake"]  (2-10-63)
241. "Banner in the Sky" [1959 feature film; Part I]  (2-17-63)
      James MacArthur, Michael Rennie
242. "Banner in the Sky: Killer Mountain" [Part II]  (2-24-63)
      as above
243. "Square Peg in a Round Hole" [animated feature with "Pro-
      fessor Ludwig Von Drake"]  (3-3-63)
244. "The Horse with the Flying Tail" [nature study]  (3-10-63)
245. "Kidnapped" [1960 feature film; Part I]  (3-17-63)  James
      MacArthur, Peter Finch
246. "Kidnapped" [Part II]  (3-24-63)  as above
247. "Stormy, the Thoroughbred" [repeat of episode of 3/14/56]
      (3-31-63)
248. "When Knighthood Was in Flower" [Part I; repeat of episode
      1/4/56]  (4-7-63)
249. "When Knighthood Was in Flower" [Part II; repeat of episode
      of 1/11/56]  (4-14-63)
250. "Three Tall Tales" [repeat of episode of 1/6/63]  (4-21-63)
251. "Prairie Seal Island" [nature study]  (4-28-63)

Tenth Season

252. "The Horse Without a Head" [feature film; Part I] (9-29-63)
     Jean Pierre Aumont, Leo McKern, Herbert Lom, Pamela
     Franklin, Lee Montague
253. "The Horse Without a Head" [Part II] (10-6-63)
254. "Fly with Von Drake" [animated feature] (10-13-63)
255. "The Wahoo Bobcat" [nature study, with Jock MacGregor,
     Bill Dunnager] (10-20-63)
256. "The Waltz King" [feature film; Part I] (10-27-63) Kerwin
     Mathews, Senta Berger, Brian Aherne, Peter Kraus
257. "The Waltz King" [Part II] (11-3-63) as above
258. "Wild Burro of the West" [repeat of episode of 1/29/60]
     (11-20-63)
259. "The Truth About Mother Goose" [animated feature] (11-17-
     63)
260. "Pollyanna" [1960 feature film; Part I] (12-1-63) Hayley
     Mills, Jane Wyman, Agnes Moorehead, Richard Egan,
     Karl Malden, James Drury, Kevin Corcoran
261. "Pollyanna" [Part II] (12-8-63) as above
262. "Pollyanna" [Part III] (12-15-63) as above
263. "From All of Us to All of You" [Christmas program] (12-
     22-63)
264. "Dumbo" [repeat of episode of 12/25/57] (12-29-63)
265. "The Ballad of Hector, the Stowaway Dog" [feature film;
     Part I] (1-5-64) Guy Stockwell, Craig Hill, John
     Stacey, Eric Pohlman
266. "The Ballad of Hector, the Stowaway Dog" [Part II] (1-12-
     64) as above
267. "Mediterranean Cruise" [with animated character "Ludwig
     Von Drake"] (1-19-64)
268. "Bristle Face" [feature film; Part I] (1-26-64) Philip Al-
     ford, Brian Keith, Slim Pickens, Wallace Ford, Jeff
     Donnell
269. "Bristle Face" [Part II] (2-2-64) as above
270. "The Scarecrow of Romney Marsh" [feature film; Part I]
     (2-9-64) Patrick McGoohan, George Cole, Geoffrey
     Keen, Sean Scully
271. "The Scarecrow of Romney Marsh" [Part II] (2-16-64) as
     above
272. "The Scarecrow of Romney Marsh" [Part III] (2-23-64) as
     above
273. "The Legend of Two Gypsy Dogs" [nature study] (3-1-64)
274. "Taste of Melon" [feature film] (3-8-64) Billy Mumy,
     Roger Mobley, John Anderson
275. "Treasure in the Haunted House" [feature film; Part I] (3-
     15-64) Ed Wynn, Billy Mumy, Roger Mobley, Michael
     McGreevey
276. "In Shape with Von Drake" [animated feature] (3-22-64)
277. "Greyfriars' Bobby" [1961 feature film; Part I] (3-29-64)
     Donald Crisp, Alex MacKenzie, Laurence Naismith, Kay
     Walsh
278. "Greyfriars' Bobby" [Part II] (4-5-64) as above

279. "Jungle Cat" [nature study] (4-12-64)
280. "Toot, Whistle, Plunk, and Boom" [repeat of episode of 3/27/59] (4-19-64)
281. "Killers of the High Country" [repeat of episode of 10/16/59] (4-26-64)
282. "Four Fabulous Characters" [animated feature] (5-3-64)
283. "Niok" [repeat of episode of 1/16/59] (5-10-64)
284. "Disneyland Goes to the World's Fair" (5-17-64)

Eleventh Season

285. "The Hound Who Thought He Was a Racoon" [nature study, with Oscar J. Busch] (9-20-64)
286. "Nikki, Wild Dog of the North" [1961 feature film; Part I] (9-27-64) Jean Coutu, Emile Genest
287. "Nikki, Wild Dog of the North" [Part II] (10-4-64) as above
288. "A Rag, a Bone, a Box of Junk" [animated musical, with "Ludwig Von Drake"] (10-11-64)
289. "The Tenderfoot" [feature film; Part I] (10-18-64) Brandon de Wilde, Brian Keith, James Whitmore, Judson Pratt, Donald May, Christopher Dark
290. "The Tenderfoot" [Part II] (10-25-64) as above
291. "The Tenderfoot" [Part III] (11-1-64) as above
292. "One Day at Teton Marsh" [nature study, narrated by Sebastian Cabot] (11-8-64)
293. a) "Ben and Me"; b) "Peter and the Wolf" [animated film, with the voice of Sterling Holloway] (11-15-64)
294. "Toby Tyler" [1960 feature film; Part I] (11-22-64) Kevin Corcoran, Bob Sweeney, Henry Calvin, Gene Sheldon
295. "Toby Tyler" [Part II] (11-29-64) as above
296. "Big Red" [1962 feature film; Part I] (12-6-64) Walter Pidgeon, Gilles Payant, Emile Genest
297. "Big Red" [Part II] (12-13-64) as above
298. "Alice in Wonderland" [repeat of episode of 11/3/54 and 1/9/57] (12-20-64)
299. "Fantasy on Skis" [repeat of episode of 2/4/62] (12-27-64)
300. "Disneyland's Tenth Anniversary" (1-3-65)
301. "Ida, the Off-Beat Eagle" [nature study] (1-10-65)
302. "Chico, the Misunderstood Coyote" [repeat of episode of 10/15/61] (1-17-65)
303. "Gallegher" [feature film; Part I] (1-24-65) Edmond O'Brien, Roger Mobley, Ray Teal, Philip Ober, Harvey Korman
304. "Gallegher" [Part II] (1-31-65) as above
305. "Gallegher" [Part III] (2-7-65) as above
306. "An Otter in the Family" [nature drama, with Tom and Mabel Beecham, Gary Beecham] (2-21-65)
307. "Almost Angels" [1962 feature film; Part I] (2-28-65) Vincent Winter, Sean Scully
308. "Almost Angels" [Part II] (3-7-65)
309. "Kilroy" [feature film; Part I] (3-14-65) Warren Berlinger, Celeste Holm, Robert Emhardt, Allyn Joslyn, Philip Abbott, Arthur Hunnicutt, Joan Blondell

310. "Kilroy" [Part II]  (3-21-65)  as above
311. "Kilroy" [Part III]  (3-28-65)  as above
312. "Kilroy" [Part IV]  (4-4-65)  as above
313. "Kids Is Kids" [repeat of episode of 12/10/61]  (4-11-65)
314. "Hans Brinker and the Silver Skates" [Part I; repeat of epi-
        sode of 1/7/62]  (4-18-65)
315. "Hans Brinker and the Silver Skates" [Part II; repeat of epi-
        sode of 1/14/62]  (4-25-65)
316. "The Wind in the Willows" [1948 animated feature, narrated
        by Basil Rathbone]  (5-2-65)
317. "One Day at Teton Marsh" [repeat of episode of 11/8/64]
        (5-9-65)
318. "The Story of Robin Hood" [1952 feature film; Part I]  (5-
        16-65)  Richard Todd
319. "The Story of Robin Hood" [Part II]  (5-23-65)  as above

Twelfth Season

320. "Yellowstone Cubs" [1963 nature study; narrated by Rex
        Allen]  (9-19-65)
321. "The Further Adventures of Gallegher: A Case of Murder"
        [Part I]  (9-26-65)  Roger Mobley, Edmond O'Brien,
        Harvey Korman, John Marley, Anne Francis, Liam Sulli-
        van, Peter Wyngarde, Victoria Shaw, James Westerfield
322. "The Further Adventures of Gallegher: The Big Swindle"
        [Part II]  (10-3-65)  as above
323. "The Further Adventures of Gallegher: The Daily Press vs.
        City Hall"  [Part III]  (10-10-65)  as above
324. "The Flight of the White Stallions" [1963 feature film; Part
        I]  (10-17-65)  Robert Taylor, Lilli Palmer, James
        Franciscus, Curt Jurgens, Eddie Albert
325. "The Flight of the White Stallions" [Part II]  (10-24-65)  as
        above
326. "The Legend of Sleepy Hollow" [repeat of episode of 10/30/
        57]  (10-31-65)
327. "Minado" [nature study, narrated by Sebastian Cabot]  (11-
        7-65)
328. "The Three Lives of Thomasina" [1963 feature film; Part I]
        (11-14-65)  Patrick McGoohan, Susan Hampshire, Karen
        Dotrice, Laurence Naismith, Alex MacKenzie, Matthew
        Garber, Jean Anderson
329. "The Three Lives of Thomasina" [Part II]  (11-21-65)  as
        above
330. "The Three Lives of Thomasina" [Part III]  (11-28-65)  as
        above
331. "Summer Magic" [1963 feature film; Part I]  (12-5-65)
        Dorothy McGuire, Hayley Mills, Burl Ives, Deborah Wal-
        ley, Una Merkel, Eddie Hodges, Michael J. Pollard
332. "Summer Magic" [Part II]  (12-12-65)  as above
333. "Country Coyote Goes Hollywood" [nature study]  (12-19-65)
334. "A Present for Donald" [repeat of episode of 12/19/56]
        (12-26-65)
335. "Searching for Nature's Mysteries" [repeat of episode of

9/26/56] (1-2-66)

336. "The Pigeon That Worked a Miracle" [repeat of episode of 10/10/58] (1-9-66)
337. "Moon Pilot" [1962 feature film; Part I] (1-16-66) Tom Tryon, Brian Keith, Edmond O'Brien, Davy Saval
338. "Moon Pilot" [Part II] (1-23-66) as above
339. "Music for Everybody" [animated musical] (1-30-66)
340. "The Legend of Young Dick Turpin" [feature film; Part I] (2-13-66) Leonard Whiting, David Weston, Bernard Lee
341. "The Legend of Young Dick Turpin" [Part II] (2-20-66) as above
342. "Ballerina" [feature film; Part I] (2-27-66) Mette Honningen, Kirsten Simone
343. "Ballerina" [Part II] (3-6-66) as above
344. "Run, Light Buck, Run" [nature study, with Al Niemela] (3-13-66)
345. "A Tiger Walks" [1964 feature film; Part I] (3-20-66) Brian Keith, Vera Miles, Pamela Franklin, Theo Marcuse, Edward Andrews, Kevin Corcoran
346. "A Tiger Walks" [Part II] (3-27-66) as above
347. "Concho, the Coyote Who Wasn't ... " [nature study, narrated by Rex Allen] (4-10-66)
348. "Comanche" [Part I; repeat of episode of 2/18/62] (4-17-66)
349. "Comanche" [Part II; repeat of episode of 2/25/62] (4-24-66)
350. "From Aesop to Hans Christian Andersen" [animated feature] (5-1-66)

Thirteenth Season

351. "Emil and the Detectives" [1964 feature film; Part I] (9-11-66) Walter Slezak, Bryan Russell, Bob Swann, Roger Mobley, Peter Ehrlich, Heinz Schubert
352. "Emil and the Detectives" [Part II] (9-18-66) as above
353. "The Legend of El Blanco" [nature study, with Alfonso Romero, José Perez] (9-25-66)
354. "Savage Sam" [1963 feature film; Part I] (10-2-66) Brian Keith, Kevin Corcoran, Rodolfo Acosta, Tommy Kirk, Jeff York, Marta Kristen
355. "Savage Sam" [Part II] (10-9-66) as above
356. "The 101 Problems of Hercules" [with Harold Reynolds, David Farrow] (10-16-66)
357. "Showdown with the Sundown Kid" [feature film; Part I] (10-23-66) Roger Mobley, Dennis Weaver, John McIntire, Ray Teal, James Gregory, Jeanette Nolan, Peter Graves
358. "Showdown with the Sundown Kid: The Crusading Reporter" [Part II] (10-30-66) as above
359. "Ranger's Guide to Nature" [with Bill Thompson, narrator] (11-13-66)
360. "The Moonspinners" [1964 feature film; Part I] (11-20-66) Hayley Mills, Peter McEnery, Eli Wallach, Irene Papas,

Pola Negri, Joan Greenwood, Michael Davis
361. "The Moonspinners" [Part II] (11-27-66) as above
362. "The Moonspinners" [Part III] (12-4-66) as above
363. "Joker, the Amiable Ocelot" [nature study, with Robert
      Becker, Jan McNabb] (12-11-66)
364. "Disneyland Around the Seasons" (12-18-66)
365. "The Truth About Mother Goose" [repeat of episode of 11/
      17/63] (12-25-66)
366. "The Silver Fox and Sam Davenport" [repeat of episode of
      10/14/62] (1-1-67)
367. "Willie and the Yank" [feature film; Part I] (1-8-67) James
      MacArthur, Kurt Russell, Jack Ging, Nick Adams,
      Donald Harron, Peggy Lipton, James Callahan, John
      Crawford
368. "Willie and the Yank" [Part II] (1-15-67) as above
369. "Willie and the Yank" [Part III] (1-22-67) as above
370. "Gallegher Goes West: Tragedy on the Trail" [feature film;
      Part I] (1-29-67) Roger Mobley, Darleen Carr, John
      McIntire, Harry Townes, Beverly Garland, Jeanette No-
      lan
371. "Gallegher Goes West: Trial by Error" [Part II] (2-5-67)
      as above
372. "The Coyote's Lament" [repeat of episode of 3/5/61] (2-12-
      67)
373. "The Boy Who Flew with Condors" [nature study, narrated by
      Leslie Nielsen] (2-19-67) Christopher Jury
374. "Atta Girl, Kelly!" [feature film; Part I] (3-5-67) Beau
      Bridges, J. D. Cannon, Billy Corcoran
375. "Atta Girl, Kelly!" [Part II] (3-12-67) as above
376. "Atta Girl, Kelly!" [Part III] (3-19-67) as above
377. "Man on Wheels" [animated feature with "Donald Duck" and
      "Goofy"] (3-26-67)
378. "A Salute to Alaska" [centennial tribute] (4-2-67)

Fourteenth Season

379. "The Tattooed Police Horse" [feature film] (9-10-67) Sandy
      Sanders, Shirley Skiles
380. "The Not So Lonely Lighthouse Keeper" [nature drama, with
      Clarence Hastings; narrated by Roy Barcroft] (9-17-67)
381. "How the West Was Lost" [animated feature with "Goofy,"
      "Pecos Bill," "Sluefoot Sue," and "Pistol Pete"; nar-
      rated by Roy Rogers and Bill Thompson] (9-24-67)
382. "The Fighting Prince of Donegal" [1966 feature film; Part I]
      (10-1-67) Peter McEnery, Susan Hampshire, Tom Adams,
      Gordon Jackson, Andrew Keir
383. "The Fighting Prince of Donegal" [Part II] (10-8-67) as
      above
384. "The Fighting Prince of Donegal" [Part III] (10-15-67) as
      above
385. "Run, Appaloosa, Run" [1966 feature film, narrated by Rex
      Allen] (10-22-67) Adele Palacios, Wilbur Plaugher
386. "Pollyanna" [Part I; repeat of episode of 12/1/63] (10-29-

67)

387. "Pollyanna" [Part II; repeat of episode of 12/8/63] (11-5-67)
388. "Pollyanna" [Part III; repeat of episode of 12/15/63] (11-12-67)
389. "One Day at Beetle Rock" [nature study, narrated by Sebastian Cabot] (11-19-67)
390. "The Monkey's Uncle" [1964 feature film; Part I] (11-26-67) Annette Funicello, Leon Ames, Frank Faylen, Arthur O'Connell, Tommy Kirk
391. "The Monkey's Uncle" [Part II] (12-3-67) as above
392. "A Boy Called Nuthin'" [feature film; Part I] (12-10-67) Andy Griffith, Ronny Howard, John Carroll, Donna Butterworth, Mickey Shaughnessy, Mary La Roche
393. "A Boy Called Nuthin'" [Part II] (12-17-67) as above
394. "From All of Us to All of You" [Christmas program] (12-24-67)
395. "Way Down Cellar" [feature film; Part I] (1-7-68) Ben Wright, Frank McHugh, Grace Lee Whitney, Richard Bakalyan, Lindy Davis, Butch Patrick, Sheldon Collins
396. "Way Down Cellar" [Part II] (1-14-68) as above
397. "Disneyland--from the Pirates of the Caribbean to the World of Tomorrow" (1-21-68)
398. "Pablo and the Dancing Chihuahua" [feature film; Part I] (1-28-68) Armando Islas
399. "Pablo and the Dancing Chihuahua" [Part II] (2-4-68)
400. "My Family Is a Menagerie" [narrated by Rex Allen] (2-11-68)
401. "The Young Loner" [feature film; Part I] (2-25-68) Butch Patrick, Kim Hunter, Edward Andrews, Frank Silvera, Jane Zachary
402. "The Young Loner" [Part II] (3-3-68) as above
403. "Wild Heart" [narrated by Leslie Nielsen] (3-10-68)
404. "The Ranger of Brownstone" [animated feature, with 'Donald Duck"] (3-17-68)
405. "The Horse with the Flying Tail" [repeat of episode of 3/10/63] (3-24-68)
406. "The Mystery of Edward Sims" [feature film; Part I] (3-31-68) Roger Mobley, John McIntire, Warren Oates
407. "The Mystery of Edward Sims" [Part II] (4-7-68) as above
408. "Ten Who Dared" [1960 feature film] (4-14-68) John Beal, James Drury, Brian Keith
409. "Jungle Cat" [repeat of episode of 4/12/64] (4-21-68)
410. "Nature's Charter Tours" [nature study] (4-28-68)

## Fifteenth Season

411. "The Legend of the Boy and the Eagle" [1967 featurette, narrated by Frank De Kova] (9-15-68) Stanford Lomakema
412. "Boomerang, Dog of Many Talents" [feature film; Part I] (9-22-68) Darren McGavin, Patricia Crowley, Darby Hinton, Russ Conway
413. "Boomerang, Dog of Many Talents" [Part II] (9-29-68) as

above
414. "Practically Reeking" [animated feature] (10-6-68)
415. "Toby Tyler" [Part I; repeat of episode of 11/22/64] (10-13-68)
416. "Toby Tyler" [Part II; repeat of episode of 11/29/64] (10-20-68)
417. "Brimstone, the Amish Horse" [feature film] (10-27-68)
      Pamela Toll, Wallace Rooney, Michael Goodwin, Phil Clark
418. "The Ugly Dachshund" [1965 feature film; Part I] (11-3-68)
      Dean Jones, Suzanne Pleshette, Charles Ruggles
419. "The Ugly Dachshund" [Part II] (11-10-68) as above
420. "The Treasure of San Bosco Reef" [feature film; Part I]
      (11-24-68) James Daly, John Van Dreelen, Roger Mobley, Nehemiah Persoff, Robert Sorrells
421. "The Treasure of San Bosco Reef" [Part II] (12-1-68) as above
422. "The Owl That Didn't Give a Hoot" [feature film] (12-8-68)
      David Potter, John Fetzer, Marian Fletcher
423. "Mickey's Fortieth Anniversary" (12-22-68)
424. "A Country Coyote Goes Hollywood" [repeat of episode of 12/19/65] (12-29-68)
425. "Solomon, the Sea Turtle" [nature study] (1-5-69)
426. "Those Calloways" [1964 feature film; Part I] (1-12-69)
      Brian Keith, Vera Miles, Brandon de Wilde, Walter Brennan, Ed Wynn
427. "Those Calloways" [Part II] (1-19-69) as above
428. "Those Calloways" [Part III] (1-26-69) as above
429. "Pancho, the Fastest Paw in the West" [nature drama, narrated by Rex Allen] (2-2-69) Frank Keith, Armando Islas, Albert Hachmeister
430. "The Secret of Boyne Castle" [1969 feature film; Part I]
      (2-9-69) Kurt Russell, Patrick Dawson, Glenn Corbett, Alfred Burke
431. "The Secret of Boyne Castle" [Part II] (2-16-69) as above
432. "The Secret of Boyne Castle" [Part III] (2-23-69) as above
433. "Nature's Better Built Homes" [nature study] (3-2-69)
434. "Ride a Northbound Horse" [feature film; Part I] (3-16-69)
      Michael Shea, Carroll O'Connor, Andy Devine
435. "Ride a Northbound Horse" [Part II] (3-23-69) as above

Sixteenth Season

436. "Wild Geese Calling" [nature drama, narrated by Steve Forrest] (9-14-69) Carl Draper, Persis Overton
437. "My Dog, the Thief" [feature film; Part I] (9-21-69) Dwayne Hickman, Elsa Lanchester, Mary Ann Mobley
438. "My Dog, the Thief" [Part II] (9-28-69) as above
439. "The Three Lives of Thomasina" [repeat of episodes 11/14/65 and 11/21/65] (10-5-69)
440. "The Three Lives of Thomasina" [repeat of episodes 11/21/65 and 11/28/65] (10-12-69)
441. "The Feather Farm" [feature film] (10-26-69) Christine

Coates, Shirley Fabricant, Mel Weiser, Nick Nolte
442. "Charlie, the Lonesome Cougar" [feature film; Part I] (11-2-69)
443. "Charlie, the Lonesome Cougar" [Part II] (11-9-69)
444. "Varda, the Peregrine Falcon" [nature study] (11-16-69)
445. "Secrets of Pirate's Inn" [feature film; Part I] (11-23-69)
Charles Aidman, Paul Fix, Ed Begley
446. "Secrets of Pirate's Inn" [Part II] (11-30-69) as above
447. "Inky, the Crow" [nature study] (12-7-69)
448. "Babes in Toyland" [1961 feature film; Part I] (12-21-69)
Annette Funicello, Ray Bolger, Tommy Sands, Henry
Calvin
449. "Babes in Toyland" [Part II] (12-28-69) as above
450. "Yellowstone Cubs" [repeat of episode of 9/19/65] (1-4-70)
451. "Bon Voyage!" [1962 feature film; Part I] (1-11-70) Fred
MacMurray, Tommy Kirk, Jane Wyman, Deborah Walley,
Michael Callan, Jessie Royce Landis
452. "Bon Voyage!" [Part II] (1-18-70) as above
453. "Bon Voyage!" [Part III] (1-25-70) as above
454. "Smoke" [feature film; Part I] (2-1-70) Ronny Howard,
Andy Devine, Earl Holliman, Jacqueline Scott, Olan Soule
455. "Smoke" [Part II] (2-8-70) as above
456. "Big Red" [Part I; repeat of episode of 12/6/64] (2-15-70)
457. "Big Red" [Part II; repeat of episode of 12/13/64] (2-22-70)
458. "Menace on the Mountain" [feature film; Part I] (3-1-70)
Charles Aidman, Albert Salmi, Mitch Vogel, Patricia
Crowley
459. "Menace on the Mountain" [Part II] (3-8-70) as above
460. "Disneyland Showtime" [with E. J. Peaker, Kurt Russell,
the Osmond Brothers] (3-22-70)
461. "Nature's Strangest Oddballs" [with "Professor Ludwig Von
Drake"] (3-29-70)

Seventeenth Season

462. "Christobalito, the Calypso Colt" [nature drama] (9-13-70)
Roberto Vigoreaux, Walter Buso
463. "The Boy Who Stole the Elephant" [feature film; Part I]
(9-20-70) Mark Lester, Tom Drake, June Havoc, David
Wayne, Dabbs Greer
464. "The Boy Who Stole the Elephant" [Part II] (9-27-70) as
above
465. "Westward Ho the Wagons" [1956 feature film; Part I] (10-4-70) Fess Parker, Kathleen Crowley
466. "Westward Ho the Wagons" [Part II] (10-11-70) as above
467. "The Wacky Zoo of Morgan City" [feature film; Part I]
(10-18-70) Cecil Kellaway, Wally Cox, Hal Holbrook,
Joe Flynn
468. "The Wacky Zoo of Morgan City" [Part II] (10-25-70) as
above
469. "Snow Bear" [feature film, narrated by John McIntire; Part
I] (11-1-70) Steve Kaleak, Rossman Peetook

470. "Snow Bear" [Part II] (11-8-70) as above
471. "Monkeys, Go Home!" [1967 feature film; Part I] (11-15-
     70) Dean Jones, Maurice Chevalier, Yvette Mimieux,
     Bernard Woringer, Clement Harari, Marcel Hillaire
472. "Monkeys, Go Home!" [Part II] (11-22-70) as above
473. "Hang Your Hat on the Wind" [feature film] (11-29-70)
     Judson Pratt, Ric Natoli, Angel Tompkins
474. "It's Tough to Be a Bird" [1969 short subject] (12-13-70)
475. "From All of Us to All of You" [Christmas program] (12-
     20-70)
476. "Minado, the Wolverine" [repeat of episode of 11/7/65]
     (12-27-70)
477. "Three Without Fear: Lost on the Baja Peninsula" [Part I;
     feature film] (1-3-71) Bart Orlando, Pablo Lopez,
     Marion Valjalo, Alex Tinne
478. "Three Without Fear: In the Land of the Desert Whales"
     [Part II] (1-10-71) as above
479. "The Adventures of Bullwhip Griffin" [1967 feature film;
     Part I] (1-17-71) Roddy McDowall, Karl Malden,
     Suzanne Pleshette, Bryan Russell, Harry Guardino,
     Mike Mazurki
480. "The Adventures of Bullwhip Griffin" [Part II] (1-24-71) as
     above
481. "The Adventures of Bullwhip Griffin" [Part III] (1-31-71)
     as above
482. "Bayou Boy" [feature film; Part I] (2-7-71) Mitch Vogel,
     Mike Lookinland, John McIntire, Jeanette Nolan, Frank
     Silvera, Paul Fix, Vito Scotti, Percy Rodriguez
483. "Bayou Boy" [Part II] (2-14-71) as above
484. "Moon Pilot" [Part I; repeat of episode of 1/16/66] (2-21-
     71)
485. "Moon Pilot" [Part II; repeat of episode of 1/23/66] (2-28-
     71)
486. "Hamad and the Pirates: The Phantom Dhow" [Part I; fea-
     ture film narrated by Michael Ansara] (3-7-71) Khalid
     Marshad, Kalifah Shaheen, Abdullah Masoud, Miriam
     Ahmed
487. "Hamad and the Pirates: The Island of the Three Palms"
     [Part II] (3-14-71) as above

Eighteenth Season

488. "Charlie Crowfoot, the Coati-Mundi" [nature study] (9-19-
     71)
489. "Hacksaw" [feature film; Part I] (9-26-71) Tab Hunter,
     Susan Bracken
490. "Hacksaw" [Part II] (10-3-71) as above
491. "Summer Magic" [Part I; repeat of episode of 12/5/65]
     (10-10-71)
492. "Summer Magic" [Part II; repeat of episode of 12/12/65]
     (10-17-71)
493. "The Strange Monster of Strawberry Cove" [feature film;
     Part I] (10-31-71) Burgess Meredith, Agnes Moorehead

494. "The Strange Monster of Strawberry Cove" [Part II] (11-7-71)
495. "The Horse in the Gray-Flannel Suit" [1968 feature film; Part I] (11-14-71) Dean Jones, Diane Baker, Lloyd Bochner, Fred Clark, Ellen Janov, Morey Amsterdam
496. "The Horse in the Gray Flannel Suit" [Part II] (11-21-71) as above
497. "Lefty, the Ding-a-Ling Lynx" [nature drama; Part I] (11-28-71) Ron Brown
498. "Lefty, the Ding-a-Ling Lynx" [Part II] (12-5-71) as above
499. "Disney on Parade" (12-19-71)
500. "Cavalcade of Songs" [repeat of episode of 9/16/62] (12-26-71)
501. "The Tattooed Police Horse" [repeat of episode of 9/10/67] (1-2-72)
502. "Mountain Born" [feature film] (1-9-72) Sam Uastin, Walter Stroud, Jolene Terr
503. "The One and Only Genuine Original Family Band" [1968 feature film; Part I] (1-23-72) Walter Brennan, Buddy Ebsen, John Davidson, Lesley Ann Warren
504. "The One and Only Genuine Original Family Band" [Part II] (1-30-72) as above
505. "Justin Morgan Had a Horse" [feature film; Part I] (2-6-72) Don Murray, R. G. Armstrong, Lana Wood, Gary Crosby
506. "Justin Morgan Had a Horse" [Part II] (2-13-72) as above
507. "The City Fox" [nature drama] (2-20-72)
508. "Banner in the Sky" [Part I; repeat of episode of 2/17/63] (3-5-72)
509. "Banner in the Sky" [Part II; repeat of episode of 2/24/63] (3-12-72)
510. "Chango, Guardian of the Mayan Treasure" [feature film] (3-19-72)
511. "Michael O'Hara the Fourth" [feature film; Part I] (3-26-72) Dan Dailey, Jo Ann Harris, Michael McGreevey, William Bramley
512. "Michael O'Hara, the Fourth" [Part II] (4-2-72) as above
513. a) 'Dad, Can I Borrow the Car?" [animated and live action satire] b) "It's Tough to Be a Bird" [repeat of episode of 12/13/70] (4-9-72)

Nineteenth Season

514. "The Computer Wore Tennis Shoes" [feature film; Part I] (9-17-72) Kurt Russell, Joe Flynn, Cesar Romero
515. "The Computer Wore Tennis Shoes" [Part II] (9-24-72) as above
516. "The Nashville Coyote" [nature drama] (10-1-72) Walter Forbes, William Garton
517. "Savage Sam" [Part I; repeat of episode of 10/2/66] (10-8-72)
518. "Savage Sam" [Part II; repeat of episode of 10/9/66] (10-15-72)

519. "High Flying Spy" [feature film; Part I] (10-22-72) Darren McGavin, Stuart Whitman
520. "High Flying Spy" [Part II] (10-29-72) as above
521. "High Flying Spy" [Part III] (11-5-72) as above
522. "Nosey, the Sweetest Skunk in the West" [nature comedy] (11-19-72) James Chandler, Janie Biddle, Walter Carlson
523. "Chandar, the Black Leopard of Ceylon" [feature film; Part I] (11-26-72)
524. "Chandar, the Black Leopard of Ceylon" [Part II] (12-3-72)
525. "Salty, the Hijacked Harbor Seal" [nature drama] (12-17-72)
526. "A Present for Donald" [repeat of episode of 12/19/56] (12-24-72)
527. "One Day on Beetle Rock" [repeat of episode of 11/19/67] (12-31-72)
528. "The Mystery in Dracula's Castle" [feature film; Part I] (1-7-73) Johnny Whitaker, Mariette Hartley, Clu Gulager, Scott Kolden
529. "The Mystery in Dracula's Castle" [Part II] (1-14-73) as above
530. "50 Happy Years" [highlights from Disney films] (1-21-73)
531. "The Monkey's Uncle" [repeat of episode of 11/26/67; Part I] (1-28-73)
532. "The Monkey's Uncle" [Part II; repeat of episode of 12/3/67] (2-4-73)
533. "Rascal" [1969 feature film; Part I] (2-11-73) Billy Mumy, Steve Forrest, Elsa Lanchester, Pamela Toll, Henry Jones, Bettye Ackerman, John Fiedler, Richard Erdman
534. "Rascal" [Part II] (2-18-73) as above
535. "Chester, Yesterday's Horse" [nature drama] (3-4-73) Jeff Tyler, Bill Williams, Barbara Hale
536. "The Little Shepherd Dog of Catalina" [nature drama] (3-11-73) Clint Rowe, William Maxwell
537. "The Boy and the Bronc Buster" [feature film; Part I] (3-18-73) Earl Holliman, Vincent Van Patten
538. "The Boy and the Bronc Buster" [Part II] (3-25-73) as above
539. "Call It Courage" [feature film narrated by Don Ho] (4-1-73) Evan Temarii

Twentieth Season

540. "The Barefoot Executive" [1971 feature film; Part I] (9-16-73) Kurt Russell, Wally Cox, Joe Flynn, Harry Morgan, Alan Hewitt, Heather North
541. "The Barefoot Executive" [Part II] (9-23-73) as above
542. "Fire on Kelly Mountain" [feature film] (9-30-73) Andrew Duggan, Larry Wilcox, Anne Lockhart, Noam Pitlik
543. "Mustang!" [nature drama narrated by Ricardo Montalban; Part I] (10-7-73) Charles Baca, Flavio Martinez, Ignacio Ramirez
544. "Mustang!" [Part II] (10-14-73) as above
545. "Stub, Best Cow Dog in the West" [nature drama, narrated

by Rex Allen] (10-21-73) Slim Pickens, Jay Sister, Mike Herbert, Luann Beach

546. "King of the Grizzlies" [1970 feature film; Part I] (10-28-73) John Yesno, Chris Wiggins

547. "King of the Grizzlies" [Part II] (11-4-73) as above

548. "The Flight of the White Stallions" [Part I; repeat of episode of 10/17/65] (11-11-73)

549. "The Flight of the White Stallions" [Part II; repeat of episode of 10/24/65] (11-18-73)

550. "Run, Cougar, Run" [feature film; Part I] (11-25-73) Stuart Whitman

551. "Run, Cougar, Run" [Part II] (12-2-73) as above

552. "The Proud Bird of Shanghai" [nature study] (12-16-73)

553. "From All of Us to All of You" [Christmas program] (12-23-73)

554. "An Otter in the Family" [repeat of episode of 2/21/65] (12-30-73)

555. "The Whiz Kid and the Mystery at Riverton" [feature film; Part I] (1-6-74) Eric Shea, Clay O'Brien, Kim Richards, Edward Andrews, John Fiedler, Lonny Chapman

556. "The Whiz Kid and the Mystery at Riverton" [Part II] (1-13-74) as above

557. "Hog Wild" [feature film; Part I] (1-20-74) John Ericson, Diana Muldaur, Clay O'Brien, Kim Richards, Denver Pyle, Shug Fisher

558. "Hog Wild" [Part II] (1-27-74)

559. "Caralo, the Sierra Coyote" [nature study] (2-3-74)

560. "The Ugly Dachshund" [Part I; repeat of episode of 11/3/68] (2-10-74)

561. "The Ugly Dachshund" [Part II; repeat of episode of 11/10/68] (2-17-74)

562. "Ringo, the Refugee Racoon" [nature study] (3-3-74)

563. "Diamonds on Wheels" [feature film; Part I] (3-10-74) Peter Firth, Patrick Allen, George Sewell, Cynthia Lund

564. "Diamonds on Wheels" [Part II] (3-17-74) as above

565. "Diamonds on Wheels" [Part III] (3-24-74) as above

566. "The Magic of Walt Disney World" (3-31-74)

Twenty-first Season

567. "The $1,000,000 Duck" [1971 feature film; Part I] (9-15-74) Dean Jones, Sandy Duncan, Joe Flynn, Tony Roberts, Lee Harcourt Montgomery, Jack Kruschen, Virginia Vincent

568. "The $1,000,000 Duck" [Part II] (9-22-74) as above

569. "Shokee, the Everglades Panther" [feature film; narrated by Michael Ansara] (9-29-74) Curtis Osceola

570. "Return of the Big Cat" [feature film; Part I] (10-6-74) Jeremy Slate, Patricia Crowley, David Wayne, Jeff East

571. "Return of the Big Cat" [Part II] (10-13-74) as above

572. "Two Against the Arctic" [nature drama, narrated by An-
     drew Duggan; Part I] (10-20-74) Susie Silook, Marty
     Smith
573. "Two Against the Arctic" [Part II] (10-27-74) as above
574. "Adventure in Satan's Canyon" [nature drama] (11-3-74)
     Richard Jaeckel, David Alan Bailey, Larry Pennell
575. "Those Calloways" [Part I; repeat of episode of 1/12/69]
     (11-10-74)
576. "Those Calloways" [Part II; repeat of episode of 1/19/69]
     (11-17-74)
577. "Those Calloways" [Part III; repeat of episode of 1/26/69]
     (11-24-74)
578. "Runaway on the Rogue River" [feature film] (12-1-74)
     Willie Aames, Denis Arndt, Slim Pickens
579. "Stub, Best Cow Dog in the West" [repeat of episode of
     10/21/73] (12-8-74)
580. "The Truth About Mother Goose" [repeat of episode of
     11/17/63] (12-22-74)
581. "The Legend of the Boy and the Eagle" [repeat of episode of
     9/15/68] (12-29-74)
582. "Greyfriars' Bobby" [repeat of episode of 3/29/64; Part I]
     (1-5-75)
583. "Greyfriars' Bobby" [Part II; repeat of episode of 4/5/64]
     (1-12-75)
584. "The Sky's the Limit" [feature film; Part I] (1-19-75)
     Lloyd Nolan, Pat O'Brien, Ike Eisenmann, Jeanette Nolan
585. "The Sky's the Limit" [Part II] (1-26-75) as above
586. "Johnny Tremain" [1957 feature film; Part I] (2-2-75) Hal
     Stalmaster
587. "Johnny Tremain" [Part II] (2-9-75) as above
588. "The Wild Country" [1971 feature film; Part I] (2-23-75)
     Vera Miles, Steve Forrest, Jack Elam, Clint Howard,
     Ronny Howard
589. "The Wild Country" [Part II] (3-2-75) as above
590. "The Footloose Goose" [nature drama] (3-9-75)
591. "Deacon, the High Noon Dog" [nature drama narrated by
     Roger Miller] (3-16-75)
592. "Welcome to the 'World'" [a tour of "Walt Disney World"
     with Lucie Arnaz, Tommy Tune and Lyle Waggoner]
     (3-23-75)

[Continuing]

PLAYHOUSE 90

The Episodes:

1. "Forbidden Area" [by Pat Frank] (10-4-56) Charles Bickford, Diana Lynn, Tab Hunter, Victor Jory, Charleton
   Heston, Vincent Price
2. "Requiem for a Heavyweight" [by Rod Serling] (10-11-56)

Jack Palance, Keenan Wynn, Ed Wynn, Kim Hunter, Max Baer, Maxie Rosenbloom

3. "Seidman and Son" [by Elick Moll] (10-18-56) Farley Granger, Eddie Kantor

4. "Rendezvous in Black" [by James P. Cavanagh from the Cornell Woolrich mystery] (10-25-56) Franchot Tone, Laraine Day, Boris Karloff, Tom Drake, Elizabeth Patterson, Viveca Lindfors

5. "The Country Husband" [by John Cheever] (11-1-56) Frank Lovejoy, Felicia Farr, Barbara Hale

6. "The Big Slide" [by Edward Beloin and Dean Reisner] (11-8-56) Red Skelton, Shirley Jones

7. "Heritage of Anger" [by Harold Jack Bloom] (11-15-56) Ralph Bellamy, Nina Foch, Lloyd Bridges, John Ericson, Tom Brown, Onslow Stevens

8. "Eloise" [by Leonard Spigelgass from the book by Kay Thompson] (11-22-56) Evelyn Rudie, Kay Thompson, Ethel Barrymore, Louis Jourdan, Monty Woolley

9. "Confession" [by Devery Freeman] (11-29-56) Dennis O'Keefe, June Lockhart, Paul Stewart

10. "Made in Heaven" [by Hagar Wilde] (12-6-56) Imogene Coca, Robert Preston, Phyllis Kirk, Eddie Mayehoff, Jacques Bergerac, Sheila Bond, Benay Venuta

11. "Sincerely, Willis Wayde" [by Frank D. Gilroy from the book by John P. Marquand] (12-13-56) Sarah Churchill, Walter Abel, Charles Bickford, Peter Lawford, Jeff Donnell, Jane Darwell

12. "The Family Nobody Wanted" [by George Bruce from Helen Doss' book] (12-20-56) Lew Ayres, Nanette Fabray

13. "Massacre at Sand Creek" [by William Sackheim] (12-27-56) John Derek, Gene Evans, Everett Sloane

14. "Snow Shoes" [by Bob Barbash] (1-3-57) Barry Sullivan, Marilyn Maxwell, Stuart Erwin, Harpo Marx, Wallace Ford, John Carradine, Kenny Delmar

15. "Mr. and Mrs. McAdam" [by Dorothy and Howard Baker] (1-10-57) John Kerr, Piper Laurie, Sir Cedric Hardwicke, Mary Astor, Victor Jory, Elizabeth Patterson

16. "So Soon to Die" [by Marc Brandel] (1-17-57) Richard Basehart, Anne Bancroft, Sebastian Cabot, Torin Thatcher

17. "The Star Wagon" [by James P. Cavanagh from the Maxwell Anderson play] (1-24-57) Eddie Bracken, Diana Lynn

18. "The Greer Case" [by Whitfield Cook from the novel by Justice David W. Peck] (1-31-57) Melvyn Douglas, Zsa Zsa Gabor, Anita Louise, Raymond Burr, Edmund Gwenn

19. "The Miracle Worker" [autobiographical story of Helen Keller] (2-7-57) Patty McCormack, Teresa Wright, John Barrymore Jr., Burl Ives, Katherine Bard

20. "The Comedian" [by Rod Serling from the Ernest Lehman novel] (2-14-57) Mickey Rooney, Edmond O'Brien, Kim Hunter, Mel Tormé, Constance Ford

21. "One Coat of White" [by Leonard Spigelgass from the H. Allen Smith romantic comedy] (2-21-57) Paul Henreid, Claudette Colbert

22. "The Blackwell Story" [adaptation of Lloyd Douglas' The First Woman Doctor] (2-28-57) Joanne Dru, Dan O'Herlihy, Charles Korvin, Marshall Thompson
23. "Invitation to a Gunfighter" (3-7-57) Hugh O'Brian, Ray Collins, Gilbert Roland
24. "The Last Tycoon" [by Don M. Mankiewicz from the F. Scott Fitzgerald novel] (3-14-57) Jack Palance, Keenan Wynn, Viveca Lindfors, Peter Lorre
25. "The Hostess with the Mostest" [by Speed Lamkin and Hagar Wilde from Perle Mesta's life story] (3-21-57) Shirley Booth, Evelyn Rudie, Perle Mesta, Shepperd Strudwick, Frank Melan, Hedda Hopper
26. "Charley's Aunt" [by Brandon Thomas] (3-28-57) Art Carney, Jeanette MacDonald, Gene Raymond, Tom Tryon, Richard Haydn, Venetia Stevenson
27. "Clipper Ship" [by Berne Giler] (4-4-57) Charles Bickford, Jan Sterling, Steve Forrest, Helmut Dantine
28. "If You Knew Elizabeth" [by Tad Mosel] (4-11-57) Claire Trevor, Gary Merrill, Ernest Truex, Natalie Schafer
29. "Three Men on a Horse" [by W. J. Russell from the Broadway comedy] (4-18-57) Jack Carson, Carol Channing, Johnny Carson
30. "Four Women in Black" [by Bernard Girard, who also produced and directed] (4-25-57) Helen Hayes, Katy Jurado, Narda Onyx, Janice Rule, Lita Milan, Ralph Meeker
31. "Child of Trouble" [by James P. Cavanagh from the magazine article by Selma Robinson] (5-2-57) Patty McCormack, Ricardo Montalban, Joan Blondell, Lillian Roth, Chester Morris, Richard Arlen
32. "Homeward Borne" [by Halsted Welles] (5-9-57) Linda Darnell, Richard Kiley, Keith Andes
33. "The Helen Morgan Story" [by Leonard Spigelgass and Paul Monash] (5-16-57) Polly Bergen, Hoagy Carmichael, Sylvia Sidney, Robert Lowery, Reginald Denny
34. "Winter Dreams" [by James P. Cavanagh from the F. Scott Fitzgerald story] (5-23-57) Dana Wynter, John Cassavetes, Edmund Gwenn, Mildred Dunnock, Phyllis Love, Darryl Hickman
35. "Circle of the Day" [by Edna Anhalt from the novel by Helen Howe] (5-30-57) Nancy Kelly, Michael Rennie, Pamela Mason, Zsa Zsa Gabor, Portland Mason, Gladys Cooper
36. "Without Incident" [by David Victor and Herbert Little Jr. from a story by Charles Marquis Warren] (6-6-57) Errol Flynn, Ann Sheridan, John Ireland, Julie London
37. "Clash by Night" [by F. M. Durkee from the Clifford Odets play] (6-13-57) Kim Stanley, E. G. Marshall, Lloyd Bridges
38. "Ain't No Time for Glory" (6-20-57) Barry Sullivan, Gene Barry, John Barrymore Jr., Bruce Bennett, Richard Jaeckel
39. "The Fabulous Irishman" [about Jewish Lord Mayor Robert Briscoe] (6-27-57) Katherine Bard, Art Carney, Eli Mintz, Charles Davis, George Matthews, Michael Higgins

Second Season

40. "The Death of Manolete" [by Barnaby Conrad and Paul Mo-
nash] (9-12-57) Jack Palance, Suzy Parker, Nehemiah
Persoff, Robert Middleton
41. "The Dark Side of the Earth" [by Rod Serling] (9-19-57)
Van Heflin, Kim Hunter
42. "Topaze" [by Marcel Pagnol] (9-26-57) Ernie Kovacs,
Sheree North, Carl Reiner, Richard Haydn
43. "A Sound of Different Drummers" [by Robert Alan Arthur]
(10-3-57) John Ireland, Diana Lynn, Sterling Hayden
44. "The Playroom" [by Tad Mosel] (10-10-57) Mildred Dunnock, Tony Randall, Nina Foch, Patricia Neal, Marilyn
Erskine
45. "Around the World in 90 Minutes" [a live party originating
from Madison Square Garden, commemorating the first anniversary of producer Mike Todd's Around the World in 80
Days] (10-17-57)
46. "The Mystery of Thirteen" [by David Shaw from the Robert
Graves novel They Hanged My Saintly Billy] (10-24-57)
Margaret O'Brien, Jack Lemmon, Gladys Cooper, Herbert
Marshall
47. "The Edge of Innocence" [by Berne Giler] (10-31-57) Joseph
Cotten, Teresa Wright, Lorne Greene, Beverly Garland,
Maureen O'Hara
48. "The Clouded Image" [by James P. Cavanagh from the novel
by Josephine Tey] (11-7-57) Farley Granger, Patty Mc-
Cormack, Judith Anderson, John Williams, Terry Moore,
Vincent Price
49. "The Jet-Propelled Couch" [by Stanley Roberts from the story
The Fifty-Minute Hour] (11-14-57) Donald O'Connor,
David Wayne, Peter Lorre
50. "The Troublemakers" [by George Bellak from his stage play]
(11-21-57) Ben Gazzara, Mary Astor, Keenan Wynn,
Robert Vaughn
51. "Panic Button" [by Rod Serling] (11-28-57) Lee J. Cobb,
Vera Miles, Robert Stack
52. "The Galvanized Yankee" [by Russell Hughes] (12-5-57)
Lloyd Nolan, James Whitmore, Martha Vickers, Victor
Jory, Neville Brand
53. "The Thundering Wave" [by Robert Alan Arthur] (12-12-57)
James Mason, Pamela Mason, Joan Bennett, Franchot
Tone
54. "For I Have Loved Strangers" [by Elick Moll from a story by
Don Murray and Fred Clasel] (12-19-57) Don Murray,
Hope Lange
55. "Lone Woman" [by Al C. Ward] (12-26-57) Scott Brady,
Vincent Price, Jack Lord, Raymond Burr, Kathryn Gray-
son
56. "Reunion" [by Merle Miller from his novel] (1-2-58) Hugh
O'Brian, Frances Farmer, Martha Hyer, Neva Patterson,
Dane Clark
57. "The Last Man" [by Aaron Spelling] (1-9-58) Sterling

Hayden, Carolyn Jones

58. "The Eighty-Yard Run" [by David Shaw from the story by Irwin Shaw] (1-16-58) Paul Newman, Joanne Woodward, "Red" Sanders

59. "Before I Die" [by Berne Giler from the story by William Sackheim and Daniel Ullman] (1-23-58) Richard Kiley, Kim Hunter, Coleen Gray, Jay C. Flippen, Joe De Santis

60. "The Gentleman from Seventh Avenue" [by Elick Moll] (1-30-58) Walter Slezak, Patricia Neal, Patricia Sidney, Robert Alda

61. "The Violent Heart" [by Leslie Stevens from the Daphne du Maurier story] (2-6-58) Dana Wynter, Ben Gazzara, Charles Korvin, Pamela Brown

62. "No Time at All" [by David Swift and Charles Einstein from Einstein's novel] (2-13-58) William Lundigan, Betsy Palmer, Jane Greer, Keenan Wynn

63. "Point of No Return" [by Frank D. Gilroy from the novel by John P. Marquand and the play by Paul Osborn] (2-20-58) Charleton Heston, Hope Lange, Katherine Bard

64. "Portrait of a Murderer" [Leslie Stevens' study of Donald Bashor, who was executed in 1957] (2-27-58) Tab Hunter, Rudy Bond, Geraldine Page, Elizabeth Patterson

65. "The Last Clear Chance" [by A. E. Hotchner] (3-6-58) Paul Muni, Luther Adler, Lee Remick, Dick York, Eithne Dunne

66. "The Male Animal" [by Don M. Mankiewicz from the James Thurber and Elliott Nugent comedy] (3-13-58) Andy Griffith, Ann Rutherford, Edmond O'Brien, Gale Gordon, Charles Ruggles, Richard Sargent

67. "The Right-Hand Man" [by Dick Berg from the story by Garson Kanin] (3-20-58) Anne Baxter, Dana Andrews

68. "Turn Left at Mount Everest" [by Del Reisman from the Lowell Barrington play] (4-3-58) Fess Parker, Peter Lorre, Paul Ford, Patricia Cutts, Arnold Stang

69. "The Dungeon" [by David Swift] (4-10-58) Paul Douglas, Agnes Moorehead, Julie Adams, Dennis Weaver, Patty McCormack

70. "Bitter Heritage" [by Joseph Landon] (4-17-58) Franchot Tone, Elizabeth Montgomery, Robert Middleton, Henry Hull, James Drury, Eva La Gallienne

71. "Verdict of Three" [by James P. Cavanagh from the novel by Raymond Postgate] (4-24-58) Gladys Cooper, Michael Wilding, Angela Lansbury, Carmen Mathews, Yvonne De Carlo

72. "Rumors of Evening" [by F. W. Durkee Jr.] (5-1-58) John Kerr, Barbara Bel Geddes, Robert Loggia, Carl Benton Reid, Pat Hitchcock, Billie Burke, Robert F. Simon

73. "Not the Glory" [by David Shaw from the Pierre Boulle story] (5-8-58) James Mason, Ann Todd, Dennis King

74. "Nightmare at Ground Zero" [by Paul Monash from the story told by Dr. John C. Clark to Robert Cahn] (5-15-58) Barry Sullivan, Jack Warden, Carl Benton Reid

75. "Bomber's Moon" [by Rod Serling] (5-22-58) Robert

Cummings, Rip Torn, Martin Balsam, Larry Gates
76. "Natchez" [by Martin M. Goldsmith from the story by E. A. Ellington] (5-29-58) Macdonald Carey, Felicia Farr, Cliff Robertson, Thomas Mitchell
77. "The Innocent Sleep" [by Tad Mosel] (6-5-58) Hope Lange, John Ericson, Buster Keaton, Hope Emerson
78. "A Town Has Turned to Dust" [by Rod Serling] (6-19-58) Rod Steiger, Fay Spain, William Shatner, James Gregory
79. "The Great Gatsby" [by David Shaw from the F. Scott Fitzgerald novel] (6-26-58) Robert Ryan, Jeanne Crain, Rod Taylor, Virginia Grey, Patricia Barry, Barry Atwater, Philip Reed

Third Season

80. "The Plot to Kill Stalin" [by David Karp] (9-25-58) Melvyn Douglas, Luther Adler, E. G. Marshall, Thomas Gomez, Eli Wallach, Oscar Homolka
81. "The Days of Wine and Roses" [by J. P. Miller] (10-2-58) Piper Laurie, Cliff Robertson, Charles Bickford
82. "The Time of Your Life" [adaptation of William Saroyan's play] (10-9-58) Jackie Gleason, Betsy Palmer, James Barton, Dick York, Bobby Van, Dina Merrill, Jack Klugman
83. "The Long March" [by Roger O. Hirson from the novel by William Styron] (10-16-58) Sterling Hayden, Jack Carson, Rod Taylor, Mona Freeman
84. "Shadows Tremble" [by Ernest Kinoy] (10-23-58) Edward G. Robinson, Beatrice Straight, Ray Walston, Frank Conroy, Parker Fennelly
85. "Word from a Sealed-Off Box" [by Mayo Simon from the New Yorker article by Henriette Roosenburg] (10-30-58) Betsy Von Furstenberg, Theodore Bikel, Jean-Pierre Aumont, Maria Schell, Vivian Nathan
86. "Heart of Darkness" [by Stewart Stern from the Joseph Conrad novel] (11-6-58) Roddy McDowall, Boris Karloff, Eartha Kitt, Oscar Homolka, Richard Haydn, Cathleen Nesbitt, Inga Swenson
87. "Old Man" [by Horton Foote from the William Faulkner story] (11-20-58) Sterling Hayden, Geraldine Page, James Westerfield, Sandy Kenyon, Malcolm Atterbury, Richard LePore, George Mitchell, Marc Lawrence, Milton Selzer
88. "The Return of Ansel Gibbs" [by David Davidson from the novel by Frederick Buechner] (11-27-58) Melvyn Douglas, Diana Lynn, Earl Holliman, Mary Astor, Loring Smith, Ilka Chase
89. "Free Week-end" [by Steven Gethers] (12-4-58) James Whitmore, Kim Hunter, Nina Foch, Charles Bickford
90. "Seven Against the Wall" [by Howard Browne from his book on the "St. Valentine's Day Massacre"] (12-11-58) Paul Lambert, Dennis Patrick, Tige Andrews; Eric Sevareid narrates
91. "The Nutcracker" [George Balanchine's ballet of the Tchaikovsky

classic, with Edward Villella and members of the New York City Ballet] (12-25-58)

92. "Face of a Hero" [by Robert Joseph from the novel by Pierre Boulle] (1-1-59) Jack Lemmon, James Gregory, Henry Hull, Ann Meacham

93. "The Wings of the Dove" [by Meade Roberts from the novel by Henry James] (1-8-59) Dana Wynter, James Donald, John Baragrey, Inga Swenson, Henry Daniell, Isabel Jeans, Lurene Tuttle

94. "The Blue Men" [by Alvin Boretz] (1-15-59) Edmond O'Brien, Jack Warden, Eileen Heckart, James Westerfield, Cameron Prud'homme, Rafael Campos

95. "The Velvet Alley" [by Rod Serling] (1-22-59) Art Carney, Leslie Nielsen, Katherine Bard, Jack Klugman, Bonita Granville, George Voskovec, Alexander Scourby

96. "A Quiet Game of Cards" [by Reginald Rose] (1-29-59) Barry Sullivan, Franchot Tone, Irene Hervey, William Bendix, E. G. Marshall, Gary Merrill

97. "Child of Our Time" [by Irving Gaynor Neiman from the autobiographical novel by Michel del Castillo] (2-5-59) Robert Crawford, Liliane Montevecchi, Maximilian Schell, Lou Jacobi

98. "The Second Man" [by Leslie Stevens from the novel by Edward Grierson] (2-12-59) James Mason, Margaret Leighton, Hugh Griffith, Kenneth Haigh, Diana Wynyard

99. "The Raider" [by Loring Mandell] (2-19-59) Rod Taylor, Paul Douglas, Frank Lovejoy, Leif Erickson, Donald Crisp, Leon Ames

100. "The Dingaling Girl" [by J. P. Miller] (2-26-59) Diane Varsi, Eddie Albert, Mort Sahl, Sam Jaffe, Harry Townes

101. "Made in Japan" [by Joseph Stefano] (3-5-59) Dean Stockwell, Harry Guardino, Dick York, Robert Vaughn, E. G. Marshall, Nobu McCarthy

102. "For Whom the Bell Tolls" [by A. E. Hotchner from the Ernest Hemingway; Part I] (3-12-59) Maria Schell, Jason Robards Jr., Maureen Stapleton, Eli Wallach, Nehemiah Persoff, Steven Hill, Vladimir Sokoloff, Milton Selzer, Marc Lawrence, Herbert Berghof, Joseph Bernard, Nick Colossanto, Sydney Pollack

103. "For Whom the Bell Tolls" [Part II] (3-19-59) as above.

104. "A Trip to Paradise" [by Adrian Spies] (3-26-59) Martha Scott, Buddy Ebsen, Susan Oliver

105. "In Lonely Expectation" [by Mayo Simon] (4-2-59) Virginia Kaye, Diane Baker

106. "The Day Before Atlanta" [by John Gay] (4-9-59) Jack Warden, Timmy Everett, Clu Gulager, Dabbs Greer, Suzi Carnell, Musa Williams, Gavin Gordon, Clinton Sundberg

107. "Judgment at Nuremberg" [by Abby Mann] (4-16-59) Claude Rains, Maximilian Schell, Melvyn Douglas

108. "A Corner of the Garden" [by Tad Mosel] (4-23-59) Eileen Heckart, Gary Merrill, Heather Sears, Tommy Kirk,

Susan Gordon
109. "Dark December" [by Merle Miller] (4-30-59) Barry Sullivan, James Whitmore, Lili Darvas, Richard Beymer
110. "Diary of a Nurse" [by Arthur Hailey] (5-7-59) Inger Stevens, Victor Jory, Mary Astor, Adam Kennedy, Mildred Dunnock
111. "A Marriage of Strangers" [by Reginald Rose] (5-14-59) Red Buttons, Diana Lynn, Joan Blondell
112. "Out of Dust" [adapted by John Gay from a drama by Lynn Riggs] (5-21-59) Wayne Morris, Gloria Talbot, Uta Hagen, Charles Bickford, Dick York
113. "The Rank and File" [by Rod Serling] (5-28-59) Van Heflin, Luther Adler, Harry Townes, Charles Bronson, Carl Benton Reid
114. "The Killers of Mussolini" [by A. E. Hotchner] (6-4-59) Nehemiah Persoff, Harry Guardino, Michael Ansara
115. "Project Immortality" [by Loring Mandell] (6-11-59) Lee J. Cobb, Kenneth Haigh, Gusti Huber, Michael Landon, Patty McCormack
116. "Dark as the Night" [by Marc Brandel from the story by James Hadley Chase; this episode was filmed in London] (6-18-59) Michael Wilding, Dennis Price Laraine Day, Hermione Baddeley
117. "The Second Happiest Day" [by Steven Gethers from the novel by John Phillips] (6-25-59) Tony Randall, Judith Anderson, Fay Wray, Margaret O'Brien, Ron Ely, Jack Mullaney

Fourth Season

118. "Target for Three" [by David Davidson] (10-1-59) Ricardo Montalban, George C. Scott, Liliane Montevecchi, Marisa Pavan
119. "The Sounds of Eden" [by George Bellak] (10-15-59) James Whitmore, Kim Hunter, Everett Sloane, Henry Jones, Dick Foran
120. "Misalliance" [by Meade Roberts from the George Bernard Shaw play] (10-29-59) Claire Bloom, Rod Taylor, Robert Morley, Kenneth Haigh, Siobhan McKenna, John Williams, Patrick Macnee, Isobel Elsom
121. "The Hidden Image" [by David Karp] (11-12-59) Franchot Tone, Martin Gabel, Nancy Marchand, George Grizzard, Frank Maxwell
122. "The Grey Nurse Said Nothing" [by Sumner Locke Elliott] (11-26-59) Hugh Griffith, Angela Lansbury, Patricia Cutts, Michael David
123. "The Tunnel" [by David Shaw] (12-10-59) Richard Boone, Onslow Stevens, Ken Lynch, Jack Weston
124. "The Silver Whistle" [by Robert E. McEnroe from his 1948 Broadway comedy] (12-24-59) Eddie Albert, Henry Jones, Bethel Leslie, Margaret Hamilton, Enid Markey
125. "A Dream of Treason" [by David Davidson from the novel by Maurice Edelman] (1-21-60) Richard Basehart,

Leora Dana, John Williams, Susan Oliver
126. "To the Sound of Trumpets" [by John Gay] (2-9-60) Dan
O'Herlihy, Sam Jaffe, Robert Coote, Stephen Boyd,
Dolores Hart, Preston Foster, Judith Anderson, Boris
Karloff
127. "The Cruel Day" [by Reginald Rose] (2-24-60) Van Heflin,
Cliff Robertson, Phyllis Thaxter, Raymond Massey, Ne-
hemiah Persoff, Peter Lorre, Charles Bronson, Thano
Rama, Miko Oscard
128. "Tomorrow" [by Horton Foote from the William Faulkner
story] (3-7-60) Richard Boone, Kim Stanley, Charles
Bickford, Chill Wills, Beulah Bondi, Andrew Prine,
Charles Aidman, Elizabeth Patterson
129. "The Hiding Place" [by Adrian Spies from the novel by
Robert Shaw] (3-22-60) James Mason, Trevor Howard,
Richard Basehart, Robert Emhardt, Helmut Dantine
130. "Alas, Babylon" [by David Shaw from a novel by Pat Frank]
(4-3-60) Dana Andrews, Don Murray, Kim Hunter,
Barbara Rush, Everett Sloane, Rita Moreno, Judith Evelyn, Don Gordon, Robert Crawford Jr., Gina Gillespie,
Burt Reynolds
131. "Journey to the Day" [by Roger O. Hirson] (4-22-60)
Janice Rule, Mike Nichols, James Gregory, Steven Hill,
Mary Dunn, James Dunn
132. "The Shape of the River" [by Harton Foote] (5-2-60) Franchot
Tone, Leif Erickson, Shirley Knight, Katherine Bard
133. "In the Presence of Mine Enemies" [by Rod Serling] (5-18-
60) Charles Laughton, Arthur Kennedy, Oscar Homolka,
Susan Kohner, George Macready, Sam Jaffe, Robert Redford, Otto Waldis

## ZANE GREY THEATRE

Above average western anthology with episodes composed by,
among many others, Sterling Silliphant ("No Man Living"), Louis
King ("Decision at Wilson's Creek") and Aaron Spelling ("Black Is
for Grief").

The Regulars: Dick Powell, host.

The Episodes:

1. "You Only Run Once" (10-5-56) Robert Ryan, Cloris Leachman
2. "The Fearful Courage" (10-12-56) James Whitmore, Ida Lupino
3. "The Long Road Home" (10-19-56) Dick Powell
4. "The Unrelenting Sky" (10-26-56) Lew Ayres, Phyllis Avery
5. "The Lariat" (11-2-56) Jack Palance, Constance Ford,
Addison Richards
6. "Death Watch" (11-9-56) Lee J. Cobb, Bobby Driscoll
7. "Stage for Tucson" (11-16-56) Eddie Albert, John Ericson,

Mona Freeman
8. "A Quiet Sunday in San Ardo" (11-23-56) Wendell Corey, Peggie Castle
9. "Vengeance Canyon" (11-30-56) Walter Brennan, Ben Cooper, Sheb Wooley
10. "Return to Nowhere" (12-7-56) John Ireland, Stephen Mc-Nally, Audrey Totter
11. "Courage Is a Gun" (12-14-56) Dick Powell, Robert Vaughn, Beverly Garland
12. "Muletown Gold Strike" (12-21-56) Rory Calhoun
13. "Stars Over Texas" (12-28-56) Ralph Bellamy, Beverly Washburn
14. "The Three Graves" (1-4-57) Jack Lemmon
15. "No Man Living" (1-11-57) Frank Lovejoy, Margaret Hayes
16. "Time of Decision" (1-18-57) Lloyd Bridges, Diane Brewster, Walter Sande
17. "Until the Man Dies" (1-25-57) Stuart Whitman, Carolyn Jones, John Payne
18. "Back Trail" (2-1-57) Dick Powell, James Anderson, Emile Meyer
19. "Dangerous Orders" (2-8-57) Mark Stevens
20. "The Necessary Breed" (2-15-57) Sterling Hayden, Jean Willes
21. "The Hanging Tree" (2-22-57) Robert Ryan, Cloris Leachman
22. "Village of Fear" (3-1-57) David Niven
23. "Black Creek Encounter" (3-8-57) Ernest Borgnine, Jan Merlin
24. "There Were Four" (3-15-57) Dean Jagger, John Derek, David Janssen
25. "A Fugitive" (3-22-57) Eddie Albert, Celeste Holm
26. "A Time to Live" (4-5-57) Ralph Meeker, Julie London
27. "Black Is for Grief" (4-12-57) Mary Astor, Tom Tryon, Beulah Bondi, Chester Morris, Mala Powers, Tom Tully
28. "Badge of Honor" (5-3-57) Robert Culp, Gary Merrill, Tom Tully
29. "Decision at Wilson's Creek" (5-17-57) John Forsythe, Marjorie Lord
30. "A Man on the Run" (6-21-57) Scott Brady

Second Season

31. "The Deserters" (10-4-57) Dick Powell, Margaret Hayes
32. "Blood in the Dust" (10-11-57) Claudette Colbert
33. "A Gun Is for Killing" (10-18-57) Edmond O'Brien, Robert Vaughn, Marsha Hunt
34. "Proud Woman" (10-25-57) Hedy Lamarr
35. "Ride a Lonely Trail" (11-2-57) Walter Brennan
36. "The Promise" (11-8-57) Gary Merrill, Tommy Sands
37. "Episode in Darkness" (11-15-57) Dewey Martin, Anne Bancroft
38. "The Open Cell" (11-22-57) Dick Powell, Marshall Thompson

39. "A Man to Look Up To" (11-29-57) Lew Ayres
40. "The Bitter Land" (12-6-57) Dan O'Herlihy, Peggy Wood
41. "Gift from a Gunman" (12-13-57) Howard Keel
42. "A Gun for My Bride" (12-27-57) Eddie Albert, Jane Greer
43. "Man Unforgiving" (1-3-58) Joseph Cotten, Johnny Crawford, Claude Akins
44. "Trial by Fear" (1-20-58) Robert Ryan, David Janssen
45. "The Freighter" (1-17-58) Barbara Stanwyck
46. "This Man Who Must Die" (1-24-58) Dan Duryea
47. "Wire" (1-31-58) Lloyd Bridges, David Opatoshu
48. "License to Kill" (2-7-58) Macdonald Carey, John Ericson
49. "Sundown at Bitter Creek" (2-14-58) Dick Powell, Cathy O'Donnell, Nick Adams, Tex Ritter
50. "The Stranger" (2-28-58) Mark Stevens
51. "The Sharpshooter" (3-7-58) Chuck Connors, Leif Erickson, Dennis Hopper, Sidney Blackmer
52. "Man of Fear" (3-14-58) Dewey Martin, Arthur Franz, Julie Adams
53. "The Doctor Keeps a Promise" (3-21-58) Cameron Mitchell
54. "Three Days to Death" (4-4-58) Michael Rennie
55. "Shadow of a Dead Man" (4-11-58) Barry Sullivan
56. "Debt of Gratitude" (4-18-58) Steve Cochran, James Whitmore
57. "A Handful of Ashes" (5-2-58) Thomas Mitchell, June Lockhart
58. "Threat of Violence" (5-23-58) Lyle Bettger, Cesar Romero
59. "Utopia, Wyoming" (6-6-58) Gary Merrill

Third Season

60. "Trail to Nowhere" (10-2-58) David Janssen, Barbara Stanwyck
61. "The Scaffold" (10-9-58) Dick Powell
62. "The Homecoming" (10-23-58) Lloyd Nolan
63. "The Accused" (10-30-58) David Niven
64. "Legacy of a Legend" (11-6-58) Lee J. Cobb
65. "To Sit in Judgment" (11-3-58) Robert Ryan
66. "The Tall Shadow" (11-20-58) Brad Dexter, John Ericson, Julie Adams
67. "The Vaunted" (11-27-58) Eddie Albert, Jane Greer
68. "Pressure Point" (12-4-58) Walter Pidgeon, Pernell Roberts
69. "Bury Me Dead" (12-11-58) Barry Sullivan
70. "Let the Man Die" (12-18-58) Marsha Hunt
71. "Medal of Valor" (12-25-58) Richard Basehart
72. "Living Is a Lonesome Thing" (1-1-59) Michael Rennie
73. "Day of the Killing" (1-8-59) Paul Douglas, Peter Breck
74. "Hang the Heart High" (1-15-59) Barbara Stanwyck, David Janssen
75. "Welcome Home, Stranger" (1-22-59) Dick Powell
76. "Trail Incident" (1-29-59) Cameron Mitchell, John Ericson
77. "Make It Look Good" (2-5-59) Arthur Kennedy
78. "A Thread of Respect" (2-12-59) Danny Thomas, James Coburn, Nick Adams

79. "Deadfall" (2-19-59) Van Johnson
80. "The Last Raid" (2-26-59) Fernando Lamas, Rita Moreno
81. "Man Alone" (3-5-59) Thomas Mitchell, Marilyn Erskine
82. "Hanging Fever" (3-12-59) Frank Lovejoy, Patrick McVey, Beverly Garland
83. "Trouble at Tres Cruces" (3-26-59) Brian Keith, Neville Brand
84. "Loyalty" (4-2-59) Edward G. Robinson, Edward G. Robinson, Jr.
85. "The Sunrise" (4-16-59) Dennis Hopper, Everett Sloane, Ben Cooper
86. "Checkmate" (4-30-59) Marsha Hunt, James Whitmore
87. "Mission to Marathon" (5-14-59) John McIntire, Stephen McNally, Mark Richman
88. "The Law and the Gun" (6-4-59) Michael Ansara, Lyle Bettger

Fourth Season

89. "Interrogation" (10-1-59) Robert Ryan, Alexander Scourby, Harry Townes
90. "Lone Woman" (10-8-59) Barbara Stanwyck, Martin Balsam
91. "Confession" (10-15-59) Dick Powell, Charles Aidman, Walter Burke
92. "The Lonely Gun" (10-22-59) Barry Sullivan
93. "Hand on the Latch" (10-29-59) Anne Baxter
94. "Showdown" (11-5-59) Frank Lovejoy
95. "Mission" (11-12-59) Sammy Davis Jr.
96. "Lonesome Road" (11-19-59) Edmond O'Brien
97. "King of the Valley" (11-26-59) Walter Pidgeon
98. "Rebel Ranger" (12-3-59) Joan Crawford
99. "Death in a Wood" (12-17-59) Dick Powell
100. "The Grubstake" (12-24-59) Cameron Mitchell
101. "The Ghost" (12-31-59) Mel Ferrer
102. "Miss Jenny" (1-7-60) Vera Miles
103. "The Reckoning" (1-14-60) Stephen McNally, Cesar Romero
104. "Wayfarers" (1-21-60) James Whitmore, Felicia Farr
105. "Picture of Sal" (1-28-60) Rod Taylor, Carolyn Jones
106. "Never Too Late" (2-4-60) Ginger Rogers
107. "Man in the Middle" (2-11-60) Richard Jaeckel, Michael Rennie
108. "Guns for Garibaldie" (2-18-60) Fernando Lamas
109. "The Sunday Man" (2-25-60) Brian Donlevy, Dean Jones, Leif Erickson
110. "Setup" (3-3-60) Steve Forrest, Phyllis Kirk
111. "A Small Town That Died" (3-10-60) Beverly Garland, Henry Hull, Dick Powell
112. "Killer Instinct" (3-17-60) Wendell Corey
113. "Sundown Smith" (3-24-60) Jack Carson
114. "Calico Bait" (3-31-60) Robert Culp, Inger Stevens
115. "Seed of Evil" (4-7-60) Raymond Massey, Cara Williams
116. "Deception" (4-14-60) Barry Nelson, Peggy Ann Garner

117. "Stagecoach to Yuma" (5-5-60) Dewey Martin, Jane Greer, Tom Drake

## Fifth Season

118. "A Gun for Willie" (10-6-60) Ernest Borgnine, Paul Birch
119. "Desert Flight" (10-13-60) Dick Powell, James Coburn
120. "Cry Hope!, Cry Hate!" (10-20-60) June Allyson, Paul Fix
121. "The Ox" (11-3-60) Burl Ives, Whit Bissell
122. "So Young the Savage Land" (11-20-60) Claudette Colbert, John Dehner
123. "Ransom" (11-17-60) Lloyd Bridges, Claude Akins
124. "The Last Bugle" (11-24-60) Robert Cummings
125. "The Black Wagon" (12-1-60) Esther Williams, Larry Pennell
126. "Knife of Hate" (12-8-60) Lloyd Nolan, Susan Oliver
127. "The Mormons" (12-15-60) Stephen McNally, Tuesday Weld, Mark Goddard
128. "The Man from Yesterday" (12-22-60) Wendell Corey, Marsha Hunt
129. "Morning Incident" (12-29-60) Robert Culp, Martha Hyer, Robert Garland
130. "Ambush" (1-5-61) Dick Powell, Don Dubbins
131. "One Must Die" (1-12-61) Philip Carey, Joan Crawford
132. "The Long Shadow" (1-19-61) Ronald Reagan, Nancy Davis
133. "Blood Red" (1-26-61) Carolyn Jones
134. "Honor Bright" (2-2-61) Danny Thomas, Marlo Thomas
135. "The Broken Wing" (2-9-61) Arthur O'Connell
136. "The Silent Sentry" (2-16-61) Don Taylor, Dick Powell
137. "The Bible Man" (2-23-61) Art Linkletter, Jack Linkletter
138. "The Scar" (3-2-61) Lew Ayres
139. "Knight of the Sun" (3-9-61) Dan Duryea, Constance Towers
140. "A Warm Day in Heaven" (3-23-61) Lon Chaney Jr., Thomas Mitchell
141. "The Empty Shell" (3-30-61) Jean Hagen, Jan Murray
142. "The Atoner" (4-6-61) Herbert Marshall
143. "Man from Everywhere" (4-13-61) Burt Reynolds, Cesar Romero
144. "The Release" (4-27-61) Gary Merrill
145. "Storm Over Eden" (5-4-61) John Derek, Nancy Gates
146. "Image of a Drawn Sword" (5-11-61) Lloyd Bridges, Beau Bridges, Susan Oliver
147. "Jericho" (5-18-61) Guy Madison, Beverly Garland


## WAGON TRAIN

In the best of Horace Greeley traditions--the odyssey West taken on by wagons under the auspices of Major Seth Adams (Ward Bond) and later Christopher Hale (John McIntire); their scouts Flint McCullough (Robert Horton), Duke Shannon (Denny Miller), Bill Hawks (Terry Wilson) and Cooper Smith (Robert Fuller).

The prodigious trek "out there" continued through 293 episodes, emptying a good share of Hollywood with a knack for unusual casting--John Barrymore Jr. a psychotic in "The Ruttledge Munroe Story," Lou Costello a derelict in "The Tobias Jones Story."

The Regulars: Major Seth Adams, Ward Bond (to episode of 3/8/61); Flint McCullough, Robert Horton (to episode of 3/20/60; then 2/15/61-5th season); Charlie Wooster, Frank McGrath; Christopher Hale, John McIntire (from 3/15/61 to conclusion); Duke Shannon, Denny "Scott" Miller (from 4/26/61 through 1963-64 season); Bill Hawks, Terry Wilson (from 1960 to conclusion); Cooper Smith, Robert Fuller (from 1963-64 season to conclusion); Barnaby West, Michael Burns (from 6/3/63 to conclusion).

The Episodes:

1. "The Willy Moran Story" (9-18-57) Ernest Borgnine, Marjorie Lord, Beverly Washburn
2. "The Jean LeBec Story" (9-25-57) Ricardo Montalban
3. "The John Cameron Story" (10-2-57) Carolyn Jones, Michael Rennie
4. "The Ruth Owens Story" (10-9-57) Shelley Winters, Dean Stockwell, Kent Smith
5. "The Les Rand Story" (10-16-57) Sterling Hayden
6. "The Nels Stack Story" (10-23-57) Mark Stevens, Joanne Dru
7. "The Emily Rossiter Story" (10-30-57) Mercedes McCambridge, Susan Oliver
8. "The John Darro Story" (11-6-57) Eddie Albert, Margo
9. "The Charles Avery Story" (11-13-57) Farley Granger, Chuck Connors, Susan Kohner
10. "The Mary Halstead Story" (11-20-57) Agnes Moorehead, Tom Laughlin
11. "The Zeke Thomas Story" (11-27-57) Gary Merrill, Janice Rule, K. T. Stevens
12. "The Riley Gratton Story" (12-4-57) Guy Madison
13. "The Clara Beauchamp Story" (12-11-57) Nina Foch, Shepperd Strudwick
14. "The Julia Gage Story" (12-18-57) Anne Jeffreys, Robert Sterling
15. "The Cliff Grundy Story" (12-25-57) Dan Duryea
16. "The Luke O'Malley Story" (1-1-58) Keenan Wynn
17. "The Jessie Cowan Story" (1-8-58) George Montgomery
18. "The Gabe Carswell Story" (1-15-58) James Whitmore, Scott Marlowe
19. "The Honorable Don Charlie Story" (1-22-58) Cesar Romero, Virginia Grey
20. "The Dora Gray Story" (1-29-58) Linda Darnell, John Carradine, Michael Connors
21. "The Annie MacGregor Story" (2-5-58) Jeannie Carson, Richard Long
22. "The Bill Tawnee Story" (2-12-58) MacDonald Carey

23. "The Mark Hanford Story" (2-26-58) Tom Tryon, Onslow Stevens, Kathleen Crowley
24. "The Bernal Sierra Story" (3-12-58) Gilbert Roland
25. "The Marie Dupree Story" (3-19-58) Debra Paget, Nick Adams, Robert Lowery
26. "A Man Called Horse" (3-26-58) Ralph Meeker, Joan Taylor
27. "The Sarah Drummond Story" (4-2-58) June Lockhart, William Talman, Gene Evans
28. "The Sally Potter Story" (4-9-58) Jocelyn Brando, Lyle Bettger, Vanessa Brown, Brad Dexter, Johnny Crawford, Martin Milner
29. "The Daniel Barrister Story" (4-16-58) Charles Bickford, Roger Smith
30. "The Major Adams Story" [Part I] (4-23-58) features Ward Bond; Virginia Grey
31. "The Major Adams Story" [Part II] (4-30-58) as above
32. "The Charles Maury Story" (5-7-58) Charles Drake, Wanda Hendrix
33. "The Dan Hogan Story" (5-14-58) Jock Mahoney, John Larch, Judith Ames
34. "The Ruttledge Munroe Story" (5-21-58) John Barrymore Jr., Mala Powers
35. "The Rex Montana Story" (5-28-58) James Dunn, Forrest Tucker, Kristine Miller
36. "The Cassie Tanner Story" (6-4-58) Marjorie Main
37. "The John Wilbot Story" (6-11-58) Dane Clark, Robert Vaughn
38. "The Monte Britton Story" (6-18-58) Ray Danton, Mona Freeman
39. "The Sacramento Story" (6-25-58) Dan Duryea, Margaret O'Brien, Linda Darnell, Marjorie Main

Second Season

40. "Around the Horn" (10-1-58) William Bendix, Ernest Borgnine, Osa Massen
41. "The Juan Ortega Story" (10-8-58) Dean Stockwell
42. "The Jennifer Churchill Story" (10-15-58) Rhonda Fleming
43. "The Tobias Jones Story" (10-22-58) Lou Costello
44. "The Liam Fitzmorgan Story" (10-29-58) Cliff Robertson
45. "The Doctor Willoughby Story" (11-5-58) Jane Wyman
46. "The Bije Wilcox Story" (11-19-58) Chill Wills
47. "The Millie Davis Story" (11-26-58) Nancy Gates, Evelyn Rudie
48. "The Sakae Ito Story" (12-3-58) Sessue Hayakawa
49. "The Tent City Story" (12-10-58) Wayne Morris, Audrey Totter, Slim Pickens
50. "The Beauty Jamison Story" (12-17-58) Virginia Mayo
51. "The Mary Ellen Thomas Story" (12-24-58) Patty McCormack
52. "The Dick Richardson Story" (12-31-58) John Ericson
53. "The Kitty Angel Story" (1-7-59) Anne Baxter, Henry Hull
54. "The Flint McCullough Story" (1-14-59) features Robert Horton; Everett Sloane

55. "The Hunter Malloy Story" (1-21-59) Lloyd Nolan
56. "The Ben Courtney Story" (1-28-59) Stephen McNally
57. "The Ella Lindstrom Story" (2-4-59) Bette Davis
58. "The Last Man" (2-11-59) Dan Duryea
59. "The Old Man Charvanaugh Story" (2-18-59) J. Carrol Naish
60. "The Annie Griffith Story" (2-25-59) Jan Sterling
61. "The Jasper Ceto Story" (3-4-59) Brian Donlevy
62. "The Vivian Carter Story" (3-11-59) Jane Darwell, Lorne
    Greene, Phyllis Thaxter
63. "The Conchita Vasquez Story" (3-18-59) Anna Maria Alber-
    ghetti
64. "The Sister Rita Story" (3-25-59) Vera Miles
65. "The Matthew Lowry Story" (4-1-59) Richard Anderson,
    Cathleen Nesbitt
66. "The Swift Cloud Story" (4-8-59) Rafael Campos
67. "The Vincent Eaglewood Story" (4-15-59) Wally Cox
68. "The Clara Duncan Story" (4-22-59) Angie Dickinson, Edu-
    ardo Ciannelli, William Reynolds
69. "The Duke LeMay Story" (4-29-59) Cameron Mitchell
70. "The Kate Parker Story" (5-6-59) Robert Fuller, Virginia
    Grey
71. "The Steve Campden Story" (5-13-59) Ben Cooper
72. "Chuck Wooster" (5-20-59) features Frank McGrath
73. "The José Maria Moran Story" (5-27-59) Robert Loggia
74. "The Andrew Hale Story" (6-3-59) John McIntire, Jane Dar-
    well
75. "The Rodney Lawrence Story" (6-10-59) Dean Stockwell
76. "The Steele Family" (6-17-59) Dan Tobin, Lee Patrick
77. "The Jenny Tanner Story" (6-24-59) Ann Blyth

Third Season

78. "The Stagecoach Story" (9-30-59) Debra Paget, Clu Gulager
79. "The Greenhorn Story" (10-7-59) Mickey Rooney
80. "The C. L. Harding Story" (10-14-59) Claire Trevor
81. "The Estaban Zamora Story" (10-21-59) Ernest Borgnine
82. "The Elizabeth McQueeney Story" (10-28-59) Bette Davis
83. "The Martha Barham Story" (11-4-59) Ann Blyth
84. "The Cappy Darrin Story" (11-11-59) Ed Wynn
85. "The Felizia Kingdom Story" (11-18-59) Dame Judith Ander-
    son
86. "The Jess MacAbee Story" (11-25-59) Andy Devine, Glenda
    Farrell
87. "The Danny Benedict Story" (12-2-59) Brandon de Wilde
88. "The Vittorio Bottecelli Story" (12-16-59) Gustavo Rojo,
    Elizabeth Montgomery
89. "The St. Nicholas Story" (12-23-59) Edward Vargas, Johnny
    Bangert
90. "The Ruth Marshall Story" (12-30-59) Luana Patten
91. "The Lita Foladaire Story" (1-6-60) Diane Brewster, Tom
    Drake, Kent Smith
92. "The Colonel Harris Story" (1-13-60) John Howard
93. "The Marie Brant Story" (1-20-60) Jean Hagen, Edward

<br>
        Platt, Richard Eyer

94. "The Larry Hanify Story" (1-27-60) Tommy Sands
95. "The Clayton Tucker Story" (2-10-60) Jeff Morrow
96. "The Benjamin Burns Story" (2-17-60) James Franciscus, J. Carrol Naish
97. "The Ricky and Laura Bell Story" (2-24-60) June Lockhart, James Gregory
98. "The Tom Tuckett Story" (3-2-60) Robert Middleton, Ben Cooper, Josephine Hutchinson
99. "The Tracy Sadler Story" (3-9-60) Elisha Cook, Elaine Stritch
100. "The Alexander Portlass Story" (3-16-60) Peter Lorre
101. "The Christine Elliot Story" (3-23-60) Henry Daniell, Phyllis Thaxter
102. "The Joshua Gilliam Story" (3-30-60) Dan Duryea, Bethel Leslie
103. "The Maggie Hamilton Story" (4-6-60) Susan Oliver
104. "The Jonas Murdock Story" (4-13-60) Noah Beery Jr.
105. "The Amos Gibbon Story" (4-20-60) Arthur Shields
106. "Trial for Murder" [Part I] (4-27-60) Henry Daniell, Henry Hull, Marshall Thompson, Dianne Foster
107. "Trial for Murder" [Part II] (5-4-60) as above
108. "The Countess Baranof Story" (5-11-60) Taina Elg
109. "The Dick Jarviss Story" (5-18-60) Tommy Nolan, Vivi Janiss, Bobby Diamond
110. "The Luke Grant Story" (6-1-60) Donald Woods, Joan O'Brien
111. "The Charlene Brenton Story" (6-8-60) Sean McClory, Jean Willes
112. "The Sam Livingston Story" (6-15-60) Charles Drake, Onslow Stevens, Anna-Lisa
113. "The Shad Bennington Story" (6-22-60) David Wayne, Maggie Pierce

Fourth Season

114. "Wagons Ho!" (9-28-60) Mickey Rooney, Ellen Corby, Olive Sturgess
115. "The Horace Best Story" (10-5-60) George Gobel, Ken Curtis
116. "The Albert Farnsworth Story" (10-12-60) Charles Laughton, James Fairfax
117. "The Allison Justis Story" (10-19-60) Gloria De Haven, Michael Burns
118. "The José Morales Story" (10-26-60) Lee Marvin, Lon Chaney Jr.
119. "Princess of a Lost Tribe" (11-2-60) Linda Lawson, Raymond Massey
120. "The Cathy Eckhardt Story" (11-9-60) Susan Oliver, Martin Landau
121. "The Bieymier Story" (11-16-60) Dan Duryea, Elen Willard
122. "The Colter Craven Story" [directed by John Ford] (11-23-60) John Carradine, Carleton Young

123. "The Jane Hawkins Story" (11-30-60) Myrna Fahey, Edgar Buchanan
124. "The Candy O'Hara Story" (12-7-60) Teddy Rooney, Jim Davis
125. "The River Crossing" (12-14-60) Michael Keep, Charles Aidman, X Brands
126. "The Roger Bigelow Story" (12-21-60) Robert Vaughn, Audrey Dalton, Claude Akins
127. "The Jeremy Dow Story" (12-28-60) Leslie Nielsen, James Lydon, Michael Burns
128. "The Earl Packer Story" (1-4-61) Ernest Borgnine, Edward Binns
129. "The Patience Miller Story" (1-11-61) Michael Ansara, Rhonda Fleming
130. "The Sam Elder Story" (1-18-61) Everett Sloane
131. "Weight of Command" (1-25-61) Tommy Rettig
132. "The Prairie Story" (2-1-61) Beulah Bondi, Jan Clayton
133. "Path of the Serpent" (2-8-61) Paul Burke, Noah Beery Jr., Melinda Plowman
134. "The Odyssey of Flint McCullough" (2-15-61) features Robert Horton; Henry Hull
135. "The Beth Pearson Story" (2-22-61) Virginia Grey
136. "The Jed Pole Story" (3-1-61) John Lasell, Joyce Meadows
137. "The Nancy Palmer Story" (3-8-61) Elisha Cook, Audrey Meadows
138. "The Christopher Hale Story" (3-15-61) features John McIntire; Lee Marvin
139. "The Tiburcio Mendez Story" (3-22-61) Nehemiah Persoff, Leonard Nimoy
140. "The Nellie Jefferson Story" (4-5-61) Janis Paige
141. "The Saul Bevins Story" (4-12-61) Rod Steiger
142. "The Joe Muharich Story" (4-19-61) Robert Blake, Akim Tamiroff
143. "The Duke Shannon Story" (4-26-61) features Scott Miller; Frank McHugh
144. "The Will Santee Story" (5-3-61) Dean Stockwell, Millie Perkins
145. "The Jim Bridger Story" (5-10-61) Karl Swenson
146. "The Eleanor Culhane Story" (5-17-61) Felicia Farr
147. "The Chalice" (5-24-61) Lon Chaney Jr., Richard Jaeckel, Argentina Brunetti
148. "The Janet Hale Story" (5-31-61) Jeanette Nolan, Bethel Leslie, Charles Aidman
149. "Wagon to Fort Anderson" (6-7-61) Albert Salmi, Carol Rossen, Don Rickles, Candy Moore
150. "The Ah Chong Story" (6-14-61) Arnold Stang
151. "The Don Alvarado Story" (6-21-61) Andra Martin

Fifth Season

152. "The Captain Dan Brady Story" (9-27-61) Joseph Cotten
153. "The Kitty Allbright Story" (10-4-61) Polly Bergen, Jocelyn Brando

154. "The Maud Frazer Story" (10-11-61) Barbara Stanwyck
155. "The Selena Hartnell Story" (10-18-61) Jan Sterling, Claude Akins
156. "The Clementine Jones Story" (10-25-61) Ann Blyth, Dick York, Willard Waterman
157. "The Jenna Douglas Story" (11-1-61) Carolyn Jones
158. "The Artie Matthewson Story" (11-8-61) Rory Calhoun, Jane Darwell, Joyce Meadows
159. "The Mark Miner Story" (11-15-61) Brandon de Wilde, Michael Burns, Barbara Parkins
160. "The Bruce Saybrook Story" (11-22-61) Brian Aherne
161. "The Lizabeth Ann Calhoun Story" (12-6-61) Dana Wynter
162. "The Traitor" (12-13-61) Nick Adams
163. "The Bettina May Story" (12-20-61) Bette Davis
164. "Clyde" (12-27-61) Harry von Zell, Nora Marlowe
165. "The Martin Onyx Story" (1-3-62) Jack Warden
166. "The Dick Pederson Story" (1-10-62) James MacArthur
167. "The Hobie Redman Story" (1-17-62) Lin McCarthy, Arch Johnson
168. "The Malachi Hobart Story" (1-24-62) Franchot Tone, Irene Ryan
169. "The Dr. Denker Story" (1-31-62) Theodore Bikel, Michael Burns
170. "The Lonnie Fallon Story" (2-7-62) Frank Overton, Gary Clarke, Lynn Loring
171. "The Jeff Hartfield Story" (2-14-62) Jack Chaplain, Roger Mobley, Dennis Rush
172. "The Daniel Clay Story" (2-21-62) Claude Rains, Fred Beir
173. "The Lieutenant Burton Story" (2-28-62) Dean Jones, Charles McGraw
174. "The Charley Shutup Story" (3-7-62) Dick York
175. "The Amos Billings Story" (3-14-62) Jon Locke, Paul Fix
176. "The Baylor Crowfoot Story" (3-21-62) Robert Culp
177. "The George B. Hanrahan Story" (3-28-62) Lee Tracy, Frank De Kova
178. "Swamp Devil" (4-4-62) Philip Bourneuf
179. "The Cole Crawford Story" (4-11-62) James Drury, Fay Wray
180. "The Levi Hale Story" (4-18-62) Trevor Bardette, Hugh Sanders
181. "The Terry Morrell Story" (4-25-62) Henry Jones, David Ladd
182. "The Jud Steele Story" (5-2-62) Arthur Franz, Edward Binns, Mary La Roche
183. "The Mary Beckett Story" (5-9-62) Anne Jeffreys, Lee Bergere
184. "The Nancy Davis Story" (5-16-62) Keith Richards
185. "The Frank Carter Story" (5-23-62) Albert Salmi, Frances Reid
186. "The John Turnbull Story" (5-30-62) Henry Silva, Steven Geray
187. "The Hiram Winthrop Story" (6-6-62) Eduard Franz

188. "The Heather Mahoney Story" (6-13-62) Jane Wyatt

Sixth Season

189. "The Wagon Train Mutiny" (9-19-62) Dan Duryea, Jane
     Wyman, Jose de Vega
190. "The Caroline Casteel Story" (9-26-62) Barbara Stanwyck,
     Barry Sullivan, Charles Drake
191. "The Madame Sagittarius Story" (10-3-62) Thelma Ritter,
     Robert Ryan, John Bernard, Perry Lopez
192. "The Martin Gatsby Story" (10-10-62) Fred Clark
193. "The John Augustus Story" (10-17-62) Joseph Cotten
194. "The Mavis Grant Story" (10-24-62) Ann Sheridan
195. "The Lisa Raincloud Story" (10-31-62) Dana Wynter
196. "The Shiloh Degnan Story" (11-7-62) Nancy Gates, Lorence
     Kerr
197. "The Levy-McGowan Story" (11-14-62) Liam Redmond, Lee
     Fuchs
198. "The John Bernard Story" (11-21-62) Robert Ryan, Perry
     Lopez
199. "The Kurt Davos Story" (11-28-62) Eddie Albert, Frances
     Reid
200. "The Eve Newhope Story" (12-5-62) Ann Blyth, Slim
     Pickens, Tudor Owen
201. "The Orly French Story" (12-12-62) Sharon Farrell, Peter
     Fonda
202. "The Donna Fuller Story" (12-19-62) Jeanne Cooper, Simon
     Oakland
203. "The Sam Darland Story" (12-26-62) Art Linkletter, Nancy
     Davis
204. "The Abel Weatherly Story" (1-2-63) J. D. Cannon, John
     Ashley
205. "The Davey Baxter Story" (1-9-63) Tommy Sands, Jeannine
     Riley
206. "The Johnny Masters Story" (1-16-63) Anthony George
207. "The Naomi Kaylor Story" (1-30-63) Joan Fontaine
208. "The Hollister John Garrison Story" (2-6-63) Charles Drake
209. "The Lily Legend Story" (2-13-63) Susan Oliver, Richard
     Jaeckel
210. "Charlie Wooster-Outlaw" (2-20-63) features Frank Mc-
     Grath; Jeanette Nolan, L. Q. Jones
211. "The Sara Proctor Story" (2-27-63) Jean Hagen, Chris
     Robinson
212. "The Emmett Lawton Story" (3-6-63) Dennis Hopper
213. "The Annie Duggan Story" (3-13-63) Arthur Franz, Carolyn
     Kearney
214. "The Michael McGoo Story" (3-20-63) Jocelyn Brando
215. "The Adam MacKenzie Story" (3-27-63) Michael Ansara
216. "The Tom Tuesday Story" (4-3-63) Brian Keith
217. "Heather and Hamish" (4-10-63) Anne Helm, Michael Parks,
     Liam Redmond
218. "The Blane Wessels Story" (4-17-63) Juanita Moore
219. "The Tom O'Neal Story" (4-24-63) Peter Helm, Brenda

Scott
220. "The Clarence Mullins Story" (5-1-63) Clu Gulager
221. "The David Garner Story" (5-8-63) Randy Boone, Susan Silo
222. "Alias Bill Hawks" (5-15-63) features Terry Wilson, Joan Freeman
223. "The Antone Rose Story" (5-22-63) Trevor Bardette, Judi Meredith, Charles Robinson
224. "The Jim Whitlow Story" (5-29-63) John Kerr
225. "The Barnaby West Story" (6-5-63) Michael Burns, Stuart Erwin

Seventh Season [as ninety minute series]

226. "The Molly Kincaid Story" (9-16-63) Barbara Stanwyck, Carolyn Jones, Ray Danton, Fabian, Brenda Scott, Pamela Austin, Harry Carey
227. "The Fort Pierce Story" (9-23-63) Ronald Reagan, Ann Blyth, John Doucette, Kathie Browne
228. "The Gus Morgan Story" (9-30-63) Peter Falk, Tommy Sands, Harry Swoger
229. "The Widow O'Rourke Story" (10-7-63) Carol Lawrence, Richard Loo
230. "The Robert Harrison Clarke Story" (10-14-63) Michael Rennie, Brian Keith, Henry Silva, Royal Dano
231. "The Myra Marshall Story" (10-21-63) Suzanne Pleshette, Charles Drake, Rex Reason, Jack Lambert
232. "The Sam Spicer Story" (10-28-63) Clu Gulager, Ed Begley, Frank Cady, Jean Inness
233. "The Sam Pulaski Story" (11-4-63) Ross Martin, Annette Funicello, Jocelyn Brando
234. "The Eli Bancroft Story" (11-11-63) Leif Erickson, Bruce Dern, David Carradine, Rachel Ames, Randy Boone
235. "The Kitty Pryor Story" (11-18-63) Diana Hyland, Bradford Dillman, Don Durant
236. "The Sandra Cummings Story" (12-2-63) Rhonda Fleming, Cynthia Pepper, Michael Conrad, John Archer
237. "The Bleeker Story" (12-9-63) Joan Blondell, Ruta Lee, Ed Nelson
238. "The Story of Cain" (12-16-63) Ron Hayes, Anne Helm
239. "The Cassie Vance Story" (12-23-63) Laraine Day, Richard Carlson, Kevin Corcoran
240. "The Fenton Canaby Story" (12-30-63) Jack Kelly, Barbara Bain, Virginia Gregg, John Hoyt, Robert Cornthwaite
241. "The Michael Malone Story" (1-6-64) Michael Parks, Dick York, Joyce Bulifant
242. "The Jed Whitmore Story" (1-13-64) Les Tremayne, Neville Brand, Karl Swenson, William Mims
243. "The Geneva Balfour Story" (1-20-64) Sherry Jackson, Robert Lansing, Peter Brown, Archie Moore
244. "The Kate Crawley Story" (1-27-64) Barbara Stanwyck
245. "The Grover Allen Story" (2-3-64) Burgess Meredith, Nancy Gates, Marshall Thompson

246. "The Andrew Elliott Story" (2-10-64) Everett Sloane, Dick
    Sargent, Alfred Ryder, Skip Homeier
247. "The Melanie Craig Story" (2-17-64) Myrna Fahey, Jim
    Davis, John Craig
248. "The Pearlie Garnet Story" (2-24-64) Sharon Farrell,
    Marilyn Maxwell, Hugh Beaumont, H. M. Wynant
249. "The Trace McCloud Story" (3-2-64) Larry Pennell, Audrey
    Dalton, Rachel Ames
250. "The Duncan McIvor Story" (3-9-64) Ron Hayes, Chris
    Robinson, Joanna Moore, John Larkin
251. "The Ben Engel Story" (3-16-64) Clu Gulager, Katherine
    Crawford, John Doucette
252. "The Whipping" (3-23-64) Martin Balsam, Jeanne Cooper
253. "The Santiago Quesada Story" (3-30-64) Joseph Wiseman,
    Edward Binns, Perry Lopez, Jena Engstrom
254. "The Stark's Bluff Story" (4-6-64) Ray Danton, Jean Hale,
    Peter Whitney, Hari Rhodes
255. "The Link Cheney Story" (4-13-64) Charles Drake, Yvonne
    Craig, Pippa Scott
256. "The Zebedee Titus Story" (4-20-64) Neville Brand, Angela
    Dorian, Robert Santon
257. "The Last Circle Up" (4-27-64) Joe De Santis, Naomi
    Stevens, Karen Green

Eighth Season [as hour series again]

258. "The Bob Stuart Story" (9-20-64) Robert Ryan, Andrew
    Prine, Vera Miles, Tommy Sands, William Smith, Stacy
    Harris
259. "The Hide Hunters" (9-27-64) Chris Robinson, Morgan
    Woodward
260. "The John Gillman Story" (10-4-64) Bobby Darin, Virginia
    Gregg, Whit Bissell, Betsy Hale
261. "The Race Town Story" (10-11-64) Dan Duryea, Allyson
    Ames, Cheryl Holdridge
262. "The Barbara Lindquist Story" (10-18-64) Dana Wynter,
    G. B. Atwater, Dave Derna
263. "The Brian Conlin Story" (10-25-64) Leslie Nielsen,
    Audrey Dalton, Paul Fix
264. "The Alice Whitetree Story" (11-1-64) Diane Baker, Ken
    Lynch, John Hoyt
265. "Those Who Stay Behind" (11-8-64) Lola Albright, Bruce
    Dern, Peter Brown, Jay North
266. "The Nancy Styles Story" (11-22-64) Deborah Walley, Ryan
    O'Neal, James Griffith
267. "The Richard Bloodgood Story" (11-29-64) Guy Stockwell,
    Reta Shaw, William Smith, David Foley
268. "The Clay Shelby Story" (12-6-64) Richard Carlson, Celia
    Kaye, Dwayne Hickman, Mort Mills
269. "Little Girl Lost" (12-13-64) Eileen Baral, John Doucette,
    Dick Cuttey
270. "The Story of Hector Heatherington" (12-20-64) Tom Ewell,
    Kim Darby, Jeanne Cooper

271. "The Echo Pass Story" (1-3-65) Jack Lord, James Caan, Diane Brewster, Susan Seaforth
272. "The Chottsie Gubenheimer Story" (1-10-65) Jeanette Nolan, Paul Stewart, John Doucette
273. "The Wanda Snow Story" (1-17-65) Marta Kristen, Arthur O'Connell, Dabbs Greer
274. "The Isaiah Quickfox Story" (1-31-65) Andrew Prine, Jan Clayton, Frank De Kova, John Doucette
275. "Herman" (2-14-65) Charles Ruggles, Tim McIntire, Linda Evans
276. "The Bonnie Brooke Story" (2-21-65) Katherine Ross, Lee Philips, Robert Emhardt
277. "The Miss Mary Lee McIntosh Story" (2-28-65) Bethel Leslie, Jack Warden
278. "The Captain Sam Story" (3-21-65) Robert Santon, Cathy Lewis
279. "The Betsy Blee Smith Story" (3-28-65) Jennifer Billingsley, Joel McCrea, Peter Whitney, Meg Wyllie
280. "The Katy Piper Story" (4-11-65) Virginia Christine, Frances Reid
281. "The Indian Girl Story" (4-18-65) Ernest Borgnine, Bruce Dern, Maggie Pierce, Michael Pate, John Lupton
282. "The Silver Lady" (4-25-65) Vera Miles, Arthur O'Connell, Henry Silva, Don Galloway
283. "The Jarbo Pierce Story" (5-2-65) Rory Calhoun, Tom Simcox, Arthur Hunnicutt, Lee Philips

## PERRY MASON

Dissertations can and should be written on how these episodes of the cases of Erle Stanley Gardner's pluperfect attorney have affected public thinking of the legal process. For Perry Mason (Raymond Burr's role--an indelible image that profoundly affected his every subsequent performance) only once lost a case to his perpetual, always bewildered opposition, District Attorney Hamilton Burger (William Talman). That singular loss occurred in the episode "The Case of the Deadly Verdict" but, never one to condescend, our redoubtable counsel launched a dynamic (and successful) appeal. He once accepted a case for thirty-seven cents (from Ruta Lee in "The Case of the Footloose Doll") while at the same time rejecting a $10,000 offer from a prominent official. But his unlimited vault of funds deriving from seemingly nowhere is but one fiction. Ponder his phenomenal speed with the trial system; his private investigator's (William Hopper as Paul Drake) veritable passport to be anywhere at any time; his ability to so clearly delineate character culpability (let alone his feeling the need to) and a celibate, surely, for so platonic was his relationship with secretary Della Street (Barbara Hale). One can only wonder how many delusions (a scenario might have an accused "Perry Mason" addict, horrified, ask his attorney: "What do you mean when you say we have to 'plea bargain'?") would have been shattered without "Perry Mason" 's nine years.

The Regulars: Perry Mason, Raymond Burr; Della Street, Barbara
Hale; Paul Drake, William Hopper; D. A. Hamilton Burg-
er, William Talman; Lt. Arthur Tragg, Ray Collins; Lt.
Andy Anderson, Wesley Lau; Lt. Steve Drumm, Richard
Anderson (last two seasons); Terrence Clay, Dan Tobin
(last season only).

The Episodes:

1. "The Case of the Restless Redhead" (9-21-57) Whitney
   Blake, Ralph Clanton, Vaughn Taylor, James Buchanon
2. "The Case of the Sleepwalker's Niece" (9-28-57) Hillary
   Brooke, Nancy Hadley, John McNamara
3. "The Case of the Nervous Accomplice" (10-5-57) Margaret
   Hayes, Greta Thyssen, William Roerick
4. "The Case of the Drowning Duck" (10-12-57) Carolyn Craig,
   Don Beddoe
5. "The Case of the Sulky Girl" (10-19-57) Olive Sturgess,
   Lillian Bronson, Raymond Greenleaf, William Schallert
6. "The Case of the Silent Partner" (10-26-57) Anne Barton,
   Mark Roberts
7. "The Case of the Angry Mourner" (11-2-57) Paul Fix,
   Barbara Eden, Joan Weldon, Peter Nelson, Malcolm Atterbury, Sylvia Field
8. "The Case of the Crimson Kiss" (11-9-57) Sue England,
   Jean Willes, Francis Bavier
9. "The Case of the Vagabond Vixen" (11-16-57) Carol Leigh
10. "The Case of the Runaway Corpse" (11-23-57) June Dayton,
    Sarah Selby, Adam Williams
11. "The Case of the Crooked Candle" (11-30-57) Doris Single-
    ton, Whit Bissell, Nancy Gates, Bruce Cowling, Henry
    Corden
12. "The Case of the Negligent Nymph" (12-7-57) Peggy Castle,
    David Lewis, James Griffith, Joan Banks
13. "The Case of the Moth-Eaten Mink" (12-14-57) Bob Oster-
    loh, Kay Faylen
14. "The Case of the Baited Hook" (12-21-57) Mary Castle,
    George Neise, Willard Sage
15. "The Case of the Fan Dancer's Horse" (12-28-57) June
    Tyler, Hugh Sanders, Susan Cummings
16. "The Case of the Demure Defendant" (1-4-58) Christine
    White, Alexander Campbell
17. "The Case of the Sunbather's Diary" (1-11-58) Susan Mor-
    row, John Locke, Paul Brinegar, Peter Leeds, Gertrude
    Michels, Nesdon Booth
18. "The Case of the Cautious Coquette" (1-18-58) Harry Jack-
    son, James Seay, Kipp Hamilton
19. "The Case of the Haunted Husband" (1-25-58) Harlan Ward,
    Helen Westcott, Patricia Hardy, Karen Steele
20. "The Case of the Lonely Heiress" (2-1-58) Robert H. Har-
    ris, L. Q. Jones, Kathleen Crowley
21. "The Case of the Green-Eyed Sister" (2-8-58) Virginia Vin-
    cent, Tina Culver

22. "The Case of the Fugitive Nurse" (2-15-58) Bethel Leslie, Maxine Cooper, Shepperd Strudwick
23. "The Case of the One-Eyed Witness" (2-22-58) Angie Dickinson, Jan Arvan, Peter Adams, Ray Kellogg, Dorothy Green, Luis Van Rooten
24. "The Case of the Deadly Double" (3-1-58) Constance Ford, Denver Pyle
25. "The Case of the Empty Tin" (3-8-58) Warren Stevens, Benson Fong, Olive Deering, Toni Gerry, Mary Shipp
26. "The Case of the Half-Wakened Wife" (3-15-58) Phyllis Avery, Tom Palmer, Claude Akins, Paul Burns, Barbara Lawrence, Jonathan Hole, Stuart Bradley
27. "The Case of the Desperate Daughter" (3-22-58) Osa Massen, Don Durant, Werner Klemperer, Gigi Perreau
28. "The Case of the Daring Decoy" (3-29-58) H. M. Wynant, Pamela Duncan, John Mack Brown, Marie Windsor
29. "The Case of the Hesitant Hostess" (4-5-58) Fred Sherman, Les Tremayne
30. "The Case of the Screaming Woman" (4-26-58) Josephine Hutchinson, Arthur Shields, Marian Seldes
31. "The Case of the Fiery Fingers" (5-3-58) Lenore Shanewise, Fay Spain, Connie Cezon, Susan Dorn, Mary La Roche
32. "The Case of the Substitute Face" (5-10-58) Theodore Newton, Maureen Cassidy
33. "The Case of the Long-Legged Models" (5-17-58) Peggy McCay
34. "The Case of the Gilded Lily" (5-24-58) Grant Withers, Richard Erdman
35. "The Case of the Lazy Lover" (5-31-58) Neil Hamilton, Ann Lee, Harry Townes
36. "The Case of the Prodigal Parent" (6-7-58) Virginia Field, John Hoyt, Fay Wray
37. "The Case of the Black-Eyed Blonde" (6-14-58) Phyllis Coates, Irene Hervey, Whitney Blake
38. "The Case of the Terrified Typist" (6-21-58) Joanna Moore, Joan Elan, Alan Marshal
39. "The Case of the Rolling Bones" (6-28-58) Edgar Stehli, Joan Camden, Mary Anderson

Second Season

40. "The Case of the Corresponding Corpse" (9-20-58) Joan Camden, Ross Elliot, Jeanne Cooper, Vaughn Taylor
41. "The Case of the Lucky Loser" (9-27-58) Heather Angel, Richard Hale, Tyler MacDuff, Bruce Bennett, Patricia Medina
42. "The Case of the Pint-Sized Client" (10-4-58) Elisha Cook, Nita Talbot, James Anderson, Bobby Clark, Eleanor Audley, Joseph Mell
43. "The Case of the Sardonic Sergeant" (10-11-58) John Dehner, Barbara Luna, Paul Picerni, Hal Torey, Lee Torrence, Kevin Hagen, Grant Richard, Rand Harper

44. "The Case of the Curious Bride" (10-18-58) Michael Emmet, James Seay, Tommy Cook, Christine White, Casey Adams, John Hoyt
45. "The Case of the Buried Clock" (11-1-58) Paul Fix, Don Beddoe
46. "The Case of the Married Moonlighter" (11-8-58) Stacy Harris, Arthur Franz, Anne Sargent
47. "The Case of the Jilted Jockey" (11-15-58) Billy Pearson, June Vincent, Barbara Lawrence
48. "The Case of the Purple Woman" (11-22-58) Bethel Leslie, Rhys Williams, George Macready
49. "The Case of the Fancy Figures" (12-13-58) William Phipps, Ralph Canton
50. "The Case of the Treacherous Toupee" (12-20-58) Robert Redford, Philip Oben, Nelson Olmstead, Peggy Converse
51. "The Case of the Credulous Quarry" (12-27-58) Russell Arms, Walter Reed, Katherine Squire, John Conwell, John Vinworth, Nathan Peterson
52. "The Case of the Shattered Dream" (1-3-59) Osa Massen, Virginia Vincent, Otto Kruger, Marion Marshall
53. "The Case of the Borrowed Brunette" (1-10-59) Joe De Santis, Maggie Mahoney
54. "The Case of the Glittering Goldfish" (1-17-59) John Hudson, Gage Clark
55. "The Case of the Footloose Doll" (1-24-59) Ruta Lee, Barton MacLane, John Bryant, Helene Stanley, Sam Buffington
56. "The Case of the Fraudulent Photo" (2-7-59) Hugh Marlowe, Bartlett Robinson
57. "The Case of the Romantic Rogue" (2-14-59) John Bryant, Marion Ross
58. "The Case of the Jaded Joker" (2-21-59) Tom Drake, Frankie Laine, Jay Norvello, Martha Vickers
59. "The Case of the Caretaker's Cat" (3-7-59) John Agar, Benson Fong
60. "The Case of the Stuttering Bishop" (3-14-59) Vaughn Taylor, Ken Lynch
61. "The Case of the Lost Last Act" (3-21-59) Stacy Harris, Jerome Cowan, Mala Powers, David Lewis
62. "The Case of the Bewildered Doctor" (4-4-59) Dick Foran, Barrie McGuire, Phillip Terry, Michael Fox
63. "The Case of the Howling Dog" (4-11-59) Ann Rutherford
64. "The Case of the Calendar Girl" (4-18-59) John Anderson, Dean Harens, Evelyn Scott
65. "The Case of the Petulant Partner" (4-25-59) R. G. Armstrong, William H. Wright
66. "The Case of the Dangerous Dowager" (5-9-59) Patricia Cutts, Michael Dante
67. "The Case of the Deadly Toy" (5-16-59) Mala Powers, Dennis Patrick, Robert Rockwell
68. "The Case of the Spanish Cross" (5-30-59) Josephine Hutchinson, Peter Miles
69. "The Case of the Dubious Bridegroom" (6-13-59) Joan

Tabor, Neil Hamilton, Patrick McVey, K. T. Stevens
70. "The Case of the Lame Canary" (6-27-59) William Kendis, Stacey Graham

## Third Season

71. "The Case of the Spurious Sister" (10-3-59) Karl Weber, Marion Marshall, Peggy Knudsen, Mary La Roche, Marianne Stewart
72. "The Case of the Watery Witness" (10-10-59) Fay Wray, John Bryant, Malcolm Atterbury, Douglas Dick
73. "The Case of the Garrulous Gambler" (10-17-59) Dick Foran, Wynn Pearce, Paula Raymond
74. "The Case of the Blushing Pearls" (10-24-59) Nobu McCarthy, Ralph Dumke, George Takei
75. "The Case of the Startled Stallion" (10-31-59) Patricia Hardy, Elliot Reed, Trevor Bardette
76. "The Case of Paul Drake's Dilemma" (11-14-59) Vanessa Brown
77. "The Case of the Golden Fraud" (11-21-59) Alan Hewitt, Arthur Franz
78. "The Case of the Bartered Bikini" (12-5-59) John Lupton, June Vincent, John Anderson, Rita Lynn, Terry Lee Huntingdon
79. "The Case of the Artful Dodger" (12-12-59) Jerome Cowen, Lurene Tuttle, Patricia Donahue
80. "The Case of the Lucky Legs" (12-19-59) Lisabeth Hush, John Archer
81. "The Case of the Violent Village" (1-2-60) Ann Rutherford, Jacqueline Scott, Ray Hemphill, Barton MacLane
82. "The Case of the Frantic Flyer" (1-9-60) Rebecca Welles, Simon Oakland, Patricia Barry
83. "The Case of the Wayward Wife" (1-23-60) Bethel Leslie, Frank Maxwell, Marshall Thompson, Richard Shannon
84. "The Case of the Prudent Prosecutor" (1-30-60) J. Pat O'Malley
85. "The Case of the Gallant Grafter" (2-6-60) Herbert Rudley, Nelson Leigh, Phillip Terry, John Stephens, Charles Aidman, Virginia Arness
86. "The Case of the Wary Wildcatter" (2-20-60) Barbara Bain, Byron Palmer, Douglas Kennedy, Harry Jackson
87. "The Case of the Mythical Monkeys" (2-27-60) Beverly Garland, Lew Gallo, Louise Fletcher, Joan Banks, Lawrence Dobkin, Norman Fell
88. "The Case of the Singing Skirt" (3-12-60) Joan O'Brien, H. M. Wynant, Chris Warfield, Henry Lascoe
89. "The Case of the Perjured Parrot" (3-19-60) Robert E. Griffin, Jody Lawrence
90. "The Case of the Bashful Burro" (3-26-60) Hugh Sanders, Sue George, George Mitchell
91. "The Case of the Crying Cherub" (4-9-60) Mala Powers, Kathryn Givney, Tom Drake, Abraham Sofaer, Joe Maross, David Lewis

92. "The Case of the Nimble Nephew" (4-23-60) Bert Convy,
    Margaret Leighton, Robert Gist, Carl Benton Reid,
    William H. Wright
93. "The Case of the Madcap Modiste" (4-30-60) Marie Wind-
    sor, John Conte, Leslie Parrish, David White, Les Tre-
    mayne
94. "The Case of the Slandered Submarine" (5-14-60) Robert
    F. Simon, Ed Platt, Hugh Marlowe, Jack Ging, Robert
    H. Harris, Ann Robinson, Mort Mills
95. "The Case of the Ominous Outcast" (5-21-60) Margaret
    Hayes, Denver Pyle, Jay Novello, Walter Burke, Robert
    Emhardt, Irene Tedrow, Jeremy Slate
96. "The Case of the Irate Inventor" (5-28-60) Ce Ce Whitney,
    Tom Coley, Kasey Rodgers, Kevin Manning
97. "The Case of the Flighty Father" (6-11-60) Anne Benton,
    Francis X. Bushman

Fourth Season

98. "The Case of the Ill-Fated Faker" (10-1-60) Sue Randall,
    Tyler Patrick, William Campbell, Ken Tobey, June Day-
    ton, Patrick McVey
99. "The Case of the Singular Double" (10-8-60) Connie Hines,
    Arch Johnson, Alan Baxter, Harry Townes, Wilton Graff,
    Andrea King
100. "The Case of the Lavendar Lipstick" (10-15-60) Patricia
    Breslin, Rita Lynn, Joe Maross, Whit Bissell, John Lup-
    ton, Dabbs Greer, James Ball
101. "The Case of the Wandering Widow" (10-22-60) Coleen
    Gray, Steven Talbot, Dean Harens, Hugh Sanders, Jay
    North, Ralph Cleton, Marguarite Chapman
102. "The Case of the Clumsy Clown" (11-5-60) Douglas Hender-
    son, Chana Eden, Walter Sande
103. "The Case of the Provocative Protege" (11-12-60) Virginia
    Field, Barry Cahill, Robert Lowery, Kathie Browne,
    Gregory Morton
104. "The Case of the Nine Dolls" (11-19-60) Laurie Perreau,
    Maggie Mahoney, Eleanor Audley, Francis X. Bushman
105. "The Case of the Loquacious Liar" (12-3-60) Regis Toomey,
    Ray Danton, Wynn Pearce
106. "The Case of the Red Riding Boots" (12-10-60) Ellen Wil-
    lard, John Archer, Reba Waters, Frank Maxwell, Shirley
    Ballard
107. "The Case of the Larcenous Lady" (12-17-60) Louise
    Fletcher, Ellen Drew, Arthur Franz, King Calder, Ed-
    ward C. Platt, Patricia Huston
108. "The Case of the Envious Editor" (1-7-61) James Coburn,
    Philip Abbott, Barbara Lawrence
109. "The Case of the Irresolute Reformer" (1-14-61) Diana
    Millay, John Hoyt, Douglas Dick, James Westerfield
110. "The Case of the Fickle Fortune" (1-21-61) Vaughn Taylor,
    Helen Brown, Virginia Christine
111. "The Case of the Waylaid Wolf" (2-4-61) Andrea Martin,

Barry Atwater, Laurie Mitchell
112. "The Case of the Wintry Wife" (2-18-61) June Vincent,
Jerome Thor
113. "The Case of the Angry Dead Man" (2-25-61) Gloria Talbot, Les Tremayne
114. "The Case of the Blind Man's Bluff" (3-11-61) John Conte,
Jack Ging, George Macready
115. "The Case of the Barefaced Witness" (3-18-61) Josephine
Hutchinson, Adam West, Ray Roberts, Paul Fix, Malcolm Atterbury, Ray Teal, Russ Conway
116. "The Case of the Difficult Detour" (3-25-61) Jeff York,
Suzanne Lloyd, Jason Evers, Mort Mills, Lee Farr
117. "The Case of the Cowardly Lion" (4-8-61) Phyllis Coates,
Carol Rossen, Paul Birch, Leslie Bradley, Fred Beir
118. "The Case of the Torrid Tapestry" (4-22-61) Conrad Nagel, Paula Raymond, Robert H. Harris
119. "The Case of the Violent Vest" (4-29-61) Myrna Fahey,
Erik Rhodes, Joe Cronine, Hayden Rorke
120. "The Case of the Misguided Missile" (5-6-61) Richard
Arlen, Jeanne Bal, Bruce Bennett, Simon Oakland,
Robert Rockwell, William Schallert
121. "The Case of the Duplicate Daughter" (5-20-61) Kaye Elhardt, Don Dubbins, Anne Helm, Walter Kinsella
122. "The Case of the Grumbling Grandfather" (5-27-61) Otto
Kruger, Gavin MacLeod, Karl Held, Patricia Barry
123. "The Case of the Guilty Clients" (6-10-61) Alan Bunce,
Faith Domergue, Guy Mitchell, Lisa Gaye, Charles Bateman, Barbara Stuart
124. "The Case of the Jealous Journalist" (6-24-61) Linden
Chiles, Jan Marlin, Irene Hervey

Fifth Season

125. "The Case of the Impatient Partner" (9-16-61) Ben Cooper,
Leslie Parrish, Lucky Prentis
126. "The Case of the Missing Melody" (9-30-61) James Drury,
Jay Novello, Bobby Troupe, Jo Morrow, Constance
Towers
126a. "The Case of the Malicious Mariner" (10-7-61) Lee Farr
127. "The Case of the Crying Comedian" (10-14-61) Tommy
Noonan, Jackie Coogan, Gloria Talbot
128. "The Case of the Meddling Medium" (10-21-61) Virginia
Field, Kent Smith, James Forrest
129. "The Case of the Pathetic Patient" (10-28-61) Skip Homeier, Frank Cady, Virginia Gregg
130. "The Case of the Traveling Treasure" (11-4-61) Lisa Gaye,
Jeff York, Arch Johnson
131. "The Case of the Posthumous Painter" (11-11-61) Stuart
Erwin, Lori March, George Macready
132. "The Case of the Injured Innocent" (11-18-61) John Conte
133. "The Case of the Left-Handed Liar" (11-25-61) Leslie
Parrish, Ed Nelson
134. "The Case of the Brazen Bequest" (12-2-61) Phyllis Avery,

Karl Weber

135. "The Case of the Renegade Refugee" (12-9-61) Dick Foran, Donna Atwood, Frank Overton

136. "The Case of the Unwelcome Bride" (12-16-61) Torin Thatcher, Diana Millay, Gerald Mohr

137. "The Case of the Roving River" (12-30-61) Bruce Bennett, Sarah Marshal

138. "The Case of the Shapely Shadow" (1-6-62) Robert Rockwell

139. "The Case of the Captain's Coins" (1-13-62) Arthur Franz, Jeremy Slate, Herbert Rudley, Joan Patrick

140. "The Case of the Tarnished Trademark" (1-20-62) Osa Massen, Marie Windsor, Karl Swenson, Dennis Patrick

141. "The Case of the Glamorous Ghost" (2-3-62) Mary Murphy

142. "The Case of the Poison Pen Pal" (2-10-62) Douglas Henderson, Patricia Breslin, Everett Sloane

143. "The Case of the Mystified Miner" (2-24-62) Josephine Hutchinson, Bartlett Robinson, Kathie Browne, Carlos Rivas, Patrick Thompson, Sheilah Bromley

144. "The Case of the Crippled Cougar" (3-3-62) Bill Williams, Noah Keen, John Bryant, Mort Mills, Rita Lynn, John Howard

145. "The Case of the Absent Artist" (3-17-62) Victor Buono, Wynn Pearce, Zasu Pitts, Mark Roberts

146. "The Case of the Melancholy Marksman" (3-24-62) Jeff Donnell, Paul Richards, Mari Blanchard, William Schallert, Ann Rutherford

147. "The Case of the Angry Astronaut" (4-7-62) James Coburn, Robert Bray, Tom Harkness

148. "The Case of the Borrowed Baby" (4-14-62) Marie Palmer, Hugh Marlowe, Corey Allen

149. "The Case of the Counterfeit Crank" (4-28-62) Otto Kruger

150. "The Case of the Skeleton's Closet" (5-5-62) Keith Andes, David Lewis, Frank Aletter, Peggy McCay, Michael Pate, Dabbs Greer

151. "The Case of the Ancient Romeo" (5-12-62) Jeff Morrow, Harry Von Zell, Antoinette Bower, Rex Reason

152. "The Case of the Promoter's Pillbox" (5-19-62) Linden Chiles, John Lasell, George Matthews, Dianne Foster, Geraldine Brooks

153. "The Case of the Lonely Eloper" (5-26-62) Danny Pierce, Jack Ging, Kathleen Crowley

## Sixth Season

154. "The Case of the Bogus Books" (9-27-62) Adam West, Phyllis Love, Maurice Manson

155. "The Case of the Capricious Corpse" (10-4-62) John Howard, Everett Glass

156. "The Case of the Playboy Pugilist" (10-11-62) Jacques Aubuchon, Gary Lockwood

157. "The Case of the Hateful Hero" (10-18-62) Robert Armstrong, Leonard Stone, Dick Davalos, Edmon Ryan,

Jeanette Nolan, Mabel Albertson

158. "The Case of the Dodging Domino" (10-25-62) David Hedison, Jeff Morrow

159. "The Case of the Double-Entry Mind" (11-1-62) Stuart Erwin, Karl Weber, Jack Betts

160. "The Case of the Unsuitable Uncle" (11-8-62) Barbara Parkins, Ford Rainey, Sean McClory, Liam Sullivan

161. "The Case of the Stand-In Sister" (11-15-62) R. G. Armstrong, Peter Whitney, Susan Seaforth

162. "The Case of the Weary Watchdog" (11-29-62) Mala Powers, Doris Dowling, Wesley Addy, John Dall

163. "The Case of the Lurid Letter" (12-6-62) Mona Freeman, Kaye Elhardt, Edgar Buchanan, Robert Rockwell

164. "The Case of the Fickle Filly" (12-13-62) Joan Freeman, Bob McQuain, Strother Martin, Jim Davis, Lisabeth Hush

165. "The Case of the Polka-Dot Pony" (12-20-62) Virginia Field, Jesse White, Melinda Plowman

166. "The Case of the Shoplifter's Shoe" (1-3-63) Leonard Nimoy, Lurene Tuttle, Margaret O'Brien

167. "The Case of the Bluffing Blast" (1-10-63) Bill Williams, Antoinette Bower

168. "The Case of the Prankish Professor" (1-17-63) Patricia Breslin, Kent Smith, Barry Atwater

169. "The Case of the Constant Doyle" (1-31-63) Bette Davis, Neil Hamilton, Peggy Ann Garner, Michael Parks

170. "The Case of the Libelous Locket" (2-7-63) Michael Rennie

171. "The Case of the Two-Faced Turnabout" (2-14-63) Hugh O'Brian

172. "The Case of the Surplus Suitor" (2-28-63) Walter Pidgeon

173. "The Case of the Golden Oranges" (3-7-63) Erin O'Brien, Arch Johnson, Arthur Hunnicutt, Natalie Trundy

174. "The Case of the Lawful Lazarus" (3-14-63) Marie Palmer, Irene Hervey, Philip Bourneuf, David McLean

175. "The Case of the Velvet Claws" (3-21-63) Wynn Pearce, Richard Webb, Anna Lisa, Virginia Gregg, Patricia Barry, James Philbrook

176. "The Case of the Lover's Leap" (4-4-63) Julie Adams, John Conte, Richard Jaeckel, Carleton Carpenter

177. "The Case of the Elusive Element" (4-11-63) George Macready, Gerald Mohr, Gloria Talbot, Douglas Henderson

178. "The Case of the Greek Goddess" (4-18-63) George Kennedy, John Larkin, Faith Domergue, John Anderson, Russell Arms, Robert Harland, Marianna Hill

179. "The Case of the Potted Planter" (5-9-63) Diane Brewster, Paul Fix, Constance Ford, Joe Maross, Mark Goddard, Robert Bray

180. "The Case of the Witless Witness" (5-16-63) Jackie Coogan, Vaughn Taylor, Robert Middleton

Seventh Season

181. "The Case of the Nebulous Nephew" (9-26-63) Hugh Marlow

Beulah Bondi, Irene Tedrow, Ron Starr, Ivan Dixon
182. "The Case of the Deadly Verdict" (10-3-63) Julie Adams, Joan Tompkins, Jan Shepard, Lee Bergere, Steve Franken
183. "The Case of the Shifty Shoebox" (10-10-63) Constance Ford, Ray Teal, Denver Pyle, Benny Baker, Billy Mumy
184. "The Case of the Drowsy Mosquito" (10-17-63) Russell Collins, Archie Moore, Robert Knapp, Arthur Hunnicutt, Strother Martin, Robert J. Wilke, Kathleen Crowley
185. "The Case of the Decadent Dean" (10-24-63) Milton Selzer, Joan Tetzel, Lloyd Corrigan, H. M. Wynant
186. "The Case of the Reluctant Model" (10-31-63) Joanna Moore, John Larkin, John Dall, Margaret Hayes, Robert Brown
187. "The Case of the Bigamous Spouse" (11-14-63) Pippa Scott, Patrick McVey, Michael Conrad, Karl Swenson
188. "The Case of the Floating Stones" (11-21-63) Joyce Jameson, Irene Tsu, Victor Maddern
189. "The Case of the Festive Falcon" (11-28-63) John Hall, Sherry Jackson, Jeff Morrow, Anne Seymour, Kathie Browne
190. "The Case of the Devious Delinquent" (12-5-63) Francis Rafferty, Otto Kruger, David Lewis, Barton MacLane, David Winters, John Washbrook, Virginia Christine
191. "The Case of the Bouncing Boomerang" (12-12-63) Diana Millay, Rod Cameron, Parley Baer, Alan Hale, Berkeley Harris
192. "The Case of the Badgered Brother" (12-19-63) Robert Harland, Nancy Kovack, Patricia Blair, Peter Walker, Patrice Wymore
193. "The Case of the Wednesday Woman" (1-2-64) Marie Windsor, Philip Pine, John Hoyt, Douglas Dick, Phyllis Hill, Lisa Gaye
194. "The Case of the Accosted Accountant" (1-9-64) Lynn Bari, Dee Hartford, Murray Matheson, Gail Kobe, Leonard Stone
195. "The Case of the Capering Camera" (1-16-64) Margo Moore, Elaine Stewart, Byron Palmer, Kurt Krueger, Mark Dempsey, Paula Raymond, Karyn Kupcinet
196. "The Case of the Ice Cold Hands" (1-23-64) Phyllis Coates, Dabbs Greer, Joyce Bulifant, Dick Davalos, Arch Johnson, Lisabeth Hush
197. "The Case of the Bountiful Beauty" (2-6-64) Ryan O'Neal, Sandra Warner, Maxwell Reed, Jean Carson, John Zaremba, Zeme North, Douglas V. Fowley, John Van Dreelen
198. "The Case of the Nervous Neighbor" (2-13-64) Paul Winchell, Jeanne Cooper, Richard Rust, Katherine Squire
199. "The Case of the Fifty Millionth Frenchman" (2-20-64) Jackie Coogan, Arthur Franz, Roxane Berard, Don Collier, David McCallum, Coleen Gray, Jacques Bergerac, Janet Lake
200. "The Case of the Frightened Fisherman" (2-27-64) Mala

Powers, Marian Collier, Lee Farr, Connie Gilchrist
201. "The Case of the Arrogant Arsonist" (3-5-64) Tom Tully, Frank Aletter, Russell Thorsen, Jeff York, Wynn Pearce
202. "The Case of the Garrulous Go-Between" (3-12-64) Mary Murphy, Lori March, Jacques Aubuchon, John Napier, Anthony Eisley, Sue Randall
203. "The Case of the Woeful Widower" (3-26-64) Harry Townes, Joan Lovejoy, Nancy Gates, Anne Carroll, Joyce Meadows, Allan Joseph
204. "The Case of the Simple Simon" (4-2-64) Virginia Field, Victor Buono, Donald Barry, Tom Conway, Sherwood Kerr, Doug Lambert, James Stacy, Jay Barnevy
205. "The Case of the Illicit Illusion" (4-9-64) Mona Freeman, Keith Andes, Ron Randall, Jena Engstrom
206. "The Case of the Antic Angel" (4-16-64) Peter Breck, Michael Ansara, Janet Day, George Tobias, Richard Erdman, Billy Halop
207. "The Case of the Careless Kidnapper" (4-30-64) Marilyn Erskine, Mark Slade, Burt Metcalfe, Tom Lowell
208. "The Case of the Drifting Dropout" (4-7-64) Carl Reindel, Vaughn Taylor, Malcolm Atterbury, Neil Hamilton, Cynthia Pepper
209. "The Case of the Tandem Target" (5-14-64) Philip Ober, Natalie Trundy, Paul Carr, Ann Rutherford
210. "The Case of the Ugly Duckling" (5-21-64) Anne Whitfield, Ford Rainey, Adam La Zarre, Reginald Gardiner, Constance Towers, Max Showalter

Eighth Season

211. "The Case of the Missing Button" (9-24-64) Julie Adams, Claire Wilcox, Ed Nelson, Dee Hartford, Anthony Eisley
212. "The Case of the Paper Bullets" (10-1-64) Lynn Loring, Jan Shepard, Patrick McVey, Ford Rainey
213. "The Case of the Scandalous Sculptor" (10-8-64) Stuart Erwin, Sean McClory, June Lockhart, Simon Scott, Sue Ane Langdon
214. "The Case of the Sleepy Slayer" (10-15-64) John Napier, Richard Hale, Gigi Perreau, Robert Brown, Hugh Marlowe, Phyllis Hill
215. "The Case of the Betrayed Bride" (10-22-64) Neil Hamilton, John Larken, Diane Foster, Guy Stockwell, Jacques Aubuchon, Jeanette Nolan
216. "The Case of the Nautical Knot" (10-29-64) Barbara Bain, Tom Tully, Whit Bissell, Lisa Gaye, Anne Whitfield
217. "The Case of the Bullied Bowler" (11-5-64) Michael Connors, Jeff Donnell, Milton Selzer, Patricia Morrow, Anne Seymour
218. "The Case of a Place Called Midnight" (11-12-64) Gerald Mohr, Fred Vincent, Harry Townes, Robert Emhardt
219. "The Case of the Tragic Trophy" (11-19-64) John Fiedler, Mimsy Farmer, George Brenlin, Paul Stewart, Constance Towers, Richard Carlson

220. "The Case of the Reckless Rock Hound" (11-26-64) Bruce
    Bennett, Jeff Corey, Audrey Totter, Elisha Cook, Ben
    Johnson, Ted De Corsia
221. "The Case of the Latent Lover" (12-3-64) Lloyd Bochner,
    Jason Evers, Douglas Dumbrille, John Lasell
222. "The Case of the Wooden Nickels" (12-10-64) Phyllis Love,
    Walter Burke, Will Kuluva, Nancy Berg, Murray Mathe-
    son
223. "The Case of the Blonde Bonanza" (12-17-64) Mary Ann
    Mobley, Vaughn Taylor, Bruce Gordon, Jonathan Lippe,
    Paul Gilbert, Michael Constantine
224. "The Case of the Ruinous Road" (12-31-64) Grant Williams,
    Bert Freed, Barton MacLane, Allan Case, Les Tremayne,
    Meg Wylie
225. "The Case of the Frustrated Folk Singer" (1-7-65) Robert
    H. Harris, Gary Crosby, Bonnie Jones, Lee Meriwether,
    Mark Goddard
226. "The Case of the Thermal Thief" [Barry Sullivan plays the
    featured attorney; the only episode in which Perry Mason
    did not appear] (1-14-65) Kathie Browne, Bert Metcalfe,
    Barry Sullivan, Robert Strauss, Bettye Ackerman, Joyce
    Van Patten
227. "The Case of the Golden Venom" (1-21-65) Francis Reid,
    Mort Mills, Lee Phillips, Carole Wells, Frank Ferguson,
    Noah Beery
228. "The Case of the Telltale Tap" (2-4-65) Ronald Winters,
    Lester Dorr, Parley Baer, Jeanne Bal, Linden Chiles,
    H. M. Wynant
229. "The Case of the Feather Cloak" (2-11-65) David Opatoshu,
    Keye Luke, Joyce Jameson, John Hall, Michael Dante,
    John Van Dreelen
230. "The Case of the Lover's Gamble" (2-18-65) Elizabeth
    Perry, June Dayton, Roy Roberts, Joan O'Brien, Donald
    Murphy, Margaret Bly
231. "The Case of the Fatal Fetish" (3-4-65) Lynn Bari, Rich-
    ard Devon, Fay Wray, Gary Collins, Karen Steele, Paul
    Smith, Alan Hewitt
232. "The Case of the Sad Sicilian" (3-11-65) Margo, Nico Min-
    ardos, Anthony Caruso, Dabbs Greer, Fabrizio Mioni,
    Paul Comi
233. "The Case of the Murderous Murder" (3-18-65) Patrice
    Wymore, Lee Bergere, Bill Williams, Jean Hale, Jess
    Barker
234. "The Case of the Careless Kitten" (3-25-65) Louise La-
    tham, Allan Melvin, Lloyd Corrigan, Julie Sommars
235. "The Case of the Deadly Debt" (4-1-65) Chris Robinson,
    Joe De Santis, Robert Quarry, Joan Huntington, Gregory
    Morton
236. "The Case of the Gambling Lady" (4-8-65) Ruta Lee,
    Myrna Fahey, Peter Breck, Kevin Hagen, Dan Seymour,
    Jesse White
237. "The Case of the Duplicate Case" (4-22-65) Martin West,
    Susan Bay, Don Dubbins, Steve Ihnat

238. "The Case of the Grinning Gorilla" (4-29-65) Charlene
     Holt, Victor Buono, Lurene Tuttle, Gavin MacLeod
239. "The Case of the Wrongful Writ" (5-6-65) Katherine Squire
     Nobu McCarthy, Bobby Troupe, Philip Abbott, Peter
     Whitney, James Shigeta
240. "The Case of the Mischievous Doll" (5-13-65) Mary
     Mitchell, Ben Cooper, Marge Redmond, Paul Lambert,
     Allyson Ames

Ninth Season

241. "The Case of the Laughing Lady" (9-12-65) John Dall,
     Jean Hale, Constance Towers
242. "The Case of the Fatal Fortune" (9-19-65) Julie Adams,
     Lee Philips, Dean Harens, Nan Martin, Ford Rainey,
     Jesse White
243. "The Case of the Candy Queen" (9-26-65) Nancy Gates,
     John Napier, Robert Rockwell, John Archer, Patricia
     Smith, H. M. Wynant
244. "The Case of the Cheating Chancellor" (10-3-65) Louise
     Latham, Peter Helm, Lee Meriwether, James Noah,
     Barry Atwater, Michael Walker
245. "The Case of the Impetuous Imp" (10-10-65) Stuart Erwin,
     Jeff Cooper, Don Dubbins, Frank Marth, Bonnie Jones,
     Hanna Landy
246. "The Case of the Carefree Coronary" (10-17-65) Bruce
     Bennett, Tracy Morgan, Whit Bissell, Robert Emhardt,
     Lawrence Montaigne
247. "The Case of the Hasty Honeymooner" (10-24-65) Hugh
     Marlowe, Noah Beery, Cathy Downs, K. T. Stevens,
     Strother Martin
248. "The Case of the 12th Wildcat" (10-31-65) Bill Williams,
     John Conte, Mona Freeman, Regis Toomey, Karl Swen-
     son, Robert Quarry
249. "The Case of the Wrathful Wraith" (11-7-65) Jeanne Bal,
     Marion Moses, Richard Eastham, Lee Farr, Walter
     Burke, Gene Lyons, Douglas Dick
250. "The Case of the Runaway Racer" (11-14-65) Anthony Ca-
     ruso, Henry Brandt, Gavin MacLeod, Jan Shepard,
     Richard Eastham, Robert H. Harris, Michael Constantine
251. "The Case of the Silent Six" (11-21-65) Virginia Gregg,
     Skip Homeier, Dianne Foster, David Macklin, Cyril Dele-
     vante, Hampton Fancher
252. "The Case of the Fraudulent Fraulein" (11-28-65) Wolfe
     Barzell, Kevin Hagen, Gregory Martin, Jeanette Nolan,
     Susanne Cramer
253. "The Case of the Baffling Bug" (12-12-65) Grant Williams,
     Dee Hartford, Gilbert Green, Ben Cooper, Alizia Gur
254. "The Case of the Golden Girls" (12-19-65) Philip Bourneuf
     Angela Dorlan
255. "The Case of the Bogus Buccaneer" (1-9-66) Rhodes Rea-
     son, Meg Wyllie, Mary Mitchell, John Milford, Leonard
     Stone, Patricia Cutts, Richard Jaeckel

256. "The Case of the Midnight Howler" (1-16-66) Myrna Fahey, Alan Baxter, Dan Travanty, Ian Wolfe, Lee Patterson
257. "The Case of the Vanishing Victim" (1-23-66) Jeanne Cooper, Lisa Gaye, Russell Arms, Carol Brewster, Richard Erdman, George Wallace
258. "The Case of the Golfer's Gambit" (1-30-66) Carl Reindel, Nancy Kovack, Dennis Patrick, Harry Townes, Bartlett Robinson
259. "The Case of the Sausalito Sunrise" (2-13-66) Donald Murphy, Allan Melvin, Elizabeth Fraser, Francine York, Peter Mamakos
260. "The Case of the Scarlet Scandal" (2-20-66) Lloyd Gough, Richard Devon, Mala Powers, Dee Pollack, Gene Evans, Will Hutchins
261. "The Case of the Twice-Told Twist" [only color episode] (2-27-66) Victor Buono, Kevin O'Neal, Lisa Seagram, Lisa Pera, Scott Graham
262. "The Case of the Avenging Angel" (3-13-66) Richard Carlson, Paul Stewart, Lurene Tuttle, Sue Ane Langdon
263. "The Case of the Tsarina's Tiara" (3-20-66) Virginia Field, Wesley Addy, Kendall Clark, Carlos Romero, Barbara Perry, Vivienne Segal
264. "The Case of the Fanciful Frail" (3-27-66) Gloria Talbott, Pippa Scott, Coleen Gray, Arch Johnson, Danielle De Metz, Joan Huntington
265. "The Case of the Unwelcome Well" (4-3-66) Wendell Corey, James Best, Les Tremayne, Gloria Talbott, Paul Brinegar, Marilyn Erskine, Danielle De Metz
266. "The Case of the Dead Ringer" (4-17-66) Stewart Moss, Tom Palmer, Indus Arthur, Henry Beckman, Oliver McGowan
267. "The Case of the Misguided Model" (4-24-66) Paul Lukather, Don Dubbins, Mary Ann Mobley, Rita Lynn, Anthony Eisley
268. "The Case of the Positive Negative" (5-1-66) Brian Donlevy, Dabbs Greer, Parley Baer, Simon Scott, Bettye Ackerman, Ted De Corsia
269. "The Case of the Crafty Kidnapper" (5-15-66) Anne Whitfield, Jay Novello, Gary Collins, Cloris Leachman, Douglas Henderson
270. "The Case of the Final Fade-Out" (5-22-66) James Stacy, Marlyn Mason, Estelle Winwood, Dick Clark, Erle Stanley Gardner, Denver Pyle

## SHIRLEY TEMPLE'S STORYBOOK

Shirley Temple entered series television as the "storyteller" and occasional star of these adaptations of classic children's fables. Noel Langley adapted his own Arabian Nights tale "The Land of Green Ginger" in a musical version with songs by Jerry Livingston and Mack David. Miss Temple introduced her children

(Charles, Lori and Susan) in another musical program, "Mother Goose."

Those who adapted the classics in straight dramatic form included Norman Lessing (for Washington Irving's "The Legend of Sleepy Hollow," and Hans Christian Andersen's "The Emperor's New Clothes"), Jean Holloway (for Hans Christian Andersen's "The Wild Swans"), Margaret Fitts (for Charles Perrault's "The Sleeping Beauty" and Charles Dickens' "The Magic Fishbone"), F. William Durkee Jr. (for the Brothers Grimm's "Rapunzel"), S. S. Schweitzer (for Maria Mulock Craik's "The Little Lame Prince"), Alvin Sapinsley (for Hans Christian Andersen's "The Nightingale"), and Noel Langley (for Washington Irving's "Rip Van Winkle").

The Regulars: Shirley Temple, hostess.

The Episodes: (telecast via NBC)

1. "Beauty and the Beast" (1-12-58) Charleton Heston, Claire Bloom, E. G. Marshall, June Lockhart, Barbara Baxley
2. "Rumpelstiltskin" (2-2-58) John Raitt, Phyllis Love, Kurt Kasznar, Shai K. Opher, Jonathan Harris
3. "The Nightingale" (2-23-58) Thomas Mitchell, Liam Sullivan, Lisa Lu, Russell Collins, Judith Braun
4. "The Legend of Sleepy Hollow" (3-5-58) Shirley Temple, John Ericson, Jules Munshin; Boris Karloff narrates
5. "Dick Whittington and His Cat" (3-23-58) Jack Diamond, Rhubarb (the cat), Judith Meredith, Martyn Green, Sebastian Cabot, Ashley Cowan
6. "The Land of Green Ginger" (4-18-58) Kuldip Singh, Sue England, Jack Albertson, Joey Faye; Shirley Temple narrates
7. "Rip Van Winkle" (5-8-58) E. G. Marshall, Leora Dana, Beverly Washburn
8. "The Sleeping Beauty" (6-8-58) Alexander Scourby, Nancy Marchand, Anne Helm, Olive Deering, Vernon Gray, Judith Evelyn
9. "The Little Lame Prince" (7-15-58) Lorne Greene, Rex Thompson
10. "The Magic Fishbone" (8-19-58) Barry Jones, Estelle Winwood, Leo G. Carroll, Lisa Daniels, Richard Lupino
11. "The Wild Swans" (9-12-58) Phyllis Love, Melville Cooper, Grant Williams
12. "Hiawatha" (10-5-58) John Ericson, Pernell Roberts, J. Carrol Naish
13. "Rapunzel" (10-27-58) Carol Lynley, Agnes Moorehead, Don Dubbins
14. "Ali Baba and the Forty Thieves" (11-12-58) Nehemiah Persoff, Thomas Gomez, Rafael Campos, Vivian Nathan, Bruce Gordon
15. "The Emperor's New Clothes" (11-25-58) Eli Wallach, Sebastian Cabot, Barbara Lord, Richard Haydn
16. "Mother Goose" (12-21-58) Elsa Lanchester, Carleton

Carpenter, Shirley Temple and her children Charles, Lori and Susan


# MAVERICK

Roy Huggins' zesty spoof of western morals, celebrating the adventures of poker-playing brothers Bret (James Garner) and Bart (Jack Kelly); later cousin Beau (Roger Moore) and brother Brent (Robert Colbert).

The Regulars: Bret Maverick, James Garner; Bart Maverick, Jack Kelly; Beau Maverick, Roger Moore (with episode of 9/18/60); Brent Maverick, Robert Colbert (with episode of 3/26/61); Dandy Jim, Efrem Zimbalist Jr. (recurring guest role); Samantha Crawford, Diane Brewster (recurring guest role).

The Episodes (chronicled from second season):

1. "The Day They Hanged Bret Maverick" (9-21-58) Whitney Blake, Ray Teal, Jay Novello
2. "Lonesome Reunion" (9-28-58)
3. "Alias Bart Maverick" (10-5-58) Richard Long, Eurlyne Howell
4. "The Belcastle Brand" (10-12-58) Reginald Owen, Joan Elan
5. "High Card Hangs" (10-19-58) Martin Landau, Efrem Zimbalist Jr.
6. "Escape to Tampico" (10-26-58)
7. "The Judas Mask" (11-2-58)
8. "The Jail at Junction Flats" (11-9-58) Patrick McVey, Jean Allison, Efrem Zimbalist Jr.
9. "The Thirty-Ninth Star" (11-16-58) Bethel Leslie
10. "Shady Deal at Sunny Acres" (11-23-58) Regis Toomey, Richard Long, Arlene Howell, John Dehner, Diane Brewster, Karl Swenson, Efrem Zimbalist Jr.
11. "Island in the Swamp" (11-30-58)
12. "Prey of the Cat" (12-7-58) Wayne Morris
13. "The Spanish Dancer" (12-14-58) Richard Long, Adele Mara, Slim Pickens, Robert Bray
14. "Holiday at Hollow Rock" (12-28-58) William Reynolds
15. "Game of Chance" (1-4-59)
16. "Gun-Shy" (1-11-59) Ben Gage, Marshall Kent
17. "Two Beggars on Horseback" (1-18-59) Ray Teal, Patricia Barry
18. "The Rivals" (1-25-59) Pat Crowley, Roger Moore
19. "Duel at Sundown" (2-1-59) Clint Eastwood, Abby Dalton, Edgar Buchanan
20. "Yellow River" (2-8-59) Pat Breslin, Robert Conrad
21. "The Saga of Waco Williams" (2-15-59) Wayde Preston, Louise Fletcher, R. G. Armstrong
22. "The Brasada Spur" (2-22-59) Hope Summers, Julie Adams,

Patrick McVey, Ken Lynch
23. "Passage to Fort Doom" (3-8-59) Nancy Gates, Diane Mc-
Bain, Arlene Howell, Fred Beir
24. "Two Tickets to Ten Strike" (3-15-59) Connie Stevens,
Adam West
25. "Betrayal" (3-22-59) Pat Crowley
26. "The Strange Journey of Jenny Hill" (3-29-59) William
Schallert, Peggy King

Third Season

27. "Pappy" (9-13-59) Henry Daniell, Mike Forest, Adam West,
Kaye Elhardt, Troy Donahue, Virginia Gregg
28. "Royal Four-Flush" (9-20-59) David Frankham, Roxane
Berard, Arch Johnson, Roberta Shore
29. "The Sheriff of Duck 'n' Shoot" (9-27-59) Peggy McCay,
Chubby Johnson
30. "You Can't Beat the Percentage" (10-4-59) Adele Mara,
Karen Steele, Gerald Mohr
31. "Cats of Paradise" (10-11-59) Mona Freeman, Lance Fuller,
Buddy Ebsen
32. "A Tale of Three Cities" (10-18-59) Pat Crowley, Edward
Kemmer
33. "Full House" (10-25-59) Robert Lowery, Gregory Walcott
34. "The Lass with the Poisonous Air" (11-1-59) Howard Petrie,
Joanna Moore
35. "The Ghost Soldiers" (11-8-59) Paul Clarke, James Westerfield
36. "Easy Mark" (11-15-59) Nita Talbot, Frank Ferguson,
Douglas Kennedy, Pippa Scott, Wynn Pearce, Edgar Buchanan
37. "A Fellow's Brother" (11-22-59) Adam West, Gary Vinson
38. "Trooper Maverick" (11-29-59) Herbert Rudley, Joe Sawyer,
Charles Cooper
39. "Maverick Springs" (12-6-59)
40. "The Goose-Drownder" (12-13-59) Richard Long, Will Wright
41. "Cure for Johnny Rain" (12-20-59) William Reynolds, John
Vivyan
42. "The Marquesa" (1-3-60) Adele Mara, Rodolfo Hoyos, Jay
Novello
43. "Cruise of the Cynthia B" (1-10-60) Mona Freeman, Jack
Livesey
44. "Maverick and Juliet" (1-17-60) Steve Terrell, Carole Wells,
Rhys Williams
45. "The White Widow" (1-24-60) Julie Adams
46. "Guatemala City" (1-31-60) Suzanne Storrs, Linda Dangcil
47. "The People's Friend" (2-7-60) John Litel, Merry Anders
48. "A Flock of Trouble" (2-14-60)
49. "The Iron Hand" (2-21-60) Susan Morrow
50. "The Resurrection of Joe November" (2-28-60) Nita Talbot
51. "The Misfortune Teller" (3-6-60) Alan Mowbray, Kathleen
Crowley
52. "Greenbacks Unlimited" (3-13-60) Wendell Holmes, Ed Dehner

Fourth Season

53.  "Bundle from Britain" (9-18-60) featuring Roger Moore
54.  "Hadley's Hunters" (9-25-60) Ty Hardin, Will Hutchins,
        Clint Walker, Peter Brown, Edgar Buchanan, Edd Byrnes,
        John Russell
55.  "The Town That Wasn't There" (10-2-60) Richard Hale,
        John Astin
56.  "Arizona Black Maria" (10-9-60) Joanna Barnes, Alan Hale,
        Gary Murray, Donald Barry
57.  "Last Wire from Stop Gap" (10-16-60) Robert Cornthwaite,
        Don Harvey, Olive Sturgess, Tol Avery
58.  "Mano Nera" (10-23-60) Gerald Mohr, Myrna Fahey
59.  "A Bullet for the Teacher" (10-30-60) Kathleen Crowley,
        Brad Johnson, Arch Johnson, Joan Tompkins
60.  "The Witch of Hound Dog" (11-6-60) Anita Sands, Wayde
        Preston, William B. Corrie
61.  "Thunder from the North" (11-13-60) Robert Warwick, An-
        dra Martin
62.  "The Maverick Line" (11-20-60) Buddy Ebsen, Will Wright,
        Peggy McCay, Chubby Johnson
63.  "Bolt from the Blue" (11-27-60) Fay Spain, Will Hutchins
64.  "Kiz" (12-4-60) Kathleen Crowley, Peggy McCay, Tristram
        Coffin, Whit Bissell, Max Baer Jr., Thomas B. Henry,
        Claude Stroud
65.  "Dodge City or Bust" (12-11-60) Diana Millay, Peter Whit-
        ney, Med Flory, Howard McNear
66.  "The Bold Fenian Men" (12-18-60) Arthur Shields, Arch
        Johnson
67.  "Destination Devil's Flat" (12-25-60) Peter Breck, Merry
        Anders
68.  "A State of Siege" (1-1-61) Ray Danton, Lisa Gaye, Joe De
        Santis
69.  "Family Pride" (1-8-61) Karl Swenson, Anita Sands, Robert
        Cornthwaite, Denver Pyle
70.  "The Cactus Switch" (1-15-61) Fay Spain, Peter Hansen,
        Edgar Buchanan, Tom Gilson
71.  "Dutchman's Gold" (1-22-61) Mala Powers, Jacques Aubu-
        chon
72.  "The Ice Man" (1-29-61) Andrew Duggan, Bruce Gordon,
        Shirley Knight, James Seay, Virginia Gregg
73.  "Diamond Flush" (2-5-61) Roxane Berard, Dan Tobin, Ann
        Lee, Carl Esmond
74.  "Last Stop: Oblivion" (2-12-61) Suzanne Lloyd, Buddy Eb-
        sen, Hampton Fancher, Maurice Manson
75.  "Flood's Folly" (2-19-61) Alan Baxter, Marlene Willis,
        Jeanne Cooper, Michael Pate
76.  "Maverick at Law" (2-26-61) Tol Avery, Gage Clarke,
        James Anderson, Ken Mayer, Kern Dobbs
77.  "Red Dog" (3-5-61) John Carradine, Mike Road, Evan Mc-
        Cord, Lee Van Cleef, Sherry Jackson
78.  "Deadly Image" (3-12-61) Gerald Mohr, Dawn Wells, Abra-
        ham Sofaer

79. "Triple Indemnity" (3-19-61) Alan Hewitt, Peter Breck, Laurie Mitchell, Charity Grace
80. "The Forbidden City" (3-26-61) Vladimir Sokoloff, Lisa Montell, Nina Shipman
81. "Substitute Gun" (4-2-61) Walter Sande, Carlos Romero, Robert Rockwell, Coleen Gray, Joan Marshall
82. "Benefit of Doubt" (4-9-61) George Wallace, Elizabeth MacRae, Trevor Bardette, Randy Stuart
83. "The Devil's Necklace" (4-23-61) John Dehner, Steve Brodie, Sharon Hugueny, John Hoyt, John Archer, Kasey Rogers

Fifth Season

84. "Dade City Dodge" (9-24-61) Kathleen Crowley, Mike Road
85. "The Art Lovers" (10-1-61) Jack Cassidy
86. "The Golden Fleecing" (10-8-61) John Qualen, Paula Raymond
87. "Three Queens Full" (11-12-61) Jim Backus
88. "Stampede" [repeat of episode of 5/25/58] (11-19-61) Efrem Zimbalist Jr.
89. "A Technical Error" (11-26-61) Reginald Owen, Peter Breck, Frank De Kova
90. "According to Hoyle" [repeat of episode of 4/6/58] (12-3-61)
91. "Two Tickets to Ten Strike" [repeat of episode of 3/15/59] (12-10-61)
92. "Stage West" [repeat of episode of 5/4/58] (12-17-61)
93. "Black Fire" [repeat of episode of 3/16/58] (12-31-61) Hans Conried, Jane Darwell, Will Wright
94. "Poker Face" (1-7-62) Carlos Rivas
95. "Shady Deal at Sunny Acres" [repeat of episode of 11/23/58] (1-21-62)
96. "Gun-Shy" [repeat of episode of 1/11/59] (1-28-62)
97. "Epitaph for a Gambler" (2-11-62) Marie Windsor
98. "A Rage for Vengeance" [repeat of episode of 1/12/58] (2-18-62) John Russell
99. "Seventh Hand" [repeat of episode of 3/2/58] (2-25-62)
100. "The Maverick Report" (3-4-62) Peter Breck, Ed Nelson, Jo Morrow
101. "Marshal Maverick" (3-11-62) John Dehner, Peter Breck
102. "Rope of Cards" [repeat of episode of 6/29/58] (3-18-62)
103. "The Saga of Waco Williams" [repeat of episode of 2/15/59] (3-25-62)
104. "The Troubled Heir" (4-1-62) Mike Road, Alan Hale
105. "The Money Machine" (4-8-62) Kathy Bennett
106. "The Belcastle Brand" [repeat of episode of 10/12/58] (4-15-62)
107. "One of Our Trains Is Missing" (4-22-62) Kathleen Crowley, Peter Breck
108. "Comstock Conspiracy" [repeat of episode of 12/29/57] (4-29-62) Werner Klemperer
109. "Seed of Deception" (5-6-62) Adele Mara

ALCOA/GOODYEAR THEATRE

The Episodes:

1. Goodyear Theatre: "The Chain and the River" (9-29-58)
   Paul Douglas, Patty McCormack
2. Alcoa Theatre: "Strange Occurrence at Rokesay" (10-6-58)
   John Kerr
3. Alcoa Theatre: "Coast to Coast" (10-20-58) Cornel Wilde
4. Goodyear Theatre: "Lazarus Walks Again" (10-27-58) Eddie
   Albert, Staats Cotsworth
5. Alcoa Theatre: "Office Party" (11-3-58) Nancy Kelly, Paul
   Richards
6. Goodyear Theatre: "The Spy" (11-10-58) Gig Young, Everett Sloane
7. Alcoa Theatre: "Eddie" (11-17-58) Mickey Rooney
8. Goodyear Theatre: "Guy in Ward 4" (11-24-58) Richard
   Kiley
9. Alcoa Theatre: "The First Star" (12-1-58) Janet Blair,
   Paul Stewart, John Cassavetes
10. Goodyear Theatre: "Points Beyond" (12-8-58) Sterling Hay-
    den, Julie Adams
11. Alcoa Theatre: "Town Budget" (12-15-58) James Whitmore,
    Marilyn Erskine
12. Goodyear Theatre: "Curtain Call" (12-22-58) Jackie Cooper,
    Barry Atwater
13. Alcoa Theatre: "The Dark File" (12-29-58) Lin McCarthy,
    Kim Hunter, Patricia Breslin
14. Goodyear Theatre: "Coogan's Reward" (1-5-59) Tony Ran-
    dall, Robert Gist
15. Alcoa Theatre: "High Class Type of Mongrel" (1-12-59)
    Jack Carson
16. Goodyear Theatre: "Afternoon of the Beast" (1-19-59) Kee-
    nan Wynn, Rafael Campos
17. Alcoa Theatre: "30 Pieces of Silver" (1-26-59) Jo Van
    Fleet, George Voskovec
18. Goodyear Theatre: "A London Affair" (2-2-59) Ray Milland,
    Gia Scala
19. Alcoa Theatre: "Goodbye Johnny" (2-9-59) Cliff Robertson
20. Goodyear Theatre: "Success Story" (2-16-59) Jim Backus,
    Virginia Gregg
21. Alcoa Theatre: "Corporal Hardy" (2-23-59) Lew Ayres,
    Tyler MacDuff
22. Goodyear Theatre: "A Good Name" (3-2-59) Edward G.
    Robinson, Lee Philips
23. Alcoa Theatre: "Man of His House" (3-9-59) Agnes Moore-
    head, Brandon De Wilde
24. Goodyear Theatre: "The Obenauf Story" (3-30-59) Kerwin
    Mathews, Herbert Anderson
25. Goodyear Theatre: "A Sword for Marius" (4-13-59) James
    Mason, Fabrizio Mioni
26. Alcoa Theatre: "Ten Miles to Doomsday" (4-20-59) Keith
    Andes, Jeff Richards, Richard Jaeckel

27. Goodyear Theatre: "A Light in the Fruit Closet" (4-27-59)
    Steve Dunne, Maggie Hayes
28. Alcoa Theatre: "The Slightly Fallen Angel" (5-4-59) Walter
    Slezak, David White, Lee Bergere
29. Goodyear Theatre: "I Remember Caviar" (5-11-59) Pat
    Crowley, Lurene Tuttle
30. Alcoa Theatre: "Boyden vs. Bunty" (5-18-59) Robert Trum-
    bull, Bert Convy
31. Goodyear Theatre: "Wait Till Spring" (5-25-59) Jeanne
    Crain, John Lupton
32. Alcoa Theatre: "Medals for Harry" (6-1-59) Eddie Ryder
33. Goodyear Theatre: "Christabel" (6-8-59) Arthur O'Connell,
    Georgann Johnson
34. Alcoa Theatre: "The Best Way to Go" (6-15-59) Gary Mer-
    rill, Joseph Sonessa, Jay C. Flippen

Second Season

35. Goodyear Theatre: "Story Without a Moral" (9-14-59) Brian
    Aherne, Kurt Kasznar, Celia Lovsky, John Abbott
36. Alcoa Theatre: "Another Day, Another Dollar" (9-21-59)
    Jack Carson, Jesse White, Flip Mark
37. Goodyear Theatre: "Hello, Charlie" (9-28-59) Tony Randall
38. Alcoa Theatre: "Operation Spark" (10-5-59) David Wayne,
    John Larch, Lamont Johnson, John Hoyt
39. Goodyear Theatre: "The Incorrigibles" (10-12-59) Paul
    Douglas, Danny Richards Jr.
40. Goodyear Theatre: "Any Friend of Julie's" (10-19-59) Les-
    lie Nielsen, Vanessa Brown, Robert F. Simon
41. Alcoa Theatre: "The Day the Devil Hid" (11-2-59) Peter
    Lind Hayes, Robert Gist, Philip Ahn
42. Goodyear Theatre: "The Golden Shanty" (11-9-59) Errol
    Flynn
43. Alcoa Theatre: "Small Bouquet" (11-16-59) Howard Duff,
    Barbara Bain
44. Goodyear Theatre: "Point of Impact" (11-23-59) Peter Law-
    ford, Dennis Patrick, Warren Stevens
45. Alcoa Theatre: "Shadow of Evil" (11-30-59) Cliff Robert-
    son, David Brian, Mary Murphy
46. Alcoa Theatre: "The Long House on Avenue A" (12-14-59)
    Henry Silva, Susan Oliver
47. Goodyear Theatre: "Lady Bug" (12-21-59) Thomas Mitchell,
    Michel Petit
48. Alcoa Theatre: "How's Business?" (12-28-59) Jack Car-
    son, Flip Mark
49. Goodyear Theatre: "Omaha Beach--Plus 15" (1-4-60)
    Cameron Mitchell, Joe Mantell
50. Alcoa Theatre: "Action Off Screen" (1-11-60) George Ma-
    haris, Patricia Owens
51. Goodyear Theatre: "Birthright" (1-18-60) Eli Wallach, Kay
    Stewart, Martin Balsam
52. Alcoa Theatre: "The Last Flight Out" (1-25-60) Dorothy
    Malone, Edward Binns, Robert Vaughn

53. Goodyear Theatre: "Capital Gains" (2-1-60) Joanne Dru, Rod Taylor, Dan Tobin
54. Alcoa Theatre: "Minister Accused" (2-8-60) Steve Forrest, Julie Adams, Olive Deering
55. Goodyear Theatre: "The Ticket" (2-15-60) Franchot Tone
56. Alcoa Theatre: "Face to Face" (2-22-60) James Gregory, Rebecca Wells
57. Goodyear Theatre: "Show Wagon" (2-29-60) Luke Anthony, Connie Hines, Jack Albertson
58. Alcoa Theatre: "Chinese Finale" (3-7-60) Jan Sterling, Hilda Plowright
59. Goodyear Theatre: "Squeeze Play" (3-14-60) Dick Shannon, William Campbell
60. Alcoa Theatre: "The Tweed Hat" (3-21-60) Don Taylor, Hazel Court
61. Goodyear Theatre: "All in the Family" (3-28-60) Pat Crowley, Lurene Tuttle, Henry Hull
62. Alcoa Theatre: "The Glorious 4th" (4-4-60) Dick York
63. Goodyear Theatre: "Author at Work" (4-11-60) Ernie Kovacs, Henry Jones
64. Alcoa Theatre: "The Observer" (4-18-60) Maximilian Schell, Werner Klemperer, George Macready
65. Goodyear Theatre: "Marked Down for Connie" (4-25-60) Elinor Donahue, Troy Travis
66. Goodyear Theatre: "The Sitter's Baby" (5-9-60) Spring Byington, Charles Ruggles, Roberta Shore
67. Alcoa Theatre: "You Should Meet My Sister" (5-16-60) Elaine Stritch, Anne Helm, Henry Corden
68. Goodyear Theatre: "The Proud Earth" (5-23-60) John Larch, Vivi Janiss

## DESILU PLAYHOUSE

Desi Arnaz was host for this anthology series, the product of his own (and wife Lucille Ball's) Desilu Productions. The "I Love Lucy" series was extended in an hour-long special format, retaining regulars William Frawley and Vivian Vance in their "Fred and Ethel Mertz" roles. Lucille Ball was the featured performer of the episode "K. O. Kitty," a comedy designed especially for her by "I Love Lucy" writers Bob Carroll Jr. and Madelyn Pugh Martin.

The most memorable of the dramas would be, of course, the classic two-part "The Untouchables," by Paul Monash from the Eliot Ness novel. In the Ness role, Robert Stack made enough of an impression to play the character repeatedly in the series begun October 15, 1959. The episode "The Untouchables" was later released as a feature film, The Scarface Mob, in 1962.

Other fine dramas were Rod Serling's "The Time Element," Paul Monash's "Debut," Aaron Spelling's "The Night the Phone

Rang, " and "Bernadette" which was adapted by Ludi Claire from Margaret Gray Blanton's biography.

The Regulars: Desi Arnaz, host.

The Episodes:

1. "The Lucille Ball-Desi Arnaz Show: Lucy Goes to Mexico" (10-6-58) Maurice Chevalier
2. "Bernadette" (10-13-58) Pier Angeli, Marian Seldes, Bruce Gordon, Ludi Claire, Jacques Aubuchon
3. "The Case for Dr. Mudd" (10-20-58) Lew Ayres
4. "Debut" (10-27-58) Susan Strasberg, Henry Daniell, Martin Milner, Maria Palmer
5. "My Father, the Fool" (11-3-58) Eli Wallach, Esther Minciotti, J. Carrol Naish, Rita Lynn
6. "K. O. Kitty" (11-17-58) Lucille Ball, William Lundigan, Aldo Ray
7. "The Time Element" (11-24-58) William Bendix, Martin Balsam
8. "The Lucille Ball-Desi Arnaz Show: Lucy Makes Room for Danny" (12-1-58) Danny Thomas, Marjorie Lord, Sherry Jackson
9. "Silent Thunder" (12-8-58) John Barrymore Jr., Wallace Ford, James Edwards, Earl Holliman
10. "The Night the Phone Rang" (12-15-58) Eddie Albert, Margo, Sidney Blackmer, Paul Dubov
11. "The Crazy Hunter" (12-29-58) Franchot Tone, Jo Van Fleet
12. "Trial at Devil's Canyon" (1-5-59) Skip Homeier, Phyllis Coates
13. "Happy Hill" (1-12-59) Royal Dano, Richard Eyer, Claire Trevor, Jay C. Flippen
14. "Ballad for a Badman" (1-26-59) Steve Forrest, Jane Russell, Jack Haley, Karen Sharpe, Mischa Auer
15. "Symbol of Authority" (2-2-59) Ernie Kovacs, Jean Hagen
16. "Lucille Ball-Desi Arnaz Show: Lucy Goes to Alaska" (2-9-59) Red Skelton
17. "Chez Rouge" (2-16-59) Ray Danton, Abel Fernandez, Harry Guardino, Dan Blocker, Herbert Berghoff, Janis Paige, Kurt Kasznar
18. "Martin's Folly" (2-23-59) Tony Randall, Carl Reiner, Maggie Mahoney
19. "Comeback" (3-2-59) Dan Duryea, Margaret Hayes, Robert Rockwell, William Frawley
20. "The Innocent Assassin" (3-16-59) Piper Laurie, James MacArthur
21. "Chain of Command" (3-23-59) Martin Milner, Hugh O'Brian
22. "The Hard Road" (3-30-59) Cliff Robertson, Barry Sullivan, Patricia Barry
23. "The Lucille Ball-Desi Arnaz Show: Lucy Wants a Career" (4-13-59) Paul Douglas
24. "The Untouchables" [Part I] (4-20-59) Robert Stack, Neville

Brand, Keenan Wynn, Barbara Nichols, Patricia Crowley, Bill Williams
25. "The Untouchables" [Part II]  (4-27-59)  as above
26. "Man in Orbit"  (5-11-59)  Lee Marvin, E. G. Marshall, Martin Balsam
27. "The Lucille Ball-Desi Arnaz Show: Lucy's Summer Vacation"  (6-8-59)  Howard Duff, Ida Lupino
28. "Perilous"  (6-22-59)  Joan Fontaine, Maximilian Schell, John Williams

## Second Season

29. "A Diamond for Carla"  (9-14-59)  Anna Maria Alberghetti, Johnny Desmond
30. "The Lucille Ball-Desi Arnaz Show: Milton Berle Hides Out at the Ricardos"  (9-25-59)  Milton Berle, Larry Keating
31. "The Day the Town Stood Up"  (10-2-59)  Joseph Cotten, James Gregory, Clu Gulager, Virginia Grey
32. "Six Guns for Donegan"  (10-16-59)  Lloyd Nolan, Jean Hagen
33. "So Tender, So Profane"  (10-30-59)  Margo, Barbara Luna
34. "Come Back to Sorrento"  (11-6-59)  Robert Loggia, Marissa Pavan
35. "Border Justice"  (11-13-59)  Gilbert Roland, Neile Adams, Bruce Gordon, Rita Lynn, Barton MacLane
36. "Lepke"  (11-20-59)  Lloyd Bridges, Sam Jaffe, Joseph Wiseman; Walter Winchell narrates
37. "The Lucille Ball-Desi Arnaz Show: The Ricardos Go to Japan"  (11-27-59)  Robert Cummings
38. "The Hanging Judge"  (12-4-59)  James Whitmore, Warren Berlinger, Jean Hagen, John McIntire, Buddy Ebsen
39. "Murder in Gratitude"  (12-11-59)  Trevor Howard, Robert Coote, Robin Hughes, Michael Pate, Patricia Driscoll
40. "The Desilu Revue" [Christmas special]  (12-25-59)  Hedda Hopper; appearing in cameos are Danny Thomas, Hugh O'Brian, Spring Byington, Ann Sothern, Lassie
41. "Meeting at Appalachia"  (1-22-60)  Cara Williams, Cameron Mitchell, Luther Adler, Jack Warden
42. "Thunder in the Night"  (2-19-60)  Rod Taylor, Desi Arnaz, George Macready, Akim Tamiroff, Marion Marshall
43. "Circle of Evil"  (3-18-60)  Hugh O'Brian, Felicia Farr, Ken Clark
44. "The Lucille Ball-Desi Arnaz Show: Lucy Meets the Moustache"  (4-1-60)  Ernie Kovacs, Edie Adams
45. "The Man in the Funny Suit"  (4-15-60)  Red Skelton, Keenan Wynn, Ed Wynn, Rod Serling
46. "City in Bondage"  (5-13-60)  Ed Begley, Barry Sullivan
47. "Murder Is a Private Affair"  (6-10-60)  David Brian, Dina Merrill, Adam West, Jack Weston, Peter Adams, Myrna Hansen, Kam Fong

THE RIFLEMAN

Moralizing western saga of a Winchester toting widower (Chuck Connors as Lucas McCain) and his son (Johnny Crawford as Mark); its episodes arrayed with would-be television superstars (but then little known): Robert Vaughn, Michael Landon and Dan Blocker among them.

The Regulars: Lucas McCain, Chuck Connors; Mark McCain, Johnny Crawford; Sheriff Micah Torrance, Paul Fix; Miss Milly Scott, Joan Taylor (as of 11/15/60); Lou Mallory, Patricia Blair (as of 10/15/62).

The Episodes:

1. "The Sharpshooter" (9-30-58) Leif Erickson, Dennis Hopper
2. "Home Ranch" (10-7-58)
3. "End of a Young Gun" (10-14-58) Michael Landon
4. "The Marshal" (10-21-58)
5. "The Brother-in-Law" (10-28-58) Jerome Courtland
6. "Eight Hours to Die" (11-4-58) George Macready
7. "Duel of Honor" (11-11-58) Cesare Danova, Jack Elam
8. "The Safe Guard" (11-18-58) Claude Akins, Marc Lawrence
9. "The Sister" (11-25-58) Sherry Jackson, Dan Blocker
10. "The Orleans Menace" (12-2-58) Akim Tamiroff
11. "The Apprentice Sheriff" (12-9-58) Robert Vaughn
12. [unknown title] (12-16-58)
13. "The Angry Gun" (12-23-58)
14. "The Gaucho" (12-30-58) Perry Lopez, Chana Eden, Lawrence Dobkin
15. "The Pet" (1-6-59) Robert J. Wilke
16. "The Sheridan Story" (1-13-59) Frank Wilcox, Bill Meigs, Lawrence Dobkin
17. "The Retired Gun" (1-20-59)
18. "The Photographer" (1-27-59) John Carradine
19. "Shivaree" (2-3-59) Luana Anders, Paul Carr, Morris Ankrum
20. "The Deadeye Kid" (2-10-59) Douglas Spencer, Kip King
21. "The Indian" (2-17-59) Michael Ansara
22. "The Boarding House" (2-24-59) Katy Jurado
23. "Second Witness" (3-3-59) Michael Pate, Hope Summers, Edgar Buchanan
24. "The Trade" (3-10-59) Paul Richards, Chris Alcaide, Katherine Bard
25. "One Went to Denver" (3-17-59) Richard Anderson, Jack Kruschen, John Goddard
26. "The Deadly Wait" (3-24-59) Lee Van Cleef
27. "The Wrong Man" (3-31-59) Lyle Bettger
28. "The Challenge" (4-7-59) Adam Williams, Les Tremayne
29. "The Hawk" (4-14-59) Patrick McVey, John Anderson
30. "Three-Legged Terror" (4-21-59) Dennis Hopper
31. "The Angry Man" (4-28-59) George Mathews, Edgar Buchanan

32. "The Woman" (5-5-59) Patricia Barry, Paul Carr, James Westerfield, Mel Carter
33. "The Money Gun" (5-12-59)
34. "A Matter of Faith" (5-19-59)
35. "Blood Brothers" (5-26-59) Rhys Williams, Ian Murray
36. "Stranger at Night" (6-2-59) Thomas Gomez
37. "The Raid" (6-9-59) Michael Ansara, Hope Summers, Robert Foulk, Pat Hogan, Michael Forest
38. "Outlaw's Inheritance" (6-16-59) William Bishop, Harlan Warde, Bartlett Robinson, Robert Foulk
39. "Boomerang" (6-23-59)
40. "The Mind Reader" (6-30-59)

## Second Season

41. "The Patsy" (9-29-59) Whit Bissell, Don Grady, John Anderson
42. "Bloodlines" (10-6-59) Buddy Hackett
43. "The Blowout" (10-13-59) John Dehner, John Milford, Hugh Sanders
44. "Obituary" (10-20-59) Alexander Scourby, Joanna Moore, Chris Alcaide
45. "Tension" (10-27-59)
46. "Eddie's Daughter" (11-3-59) Gloria De Haven
47. "Panic" (11-10-59) Dabbs Greer, Hope Summers
48. "Ordeal" (11-17-59)
49. "The Spiked Rifle" (11-24-59) Harlan Warde
50. "Letter of the Law" (12-1-59)
51. "The Legacy" (12-8-59) James Barton, James Franciscus
52. "The Baby Sitter" (12-15-59) Phyllis Avery, John Dehner
53. "The Coward" (12-22-59) John Milford, Carleton Carpenter
54. "Surveyors" (12-29-59) Harlan Warde, Mike Kellin
55. "Day of the Hunter" (1-5-60) John Anderson
56. "Mail Order Groom" (1-12-60) Peter Whitney, Sandy Kenyon, John Anderson
57. "A Case of Identity" (1-19-60) Royal Dano, Herbert Rudley
58. "The Visitors" (1-26-60) Christine White, June Vincent, Michael Pate, Wally Bennett
59. "Hero" (2-2-60) Robert Culp, Frank Ferguson
60. "The Horsetraders" (2-9-60)
61. "The Spoiler" (2-16-60) Skip Homeier
62. "Heller" (2-23-60) Gigi Perreau, Sid Gillman
63. "The Grasshopper" (3-1-60) Arthur Hunnicutt, Arthur Space, Richard Devon, Stuart Randall
64. "A Time for Singing" (3-8-60) Robert Knapp, Chris Alcaide
65. "The Deserter" (3-15-60) Ron Hagerthy, Robert Cornthwaite
66. "The Vision" (3-22-60) Marian Seldes, Milton Parsons
67. "The Lariat" (3-29-60) Harlan Warde, Bill Quinn, Richard Anderson
68. "Smoke Screen" (4-5-60) Jennifer Lea, Paul Carr, Douglas Kennedy
69. "Shotgun Man" (4-12-60) John Harmon, Jack Elam, John Anderson

70. "Sins of the Father" (4-19-60) George Wallace, Eugene Martin
71. "The Prodigal" (4-26-60) Josephine Hutchinson, Kevin Hagen
72. "The Fourflusher" (5-3-60) Whit Bissell, K. T. Stevens
73. "The Jailbird" (5-10-60) Dabbs Greer, Karl Swenson
74. "Meeting at Midnight" (5-17-60) Claude Akins, Frank De Kova, Marilyn Maxwell
75. "Nora" (5-24-60) Chad Morgan, Julie Adams, Michael Stefani
76. "The Hangman" (5-31-60) Whit Bissell, Michael Fox, Richard Deacon

Third Season

77. "Trail of Hate" (9-27-60) Harold J. Stone, Marc Lawrence
78. "Woman from Hog Ridge" (10-4-60) Bill Quinn, Dee J. Thompson
79. "Seven" (10-11-60)
80. "The Pitchman" (10-18-60) Bob Sweeney, John Milford, Danny Richards Jr.
81. "Strange Town" (10-25-60) Claude Akins
82. "Baranca" (11-1-60) Cesare Danova, John Milford
83. "The Martinet" (11-8-60) John Hoyt, Don Dubbins
84. "Miss Milly" (11-15-60) Warren Oates, Richard Devon
85. "Dead Cold Cash" (11-22-60) Sara Taft
86. "The Schoolmaster" (11-29-60) Arnold Moss, Pamela Cole, Jimmy Fields
87. "The Promoter" (12-6-60) Dabbs Greer, Danny Miller
88. "The Illustrator" (12-13-60)
89. "The Silent Knife" (12-20-60) Brad Weston, Richard Devon, Hope Summers
90. "Miss Bertie" (12-27-60) Agnes Moorehead, Bill Quinn, Richard Anderson, Glenn Strange
91. "Six Years and a Day" (1-3-61) James Gavin, Regina Gleason
92. "Flowers by the Door" (1-10-61) Pat Breslin
93. "Long Trek" (1-17-61) Lonny Chapman
94. "The Actress" (1-24-61) Diana Millay, Ralph Moody
95. "Face of Yesterday" (1-31-61) Ben Cooper, John Anderson
96. "Wyoming Story" [Part I] (2-7-61) Russell Thorson, Dabbs Greer, Chris Alcaide, Kent Taylor, Enid Janes
97. "Wyoming Story" [Part II] (2-14-61) as above
98. "Closer than a Brother" (2-21-61) Rex Ingram, Berry Kroeger
99. "The Lost Treasure of Canyon Town" (2-28-61) William Fawcett, Robert Foulk
100. "Dark Day at North Folk" (3-7-61) Ralph Moody, John Milford
101. "The Prisoner" (3-14-61) John Dehner, Bill Quinn, Adam Williams
102. "Assault" (3-21-61) Bob Sweeney, Linda Lawson, King Calder

103. "Short Rope for a Tall Man" (3-28-61) William Schallert, Bert Freed
104. "The Clarence Bibs Story" (4-4-61) Buddy Hackett, Denver Pyle, Lee Van Cleef, X Brands, John Milford
105. "The Score Is Even" (4-11-61) Adam Williams
106. "The Mescalero Curse" (4-18-61) Michael Pate, Ralph Moody
107. "Stopover" (4-25-61) Bethel Leslie, Adam West, Gordon Jones
108. "The Lonesome Bride" (5-2-61) Kay Kuter, Bill Quinn, Joan Shawlee
109. "Death Trap" (5-9-61) Philip Carey, James Drury, Gigi Perreau
110. "The Queue" (5-16-61) Peter Whitney, Victor Sen Yung

Fourth Season

111. "The Vaqueros" (10-2-61) Martin Landau, Than Wyenn, Ziva Rodann
112. "First Wages" (10-9-61) Ed Nelson
113. "Sheer Terror" (10-16-61) Harlan Warde, Charles Macauley
114. "The Stand In" (10-23-61) Dabbs Greer, Bert Taylor, Richard Devon, Charles Cooper
115. "The Journey Back" (10-30-61) John Anderson, John Milford, Mel Carter, Chris Alcaide
116. "The Decision" (11-6-61) Denver Pyle, Richard Kiel, Hampton Fancher, Kevin Hagen
117. "Knight Errant" (11-13-61) Jack Elam, Lawrence Dobkin
118. "Honest Abe" (11-20-61) Royal Dano
119. "The Long Goodbye" (11-27-61) Edgar Buchanan, Teddy Rooney
120. "The Shattered Idol" (12-4-61) Kevin McCarthy
121. "Long Gun from Tucson" (12-11-61) Peter Whitney
122. "The High Country" (12-18-61) James Coburn, Ellen Corby
123. "A Friend in Need" (12-25-61) Parley Baer
124. "Skull" (1-1-62) Lyle Bettger, John Alvin
125. "The Princess" (1-8-62) Annie Farge
126. "Gunfire" (1-15-62) Lon Chaney Jr.
127. "The Quiet Fear" (1-22-62) Patrick McVey, Enid Janes
128. "Sporting Chance" (1-29-62) Arthur Malet
129. "A Young Man's Fancy" (2-5-62) Cheryl Holdridge
130. "The Man from Salinas" (2-12-62) Robert Culp, Jack Hogan
131. "Two Ounces of Tin" (2-19-62) Sammy Davis Jr.
132. "Deadly Image" (2-26-62) Leonard Stone, Bill Quinn, Robert Bice, Troy Melton
133. "The Debut" (3-5-62) Keith Andes
134. "The Tin Horn" (3-12-62) Grant Richards, Grace Lee Whitney
135. "None So Blind" (3-19-62) Cliff Osmond, Jeff York
136. "Jealous Man" (3-26-62) Mort Mills, Diana Brewster
137. "Guilty Conscience" (4-2-62) Lee Patrick, Tommy Nolan, Argentina Brunetti

138. "Day of Reckoning" (4-9-62) Warren Oates, Royal Dano
139. "The Day a Town Slept" (4-16-62) James Best, Lawrence Dobkin
140. "Milly's Brother" (4-23-62) Richard Anderson
141. "Outlaw Shoes" (4-30-62) Michael Green, Tom Gilson, Mel Carter, Roy Barcroft
142. "The Executioner" (5-7-62) Adam Williams, Michael Pate

Fifth Season

143. "The Wanted Man" (9-25-62) Dick Foran
144. "Waste" [Part I] (10-1-62) Vito Scotti, Tony Rose, Pepe Hern, Robert Culp
145. "Waste" [Part II] (10-8-62) as above
146. "Lou Mallory" (10-15-62)
147. "Quiet Night, Deadly Night" (10-22-62) Carol Leigh, Ed Ames
148. "Death Never Rides Alone" (10-29-62) Lee Van Cleef, Rex Holman
149. "I Take This Woman" (11-5-62) Sean McClory
150. "The Assailants" (11-12-62) John Milford, Steven Marlo
151. "Mark's Rifle" (11-19-62) Mark Goddard
152. "The Most Amazing Man" (11-26-62) Sammy Davis Jr., Richard Devon
153. "Squeeze Play" (12-3-62) Gerald Mohr
154. "Gun Shy" (12-10-62) Peter Whitney, Pat Golden
155. "The Anvil Chorus" (12-17-62) Joe Higgins
156. "Conflict" (12-24-62) Rhodes Reason
157. "Incident at Line Shack Six" (1-7-63) John Anderson, Ray Kellogg
158. "Suspicion" (1-14-63) Kevin McCarthy
159. "The Sidewinder" (1-21-63) Billy Hughes
160. "The Sixteenth Cousin" (1-28-63) Vito Scotti
161. "Hostages to Fortune" (2-4-63) Tony Haig
162. "And the Devil Makes Five" (2-11-63)
163. "End of the Hunt" (2-18-63) Jeff Morrow
164. "The Bullet" (2-25-63) Harold J. Stone, Asa Maynor, Richard Anderson
165. [unknown title] (3-4-63) George Lindsey, Dal Jenkins
166. "The Guest" (3-11-63) Cesare Danova
167. "Which Way'd They Go?" (4-1-63) Vito Scotti
168. "Old Tony" (4-8-63) Stefan Schabel

77 SUNSET STRIP

Producer Roy Huggins ingratiated a generation of American youth with this trend-setter, inspired by his own novel The Double Take (New York: William Morrow & Co., 1946). The plot concerns a private detective agency of two (Efrem Zimbalist Jr. as the urbane Stuart Bailey; Roger Smith as Bailey's piquant younger colleague Jeff Spencer) and their frequently eccentric clientele.

Edward Byrnes made a lasting impression as the parking lot attendant for the mythical "77 Sunset Strip"--the role of "Kookie," who stylishly ran a readily accessible comb through his hair. Byrnes, incidentally, was a villain in the initial teleplay by Marion Hargrove. This pilot was subsequently released as the feature film Girl on the Run (1958).

Certainly the most unusual of the teleplays was that composed and directed by Roger Smith, The Silent Caper, a mystery without a single line of dialogue.

Other regulars were Jacqueline Beer as the agency secretary Suzanne Fabry, Louis Quinn as the perpetual gambler "Roscoe," and, joining in the detective work in later seasons, Richard Long as Rex Randolph and Robert Logan as J. R. Hale.

Mack David composed the theme lyrics, replete with fingersnaps.

The Regulars: Stuart Bailey, Efrem Zimbalist Jr.; Jeff Spencer, Roger Smith; Kookie, Edward Byrnes; Suzanne, Jacqueline Beer; Roscoe, Louis Quinn; Rex Randolph (with the 1960 season), Richard Long; J. R. Hale (with 10/13/61), Robert Logan.

The Episodes:

1. "Girl on the Run" [ninety minute pilot episode released as a telefeature] (10-10-58) Shepperd Strudwick, Erin O'Brien, Ray Teal, Barton MacLane
2. "Lovely Lady, Pity Me" (10-17-58) Kathleen Crowley, Peter Breck, Jeanne Cooper
3. "A Nice, Social Evening" (10-24-58) Ray Danton
4. "Casualty" (10-31-58) Dolores Donlon
5. "The Bouncing Chip" (11-7-58) Brad Dexter, Ruta Lee, Ray Teal, Russ Conway
6. "Two and Two Make Six" (11-14-58) Karl Swenson, Adam West
7. "All Our Yesterdays" (11-21-58) Francis X. Bushman, Doris Kenyon, John Carradine, Merry Anders
8. "A Well-Selected Frame" (11-28-58) Peggie Castle
9. "The Iron Curtain Caper" (12-5-58)
10. "Vicious Circle" (12-12-58) Bert Convy
11. "One False Step" (12-19-58) Richard Long, Connie Stevens, Edward Kemmer
12. [unknown title] (12-26-58) Bruce Bennett
13. "Hit and Run" (1-2-59) Robert H. Harris
14. "Not an Enemy in the World" (1-9-59) Carole Mathews, Phil Terry
15. "The Secret of Adam Cain" (1-16-59) David Frankham, Berry Kroeger
16. "The Girl Who Couldn't Remember" (1-23-59) Nancy Gates, John Vivyan

17. "Dark Vengeance" (1-30-59) Jerome Thor
18. "Conspiracy of Silence" (2-6-59) Patricia Crowley, Gerald Mohr
19. "Eye Witness" (2-13-59) Robert Douglas, Jay North, Patricia Barry
20. "Lovely Alibi" (2-20-59) Steve Brodie, Claude Akins, Andra Martin
21. "In Memoriam" (2-27-59) Alan Marshal, Joe De Santis
22. "The Fifth Stair" (3-6-59) Julie Adams, Richard Long
23. "Pasadena Caper" (3-13-59) Elizabeth Patterson, Hallene Hill
24. "Hong Kong Caper" (3-20-59) Neil Hamilton, Karen Steele, Frank Wilcox
25. "A Check Will Do Nicely" (3-27-59) Janet Lake, Robin Hughes
26. "The Grandma Caper" (4-3-59) Frances Bavier, Jerome Cowan
27. "Honey from the Bee" (4-10-59) Connie Stevens, Jay Novello, Celia Lovsky
28. "Abra-Cadaver" (4-17-59) Fay Spain
29. "A Bargain in Tombs" (4-24-59) Ray Danton, Linda Watkins, Louise Fletcher
30. "The Widow Wouldn't Weep" (5-1-59) Valerie Allen, Raymond Bailey
31. "Downbeat" (5-8-59) James Garner (with guest appearance by Hollywood reporter James Bacon), Dorothy Provine
32. "The Canine Caper" (5-15-59) Julie Adams, Roxanne Berard
33. "Mr. Paradise" (5-22-59)
34. "Strange Girl in Town" (5-29-59) Jack Mulhall

Second Season

35. "Only Zeroes Count" (10-2-59) Robert Conrad, Poncie Ponce
36. "The Kookie Caper" (10-9-59) Will Hutchins, Sherry Jackson
37. "Six Superior Skirts" (10-16-59) Abraham Sofaer (with appearances by the Mary Kaye Trio and the Frankie Ortego group)
38. "Clay Pigeon" (10-23-59) Paula Raymond, Dan Tobin
39. "Thanks for Tomorrow" (10-30-59) Brad Dexter, Adam West
40. "Sing Something Simple" (11-6-59) Linda Darnell
41. "Treehouse Caper" (11-13-59) Tom Drake, Donald Barry, Bunny Cooper
42. "Out of the Past" (11-20-59)
43. "The Widow and the Web" (11-27-59)
44. "Secret Island" (12-4-59) Jacques Bergerac, Kathleen Crowley, Tuesday Weld, Catherine McLeod
45. "Texas Doll" (12-11-59) Sherry Jackson
46. "Vacation with Pay" (12-18-59) Herbert Rudley
47. "The Juke-Box Caper" (12-25-59) Ted de Corsia
48. "Created He Them" (1-1-60) Adele Mara, Jean Byron
49. "Collector's Item" (1-8-60) Marie Windsor, Jim Backus
50. "Switchburg" (1-15-60) Dolores Donlon, Jean Allison

51. "The One That Got Away" (1-22-60) Whitney Blake, Lisa Montell
52. "Ten Cents a Dance" (1-29-60) Bea Benaderet, Linda Lawson, Tony George
53. "Who Killed Cock Robin?" (2-5-60) Robert Conrad, Jacques Aubuchon, Fay Wray
54. "Condor's Lair" (2-12-60) Troy Donahue, Tuesday Weld
55. "The Starlet" (2-26-60) Diane McBain, Jean Blake
56. "Safari" (3-4-60) Julie Adams, Arch Johnson
57. "Blackout" (3-11-60) Warren Oates, Donald May, Rex Reason
58. "Return to San Dede: The Desert Story" [Part I] (3-18-60) Andra Martin, Luis Van Rooten, Rodolfo Hoyos
59. "Return to San Dede: The Capital City" [Part II] (3-25-60) as above
60. "Publicity Brat" (4-1-60) Evelyn Rudie, Billie Burke
61. "The Fix" (4-8-60) Mary Tyler Moore, Rhodes Reason
62. "Legend of the Crystal Dart" (4-15-60) Marilyn Maxwell, William Schallert, Kurt Kreuger
63. "Stranger than Fiction" (4-22-60) John Howard, Suzanne Lloyd
64. "Genesis of Treason" (4-29-60) Dianne Foster, Donald May
65. "Fraternity of Fear" (5-6-60) Shirley Knight, Gary Vinson
66. "Spark of Freedom" (5-13-60) Anna-Lisa, Marcel Dalio
67. "Perfect Set-Up" (5-20-60) Anthony Eisley, Connie Stevens, Poncie Ponce, Warren Stevens
68. "Sierra" (5-27-60) Horace MacMahon
69. "The Silent Caper" (6-3-60) Ann Duncan, Dale Van Sickel
70. "Family Skeleton" (6-10-60) Suzanne Storrs, Walter Reed

Third Season

71. "The Attic" (9-16-60) Lee Van Cleef
72. "The Fanatics" (9-23-60) Tristram Coffin, Margaret Thomas
73. "The President's Daughter" (9-30-60) Jacqueline Ravell, George Tobias
74. "The Office Caper" (10-7-60) Sherry Jackson, Richard Jaeckel
75. "The Wide Screen Caper" (10-14-60) James Milhollin
76. "The Negotiable Blonde" (10-21-60) Karen Steele, Jay Novello, Rhodes Reason
77. "The Laurel Canyon Caper" (10-28-60) Jock Mahoney, Kaye Elhardt
78. "Double Trouble" (11-4-60) Bruce Cabot
79. "Trouble in the Middle East" (11-11-60) Sherry Jackson
80. "The Duncan Shrine" (11-18-60) Marjorie Bennett, Donald Woods
81. "The Double Death of Benjamin Markham" (11-25-60) Walter Burke, Eddie Forster
82. "Antwerp Caper" (12-2-60) Karen Steele, John Van Dreelen
83. "The Affairs of Adam Gallante" (12-9-60) Alvy Moore, Sue Randall, Carmen Phillips
84. "The Valley Caper" (12-16-60) Kathleen Crowley

85. "The Dresden Doll" (12-23-60) Myrna Fahey, H. M. Wynant, Raymond Bailey
86. "The Rice Estate" (12-30-60) Peggy McCay, Gary Conway
87. "The Hamlet Caper" (1-6-61) Andrew Duggan, Faith Domergue, Nina Shipman
88. "The Man in the Mirror" (1-13-61) Karl Swenson, Robert Colbert, Tristram Coffin
89. "The College Caper" (1-20-61) Chad Everett, Alan Baxter
90. "The Positive Negative" (1-27-61) John Conte, Leslie Parrish, Kurt Kreuger
91. "The Corsican Caper" (2-3-61) Max Baer, Byron Keith
92. "Once Upon a Caper" (2-10-61) John Hubbard, Joan Staley, Byron Keith
93. "Strange Bedfellows" (2-17-61) Ty Hardin, Kathleen Crowley
94. "A Face in the Window" (2-24-61) Paula Raymond, Peter Breck, Merry Anders
95. "Tiger by the Tail" (3-3-61) Roger Moore (as himself), Merry Anders (as herself), John Van Dreelen
96. "The Space Caper" (3-10-61) Arthur Franz, Coleen Gray
97. "Open and Close in One" (3-17-61) Julie Adams, Buddy Ebsen, Joel Grey
98. "The Legend of Leckonby" (3-24-61) Rochelle Hudson, Richard Carlyle, Jean Allison
99. "Old Card Sharps Never Die" (3-31-61) Lisa Gaye, Robert Colbert, Robert Lowery
100. "Vamp Till Ready" (4-7-61) Bert Convy, Janet Lake, John Van Dreelen
101. "Common Denominator" (4-14-61) Philip Terry, Connie Davis
102. "The Six Out of Eight Caper" (4-21-61) Robert Hutton, Patrice Wymore
103. "The Celluloid Cowboy" (4-28-61) Andrew Duggan, Peggy McCay, Donna Douglas, Kent Taylor
104. "The Eyes of Love" (5-5-61) John Conte
105. "Designing Eye" (5-12-61) Rebecca Welles, Robert H. Harris
106. "Caper in E Flat" (5-19-61) Cloris Leachman
107. "The Hot Tamale Caper" [Part I] (5-26-61) Troy Donahue, Joe De Santis, Donna Martell, Carlos Romero
108. "The Hot Tamale Caper" [Part II] (6-2-61) as above

Fourth Season

109. "The Rival Eye Caper" (9-22-61) Chad Everett, Virginia Gregg
110. "The Desert Spa Caper" (9-29-61) Kathleen Crowley, Lisa Gaye
111. "The Man in the Crowd" (10-6-61) Robert Colbert, Tim Graham
112. "The Inverness Cape Caper" (10-13-61) Jay Novello, Elisha Cook
113. "The Lady Has the Answers" (10-20-61) Merry Anders,

Linda Watkins, Nina Shipman, Tom Brown, Charles Herbert
114. "The Unremembered" (10-27-61) John Dehner, Tristram Coffin
115. "Big Boy Blue" (11-3-61) Biff Elliot
116. "The Cold-Cash Caper" (11-10-61) Mikki Jamison, Mari Blanchard
117. "The Missing Daddy Caper" (11-17-61) Bernie Fein, Grace Lee Whitney, Bob Hogan
118. "The Turning Point" (11-24-61) David Winters, Kathie Browne
119. "The Deadly Solo" (12-1-61) Lee Philips, Kaye Elhardt
120. "Reserved for Mr. Bailey" (12-8-61)
121. "The Navy Caper" (12-15-61) Ellen McRae, Simon Scott
122. "Bullets for Santa" (12-22-61) Victor Buono, Gerald Mohr, Marilyn Maxwell, Yvonne Craig
123. "The Chrome Coffin" (12-29-61) Charles Robinson, Vaughn Taylor, Max Baer
124. "The Down Under Caper" [scripted by Roger Smith] (1-5-62) Victoria Shaw
125. "Mr. Bailey's Honeymoon" (1-12-62) William Windom, Elizabeth MacRae
126. "Penthouse on Skid Row" (1-19-62)
127. "The Diplomatic Caper" (1-26-62) Chad Everett, Carolyn Craig
128. "The Bridal Trail Caper" (2-2-62) Dyan Cannon, Jack Cassidy
129. "Brass Ring Caper" (2-9-62) Joan Tabor, Simon Scott
130. "The Bell Air Hermit" (2-16-62) Jackie Russell, Wynn Pearce
131. "The Parallel Caper" (2-23-62) Allison Hayes, Danielle de Metz
132. "Twice Dead" (3-2-62) Margaret Hayes, Sharon Hugueny
133. "Jennifer" (3-9-62) Claire Griswold, Donald Woods
134. "Baker Street Caper" (3-16-62) Andrew Duggan
135. "The Long Shot Caper" (3-23-62) James Best, Christine Nelson
136. "Violence for Your Furs" (3-30-62) Philip Carey, Mala Powers
137. "The Pet Shop Caper" (4-6-62) Michael Pate
138. "The Steerer" (4-13-62) Pamela Austin
139. "Ghost of a Memory" (4-20-62) Kathie Browne, Chick Chandler, Jennifer West
140. "The Disappearance" (4-27-62) John Litel, John Dehner
141. "The Lovely American" (5-4-62) Lisa Gaye, Renzo Cesana
142. "The Gemologist Caper" (5-11-62) Joanna Moore, Marcel Hillaire
143. "Flight from Escondido" (5-18-62) Philip Carey, Joe De Santis
144. "Dress Rehearsal" (5-25-62) Diane Jergens, Natalie Schafer
145. "Framework for a Badge" (6-1-62) Richard Devon, Irene Hervey, Tom Drake

146. "Pattern for a Bomb" (6-8-62) Larry Ward, Frank de Kova
147. "Upbeat" (6-15-62) Andrew Duggan, Dorothy Provine, John Van Dreelen
148. "Nightmare" (6-22-62) Peter Breck, Anna-Lisa
149. "The Gang's All Here" (6-29-62) Sammy Davis Jr., Peter Brown, Dick Foran

Fifth Season

150. "The Reluctant Spy" (10-12-62) Randy Stuart, Ned Glass
151. "Leap, My Lovely" (10-19-62) Neil Hamilton
152. "Terror in a Small Town" (10-26-62) Warren Oates, Frank Ferguson, Kevin Hagen, Don O'Kelly
153. "The Raiders" (11-2-62) Lee Bowman, Kathie Browne
154. "The Floating Man" (11-9-62) Henry Daniell, Coleen Gray
155. "The Catspaw Caper" (11-16-62) Valerie Varda, Charles H. Radilao
156. "Wolf! Cried the Blonde" (11-23-62) Jo Morrow
157. "The Dark Wood" (11-30-62) Diane Brewster, Dennis James
158. "Shadow on Your Shoulder" (12-7-62) Cloris Leachman
159. "Adventure in San Dede" (12-14-62) Joe De Santis
160. "The Odds on Odette" (12-21-62) Henry Daniell
161. "The Snow Job Caper" (12-28-62) Bill Williams
162. "Falling Stars" (1-4-63) Paul Winchell, Jerry Paris
163. "The Tarnished Idol" (1-11-63) Van Williams, Dana Howard
164. "Scream Softly, Dear" (1-18-63) Elinor Donahue
165. "Terror in Silence" (1-25-63) Strother Martin
166. "Crashout" (2-1-63) Michael Parks
167. "The Night Was Six Years Long" (2-8-63) Myrna Fahey, Philip Carey
168. "Six Feet Under" (2-15-63) Karen Sharpe, Malachi Throne
169. "Escape to Freedom" (2-22-63) Ursula Theiss, Werner Klemperer
170. "Dial S for Spencer" (3-1-63) Tom Drake
171. "Nine to Five" (3-8-63) Diane McBain, Maggie Pierce
172. "Stranger from the Sea" (3-15-63) Robert J. Wilke, Mako
173. "The Man Who Wasn't There" (3-22-63) Don Dubbins, Grace Raynor
174. "Flight 307" (3-29-63) Philip Carey, Gena Rowlands
175. "Target Island" (4-5-63) Jenny Maxwell
176. "Reunion at Balboa" (4-12-63) Arthur Franz, John Dehner, Walter Slezak, Karen Sharpe, Robert Strauss
177. "Walk Among Tigers" (4-19-63) Allen Jones, Warren Stevens, Kaye Elhardt
178. "The Left Field Caper" (4-26-63) Ed Nelson, Diane Ladd, Bo Belinsky, Ronnie Dapo
179. "The Heartbeat Caper" (5-3-63) Carl Reindell
180. "To Catch a Mink" (5-10-63) Dianne Foster, Robert Armstrong
181. "Lady in the Sun" (5-17-63) Karen Sharpe
182. "Our Man in Switzerland" (5-24-63) Kurt Kreuger, Albert Paulsen

183. "Your Fortune for a Penny" (5-31-63) Robert Vaughn,
Susan Oliver
184. "The Checkmate Caper" (6-7-63) William Windom, Nancy
Kulp
185. "Never to Have Loved" (6-14-63) Albert Paulsen, Philip
Abbott


77 SUNSET STRIP (new format)

All that remained of the original series in the fall of 1963
was its title and Stuart Bailey, now searching for a lost heir.

The Regulars: Stuart Bailey, Efrem Zimbalist Jr.

The Episodes:

1. "5" [Part I] (9-20-63) Burgess Meredith, Keenan Wynn,
Joseph Schildkraut, Peter Lorre, Herbert Marshall,
Wally Cox, Richard Conte, William Shatner, Walter Sle-
zak, Ed Wynn
2. "5" [Part II] (9-27-63) Burgess Meredith, Keenan Wynn,
Joseph Schildkraut, Wally Cox, Richard Conte, William
Shatner, Walter Slezak, Victor Buono, George Jessel,
Clint Walker, Diane McBain, Gene Nelson
3. "5" [Part III] (10-4-63) Burgess Meredith, Keenan Wynn,
Joseph Schildkraut, Richard Conte, William Shatner,
Walter Slezak, Gene Nelson, Lloyd Nolan, Luther Adler
4. "5" [Part IV] (10-11-63) Burgess Meredith, Richard Conte,
Walter Slezak, Lloyd Nolan, Cesar Romero, Jacques
Bergerac, Telly Savalas, Marisa Pavan, Tony Bennett
5. "5" [Part V] (10-18-63) Burgess Meredith, Richard Conte,
Walter Slezak, Clint Walker, Gene Nelson, Lloyd Nolan,
Brian Keith, Charles Radilac, Lawrence Mann
6. "White Lie" (10-25-63) Elizabeth Montgomery, Gene Evans,
Kim Hamilton
7. "88 Bars" (11-1-63) Cloris Leachman, Joanna Barnes,
Bobby Troup, DeForest Kelley
8. "Don't Wait for Me" (11-8-63) Jo Van Fleet, Brenda Scott,
Philip Pine, Joe De Santis, Gus Trikonis
9. "By His Own Verdict" (11-15-63) Nick Adams, Joseph
Cotten, Barbara Bain, Karl Swenson
10. "Deposit with Caution" (11-29-63) Harold J. Stone, Nancy
Malone, Virginia Gregg
11. "The Toy Jungle" (12-6-63) Patricia Crowley, Russell
Johnson
12. "The Fumble" (12-13-63) Richard Long, Gail Kobe, Sue
Ane Langdon, Robert F. Simon
13. "Bonus Baby" (12-20-63) Simon Oakland, Frank de Kova,
Michael Constantine, James Farentino
14. "Paper Chase" (12-27-63) Elena Verdugo, Lisa Gaye,
David White

15. "Lover's Lane" (1-3-64) Charles McGraw, Bruce Dern, Beverly Washburn, Preston Foster
16. "Alimony League" (1-10-64) Julie Adams, Diana Millay, Kathie Browne, Lloyd Corrigan
17. "Not Such a Simple Knot" (1-17-64) Dan Tobin, Ruta Lee
18. "The Target" (1-24-64) Keith Andes, Jeanne Cooper, Les Tremayne
19. "Dead as in Dude" (1-31-64) Reginald Gardiner
20. "Queen of the Cats" (2-7-64) Jean Engstrom, Virginia Gregg, Parley Baer, Steve Ihnat


THE LORETTA YOUNG SHOW

The Regulars: Loretta Young, hostess.

The Episodes (chronicled from January 1959):

1. "The Break-off" (1-4-59) Ralph Meeker
2. "Sister Ann" (1-11-59) Loretta Young, Claude Akins, Hope Summers
3. "This Is the Moment" (1-18-59) James Daly, Chris White
4. "Incident in India" (1-25-59) Loretta Young, Richard Devon
5. "Seed from the East" (2-1-59) Virginia Christine, Dean Jagger
6. "The Black Lace Valentine" (2-8-59) Loretta Young, Joe Maross
7. "Marriage Crisis" (2-15-59) Elizabeth Montgomery, Jack Lord
8. "The Portrait" (2-22-59) Loretta Young, Richard Garland, George Macready
9. "810 Franklin Street" (3-1-59) Royal Dano, Jackie Coogan
10. "The Prettiest Girl in Town" (3-8-59) Loretta Young, James Philbrook
11. "The Tenderizer" (3-22-59) Loretta Young, Joe Maross
12. "Each Man's Island" (3-29-59) Ricardo Montalban, Don Beddoe, Chris White
13. "Mr. Wilson's Wife" [Part I] (4-5-59) Joseph Wiseman, Loretta Young, Claude Akins
14. "Mr. Wilson's Wife" [Part II] (4-12-59) as above
15. "Strictly Personal" (4-19-59) Steve Cochran, Whitney Blake
16. "Accused" (4-26-59) Loretta Young, Ann Doran, Dabbs Greer
17. "Trouble in Fenton Valley" (5-10-59) Claude Akins

Eighth Season

18. "The Road" (9-20-59) Loretta Young, Joseph Cuby
19. "One Beautiful Moment" (9-27-59) Loretta Young, Barry Atwater
20. "The Strangers that Came to Town" (10-4-59) John Beal, David Duval

21. "Mask of Violence" (10-11-59) Loretta Young, Barry Atwater
22. "Circles of Panic" (10-25-59) Frank Lovejoy, Dick Wilson
23. "The Red Dress" (11-1-59) Nina Foch, Dabbs Greer
24. "A New Step" (11-8-59) Elizabeth Fielding, Loretta Young
25. [unknown title] (11-15-59)
26. "Lady in the Fish Bowl" (11-22-59) Loretta Young, Jeffrey Stone
27. "Vengeance Is Thine" (11-29-59) Marshall Thompson
28. "The Penthouse" (12-6-59) Loretta Young, Elliott Reid
29. "Alien Love" (12-13-59) Loretta Young, Walter Slezak
30. "Christmas Stopover" (12-20-59) Loretta Young, John Larch, Bobby Clark
31. "Shower of Ashes" (12-27-59) Everett Sloane, Eduard Franz
32. "The Grenade" (1-3-60) John Ericson, Dabbs Greer
33. "Little Mister Tall Tales" (1-10-60) Clement Brace, Charles Herbert
34. "Off-Duty Affair" (1-17-60) Marshall Thompson, Chris White
35. "Mrs. Minton" (1-24-60) Loretta Young, Henry Brandon
36. "The Hired Hand" (2-7-60) Ricardo Montalban, William Fawcett, Chris White
37. "Slight Delay" (2-14-60) Skip Homeier, Mary Young
38. "Second Spring" (2-21-60) Loretta Young, Don Haggerty
38a. "A Greater Strength" [repeat of episode of 2/23/58] (2-28-60) Loretta Young, Mae Clark
39. "Crisis in 114" (3-6-60) Everett Sloane, Bill Tennant, Don Haggerty
40. "The Trouble with Laury's Men" (3-13-60) Loretta Young, Julie Sommars
41. "The Trial" (3-20-60) Regis Toomey, Mary Monday
42. "Plain, Unmarked Envelope" (4-3-60) Don DeFore, Bethel Leslie
43. "The Best Season" (4-17-60) Richard Carlson, June Vincent
44. "The Unwanted" (5-1-60) Anna Lee, Robert Bray
45. "Faith, Hope, and Mr. Flaherty" (5-8-60) Loretta Young, Virginia Christine
46. "Eternal Vow" [Part I] (5-15-60) Loretta Young, Jean Pierre Aumont
47. "Eternal Vow" [Part II] (5-22-60) as above
48. "The Misfit" (6-5-60) Everett Sloane, Henry Jones, Patricia Donahue

Ninth Season

49. "The Long Night" (9-18-60) Loretta Young, Robert Richards
50. "At the Edge of the Desert" (9-25-60) Ricardo Montalban, Patricia Donahue
51. "Fair Exchange" (10-2-60) Loretta Young, Ruth Brady
52. "Linda" (10-9-60) Karen Sharpe, Jack Ging, James Drury
53. "Switchblade" (10-16-60) Everett Sloane (narrator), James Barton, Bill Tennant
54. "Love Between the Acts" (10-23-60) Loretta Young, Isobel Elson, James Philbrook
55. "The Glass Cage" (10-30-60) Audrey Totter, Bill Tennant, Charlotte Stewart

56. "The Seducer" (11-6-60) Loretta Young, John Newland, Marlene Willis, Peter Leeds, Jack Lester, Kitty Kelly
57. "No Margin for Error" (11-13-60) Ricardo Montalban, Henry Hunter, Olan Soule, Marion Ross
58. "Unconditional Surrender" (11-20-60) Loretta Young, John Newland
59. "The Night the Doorbell Rang" (11-27-60) Ruth Storey, Charles Korvin
60. "These Few Years" (12-11-60) Loretta Young, Preston Hanson
61. "My Own Master" (12-18-60) Cloris Leachman, Billy Mumy, Mark Roberts
62. "Enter at Your Own Risk" (1-8-61) Ralph Meeker, Merry Anders, Ross Elliott, Charles Steel
63. "The Subtle Danger" (1-15-61) Richard Coogan, Loretta Young, Barney Phillips
64. "The Lie" (1-22-61) Loretta Young, Lucy Prentis, Marlene De Lamater
65. "Quiet Desperation" (2-5-61) Loretta Young, Byron Morrow, H. M. Wynant, Michael Burns
66. "The Golden Cord" (2-12-61) Darryl Hickman, Vito Scotti, Frank Puglia, Joe Abdulloh
67. "Double Edge" (2-19-61) Larry Blyden, Jean Howell, Frank Jenks
68. "The Choice" (2-26-61) Loretta Young, Richard Ney, George Nader, Jean Gillespie
69. "When Queens Ride By" (3-12-61) Lois Smith, June Vincent, John Milford, Charles Seel
70. "The Preliminaries" (3-19-61) James Drury, George Macready, Katherine Squire, Lory Patrick
71. "Woodlot" (3-26-61) Charles Bronson, Ellen McRae, Ted Stanhope, John Clarke
72. "Doesn't Everybody?" (4-2-61) Loretta Young, Mary Adams, James Philbrook, Peter Forster
73. "The Man Who Couldn't Smile" (4-9-61) Ricardo Montalban, Rico Alaniz, Alma Beltran
74. "Emergency in 114" (4-23-61) Loretta Young, Alf Kjellin, Ted De Corsia, Larry Adare
75. "13 Donner Street" (4-30-61) Larry Blyden, Johnny Seven, Barney Phillips, Jean Howell
76. "Those at the Top" (5-7-61) James Gregory, Nestor Paiva, Addison Richards, Catherine MacLeod, Scott Wells
77. "The Wedding" (5-21-61) Cloris Leachman, Harry Townes, Linda Watkins, Gertrude Flynn, Camille Franklin
78. "The Forbidden Guests" (5-28-61) Loretta Young, Candy Moore, Steve Hammer, Richard Garland


TALES OF WELLS FARGO

It was inevitable that the stage routes and an agent (Dale Robertson as Jim Hardie) would have their legends told; this western expanded to a full hour in 1961.

The Regulars: Jim Hardie, Dale Robertson.

The Episodes (chronicled from January, 1959):

1. "Showdown Trail" (1-5-59) Will Wright
2. "Wild Cargo" (1-19-59) Adele Mara
3. "The Cleanup" (1-26-59) James Bell
4. "Fort Massacre" (2-2-59)
5. "The Town That Wouldn't Talk" (2-9-59) Linda Leighton
6. "Lola Montez" (2-16-59) Rita Moreno
7. "The Branding Iron" (2-23-59) Ann Rutherford, Willard Sage
8. "The House I Enter" (3-2-59) Michael Hinn, Alan Baxter
9. "The Legacy" (3-9-59) William Joyce, Sandra Knight
10. "The Rawhide Kid" (3-16-59) Troy Donahue
11. "Toll Road" (3-23-59) Frank Ferguson, Will White
12. "The Tired Gun" (3-30-59) Jeanette Nolan, Morgan Woodward
13. "Terry" (4-6-59) Steven Ritch, Judi Meredith, Trevor Bardette
14. "The Last Stand" (4-13-59) Eddy Walker, John Harmon
15. "Bob Dawson" (4-20-59) Edgar Buchanan
16. "The Tall Texan" (4-27-59)
17. "Doc Holliday" (5-4-59) Martin Landau, Whitney Blake
18. "Kid Curry" (5-11-59) Phillip Pine
19. "Little Man" (5-18-59)
20. "The Daltons" (5-25-59)
21. "The Bounty Hunter" (6-1-59)
22. "Clay Allison" (6-15-59) Warren Stevens

Fourth Season

23. "Young Jim Hardie" (9-7-59) Walter Sande, John Dehner, Vito Scotti
24. "Desert Showdown" (9-14-59) Gregory Walcott
25. "The Warrior's Return" (9-21-59) Don McGowan
26. "The Stage Line" (9-28-59) Carolyn Craig, James Franciscus
27. "Long Odds" (10-5-59) Mary La Roche, Russ Conway
28. "The Train Robbery" (10-12-59) Jeanne Bates, John Doucette
29. "Double Reverse" (10-19-59) Denver Pyle, Judith Evelyn
30. "Tom Horn" (10-26-59) Les Johnson
31. "The Quiet Village" (11-2-59) Katherine Squire, Tom Laughlin
32. "Home Town" (11-16-59)
33. "End of a Legend" (11-23-59) Philip Coolidge, John Larch
34. "Return of Doc Bell" (11-30-59) Edward C. Platt
35. "Woman with a Gun" (12-7-59)
36. "Long Odds" (12-14-59)
37. "Wanted: Jim Hardie" (12-21-59) Beverly Tyler
38. "Relay Station" (12-28-59) Lori Nelson, Wynn Pearce
39. "Cole Younger" (1-4-60) Royal Dano

40.  "The Easterner" (1-11-60) Gerald Mohr, Joanna Moore
41.  "The Governor's Visit" (1-18-60) Wendell Holmes, Tom McKee
42.  "The Journey" (1-25-60)
43.  "The Canyon" (2-1-60) Bruce Gordon, Jean Ingram
44.  "Red Ransom" (2-8-60)
45.  "The English Woman" (2-15-60)
46.  "Forty-Four Forty" (2-29-60)
47.  "The Late Mayor Brown" (3-7-60) Gail Kobe
48.  "Black Trail" (3-14-60) Diane Foster
49.  "The Great Bullion Robbery" (3-21-60) Edward Kemmer, Joyce Taylor
50.  "The Outlaw's Wife" (3-28-60) Bob Strong, Cassie Case
51.  "The Town" (4-4-60) Mary Webster, Rhys Williams
52.  "The Trading Post" (4-11-60) Mort Mills
53.  "Dead Man's Street" (4-18-60) Barney Phillips, Buddy Ebsen, Wallace Ford, Robert Bray
54.  "Threat of Death" (4-25-60) Robert Middleton, William Campbell
55.  "Dealer's Choice" (5-2-60) Patricia Barry, Robert Lowery
56.  "Pearl Hart" (5-9-60) Beverly Garland, Michael Pate
57.  "Vasquez" (5-16-60) Cesare Danova, Barbara Luna, Rodolfo Hoyos
58.  "Kid Brother" (5-23-60) Larry Pennell, Lucy Marlow
59.  "Man for the Job" (5-30-60) Harold J. Stone, Ken Lynch

Fifth Season

60.  "Day of Judgment" (9-5-60) John Dehner, John Lupton, Doris Dowling
61.  "Doc Dawson" (9-19-60) Edgar Buchanan
62.  "The Kinfolk" (9-26-60) Richard Jaeckel, Dan Riss, Logan Field
63.  "All That Glitters" (10-24-60) Ken Lynch, Barbara Stuart, Ron Harper
64.  "Run for the River" (11-7-60) Ron Hayes, John Damier
65.  "Leading Citizen" (11-14-60) Wesley Lau, Robert Middleton, Robert Carricart
66.  "The Killing of Johnny Lash" (11-21-60)
67.  "The Wade Place" (11-28-60) Robert J. Wilke, Vaughn Taylor, Russell Thorson
68.  "Jeff Davis' Treasure" (12-5-60) John Dehner, John McLiam
69.  "The Bride and the Bandit" (12-12-60) Jan Clayton, Dabbs Greer
70.  "Escort to Santa Fe" (12-19-60) Gregory Walcott, Alex Montoya, Linda Lawson
71.  "Frightened Witness" (12-26-60) John Milford, Michael Burns
72.  "The Border Renegade" (1-2-61) Ernest Sarracino, Elaine Davis
73.  "Captain Scoville" (1-9-61) William Tannen, John Craig
74.  "The Has-Been" (1-16-61) Adam West, J. Pat O'Malley
75.  "Town Against a Man" (1-23-61) Val Avery, Lurene Tuttle

76. "The Barefoot Bandit" (1-30-61) Tom Hennesy, John Marshall
77. "The Hand That Shook the Hand" (2-6-61) Vito Scotti, Claude Akins
78. "That Washburn Girl" (2-13-61) Jack Nicholson, Mari Aldon, John Archer
79. [unknown title] (2-27-61) Robert Middleton
80. "A Show from Silver Lode" (3-6-61) Patrice Wymore, Jerry O'Sullivan
81. "Fraud" (3-13-61) Earl Hansen, Michael Whalen
82. "Stage from Yuma" (3-20-61) Brad Dexter, Harry Harvey Jr.
83. "Prince Jim" (3-27-61) Norman Leavitt, J. Pat O'Malley, Gina Gillespie
84. "The Remittance Man" (4-3-61) David Frankham, Yvonne Craig
85. "The Jealous Man" (4-10-61) Faith Domergue, Ed Nelson
86. "Something Pretty" (4-17-61) Peter Whitney, Margo Lorenz
87. "Lady Trouble" (4-24-61) Josephine Hutchinson, Robert Armstrong
88. "Moment of Glory" (5-1-61) Bryan Russell, Eddy Waller
89. "The Lobo" (5-8-61) Jim Davis, Betsy Hale
90. "Rifles for Red Hand" (5-15-61) Ziva Rodann, Harp McGuire
91. "Gunman's Revenge" (5-22-61) Harry Carey Jr., Robert Foulk
92. "The Repentant Outlaw" (5-29-61) Edgar Buchanan, Lew Gallo
93. "A Quiet Little Town" (6-5-61) John Dehner
94. "Bitter Vengeance" (6-12-61) Tom Gilson, Nina Shipman

Sixth Season

95. "Casket 7.3" (9-30-61) Jack Ging, Howard Keel, Suzanne Lloyd
96. "The Dodger" (10-7-61) Claude Akins, Philip Carey
97. "Treasure Coach" (10-14-61) Robert Vaughn, Pat Crowley, J. Pat O'Malley
98. "Death Raffle" (10-21-61) Gary Clarke
99. "Mr. Mute" (11-4-61) Vito Scotti
100. "Jeremiah" (11-11-61) Stuart Erwin, Nancy Gates, George Macready
101. "A Fistful of Pride" (11-18-61) Eddie Albert, Ed Nelson, David White
102. "Defiant at the Gate" (11-25-61) Tom Tully, Gloria Talbot
103. "Man of Another Breed" (12-2-61) Debra Paget, Robert Middleton
104. "Kelly's Clover Girls" (12-9-61) Virginia Field, Dawn Wells
105. "A Killing in Calico" (12-16-61) Dean Jones, John Larch
106. "New Orleans Trackdown" (12-23-61) Tina Louise
107. "Trackback" (12-30-61) Richard Rust, Leo Gordon
108. "Money Run" (1-6-62) Michael Ansara

109. "Reward for Gaine" (1-20-62) John Doucette, Brad Weston, John Anderson
110. "Assignment in Gloribee" (1-27-62) Rod Cameron, George Kennedy, Stafford Repp
111. "Incident at Crossbow" (2-3-62) Robert Sampson, Dara Howard
112. "Portrait of Teresa" (2-10-62) Arthur Franz, Simon Oakland
113. "Hometown Doctor" (2-17-62) Richard Long
114. "The Traveler" (2-24-62) Jack Warden
115. "Winter Storm" (3-3-62) Dan Duryea, R. G. Armstrong
116. "Chauncey" (3-17-62) Burt Brinckerhoff
117. "Who Lives by the Gun" (3-24-62) Burt Patton, Judith Evelyn
118. "To Kill a Town" (3-31-62) Buddy Ebsen, Joan Staley, Russell Johnson
119. "End of a Minor God" (4-7-62) Eileen Ryan
120. "Remember the Yazoo" (4-14-62) Jason Evers
121. "The Angry Sky" (4-21-62) Arch Johnson
122. "Royal Maroon" (4-28-62) William Demarest, Kathleen Crowley, Harold J. Stone
123. "The Gold Witch" (5-5-62) Frank Ferguson, Ron Randall
124. "Don't Wake a Tiger" (5-12-62) Royal Dano, Robert Rockwell, Marjorie Reynolds
125. "The Wayfarers" (5-19-62) James Coburn, Roxane Berard
126. "Vignette of a Sinner" (6-2-62) Jeff Morrow, Edward C. Platt

# RAWHIDE

Downbeat tale of cattle herdsmen; Clint Eastwood rocketing to fame as Rowdy Yates.

The Regulars: Rowdy Yates, Clint Eastwood; Gil Favor, Eric Fleming; Pete Nolan, Sheb Wooley; Wishbone, Paul Brinegar; Jim Quince, Steve Raines; Sheriff, Grant Richards; Mushy, James Murdock; Scarlett, Rocky Shahan; Hey Soos, Robert Cabal; Toothless, William Thompkins; Jed Colby, John Ireland (with episode of 9/28/65); Simon Blake, Raymond St. Jacques (last season only); Ian Cabot, David Watson (last season only).

The Episodes:

1. "Incident of the Tumbleweed Wagon" (1-9-59) Terry Moore, Tom Conway
2. "Incident at Alabaster Plain" (1-16-59)
3. "Incident with an Executioner" (1-23-59) Dan Duryea, Marguerite Chapman
4. "Incident of the Widowed Dove" (1-30-59) Sally Forrest
5. "Incident on the Edge of Madness" (2-6-59) Lon Chaney Jr.

Marie Windsor

6. "Incident of the Power and the Plow" (2-13-59) Brian Donlevy, Michael Pate, Dick Van Patten
7. "Incident at Barker Springs" (2-20-59) Paul Richards, June Lockhart
8. "Incident West of Lano" (2-27-59) Martha Hyer, Abby Dalton
9. "Incident of the Town in Terror" (3-6-59) Margaret O'Brien
10. "Incident of the Golden Calf" (3-13-59) Macdonald Carey
11. "Incident of the Coyote Weed" (3-20-59) Rick Jason
12. "Incident at Chubasco" (4-3-59) George Brent, John Ericson
13. "Incident of the Curious Street" (4-10-59) Mercedes McCambridge, James Westerfield
14. "Incident of the Dog Days" (4-17-59) Don Dubbins
15. "Incident of the Calico Gun" (4-24-59) Jack Lord
16. "Incident of the Misplaced Indians" (5-8-59) Kim Hunter
17. "Incident Below the Brazos" (5-15-59) Leslie Nielsen, Martin Landau
18. "Incident of the Dry Drive" (5-22-59) Victor Jory
19. "Incident of the Judas Trap" (6-5-69) Nina Foch, Phyllis Coates, Jane Nigh
20. "Incident in No Man's Land" (6-12-59) Brian Keith, Phyllis Avery
21. "Incident of a Burst of Evil" (6-26-59) Linda Crystal, Elisha Cook
22. "Incident of the Roman Candles" (7-10-59) Beverly Garland, Richard Eyer

Second Season

23. "Incident of the Day of the Dead" (9-18-59) Viveca Lindfors, Alexander Scourby
24. "Incident at Dangerfield Dip" (10-2-59)
25. "Incident of the Shambling Man" (10-9-59) Victor McLaglen, Anne Francis, Gene Nelson
26. "Incident at Jacob's Well" (10-16-59) David Brian
27. "The Thirteenth Man" (10-23-59) Robert Anderson
28. "Incident at the Buffalo Smoke House" (10-30-59) Vera Miles, Leif Erickson, Gene Evans
29. "Incident of the Haunted Hills" (11-6-59) John Barrymore Jr.
30. "Incident of the Stalking Death" (11-13-59) Cesar Romero, Mari Blanchard, Regis Toomey
31. "Incident of the Valley in Shadow" (11-20-59) Rick Jason, Fay Spain
32. "Incident of the Blue Fire" (12-11-59) Skip Homeier
33. "Incident at Spanish Rock" (12-18-59) Elena Verdugo
34. "Incident of the Druid Curse" (1-8-60) Claude Akins, Luana Patten
35. "Incident at Red River Station" (1-15-60) James Dunn
36. "Incident of the Devil and His Due" (1-22-60) Neville Brand
37. "Incident of the Wanted Painter" (1-29-60) Steve Brodie, Arthur Franz

38. "Incident at Tinker's Dam" (2-5-60) Anthony Dexter, Regis Toomey
39. "Incident of the Night Horse" (2-19-60) George Wallace
40. "Incident of the Sharpshooter" (2-26-60) Jock Mahoney
41. "Incident of the Dust Flower" (3-4-60) Margaret Phillips
42. "Incident at Sulphur Creek" (3-11-60) John Dehner, Jan Shepard
43. "Incident of the Champagne Bottles" (3-18-60) Hugh Marlowe, Patricia Barry
44. "Incident of the Stargazer" (4-1-60) Buddy Ebsen
45. "Incident of the Dancing Death" (4-8-60) Kipp Hamilton, Mabel Albertson
46. "Arana Sacar" (4-22-60) Cloris Leachman
47. "Incident of the Deserter" (4-29-60) Sheila Bromley
48. "Incident of the One Hundred Amulets" (5-6-60)
49. "Incident of the Murder Steer" (5-13-60) James Franciscus, Whitney Blake
50. "Incident of the Music Maker" (5-20-60) Lili Kardell, Werner Klemperer
51. "Incident of the Silent Web" (6-3-60) Don Haggerty
52. "Incident of the Last Chance" (6-10-60) John Kerr, Roxane Berard
53. "Incident in the Garden of Eden" (6-17-60) John Ireland, Debra Paget, Robert Coote

Third Season

54. "Incident at Rojo Canyon" (9-30-60) Julie London, Bobby Troup, Frank Maxwell, John Pickard
55. "Incident of the Challenge" (10-14-60) Lyle Bettger, Michael Pate
56. "Incident at Dragoon Crossing" (10-21-60) Dan O'Herlihy, Garry Walberg
57. "Incident of the Night Visitor" (11-4-60) Dane Clark, Tommy Nolan
58. "Incident of the Slavemaster" (11-11-60) John Agar, Peter Lorre
59. "Incident on the Road to Yesterday" (11-18-60) Frankie Lane, Chester Morris
60. "Incident at Superstition Prairie" (12-2-60) Rodolfo Acosta, Michael Pate
61. "Incident at Poco Tiempo" (12-9-60) Gigi Perreau, Agnes Moorehead, Stewart Bradley
62. "Incident of the Captive" (12-16-60) Mercedes McCambridge, Albert Salmi, Joe De Santis
63. "Incident of the Buffalo Soldier" (1-6-61) Woody Strode, Ray Montgomery
64. "Incident of the Broken Word" (1-20-61) E. G. Marshall, Dick York
65. "Incident at the Top of the World" (1-27-61) Robert Culp
66. "Incident of the Promised Land" (2-3-61) Mary Astor
67. "Incident of the Big Blowout" (2-10-61) Mari Blanchard
68. "Incident of the Fish Out of the Water" (2-17-61) Dorothy

Green, Jock Gaynor
69. "Incident on the Road Back" (2-24-61) Gene Evans, Jeanne Cooper, Arch Johnson
70. "Incident of the New Start" (3-3-61) John Dehner
71. "Incident of the Running Iron" (3-10-61) Darryl Hickman
72. "Incident Near Gloomy River" (3-17-61) John Cassavetes, Leif Erickson, John Ericson
73. "Incident of the Boomerang" (3-24-61) James Drury, Patricia Medina, Woody Strode
74. "Incident of His Brother's Keeper" (3-31-61) Jack Lord, Susan Oliver
75. "Incident in the Middle of Nowhere" (4-7-61) Cecil Kellaway, Fay Spain
76. "Incident of the Phantom Burglar" (4-14-61) Jock Mahoney
77. "Incident of the Lost Idol" (4-28-61) Claude Akins
78. "Incident of the Running Man" (5-5-61) Lloyd Corrigan, Robert Wilke
79. "Incident of the Painted Lady" (5-12-61) Marie Windsor, David Brian
80. "Incident Before Black Pass" (5-19-61) Zachary Scott, Robert Armstrong, Cathy Downs
81. "Incident of the Black Storms" (5-26-61) Stephen McNally
82. "Incident of the Night on the Town" (6-2-61) Harry Townes, James Drury
83. "Incident of the Wagon on Payday" (6-16-61) Stephen Joyce, Ford Rainey
84. "Incident of Fear in the Streets" (6-23-61) Gary Merrill

Fourth Season

85. "Incident at Rio Salado" (9-29-61) Tom Tully
86. "The Sendoff" (10-6-61) Darren McGavin, Claude Akins
87. "The Long Shakedown" (10-13-61) Skip Homeier, Lew Gallo
88. "Judgment at Hondo Seco" (10-20-61) Ralph Bellamy
89. "The Lost Tribe" (10-27-61) Abraham Sofaer
90. "Incident of the Inside Man" (11-3-61) Charlie Gray, Anne Helm, Chris Alcaide
91. "The Black Sheep" (11-10-61) Richard Basehart
92. "The Prairie Elephant" (11-17-61) Lawrence Dobkin, Gloria Talbott
93. "The Little Fishes" (11-24-61) Burgess Meredith, Phyllis Coates, Richard Webb
94. "The Blue Sky" (12-8-61) Phyllis Thaxter
95. "The Gentleman's Gentleman" (12-15-61) Brian Aherne
96. "Twenty-five Santa Clauses" (12-22-61) Ed Wynn, Anne Seymour
97. "The Long Count" (1-5-62) Bethel Leslie, Kevin Hagen
98. "The Captain's Wife" (1-12-62) Barbara Stanwyck
99. "The Peddler" (1-19-62) George Kennedy
100. "Incident of the Woman Trap" (1-26-62) Robert Gist, Alan Hale
101. "The Bosses' Daughters" (2-2-62) Paul Richards, Dorothy Green, Alan Hale
102. [unknown title] (2-9-62) Jock Gaynor, Russell Arms

103. "The Greedy Town" (2-16-62) Mercedes McCambridge, Diana Millay, Charles Gray
104. "Grandma's Money" (2-23-62) Josephine Hutchinson, Frank Maxwell
105. "The Pitchwagon" (3-2-62) Buddy Ebsen, Joan O'Brien, Hugh Marlowe
106. "The Hostile Child" (3-9-62) Debra Paget
107. "The Immigrants" (3-16-62) Maria Palmer, John Van Dreelen
108. "The Child Woman" (3-23-62) Cesar Romero, Jena Engstrom, Dorothy Morris, Julian Burton
109. "A Woman's Place" (3-30-62) Gail Kobe, Mala Powers
110. "The Reunion" (4-6-62) Darryl Hickman, Walter Pidgeon
111. "The House of the Hunter" (4-20-62) Robert F. Simon, Rosemary De Camp
112. "Gold Fever" (5-4-62) Victor Jory, Karen Sharpe, Marion Ross
113. "The Devil and the Deep Blue" (5-11-62) Coleen Gray
114. "Abilene" (5-18-62) Audrey Totter, Ken Lynch, John Pickard

Fifth Season

115. "Incident of the Hunter" (9-28-62) Mark Stevens, Hal Baylor
116. "Incident of the Portrait" (10-5-62) John Ireland
117. "Incident at Cactus Wells" (10-12-62) Keenan Wynn
118. "Incident of the Prodigal Son" (10-19-62) Carl Reindel, Gene Evans
119. "Incident of the Four Horsemen" (10-26-62) Claude Akins
120. "Incident of the Lost Woman" (11-2-62) Fay Spain
121. "Incident of the Dogfaces" (11-9-62) James Whitmore
122. "Incident of the Wolvers" (11-16-62) Dan Duryea, Patty McCormack
123. "Incident at Sugar Creek" (11-23-62) Beverly Garland, Everett Sloane
124. "Incident of the Reluctant Bridegroom" (11-30-62) Ruta Lee, Ed Nelson
125. "Incident of the Querencias" (12-7-62) Edward Andrews
126. "Incident at Quivira" (12-14-62) Royal Dano, Claude Akins
127. "Incident of Decision" (12-28-62) Carlos Romero
128. "Incident of the Buryin' Man" (1-4-63) Constance Ford
129. "Incident at the Trail's End" (1-11-63) Harold J. Stone
130. "Incident at Spider Rock" (1-18-63) Mary Beth Hughes, Lon Chaney Jr., Peggy Ann Garner
131. "Incident of the Mountain Man" (1-25-63) Patricia Crowley
132. "Incident at Crooked Hat" (2-1-63) James Gregory, Jeanne Cooper
133. "Incident of Judgment Day" (2-8-63) Claude Rains, John Dehner
134. "Incident of the Black Sheep" (2-15-63) Richard Basehart
135. "Incident of the Gallows Tree" (2-22-63) Beverly Garland, Judson Pratt

136. "Incident of the Married Widow" (3-1-63) Patricia Barry, Dabbs Greer
137. "Incident of the Pale Rider" (3-15-63) Albert Salmi
138. "Incident of the Commanchero" (3-22-63) Robert Loggia
139. "Incident of the Clown" (3-29-63) Eddie Bracken
140. "Incident of the Black Ace" (4-12-63) Walter Slezak, Karen Sharpe, Robert Strauss
141. "Incident of the Hostages" (4-19-63) Suzanne Cupito, Tony Haig, Leslie Wales
142. "Incident of the White Eyes" (5-3-63) Nita Talbot, Nehemiah Persoff
143. "Incident at Rio Doloroso" (5-10-63) Michael Ansara, Cesar Romero
144. "Incident at Alkali Sink" (5-24-63) Russell Johnson, Ruta Lee

Sixth Season

145. "Incident of the Red Wind" (9-26-63) Neville Brand
146. "Incident of Iron Bull" (10-3-63) James Whitmore, Michael Ansara, Richard X. Slattery
147. "Incident at El Crucero" (10-10-63) Gene Evans, Elizabeth Montgomery
148. "Incident of the Travelin' Man" (10-17-63) Robert Middleton, Simon Oakland, Robert Donner
149. "Incident at Paradise" (10-24-63) Burgess Meredith, Patty McCormack, Beau Bridges, Arch Johnson
150. "Incident at Farragut Pass" (10-31-63) Frankie Avalon, Glenda Farrell, Tommy Farrell, John Pickard
151. "Incident at Two Graves" (11-7-63) Bill Travers, Steve Brodie
152. "Incident of the Rawhiders" (11-14-63) Denver Pyle, Nina Shipman, James Best
153. "Incident of the Prophecy" (11-21-63) Dan Duryea, Warren Oates
154. "Incident at Confidence Creek" (11-28-63) Dick York, Barbara Eden
155. "Incident of the Death Dancer" (12-5-63) Forrest Tucker
156. "Incident of the Wild Deuces" (12-12-63) George Chandler, Barbara Stuart
157. "Incident of the Geisha" (12-19-63) Miyoshi Umeki, Joseph Perry
158. "Incident at Ten Trees" (1-2-64) Royal Dano, Susan Kohner
159. "Incident of the Rusty Shotgun" (1-9-64) Claude Akins, Marie Windsor
160. "Incident of Midnight Cave" (1-16-64) Edward Kemmer
161. "Incident of the Dowry Dundee" (1-23-64) Lyle Bettger, Hazel Court
162. "Incident at Gila Flats" (1-30-64)
163. "Incident of the Pied Piper" (2-6-64) Arch Johnson, Eddie Bracken, Everett Sloane
164. "Incident of the Swindler" (2-20-64) John Dehner, Peter Leeds, Sally Forrest

165. "Incident of the Wanderer" (2-27-64) Nehemiah Persoff
166. "Incident at Zebulon" (3-5-64) Robert Cornthwaite, John Lupton
167. "Incident at Hourglass" (3-12-64) Jay C. Flippen, John Anderson, Elizabeth MacRae
168. "Incident at the Odyssey" (3-26-64) Mickey Rooney, Carole Matthews
169. [unknown title] (4-2-64) Allyn Joslyn, Lola Albright, Virginia Gregg
170. "Incident at El Toro" (4-9-64) James Best, Hal Baylor, John Cole
171. "Incident at Deadhorse" [Part I] (4-16-64) Broderick Crawford, Chill Wills, Burgess Meredith, Robert Middleton
172. "Incident at Deadhorse" [Part II] (4-23-64) as above
173. "Incident of the Gilded Goddess" (4-30-64) Dina Merrill
174. "Incident at Seven Fingers" (5-7-64) Hari Rhodes, Harry Townes, William Marshall
175. "Incident of the Peyote Cup" (5-14-64) James Gregory, Ted De Corsia

Seventh Season

176. "The Race" (9-25-64) Warren Oates, William Bryant
177. "The Enormous Fist" (10-2-64) Brenda Scott, Mark Slade
178. "Piney" (10-9-64) Lee Van Cleef, Ed Begley, Elisha Cook, J. D. Cannon
179. "The Lost Herd" (10-16-64) Bill Williams, Harry Townes, Royal Dano
180. "A Man Called Mushy" (10-23-64) Paul Comi, Margo, Mike Kellin, Sondra Kerr
181. "Canliss" (10-30-64) Dean Martin, Laura Devon, Scott Marlowe, Michael Ansara, Theodore Bikel, Ramon Novarro
182. "Damon's Road" [Part I] (11-13-64) Fritz Weaver, Sean McClory, Barbara Eden, Paul Comi
183. "Damon's Road" [Part II] (11-20-64) as above
184. "The Backshooter" (11-27-64) Kathryn Hays, Louis Hayward, Slim Pickens, Terry Becker
185. "Corporal Dasovik" (12-4-64) John Barrymore Jr., Nick Adams, G. B. Atwater
186. "The Photographer" (12-11-64) Eddie Albert, Morgan Woodward, Ben Cooper
187. "No Dogs or Drovers" (12-18-64) Philip Abbott, Dabbs Greer, Gilbert Green, Zeme North
188. "The Book" (1-8-65) Pat Hingle, J. D. Cannon, Leonard Strong
189. "Josh" (1-15-65) Albert Dekker, Jay C. Flippen, John Doucette, John Pickard
190. "A Time for Waiting" (1-22-65) George Grizzard, Ken Berry, Lisabeth Hush
191. "Moment in the Sun" (1-29-65) Billy Gray, Sherry Jackson, Pat Conway, Gene Evans
192. "Texas Fever" (2-5-65) Royal Dano, Christopher Dark,

Judi Meredith, Frank Maxwell

193. "Blood Harvest" (2-12-65) Steve Forrest, Tom Tully, Michel Petit, Richard X. Slattery
194. "The Violent Land" (3-5-65) Michael Forest, Davey Davison
195. "The Winter Soldier" (3-12-65) Robert Blake, Brooke Bundy, Liam Sullivan
196. "Prairie Fire" (3-19-65) Michael Conrad, Anthony Caruso
197. "Retreat" (3-26-65) John Anderson, Steve Ihnat, John Lasell
198. "The Empty Sleeve" (4-2-65) Everett Sloane, Burt Douglas, Nancy Rennick
199. "The Diehard" (4-9-65) Efrem Zimbalist Jr., Lawrence Dobkin
200. "Mrs. Harmon" (4-16-65) Barbara Barrie, Paul Lambert
201. "The Calf Women" (4-30-65) Julie Harris, Betty Conner, Roger Ewing
202. "The Spanish Camp" (5-7-65) John Ireland, Brock Peters
203. "El Hombre Bravo" (5-14-65) Frank Silvera, Malachi Throne, Henry Corden
204. "The Gray Rock Hotel" (5-21-65) Lola Albright, Steven Hill, Strother Martin

Eighth Season

205. "Encounter at Boot Hill" (9-14-65) Simon Oakland, Peter Haskell, Timothy Carey, Malcolm Atterbury, Dal Jenkins, Jeff Corey
206. "Six Weeks to Bent Fork" (9-28-65) James Gregory, R. G. Armstrong, Vaughn Taylor
207. "Walk into Terror" (10-5-65) Claude Akins, Bruce Dern, Roy Barcroft
208. "Escape to Doom" (10-12-65) Rip Torn, Christopher Dark
209. "Hostage for Hanging" (10-19-65) Mercedes McCambridge, Robert Blake, Sharon Farrell, Warren Oates
210. "The Vasquez Woman" (10-26-65) Cesar Romero, Carol Lawrence, Malachi Throne
211. "Clash at Broken Bluff" (11-2-65) Warren Stevens, Nancy Gates, Ron Randell
212. "The Pursuit" (11-9-65) Ralph Bellamy, Jim Davis
213. "Duel at Daybreak" (11-16-65) Charles Bronson, Jill Haworth, Joe di Reda
214. "Brush War at Buford" (11-23-65) Richard Carlson, Robert Middleton, Skip Homeier, Tim McIntire
215. "The Testing Post" (11-30-65) Rory Calhoun, Dick Foran, Burt Brinckerhoff, K. L. Smith
216. "Crossing at White Feather" (12-7-65) Johnny Crawford, Albert Dekker, G. B. Atwater

ALCOA PRESENTS

The Regulars: John Newland, host.

The Episodes:

1. "The Bride Possessed" (1-20-59) Virginia Leith, Skip Homeier, Harry Townes
2. "The Night of April 14th" (1-27-59) Barbara Lord, Patricia Macnee
3. "Emergency Only" (2-3-59) Jocelyn Brando, Lin McCarthy, Paula Raymond
4. "The Dark Room" (2-10-59) Cloris Leachman, Marcel Dallo
5. "Twelve Hours to Live" (2-17-59) Jean Allison, Paul Richards
6. "Epilogue" (2-24-59) Charles Aidman, Julie Adams
7. "The Dream" (3-3-59) Reginald Owen
8. "Premonition" (3-10-59) Beverly Washburn, Pamela Lincoln
9. "The Dead Part of the House" (3-17-59) Mimi Gibson
10. "The Vision" (3-24-59) Bruce Gordon, Pernell Roberts
11. "The Devil's Laughter" (3-31-59) Alfred Ryder
12. "The Return of Mitchell Campion" (4-7-59) Patrick O'Neal
13. "The Navigator" (4-14-59) Don Dubbins
14. "The Secret" (4-21-59) Maria Palmer, Robert Douglas
15. "The Angry Man" (4-28-59) George Mathews, Edgar Buchanan
16. "The Burning Girl" (5-5-59) Luana Anders, Sandra Knight, Olive Deering
17. "Haunted U-Boat" (5-12-59) Enid Feldary, Werner Klemperer, Wesley Lau
18. "Image of Death" (5-19-59) Max Adrian, Doris Dowling
19. "The Captain's Guests" (5-26-59) Robert Webber, Nancy Hadley
20. "Echo" (6-2-59) Ross Martin, Edward Kemmer, Leslie Barrett
21. "Front Runner" (6-9-59) Ben Cooper, Walter Burke
22. "The Riddle" (6-16-59) Warren Stevens, Bethel Leslie

Second Season

23. "Delusion" (9-15-59) Norman Lloyd
24. "Ordeal on Locust Street" (9-22-59) Suzanne Lloyd, Augusta Dabney
25. "Brainwave" (10-6-59) George Grizzard, Whit Bissell
26. "Doomsday" (10-13-59) Torin Thatcher, Donald Harron
27. "Night of the Kill" (10-20-59) Dennis Holmes, Fred Beir
28. "The Inheritance" (10-27-59) Sean McClory
29. "The Open Window" (11-3-59) Michael Harris
30. "Message from Clara" (11-10-59) Barbara Baxley, Robert Ellenstein, Celia Lovsky
31. "Forked Lightning" (11-17-59) Ralph Nelson, Frank Maxwell
32. "Reunion" (11-24-59) Betsy Von Furstenberg, Paul Carr
33. "Dead Ringer" (12-1-59) Norma Crane, Grant Williams

34. "The Stone Cutter" (12-8-59) Walter Burke, Joe Mantell, Arthur Sheilds
35. "Father Image" (12-15-59) Jack Lord, Cee Cee Whitney, Ian Wolfe
36. "Make Me Not a Witch" (12-22-59) Patty McCormack, Eileen Ryan, Leo Penn
37. "The Hand" (12-29-59) Robert Loggia, Miriam Colon, Pete Candoli
38. "The Justice Tree" (1-5-60) Frank Overton, Sallie Brophy
39. "Earthquake" (1-12-60) David Opatoshu, Olan Soule
40. "Forests of the Night" (1-19-60) Alfred Ryder, Mark Roberts
41. "Call from Tomorrow" (1-26-60) Margaret Phillips, Arthur Franz
42. "Who Are You?" (2-2-60) Reba Waters, Philip Bourneuf, Anna Lee
43. "The Day the World Wept" (2-9-60) Barry Atwater, Jeanne Bates
44. "The Lovers" (2-16-60) Vanessa Brown, John Beal
45. "Vanishing Point" (2-23-60) Edward Binns
46. "The Mask" (3-1-60) Wesley Lau, Luis Van Rooten
47. "The Haunting" (3-8-60) Ronald Howard, Christine White
48. "The Explorer" (3-15-60) Gregory Morton, Bert Convy
49. "The Clown" (3-22-60) Mickey Shaughnessy, Yvette Mimieux, Christopher Dark
50. "I Saw You Tomorrow" (4-5-60) John Hudson, Rosemary Murphy
51. "Encounter" (4-12-60) Robert Douglas, Mike Forest
52. "The Peter Hurkos Story" [Part I] (4-19-60) Albert Salmi, Betty Garde, Alf Kjellin, Andrew Prine
53. "The Peter Hurkos Story" [Part II] (4-26-60) as above
54. "Delia" (5-3-60) Lee Philips, Barbara Lord
55. "The Visitor" (5-10-60) Joan Fontaine
56. "Gypsy" (5-17-60) Johnny Seven, Robert Blake, John Kellogg
57. "Contract" (5-24-60) Ron Randell, Catherine McLeod
58. "The Lonely Room" (5-31-60) Fabrizio Mioni
59. "House of the Dead" (6-7-60) Mario Alcaide
60. "Good-bye, Grandpa" (6-14-60) Edgar Stehli, Anna Karen
61. "The Storm" (6-21-60) Lee Bergere, Rebecca Welles

Third Season

62. "Anniversary of a Murder" (9-27-60) Harry Townes, Randy Stuart
63. "The Death Waltz" (10-4-60) Elizabeth Montgomery, Joe Cronin, K. T. Stevens
64. "The Return" (10-11-60) Dick Davalos, Jack Mullaney
65. "If You See Sally" (10-18-60) Ann Whitfield
66. "Moment of Hate" (10-25-60) Joanne Linville, John Kellogg
67. "To Know the End" (11-1-60) Elen Willard
68. "The Trap" (11-15-60) Mike Kellin, Francis DeSales
69. "The Voice" (11-22-60) Robert Lansing, Luana Anders
70. "The Promise" (11-29-60) William Shatner, Ben Wright

71. "Tonight at 12:17!" (12-6-60) Peggy Ann Garner, John Lasell
72. "Where Are They?" (12-13-60) Philip Pine, Joan Tompkins
73. "Legacy of Love" (12-20-60) Norma Crane, Charles Aidman
74. "Rendezvous" (12-27-60) Georgann Johnson, Donald Murphy
75. "The Executioner" (1-3-61) Buzz Martin, Crahan Denton
76. "The Last Round" (1-10-61) Charles Bronson
77. "Dead Man's Tale" (1-17-61) Lonny Chapman, Jean Engstrom
78. "The Sacred Mushroom" (1-24-61)
79. "The Gift" (1-31-61) Scott Marlowe, Betty Garde, Mary Sinclair
80. "Persons Unknown" (2-7-61) David Stewart, Jay Novello
81. "Tidal Wave" (2-14-61) Jean Allison, Dennis Patrick
82. "Night of Decision" (2-21-61) Robert Douglas, Richard Hale, Donald Buka
83. "The Stranger" (2-28-61) Peter Dyneley, Bill Nagy, Patrick MacAlinney, Graham Stark
84. "Justice" (3-7-61) Meredith Edwards, Clifford Evans
85. "The Face" (3-14-61) Sean Kelly, Penelope Horner, John Brown
86. "That Room Upstairs" (3-21-61) Lois Maxwell, David Knight
87. "Signal Received" (4-4-61) Mark Eden, Terry Palmer, Richard Gale
88. "The Confession" (4-11-61) Donald Pleasence, Adrienne Corri, Robert Raglan
89. "The Avengers" (4-25-61) Andre Morell, Lisa Gastoni, Stanley Van Beers, Carl Jaffe
90. "The Prisoner" (5-2-61) Catherine Feller, Anton Diffring, Faith Brook
91. "Blood Flower" (5-16-61) Larry Gates, Eugene Iglesias
92. "The Sorcerer" (5-23-61) Christopher Lee, Martin Benson, Gabrielli Lucudi
93. "The Villa" (6-6-61) Elizabeth Sellars, Geoffrey Toone, Michael Crawford, Maria Landi
94. "The Tiger" (6-20-61) Pamela Brown, Pauline Challenor, Elspeth March, Patsy Smart
95. "Nightmare" (6-27-61) Peter Wyngarde, Mary Peach, Ambrosine Phillpotts, Ferdy Mayne
96. "Eye Witness" (7-4-61) John Meillon

CHEYENNE

Warner Brothers' classic western of the peregrinations of Cheyenne Bodie who, as recalled in the episode "Legacy of the Lost," was born of a white man, Lionel Abbott, but bred by Indian Chief Red Cloud. The hour western, begun September 20, 1955, and initially alternating with the dramas "Casablanca" and "King's Row" (with the drama "Conflict" in its second year) did much to popularize the western ballad--used religiously in WB dramas of the genre thereafter.

The Regulars: Cheyenne Bodie, Clint Walker; Bronco Layne, Ty Hardin; Tom Brewster ("Sugarfoot"), Will Hutchins.

The Episodes (chronicled from 1959):

1.  Cheyenne: "Blind Spot" (9-21-59) Robert Crawford, Jean Byron, Barry Kelly
2.  Cheyenne: "Reprieve" (10-5-59) Connie Stevens
3.  Cheyenne: "The Rebellion" (10-12-59) Rodolfo Acosta, Frank De Kova, Joe De Santis, Faith Domergue
4.  Cheyenne: "Trial by Conscience" (10-26-59) Jeff York, Pat Crowley
5.  Cheyenne: "The Imposter" (11-2-59) Robert McQueeney, Peter Whitney, James Drury
6.  Cheyenne: "Prisoner of Moon Mesa" (11-16-59)
7.  Cheyenne: "The Long Winter" [repeat of episode of 9/25/56] (11-23-59) Robert J. Wilke, Tom Pittman
8.  Cheyenne: "The Iron Trail" [repeat of episode of 1/1/57] (12-7-59) Dani Crayne
9.  Cheyenne: "Hard Bargain" [repeat of episode of 5/21/57] (12-14-59) Regis Toomey, Richard Crenna
10. Cheyenne: "The Long Search" [repeat of episode of 4/22/58] (12-28-59) Norman Frederic, Claude Akins
11. Cheyenne: "Gold, Glory, and Custer--Prelude" [Part I] (1-4-60) Julie Adams, Liam Sullivan, Lorne Greene
12. Cheyenne: "Gold, Glory, and Custer--Requiem" [Part II] (1-11-60) as above
13. Cheyenne: "The Brand" [repeat of episode of 4/9/57] (1-18-60) Edward Byrnes, Sue George
14. Cheyenne: "Ghost of Cimarron" [repeat of episode of 3/25/58] (1-25-60) Peter Brown, Patrick McVey
15. Cheyenne: "Riot at Arroyo Soco" (2-1-60) Wynn Pearce, Frank Ferguson, Whitney Blake, Harry Lauter, Don Haggerty
16. Cheyenne: "Apache Blood" (2-8-60) Scott Marlowe
17. Cheyenne: "The Mutton Puncher" [repeat of episode of 10/22/57] (2-15-60) Billy Gray, Laurie Chapman, Marie Windsor
18. Cheyenne: "White Warrior" [repeat of episode of 3/11/58] (2-22-60) Michael Landon, Randy Stuart
19. Cheyenne: "Outcast of Cripple Creek" (2-29-60) Whit Bissell, Rhodes Reason, Robert J. Wilke, Lisa Gaye, Tol Avery
20. Cheyenne: "Alibi for a Scalped Man" (3-7-60) Mala Powers, Richard Coogan, R. G. Armstrong
21. Cheyenne: "Home Is the Brave" (3-14-60) John Howard, John Archer, Paula Raymond
22. Cheyenne: "Deadline" [repeat of episode of 2/26/57] (3-21-60) Mark Roberts, John Qualen
23. Cheyenne: "The Last Comanchero" [repeat of episode of 1/14/58] (3-28-60) Edward Byrnes, Harold J. Stone,

Virginia Aldridge
24. Cheyenne: "Lone Gun" [repeat of episode of 12/4/56] (4-4-60) Paul Brinegar, Nancy Hale
25. Cheyenne: "Born Bad" [repeat of episode of 3/26/57] (4-11-60) Jill Jarmyn, Wright King, Robert F. Simon
26. Cheyenne: "Border Affair" (4-18-60) Erin O'Brien, Michael Pate, Sebastian Cabot, Joy Page
27. Cheyenne: "Incident at Indian Springs" [repeat of episode of 9/24/57] (4-25-60) Dan Barton, Bonnie Bolding
28. Cheyenne: "The Broken Pledge" [repeat of episode of 6/4/57] (5-2-60) Jean Byrin, John Dehner, Norman Frederic, Paul Birch
29. Cheyenne: "The Conspirators" [repeat of episode of 10/8/57] (5-9-60) Tom Conway, Joan Weldon
30. Cheyenne: "Test of Courage" [repeat of episode of 1/29/57] (5-16-60) Mary Castle, John Archer, George Neise
31. Cheyenne: "The Law Man" [repeat of episode of 11/6/56] (5-23-60) Andrea King, Paul Engle, Grant Williams
32. Cheyenne: "Town of Fear" [repeat of episode of 12/3/57] (5-30-60) Walter Coy, Alan Wells
33. Cheyenne: "Standoff" [repeat of episode of 5/6/58] (6-6-60) Rodolfo Acosta, Richard Garland
34. Cheyenne: "Hired Gun" [repeat of episode of 12/17/57] (6-13-60) Don Megowan, Alan Hale
35. Cheyenne: "Strange Request" (6-20-60) Jan Sterling, Rhys Williams, Laurence Dobkin
36. Cheyenne: "Decision at Gunsight" [repeat of episode of 4/23/57] (6-27-60) John Carradine, Patrick McVey, Marie Windsor
37. Cheyenne: "Noose at Noon" [repeat of episode of 6/3/58] (7-4-60) Charles Quinlivan, Theona Bryant
38. Cheyenne: "Death Deals the Hand" [repeat of episode of 10/9/56] (7-18-60) Arthur Hunnicutt, Pat Tiernan

Sixth Season

39. Sugarfoot: "Shadow Catcher" (9-26-60)
40. Cheyenne: "The Long Rope" (10-3-60) Donald May, Merry Anders, Peter Whitney, Frank Albertson
41. Cheyenne: "Counterfeit Gun" (10-10-60) Robert Lowery, Lisa Gaye, Vito Scotti, Ray Teal
42. Bronco: "The Mustangers" (10-17-60) Mike Keene, Whitney Blake
43. Sugarfoot: "A Noose for Nora" (10-24-60) Madlyn Rhue
44. Cheyenne: "Road to Three Graves" (10-31-60) Alan Hale
45. Bronco: "Apache Treasure" (11-7-60) Mort Mills, Richard Hale
46. Sugarfoot: "Man from Medora" (11-21-60) Albert Carrier, Peter Breck, Ray Walker
47. Cheyenne: "Two Trails to Santa Fe" (11-28-60) Sonja Wilde, Robert Colbert, Richard Webb
48. Bronco: "Seminole War Pipe" (12-12-60) Robert Palmer, Anna Kashfi, Dean Fredericks
49. Cheyenne: "Savage Breed" (12-19-60) Ray Danton, Charlie

Briggs
50. Sugarfoot: "Welcome Enemy" (12-26-60) Glenn Strange, Suzanne Lloyd
51. Bronco: "Ordeal at Dead Tree" (1-2-61) Dorothy Neumann, Frank Ferguson
52. Cheyenne: "Incident at Dawson Flats" (1-9-61) Gerald Mohr, Joan O'Brien, Jock Gaynor
53. Sugarfoot: "Toothy Thompson" (1-16-61) Jack Elam, John Marley
54. Bronco: "The Invaders" (1-23-61) Gerald Mohr, Walter Sande, Shirley Knight
55. Cheyenne: "Duel at Judas Basin" [Ty Hardin and Will Hutchins appeared in their "Bronco" and "Sugarfoot" roles] (1-30-61) Jacques Aubuchon, Alan Caillou, Sheldon Allman
56. Sugarfoot: "Shepherd with a Gun" (2-6-61) Raoul De Leon, Regis Toomey, Rafael Campos
57. Cheyenne: "The Return of Mr. Grimm" (2-13-61) R. G. Armstrong, Anita Sands
58. Bronco: "The Buckbrier Trail" (2-20-61) Michael Keep, Ray Danton, Mike Road
59. Cheyenne: "The Beholden" (2-27-61) Don Megowan, Patrice Wymore
60. Sugarfoot: "Angel" [Ty Hardin appeared in his "Bronco" role] (3-6-61) Cathy O'Donnell, Jack Elam, Frank Albertson
61. Bronco: "Yankee Tornado" [Will Hutchins appeared in his "Sugarfoot" role] (3-13-61) Tristram Coffin, Peter Breck
62. Cheyenne: "The Frightened Town" (3-20-61) Andrew Duggan, James Griffith
63. Sugarfoot: "Stranger in Town" (3-27-61) Jacques Aubuchon, Stephen Lander, Erika Peters
64. Bronco: "Manitoba Manhunt" (4-3-61) Richard Garland, Jacqueline Beer
65. Cheyenne: "Lone Patrol" (4-10-61) Robert McQueeney, Evan McCord
66. Sugarfoot: "Trouble at Sand Springs" (4-17-61) Suzanne Storrs, Craig Hill, Tommy Rettig
67. Bronco: "Stage to the Sky" (4-24-61) Joan Marshall, Kent Taylor, Bing Russell
68. Cheyenne: "Massacre at Gunsight Pass" (5-1-61) Sherwood Price, X Brands, Jack Elam
69. Bronco: "Guns of the Lawless" (5-8-61) Denver Pyle, Fred Beir, Morris Ankrum
70. Cheyenne: "The Greater Glory" (5-15-61) William Sargent, Susan Crane

Seventh Season

71. Cheyenne: "Winchester Quarantine" (9-25-61) Denver Pyle, Steve Brodie
72. Bronco: "Trouble Street" (10-2-61) Tom Drake, James Coburn, Mala Powers
73. Cheyenne: "Cross Purpose" (10-9-61) Michael Forest
74. Bronco: "Cousin from Atlanta" (10-16-61) Anne Helm

75. Cheyenne: "The Young Fugitives" (10-23-61) Richard Evans
76. Cheyenne: "Day's Pay" (10-30-61)
77. Bronco: "The Prince of Darkness" (11-6-61) Efrem Zim-
    balist Jr., Edwin Booth
78. Cheyenne: "Retaliation" (11-13-61) John Anderson, Jason
    Evers, Randy Stuart
79. Cheyenne: "Storm Center" (11-20-61) Robert Crawford Jr.
80. Bronco: "One Came Back" (11-27-61) Robert McQueeney,
    Karen Steele
81. Cheyenne: "Legacy of the Lost" (12-4-61) Richard Hale,
    Peter Breck, Peter Whitney
82. Cheyenne: "The Brahma Bull" (12-11-61) Kevin Hagen
83. Bronco: "The Equalizer" (12-18-61) Jack Nicholson,
    Marie Windsor, Steve Brodie, Frank Albertson
84. Bronco: "The Harrigan" (12-25-61) Jack Cassidy, Kathie
    Browne
85. Bronco: "Beginner's Luck" (1-1-62) Hayden Rourke
86. Cheyenne: "The Wedding Rings" (1-8-62) Harold J. Stone
87. Bronco: "Ride the Whirlwind" (1-15-62) Vaughn Taylor
88. Bronco: "A Sure Thing" (1-22-62) Alan Hale
89. Cheyenne: "The Idol" (1-29-62) Jeff Morrow, Leo Gordon
90. Bronco: "Trail of Hatred" (2-5-62) Kent Smith, Rian Gar-
    rick
91. Bronco: "Rendezvous with a Miracle" (2-12-62) Gloria
    Talbott
92. Cheyenne: "One Way Ticket" (2-19-62) Philip Carey
93. Bronco: "Destinies West" (2-26-62) Kathleen Crowley
94. Bronco: "The Last Letter" (3-5-62) Ernest Sarracino
95. Cheyenne: "The Bad Penny" (3-12-62) Susan Seaforth,
    Robert Hogan, Richard Webb, Don Haggerty
96. Bronco: "One Evening in Abilene" (3-19-62) Lisa Gaye,
    Jack Cassidy, Lee Van Cleef
97. Bronco: "Until Kingdom Come" (3-26-62) Philip Carey,
    Jacqueline Beer
98. Bronco: "Moment of Doubt" (4-2-62) Roxane Berard
99. Bronco: "A Town That Lived and Died" (4-9-62) John
    Russell, Anna Capri, Jolene Brand
100. Bronco: "The Immovable Object" (4-16-62) William Faw-
     cett, Mike Road, Maggie Pierce
101. Cheyenne: "A Man Called Ragan" (4-23-62) Arch Johnson,
     Chad Everett, Jack Elam
102. Bronco: "Then the Mountains" (4-30-62) Susan Seaforth,
     Gerald Mohr

Eighth Season

103. Cheyenne: "The Durango Brothers" (9-24-62) Sally Keller-
     man, Jack Elam
104. Cheyenne: "Satonka" (10-1-62) Andrew Duggan, Susan Sea-
     forth
105. Cheyenne: "Sweet Sam" (10-8-62) Robert McQueeney,
     James Best, Denver Pyle
106. Cheyenne: "Man Alone" (10-15-62) Kathy Bennett

107. Cheyenne: "The Quick and the Deadly" (10-22-62) Mike
     Road, Jeanne Cooper
108. Cheyenne: "Indian Gold" (10-29-62) Peter Breck
109. Cheyenne: "Dark Decision" (11-5-62) Diane Brewster,
     Peter Breck
110. Cheyenne: "Pocketful of Stars" (11-12-62) Peter Brown
111. Cheyenne: "The Vanishing Breed" (11-19-62) Regis Toomey
112. Cheyenne: "Vengeance Is Mine" (11-26-62) Van Williams
113. Cheyenne: "Johnny Brassbuttons" (12-3-62) Philip Carey
114. Cheyenne: "Wanted for the Murder of Cheyenne Bodie"
     (12-10-62) Richard Webb, Ruta Lee
115. Cheyenne: "Showdown at Oxbend" (12-17-62) Joan Caulfield


PETER GUNN

     Blake Edwards' private eye yarn significant for the fact that
Craig Stevens was indelibly associated with his role as the hero,
Peter Gunn, and for Henry Mancini's palpitating jazz theme.

The Regulars: Peter Gunn, Craig Stevens; Edie Hart, Lola Al-
          bright; Lieutenant Jacobi, Hershel Bernardi; Mother,
          Hope Summers (first season only); Mother, Minerva Ure-
          cal (with second season).

The Episodes (chronicled from second season):

  1. "Protection" (9-21-59) Cyril Delevanti
  2. "Crisscross" (9-28-59)
  3. "Edge of the Knife" (10-5-59)
  4. "The Comic" (10-12-59) Shelley Berman, Patricia Donahue
  5. "Death Is a Red Rose" (10-19-59) Henry Beckman
  6. "The Young Assassins" (10-26-59) Dan Easton
  7. "The Feathered Doll" (11-2-59)
  8. "Kidnap" (11-16-59)
  9. "The Rifle" (11-23-59) Paul Comi
 10. "The Game" (11-30-59) Robert Emhardt
 11. "Baby Shoes" (12-7-59) Billy Barty
 12. "The Price Is Murder" (12-14-59) Robert Carricart, Den-
     nis Patrick
 13. "Terror on the Campus" (12-21-59) Anne Seymour
 14. "The Wolfe Case" (12-28-59)
 15. "Hot Money" (1-4-60) Dan Barton
 16. "Spell of Murder" (1-11-60) Malcolm Atterbury
 17. "The Grudge" (1-18-60) Robert Gist
 18. "Fill the Cup" (1-25-60) John McIntire
 19. "See No Evil" (2-1-60) Walter Burke
 20. "Sentenced" (2-8-60) Peter Adams, George Eldredge,
     Robert Ellenstein
 21. "The Hunt" (2-15-60)
 22. "Hollywood Calling" (2-29-60)
 23. "Sing a Song of Murder" (3-7-60) Diahann Carroll, James

Edwards
24. "The Long, Long Ride" (3-14-60) Robert J. Wilke
25. "The Deadly Proposition" (3-21-60) Frank Maxwell, David White
26. "The Murder Clause" (3-28-60) James Coburn, Cece Whitney
27. "The Dummy" (4-4-60) Maurice Marsac
28. "A Slight Touch of Homicide" (4-11-60) Terence DeMarney, Marcel Hillaire
29. "Wings of an Angel" (4-18-60) Sandy Kenyon
30. "The Death Watch" (4-25-60) Christopher Dark
31. "Witness in the Window" (5-2-60) Charles Aidman
32. "The Best Laid Plans" (5-9-60) Herb Ellis, Peter Whitney
33. "Send a Thief" (5-16-60) Phyllis Avery
34. "The Semi-Private Eye" (5-23-60) Billy Gray, Edward C. Platt
35. "Letter of the Law" (5-30-60) Frank Overton
36. "The Crossbow" (6-6-60) Henry Daniell
37. "The Heiress" (6-13-60) Selette Cole

Third Season

38. "The Passenger" (10-3-60) Forrest Lewis, Ted De Corsia
39. "Mask of Murder" (10-10-60) Dianne Foster
40. "The Maitre D" (10-17-60) James Lamphier
41. "The Candidate" (10-24-60)
42. "The Judgment" (10-31-60)
43. "The Death Frame" (11-7-60) Wesley Lau, Harry Clenn
44. "Death Across the Board" (11-14-60) Robert Warwick, Ned Glass
45. "Tramp Steamer" (11-21-60) Bert Freed, Peggy Taylor
46. "The Long Green Kill" (11-28-60) Patricia Huston, Diane Storm
47. "Take Five for Murder" (12-5-60) David Howe, Millicent Deming
48. "Dream Big, Dream Deadly" (12-12-60) Regis Toomey, Jimmy Fairfax
49. "Sepi" (12-19-60) Eugene Martin, June Vincent
50. "The Tender Touch" (12-26-60) Howard McNear, Joey Faye
51. "The Royal Roust" (1-2-61) Leonard Strong, Warren Kemmerling
52. "Bullet in Escrow" (1-9-61) Leonard Stone, Cegg Hoyt
53. "Jacoby's Vacation" (1-16-61) George Ives, Troy Melton, Mary Munday, Tom Palmer
54. "Blind Item" (1-23-61) Richard Ney, Mark Allen, Irene Hervey
55. "Death Is a Sore Loser" (1-30-61) Morris Erby, Jack Bernardi, Barbara English, Shirley Cytron
56. "I Know It's Murder" (2-13-61) Tommy Rettig, Jean Engstrom, Hayden Rorke, Alex Sharpe
57. "A Kill and a Half" (2-20-61) Norman Fell, Bruce Gordon, Virginia Vincent, Billy Curtis
58. "... Than a Serpent's Tooth" (2-27-61) Pamela Britton,

Clarke Gordon, Anne Whitfield
59. "The Deep End" (3-6-61) William Bryant, John Fiedler,
Billy Bakewell
60. "Portrait in Leather" (3-13-61) Herb Armstrong, Ann Robinson, William Fawcett
61. [unknown title] (3-20-61) Patti Saunders, Harry Swoger,
Barbara Stuart, Robert Lieb
62. "Cry Love--Cry Murder" (3-27-61) Joseph Sonessa, Raoul
De Leon, Eugene Igleseas
63. "A Penny Saved" (4-3-61) Oleg Tupine, Lillian Adams,
Abraham Sofaer, Joyce Vanderveen
64. "Short Motive" (4-10-61) Jimmy Murphy, Jo Helton, John
Dierkes, Fredric Villani
65. "The Murder Bond" (4-24-61) Russell Collins, Al Christy,
Ray Jenson
66. "The Most Deadly Angel" (5-1-61) Mary Sinclair, Tom Newman, Harold J. Stone, Bob Wiensko
67. "Till Death Do Us Part" (5-8-61) Robert Gibbons, Bill Lund-
mark, Anne Bellamy
68. "Last Resort" (5-15-61) Francis X. Bushman, Randy Stuart,
Sherwood Price
69. [unknown title] (5-22-61) Peter Mamakos, Bert Remsen,
Anna Navarro
70. "A Bullet for the Boy" (5-29-61) Peter Mamakos, Buzz
Martin, John Eldredge, Linda Watkins
71. "Death Is a Four-Letter Word" (6-5-61) Virginia Grey, Ned
Glass, Patric Knowles, J. Pat O'Malley
72. "Deadly Intrusion" (6-12-61) Britt Lomand, Erica Elliot,
Bill Berger, Nesdon Booth
73. "Voodoo" (6-19-61) Al Ruscio, Norbert Schiller, Donald
Long, Anthony De Marro, Greta Granstedt
74. "Down the Drain" (6-26-61) Jane Morgan, Eugene Borden,
James Waters, Burt Mustin


## BAT MASTERSON

The urbane legendary western hero was played to a polished
peak by Gene Barry in the title role.

The Regulars: Bat Masterson, Gene Barry.

The Episodes (chronicled from second season):

1. "To the Manner Born" (10-1-59) Ernestine Barrier
2. "Wanted--Dead" (10-15-59) Bethel Leslie, John Dehner
3. "No Funeral for Thorn" (10-22-59) Elisha Cook, Ray Teal,
Joi Lansing
4. "Shakedown at St. Joe" (10-29-59) Bruce Gordon, Joan
O'Brien
5. "Lady Luck" (11-5-59) Dyan Cannon, Pamela Duncan, Don
Haggerty

6. "Who'll Bury My Violence?" (11-12-59) Mort Mills
7. "Dead Men Don't Pay Debts" (11-19-59)
8. "Death and Taxes" (11-26-59) Richard Arlen, Don Kennedy, Susan Cummings
9. "Bat Plays a Dead Man's Hand" (12-3-59) Guy Prescott, Jan Harrison
10. "Garrison Finish" (12-10-59)
11. "The Canvas and the Cane" (12-17-59)
12. "The Inner Circle" (12-31-59) Jean Willes
13. "The Pied Piper of Dodge City" (1-7-60) Donald Barry
14. "A Picture of Death" (1-14-60) Patricia Donahue, Donald Woods
15. "Pigeon and Hawk" (1-21-60) Howard Petrie, Hugh Sanders
16. "Flume to the Mother Lode" (1-28-60) Paul Lambert, Jerome Cowan
17. "Death by the Half Dozen" (2-4-60) Ted De Corsia, Patrick Waltz
18. "Deadly Diamonds" (2-11-60)
19. "Mr. Fourpaws" (2-18-60)
20. "Six Feet of Gold" (2-25-60)
21. "Cattle and Cane" (3-3-60) Brad Dexter
22. "The Disappearance of Bat Masterson" (3-10-60) Oscar Beregi
23. "The Snare" (3-17-60) Robert Ivers
24. "Three Bullets for Bat" (3-24-60) Kent Taylor, Suzanne Lloyd
25. "The Reluctant Witness" (3-31-60) Allison Hayes, Ronald Hayes
26. "Come Out Fighting" (4-7-60) Rhys Williams
27. "Stage to Nowhere" (4-14-60) Constance Ford
28. "Incident at Fort Bowie" (4-21-60) Cathy Downs
29. "Masterson's Arcadia Club" (4-28-60) Morgan Jones, X Brands
30. "Welcome to Paradise" (5-5-60) Robert Foulk, James Parnell
31. "A Grave Situation" (5-12-60) John Doucette
32. "Wanted--Alive Please" (5-26-60) Steve Darrell
33. "The Elusive Baguette" (6-2-60) Leslie Parrish, Allison Hayes
34. "The Big Gamble" (6-16-60) Evan Thompson, Arch Johnson
35. "Blood on the Money" (6-23-60) Walter Coy
36. "Barbary Castle" (6-30-60) Jay Novello, Gloria Talbott

Third Season

37. "Debt of Honor" (9-29-60) Paul Langton, Gordon Hall
38. "Law of the Land" (10-6-60) Howard Petrie, Leo Gordon, Barbara Lawrence, Ray Teal, Allan Jaffe
39. "Bat Trap" (10-13-60) Lon Chaney
40. "The Rage of Princess Ann" (10-20-60) Ron Hayes, Paul Lambert
41. "The Hunter" (10-27-60) Sue Randall, Gerald Melton, Mickey Simpson, Brett King, John Vivyan

42. "Murder Can Be Dangerous" (11-3-60)
43. "High Card Loses" (11-10-60) Joan O'Brien, Jean Blake
44. "Dakota Showdown" (11-17-60) Tom Gilson, Kasey Rogers
45. "The Last of the Night Raiders" (11-24-60) Paula Raymond, Don O'Kelly
46. "Last Stop to Austin" (12-1-60) Jan Merlin, Charles Reade, Robert Karnes, Susan Cummings, Charles Fredericks
47. "A Time to Die" (12-15-60) Robert Strauss, William Tanner
48. "Death by Decree" (12-22-60) Paul Richards, June Blair, Allan Jaffe, Raymond Bailey, Robert F. Simon
49. "The Lady Plays Her Hand" (12-29-60) Wandra Hendrix, William Schallert
50. "Tempest at Tioga Pass" (1-5-61) Hank Patterson, George Macready
51. "The Court Martial of Major Mars" (1-12-61) John Anderson, Peggy Knudsen
52. "The Price of Paradise" (1-19-61) Richard Arlen, Diane Cannon, Lance Fuller
53. "End of the Line" (1-26-61) Liam Sullivan, Denver Pyle, Thorn Carney
54. "The Prescott Campaign" (2-2-61) John Dehner, Philip Ober, George Sawaya
55. "Bullwhacker's Bounty" (2-16-61) Jack Lambert, Will Wright, Jan Shepard, J. L. Smith
56. "A Lesson in Violence" (2-23-61) Virginia Gregg, Allan Jaffe, Larry Darr, Richard Eastham
57. "Run for Your Money" (3-2-61) Ray Hamilton, Gerald Mohr, Jan Harrison, Carlyle Mitchell
58. "Terror on the Trinity" (3-9-61) William Conrad, Lisa Lu, Mickey Morton
59. "Episode in Eden" (3-16-61) Bek Nelson, Bob Rice
60. "The Good and the Bad" (3-23-61) Robert Ivers, Anna Navarro, Jeanette Nolan, Grace Lee Whitney
61. "No Amnesty for Death" (3-30-61) Robert Blake, DeForest Kelly, R. G. Armstrong, Betty Barry
62. [unknown title] (4-6-61) Jean Allison, Jack Hogan, Don Wilbanks, Barry Kelley
63. "Meeting at Mimbers" (4-13-61) Warren Oates, John Burns, Harry Shannon
64. "Dagger Dance" (4-20-61) George Eldredge, Ken Mayer, Marya Stevens, William Tannen
65. "The Fourth Man" (4-27-61) George Kennedy, Dehi Berti, Audrey Dalton, Mickey Finn
66. "Dead Man's Claim" (5-4-61) Charles Maxwell, Taffy Paul, Craig Duncan, Chuck Webster
67. "The Marble Slab" (5-11-61) Erin O'Brien, Marvin Miller, Bob Rice, Rick Vallen
68. "Farmer with a Badge" (5-18-61) John Agar, Gregory Walcott, King Calder, Jackie Loughery
69. "The Fatal Garment" (5-25-61) Ron Hayes, Ed Nelson, Lisa Gaye, Les Hillman
70. "Jeopardy at Jackson Hole" (6-1-61) Joan Tabor, Larry Pennell, Ron Foster, Paul Dubov, Harry Fileer

LAWMAN

Slight western drama of a Laramie marshal (John Russell as Dan Troup), his deputy (Peter Brown as Johnny McCay) and saloon owner Lily Merrill (Peggie Castle).

The Regulars: Marshal Dan Troup, John Russell; Deputy Johnny McCay, Peter Brown; Lily Merrill, Peggie Castle (with episode of 10/4/59).

The Episodes (chronicled from second season):

1. "Lily" (10-4-59) Ray Danton
2. "The Hunch" (10-11-59) Tom Drake
3. "Shackled" (10-18-59) Robert McQueeney
4. "The Exchange" (10-25-59) Mike Road
5. "The Last Man" (11-1-59) Henry Brandon
6. "The Breakup" (11-8-59) Donald Buka
7. "Shadow Witness" (11-15-59)
8. "The Prodigal" (11-22-59) Tony Young
9. "The Press" (11-29-59) Robert J. Wilke
10. "9:05 to North Platte" (12-6-59)
11. "The Hoax" (12-20-59) Willard Waterman, John Hubbard
12. "The Shelter" (12-27-59) Chris Alcaide
13. "Last Stop" (1-3-60) Richard Arlen, Jonathan Gilmore
14. "The Showdown" (1-10-60) James Coburn, John Howard
15. "The Stranger" (1-17-60) Ian Wolfe, Clancy Cooper, Roscoe Ates
16. "The Wolfer" (1-24-60)
17. "The Hardcase" (1-31-60) Dody Heath, Don Drysdale
18. "To Capture the West" (2-7-60) Warren Stevens, Henry Brandon
19. "The Ugly Man" (2-14-60)
20. "The Kids" (2-21-60) Evelyn Rudie
21. "The Thimblerigger" (2-28-60)
22. "The Truce" (3-6-60) Don O'Kelly, Robert McQueeney
23. "Reunion in Laramie" (3-13-60) William Schallert
24. "Thirty Minutes" (3-20-60) Jack Elam
25. "Left Hand of the Law" (3-27-60) John Anderson, Robert Reed
26. "Belding's Girl" (4-3-60) Susan Morrow, Donald Barry
27. "Girl from Grantsville" (4-10-60) Suzanne Lloyd, Burt Douglas
28. "The Surface of Truth" (4-17-60) Peter Whitney, Richard Hale
29. "The Salvation of Owny O'Reilly" (4-24-60) Joel Grey, Donald Murphy
30. "The Lady Belle" (5-1-60) Joan Marshall, Vinton Hayworth
31. "The Payment" (5-8-60) Troy Donahue, Robert McQueeney
32. "The Judge" (5-15-60) John Hoyt, Diane McBain
33. "Man on a Wire" (5-22-60) Gustavo Rojo, Karen Steele
34. "The Parting" (5-29-60) Kenneth Tobey, Nancy Wickwire
35. "The Swamper" (6-5-60) Luana Anders, J. Pat O'Malley

36. "Man on a Mountain" (6-12-60) Richard Garland, Lee Van Cleef
37. "Fast Trip to Cheyenne" (6-19-60) King Calder, Suzanne Storrs

Third Season

38. "The Town Boys" (9-18-60) Tom Rettig, Richard Evans
39. "The Go-Between" (9-25-60) Paul Comi, Tom Gilson
40. "The Mad Bunch" (10-2-60) Edward Byrnes, Nick Dennis, Asa Maynor, Frank Ferguson
41. "The Old War Horse" (10-9-60) Lee Patrick, Arch Johnson
42. "The Return of Owny O'Reilly" (10-16-60) Joel Grey, Lee Van Cleef, William Fawcett
43. "Yawkey" (10-23-60) Ray Danton, Dan Sheridan
44. "Dilemma" (10-30-60) Tom Drake, John Beradino
45. "The Post" (11-6-60) Don Megowan, Bernard Fein
46. "Chantay" (11-13-60) Sharon Hugueny, Dean Fredericks
47. "Samson the Great" (11-20-60) Walter Burke, Mickey Simpson
48. "The Second Son" (11-27-60) Kimm Charney, Warren Oates
49. "The Catcher" (12-4-60) James Coburn, Robert Armstrong
50. "Cornered" (12-11-60) Frank De Kova, Tom Troupe
51. "The Escape of Joe Kilmer" (12-18-60) Lenore Roberts, Ken Lynch, Wynn Pearce, Joe Ruskin
52. "Old Stefano" (12-25-60) Gregg Palmer, John Qualen, Vladimir Sokoloff
53. "The Robbery" (1-1-61) Robert Ridgly, Hal Torey
54. "Firehouse Lil" (1-8-61) Vinton Hayworth, Dan Sheridan
55. "The Frame-Up" (1-15-61) Randy Stuart, Dabbs Greer
56. "Marked Man" (1-22-61) Jeff De Benning, Andrew Duggan, Miranda Jones
57. "The Squatters" (1-29-61) DeForest Kelly, Tom Gilson, Nina Shipman
58. "Homecoming" (2-5-61) Marc Lawrence, Ray Stricklyn
59. "Hassayampa" (2-12-61) John Anderson, Donald Barry, George Wallace
60. "The Promoter" (2-19-61) John Van Dreelen, Don Beddoe
61. "Detweiler's Kid" (2-26-61) Otto Waldis, Joyce Meadows
62. "The Inheritance" (3-5-61) Will Wright, Lurene Tuttle, Rex Holman
63. "Blue Boss and Willie Shay" (3-12-61) Sammy Davis Jr., Richard Jaeckel
64. "The Man from New York" (3-19-61) Mike Road, Richard Arlen
65. "Mark of Cain" (3-26-61) Coleen Gray, John Kellogg
66. "Fugitive" (4-2-61) Keith Richards, Catherine McLeod
67. "The Persecuted" (4-9-61) Adam Williams, Jean Willis, Evan McCord
68. "The Grubstake" (4-16-61) Frank Ferguson, Dan Sheridan, Heather Angel
69. "Whiphand" (4-23-61) Med Florey, Peggy McCay, Leo Gordon

70. "The Threat" (4-30-61) Whit Bissell, Russ Conway, Don O'Reilly
71. "The Trial" (5-7-61) Richard Sakai, Ray Teal, Shirley Knight
72. "Blind Date" (5-14-61) Mala Powers, Ted De Corsia, Jason Evers
73. "The Break-In" (5-21-61) Sheldon Allman, James Anderson
74. "Conditional Surrender" (5-28-61) Robert F. Simon, Claire Griswold
75. "Cold Fear" (6-4-61) Frank Overton, Chris Alcaide, Maggie Mahoney
76. "The Promise" (6-11-61) Robert Palmer, Ben Wright

Fourth Season

77. "Trapped" (9-17-61) Peter Breck
78. "The Juror" (9-24-61) Jack Hogan
79. "The Four" (10-1-61) Jack Elam
80. "The Son" (10-8-61) Chad Everett
81. "Owny O'Reilly, Esq." (10-15-61) Michael Greer
82. "The Substitute" (10-22-61) Kathleen Freeman
83. "The Stalker" (10-29-61) Peter Whitney, Donald Barry
84. "The Catalogue Woman" (11-5-61) Herb Vigran
85. "The Cold One" (11-12-61) Michael Pate
86. "Parphyrias Lover" (11-19-61) Lance Fuller
87. "The Appointment" (11-26-61) Kent Smith
88. "The Lords of Darkness" (12-3-61) Arch Johnson
89. "Tarot" (12-10-61) Robert McQueeney
90. "The Prodigal Mother" (12-17-61) Catherine McLeod
91. "By the Book" (12-24-61) Lyle Talbot
92. "The Trojan Horse" (12-31-61) Ken Tobey
93. "The Locket" (1-7-62) Julie Van Zandt
94. "A Friend of the Family" (1-14-62) Frank Ferguson, Vinton Hayworth
95. "The Vintage" (1-21-62) Kevin Hagen
96. "The Tarnished Badge" (1-28-62) Lon Chaney Jr.
97. "No Contest" (2-4-62) Guy Stockwell, Dawn Wells
98. "Change of Venue" (2-11-62) Philip Carey
99. "The Hold-Out" (2-18-62) Arch Johnson
100. "The Barber" (2-25-62) Pitt Herbert
101. "The Long Gun" (3-4-62) John Dehner
102. "Clooty Hutter" (3-11-62) Virginia Gregg, Jack Hogan
103. "Heritage of Hate" (3-18-62) Kathie Browne
104. "Mountain Man" (3-25-62) Med Florey
105. "The Bride" (4-1-62) Jo Morrow, L. Q. Jones
106. "The Wanted Man" (4-8-62) Marie Windsor

## BONANZA

The series that carved a niche in the hearts of millions of Americans for fourteen years (and beyond--it is still a syndication smash) is actually a giant soap opera fashioned very much in the manner of "Father Knows Best." There was paragon of virtue "Pa" Cartwright (Lorne Greene) who, when the moral situation arose, unlike "Father Knows Best"'s Jim Anderson, dispensed his dictums with all the ferocity of Zeus dispensing thunderbolts. And there was eldest son Adam (Pernell Roberts), the wiser (of course) and so most disciplined. In many ways Adam's antithesis was impetuous youngest son Joseph, appropriately called (as if to confirm his youthful misgivings) "Little Joe" (Michael Landon). The remaining son (Dan Blocker) was nicknamed "Hoss" (frequently confused with "horse" whenever unknowning strangers pondered his large frame). As the good-natured middle brother, "Hoss" more often opted for the antics of "Little Joe" over the certain courses of Adam. Add to this basic formula the grand image of the family spread "The Ponderosa" and, after a prime time change made the series accessible to a greater number of living rooms, a long-running track record was inevitable.

Above all else, "Bonanza" was a western, and so entitled to the genre's liberties with historical record. Charles Dickens (Jonathan Harris' role in "A Passion for Justice"), Samuel Clemens (Howard Duff's role in "Enter Mark Twain"), and Nobel Prize scientist Albert Abraham Michelson (played as a youth by Douglas Lambert in "Look to the Stars") were a few of the luminaries who passed the Cartwrights Virginia City way, the lives of the contemporaries dubiously intertwined.

Three episodes recalled widower Ben Cartwright's three wives: Bostonian Elizabeth (Geraldine Brooks' role in "Elizabeth, My Love"), who mothered Adam; Swedish Inger (Inga Swenson's role in "Inger, My Love") who mothered "Hoss," and Marie (Felicia Farr's role in "Marie, My Love"), who hailed from New Orleans' French Quarter and who mothered "Little Joe."

Several of Hollywood's better-known character actors did deliver fine performances; the gunplay in these particular episodes being restrained. Henry Jones was in fine form as the resurrected

Don Quixote of "A Knight to Remember." Edward Andrews was a perfectly mad "minister of the gospel" in "Song in the Dark." And Ellen Corby and Henry Hull were properly enmeshed in the affairs of the feuding factions of "The Gunmen."

Series star Michael Landon eventually tried his hand at writing (and subsequently directing) several of the teleplays. One of his best directing efforts was for Suzanne Clauser's "The Stillness Within," with Jo Van Fleet exceptional as blind teacher Ellen Dobbs.

The death of Dan Blocker on May 14, 1972 and a shift in days (from Sundays to Tuesdays) were blows too great to withstand; the series made its network exodus in January of 1973.

The Regulars: Ben Cartwright, Lorne Greene; Adam Cartwright, Pernell Roberts; Hoss (Eric) Cartwright, Dan Blocker; Joseph ("Little Joe") Cartwright, Michael Landon; Sheriff Roy Coffee, Ray Teal; Hop Sing, Victor Sen Yung; Candy, David Canary (later seasons); Griff King, Tim Matheson (1972 season); Jamie, Mitch Vogel (from twelfth season).

The Episodes:

1. "A Rose for Lotta" (9-12-59) Yvonne DeCarlo, George Macready
2. "The Sun Mountain Herd" (9-19-59) Barry Sullivan, Leo Gordon
3. "The Newcomers" (9-26-59) Inger Stevens, John Larch
4. "The Paiute War" (10-3-59) Jack Warden, Anthony Caruso, Mike Forest
5. "Enter Mark Twain" (10-10-59) Howard Duff, John Litel, Dorothy Green
6. "The Julia Bulette Story" (10-17-59) Jane Greer, Alexander Scourby
7. "The Saga of Annie O'Toole" (10-24-59) Ida Lupino, Alan Hale, Jon Patrick
8. "The Philip Diedeshiemer Story" (10-31-59) John Beal, Mala Powers, Mae Marsh, R. G. Armstrong, Charles Cooper
9. "Mr. Henry Comstock" (11-7-59) Jack Carson
10. "The Magnificent Adah" (11-14-59) Ruth Roman
11. "The Truckee Strip" (11-21-59) James Coburn, Carl Benton Reid, S. John Launer
12. "The Hanging Posse" (11-28-59) Onslow Stevens
13. "Vendetta" (12-5-59) Mort Mills
14. "The Sisters" (12-12-59) Fay Spain
15. "The Last Hunt" (12-19-59) Chana Eden, Steven Terrell
16. "El Toro Grande" (1-2-60) Barbara Luna, Ricardo Cortez
17. "The Outcast" (1-9-60) Susan Oliver, Jack Lord
18. "House Divided" (1-16-60) Cameron Mitchell, Stacy Harris, Mickey Simpson, Marianne Stewart
19. "The Gunmen" (1-23-60) Henry Hull, Ellen Corby

20. "The Fear Merchants" (1-30-60) Gene Evans, Buddy Lee, Pat Michon
21. "The Spanish Grant" (2-6-60) Patricia Medina, Sebastian Cabot
22. "Blood on the Land" (2-13-60) Everett Sloane
23. "Desert Justice" (2-20-60) Claude Akins, Wesley Lau
24. "The Stranger" (2-27-60) Lloyd Nolan
25. "Escape to the Ponderosa" (3-5-60) Joe Maross, Grant Williams, James Parnell, Gloria Talbott, Chris Alcaide
26. "The Avenger" (3-19-60) Vic Morrow, Jean Allison
27. "The Last Trophy" (3-26-60) Hazel Court, Edward Ashley
28. "San Francisco Holiday" (4-2-60) Robert Nichols, O. Z. Whitehead
29. "Bitter Water" (4-9-60) Don Dubbins, Merry Anders, Robert F. Simon
30. "Feet of Clay" (4-16-60) David Ladd, Logan Field
31. "Dark Star" (4-23-60) Hugo Haas, Susan Harrison
32. "Death at Dawn" (4-30-60) Robert Middleton, Gregory Walcott

## Second Season

33. "Showdown" (9-10-60) Ben Cooper, Jack Lambert
34. "The Mission" (9-17-60) Henry Hull, Peter Whitney, John Dehner, Harry Carey Jr.
35. "Badge Without Honor" (9-24-60) Dan Duryea, Fred Beir, Christine White
36. "The Mill" (10-1-60) Claude Akins, Harry Townes, Dianne Foster
37. "The Hopefuls" (10-8-60) Larry Gates, Patricia Donahue, Dennis Patrick
38. "Denver McKee" (10-15-60) Franchot Tone, Natalie Trundy
39. "Day of Reckoning" (10-22-60) Ricardo Montalban
40. "The Abduction" (10-29-60) Gerald Mohr, Jackie Russell
41. "Breed of Violence" (11-5-60) John Ericson, Myrna Fahey, Val Avery
42. "The Last Viking" (11-12-60) Neville Brand, Sonja Wilde, Al Ruscio
43. "The Trail Gang" (11-26-60) Dick Davalos, James Westerfield, Edgar Buchanan, Robert J. Wilke
44. "The Savage" (12-3-60) Anna-Lisa, Hal Jon Norman
45. "Silent Thunder" (12-10-60) Stella Stevens, Albert Salmi, James Griffith, Kenneth MacKenna, Sherwood Price
46. "The Ape" (12-17-60) Leonard Nimoy, Cal Bolder
47. "The Blood Line" (12-31-60) Lee Van Cleef, Jan Sterling, David Macklin
48. "The Courtship" (1-7-61) Julie Adams
49. "The Spitfire" (1-14-61) Katherine Warren, Jack Elam
50. "The Bride" (1-28-61) John McIntire, Suzanne Lloyd, Adam West
51. "The Fugitive" (2-4-61) Frank Silvera
52. "Vengeance" (2-11-61) Adam Williams, Beverly Tyler
53. "Tax Collector" (2-18-61) Eddie Firestone, Kathie Browne

54. "The Rescue" (2-25-61) Leif Erickson, Richard Coogan
55. "The Dark Gate" (3-4-61) James Coburn, CeCe Whitney
56. "The Duke" (3-11-61) Maxwell Reed, Randy Stuart, J. Pat O'Malley, Jason Evers
57. "Cut-throat Junction" (3-18-61) Robert Lansing, Shirley Ballard
58. "The Gift" (4-1-61) Martin Landau, Jim Davis
59. "The Rival" (4-15-61) Peggy Ann Garner, Charles Aidman
60. "The Infernal Machine" (4-22-61) George Kennedy, Eddie Ryder
61. "Thunderhead Swindle" (4-29-61) Parley Baer, Vito Scotti
62. "The Secret" (5-6-61) Russell Collins, Morgan Woodward
63. "The Dream Riders" (5-20-61) Sidney Blackmer, Burt Douglas
64. "Elizabeth, My Love" (5-27-61) Geraldine Brooks, Torin Thatcher
65. "Sam Hill" (6-3-61) Claude Akins, Ford Rainey

Third Season

66. "The Smiler" (9-24-61) Hershel Bernardi, Scatman Crothers
67. "Springtime" (10-1-61) John Carradine, John Qualen
68. "The Honor of Cochise" (10-8-61) Jeff Morrow, DeForest Kelley
69. "The Lonely House" (10-15-61) Paul Richards, Faith Domergue
70. "The Burma Rarity" (10-22-61) Beatrice Kay, Wally Brown
71. "Broken Ballad" (10-29-61) Robert Culp
72. "The Many Faces of Gideon Flinch" (11-5-61) Ian Wolfe, Arnold Stang, Sue Ane Langdon
73. "The Friendship" (11-12-61) Dean Jones, Janet Lake
74. "The Countess" (11-19-61) Margaret Hayes, John Anderson
75. "The Horse Breaker" (11-26-61) Ben Cooper, R. G. Armstrong
76. "Day of the Dragon" (12-3-61) Lisa Lu, Richard Loo, Philip Ahn, Mort Mills
77. "The Frenchman" (12-10-61) Andre Philippe, Erika Peters
78. "The Tin Badge" (12-17-61) Vic Morrow, Karen Steele
79. "Gabrielle" (12-24-61) Diane Mountford, John Abbott
80. "Land Grab" (12-31-61) John McGiver, George Mitchell
81. "The Tall Stranger" (1-7-62) Sean McClory, Kathie Browne
82. "The Lady from Baltimore" (1-14-62) Mercedes McCambridge
83. "The Ride" (1-21-62) Jan Merlin, Grace Gaynor
84. "The Storm" (1-28-62) Brooke Hayward, Frank Overton
85. "The Auld Sod" (2-4-62) Cheerio Meredith, James Dunn
86. "Gift of Water" (2-11-62) Royal Dano, Pam Smith
87. "The Jacknife" (2-18-62) Bethel Leslie
88. "The Guilty" (2-25-62) Lyle Bettger, Charles Maxwell
89. "The Wooing of Abigail Jones" (3-4-62) Eileen Ryan, Vaughn Monroe
90. "The Law Maker" (3-11-62) Arthur Franz, Les Tremayne
91. "Look to the Stars" (3-18-62) Douglas Lambert, William Schallert

92. "The Gamble" (4-1-62) Charles McGraw, Ben Johnson
93. "Crucible" (4-8-62) Lee Marvin
94. "Inger, My Love" (4-15-62) Inga Swenson, James Philbrook
95. "Blessed Are They" (4-22-62) Robert Brown, Ford Rainey
96. "The Dowry" (4-29-62) Steven Geray
97. "The Long Night" (5-6-62) James Coburn, Bing Russell
98. "The Mountain Girl" (5-13-62) Nina Shipman, Warren Oates
99. "The Miracle Worker" (5-20-62) Ed Nelson, Patricia Breslin, Mort Mills

Fourth Season

100. "The First Born" (9-23-62) Barry Coe, Eddy Waller
101. "The Quest" (9-30-62) Grant Richards
102. "The Artist" (10-7-62) Virginia Grey, Dan O'Herlihy
103. "A Hot Day for a Hanging" (10-14-62) Denver Pyle
104. "The Deserter" (10-21-62) Claude Akins, Robert Sampson
105. "The Way Station" (10-29-62) Robert Vaughn, Dawn Wells
106. "The War Comes to Washoe" (11-4-62) Harry Townes, Joyce Taylor
107. "Knight Errant" (11-18-62) John Doucette, Judi Meredith
108. "The Beginning" (11-25-62) Ken Lynch, Carl Reindel
109. "The Deadly Ones" (12-2-62) Leo Gordon
110. "Gallagher Sons" (12-9-62) Eileen Chesis, Robert Strauss
111. "The Decision" (12-16-62) DeForest Kelley
112. "The Good Samaritan" (12-23-62) Jeanne Cooper
113. "The Jury" (12-30-62) Jack Betts
114. "The Colonel" (1-6-63) John Larkin
115. "Song in the Dark" (1-13-63) Edward Andrews, Gregory Walcott
116. "Elegy for a Hangman" (1-20-63) Keir Dullea, Otto Kruger
117. "Half a Rogue" (1-27-63) Slim Pickens
118. "The Last Haircut" (2-3-63) Perry Lopez
119. "Marie, My Love" (2-10-63) Felicia Farr
120. "The Hayburner" (2-17-63) William Demarest, Ellen Corby
121. "The Actress" (2-24-63) Patricia Crowley, Joey Scott
122. "A Stranger Passed This Way" (3-3-63) Signe Hasso, Robert Emhardt
123. "The Way of Aaron" (3-10-63) Aneta Corseaut, Ludwig Donath
124. "A Woman Lost" (3-17-63) Ruta Lee
125. "Any Friend of Walter's" (3-24-63) Arthur Hunnicutt
126. "Mirror of a Man" (3-31-63) Ron Hayes, Ford Rainey
127. "My Brother's Keeper" (4-7-63) Carolyn Kearney
128. "Five into the Wind" (4-21-63) Kathleen Crowley, Dabbs Greer
129. "The Saga of Whizzer McGee" (4-28-63) George Brenlin, Jeanne Bal
130. "The Thunder Man" (5-5-63) Simon Oakland, Evelyn Scott
131. "Rich Man, Poor Man" (5-12-63) J. Pat O'Malley, John Fiedler
132. "The Boss" (5-19-63) Carroll O'Connor, Denver Pyle
133. "Little Man--Ten Feet Tall" (5-26-63) Ross Martin, Denver

Pyle

Fifth Season

134. "She Walks in Beauty" (9-22-63) Gena Rowlands, Jeanne
     Cooper
135. "A Passion for Justice" (9-29-63) Jonathan Harris, Victor
     Maddern
136. "Rain from Heaven" (10-6-63) John Anderson
137. "Twilight Town" (10-13-63) Davey Davison, Stacy Harris
138. "The Toy Soldier" (10-20-63) Philip Abbott, Morgan Wood-
     ward
139. "A Question of Strength" (10-27-63) Judy Carne, Ilka
     Windish, John Kellogg
140. "Calamity Over the Comstock" (11-3-63) Stefanie Powers,
     Christopher Dark
141. "Journey Remembered" (11-10-63) Inga Swenson, Gene
     Evans, Kevin Hagen
142. [title unknown] (11-17-63)
143. "The Waiting Game" (12-8-63) Kathie Browne, Katie Sweet
144. "The Legacy" (12-15-63) Robert H. Harris, James Best,
     Philip Pine
145. "Hoss and the Leprechauns" (12-22-63) Sean McClory
146. "The Prime of Life" (12-29-63) Jay C. Flippen, Melora
     Conway
147. "The Lila Conrad Story" (1-5-64) Andrew Duggan, Patricia
     Blair
148. "Ponderosa Matador" (1-12-64) Marianna Hill, Nestor
     Paiva
149. "My Son, My Son" (1-19-64) Teresa Wright, Dee Pollack
150. "Alias Joe Cartwright" (1-26-64) Keenan Wynn
151. "The Gentleman from New Orleans" (2-2-64) John Dehner,
     Sheldon Allman
152. "The Cheating Game" (2-9-64) Kathie Browne, Peter Breck
153. "Bullet for a Bride" (2-16-64) Marlyn Mason, Denver Pyle
154. "King of the Mountain" (2-23-64) Robert Middleton, Slim
     Pickens, Laurie Mitchell
155. "Love Me Not" (3-1-64) Anjanette Comer
156. "The Pure Truth" (3-8-64) Glenda Farrell, Lloyd Corrigan
157. "No Less a Man" (3-15-64) Parley Baer, John Kellogg
158. "Return to Honor" (3-22-64) Guy Williams, Arch Johnson
159. "The Saga of Muley Jones" (3-29-64) Bruce Yarnell, Jesse
     White
160. "The Roper" (4-5-64) Scott Marlowe, Julie Sommars
161. "Pink Cloud Comes from Old Cathay" (4-12-64) Marlo
     Thomas, Philip Ahn, Benson Fong
162. "The Campaneros" (4-19-64) Faith Domergue, Frank Silvera
163. "Enter Thomas Bowers" (4-26-64) William Marshall
164. "The Dark Past" (5-3-64) Dennis Hopper, Susan Seaforth
165. "The Pressure Game" (5-10-64) Kathie Browne, Joan Blon-
     dell
166. "Triangle" (5-17-64) Kathie Browne, Guy Williams
167. "Walter and the Outlaws" (5-24-64) Arthur Hunnicutt, Steve

Brodie, James Luisi

## Sixth Season

168. "Invention of a Gunfighter" (9-20-64) Guy Stockwell, Valerie Allen, Ron Foster
169. "The Hostage" (9-27-64) Harold J. Stone, Conlan Carter, Jacqueline Scott
170. "The Wild One" (10-4-64) Aldo Ray, Kathryn Hays
171. "Thanks for Everything, Friend" (10-11-64) Rory Calhoun, Linda Foster
172. "Logan's Treasure" (10-18-64) Dan Duryea, John Kellogg, Virginia Gregg
173. "The Scapegoat" (10-25-64) George Kennedy, Richard Devon, Sandra Warner
174. "A Dime's Worth of Glory" (11-1-64) Walter Brooke, Bruce Cabot
175. "Square Deal Sam" (11-8-64) Ernest Truex, Sandy Kenyon, Nydia Westman
176. "Between Heaven and Earth" (11-15-64) Richard Jaeckel
177. "Old Sheba" (11-22-64) William Demarest, Clegg Hoyt
178. "A Man to Admire" (12-6-64) James Gregory, Michel Petit, Booth Colman
179. "The Underdog" (12-13-64) Charles Bronson, Tom Reese, Bill Clark
180. "A Knight to Remember" (12-20-64) Henry Jones, Robert Sorrells
181. "The Saga of Squaw Charlie" (12-27-64) Anthony Caruso, Virginia Christine, Don Barry
182. "The Flapjack Contest" (1-3-65) Johnny Seven, Joan Huntington, Mel Bergen
183. "The Far, Far, Better Thing" (1-10-65) Brenda Scott, X Brands
184. "Woman of Fire" (1-17-65) Joan Hackett, Jay Novello, Cesare Danova
185. "The Ballerina" (1-24-65) Barrie Chase, Warren Stevens
186. "The Flannel-Mouth Gun" (1-31-65) Earl Holliman, Robert Wilke, Don Collier, Harry Carey
187. "Ponderosa Birdman" (2-7-65) Ed Wynn, Marlyn Mason
188. "The Search" (2-14-65) Lola Albright, Kelly Thordsen
189. "The Deadliest Game" (2-21-65) Cesar Romero, Ilze Taurins
190. "Once a Doctor" (2-28-65) Michael Rennie, Ashley Cowen
191. "Right Is the Fourth R" (3-7-65) Mariette Hartley, Everett Sloane
192. "Hound Dog" (3-21-65) Bruce Yarnell, Sue Ane Langdon
193. "The Trap" (3-28-65) Joan Freeman, Steve Cochran
194. "Dead and Gone" (4-4-65) Hoyt Axton, Susanne Cramer
195. "A Good Night's Rest" (4-11-65) Abigail Skelton, Robert Ridgley, Jean Willes, Lloyd Corrigan, Jay Ripley
196. "To Own the World" (4-18-65) Telly Savalas, Linda Lawson
197. "Lothario Larkin" (4-25-65) Noah Beery Jr., Dorothy Green
198. "The Return" (5-2-65) Tony Young, Joan Blackman, John

    Conte
199. "The Jonah" (5-9-65) Angela Clark, Erin O'Donnell, Dean
    Harens
200. "The Spotlight" (5-16-65) Viveca Lindfors, Ron Randell
201. "Patchwork Man" (5-23-65) Grant Williams, Bruce Gordon,
    Sue Randall, Lane Bradford

Seventh Season

202. "The Debt" (9-12-65) Tommy Sands, Brooke Bundy
203. "The Dilemma" (9-19-65) Tom Tully, Anthony Call
204. "The Brass Box" (9-26-65) Ramon Novarro, Michael Dante
205. "The Other Son" (10-3-65) Ed Begley, Bing Russell, Tom
    Simcox
206. "The Lonely Runner" (10-10-65) Gilbert Roland, Pat Con-
    way, Ken Lynch
207. "Devil on Her Shoulder" (10-17-65) Ina Balin, John Dou-
    cette
208. "Found Child" (10-24-65) Eileen Baral, Gerald Mohr
209. "The Meredith Smith" (10-31-65) Strother Martin, Anne
    Helm, Robert Colbert
210. "Mighty Is the Word" (11-7-65) Glenn Corbett, Michael
    Whitney, Sue Randall
211. "The Strange One" (11-14-65) Louise Sorel, Robert
    McQueeney, Willard Sage
212. "The Reluctant Rebel" (11-21-65) Tim Considine, Royal
    Dano
213. "Five Sundowns to Sunup" (12-5-65) Marie Windsor, Doug-
    las Henderson, John Hoyt
214. "A Natural Wizard" (12-12-65) Eddie Hodges, Douglas Ken-
    nedy, Jacqueline Scott
215. "All Ye His Saints" (12-19-65) Clint Howard, Leif Erick-
    son
216. "A Dublin Lad" (1-2-66) Liam Sullivan, Maggie Mahoney
217. "To Kill a Buffalo" (1-9-66) Jose De Vega, Steven Gravers
218. "Ride the Wind" [Part I] (1-16-66) Victor Jory, Rod
    Cameron, DeForest Kelley
219. "Ride the Wind" [Part II] (1-23-66) as above
220. "Destiny's Child" (1-30-66) Dick Peabody, Walter Burke
221. "Peace Officer" (2-6-66) Eric Fleming, Ron Foster
222. "The Code" (2-13-66) George Montgomery, Robert Ellen-
    stein
223. "Three Brides for Hoss" (2-20-66) Stuart Erwin, Wynn
    Pearce
224. "The Emperor Norton" (2-27-66) Sam Jaffe, Parley Baer
225. "Her Brother's Keeper" (3-6-66) Nancy Gates, Wesley
    Lau
226. "The Trouble with Jamie" (3-20-66) Michael Burns, Ross
    Elliott
227. "Shining in Spain" (3-27-66) Judi Rolin, Woodrow Parfrey
228. "The Genius" (4-3-66) Lonny Chapman
229. "The Unwritten Commandment" (4-10-66) Wayne Newton,
    Anne Jeffreys, Malcolm Atterbury

230. "Big Shadows on the Land" (4-17-65) Jack Kruschen, Brioni Farrell
231. "The Fighters" (4-24-66) Philip Pine, Michael Conrad
232. "Home from the Sea" (5-1-66) Alan Bergmann, Ivor Barry
233. "The Last Mission" (5-8-66) R. G. Armstrong, Tom Reese
234. "A Dollar's Worth of Trouble" (5-15-66) Sally Kellerman, Mabel Anderson, Elisha Cook

Eighth Season

235. "Something Hurt, Something Wild" (9-11-66) Lyle Bettger, Lynn Loring
236. "Horse of a Different Hue" (9-18-66) Charles Ruggles, Skip Homeier, Julie Parrish
237. "A Time to Step Down" (9-25-66) Ed Begley, Audrey Totter
238. "The Pursued" [Part I] (10-2-66) Eric Fleming, Dina Merrill, Lois Nettleton
239. "The Pursued" [Part II] (10-9-66) as above
240. "To Bloom for Thee" (10-16-66) Geraldine Brooks, Don Haggerty
241. "Credit for a Kill" (10-23-66) Don Collier, Dean Harens
242. "Four Sisters from Boston" (10-30-66) Vera Miles, Morgan Woodward
243. "Old Charlie" (11-6-66) John McIntire, Jeanette Nolan
244. "Ballad of the Ponderosa" (11-13-66) Randy Boone, Ann Doran, Roger Davis, John Archer
245. "The Oath" (11-20-66) Tony Bill, Douglas Kennedy
246. "A Real Nice, Friendly Little Town" (11-27-66) Louise Latham, Mark Slade
247. "The Bridegroom" (12-4-66) Ron Hayes, Joanne Linville
248. "Tommy" (12-18-66) Teddy Quinn, Janet DeGore
249. "A Christmas Story" (12-25-66) Wayne Newton, Jack Oakie
250. "Ponderosa Explosion" (1-1-67) Dub Taylor, Chick Chandler
251. "Justice" (1-8-67) Beau Bridges
252. "A Bride for Buford" (1-15-67) Lola Albright, Jack Elam
253. "Black Friday" (1-22-67) John Saxon, Ford Rainey
254. "The Unseen Wound" (1-29-67) Leslie Nielsen, Nancy Malone
255. "Journey to Terror" (2-5-67) John Ericson, Jason Evers
256. "Amigo" (2-12-67) Henry Darrow, Gregory Walcott
257. "A Woman in the House" (2-19-67) Diane Baker, Paul Richards
258. "Judgment at Red Creek" (2-26-67) John Ireland, Harry Carey
259. "Joe Cartwright, Detective" (3-5-67) Mort Mills, Ken Lynch, Bing Russell
260. "Dark Enough to See the Stars" (3-12-67) Richard Evans, Linda Foster
261. "The Deed and the Dilemma" (3-26-67) Jack Kruschen, Donald Woods
262. "The Prince" (4-2-67) Lloyd Bochner, Claire Griswold,

Warren Stevens
263. "A Man Without Land" (4-9-67) Jeremy Slate, Royal Dano
264. "Napoleon's Children" (4-16-67) Michael Burns, Robert
      Biheller
265. "The Wormwood Cup" (4-23-67) Frank Overton, Judi Mere-
      dith
266. "Clarissa" (4-30-67) Nina Foch, Roy Roberts
267. "Maestro Hoss" (5-7-67) Zsa Zsa Gabor, Kathleen Freeman
268. "The Greedy Ones" (5-14-67) Robert Middleton, George
      Chandler

Ninth Season

269. "Second Chance" (9-17-67) James Gregory, Joe De Santis,
      Bettye Ackerman
270. "Sense of Duty" (9-24-67) Gene Rutherford, Michael Forest,
      Ron Foster
271. "The Conquistadors" (10-1-67) John Saxon, Eddie Ryder,
      John Kellogg, Mike De Anda
272. "Judgment at Olympus" (10-8-67) Barry Sullivan
273. "Night of Reckoning" (10-15-67) Richard Jaeckel, Ron
      Hayes, Joan Freeman
274. "False Witness" (10-22-67) Davey Davison, Michael Blod-
      gett, Robert McQueeney
275. "The Gentle Ones" (10-29-67) Robert Walker Jr., Lana
      Wood
276. "Desperate Passage" (11-5-67) Tina Louise, Steve Forrest
277. "The Sure Thing" (11-12-67) Kim Darby
278. "Showdown at Tahoe" (11-19-67) Richard Anderson, Sheila
      Larken, Karl Swenson
279. "Six Black Horses" (11-26-67) Burgess Meredith, David
      Lewis, Judy Parker, Richard X. Slattery, Don Haggerty,
      Hal Baylor
280. "Check Rein" (12-3-67) Patricia Hyland, Ford Rainey,
      James MacArthur, Charles Maxwell, Robert Karnes
281. "Justice Deferred" (12-17-67) Simon Oakland, Nita Talbot
282. "The Gold Detector" (12-24-67) Wally Cox, Paul Fix, Dub
      Taylor, Kelly Thordsen
283. "The Trackers" (1-7-68) Warren Stevens, Bruce Dern,
      Warren Vanders, Ted Gehring
284. "A Girl Named George" (1-14-68) Sheilah Wells, Jack
      Albertson, Gerald Mohr
285. "The Thirteenth Man" (1-21-68) Albert Salmi, Richard
      Carlson, Ken Tobey, Myron Healey, Bill Quinn, Anna
      Navarro
286. "The Burning Sky" (1-28-68) Dawn Wells, Michael Murphy
287. "The Price of Salt" (2-4-68) Kim Hunter, John Doucette,
      James Best
288. "Blood Tie" (2-18-68) Robert Drivas, Conlan Carter
289. "The Crime of Johnny Mule" (2-25-68) Noah Beery
290. "The Late Ben Cartwright" (3-3-68) Sidney Blackmer,
      Bert Freed, William Campbell, Simon Scott
291. "Star Crossed" (3-10-68) Tisha Sterling, William Windom

292. "Trouble Town" (3-17-68) Robert Wilke, Elizabeth MacRae, Steve Brodie
293. "Commitment at Angelus" (4-7-68) Peter Whitney, Marj Dusay, Ken Lynch, Ivan Triesault
294. "A Dream to Dream" (4-14-68) Steve Ihnat, Julie Harris
295. "In Defense of Honor" (4-28-68) Lou Antonio, Arnold Moss, Ned Romero, Lane Bradford, Cherie Latimer, Troy Melton
296. "To Die in Darkness" [Michael Landon made his directorial debut with this episode, which he scripted] (5-5-68) James Whitmore
297. "The Bottle Fighter" (5-12-68) Albert Dekker
298. "The Arrival of Eddie" (5-19-68) Michael Vincent
299. "The Stronghold" (5-26-68) Michael Witney, Paul Mantee, Lynda Day, James Davidson
300. "Pride of Man" (6-2-68) Morgan Woodward
301. "A Severe Case of Matrimony" (7-7-68) J. Carrol Naish
302. "Stage Door Johnnies" (7-28-68) Kathleen Crowley, Walter Brooke, Mike Mazurki

Tenth Season

303. "Different Pines, Same Wind" (9-15-68) Irene Tedrow, John Randolph, Herbert Voland, G. D. Spradlin, George Murdock, John L. Wheeler
304. "Child" (9-22-68) John Marley, Harry Hickok, Yaphet Kotto, Henry Beckman, Frank DeVol, Robert Ball, Charles Maxwell, Bruce Kirby
305. "Salute to Yesterday" (9-29-68) Pat Conway, Sandra Smith, John Kellogg, Carlos Rivas
306. "The Real People of Muddy Creek" (10-6-68) Joe Don Baker, Clifton James, Jean Hale, Ann Doran, Hal Lynch, Russell Thorson
307. "The Passing of a King" (10-13-68) Jeremy Slate, Denver Pyle, Diana Muldaur, Dan Tobin, Russ Conway
308. "The Last Vote" (10-20-68) Tom Bosley, Wally Cox, Robert Emhardt, Bing Russell, Don Haggerty, Lane Bradford, Bruno Ve Sota
309. "Catch as Catch Can" (10-27-68) Paul Richards, Slim Pickens, Robert Yuro, Richard Eric Winter, Arthur Malet
310. "Little Girl Lost" (11-3-68) Linda Sue Risk, Antoinette Bower
311. "The Survivors" (11-10-68) Mariette Hartley, John Carter, Martin Ashe, Harriet Medin
312. "The Sound of Drums" (11-17-68) Jack Kruschen, Penny Santon, Brioni Farrell, Michael Stefani
313. "Queen High" (12-1-68) Celeste Yarnell, Paul Lambert, Sandor Szabo, Dabney Coleman, Ken Drake, Edward Schaaf
314. "Yonder Man" (12-8-68) John Vernon, Melissa Murphy, Rodolfo Acosta, Larry Ward
315. "Mark of Guilt" (12-15-68) Dick Foran, Michael Vandever,

Alan Bergmann, Lou Frissell, Gordon Dilworth

316. "A World Full of Cannibals" (12-22-68) James Patterson
317. "Sweet Annie Laurie" (1-5-69) Joan Van Ark, James Olson
318. "My Friend, My Enemy" (1-12-69) John Saxon, Woodrow
     Parfrey, Chick Chandler, Gregory Walcott, Ben Hammer
319. "Mrs. Wharton and the Lesser Breeds" (1-19-69) Mildred
     Natwick, Oren Stevens
320. "Erin" (1-26-69) Mary Fickett, Don Briggs, Michael Keep,
     Joan Tompkins
321. "Company of Forgotten Men" (2-2-69) James Gregory,
     Charles Maxwell, John Pickard, Ken Lynch, William
     Bryant
322. "The Clarion" (2-9-69) Phyllis Thaxter, Simon Oakland,
     William Jordan, Hamilton Camp, Philip Kennally, Ken
     Mayer, Connie Sawyer, James Jeter, Arthur Peterson
323. "The Lady and the Mountain Lion" (2-23-69) Richard
     Haydn, Michael Keep
324. "Five Candles" (3-2-69) Scott Thomas, Don Knight
325. "The Wish" (3-9-69) Ossie Davis, George Spell
326. "The Deserter" (3-16-69) Ford Rainey, Ellen Davalos
327. "Emily" (3-23-69) Beth Brickell, Ron Hayes
328. "The Running Man" (3-30-69) Robert Pine, Will Geer
329. "The Unwanted" (4-6-69) Bonnie Bedelia, Charles McGraw,
     Michael Vincent
330. "Speak No Evil" (4-20-69) Patricia Smith, Kevin Burchett,
     Dana Elcar
331. "The Fence" (4-27-69) J. D. Cannon, John Anderson
332. "A Ride in the Sun" (5-11-69) Robert Hogan, Anthony
     Zerbe, Marj Dusay, Jack Collins

Eleventh Season

333. "Another Windmill to Go" (9-14-69) Laurence Naismith,
     Jill Townsend
334. "The Witness" (9-21-69) Stefan Gierasch, Melissa Murphy
335. "Silence at Stillwater" (9-28-69) Pat Hingle, Strother
     Martin
336. "A Lawman's Lot Is Not a Happy One" (10-5-69) Tom
     Bosley, Robert Emhardt
337. "Anatomy of a Lynching" (10-12-69) Guy Stockwell, Tyler
     McVey
338. "To Stop a War" (10-19-69) Steve Forrest, Miriam Colon,
     Warren Kemmerling, Bing Russell
339. "The Medal" (10-26-69) Dean Stockwell, Harry Townes,
     Susan Howard, Charles Briles
340. "The Stalker" (11-2-69) Charlotte Stewart, Lloyd Battista,
     John Perak
341. "Meena" (11-16-69) Ann Prentiss, Victor French, Dub
     Taylor, Robert Donner
342. "A Darker Shadow" (11-23-69) Gregory Walcott
343. "Dead Wrong" (12-7-69) Mike Mazurki, Robert Sorrells
344. "Old Friends" (12-14-69) Robert J. Wilke, Morgan Wood-
     ward

345. "Abner Willoughby's Return" (12-21-69) John Astin, Emmaline Henry
346. "The Fence" (12-28-69) John Anderson, J. D. Cannon, Verna Bloom, Lawrence Linville
347. "It's a Small World" (1-4-70) Michael Dunn, Edward Binns, Bing Russell, Angela Clarke
348. "Danger Road" (1-11-70) Robert Lansing, Anna Novarro, William Sylvester
349. "The Big Jackpot" (1-18-70) Walter Brooke, Robert F. Simon, Alan Caillou
350. "The Trouble with Amy" (1-25-70) Jo Van Fleet, John Crawford, Donald Moffatt
351. "The Lady and the Mark" (2-1-70) Elaine Giftos, James Westerfield, Christopher Connelly
352. "Is There Any Man Here?" (2-8-70) John McLiam, Mariette Hartley, Burr DeBenning
353. "The Law and Billy Burgess" (2-15-70) Mercedes McCambridge, Les Tremayne, David Cassidy
354. "Long Way to Ogden" (2-22-70) Kathleen Freeman, Walter Barnes
355. "Return Engagement" (3-1-70) Joyce Bulifant, Sally Kellerman, Morgan Sterne
356. "The Gold Mine" (3-8-70) Tony De Costa, Bruce Dern
357. "Decision at Los Robles" (3-22-70) William H. Bassett, Joe De Santis, Ted Cassidy
358. "Caution, Easter Bunny Crossing" (3-29-70) Marc Lawrence, Len Lesser
359. "The Horse Traders" (4-5-70) Dub Taylor, Ann Prentiss, Victor French, Lou Frizzell
360. "What Are Pardners For?" (4-12-70) Slim Pickens, Dabbs Greer, John Beck, Richard Evans
361. "A Matter of Circumstance" (4-19-70) Ted Gehring, Vincent Van Patten

Twelfth Season

362. "The Night Virginia City Died" (9-13-70) Angel Tompkins, Bing Russell, Phil Brown, Edith Atwater
363. "A Matter of Faith" (9-20-70) Lou Frizzell, Bruce Gordon
364. "The Weary Willies" (9-27-70) Richard Thomas, Lee Purcell, Lonny Chapman, Elisha Cook
365. "The Wagon" (10-5-70) Denver Pyle, Salome Jens, George Murdock
366. "The Power of Life and Death" (10-11-70) Rupert Crosse, Lou Frizzell
367. "Gideon, the Good" (10-18-70) Richard Kiley, Terry Moore, A. Martinez, Carmen Zapata
368. "The Trouble with Trouble" (10-25-70) Gene Evans, E. J. Andre, G. D. Spradlin
369. "Thorton's Account" (11-1-70) Gregory Walcot, Carl Reindel, Heather Menzies, Scott Walker
370. "The Love Child" (11-8-70) Carol Lawson, Will Geer, Josephine Hutchinson

371. "El Jefe" (11-15-70) Rodolfo Acosta, Warren Stevens, Jaime Sanchez
372. "The Luck of Pepper Shannon" (11-22-70) Neville Brand, Walter Brooke, Dan Tobin
373. "The Imposters" (12-13-70) Strother Martin, Anthony Colti, Anthony James
374. "Honest John" (12-20-70) Jack Elam
375. "For a Young Lady" (12-27-70) Jewel Blanch, Paul Fix, Madeleine Sherwood
376. "A Single Pilgrim" (1-3-71) Beth Brickell, Jeff Corey, John Schuck
377. "The Gold-Plated Rifle" (1-10-71) regulars
378. "Top Hand" (1-17-71) Ben Johnson, Roger Davis
379. "A Deck of Aces" (1-31-71) Alan Oppenheimer, Linda Gaye Scott, Charles Dierkop
380. "The Desperado" (2-7-71) Lou Gossett, Marlene Clark, Ramon Bieri
381. "The Reluctant American" (2-14-71) Daniel Massey, Jill Haworth, J. Pat O'Malley, Daniel Kemp
382. "Shadow of a Hero" (2-21-71) Laurence Luckinbill, John Randolph, Linda Watkins
383. "The Silent Killers" (2-28-71) Meg Foster, Harry Holcombe, Louise Latham
384. "Terror at 2:00" (3-7-71) Steve Ihnat, Dabbs Greer, Byron Mabe
385. "The Stillness Within" (3-14-71) Jo Van Fleet, Harry Holcombe, Jeannine Brown
386. "A Time to Die" (3-21-71) Vera Miles, Henry Beckman, Melissa Newman
387. "Winter Kill" (3-28-71) Glenn Corbett, Clifton James, Sheilah Wells
388. "Kingdom of Fear" (4-4-71) Alfred Ryder, Richard Mulligan, Luke Askew
389. "An Earthquake Called Callahan" (4-11-71) Victor French, Sandy Duncan, Lou Frizzell, Dub Taylor

Thirteenth Season

390. "The Grand Swing" (9-19-71) Ralph Moody, Charlotte Stewart, Med Flory, Ted Gehring
391. "Fallen Woman" (9-26-71) Susan Tyrrell, Arthur O'Connell, Ford Rainey
392. "Bushwacked" (10-3-71) Richard O'Brien, Peggy McCay, David Huddleston
393. "Rock-a-Bye Hoss" (10-10-71) Edward Andrews, Patricia Harty, Ellen Moss
394. "The Prisoners" (10-17-71) Michael Witney, Morgan Woodward, Manuel Padilla
395. "Cassie" (10-27-71) Lisa Gerritsen, Diane Baker, Jack Cassidy
396. "Don't Cry, My Son" (10-31-71) Richard Mulligan, Diana Shalet, Dan Ferrone
397. "Face of Fear" (11-14-71) Bradford Dillman, Chick Chandl

Donald Moffatt
398. "Blind Hunch" (11-21-71) Rip Torn, Don Knight, Loretta Leversee, Charles Maxwell
399. "The Iron Butterfly" (11-28-71) Mariette Hartley, Stefan Gierasch
400. "The Rattlesnake Brigade" (12-5-71) Neville Brand, David Sheiner, Severn Darden
401. "Easy Come, Easy Go" (12-12-71) Ann Prentiss
402. "A Home for Jamie" (12-19-71) regulars
403. "Warbonnet" (12-26-71) Chief Dan George, Forrest Tucker, Linda Cristal
404. "A Lonely Man" (1-2-72) Kelly Jean Peters, Peter Hobbs
405. "Second Sight" (1-9-72) Joan Hackett
406. "Saddle Stiff" (1-16-72) Buddy Ebsen
407. "Frenzy" (1-30-72) Kathleen Widdoes, Jason Karpf, Michael Pataki
408. "Customs of the Country" (2-6-72) Alan Oppenheimer, Pilar Seurat
409. "Shanklin" (2-13-72) Charles Cioffi, Woodrow Parfrey, Kara Lukas
410. "Search in Limbo" (2-20-72) Albert Salmi, Lawrence Montaigne, Pamela Payton-Wright
411. "He Was Only Seven" (3-5-72) Roscoe Lee Browne, William Watson, Robert Doyle
412. "The Younger Brothers" (3-12-72) Strother Martin, Doc Severinsen, Chuck McCann, Henry Jones
413. "A Place to Hide" (3-19-72) Suzanne Pleshette, Hurd Hatfield, Jodie Foster, Jon Cypher
414. "A Visit to Upright" (3-26-72) Alan Oppenheimer, Loretta Swit, Anne Seymour
415. "One Ace Too Many" (4-2-72) Greg Mullavey, Kate Jackson, William Mims

Fourteenth Season

416. "Forever" [special two-hour episode] (9-12-72) Bonnie Bedelia, Roy Jenson, Andy Robinson, Larry Golden
417. "Heritage of Anger" (9-19-72) Robert Lansing, Fionnuala Flanagan, Warren Kemmerling, Len Lesser
418. "The Initiation" (9-26-72) Ronny Howard, James Chandler, Ed Bakey, Sean Kelly, Biff Elliot
419. "Riot!" (10-3-72) Aldo Ray, Tim Matheson, Marco St. John
420. "New Man" (10-10-72) Ronny Cox, Charles Dierkop
421. "Ambush at Rio Lobo" (10-24-72) James Olson, Albert Salmi, Sian Barbara Allen, Murray MacLeod
422. "The 26th Grave" (10-31-72) Ken Howard, Dana Elcar, Stacy Keach Jr., Phil Kenneally, Walter Burke
423. "Stallion" (11-14-72) Clu Gulager, Mitzi Hoag, Vincent Van Patten
424. "The Hidden Enemy" (11-28-72) Mike Farrell, Melissa Murphy, Jason Wingreen, David Huddleston, Russell Thorsen

425. "The Sound of Loneliness" (12-5-72) Jack Albertson, Timothy Marshall, Dan Feronne, John Randolph, Carol Lawson
426. "The Bucket Dog" (12-19-72) William Sylvester, John Zaremba, Don Knight, Ivan Bonar
427. "First Love" (12-26-72) Pamela Franklin, Jordan Rhodes, Lisa Eilbacher
428. "The Witness" (1-2-73) regulars
429. "The Marriage of Theodora Duffy" (1-9-73) Richard Eatham, Ramon Bieri, Karen Carlson, Robert Yuro
430. "The Hunter" (1-16-73) Tom Skerritt, Phillip Avenetti


## THE MAN AND THE CHALLENGE

Highway hypnosis was but one of the phenomena investigated by government scientist Glenn Barton (George Nader) in this Ivan Tors entry.

The Regulars: Glenn Barton, George Nader.

The Episodes:

1. "The Sphere of No Return" (9-12-59) Paul Burke, Joyce Meadows, Raymond Bailey
2. "Maximum Capacity" (9-19-59) James Best, Robert Conrad, Paula Raymond
3. "Odds Against Survival" (9-26-59)
4. "Sky Diving" (10-3-59) Daniele Aubrey, John Van Dreelen
5. "Experiments in Terror" (10-10-59) Otto Kruger, Julie Adams
6. "Invisible Force" (10-17-59) Debra Paget, William Conrad
7. "Escape to Nepal" (10-24-59)
8. "Border to Border" (10-31-59) Edward Kemmer
9. "Trial by Fire" (11-7-59) H. M. Wynant, Joyce Taylor
10. "White Out" (11-14-59) Jan Shepard, Phil Terry
11. "The Breaking Point" (11-28-59) Alfred Ryder, John Marley
12. "Jungle Survival" (12-5-59) Dean Harens
13. "I've Killed Seven Men" (12-12-59) Lin McCarthy
14. "Man Without Fear" (12-19-59) John Daly, Tracey Roberts
15. "The Visitors" (12-26-59) Jack Ging, Bert Remsen
16. "The Storm" (1-2-60) Fred Gabourie, Roberta Haynes
17. "Killer River" (1-9-60) John Archer, Michael Keith
18. "Rodeo" (1-23-60) Ann Robinson, Myron Healey
19. "The Windowless Room" (1-30-60) Jack Ging, Sue Randall
20. "Nightmare Crossing" (2-6-60) Keith Larsen, Tony Monaco
21. "The Lure of Danger" (2-13-60) Miguel Landa, Felipe Turich
22. "Recovery" (2-20-60) Eloise Hardt
23. "Buried Alive" (2-27-60) Joyce Meadows, Robert Gothie
24. "Recondo" (3-5-60) Jack Harris, Marianne Hill

25. "Flying Lab" (3-12-60) Keith Vincent
26. "Hurricane Mesa" (3-19-60) Jack Ging, Bob Bice
27. "Astro Female" (3-26-60) Maureen Leeds, Adrienne Hayes
28. "The Extra Sense" (4-2-60) Frank Maxwell, Paul Comi
29. "Man in the Capsule" (4-9-60) Darryl Hickman, Fred Beir
30. "The Dropper" (4-23-60) Jack O'Brien, Arthur Heller
31. "High Dive" (4-30-60) Olive Sturgess, Charles Alvin Bell
32. "Daredevils" (5-7-60) Don Kennedy, Christine White
33. "Shooter McLaine" (5-21-60) Mala Powers, John Milford
34. "Early Warning" (5-28-60) Philip Ober, Bethel Leslie
35. "Breakoff" (6-4-60) Karl Swenson, Miranda Jones
36. "Highway to Danger" (6-11-60) Karen Scott, Hank Patterson


## THE DEPUTY

A vehicle for Henry Fonda was this western in which he was an Arizona marshal; Allen Case his reluctant deputy.

The Regulars: Marshal Simon Fry, Henry Fonda; Clay McCord, Allen Case; Marshal Herk Lamson, Wallace Ford; Fran McCord, Betty Lou Keim; Sargeant Tasker, Read Morgan (with episode of 10/1/60).

The Episodes:

1. [Fry pursues two bank robbers] (9-12-59)
2. "The Wild Wind" (9-19-59) Richard Shannon, Gary Vinson
3. "Back to Glory" (9-26-59) Frank De Kova, Marie Windsor
4. "Shadow of the Noose" (10-3-59) Clu Gulager, Denver Pyle
5. "Powder Keg" (10-10-59) Onslow Stevens, Read Morgan, Christopher Dark
6. "Like Father" (10-17-59) Fred Beir, James Westerfield
7. "Proof of Guilt" (10-24-59)
8. "The Johnny Shanks Story" (10-31-59) Skip Homeier
9. "Focus of Doom" (11-7-59) Eduard Franz, Dennis Patrick
10. "The Big Four" (11-14-59) Henry Brandon, Richard Bakalyan
11. "The Next Bullet" (11-28-59)
12. "The Deal" (12-5-59) Kelly Thordson, Mel Welles
13. "Land Greed" (12-12-59) Vivian Vance
14. "Man of Peace" (12-19-59) Robert Warwick, Edgar Buchanan
15. "The Orphans" (12-26-59)
16. "Backfire" (1-2-60) Paula Raymond, Charles Cooper
17. "Hang the Law" (1-9-60) Martha Hyer
18. "Silent Gun" (1-23-60)
19. "The Hidden Motive" (1-30-60) Roxanne Berard, Jeremy Slate
20. "Lawman's Blood" (2-6-60) Philip Pine
21. "The Return of Simon Fry" (2-13-60) Stacy Keach, Peter Mamakos
22. "Queen Bea" (2-20-60)
23. "The Two Faces of Bob Claxton" (2-27-60) Robert

Montgomery Jr.
24. "Lady with a Mission" (3-5-60) Jan Clayton
25. "The Border Between" (3-12-60) Anna Kashfi, Leo Gordon
26. "Final Payment" (3-19-60)
27. "Dark Reward" (3-26-60) Jean Willes, Richard Garland
28. "Marked for Bounty" (4-2-60) Ron Hayes, Alan Baxter
29. "The Truly Yours" (4-9-60) Harry Townes, James Coburn, Arthur Batanides, Miriam Colon
30. "A Time to Sow" (4-23-60) Richard Crenna, Coleen Gray
31. "Last Gunfight" (4-30-60) Charles McGraw
32. "The Chain of Action" (5-7-60) Lee Patterson
33. "Lucifer Urge" (5-14-60) George Tobias, Nancy Valentine
34. "Palace of Chance" (5-21-60) Karen Steele, Lee Van Cleef
35. "The X Game" (5-28-60) John Hoyt
36. "Trail of Darkness" (6-4-60) Donald Woods, Gregg Palmer
37. "The Standoff" (6-11-60) Alan Hale
38. "The Choice" (6-25-60) Rex Holman
39. "Ma Mack" (7-9-60) Nina Varela, Jack Hogan

Second Season

40. "The Deadly Breed" (9-24-60) Susan Oliver, Lyle Bettger
41. "Meet Sergeant Tasker" (10-1-60)
42. "The Jason Harris Story" (10-8-60) Jeff Morrow, Dianne Foster
43. "The Fatal Urge" (10-15-60) Kathleen Crowley, Ron Starr
44. "Mother and Son" (10-29-60) James Franciscus, Josephine Hutchinson
45. "Bitter Root" (11-5-60) Virginia Gregg, Don Megowan
46. "The Higher Law" (11-12-60) H. M. Wynant, John Larch
47. "Passage to New Orleans" (11-19-60) Patrice Wymore, Carl Benton Reid
48. "The World Against Me" (11-26-60) Dennis Joel, Joseph Bassett
49. [unknown title] (12-3-60) Fay Spain, William Fawcett
50. "Three Brothers" (12-10-60) Cathy Case, Jack Ging, Lew Gallo
51. "Day of Fear" (12-17-60) Tyler McVey, Mary Tyler Moore
52. "Second Cousin to the Czar" (12-24-60) Carl Esmond
53. "Judas Town" (12-31-60) Roy Roberts, Ed Nelson
54. "Duty Bound" (1-7-61) Frank Maxwell, Ron Harper
55. "The Lesson" (1-14-61) Harry Lauter, Wanda Hendrix
56. "Past and Present" (1-21-61) Arthur Franz, Mary Beth Hughes
57. "The Hard Decision" (1-28-61) Marc Lawrence
58. "The Dream" (2-4-61) Dick Foran, Carolyn Craig
59. "The Shackled Town" (2-11-61) Robert Brubaker, Reed Hadley
60. "The Lonely Road" (2-18-61) Edward Binns, Constance Ford
61. "The Challenger" (2-25-61) Hal Baylor
62. "The Edge of Doubt" (3-4-61) Richard Chamberlain
63. "Two-way Deal" (3-11-61) Billy Gray, Ted De Corsia
64. "The Means and the End" (3-18-61) Phyllis Love, DeForest

Kelley
65. "The Example" (3-25-61) Denver Pyle
66. 'Cherchez la Femme" (4-1-61) Lisa Montell
67. "Tension Point" (4-8-61) John Marley, Jerome Thor, Virginia Christine
68. "Brother in Arms" (4-15-61) Lon Chaney, Denny Miller
69. "The Return of Widow Brown" (4-22-61) Norma Crane, Richard Shannon
70. "Spoken in Silence" (4-29-61) Robert Burton, Frances Helm
71. "Enemy of the Town" (5-6-61) Whit Bissell, Ray Kellogg
72. "The Legend of Dixie" (5-20-61) Gregory Walcott, Stanley Adams
73. "The Deathly Quiet" (5-27-61) Johnny Cash, Robert Foulk, Michael Garrett
74. "Brand of Honesty" (6-10-61) George Dolenz, Elisha Cook
75. "Lorinda Belle" (6-24-61) Claude Akins, Frank Overton
76. "Lawman's Conscience" (7-1-61) Russell Johnson, Tracey Roberts, Jason Robards Sr.


## FIVE FINGERS

Not of the calibre of its 1952 film predecessor was this television adaptation of L. C. Moyzisch's book Operation: Cicero (New York: Coward-McCann, 1950).

The Regulars: Victor Sebastion, David Hedison; Simone Genet, Luciana Paluzzi; Robertson, Paul Burke.

The Episodes:

1. "Station Break" (10-3-59) Eva Gabor, David Opatoshu
2. "Dossier" (10-10-59) Edgar Bergen
3. "Moment of Truth" (10-17-59) Nehemiah Persoff
4. "The Unknown Town" (10-24-59)
5. "The Man with the Triangle Heads" (10-31-59) Monty Wooley
6. "The Assassin" (11-7-59) John McGiver
7. "The Man Who Got Away" (11-14-59) Arlene Francis
8. "The Emerald Curtain" (11-21-59) Michael David
9. "Temple of the Swinging Doll" (11-28-59) Viveca Lindfors
10. "Final Dream" (12-5-59) Cesare Danova
11. "Thin Ice" (12-19-59) Peter Lorre, Alan Young
12. "Operation Ramrod" (12-26-59) Oscar Homolka, Ray Anthony, Eric O'Brien
13. "The Judas Goat" (1-2-60) Margaret Lindsay
14. "Search for Edward Stoyan" (1-9-60) Hugo Haas, Margaret Phillips, Martin Balsam

RIVERBOAT

Voluminous NBC answer to "Wagon Train"; a study of Mississippi riverboat life in the 1840s, featuring Darren McGavin as Captain Grey Holden, Burt Reynolds his pilot Ben Frazer and an all-star guest cast.

The Regulars: Capt. Grey Holden, Darren McGavin (Dan Duryea filled in for McGavin temporarily in the latter part of the first season); pilot Ben Frazer, Burt Reynolds; pilot Bill Blake (second season), Noah Beery; Carney, Dick Wessel.

The Episodes:

1.  "Payment in Full" (9-13-59) Nancy Gates, Aldo Ray, Louis Hayward, Barbara Bel Geddes
2.  "The Barrier" (9-20-59) Elizabeth Montgomery, John Kerr, William Bendix
3.  "About Roger Mowbray" (9-27-59) Robert Vaughn, Vera Miles
4.  "Race to Cincinnati" (10-4-59) Anne Baxter, Monica Lewis, Robert Lowery
5.  "The Unwilling" (10-11-59) Eddie Albert, Debra Paget
6.  "The Fight Back" (10-18-59) John Ireland, Karl Swenson
7.  "Escape to Memphis" (10-25-59) Jeanne Crain, Claude Akins
8.  "Witness No Evil" (11-1-59) Vincent Price
9.  "A Night at Trapper's Landing" (11-8-59) Ricardo Montalban, Peter Whitney, Judson Pratt
10. "The Faithless" (11-22-59) Richard Carlson, Bethel Leslie, Bert Freed
11. "The Boy from Pittsburgh" (11-29-59) Tommy Nolan, Mona Freeman
12. "Jessie Quinn" (12-6-59) Mercedes McCambridge
13. "Strange Request" (12-13-59) Jan Sterling
14. "Guns for Empire" (12-20-59) George Macready, Gena Rowlands
15. "Face of Courage" (12-27-59) Doug McClure, Tom Drake, Tracey Roberts
16. "Tampico Raid" (1-3-60) Patricia Crowley, Edward Colmans
17. "Landlubbers" (1-10-60) Gloria Talbott, Richard Devon
18. "The Blowup" (1-17-60) Whitney Blake
19. "Forbidden Island" (1-24-60)
20. "Salvage Pirates" (1-31-60) Judi Meredith, Richard Garland
21. "Path of an Eagle" (2-1-60) Dianne Foster
22. "The Treasure of Hawk Hill" (2-8-60) Kent Taylor
23. "The Wichita Arrows" (2-29-60) Dan Duryea
24. "Fort Epitaph" (3-7-60) Dan Duryea, Joan Camden
25. "Three Graves" (3-14-60) Beverly Garland
26. "Hang the Men High" (3-21-60) Stephen McNally
27. "The Night of the Faceless Men" (3-28-60) Hugh Downs, Patricia Medina, Jocelyn Brando
28. "The Long Trail" (4-4-60) Perry Lopez, Abraham Sofaer
29. "The Quick Noose" (4-11-60) Nan Leslie, Ed Nelson

30. "The Sellout" (4-18-60) Frank Overton, Barbara Stuart

Second Season

31. "End of a Dream" (9-19-60) Cliff Robertson, Susan Cummings
32. "That Taylor Affair" (9-26-60) Arlene Dahl, Robert Ellenstein, Stanley Adams, Paul Fix
33. "The Two Faces of Grey Holden" (10-3-60) Suzanne Pleshette, Thomas Gomez, Celia Lovsky
34. "River Champion" (10-10-60) Dennis O'Keefe, George Kennedy, Slim Pickens, Norma Crane
35. "No Bridge on the River" (10-24-60) Sandy Kenyon
36. "Trunk Full of Dreams" (10-31-60) Raymond Massey, Bethel
Leslie
37. "The Water of Gorgeous Springs" (11-7-60)
38. "Devil in Skirts" (11-21-60) Gloria Talbott, Frank Silvera
39. "The Quota" (11-28-60) Gene Evans, James Griffith
40. "Chicota Landing" (12-5-60) Joe De Santis, Connie Hines
41. "Duel on the River" (12-12-60) Fay Spain, Claude Akins
42. "Zigzag" (12-26-60) Charles Bronson, Stella Stevens
43. "Listen to the Nightingale" (1-2-61) Jeanne Bal, Jack Albertson


SUNDAY SHOWCASE

The Episodes:

1. "People Kill People Sometimes" [by S. Lee Pogostin; directed
by John Frankenheimer] (9-20-59) Geraldine Page, Jason
Robards Jr. , George C. Scott, Zina Bethune
2. "What Makes Sammy Run?" [Part I: adapted by Budd Schulberg from his novel; directed by Delbert Mann] (9-27-59)
Larry Blyden, David Opatoshu, Barbara Rush, John Forsythe, Dina Merrill
3. "What Makes Sammy Run?" [Part II] (10-4-59) as above
4. "Our American Heritage: Divided We Stand: A Crucial Year
in the Life of Thomas Jefferson" [by Morton Wishengrad]
(10-18-59) Ralph Bellamy, Arthur Kennedy, Elizabeth Hubbard, Howard St. John, Lori March, House Jameson, Sarah
Marshall
5. "A Tribute to Mrs. Franklin D. Roosevelt" (10-25-59) appearances by Henry Morgan, Helen Hayes, Marian Anderson, Lauren Bacall, Ralph Bellamy, Maurice Chevalier,
Jimmy Durante, Eddie Cantor, Henry Fonda, Sidney Poitier, Gertrude Berg, Elizabeth Taylor, Bob Hope
6. "Murder and the Android" [by Alfred Bester] (11-8-59) Kevin
McCarthy, Rip Torn, Vladimir Sokoloff, Suzanne Pleshette,
Sono Osato
7. "Our American Heritage: The Practical Dreamer" (11-22-
59) Burgess Meredith, Betsy Palmer, Mark Stevens, Ed

Whitney, Peggy Ann Garner
8. "The National Academy of Recording Arts and Sciences" (11-29-59) Meredith Willson, host.
9. "Give My Regards to Broadway" (12-6-59) Jimmy Durante, Ray Bolger, Jane Powell, Jimmie Rodgers, Eddie Hodges
10. "The Indestructible Mr. Gore" [by Gore Vidal; about the late Senator Thomas Pryor Gore] (12-13-59) William Shatner, E. G. Marshall, Inger Stevens, Nancy Marchand
11. "The Margaret Bourke White Story" [by Joseph Liss] (1-3-60) Teresa Wright, Eli Wallach, Philip Bourneuf
12. "Hedda Hopper's Hollywood" (1-10-60)
13. "One Loud Clear Voice" [by Roger O. Hirson] (1-17-60) Wendell Corey, Larry Blyden, Jack Klugman, Joseph Sweeney, Mary Fickett, Frank Conroy
14. "Our American Heritage: Destiny West" [by William Altman] (1-24-60) James Daly, Jeffrey Hunter, Susan Strasberg, Howard St. John
15. "After Hours" [romantic comedy by Tony Webster] (2-7-60) Christopher Plummer, Sally Ann Howes, Buster Keaton
16. "Our American Heritage: Shadow of a Soldier" [by John Whedon] (2-21-60) James Whitmore, Melvyn Douglas, Teresa Wright, John Baragrey
17. "The Secret of Freedom" [by Archibald MacLeish] (2-28-60) Thomas Mitchell, John McGiver, Tony Randall, Kim Hunter
18. "Turn the Key Deftly" [by Alfred Bester] (3-6-60) Julie Harris, Maximilian Schell, Francis Lederer, Humphrey Davis, Louis Edmonds
19. "Our American Heritage: Autocrat and Son" [by Ernest Kinoy] (3-20-60) Christopher Plummer, Anne Francis, Cedric Hardwicke, Ann Harding, Bramwell Fletcher
20. "The American" [by Merle Miller; directed by John Frankenheimer] (3-27-60) Steven Hill, Lee Marvin, Milton Selzer, Frank Overton, Frank Corsaro, Thomas Carlin
21. "Hollywood Sings" [musical review] (4-3-60) Tammy Grimes, Eddie Albert, Boris Karloff
22. "Our American Heritage: Millionaire's Mite" [by Ernest Kinoy; Jack Smight directed] (4-10-60) David Wayne, Judith Anderson, Eddie Hodges, Neva Patterson, Mark O'Daniels, Roy Poole

THE REBEL

Andrew J. Fenady's study of an Appomattox veteran (Nick Adams as Johnny Yuma) who wrestles with his conscience and assorted reprobates in the post-Civil War West.

The Regulars: Johnny Yuma, Nick Adams.

The Episodes:

1. [unknown title] (10-4-59) John Carradine, Dan Blocker,

Strother Martin, Jeanette Nolan
2. [unknown title] (10-11-59) Sue Randall, Bob Steele, J. Pat O'Malley
3. [unknown title] (10-18-59) Royal Dano, Carol Nugent, Rodolfo Acosta
4. "Vicious Circle" (10-25-59) George Macready, Ed Ryder, Ed Nelson
5. [unknown title] (11-1-59) Karl Swenson, J. Pat O'Malley
6. "The Scavengers" (11-8-59) James Westerfield, Olive Sturgess
7. [unknown title] (11-15-59) Malcolm Cassell
8. "Dark Secret" (11-22-59) Tyler McVey, N. J. Davis
9. [unknown title] (11-29-59) Hampton Fancher, Hal Stalmaster
10. [unknown title] (12-6-59) Agnes Moorehead, Madlyn Rhue
11. "The Vagrants" (12-20-59) Robert Foulk, Wright King
12. "Gun City" (12-27-59) Otto Kruger, Dan Sheridan
13. "The Death of Gray" (1-3-60) Harry Townes, Johnny Cash
14. "Angry Town" (1-10-60) Perry Cook, Jose Sanchez
15. "Gold Seeker" (1-17-60) John Sutton, Eddie Little Sky
16. [Yuma encounters girls stranded in desert left to die] (1-24-60)
17. "The Unwanted" (1-31-60) Trevor Bardette
18. "The Crime" (2-7-60) Walter Sande
19. "Noblesse Oblige" (2-14-60) Robert Vaughn, Gail Russell
20. "Land" (2-21-60) Rudolph Anders, Ralph Moody
21. "He's Only a Boy" (2-28-60) Robert Blake, Michael Vanderver
22. "Take Dead Aim" (3-6-60) Edgar Barrier, Mala Powers
23. "The Rattler" (3-13-60) Martha Vickers, Tony Haig
24. "You Steal My Eyes" (3-20-60) Cathy O'Donnell, William Bryant
25. "Fair Game" (3-27-60) James Drury, Patricia Medina
26. "Unsurrendered Sword" (4-3-60) Jay Novello, Paul Picerni
27. "The Captive of Temblor" (4-10-60) Robert Brubaker, James Seay
28. "Blind Marriage" (4-17-60) Lisa Lu, Philip Ahn
29. "Absolution" (4-24-60) Gloria Talbott, Barry Atwater
30. "A Grave for Johnny Yuma" (5-1-60) Fred Beir, John Brinkley
31. "In Memory of a Son" (5-8-60) Harry Bartell, Jack Hogan
32. "Paint a House With Scarlet" (5-15-60) Clu Gulager, Maggie Mahoney, John Anderson
33. "Grant of Land" (5-22-60) Paul Richards, Ruta Lee
34. "Night on a Rainbow" (5-29-60) James Best, Gail Kobe, Perry Cook
35. "Lady of Quality" (6-5-60) Joanna Moore, Edward Kemmer
36. "The Earl of Durango" (6-12-60) Patricia Medina, John Sutton, George Tobias, L. Q. Jones

Second Season

37. "Johnny Yuma at Appomattox" (9-18-60) George Macready, Ed Nelson, William Bryant, J. Pat O'Malley, Andrew J.

Fenady

38. "The Bequest" (9-25-60) Elisha Cook, John Carradine
39. "The Champ" (10-2-60) Michael Ansara
40. "The Waiting" (10-9-60) Claude Akins, Joan Evans
41. "To See the Elephant" (10-16-60) Mark Goddard, Ron Soble
42. "Deathwatch" (10-23-60) James Best, Frank Silvera
43. "Run, Killer, Run" (10-30-60) Richard Jaeckel, Ed Nelson
44. "The Hunted" (11-6-60) Leonard Nimoy, Arline Sax
45. "The Legacy" (11-13-60) Jon Lormer, James Chandler
46. "Don Gringo" (11-20-60) Gigi Perreau, Rosa Turich
47. "Explosion" (11-27-60) L. Q. Jones, Denny Miller
48. "Vindication" (12-4-60) James Drury, Martha Vickers
49. "The Scalp Hunter" (12-11-60) John Dehner, Earl Parker
50. "Berserk" (12-18-60) Tom Drake
51. [unknown title] (12-25-60) William Demarest, Soupy Sales, Cathy O'Donnell
52. "The Liberators" (1-1-61) Nico Minardos
53. "The Guard" (1-8-61) Ed Nelson, Dee Pollock
54. "The Promise" (1-15-61) Gigi Perreau, Peter Whitney
55. "Jerkwater" (1-22-61) John Dehner, John Marley
56. "Paperback Hero" (1-29-61) Virginia Gregg, Robert Palmer
57. "The Actress" (2-5-61) Virginia Field, Sandra Knight
58. "The Threat" (2-12-61) Aladdin Pallante, Trevor Bardette
59. "The Road to Jericho" (2-19-61) Robert Middleton, Warren Stevens
60. "The Last Drink" (2-26-61) Tom Drake
61. "The Burying of Sammy Hart" (3-5-61) Iron Eyes Cody, George Wallace
62. "The Pit" (3-12-61) Olive Sturgess, Myron Healey
63. "Shriek of Silence" (3-19-61) Tommy Noonan, Yvette Vickers
64. [unknown title] (3-26-61) Frank Overton, Jaime Farr
65. "Miz Purdy" (4-2-61) Patricia Breslin, Jason Evers
66. "The Ballad of Danny Brown" (4-9-61) Tex Ritter, Gail Kobe
67. "The Proxy" (4-16-61) Vic Damone, Royal Dano
68. "Decision at Sweetwater" (4-23-61) Yvette Vickers, William Phipps
69. "Helping Hand" (4-30-61) Leif Erickson, Jack Elam, Eddie Ryder
70. "The Uncourageous" (5-7-61) George Dolenz, Eugene Iglesias
71. "Mission--Varina" (5-14-61) Frieda Inescort, William Schallert
72. "The Calley Kid" (5-21-61) Richard Bakalyan, Michael Vanderver
73. "Ben White" (5-28-61) Mary Murphy, Charles Aidman
74. "The Found" (6-4-61) Peggy Campbell
75. "The Hostage" (6-11-61) Lon McCallister, Jean Inness
76. "The Executioner" (6-18-61) Terry Moore, Barry Atwater

## THE ALASKANS

This series was advertised with the line "Television, for the first time, lays bare the raw emotions and unbridled lust of the Yukon gold ruoh." The Alaska of 1889 found principals Silky Harris (Roger Moore) and Reno McKee (Jeff York) variously involved with dancing girls in "The Petticoat Crew," and of course the more conventional discovery of a gold mine in "Black Sand." Dorothy Provine, then at a pinnacle of popularity, was the morale-boosting saloon singer Rocky Shaw.

The Regulars: Silky Harris, Roger Moore; Reno McKee, Jeff York; Rocky Shaw, Dorothy Provine.

The Episodes:

1. "Gold Sled" (10-4-59) Allyn Joslyn, Hank Patterson
2. "Cheating Cheaters" (10-11-59) Ray Danton, Frank Ferguson, Frank De Kova
3. [unknown title] (10-18-59) Andrea King, John Dehner
4. "The Petticoat Crew" (10-25-59)
5. "Starvation Stampede" (11-1-59) James Westerfield
6. "Big Deal" (11-8-59) John Dehner, Jesse White
7. "Contest at Gold Bottom" (11-15-59) Ray Danton, Frank De Kova
8. "Winter Song" (11-22-59) Marie Windsor, Alan Baxter
9. "The Golden Fleece" (11-29-59) Ray Danton, Beatrice Kay, Theodore Marcuse
10. "Doc Booker" (12-6-59) Julie Adams
11. "The Abominable Snowman" (12-13-59) Ruta Lee, Ray Teal, Robert Boon
12. "Remember the Maine" (12-20-59) John Dehner
13. "Million Dollar Kid" (1-3-60) Bart Bradley, Mort Mills
14. "The Trial of Reno McKee" (1-10-60) Efrem Zimbalist Jr., Karen Steele
15. "Gold Fever" (1-17-60) Gerald Mohr, Werner Klemperer
16. "The Challenge" (1-24-60) Don Dubbins, Robert Colbert, John Hoyt
17. "The Long Pursuit" (1-31-60) Ruta Lee
18. "Spring Fever" (2-7-60) Rex Reason, Lynn Statten
19. "Black Sand" (2-14-60)
20. "The Seal Skin-Game" (2-21-60) Ray Danton
21. "Peril at Caribou Crossing" (2-28-60) Lee Van Cleef, Jerry Paris, Steve Brodie, Fay Spain
22. "Behind the Moon" (3-6-60) Lee Patterson, Michael Forest, Andra Martin
23. "Partners" (3-13-60) Jimmy Carter, Alan Hale Jr.
24. "Disaster at Gold Hill" (3-20-60) Madlyn Rhue, Rex Reason, Mike Road
25. "The Last Bullet" (3-27-60) Frank Cady, Andra Martin
26. "A Barrel of Gold" (4-3-60) Jean Allison, Edward Kemmer, Michael Forest
27. "The Bride Wore Black" (4-10-60) John Beal, Lee Bergere,

Fay Spain
28. "Odd Man Hangs" (4-17-60) Michael Forest, Valerie French
29. "Counterblow" (4-24-60) Karen Steele, Horace MacMahon, Robert McQueeney
30. "Heart of Gold" (5-1-60) Michael Forest, Troy Donahue
31. "Kangaroo Court" (5-8-60) Larry Pennell, Joan O'Brien
32. "The Silent Land" (5-15-60) Michael Forest, Claude Akins, Richard Carlyle, Arthur Franz
33. "Calico" (5-22-60) Myrna Fahey, Rex Reason, Richard Webb, Tristram Coffin
34. "Sign of the Kodiak" (5-29-60) Michael Forest, Lee Patterson, Pippa Scott
35. "White Vengeance" (6-5-60) Andra Martin, Peter Whitney, Robert Colbert
36. "The Ballad of Whitehorse" (6-12-60) Rex Reason, James Parnell, Jean Allison
37. "The Devil Made Five" (6-19-60) Andrea King, Walter Burke


BOURBON STREET BEAT

Effectively filmed private detective series, the locale being New Orleans' French Quarter. Richard Long (as Rex Randolph), Andrew Duggan (as Cal Calhoun) and Van Williams (as Ken Madison) were the sleuths; Arlene Howell (as Melody Lee Mercer) their secretary.

The Regulars: Rex Randolph, Richard Long; Cal Calhoun, Andrew Duggan; Melody Lee Mercer, Arlene Howell; Kenny Madison, Van Williams.

The Episodes:

1. "The Taste of Ashes" (10-5-59)
2. "The Mourning Cloak" (10-12-59) Maggie Hayes, John Hoyt
3. "Torch Song for Trumpet" (10-19-59) Richard Rust, Suzanne Lloyd
4. "Woman in the River" (10-26-59)
5. "Girl in Trouble" (11-2-59) Faith Domergue, Robert J. Wilke
6. "Tiger Moth" (11-9-59)
7. "Secret of Hyacinth Bayou" (11-16-59) Rusty Lane
8. "Invitation to Murder" (11-23-59) Kathleen Crowley
9. "Mrs. Viner Vanishes" (11-30-59) Nita Talbot, Wayne Morris
10. "The Light Touch of Terror" (12-7-59) Sue Ane Langdon
11. "The Golden Beetle" (12-14-59) Mala Powers
12. "The Black Magnolia" (12-21-59) Mary Tyler Moore, Sara Haden
13. "Portrait of Lenore" (12-28-59) Madlyn Rhue
14. "Kill with Kindness" (1-4-60) Nancy Gates, Isobel Elsom
15. "Inside Man" (1-11-60) Richard Carlyle, Dolores Donlon

16. "Find My Face" (1-19-60) Nita Talbot
17. "Knock on Any Tombstone" (1-25-60)
18. "Key to the City" (2-1-60) Shirley Knight
19. "The Ten Percent Blues" (2-8-60) Nita Talbot, Marie Windsor, Eddie Cole
20. "Melody in Diamonds" (2-15-60)
21. "The House of Ledezan" (2-22-60)
22. "Target of Hate" (3-7-60) James Coburn, Richard Chamberlain, John Marley
23. "The Missing Queen" (3-14-60) Eddie Cole
24. "Neon Nightmare" (3-21-60) Randy Stuart
25. "Wall of Silence" (3-28-60) Roxanne Berard, James Drury
26. "Twice Betrayed" (4-4-60) Judson Pratt, Laurie Mitchell, Grant Richards
27. "Swamp Fire" (4-11-60) Rex Reason, Donald Barry
28. "If a Body" (4-18-60) Nita Talbot, Maureen Arthur, John Milford
29. "Six Hours to Midnight" (4-25-60) George Wallace, Melora Conway
30. "Last Exit" (5-2-60) Ray Danton, Madlyn Rhue
31. "Deadly Persuasion" (5-9-60) Arthur Franz
32. "Suitable for Framing" (5-16-60) Rita Moreno, Barbara Lord
33. "False Identity" (5-23-60) Irene Hervey
34. "Green Hell" (5-30-60) Suzanne Lloyd, Joe De Santis
35. "Ferry to Algiers" (6-6-60) Estelle Winwood
36. "Show Wagon" (6-13-60) Horace MacMahon
37. "Interrupted Wedding" (6-20-60) Randy Stuart, Whit Bissell
38. "Reunion" (6-27-60) Marlene Willis, Dianne Foster
39. "Teresa" (7-4-60) Andra Martin, Marie Windsor, Karen Steele

## ADVENTURES IN PARADISE

Exhilarating topical adventure-romance from the pen of James Michener, with Gardner McKay attaining star status as the island drifter and schooner Captain Adam Troy.

The Regulars: Capt. Adam Troy, Gardner McKay; Clay Baker (first mate, second season and innkeeper of Bali Miki third season), James Holden; Sondi, Sondi Sodsai; Kelly, Lani Kai; Chris Parker (first mate, last season only), Guy Stockwell; Trader Penrose (hotel operator), George Tobias; Oliver Kee, Weaver Levy; Bouchard, Marcel Hillaire.

The Episodes:

1. "The Pit of Silence" (10-5-59) Teresa Wright, Hazel Court, Robert F. Simon
2. "The Black Pearl" (10-12-59) Patricia Medina, Lon Chaney Jr., Kurt Kasznar, Anthony Steele
3. "Paradise Lost" (10-26-59) Gladys Cooper, Robert Middleton,

Fay Spain
4. "Lady from South Chicago" (11-2-59) Suzanne Pleshette, Paulette Goddard
5. "The Derelict" (11-9-59) Lilliane Montevecci, Ricardo Montalban
6. "Safari at Sea" (11-16-59) John Ericson, Diana Lynn
7. "Mission to Manila" (11-23-59) Thomas Gomez, Julie London
8. "The Raft" (11-30-59) Patricia Owens, Edward Andrews
9. "Peril at Pitcairn" (12-7-59) Eva Gabor
10. "The Bamboo Curtain" (12-14-59) David Opatoshu, Anne Francis
11. "The Haunted" (12-21-59) Kim Hunter, Elaine Stritch, Linda Lawson
12. "Somewhere South of Suva" (12-28-59) Alexis Smith
13. "Castaways" (1-4-60) Fifi D'Orsay, Viveca Lindfors
14. "Archer's Ring" (1-11-60) Wayne Morris, Anna Kashfi
15. "Nightmare on Napuka" (1-18-60) Martin Landau, Herbert Marshall
16. "Walk Through the Night" (1-25-60) Mara Corday, Lawrence Tierney
17. "Judith" (2-1-60) Dan Duryea, Gloria Vanderbilt
18. "The Color of Venom" (2-8-60) Vincent Price, Chana Eden
19. "Isle of Eden" (2-22-60) Yvonne DeCarlo, Hugo Haas
20. "Prisoner in Paradise" (2-29-60) Fay Bainter, Barbara Bain, Patricia Cutts
21. "The Siege of Troy" (3-7-60) Ron Randell, Joanna Moore
22. "There Is an Island" (3-14-60) Herbert Marshall, Henry Slate
23. "The Amazon" (3-21-60) Tom Drake, Lizabeth Scott
24. "The Violent Journey" (3-28-60) Natalie Trundy, Jeff Richards
25. "Forbidden Sea" (4-4-60) Joan Blondell, Henry Silva
26. "Passage to Tua" (4-11-60) Diane Baker, Brett Halsey, John Van Dreelen
27. "Heads You Lose" (4-18-60) Luciana Paluzzi, Sean McClory
28. "The Death-Divers" (4-25-60) Gena Rowlands, Chana Eden
29. "Beached" (5-2-60) Marilyn Maxwell, Simon Oakland, Read Morgan
30. "Whip Fight" (5-9-60) Geoffrey Horne, Susan Oliver

Second Season

31. "Open for Diving" (10-3-60) Julie Newmar, Ken Renard
32. "The Intruders" (10-10-60) Cecil Kellaway, Elsa Lanchester
33. "Once Around the Circuit" (10-17-60) Peggy Ann Garner, Mike Kellin
34. "Away from It All" (10-24-60) Barbara Luna, Henry Jones
35. "The Krishmen" (10-31-60) Agnes Moorehead
36. "A Whale of a Tale" (11-7-60) Juliet Prowse, Cal Bolder, Rhys Williams
37. "Hangman's Island" (11-21-60) Carroll O'Connor
38. "One Little Pearl" (11-28-60) Philip Ahn, France Nuyen

39. "The Big Surf" (12-5-60) Betsy Von Furstenberg
40. "Daughter of Illusion" (12-12-60) Barbara Steele, Alan Napier
41. "Sink or Swim" (12-19-60) Danielle de Metz, Barbara Stuart, Constance Towers
42. "Incident in Suva" (12-26-60) Joanna Barnes, Abraham Sofaer
43. "Treasure Hunt" (1-9-61) Cesare Danova, Marc Alcalde
44. "The Perils of Penrose" (1-16-61) Murray Matheson
45. "Mr. Flotsam" (1-23-61) Reginald Gardiner, Martin Landau
46. "The Good Killing" (1-30-61) Juano Hernandez, John Van Dreelen, Rafael Campos, Al Freeman Jr.
47. "Man Eater" (2-6-61) Bethel Leslie, Kent Smith, Michael Pate, John Fiedler
48. "Act of Piracy" (2-13-61) Steven Hill, Joanne Linville, Milton Selzer
49. "Captain Butcher" (2-20-61) Alan Hale, John Anderson, Fay Spain
50. "The Feather Cloak" (2-27-61) George Macready, Pippa Scott, Philip Pine
51. "Angel of Death" (3-6-61) Inger Stevens, Paul Langton, Michael Forest
52. "Who Is Sylvia?" (3-13-61) Geraldine Brooks, Elana Eden, Jeanette Nolan
53. "The Wonderful Nightingale" (3-27-61) Michael O'Shea, Nobu McCarthy
54. "The Jonah Stone" (4-3-61) Gloria DeHaven, Hans Conried, J. Pat O'Malley
55. "A Touch of Genius" (4-10-61) Jessie Royce Landis, John Abbott, Cecil Kellaway, Warren Stevens
56. "The Serpent in the Garden" (4-17-61) Marilyn Maxwell, Alan Hale, Ken Renard
57. "A Penny a Day" (4-24-61) Thomas Mitchell, Estelle Winwood, Reginald Denny, Finton Meyler
58. "Adam Sam" (5-1-61) Dan O'Herlihy, Vladimir Sokoloff, Bruce Gordon
59. "Wild Mangoes" (5-8-61) Simon Oakland, Tige Andrews, Gail Kobe, Joan O'Brien, Lisa Gaye
60. "Hill of Ghosts" (5-15-61) Susan Oliver, James Barton, John Hoyt
61. "Flamin' Lady" (5-22-61) Cathleen Nesbitt, Patricia Cutts, Vaughn Taylor
62. "Errand of Mercy" (5-29-61) Skip Homeier, Jan Sterling, Alan Caillou, Jacqueline Scott, Parley Baer, Dabbs Greer
63. "Command at Sea" (6-5-61) Philip Ahn, Raymond Massey, Antoinette Bower, Miriam Colon
64. "Beach Head" (6-12-61) Glynis Johns, Torin Thatcher, Paul Mantee
65. "Nightmare in the Sun" (6-19-61) Bethel Leslie, Charles Aidman, Noah Beery, Barbara Bain

Third Season

66. "Appointment at Tara-Bi" (10-1-61) Don Dubbins, Sean

McClory, Susan Hampshire
67. "The Reluctant Hero" (10-8-61) Dick York, Susan Oliver
68. "Vendetta" (10-15-61) Diane Baker, Rita Moreno, Carmen Mathews
69. "Queens Back" (10-22-61) Fritz Feld, Jo Morrow
70. "The Closing Circle" (10-29-61) Joanne Linville, Arch Johnson
71. "Show Me a Hero" (11-5-61) David Janssen, George Macready
72. "The Pretender" (11-12-61) Cecil Kellaway, Anne Helm, Anne Seymour, Virginia Gregg
73. "The Fires of Kanau" (11-19-61) Nancy Gates, Barry Morse
74. "The Assassins" (11-26-61) Madlyn Rhue, Judson Pratt
75. "One Way Ticket" (12-3-61) Lola Albright, Fifi D'Orsay, Buddy Ebsen
76. "The Trial of Adam Troy" (12-17-61) Margaret O'Brien, Ben Cooper
77. "The Inheritance" (12-24-61) Barbara Eden, Cathleen Nesbitt
78. "Survival" (12-31-61) Charles Bronson, Russell Johnson, Pippa Scott
79. "Hurricane Audrey" (1-7-62) Janice Rule, Lawrence Dobkin
80. "Once There Was a Princess" (1-14-62) Ina Balin, Paul Hartman
81. "The Velvet Trap" (1-21-62) Tuesday Weld, Bert Freed
82. "Policeman's Holiday" (1-28-62) Reginald Denny, Virginia Field
83. "Please Believe Me" (2-4-62) Kent Smith, Jacqueline Scott, Jason Evers
84. "The Quest of Ambrose Feather" (2-11-62) Reginald Owen, Jesse White, Pippa Scott
85. "Build My Gallows Low" (2-18-62) Peggy Ann Garner, James Hong, Steven Geray
86. "The Secret Place" (2-25-62) Dan O'Herlihy, Donald Losby, Robert Cornthwaite
87. "The Beach at Belle Anse" (3-4-62) Simon Oakland, Phyllis Avery, Greta Chi
88. "A Bride for the Captain" (3-11-62) Ray Walston, Maggie Pierce, J. Pat O'Malley
89. "The Dream Merchant" (3-18-62) Constance Ford, Larry Blyden, Patricia Breslin
90. "The Baby Sitters" (3-25-62) Erika Peters, Lee Patrick
91. "Blueprint for Paradise" (4-1-62) Pilar Seurat, John Fiedler

## THE JUNE ALLYSON SHOW

Wildly varying series of dramas, several of them expressly composed for Miss Allyson. In David Fielder's comedy episode "The Old Fashioned Way" she is the incessantly active pregnant wife of actor Dick Shawn. In "Child Lost" she is the sitter for a very young Ronny Howard who has apparently been kidnapped. In

"Sister Mary Slugger" she is the much loved nun who is both support-
er of and player on a boys' softball team, much to the distress of
her Mother Superior.

Far better were those dramas not labored around the featured actress. "Suspected" has Ann Blyth as a lady falsely accused
of murder and is notable for at least one scene--that in which Miss
Blyth makes her "one phone call" to her sister and, rather than
sympathy, gains only a sibling's fear for the family reputation.
Irving Elman's drama title "The Pledge" refers to Dewey Martin's
promise to a wartime orphan boy that he become an adopted child.
Martin's wife (Mona Freeman) is expecting, however, and resents
her husband's commitment--to the boy's knowledge. Guilt-ridden
at the time of her delivery, she deludes herself into thinking her
baby dead.

Lloyd Bridges' virtuoso performance distinguishes the drama
"The Death of the Temple Bay" in which he is a sea captain who
dies questioning his motives for going down with his ship.

The Regulars: June Allyson, hostess.

The Episodes:

1. "Ruth and Naomi" (9-21-59) June Allyson, Ann Harding,
   Mark Richman
2. "Dark Morning" (9-28-59) Bette Davis, Leif Erickson
3. "The Opening Door" (10-5-59) Irene Dunne
4. "A Summer's Ending" (10-12-59) Dick Powell, June Allyson,
   Les Tremayne
5. "The Tender Shoot" (10-19-59) Ginger Rogers, Paul Carr
6. "The Pledge" (10-26-59) Mona Freeman, Dewey Martin
7. "Love Is a Headache" (11-2-59) Akim Tamiroff
8. "Child Lost" (11-16-59) June Allyson, Steve Brodie, Ronny
   Howard
9. "Night Out" (11-23-59) Ann Sothern, Pat Carroll
10. "The Girl" (11-30-59) Jane Powell
11. "The Wall Between" (12-7-59) Kevin McCarthy
12. "The Crossing" (12-14-59) Barry Sullivan, Dolores Hart
13. "No Place to Hide" (12-21-59) Debra Paget
14. "Suspected" (12-28-59) Ann Blyth, Gerald Mohr
15. "Edge of Fury" (1-4-60) Dan O'Herlihy
16. "The Trench Coat" (1-11-60) David Niven, Phyllis Coates
17. "The Way Home" (1-18-60) Eugenie Leontovich, Ronald
    Reagan
18. "Moment of Truth" (1-25-60) Edgar Bergen, Stephen McNal-
    ly, Lyle Bettger, Darryl Hickman
19. "So Dim the Light" (2-1-60) Robert Culp, June Allyson
20. "Trial by Fear" (2-8-60) Pippa Scott, Chuck Connors
21. "Threat of Evil" (2-15-60) Patricia Crowley, Barry Nelson
22. "Escape" (2-22-60) Sylvia Sidney, Brian Donlevy, Frank
    Lovejoy, Margaret O'Brien
23. "Piano Man" (2-29-60) Vic Damone, Keenan Wynn

24. "Sister Mary Slugger" (3-14-60) June Allyson, Sean McClory
25. "The Blue Goose" (3-21-60) Joseph Cotten, Susan Oliver, Mary Sinclair
26. "Once Upon a Knight" (3-28-60) Jean Hagen, James Mason
27. "Slip of the Tongue" (4-11-60) Rossano Brazzi, Virginia Grey
28. "Surprise Party" (4-18-60) Shepperd Strudwick, Myrna Loy, Susan Crane, Mark Goddard
29. "The Doctor and the Redhead" (4-25-60) Dick Powell, Regis Toomey
30. "Intermission" (5-2-60) Russell Johnson

Second Season

31. "The Lie" (9-29-60) June Allyson
32. "The Dance Man" (10-6-60) Dean Stockwell, Anne Baxter
33. "Dark Fear" (10-13-60) Joseph Cotten
34. "The Test" (10-20-60) Robert Knapp, Eduard Franz, Vaughn Taylor
35. "Play Acting" (10-27-60) Steve Allen
36. "The Woman Who" (11-3-60) Van Johnson, June Allyson
37. "I Hit and Ran" (11-20-60) James Gregory
38. "Love on Credit" (11-17-60) Carolyn Jones
39. "The Visitor" (11-24-60) Katherine Bard, Harry Townes
40. "A Thief or Two" (12-1-60) Lew Ayres, Jeff Donnell, Anne Helm
41. "Emergency" (12-8-60) Robert Vaughn, James Komack
42. "The Desperate Challenge" (12-15-60) June Allyson, John Lasell
43. "Silent Panic" (12-22-60) Harpo Marx, Ernest Truex
44. "End of a Mission" (1-2-61) Steve Forrest, Lili Darvas
45. "The Defense Is Restless" (1-9-61) June Allyson, John Lasell
46. "The Guilty Heart" (1-16-61) James Franciscus, Susan Kohner
47. "Affair in Athens" (1-23-61) June Allyson, Michael Davis
48. "School of the Soldier" (1-30-61) Lee J. Cobb, Dick York
49. "Without Fear" (2-6-61) June Allyson, Edward Binns
50. "A Great Day for a Scoundrel" (2-13-61) Hans Conried, John Abbott, K. T. Stevens
51. "The Old Fashioned Way" (2-20-61) June Allyson, Dick Shaw
52. "The Moth" (2-27-61) June Allyson, Joe Maross
53. "The Haven" (3-6-61) Ralph Bellamy, Patricia Breslin
54. "The Man Who Wanted Everything Perfect" (3-13-61) Russell Nype
55. "The Secret Life of James Thurber" (3-20-61) Orson Bean, Adolphe Menjou
56. "Our Man in Rome" (3-27-61) Rossano Brazzi, Eugenie Leontovich
57. "The Death of the Temple Bay" (4-3-61) Lloyd Bridges

LARAMIE

Rather cumbersome color western, not restricted to drama and featuring Robert Fuller--who would subsequently appear regularly in "Wagon Train"--as Jess Harper.

The Regulars:  Jess Harper, Robert Fuller; Slim Sherman, John Smith; Andy Sherman, Bobby Crawford Jr.; Jonesy, Hoagy Carmichael; Mike, Dennis Holmes (from third season); Daisy, Spring Byington (from third season).

The Episodes:

1.  "Stage Stop" (9-15-59) Dan Duryea, Everett Sloane
2.  "Glory Road" (9-22-59) Eddie Albert, Nanette Fabray, Ray Teal
3.  "Circle of Fire" (9-29-59) Marsha Hunt, Ernest Borgnine
4.  "Fugitive Road" (10-6-59) Clu Gulager
5.  "The Star Trail" (10-13-59) Lloyd Nolan, Patricia Barry
6.  "The Lawbreakers" (10-20-59) James Best, John McIntire
7.  "The Iron Captain" (10-27-59) Edmond O'Brien
8.  "General Delivery" (11-3-59) Rod Cameron
9.  "The Run to Tumavaca" (11-10-59) Gena Rowlands
10. "The General Must Die" (11-17-59) Brian Keith
11. "Dark Verdict" (11-24-59) Thomas Mitchell
12. "Man of God" (12-1-59) James Gregory
13. "Bare Knuckles" (12-8-59) Dan Megowan, Wally Brown
14. "The Lonesome Gun" (12-15-59) Gary Merrill
15. "Night of the Quiet Man" (12-22-59) Lyle Bettger
16. "The Pass" (12-29-59) Madlyn Rhue
17. "Trail Drive" (1-12-60) Jim Davis
18. "Day of Vengeance" (1-19-60) John Larch, Adele Mara
19. "The Legend of Lily" (1-26-60) Kent Taylor, Patsy Kelly, George Tobias, Constance Moore
20. "Death Wind" (2-2-60) Claude Akins, Nancy Gates
21. "Company Man" (2-9-60) John Dehner
22. "Rope of Steel" (2-16-60) Harry Townes, Mari Blanchard
23. "Duel at Alta Mesa" (2-23-60) Douglas Dumbrille, Tom Drake, Fay Spain
24. "Street of Hate" (3-1-60) Charles Bronson, Joel Smith
25. "Ride or Die" (3-8-60) Simon Oakland, Robert Clark
26. "Hour After Dawn" (3-15-60) Bruce Bennett, Ben Johnson
27. "The Protectors" (3-22-60) Vince Edwards, Herbert Rudley
28. "Saddle and Spur" (3-29-60) Beverly Garland, George Neise
29. "Midnight Rebellion" (4-5-60) Bruce Gordon
30. "Cemetery Road" (4-12-60) Dennis Patrick
31. "Defiance" (4-19-60) Bing Russell

Second Season

32. "The Track of the Jackal" (9-27-60) Stephen McNally, Robert J. Wilke
33. "Three Road West" (10-4-60) Vera Miles, Myron Healy

34. "Ride the Wild Wind" (10-11-60) Ernest Borgnine
35. "Ride Into Darkness" (10-18-60) Charles Drake, Phyllis Avery
36. "The Long Riders" (10-25-60) Dan Duryea
37. "The Dark Trail" (11-1-60) Robert Vaughn, Gigi Perreau
38. ".45 Calibre" (11-15-60) George Nader, Anna-Lisa, Lee Van Cleef
39. "License to Kill" (11-22-60) R. G. Armstrong
40. "Drifter's Gold" (11-29-60) Rod Cameron, Judi Meredith
41. "No Second Chance" (12-6-60) Jeff Richards
42. "Duel at Parkinson Town" (12-13-60) Henry Hull, Murray Matheson
43. "A Sound of Bells" (12-27-60) Kim Hector, Ross Martin, Dick Foran, Mara Corday, Rachel Ames, Ben Johnson
44. "The Passing of Kula Smith" (1-3-61) John McIntire, Walter Sande
45. "Man from Kansas" (1-10-61) Jock Mahoney, Jocelyn Brando
46. "Killer Without Cause" (1-24-61) Patricia Collinge
47. "Stolen Tribute" (1-31-61) Jan Merlin
48. "The Lost Dutchman" (2-14-61) Robert Emhardt, Robert Armstrong, Karen Steele
49. "Cactus Lady" (2-21-61) Anita Sands, Arthur Hunnicutt
50. "Riders of the Night" (3-7-61) Richard Coogan, Mary Murphy
51. "The Mark of the Maneaters" (3-14-61) James Coburn, Charles McGraw
52. "Rimrock" (3-21-61) Lyle Bettger, Mort Mills
53. "Run of the Hunted" (4-4-61) Charles Bronson
54. "Two for the Gallows" (4-11-61) Warren Oates, Donald Woods
55. "The Debt" (4-18-61) Harry Carey Jr., Jason Evers, Vaughn Taylor
56. "Killer's Odds" (4-25-61) John Lupton, Russell Johnson, Lee Van Cleef
57. "Bitter Glory" (5-2-61) Dick Foran, Ed Nelson, Dianne Foster
58. "The Tumbleweed Wagon" (5-9-61) Jack Elam, Elisha Cook
59. "Trigger Point" (5-16-61) Gregory Walcott, Mary Murphy
60. "Badge of the Outsider" (5-23-61) Roy Barcroft
61. "Men in Shadows" (5-30-61) Rod Cameron, Joan Tabor, Dennis Patrick
62. "Strange Company" (6-6-61) Bill Tennant
63. "Widow in White" (6-13-61) Sue England

Third Season

64. "Dragon at the Door" (9-26-61) Robert Kino, Anita Loo
65. "Ladies Day" (10-3-61) Jock Mahoney
66. "Siege at Jubilee" (10-10-61) Lin McCarthy
67. "The Mountain Men" (10-17-61) Dan Duryea
68. "The Fatal Step" (10-24-61) Gary Clarke, Dennis Patrick
69. "The Last Journey" (10-31-61) Rod Cameron, Sandra Knight, Dick Davalos, Mort Mills, Gene Roth
70. "The Accusers" (11-14-61) Charles Drake
71. "Wolf Cub" (11-21-61) Robert Blake

72. "Handful of Fire" (12-5-61) George Macready
73. "The Killer Legend" (12-12-61) Pat Conway, Dick Foran, Joan Evans
74. "The Jailbreakers" (12-19-61) Charles Aidman, R. G. Armstrong, Jan Shepard
75. "The Lawless Seven" (12-26-61) Lyle Bettger
76. "The Perfect Gift" (1-2-62) Lisa Gaye, John Anderson, Russell Johnson
77. "The Barefoot Kid" (1-9-62) Mary Sinclair
78. "Shadows in the Dust" (1-16-62) Susan Oliver
79. "The Runaway" (1-23-62) James Best, Jack Chaplain
80. "The Confederate Express" (1-30-62) John Larch, Steve Brodie
81. "The High Country" (2-6-62) Barton MacLane, Frank Overton
82. "A Grave for Cully Brown" (2-13-62) David McLean, Karen Steele, Karl Swenson
83. "The Runt" (2-20-62) Leonard Nimoy, Ben Cooper
84. "The Dynamiters" (3-6-62) Russell Johnson, Mark Andrews
85. "The Day of the Savage" (3-13-62) John Lupton
86. "Justice in a Hurry" (3-20-62) Diana Millay, Hugh Sanders
87. "The Replacement" (3-27-62) Richard Coogan, L. Q. Jones, Roberta Shore, Stuart Randall
88. "The Turn of the Wheel" (4-3-62) Lyle Bettger, Erin O'Brien, Anthony Caruso
89. "Trial by Fire" (4-10-62) Cloris Leachman
90. "Fall Into Darkness" (4-17-62) Jean Byron, Harry Lauter
91. "Deadly Is the Night" (5-15-62) Lloyd Nolan

Fourth Season

92. "Among the Missing" (9-25-62) Ivan Dixon, Claude Akins
93. "War Hero" (10-2-62) Lloyd Nolan, Joanna Barnes
94. "The Fortune Hunter" (10-9-62) Ray Danton
95. "Shadow of the Past" (10-16-62) Jeffrey Hunter
96. "The Long Road Back" (10-23-62) Yvonne Craig, Edgar Buchanan
97. "Lost Allegiance" (10-30-62) Rod Cameron
98. "The Sunday Shoot" (11-13-62) Stuart Randall
99. "Double Eagles" (11-20-62) Russell Johnson, Dick Foran
100. "Beyond Justice" (11-27-62) Lyle Bettger
101. "Bad Blood" (12-4-62) Jean Byron, John Anderson
102. "Time of the Traitor" (12-11-62) Lew Ayres
103. "Gun Duel" (12-25-62) DeForest Kelley
104. "Naked Steel" (1-1-63) John Doucette
105. "Vengeance" (1-8-63) Fay Spain, Denver Pyle
106. "Protective Custody" (1-15-63) David Brian
107. "The Betrayers" (1-22-63) Adam West
108. "The Wedding Party" (1-29-63) Jacqueline Scott
109. "No Place to Run" (2-5-63) Don Durant
110. "The Fugitives" (2-12-63) Phyllis Avery
111. "The Dispossessed" (2-19-63)
112. "The Renegade Brand" (2-26-63) Lori Patrick, Jeanette

Nolan
113. "The Violent Ones" (3-5-63) John Anderson, Dawn Wells, Paul Carr
114. "The Unvanquished" (3-12-63) Frank De Kova
115. "The Sometime Gambler" (3-19-63) James Gregory, Jacqueline Scott
116. "Edge of Evil" (4-2-63) Ron Harper
117. "Broken Honor" (4-9-63) Rod Cameron
118. "The Last Battleground" (4-16-63) John Hoyt
119. "The Stranger" (4-23-63) Geraldine Brooks, Dewey Martin
120. "The Marshals" (4-30-63) Reginald Gardiner, David McLean
121. "Badge of Glory" (5-7-63) Lin McCarthy, Jo Morrow
122. "Trapped" (5-14-63) Tommy Sands
123. "The Road to Helena" (5-21-63) Henry Hull

## SUGARFOOT/BRONCO HOUR

Two hour-long Warner Brothers westerns both of which first appeared on "Cheyenne"--Sugarfoot being the nickname for Tom Brewster, the drifter whose Scottish relatives made an appearance in, for one, "MacBrewster the Bold"; "Bronco" being the protagonist of a post-Civil War tale.

The Regulars: Tom Brewster ("Sugarfoot"), Will Hutchins; Bronco Layne, Ty Hardin.

The Episodes:

1. Sugarfoot: "The Trial of the Canary Kid" (9-15-59) Wayde Preston, Peter Brown, Ty Hardin
2. Bronco: "Game at the Beacon Club" (9-22-59) Patricia Crowley, Barry Kelly
3. Sugarfoot: "The Wild Bunch" (9-29-59) Ray Danton, Connie Stevens
4. Bronco: "The Burning Springs" (10-6-59) Rhodes Reason
5. Sugarfoot: "MacBrewster the Bold" (10-13-59) Myron Healy
6. Bronco: "Bodyguard" (10-20-59) Alan Hale, Alan Baxter
7. Sugarfoot: "The Gitanos" (10-27-59) Suzanne Lloyd
8. Bronco: "The Soft Answer" (11-3-59) Ray Stricklyn, Leo Gordon
9. Sugarfoot: "The Canary Kid, Inc." (11-10-59) Wayde Preston, Fredd Wayne
10. Bronco: "The Last Resort" (11-17-59) Kent Taylor, Marshall Thompson
11. Sugarfoot: "Outlaw Island" (11-24-59) Merry Anders, Gerald Mohr
12. Bronco: "The Devil's Spawn" (12-1-59) Troy Donahue, Mike Keene
13. Sugarfoot: "Apollo with a Gun" (12-8-59) Mari Blanchard, Joe Sawyer

14. Bronco: "Flight from an Empire" (12-15-59) Karen Verne, Sasha Harden
15. Sugarfoot: "The Gaucho" (12-22-59) Carlos Rivas, Lori Nelson
16. Bronco: "Night Train to Denver" (12-29-59) Brad Dexter, Robert Colbert, Jacqueline McKeever
17. Sugarfoot: "Journey to Provision" (1-5-60) Mort Mills, Maurice Manson
18. Bronco: "Shadow of Jesse James" (1-12-60) James Coburn, Jeanne Cooper
19. Sugarfoot: "The Highbinder" (1-19-60) H. T. Tsiang, James Hong, Don Haggerty
20. Bronco: "The Masquerade" (1-26-60) Joel Grey, Cathleen Nesbitt, Jennifer West
21. Sugarfoot: "Wolf Pack" (2-2-60) Richard Coogan
22. Bronco: "Volunteers from Aberdeen" (2-9-60) Regis Toomey, Robert Reed
23. Sugarfoot: "Fernando" (2-16-60) Pat Comiskey
24. Bronco: "Every Man a Hero" (2-23-60)
25. Sugarfoot: "Blackwater Swamp" (3-1-60) cameo appearance by Chuck Essegian of the L. A. Dodgers
26. Bronco: "Death of an Outlaw" (3-8-60) Stephen Yoce, Rhodes Reason
27. Sugarfoot: "Return to Boot Hill" (3-15-60) Gary Vinson, Alan Hewitt
28. Bronco: "The Human Equation" (3-22-60) Lawrence Dobkin, Herbert Rudley
29. Sugarfoot: "Vinegaroom" (3-29-60) Richard Devon, Frank Ferguson
30. Bronco: "Montana Passage" (4-5-60) Mala Powers, Mari Blanchard
31. Sugarfoot: "The Corsican" (4-12-60) Mala Powers, Harry Shannon
32. Bronco: "Legacy of Twisted Creek" (4-19-60) Gustavo Rojo, Carleton Young
33. Sugarfoot: "Blue Bonnet Stray" (4-26-60) Alan Baxter, Janet De Gore
34. Bronco: "Tangled Trail" (5-3-60) Randy Stuart, Marc Lawrence
35. Sugarfoot: "The Long Dry" (5-10-60) Jennifer West
36. Bronco: "La Rubia" (5-17-60) Faith Domergue
37. Sugarfoot: "Funeral at Forty Mile" (5-24-60) Donald May, Kent Taylor, John Qualen
38. Bronco: "Winter Kill" (5-31-60) Virginia Gregg, Richard Rust, John Lita
39. Sugarfoot: "The Captive Locomotive" (6-7-60) Jeanne Cooper, Horace MacMahon, Rex Reason
40. Bronco: "End of a Rope" (6-14-60) Robert Colbert, James Lydon, Horace MacMahon

TIGHTROPE!

Trite law and order tale of an undercover police detective simply called "Nick."

The Regulars: Michael Connors as a nameless undercover member of police department.

The Episodes:

1. "Getaway Day" (9-8-59) Raymond Bailey, Ann McCrea, Ed Nelson
2. "The Casino" (9-15-59) Alan Reed
3. "The Frame" (9-22-59) Dave Morick, John Marley, L. Q. Jones
4. "Stand on Velvet" (9-29-59)
5. "The Cracking Point" (10-6-59) Richard Jaeckel, Simon Oakland
6. "The Thousand Dollar Bill" (10-13-59) Bert Freed, Suzanne Lloyd
7. "Music and Mink" (10-20-59) Murvyn Vye, Carol Kelly, Roy Engel
8. "Man in the Middle" (11-3-59) Gerald Mohr, Marc Lawrence
9. "The Patsy" (11-10-59) Ted de Corsia, James Westerfield, Vaughn Taylor
10. "The Money Fight" (11-17-59)
11. "Black Tie Kill" (11-24-59) Nestor Paiva, Dan Barton
12. "The Perfect Circle" (12-1-59) Jack Hogan, Dennis Patrick
13. "The Lady" (12-8-59) George Macready, Russ Conway, June Vincent
14. "Cold Kill" (12-15-59) Frank Puglia, Stacy Harris
15. "The Neon Wheel" (12-22-59) Kent Taylor, Barbara Lawrence
16. "Two Private Eyes" (12-29-59) Patric Knowles, Sandy Kenyon
17. "Night of the Gun" (1-5-60) Whit Bissell
18. "Broken Rope" (1-12-60) Brad Dexter, Regis Toomey, Jack Elam, Ken Lynch
19. [unknown title] (1-19-60) Whitney Blake, John Abbott, Vladimir Sokoloff
20. "Assignment in Jericho" (1-26-60) Donald Woods, Jean Byron
21. "Three to Make Ready" (2-2-60) Jerome Cowan
22. "The Model and the Mob" (2-9-60) Jean Ingram
23. "The Long Odds" (2-16-60) Elisha Cook
24. "The Brave Pigeon" (2-23-60)
25. "First Time Out" (3-1-60)
26. "Park Avenue Story" (3-8-60) Eduardo Ciannelli, Beverly Tyler
27. "Big Business" (3-15-60) Leo Gordon, George Tobias
28. "The Chinese Pendant" (3-29-60) Ted de Corsia, Philip Ahn
29. "Achilles and His Heels" (4-5-60) Harry Bellaver, Edward Ryder

30. "Gangster's Daughter" (4-12-60) Leslie Parrish, Joe De Santis
31. "The Penthouse Story" (4-19-60) Myron Healey, Dolores Donlan
32. "The Shark" (4-26-60) Jesse White, Stanley Adams
33. "The Horse Runs High" (5-3-60) Robert Lowery, Karen Steele
34. "The Hired Guns" (5-10-60) Barry Atwater, John Kellogg
35. "Borderline" (5-17-60) Paula Raymond
36. "A Matter of Money" (5-24-60)
37. "Bullets and Ballet" (5-31-60) John Beradino, Cindy Robbins

FORD STARTIME

The Episodes:
1. "The Wonderful World of Entertainment" (10-6-59) Rosalind Russell, Kate Smith, Polly Bergen, Ernie Kovacs, Eddie Hodges, Jack Parr, Arthur O'Connell, Maurice Chevalier, Eddie Foy Jr.
2. "The Jazz Singer" [adapted and modernized by Ralph Nelson] (10-13-59) Jerry Lewis, Molly Picon, Anna Maria Alberghetti
3. "The Turn of the Screw" [adapted by James Costigan from Henry James' novella; directed by John Frankenheimer] (10-20-59) Ingrid Bergman, Paul Stevens, Isobel Elsom, Hayward Morse, Alexandra Wager
4. "The Secret World of Kids" [Art Linkletter Special] (10-27-59) Vincent Price, Mickey Rooney, Ann Blyth, Angela Cartwright, appearances by Richard Nixon and mother.
5. "The Dean Martin Show" (11-3-59) Frank Sinatra, Mickey Rooney
6. "The Wicked Scheme of Jebel Deeks" [by John D. Hess] (11-10-59) Alec Guinness, Henry Jones, Patricia Barry, Roland Winters, William Redfield
7. "George Burns in the Big Time" (11-17-59) guests: Jack Benny, Eddie Cantor, George Jessel, Bobby Darin, The Kingston Trio
8. "Merman on Boradway" (11-24-59) Ethel Merman, Tab Hunter, Tom Poston, Fess Parker, Bobby Sherwood
9. "Something Special" [comedy by Sol Saks] (12-1-59) Jeannie Carson, Jack Carson, Red Buttons
10. "My Three Angels" [adapted by Sam and Bella Spewack from their Broadway play] (12-8-59) Walter Slezak, George Grizzard, Barry Sullivan
11. "Cindy's Fella" [western version of "Cinderella" by Jameson Brewer; adapted from story by Frank Burt] (12-15-59) James Stewart, George Gobel, Lois Smith, James Best
12. "Christmas Startime with Leonard Bernstein" (12-22-59) with Marian Anderson, St. Paul's Cathedral Boys Choir of London
13. "Meet Cyd Charisse" (12-29-59) guests: Tony Martin, Eve

Arden, James Mitchell

14. "The Man" [adapted by James P. Cavanagh from play by Mel Dinelli] (1-5-60) Audie Murphy, Michael J. Pollard, Thelma Ritter

15. "The Dean Martin Show" (1-12-60) Andre Previn, Nanette Fabray, Fabian

16. "Crime, Inc." [documentary with Lloyd Nolan as narrator] (1-19-60)

17. "The Wonderful World of Jack Parr" (1-26-60) Jonathan Winters, Betty Bruce, Alice Pearce, Harry Mimmo, Pat Suzuki

18. "The Greatest Man Alive" [adapted by Tony Webster from his Broadway comedy] (2-2-60) Bert Lahr, Ed Wynn, Nancy Olson, Russell Nype

19. "The Swingin' Years" (2-9-60) with Gene Krupa, Woody Herman, Count Basie, Anita O'Day, Guy Lombardo, Helen O'Connell

20. "Closed Set" [by Gavin Lambert] (2-16-60) Agnes Moorehead Joan Fontaine, John Ireland

21. "Talent Scouts Program" [with Dave Garroway] (2-23-60)

22. "Jeff McCleod, the Last Reb" [by Douglas Heyes and William D. Gordon] (3-1-60) Robert Horton, Ricardo Montalban, Anne Francis, Marshall Thompson

23. "The Swingin' Singin' Years" (3-8-60) with Jo Stafford, Woody Herman

24. "Academy Award Songs" (3-15-60) with Nat King Cole, Gogi Grant

25. "Dear Arthur" [Gore Vidal adapted from "Arthur" by P. G. Woodhouse] (3-22-60) Rex Harrison, Hermione Baddeley, Sarah Marshall, Nicholas Pryor

26. "The Young Juggler" [from the Anatole France story "Le Jongleur de Notre Dame" from the French legend] (3-29-60) Tony Curtis, Patricia Medina, Nehemiah Persoff, Elisha Cook

27. "Incident at the Corner" [Charlotte Armstrong adapted from her novella; Alfred Hitchcock directed] (4-5-60) Vera Miles, George Peppard, Paul Hartman

28. "Soldiers in Greasepaint" [U.S.O. tribute] (4-26-60) with Don Adams, Jane Adams

29. "Fun Fair" [salute to the American county fair] (5-3-60) with Celeste Holm, Margaret Hamilton, Jaye P. Morgan

30. "Tennessee Ernie Ford Meets King Arthur" (5-10-60) Alan Young, Vincent Price, Alan Mowbray

31. "Sing Along With Mitch" (5-24-60) Mitch Miller, Diana Trask, Leslie Uggams

32. "The Nanette Fabray Show" (5-31-60) with Stubby Kaye, Tony Randall, Robert Strauss, Jean Pierre Aumont

PHILIP MARLOWE

Standard video treatment of the Raymond Chandler private

detective; Marlowe lacking the fascination he once evoked in the 1946 feature film The Big Sleep (no wonder--one scenarist for the film being William Faulkner).

The Regulars: Philip Marlowe, Philip Carey.

The Episodes:

1. "The Ugly Duckling" (10-6-59) Rhys Williams, Virginia Gregg
2. "Prescription for Murder" (10-13-59) Marianne Stewart, Alexander Scourby
3. "Buddy Boy" (10-20-59) Ce Ce Whitney
4. 'Death in the Family" (10-27-59) Robert Brubaker, Joan Banks
5. "Mama's Boy" (11-3-59) Joan Taylor
6. "Child of Virtue" (11-10-59) Joe De Santis, Yvonne Craig
7. "Bum Wrap" (11-17-59) Stacy Harris, William Swan
8. "The Temple of Love" (11-24-59) John Dehner, Richard Hale
9. "The Mogul" (12-1-59) William Schallert, Rhodes Reason
10. "Hit and Run" (12-8-59) Richard Crane, Kaye Elhardt
11. "Mother Dear" (12-15-59) Franco Corsaro
12. "The Hunger" (12-22-59) Mercedes Shirley, Kathryn Card
13. "Ricochet" (12-29-59) Mark Roberts, Patricia Donahue
14. "The Scarlet A" (1-5-60) Suzanne Lloyd, Frank Ferguson
15. "A Standard for Murder" (1-12-60) Edward Kemmer
16. "Poor Lilli, Sweet Lilli" (1-19-60) Norm Alden
17. 'Death Takes a Lover" (1-26-60) John Hudson, Gale Robbins
18. 'One Ring for Murder" (2-2-60) Rebecca Welles
19. "Gem of a Murder" (2-9-60) William Schallert
20. "Time to Kill" (2-16-60)
21. "Murder in the Stars" (2-23-60)
22. "Murder by the Book" (3-1-60) William Schallert
23. "Murder Is a Grave Affair" (3-8-60) Gene Nelson, Betsy Jones-Moreland
24. "Murder Is Dead Wrong" (3-15-60) Paul Richards, Tom Drake
25. "Last Call for Murder" (3-22-60) James Douglas, Jan Shepard
26. "You Kill Me" (3-29-60) Edward Kemmer, Marion Ross

THE LINEUP

In this reworked format for the long-running series begun October 1, 1954, about the cases of two San Francisco police detectives, only Lt. Ben Guthrie (Warner Anderson) remains of the courageous pair. Guthrie's partner, Inspector Matt Grebb (Tom Tully), returned for the episode of November 4, 1959.

With the police force now expanded and the drama running time lengthened to a full hour, characterizations became more interesting. It is the motives behind (rather than merely the criminal act of) robbery in "Prelude to Violence" that renders Robert Vaughn's portrayal as the man in question a sympathetic one. And juvenile delinquency--too often purely exploited for sensational effect--is handled well in the episodes "Wake Up to Terror" and "Run to the City."

The Regulars: Lt. Ben Guthrie, Warner Anderson; Inspector Dan Delaney, William Leslie; Inspector Charlie Summers, Tod Barton; Inspector Al Quine, Robert Palmer; Pete Larkins, Skip Ward; Sandy McCallister, Rachel Ames.

The Episodes:

1. "Wake Up to Terror" (9-30-59) Dennis Hopper, Jackie Coogan, Marguerite Chapman
2. "The Strange Return of Army Armitage" (10-7-59) Jack Lord, Steven Hill, Kim Hunter
3. "My Son Is a Stranger" (10-14-59) Frank Silvera, Vic Morrow, Robert Morris
4. "Death of a Puppet" (10-21-59) Paul Winchell
5. "Thrills" (10-28-59) Peggy Ann Garner, Diane Brewster, Rick Jason
6. "Prelude to Violence" (11-4-59) Robert Vaughn, Tom Tully
7. "Run to the City" (11-11-59) Susan Oliver, Jonathan Gilmore
8. "Lonesome as Midnight" (11-18-59) James Best, Nita Talbot, Fred Beir
9. "The Counterfeit Citizens" (12-2-59) Fabrizio Mioni, Chana Mioni, Chana Eden
10. "The Chinatown Story" (12-9-59) Neva Aki, Mark Damon
11. "Vengeful Knife" (12-16-59) Vic Morrow
12. "Prince of Penmen" (1-6-60) Paul Lambert, Nancy Gates, Marie Windsor
13. "The Woman on the Ledge" (1-13-60) Virginia Vincent, Joe Maross
14. "Seven Sinners" (1-20-60) Clu Gulager, Barbara Turner, Richard Shannon

HAWAIIAN EYE

Warner Brothers' island successor to "77 Sunset Strip" (perhaps a matched bookend--inasmuch as principals at times interchanged episodes), the private eyes being Tom Lopaka (Robert Conrad), Tracy Steele (Anthony Eisley) and Greg MacKenzie (Grant Williams). Connie Stevens was the flighty night club singer Cricket Blake; Troy Donahue was given a continuing role once his WB entry--"Surfside 6"--had been canceled.

The Regulars: Tom Lopaka, Robert Conrad; Cricket Blake, Connie Stevens; Tracy Steele, Anthony Eisley; Kim, Poncie Ponce; Moke, Doug Mossman; Quon, Mel Prestlidge; Greg MacKenzie (since 12/21/60), Grant Williams; Philip Barton (fourth season), Troy Donahue.

The Episodes:

1. "Malihini Holiday" (10-7-59) Patricia Driscoll, Duncan LaMont, Edward Kemmer
2. "Waikiki Widow" (10-14-59) Paula Raymond, Robert McQueeney
3. "Second Day of Infamy" (10-21-59) Yuki Shimoda
4. "All Expenses Paid" (10-28-59) Karen Steele, Anthony George, Mary Adams
5. "Dangerous Eden" (11-4-59) Jackie Coogan, Audrey Totter, Myrna Fahey
6. "Cloud Over Koala" (11-11-59) Jack Orrison, Joanna Moore
7. "Beach Boy" (11-18-59) Troy Donahue, Anna Lee, Faith Domergue
8. "Three Tickets to Lani" (11-25-59) Efrem Zimbalist Jr. (in the role of Stuart Bailey)
9. "Quick Return" (12-2-59) Adam West, Hugh Sanders
10. "Secret of the Second Door" (12-9-59) Christine White
11. "Shipment from Kihei" (12-16-59) Beverly Garland
12. "A Dime a Dozen" (12-23-59) Shirley Knight, Joanna Barnes
13. "The Koa Man" (12-30-59) Barbara Luna, Suzanne Storrs, Adam Williams
14. "Stamped for Danger" (1-6-60) Ruta Lee
15. "Kamehameha Cloak" (1-13-60) Kathleen Crowley, Tris Coffin, Robert Colbert, Paul Picerni
16. "The Kikiki Kid" (1-20-60) John Gabriel, Jean Byron
17. "Then There Were Three" (1-27-60) Nancy Gates
18. "Sword of the Samurai" (2-3-60) George Takei, James Yagi
19. "Hong Kong Passage" (2-10-60) Merry Anders, Whit Bissell
20. "Cut of Ice" (2-17-60) Roberta Haynes, Frank Albertson, Donald Lawton
21. "Fatal Cruise" (2-24-60) Shirley Knight, Gary Conway
22. "Danger on Credit" (3-2-60) Gary Vinson
23. "Bequest of Arthur Goodwin" (3-9-60) Fay Wray, Andrea King
24. "A Birthday Boy" (3-16-60) Troy Donahue, Fay Spain
25. "Second Fiddle" (3-23-60) John Van Dreelen, Myrna Fahey
26. "Kim Quixote" (3-30-60) Mala Powers, Don Gordon
27. "The Lady's Not for Traveling" (4-6-60) Peggy McCay, Richard Shannon
28. "Murder Anyone?" (4-13-60) Julie Adams, Ray Danton, Richard Garland, Herbert Rudley
29. "The Typhoon" (4-27-60) Mary Tyler Moore, Jean Allison
30. "Shadow of the Blade" (5-4-60) Lisa Lu, Fred Beir
31. "Dead Ringer" (5-11-60) Dianne Foster, Warren Stevens
32. "Little Blalah" (5-18-60) Andra Martin, Mike Road
33. "Assignment: Manila" (5-25-60) Lisa Gaye, Janet Lake

Second Season

34. "I Wed Three Wives" (9-14-60) Ray Danton, Tommy Farrell, Barney Phillips, Roger Smith and Efrem Zimbalist Jr. (in Jeff Spencer and Stuart Bailey roles)
35. "Princess from Manhattan" (9-21-60) Janet Lake, John van Dreelen
36. "With This Ring" (9-28-60) Paul Richards, Ruta Lee, Terry Burnham
37. "Sea Fire" (10-5-60) Anthony Caruso, Andrea Martin, Fred Beir, John Marley
38. "Jade Song" (10-12-60) James Hong, George Takei, Lisa Lu
39. "The Blue Goddess" (10-19-60) Burt Douglas, Suzanne Lloyd
40. "White Pigeon Ticket" (10-26-60) Harry Jackson, Warren Stevens, Joan Marshall
41. "Vanessa Vanishes" (11-2-60) Mary Tyler Moore
42. "The Kahuma Curtain" (11-9-60) Chad Everett, Shirley Knight
43. "Girl on a String" (11-16-60) Joan Staley, Linda Lawson
44. "Kakua Woman" (11-23-60) Stella Stevens, Anita Loo, Mike Road
45. "The Contenders" (11-30-60) Myrna Fahey, Frank De Kova
46. "Swan Song for a Hero" (12-7-60) John Van Dreelen, Robert Lowery
47. "The Money Blossom" (12-14-60) Gerald Mohr, Jean Willes
48. "Services Rendered" (12-21-60) Leslie Parrish
49. "Baker's Half Dozen" (12-28-60) Peter Breck, Lee Kinsolving
50. "Made in Japan" (1-4-61) Brad Dexter, Frank Ferguson, Anne Whitfield
51. "A Touch of Velvet" (1-11-61) Robert Hutton, Dick Davalos
52. "Talk and You're Dead" (1-18-61) Lisa Gaye, Walter Burke
53. "Robinson Koyote" (1-25-61) Julie Adams
54. "The Manabi Figurine" (2-1-61) Mike Road, Paula Raymond
55. "Caves of Pele" (2-8-61) Claire Griswold, Mark Damon
56. "Man in a Rage" (2-15-61) Robert Colbert, Cloris Leachman
57. "The Stanhope Brand" (2-22-61) Arch Johnson, Lee Van Cleef, Inger Stevens, John Zaremba
58. "The Trouble with Murder" (3-1-61) Arthur Franz
59. "Man from Manila" (3-8-61) Kent Taylor, Jean Gillespie, Robert Palmer
60. "Her Father's House" (3-15-61) Ellen Davalos, Craig Hill
61. "The Humukumunukunukuapuaa Kid" (3-22-61) Bert Convy, Anne Helm
62. "Don't Kiss Me Goodbye" (3-29-61) Merry Anders, Anita Loo
63. "Dragon Road" (4-5-61) Frances Fong, Alan Hale
64. "It Ain't Cricket" (4-12-61) Gigi Perreau
65. "The Comics" (4-19-61) Mary Tyler Moore, Marie Windsor
66. "Father, Dear Father" (4-26-61) Lawrence Dobkin, Judy Bamber
67. "The Manchu Formula" (5-3-61) Philip Ahn, Lisa Lu,

George Takei
68. "The Pretty People" (5-10-61) Maria Palmer
69. "The Big Dealer" (5-17-61) Dyan Cannon
70. "Maid in America" (5-24-61) Anita Loo, Aki Aleong
71. "A Taste for Money" (5-31-61) Robert Colbert, Vaughn Taylor

Third Season

72. "Satan City" (9-27-61) Arthur Franz, Virginia Gregg
73. "The Kapua of Coconut Bay" (10-4-61) Anne Seymour, Arch Johnson, Mari Blanchard
74. "The Moon of Mindanao" (10-11-61) Diana Millay, Robert Brubaker, Russ Conway, Cayla Graves
75. "The Doctor's Lady" (10-18-61) Dorothy Green, Lisa Gaye
76. "Thomas Jefferson Chu" (10-25-61) George Takei, Frances Fong, Dabbs Greer
77. "Pill in a Box" (11-1-61) Lewis Charles
78. "Kill a Grey Fox" (11-8-61) David White, Robert Colbert, Jo Morrow
79. "The Reluctant Visit" (11-15-61) Richard Carlyle, Beatrice Kay, Victor Buono, Chad Everett
80. "Queen from Kern County" (11-22-61) Marie Windsor, Gale Page, Jerome Cowan
81. "Two for the Money" (12-6-61) Mary Tyler Moore, Irene Hervey, Roger Smith
82. "Tusitala" (12-13-61) Kent Taylor, Susan Silo, Ronald Long
83. "The Classic Cab" (12-20-61) Kathleen Crowley, Tris Coffin
84. "Concert in Hawaii" (12-27-61) Faith Domergue, Jack Cassidy, K. T. Stevens
85. "The Missile Rogues" (1-3-62) Warren Stevens, Jesse White, Joan Marshall
86. "Little Miss Rich Witch" (1-10-62) Janet Lake, Robert Colbert
87. "Big Fever" (1-17-62) Tom Drake, Alan Baxter, Andrew King
88. "Year of Grace" (1-24-62) Lisa Gaye, Nico Minardos, Paula Raymond, Patric Knowles
89. "My Love, But Lightly" (1-31-62) Ziva Rodann, John van Dreelen
90. "Cricket's Millionaire" (2-7-62) Anne Whitfield, Andre Phillipe
91. "Four-Cornered Triangle" (2-14-62) Chad Everett
92. "Total Eclipse" (2-21-62) Kathryn Hays
93. "Blackmail in Satin" (2-28-62) Efrem Zimbalist Jr., Susan Seaforth, Linda Watkins, Bernard Fein, Bob Hogan
94. "A Scent of Whales" (3-7-62) John Dehner, Sherry Jackson, Dennis Patrick
95. "A Likely Story" (3-14-62) Dorothy Provine, Fred Beir
96. "The Meeting at Molokai" (3-21-62) Mala Powers, Dorothy Green, Neil Hamilton
97. "The Payoff" (3-28-62) Barbara Luna, Fay Spain, Paul

Mantee
98. "An Echo of Honor" (4-4-62) Philip Reed
99. "Nightmare in Paradise" (4-11-62) Abby Dalton
100. "Aloha, Cricket" (4-18-62) Peter Breck, Claire Carleton, Tita Marsell
101. "The Last Samurai" (4-25-62) Irene Hervey, Evan McCord
102. "Rx Cricket" (5-2-62) Paula Raymond, Chad Everett
103. "Location Shooting" (5-9-62) Joan Staley, Bill Williams, Donald Woods
104. "Across the River Lethe" (5-16-62) Janet Lake, Kathy Bennett
105. "Scene of the Crime" (5-23-62) Arch Johnson, Angela Greene, Kaye Elhardt
106. "Among the Living" (5-30-62) Edward Byrnes, Mike Road, Grace Gaynor, Robert Lowery, Roxanne Arlen
107. "V is for Victim" (6-6-62) Antoinette Bower, Isobel Elsom
108. "Koko Kate" (6-13-62) Chad Everett, Virginia Gregg, Merry Anders
109. "Lalama Lady" (6-20-62) Peter Brown, Randy Stuart, Pamela Austin, Whit Bissell

Fourth Season

110. "Day in the Sun" (10-2-62) Marie Windsor, James Best
111. "Somewhere There's Music" (10-9-62) John Wengraf
112. "There'll Be Some Changes Made" (10-16-62) Victor Jory, Claude Akins
113. "The Broken Thread" (10-23-62) Philip Ahn
114. "Lament for a Saturday Warrior" (10-30-62) Dick Davalos
115. "The After Hours Heart" (11-13-62) Peggy McKay
116. "The Sign-Off" (11-20-62) Dawn Wells
117. "A Night with Nora Stewart" (11-27-62) Dorothy Provine
118. "To See, Perchance to Dream" (12-4-62) Jack Hogan
119. "Pursuit of a Lady" (12-11-62) Diane McBain
120. "Shannon Malloy" (12-18-62) Susan Silo, Virginia Gregg
121. "Go Steady with Danger" (1-1-63) Michael Dante, Jeanette Nolan
122. "Kupikio Kid" (1-8-63) Irene Hervey, Anita Loo
123. "Maybe Menehunes" (1-15-63) Mala Powers
124. "Pretty Pigeon" (1-22-63) Diane McBain
125. "Two Too Many" (1-29-63) Ray Danton, Richard Loo, Rudy Solari
126. "Boar Hunt" (2-5-63) George Montgomery
127. "Go For Baroque" (2-12-63) Joanna Moore
128. "The Long Way Home" (2-19-63) Jeanne Cooper, Susan Seaforth
129. "Two Million Too Much" (2-26-63) Van Williams, Barbara Bain, Karen Sharpe
130. "Blow Low, Blow Blue" (3-5-63) Joan Freeman, Victor Sen Yung
131. "Gift of Love" (3-19-63) Peggy McKay, Kevin Hagen
132. "The Sisters" (3-26-63) Myrna Fahey, Maggie Pierce
133. "Passport" (4-2-63) Randy Stuart

WICHITA TOWN

Western vehicle for the father and son Joel and Jody McCrea, as the sheriff and deputy of "Wichita Town."

The Regulars: Mike Dunbar, Joel McCrea; Ben Matheson, Jody McCrea; Aeneas MacLinahan, Bob Anderson.

The Episodes:

1. "The Night the Cowboys Roared" (9-30-59) Tony Montenaro, Frank Ferguson
2. "Wyndham's Way" (10-7-59) George Neise
3. "Bullet for a Friend" (10-14-59) Carlos Romero
4. "They Won't Hang Jimmy Relson" (10-21-59) Vic Morrow
5. "Drifting" (10-28-59) John Larch, John McIntire
6. "Man on the Hill" (11-4-59) Mort Mills
7. "Day of Battle" (11-18-59) Robert Foulk, Carlos Romero
8. "Passage to the Enemy" (12-2-59) Robert Vaughn, Jean Inness
9. "Out of the Past" (12-9-59) Skip Homeier
10. "Death Watch" (12-16-59)
11. "The Devil's Choice" (12-23-59) Robert Bray, Richard Coogan
12. "Biggest Man in Town" (12-30-59) Don Dubbins, Yvonne Line, Ron Hagerthy
13. "Ruby Dawes" (1-6-60) Marilyn Erskine, Charles Aidman
14. "Bought" (1-13-60) Robert Middleton, Enid Janes, George Neise
15. "The Long Night" (1-20-60) Charles Seel, Sherwood Price
16. "Seed of Hate" (1-27-60) Keith Larsen
17. "The Avengers" (2-3-60) Emile Meyer, Tom Gilson
18. "Brothers of the Knife" (2-10-60) Anthony Caruso, Abraham Sofaer
19. "Afternoon in Town" (2-17-60) Alan Hale, Ron Hayes
20. "The Frontiersman" (3-2-60) Gene Evans, Frank Ferguson
21. "The Hanging Judge" (3-9-60) Frank Lovejoy, Carl Benton Reid
22. "Second Chance" (3-16-60) Tom Drake, Robert F. Simon
23. "Paid in Full" (3-23-60) John McIntire, I. Stanford Jolley
24. "The Legend of Tom Horn" (3-30-60) Nancy Gates, Michael Pate

THE LAW OF THE PLAINSMAN

Tough, frequently penetrating western tale of a well-educated Indian and New Mexico deputy marshal (Michael Ansara as Sam Buckhart).

The Regulars: Deputy Sam Buckhart, Michael Ansara; Marshal Morrison, Dayton Lummis; Tess, Gina Gillespie.

The Episodes:

1. "Prairie Incident" (10-1-59)
2. "Full Circle" (10-8-59) Lyle Bettger, Gail Kobe, Wayne Rogers
3. "A Matter of Life or Death" (10-15-59) Gustavo Rojo, Jean Allison
4. "The Hostiles" (10-22-59)
5. "Passenger to Mescalero" (10-29-59) Brian G. Hutton
6. "Blood Trails" (11-5-59) Chris Alcaide
7. "Desperate Decision" (11-12-59) Robert Wilke
8. "Appointment in Sante Fe" (11-19-59) John Anderson
9. "The Gibbet" (11-26-59) Robert F. Simon, Mort Mills
10. "The Dude" (12-3-59) Robert Vaughn
11. "The Innocent" (12-10-59) Robert Vaughn, Elena Verdugo
12. "Clear Title" (12-17-59) John Dehner, Lee Van Cleef
13. "Toll Road" (12-24-59) Bert Freed, Maggie Pierce
14. "Calculated Risk" (12-31-59) Don Grady, Chris Alcaide
15. "Fear" (1-7-60) Stephen Talbot
16. "Endurance" (1-14-60)
17. "The Comet" (1-21-60) Jacques Aubuchon, Ned Glass
18. "The Rawhiders" (1-28-60) John Milford, Joe De Santis
19. "The Imposter" (2-4-60) Harry Landers
20. "Common Ground" (2-11-60) Michael Pate
21. "The Matriarch" (2-18-60) Lynn Bari
22. "A Question of Courage" (2-25-60) Claude Akins, Patricia Donahue
23. "Dangerous Barriers" (3-10-60) Arch Johnson, Steve Marlo
24. "The Show-Off" (3-17-60) Scott Marlowe, Leo Gordon
25. "Rabbit's Fang" (3-24-60) Don Dubbins, Constance Ford
26. "Stella" (3-31-60) Gloria Talbot, Richard Devon
27. "Amnesty" (4-7-60) Chris Alcaide, Robert Warwick
28. "Jeb's Daughter" (4-14-60) John Anderson, Suzanne Lloyd
29. "Cavern of the Wind" (4-21-60) Paul Langton, Richard Anderson
30. "Trojan Horse" (5-5-60) Gene Nelson

## JOHNNY STACCATO

Elmer Bernstein's musical score and interesting Greenwich Village locale heighten this private detective yarn, with John Cassavetes as the jazz pianist turned sleuth and Eduardo Ciannelli as his confidant, night club owner Waldo.

The Regulars: Johnny Staccato, John Cassavetes; Waldo, Eduardo Ciannelli.

The Episodes:
1. "The Naked Truth" (9-10-59) Michael Landon, Chick Chandler, Stacy Harris; appearances by musicians Pete Candoli, Red Norvo, Red Mitchell, Johnny Williams, Barney Kessel

Shelly Manne
2. "Murder for Credit" (9-17-59) Charles McGraw, Martin Landau
3. "The Parents" (9-24-59) Shirley Knight
4. "The Shop of the Four Winds" (10-1-59)
5. "The Nature of the Night" (10-15-59) Dean Stockwell
6. "Viva Paco" (10-22-59) Jimmy Murphy
7. "Evil" (10-29-59) Elizabeth Patterson
8. "Murder in Hi Fi" (11-5-59)
9. "Fly, Baby, Fly" (11-12-59) Gena Rowlands
10. "Tempted" (11-19-59) Elizabeth Montgomery
11. "The Poet's Touch" (11-26-59) Ken Walken
12. "The Unwise Men" (12-3-59)
13. "A Piece of Paradise" (12-10-59)
14. "The Return" (12-17-59) Tom Allen, Virginia Vincent, Ben Hammer
15. "Collector's Item" (12-31-59) Rupert Crosse, Juano Hernandez
16. "Man in the Pit" (1-7-60) Buzz Martin
17. "The Only Witness" (1-14-60) Geraldine Brooks
18. "Night of Jeopardy" (1-21-60) Frank de Kova
19. "Double Feature" (1-28-60) Martin Mason
20. "The List of Death" (2-4-60) Monica Lewis, Paul Stewart
21. "Jessica Winthrop" (2-11-60) Cloris Leachman
22. "An Act of Terror" (2-18-60)
23. "An Angry Young Man" (2-25-60) Warren Berlinger
24. "The Mask of Jason" (3-3-60) Mary Tyler Moore
25. "A Nice Little Town" (3-10-60)
26. "Swinging Longhair" (3-17-60) George Voskovec
27. "The Wild Reed" (3-24-60) Bethel Leslie, Harry Guardino

## THE UNTOUCHABLES

This relentless examination of the Chicago cesspool of the Prohibition Era--perhaps the most celebrated study in any medium before or since--has an eerie quality about it; one that transcends the hefty doses of violence that interlace its episodes into a genuine art form. Eliot Ness, as the archetypal good, is a full-bodied character as portrayed by Robert Stack, to be sure. But neither Ness nor his seemingly endless parade of underworld nemeses are as important as is the change in climate, or mood that follows through in the duration of a single episode. Look no further than The Untouchables for an exegesis on the unsteady balance of Good and Evil. Ness triumphs only in the physical sense, but the cesspool triumphs spiritually.

In what may be this series' finest episode, The White Slavers, in which Betty Field was extraordinary as a former procuress for the mob, evil runs rampant and we are actually relieved when the teleplay has concluded. One scene alone has the mob sweeping up innocent young women south of the Mexican border to be sold into prostitution, only to be tipped that Ness is on their trail and so getting rid of the evidence, literally, by machine-gunning to death the whole of their hapless victims. More than a decade after its initial showing, the denouement still disturbs. The principal mafioso in this case is entrapped in the cellar of his hideaway by several of the women whose lives he has mutilated. The women approach closer and closer--as if to consume their captive--while his screams are muted by the gunplay going on on the floor above.

Quinn Martin's conception--his finest hour--was much enhanced by the documentary-like narrative of Walter Winchell whose nasal oratory was widely satirized. Add to this some fine camera work, editing and art direction and the throbbing musical score of Nelson Riddle.

The Regulars: Eliot Ness, Robert Stack; Cam Allison, Anthony George (first season); Rossi, Nicholas Georgiade; Flaherty, Jerry Paris; Rossman, Steve London; Lee Hobson, Paul Picerni (from second season); Youngfellow, Abel Fernandez (from second season). Narrated by Walter Winchell.

The Episodes:

1. "The Empty Chair" (10-15-59) Nehemiah Persoff, Bruce Gordon, Barbara Nichols
2. "Ma Barker and Her Boys" (10-22-59) Claire Trevor, Adam Williams, Joe Di Reda
3. "The Jake Lingle Story" (10-29-59) J. Carrol Naish, Rita Lynn
4. "The George 'Bugs' Moran Story" (11-5-59) Lloyd Nolan, Jack Warden
5. "Ain't We Got Fun?" (11-12-59) Cameron Mitchell, Joseph Buloff, Ted de Corsia
6. "The Vincent 'Mad Dog' Coll Story" (11-19-59) Lawrence Dobkin, Clu Gulager
7. "Mexican Standoff" (11-26-59) Vince Edwards, Martin Landau
8. "The Artichoke King" (12-3-59) Jack Weston, Robert Ellenstein
9. "Tri-State Gang" (12-10-59) William Bendix
10. "The Dutch Schultz Story" (12-17-59) Lawrence Dobkin, Mort Mills
11. "You Can't Pick the Number" (12-24-59) Darryl Hickman, Jay C. Flippen
12. "Underground Railway" (12-31-59) Cliff Robertson, Virginia Vincent
13. "Syndicate Sanctuary" (1-7-60) Mike Kellin, Anthony Caruso, Gail Kobe, Jack Elam
14. "The Noise of Death" (1-14-60) J. Carrol Naish, Rita Lynn
15. "Star Witness" (1-21-60) Jim Backus, Marc Lawrence
16. "The St. Louis Story" (1-28-60) David Brian, Leo Gordon
17. "One-Armed Bandit" (2-4-60) Harry Guardino, John Beradino

18. "Little Egypt" (2-11-60) Fred Clark
19. "The Big Squeeze" (2-18-60) Dan O'Herlihy
20. "The Unhired Assassin" [Part I] (2-25-60) Robert Middleton, Lee Van Cleef, Bruce Gordon, Joe Mantell
21. "The Unhired Assassin" [Part II] (3-3-60) as above
22. "The White Slavers" (3-10-60) Betty Field, Dick York
23. "Three Thousand Suspects" (3-24-60) Leslie Nielsen, Peter Leeds
24. "The Doreen Maney Story" (3-31-60) Anne Francis, Connie Hines, Christopher Dark
25. "Portrait of a Thief" (4-7-60) Charles McGraw, Henry Jones, Frank Wilcox, Edward Andrews
26. "Underworld Bank" (4-14-60) Thomas Mitchell, Peter Falk
27. "Head of Fire, Feet of Clay" (4-21-60) Nehemiah Persoff, Jack Warden, Madlyn Rhue
28. "The Frank Nitti Story" (4-28-60) Myron McCormick

Second Season

29. "The Rusty Heller Story" (10-13-60) Elizabeth Montgomery, David White, Harold J. Stone
30. "Clay Pigeon: The Jack 'Legs' Diamond Story" (10-20-60) Steven Hill, Lawrence Dobkin, Robert Carricart, Suzanne Storrs, Norma Crane
31. "Nicky" (11-3-60) Luther Adler, Michael Ansara
32. "The Waxey Gordon Story" (11-10-60) Nehemiah Persoff, Sam Gilman
33. "The Mark of Cain" (11-17-60) Henry Silva
34. "A Seat on the Fence" (11-24-60) Frank Silvera, John McIntire
35. "The Purple Gang" (12-1-60) Steve Cochran, Bruce Gordon
36. "Kiss of Death Girl" (12-8-60) Jan Sterling, Mickey Shaughnessy
37. "The Larry Fay Story" (12-15-60) Sam Levene, Robert Emhardt, June Havoc
38. "The Otto Frick Story" (12-22-60) Francis Lederer, Richard Jaeckel, Jack Warden
39. "The Tommy Karpeles Story" (12-29-60) Joseph Wiseman, Harold J. Stone, Madlyn Rhue, Murray Hamilton, Vic Morrow
40. "The Big Train" [Part I] (1-5-61) Neville Brand, Bruce Gordon, Robert F. Simon, James Westerfield
41. "The Big Train" [Part II] (1-12-61) as above
42. "The Masterpiece" (1-19-61) Robert Middleton, Rip Torn, George Voskovec, Joseph Ruskin, Bruce Gordon
43. "The Organization" (1-26-61) Richard Conte, Susan Oliver, Milton Selzer
44. "Jamaica Ginger" (2-2-61) Brian Keith, Michael Ansara, Alfred Ryder
45. "Augie 'The Banker' Ciamino" (2-9-61) Sam Jaffe, Keenan Wynn, Will Kuluva, Lee Philips
46. "The Underground Court" (2-16-61) Joan Blondell, Richard Devon, Eddie Firestone, Frank de Kova

47. "The Nick Moses Story" (2-23-61) Harry Guardino, Joe De Santis, Michael Constantine, Bruce Gordon
48. "The Antidote" (3-9-61) Telly Savalas, Joseph Wiseman, Bruce Gordon
49. "The Lily Dallas Story" (3-16-61) June Vincent, Norma Crane, Barbara Parkins, Larry Parks, Dabbs Greer
50. "Murder Under Glass" (3-23-61) Luther Adler, Bruce Gordon, Dennis Patrick
51. "Testimony of Evil" (3-30-61) David Brian, Fay Spain, John Marley
52. "Ring of Terror" (4-13-61) Viveca Lindfors, Harold J. Stone, John Crawford
53. "Mr. Moon" (4-20-61) Victor Buono, Karl Swenson, Bruce Gordon
54. "Death for Sale" (4-27-61) James MacArthur, Lou Polan
55. "Stranglehold" (5-4-61) Ricardo Montalban, Philip Pine, Kevin Hagen, Trevor Bardette
56. "The Nero Rankin Story" (5-11-61) Will Kuluva, John Dehner, Joanna Moore
57. "The Seventh Vote" (5-18-61) Nehemiah Persoff, Bruce Gordon, Joseph Ruskin, George Neise
58. "The King of Champagne" (5-25-61) Robert Middleton, Michael Constantine, Barry Morse, Grant Richards
59. "The Nick Acropolis Story" (6-1-61) Lee Marvin, Bruce Gordon, Constance Ford
60. "The 90-Proof Dame" (6-8-61) Steve Cochran, Warren Stevens, Joanna Barnes, Steven Geray

Third Season

61. "The Troubleshooter" (10-12-61) Peter Falk, Murray Hamilton, Ned Glass
62. "Powerplay" (10-19-61) Wendell Corey, Carroll O'Connor, Albert Salmi
63. "Tunnel of Horrors" (10-26-61) Martin Balsam, Bruce Gordon, Joseph Ruskin
64. "The Genna Brothers" (11-2-61) Marc Lawrence, Anthony Carbone
65. "The Matt Bass Scheme" (11-9-61) Telly Savalas, Bruce Gordon
66. "Loophole" (11-16-61) Jack Klugman, Martin Landau, George Tobias, Gavin MacLeod
67. "Jigsaw" (11-23-61) James Gregory, Cloris Leachman, Bruce Gordon, Alan Baxter
68. "Mankiller" (12-7-61) Bruce Gordon, Ruth Roman
69. "City Without a Name" (12-14-61) Paul Richards, Mike Kellin, Theodore Marcuse, Bruce Gordon
70. "Hammerlock" (12-21-61) Harold J. Stone, Joan Staley, Will Kuluva, John Larch
71. "Canada Run" (1-4-62) Simon Oakland, Arthur Hill, Bruce Gordon
72. "Fall Guy" (1-11-62) Hershel Bernardi, Don Gordon, Robert Emhardt, Jay C. Flippen

73. "The Gang War" (1-18-62) Victor Buono, Bruce Gordon
74. "The Silent Partner" (2-1-62) Charles McGraw, Dyan Cannon, Allyn Joslyn
75. "The Whitey Steele Story" (2-8-62) Henry Silva, Murray Hamilton, Eduardo Ciannelli
76. "The Death Tree" (2-15-62) Charles Bronson, Barbara Luna
77. "Takeover" (3-1-62) Luther Adler, Robert Loggia
78. "The Stryker Brothers" (3-8-62) Nehemiah Persoff, Frank Sutton, Michael Strong
79. "Element of Danger" (3-22-62) Lee Marvin, Victor Jory
80. "The Maggie Storm Story" (3-29-62) Patricia Neal, Vic Morrow, John Kellogg
81. "Man in the Middle" (4-5-62) Martin Balsam, Tom Drake, Cloris Leachman
82. "Downfall" (5-3-62) Steven Hill, Simon Oakland
83. "The Case Against Eliot Ness" (5-10-62) Pat Hingle
84. "The Ginnie Littlesmith Story" (5-17-62) Phyllis Love
85. "The Contract" (5-31-62) Harry Guardino, Gloria Talbott, Frank Sutton
86. "Pressure" (6-14-62) Harold J. Stone, Warren Oates, Darryl Hickman
87. "Arsenal" (6-28-62) Salome Jens, George Mathews, Bruce Gordon
88. "The Monkey Wrench" (7-5-62) Claude Akins, Oscar Beregi, Dolores Dorn, Bruce Gordon

## Fourth Season

89. "The Night They Shot Santa Claus" (9-25-62) Nita Talbot, Ruth White
90. "Cooker in the Sky" (10-2-62) Anne Jackson
91. "The Chess Game" (10-9-62) Richard Conte
92. "The Economist" (10-16-62) Joseph Sirola
93. "The Pea" (10-23-62) Frank Gorshin
94. "Bird in the Hand" (10-30-62) Dane Clark, Carroll O'Connor, Hershel Bernardi
95. "The Eddie O'Gara Story" (11-13-62) Michael Connors
96. "Elegy" (11-20-62) Barbara Stanwyck, Peggy Ann Garner, John Larch
97. "Come and Kill Me" (11-27-62) Dan Dailey
98. "A Fist of Five" (12-4-62) Lee Marvin, Phyllis Coates, James Caan, Roy Thinnes
99. "The Floyd Gibbons Story" (12-11-62) Scott Brady, Dorothy Malone, Stuart Erwin
100. "Double Cross" (12-18-62) Harry Morgan
101. "Search for a Dead Man" (1-1-63) Barbara Stanwyck
102. "The Speculator" (1-8-63) Telly Savalas, Bruce Gordon, Frank Sutton, Ted Knight
103. "Snowball" (1-15-63) Robert Redford, Bruce Gordon
104. "Jake Dance" (1-22-63) Dane Clark
105. "Blues for a Gone Goose" (1-29-63) Robert Duvall, Kathy Nolan

106. "Globe of Death" (2-5-63) Bruce Gordon
107. "An Eye for an Eye" (2-19-63) Jack Klugman
108. "Junk Man" (2-26-63) Pat Hingle
109. "Man in the Cooler" (3-5-63) Salome Jens, J. D. Cannon, Peter Whitney
110. "The Butcher's Boy" (3-12-63) John Larkin, Frank Sutton
111. "The Spoiler" (3-26-63) Claude Akins, Rip Torn
112. "One Last Killing" (4-2-63) Don Gordon
113. "The Giant Killer" (4-9-63) Paul Richards, Torin Thatcher, Peggy Ann Garner
114. "The Charlie Argos Story" (4-16-63) Robert Vaughn, Kent Smith, Patricia Owens
115. "The Jazz Man" (4-30-63) Simon Oakland, Robert Emhardt, Jacqueline Scott
116. "The Torpedo" (5-7-63) Charles McGraw
117. "Line of Fire" (5-14-63) Sherwood Price
118. "A Taste for Pineapple" (5-21-63) Tom Tully, Edward Binns

## TROUBLESHOOTERS

Unlikely study of a team of globe-trotting construction workers, with durable Keenan Wynn featured as Kodiak and Olympic star Bob Mathias as Dugan.

The Regulars: Kodiak, Keenan Wynn; Dugan, Bob Mathias; Scotti, Bob Fortier; Skinner, Carey Loftin; Jim, Bob Harris; Slats, Chet Allen.

The Episodes:

1. "Liquid Death" (9-11-59)
2. 'Disaster" (9-18-59) Peter Miller
3. "Trouble at Elbow Bend" (9-25-59)
4. "Lower Depths" (10-2-59)
5. "Tiger Culhane" (10-9-59)
6. "Moment of Terror" (10-16-59)
7. "Gino" (10-23-59) Marc Cavell, John Larch
8. "Pipeline" (11-6-59) Philip Pine, Ruta Lee
9. "Trapped" (11-13-59)
10. "The Big Squeeze" (11-20-59) Edgar Stehli
11. 'Downrange" (11-27-59) Charles McGraw
12. "Tunnel to Yesterday" (12-4-59) Werner Klemperer
13. "The Chain" (12-11-59) Rebecca Welles
14. 'Swing Shift" (12-25-59) Fintan Meyler
15. "The Mountain That Moved" (1-1-60) Abraham Sofaer, Sandra Marsh
16. 'High Steel" (1-15-60) Marc Lawrence
17. [unknown title] (1-22-60) Howard Caine
18. "The Big Blaze" (1-29-60) Chana Eden, Perry Lopez
19. "Head-Hunter Road" (2-12-60) Joe Ruskin

20. "The Town That Wouldn't Die" (2-19-60)
21. "Incident at Rain Mountain" (2-26-60) Sam Gilman, Madlyn Rhue, Tom Palmer
22. "Senorita" (3-4-60)
23. "The Landmark" (3-11-60) Louise Fletcher, Ron Hayes
24. "Fire in the Hole" (3-18-60) Rhys Williams
25. "No Stone Unturned" (3-25-60) Jacques Aubuchon, James Hong
26. "The Carnival" (4-1-60) Robert Eyer, Edgar Buchanan


HOTEL DE PAREE

Law and order was achieved by the glare of the sun in this western entry of a troubleshooter whose glistening silver hatband left the gunfighters dazed and helpless. Earl Holliman was the hero Sundance of a Colorado town.

The Regulars: Sundance, Earl Holliman; Annette, Jeanette Nolan; Monique, Judi Meredith; Aaron, Strother Martin.

The Episodes:

1. [unknown title] (10-2-59) Theodore Bikel
2. "Juggernaut" (10-9-59) Brian Donlevy
3. "Vein of Ore" (10-16-59) John Mills, Pat Williams
4. "The High Cost of Justice" (10-23-59) Leif Erickson
5. "Return of Monique" (10-30-59) Mark Richman
6. "A Rope Is for Hanging" (11-6-59) James Barton, Peter Whitney
7. "A Fool and His Gold" (11-13-59) Sebastian Cabot, James Barton
8. "The Only Wheel in Town" (11-20-59)
9. "The Man Who Believed in Law" (11-27-59) Charles McGraw, Alice Frost
10. "Sundance and the Hostiles" (12-11-59) Allyn Joslyn, John Pickard
11. "Sundance and the Violent Siege" (12-18-59)
12. "Sundance and the Blood Money" (1-1-60) Darryl Richard
13. "Sundance and the Bare-Knuckled Fighters" (1-8-60)
14. "Sundance and the Kid from Nowhere" (1-15-60) Scott Marlowe
15. "Sundance Goes to Kill" (1-22-60) Ron Hayes, Madlyn Rhue
16. "Sundance and the Best Soldier" (2-5-60) Judson Pratt
17. "Sundance and the Man in Room Seven" (2-12-60) Lee Van Cleef
18. "Hard Luck for Sundance" (2-19-60)
19. "Sundance and the Greenhorn Trader" (2-26-60) Richard Ney, Richard Devon
20. "Sundance and Useless" (3-4-60) Bruce Gordon, Read Morgan
21. "Sundance and the Hero of Bloody Blue Creek" (3-11-60)

        Jerome Cowan, Frank De Kova
22. "Sundance and the Marshal of Water's End" (3-18-60) Karl
     Swenson
23. "Sundance and the Black Widow" (4-1-60) Patricia Medina,
     Dennis Cross
24. "Vengeance for Sundance" (4-8-60) J. Pat O'Malley, Lane
     Bradford
25. "Sundance and the Man in the Shadows" (4-15-60) Philip
     Abbott, Oliver McGowan
26. "Sundance and the Long Trek" (4-22-60) Denver Pyle, Paul
     Burke, Harry Carey Jr.
27. "Bounty for Sundance" (4-29-60) King Donovan, Richard
     Shannon
28. "Sundance and the Good-Luck Coat" (5-6-60) Russ Bender,
     Robert Gist
29. [unknown title] (5-13-60) Brad Trumbull, David White
30. "Sundance and the Barren Soil" (5-20-60) Joanne Linville,
     James Lydon
31. "Sundance and the Fallen Sparrow" (5-27-60) Patricia Bres-
     lin, Kevin Hagen
32. "Sundance and the Delayed Gun" (6-3-60) Henry Silva, Al-
     bert Salmi


MAN FROM BLACKHAWK

       Unconventional Herb Meadows tale of a nineteenth-century
insurance investigator (Robert Rockwell as Sam Logan) going after
the western swindlers.

The Regulars: Sam Logan, Robert Rockwell.

The Episodes:

1. "Logan's Policy" (10-9-59) Beverly Garland, Richard Rust
2. "The Trouble with Tolliver" (10-16-59) Vaughn Taylor,
     Robert Bray
3. "The New Semaria Story" (10-23-59) Karl Swenson, Paul
     Carr
4. "The Man Who Stole Happiness" (10-30-59) Jean Willes
5. "The Gypsy Story" (11-6-59) Frank Silvera, Marianne
     Stewart
6. "Station Six" (11-13-59) Mary LaRoche, Mort Mills
7. "Vendetta for the Lovelorn" (11-20-59)
8. "The Winthrop Woman" (11-27-59) Louis Jean Heyde
9. "Contraband Cargo" (12-4-59) John Sutton, Mara Corday
10. "A Matter of Conscience" (12-11-59) Bethel Leslie, Robert
     Burton
11. "Death Is the Best Policy" (12-18-59) Walter Burke, Vir-
     ginia Christine
12. "The Legacy" (12-25-59) Ruta Lee, Joe di Reda
13. "The Biggest Legend" (1-1-60) Joe Mantell, Arthur Hunnicutt

14. "Death at Noon" (1-8-60) Charles McGraw, Jeanne Cooper
15. "The Savage" (1-15-60) Sean McClory
16. "The Hundred Thousand Dollar Policy" (1-22-60) Alan Hale, Barbara Lawrence
17. "Portrait of Cynthia" (1-29-60) Robert Lowery, Maria Winter
18. "El Patron" (2-5-60) Eduardo Noriega
19. "Drawing Account" (2-12-60) Judson Pratt, Kathie Browne
20. "The Ghost of Lafitte" (2-26-60) Tom Rettig
21. "Execution Day" (3-4-60)
22. "Destination Death" (3-11-60) Robert H. Harris, Billy Curtis
23. "Diamond Cut Diamond" (3-18-60) Robert F. Simon
24. "Death by Northwest" (3-25-60) Forrest Lewis, Hollis Irving
25. "The Last Days of Jessie Turnbull" (4-1-60) Virginia Gregg
26. "The Search for Cape Borden" (4-15-60) Sandra Knight, George Neise
27. "The Sons of Don Antonio" (4-22-60) Jacques Aubuchon, Gustavo Rojo
28. "Incident at Tupelo" (4-29-60) Betsy Jones-Moreland, George Milan
29. "The Harpoon Story" (5-6-60) Gil Rankin, Rebecca Welles
30. "The Montreal Story" (5-13-60) Marie Aldon, Robert Eyer
31. "In His Steps" (5-20-60) Nita Talbot, Richard Shannon
32. "Trial by Combat" (5-27-60) Robert Brubaker, Russell Thorson
33. "The Man Who Wanted Everything" (6-3-60) Patricia Donahue, Denver Pyle
34. [unknown title] (6-10-60)
35. "The Lady in Yellow" (6-17-60) Neil Hamilton, Regis Toomey, Bethel Leslie
36. "Gold Is Where You Find It" (6-24-60) Logan Field, Lyn Thomas
37. "Remember Me Not" (9-9-60) Peter Adams, Joanna Barnes

## THE DETECTIVES

Robert Taylor entered series television dutifully cast as police Captain Matt Holbrook, who supervises the workings of middle-aged family man Lieutenant Johnny Russo (Tige Andrews), veteran Lieutenants Otto Lindstrom (Russell Thorson) and Jim Conway (Lee Tharr) and young bachelors Sergeants Chris Ballard (Mark Goddard) and Steve Nelson (Adam West).

What must have been an effort toward realism failed; teleplays pretentiously examined such contemporary themes as the beatnik cult (in Michael Morris' "Tobey's Place") and juvenile delinquency (in Herman Groves' "Beyond a Reasonable Doubt"). Yet this failure at realism may have been to the series' advantage. Arthur Hiller's direction of Calvin Clements' "Night Boat," in which Scott Marlowe is cast as a psychotic strangler, is artfully illusory.

The Regulars: Captain Matt Holbrook, Robert Taylor; Lieutenant Johnny Russo, Tige Andrews; Lieutenant Jim Conway, Lee Tharr (first season); Lieutenant Otto Lindstrom, Russell Thorson (last two seasons); Sergeant Chris Ballard, Mark Goddard (last two seasons); Sergeant Steve Nelson, Adam West (last two seasons); Lisa, Ursula Thiess.

The Episodes:

1. "The Streger Affair" (10-16-59) Jean Hagen, Johnny Seven
2. "Shot in the Dark" (10-23-59) Lin McCarthy, Robert Carricart
3. "The Hiding Place" (10-30-59) Jay North
4. "Decoy" (11-6-59)
5. "Murderous Deadline" (11-13-59) Lawrence Dobkin, Hollis Irving
6. "The Bait" (11-20-59)
7. "My Name Is Tommy" (11-27-59) Eugene Martin, Jan Arvan
8. "Back-Seat Driver" (12-4-59) Richard Evans, Richard Devon
9. "Two-Time Loser" (12-11-59) Bruce Gordon
10. "The Long Drive" (12-18-59) Virginia Vincent
11. "Masquerade" (12-25-59) Mary Murphy
12. "Life in the Balance" (1-1-60) Arthur Batanides, Arline Sax
13. "Karate" (1-8-60) John Anderson
14. "Blue Fire" (1-15-60)
15. "My Brother's Keeper" (1-22-60) Olan Soule, Della Sharman
16. "House Call" (1-29-60) Fay Spain, Pernell Roberts
17. "The Trap" (2-5-60) Cathy O'Donnell
18. "Conspiracy of Silence" (2-12-60) Simon Oakland, Bert Freed
19. "Twelve Hours to Live" (2-19-60)
20. "Anatomy of Fear" (2-26-60)
21. "Armed and Dangerous" (3-4-60)
22. "The Bad Eye of Rose Rosetti" (3-11-60) Frank Puglia, Augusta Merighi
23. "Time and Tide" (3-18-60) Robert Middleton, Linda Watkins
24. "Little Girl Lost" (3-25-60) George Mitchell, Eileen Chesis
25. "The Chameleon Truck" (4-1-60) James Bell, Burt Metcalfe
26. "The Old Gang" (4-8-60) John Apone, Sheridan Comerate
27. "The Bodyguards" (4-15-60) Charles McGraw, J. Pat O'Maley
28. "The Prowler" (4-22-60) Marsha Hunt, John Anderson
29. "Face Down, Floating" (4-29-60) Spring Byington, Harry Ellerbe
30. "The Long Jump" (5-6-60) Adam Williams, Enid Janes
31. "Trial by Fire" (5-13-60) Darryl Hickman, Jack Weston
32. "The Retirement of Maria Muir" (5-20-60) Eva Gabor, John Van Dreelen
33. "Song of Songs" (5-27-60)

Second Season

34. "The New Man" (9-16-60) Roxanne Arlen
35. "Longshot" (9-23-60) Jack Grimes
36. "The Sports Job" (9-30-60)
37. "Alibis" (10-7-60) Joe Mantell, Eddie Firestone, Donna
    Douglas
38. "Shuttle" (10-14-60) Johnny Seven, John Newton
39. "Cop on Trial" (11-4-60) Herman Rudin, Gilbert Green
40. "The Little Witness" (11-11-60) Billy Hughes, Alice Backes
41. "You Only Die Once" (11-18-60) Al Ruscio, Jean Allison
42. "Adopted" (11-25-60) Eddie Ryder, Patricia Breslin
43. "The Other Side" (12-2-60) Marc Lawrence, John Zaccaro
44. "The Scalpel" (12-9-60) Mort Mills
45. "Big Poison" (12-16-60) Edward Binns, Eddie Ryder
46. "The Informer" (12-23-60) Joe Mantell, George Conrad
47. "Razor's Edge" (12-30-60) Richard Evans
48. "The Frightened Ones" (1-6-61) James Coburn, Chris Robin-
    son, Michael Parks
49. "Power Failure" (1-13-61) Joe Turkel
50. "Kinfolk" (1-20-61) Dabbs Greer, Lonny Chapman, L. Q.
    Jones
51. "Quiet Night" (1-27-61) Yvonne Craig, Rudy Solari
52. "See No Evil" (2-3-61) Jacqueline Scott, Grant Richards
53. "Personal Enemy" (2-10-61) Michael Parks, Floy Dean
    Scott
54. "Matt's Woman" (2-17-61) Joan Taylor
55. "An Eye for an Eye" (2-24-61) Eduardo Ciannelli, Arline
    Sax
56. "Bad Apple" (3-3-61) Robert Culp, Rudy Donlan
57. "Not So Long Ago" (3-10-61) Virginia Vincent, Baruch Lu-
    met
58. "The Reason" (3-17-61)
59. "Secret Assignment" (3-24-61) Anthony Caruso, Jack Kru-
    schen
60. "Time for Decision" (3-31-61) Sue Randall, Rita Lynn
61. "Terror on Ice" (4-7-61) Douglas Lambert, Adam Williams
62. "Little Boy Clue" (4-14-61) Dennis Joel, Robert Karnes
63. "The Short Way Home" (4-21-61) Don Quine, Enid Janes,
    Johnny Seven
64. "Other Cheek" (4-28-61) Lee Kinsolving, Joan Marshall
65. "The Airtight Case" (5-5-61) Philip Abbott, Edward Knight
66. "Duty Date" (5-12-61) Barbara Nichols, Steve Graves
67. "The Champ" (5-19-61) Michael Dante

Third Season [as hour series]

68. "Tobey's Place" (9-29-61) Peter Whitney, Anita Sands,
    William Windom, Marty Ingalls
69. "The Legend of Jim Riva" (10-6-61) Edward G. Robinson
70. "Shadow of His Brother" (10-13-61) Martin Landau, William
    Sargent
71. "A Barrel Full of Monkeys" (10-27-61) Arthur Malet, Nancy

Gates, Sue Ane Langdon, Dabbs Greer
72. "One Lucky Break" (11-3-61) Whit Bissell, Jonathan Hole
73. "A Piece of Tomorrow" (11-10-61) Michael Constantine, Victor Buono, Charles Aidman
74. "Beyond a Reasonable Doubt" (11-17-61) David Winters, Michael Parks, Denver Pyle
75. "Hit and Miss" (12-1-61) Joe Mantell, Grace Lee Whitney
76. "Song of the Guilty Heart" (12-8-61) Inger Stevens, Leo Penn
77. "Escort" (12-15-61) Telly Savalas, Patricia Crowley, Ed Nelson
78. "The Queen of Craven Point" (12-22-61) Lola Albright, Russell Johnson, Michael Forest
79. "Act of God" (12-29-61) Bruce Dern, James Whitmore
80. "Point of No Return" (1-12-62) Robert Gist, Jerry Paris
81. "Crossed Wires" (1-19-62) Diane Foster, Ed Nelson, Frank Sutton
82. "Night on the Town" (1-26-62) Mari Blanchard, Arthur Malet, John Abbott
83. "Pandora's Box" (2-2-62) Rita Lynn, Kathleen Freeman, Ford Rainey
84. "The Jagged Edge" (2-9-62) Chris Robinson, Jean Allison, Harvey Korman
85. "The Outsider" (2-16-62) Dabbs Greer, Patricia Huston
86. "Walk a Crooked Line" (2-23-62) James Drury, Leonard Stone
87. "Night Boat" (3-2-62) Scott Marlowe, Joyce Van Patten, Jean Engstrom
88. "One Lousy Wednesday" (3-9-62) Sean McClory, Rita Lynn
89. "The Con Man" (3-16-62) Hershel Bernardi, Lillian Bronson, Natalie Norwick
90. "Never the Twain" (3-23-62) Bob Okazaki, Enid Jaynes, Ed Nelson
91. "Three Blind Mice" [Part I] (3-30-62) Vera Miles, Harold J. Stone, Philip Bourneuf, Marc Lawrence
92. "Three Blind Mice" [Part II] (4-6-62) as above
93. "Finders Keepers" (4-13-62) Richard Devon, Diane Mountford
94. "The Fourth Commandment" (4-20-62) James Douglas, Ben Wright
95. "The Walls Have Eyes" (4-27-62) John Larkin, Ellen McCrae, Johnny Seven
96. "Strangers in the House" (5-4-62) Chris Robinson, John Karlen, David Sheiner
97. "Saturday Edition" (5-18-62) John Larkin, Joseph Ruskin

THE TWILIGHT ZONE

Rod Serling's classic anthology so beautifully blended the sense of foreboding with character and with the elements that, if there is not a "twilight zone," there is a good case there ought to be. Two remarkable performances: that delivered by Ed Wynn, as the man who encounters "Mr. Death" in "One for the Angels"; Agnes Moorehead's virtuoso, as the woman who has discovered "tiny aliens" (but are they?) in her solitary home in Richard Matheson's superlative "The Invaders." Composers, in addition to Serling, included Ray Bradbury ("I Sing of the Body Electric") and Lucille Fletcher ("The Hitchhiker").

The Regulars: Rod Serling, host.

The Episodes:

1. "Where Is Everybody?" (10-2-59) Earl Holliman, James Gregory
2. "One for the Angels" (10-9-59) Ed Wynn, Murray Hamilton
3. "Mr. Denton on Doomsday" (10-16-59) Dan Duryea, Martin Landau
4. "The 16mm. Shrine" (10-23-59) Martin Balsam, Ida Lupino
5. "Walking Distance" (10-30-59) Gig Young
6. "Escape Clause" (11-6-59) Thomas Gomez, David Wayne, Virginia Christine, Wendell Holmes
7. "The Lonely" (11-13-59) Jack Warden
8. "Time Enough at Last" (11-20-59) Burgess Meredith, Jacqueline DeWitt
9. "Perchance to Dream" (11-27-59) Richard Conte, Suzanne Lloyd
10. "Judgment Night" (12-4-59) Nehemiah Persoff
11. "And When the Sky Was Opened" (12-11-59) Rod Taylor, Charles Aidman
12. "What You Need" (12-25-59) Ernest Truex, Steve Cochran
13. "The Four of Us Are Dying" (1-1-60) Harry Townes, Ross Martin
14. "Third from the Sun" (1-8-60) Fritz Weaver, Joe Maross, Edward Andrews
15. "I Shot an Arrow into the Air" (1-15-60) Dewey Martin, Edward Binns, Ted Otis
16. "The Hitchhiker" (1-22-60) Inger Stevens, Leonard Strong, Adam Williams
17. "The Fever" (1-29-60) Everett Sloane, Vivi Janiss
18. "The Last Flight" (2-5-60) Kenneth Haigh, Alexander Scourby
19. "The Purple Testament" (2-12-60) Dick York, William Reynolds
20. "Elegy" (2-19-60) Cecil Kellaway, Jeff Morrow
21. "Mirror Image" (2-26-60) Vera Miles, Martin Milner
22. "The Monsters Are Due on Maple Street" (3-4-60) Claude Akins, Jack Weston
23. "A World of Difference" (3-11-60) Howard Duff, Eileen Ryan
24. "Long Live Walter Jameson" (3-18-60) Estelle Winwood, Kevin McCarthy
25. "People Are Alike All Over" (3-25-60) Roddy McDowall, Susan Oliver
26. "Execution" (4-1-60) Albert Salmi, Russell Johnson

27. "Big, Tall Wish" (4-8-60) Ivan Dixon, Steven Perry
28. "A Nice Place to Visit" (4-15-60) Larry Blyden, Sebastian Cabot
29. "Nightmare as a Child" (4-29-60) Janice Rule, Shepperd Strudwick
30. "A Stop at Willoughby" (5-6-60) James Daly, James Maloney, Patricia Donahue
31. "The Chaser" (5-13-60) George Grizzard, John McIntire, Patricia Barry
32. "A Passage for Trumpet" (5-20-60) Jack Klugman, Mary Willister
33. "Mr. Bevis" (6-3-60) Orson Bean, Henry Jones
34. "The After Hours" (6-10-60) Anne Francis
35. "The Mighty Casey" (6-17-60) Robert Sorrella, Jack Warden

Second Season

36. "King Nine Will Not Return" (9-30-60) Robert Cummings
37. "Man in a Bottle" (10-7-60) Luther Adler
38. "Nervous Man in a Four Dollar Room" (10-14-60) Joe Mantell
39. "A Thing About Machines" (10-28-60) Richard Haydn, Barney Phillips
40. "The Howling Man" (11-4-60) John Carradine
41. "The Eye of the Beholder" (11-11-60) William Gordon, Jennifer Howard
42. "Nick of Time" (11-18-60) William Shatner, Patricia Breslin
43. "The Lateness of the Hour" (12-2-60) Inger Stevens, John Hoyt
44. "The Trouble with Templeton" (12-9-60) Brian Aherne
45. "A Most Unusual Camera" (12-16-60) Fred Clark, Jean Carson
46. "Night of the Meek" (12-23-60) Art Carney
47. "Dust" (1-6-61) Thomas Gomez, Vladimir Sokoloff, John Larch
48. "Back There" (1-13-61) Paul Hartman, Russell Johnson
49. "The Whole Truth" (1-20-61) Jack Carson, Jack Ging, Loring Smith
50. "The Invaders" (1-27-61) Agnes Moorehead
51. "A Penny for Your Thoughts" (2-3-61) Dick York
52. "Twenty-Two" (2-10-61) Barbara Nichols
53. "The Odyssey of Flight 33" (2-24-61) John Anderson, Paul Comi
54. "Mr. Dingle, the Strong" (3-3-61) Burgess Meredith
55. "Static" (3-10-61) Dean Jagger, Carmen Matthews, Robert Emhardt
56. "The Prime Mover" (3-24-61) Dane Clark, Buddy Ebsen, Christine White
57. "A Long Distance Call" (3-31-61) Billy Mumy, Lili Darvas, Patricia Smith
58. "A Hundred Yards Over the Rim" (4-7-61) Cliff Robertson
59. "The Rip Van Winkle Caper" (4-21-61) Oscar Beregi, Simon Oakland

30. "The Silence" (4-28-61) Franchot Tone
31. "Shadow Play" (5-5-61) Dennis Weaver, Bernie Hamilton
32. "The Mind and the Matter" (5-12-61) Shelley Berman
33. "Will the Real Martian Please Stand Up?" (5-26-61) John
    Hoyt, Jack Elam, Morgan Jones, John Archer, Jean
    Willes
34. "The Obsolete Man" (6-2-61) Burgess Meredith, Fritz
    Weaver

Third Season

55. "The Arrival" (9-22-61) Harold J. Stone, Fred Wayne,
    Noah Keen
56. "The Shelter" (9-29-61) Michael Burns, Larry Gates, Peggy
    Stewart
57. "The Passerby" (10-6-61) James Gregory
58. "A Game of Pool" (10-13-61) Jack Klugman, Jonathan Win-
    ters
59. "The Mirror" (10-20-61) Peter Falk
70. "The Grave" (10-27-61) Lee Marvin
71. "It's a Good Life" (11-3-61) Cloris Leachman, Billy Mumy
72. "Death's-Head Revisited" (11-10-61) Joseph Schildkraut,
    Karen Verne
73. "The Midnight Sun" (11-17-61) Lois Nettleton, Betty Garde
74. "Still Valley" (11-24-61) Gary Merrill, Vaughn Taylor, Ben
    Cooper
75. "The Jungle" (12-1-61) John Dehner
76. "Once Upon a Time" (12-15-61) Buster Keaton, Stanley
    Adams
77. "Five Characters in Search of an Exit" (12-22-61) William
    Windom, Susan Harrison, Murray Matheson
78. "A Quality of Mercy" (12-29-61) Dean Stockwell, Albert
    Salmi
79. "Nothing in the Dark" (1-5-62) Gladys Cooper, Robert Red-
    ford
80. "One More Pallbearer" (1-12-62) Joseph Wiseman
81. "Dead Man's Shoes" (1-19-62) Warren Stevens, Joe Mar-
    shall
82. "The Hunt" (1-26-62) Jeanette Nolan, Arthur Hunnicutt
83. "Showdown with Rance McGrew" (2-2-62) Larry Blyden,
    Arch Johnson
84. "Kick the Can" (2-9-62) Ernest Truex, John Marley, Rus-
    sell Collins, Hank Peterson
85. "A Piano in the House" (2-16-62) Joan Hackett, Barry
    Morse
86. "The Last Rites of Jeff Myrtlebank" (2-23-62) Sherry Jack-
    son, James Best
87. "To Serve Man" (3-2-62) Lloyd Bochner, Susan Cummings
88. "The Fugitive" (3-9-62) J. Pat O'Malley, Susan Gordon
89. "Little Girl Lost" (3-16-62) Sarah Marshall
90. "Person or Persons Unknown" (3-23-62) Richard Long,
    Frank Silvera
91. "The Little People" (3-30-62) Claude Akins, Joe Maross,

Michael Ford
92. "Four O'Clock" (4-6-62) Theodore Bikel
93. "Hocus-Pocus and Frisby" (4-13-62) Andy Devine
94. "The Trade-Ins" (4-20-62) Joseph Schildkraut
95. "The Gift" (4-27-62) Geoffrey Horne
96. "The Dummy" (5-4-62) Cliff Robertson
97. "A Young Man's Fancy" (5-11-62) Alex Nicol, Phyllis Thaxter
98. "I Sing of the Body Electric" (5-18-62) Josephine Hutchinson
99. "Cavender Is Coming" (5-25-62) Carol Burnett, Jesse White, Howard Smith, John Fiedler
100. "The Changing of the Guard" (6-1-62) Donald Pleasence
101. "The Private World of Darkness" (6-15-62) William D. Gordon

Fourth Season [as hour series]

102. "In His Image" (1-3-63) George Grizzard, Gail Kobe, Katherine Squire
103. "The Thirty Fathom Grave" (1-10-63) Diana Millay, Pat Conway
104. "Valley of the Shadow" (1-17-63) David Opatoshu, Natalie Trundy, Ed Nelson
105. "He's Alive" (1-24-63) Dennis Hopper
106. "The Mute" (1-31-63) Barbara Baxley, Frank Overton
107. "Death Ship" (2-7-63) Jack Klugman, Ross Martin
108. "Jess-Belle" (2-14-63) Anne Francis, James Best, Jeanette Nolan
109. "Miniature" (2-21-63) Robert Duvall, William Windom, Barbara Barrie
110. "Printer's Devil" (2-28-63) Patricia Crowley, Robert Sterling, Burgess Meredith
111. "No Time Like the Past" (3-7-63) Dana Andrews, Patricia Breslin
112. "The Parallel" (3-14-63) Steve Forrest, Jacqueline Scott
113. "I Dream of Genie" (3-21-63) Howard Morris, Patricia Barry
114. "The New Exhibit" (4-4-63) Martin Balsam, Maggie Mahoney, Will Kuluva
115. "Of Late, I Think of Cliffordville" (4-11-63) Albert Salmi, Julie Newmar, John Anderson
116. "The Incredible World of Horace Ford" (4-18-63) Pat Hingle, Nan Martin
117. "On Thursday We Leave for Home" (5-2-63) James Whitmore, James Broderick, Tim O'Connor
118. "Passage on the Lady Anne" (5-9-63) Gladys Cooper, Wilfrid Hyde-White, Cecil Kellaway, Lee Philips, Joyce Van Patten
119. "The Bard" (5-23-63) Jack Weston, John Williams

Fifth Season [again as half hour]

120. "In Praise of Pip" (9-27-63) Jack Klugman, Robert Diamond, Connie Gilchrist
121. "Steele" (10-4-63) Lee Marvin, Joe Mantell
122. "Nightmare at 20,000 Feet" (10-11-63) William Shatner, Christine White, Asa Maynor, Nick Cravat
123. "A Kind of Stop Watch" (10-18-63) Richard Erdman, Doris Singleton, Roy Roberts
124. "The Last Night of a Jockey" (10-25-63) Mickey Rooney
125. "The Living Doll" (11-1-63) Telly Savalas, Mary LaRoche
126. "The Old Man in the Cave" (11-8-63) James Coburn, John Anderson, John Marley
127. "Uncle Simon" (11-15-63) Sir Cedric Hardwicke, Ian Wolfe, Constance Ford
128. "Probe 7, Over and Out" (11-29-63) Richard Basehart, Antoinette Bower, Harold Gould
129. "The 7th Is Made Up of Phantoms" (12-6-63) Randy Boone, Ron Foster, Warren Oates
130. "A Short Drink from a Certain Fountain" (12-13-63) Patrick O'Neal, Ruta Lee, Walter Brooke
131. "Ninety Years Without Slumbering" (12-20-63) Ed Wynn, James Callahan, William Sargent
132. "Ring-a-Ding Girl" (12-27-63) Maggie McNamara, David Macklin
133. "You Drive" (1-3-64) Edward Andrews, Kevin Hagen
134. "The Long Morrow" (1-10-64) Robert Lansing, Mariette Hartley, George Macready, Edward Binns
135. "The Self-Improvement of Salvadore Ross" (1-17-64) Vaughn Taylor, Don Gordon, Gail Kobe, Douglass Dumbrille
136. "Number Twelve Looks Just Like You" (1-24-64) Richard Long, Suzy Parker, Collin Wilcox
137. "Black Leather Jackets" (1-31-64) Lee Kinsolving, Michael Forest, Shelley Fabares
138. "Night Call" (2-7-64) Gladys Cooper, Nora Marlowe, Martine Bartlett
139. "From Agnes--With Love" (2-14-64) Wally Cox, Sue Randell, Ralph Taeger
140. "Spur of the Moment" (2-21-64) Diana Hyland, Roger Davis, Marsha Hunt, Philip Ober
141. "An Occurrence at Owl Creek Bridge" (2-28-64) Roger Jacquet, Anne Cornaly
142. "Queen of the Nile" (3-6-64) Ann Blyth, Lee Philips
143. "What's in the Box?" (3-13-64) Joan Blondell, Sterling Holloway, William Demarest, Sandra Gould
144. "The Masks" (3-20-64) Robert Keith, Milton Selzer, Alan Sues, Virginia Gregg
145. "I Am the Night--Color Me Black" (3-27-64) Michael Constantine, Paul Fix, Terry Becker, Ivan Dixon
146. "Sounds and Silences" (4-3-64) John McGiver, Penny Singleton
147. "Caesar and Me" (4-10-64) Jackie Cooper, Susanne Cupito
148. "The Jeopardy Room" (4-17-64) Martin Landau, John Van

Dreelen
149. "Stopover in a Quiet Town" (4-24-64) Barry Nelson, Nancy Malone
150. "The Encounter" (5-1-64) Neville Brand, George Takei
151. "Garrity and the Graves" (5-8-64) John Dehner, J. Pat O'Malley
152. "The Brain Center at Whipple's" (5-15-64) Richard Devon, Paul Newlan
153. "Come Wander with Me" (5-22-64) Gary Crosby, John Bolt
154. "The Fear" (5-29-64) Mark Richman, Hazel Court
155. "The Bewitchin' Pool" (6-19-64) Mary Badham, Tim Stafford

THE MAN FROM INTERPOL

Typical Scotland Yard mystery tale featuring Richard Wyler as agent Anthony Smith.

The Regulars: Anthony Smith, Richard Wyler; Inspector Mercer, John Longden.

The Episodes:

1. "Nest of Vipers" (1-30-60)
2. "The Feathered Friend" (2-6-60)
3. "Soul Peddlers" (2-13-60)
4. "Odds on Murder" (2-20-60)
5. "The Key Witness" (2-27-60)
6. "Escape Route" (3-5-60)
7. [unknown title] (3-12-60)
8. "Love by Extortion" (3-19-60)
9. "The Dollmaker" (3-26-60)
10. "No Other Way" (4-2-60)
11. "The Trap" (4-9-60) Peter Reynolds, Inia Te Wiata
12. "The Man Who Sold Hope" (4-16-60) Walter Gotell, Jacques Cey
13. "The Murder Racket" (4-23-60) Douglas Jones
14. "Death Via Parcel Post" (4-30-60) Arnold Bell
15. "Out of Thin Air" (5-7-60) Brian Worth
16. "The Case of Mike Krello" (5-14-60) Bill O'Connor
17. "Killer with a Long Arm" (5-21-60) Robert Sansom
18. "Murder in the Smart Set" (5-28-60) Hariette Johns, Shirley Cain
19. "The Front Man" (6-4-60) Peter Dyneley
20. "Murder Below Decks" (6-11-60) Mahmood Mall, Michael Peake
21. "International Diamond Incident" (6-18-60) Paul Carpenter, Jill Melford
22. "The Last Words" (6-25-60) Peter Murray
23. "The Maharajah of Den" (7-2-60) Francis Mathews, George Pastell

24.   "Diplomatic Courier"   (7-9-60)   John McLean
25.   "Inside Job"   (7-16-60)   Graham Ashley
26.   "A Woman in Paris"   (7-23-60)   Martine Alexis, Francis
        Mathews
27.   "Mistaken Identity"   (7-30-60)
28.   "Man Alone"   (8-6-60)   Michael Balfour
29.   "Missing Child"   (8-13-60)
30.   "The Big Thirst"   (8-20-60)
31.   "My Brother's Keeper"   (8-27-60)   John Martin
32.   "Death in Oils"   (9-3-60)   Ralph Michael, Robert Ayres
33.   "Multi Murder"   (9-20-60)
34.   "Latest Fashions in Crime"   (9-17-60)   Ferdy Mayne, Mark
        Singleton
35.   "The Art of Murder"   (9-24-60)   William Marshall, Lionel
        Ngakane
36.   "The Child of Eve"   (10-1-60)   Lisa Daniely, Peter Sinclair
37.   "Tight Secret"   (10-8-60)   Richard Thorpe, Eira Heath
38.   "The Big Racket"   (10-15-60)
39.   "The Golden Shirri"   (10-22-60)


THE OVERLAND TRAIL

        Trite stagecoach drama, the line under the aegis of Fred-
erick Thomas Kelly (William Bendix).

The Regulars:  Frederick Thomas Kelly, William Bendix; Frank
        ("Flip") Flippen, Doug McClure.

The Episodes:

1.   "Perilous Passage"   (2-7-60)   Lynn Bari
2.   "The O'Mara's Ladies"   (2-14-60)   Sean McClory, Maggie
        Pierce
3.   "West of Boston"   (2-21-60)   Caroline Craig, Guy Mitchell
4.   "High Bridge"   (2-28-60)   Whitney Blake
5.   "Westbound Stage"   (3-6-60)   Suzanne Lloyd
6.   "All the O'Mara's Horses"   (3-13-60)   Sean McClory, Karen
        Sharpe
7.   "Daughter of the Sioux"   (3-20-60)   Harry Guardino
8.   "Lawyer in Petticoats"   (3-27-60)   Diane Foster, Barton
        MacLane, George Tobias
9.   "Vigilantes of Montana"   (4-3-60)   Werner Klemperer, Myrna
        Fahey
10.   "Fire in the Hole"   (4-17-60)   Claude Akins, Susan Cummings
11.   "Mission to Mexico"   (4-24-60)   Robert Loggia, Barbara Lord
12.   "First Stage to Denver"   (5-1-60)   Sue George, Peter Whitney
13.   "Sour Annie"   (5-8-60)   Mercedes McCambridge, Richard
        Devon
14.   "The Baron Comes Back"   (5-15-60)   Lucy Marlowe, Gerald
        Mohr, Denver Pyle
15.   "Escort Detail"   (5-22-60)   David Wayne

16. "The Reckoning" (5-29-60) Monica Lewis, John Carradine
17. "The Most Dangerous Gentleman" (6-5-60) Ron Randell,
    John McIntire, Jeff Donnell, Onslow Stevens


DOW HOUR OF GREAT MYSTERIES

The Regulars: Joseph Welch, host.

The Episodes:

1. "The Bat" [Walter Kerr adapted from the 1920 play by Mary
   Roberts Rinehart and Avery Hopwood] (3-31-60) Helen
   Hayes, Jason Robards Jr., Margaret Hamilton, Martin
   Brooks, Bethel Leslie, Shepperd Strudwick, Karl Light,
   Mark Satow
2. "The Burning Court" [adapted by Kelly Ross from the novel
   by John Dickson Carr] (4-24-60) Barbara Bel Geddes,
   George C. Scott, Robert Lansing
3. "The Woman in White" [adapted by Frank Ford from Wilkie
   Collins' 1860 novel] (5-23-60) Siobhan McKenna, Robert
   Flemyng, Arthur Hill, Lois Nettleton, Rita Vale, Catherine
   Proctor
4. "The Dachet Diamonds" [adapted by Walter Kerr from Richard
   Marsh's book] (9-20-60) Rex Harrison, Tammy Grimes,
   Robert Flemyng, David Hurst, Alice Ghostley, Reginald
   Denny, Melville Cooper, Laurie Main
5. "The Cat and the Canary" [Audrey and William Roos adapted
   from the John Willard novel] (9-27-60) Collin Wilcox,
   Sarah Marshall, Andrew Duggan, Hortense Alden, Jack
   Betts, Louis Edmonds, George Macready, Telly Savalas
6. "The Inn of the Flying Dragon" [adapted by Sheldon Reynolds]
   (10-18-60) Farley Granger, Hugh Griffith, Barry Morse,
   Macha Meril
7. "The Great Impersonation" [adapted by William and Audrey
   Roos from the novel by E. Phillips Oppenheim] (11-15-60)
   Eva Gabor, Keith Michell, Jeanette Sterke, Theodore Marcuse; Alistair Cooke narrates


MYSTERY SHOW

The Regulars: Walter Slezak, host; Vincent Price hosted the last
    two episodes.

The Episodes:

1. "The Machine Calls It Murder" (5-29-60) Larry Blyden,
   Everett Sloane, Betsy Von Furstenberg
2. "Thunder of Silence" [by Adrian Spies] (6-5-60) James Whitmore, John Hoyt, Sandy Kenyon, Jean Carson

3. "Summer Hero" [by Charlotte Armstrong] (6-12-60) Zachary Scott, Patty McCormack, Ruth Ford, Bobby Driscoll
4. "Dark Possession" [by Gore Vidal; a revision of his own 1954 "Studio One" drama] (6-19-60) Diana Lynn, Anne Seymour, Marion Ross, W. H. Bassett, Berry Kroeger
5. "Fear Is the Parent" (6-26-60) Mona Freeman, Arthur Franz, Chet Stratton
6. "Murder Me Nicely" [by Mann Rubin] (7-3-60) Everett Sloane, Mark Goddard, Sylvia Field, Doreen Lang, Yvonne Craig
7. "Dead Man's Walk" [by Stephen Kandel] (7-10-60) Abby Dalton, Robert Culp, Bruce Gordon, Arthur Batanides, Ellen Corby
8. "The Last Six Blocks" [by Adrian Spies] (7-17-60) Dane Clark, Margarita Cordova, Jerome Cowan
9. "I Know What I'd Have Done" [by Charles Larson] (7-24-60) George Brent, Maggie Hayes, Nancy Rennick
10. "Enough Rope" [by William Link and Richard Levinson] (7-31-60) Richard Carlson, Bert Freed
11. "Trial by Fury" [by Stephen Kandel] (8-7-60) Agnes Moorehead, Warren Stevens
12. "Run-Around" [by Mort R. Lewis] (8-14-60) Vincent Price, Everett Sloane, Nelson Holmes, John Milford
13. "The Inspector Vanishes" [by Norman Lessing from a story by A. E. Hotchner] (8-21-60) Walter Slezak, Berry Kroeger, Erin O'Brien, Doris Dowling, Barbara Stuart
14. "Femme Fatale" [by John McGreevey] (8-28-60) Janet Blair, Tracey Roberts, Joe De Santis, Doris Lloyd
15. "Murder by the Book" [by Stephen Kandel] (9-4-60) Vanessa Brown, Jeff Morrow, Carol Ohmart, Nelson Olmsted, Hugh Sanders
16. "Blind Man's Bluff" [by Alan Armer and Walter Grauman] (9-11-60) John Ericson, Joan Evans, Jerome Cowan
17. "The Suicide Club" [adapted by producer Norman Lessing from the story by Robert Louis Stevenson] (9-18-60) Cesar Romero, Everett Sloane
18. "A Perfect Alibi" (9-25-60) Janet Blair

## TATE

Slight western about a moralizing one-armed gunfighter.

The Regulars: Tate, David McLean.

The Episodes:

1. "Home Town" (6-8-60) Royal Dano, James Coburn, Sandra Knight
2. "Stopover" (6-15-60) King Calder
3. "The Bounty Hunter" (6-22-60) Robert Culp, Louise Fletcher
4. "Voices of the Town" (7-6-60) Paul Richards

5. "A Lethal Pride" (7-20-60) Ronald Nicholas, Marianna Hill
6. "Tigero" (8-3-60) Martin Landau, Ted Markland
7. "Comanche Scalps" (8-10-60) Frank Overton, Robert Redford, Leonard Nimoy, Lane Bradford
8. "Before Sunup" (8-17-60) Robert Boon, Jean Allison, Warren Oates
9. "The Reckoning" (8-24-60) Phyllis Avery, Crahan Denton, Bing Russell
10. "The Gunfighters" (8-31-60) Jack Hogan, Elizabeth Perry
11. "Quiet After the Storm" (9-7-60) Cathy O'Donnell, Hampton Fancher
12. "The Return of Jessica Jackson" (9-14-60) Patricia Breslin, John Kellogg, Jock Gaynor
13. "The Mary Hardin Story" (9-21-60) Julie Adams

## MOMENT OF FEAR

Ernest Kinoy ("The Accomplice"; from the novel by Fritz Leiber, "Conjure Wife"), David Shaw ("Total Recall") and James Yaffe ("The Third Party") were among the first-class composers of this mystery anthology.

The Episodes:

1. "The Golden Deed" (7-1-60) Macdonald Carey, Robert Redford, Nina Foch
2. "Conjure Wife" (7-8-60) Larry Blyden
3. "Fire by Night" (7-22-60) Mark Richman, Fay Spain, Phyllis Hill
4. "Total Recall" (7-29-60) Inger Stevens, Leslie Nielsen, Neva Patterson
5. "The Third Party" (8-12-60) E. G. Marshall, James Gregory
6. "If I Should Die" (8-19-60) Donald Harron, Tim O'Connor, Olive Deering, Scott McKay
7. "The Accomplice" (8-26-60) Nehemiah Persoff, Geoffrey Horne, Will Kuluva, Robert Dowdell, Lilia Skala
8. "Cage of Air" (9-9-60) Laraine Day, Robert Lansing, Meg Mundy

## THE WRANGLER

Jason Evers starred as the peregrinating cowboy Pitcairn.

The Regulars: Pitcairn, Jason Evers.

The Episodes:

1. "Incident at the Bar M" (8-4-60) Susan Oliver, Bing Russell

2. "A Time for Hanging" (8-11-60) Robert Middleton
3. "Affair at the Trading Post" (8-18-60) Suzanne Lloyd, Warren Oates
4. "The Affair with Browning's Woman" (8-25-60) Julie Adams, Michael Burns
5. "Incident of the Wide Lop" (9-1-60) Harry Townes
6. "Encounter at Elephant Butte" (9-15-60) Robert Emhardt, Robert Carricart

1960-1961 SEASON

THE ROARING TWENTIES

A rowdy period piece of the jazz era (for which the early 1960s video held a certain fascination); newspaper reporters Scott Norris (Rex Reason) and Pat Garrison (Donald May) are those who carry us through the flamboyance.

The Regulars: Scott Norris, Rex Reason; Pat Garrison, Donald May; Pinky Pinkham, Dorothy Provine; Chris Higbee, Gary Vinson; MacDonald, Emile Meyer; Dixie, Carolyn Komant; the bartender, Wally Brown; Switolski, Mike Road.

The Episodes:

1. "Burnett's Woman" (10-15-60) Madlyn Rhue, Lawrence Dobkin
2. "Champagne Lady" (10-22-60) Robert Lowery, Leslie Parrish
3. "The Velvet Frame" (10-29-60) Gloria Talbott, John Banner
4. "Vendetta on Beecker Street" (11-5-60) Andra Martin, Peter Mamakos
5. "The Prairie Flower" (11-12-60) Patricia Crowley, Patrice Wymore
6. "Brother's Keeper" (11-19-60) Andrew Duggan
7. "Judge Seward's Secret" (11-26-60) Whit Bissell
8. "The White Carnation" (12-3-60) Frank DeKova, Ray Danton
9. "Bold Edition" (12-10-60) Joe Mantell
10. "Layoff Charlie" (12-17-60) Parley Baer, Theodore Marcuse
11. "The Maestro" (1-7-61) Marc Alcalde, Anthony Caruso
12. "Dance Marathon" (1-14-61) Peggy McKay
13. "Big Town Blues" (1-21-61) Peter Breck, Shirley Knight, Karen Steele
14. "Coney Red Hots" (1-28-61) Joe Gallison, Judi Meredith
15. "Two a Day" (2-4-61) Randy Stuart, John Van Dreelen
16. "Lucky Charm" (2-11-61) Cesare Danova
17. "Black Saturday" (2-18-61) Robert H. Harris
18. "Pie in the Sky" (2-25-61) Will Hutchins
19. "The Vamp" (3-4-61) Ray Danton
20. "War with the Night Hawkers" (3-11-61) Robert Lowery, Dawn Wells
21. "Twelfth Hour" (3-18-61) Gigi Perreau, Evan McCord
22. "The Salvation of Killer McFadden" (4-1-61) Biff Elliott,

John Hoyt, Robert Carricart, Jean Allison
23. "The Fifth Pin" (4-8-61) Claire Griswold, Michael Pate
24. "The Red Carpet" (4-15-61) Christine White, Robert Corn-thwaite
25. "Scandal Sheet" (4-22-61) Berry Kroeger, Ellen Corby, Guy Stockwell
26. "Mademoiselle from Armentieres" (4-29-61) Elliott Reid, Gladys Holland
27. "Among the Missing" (5-6-61) Jack Ging, Robert F. Simon
28. "Right Off the Boat" [Part I] (5-13-61) Roger Moore, Sher-wood Price, Joan Marshall, John Kellogg
29. "Right Off the Boat" [Part II] (5-20-61) as above
30. "Million-Dollar Suit" (5-27-61) Rudy Solari, Frank De Kova
31. "Royal Tour" (6-3-61) Alex Davion, Oscar Beregi

## Second Season

32. "No Exit" (10-7-61)
33. "Kitty Goes West" (10-14-61) Glynis Johns, Philip Carey
34. "Nobody's Millions" (10-21-61) William Reynolds, Frank Ferguson
35. "Standing Room Only" (10-28-61) Keenan Wynn
36. "Another Time, Another War" (11-4-61) Grace Lee Whitney, Eddie Bracken
37. "Everybody Loves Benny" (11-11-61) Peter Breck, Pamela Curran
38. "Duke on the Bum" (11-18-61) Ruta Lee, Robert Strauss
39. "Pinky Goes to College" (11-25-61) Joby Baker, Jesse White
40. "So's Your Old Man" (12-2-61) Claude Akins, Mabel Ander-son
41. "Asparagus Tipps" (12-9-61) Jeanne Cooper
42. "Blondes Prefer Gentlemen" (12-16-61) Keith Larsen, Robert Carricart
43. "You Can't Fight City Hall" (1-6-62) Robert Crawford Jr., Donald Woods
44. "Footlights" (1-13-62) Robert Colbert, Harold J. Stone
45. "The People People Marry" (1-20-62) Jack Carter, Jesse White, Roxanne Arlen, Eddie Ryder

## THE TALL MAN

Barry Sullivan as Sheriff Pat Garrett makes worthwhile this conventional western, with Clu Gulager as William H. Bonney ("Billy the Kid").

The Regulars: Pat Garrett, Barry Sullivan; William H. Bonney ("Billy the Kid"), Clu Gulager.

The Episodes:

1. "Garrett and the Kid" (9-10-60) Robert Middleton, Denver

Pyle
2. "Forty-Dollar Boots" (9-17-60) Ron Soble, Ken Lynch
3. "Bad Company" (9-24-60) Otto Waldis
4. "The Shawl" (10-1-60) Frank Killmond, Gregory Walcott
5. "The Lonely Star" (10-8-60) Jim Davis, Ken Lynch, Ford Rainey
6. "A Bounty for Billy" (10-15-60) Leonard Nimoy
7. "The Parson" (10-29-60) Harold J. Stone, Robert Shawley
8. "Night Train to Tularosa" (11-5-60) Claude Akins, Robert McQueeney
9. "Larceny and Young Ladies" (11-12-60) Cindy Robbins, Jud Nugent
10. "Counterfeit Law" (11-19-60) George Macready
11. "And the Beast" (11-26-60)
12. "Bitter Ashes" (12-3-60) Narda Onyx, R. G. Armstrong
13. "McBean Rides Again" (12-10-60) Judy Nugent, Olive Sturgess
14. "Tiger Eye" (12-17-60) Paul Brinegar
15. "Billy's Baby" (12-24-60) Marianna Hill, K. L. Smith
16. "One of One Thousand" (12-31-60) George Wallace, Harry Carey Jr.
17. "First Blood" (1-7-61) Jan Merlin, Robert Montgomery Jr.
18. "A Gun Is for Killing" (1-14-61) Gregg Palmer, Leonard Nimoy
19. "The Grudge Fight" (1-21-61) Richard Jaeckel
20. "The Best Policy" (1-28-61) James Coburn, Ron Harper
21. "The Reversed Blade" (2-4-61) John Archer, Jeanne Cooper
22. "Dark Moment" (2-11-61) Martin Landau
23. "The Reluctant Bridegroom" (2-18-61) Judy Nugent, Olive Sturgess, Andy Clyde
24. "Maria's Little Lamb" (2-25-61) Pat Michon
25. "Big Sam's Boy" (3-4-61) Russell Collins, Paul Carr, Lew Gallo
26. "The Last Resource" (3-11-61) Robert J. Wilke, Marianna Hill
27. "Rovin' Gambler" (3-18-61) Faith Domergue, Robert Lansing, X Brands
28. "Hard Justice" (3-25-61) Lyle Bettger, Steve Warren
29. "The Legend and the Gun" (4-1-61) Michael Pate, Jocelyn Brando, Tom Gilson
30. "A Kind of Courage" (4-8-61) James Griffith
31. "Millionaire McBean" (4-15-61) Judy Nugent, Olive Sturgess
32. "A Scheme of Hearts" (4-22-61) Kathleen Hughes, John Lasell
33. "The Cloudbuster" (4-29-61) Sue George, Frank de Kova
34. "Ransom of a Town" (5-6-61) Michael Forest, Michael Burns, Eduardo Ciannelli
35. "Ladies of the Town" (5-20-61) Monica Lewis, Wesley Lau
36. "Death or Taxes" (5-27-61) Alan Baxter, Joe De Santis
37. "The Great Western" (6-3-61) Connie Gilchrist, Frank Ferguson

Second Season

38. "The Liberty Belle" (9-16-61) Patricia Donahue, Chris Al-
     caide
39. "Where Is Sylvia?" (9-23-61) Patricia Barry
40. "The Female Artillery" (9-30-61) Nan Leslie, Joan Evans
41. "Shadow of the Past" (10-7-61) Charles Aidman, Barbara
     Perkins
42. "An Item for Sale" (10-14-61) Sandy Kenyon
43. "The Judas Palm" (10-21-61) Edgar Buchanan
44. "The Woman" (10-28-61) Don Harvey, Julie Sommars, Coleen
     Gray
45. "Trial by Hanging" (11-4-61) George Kennedy
46. "The Leopard's Spots" (11-11-61) Paul Birch
47. "Petticoat Crusade" (11-18-61) Mona Freeman
48. "Time of Foreshadowing" (11-25-61) Vic Morrow, Judi
     Meredith
49. "Fool's Play" (12-2-61) Paul Comi
50. "Legend of Billy" (12-9-61) Berry Kroeger
51. "A Tombstone for Billy" (12-16-61) Howard McNear
52. "Sidekick" (12-23-61) Rafael Lopez
53. "Apache Daughter" (12-30-61) Sherry Jackson, J. Pat O'Mal-
     ley
54. "Substitute Sheriff" (1-6-62) Andy Clyde
55. [unknown title] (1-13-62)
56. "St. Louis Woman" (1-20-62) Jan Clayton
57. "The Hunt" (1-27-62) Richard Ney
58. "The Impatient Brides" (2-3-62) Joan O'Brien, Hollis Irving
59. "Rio Doloroso" (2-10-62) Dennis Patrick
60. "An Hour to Die" (2-17-62) Pamela Duncan
61. "Property of the Crown" (2-24-62) Mark Miller
62. "Night of the Hawk" (3-3-62) John Anderson
63. "Three for All" (3-10-62) George Kennedy
64. "Quarantine" (3-17-62) Gary Clarke
65. "The Four Queens" (3-24-62) Monica Lewis
66. "The Long Way Home" (3-31-62) Doris Dowling
67. "A Time to Run" (4-7-62) Sandra Knight, John Fiedler
68. "Trial by Fury" (4-14-62) Robert Emhardt, Barbara Law-
     rence
69. "The Frame" (4-21-62) Lori March
70. "The Run Away Groom" (4-28-62) Roberta Shore, Gary Vin-
     son
71. "The Black Robe" (5-5-62)
72. "The Woman in Black" (5-12-62) Gregory Marton, Adele Mara
73. "G.P." (5-19-62) Ed Nelson
74. [unknown title] (5-26-62) George Macready, Floy Dean Smith

CHECKMATE

     Eric Ambler's generally exciting mystery tale of private in-
vestigators Don Corey (Anthony George) and Jed Sills (Doug McClure)

and their criminologist mentor Dr. Carl Hyatt (Sebastian Cabot).

The Regulars: Don Corey, Anthony George; Jed Sills, Doug Mc-
Clure; Dr. Carl Hyatt, Sebastian Cabot.

The Episodes:

1. "Death Runs Wild" (9-17-60) Frankie Darro, Anne Baxter
2. "Interrupted Honeymoon" (9-24-60) Inger Stevens, Robert
Vaughn
3. "The Cyanide Touch" (10-1-60) Henry Jones, Dean Stockwell, Yvonne Craig, Ken Lynch
4. "Lady on the Brink" (10-15-60) Jane Wyman, Ken Lynch
5. "Face in the Window" (10-22-60) Julie Adams, Joseph Cotten
6. "Runaway" (10-29-60) Anna Maria Alberghetti
7. "Target ... Tycoon" (11-5-60) Charles Bickford, Madlyn
Rhue, Robert J. Wilke
8. "Deadly Shadow" (11-12-60) Margaret O'Brien, Ken Lynch
9. "The Dark Divide" (11-19-60) Barbara Rush
10. "Moment of Truth" (11-26-60) Martin Landau, Richard
Conte, Victor Buono
11. "The Mask of Vengeance" (12-3-60) Janice Rule, Cloris
Leachman
12. "Murder Game" (12-17-60) John Williams, Joe Mantell,
Richard Anderson, Joyce Jameson
13. "The Princess in the Tower" (12-31-60) Terry Moore,
Philip Ober
14. "Terror from the East" (1-7-61) Charles Laughton, Lisa Lu
15. "The Human Touch" (1-14-61) Peter Lorre, June Vincent,
Ronald Long, Ken Lynch
16. "Hour of the Execution" (1-21-61) James Gregory, Norma
Crane, Virginia Gregg, Larry Kert
17. "Don't Believe a Word She Says" (1-28-61) Mona Freeman,
Russell Collins, Reta Shaw
18. "Laugh Till I Die" (2-4-61) Dick Shawn, Robert Emhardt,
Joanne Linville
19. "Between Two Guns" (2-11-61) Beverly Garland, Jack Ward-
en, Ed Nelson
20. "A Matter of Conscience" (2-18-61) Josephine Hutchinson,
Ron Nicholas, Gary Merrill
21. "Melody for Murder" (2-25-61) Everett Sloane, Jimmie Rodgers
22. "Phantom Lover" (3-4-61) Robert Lansing, Bethel Leslie
23. "The Gift" (3-11-61) Patrice Munsel, Dorothy Green, Frank
Albertson, Celia Lovsky
24. "One for the Book" (3-18-61) Jocelyn Brando, Audrey
Meadows, Donald Woods
25. "The Paper Killer" (3-25-61) Mickey Rooney, Dianne Foster
William Schallert, Donna Douglas, Dennis Patrick
26. "Jungle Castle" (4-1-61) Lee Marvin, Patricia Donahue,
Denver Pyle
27. "The Deadly Silence" (4-8-61) Diana Lynn, Parley Baer,
Donna Douglas
28. "Goodbye Griff" (4-15-61) Julie London, Lynn Bari, Harry
Guardino

29. "Dance of Death" (4-22-61) Cyd Charisse, Carlos Romero, John Emery
30. "Voyage into Fear" (5-6-61) Joan Fontaine, Scott Brady
31. "Tight as a Drum" (5-13-61) Dan Duryea, Peter Lazer
32. "Death by Design" (5-20-61) Eve Arden, Larry Gates
33. "The Thrill-Seeker" (5-27-61) Susan Oliver, Paul Hartman
34. "Hot Wind in a Cold Town" (6-10-61) Ricardo Montalban, Jerome Thor, Martin Landau, Norman Fell, Betty Garde
35. "A Slight Touch of Venom" (6-17-61) Keenan Wynn, Susan Cummings, John Fiedler
36. "State of Shock" (6-24-61) Nina Foch, Warren Stevens, Jeanne Bal

Second Season

37. "Portrait of a Man Running" (10-4-61) Ralph Bellamy, Chester Morris, Wright King
38. "The Button-Down Break" (10-11-61) Tony Randall, Ken Lynch
39. "The Heat of Passion" (10-18-61) Dorothy Malone, John Dehner, Ed Nelson
40. "Waiting for Jocko" (10-25-61) Jeffrey Hunter
41. "Through a Dark Glass" (11-1-61) Claire Bloom, William Windom
42. "Juan Moreno's Body" (11-8-61) Henry Jones, Diana Lynn
43. "Kill the Sound" (11-15-61) Sid Caesar, Dianne Foster
44. "The Crimson Pool" (11-22-61) Vera Miles, John Kerr, Jacques Aubuchon
45. "The Two of Us" (11-29-61) Lloyd Bridges, Audrey Dalton
46. "Nice Guys Finish Last" (12-13-61) James Whitmore, Diana Van Der Vlis
47. "To the Best of My Recollection" (12-27-61) Bill Bixby, Laraine Day, Charles Drake
48. "A Funny Thing Happened to Me on the Way to the Game" (1-3-62) Jack Benny, Otto Kruger, Tina Louise
49. "The Star System" (1-10-62) Jack Lord, Elizabeth Montgomery
50. "The Renaissance of Gussie Hill" (1-17-62) Hershel Bernardi, Eleanor Parker
51. "A Very Rough Sketch" (1-24-62) Dina Merrill, Keir Dullea
52. "The Yacht Club Gang" (1-31-62) John Baragrey, Patricia Neal, Stephen Franken
53. "Death Beyond Recall" (2-7-62) Kent Smith, Walter Pidgeon, Mary LaRoche, Stefford Repp
54. "The Sound of Nervous Laughter" (2-14-62) Margaret Phillips, George Sanders
55. "An Assassin Arrives, Andante" (2-21-62) Richard Conte, Signe Hasso
56. "Remembrance of Crimes Past" (2-28-62) Angie Dickinson, Warren Stevens
57. "The Heart Is a Handout" (3-7-62) Myron McCormick
58. "A Brooding Fixation" (3-14-62) Mary Astor, Scott Marlowe
59. "A Chant of Silence" (3-21-62) Nick Adams, James Coburn,

Alan Napier
60. "Trial by Midnight" (3-28-62) Dana Andrews, Lori March
61. "Ride a Wild Horse" (4-4-62) David Janssen, Suzanne Lloyd
62. "So Beats My Plastic Heart" (4-11-62) Celeste Holm, Susan Oliver
63. "In a Foreign Quarter" (4-18-62) Tod Andrews, Nobu McCarthy
64. "Referendum on Murder" (4-25-62) Bethel Leslie, Dan O'Herlihy
65. "The Someday Man" (5-2-62) Ron Randell, Julie Adams, Don Taylor
66. "Rendezvous in Washington" (5-9-62) Macdonald Carey, Kathleen Crowley
67. "The Bold and the Tough" (5-16-62) Earl Holliman, Edward Binns
68. "Will the Real Killer Please Stand Up?" (5-23-62) Milton Selzer
69. "Down the Gardenia Path" (6-6-62) Ilka Chase, Susan Kohner
70. "Side by Side" (6-13-62) Buddy Ebsen, Ed Nelson

## SHIRLEY TEMPLE THEATRE

An admirable staging of Jules Verne's classic The Watch's Soul with the episode "The Terrible Clockman," by Bernard Schoenfeld, highlighted Miss Temple's return to television, with yet another series of children's classics.

The Regulars: Shirley Temple, hostess.

The Episodes:

1. "The Land of Oz" (9-18-60) Agnes Moorehead, Arthur Treacher, Shirley Temple, Ben Blue, Sterling Holloway, Frances Bergen, Jonathan Winters
2. "Kim" (9-25-60) Tony Haig, Michael Rennie, Joseph Wiseman, Arnold Moss
3. "Winnie-the-Pooh" (10-2-60) Shirley Temple, Teddy Eccles, Bill Baird's marionettes
4. "Tom and Huck" (10-9-60) Dan Duryea, Janet Blair, Jackie Coogan, Teddy Rooney, David Ladd
5. "Madeline" (10-16-60) Imogene Coca, Billy Gilbert, Gina Gillespie
6. "Little Men" (10-23-60) Shirley Temple, Fernando Lamas, Bobby Crawford
7. "The Prince and the Pauper" (10-30-60) Gig Young, Peter Lazer, Richard Ney
8. "Enemy Lou" (11-6-60) Fred Clark, Marjorie Reynolds, Frankie Avalon, Bernadette Withers, Jimmy Boyd
9. "The Reluctant Dragon" (11-13-60) John Raitt, Shirley Temple, Jack Weston, J. Pat O'Malley

10. "The Black Arrow" (11-27-60) Henry Daniell, Sean McClory, Tony Haig, Jacques Aubuchon
11. "The Indian Captive" (12-4-60) Steve Cochran, Cloris Leachman, Jenny Lynn, Anne Seymour, Doris Dowlen
12. "The House of the Seven Gables" (12-11-60) Robert Culp, Agnes Moorehead, Martin Landau, Jonathan Harris, John Abbott
13. "Baa, Baa, Black Sheep" (12-18-60) Geraldine Fitzgerald, Dennis Kohler, Gloria Vanderbilt, Liam Redmond
14. "Babes in Toyland" (12-25-60) Jonathan Winters, Jerry Colonna, Carl Ballantine
15. "Pippi Longstocking" (1-8-61) Gina Gillespie
16. "King Midas" (1-15-61) Wally Cox, Paul Ford, Anne Helm, Arthur Treacher, Julius LaRosa
17. "Rebel Gun" (1-22-61) Robert Morse, Jackie Coogan, Robert Sampson
18. "The Terrible Clockman" (1-29-61) Sam Jaffe, Eric Portman, Shirley Temple, Jacques Aubuchon
19. "The Pawn" (2-5-61) Jane Darwell, Charles McGraw, Robert Crawford Jr.
20. "Onawandah" (2-12-61) David Kent, Harry Townes
21. "The Return of Long John Silver" (2-19-61) James Westerfield, Tim O'Connor
22. "The Little Mermaid" (3-5-61) Nina Foch, Cathleen Nesbitt
23. "The Peg Leg Pirate of Sulu" (3-12-61) Claude Akins, Eugene Martin, Miriam Colon, Edgar Stehli
24. "The Princess and the Goblins" (3-19-61) Irene Hervey, Jack Ging

## THE ISLANDERS

Topical adventure yarn of island drifters Sandy Wade (William Reynolds) and Zack Malloy (James Philbrook); Diane Brewster had the role of a crafty pursuer.

The Regulars: Sandy Wade, William Reynolds; Zack Malloy, James Philbrook; Wilhemina Vandeveer, Diane Brewster.

The Episodes:

1. "Five O'Clock Friday" (10-2-60) Sebastian Cabot, Robert Carricart, Daria Massey, Theodore Marcuse, Peter Mamakos
2. "Flight from Terror" (10-9-60) Warren Hsieh, Gigi Perreau, Fay Wray
3. "The Terrified Blonde" (10-16-60) Joan O'Brien, Peter Whitney, Teru Shimada
4. "Talent for Danger" (10-23-60) Nobu McCarthy, Sean McLory, Christopher Dark
5. "Operation Dollar Sign" (10-30-60) Jacques Aubuchon, Michael Pate, Richard Devon

6.  "Hostage Island" (11-6-60) Steven Geray, Peter Falk, Jan
    Merlin, George Kennedy
7.  "The Phantom Captain" (11-13-60) Walter Burke, Mario
    Alcaide, Harold J. Stone, Lisa Lu
8.  "Our Girl in Saigon" (11-20-60) Roy Wright, Anna-Lisa
9.  "Forbidden Cargo" (11-27-60) E. G. Marshall, Thomas
    Gomez, Eduardo Ciannelli
10. "The Cold War of Adam Smith" (12-4-60) Charles Bickford,
    Keenan Wynn, Ronald Long
11. "Deadly Tomorrow" (12-11-60) Thomas Mitchell, Norma
    Crane
12. "The Widow from Richmond" (12-18-60) Glenda Farrell,
    Frank de Kova
13. "Duel of Strangers" (12-25-60) Howard St. John, Gia Scala
14. "The Twenty-Six Paper" (1-8-61) Gloria Talbott, Henry
    Silva, Betty Garde, Elisha Cook
15. "The Generous Politician" (1-15-61) Philip Ahn, Charles
    Bronson, J. Pat O'Malley, Benson Fong
16. "Escape from Kaledau" (1-29-61) Luther Adler, Hans Con-
    ried, Wendy Barrie, Henry Daniell, John Abbott
17. "To Bell a Cat" (2-5-61) Sam Jaffe, Harry Townes, Luana
    Anders, Jay Novello
18. "Willy's Millionaire" (2-12-61) Leslie Nielsen, George
    Macready, Anthony Caruso
19. "The Strange Courtship of Danny Koo" (2-19-61) Aki Aleong
    Pilar Seurat, James Hong, Teru Shimada
20. "Island Witness" (2-26-61) Gena Rowlands, Darren McGavin
    Karl Swenson
21. "A Rope for Charlie Munday" (3-5-61) Murray Matheson,
    Russell Collins, Jay Novello
22. "The World Is Her Oyster" (3-12-61) Leo Penn, Mike Kel-
    lin, Arthur Batanides
23. "The Pearls of Ratu" (3-19-61) Bert Remsen, Christine
    White, Chana Eden, Werner Klemperer
24. "La Costa Vendetta" (3-26-61) Patric Knowles, Al Ruscio,
    Linda Wong

SURFSIDE SIX

　　　Intriguing photography distinguishes this private detective
yarn, the principals (Van Williams as Ken Madison; Lee Patterson
as David Thorne; Troy Donahue as Sandy Winfield) residing on a
houseboat. As the fiery night club performer Cha Cha O'Brien,
Margarita Sierra (who tragically died in 1963) frequently stole the
show.

The Regulars: Sandy Winfield, Troy Donahue; Ken Madison, Van
　　　　　Williams; David Thorne, Lee Patterson; Daphne DeWitt
　　　　　Dutton, Diane McBain; Cha Cha O'Brien, Margarita Sierra

The Episodes:

1. "Country Gentleman" (10-3-60) Fred Wayne, Ray Danton, Frank de Kova
2. "High Tide" (10-10-60) Sherry Jackson, Gregg Palmer
3. "The Clown" (10-17-60) Vito Scotti, Joe De Santis, Ted de Corsia
4. "According to Our Files" (10-24-60) Alvy Moore
5. "Local Girl" (10-31-60) Sue Ane Langdon, Frank Ferguson
6. "Par-a-kee" (11-7-60) Lyle Talbot, Raymond Bailey
7. "Deadly Male" (11-14-60) Nancy Hadley, George Wallace, Robert Colbert
8. "Power of Suggestion" (11-21-60) Shirley Knight, Stephen Bekassy
9. "The International Set" (12-5-60) Claude Akins, Vaughn Taylor, Russell Thorson
10. "The Frightened Canary" (12-12-60) Nina Shipman, Ray Danton
11. "Girl in the Galleon" (12-19-60) Andra Martin, Dean Fredericks
12. "Bride and Seek" (12-26-60) Grant Williams, Warren Stevens, Kaye Elhardt
13. "Little Star Lost" (1-2-61) Shirley Knight, Constance Ford
14. "Heels Over Head" (1-9-61) Carlos Romero, Berry Kroeger
15. "The Facts on the Fire" (1-16-61) Julie Adams, Richard Webb
16. "Yesterday's Hero" (1-23-61) Merry Anders, Joe De Santis
17. "Thieves Among Honor" (1-30-61) Peter Breck, Alex Gerry
18. "License to Steal" (2-6-61) Jil Jarmyn, Vito Scotti, Joseph Ruskin
19. "Race Against Time" (2-13-61) Angela Greene, Nancy McCarthy
20. "Black Orange Blossoms" (2-20-61) Kathleen Crowley, David Frankham
21. "The Chase" [co-scripted by Roger Smith] (2-27-61) Reggie Nalder, Tim Graham
22. "Ghost of a Chance" (3-6-61) Claire Kelly, John Gabriel
23. "The Impractical Joker" (3-13-61) Harold J. Stone, Karen Steele, Mala Powers
24. "Inside Job" (3-20-61) Mary Tyler Moore, Jeffrey Stone, Dolores Donlon
25. "Invitation to a Party" (3-27-61) Kaye Elhardt, Ed Nelson
26. "Spring Training" (4-3-61) Will Hutchins, Gigi Perreau, Bing Russell
27. "Double Image" (4-10-61) Ellen McRae, Brad Dexter
28. "Circumstantial Evidence" (4-17-61) Lisa Gaye, John Lupton, John Beradino
29. "Vengeance Is Bitter" (4-24-61) Guy Stockwell, Claire Griswold, Peggy McCay, James Seay
30. "Little Mister Kelly" (5-1-61) Biff Elliott, Ronnie Dapo
31. "Spinout at Sebring" (5-8-61) Sue Randall, John Van Dreelen, Alejandro Rey
32. "The Bhoyo and the Blonde" (5-15-61) Paula Raymond, Sean

McClory, Sue Ane Langdon, Anthony Caruso
33.  "An Overdose of Justice" (5-22-61) Mara Corday, Edward
     Platt

Second Season

34.  "Count Seven" (9-18-61) Jason Evers, Shirley Balkard
35.  "The Wedding Guest" (9-25-61) Kaye Elhardt, Joan Mar-
     shall
36.  "One for the Road" (10-2-61) James Best, Elizabeth Mac-
     Rae
37.  "Daphne, Girl Detective" (10-9-61) Bruce Dern, Grace
     Gaynor
38.  "The Empty House" (10-16-61) Susan Seaforth, Sherwood
     Price
39.  "Witness for the Defense" (10-23-61) Lon Chaney, Elisha
     Cook
40.  "Laugh for the Lady" (10-30-61) Julie Adams
41.  "Affairs at Hotel Delight" (11-6-61) Leslie Parrish, William
     Windom, Dub Taylor, Jock Gaynor
42.  "Jonathan Wembley Is Missing" (11-13-61) Elliott Reid,
     Joan O'Brien, Donna Douglas
43.  "The Old School Tie" (11-20-61) Gloria Talbott, Margaret
     Lindsay, John Howard
44.  "A Matter of Seconds" (11-27-61) Claude Akins, Steve
     Brodie, William Schallert
45.  "Prescription for Panic" (12-4-61) Kathleen Crowley, Doug-
     las Henderson
46.  "A Slight Case of Chivalry" (12-18-61) John Dehner, Rox-
     anne Arlen
47.  "Pattern for a Frame" (12-25-61) Myrna Fahey, Robert
     Cornthwaite
48.  "The Roust" (1-1-62) David White, Vito Scotti, Elizabeth
     MacRae
49.  "The Quarterback" (1-8-62) Janet Lake, Sandy Kevin, Tucker
     Smith, Al Alvalon
50.  "Separate Checks" (1-15-62)
51.  "The Artful Deceit" (1-22-62) Chad Everett, Angela Greene
52.  "Anniversary Special" (1-29-62) William Windom, Jeanne
     Cooper, Sally Jones
53.  "The Surfside Swindle" (2-5-62) Gerald Mohr, Dabbs Greer,
     Lisa Montell
54.  "Who Is Sylvia?" (2-12-62) Karen Steele, Karl Swenson,
     Jack Cassidy, Joan Marshall
55.  "Find Leroy Burdette" (2-19-62) Susan Seaforth, Nancy Val-
     entine
56.  "Many a Slip" (2-26-62) Kathryn Hays, Edward Kemmer,
     Cathy Downs
57.  "The Green Beret" (3-5-62) Adam Williams, Bart Burns,
     Richard Benedict
58.  "Vendetta Arms" (3-12-62) Dennis Hopper, Robert H. Har-
     ris, John Marley
59.  "A Piece of Tommy Minor" (3-19-62) Lee Philips, Tom

Drake
60. "Portrait of Nicole" (3-26-62) Peggy McCay, Peter Breck, Francine York
61. "Elegy for a Bookkeeper" (4-2-62) Shirley Knight, Arch Johnson
62. "The Money Game" (4-9-62) Gerald Mohr, Nico Minardos
63. "Irish Pride" (4-16-62) Malachy McCort, Richard Karlen
64. "Green Bay Riddle" (4-23-62) Donald May, Lisa Gaye, Lee Farr
65. "Love Song for a Deadly Redhead" (4-30-62) Shary Marshall, (Edward Byrnes and Roger Smith in roles as Kookie and Jeff Spencer)
66. "Dead Heat" (5-7-62) Jeanne Cooper, Warren Stevens
67. "Squeeze Play" (5-14-62) Peter Breck, Andrea King, Laraine Stephens
68. "A Private Eye for Beauty" (5-21-62) John Dehner, Dawn Wells
69. "Masquerade" (5-28-62) Eva Norde, Willard Sage, Robert Dowdell, Charles Radilac
70. "Pawn's Gambit" (6-4-62) Kathie Browne, Otto Waldis, Lucy Prentis
71. "Neutral Corner" (6-11-62) Chad Everett, Allison Ames, Grace Lee Whitney
72. "House on Boca Key" (6-18-62) Patricia Blair, Alan Baxter, Anna Capri
73. "Midnight for Prince Charming" (6-25-62) Mike Road, R. G. Armstrong, Jo Morrow, Richard Benedict


KLONDIKE

Drawn from Pierre Berton's The Klondike Fever is this zesty tale of the Alaska gold rush period.

The Regulars: Mike Halliday, Ralph Taeger; Kathy O'Hara, Marie Blanchard; Jeff Durain, James Coburn; Goldie, Joi Lansing; Joe Teel, L. Q. Jones.

The Episodes:

1. "Klondike Fever" (10-10-60) Karl Swenson, Ray Teal
2. "River of Gold" (10-24-60) Forrest Lewis
3. "Saints and Stickups" (10-31-60) Whit Bissell, Virginia Gregg
4. "The Unexpected Candidate" (11-7-60) Judson Pratt, Robert E. Griffin
5. "88 Keys to Trouble" (11-14-60) Wallace Ford, Charles Fredericks
6. "Swoger's Mules" (11-21-60) Claude Akins
7. "Sure Thing, Men" (11-28-60) Larry Pennell, Tyler McVey, Jack Albertson
8. "Taste of Danger" (12-5-60)

9. "Bare Knuckles" (12-12-60) J. Pat O'Malley, Richard Kiel
10. "Halliday's Club" (12-19-60) Jackie Coogan, Hugh Sanders
11. "Bathhouse Justice" (12-26-60) Walter Burke, Nora Marlowe
12. "Swing on Your Partner" (1-9-61)
13. "The Golden Burro" (1-16-61) Edgar Buchanan, Robert F. Simon
14. "Queen of the Klondike" (1-23-61) Hank Patterson, Jack Elam, Lane Bradford
15. "The Man Who Owned Skagway" (1-30-61) Lawrence Dobkin, Emory Parnell, Ralph Moody
16. "Sitka Madonna" (2-6-61) Patric Knowles, Ron Hayes
17. "The Hostages" (2-13-61) Lon Chaney, Chris Alcaide, Michael Raffetto

DANTE'S INFERNO

Not even the presence of a fine actor, Howard Duff, in the lead role of Willie Dante could uplift this banal tale of a hard-as-nails investigator and owner of a night club called 'Dante's Inferno.'"

The Regulars: Willie Dante, Howard Duff; Police Lieutenant Bob Malone, Mort Mills; Stewart Styles, Alan Mowbray; Biff, Tom D'Andrea.

The Episodes:

1. "One for the Birds" (10-3-60) Joanna Barnes
2. "Opening Night" (10-10-60) Robert F. Simon
3. "The Feline Traveler" (10-17-60) Patricia Medina
4. "Dante's Dilemma" (10-31-60) William Hudson
5. "The Misfortune Cookie" (11-7-60) Lisa Lu
6. "San Quentin Quill" (11-14-60) Carolyn Kearney
7. "The Unclean Green" (11-21-60) Dolores Donlon
8. "The Bavarian Barbarians" (11-28-60) Carol Ohmart
9. "My Pal, the Bullseye" (12-5-60) Joyce Jameson
10. "The Jolly Rogers Cocktail" (12-19-60) Edward C. Platt, Chana Eden
11. "A Punch from Judy" (12-26-60) Joan Tabor
12. "Don't Come On'a My House" (1-2-61) Audrey Dalton, Hayden Rorke
13. "Wine, Women, and Willie" (1-9-61) Robert Strauss, Jacqueline Scott
14. "Dial D for Dante" (1-16-61) Jan Shepard, Lori Nelson
15. "The Devil to Pay" (1-23-61) Tracey Roberts, Joseph Ruskin
16. "Dante Rides Again" (1-30-61) Nita Talbot
17. "Dante's Fickle Fate" (2-6-61) Ruta Lee, Theodore Marcuse
18. "Aces and Eights" (2-13-61) Dick Foran
19. "Light Lady, Dark Room" (2-20-61) Christopher Dark, Tina Carver

20. "Not as a Canary" (2-27-61) Adele Mara, John Beradino
21. "Pick a Peck of Diamonds" (3-6-61) Bek Nelson
22. "Dante in the Dark" (3-13-61) Bert Freed, Marion Ross
23. "Hunter with a Badge" (3-20-61) Charles McGraw, Eddie Firestone
24. "Friendly Assassin" (3-27-61) Karen Steele, Leonard Strong
25. "The Sesame Key" (4-3-61) Nora Hayden
26. "Around a Dark Corner" (4-10-61) Diana Millay, Paul Fix


BARBARA STANWYCK THEATRE

The Regulars: Barbara Stanwyck, hostess.

The Episodes:

1. "The Mink Coat" (9-19-60) Stephen McNally, Barbara Stanwyck
2. "Good Citizen" (10-3-60) Hume Cronyn
3. "Discreet Deception" (10-10-60) Patric Knowles
4. "The Seventh Miracle" (10-17-60) Lloyd Nolan
5. "The Key to a Killer" (10-31-60) Vic Morrow
6. "House in Order" (11-7-60) Shepperd Strudwick
7. "The Miraculous Journey of Tadpole Chan" (11-14-60) Ralph Bellamy, Dick Kay Hong
8. "The Secret of Mrs. Randall" (11-21-60) Barbara Stanwyck
9. "Ironback's Bride" (11-28-60) Charles Bickford, Barbara Stanwyck
10. "We Are the Women Who Wait" (12-5-60) Barbara Stanwyck, John Kellogg, Marion Ross
11. "Out of the Shadows" (12-19-60) Barbara Stanwyck, William Stephens
12. "No One" (12-26-60) Dennis Hopper, Susan Oliver
13. "The Cornerstone" (1-2-61) Barbara Stanwyck, Rafael Campos
14. "Night Visitor" (1-9-61) Michael Ansara, Julie London
15. "Size 10" (1-16-61) Robert Paige, Barbara Stanwyck
16. "Dear Charlie" (1-23-61) Milton Berle, Lurene Tuttle
17. "Dragon by the Tail" (1-30-61) Anna May Wong, Barbara Stanwyck
18. "The Sisters" (2-6-61) Michael Rennie, Barbara Stanwyck
19. "Big Career" (2-13-61) Elizabeth Patterson, Gene Raymond
20. "Confession" (2-20-61) Barbara Stanwyck, Lee Marvin
21. "Along the Barbary Coast" (2-27-61) Jerome Thor, Barbara Stanwyck
22. "Shock" (3-6-61) Eduard Franz
23. "The Golden Acres" (3-13-61) Kent Smith
24. "Adventure on Happiness Street" (3-20-61) Robert Culp, Lew Ayres, Barbara Stanwyck
25. "High Tension" (3-27-61) Tony Maxwell, Nora Marlowe, Barbara Stanwyck
26. "Sign of the Zodiac" (4-3-61) Joan Blondell, Dan Duryea

27.  "Call Me Annie" (4-10-61)  Peggy Cass
28.  "The Choice" (4-17-61)  Robert Horton, James Best
29.  "Frightened Doll" (4-24-61)  Wallace Ford, Harold J. Stone, Barbara Stanwyck
30.  "Yanqui Go Home" (5-1-61)  Dana Andrews
31.  "Little Big Mouth" (5-8-61)  Barbara Stanwyck, Buddy Ebsen
32.  "The Assassin" (5-15-61)  Leon Ames, Peter Falk
33.  "The Triple C" (5-22-61)  James Philbrook, Barbara Stanwyck
34.  "The Hitch-Hiker" (5-29-61)  Joseph Cotten, Elana Eden, Barbara Stanwyck
35.  "Big Jake" (6-5-61)  Andy Devine, John Qualen
36.  "A Man's Game" (7-3-61)  Charles Drake


STAGECOACH WEST

This western of a stagecoach line run jointly by Luke Parry (Wayne Rogers) and Simon Kane (Robert Bray) suffers by its incessant (even considering the genre) moralizing. When Kane's son Davey (Richard Eyer), who is made to be incredibly suppliant in this, asks about his late (he's been led to believe) mother, the truth must stay concealed. It seems that Davey's mother was a "saloon woman" (they always are), so what was to stop Simon from continuing the lie, despite the fact that Mrs. Kane sacrifices her life for Davey in the initial episode?

The Regulars:  Luke Parry, Wayne Rogers; Simon Kane, Robert Bray; Davey Kane, Richard Eyer; Zeke Bonner, James Burke.

The Episodes:

1.  "High Lonesome" (10-4-60)  Jane Greer, James Best, Robert F. Simon
2.  "The Land Beyond" (10-11-60)  Gigi Perreau
3.  "Dark Return" (10-18-60)  Billy Gray, John Kellogg
4.  "The Unwanted" (10-25-60)  Tammy Marihugh, Bethel Leslie
5.  "A Fork in the Road" (11-1-60)  Jack Warden
6.  "A Time to Run" (11-15-60)  Cesar Romero, Barbara Nichols
7.  "Red Sand" (11-22-60)  Dean Jones, Harold J. Stone, Edgar Buchanan, Diana Millay
8.  "The Saga of Jeremy Boone" (11-29-60)  Mark Stevens, Ben Cooper
9.  "Life Sentence" (12-6-60)  Virginia Grey, Bruce Gordon, Harry Townes
10.  "The Storm" (12-13-60)  Beverly Garland, Tom Drake, J. Pat O'Malley
11.  "Three Wise Men" (12-20-60)  Dick York, Ellen Clark, Denver Pyle
12.  "By the Deep Six" (12-27-60)  Ashley Cowan, Mort Mills

13. "Object: Patrimony" (1-3-61) Pippa Scott, George Neise, Robert Vaughn
14. "Come Home Again" (1-10-61) James Coburn, Lisa Kirk
15. "The Brass Lily" (1-17-61) Jean Hagen, John Litel
16. "Finn McCool" (1-24-61) Sean McClory, Hazel Court
17. "Image of a Man" (1-31-61) Thomas Mitchell, John Dehner, DeForest Kelley
18. "Not in Our Stars" (2-7-61) Lon Chaney Jr., Jay C. Flippen
19. "The Arsonist" (2-14-61) James Dunn, Adele Mara, James Best
20. "Songs My Mother Told Me" (2-21-61) Arthur O'Connell, Richard Devon, Rachel Ames
21. "The Root of Evil" (2-28-61) Philip Carey, John Dehner, Rachel Ames
22. "The Outcasts" (3-7-61) Don Dubbins, Joanna Barnes
23. "The Remounts" (3-14-61) Richard Devon, Mort Mills
24. "House of Violence" (3-21-61) Jack Lord
25. "The Butcher" (3-28-61) Rodolfo Hoyos, John Dehner, Jack Lord
26. "Fort Wyatt Crossing" (4-4-61) Steven Terrell, Madlyn Rhue
27. "A Place of Still Waters" (4-11-61) Darren McGavin, Edward Binns
28. "Never Walk Alone" (4-18-61) William Campbell, Lee Van Cleef, Karen Sharpe
29. "The Big Gun" (4-25-61) Cesar Romero, Barbara Luna, DeForest Kelley
30. "The Dead Don't Cry" (5-2-61) James Best, Tod Lasswell
31. "The Raider" (5-9-61) Henry Silva, Jan Shepard, James Lydon
32. "Blind Man's Bluff" (5-16-61) James Drury, Ruta Lee, Whit Bissell
33. "The Bold Whip" (5-23-61) John Kellogg, Carolyn Kearney
34. "The Orphans" (5-30-61) Robert Cabal, Linda Dangcil
35. "The Guardian Angels" (6-6-61) Casey Adams, Malcolm Atterbury, Steve Brodie
36. "The Swindler" (6-13-61) Dennis Patrick, John Litel
37. "The Renegades" (6-20-61) Richard Devon, Warren Oates
38. "The Marker" (6-27-61) Mort Mills, Ruta Lee

THRILLER

Splendid, atmospheric tales of the macabre, with Boris Karloff as host and occasional star.

The Regulars: Boris Karloff, host.

The Episodes:

1. "The Twisted Image" (9-13-60) Constance Ford, Leslie Nielsen, Boris Karloff, George Grizzard

2. "Child's Play" (9-20-60) Bethel Leslie, Tommy Nolan, Frank Overton
3. "Worse Than Murder" (9-27-60) Constance Ford, Christine White
4. "The Mark of the Hand" (10-4-60) Shepperd Strudwick, Mona Freeman, Woody Strode, Jessie Royce Landis
5. "Rose's Last Summer" (10-11-60) Mary Astor
6. "The Guilty Men" (10-18-60) Jay C. Flippen, Anne Barton, Everett Sloane, Frank Silvera, Frank Dana
7. "The Purple Room" (10-25-60) Rip Torn, Patricia Barry, Ray Teal, Richard Anderson, Alan Napier
8. "The Watcher" (11-1-60) Richard Chamberlain, Martin Gabel, Stuart Erwin
9. "Girl with a Secret" (11-15-60) Fay Bainter, Rhodes Reason, Myrna Fahey, Cloris Leachman
10. "The Prediction" (11-22-60) Boris Karloff, Audrey Dalton
11. "The Fatal Impulse" (11-29-60) Elisha Cook, Mary Tyler Moore, Robert Lansing, Conrad Nagel
12. "The Big Blackout" (12-6-60) Charles McGraw, Jack Carson
13. "Knock Three--One--Two" (12-13-60) Charles Aidman, Beverly Garland, Warren Oates, Joe Maross
14. "Man in the Middle" (12-20-60) Mort Sahl, Sue Randall
15. "The Cheaters" (12-27-60) Henry Daniell, Mildred Dunnock, Harry Townes, Paul Newlan
16. "The Hungry Glass" (1-3-61) William Shatner, Elizabeth Allen, Russell Johnson, Joanna Heyes
17. "The Poisoner" (1-10-61) Murray Matheson, Sarah Marshall, Brenda Forbes
18. "Man in the Cage" (1-17-61) Philip Carey, Diana Millay, Guy Stockwell, Eduardo Ciannelli
19. "Choose a Victim" (1-24-61) Larry Blyden, Susan Oliver, Vaughn Taylor, Tracey Roberts
20. "Hay-Fork and Bill-Hook" (2-7-61) Kenneth Haig, Allan Caillou, Audrey Dalton, Alan Napier, J. Pat O'Malley
21. "The Merriweather File" (2-14-61) James Gregory, Bethel Leslie, Edward Binns, Ross Elliott
22. "The Fingers of Fear" (2-21-61) Nehemiah Persoff, H. M. Wynant, Robert Middleton, Kevin Hagen
23. "Well of Doom" (2-28-61) Ronald Howard, Henry Daniell, Torin Thatcher, Richard Kiel, Fenton Meyler
24. "The Ordeal of Dr. Cordell" (3-7-61) Robert Vaughn, Kathleen Crowley, Russ Conway, Marlo Thomas, Robert Ellenstein
25. "Trio for Terror" (3-14-61) [Act I] Richard Lupino, [Act II] Reginald Owen, [Act III] Michael Pate
26. "Papa Benjamin" (3-21-61) John Ireland, Jeanne Bal, Robert H. Harris, Jester Hairston
27. "Late Date" (4-4-61) Larry Pennell, Edward C. Platt, Jody Fair, Chris Seitz
28. "Yours Truly, Jack the Ripper" (4-11-61) John Williams, Donald Woods
29. "The Devil's Ticket" (4-18-61) Macdonald Carey, John Emery, Joan Fertzei, Patricia Medina

30. "Parasite Mansion" (4-25-61) Pippa Scott, James Griffith, Jeanette Nolan, Tommy Nolan
31. "A Good Imagination" (5-2-61) Patricia Barry, Edward Andrews, Ed Nelson, William Allyn
32. "Mr. George" (5-9-61) Gina Gillespie, Virginia Gregg, Howard Freeman, Lillian Bronson
33. "Terror in Teakwood" (5-16-61) Guy Rolfe, Hazel Court, Charles Aidman, Vladimir Sokoloff, Reggie Nalder
34. "The Prisoner in the Mirror" (5-23-61) Lloyd Bochner, Marion Ross, Jack Mullaney, Pat Michon, David Frankham
35. "Dark Legacy" (5-30-61) Henry Silva, Harry Townes, Ilka Windish, Alan Napier, Richard Hale
36. "Pigeons from Hell" (6-6-61) Brandon de Wilde, Crahan Denton, Ken Renard, David Whorf
37. "The Grim Reaper" (6-13-61) William Shatner, Natalie Schafer, Elizabeth Allen, Scott Merrill

Second Season

38. "What Beckoning Ghost?" (9-18-61) Judith Evelyn, Tom Helmore, Adele Mara
39. "Guillotine" (9-25-61) Robert Middleton, Alejandro Rey
40. "The Premature Burial" (10-2-61) Boris Karloff, Sidney Blackmer, Scott Marlowe, Patricia Medina
41. "The Weird Tailor" (10-16-61) Henry Jones, George Macready, Abraham Sofaer
42. "God Grant that She Lye Stille" (10-23-61) Henry Daniell, Sarah Marshall, Ronald Howard
43. "Masquerade" (10-30-61) Elizabeth Montgomery, Tom Poston, John Carradine
44. "The Last of the Sommervilles" (11-6-61) Phyllis Thaxter, Martita Hunt, Boris Karloff
45. "Letter to a Lover" (11-13-61) Ann Todd, Murray Matheson
46. "A Third for Pinochle" (11-20-61) Edward Andrews, Ann Shoemaker, Doro Merande, June Walker
47. "The Closed Cabinet" (11-27-61) Olive Sturgess, David Frankham, Peter Forster, Jennifer Raine
48. "Dialogues with Death" (12-4-61) a) "Welcome Home" Estelle Winwood, Ed Nelson, Boris Karloff; b) "Friend of the Dead"
49. "The Return of Andrew Bentley" (12-11-61) John Newland, Antoinette Bower, Norma Crane
50. "The Remarkable Mrs. Hawk" (12-18-61) Jo Van Fleet, John Carradine, Paul Newlan
51. "Portrait Without a Face" (12-25-61) Jane Greer, John Newland, Robert Webber
52. "An Attractive Family" (1-1-62) Otto Kruger, Richard Long, Joan Tetzel, Leo G. Carroll
53. "Waxworks" (1-8-62) Oscar Homolka, Antoinette Bower, Alan Baxter, Booth Colman
54. "La Strega" (1-15-62) Ursula Andress, Alejandro Rey, Jeanette Nolan
55. "The Storm" (1-22-62) Nancy Kelly, David McLean, David

Janssen
56. "A Wig for Miss Devore" (1-29-62) John Baragrey, Patricia Barry, John Fielder
57. "The Hollow Watcher" (2-12-62) Warren Oates, Denver Pyle, Sean McClory, Audrey Dalton
58. "Cousin Tundifer" (2-19-62) Edward Andrews, Vaughn Taylo Sue Ane Langdon, Howard McNear
59. "The Incredible Doctor Markesan" (2-26-62) Dick York, Carolyn Kearney
60. "Flowers of Evil" (3-5-62) Luciana Paluzzi, Kevin Hagen, Vladimir Sokoloff, Jack Eston
61. "Till Death Do Us Part" (3-12-62) Henry Jones, Jocelyn Brando, Reta Shaw, Edgar Buchanan, Philip Ober
62. "The Bride Who Died Twice" (3-19-62) Mala Powers, Eduardo Ciannelli, Robert Colbert, Joe De Santis
63. "Kill My Love" (3-26-62) Richard Carlson, Patricia Breslin David Kent, K. T. Stevens
64. "Men of Mystery" (4-2-62) Mary Tyler Moore, William Windom
65. "The Innocent Bystanders" (4-9-62) George Kennedy, John Anderson, Steven Terrell, Janet Lake
66. "Lethal Ladies" (4-16-62) Howard Morris, Rosemary Murph
67. "The Specialists" (4-30-62) Lin McCarthy, Sean McClory, David Frankham

THE AQUANAUTS

A further celebration of youthful vigor, this Ivan Tors serie appropriately immerses its heroes in that eternal symbol of intran igence--the sea. Aquanauts Drake Andrews (Keith Larsen), Larry Lahr (Jeremy Slate) and Mike Madison (Ron Ely) expectedly do battle with both man and nature, once with an underwater earthquake (in "The Landslide Adventure"), once armed with spears in an underwater duel with counterfeiters (in "The Stakeout Adventure once, in the fifth episode, in the quest for that enigmatic stand-by --Atlantis.

The Regulars: Drake Andrews, Keith Larsen (to episode of 2/22/ 61); Larry Lahr, Jeremy Slate; Mike Madison, Ron Ely (with episode of 3/1/61); the Captain, Charles Thompson.

The Episodes:

1. [unknown title] (9-14-60) Larry Pennell, Edward Binns, Sarah Marshall
2. [unknown title] (9-21-60) Harry Townes, Leslie Parrish
3. [unknown title] (9-28-60) Richard Carlson, Gerald Mohr
4. [unknown title] (10-5-60) Keenan Wynn, Patricia Cutts, Joh Sutton
5. [unknown title] (10-12-60) Lynn Bari, Paul Henreid, Mort Mills, Joyce Meadows

6.  [unknown title] (10-19-60) Dean Jones, Alfred Ryder, Pippa Scott
7.  [unknown title] (10-26-60) Richard Eastham
8.  [unknown title] (11-9-60) Everett Sloane, Chana Eden, Thomas Gomez, Ned Glass
9.  [unknown title] (11-16-60) Jennifer West, Diana Millay, Robert Gothie, Sue Randall, Frank Albertson, Sam Levene
10. "The Cavedivers" (12-7-60) Charles Bronson, Paula Raymond, Robert Knapp
11. "The Big Swim" (12-14-60) Brad Dexter, Burt Reynolds, Annette Driggers, Donna Douglas, Valerie Allen
12. "Underwater Demolition" (12-21-60) Robert Strauss, John Dierkes, Annelle Hayes, Stephen Roberts
13. "River Gold" (1-4-61) James Coburn, Margaret O'Brien
14. "Niagara Dive" (1-11-61) Whitney Blake, Gina Gillespie
15. [unknown title] (1-25-61) Mary Tyler Moore, William Conrad
16. "Secret at Half Moon Key" (2-1-61) Erin O'Brien, Ken Drake, Frank McDonald, Charles Cooper
17. "The Storm Adventure" (2-8-61) Telly Savalas, Susan Oliver, John Marley, Russ Conway
18. "The Armored Truck Adventure" (2-15-61) Ray Walston, Ron Soble, Leo Penn
19. "The Defective Tank Adventure" (2-22-61) June Blair, William Bramley, John Fiedler, Nora Hayden, Isabel Jewell, Neil Hamilton

[Hereafter with the title MALIBU RUN]

20. "The Jeremiah Adventure" (3-1-61) Peter Falk, Edgar Stehli, Joyce Meadows, Milton Selzer
21. "The Tidal Wave Adventure" (3-8-61) Cecil Parker, Antoinette Bower, Russell Nype, John McGiver
22. "The Radioactive Object Adventure" (3-22-61) John Williams, Diane Cannon, Ken Lynch
23. "The Double Adventure" (3-29-61) Peter Falk, Lewis Charles, Al Ruscio, Shary Layne
24. "The Rainbow Adventure" (4-19-61) Ray Hamilton, Yvonne Craig, Norman Fell
25. "The Frankie Adventure" (4-26-61) Alan Baxter, Anne Helm, Scott Marlowe, Jane Withers
26. "The Guilty Adventure" (5-3-61) Robert Strauss, Robert Gist, Milton Selzer, Phyllis Hill
27. "The Landslide Adventure" (5-10-61) Robert Vaughn, Dan Tobin, Kaye Elhardt, Barney Phillips
28. "The Kidnap Adventure" (5-17-61) John Lupton, Burt Reynolds, Joe Maross, Nina Shipman
29. "The Stakeout Adventure" (5-24-61) John Dehner, Dabbs Greer, Donna Douglas
30. "The Scavenger Adventure" (5-31-61) Dan Tobin, Linden Chiles, Kay Hughes, Ann Hughes, Florence Sundstrom, Fred Sherman, Don Welbanks

31. "The Diana Adventure" (6-7-61) Jim Davis, Diane Cannon,
    Ken Curtis, Jerry Riggio


HONG KONG

      Expectedly exotic adventure drama with Rod Taylor as Glenn
Evans, the reporter stationed in Hong Kong.

The Regulars: Glenn Evans, Rod Taylor; Neil Campbell, Chief of
      Police, Lloyd Bochner; Tully, Jack Kruschen; Fong,
      Harold Fong.

The Episodes:

1. "Clear for Action" (9-28-60) France Nuyen, Burt Brinckerhoff
2. "Murder Royal" (10-5-60) Frederic Worlock
3. "Pearl Flower" (10-12-60) Inger Stevens, Thomas Gomez
4. "Freebooter" (10-19-60) Beverly Garland, Frank Silvera,
   Arch Johnson
5. "The Jade Empress" (10-26-60) Patricia Crowley, Richard
   Grey
6. "The Jumping Dragon" (11-2-60) Jerome Thor, Taina Elg
7. "Blind Bargain" (11-9-60) Joanna Moore, Daria Massey
8. "Colonel Cat" (11-16-60) Herbert Marshall, Sarah Marshall
9. "The Turncoat" (11-23-60) Lisa Lu, Christopher Dark
10. "To Catch a Star" (11-30-60) Luciana Paluzzi, Edward
    Andrews
11. "Nine Lives" (12-7-60) Harry Townes, Terence de Marney
12. "The Dragon Cup" (12-14-60) Philip Ahn, Bethel Leslie,
    Harold J. Stone
13. "When Strangers Meet" (12-21-60) Pippa Scott, Kenneth
    MacKenna, Clarence Lung
14. "Suitable for Framing" (1-4-61) Julie London, Jason Evers
15. "Lesson in Fear" (1-11-61) Suzanne Pleshette, David Hedi-
    son
16. "The Survivor" (1-18-61) Coleen Gray, June Dayton
17. "Night Cry" (1-25-61) Liam Redmond, Tommy Rettig, Denny
    Miller
18. "Double Jeopardy" (2-1-61) Felicia Farr, Frank De Kova
19. "Lady Godiva" (2-8-61) Dina Merrill, Philip Ahn
20. "The Hunted" (2-15-61) John Abbott, Arline Sax
21. "With Deadly Sorrow" (2-22-61) Anne Francis, Benson Fong,
    Mary Murphy
22. "Murder by Proxy" (3-1-61) Nancy Gates, Richard Ander-
    son, Paul Richards
23. "The Woman in Gray" (3-8-61) Rhonda Fleming, J. Pat
    O'Malley
24. "Love, Honor, and Perish" (3-15-61) Joan Caulfield, Warren
    Stevens
25. "The Innocent Exile" (3-22-61) Susan Kohner, Jay Novello,

    Joe De Santis
26. "The Runaway" (3-29-61) Gia Scala, Lawrence Dobkin


THE NAKED CITY

  Mark Hellinger's brilliant conception, having been the basis
for the 1948 Jules Dassin film, was transformed into first a half-
hour television series (39 episodes) in 1958; subsequently into this
equally brilliant hour series which follows.

  One never had reason to fault the thesis that there are indeed "eight million stories in the naked city," for characters
seemed to fuse with the tenements of New York City--as though the
city were expressing itself. In Abram S. Ginnes' extraordinary
teleplay "And By the Sweat of Thy Brow," the hero stays concealed
in shadows while sermonizing a girl companion on the state of his
environs. Much more than just a detective story, episodes examined
both the bizarre types (neo-Nazis in the chilling "Tombstone for a
Derelict") and those unembellished by the sensational (the junior
executive of "Alive and Still a Second Lieutenant," the dreamy
spinster of "To Dream Without Sleep," the overprotective parent
of "Daughter, Am I in My Father's House?"). The writers were
of the highest calibre: Ernest Kinoy ("Golden Lads and Girls"),
Joel Carpenter ("One, Two, Three, Rita Rakahowski"), Shimon
Wincelberg ("Barefoot on a Bed of Coals") and Abram S. Ginnes
(the comedy "No Naked Ladies in Front of Giovanni's House!" in
addition to the aforementioned drama "And By the Sweat of Thy
Brow").

  Fine performances were delivered by Paul Burke, Horace
MacMahon and Harry Bellaver as Detective Adam Flint, Lieutenant
Mike Parker and Sergeant Frank Arcaro, respectively and by Nancy
Malone as Libby.

The Regulars: Detective Adam Flint, Paul Burke; Lieutenant Mike
    Parker, Horace MacMahon; Sergeant Frank Arcaro, Harry
    Bellaver; Libby, Nancy Malone.

The Episodes:

1. "A Death of Princes" (10-12-60) George Maharis, John
   Baragrey, Eli Wallach, Jan Miner
2. "The Pedigree Sheet" (10-19-60) Suzanne Pleshette, Eric
   Portman, Murray Hamilton, Roger C. Carmel
3. "A Succession of Heartbeats" (10-26-60) Felicia Farr, Fay
   Spain
4. "Down the Long Night" (11-2-60) Leslie Nielsen, Nehemiah
   Persoff, Geraldine Brooks
5. "To Walk in Silence" (11-9-60) Claude Rains, Telly Savalas
6. "Killer with a Kiss" (11-16-60) Burt Brinckerhoff, Carmen
   Mathews, Clifton James, Norma Connolly

7. "Debt of Honor" (11-23-60) Lois Nettleton, Steve Cochran
8. "The Human Trap" (11-30-60) Ruth Roman, Zina Bethune
9. "The Man Who Bit the Diamond in Half" (12-14-60) Luther
   Adler, Walter Matthau, Elizabeth Allen
10. "Bullets Cost Too Much" (1-4-61) Dick York, Betty Field,
    Bruce Dern
11. "Murder Is a Face I Know" (1-11-61) Theodore Bikel, Keir
    Dullea
12. "Landscape with Dead Figures" (1-18-61) Myron McCormick,
    Conrad Nagel, Alfred Ryder
13. "A Hole in the City" (2-1-61) Sylvia Sidney, Robert Duvall
14. "The Well-Dressed Termites" (2-8-61) Jack Klugman, John
    Baragrey, House Jameson, Philip Abbott, Norma Crane
15. "The Day It Rained Mink" (2-15-61) Keenan Wynn, Abbe
    Lane
16. "Button in a Haystack" (2-22-61) Albert Salmi, Peggy Ann
    Garner
17. "Shoes for Vinnie Winford" (3-1-61) Dennis Hopper, Hilda
    Brawner, Geoffrey Lumb
18. "The Deadly Guinea-Pig" (3-8-61) Eugenie Leontovich,
    Viveca Lindfors
19. "Vengeance Is a Wheel" (3-15-61) Ben Piazza, Paul Stevens,
    Frank Marth
20. "The Fault in Our Stars" (3-22-61) Roddy McDowall, Mary
    Fickett
21. "Tombstone for a Derelict" (4-5-61) Robert Redford, Polly
    Rowles
22. "A Memory of Crying" (4-12-61) Susan Oliver, Luther
    Adler, Betty Field
23. "New York to L.A." (4-19-61) Martin Balsam, Robert Blake
24. "A Very Cautious Boy" (4-26-61) Peter Falk, Ruth White
25. "An Economy of Death" (5-3-61) Sam Jaffe, Sandor Szabo
26. "$C_3H_5(NO_3)^3$" (5-10-61) Hume Cronyn, J. D. Cannon
27. "Make-Believe Man" (5-17-61) Chester Morris, Nehemiah
    Persoff, Eduardo Ciannelli
28. "To Dream Without Sleep" (5-24-61) Lois Nettleton, Bibi
    Osterwald, Valerie Bettis, Eddie Holmes
29. "A Kettle of Precious Fish" (5-31-61) Albert Dekker,
    Woodrow Parfrey, Russell Collins
30. "Sweet Prince of Delancey Street" (6-7-61) Robert Morse,
    James Dunn, Dustin Hoffman, Jan Miner
31. "The Day the Island Almost Sank" (6-14-61) Paul Hartman,
    Roger C. Carmel
32. "Take and Put" (6-21-61) Mildred Natwick, Ronald Winters,
    Nancy Carroll

Second Season

33. "Take Off Your Hat When a Funeral Passes By" (9-27-61)
    Lee J. Cobb, Geraldine Fitzgerald
34. "Dead on the Field of Honor" (10-4-61) Cathleen Nesbitt,
    Logan Ramsey, Ann Williams
35. "A Corpse Ran Down Mulberry Street" (10-11-61) Nehemiah

Persoff, Sorrell Booke, Joe De Santis

36. "The Fingers of Henri Tourelle" (10-18-61) Luther Adler, Nina Foch, Michael Tolan, Robert Loggia

37. "A Wednesday Night Story" (11-1-61) Constance Ford, David Janssen, Ulla Jacobsson

38. "The Tragic Success of Alfred Tiloff" (11-8-61) Jack Klugman, Jan Sterling

39. "Which Is Joseph Creeley?" (11-15-61) Martin Balsam, Jack Kruschen, Murray Hamilton

40. "Show Me the Way to Go Home" (11-22-61) Burt Brinckerhoff, Louise Albritton, Celia Adler

41. "The Hot Minerva" (11-29-61) Kurt Kasznar, Glynis Johns

42. "Requiem for a Sunday Afternoon" (12-6-61) Marissa Pavan, Jay Novello

43. "Ooftus Goofus" (12-13-61) Mickey Rooney, Maureen Stapleton

44. "Bridge Party" (12-27-61) Fred Clark, Albert Dekker, House Jameson, James Barton

45. "The Face of the Enemy" (1-3-62) Kim Hunter, Jack Warden

46. "Portrait of a Painter" (1-10-62) William Shatner, Theodore Bikel

47. "The Night the Saints Lost Their Halos" (1-17-62) Jo Van Fleet, Peter Fonda

48. "The Contract" (1-24-62) James Shigeta, Pilar Seurat, Abraham Sofaer

49. "One of the Most Important Men in the Whole World" (1-31-62) Myron McCormick, Anne Seymour, Richard Conte

50. "A Case Study of Two Savages" (2-7-62) Tuesday Weld, Rip Torn

51. "Let Me Die Before I Wake" (2-14-62) Jack Klugman, Joanne Linville, Michael Constantine

52. "To Walk Like a Lion" (2-28-62) Orson Bean, Karen Steele, Barbara Barrie

53. "Today the Man Who Kills the Ants Is Coming" (3-7-62) Milt Kamen, John Larch, Geraldine Fitzgerald

54. "A Run for the Money" (3-14-62) Lois Nettleton, Eli Wallach, Keenan Wynn

55. "The One Marked Hot Gives Cold" (3-21-62) Madeleine Sherwood, Robert Duvall

56. "Without Stick or Sword" (3-28-62) William Shatner, Martin Balsam

57. "Lament for a Dead Indian" (4-11-62) Neville Brand, Peter Falk

58. "The Sweetly Smiling Face of Truth" (4-25-62) Nina Foch, Patrick O'Neal

59. "And If Any Are Frozen, Warm Them" (5-9-62) Nehemiah Persoff, Akim Tamiroff, Lilia Skala

60. "Strike a Statue" (5-16-62) George C. Scott, Lois Smith

61. "The Multiplicity of Herbert Konish" (5-23-62) David Wayne, Nancy Marchand

62. "The King of Venus Will Take Care of You" (5-30-62) Jack Warden, Barbara Baxley, Mike McGreevey

63. "The Rydecker Case" (6-6-62) Martin Gabel, Kathryn Hays,

Michael Tolan
64. "Memory of a Red Trolley Car" (6-13-62) Beatrice Straight, Barry Morse, Gladys Cooper
65. "Goodbye Mama, Hello Auntie Maud" (6-20-62) Salome Jens, James Coburn
66. "Daughter, Am I in My Father's House?" (6-27-62) Dan Duryea, Barbara Harris, Joe Silver, Marco St. John

Third Season

67. "Hold for Gloria Christmas" (9-19-62) Hershel Bernardi, Burgess Meredith, Eileen Heckart, Sanford Meisner
68. "Idylls of a Running Back" (9-26-62) Sandy Dennis, Aldo Ray, Joe Silver
69. "And by the Sweat of Thy Brow" (10-10-62) Richard Jordan, Michael Gorrin, Barbara Barrie
70. "Kill Me While I'm Young So I Can Die Happy" (10-17-62) Maureen Stapleton, Carl Byrd, Rosetta Veneziani
71. "Five Cranks for Winter ... Ten Cranks for Spring" (10-24-62) Hershel Bernardi, Robert Duvall, Shirley Knight, Ludwig Donath
72. "So Fight City Hall" (10-31-62) Joseph Buloff, George Rose, Sally Gracie
73. "Torment Him Much and Hold Him Long" (11-7-62) Robert Duvall, Barbara Loden, Dan Morgan, Sandy Barron, Jesse White, Alfred Ryder
74. "Make It Fifty Dollars and Add Love to Nona" (11-14-62) Luther Adler, Ed Begley, Alex Viespi, Roxanne Arlen
75. "A Horse Has a Big Head--Let Him Worry!" (11-21-62) Diahann Carroll, John Megna, Audrey Lindley
76. "Dust Devil on a Quiet Street" (11-28-62) Richard Basehart, Robert Walker Jr., Peter Helm
77. "The Virtues of Madame Douvay" (12-5-62) Chana Eden, Denise Darcel, Claude Dauphin, Nico Minardos
78. "King Stanislaus and the Knights of the Round Table" (12-12-62) Jack Klugman, John Larch, Joanna Merlin
79. "Spectre of the Rose Street Gang" (12-19-62) Bethel Leslie, Carroll O'Connor, Jack Warden, Roger C. Carmel
80. "Don't Knock It Till You've Tried It" (12-26-62) Walter Matthau, Pat Englund, Sally Gracie
81. "Her Life in Moving Pictures" (1-2-63) Eileen Heckart, Bradford Dillman, House Jameson, Frances Heflin
82. "Robin Hood and Clarence Darrow, They Went Out with Bow and Arrow" (1-9-63) Eddie Albert, Paul O'Keefe, Ronnie Walken
83. "The Apple Falls Not Far from the Tree" (1-23-63) Keir Dullea, Louise Platt, Alexander Scourby, Roy Poole
84. "Beyond This Place There Be Dragons" (1-30-63) Frank Gorshin, Val Avery, Sorrell Booke, Hilda Brawner, Richard Shepard
85. "A Man Without a Skin" (2-6-63) Gabriel Dell, George Segal, Dana Elcar, Barbara Hayes
86. "Bringing Far Places Together" (2-20-63) Alejandro Rey,

Coco Ramirez, Victor Gabriel Junquera
87. "The Highest of Prizes" (2-27-63) Robert Culp, Akim Tamiroff, Joanne Linville
88. "Alive and Still a Second Lieutenant" (3-6-63) Robert Sterling, Jon Voight, Hilda Brawner
89. "Stop the Parade!, A Baby Is Crying!" (3-20-63) Jack
Klugman, Diana Hyland, James Patterson, Alex Viespi
90. "On the Battlefront, Every Minute Is Important" (3-27-63)
David Janssen, Kurt Kasznar, Leonardo Cimino, Margaret
O'Neill
91. "Howard Running Bear Is a Turtle" (4-3-63) Piper Laurie,
Juano Hernandez, Perry Lopez, Felice Orlandi
92. "No Naked Ladies in Front of Giovanni's House!" (4-17-63)
Harry Guardino, Marissa Pavan, Al Lewis
93. "Carrier" (4-24-63) Sandy Dennis, Bruce Gordon, Peter
Morelli
94. "Color Schemes Like Never Before" (5-1-63) Lou Antonio,
Carol Rossen, Neva Patterson, Johnny Seven, Gene Roche
95. "The S.S. American Dream" (5-8-63) Madeleine Sherwood,
John Larch, Gretchen Wyler, Roger C. Carmel, Percy
Rodriguez
96. "One, Two, Three, Rita Rakahowski" (5-15-63) Nehemiah
Persoff, Carol Rossen, Anthony Franciosa, Alice Ghostley
97. "Golden Lads and Girls" (5-22-63) Elizabeth Allen, Tom
Bosley, Robert Webber, Mike Kellin, Norma Connolly,
Murray Matheson
98. "Barefoot on a Bed of Coals" (5-29-63) Steven Hill, Zohra
Lampert, Elizabeth Allen, Henry Kascoe


THE OUTLAWS

Not in the usual western mold was this weekly confessional
by an illustrious lawbreaker who owed his downfall to the skill of
Oklahoma Marshal Frank Caine (Barton MacLane).

The Regulars: Marshal Frank Caine, Barton MacLane; Deputy Will
Foreman, Don Collier; Deputy Heck Martin, Jock Gaynor;
Deputy Chalk Breeson, Bruce Yarnell (joined in second
season).

The Episodes:

1. "Thirty a Month" (9-29-60) Steve Forrest, Robert Culp
2. "Ballad for a Badman" (10-6-60) Cliff Robertson, Madlyn
Rhue, Charles Aidman, Paul Hartman, Patricia Breslin
3. "Beat the Drum Slowly" (10-20-60) Vic Morrow, Dean Jones
4. "Rape of Red Sky" (10-27-60) Skip Homeier, Gerald Mohr,
Jackie Coogan, Leo Gordon
5. "Shorty" (11-3-60) Alfred Ryder, Hampton Fancher
6. "Last Chance" (11-10-60) Jack Mullaney, John Larch, Ellen
Willard

7. "Starfall" [Part I] (11-24-60) William Shatner, John Hoyt, Adam Williams, David White, Edgar Buchanan, Pippa Scott, Paul Richards, Jack Warden
8. "Starfall" [Part II] (12-1-60) as above
9. "The Fortune Stone" (12-15-60) Gerald Mohr, Dianne Foster, Edward Atienza
10. "The Quiet Killer" (12-29-60) Gene Evans
11. "The Waiting Game" (1-19-61) Alan Hale, Edward Andrews, Larry Gates, Fred Beir
12. "The Daltons Must Die" [Part I] (1-26-61) Larry Pennell, Joan Evans, Robert Lansing, Charles Carlson, Chris Robinson
13. "The Daltons Must Die" [Part II] (2-2-61) as above
14. "Assassin" (2-9-61) Dean Stockwell, Kevin Hagen, Jennifer West
15. "Culley" (2-16-61) Henry Hull, James Coburn, John Milford, Sue Ane Langdon
16. "The Bill Doolin Story" (3-2-61) Joe Maross, Jean Allison, Jacques Aubuchon, Wright King
17. "The Bell" (3-9-61) Simon Oakland, Jack Lord, John Howard
18. "No More Pencils--No More Books" (3-16-61) David Wayne, Tom Gilson
19. "Blind Spot" (3-30-61) Gary Merrill, Roger Mobley
20. "Outrage at Pawnee Bend" (4-6-61) Paul Ford, Frank McHugh, Jonathan Harris
21. [unknown title] (4-13-61) Vic Morrow, Jeanette Nolan, Martin Landau, Randy Sparks
22. "The Sooner" (4-27-61) Cesare Danova, Stacy Harris, James Chandler, Joan Tetzel
23. "Sam Bass" (5-4-61) Jack Chaplain, Dennis Patrick
24. "The Brothers" (5-11-61) Richard Rust, Charles Briggs, Christine White, Jim Davis
25. "The Little Colonel" (5-18-61) Ralph Manza, Craig Curtis, Rafael Campos
26. "Return to New March" (6-22-61) Julie Adams, Preston Foster

Second Season

27. "Chalk's Lot" (10-5-61) David White
28. "The Connie Masters Story" (10-12-61) Cliff Robertson, Judy Lewis
29. "My Friend, the Horse Thief" (10-19-61) Brian Keith
30. "The Cut Pups" (10-26-61) Ray Walston
31. "Night Riders" (11-2-61) Dick York
32. "The Brathwaite Brothers" (11-9-61) Lonny Chapman
33. "Walk Tall" (11-16-61) Paul Carr
34. "Roly" (11-23-61) David Wayne
35. "No Luck on Friday" (11-30-61) Vic Morrow
36. "The Outlaw Marshals" (12-14-61) Myron McCormick
37. "Masterpiece" (12-21-61) Walter Slezak
38. "The Dark Sunrise of Griff Kincaid" (1-4-62) Cliff Robertson,

Elisha Cook
39. "The Verdict" (1-18-62) Pippa Scott, Russell Thorsen, Jan Merlin
40. "Buck Breeson Rides Again" (1-25-62) Lloyd Nolan
41. "A Bit of Glory" (2-1-62) Eli Wallach
42. "Horse of a Similar Color" (2-8-62) Tony Terry
43. "The Sisters" (2-15-62) Olive Sturgess, Gina Gillespie, Jackie Coogan
44. "A Day to Kill" (2-22-62) Alejandro Rey
45. "No More Horses" (3-1-62) Richard Long
46. "Ride the Man Down" (3-8-62) Henry Jones
47. "Farewell Performance" (3-15-62) Myron McCormick
48. "Charge!" (3-22-62) Claude Akins, Frank De Kova


THE WITNESS

David Susskind's excellent blend of drama and documentary in which a celebrated reprobate of the past was made to appear before a simulated congressional panel composed of actual attorneys.

The Regulars: Real-life lawyers Richard Steel, William F. X. Geoghan Jr. , Charles Haydon, and Benedict Ginsberg portray congressional panel members. Verne Collett plays the reporter for the hearings.

The Episodes:

1. "Lucky Luciano" (9-29-60) Telly Savalas, Anita Dangler
2. "Huey P. Long" (10-6-60) Clifton James, William Hanson, Vincent Gardenia
3. "Arnold Rothstein" (10-20-60) David J. Stewart, Fred J. Scollay
4. "Benjamin (Bugsy) Siegel" (10-27-60) Larry Blyden
5. "Roger (The Terrible) Touhy" (11-3-60) Myron McCormick
6. "James M. Curley" (11-20-60) Arthur O'Connell
7. "Mayor James J. Walker" (11-17-60) Murray Hamilton
8. "Lieutenant Charles Becker" (11-24-60) Nehemiah Persoff
9. [unknown title] (12-8-60)
10. " 'Legs' Diamond" (12-15-60)
11. "Kid Twist" (12-22-60) Peter Falk, William Smithers
12. "Dutch Schultz" (12-29-60) Lillian Roth, Val Avery, Lonny Chapman
13. "James J. Hines" (1-5-61) Albert Dekker
14. "Ma Barker" (1-12-61) Joan Blondell, William Smithers
15. "John Herbert Dillinger" (1-19-61)
16. "Shoeless Joe Jackson" (1-26-61) Biff McGuire, Royal Beal

DAN RAVEN

Tedious detective yarn straining through the neuroses of several Hollywood types against its Sunset Strip locale and featuring Skip Homeier in the lead as Dan Raven.

The Regulars: Lieutenant Detective Dan Raven, Skip Homeier; Detective Sergeant Burke, Dan Barton; Perrey Levitt, Quinn Redeker.

The Episodes:

1.  "The High Cost of Fame" (9-23-60) Bobby Darin (as himself); Corey Allen, Richard Carlyle
2.  "The Mechanic" (9-30-60) Buddy Hackett, Eddie Ryder
3.  "L. A. 46" (10-14-60) Asa Maynor
4.  "Penny" (10-28-60) Gogi Grant, Paul Richards
5.  "The Empty Frame" (11-4-60)
6.  "The Night Is Numbered" (11-11-60) Kent Smith, Bob Crewe (as himself)
7.  "Japanese Sandbag" (11-18-60) Theodore Marcuse, Leo Gordon
8.  "The Junket" (11-25-60) Mel Torme, Dick Whittinghill (a Los Angeles radio announcer as himself)
9.  "Man on the Ledge" (12-2-60) Paul Winchell, Allen Pinson, Rita Lynn
10. "Amateur Night" (12-9-60) Jan Arvan, Sid Tomack, Asa Maynor, Marty Ingels
11. "Tinge of Red" (12-16-60) Julie London, Gavin MacLeod, Judson Pratt
12. "The Satchel Man" (12-30-60) Paul Anka (as himself), Parley Baer, Marty Ingels, Jocelyn Somers, Richard Bakalyan, Enid Janes
13. "Buy a Nightmare" (1-6-61) Claude Johnson, Harvey Lembeck, Tony Call


ROUTE 66

Stirling Silliphant's downbeat tale of two cross-country drifters, Tod Stiles (Martin Milner) and Buz Murdock (George Maharis) --the latter subsequently replaced by Glenn Corbett as Linc Case.

The Regulars: Tod Stiles, Martin Milner; Buz Murdock, George Maharis; Linc Case, Glenn Corbett (last season only).

The Episodes:

1.  "Black November" (10-7-60) Patty McCormack, Everett Sloane
2.  "A Lance of Straw" (10-14-60) Thomas Gomez, Janice Rule, Nico Minardos

3. "The Swan Bed" (10-21-60) Zina Bethune, Betty Field, Murray Hamilton, Henry Hull
4. "The Man on the Monkey Board" (10-28-60) Lew Ayres, Alfred Ryder, Frank Overton
5. "The Strengthening Angels" (11-4-60) Suzanne Pleshette, Warren Stevens, John Larch, Harry Townes
6. "Ten Drops of Water" (11-11-60) Burt Brinckerhoff, Deborah Walley
7. "Three Sides of a Coin" (11-18-60) E. G. Marshall, Joey Heatherton, Stephen Boister
8. "Legacy for Lucia" (11-25-60) Jay C. Flippen, Arline Sax
9. "Layout at Glen Canyon" (12-2-60) Charles McGraw, Bethel Leslie
10. "The Beryllium Eater" (12-9-60) Inger Stevens, Edgar Buchanan, Edward Binns
11. "A Fury Slinging Flame" (12-30-60) Leslie Nielsen, Conrad Nagel, James Brown, Fay Spain
12. "Sheba" (1-6-61) Lee Marvin, Whitney Blake
13. "The Quick and the Dead" (1-13-61) Regis Toomey, Susan Kohner, Betsy Jones-Moreland, Frank Overton
14. "Play It Glissando" (1-20-61) Jack Lord, Anne Francis
15. "The Clover Throne" (1-27-61) Jack Warden, Anne Helm, Arthur Batanides
16. "Fly Away Home" [Part I] (2-10-61) Michael Rennie, Dorothy Malone, Cathy Lewis, Jenny Maxwell
17. "Fly Away Home" [Part II] (2-17-61) as above
18. "Sleep on Four Pillows" (2-24-61) Patty McCormack, Larry Gates, John Beradino, Marianne Stewart
19. "An Absence of Tears" (3-3-61) Wilfrid Hyde-White, Martha Hyer, Mary Webster, Rin Tin Tin
20. "Like a Motherless Child" (3-17-61) Sylvia Sidney
21. "Effigy in Snow" (3-24-61) Scott Marlowe, Jeanne Bal, Kurt Kreuger
22. "Eleven, the Hard Way" (4-7-61) Walter Matthau, Edward Andrews, Guy Raymond
23. "Most Vanquished, Most Victorious" (4-14-61) Beatrice Straight, Royal Dano, Frank De Kova
24. "Don't Count Stars" (4-28-61) Dan Duryea, Susan Melvin
25. "The Newborn" (5-5-61) Robert Duvall, Albert Dekker, Arline Sax, Whitney Blake
26. "A Skill for Hunting" (5-12-61) Gene Evans, Joanna Moore, Harold J. Stone
27. "Trap at Cordova" (5-26-61) Thomas Gomez, Dianne Foster
28. "The Opponent" (6-2-61) Darren McGavin, Lois Nettleton, Edward Asner
29. "Welcome to Amity" (6-9-61) Susan Oliver, Martha Scott
30. "Incident on a Bridge" (6-16-61) Alexis Smith, Nehemiah Persoff, Lois Smith

## Second Season

31. "A Month of Sundays" (9-22-61) Anne Francis, Conrad Nagel, Betty Garde

32. "Blue Murder" (9-29-61) Suzanne Pleshette, Harry Townes, Claude Akins
33. "Good Night, Sweet Blues" (10-6-61) Ethel Waters, Juano Hernandez, Coleman Hawkins, Roy Eldridge
34. "Birdcage on My Foot" (10-13-61) Robert Duvall, Diane Mallory
35. "First Class Mouliak" (10-20-61) Nehemiah Persoff, Robert Redford, Martin Balsam
36. "Once to Every Man" (10-27-61) Janice Rule, Murray Matheson
37. "The Mud Nest" (11-10-61) Lon Chaney Jr. , Betty Field, Sylvia Miles
38. "Bridge Across Five Days" (11-17-61) James Dunn, Nina Foch, Jean Muir
39. "Mon Petit Chou" (11-24-61) Lee Marvin, Macha Meril
40. "Some of the People, Some of the Time" (12-1-61) Shirl Conway, Keenan Wynn, Lois Nettleton
41. "The Thin White Line" (12-8-61)
42. "And the Cat Jumped Over the Moon" (12-15-61) Martin Sheen, Jimmy Caan, Susan Silo, Milt Kamen
43. "Burning for Burning" (12-29-61) Beulah Bondi, Pat Hingle, Inger Stevens
44. "To Walk with the Serpent" (1-5-62) Dan O'Herlihy, Judson Laire
45. "A Long Piece of Mischief" (1-19-62) Albert Salmi, Ben Johnson, Slim Pickens, Audrey Totter
46. "1,800 Days to Justice" (1-26-62) DeForest Kelley, John Ericson, Noah Beery Jr. , Marion Ross
47. "A City of Wheels" (2-2-62) Bethel Leslie, Steven Hill, James Callahan
48. "How Much a Pound Is Albatross?" (2-9-62) Frank McHugh, Julie Newmar
49. "Aren't You Surprised to See Me?" (2-16-62) David Wayne, James Brown
50. "You Never Had It So Good" (2-23-62) Peter Graves, Patricia Barry
51. "Shoulder the Sky, My Lad" (3-2-62) Lili Darvas, Edward Asner
52. "Blues for the Left Foot" (3-9-62) Elizabeth Seal, Akim Tamiroff, Zack Matalon, Harvey Lembeck
53. "Go Read the River" (3-16-62) Lois Smith, John Larch, Harold Gould
54. "Even Stones Have Eyes" (3-30-62) Barbara Barrie, Paul Tripp
55. "Love Is a Skinny Kid" (4-6-62) Tuesday Weld, Burt Reynolds, Cloris Leachman, Margaret Phillips
56. "Kiss the Maiden, All Forlorn" (4-13-62) Douglas Fairbanks Jr. , Arthur Hill, Zina Bethune, Elena Verdugo
57. "Two on the House" (4-20-62) Ralph Meeker, Henry Silva, Patricia Smith
58. "There I Am--There I Always Am" (5-4-62) Joanna Moore, Emile Genest, Joe Queens
59. "Between Hello and Goodbye" (5-11-62) Hershel Bernardi,

Susan Oliver
60. "A Feat of Strength" (5-18-62) Jack Warden, Signe Hasso, Joe De Santis
61. "Hell Is Empty, All the Devils Are Here" (5-25-62) Peter Graves, Eva Stern
62. "From an Enchantress Fleeing" (6-1-62) Arthur O'Connell, Anne Helm, Biff Elliott, June Vincent

Third Season

63. "One Tiger to a Hill" (9-21-62) Signe Hasso, David Janssen, Laura Devon
64. "Journey to Nineveh" (9-28-62) Joe E. Brown, John Astin, Buster Keaton, Gene Raymond
65. "Man Out of Time" (10-5-62) Luther Adler, Glenda Farrell Frank McHugh, Bruce Gordon
66. "Ever Ride the Waves in Oklahoma?" (10-12-62) Jeremy Slate
67. "Voice at the End of the Line" (10-19-62) Sorrell Booke, Frank Campanella
68. "Lizard's Leg and Owlet's Wing" (10-26-62) Conrad Nagel, Peter Lorre, Lon Chaney Jr., Boris Karloff
69. "Across Walnuts and Wine" (11-2-62) Nina Foch, James Dunn, Betty Field, Robert Walker Jr.
70. "Welcome to the Wedding" (11-9-62) Rod Steiger
71. "Every Father's Daughter Must Weave Her Own" (11-16-62) Madlyn Rhue, Jack Kruschen
72. "Poor Little Kangaroo Rat" (11-23-62) Leslie Nielsen, Joanne Linville
73. "Hey Moth, Come Eat the Flame" (11-30-62) Harry Guardino, Mike Kellin
74. "Only by Cunning Glimpses" (12-7-62) Lois Smith, Theodore Bikel
75. "Where Is Chick Lorimer?, Where Has She Gone?" (12-14-62) Vera Miles, Martha Scott
76. "Give the Old Cat a Tender Mouse" (12-21-62) Julie Newmar, Robert Webber
77. "A Bunch of Lovely Pagliaccis" (1-4-63) Vivian Blaine, Barry Sullivan
78. "You Can't Pick Cotton in Tahiti" (1-11-63) Richard Basehart, Jena Engstrom
79. "A Gift for a Warrior" (1-18-63) James Whitmore
80. "Suppose I Said I Was the Queen of Spain" (2-8-63) Lois Nettleton, Robert Duvall, Harvey Korman, Philip Abbott
81. "Somehow It Gets to Be Tomorrow" (2-15-63) Martin Balsam
82. "Shall Forfeit His Dog and Ten Shillings to the King" (2-22-63) Steve Cochran, Kathleen Crowley
83. "In the Closing of a Trunk" (3-8-63) Ed Begley, Ruth Roman
84. "Fifty Miles from Home" (3-22-63) Susan Oliver, Glenn Corbett
85. "Narcissus on an Old Red Fire Engine" (3-29-63) Anne Helm, Alan Hale

86. "The Cruelest Sea of All" (4-5-63) Diane Baker, Edward Binns
87. "Peace, Pity, Pardon" (4-12-63) Michael Tolan, Alejandro Rey
88. "What a Shining Young Man Was Our Gallant Lieutenant" (4-26-63) Dick York
89. "But What Do You Do in March?" (5-3-63) Susan Kohner, Janice Rule, Guy Lombardo, Carmen Lombardo, Sammy Shore, Kay Medford
90. "Who Will Cheer My Bonnie Bride?" (5-10-63) Rip Torn, Albert Salmi
91. "Shadows of an Afternoon" (5-17-63) Ralph Meeker, Kathryn Hays, Miriam Hopkins
92. "Soda Pop and Paper Flags" (5-31-63) Chester Morris, Joseph Campanella, Alan Alda, Tom Bosley

Fourth Season

93. "Two Strangers and an Old Enemy" (9-27-63) Ray Milland, Jack Warden, Anthony Zerbe, Sessue Hayakawa
94. "Same Picture, Different Frame" (10-4-63) Joan Crawford, Patrick O'Neal, Tom Bosley
95. "Come Out, Come Out Wherever You Are" (10-11-63) Diane Baker, Lon Chaney Jr.
96. "Where Are the Sounds of Celli Brahms?" (10-18-63) Tammy Grimes, Horace MacMahon, Harry Bellaver
97. "Build Your Own House with Their Back to the Sea" (10-25-63) William Shatner, Pat Hingle
98. "And Make Thunder His Tribute" (11-1-63) J. Carrol Naish, Alfred Ryder, Lou Antonio, Michael J. Pollard
99. "The Stone Guest" (11-8-63) Jo Van Fleet, Lee Philips
100. "I Wouldn't Start from Here" (11-15-63) Parker Fennelly, Rosemary Forsyth
101. "I'm Here to Kill a King" (11-29-63) Robert Loggia, Tina Louise, Frank Campanella, Arnold Moss
102. "A Long Way from St. Louis" (12-6-63) Jessica Walter, Virginia Wing, Lynda Day, Hedley Mattingly
103. "Come Home, Greta Inger Gruenschaffen" (12-13-63) Chad Everett, Tammy Grimes
104. "93 Percent in Smiling" (12-20-63) Albert Salmi, David Howell, Susan Howell
105. "Child of a Night" (1-3-64) Sylvia Sidney, Chester Morris, Hershel Bernardi, Joanna Pettet, Percy Rodriguez, Diana Van Der Vlis
106. "Is It True There Are Poxies at the Bottom of Landfair Lake?" (1-10-64) Geoffrey Horne, Collin Wilcox
107. "Like This It Means Father---Like This--Bitter--Like This-Tiger" (1-17-64) Larry Blyden, Frances Helm
108. "Kiss the Monster, Make Him Sleep" (1-24-64) James Coburn, Linda Watkins, Barbara Mattes
109. "Cries of a Person Close to One" (1-31-64) Michael Parks
110. "Who in His Right Mind Needs a Nice Girl?" (2-7-64) Dan Frazer, Ruth McDevitt, Lee Philips, Lois Smith

111. "This Is Going to Hurt Me More Than It Hurts You" (2-14-64) Soupy Sales, Roland Winters, Lee Meriwether
112. "Follow the White Dove with the Broken Wing" (2-21-64) Lee Kinsolving, Grayson Hall, Bert Freed
113. "Where There's a Will, There's a Way" [Part I] (3-6-64) Nina Foch, Patrick O'Neal, Barbara Eden, Chill Wills, Roger C. Carmel, Alex Viespi
114. "Where There's a Will, There's a Way" [Part II] (3-13-64) as above

THE WESTERNER

Sam Peckinpah's compelling, offbeat western properly casts Brian Keith as the solitary hero Dave Blasingame. The musical score is by Hershel Burke Gilbert.

The Regulars: Dave Blasingame, Brian Keith.

The Episodes:

1. "Jeff" (9-30-60) Diana Millay, Geoffrey Toone
2. "School Days" (10-7-60) R. G. Armstrong, John Anderson, Richard Rust
3. "Brown" (10-21-60) John Dehner, Harry Swoger
4. "Mrs. Kennedy" (10-28-60) Paul Richards
5. "Dos Pinos" (11-4-60) Read Morgan, Malcolm Atterbury, Adam Williams
6. "The Courting of Libby" (11-11-60)

Episodes continued through 12/30/60]

MICHAEL SHAYNE

Undistinguished private detective yarn based in Miami Beach and featuring Richard Denning in the title role.

The Regulars: Michael Shayne, Richard Denning; Lucy Hamilton, Patricia Donahue; Tim Rourke, Jerry Paris; Will Gentry, Chief of Police, Herbert Rudley; Dick Hamilton, Gary Clarke.

The Episodes:

1. "Dolls Are Deadly" (9-30-60) Howard Caine, Jack Albertson
2. "A Night with Nora" (10-7-60) Everett Sloane, Alexis Smith
3. "Die Like a Dog" (10-14-60) Julie London
4. "Framed in Blood" (10-28-60) Lola Albright, Joe Ruskin
5. "Call for Michael Shayne" (11-4-60) Fay Spain, Eduard

Franz
6.  "Shoot the Works" (11-11-60) Philip Carey, Kent Smith
7.  "This Is It, Michael Shayne" (11-18-60) Julie Adams, Hillary Brooke
8.  "The Poison Pen Club" (11-25-60) Hugh Marlowe
9.  "Blood on Biscayne Bay" (12-2-60) Mona Freeman
10. "Murder Plays Charades" (12-9-60)
11. "Murder and the Wanton Bride" (12-16-60) Beverly Garland
12. "Death Selects the Winner" (12-23-60) Diana Millay, Howard Caine
13. "Murder in Wonderland" (12-30-60) Carolyn Kearney, Anthony Caruso
14. "Man with a Cane" (1-6-61) Thomas Gomez, Carol Rossen
15. "Spotlight on a Corpse" (1-13-61) Herbert Marshall
16. "Murder Round My Wrist" (1-20-61) Helen Hayes
17. "The Badge" (1-27-61) Ken Patterson, Milton Selzer, Joey Walsh
18. "The Heiress" (2-3-61) Lynn Bari, Susan Oliver
19. "Final Settlement" (2-10-61) Patricia Huston, Allyn Joslyn
20. "Four Lethal Ladies" (2-17-61) Roy Roberts, Grace Lee Whitney
21. "The Ancient Art of Murder" (2-24-61) Parley Baer, Gil Frye
22. "Murder at the Convention" (3-3-61) Mari Aldon, Marianne Hill
23. "Strike Out" (3-10-61) James Best, Peter Baldwin
24. "Murder Is a Fine Art" (3-17-61) Ross Martin
25. "The Body Beautiful" (3-24-61) Patricia Crowley
26. "Marriage Can Be Fatal" (3-31-61) Barbara Nichols
27. "The Boat Caper" (4-7-61) Stephen McNally, Joyce Meadows
28. "Date with Death" (4-14-61) Jack Kruschen
29. "The Trouble with Ernie" (4-21-61) Sue Randall, Dick Sharp
30. "No Shroud for Shayne" (5-5-61) James Drury, Rita Moreno
31. "It Takes a Heap O'Dyin' " (5-12-61) Jack Ging
32. "Dead Air" (5-19-61) Merry Anders, Audrey Dalton

THE LAW AND MR. JONES

Sy Gomberg's frequently well-written account of the cases taken by a vivacious and loquacious attorney, Abraham Lincoln Jones (James Whitmore). Gomberg's own "The Cooperatives" has the distinction of allowing hero Jones' imperfections to become glaringly apparent. An elderly man wishes to lease an apartment to three former convicts over the firm objections of his neighbors. "And what's your problem, Mr. Jones?," the lessor asks, when Jones initially joins forces with other apartment owners to have the former convicts removed. Frustrated by the prejudice that greeted them, the new renters vandalize the apartment building then recant offering to pay the damages. Jones comes to see the end result his prejudice, of course. But if this appears a tired theme, Gomberg's teleplay clearly wasn't, what with Jones' failings--no sacrilege here--made manifest at last.

Other regulars were Janet De Gore as Jones' secretary
Marsha Spear and Conlan Carter as law clerk C. E. Carruthers.

The Regulars: Abraham Lincoln Jones, James Whitmore; Marsha
Spear, Janet De Gore; C. E. Carruthers, Conlan Carter.

The Episodes:

1. "What's in a Name?" (10-7-60) Dennis Patrick, Franz
Roehn, Charles Drake, Carl Benton Reid, J. Pat O'Malley
2. "Music to Hurt By" (10-14-60)
3. "The Baby" (10-28-60) William Sargent, Dinah Anne Rodgers
4. "Drivel" (11-4-60) Russ Brown, Parley Baer
5. "Semper Fidelis" (11-11-60) Philip Pine
6. "The Promise of Life" (11-18-60) Liam Sullivan, Billy
Hughes
7. "The Storyville Gang" (11-25-60) Rex Ingram, Gene Benton
8. "No Sale" (12-2-60) Sam Jaffe, Robert H. Harris
9. "A Question of Guilt" (12-16-60) Beverly Washburn, Barney
Phillips, Doug Lambert
10. "Christmas Is a Legal Holiday" (12-23-60) Charity Grace,
Wesley Lau, Barbara Bain
11. "The Long Echo" (12-30-60) Lee Bergere, Nancy Marchand
12. "The Big Gambling Raid" (1-6-61) Stanley Adams, William
Fawcett, James Westerfield
13. "The Trophy" (1-13-61) Mary La Roche, Lyle Bettger
14. "Indian War" (1-20-61) Russ Brown, Susan Dorn, Bryon
Morrow
15. "Exit" (1-27-61) Robert Warwick, Jonathan Harris
16. "Unbury the Dead" (2-3-61) Paul Richards, Ralph Moody
17. "The End Justifies the End" (2-10-61) John Marley
18. "Lethal Weapons" (2-17-61) Bernie Hamilton
19. "One for the Money" (2-24-61)
20. "Cold Turkey" (3-3-61) Peter Falk, Leo Penn, Joyce Van
Patten
21. [unknown title] (3-10-61) Jack Mullaney
22. "Everybody vs. Timmy Drayton" (3-17-61) Dick Powell
23. [unknown title] (3-24-61) Vic Morrow, Joey Walsh
24. "Accidental Jeopardy" (3-31-61) Robert Middleton
25. "Mea Culpa" (4-7-61) John Bleifer, Charles Aidman
26. "A Fool for a Client" (4-21-61) Otto Kruger, Stanja Lowe
27. "The Enemy" (4-28-61) Dean Stanton
28. "One by One" (5-5-61) David Winters, Mike Parks, Gus
Trikonis, Bernard Fein
29. "The Quiet Town" (5-12-61) John Brinkley
30. "The Last Commencement" (5-19-61) Rhys Williams
31. "No Law for Ghosts" (5-26-61) Robert Gist, June Dayton
32. "The Broken Hand" (6-2-61) Sam Jaffe

## THE AMERICANS

The principals here were on opposing sides of the American Civil War.

The Regulars: Ben Canfield, Darryl Hickman; Jeff Canfield, Dick Davalos.

The Episodes:

1. "Harpers Ferry: 1861" (1-23-61) Ron Randell, John McIntire, Kenneth Tobey
2. "Rebellion at Blazing Rock" (1-30-61) Michael Rennie, John Howard, Karen Sharpe
3. "The Regular" (2-6-61) Kent Smith, John Doucette, Kathleen Crowley, Sandy Kenyon, Wynn Pearce
4. "The Rebellious Rose" (2-13-61) Nina Foch, Martin Gabel, Charles Aidman, Robert J. Wilke
5. "On to Richmond" (2-20-61) John Doucette, Diana Millay, Wynn Pearce
6. "Half Moon Road" (2-27-61) Jack Lord, James Barton, Enid Janes, George Mitchell, Susan Silo
7. "The Reconnaissance" (3-6-61) Lee Marvin, Don Megowan, Diane Jergens, Brad Weston
8. "The Escape" (3-13-61) Dan O'Herlihy, Slim Pickens, Dayton Lummis
9. "The Guerrillas" (3-20-61) Robert Culp, Berry Kroeger, Paul Lambert, Sonya Wilde
10. "The Invaders" (3-27-61) James Franciscus, Myrna Fahey, Steve Brodie, Paul Carr, Slim Pickens, Ian Wolfe
11. "The Gun" (4-3-61) Susan Oliver, Lonny Chapman, Richard Carlyle, Jack Elam
12. "The Sentry" (4-10-61) Brian Keith, Ben Cooper, Judson Pratt, Robert Hastings
13. "The Bounty Jumpers" (4-17-61) Ray Walston, Anne Helm, Larry Gates, Gene Lyons
14. "The Long Way Back" (4-24-61) Charles Bickford, Patricia Barry, Walter Sande
15. "The War Between the States" (5-1-61) Dick York, Lisabeth Hush, John McGiver, Lloyd Bochner, Lurene Tuttle
16. "The Coward" (5-8-61) Robert Redford, Carroll O'Connor, Jackie Coogan, L. Q. Jones
17. "The Inquisitors" (5-15-61) Marsha Hunt, Robert Middleton, Kent Smith, Robert Gist

## THE GUNSLINGER

Moody, "adult" post-Civil War western of a cavalry agent (Tony Young as "Cord") and his commander, Captain Zachary Wingate (Preston Foster).

The Regulars: Cord, Tony Young; Captain Zachary Wingate, Preston Foster; Pico McGuire, Charles Gray; Billy Urchin, Dee Pollock.

The Episodes:

1. "Border Incident" (2-9-61) Royal Dano, Fay Spain
2. "The Hostage Fort" (2-16-61) Jack Elam, Jena Engstrom, Vaughn Taylor
3. "Appointment in Cascabel" (2-23-61) Anthony Caruso, Midge Ware
4. "The Zone" (3-2-61) Addison Richards, Sandy Kenyon, Anne Graves
5. "Rampage" (3-16-61) Jock Mahoney, Jan Shepard, Lew Gallo
6. "The Recruit" (3-23-61) Gene Evans, John Howard
7. "Road of the Dead" (3-30-61) Mari Blanchard, Paul Lambert, Carlos Romero
8. "Golden Circle" (4-13-61) Buddy Ebsen, John Hoyt
9. "The Diehards" (4-20-61) Lloyd Corrigan, Arlene Sax
10. "Johnny Sergeant" (5-4-61) Jock Gaynor, Phyllis Coates, Sonya Wilde
11. "The Death of Yellow Singer" (5-11-61) Henry Brandon, Barbara Luna
12. "The New Savannah Story" (5-18-61) Dorothy Green, Anne Helm, Frank De Kova


## ACAPULCO

In this "Klondike" metamorphosis, not only the locale evident by the title has changed, so have the principals--Ralph Taeger and James Coburn becoming beachcombers Patrick Malone and Gregg Miles.

The Regulars: Patrick Malone, Ralph Taeger; Gregg Miles, James Coburn; Attorney (retired) Carver, Telly Savalas; Chloe (bar hostess), Allison Hayes; Bobby (night club owner), Bobby Troup.

The Episodes:

1. "Bell's Half Acre" (2-27-61) Leslie Parrish
2. "The Gentleman from Brazil" (3-13-61) Martin Landau, Alan Hale Jr., Diane Cannon, Robert Cornthwaite
3. [unknown title] (3-20-61) Joanna Barnes, Grace Lee Whitney, Russell Collins
4. [unknown title] (3-27-61) James Dunn, Myrna Fahey, Ron Hayes, Ben Young
5. "Fisher's Daughter" (4-3-61) George Kennedy, Jan Harrison
6. "Blood Money" (4-10-61) Michael Pate, Audrey Dalton

[Episodes continued through 4/24/61]

'WAY OUT

Sumner Locke Elliott ("I Heard You Calling Me"), Roald Dahl ("William and Mary"), and Irving Gaynor Neiman ("Dissolve to Black") were among the high calibre writers whose suspense tales formed this anthology series, very much in the tradition of Rod Serling's "The Twilight Zone."

The Episodes:

1. "William and Mary" (3-31-61)
2. [unknown title] (4-7-61)
3. "The Sisters" (4-14-61) Lois Smith, Carmen Mathews
4. "Button, Button" (4-28-61) Warren Finnerty, Dick O'Neill
5. "I Heard You Calling Me" (5-5-61) Constance Ford, Anthony Dawson
6. "The Croaker" (5-12-61) John McGiver, Richard Thomas
7. "False Face" (5-26-61) Alfred Ryder, Martin Brooks
8. "Dissolve to Black" (6-2-61) Kathleen Widdoes
9. "Death Wish" (6-9-61) Charlotte Rae, Don Keefer
10. "The Overnight Case" (6-16-61) Martin Balsam, Barbara Baxley, Kevin McCarthy
11. "Hush, Hush" (6-23-61) Woodrow Parfrey, Barry Newman, Rosemary Murphy
12. "Side Show" (6-30-61) Myron McCormick, Margaret Phillips
13. "Soft Focus" (7-7-61) Barry Morse, Joan Hotchkis
14. "20/20" (7-14-61) Walter Slezak, Ruth White


THE ASPHALT JUNGLE

Not up to par with its splendid 1950 John Huston film predecessor from the novel by W. R. Burnett is this nonetheless grim police detective drama--Robert Vaughn excellent as the Nazi advocate of the concluding teleplay.

The Regulars: Deputy Police Commissioner Matthew Gower, Jack Warden; Captain Gus Honochek, Arch Johnson; Sergeant Danny Keller, Bill Smith.

The Episodes:

1. "The Burglary Ring" (4-2-61) John Harmon, James Westerfield
2. "The Lady and the Lawyer" (4-9-61) Vera Miles
3. "The Friendly Gesture" (4-16-61) Milton Selzer, George Kennedy
4. "The Gomez Affair" (4-23-61) Everett Sloane
5. "The Sniper" (4-30-61) Leo Penn, Michael Parks, Virginia Christine
6. "The Last Way Out" (5-7-61) John Ireland
7. "The McMasters Story" (5-14-61) Erin O'Brien

8.  "The Nine-Twenty Hero" (5-21-61) Skip Homeier
9.  "The Professor" (5-28-61) Milton Selzer, Frank Overton
0.  "The Fighter" (6-4-61) Gerald O'Laughlin, Michael Constantine
1.  "The Kidnapping" (6-11-61) Paul Stewart, Alexander Scourby
2.  'Dark Night" (6-18-61) Fritz Weaver, Joyce Meadows, Morgan Woodward
3.  "The Scott Machine" (6-25-61) Robert Vaughn, Leora Dana


ANGER MAN

Patrick McGoohan's first outing as security agent John Drake; restrained, literate espionage yarn.

The Regulars: John Drake, Patrick McGoohan.

The Episodes:

1.  "Handcuffed" (4-5-61)
2.  [unknown title] (4-12-61)
3.  "The Lonely Chair" (4-19-61) Sam Wanamaker
4.  "The Sisters" (4-26-61) Mai Zetterling
5.  [unknown title] (5-3-61)
6.  "View from the Villa" (5-10-61) Barbara Shelley, John Lee, Delphi Lawrence, Colen Douglas
7.  "The Conspirators" (5-17-61) Terrance Logdon, Hugh Money
8.  "The Journey Ends Halfway" (5-24-61) Paul Daneman, Anna May Wong, Willoughby Goddard, Paul Hardmuth
9.  "Vacation" (5-31-61) Jacqueline Ellis, Barrie Ingham, Esmond Knight, Lawrence Davidson
10. "The Lovers" (6-7-61) Michael Ripper, Ewen Solon, Maxine Audley, Martin Miller
.   "The Brothers" (6-14-61) Lisa Gastoni, Ronald Fraser, Derren Nesbitt, John Woodvine, George Coulouris
2.  "The Girl Who Likes G.I.s" (6-21-61) Anna Gaylor, Nigel Green, Anthony Busheli
.   "The Nurse" (6-28-61) Eileen Moore, Robert Ayres, Jock McGowran, Harold Kasket, Eric Pohlmann, Heather Chasen
.   "Position of Trust" (7-5-61) Lois Maxwell, Irene Prador, Donald Pleasence, John Phillips
.   "The Gallows Tree" (7-12-61) Paul Rogers, Wendy Craig, Raymond Huntley
.   "The Sanctuary" (7-19-61) Kieron Moore, Wendy Williams, Barry Keegan, Charles Farrell
.   [unknown title] (7-26-61) Lee Montague, Ronald Allen
.   "The Leak" (8-2-61) Zena Marshall, Bernard Archard
.   [unknown title] (8-9-61) Jeanne Moody, Marie Burke, Noel Trevarthen, Alan Gifford
.   "The Key" (8-16-61) Robert Flemying, Monique Ahrend, Charles Gray, Charles Carson, Peter Swanwick
.   "Find and Return" (8-23-61) Moira Lister, Richard Wattis,

Donald Pleasence, Paul Stussino
22. "Deadline" (8-30-61) William Marshall, Barbara Chilcott, Christopher Carlos, Erdic Connor
23. "The Island" (9-6-61) Allen Cuthbertson, Peter Stephens, Ann Firbank, Michael Ripper
24. "The Girl in Pink Pajamas" (9-13-61) Angela Browne, Alan Tilvern, John Crawford, Robert Raglan

## WHISPERING SMITH

Cumbersome western, essentially an anachronistic detective yarn, with Audie Murphy as the sleuth Tom Smith.

The Regulars: Detective Tom Smith, Audie Murphy; Detective George Romack, Guy Mitchell; Chief John Richards, Sam Buffington.

The Episodes:

1. "The Blind Gun" (5-8-61) Jan Merlin, Earl Hansen, Robert Osterloh
2. "The Grudge" (5-15-61) Robert Redford, June Walker, Gloi Talbott
3. "The Devil's Share" (5-22-61) Clu Gulager, Rosemary Day James Lydon
4. "Stakeout" (5-29-61) John Cliff, Troy Melton, Joyce Taylor
5. "Safety Value" (6-5-61) Della Sharman, Les Tremayne, Harry Carey Jr.
6. "Stain of Justice" (6-12-61) Richard Chamberlain, Patric Knowles, Nancy Valentine
7. "The Deadliest Weapon" (6-19-61) Aline Towne, Paul Lees Bartlett Robinson, Don Keefer
8. "The Quest" (6-26-61) Ellen Willard, John Harmon
9. "Three for One" (7-3-61) Richard Crane, Ken Mayer, Roscoe Ates, Pamela Duncan
10. "Death at Even Money" (7-10-61) Marc Lawrence, Robert Lowery, John Day, Sandy Sanders, Sherwood Price
11. "The Hemp Reeger Case" (7-17-61) James Best, Patricia Medina, Edward C. Platt
12. "The Mortal Coil" (7-24-61) Henry Brandon, Hugh Sanders
13. "Cross Cut" (7-31-61) Audrey Dalton, Colin Male, Jim Hayward
14. "Double Edge" (8-7-61) Myron Healey, Lori Nelson, Read Morgan
15. "The Trademark" (8-14-61) Marie Windsor, Donald Buka, Forrest Tucker, Andrew Winberg
16. "The Jodie Tyler Story" (8-21-61) Rachel Fougler, Read Morgan, Jimmy Carter
17. "Poet and Peasant Case" (8-28-61) Alan Mowbray, Jack Catron, Yvonne Adrian
18. "Dark Circle" (9-4-61) E. J. Andre, Diana Millay, Carlet

Young, Adam Williams
19. "Swift Justice" (9-11-61) Monte Burkhart, Minerva Urecal, William Tannen
20. "The Idol" (9-18-61) Joan O'Brien, Alan Hale, John Stephenson


KRAFT MYSTERY THEATRE

The Episodes:

1. "The Professionals" (6-14-61) William Lucas, Andrew Faulds, Colette Wilde, Stratford Jones, Vilma Ann Leslie, Edward Cust, Charles Vince
2. "Deadly Record" (6-21-61) Lee Patterson, Barbara Shelley, Peter Dyneley, Jane Hylton, Geoffrey Keen, Ferdy Mayne, April Orlich
3. "Account Rendered" (6-28-61) Griffith Jones, Ursula Howells, Honor Blackman, Ewen Solon
4. "Breakout" (7-5-61) Lee Patterson, Billy Whitelaw, Hazel Court, Terence Alexander
5. "Danger Tomorrow" (7-12-61) Robert Urquhart, Zena Walker, Lisa Daniely, Rupert Davies
6. "The Hideout" (7-19-61) Ronald Howard, Dermot Walsh, Rona Anderson, Sam Kydd
7. "The White Trap" (7-26-61) Lee Patterson, Felicity Young, Conrad Phillips, Yvette Wyatt
8. "Witness in the Dark" (8-2-61) Patricia Dainton, Conrad Phillips, Madge Ryan, Enid Lorimer
9. "The Spider's Web" (8-9-61) Glynis Johns, John Justin, Jack Hulbert, Cicely Courtneidge, David Nixon
10. "House of Mystery" (8-16-61) Jane Hylton, Peter Dyneley, Nanette Newman, Maurice Kaufmann, Colin Gordon
11. "The Desperate Man" (8-23-61) Jill Ireland, Conrad Phillips, William Hartnell
12. "The House of Rue Riviera" (8-30-61) Jayne Mansfield, Diana Trask, John Ericson, Richard Anderson
13. "Flight from Treason" (9-6-61) John Gregson, Ian Hendry, Robert Brown, Avril Elgar
14. "Port of Revenge" (9-13-61) Dan O'Herlihy, Francoise Prevost, Maurice Teymas
15. "The Third Alibi" (9-20-61) Laurence Payne, Patricia Dainton, Ian Griffiths
16. "Death and the Sky Above" (9-27-61) Peter Williams, Petra Davies

Second Season

17. "In Close Pursuit" (6-13-62) Beverly Garland, Jan Sterling, William Windom
18. "Death of a Dream" (6-20-62) Robert Vaughn, Dianne

Foster, Sherwood Price
19. "Perilous" [repeat of "Desilu Playhouse" episode of 6/22/59] (6-27-62)
20. "Dead on Nine" (7-4-62) Louis Hayward, Signe Hasso, Leo G. Carroll, Audrey Dalton
21. "Two Counts of Murder" (7-11-62) Raymond Massey, David Janssen, Whitney Blake, Robert Emhardt, Lawrence Dobkin
22. "Night Panic" (7-18-62) Cloris Leachman, John Ericson, Marion Ross, Gordon Jones, S. John Launer
23. "Murder Is a Private Affair" [repeat of "Desilu Playhouse" episode of 6/10/60] (7-25-62)
24. "Sound of Murder" (8-1-62) Alex Davion, Liam Redmond, Antoinette Bower, Ronald Long
25. "Chez Rouge" [repeat of "Desilu Playhouse" episode of 2/16/59] (8-8-62)
26. "Cry Ruin" (8-15-62) Keir Dullea, Larry Gates, Richard Anderson, Ellen McRae, Denver Pyle, Robert F. Simon, Leonard Stone
27. "Thunder in the Night" [repeat of "Desilu Playhouse" episode of 2/19/60] (8-22-62)
28. "The Problem in Cell 13" (8-29-62) Everett Sloane, Claude Dauphin, Philip Pine, June Walker, Joseph Ruskin
29. "The Night the Phone Rang" [repeat of "Desilu Playhouse" episode of 12/15/58] (9-5-62)
30. "Change of Heart" (9-12-62) Robert Middleton, Donald May, Russ Conway, Evans Evans, Dick Sargent, Allison Hayes, Karl Swenson
31. "Murder in Gratitude" [repeat of "Desilu Playhouse" episode of 12/11/59] (9-19-62)
32. "Circle of Evil" [repeat of "Desilu Playhouse" episode of 3/18/60] (9-26-62)

Third Season

33. "Shadow of a Man" (6-19-63) Broderick Crawford, Jack Kelly, Beverly Owen, Michael Burns, John Anderson, Berkely Harris
34. "The Image Merchants" (6-26-63) Melvyn Douglas, Macdonald Carey, Ronald Foster, Geraldine Brooks, Dianne Foster
35. "The Rules of the Game" [repeat of "Alcoa Premiere" episode of 5/1/62] (7-3-63)
36. "Catch Fear By the Throat" (7-10-63) Steve Forrest, Bradford Dillman, Linden Chiles
37. "The Fugitive Eye" [repeat of "Alcoa Premiere" episode of 10/17/61] (7-17-63)
38. "The Fortress" [repeat of "Alcoa Premiere" episode of 10/24/61] (7-24-63)
39. "Of Struggle and Flight" [repeat of "Alcoa Premiere" episode of 3/28/63] (7-31-63)
40. "The Boy Who Wasn't Wanted" [repeat of "Alcoa Premiere" episode of 6/5/62] (8-7-63)

41. "The Dark Labyrinth" [repeat of "Alcoa Premiere" episode of 3/21/63] (8-14-63)
42. "The Hour of the Bath" [repeat of "Alcoa Premiere" episode of 1/16/62] (8-21-63)
43. "Talk to My Partner" (8-28-63) Ray Danton, Joanna Moore
44. "Ordeal in Darkness" [repeat of "Alcoa Premiere" episode of 11/15/62] (9-4-63)
45. "Go Look at Roses" (9-11-63) John Forsythe, Lola Albright, Cathleen Nesbitt, Norman Fell


GREAT GHOST TALES

The Episodes:

1. "William Wilson" (7-6-61) Peter Brandon, Robert Duvall, Joanne Linville
2. "Lucy" (7-13-61) Lee Grant, Kevin McCarthy
3. "The Monkey's Paw" (7-20-61) Mildred Dunnock, R. G. Armstrong
4. "Bye Bye Baby" (7-27-61) Janet Ward, Collin Wilcox, David J. Stewart, Edmon Ryan
5. "August Heat" (8-3-61) James Broderick, Vincent Gardenia, Virginia Leith, Herbert Voland
6. "Summer Rental" (8-10-61) Harry Millard, Cynthia Baxter
7. "Mr. Arcularis" (8-17-61) Lois Nettleton, John Abbott
8. "Sredni Vashtar" (8-24-61) Richard Thomas, Judith Evelyn
9. "Phantom of Delight" (8-31-61) Blanche Yurka, Eric Berry, Clifford David, Anne Williams
10. "Room 13" (9-7-61) William Redfield, Diana Van Der Vlis
11. "The Wendigo" (9-14-61)
12. "Who's the Fairest One of All?" (9-21-61) Salome Jens, Arthur Hill, Ruth White

## THE DEFENDERS

Magnificent Herbert Brodkin-Reginald Rose journey through the vicissitudes of the legal process with E. G. Marshall and Robert Reed as the father and son exemplary defense counsels. Stunning guest performances with provocative situations; glorious teleplays by veterans of the golden age, a part of which was now recalled to life.

The Regulars: Atty. Lawrence Preston, E. G. Marshall; Atty. Kenneth Preston, Robert Reed; Helen Donaldson, Polly Rowles; Joan Miller, Joan Hackett.

The Episodes:

1. "Quality of Mercy" (9-16-61) Gene Hackman, Jack Klugman, Philip Abbott, Michael Lipton
2. "Killer Instinct" (9-23-61) William Shatner
3. "Death Across the Counter" (9-30-61) Clu Gulager, Frank McHugh, Harry Townes
4. "The Riot" (10-7-61) Ossie Davis, Fritz Weaver
5. "Young Lovers" (10-14-61) Lynn Loring, Burt Brinckerhoff
6. "The Boy Between" (10-21-61) Ilka Chase, Arthur Hill, Norma Crane
7. "The Hundred Lives of Harry Simms" (10-28-61) Sam Wanamaker, Frank Gorshin, Frank Overton
8. "The Accident" (11-4-61) Evans Evans, Lonnie Chapman
9. "The Trial of Jenny Scott" (11-11-61) Pat Hingle, Mary Fickett
10. "The Man with the Concrete Thumb" (11-18-61)
11. "The Treadmill" (11-25-61) Leora Dana, Judson Laire, Alfred Ryder, Edward Binns
12. "Perjury" (12-2-61) Robert Duvall, Robert Loggia
13. "The Attack" (12-9-61) Richard Kiley, Martin Sheen, Nancy Marchand
14. "The Prowler" (12-16-61) Zohra Lampert, Kent Smith, Elizabeth Ashley
15. "Gideon's Follies" (12-23-61) Shirl Conway, Julie Newmar, Zohra Lampert
16. "The Best Defense" (12-30-61) Martin Balsam, Edward Andrews

17. "The Bedside Murder" (1-6-62) Murray Hamilton, Sam Jaffe, Alexander Scourby
18. "The Search" (1-20-62) Jack Klugman, Judson Laire, James Congdon, Harry Millard
19. "Storm at Birch Glen" (1-27-62) James Broderick, Dolores Sutton
20. "The Point Shaver" (2-3-62) Andrew Prine, Paul Prokop
21. "The Locked Room" (2-10-62) Viveca Lindfors, Inga Swenson, Zachary Scott
22. "The Empty Chute" (2-17-62) Neva Patterson, Chester Morris
23. "The Crusader" (2-24-62) Warren Stevens, Alan Bunce, Ronald Winters, Anne Meacham
24. "The Hickory Indian" (3-3-62) George Voskovec, Larry Gates
25. "The Iron Man" (3-10-62) Ben Piazza
26. "The Tarnished Cross" (3-17-62) Martin Sheen, Biff McGuire
27. "The Last Six Months" (3-31-62) Arthur Hill, Louisa Horton
28. "The Naked Heiress" (4-7-62) Glenda Farrell, Conrad Nagel, Salome Jens
29. "Reunion with Death" (4-21-62) Robert Webber
30. "The Benefactor" (4-28-62) Judson Laire, Robert F. Simon
31. "Along Came a Spider" (5-5-62) Paul Hartman
32. "The Broken Barrelhead" (5-26-62) Harold J. Stone

## Second Season

33. "The Voices of Death" (9-15-62) Judson Laire, Ruth Roman, J. D. Cannon
34. "Blood Country" (9-22-62) James Broderick, James Olsen
35. "The Indelible Silence" (9-29-62) Shepperd Strudwick, Dennis Hopper
36. "The Seven Ghosts of Simon Gray" (10-6-62) Ed Begley, Barbara Baxley
37. "The Unwanted" (10-13-62) Diana Hyland, Milton Selzer
38. "Madman" [Part I] (10-20-62) John Beal, Sylvia Sidney, Don Gordon
39. "Madman" [Part II] (10-27-62) as above
40. "The Bigamist" (11-3-62) Jason Evers
41. "The Avenger" (11-17-62) Murray Hamilton, Ludwig Donath, Peter Von Zerneck
42. "The Invisible Badge" (11-24-62) William Shatner, Lois Smith, Joe Maross, Bert Wheeler
43. "The Hidden Jungle" (12-1-62) Jean Stapleton, Carroll O'Connor, Frank Overton
44. "The Savage Infant" (12-8-62) Juano Hernandez, John Costopoulos
45. "The Apostle" (12-15-62) John Kerr, Albert Salmi
46. "Grandma TNT" (12-22-62) Lillian Gish, Enid Markey
47. "Don't Take the Stand" (12-29-62) Jeremy Slate
48. "Kill or Be Killed" (1-5-63) Joanne Linville, Simon Oakland, Gerald S. O'Loughlin

49. "Man Against Himself" (1-12-63) Marc Connelly, Ivan Dixon
50. "The Poisoned Fruit Doctrine" (1-19-63) Stuart Erwin, Virginia Gilmore
51. "Poltergeist" (1-26-63) Mary Astor, Patrick O'Neal
52. "Ordeal" (2-2-63) Robert Webber
53. "The Hour Before Doomsday" (2-9-63) Kevin McCarthy
54. "The Traitor" (2-16-63) Fritz Weaver, Tim O'Connor
55. "The Eye of Fear" (2-23-63) Robert Loggia
56. "Metamorphosis" (3-2-63) Ossie Davis, Robert Duvall
57. "The Last Illusion" (3-9-63) James Farentino, Betsy Von Furstenberg, Frank Silvera
58. "The Heathen" (3-23-63) Gerald Hiken
59. "A Book for Burning" (3-30-63) Walter Abel, Alexander Scourby
60. "A Taste of Vengeance" (4-6-63) Ann Harding, Marc Connelly, Edward Binns, Collin Wilcox
61. "The Colossus" (4-13-63) Leo Genn
62. "Judgment Eve" (4-20-63) Gene Hackman
63. "The Noose" (4-27-63) Bruce Gordon, Larry Hagman
64. "Everybody Else Is Dead" (5-11-63) Geraldine Brooks, Darren McGavin
65. "The Trial of Twenty-Two" (5-18-63) Lilia Skala, Akim Tamiroff
66. "The Brother Killers" (5-25-63) Gene Raymond, Peter Fonda, Conrad Nagel, Jon Voight

Third Season

67. "The Weeping Baboon" (9-28-63) Dennis Hopper, Judson Laire, Edward Binns, Michael Strong
68. "The Empty Heart" (10-5-63) Murray Hamilton, Lee Grant, Sidney Blackmer
69. "The Captive" (10-12-63) Andrew Duggan, Mary Ficket, Ludwig Donath, Tim O'Connor, Robert Ellenstein, Dana Elcar
70. "The Bagman" (10-19-63) Howard da Silva, Chester Morris
71. "Conspiracy of Silence" (10-26-63) Jerome Olson, Janet Ward, Carroll O'Connor, Louise Sorel, Eugene Patterson
72. "The Cruel Hook" (11-2-63) William Shatner, Ed Asner
73. "Star-Spangled Ghetto" (11-9-63) Richard Jordon, Ossie Davis, Gerald Hiken, Kathleen Widdoes, Vincent Gardenia
74. "Loophole" (11-16-63) James Patterson, Harold J. Stone
75. "The Seal of Confession" (11-30-63) Robert Webber, Biff McGuire, Malachi Throne, House Jameson
76. "Climate of Evil" (12-7-63) Dean Stockwell, Nan Martin, Warren Finnerty, Roland Winters
77. "The Crowd Pleaser" (12-14-63) Stephen Brooks, Lou Antonio, Ellen Madison
78. "Old Lady Ironsides" (12-21-63) Janet Margolin, Mart Hulswit, Aline MacMahon
79. "Fugue for Trumpet and Small Boy" (12-28-63) Peter Lazer, Patrick O'Neal, Joyce Van Patten
80. "Claire Cheval Died in Boston" (1-4-64) Barbara Harris,

Barbara Baxley, Hershel Bernardi
81. "The Last Day" (1-11-64) Ralph Meeker, Larry Hagman, Richard Kiley
82. "Blacklist" (1-18-64) John Baragrey, Brett Somers, Jack Klugman, Robert Drivas, Margaret Hayes, Neva Patterson
83. "Who'll Dig His Grave?" (1-25-64) Barry Morse
84. "All the Silent Voices" (2-1-64) James Gregory, Dana Elcar, Eileen Heckart
85. "The Secret" (2-8-64) Martin Landau, Tim O'Connor, George Voskovec
86. "The Pill Man" (2-22-64) Teresa Wright, Edward Binns, Douglas Campbell
87. "Drink Like a Lady" (2-29-64) Janice Rule, J. D. Cannon, Murray Hamilton
88. "Survival" (3-14-64) Bert Convy, Leslie Nielsen, George Wallace, Peter Duryea, Billy Dee Williams
89. "Moment of Truth" (3-21-64) Jack Gilford, Norman Fell, Anne Jackson
90. "The Hidden Fury" (3-28-64) Susan Oliver, Joseph Anthony
91. "Die Laughing" (4-11-64) Milton Berle, Marsha Hunt, Jan Murray, Lynn Loring
92. "May Day! May Day!" (4-18-64) Torin Thatcher, Tim O'Connor, Skip Homeier
93. "The Thief" (4-25-64) Laurence Naismith, Glynis Johns
94. "Yankee Go Home" (5-2-64) Richard Kiley, Frank Overton
95. "The Man Who Saved His Country" (5-9-64) James Coburn,
96. "Mind Over Murder" (5-16-64) Ossie Davis, Emlyn Williams
97. "The Sixth Alarm" (5-23-64) Hershel Bernardi, Simon Oakland, Marian Seldes
98. "The Fine Line" (5-30-64) Martin Balsam, Jessica Walter, Nancy Wickwire
99. "The Non-Violent" (6-6-64) Ivan Dixon, James Earl Jones, Sam Groom, Gene Raymond
100. "Stowaway" (6-13-64) Lillian Gish, Cliff Carpenter
101. "Hollow Triumph" (6-20-64) Brenda Vaccaro, Sam Wanamaker, Nancy Marchand
102. "The Uncivil War" (6-27-64) William Shatner, Ina Balin, Diana Van Der Vlis, Milton Selzer

Fourth Season

103. "The Seven Hundred-Year-Old Gang" [Part I] (9-24-64) Jack Gilford, Tom Poston, Martin Balsam, David Doyle, Barbara Barrie
104. "The Seven Hundred-Year-Old Gang" [Part II] (10-1-64) as above
105. "Hero of the People" (10-8-64) Edward Asner, J. D. Cannon, Ann Wedgeworth, Dorrit Helton
106. "Go-Between" (10-15-64) Arthur Hill, Phyllis Thaxter, John Randolph
107. "Conflict of Interests" (10-22-64) Cloris Leachman, Marc

Connelly, Edward Woodward
108. "The Man Who" (10-29-64) Howard Da Silva, Patrick O'Neal
109. "Turning Point" (11-5-64) Martin Sheen, Ossie Davis, Alfred Ryder
110. "A Taste of Ashes" (11-12-64) Betty Field, Martin Sheen, Darren McGavin
111. "Comeback" (11-26-64) Viveca Lindfors, Charlotte Rae, Lonny Chapman
112. "The Siege" (12-3-64) Robert Redford, Jennifer West, Dan Travanty
113. "Whitewash" (12-10-64) Alan Bunce, Lonny Chapman, Ricardo Montalban, Michael Gazzo
114. "A Voice Loud and Clear" (12-17-64) Paul Stevens, Shirley Knight, Geraldine Fitzgerald, Lonny Chapman
115. "King of the Hill" (12-31-64) Albert Dekker, Aline MacMahon, Kathryn Hays
116. "Whipping Boy" (1-7-65) William Shatner, Madlyn Rhue, Ben Piazza, Philip Bosco
117. "Eyewitness" (1-14-65) Robert Walker Jr., Philip Vandervort, Rosemary Murphy, Lonny Chapman
118. "The Silent Killers" (1-21-65) Dane Clark, Norma Crane, John Colicos, Diana Van Der Vlis
119. "Death on Wheels" (1-28-65) Judson Laire, Leslie Nielsen, Nancy Wickwire, Andrew Duggan
120. "The Unwritten Law" (2-4-65) David Opatoshu, Kim Hunter, J. D. Cannon, Jessica Walter
121. "The Objector" (2-11-65) Brandon de Wilde, Dana Elcar, Jack Albertson, Rochelle Oliver
122. "Fires of the Mind" (2-18-65) Vincent Gardenia, Ossie Davis, Donald Pleasence, Robert Mall
123. "No-Knock" (2-25-65) Carol Rossen, Jack Gilford, Frank Cavestani, William Smithers, John Randolph
124. "The Merry-Go-Round Murder" (3-4-65) Bethel Leslie, Ruth White, John Cullum
125. "Nobody Asks What Side You're On..." (3-11-65) Ossie Davis, Al Freeman Jr., Lee Grant, George Pettace
126. "Impeachment" (3-18-65) Dan O'Herlihy, Tom Carlin, Alexis Smith
127. "The Sworn Twelve" (3-25-65) Ossie Davis, Brenda Vaccaro, Ruby Dee, Murray Hamilton
128. "A Matter of Law and Disorder" (4-8-65) Pat Hingle, Dustin Hoffman, Chester Morris, John Baragrey
129. "Youths and Maidens on an Evening Walk" (4-15-65) Joan Darling, Murray Matheson
130. "The Prosecutor" (4-29-65) Larry Blyden, Teresa Wright, Frank Overton
131. "The Bum's Rush" (5-6-65) Tom Bosley, Terry Carter
132. "Only a Child" (5-13-65) Robert Duvall, Collin Wilcox, Joel Crothers, Dennis Patrick

# FOLLOW THE SUN

Another in the period vogue of adventure yarns with Hawaiian settings, this one had its principals magazine writers (Barry Coe as Ben Gregory and Brett Halsey as Paul Templin), investigator (Gary Lockwood as Eric Jason) and secretary (Gigi Perreau as Katherine Ann Richards).

Guest performances were not always relegated to the sun and sand and surf. Jane Darwell was fine as the domineering island matriarch of "The Far Side of Nowhere." And Inger Stevens made palatable the espionage tale "The Girl from the Brandenburg Gate." Yet there is an appealing quality to this series, not easily expressed. In its celebration of Kennedy administration "vigah," this, perhaps more than any other series of its day, beckoned us to share in the vitality of the characters; to plunge into joie de vivre before the last breathless years of ephemeral youth passed by.

The Regulars: Ben Gregory, Barry Coe; Paul Templin, Brett Halsey; Katherine Ann Richards, Gigi Perreau; Eric Jason, Gary Lockwood; Lt. Frank Roper, Jay Lanin.

The Episodes:

1. "A Rage for Justice" (9-17-61) Nita Talbot, Robert Vaughn, Torin Thatcher, Ilka Windish, Howard Caine
2. "Cry Fraud" (9-24-61) Inger Stevens, Philip Ahn, Everett Sloane, Peter Baldwin
3. "The Highest Wall" (10-1-61) Bartlett Robinson, Tuesday Weld, Charles Ruggles
4. "Journey into Darkness" (10-8-61) Diane Baker, Ken Lynch, David Brandon, Frank Maxwell, Raymond Bailey
5. "The Woman Who Never Was" (10-15-61) Henry Jones, Richard Loo, Bethel Leslie, Diane Cannon
6. "Busman's Holliday" (10-22-61) Jack Klugman, Leslie Parrish, Arthur Batanides, Don Beddoe
7. "Another Part of the Jungle" (10-29-61) Patricia Owens, David McLean, Harold Gould, Guy Doleman
8. "The Longest Crap Game in History" (11-5-61) Dennis O'Keefe, Nobu McCarthy, Yvonne DeCarlo
9. "The Hunters" (11-12-61) Mark Miller, Skip Homeier, Hari Rhodes, Ivan Dixon, Lee Philips, Susan Harrison
10. "Little Girl Lost" (11-19-61) Keye Luke, Tom Palmer, Tsuruko Kobayaski
11. "Night Song" (11-26-61) Julie London, Charles McGraw, Lawrence Tierney
12. "The Primitive Clay" (12-3-61) Joanna Barnes, Larry Gates, Karen Steele
13. "Conspiracy of Silence" (12-10-61) Neil Hamilton, Vivi Janiss, Simon Oakland, Stella Stevens
14. "The Far Side of Nowhere" (12-17-61) Jane Darwell, Robert Vaughn, Joanna Moore, Jud Taylor, Tom Drake
15. "Mele Kalikimaka to You" (12-24-61) Edward Andrews, Ellen

Corby, Walter Hong Jr., William Schallert
16. "The Girl from the Brandenberg Gate" (12-31-61) Inger
    Stevens, Rex Holman, Abraham Sofaer
17. "Chicago Style" (1-7-62) Keenan Wynn, Cecily Parker,
    Eduardo Ciannelli, Eddie Firestone, Lee Patrick
18. "The Last of the Big Spenders" (1-14-62) Irene Hervey,
    Lee Tracy, Jay C. Flippen
19. "Ghost Story" (1-21-62) Martha Scott, Gene Evans, Philip Ahn
20. "Sergeant Kolchak Fades Away" (1-28-62) William Bendix,
    Howard Smith, Nobu McCarthy
21. "The Dumbest Blonde" (2-4-62) Brian Keith, Tom Palmer,
    Jayne Mansfield
22. "Annie Beeler's Place" (2-11-62) Yvonne DeCarlo, Alan
    Napier, Joan O'Brien, Dennis O'Keefe, Victor Sen Yung,
    Jerry Oddo
23. "The Irresistible Miss Bullfinch" (2-18-62) Celeste Holm,
    Alan Hale, Reta Shaw
24. "A Choice of Weapons" (2-25-62) Jackie Coogan, Ned Glass
    Anne Helm, David Janssen, Max Baer, Jr.
25. "Marine of the Month" (3-4-62) Rhonda Fleming, Keith
    Andes, Dabbs Greer
26. "The Inhuman Equation" (3-11-62) Jim Backus, Wally Cox,
    Cecil Kellaway, Sue Ane Langdon
27. "A Ghost in Her Gazebo" (3-18-62) Cesar Romero, Yvonne
    Craig, William Windom, Elsa Lanchester
28. "Not Aunt Charlotte!" (3-25-62) Laraine Day, Gene Nelson
    Diane Jergens
29. "Run, Clown, Run" (4-1-62) Pippa Scott, James Dunn,
    Rory O'Brien, Mark Roberts
30. "Chalk One Up for Johnny" (4-8-62) Rosemary DeCamp,
    Lew Gallo, Joanne Gilbert, Lee Tracy

BUS STOP

This series of dramas bears the impeccable stamp of William Inge, who served as script supervisor. Based loosely on Inge's own play of the same title (the Inge original was the basis for the episode "Cherie," adapted by Robert Blees), each segment recounts the life of those who pass through Sunrise, Colorado. Town residents include Grace Sherwood (Marilyn Maxwell), owner of the diner where much of the action is played out, waitress Elm Gahringer (Joan Freeman), Sheriff Will Mayberry (Rhodes Reason and District Attorney Glenn Wagner (Richard Anderson).

Diane Baker's subtle evocation of déjà vu distinguishes th episode "The Resurrection of Annie Ahearn," which was acclaime by the Los Angeles Times as "moving, memorable ... an hour o truth and beauty and power." George Grizzard and Joanne Linvil were the lovers of an intriguing play with an even more intriguing title--"I Kiss Your Shadow." But the most memorable of the tel plays was the much discussed, just as much condemned, "A Lion

Walks Among Us," in which Fabian Forte was cast as Mephistophe-
les in the flesh. The Ellis Kadison teleplay from a Tom Wicker
novel was given a first-class director in the person of Robert Altman. Yet the segment was called "cheaper than anything yet seen
on television" by reviewer Jack Gould ("An Hour of Ugliness:
A.B.C. 'Bus Stop' Presents Study of Pure Evil in 'A Lion Walks
Among Us,'" New York Times, 4 December 1961, p. 75). A
Newsweek (18 December 1961, p. 62) piece commented on the controversy generated by the telecast.

The Regulars: Grace Sherwood, Marilyn Maxwell; Sheriff Will
        Mayberry, Rhodes Reason; Elma Gahringer, Joan Freeman;
        District Attorney Glenn Wagner, Richard Anderson; Jeff
        (assistant to Sheriff Mayberry), Billy Tyler (with episode
        of 11/5/61).

The Episodes:

1.  "Afternoon of a Cowboy" (10-1-61) Steve Cochran, Dean
     Stockwell, Chris Robinson, Bethel Leslie, Anne Helm
2.  "The Resurrection of Annie Ahearn" (10-15-61) Diane Baker,
     Anne Seymour, Alice Frost, James Brolin, Jered Barclay,
     Thomas C. Allen
3.  "The Covering Darkness" (10-22-61) Robert Redford, Bar-
     bara Baxley, June Walker, Mary Gregory
4.  "Portrait of a Hero" (10-29-61) Rod Taylor, Nina Foch
5.  "The Glass Jungle" (11-5-61) Lloyd Nolan, Nehemiah Per-
     soff, Patricia Donahue
6.  "Cherie" (11-12-61) Tuesday Weld, Gary Lockwood, Joseph
     Cotten, Buddy Ebsen
7.  "Accessory by Consent" (11-19-61) Nancy Gates, Jack Ward-
     en, John Williams, John Newlan
8.  "The Man from Bootstrap" (11-26-61) Buddy Ebsen, Jack
     Carson, Edgar Buchanan, Kathleen Freeman
9.  "A Lion Walks Among Us" (12-3-61) Fabian Forte, Dianne
     Foster, Philip Abbott, Jenny Maxwell, Dabbs Greer, Roy
     Engel, Bernard Kates, Robert Ridgely, Perry Ivins, Owen
     Bush
10.  "Call Back Yesterday" (12-10-61) David Hedison, Geraldine
     Brooks, Frank Overton, Katherine Squire
11.  "And the Pursuit of Evil" (12-17-61) James MacArthur,
     Keenan Wynn, Crahan Denton
12.  "The Runaways" (12-24-61) Fred Clark, David Winters,
     Lynn Loring, Parley Baer, Joan Tompkins, Isobel Ran-
     dolph
13.  "Jaws of Darkness" (12-31-61) Madlyn Rhue, Coleen Gray,
     Jennifer Gillespie, Stewart Bradley
14.  "Summer Lightning" (1-7-62) Steve Forrest, Phyllis Love,
     Beverly Garland, Paul Langton
15.  "Cry to Heaven" (1-14-62) Nina Foch
16.  "The Stubborn Stumbos" (1-21-62) Earl Holliman, Claude
     Akins, Don Megowan
17.  "Turn Again Home" (1-28-62) Wendell Corey, Ruth Roman,

Joyce Van Patten, Grant Richards
18. "How Does Charley Feel?" (2-4-62) Cliff Robertson, Diana Lynn
19. "Put Your Dreams Away" (2-11-62) Gary Merrill, Felicia Farr
20. "The Opposite Virtues" (2-18-62) Lew Ayres, Leora Dana, Robert F. Simon, George Hamilton, Jeanette Nolan, Michael Parks
21. "The Ordeal of Kevin Brooke" (2-25-62) Mark Stevens, William Windom, Patricia Owens, Lawrence Tierney
22. "Door Without a Key" (3-4-62) Howard Duff, Pippa Scott, Robert Colbert, Richard Slattery, John de la Vallee, George Kane, John Zaremba, Anne Loos
23. "Verdict of Twelve" (3-11-62) Everett Sloane, John Kerr, Richard Carlson, Jay C. Flippen, Steve Harris, Barbara Dana
24. "County General" (3-18-62) Frank Lovejoy, Donald May, Dianne Foster
25. "I Kiss Your Shadow" (3-25-62) George Grizzard, Joanne Linville, Alfred Ryder

THE DUPONT SHOW OF THE WEEK

Dupont's superb successor to its "Show of the Month," with dramas, documentaries and musical programs. Perhaps the most memorable drama was Nicholas E. Baehr's study of helpless and terrified subway passengers, mercilessly intimidated by a pair of sadistic hoodlums--"Ride with Terror," which Baehr adapted for the 1967 feature film "The Incident."

The Episodes:

1. "Laughter, U.S.A." [variety program] (9-17-61) Phil Silvers, Bob Hope, Jimmy Durante, Milton Berle, Jerry Lewis, Dick Martin
2. "Happy with the Blues" [musical tribute to Harold Arlen] (9-24-61) Peggy Lee, Vic Damone, Robert Strauss, Joanie Summers
3. "Hemingway" [narrated by Chet Huntley] (10-1-61)
4. "USO--Wherever They Go!" [a tribute] (10-8-61)
5. "The Battle of the Paper Bullets" (10-15-61) Frank Lovejoy, Cesar Romero, Cliff Norton, Jerry Lester, Russell Collins
6. "Merrily We Roll Along" [a comical look at the auto; narrated by Groucho Marx] (10-22-61)
7. "The Ziegfeld Touch" [musical program narrated by Joan Crawford] (10-29-61) Barbara Cook, Jack Irvin, Danny Meehan, Marilyn Lovell
8. "Music of the Thirties" [musical program narrated by Paul Whiteman] (11-5-61) Count Basie, Bill Hayes
9. "The Wonderful World of Toys" [variety program] (11-12-61) Carol Burnett, Harpo Marx

10. "Chicago and All That Jazz" [narrated by Garry Moore] (11-26-61)
11. "Trick or Treason" (12-17-61) Martin Gabel, Monique Van Vooren
12. "Fred Waring's Unforgetables" [musical program] (12-24-61)
13. "Hollywood, My Home Town" [with Ken Murray] (1-7-62)
14. "Circus" [a history, both off stage and on, with Emmett Kelly] (1-21-62)
15. "The Forgery" (2-4-62) Arthur Kennedy, Arnold Marle
16. "Police Emergency" [narrated by Walter Matthau] (2-18-62)
17. "Regards to George M. Cohan" [a tribute narrated by Peter Lind Hayes] (3-4-62) Dorothy Louden, Paula Hayden, Lester James, Danny Meehan
18. "The Beauty of Woman" (4-1-62) Cyril Ritchard, Hermione Gingold, Katherine Anne Porter, Ruby Dee, Zsa Zsa Gabor, Lillian Gish, Anita Colby; film clips of beautiful women
19. "The Action in New Orleans" (4-15-62) Robert Cummings, Audrey Meadows
20. "The World's Greatest Robbery" [Part I] (4-29-62) R. G. Armstrong, John Cliff, Gavin MacLeod, Milton Selzer
21. "The World's Greatest Robbery" [Part II] (5-6-62) as above
22. "America's Fads and Foibles" [musical program conducted and arranged by Robert Russell Bennett] (5-13-62) Art Carney, host; Barbara Cook, Alice Ghostley, Eileen Rodgers, James Hurst
23. "A Sound of Hunting" (5-20-62) Sal Mineo, Peter Falk, Robert Lansing
24. "Hurricane" [documentary on Hurricane Carla; narrated by Dane Clark] (5-27-62)
25. "D-Day" (6-3-62)
26. "The Movie Star" (6-10-62) Dane Clark, Kathleen Widdoes, Nancy Marchand, Harry Townes, Norma Crane
27. "The Richest Man in Bogota" (6-17-62) Lee Marvin, Richard Eastham, Miriam Colon
28. "Seven Keyes to Baldpate" (6-24-62) Fred Gwynne, Joe E. Ross, Joyce Meadows, Bruce Gordon, Pat Stanley

## Second Season

29. "The Outpost" [by Roger O. Hirson; Fielder Cook directed] (9-16-62) Neville Brand, Claude Rains, Richard Conte, Keir Dullea, Everett Sloane
30. "The Interrogator" (9-23-62) Ina Balin, John Mills, Robert Loggia, Betty Garde, Murray Matheson, Jose Perez
31. "Fire Rescue" [documentary on the New York City Fire Department Rescue Company One; Walter Matthau narrated] (9-30-62)
32. "Big Deal in Laredo" [by Sidney Carroll] (10-7-62) Walter Matthau, John McGiver, Teresa Wright, Zachary Scott, John Megna, Roland Winters, Dana Elcar, William Hansen
33. "The Betrayal" [adapted by Ernest Pendrell from Joseph Conrad's Under Western Eyes] (10-21-62) Franchot Tone, Burt Brinckerhoff, Margaret O'Brien, Blanche Yurka,

John Abbott, Maureen Stapleton, John Alderman

34. "The Shadowed Affair" [by Edward Essex from the story by Michael Dyne and Helen Airoff] (11-4-62) Douglas Fairbanks Jr., Greer Garson, Lois Nettleton

35. "Emergency Ward" [documentary on the experiences of Dr. Martein Mulder, a New York Bellevue Hospital intern; narrated by Dana Andrews] (11-18-62)

36. "Mutiny" [by Jerome Ross; directed by Jack Smight] (12-2-62) Dana Andrews, Robert Walker Jr., John Baragrey, Dirk Koolman, Staats Cotsworth, Lonnie Chapman, Fred Stewart, Allen Nourse, Dick Haymes Jr.

37. "The Ordeal of Dr. Shannon" [by Robert Stewart from A. J. Cronin's Shannon's Way; Joan Kemp-Welch directed] (12-16-62) Rod Taylor, Finlay Currie, Ronald Fraser, Elizabeth MacLennan

38. "Windfall" [by Roger O. Hirson] (1-13-63) Eddie Albert, Glynis Johns, Murray Hamilton, Milton Selzer

39. "Two Faces of Treason" [by Phil Reisman Jr.; Franklin Schaffner directed] (2-10-62) Lloyd Nolan, Larry Blyden, James Daly, Martha Scott, James Patterson, Frank Campanella

40. "Comedian Backstage" [documentary focuses on Shelley Berman; Frank McGee narrates] (3-10-63)

41. "Diamond Fever" [by Jerome Ross] (3-24-63) Theodore Bikel, Peter Lorre, Martin Brooks, Sidney Blackmer, Jeri Archer

42. "The Shark" [by Larry Marcus] (4-7-63) Anthony Franciosa, Skip Homeier, Diana Hyland, Fred Stewart

43. "Prisoner at Large" [documentary] (4-21-63)

44. "Something to Hide" [by Leslie Sands] (5-5-63) Coleen Dewhurst, Henry Jones, Dirk Koolman, Hilda Brawner

45. "The Legend of Lylah Clare" [by Robert Thom; Franklin Schaffner directed] (5-19-63) Tuesday Weld, Alfred Drake, Sorrell Booke, Michael Tolan, Johnny Haymer

46. "The Triumph of Gerald Q. Wert" [by Ernestine Barton] (6-9-63) Art Carney, John Megna, David Opatoshu, Dana Elcar, Joe E. Marks, Sada Thompson, Logan Ramsey, Charles White

47. "San Francisco Detective" [documentary] (6-16-63)

48. "A Dozen Deadly Roses" [by Leonard Kantor] (6-23-63) Lauren Bacall, Walter Matthau, Robert Alda, Vincent Gardenia, Addison Powell

49. "Opening Night" [a theatre documentary narrated by Jason Robards Jr.] (6-30-63)

50. "To Bury Caesar" (7-7-63) Jack Hawkins, Pamela Brown, Nigel Davenport

Third Season

51. "The Last Hangman" (9-15-63) Ed Begley, Noel Purcell, Finlay Currie, Clive Revill

52. "Holdup" (9-22-63) Hans Conried, Hal March, Charlotte Rae

3. "The Bachelor Game" (9-29-63) Barry Nelson, Elliott Reid, Diana Van Der Vlis
4. "The Takers" (10-13-63) Walter Matthau, Shirley Knight, Nancy Barrett, Claude Rains
5. "Manhattan Battleground" [documentary narrated by Dane Clark] (10-20-63)
6. "The Silver Burro" (11-3-63) Ray Milland, Carroll O'Connor, Larry Hagman
7. "Miss America--Behind the Scenes" [narrated by Frank McGee] (11-17-63)
8. "Ride with Terror" [by Nicholas E. Baehr] (12-1-63) Tony Musante, Gregory Rozakis, Gene Hackman, Vincent Gardenia, Loretta Leversee
9. "The Gambling Heart" [by Horton Foote] (2-23-64) Ruth White, Tom Bosley, Sarah Marshall, Estelle Parsons
0. "Hell Walkers" (3-8-64) John Mills, Curt Jergens, George Voskovec
1. "High Wire--The Great Wallendas" [circus documentary] (3-22-64)
2. "Jeremy Rabbitt, the Secret Avenger" (4-5-64) Frank Gorshin, Jim Backus, Brian Donlevy, Carolyn Jones, Walter Matthau, Franchot Tone
3. "A Day Like Today" (4-19-64) Art Carney, Kathleen Maguire, Janice Hanson, Dennis Cooney
4. "Incident on Wilson Street" [narrated by Frank McGee] (5-3-64)
5. "Don't Go Upstairs" (5-17-64) Connie Scott, James Daly, Charles Aidman
6. "More, More, More, More" (5-31-64) Fred Clark, Martin Milner, Patricia Barry
7. "The Patient in Room 601" [by Fred Freed; the story of Lita Levine, who was burned in a 1958 Massachusetts plane crash] (6-7-64)
8. "Ambassador at Large" (6-14-64) Arthur Kennedy, Larry Hagman, Peter Falk, Andrew Duggan, Oscar Homolka
9. "The Missing Bank of Rupert X. Humperdink" (6-21-64) John McGiver, Gerald Hiken
0. "Flight Deck" (6-28-64)

7th PRECINCT

Well-composed dramas from the Ed McBain detective stories New York's "87th Precinct"; volatile and at times fascinating ysteries with Gena Rowlands wonderful as the deaf mute wife of etective Steve Carella (Robert Lansing).

he Regulars: Detective Steve Carella, Robert Lansing; Teddy Carella, Gena Rowlands; Detective Meyer Meyer, Norman Fell; Detective Bert Kling, Ron Harper; Detective Roger Havilland, Gregory Walcott.

The Episodes:

1. "The Floater" (9-25-61) Robert Culp, Natalie Norwick
2. "Lady in Waiting" (10-2-61) Constance Ford, Margarita Cordova
3. "Lady Killer" (10-9-61) Peter Leeds, Marion Collier, Patricia Donahue
4. "The Modus Man" (10-16-61) John Anderson, Jena Engstrom
5. "Line of Duty" (10-23-61) Richard Le Pore, Anita Sands, Vivi Janiss, Walter Burke
6. "Occupation: Citizen" (10-30-61) Ross Martin, Caren Lenay, John Dennis
7. "Killer's Payoff" (11-6-61) Beverly Garland, Jeanne Cooper, Paul Richards, Jack Albertson, William Fawcett
8. "The Guilt" (11-13-61) Mike Kellin, Norma Crane
9. "Empty Hours" (11-20-61) Patricia Crowley, Tom Fadden, William Schallert
10. "My Friend, My Enemy" (11-27-61) Dennis Hopper, Carol Rossen, Jocelyn Brando, Ann Whitfield, Gary Clarke
11. "The Very Hard Sell" (12-4-61) Leonard Nimoy, Peter Helm, Alice Frost
12. "'Til Death" (12-11-61) Darryl Hickman, Judi Meredith, Johnny Seven
13. "The Heckler" (12-18-61) Robert Vaughn, Mary La Roche, Joe Perry
14. "Run, Rabbit, Run" (12-25-61) Alfred Ryder, Barbara Stuart
15. "Main Event" (1-1-62) Myron McCormick, Robert Carricart, Arch Johnson, Maggie Pierce
16. "Man in a Jam" (1-8-62) Lin McCarthy, Joey Walsh
17. [unknown title] (1-15-62)
18. "Out of Order" (1-22-62) Charles Robinson, Paul E. Burns, Dawn Wells
19. "The Pigeon" (1-29-62) Peter Falk, Roxane Berard, Arthur Batanides, Morgan Woodward
20. "Bullet for Katie" (2-12-62) Ed Nelson, Roger Mobley
21. "King's Ransom" (2-19-62) Charles McGraw, Charles Aidman, Dan Tobin, Nancy Davis
22. "Feel of the Trigger" (2-26-62) Neil Nephew, Bernie Hamilton, Ted De Corsia, Ellen Corby
23. "Killer's Choice" (3-5-62) Gloria Talbott, R. G. Armstrong, Rosemary DeCamp, Katherine Warren
24. "Square Cop" (3-12-62) Lee Tracy, Jack Hogan
25. "Step Forward" (3-26-62) Ruth Storey, Philip Bourneuf
26. "Idol in the Dust" (4-2-62) Michael Dante, Jeanette Nolan
27. "Ramon" (4-9-62) Danny Bravo, Edward Colmans
28. "New Man in the Precinct" (4-16-62) Ray Montgomery, Robert Colbert, Fred Beir
29. "Dawns an Evil Day" (4-23-62) Victor Jory, Paul George
30. "The Lover" (4-30-62) Janis Paige, Russell Collins

BEN CASEY

James Moser's classic study of life at County General Hospital, honoring the dynamic spirit--Vince Edwards as neurosurgeon Ben Casey--and the conscience of the hospital (and Casey's mentor) Dr. David Zorba (Sam Jaffe), whose recitation and blackboard drawing of the life cycle commenced each teleplay. There were at least 153 physiological and/or psychological difficulties, all foretold with great reverence and with literary inspiration as varied as Julia A. Fletcher Carney ("Little Drops of Water, Little Grains of Sand"), Lewis Carroll ("Six Impossible Things Before Breakfast"), Algernon Charles Swinburne ("The Light that Loses, the Night that Wins"), John Webster ("Weave Nets to Catch the Wind"), Shakespeare and the Bible. One of the greats.

The Regulars: Dr. Ben Casey, Vincent Edwards; Dr. David Zorba, Sam Jaffe; Dr. Maggie Graham, Bettye Ackerman; Nick Kanavaras, Nick Dennis; Nurse Wills, Jeanne Bates; Hoffman, Harry Landers. Semi-regular 64-65 season: Stella Stevens as Jane Hancock; Dr. David Niles Freeland, Franchot Tone (last season).

The Episodes:

1. "To the Pure" (10-2-61) Barton Heyman, Rafael Lopez
2. "But Linda Only Smiled" (10-9-61) Jeanne Cooper, Susan Gordon
3. "The Insolent Heart" (10-16-61) Luther Adler, Carl Benton Reid
4. "I Remember a Lemon Tree" (10-23-61) George C. Scott, Colleen Dewhurst
5. "An Expensive Glass of Water" (10-30-61) Chester Morris, Neva Patterson
6. "The Sound of Laughter" (11-6-61) Stanley Adams, Edward Colmans
7. "A Few Brief Lines for Dave" (11-13-61) Kevin McCarthy, Phyllis Love
8. "Pavane for a Gentle Lady" (11-20-61) Bethel Leslie, Nellie Burt
9. "My Good Friend Krikor" (11-27-61) Abraham Sofaer, Robert Ellenstein
10. "The Sweet Kiss of Madness" (12-4-61) Arthur Hill, William Windom, Patricia Barry
11. "A Certain Time, a Certain Darkness" (12-11-61) Donald Woods, Joan Hackett, Lynn Bari
12. "A Dark Night for Billy Harris" (12-18-61) Telly Savalas, Bruce Dern
13. "And If I Die" (1-1-62) Brett Somers, John Larch
14. "A Memory of Candy Stripes" (1-8-62) Franchot Tone, Denise Alexander
15. "Imagine a Long, Bright Corridor" (1-15-62) Vivi Janiss, Robert Blake
16. "A Story to Be Told Softly" (1-22-62) Jean Hagen, Lee

Marvin

17. "The Big Trouble with Charlie" (1-29-62) Jack Warden, My-
    ron McCormick
18. "Give My Hands an Epitaph" (2-5-62) Jack Klugman, Eileen
    Ryan
19. "Victory Wears a Cruel Smile" (2-12-62) Ed Begley, Alfred
    Ryder
20. "Odyssey of a Proud Suitcase" (2-19-62) Francis Lederer,
    Fay Spain
21. "Behold a Pale Horse" (2-26-62) Suzanne Pleshette, Keenan
    Wynn, Paul Hartman
22. "For the Ladybug, One Dozen Roses" (3-5-62) Cliff Robert-
    son, Michael Davis
23. "To a Grand and Natural Finale" (3-12-62) Hari Rhodes,
    Gina Gillespie
24. "Monument to an Aged Hunter" (3-19-62) Wilfrid Hyde-
    White, Robert F. Simon, Chris Robinson
25. "All the Clocks Are Ticking" (3-26-62) Nan Martin
26. "Among Others, a Girl Named Abilene" (4-2-62) Ronnie
    Haran, Denver Pyle
27. "A Pleasant Thing for the Eyes" (4-16-62) Yoko Tani, Eddie
    Firestone
28. "And Eve Wore a Veil of Tears" (4-23-62) Betty Field,
    Carmen Matthews
29. "Preferably, the Less-Used Arm" (4-30-62) Joe Perry,
    Chal Johnson
30. "An Uncommonly Innocent Killing" (5-7-62) Eddie Albert,
    Conrad Nagel, Andrew Prine
31. "So Oft It Chances in Particular Men" (5-21-62) James Fran-
    ciscus, Carol Rossen
32. "When You See an Evil Man" (5-28-62) Tuesday Weld, Si-
    mon Oakland, Jeanette Nolan

Second Season

33. "Mrs. McBroom and the Cloud Watcher" (10-1-62) Patty
    Duke, Joanne Linville
34. "The Night That Nothing Happened" (10-8-62) Michael Con-
    stantine, Jerry Paris
35. "In the Name of Love, a Small Corruption" (10-15-62) Rod
    Steiger, Felicia Farr
36. "Legacy from a Stranger" (10-22-62) Janet Margolin, Jud-
    son Laire, Steven Hill
37. "Go Not Gently into the Night" (10-29-62) Pat Rosson
38. "Behold!, They Walk an Ancient Road" (11-5-62) Carroll
    O'Connor, Ludwig Donath
39. "Of All Save Pain Bereft" (11-12-62) Gerald S. O'Loughlin
40. "And Even Death Shall Die" (11-19-62) Elizabeth Allen,
    Robert Walker Jr.
41. "The Fireman Who Raised Rabbits" (11-26-62) Strother
    Martin, L. Q. Jones, Walter Burke, Rosemary Murphy
42. "Between Summer and Winter, the Glorious Season" (12-3-
    62) Nellie Burt

43. "I Hear America Singing" (12-10-62) Jack Warden
44. "Pack Up All My Cares and Woes" (12-17-62) Burgess Meredith
45. "Saturday, Surgery and Stanley Schultz" (12-31-62) James Dunn, Eli Mintz
46. "I'll Be Alright in the Morning" (1-7-63) Steven Hill, Bethel Leslie
47. "A Cardinal Act of Mercy" [Part I] (1-14-63) Glenda Farrell, Kim Stanley, Gary Crosby
48. "A Cardinal Act of Mercy" [Part II] (1-21-63) as above
49. "Use Neon for My Epitaph" (1-28-63) Gary Merrill
50. "He Thought He Saw an Albatross" (2-4-63) Leslie Nielsen
51. "A Short Biographical Sketch of James Tuttle Peabody M.D." (2-11-63) Fred Vincent
52. "A Hundred More Pipers" (2-18-63) James Donald, Harold J. Stone
53. "Suffer the Little Children" (2-25-63) Elizabeth Allen, Jacqueline Scott
54. "Rigadoon for Three Pianos" (3-4-63) Diana Hyland, Beatrice Straight
55. "The White Ones Are Dolphins" (3-11-63) Luther Adler, Sharon Farrell, Ray Walston, John Qualen
56. "Will Everyone Who Believes in Terry Dunne Please Applaud?" (3-18-63) Neville Brand
57. "For I Will Plait Thy Hair with Gold" (3-25-63) Dan O'Herlihy
58. "Father Was an Intern" (4-1-63) Michael Parks, James Whitmore
59. "Rage Against the Dying Light" (4-15-63) Melvyn Douglas
60. "La Vie, La Vie Interieur" (4-22-63) Olive Deering
61. "My Enemy Is a Bright Green Sparrow" (4-29-63) Patricia Neal
62. "Lullaby for Billy Digman" (5-6-63) Philip Abbott, Barbara Barrie
63. "Hang No Hats on Dreams" (5-13-63) Ed Begley, Kathy Nolan
64. "For This Relief, Much Thanks" [Part I] [conclusion on initial episode of series "The Breaking Point" of 9/16/63] (9-9-63) Eduard Franz, Paul Richards, Scott Marlowe, Oscar Homolka, Sheree North

Third Season

65. "Justice to a Microbe" (9-18-63) James Caan, Robert Loggia
66. "With the Rich and the Mighty, Always a Little Patience" (9-25-63) Frederick Beir, Anne Francis, Frank Aletter
67. "Allie" (10-2-63) Sammy Davis Jr., Greg Morris
68. "If There Were Dreams to Sell" (10-9-63) Suzy Somers, Kay Medford, Cecil Kellaway
69. "The Echo of a Silent Cheer" [Part I] (10-16-63) Barry Sullivan, Beau Bridges, Carole Wells
70. "The Echo of a Silent Cheer" [Part II] (10-23-63) as above

71. "Little Drops of Water, Little Grains of Sand" (10-30-63) Aldo Ray, Norma Crane, Harry Townes
72. "Light Up the Dark Corners" (11-6-63) Richard Basehart, Piper Laurie, J. Pat O'Malley
73. "Six Impossible Things Before Breakfast" (11-13-63) Ricardo Montalban, James Best
74. "Fire in a Sacred Fruit Tree" (11-20-63) Dean Jones, Ulla Jacobsson
75. "Dispel the Black Cyclone That Shakes the Throne" (11-27-63) Mary Astor, Eileen Heckart, Wilton Graff, James Dunn
76. "My Love, My Love" (12-4-63) Barry Nelson, Anjanette Comer, Anna-Lisa
77. "From Too Much Love of Living" (12-11-63) Barbara Rush, Mark Richman
78. "It is Getting Dark ... And We Are Lost" (12-18-63) Gene Lyons, Ann Julliann, Robert Webber
79. "The Last Splintered Spoke on the Old Burlesque Wheel" (12-25-63) Maggie McNamara, George Grizzard
80. "The Light That Loses, the Night That Wins" (1-1-64) Dana Andrews, Peggy McCay, Don Spruance
81. "I'll Get On My Icefloe and Wave Goodbye" (1-8-64) Rachel Ames, Charles Ruggles, Joseph Buloff, Norman Fell
82. "The Only Place Where They Know My Name" (1-15-64) Michael Higgins, Phil Harris
83. "There Was Once a Man in the Land of Uz" (1-22-64) Robert Walker Jr., James Gregory, Royal Dano
84. "One Nation Indivisible" (1-29-64) Susan Gordon
85. "Goodbye to Blue Elephants and Such" (2-5-64) Davey Davison, Virginia Christine, James Callahan
86. "The Bark of a Three-Headed Hound" (2-12-64) Bradford Dillman, Jeff Morris, Sally Kellerman
87. "The Sound of One Hand Clapping" (2-19-64) Robert Culp, Milton Selzer, Richard Evans
88. "A Falcon's Eye, a Lion's Heart, a Girl's Hand" (2-26-64) Harry Guardino, John Zaremba, Tom Troupe
89. "The Lonely Ones" (3-4-64) Jill Ireland, Dennis Crosby, Cherylene Lee
90. "Keep Out of Reach of Adults" (3-11-64) Geraldine Brooks, Richard Kiley
91. "Dress My Doll Pretty" (3-18-64) Sheree North, Betsy Hale, Dean Harens, Kathleen Freeman
92. "Onions and Mustard Seed Will Make Her Weep" (3-25-64) Noreen Corcoran, William Arvin
93. "Make Me the First American" (4-1-64) Frank De Kova, Mario Alcalde
94. "Heap Logs and Let the Blaze Laugh Out" (4-8-64) Irene Dailey, Charles Robinson, Gail Kobe
95. "For a Just Man Falleth Seven Times" (4-15-64) Lew Ayres, Sharon Farrell, Lee Grant
96. "Evidence of Things Not Seen" (4-22-64) Wilfrid Hyde-White, James Shigeta, Katherine Ross, Ben Wright

Fourth Season

97. "August Is the Month Before Christmas" (9-14-64) Margaret Leighton, Jessica Walter, Ted Bessell
98. "A Bird in the Solitude Singing" (9-21-64) Anne Francis
99. "But Who Shall Beat the Drums?" (9-28-64) Rip Torn, Eduard Franz, Susan Bay, John Anderson
100. "Autumn Without Red Leaves" (10-5-64) Robert Culp, Collin Wilcox
101. "You Fish or You Cut Bait" (10-12-64) Ben Piazza, John Anderson
102. "For Jimmy, the Best of Everything" (10-19-64) Peter Falk, Lee Grant, Malachi Throne
103. "A Woods Full of Question Marks" (10-26-64) Dane Clark, Ellen Corby, June Reed, Nancy Rennick
104. "A Thousand Words Are Mute" (11-9-64) Pippa Scott, Tyler McVey, Robert Sampson
105. "Money, a Horse, and a Knowledge of Latin" (11-16-64) Barry Sullivan, Walter Brooke
106. "A Disease of the Heart Called Love" (11-23-64) Shelley Winters, Milt Kamen
107. "Kill the Dream, but Spare the Dreamer" (11-30-64) Darren McGavin, Peggy McCay, John Harding
108. "Courage at 3 A.M." (12-7-64) Janice Rule, Lloyd Gough, Booth Colman
109. "The Wild, Wild, Wild, Waltzing World" (12-14-64) Joan Hackett, Robert Loggia
110. "A Boy Is Standing Outside the Door" (1-4-65) Tony Bill, Elsa Lanchester, Maureen O'Sullivan, William Marshall
111. "Where Does the Boomerang Go?" (1-11-65) George Hamilton, Charles McGraw, Norman Fell
112. "Pas de Deux" (1-18-65) Susan Oliver, Harvey Lembeck, Dan Tobin, Alfred Ryder
113. "Every Other Minute, It's the End of the World" (1-25-65) Francis Lederer, Patricia Hyland, John Zaremba
114. "A Rambling Discourse on Egyptian Water Clocks" (2-1-65) Peter Haskell, Barbara Barrie, Walter Koenig
115. "When I Am Grown to Man's Estate" (2-8-65) Roddy McDowall, Madeleine Sherwood
116. "A Man, a Maid, and a Marionette" (2-22-65) Van Johnson, Marsha Hunt
117. "A Dipperful of Water from a Poisoned Well" (3-1-65) Viveca Lindfors, Hans Conried
118. "A Little Fun to Match the Sorrow" (3-8-65) Jerry Lewis, Robert H. Harris, James Best, Dianne Foster
119. "Minus That Old Rusty Hacksaw" (3-15-65) Gloria Swanson, Joe De Santis
120. "Eulogy in Four Flats" (3-22-65) Tom Drake, Lee Tracy, Norma Connolly, Donna Anderson
121. "Three L'il Lambs" (3-29-65) Nick Adams, Carroll O'Connor, Marlo Thomas, Norman Alden
122. "A Slave Is on the Throne" (4-12-65) Jack Klugman, Pippa Scott, John Zaremba

123. "Journeys End in Lovers Meeting" (4-19-65) Antoinette
     Bower, Red Buttons, Julie Parish
124. "The Day They Stole County General" (4-26-65) Howard Da
     Silva, Sharon Farrell, Cliff Norton
125. 'Did Your Mother Come from Ireland?" (5-3-65) Cesar
     Romero, Tom Bosley
126. "From Sutter's Crick ... and Beyond Farewell" (5-10-65)
     Wilfrid Hyde-White, John Megna, K. L. Smith
127. "A Horse Named Stravinsky" (5-17-65) Eartha Kitt, Percy
     Rodriguez, Everett Sloane, John Qualen

Fifth Season

128. "A War of Nerves" (9-13-65) Leslie Nielsen, Antoinette
     Bower, Marlyn Mason, Jim McMullan
129. 'O' the Big Wheel Turns by Faith" (9-20-65) James Far-
     entino, Stephen McNally
130. "A Nightingale Named Nathan" (9-27-65) Howard Da Silva,
     Barbara Turner, Marlyn Mason, Stephen McNally, Don
     Marshall
131. "Run for Your Lives, Dr. Galanos Practices Here" (10-4-
     63) Nehemiah Persoff, Michael Ansara, Marlyn Mason,
     Bob Random
132. "Because of the Needle, the Haystack Was Lost" (10-11-65)
     Gladys Cooper, Ann Harding, Marlyn Mason, Malachi
     Throne, Hari Rhodes
133. 'What to Her Is Plato?" (10-18-65) Julie Sommers, Mar-
     lyn Mason, Malachi Throne, Bernie Kopell
134. "Francini? Who Is Francini?" (10-25-65) Gabriel Dell,
     Pippa Scott, Marlyn Mason
135. "Then I, and You, and All of Us Fall Down" (11-1-65)
     Dick Clark, Brian Bedford, Jim McMullan, Steven Marlo
136. 'No More, Cried the Rooster--There Will Be Truth" (11-8-
     65) James Shigeta, Malachi Throne, Antoinette Bower,
     Benson Fong
137. "The Importance of Being 65937" (11-15-65) Macdonald
     Carey, Linda Gaye Scott, Ned Glass
138. 'When Givers Prove Unkind" (11-22-65) Wilfrid Hyde-
     White, Allyn Joslyn, Linda Marsh
139. "The Man from Quasilia" (11-29-65) Nico Minardos, Bar-
     bara Luna, Wilfrid Hyde-White, Ned Glass, Victor Frenc
140. 'Why Did the Day Go Backwards?" (12-6-65) Wilfrid Hyde-
     White, Lainie Kazan
141. 'If You Really Want to Know What Goes on in a Hospital....
     (12-20-65) Sally Kellerman, Don Francks
142. 'If You Play Your Cards Right, You Too Can Be a Loser"
     (12-27-65) Yvonne Craig
143. "In Case of Emergency, Cry Havoc" (1-3-66) Geraldine
     Brooks, Henry Beckman
144. "Meantime, We Shall Express Our Darker Purpose" (1-20-
     66) Alfred Ryder, Virginia Gregg, Robert Burr
145. "For San Diego You Need a Different Bus" (1-17-66) Dane
     Clark, Sidney Blackmer

146. "Smile, Baby, Smile, It's Only Twenty Dols. of Pain" (1-24-66) Sidney Blackmer, Dana Wynter
147. "Fun and Games and Other Tragic Things" (1-31-66) Sidney Blackmer, Heidy Hunt
148. "Weave Nets to Catch the Wind" (2-7-66) Sidney Blackmer, Jeanne Cooper
149. "Lullaby for a Wind-Up Toy" (2-14-66) Jack Carter, Brooke Bundy
150. "Where Did All the Roses Go?" (2-21-66) Viveca Lindfors, Sherwood Price, Joe Maross
151. "Twenty-Six Ways to Spell Heartbreak, A.B.--C.D...." (2-28-66) Christopher Harris, Peter Haskell
152. "Pull the Wool Over Your Eyes, Here Comes the Cold Wind of Truth" (3-14-66) Robert Lipton, Juliet Mills, Sam Groom
153. "Then, Suddenly, Panic!" (3-12-66) Janet Blair, Kathryn Crosby, Gavin MacLeod


THE NEW BREED

Absorbing Quinn Martin study of a crackerjack police squad in contemporary Los Angeles--all in the classic tradition of Martin's "The Untouchables."

The Regulars: Lieutenant Price Adams, Leslie Nielsen; Sgt. Vince Cavelli, John Beradino; Patrolman Joe Huddleston, John Clarke; Patrolman Peter Garcia, Greg Roman; Capt. Keith Gregory, Byron Morrow.

The Episodes:

1. "No Fat Cops" (10-3-61) June Dayton, Charles Aidman
2. "Prime Target" (10-10-61) Keir Dullea, James Gregory, Pilar Seurat
3. "Death of a Ghost" (10-17-61) Fritz Weaver
4. "To None a Deadly Drug" (10-24-61) Gary Merrill, Barbara Baxley
5. "The Compulsion to Confess" (10-31-61) Telly Savalas
6. " 'Til Death Do Us Part" (11-7-61) Eileen Heckart, Wendell Corey, Michael Allinson
7. "The Butcher" (11-14-61) Lynn Bari, Jeanne Cooper, Charles Carlson, Peter Whitney
8. "Wave Goodbye to Grandpa" (11-21-61) Dennis King
9. "Sweet Bloom of Death" (11-28-61) Cathleen Nesbitt, Patricia Breslin, Henry Jones, Lee Bergere, Phil Coolidge
10. "The Valley of the Three Charlies" (12-5-61) Charles Bronson, Keenan Wynn, Mike Kellin
11. "Lady Killer" (12-12-61) Martin Balsam, Anne Francis, Robert Redford
12. "Blood Money" (12-19-61) Charles McGraw, Gloria

Grahame, Jack Oakie, Diana Millay
13. "I Remember Murder" (12-26-61) Ilka Chase, Tina Louise, Robert Middleton, Virginia Field
14. "The All-American Boy" (1-2-62) Edward Binns, Paul Carr, Burt Brinckerhoff
15. "Cross the Little Line" (1-9-62) Peter Falk, Joan Hackett, Victor Jory
16. "To Sell a Human Being" (1-16-62) Paul Richards, Richard Arlen, Jean Engstrom, Jena Engstrom
17. "Care Is No Cure" (1-23-62) Faye Emerson, Royal Dano, Sherry Jackson, Leif Erickson, Mario Alcaide
18. "Policemen Die Alone" [Part I] (1-30-62) Zachary Scott, Margaret Hayes, Ed Begley, Victor Jory
19. "Policemen Die Alone" [Part II] (2-6-62) as above
20. "Mr. Weltschmerz" (2-13-62) Cecil Kellaway, Josephine Hutchinson
21. "Wings for a Plush Horse" (2-20-62) Barry Morse, Nan Martin, John Baragrey
22. "How Proud the Guilty" (2-27-62) Nehemiah Persoff, Diane Mountford, Robert Eyer
23. "The Torch" (3-6-62) Stanley Adams, Les Tremayne
24. "All the Dead Faces" (3-13-62) Jack Klugman, Brett Somers, Arnold Moss
25. "The Deadlier Sex" (3-20-62) Judi Meredith, Paula Raymond, Betsy Jones-Moreland
26. "Edge of Violence" (3-27-62) Les Damon, John Brinkley
27. "Echoes of Hate" (4-3-62) Andrew Prine, Cameron Prud'-homme, Natalie Trundy
28. "The Man with the Other Face" (4-10-62) Eduardo Ciannelli
29. "Thousands and Thousands of Miles" (4-17-62) Patty McCormack, Peter Fonda
30. "Hail, Hail, the Gang's All Here" (4-24-62) Edward Andrews, John Larkin, Yvonne Craig
31. "My Brother's Keeper" (5-1-62) Margo, Robert Blake, Frank Silvera
32. "A Motive Named Walter" (5-8-62) Eddie Albert, Laraine Day, Bea Benaderet
33. "Wherefore Art Thou, Romeo?" (5-15-62) Joseph Wiseman, Carmen Matthews
34. "Judgment at San Belito" (5-22-62) Arthur O'Connell, Cloris Leachman
35. "So Dark the Night" (5-29-62) Dina Merrill, Don Taylor
36. "Walk This Street Lightly" (6-5-62) Barry Morse

THE DICK POWELL SHOW

Series host Dick Powell also appeared in several of these teleplays, distinguished by some strong performances from a number of big-name guest stars. Peter Falk justly received an Emmy for his role as Aristede Fresco, the Greek truckdriver whose tomato delivery schedule is abruptly interrupted by a pregnant young woman. Powell himself was fine as the prosecutor Major Ed Clayborn of Harry Julian Fink's essentially Cold War piece "The Court-Martial of Captain Wycliff. " Writers for the series included Allan Sloane ("330 Independence S. W. ") and Walter Doniger ("Squadron").

The Regulars: Dick Powell, host.

The Episodes:

1. "Who Killed Julie Greer?" (9-26-61) Lloyd Bridges, Nick Adams, Mickey Rooney, Dean Jones, Carolyn Jones, Jack Carson, Edgar Bergen, Ronald Reagan, Kay Thompson, Dick Powell
2. "Ricochet" (10-3-61) Van Heflin, Ellen McRae, John Chandler
3. "Killer in the House" (10-10-61) Earl Holliman, Edmond O'Brien, Claire Griswold
4. "John J. Diggs" (10-17-61) Rhonda Fleming, Dick Powell, Wilton Kriff
5. "Doyle Against the House" (10-24-61) Milton Berle, Jan Sterling
6. "Out of the Night" (10-31-61) Dick Powell, Ziva Rodann, John Van Dreelen
7. "Somebody's Waiting" (11-7-61) Susan Oliver
8. "The Geetas Box" (11-14-61) Charles Bickford, Dean Stockwell, Cliff Robertson
9. "Goodbye, Hannah" (11-21-61) Carolyn Jones, Dick Powell
10. "Up Jumped the Devil" (11-28-61) Otto Kruger, Hugh O'Brian
11. "Three Soldiers" (12-5-61) Telly Savalas, Robert Webber, James Donald
12. "A Swiss Affair" (12-12-61) Cecil Kellaway, Hazel Court
13. "The Fifth Caller" (12-19-61) Michael Rennie, Tom Conway, Eva Gabor, Elsa Lanchester, George Macready
14. "Open Season" (12-26-61) Thomas Gomez, Dorothy Malone, Dennis O'Keefe, Paul Richards
15. "Death in a Village" (1-2-62) Nehemiah Persoff, Thomas Gomez, Gilbert Roland
16. "A Time to Die" (1-9-62) June Allyson, Dick Powell, Ernest Truex, Tuesday Weld, John Saxon, Edgar Bergen, Andy Williams
17. "The Price of Tomatoes" (1-16-62) Peter Falk, Inger Stevens, Alejandro Rey
18. "Obituary for Mr. 'X'" (1-23-62) Steve Cochran, Nancy Davis, John Ireland, Dina Merrill, Gary Merrill
19. "Squadron" (1-30-62) Dick Powell, Pat Conway, Joanna Moore, Robert Boon, Hershel Bernardi
20. "The Prison" (2-6-62) Theodore Bikel, Charles Boyer
21. "Seeds of April" (2-13-62) Gene Barry, Keenan Wynn, Nina Foch, Beverly Garland
22. "The Legend" (2-20-62) Sammy Davis Jr., Everett Sloane, Lawrence Dobkin
23. "The Hook" (3-6-62) Robert Loggia, Ed Begley, Ray Danton, David Lewis, Ted De Corsia, Joan Taylor, Anthony Caruso

24. "The View from the Eiffel Tower" (3-13-62) Akim Tamiroff, Jane Powell, Bella Darvi
25. "330 Independence S.W." (3-20-62) William Bendix, Julie Adams, David McLean
26. "The Clocks" (3-27-62) Charles Drake, Joan Fontaine, Wayne Rogers, David Farrar
27. "Safari" (4-3-62) Juano Hernandez, Glynis Johns
28. "The Boston Terrier" (4-10-62) John McGiver, Robert Vaughn
29. "No Strings Attached" (4-24-62) Barbara Nichols, Angie Dickinson, Mamie Van Doren
30. "Savage Sunday" (5-1-62) Nick Adams, Ann Blyth

Second Season

31. "Special Assignment" (9-25-62) Barbara Stanwyck, Dick Powell, Edgar Bergen, Frances Bergen, Jackie Cooper, Lloyd Nolan, Mickey Rooney, June Allyson
32. "Tomorrow, the Man" (10-2-62) Larry Blyden, Kim Hunter, Peter Lazer, Eli Wallach, Susan Kohner
33. "Run Till It's Dark" (10-9-62) Fabian Forte, Tuesday Weld
34. "The Doomsday Boys" (10-16-62) Peter Falk, Alejandro Rey
35. "The Sea Witch" (10-23-62) John Ericson, Carolyn Jones, Harry Guardino, Gerald Mohr, Rex Ingram, Ralph Manza
36. "The Great Anatole" (10-30-62) Curt Jergens, Dana Wynter Lee Philips
37. "Days of Glory" (11-13-62) Charles Boyer, Suzanne Pleshette, Lloyd Bochner
38. "In Search of a Son" (11-20-62) Dick Powell, Gladys Cooper Sebastian Cabot, Dean Stockwell
39. "Borderline" (11-27-62) John Payne, Elisha Cook, Hazel Court, Frank Silvera, Michael Davis
40. "Pericles on 31st Street" (12-4-62) Theodore Bikel, Carrol O'Connor, Arthur O'Connell
41. "The Court-Martial of Captain Wycliff" (12-11-62) Dick Powell, Dina Merrill, Robert Webber, Ed Begley, Edward Andrews, James MacArthur, Charles Ruggles, Alexander Scourby, Robert Keith, Martin Brandt
42. "Crazy Sunday" (12-18-62) Rip Torn, Vera Miles, Dana Andrews, Barry Sullivan
43. "The Big Day" (12-25-62) Robert Morley, Jack Cassidy, Joan Blondell
44. "The Honorable Albert Higgins" (1-1-63) Tom Ewell, Barbara Rush
45. "Project 'X'" (1-8-63) Michael Rennie, Steve Forrest, Gregory Peck, Gena Rowlands
46. "The Losers" (1-15-63) Rosemary Clooney, Lee Marvin, Keenan Wynn
47. "Everybody Loves Sweeney" (1-22-63) Mickey Rooney, Frank Sinatra
48. "The Rage of Silence" (1-29-63) Carol Lynley
49. "The Judge" (2-5-63) Richard Basehart, Otto Kruger
50. "Luxury Liner" (2-12-63) Rory Calhoun, Jan Sterling, Carroll O'Connor

51. "Apples Don't Fall Far" (2-19-63) Johnny Crawford, David Wayne
52. "Tissue of Hate" (2-26-63) Polly Bergen, Henry Fonda
53. "Thunder in a Forgotten Town" (3-5-63) Edie Adams, Jackie Coogan, Jackie Cooper, Joey Bishop, David Janssen, Pat O'Brien, Susan Oliver, Dewey Martin
54. "Colossus" (3-12-63) William Shatner, Geraldine Brooks
55. "Charlie's Duet" (3-19-63) Jim Backus, Julie London, Zsa Zsa Gabor
56. "The Third Side of the Coin" (3-26-63) Hugh Marlowe, John Forsythe, June Allyson
57. "Epilogue" (4-2-63) Claude Akins, Lee Marvin, Pat Boone, Ricardo Montalban
58. "The Last of the Big Spenders" (4-16-63) Hershel Bernardi, Robert Redford, Inger Stevens
59. "The Old Man and the City" (4-23-63) Charles Ruggles, Dennis Morgan, Charles Bickford, June Allyson, Edward Binns, Gene Raymond
60. "The Last of the Private Eyes" (4-30-63) Macdonald Carey, William Bendix, Sebastian Cabot, Eddie Anderson, Robert Cummings, Jeanne Crain, Keenan Wynn, William Lundigan, Janis Paige, Arnold Stang, Jay C. Flippen, Linda Christian


CAIN'S HUNDRED

Contemporary law and order tale of a syndicate attorney who apostatizes, seeking moral restitution for crimes past by going after one hundred underworld figures.

The Regulars: Nicholas Cain, Mark Richman.

The Episodes:

1. "Crime and Commitment" [Part I] (9-19-61) Martin Gabel, Carol Rossen, Gavin MacLeod
2. "Rules of Evidence" [Part II] (9-26-61) as above
3. "Blue Water, White Beach" (10-3-61) Patricia Medina, Ed Begley
4. "Markdown on a Man" (10-10-61) John McGiver, Phyllis Love
5. "Degrees of Guilt" (10-17-61) David Brian, Janet Lake
6. "King of the Mountain" (10-24-61) Barbara Baxley, Edward Andrews
7. "Penitent" (10-31-61) Hershel Bernardi
8. "Comeback" (11-7-61) Clifton James
9. "Dead Load" (11-21-61) Charles Bronson, Harold J. Stone
10. "In the Balance" (11-28-61) Telly Savalas, Alexander Scourby
11. "Five for One" (12-5-61) Jim Backus
12. "The Fixer" (12-12-61) Pat Hingle, Cloris Leachman
13. "Cain's Final Judgment" (12-19-61) Sam Jaffe, Paul Stewart

14. "The Plush Jungle" (1-2-62) Robert Culp, John Larch
15. "Take a Number" (1-9-62) Frank McHugh, Martin Balsam, Shirley Ballard
16. "The Debasers" (1-16-62) Robert Vaughn, Neville Brand, Marsha Hunt
17. "The Schemer" (1-23-62) Richard Kiley, Paul Richards, Bert Freed, Carolyn Kearney
18. "The Manipulator" (1-30-62) Fritz Weaver, Sidney Blackmer, Jacques Aubuchon, George Voskovec
19. "Marked by Proxy" (2-6-62) Charles McGraw, Regis Toomey, Fay Spain
20. "Blood Money" (2-13-62) Ed Begley, Everett Sloane, Larry Blyden, Don Rickles
21. "Blues for a Junkman" (2-27-62) James Coburn, Dorothy Dandridge, Ivan Dixon
22. "The New Order" (3-6-62) Simon Oakland, Lin McCarthy, Jack Ging
23. "The Cost of Living" (3-20-62) Susan Oliver, Walter Slezak
24. "Savage in Darkness" (3-27-62) Harold J. Stone, Telly Savalas, Barbara Eden
25. "The Swinger" (4-3-62) Robert Culp, Sammy Davis Jr., Zina Bethune, Jersey Joe Walcot
26. "Inside Track" (4-10-62) Lloyd Bochner, David Janssen, Bethel Leslie
27. "A Creature Lurks in Ambush" (4-17-62) Ricardo Montalban, Keir Dullea, Robert Blake, Ted De Corsia
28. "Woman of Silence" (4-24-62) Madlyn Rhue, Jack Klugman, Perry Lopez
29. "The Left Side of Canada" (5-1-62) Harry Guardino, Beverly Garland
30. "The Quick Brown Fox" (5-15-62) Patricia Crowley, Edward Binns, Alex Nicol

ALCOA PREMIERE

Generally intriguing drama anthology boasting first-class composers (Larry Marcus for an adaptation of Lionel Trilling's short story "Of This Time, Of That Place"; Ray Bradbury for "The Jail"; Gene L. Coon for "The Hat of Sergeant Martin"; John Furia Jr. for "The Broken Year") and one episode, "Flashing Spikes" (by Jameson Brewer from the Frank O'Rourke novel), directed by John Ford.

The Regulars: Fred Astaire, host.

The Episodes:

1. "People Need People" (10-10-61) Arthur Kennedy, Lee Marvin, James Gregory, Keir Dullea, Katherine Squire, Jocelyn Brando
2. "The Fugitive Eye" (10-17-61) Charleton Heston, Leo G.

Carroll
3. "The Fortress" (10-24-61) Lloyd Bridges, Philip Ahn, James Shigeta
4. "Moment of Decision" (11-7-61) Fred Astaire, Harry Townes, Maureen O'Sullivan
5. "Family Outing" (11-14-61) Lin McCarthy, Nancy Olson, Michael Burns
6. "The Witch Next Door" (11-28-61) Susan Gordon, Mary La Roche, James Whitmore
7. "The Breaking Point" (12-5-61) Brian Keith, Mary Murphy, Brad Dexter
8. "Delbert, Texas" (12-12-61) David Wayne
9. "The End of a World" (12-19-61) Robert Loggia, Andrew Prine, Robert Ellenstein
10. "The Cake Baker" (1-2-62) Shelley Winters, Ed Nelson, Marjorie Reynolds
11. "Pattern of Guilt" (1-9-62) Ray Milland, Myron McCormick, Joanna Moore
12. "The Hour Of the Bath" (1-16-62) Barbara Luna, Robert Fuller
13. "The Jail" (2-6-62) John Gavin, James Barton, Bettye Ackerman, Noah Keen, Barry Morse
14. "Mr. Easy" (2-13-62) Fred Astaire, Joanna Barnes
15. "The Man with the Shine on His Shoes" (2-20-62) Henry Hull, Peter Helm
16. "The Doctor" (2-27-62) Richard Kiley, Don Keefer, Cloris Leachman, Ken Lynch
17. "Of This Time, Of That Place" (3-6-62) Jason Evers, Henry Jones, Burt Brinckerhoff, Nancy Hadley
8. "Second Chance" (3-13-62) Cliff Robertson, Earl Holliman, Andrew Prine
9. "Tiger" (3-20-62) Keir Dullea, Robert Shore, Gary Merrill
20. "Seven Against the Sea" (4-3-62) Ernest Borgnine, Ron Foster
1. "The Very Custom Special" (4-10-62) Robert Strauss, J. Pat O'Malley
2. "All My Clients Are Innocent" (4-17-62) Barry Morse, Joan Staley, Dick Davalos
3. "The Rules of the Game" (5-1-62) Hugh O'Brian, Bethel Leslie, Edgar Stehli, Roland Winters
4. "Cry Out of Silence" (5-15-62) Celeste Holm, David McLean, Philip Bourneuf
5. "A Place to Hide" (5-22-62) Joan Hackett, Dean Stockwell, Frank Ferguson
6. "The Boy Who Wasn't Wanted" (6-5-62) Dana Andrews, Billy Mumy, Marilyn Erskine, Barbara Loden
7. "It Takes a Thief" (6-19-62) Edward Andrews, Constance Ford
8. "The Time of the Tonsils" (6-26-62) Eddie Albert, Howard McNear

Second Season

29. "Flashing Spikes" (10-4-62) Tige Andrews, Jack Warden, Patrick Wayne, Stefanie Hill, Carleton Young, Edgar Buchanan, Don Drysdale

30. "Guest in the House" (10-11-62) Fred Astaire, Lloyd Bochner, Philip Abbott, Phyllis Avery

31. "The Long Walk Home" (10-18-62) Lin McCarthy, Nancy Rennick, R. G. Armstrong, Ken Lynch

32. "The Voice of Charlie Pont" (10-25-62) Bradford Dillman, Diana Hyland, Robert Redford, Bill Bixby, Cathie Merchant, Tammy Locke, Bob Hopkins, Joey Russo

33. "Mr. Lucifer" (11-1-62) Fred Astaire, Elizabeth Montgomery, Frank Aletter, Hal Smith, Joyce Bulifant, George Petrie

34. "The Masked Marine" (11-8-62) Harry Guardino, James Caan, Chris Robinson, George Brenlin, James McMullan

35. "Ordeal in Darkness" (11-15-62) Keir Dullea, Richard Conte, Dorothy Green

36. "Whatever Happened to Miss Illinois?" (11-22-62) Carol Lynley, Anthony George, Arch Johnson

37. "The Hands of Danofrio" (11-29-62) Telly Savalas, John Williams, Joseph Campanella, Beulah Bondi

38. "The Contenders" (12-6-62) Suzanne Pleshette, Signe Hasso, Elen Willard, Edward Asner, Chester Morris, James Patterson

39. "The Way from Darkness" (12-13-62) Shelley Winters, Joan Hackett, Donald Harron, George Furth

40. "The Potentate" (12-20-62) Theodore Bikel, Milton Selzer, Carol Rossen, David Opatoshu

41. "Blues for a Hanging" (12-27-62) Janis Paige, Lurene Tuttle Lory Patrick, Shelly Manne

42. "Impact of an Execution" (1-3-63) Ralph Bellamy, Ruby Dee Peggy Ann Garner, Robert Colbert

43. "Lollipop Louie" (1-10-63) Aldo Ray, Barbara Turner, Ralph Manza, Edmund Vargas, Paul Comi, Betty Hardford

44. "The Glass Palace" (1-17-63) Ricardo Montalban, Anne Francis, Joanna Barnes, Don Hamner

45. "Five, Six, Pick Up Sticks" (1-24-63) John Forsythe, Mickey Rooney, Barbara Nichols, John Lupton, Geraldine Brooks Bibi Osterwald

46. "The Hat of Sergeant Martin" (2-7-63) Claude Akins, Roger Perry, Rafael Campos, Carlos Romero, Will Kuluva

47. "Blow High, Blow Clear" [unsold pilot film for projected fall series] (2-14-63) Tommy Sands, Jane Wyatt, Dan Duryea Chris Robinson, John Anderson

48. "Chain Reaction" (2-21-63) Ralph Bellamy, Charles Drake, Bradford Dillman, Bettye Ackerman

49. "Hornblower" (2-28-63) David Buck, Terence Longdon, Peter Arne, Nigel Green, Sean Kelly

50. "Jeeney Ray" (3-14-63) Brenda Scott, Joanna Moore, Ron Hayes, Jim Davis, Olive Carey

51. "The Dark Labyrinth" (3-21-63) Patrick O'Neal, Salome

Jens, Carroll O'Connor, Arthur Malet, Barbara Barrie
52. "Of Struggle and Flight" (3-28-63) Janice Rule, Jack Kruschen, Dabney Coleman, Tod Andrews, Gerald O'Loughlin
53. "The Broken Year" (4-4-63) Keir Dullea, Shirley Knight,
Leif Erickson, Katherine Bard, George Kennedy
54. "This Will Kill You" (4-11-63) Louis Nye, Howard Morris,
Frances Rafferty, Ernest Borgnine (as himself in cameo)
55. "Million Dollar Hospital" (4-18-63) Charles Bickford,
William Shatner, Reta Shaw, Nancy Rennick, Arthur Batanides
56. "The Town That Died" (4-25-63) Dana Andrews, Gene Evans,
Mary La Roche, William Schallert

## FRONTIER CIRCUS

Western tale of a traveling circus, periodically enmeshed,
of course, with the problems of staging performances--the series
itself relying upon the star quality of its guests.

The Regulars: Col. Casey Thompson, Chill Wills; Ben Travis,
John Derek; Tony Gentry, Richard Jaeckel.

The Episodes:

1. "The Depths of Fear" (10-5-61) Aldo Ray, James Gregory,
Bethel Leslie, Vito Scotti
2. "The Smallest Target" (10-12-61) Barbara Rush, Brian
Keith
3. "Lippizan" (10-19-61) Vera Miles
4. "Dr. Sam" (10-26-61) Irene Dunne, Ellen Corby, J. Pat
O'Malley
5. "The Hunter and the Hunted" (11-2-61) Eddie Albert, Rip
Torn, Jocelyn Brando
6. "Karina" (11-9-61) Elizabeth Montgomery
7. "Journey from Hannibal" (11-16-61) Thelma Ritter
8. "Winter Quarters" (11-23-61) Robert J. Wilke
9. "The Patriarch of Purgatory" (11-30-61) Royal Dano,
Robert Sampson, Carolyn Kearney
10. "The Shaggy Kings" (12-7-61) Dick York, Dan Duryea,
Michael Pate
11. "Coals of Fire" (1-4-62) Sammy Davis Jr.
12. "The Balloon Girl" (1-11-62) Stella Stevens, Claude Akins,
Chick Chandler
13. "Mr. O'Grady Regrets" (1-25-62) Charles Ruggles, Anne
Helm
14. "Quick Shuffle" (2-1-62) Gilbert Roland, Patricia Barry
15. "The Courtship" (2-15-62) Jo Van Fleet, Henry Jones
16. "Stopover in Paradise" (2-22-62) Carolyn Jones, Robert
Simon
17. "Naomi Champagne" (3-1-62) Constance Ford
18. "Calamity Circus" (3-8-62) Mickey Rooney, Nico Minardos

19. "The Inheritance" (3-15-62) Marc Marno, Alan Hale, J. Pat O'Malley
20. "Mighty Like Rogues" (3-29-62) Glenda Farrell, Joby Baker, Roger Mobley, Jena Engstrom, J. Pat O'Malley
21. "Never Won Fair Lady" (4-5-62) Red Buttons, Gloria Talbot
22. "The Good Fight" (4-19-62) Ray Daley, George Macready
23. "The Clan MacDuff" (4-26-62) James Barton
24. "The Race" (5-3-62) Edward Andrews, Skip Homeier
25. "The Daring Durandos" (5-17-62) Nehemiah Persoff

DR. KILDARE

Satisfying television adaptation of the popular motion picture serial but lacking the gusto of its contemporary medical entry, "Ben Casey." 'Dr. Kildare' 's initial film is the composition of E. Jack Neuman, veteran of the radio series of the intern Kildare and Chief of Medical Services Dr. Gillespie at Blair General Hospital.

The Regulars: Dr. James Kildare, Richard Chamberlain; Dr. Gillespie, Raymond Massey; Dr. Thomas Gerson, Jud Taylor; Dr. Simon Agurski, Eddie Ryder; Susan Deigh, Joan Patrick; Nurse Fain, Jean Inness; Nurse Zoe Lawton, Lee Kurty (last season).

The Episodes:

1. "Twenty-Four Hours" (9-28-61) Beverly Garland, Jack Weston, Carol Rossen
2. "Immunity" (10-5-61) Gail Kobe, Ted Knight
3. "Shining Image" (10-12-61) Suzanne Pleshette, Edward Andrews
4. "Winter Harvest" (10-19-61) Charles Bickford, Hershel Bernardi
5. "A Million Dollar Property" (10-26-61) Cathleen Nesbitt, Anne Francis, Jan Murray
6. "Admitting Service" (11-2-61) William Shatner
7. "The Lonely Ones" (11-9-61) Dick York, Carolyn Kearney
8. "Holiday Weekend" (11-16-61) Dick Sargent
9. "The Patient" (11-23-61) Jean Stapleton, Jenny Maxwell
10. "For the Living" (11-30-61) Charles McGraw, Beatrice Straight
11. "Second Chance" (12-7-61) Ross Martin
12. "Hit and Run" (12-14-61) Dick Foran, Richard Kiley
13. "Season to Be Jolly" (12-21-61) Dan O'Herlihy
14. "Johnny Temple" (12-28-61) Doug Lambert, Virginia Gregg, Peter Whitney
15. "My Brother, the Doctor" (1-4-62) Eddie Ryder, Hershel Bernardi
16. "The Administrator" (1-11-62) Joseph Cotten, Dorothy

Malone
17.   "Oh, My Daughter" (1-25-62) Victor Jory, Dina Merrill
18.   "The Search" (2-1-62) Jeremy Slate, Pippa Scott
19.   "The Glory Hunter" (2-8-62) Martin Balsam, Alfred Ryder
20.   "The Dragon" (2-15-62) Margaret O'Brien, Scott Marlowe
21.   "The Stepping Stone" (2-22-62) Eduardo Ciannelli, Joseph
        Schildkraut
22.   "The Bronc Buster" (3-1-62) Arch Johnson
23.   "The Witch Doctor" (3-8-62) Joan Hackett, Pat Hingle
24.   "The Roaring Boy-O" (3-15-62) Dan O'Herlihy, Fay Spain
25.   "Solomon's Choice" (3-29-62) Barbara Baxley, Collin Wilcox
26.   "A Very Present Help" (4-5-62) Patricia Crowley, Glynis
        Johns
27.   "One for the Road" (4-12-62) Lee Marvin
28.   "Horn of Plenty" (4-19-62) Ellen Willard, Julie Adams
29.   "The Chemistry of Anger" (4-26-62) Rip Torn
30.   "Something of Importance" (5-3-62) George Voskovec, Ivan
        Dixon
31.   "A Distant Thunder" (5-10-62) Dean Jagger
32.   "Road to the Heart" (5-17-62) Rory O'Brien, Joanne Lin-
        ville
33.   "Operation Lazarus" (5-24-62) Mary Astor, Sidney Blackmer

## Second Season

34.   "Gravida One" (9-27-62) Patricia Barry, Otto Kruger
35.   "The Burning Sky" (10-4-62) Carroll O'Connor, Robert Red-
        ford, Harriet Day
36.   "The Visitors" (10-11-62) Theodore Bikel, John Cassavetes
37.   "The Mask Makers" (10-18-62) Carolyn Jones
38.   "Guest Appearance" (10-25-62) Jack Carter
39.   "Hastings' Farewell" (11-1-62) Beverly Garland, Harry
        Guardino
40.   "Breakdown" (11-8-62) Larry Parks, Inga Swenson
41.   "Cobweb Chain" (11-15-62) Steven Hill, Miriam Colon
42.   "The Soul Killer" (11-22-62) Eileen Heckart, Barbara Park-
        ins, Suzanne Pleshette
43.   "An Ancient Office" (12-6-62) Ed Begley, Joan Freeman,
        Peggy Wood, Dick Davalos, Irene Hervey, Henderson
        Forsythe
44.   "The Legacy" (12-13-62) Olympia Dukakis, Edward Asner
45.   "The Bed I've Made" (12-20-62) Dan Tobin
46.   "A Time for Every Purpose" (12-27-62) Betty Field
47.   "Love Is a Sad Song" (1-3-62) Diana Hyland, Dan Tobin
48.   "The Thing Speaks for Itself" (1-10-63) George Macready,
        Zohra Lampert, Fritz Weaver
49.   "The Great Guy" (1-17-63) Constance Ford
50.   "The Mosaic" (1-31-63) James Caan, Tom Tryon
51.   "The Good Luck Charm" (2-7-63) Gloria Swanson
52.   "Jail Ward" (2-14-63) James Franciscus, Henry Silva
53.   "A Trip to Niagara" (2-21-63) Irene Dailey, John Larch
54.   "A Place Among the Monuments" (2-28-63) Harold J. Stone,
        Zohra Lampert

55. "Face of Fear" (3-7-63) Mary Astor, Robert Culp
56. "Sister Mike" (3-14-63) Fay Bainter
57. "A Very Infectious Disease" (3-21-63) Dan O'Herlihy, Jean Hagen
58. "The Dark Side of the Mirror" (3-28-63) Alex Nicol, Polly Bergen
59. "Sleeping Princess" (4-11-63) June Harding
60. "Ship's Doctor" (4-18-63) Patrick O'Neal, Elinor Donahue
61. "Tight-rope into Nowhere" (4-25-63) Mary Murphy, Edward Asner
62. "The Balance and the Crucible" (5-2-63) Peter Falk
63. "The Gift of the Koodjanuk" (5-9-63) Brian Keith, Greg Morris
64. "An Island Like a Peacock" (5-16-63) Kathryn Hays, Forrest Tucker
65. "To Each His Prison" (5-23-63) Ross Martin, Lois Smith
66. "A Hand Held Out in Darkness" (5-30-63) Vicki Cos, Philip Abbott

Third Season

67. "Who Ever Heard of a Two-Headed Doll?" (9-26-63) Charles Bronson, Janice Rule, Richard Anderson, Steven Bell
68. "The Good Samaritan" (10-3-63) Thomas Gomez, Ruth White, John Anderson
69. "If You Can't Believe the Truth... " (10-10-63) Barbara Eden, James Whitmore
70. "The Heart, an Imperfect Machine" (10-17-63) Pat Hingle, Diane Baker, Charles McGraw
71. "A Game for Three" (10-24-63) Andrew Prine, Susan Strasberg
72. "The Exploiters" (10-31-63) Nancy Malone, Judson Laire, Glenda Farrell
73. "One Clear, Bright Thursday Morning" (11-7-63) Miyoshi Umecki, James Shigeta
74. "The Eleventh Commandment" (11-14-63) Molly Picon, Michael Forrest, Susan Oliver
75. "Four Feet in the Morning" [Part I; concluded with "The Eleventh Hour" episode of 11/27/63] (11-21-63) Ralph Bellamy, Jack Ging, Tony Dow, Andrew Duggan, Ruth Roman, Marta Kristen, Phyllis Avery
76. "The Pack Rat and the Prima Donna" (11-28-63) Celeste Holm, Ed Nelson, Charles Fredericks
77. "The Backslider" (12-5-63) Kevin McCarthy, Anne Helm, Lori March
78. "Charles Wade Makes Lots of Shade" (12-12-63) Frank Overton, Dale Melone, Mary La Roche, Marion Ross
79. "The Oracle" (12-19-63) Lauren Bacall, Brenda Scott
80. "Vote of Confidence" (12-26-63) Eddie Albert, Frank Aletter, Patricia Breslin, Carl Benton Reid, Lee Meriwether
81. "A Willing Suspension of Disbelief" (1-9-64) Jack Lord, Mala Powers, Denver Pyle
82. "Tyger, Tyger... " [Part I] (1-16-64) Yvette Mimieux, Clu

Gulager, Anjanette Comer, John Newland
83. "Tyger, Tyger..." [Part II] (1-23-64) as above
84. "Never Too Old for the Circus" (1-30-64) Ann Harding, Walter Pidgeon
85. "Onions, Garlic, and Flowers That Bloom in the Spring" (2-6-64) Cesar Romero, Audrey Dalton, Joe De Santis
86. "To Walk in Grace" (2-13-64) Gena Rowlands, Joan Tompkins
87. "Goodbye, Mr. Jersey" (2-20-64) Suzanne Pleshette, J. Pat O'Malley
88. "Why Won't Anybody Listen?" (2-27-64) Claude Rains, William Demarest
89. "The Child Between" (3-5-64) Beau Bridges, Jeanne Cooper, Lee Philips
90. "A Hundred Million Tomorrows" (3-12-64) George Grizzard, Paul Burke, Diana Van Der Vlis
91. "Tomorrow Is a Fickle Girl" (3-19-64) Sal Mineo, Naomi Stevens
92. "Quid Pro Quo" (3-26-64) Michael Callan, Robert Walker Jr.
93. "A Day to Remember" (4-2-64) Anne Baxter, Yvonne Craig, Michel Petit
94. "An Ungodly Act" (4-9-64) Douglas Fairbanks Jr., Shelley Morrison
95. "A Nickel's Worth of Prayer" (4-16-64) Ed Begley, Kim Darby, Lola Albright
96. "Night of the Beast" (4-23-64) Bradford Dillman, Carol Rossen, Sharon Farrell, John Ashley
97. "The Middle of Ernie Mann" (4-30-64)
98. "A Sense of Tempo" (5-7-64) Patricia Crowley, Cyril Ritchard, Jeanette Nolan
99. "Speak Not in Angry Whispers" (5-14-64) Lois Nettleton, Gerald S. O'Loughlin
100. "Dolly's Dilemma" (5-21-64) Joan Blondell, Chester Morris

Fourth Season

101. "Man Is a Rock" (9-24-64) Walter Matthau, Georgann Johnson, Richard Evans, Lana Wood, Ken Lynch
102. "Maybe Love Will Save My Apartment House" (10-1-64) Suzy Parker, Barry Nelson, Lisa Loring
103. "The Hand that Hurts, the Hand that Heels" (10-8-64) Steve Ihnat, Janice Rule, Jeanette Nolan
104. "The Last Leaves on the Tree" (10-15-64) Hans Conried, Estelle Winwood, Josephine Hutchinson
105. "What's Different About Today?" (10-22-64) Kim Darby, Kelly Corcoran, John Lasell
106. "The Sound of a Faraway Hill" (10-29-64) Lee Marvin, David Sheiner, John Megna
107. "A Candle in the Window" (11-5-64) Ronny Howard, Ruth Roman, Walter Burke
108. "Rome Will Never Leave You" [Part I] (11-12-64) Ramon

Novarro, Alida Valli, Mercedes McCambridge, Paul Stewart, Daniela Bianchi

109. "Rome Will Never Leave You" [Part II] (11-19-64) as above

110. "Rome Will Never Leave You" [Part III] (11-26-64) as above

111. "The Elusive Dik-Dik" (12-3-64) Geraldine Brooks, Barbara McNair, Tom Helmore, Michel Petit

112. "Catch a Crooked Mouse" (12-17-64) Harold J. Stone, Andrew Prine, Joe Maross, Fay Spain, Joe Mantell

113. "An Exchange of Gifts" (12-24-64) Rip Torn, John Qualen, Sam Weston

114. "Never Is a Long Day" (12-31-64) Walter Slezak, Davey Davison, Hanna Landy

115. "Lullaby for an Indian Summer" (1-7-65) Margaret Leighton, Tisha Sterling, Robert Young, Peter Duryea

116. "Take Care of My Little Girl" (1-14-65) Gail Kobe, Larry Blyden, Stuart Erwin, Veronica Cartwright

117. "My Name Is Lisa, and I Am Lost" (1-21-65) Nina Foch, Lois Nettleton, Carmen Matthews, Harry Townes

118. "Please Let My Baby Live" (1-28-65) Diana Hyland, Marge Redmond, Peter Haskell, Harold Gould

119. "No Mother to Guide Them" (2-4-65) Jack Warden, Patricia Hyland, Joan Tompkins

120. "Marriage of Convenience" (2-11-65) Burt Brinckerhoff, Louise Sorel, Rodolfo Hoyos

121. "Make Way for Tomorrow" (2-18-65) Ed Begley, Joanna Barnes, Mabel Albertson

122. "Miracle for Margaret" (2-25-65) Barbara Bel Geddes, Ford Rainey, Betsy Hale

123. "Do You Trust Your Doctor?" (3-4-65) Robert Culp, Leslie Nielsen, Angie Dickinson, Alma Platt

124. "All Brides Should Be Beautiful" (3-11-65) Colleen Dewhurst, Tom Bosley, Rusty Lane

125. "She Loves Me, She Loves Me Not" [Part I] (3-18-65) Angie Dickinson, Leslie Nielsen, Jan Peters

126. "She Loves Me, She Loves Me Not" [Part II] (3-25-65) as above

127. "A Journey to Sunrise" (4-1-65) Don Quine, Malcolm Atterbury

128. "The Time Buyers" (4-8-65) Carroll O'Connor, Patricia Barry, Donnelly Rhodes, Les Tremayne

129. "Music Hath Charms" (4-15-65) Dorothy Provine, Darryl Hickman, Rosemary DeCamp

130. "Believe and Live" (4-22-65) Dan O'Herlihy, Conrad Nagel, Anne Jeffreys, Kevin McCarthy

131. "A Reverence for Life" (4-29-65) Dennis Weaver, Phyllis Love, Norman Fell, Frank Maxwell

132. "Wings of Hope" (5-13-65) Sharon Farrell, Earl Holliman, Whit Bissell

Fifth Season [now as half hour series]

133. "Behold the Great Man" [Part I] (9-13-65) James Mason,
    Margaret Leighton, Burt Brinckerhoff, Naomi Stevens,
    Robert Cornthwaite, Sara Haden, Mark Vance, Christo-
    pher West, John Lodge, Rodolfo Hoyos
134. "A Life for a Life" [Part II] (9-14-65) as above
135. "Web of Hate" [Part III] (9-20-65) as above
136. "The Horizontal Hero" [Part IV] (9-21-65) as above
137. "The Bell in the Schoolhouse Tolls for Thee, Kildare" [Part
    I] (9-27-65) Dean Stockwell, Tony Bill, Andrew Prine,
    Sheila Wells, Francis X. Bushman, William Bramley
138. "Life in the Dance Hall: F-U-N" [Part II] (9-28-65) as
    above
139. "Some Doors Are Slamming" [Part III] (10-5-65) as above
140. "Enough La Bohème for Everybody" [Part IV] (10-11-65)
    as above
141. "Now, the Mummy" [Part V] (10-12-65) as above
142. "A Pyrotechnic Display" [Part VI] (10-18-65) as above
143. "With Hellfire and Thunder" [Part I] (10-19-65) James
    Daly, Barbara Rush, Sorrell Booke, Bert Freed, George
    Savalas, James Dawson
144. "Daily Flights to Olympus" [Part II] (10-25-65) as above
145. "The Life Machine" [Part I] (10-26-65) Leslie Nielsen,
    David Opatoshu, Marlyn Mason, Robert Reed, Cloris
    Leachman, Barbara Rush, Philip Bourneuf, Hazel Court,
    Hayden Rorke, Donna Loren
146. "Toast the Golden Couple" [Part II] (11-1-65) as above
147. "Wives and Losers" [Part III] (11-2-65) as above
148. "Welcome Home, Dear Anna" [Part IV] (11-8-65) as above
149. "A Little Child Shall Lead Them" [Part V] (11-9-65) as
    above
150. "Hour of Decision" [Part VI] (11-15-65) as above
151. "Aftermath" [Part VII] (11-16-65) as above
152. "Fathers and Daughters" [Part I] (11-22-65) Fred Astaire,
    Audrey Totter, Spring Byington, Laura Devon, Harry
    Morgan, Kathy Garver, Norman Fell, Alan Hewitt
153. "A Gift of Love" [Part II] (11-23-65) as above
154. "The Tent-Dwellers" [Part III] (11-29-65) as above
155. "Going Home" [Part IV] (11-30-65) as above
156. "Something Old, Something New" [Part I] (12-6-65) Kim
    Hunter, Sharon Farrell
157. "To Visit One More Spring" [Part II] (12-7-65) as above
158. "From Niagara with Love" [Part I] (12-13-65) Darren
    McGavin, Patricia Barry, Tippy Walker
159. "In the Roman Candle's Bright Glare" [Part II] (12-14-65)
    as above
160. "When Shadows Fall" [Part III] (12-20-65) as above
161. "Rage, Rage Against the Dying of the Light" [Part IV] (12-
    21-65) as above
162. "Perfect Is Hard to Be" [Part I] (12-27-65) Basil Rath-
    bone, Susan Oliver, Frances Reid
163. "Duet for One Hand" [Part II] (12-28-65) as above

164. "The Atheist and the True Believer" [Part I] (1-3-66) Jack
     Hawkins, Bradford Dillman, Diane Baker, Donald Madden
165. "A Quick Look at Glory" [Part II] (1-4-66) as above
166. "A Sort of Falling in Love" [Part III] (1-10-66) as above
167. "The Last to Believe in Miracles" [Part IV] (1-11-66) as
     above
168. "The Next Thing to Murder" [Part V] (1-17-66) as above
169. "Never So Happy" [Part VI] (1-18-66) as above
170. "A Cry from the Streets" [Part I] (1-24-66) James Earl
     Jones, Diana Sands, Eduardo Ciannelli, G. B. Atwater,
     Beah Richards
171. "Gratitude Won't Pay the Bills" [Part II] (1-25-66) as above
172. "Adrift in a Sea of Confusion" [Part III] (1-31-66) as above
173. "With These Hands" [Part IV] (2-1-66) as above
174. "A Few Hearts, a Few Flowers" [Part I] (2-7-66) Ri-
     cardo Montalban, Elizabeth Allen
175. "Some Tales for Halloween" [Part II] (2-8-66) as above
176. "We Dance to the Tango of Love" [Part III] (2-14-66) as
     above
177. "You Got to Walk That Lonesome Valley" [Part IV] (2-15-
     66) as above
178. "The Encroachment" [Part I] (2-21-66) William Shatner,
     Martin Balsam, Diana Muldaur, Joanna Pettet, Jack
     Nicholson
179. "A Patient Lost" [Part II] (2-22-66) as above
180. "What Happened to All the Sunshine and Roses?" [Part III]
     (2-28-66) as above
181. "The Taste of Crow" [Part IV] (3-7-66) as above
182. "Out of a Concrete Tower" [Part V] (3-8-66) as above
183. "The Art of Taking a Powder" [Part I] (3-14-66) John
     Saxon, Joan Marshall, Angela Clarke, Joe De Santis
184. "Read the Book, Then See the Picture" [Part II] (3-15-66)
     as above
185. "A Sometimes Distant Spring" [Part I] (3-21-66) Diane
     Varsi, Kim Karath, Gloria McMillan, Virginia Gregg
186. "Travel a Crooked Road" [Part II] (3-22-66) as above
187. "Mercy or Murder?" [Part I] (3-28-66) Richard Beymer,
     George Kennedy, Murray Hamilton, Mart Hulswit
188. "A Strange Sort of Accident" [Part II] (3-29-66) as above
189. "New Doctor in Town" [Part III] (4-4-66) as above
190. "Reckoning" [Part IV] (4-5-66) as above


THE INVESTIGATORS

Trite mystery series of insurance investigators.

The Regulars: Russ Andrews, James Franciscus; Steve Banks,
     James Philbrook; Maggie Peters, Mary Murphy; Bill
     Davis, Al Austin; Polly Walters, June Kenny.

The Episodes:

1. "Murder on Order" (10-5-61) Rhonda Fleming, Brad Dexter, June Dayton
2. "The Oracle" (10-12-61) Lee Marvin, Audrey Dalton, John Williams
3. "New Sound for the Blues" (10-19-61) Claire Trevor, Bill Williams
4. "I Thee Kill" (10-26-61) Mickey Rooney, Claire Griswold, Richard Rust
5. "Quite a Woman" (11-2-61) Miriam Hopkins, Otto Kruger, Alan Mowbray, Abraham Sofaer
6. "Style of Living" (11-9-61) Dina Merrill, Edward Binns, Bethel Leslie, Gavin MacLeod
7. "In a Mirror, Darkly" (11-16-61) Diana Lynn, Miriam Hopkins, Harry Townes, Joanna Barnes
8. "De Luca" (11-23-61) Robert Middleton, Judi Meredith, Vito Scotti, Mario Alcaide
9. "Death Leaves a Tip" (11-30-61) Jane Wyman
10. "Panic Wagon" (12-7-61) Albert Salmi, Robert Webber, Jean Engstrom
11. "The Mind's Own Fire" (12-14-61) Dennis Hopper, Mildred Dunnock, James Dunn
12. "Something for Charity" (12-21-61) Ida Lupino, Linda Watkins, Val Avery
13. "The Dead End Man" (12-28-61) Henry Jones, Pat Carroll, Dorothy Green, Philip Ober, William Fawcett


STRAIGHTAWAY

Again, a tribute to the youthful spirit--this one of the adventures of race car drivers.

The Regulars: Scott Ross, Brian Kelly; Clipper Hamilton, John Ashley.

The Episodes:

1. "The Leather Dollar" (10-6-61) Luther Adler
2. "The Tin Caesar" (10-13-61) Neville Brand
3. "The Nobles Oblige" (10-20-61)
4. "Heat Wave" (10-27-61) Malcolm Atterbury
5. "Die Laughing" (11-3-61) Jack Klugman, Scott Marlowe
6. "The Heist" (11-10-61) Peter Whitney, Gavin MacLeod
7. "The Stranger" (11-17-61) Bethel Leslie, Kevin Hagen, Patricia O'Neal
8. "The Racer and the Lady" (11-24-61) Joan Tabor
9. "Pledge a Nightmare" (12-1-61) Michael Parks
10. "The Sportscar Breed" (12-8-61) Diana Dors
11. "A Toast to Yesterday" (12-15-61) Gloria Swanson
12. "Troubleshooter" (12-22-61) Myrna Fahey

13. "The Bribe" (12-29-61) John Considine
14. "Last Chance" (1-10-62)
15. "A Moment in the Sun" (1-17-62) Robert Blake
16. "The Drag Strip" (1-24-62) Richard Miles, Asa Maynor
17. "Crossroad" (1-31-62) Michael Pagan, Lew Gallo
18. "Sounds of Fury" (2-7-62) Mary Tyler Moore, Robert F. Simon
19. "Escape from Darkness" (2-14-62) William Bramley
20. "Tiger by the Tail" (2-21-62) Eddie Foy III, Asa Maynor
21. "The Ledge" (2-28-62) Leo Penn, Ken Lynch
22. "The Longest Night" (3-7-62) Paul Richards
23. "Full Circle" (3-14-62) Howard Caine
24. "The Craziest Race in Town" (3-21-62) Barbara Bain, Asa
    Maynor, Don Beddoe
25. "To Climb Steep Hills" (3-28-62) Paul Carr
26. "The Hoax" (4-4-62) Tod Andrews


TARGET!: THE CORRUPTORS

Initially titled "Exposé," the basis for this series was the muckraking journalism of co-producer (along with Dan Burrows and Leonard Ackerman) Lester Velie. The episodes were hard-hitting drama, with an uncompromising emphasis on the all-too-frequent failings of our legal system. In "The Poppy Vendor," by Les Pine, the higher-ups in the narcotics racket get away, with protagonist Gena Rowlands, in constant need of a "fix," giving birth to an addicted child--a fact which in no way impairs her insatiable desire to "come back for more." In "Play It Blue," by Alexander Richards, Richard Landau and Harry Essex, syndicate control of the recording industry leads pop singer Dean Jones to inadvertently cause the death of his fianceé, for which reason he will ever more "play his songs blue." Robert Vaughn was a perfect villain in Harry Essex's and Gene Roddenberry's "To Wear a Badge," serenely corrupting a seemingly uncorruptible policeman Robert Culp. But perhaps the best of all the episodes, if only because it was a sincere plea for reform of our prison system, was Gilbert Ralston's "Fortress of Despair," in which seventeen-year-old Lynn Loring is incarcerated with hardened criminals, innocently "taking a rap" as an accomplice to the crime of her burglar fiancé. Before the dawn of her eighteenth birthday, she has undergone a metamorphosis, emerging as a woman about to embark on a life of crime. Arthur Hiller did a fine job of direction for the episode.

One flaw with the series, however, was in its hero-worship of principal character Paul Mareno (Stephen McNally) who carried on his muckraking with a fierce mien too long the stereotype of the roving reporter, and a totally uncorruptible conviction which seemed out of place against the rampant evil which somehow found its way into the minds of most every guest star.

The Regulars: Paul Mareno, Stephen McNally; Jack Flood, Robert
    Harland.

The Episodes:

1.  "The Million Dollar Dump" (9-29-61)  Peter Falk, Walter
    Matthau, Robert Middleton
2.  "Pier 60" (10-6-61)  Jack Klugman, Vic Morrow
3.  "The Platinum Highway" (10-13-61)  Dan O'Herlihy
4.  "The Invisible Government" (10-20-61)  Edmond O'Brien
5.  "The Poppy Vendor" (10-27-61)  Gena Rowlands, Robert
    Loggia, John Marley, Don Gordon, David White
6.  "Bite of a Tiger" (11-3-61)  Thomas Gomez, Ed Begley,
    Lee Philips
7.  "Touch of Evil" (11-10-61)  Ray Walston, Lee Kinsolving
8.  "Mr. Megalomania" (11-17-61)  Wendell Corey
9.  "The Golden Carpet" (11-24-61)  Larry Blyden, Edward As-
    ner
10. "To Wear a Badge" (12-1-61)  Robert Vaughn, Robert Culp,
    Jacqueline Scott, Royal Dano, Michael Constantine, John
    Kellogg
11. "Silent Partner" (12-8-61)  Robert H. Harris, Luther Adler
12. "Prison Empire" (12-15-61)  Preston Foster
13. "The Fix" (12-22-61)  Frank Lovejoy, Harry Townes
14. "Quicksand" (12-29-61)  Steve Forrest, Richard Long,
    Eduardo Ciannelli, Sarah Marshall
15. "A Man Is Waiting to Be Murdered" (1-5-62)  Burt Brincker-
    hoff, Brian Donlevy, Jacques Aubuchon
16. "One for the Road" (1-12-62)  Irene Hervey, David Brian,
    Constance Ford, Walter Matthau
17. "Play It Blue" (1-19-62)  Dean Jones, Harold J. Stone
18. "Chase the Dragon" (1-26-62)  Jack Klugman, Keye Luke,
    Cely Carrillo
19. "The Middle Man" (2-2-62)  David Janssen
20. "Viva Vegas" (2-9-62)  Suzanne Pleshette, Jack Oakie
21. "Fortress of Despair" (2-16-62)  Lynn Loring, Joyce Van
    Patten
22. "The Wrecker" (3-2-62)  Luther Adler, Cloris Leachman,
    Linden Chiles
23. "Babes in Wall Street" (3-9-62)  Harry Guardino, Barbara
    Eden
24. "My Native Land" (3-16-62)  Cesar Romero, Ilka Windish,
    Jerome Cowan, Will Kuluva
25. "The Malignant Hearts" (3-23-62)  Sidney Blackmer, James
    Gregory
26. "A Man's Castle" (3-30-62)  Scott Marlowe, Robert Emhardt
27. "Journey into Mourning" (4-13-62)  Keenan Wynn, Ivan Dixon,
    Warren Oates, Royal Dano
28. "The Blind Goddess" (4-20-62)  Margaret Hayes, Macdonald
    Carey, Robert Middleton
29. "A Book of Faces" (4-27-62)  Martin Balsam, Shirley Knight,
    Constance Ford, Jeanette Nolan, Virginia Christine
30. "License to Steal" (5-4-62)  Harold J. Stone, Gene Evans,
    Sonya Wilde
31. "Yankee Dollar" (5-11-62)  Robert F. Simon, Hope Holiday,
    Alan Hale Jr., Alfred Ryder, William Conrad

32. "The Organizer" [Part I]  (5-18-62)  Brian Keith, Burt
     Brinckerhoff, Jack Warden
33. "The Organizer" [Part II]  (5-25-62)  as above
34. "Nobody Gets Hurt"  (6-1-62)  Kevin McCarthy, Michael
     Parks, Russell Collins
35. "Goodbye, Children"  (6-8-62)  John Ericson, Bethel Leslie

1962-1963 SEASON

SAM BENEDICT

Drawn from the experiences of renowned trial lawyer Jacob W. Ehrlich, who served as technical consultant for the series, this attained some interesting performances from several actors in even more interesting situations. Robert Lansing was in fine form in "Read No Evil," about a high school teacher who battles censorship and accordingly suffers a town's intolerance. "So Various, So Beautiful"--a title from Matthew Arnold's 1867 masterpiece Dover Beach--dealt with a potential false testimony (by Hazel Court in the role of Deborah Bowman) in a murder case in which the accused had already been administered his capital punishment. Edmond O'Brien brought stature and substance to the Sam Benedict/Ehrlich role.

The Regulars: Sam Benedict, Edmond O'Brien; Hank Tabor (assistant to Benedict), Richard Rust; Trudy Wagner (secretary), Joan Tompkins.

The Episodes:

1. "Hannigan" (9-15-62) Lloyd Bochner, Gene Raymond, Tammy Marihugh, Katherine Bard, Donna Douglas
2. "A Split Week in San Quentin" (9-22-62) Jack Weston, Katherine Ross, Rex Ingram, Joe De Santis
3. "Nor Practice Makes Perfect" (9-29-62) Claude Rains, John Anderson, Linda Watkins, Narda Onyx
4. "Nothing Equals Nothing" (10-6-62) Constance Ford, Nancy Kelly, Otto Kruger
5. "Tears for a Nobody Doll" (10-13-62) Miyoshi Umeki, Michael Constantine, Joanna Barnes
6. "Twenty Aching Years" (10-20-62) Hershel Bernardi, Joanne Linville, Harry Townes
7. "Maddon's Folly" (10-27-62) Robert Lansing, Vera Miles, Paul Newlan
8. "Hear the Mellow Wedding Bells" (11-3-62) Joseph Schildkraut, Larry Blyden, Zohra Lampert
9. "Life Is a Lie, Love Is a Cheat" (11-10-62) Audrey Meadows, Ed Nelson, Joe Mantell
10. "The Bird of Warning" (11-17-62) Diana Hyland, Maria Palmer, George Tobias

11. "The View from an Ivory Tower" (11-24-62) Dan O'Herlihy, Phyllis Avery, Lawrence Dobkin
12. "Everybody's Playing Polo" (12-1-62) Burgess Meredith, Irene Dailey, Joby Baker
13. "Too Many Strangers" (12-8-62) Gloria Grahame, Marsha Hunt, Michael Parks
14. "So Various, So Beautiful" (12-15-62) Theodore Bikel, Hazel Court, Murray Matheson, Noah Keen
15. "Where There's a Will" (12-22-62) Geraldine Brooks, Frank Overton, Norman Fell, Jean Inness
16. "The Target Over the Hill" (12-29-62) Inger Stevens, Everett Sloane, Arch Johnson, Dolores Sutton
17. "Not Even the Gulls Shall Weep" (1-5-63) Howard Duff, Ida Lupino, J. Pat O'Malley, Karl Swenson, David Sheiner
18. "The Boiling Point" (1-12-63) Gary Merrill, David Wayne, Elizabeth MacRae
19. "Green Room, Grey Morning" (1-19-63) Ruth Roman, Frank Albertson, Tige Andrews
20. "Run Softly, Oh Softly" (1-26-63) Brian Keith, Barbara Stuart, Lori Martin, Philip Ober
21. "Sugar and Spice and Everything" (2-2-63) Arthur O'Connell, Yvonne Craig, William Schallert, Robert Emhardt, Gail Kobe
22. "Some Fires Die Slowly" (2-16-63) James MacArthur, Barry Sullivan, Karl Swenson, George Mitchell, Gage Clarke
23. "Image of a Toad" (2-23-63) Beverly Garland, Nehemiah Persoff, Russell Collins, Doro Merande, Patricia Huston
24. "Seventeen Gypsies and a Sinner Named Charlie" (3-2-63) Edmond O'Brien in a dual role; Maria O'Brien, Katie Sweet, Rory Stevens, Kyle Johnson
25. "Accomplice" (3-9-63) Eddie Albert, Brock Peters, Roger Perry, Ellen Holly
26. "Read No Evil" (3-16-63) Robert Lansing, Olive Deering, Susan Silo, Frank Sinatra Jr., Shirley O'Hara
27. "Of Rusted Cannons and Fallen Sparrows" (3-23-63) James Gregory, Nina Foch, Russell Thorson, Lisabeth Hush
28. "Season of Vengeance" (3-30-63) Elizabeth Ashley, Lou Jacobi, Paul Lucas, Gusti Huber

G. E. TRUE

The Regulars: Jack Webb, host.

The Episodes:

1. "Circle of Death" (9-30-62) William Conrad, Rachel Ames
2. "V--Victor 5" (10-7-62) Karl Held, Barbara Wilkin
3. "Harris vs. Castro" (10-14-62) Robert Knapp
4. "Code Name--Christopher" [Part I] (10-21-62) Jack Webb, Lloyd Bochner
5. "Code Name--Christopher" [Part II] (10-28-62) as above

6.  "The Handmade Private" (11-4-62) Jerry Van Dyke, Arte Johnson
7.  "The Last Day" (11-11-62) Mark Dempsey, Joan Huntington
8.  "Man with a Suitcase" (11-18-62) Bill Berger, Erika Peters, Werner Klemperer
9.  "Mile-Long Shot to Kill" (11-25-62) James Griffith, Russell Johnson
10. "Cheating Cheaters" (12-2-62) Dan MacFarland, Jack Hogan, Charlotte Austin
11. "U. X. B. " (12-9-62) Michael Evans
12. "The Wrong Nickel" (12-16-62) Albert Paulsen, Malachi Throne
13. "Little Richard" (12-23-62) Hampton Fancher
14. "The Amateurs" (12-30-62) Jonathan Hole
15. "Open Season" (1-6-63) James Best, Shirley Ballard, David McLean, Walter Reed
16. "Defendant: Clarence Darrow" (1-13-63) Robert Vaughn
17. "OSI" (1-20-63) Eric Feldary
18. "Firebug" (1-27-63) Keith Andes, Victor Buono
19. "Escape" [Part I] (2-10-63) Ben Wright
20. "Escape" [Part II] (2-17-63) as above
21. "The Moonshiners" (2-24-63) Gene Evans, Robert Emhardt
22. "Security Risk" (3-3-63) Erika Peters, Charles Aidman
23. "The Black-Robed Ghost" (3-10-63) Josephine Hutchinson, Jeanette Nolan
24. "Ordeal" (3-17-63) Chris Robinson
25. "The Tenth Mona Lisa" (3-31-63) Vito Scotti
26. "Gertie the Great" (4-14-63) Robert Brubaker
27. "Black Market" (4-21-63) Jan Shepard, John Marley, John Banner
28. "Nitro" (4-28-63) Philip Carey, Jacqueline Scott
29. "Heydrich" [Part I] (5-5-63) Albert Paulsen, Kurt Kreuger
30. "Heydrich" [Part II] (5-12-63) as above
31. "Commando" (5-19-63) Sean McClory, Lloyd Bochner
32. "Five Tickets to Hell" (5-26-63) Barbara Luna, Cesar Romano


## IT'S A MAN'S WORLD

Family drama of siblings surviving on an Ohio River houseboat.

The Regulars: Wes Macauley, Glenn Corbett; Howie Macauley, Michael Burns; Tom-Tom DeWitt, Ted Bessell; Verne Hodges, Randy Boone; Irene Hoff, Jan Norris; Mrs. Dobson, Kate Murtagh; Virgil Dobson, Scott White; Nora Fitzgerald, Anne Schuyler; Houghton Scott, Harry Harvey Jr.; Sue, Cathy Birch.

The Episodes:

1. "Four to Go" (9-17-62) regulars
2. "Stir Crazy" (9-24-62) regulars
3. "Molly Pitcher and the Green-Eyed Monster" (10-1-62) regulars
4. "Winning His Way" (10-15-62) Michael Garrett, Tim Graham
5. "Drive Over to Exeter" (10-22-62) Max Baer, Hope Summers, George Taylor
6. "The Beavers and the Otters" (10-29-62) Sally Mills, Amzie Strickland
7. "Howie's Adventure" (11-5-62) Doris Karnes, Kay Parker
8. "The Bravest Man in Cordella" (11-12-62) Dawn Wells, Gary Conway
9. "The Man on the Second Floor" (11-19-62) Dan Sheridan, Charles Thompson
10. "I Count My Life in Coffee Cups" (11-26-62) Diane Sayer, Arch Whiting
11. "Chicago Gains a Number" (12-3-62) Karl Swenson, Dawn Wells
12. "The Macauley Profile" (12-10-62) Lenore Kingston, Paul Comi
13. "The Long Short Cut" (12-17-62) Harold Gould, Joan Tewksbury
14. "The Long Way Around" (12-24-62) Judy Thompson, Bernadette Withers
15. "Night Beat of the Tom-Tom" (12-31-62) Buck Young, Russell Johnson, Ford Rainey
16. "Hour of Truth" (1-7-63) Lory Patrick
17. "The Unbalanced Line" (1-14-63) Paul Comi, R. G. Armstrong
18. "Mutiny on the Elephant" (1-21-63) regulars
19. "Winter Song" (1-28-63) regulars

## SAINTS AND SINNERS

This fine series with the newsroom as a backdrop functioned on a variety of dramatic levels. It was, for one, a weekly sociology lesson on the foibles and failings (on the saints and the sinners) of the subjects covered by reporter Nick Alexander (Nick Adams). It was, as well, an episodic adventure in the coming of age of the young, idealistic Alexander--a trite theme which was somehow made palatable by a believability in the character, more epitomized by the real-life Adams than by the fictional protagonist. It was, moreover, a weekly morality play where at least one subject--one Fallen Angel--surmounted, if but briefly, his foibles.

Without question the most sympathetic character was that played by Charles Ruggles, perfectly suited to the role of an aging politician making his last political stand for governor of New York. In the character Jerry Archer, Ruggles poignantly captured the despair of the has-been, of whom one party pro has commented: "After a period of mourning, you gotta bury the dead." Alexander, sent to cover the convention's proceedings, revives the viability of Archer, who had been idealized by Alexander in his younger years. When Archer learns of the possible existence of a slush fund by a prominent rival, he is at first reluctant to use the information, delivering a sermon on the code of fair play. Later, however, he momentarily succumbs to the temptation of using the information, overly zealous in his final quest. The last scene has Ruggles addressing the convention. Making no reference to the possible slush, he endorses his opposition, and, over the protestations of his dedicated following ("To whom are you shouting no? Inexorable Time?") withdraws his candidacy. He concludes by paraphrasing the Bible: "I had rather be a servant in the house of my party than to sit in the seats of the mighty." "Servant in the House of My Party," as the teleplay was appropriately titled, was written by Adrian Spies and Allen Rivkin and directed by Paul Wendkos.

Yet another good episode was "Judgment in a Jazz Alley," in which Lew Ayres played a judge with an above reproach reputation, now affected by personal tragedy--thus faltering while at the bench. An opportunistic attorney seeks to end the judge's career, but the realization that occurs to Ayres while pursuing the youth who had beaten his daughter (a sort of "judgment in a jazz alley") --that he has lost his capacity to reason fairly--convinces him to resign. Jo Pagano's script was convincing, if sentimental; Sutton Rolley directed. A final episode of merit worth mentioning (there are others) was "The Home-Coming Bit" by Mel Goldberg and directed by John Peysner. In that drama, Elizabeth Montgomery, a former thief now on parole, is the subject of an undercover assignment for reporter Barbara Rush (she guest starred in other segments as well). A suspicious family greets Montgomery returning home. When her sister-in-law's wristwatch is discovered missing, Montgomery is falsely accused and runs from the house, determined to leave town. She returns for her baby (the real watch thief, it turns out) and is prepared to board a bus with a down-on-is-luck boyfriend when the philosophy of reporter Rush keeps her from doing so.

No review of this series would be complete without citing the nice camera work of Lucien Ballard and Wilfred M. Cline. Each scenario greatly benefited from the effective, beautiful musical score of Elmer Bernstein.

The Regulars: Nick Alexander, Nick Adams; Mark Grainger, John Larkin; Dave Tabak, Robert F. Simon; Klugie, Richard Erdman; Polly Holeran, Sharon Farrell; Charlie, Nicky Blair; Lizzie Hogan, Barbara Rush (recurring guest star).

The Episodes:

1. "Dear George, the Siamese Cat Is Missing" (9-17-62) Barbara Rush; Gary Lockwood, Brian Donlevy, Lola Albright

2. "All the Hard Young Men" (9-24-62) Red Buttons, Everett Sloane, Doug Lambert, Jack Albertson, Frank Sutton
3. "The Man on the Rim" (10-1-62) Joseph Cotten, Kathy Nolan, Alan Baxter
4. "Judgment in a Jazz Alley" (10-8-62) Lew Ayres, Ray Walston, Larry Gates, James Callahan
5. "Source of Information" (10-15-62) Dennis Morgan, Scott Marlowe, Irene Dunne, Hayden Rorke
6. "Three Columns of Anger" (10-22-62) Albert Salmi, Tab Hunter, Jean Allison, Arch Johnson
7. "A Servant in the House of My Party" (11-5-62) Charles Ruggles, J. Pat O'Malley, Patricia Breslin, Simon Scott, Judson Pratt, J. Edward McKinley
8. "Daddy's Girl" (11-12-62) Barbara Eden, Warren Stevens, Jeanette Nolan, Mike Masters
9. "Luscious Lois" (11-19-62) Barbara Rush; Glynis Johns, Edward Binns, Ellen Case
10. "A Shame for a Diamond Wedding" (11-26-62) Paul Muni, Lili Darvas, Edward Andrews, Florence Halop, Noreen Corcoran, Cliff Norton, Alan Hewitt, Edgar Stehli, Jack Mullaney, Chet Stratton
11. "Judith Was a Lady" (12-3-62) Arthur Franz, Simon Oakland, David White, Dan Tobin, Paul Tripp, Constance Dane
12. "A Night of Horns and Bells" (12-24-62) Edward Everett Horton, Michael Wilding, Cloris Leachman, Philip Abbott, Shary Marshall
13. "Taste of Evil" (12-31-62) Paul Carr, John Kellogg, Craig Curtis, Ron Hagerthy, Lurene Tuttle, John Marley
14. "The Home-Coming Bit" (1-7-63) Barbara Rush; Elizabeth Montgomery, Ed Nelson, Norm Alden, Penny Santon, Everett Sloane
15. "Slug It, Miss Joyous" (1-14-63) Kathie Browne, Michael Strong, Paul Lambert
16. "The Year Joan Crawford Won the Oscar" (1-21-63) Robert Lansing, Ann Blyth, Robert Elston, Harvey Korman, Ellen Corby, Leon Askin
17. "New Lead Berlin" (1-28-63) Barbara Rush; Richard Webb, Martin Kosleck, Lew Gallo, Eva Sorney

STONEY BURKE

Leslie Stevens' rather titillating study of a rodeo cowboy; Jack Lord having the title role.

The Regulars: Stoney Burke, Jack Lord; Ves Painter, Warren Oates; Cody Bristol, Robert Dowdell; E. J. Stocker, Bruc Dern; Red, Bill Hart.

The Episodes:

1. "The Contender" (10-1-62) Philip Abbott

2. "Fight Night" (10-8-62) Alan Bunce, Edgar Buchanan
3. "Child of Luxury" (10-15-62) Judson Laire, Ina Balin, Eduard Franz
4. "Point of Honor" (10-22-62) Scott Marlowe, Patricia Breslin
5. "The Mob Riders" (10-29-62) Michael Parks
6. "A Matter of Pride" (11-5-62) William Windom, Jena Engstrom
7. "Sidewinder" (11-12-62) Edward Binns, Mark Miller
8. "The Scavenger" (11-19-62) John Kellogg, James Mason
9. "Spin a Golden Web" (11-26-62) Robert Webber, Salome Jens, John Anderson
10. "The Wanderer" (12-3-62) Albert Salmi, Jacqueline Scott
11. "Five by Eight" (12-10-62) Ed Nelson, William Schallert
12. "Bandwagon" (12-17-62) Mariette Hartley
13. "Cousin Eunice" (12-24-62) Cloris Leachman
14. "Gold Plated Maverick" (1-7-63) Michael Anderson Jr., Buck Taylor, John Larch
15. "Death Rides a Pale Horse" (1-14-63) Steve Cochran, Dyan Cannon
16. "King of the Hill" (1-21-63) John Dehner, Leora Dana
17. "A Matter of Percentage" (1-28-63) Jack Weston
18. "Image of Glory" (2-4-63) Simon Oakland
19. "Cat's Eyes" (2-11-63) Fay Spain
20. "Webb of Fear" (2-18-63) Carroll O'Connor, Jeanne Cooper
21. "Point of Entry" (3-4-63) Cesare Danova, Antoinette Bower, William Smith
22. "To Catch the Kaiser" (3-11-63) Diana Hyland
23. "Joby" (3-18-63) Robert Duvall
24. "Forget No More" (3-25-63) Laura Devon
25. "Color Him Lucky" (4-1-63) Charles Robinson
26. "Weapons Man" (4-8-63) J. D. Cannon, Henry Silva
27. "Kelly's Place" (4-15-63) Elizabeth Allen, Vince Patterson
28. "Kincaid" (4-22-63) Dick Clark, David Winters
29. "A Girl Named Amy" (4-29-63) June Harding, Chris Robinson, Donald Woods
30. "Tigress by the Tail" (5-6-63) Elizabeth Ashley
31. "The Test" (5-13-63) Richard Eyer, Ivan Dixon, James Coburn
32. "The Journey" (5-20-63) Mark Richman

## COMBAT!

"Combat!" emerges as television's most significant dramatic statement on the ravages of war--the dysphoria that lingers in the memory of every one of its surviving participants long after the armistice is signed; a searing glance at the human condition bereft of its human quality. One episode in particular will haunt eternally. A frightened young soldier has entered an abandoned church, and genuflects at the altar. He cries to heaven for protection while a shadowy figure reveals itself. The sniper's bullet reaches its destiny and a tearful soldier lies crumpled over at the foot of a crucifix, the study of the wasted youth a brilliant irony against the reverberating battle rhythms in the distance.

If, within its five-year duration on the network, "Combat!" never grew maudlin or tedious, it is because it never forgot that war was, after all, hell, and hell cannot be compromised even for the whims of Hollywood scenarists. And so it remained, in its conflict of personalities (of unrelenting officers and the earthiest of privates), in as bleak and desolate landscapes as art directors could develop, a morality play that gained our tears for every other frame.

The Regulars: Lt. Gil Hanley, Rick Jason; Sgt. Chip Saunders, Vic Morrow; Doc Walton, Steven Rogers; Caje, Pierre Jalbert; Kirby, Jack Hogan; Littlejohn, Dick Peabody; Nelson, Tom Lowell; Doc, Conlan Carter (with second season); Braddock, Shecky Greene (first season).

The Episodes:

1. "Forgotten Front" (10-2-62) Albert Paulsen
2. "Rear Echelon Commandos" (10-9-62) Stephen Coit
3. "Lost Sheep, Lost Shepherd" (10-16-62) Jeffrey Hunter, Joby Baker
4. "Any Second Now" (10-23-62) Alex Davion, Donald May
5. "Far from the Brave" (10-30-62) Joe Mantell, Joyce Van Patten
6. "Missing in Action" (11-13-62) Howard Duff
7. "Escape to Nowhere" (11-20-62) Albert Paulsen
8. "The Celebrity" (11-27-62) Tab Hunter
9. "Cat and Mouse" (12-4-62) Albert Salmi
10. "I Swear by Apollo" (12-11-62) Gunnar Hellstrom
11. "A Day in June" (12-18-62) Max Dommar
12. "The Prisoner" (12-25-62) Keenan Wynn
13. "Reunion" (1-1-63) Fifi D'Orsay
14. "The Medal" (1-8-63) Joseph Campanella, Frank Gorshin
15. "Just for the Record" (1-15-63) Alf Kjellin, Micheline Presle
16. "The Volunteer" (1-22-63) Sergei Prieur
17. "The Squad" (1-29-63) Jonathan Bolt
18. "Next in Command" (2-5-63) Ben Cooper
19. "The Chateau" (2-12-63) Dan O'Herlihy, Joan Hackett
20. "Off Limits" (2-19-63) Peggy Ann Garner, Jeremy Slate
21. "No Time for Pity" (2-26-63) Denise Alexander, Gunnar Hellstrom
22. "Night Patrol" (3-5-63) regulars only
23. "Survival" (3-12-63) regulars only
24. "No Hallelujah for Glory" (3-19-63) Elizabeth Allen
25. "The Quiet Warrior" (3-26-63) J. D. Cannon
26. "The Battle of the Ropes" (4-2-63) Antoinette Bower, Penny Santon
27. "Hill 256" (4-9-63) Robert Culp
28. "The Sniper" (4-16-63) regulars only

29. "One More for the Road" (4-23-63) Don Edmonds
30. "The Walking Wounded" (4-30-63) Gary Merrill, Geraldine Brooks
31. "High Named Today" (5-7-63) Dean Stockwell
32. "No Trumpets, No Drums" (5-14-63) Andrea Darvi

Second Season

33. "The Bridge at Chalons" (9-17-63) Lee Marvin, Lee Krueger
34. "Bridgehead" (9-24-63) Nick Adams, Noam Pitlik, Paul Busch
35. "Masquerade" (10-1-63) Rocky Marciano, James Coburn, Dan Stafford
36. "The Long Way Home" [Part I] (10-8-63) Richard Basehart, Simon Oakland, Woodrow Parfrey
37. "The Long Way Home" [Part II] (10-15-63) as above
38. "The Wounded Don't Cry" (10-22-63) Karl Boehm, Leonard Nimoy
39. "Doughboy" (10-29-63) Eddie Albert, Paul Busch, Bill Harlow, Alida Valli
40. "Glow Against the Sky" (11-5-63) Kurt Kreuger, Bill Sargent
41. "The Little Jewel" (11-12-63) Michel Petit, Paul Busch, Ed Tierney
42. "A Distant Drum" (11-19-63) Denise Darcel, Holly McIntire
43. "Anatomy of a Patrol" (11-26-63) James Caan, Bill Smith, William Sargent
44. "Ambush" (12-3-63) Marisa Pavan, Charles Macaulay
45. "Barrage" (12-10-63) Alf Kjellin
46. "Thunder from the Hill" (12-17-63) Peter Whitney, Robert Carricart
47. "The Party" (12-24-63) Danielle DeMetz, Terry Becker, Biff Elliot
48. "Gideon's Army" (12-31-63) Milton Selzer, Richard Jaeckel, Albert Szabo
49. "The Pillbox" (1-7-64) Warren Oates, Albert Paulsen
50. "The General and the Sergeant" (1-14-64) John Dehner, Denise Alexander
51. "The Eyes of the Hunter" (1-21-64) Ed Nelson, Joe Sirola
52. "The Hostages" (1-28-64) Mark Richman
53. "Mail Call" (2-4-64) James Best, Fred Harris, Ray Fulmer
54. "Counter-punch" (2-11-64) Steve Gravers, George Savalas, Malachi Throne
55. "A Silent Cry" (2-18-64) Richard Anderson, Robert Crawford Jr.
56. "The Hunter" (2-25-64) Alfred Ryder, Ed Tierney
57. "What Are the Bugles Blowin' For?" [Part I] (3-3-64) Ronald Howard, John Alderson
58. "What Are the Bugles Blowin' For?" [Part II] (3-10-64) as above
59. "Weep No More" (3-17-64) Anjanette Comer, Ted Knight
60. "The Short Day of Private Putnam" (3-24-64) Beau Bridges,

Robert Sampson
61. "Rescue" (3-31-64) Guy Stockwell, Edward Binns
62. "Command" (4-7-64) Joseph Campanella, William Arvin
63. "Infant of Prague" (4-14-64) Jeanette Nolan, Jeanne Rainer
64. "The Glory Among Men" (4-21-64) Eddie Ryder, Peter Helm

Third Season

65. "Mountain Men" (9-15-64) Theodore Bikel, Henry Brandon
66. "Vendetta" (9-22-64) Peter Deuel, Telly Savalas, Athan
     Karras
67. "Point of View" (9-29-64) Paul Burke, H. M. Wynant
68. "The Duel" (10-6-64) Bobby Rydell, Tram Tyson
69. "The Silver Service" (10-13-64) Claudine Longet, Mickey
     Rooney, Ramon Novarro, Norm Alden
70. "The Hard Way Back" (10-20-64) Sal Mineo, Erik Holland
71. "Operation Fly Trap" (10-27-64) Gary Lockwood
72. "The Little Carousel" (11-10-64) Sylviane Margolle, Warren
     Vanders
73. "Fly Away Home" (11-17-64) Neville Brand, Stephen Joyce
74. "The Imposter" (11-24-64) Alan Baxter, Skip Homeier,
     Warren Stevens, James Dobson
75. "A Gift of Hope" (12-1-64) Rip Torn, Anthony Eisley,
     Robert Yuro
76. "A Rare Vintage" (12-8-64) Lyle Bettger, Marcel Hillaire
77. "The Long Walk" (12-15-64) Roddy McDowall, Peter Brocco,
     Chris Howard
78. "The Town That Went Away" (12-22-64) Jay Novello, Susan
     Silo, Billy Beck
79. "Birthday Cake" (12-29-64) Philip Pine
80. "The Enemy" (1-5-65) Robert Duvall, Anne Lee
81. "The Cossack" (1-12-65) James Whitmore, Glen Stensel
82. "Losers Cry Deal" (1-19-65) Mike Kellin, Dee Pollack
83. "More Than a Soldier" (1-26-65) Tommy Sands, Ron Soble
84. "Brother, Brother" (2-2-65) Frankie Avalon, Charles A.
     Bastin
85. "The Steeple" (2-9-65) David Sheiner, Robert Cornthwaite
86. "The Convict" (2-16-65) Gilbert Roland, Clive Clerk,
     Robert Carricart
87. "Dateline" (2-23-65) Dan Duryea, Henry Beckman
88. "A Walk with an Eagle" (3-2-65) Lee Philips, Pat Colby
89. "The Long Wait" (3-9-65) Terry Carter, William Wellman
90. "The Tree of Moray" (3-16-65) Robert Loggia, Robert
     Ellenstein, Emile Genest
91. "A Cry in the Ruins" (3-23-65) Lisa Pera, William Smith-
     ers, Glenn Cannon
92. "The Hell Machine" (3-30-65) Frank Gorshin, Than Wyenn,
     Lou Robb
93. "Billy the Kid" (4-6-65) Andrew Prine, John Milford
94. "Heritage" (4-13-65) Charles Bronson, Robert Fortier
95. "Odyssey" (4-20-65) Bert Freed, Teno Pollick
96. "Beneath the Ashes" (4-27-65) Chad Everett, Noam Pitlik

Fourth Season

97. "Main Event" (9-14-65) Jack Carter, Ben Cooper, Vic Werber, Hans Difflipp, Todd Lasswell
98. "The First Day" (9-21-65) Dee Pollack, Buck Taylor, Kevin Coughlin, Rick Weber
99. "S. I. W. " (9-28-65) John Cassavetes, William Stevens, Paul Sheriff
100. "The Linesman" (10-5-65) Jack Lord, Peter Duryea, Heinz Brinkman
101. "The Farmer" (10-12-65) Dennis Weaver, Felix Lochar, Dina Harmsen
102. "Evasion" (10-19-65) Lloyd Bochner, Jacques Aubuchon, John Lodge
103. "Hear No Evil" (10-26-65) Peter Haskell, Richard Tretter
104. "Crossfire" (11-2-65) Don Gordon, Burt Douglas, Ron Foster
105. "Nine Place Vendee" (11-9-65) Lee Patterson, Christopher Dark, Patrick Michenaud, William Leslie
106. "The Old Men" (11-16-65) Tom Drake, Simon Oakland, William Phipps, Paul Busch
107. "Soldier of Fortune" (11-23-65) Burt Brinckerhoff, Wesley Lau, William Campbell, Ed Deemer
108. "The Casket" (11-30-65) Nina Foch, Raymond Cavaleri, Henry Brandt
109. "Luck with Rainbows" (12-7-65) Michael Evans, Bill Glover, Roy Dean
110. "Breakout" (12-14-65) Fernando Lamas
111. "The Finest Hour" (12-21-65) Luise Rainer, Ramon Novarro
112. "The Raider" (12-28-65) Martin Brooks
113. "The Mockingbird" (1-4-66) John Agar, Jeremy Slate
114. "The Good Samaritan" (1-11-66) Tom Simcox, Hank Brandt
115. "Retribution" (1-18-66) Albert Paulsen
116. "Counterplay" (1-25-66) Mark Richman, H. M. Wynant
117. "Nothing to Lose" (2-1-66) Sal Mineo, Tom Skerritt
118. "Ask Me No Questions" (2-8-66) Claude Akins, Ed Peck
119. "The Ringer" (2-15-66) Tom Pace, Mort Hulswit
120. "The Flying Machine" (2-22-66) Keenan Wynn, Peter Coe
121. "Hills Are for Heroes" [Part I] (3-1-66) Paul Carr, Joe Walsh
122. "Hills Are for Heroes" [Part II] (3-8-66) as above
123. "Gitty" (3-15-66) Andrea Darvi
124. "One at a Time" (3-22-66) Larry Kert, Jan Merlin, Rod Lauren, Robert Yuro, Ronnie Welsh
125. "A Sudden Terror" (3-29-64) Brandon de Wilde, David Moss
126. "Run, Sheep, Run" (4-5-66) Dwayne Hickman, Frank Marth
127. "The Leader" (4-12-66) William Bryant, Michael Vandever

Fifth Season

128. "The Gun" (9-13-66) Warren Stevens, Wayne Rogers, Tim

Felix
129. "The Losers" (9-20-66) Bill Bixby, Rafael Campos, John Considine, Bill Gray
130. "Ollie Joe" (9-27-66) Robert Walker Jr., Claude Akins, William Bryant, Warren Vanders
131. "The Brothers" (10-4-66) Fernando Lamas, Sal Mineo, Ted Knight, Kurt Landen
132. "The Chapel at Able-Five" (10-11-66) Fritz Weaver, John Hudson, George Sawaya, Jan Malmajo
133. "A Child's Game" (10-18-66) Peter Haskell, Dennis Olivieri, John Maurer
134. "The Letter" (10-25-66) Randy Boone, Barry Russo, John Nealson
135. "Headcount" (11-1-66) Jan Merlin, Ron Soble, Tom Pace, Ray Stricklyn, William Schallert
136. "Decision" (11-15-66) James Franciscus
137. "The Outsider" (11-22-66) Jason Evers, William Bryant
138. "Conflict" (11-29-66) William Bryant
139. "Gulliver" (12-6-66) Stefan Arngrim, Vicki Malkin, William Bramley, Jeremie Paul André
140. "The Bankroll" (12-13-66) James Stacy, Buck Taylor, Mike Farrell, Steven Marlo, Norbert Meisel
141. "Cry for Help" (12-20-66) Robert Duvall, Faith Domergue, Gene Kirkwood, Chris Howard
142. "The Furlough" (12-27-66) Carol Lawrence, John Williams, Paul Picerni, Jon Walmsley, Tony Fraser, Chris Charney
143. "Entombed" (1-3-67) Margaret O'Brien, Skip Homeier, Michael Constantine, Tom Fielding, King Moody
144. "Gadjo" (1-17-67) Ricardo Montalban, David Sheiner, Eugene Iglesias, Pat Renella, Anthony Benson, Hank Brandt
145. "Anniversary" (1-24-67) Telly Savalas, John Van Dreelen, Sofia Marie, Anne Wakefield
146. "Encounter" (1-31-67) James MacArthur, James Daly, Richard Eyer
147. "The Gantlet" (2-7-67) Tom Skerritt, Bill Glover, Tom P. Pace
148. "The Masquers" (2-14-67) Nick Adams, Roger Perry, Gavin MacLeod, Maurice Marsac
149. "A Little Jazz" (2-21-67) Dan Duryea, Dennis Hopper, Noah Beery, Joe Maross, Robert Easton
150. "Nightmare on the Red Ball Run" (2-28-67) Claude Akins, William Campbell
151. "Jonah" (3-7-67) Peter Duryea
152. "The Partisan" (3-14-67) Robert Duvall, Claudine Longet

---

## THE LLOYD BRIDGES SHOW

This anthology series showcasing the talents of Lloyd Bridges (he is both journalist Adam Shepherd and a second character he creates while in a pensive mood) contains the highly acclaimed drama "A Pair of Boots," a Civil War tale composed by Mort R. Lewis and directed by John Cassavetes.

The Regulars: Adam Shepherd (and second character), Lloyd Bridges.

1. "Wheresoever I Enter" (9-11-62) Harry Guardino, Michael Constantine, Alejandro Rey, Nick Alekos
2. "El Medico" (9-18-62) John Cassavetes, Mario Alcaide, Gary Walberg
3. "My Child Is Yet a Stranger" (9-25-62) Bethel Leslie, Suzanne Cupito
4. "A Pair of Boots" (10-2-62) Royal Dano, Beau Bridges, Lawrence Tierney, Gene Darfler, George Dunn, Fred Draper
5. "Mr. Pennington's Machine" (10-9-62) Betty Garrett, Lee Philips, James Hong, H. T. Tsiang
6. "Just Married" (10-16-62) Carolyn Jones, Edgar Buchanan
7. "The Testing Ground" (10-23-62) Paul Richards, James Edwards, Frank Aletter
8. "War Song" (10-30-62) Ricardo Montalban, Frank London, Noam Pitlik
9. "Yankee Stay Here" (11-13-62) David White, Mako, William Murray
10. "Miracle of Mesa Verde" (11-20-62) John Kerr
11. "Little Man, Big Bridge" (11-27-62) Eduardo Ciannelli, Ed Peck, Jerry Paris, Barry Kelley
12. "Permission Granted" (12-4-62) Robert Simon, Terry Becker, Linda Ho, James Hong
13. "Gentleman in Blue" (12-11-62) Jeff Bridges, Dianne Foster, Rex Ingram
14. "The Sound of Angels" (12-18-62) Cindy Bridges (Lloyd's daughter in her acting debut); J. Pat O'Malley, Nancy Gates, Bert Remsen
15. "Now You Take Your Average Rock" (12-25-62) Paul Ford, Marie Windsor, Robert Gibbons
16. "The Scapegoat" (1-1-63) Michael Constantine, Doug Lambert, Richard Chambers
17. "The Wonder of Wanda" (1-8-63) Anna-Lisa, Hanna Landy, Werner Klemperer, Suzanne Cupito, Oscar Beregi
18. "My Daddy Can Lick Your Daddy" (1-22-63) Gary Lockwood, Mary Murphy, Morris Buchanan
19. "A Game for Alternate Mondays" (1-29-63) Glynis Johns, Leslye Hunter
20. "A Personal Matter" (2-5-63) Gena Rowlands, Robert Carricart, Lester Fletcher
21. [unknown title] (2-12-63) Beau Bridges, Tony Fasce, Mickey Freeman; Bo Belinsky and Ed Sadowski of the L.A. Dodgers appear as themselves
22. "The Rising of the Moon" (2-19-63) Kathy Nolan, Maurice Dallimore
23. "To Walk with the Stars" (2-26-63) Jeff Bridges, Virginia

        Vincent, Dolores Michaels
24.  "The Courtship" (3-5-63) Diane Baker, Lonny Chapman
25.  "The Sheridan Square" (3-12-63) Gogi Grant, Alan Napier
26.  "Gym in January" (3-19-63) Gloria DeHaven, Norman Fell, Elizabeth Fraser
27.  "The Last Lion" (4-2-63) Barbara Shelley, Morris Buchanan
28.  "The Tyrees of Capitol Hill" [unsold pilot film for projected fall series] (4-9-63) Edgar Buchanan, Philip Alford
29.  "Waltz of the Two Commuters" (4-16-63) Linda Christian, Nancy Gates
30.  "Freedom Is for Those Who Want It" (4-30-63) Albert Paulsen, Ben Ari, Nancy Neumann
31.  "The Ramp" (5-7-63) Don Dubbins, Rhys Williams, Bennye Gatteys, Norma Connolly
32.  "Without Wheat, There Is No Bread" (5-14-63) Don Gordon, Eduardo Ciannelli, Robert Carricart
33.  "The Epidemic" (5-21-63) Wanda Hendrix, Gary Walberg, Athan Karras, John Marley
34.  "Afternoon of a Champion" (5-28-63) Jan Harrison, Fabrizio Mioni, Russ Conway, Robert Herrman; 1962 "Indianapolis 500" winner Roger Ward appears

## EMPIRE

This series initially functioned in much the same style as did the 1956 George Stevens film <u>Giant</u> which in turn was derived from Edna Ferber's 1952 novel. The wealthy Garrets of New Mexico (with Anne Seymour as matriarch Lucia; Terry Moore as her daughter Connie and Ryan O'Neal as son Tal) endure the tribulations that necessarily follow when one is married to the land (the land is the real player in series of this kind), condescending to no one save ranch foreman Jim Redigo. So dominating was the character Redigo indeed, that by the twenty-first episode, Terry Moore's role was written out of the series and by the second season Redigo had inherited the series itself. Thereafter Ryan O'Neal solitarily retained his familial role.

The Regulars: Jim Redigo, Richard Egan; Lucia Garret, Anne Seymour (first season only); Connie Garret, Terry Moore (to episode of 2/19/63); Tal Garret, Ryan O'Neal; Paul Moreno, Charles Bronson (regular as of 2/26/63); Frank, Rudy Solari (last season); Mike, Roger Davis (last season); Linda, Nina Martinez (last season); Gerry, Elena Verdugo (last season).

The Episodes:

1.  "The Day the Empire Stood Still" (9-25-62) Charles Bronson, Denver Pyle, Oliver McGowan
2.  "Ballard Number One" (10-2-62) Ed Begley, George Matthews, Gilbert Green

3. "A Place to Put a Life" (10-9-62) Chris Robinson, James Griffith, Cathy Lewis
4. "Ride to a Fall" (10-16-62) Victor Jory, Claude Akins
5. "Long Past, Long Remembered" (10-23-62) Tom Tully, Richard Jordan, Paul Birch
6. "Walk Like a King" (10-30-62) Ralph Meeker, Joanne Linville
7. "The Fire Dancer" (11-13-62) Frank Gorshin, Roy Barcroft, Susan Silo
8. "The Tall Shadow" (11-20-62) Bethel Leslie, Frank Overton, Mickey Sholdar
9. "The Earth Mover" (11-27-62) Dan O'Herlihy, Linda Bennett, Eddie Waller, Max Showalter
10. "Pressure Lock" (12-4-62) Cathleen Nesbitt, Carolyn Kearney, Ford Rainey
11. "Echo of a Man" (12-11-62) John Dehner, Glenn Turnbull, Claire Griswold
12. "When the Gods Laugh" (12-18-62) James Gregory, Roger Mobley, Jenny Maxwell
13. "Green, Green, Hills" (12-25-62) Arthur O'Connell, Joanna Moore, Leonard Stone
14. "Stopover on the Way to the Moon" (1-1-63) Keir Dullea, Sharon Farrell, Mark Allen, Harold Gould
15. "The Four Thumbs Story" (1-8-63) Ray Danton, Rudy Solari, Barry Atwater
16. "End of an Image" (1-15-63) Richard Gordon, Gail Kobe
17. "The Loner" (1-22-63) Jeremy Slate, Clarke Gordon, Warren Vanders
18. "Where the Hawk Is Wheeling" (1-29-63) Robert Culp, Walter Burke, John Duke
19. "No Small Wars" (2-5-63) Robert Vaughn, Walter Brooke, Otis Greene
20. "The Tiger Inside" (2-12-63) Harold J. Stone, Joyce Bulifant, Philip Abbott, Richard Evans
21. "Season of Growth" (2-19-63) Pat Conway, James Stapleton, Arch Johnson
22. "Seven Days on Rough Street" (2-26-63) Frank Sutton, Clegg Hoyt
23. "A House In Order" (3-5-63) Virginia Gregg, James Callahan, Oliver McGowan, Russell Thorson
24. [unknown title] (3-12-63) Joanna Barnes, John Vivyan, Dayton Lummis
25. "Burnout" (3-19-63) Gunnar Hellstrom, John Milford, Karen Steele
26. "Hidden Asset" (3-26-63) Lon Chaney Jr., William Windom, Barbara Bain, John Matthews
27. "Arrow in the Blue" (4-9-63) Telly Savalas, Russell Johnson, Ilka Windish
28. "Breakout" (4-16-63) William Schallert, Dean Stanton, Don Gordon
29. "65 Miles Is a Long, Long Way" (4-23-63) Claude Akins, Jean Engstrom, Woodrow Parfrey, Ann Carroll
30. "Duet for Eight Wheels" (4-30-63) Inger Stevens, Lawrence

Dobkin, Noah Keen
31. "Between Friday and Monday" (5-7-63) Joan Hackett, William Mims, Naomi Stevens, Dort Clark
32. "The Convention" (5-14-63) Diane Brewster, Rudy Bond, Alan Hale, Anne Helm, L. Q. Jones

Second Season [now as REDIGO]

33. "Lady War-Bonnet" (9-24-63) Mary Murphy
34. "The Blooded Bull" (10-1-63) Peter Brown, Richard Evans
35. "Boy from the Rio Bravo" (10-8-63) Michael Davis
36. "Prince Among Men" (10-15-63) Nico Minardos, Pim Grala
37. "The Crooked Circle" (10-22-63) Pippa Scott, Richard Anderson
38. "Little Angel Blue Eyes" (10-29-63) Kathie Browne, James Best
39. "Man in a Blackout" (11-5-63) Albert Salmi, Evans Evans, Harry Carey
40. "Papa-San" (11-12-63) Anita Loo, Chad Everett, Ed Peck
41. [unknown title] (11-19-63)
42. "Shadow of the Cougar" (11-26-63) Kathleen Crowley, Mike Connors
43. "The Thin Line" (12-3-63) Ray Danton, Jim Drum
44. "Hostage Hero Hiding" (12-10-63) Ed Nelson, Elinor Donah
45. "Privilege of a Man" (12-17-63) Arch Johnson, Peggy McC
46. "The Hunters" (12-31-63) Perry Lopez, Walter Sande

THE VIRGINIAN

Based loosely on the Owen Wister classic, this first of tele vision's ninety-minute westerns only finally surrenders (in its late seasons) to the genre's knack for suffocating characterizations in the resonance of gunplay. Its greatest triumph was Roland Kibbee's "The Brazen Bell," in which George C. Scott delivers one o the most potent performances in television history. Kibbee's teleplay title is taken from Oscar Wilde's 1898 poem The Ballad of Reading Gaol, a reading of which figures prominently in the drama outcome. The plot has Scott as a newcomer schoolteacher whose refinements and passivity are mistaken by the townspeople as cow ardice. When two escaped convicts take over the schoolhouse, threatening the lives of the children, the teacher's aversion to vio lence becomes a major concern. Efforts at instructing the schola once his captors have released him to acquire supplies, appear fu tile. It is teacher Scott, however, whose elaborate scheme saves the children. His wife already dead of the younger convict's trigger, he movingly reads from the Wilde poem in the hope that the older and more sympathetic convict will grasp in the work a personal meaning. The plan being successful, the convict abruptly turns from his position as lookout, making him an easy victim for Judge Henry Garth (series regular Lee J. Cobb) who has been ar and waiting outside. Thanks to the Scott performance and to Jam

Sheldon's sensitive direction, the tired and dubious western theme of nobility through action is mercifully restrained.

Percy Faith composed the musical theme. The series boasted brilliant photography (Lionel Lindon and Neil Beckner) and art direction (George Patrick).

The Regulars: The Virginian, James Drury; Judge Henry Garth, Lee J. Cobb (through 1965-66 season); Trampas, Doug McClure; Molly Wood, Pippa Scott (first season); Steve, Gary Clarke; Betsy, Roberta Shore; Deputy Emmett Ryker (from third season), Clu Gulager; Morgan Starr (with episode of 2/9/66 through season), John Dehner; Grainger (from 1966-67 season through 10/25/67), Charles Bickford; Stacey Grainger (from 1966-67 season), Don Quine; Holly Grainger (from 11/1/67), Jeanette Nolan; Jennifer (with 11/3/65 through season), Diane Roter; Elizabeth (from 1966-67 season), Sara Lane; Clay Grainger (from 11/1/67 through 1969-70 season), John McIntire; Randy, Randy Boone; David Sutton (1968-69 season), David Hartman; Jim Horn (1969-70 season), Tim Matheson; Sheriff Abbott, Ross Elliott.

The Episodes:

1. "The Executioners" (9-19-62) Hugh O'Brian, Colleen Dewhurst, John Lodge
2. "Woman from White Wing" (9-26-62) Barry Sullivan, Robert Sampson
3. "Throw a Long Rope" (10-3-62) Jack Warden, Jacqueline Scott, Ted Knight, John Anderson, Roger Mobley, Lew Brown
4. "The Big Deal" (10-10-62) Ricardo Montalban
5. "The Brazen Bell" (10-17-62) George C. Scott, Ann Meacham, Royal Dano, John Davis Chandler
6. "Big Day, Great Day" (10-24-62) Aldo Ray
7. "Riff-Raff" (11-7-62) Ray Danton, Don Durant, Karl Swenson
8. "Impasse" (11-14-62) Eddie Albert
9. "It Tolls for Thee" (11-21-62) Lee Marvin, Albert Salmi
10. "West" (11-28-62) Claude Akins, Steve Cochran, Russell Thorson, Richard Reeves, James Brown, Allen Case, Leo Gordon
11. "The Devil's Children" (12-5-62) Charles Bickford, Joan Freeman, Burt Brinckerhoff
12. "Fifty Days to Moose Jaw" (12-12-62) Brandon de Wilde
13. "The Accomplice" (12-19-62) Bette Davis
14. "Man from the Sea" (12-26-62) Tom Tryon, Shirley Knight, Carol Lynley
15. "Duel at Shiloh" (1-2-63) Geraldine Brooks, Brian Keith, Ben Johnson, Christopher King, DeForest Kelley, Russell Thorson, Mort Mills
16. "The Exiles" (1-9-63) Tammy Grimes, Ken Lynch
17. "The Judgment" (1-16-63) John Kerr

18. "Say Goodbye to All That" (1-23-63) Charles McGraw, Fabian
19. "The Man Who Couldn't Die" (1-30-63) Vera Miles
20. "If You Have Tears" (2-13-63) Robert Vaughn, Phyllis Avery, Dana Wynter, Nancy Sinatra
21. "The Small Parade" (2-20-63) David Wayne
22. "Vengeance Is the Spur" (2-27-63) Nina Foch, Michael Rennie
23. "The Money Cage" (3-6-63) Steve Forrest, Bethel Leslie
24. "The Golden Door" (3-13-63) Karl Boehm, Robert Duvall
25. "A Distant Fury" (3-20-63) Howard Duff, Ida Lupino, Joey Heatherton
26. "Echo from Another Day" (3-27-63) Bradford Dillman, Edward Asner, John Dehner
27. "Strangers at Sundown" (4-3-63) Harry Morgan, Skip Homeier
28. "Mountain of the Sun" (4-17-63) Jeanette Nolan, Dolores Hart
29. "Run Away Home" (4-24-63) Russ Conway, Jeannine Riley, Karl Swenson
30. "The Final Hour" (5-1-63) Jacques Aubuchon, Ulla Jacobsson

Second Season

31. "Ride a Dark Trail" (9-18-63) Sonny Tufts, Stuart Randall, Charles Fredericks, Hal Baylor
32. "To Make This Place Remember" (9-25-63) Joan Blondell, Sunny Jordan, John Dehner, Jocelyn Brando
33. "No Tears for Savannah" (10-2-63) Everett Sloane, Gena Rowlands, Stephen McNally, Arthur Franz, Joanna Moore, Robert Coleman, Vaughn Taylor
34. "A Killer in Town" (10-9-63) Broderick Crawford, Arch Johnson
35. "The Evil That Men Do" (10-16-63) Robert Redford, Patrici Blair, L. Q. Jones, Simon Scott
36. "It Takes a Big Man" (10-23-63) Lloyd Nolan, Chris Robinson, Ryan O'Neal, Pamela Austin, Bobs Watson
37. "Brother Thaddeus" (10-30-63) Albert Salmi, Joe Maross, Kathie Browne, Richard Devon
38. "A Portrait of Marie Valonne" (11-6-63) Madlyn Rhue, Mar Richman, Skip Homeier, Marge Redmond
39. "Run Quiet" (11-13-63) Clu Gulager, Gail Kobe, L. Q. Jones, Slim Pickens
40. "Stopover in a Western Town" (11-27-63) Warren Oates, Dick York, Joan Freeman, Robert Simon
41. "The Fatal Journey" (12-4-63) Robert Lansing
42. "A Time Remembered" (12-11-63) Yvonne DeCarlo, Melinda Plowman
43. "Siege" (12-18-63) Philip Carey, Elinor Donahue, Joseph Campanella, Ron Hayes
44. "Man of Violence" (12-25-63) Michael Pate, Leonard Nimoy Peggy McCay, DeForest Kelley
45. "The Invaders" (1-1-64) Ed Begley, Beverly Owen, James McMullan, Roy Engle

46. "Roar from the Mountain" (1-8-64) Jack Klugman, Joyce
    Bulifant, Emile Genest, Blair Davies
47. "The Fortunes of J. Jimerson Jones" (1-15-64) Pat O'Brien,
    Jeanne Cooper, Peter Adams, Ann Doran
48. "The Thirty Days of Gavin Heath" (1-22-64) Leo Genn,
    Brendon Dillon
49. "The Drifter" (1-29-64) Leif Erickson, Michael Forest
50. "First to Thine Own Self" (2-12-64) Claire Wilcox, Mary
    La Roche, Frank Maxwell
51. "A Matter of Destiny" (2-19-64) Peter Graves, Richard
    Jaeckel, Jean Hale
52. "Smile of a Dragon" (2-26-64) Richard Carlson, Miyoshi
    Umecki, Frank Overton
53. "The Intruders" (3-4-64) Darren McGavin, Hugh Marlowe,
    David Carradine
54. "Walk in Another's Footsteps" (3-11-64) John Agar, Sheree
    North, Dennis Holmes
55. "Rope of Lies" (3-25-64) Diana Millay, Peter Breck
56. "The Secret of Brynmar Hall" (4-1-64) Jane Wyatt, Mark
    Goddard, Brooke Bundy
57. "The Long Quest" (4-8-64) Patricia Breslin, Ruta Lee,
    Joseph Campanella
58. "A Bride for Lars" (4-15-64) Peter Whitney, Katherine
    Crawford
59. "Dark Destiny" (4-29-64) Brenda Scott, Robert Wilke
60. "A Man Called Kane" (5-6-64) Dick Foran, Jeremy Slate

## Third Season

61. "Ryker" (9-16-64) Clu Gulager (hereafter in series), Anne
    Helm, Leslie Nielsen, Jan Merlin, Russ Conway
62. "The Dark Challenge" (9-23-64) Victor Jory, Katherine
    Ross, Joan O'Brien, Chris Robinson, Than Wyenn
63. "The Black Stallion" (9-30-64) Robert Culp, Jena Engstrom,
    Donald Barry
64. "The Hero" (10-7-64) Steve Forrest, Warren Stevens
65. "Felicity's Spring" (10-14-64) Katherine Crawford, Dean
    Harens, Carl Benton Reid, Mariette Hartley
66. "The Brazos Kid" (10-21-64) Barbara Eden, Skip Homeier,
    Alvy Moore, George Petrie
67. "Big Image ... Little Man" (10-28-64) Slim Pickens, Linden
    Chiles, Olive Sturgess
68. "A Father for Toby" (11-4-64) Rory Calhoun, Kurt Russell,
    Joanna Moore
69. "The Girl from Yesterday" (11-11-64) Mark Richman, Ruta
    Lee, Don Collier
70. "Return a Stranger" (11-18-64) Leif Erickson, Peter Brown,
    Whit Bissell, William Fawcett
71. "All Nice and Legal" (11-25-64) Anne Francis, Ellen Corby,
    Seth Potter, Paul Comi, John Kellogg
72. "A Gallows for Sam Horn" (12-2-64) John Lupton, Edward
    Binns, George Kennedy
73. "Portrait of a Widow" (12-9-64) Vera Miles, Nancy Gates,

John Gavin, Ann Doran

74. "The Payment" (12-16-64) Lloyd Nolan, Bruce Dern, Lisabeth Hush
75. "Man of the People" (12-23-64) James Dunn, Martin West, Roy Engel, Alvy Moore
76. "The Hour of the Tiger" (12-30-64) Tom Tully, Cely Carrillo, Leo Gordon
77. "Two Men Named Laredo" (1-6-65) Fabian, Ford Rainey, Elizabeth Macrae, Paul Comi
78. "Hideout" (1-13-65) Forrest Tucker, Andrew Prine, Douglas Fowley
79. "Six Graves at Cripple Creek" (1-27-65) John Doucette, Sheilah Wells, Walter Reed, Paul Buck
80. "Lost Yesterday" (2-3-65) Shirley Knight, Monica Lewis, Simon Scott, John Kellogg
81. "A Slight Case of Charity" (2-10-65) Kathryn Hays, Les Tremayne, Jerome Courtland, E. J. Andre
82. "You Take the High Road" (2-17-65) Richard Beymer, Diana Lynn, Roy Engel
83. "Shadows of the Past" (2-24-65) Jack Warden, Marilyn Erskine, John Milford, James Beck
84. "Legend for a Lawman" (3-3-65) Adam West, Ford Rainey, William Mims, John Litel
85. "Timberland" (3-10-65) Martin Milner, Joan Freeman, William Smith, Arch Johnson
86. "Dangerous Road" (3-17-65) Simon Oakland, Tom Simcox, Marilyn Wayne, Robert Pine, Ben Johnson
87. "Farewell to Honesty" (3-24-65) Kathleen Crowley, Richard Carlson, Harold Gould, Herbert Voland
88. "The Old Cowboy" (3-31-65) Franchot Tone, Billy Mumy, Alan Baxter
89. "The Showdown" (4-14-65) Michael Ansara, Peter Whitney, Tom Skerritt, Leonard Nimoy
90. "We've Lost a Train" (4-21-65) Ida Lupino, Fernando Lamas, William Smith, Rhonda Fleming, Philip Carey, Neville Brand, Peter Brown

Fourth Season

91. "The Brothers" (9-15-65) Robert Lansing, Andrew Prine, Kurt Russell, Jan Shepard, Myron Healey, Loyal Lucas, Bill Quinn, Stuart Randall, Henry Hunter, Fred Carson, Hal Baylor
92. "Day of the Scorpion" (9-22-65) John Anderson, Sean McClory
93. "A Little Learning" (9-29-65) Susan Oliver, Albert Salmi, Bruce Dern
94. "The Claim" (10-6-65) William Shatner
95. "The Awakening" (10-13-65) Glenn Corbett
96. "Ring of Silence" (10-27-65) Earl Holliman
97. "Jennifer" (11-3-65) Diane Roter, James MacArthur
98. "Nobility of Kings" (11-10-65) Charles Bronson, Lois Nettleton, George Kennedy, Vito Scotti, Bob Random

99. "Show Me a Hero" (11-17-65) Richard Beymer, Leonard
    Nimoy, Sherry Jackson
100. "Beyond the Border" (11-24-65) Thomas Gomez, Joan
    Staley
101. "The Dream of Stavros Karas" (12-1-65) Michael Constan-
    tine, Louise Sorel
102. "The Laramie Road" (12-8-65) Leslie Nielsen, Claude
    Akins, Harold J. Stone, Margaret Blye, Berkeley Harris,
    Marge Redmond, Rory Stevens, Harlan Warde
103. "The Horse Fighter" (12-15-65) Harry Guardino
104. "Letter of the Law" (12-22-65) Simon Oakland, James Best
105. "Blaze of Glory" (12-29-65) Leif Erickson, Joan Freeman
106. "Nobody Said Hello" (1-5-66) Virginia Grey, James Whit-
    more, Steve Carlson
107. "Men with Guns" (1-12-66) Telly Savalas, Robert F. Simon
108. "Long Ride to Wind River" (1-19-66) Michael Burns, Pilar
    Seurat, John Cassavetes
109. "Chaff in the Wind" (1-26-66) Ed Begley, Tony Bill, Linda
    Lawson
110. "The Inchworm's Got No Wings at All" (2-2-66) Stacy
    Maxwell, Lou Antonio, Anthony Caruso
111. "Morgan Starr" (2-9-66) features John Dehner, hereafter
    in series; Peggy Castle, George Mitchell
112. "Harvest of Strangers" (2-16-66) Geoffrey Horne, John An-
    derson, Barbara Turner, Jan Shepard
113. "Ride a Cock-Horse to Laramie Cross" (2-23-66) Nita
    Talbot, Clint Howard
114. "One Spring Like Long Ago" (3-2-66) Eduard Franz, War-
    ren Oates, Clive Clerk, Martine Bartlett
115. "The Return of Golden Tom" (3-9-66) Victor Jory, Linden
    Chiles, Jean Inness, Kelly Thordsen
116. "The Wolves Up Front, the Jackals Behind" (3-23-66)
    James Farentino, Jay C. Flippen, Michael J. Pollard,
    Peggy Lipton, Jack Ragotzy, Donnelly Rhodes
117. "That Saunders Woman" (3-30-66) Sheree North, Liam Sul-
    livan
118. "No Drums, No Trumpets" (4-6-66) Julie Adams, Leslie
    Nielsen, Eduardo Ciannelli
119. "A Bald-Faced Boy" (4-13-66) Andrew Prine, Royal Dano
120. "The Mark of a Man" (4-20-66) Harold J. Stone, Brooke
    Bundy, Barry Primus

Fifth Season

21. "Legacy of Hate" (9-14-66) Jo Van Fleet
22. "Ride to Delphi" (9-21-66) Harold J. Stone, Angie Dickin-
    son, Warren Oates, Bernie Hamilton
23. "The Captive" (9-28-66) Susan Strasberg
24. "An Echo of Thunder" (10-5-66) Jason Evers, Linden
    Chiles, Indus Arthur, Mark Miranda, John Anderson
25. "Jacob Was a Plain Man" (10-12-66) Aldo Ray, Peter
    Duryea
26. "The Challenge" (10-19-66) Barbara Anderson, Dan Duryea,

Michael Burns
127. "Outcast" (10-26-66) Fabian
128. "Trail to Ashley Mountain" (11-2-66) Martin Milner, Hugh
Marlowe
129. "Dead Eye Dick" (11-9-66) Alice Rawlings
130. "High Stakes" (11-16-66) Terry Moore, Jack Lord, Michael
Ansara, Dirk Rambo
131. "Beloved Outlaw" (11-23-66) features Sara Lane
132. "Linda" (11-30-66) Diane Baker
133. "Long Journey Home" (12-14-66) Pernell Roberts, Michael
Burns, Noah Beery, Jan Shepard
134. "Girl on the Glass Mountain" (12-28-66) Tom Tryon, Hugh
Beaumont, Laurie Mitchell, Pamela Austin, Dorothy
Green, Brian Avery, Michael Greene, John Archer,
Steve Raines, Ed Prentiss
135. "Vengeance Trail" (1-4-67) Ron Russell
136. "Sue Ann" (1-11-67) Patty Duke
137. "Yesterday's Timepiece" (1-18-67) Audrey Totter, Stuart
Erwin, Pat O'Brien, Andy Devine, Bruce Bennett
138. "Requiem for a Country Doctor" (1-25-67) Dick Foran,
Cloris Leachman
139. "The Modoc Kid" (2-1-67) John Saxon
140. "The Gauntlet" (2-8-67) Mark Richman, Bruce Bennett,
Marian Moses, Stefan Arngrim
141. "Without Mercy" (2-15-67) James Gregory, Katherine
Walsh
142. "Melanie" (2-22-67) Susan Clark, Victor Jory
143. "Doctor Pat" (3-1-67) Jill Donohue, John Bryant, Mari
Blanchard, Jean Inness, Donald Barry, Walter Coy
144. "Nightmare at Fort Killman" (3-8-67) James Daly, Johnny
Seven, Les Crane, Don Mitchell, Wally Strauss
145. "Bitter Harvest" (3-15-67) Whitney Blake, Larry Pennell
146. [unknown title] (3-22-67) Robert Fuller, Jocelyn Brando
147. "The Girl on the Pinto" (3-29-67) Valora Noland
148. "Lady of the House" (4-5-67) Myrna Loy
149. "The Strange Quest of Claire Bingham" (4-12-67) Andrew
Prine, Sandra Smith

Sixth Season

150. "Reckoning" (9-13-67) Dick Foran, Charles Bronson
151. "The Deadly Past" (9-20-67) Darren McGavin, Linden
Chiles, Mary Robin-Redd, Bing Russell, Alan Baxter,
Robert Strauss
152. "The Lady from Witchita" (9-27-67) Joan Collins, Rose
Marie, Harry Lauter
153. "Star Crossed" (10-4-67) Tom Tryon, Lisabeth Hush,
Kiel Martin, Brian Nash
154. "Johnny Moon" (10-11-67) Tom Bell, Ben Johnson, Michael
Higgins, Bo Hopkins, Cliff Potter, George Brenlin
155. "The Masquerade" (10-18-67) Lloyd Nolan, David Hartman,
Diana Muldaur, Bobby Buntrock, Ed Prentiss, Harry
Hickox

156. "Ah Sing vs. Wyoming" (10-25-67) Edmond O'Brien, Aki
     Aleong, Lloyd Bochner, Robert Ellenstein, Bartlett
     Robinson, Roy Engel, Jill Donohue, John Hoyt
157. "Bitter Autumn" (11-1-67) John Anderson
158. "A Bad Place to Die" (11-8-67) Victor Jory, Susanne
     Benton, Myron Healey, Henry Beckman
159. "Paid in Full" (11-22-67) James Whitmore, Don Stroud,
     Douglas Kennedy, Robert Yuro
160. "To Bear Witness" (11-29-67) William Windom, Joanna
     Moore, Malachi Throne, Paul Carr
161. "The Barren Ground" (12-6-67) Jay C. Flippen, Collin
     Wilcox, Byron Mabe, Christopher Horne, Noah Keen
162. "Execution at Triste" (12-13-67) Sharon Farrell, Robert
     Lansing, Kelly Thordsen, Burt Douglas, Cyril Delevanti,
     Steve Raines, Nate Esformes, Philip Chapin, Percy Hel-
     ton, Bert Freed
163. "A Small Taste of Justice" (12-20-67) Susan Oliver, Peter
     Brown, John Lupton, Virginia Christine, Vaughn Taylor,
     Judson Pratt, James Gammon, Stephen Coit, Quent Son-
     dergaard, Stuart Nisbet
164. "The Fortress" (12-27-67) Leslie Nielsen, Kipp Hamilton,
     Barbara Bouchet, Willard Sage, H. M. Wynant, Paul
     Picerni
165. "The Death Wagon" (1-3-68) Albert Salmi, Bill Baldwin,
     Jeff Malloy, Nicolas Beauvy, Adam O'Neil, Tim McIntire,
     Ken Swofford
166. "Jed" (1-20-68) Steve Ihnat, Brenda Scott, Sammy Jackson,
     Stuart Margolin
167. "With Help from Ulysses" (1-17-68) Hugh Beaumont, J. Pat
     O'Malley, Jill Donohue, Barbara Rhoadig
168. "The Gentle Tamers" (1-24-68) Anthony Call, Darwin Jos-
     ton, Paul Comi, Wesley Lau, James Griffith, Don Pedro
     Colley
169. "The Good-Hearted Badman" (2-7-68) Peter Deuel, Anthony
     Zerbe, John Larch
170. "The Hell Wind" (2-14-68) Patricia Crowley, Ford Rainey,
     Woodrow Parfrey, Kiel Martin
171. "The Crooked Path" (2-21-68) Tom Skerritt, Kevin Cough-
     lin, John Marley, Ellen Moss
172. "Stacey" (2-28-68) Robert H. Harris, Lee Kroeger, Bar-
     bara Werle
173. "The Handy Man" (3-6-68) Mel Tormé, Tom Simcox,
     Paul Mantee
174. "The Decision" (3-13-68) Steve Carlson, Kenneth Tobey
175. "Seth" (3-20-68) Michael Burns, Kevin Hagen, Richard
     LePore

## Seventh Season

176. "The Saddle Warmer" (9-18-68) Ralph Bellamy, Tom Sker-
     ritt, Quentin Dean
177. "Silver Image" (9-25-68) Geraldine Brooks, James Daly,
     William Smith, Red Morgan, Harry Harvey Sr., Harper

        Flaherty, Tim Graham, Donald Barry

178. "The Orchard" (10-2-68) William Windom, Burgess Meredith, Brandon de Wilde, Ben Wright, William Phipps, Lew Brown, Ben Murphy

179. "Vision of Blindness" (10-9-68) John Saxon, Ben Johnson

180. "The Wind of Outrage" (10-16-68) Ricardo Montalban, Lois Nettleton, Lawrence Dane

181. "Image of an Outlaw" (10-23-68) Don Stroud, Amy Thomson, Sandy Kenyon

182. "The Heritage" (10-30-68) Buffy Sainte-Marie, Ned Romero, Jim Davis, Karl Swenson, Jay Silverheels

183. "Ride the Misadventure" (11-6-68) Joseph Campanella, Katherine Justice

184. "The Storm Gate" (11-13-68) Burr De Benning, Susan Oliver, Scott Brady, Robert F. Simon, Roy Jenson

185. 'Dark Corridor" (11-27-68) Judy Lang, Paul Smith, Paul Winchell

186. "The Mustangers" (12-4-68) John Agar, James Edwards, Don Knight, Chuck Daniel, William Burns, Marjorie Bennett, Grace Lee Whitney

187. 'Nora" (12-11-68) Anne Baxter, Hugh Beaumont, Tim McIntire, Ken Renard, Harry Lauter

188. "Big Tiny" (12-18-68) Roger Torrey, Dick Foran, David Sutton, Julie Sommars, Mabel Albertson

189. 'Stopover" (1-8-69) Jay C. Flippen, Herb Jeffries, Douglas Henderson, Kevin Hagen, John Kellogg, Jan Shepard, William Fawcett

190. 'Death Wait" (1-15-69) Harold J. Stone, Sheila Larkin, Conlan Carter, Murray MacLeod

191. "Last Grave at Socorro Creek" (1-22-69) Kevin Coughlin, Steve Ihnat

192. "Crime Wave at Buffalo Springs" (1-29-69) Carrie Snodgrass, Tom Bosley, Yvonne DeCarlo, James Brolin, Ann Prentiss, Gary Vinson

193. "The Price of Love" (2-12-69) Peter Deuel, James Gregory, Skip Homeier

194. "The Ordeal" (2-19-69) Robert Pine, Michael Masters, Jennifer Gan

195. "The Land Dreamer" (2-26-69) Don Francks, James Olson, Cloris Leachman, Ford Rainey, John Daniels

196. "Eileen" (3-5-69) Debbie Watson, Richard van Vleet

197. 'Incident at Diablo Crossing" (3-12-69) Gary Collins, Bernie Hamilton

198. "Storm Over Shiloh" (3-19-69) Harper Flaherty

199. "The Girl in the Shadows" (3-26-69) Jack Albertson, Brenda Scott, Greg Mullavey

200. "Fox, Hound, and the Widow McCloud" (4-2-69) Troy Donahue, Jean Inness, Victor Jory

201. "The Stranger" (4-9-69) Shelly Novack, John Doucette

Eighth Season

202. "The Long Ride Home" (9-17-69) Leslie Nielsen, Lonny

Chapman, Joyce Jameson, Patrick Tovatt
203. "A Flash of Darkness" (9-24-69) James Whitmore, Pamela McMyler
204. "Halfway Back from Hell" (10-1-69) William Windom, John Dehner
205. "The Power Seekers" (10-8-69) Barry Sullivan, Andrew Prine
206. "Family Man" (10-15-69) Frank Webb, Darleen Carr
207. "The Runaway Boy" (10-22-69) Guy Stockwell, Johnny Whitaker
208. "A Love to Remember" (10-29-69) Diane Baker, Fred Beir
209. "The Substitute" (11-5-69) Dennis Cooney, Beverly McKinsey
210. "The Bugler" (11-19-69) Michael Burns, Morgan Woodward
211. "Home to Methuselah" (11-26-69) Audrey Totter, John Anderson, Anthony Call
212. "A Touch of Hands" (12-3-69) Belinda Montgomery, Michael Constantine
213. "Journey to Scathelock" (12-10-69) Burr De Benning, Anne Helm, Frank Campanella, Lawrence Dane
214. "A Woman of Stone" (12-17-69) Bethel Leslie, Charles Drake
215. "Black Jade" (12-31-69) William Shatner, Jill Townsend, James Watson
216. "You Can Lead a Horse to Water" (1-7-70) Elizabeth Hubbard, Strother Martin
217. "Nightmare" (1-21-70) Joan Crawford, Steve Sandor
218. "The Shiloh Years" (1-28-70) Anthony Franciosa, Harold J. Stone
219. "Train of Darkness" (2-4-70) Dennis Weaver, Charlotte Stewart
220. "A Time of Terror" (2-11-70) Joseph Cotten, Shelly Novack
221. "No War for the Warrior" (2-18-70) Henry Jones, Charles Robinson, Charles Aidman
222. "A King's Ransom" (2-25-70) Jackie DeShannon, Patrick Macnee
223. "The Sins of the Fathers" (3-4-70) Robert Lipton, Tim McIntire
224. "Rich Man, Poor Man" (3-11-70) Jack Elam, Patricia Morrow
225. "The Gift" (3-18-70) Tab Hunter, Julie Gregg, Frank Marth

## THE MEN FROM SHILOH

This new title was given to "The Virginian." James Drury and Doug McClure were the only regulars to remain.

The Regulars: Col. Alan MacKenzie, Stewart Granger; Tate, Lee Majors; Virginian, James Drury; Trampas, Doug McClure.

The Episodes:

1. "The West vs. Colonel MacKenzie" (9-16-70) Martha Hyer, Elizabeth Ashley, Don De Fore, John Larch
2. "The Best Man" (9-23-70) Desi Arnaz, Katy Jurado, James Farentino
3. "Jenny" (9-30-70) Janet Leigh, Charles Drake, John Ireland, Jo Ann Harris, Christopher Dark, Myron Healey, Lew Brown
4. "With Love, Bullets, and Valentines" (10-7-70) Art Carney, Tom Ewell, Deborah Walley, Jack Albertson
5. "The Mysterious Mr. Tate" (10-14-70) Robert Webber, Dane Clark, Annette O'Toole
6. "Gun Quest" (10-21-70) Anne Francis, Neville Brand, Brandon de Wilde, Agnes Moorehead, Joseph Cotten, Rod Cameron, Monte Markham, John Smith, Sally Shockley
7. "Crooked Corner" (10-28-70) Susan Strasberg, Kurt Kasznar, Brock Peters, Walter Koenig, Lloyd Battista
8. "Lady at the Bar" (11-4-70) Greer Garson, James Whitmore, E. G. Marshall, Jay Robinson, Kenneth Tobey
9. "The Price of the Hanging" (11-11-70) Jane Wyatt, Lew Ayres, Edward Binns, Tom Tryon, Patricia Harty
10. "Experiment at New Life" (11-18-70) Lyle Bettger, Vera Miles, Ralph Meeker, Patricia Medina, Sue Lyon
11. "Follow the Leader" (12-2-70) Anthony Franciosa, Frank Gorshin
12. "Last of the Comancheros" (12-9-70) Ricardo Montalban
13. "Hannah" (12-30-70) Lisa Gerritsen, Susan Oliver
14. "Nan Allen" (1-6-71) Diane Baker, E. G. Marshall, Tom Skerritt, Eric Christmas, Read Morgan, Arch Johnson
15. "The Politician" (1-13-71) John Ericson, William Windom, Diana Muldaur, Jean Hale, Denny Miller, Jim Davis
16. "The Animal" (1-20-71) Jack Ging, Scott Brady, Andy Devine, Chuck Connors
17. "The Legacy of Spencer Flats" (1-27-71) Ann Sothern, Carolyn Jones, Bradford Dillman, Edgar Buchanan
18. "The Angus Killer" (2-10-71) Dina Merrill, Van Johnson, Ruth Roman, Andrew Parks, Chill Wills, Stephen McNally
19. "Flight from Memory" (2-17-71) Burgess Meredith, Robert Fuller, Tisha Sterling, Roger Cudney
20. "Tate, Ramrod" (2-24-71) Michael Burns, Sally Ann Howes, Craig Stevens, Joan Harris, Alan Hale Jr. , George Paulsin, Rex Allen
21. "The Regimental Line" (3-3-71) John Saxon, Eric Christmas, Eddie Little Sky
22. "The Town Killer" (3-10-71) Howard Duff, Peter Lawford, Lloyd Bochner, Brenda Benet
23. "Wolf Track" (3-17-71) Julie Harris, Pernell Roberts, Clint Howard, Arthur O'Connell
24. "Jump-Up" (3-24-71) John McGiver, Madlyn Rhue, John Astin

THE ELEVENTH HOUR

Beautiful, highly literate series of dramas of a forensic psychiatrist (Wendell Corey as Dr. Theodore Bassett; subsequently Ralph Bellamy as Dr. Starke), a psychologist (Jack Ging as Dr. Paul Graham) and their patients. Elaborate episode titles are drawn from an abundance of literary origins. "Where Have You Been, Lord Randall, My Son?," about a young man's extreme mother attachment, derives from the anonymous ballad Lord Randall, with a stanza which perfectly accrues to the teleplay's theme: "O where hae ye been, Lord Randall, my son?/O where hae ye been, my handsome young man?"/"I hae been to the wildwood; mother, make my bed soon,/For I'm weary wi' hunting, and fain wald lie down."

"Where Ignorant Armies Clash by Night," with Nan Martin in the role of a married woman who believes she has spoken with her dead lover, is taken from Matthew Arnold's 1867 Dover Beach, while of course "The Wings of the Morning" is Biblical (Psalms 139:9) in origin.

Whatever the theme (post-natal depression in Alfred Brenner's "The Blues My Baby Gave to Me," war desertion in Theodore Apstein's "There Are Dragons in This Forest," and child pregnancy in Apstein's "Of Roses and Nightingales and Other Lovely Things"), the treatment was inspired; the quality of writing excellent. Producer Sam Rolfe in conjunction with associate producer Irving Elman composed the theme. Harry Sukman was musical director for the series.

The Regulars: Dr. Theodore Bassett, Wendell Corey (first season only); Dr. Paul Graham, Jack Ging; Dr. Starke, Ralph Bellamy (second season only).

The Episodes:

1. "Ann Costigan: A Duel on a Field of White" (10-3-62) Vera Miles, Murray Hamilton, Roger Perry
2. "There Are Dragons in This Forest" (10-10-62) Steven Hill, Mai Zetterling, Lloyd Bochner
3. "Make Me a Place" (10-17-62) David Janssen, Barbara Rush, Susan Gordon
4. "I Don't Belong in a White-Painted House" (10-24-62) George C. Scott, Colleen Dewhurst, John Anderson, Michael Strong
5. "The 7th Day of Creation" (10-31-62) Katy Jurado, Teno Pollick, John McGiver, Emily McLaughlin, Noah Keen
6. "Of Roses and Nightingales and Other Lovely Things" (11-7-62) Kim Hunter, Pat Hingle, Davey Davison, Donald Losby
7. "Angie, You Made My Heart Stop" (11-14-62) Collin Wilcox, Albert Salmi, Dabbs Greer, David Sheiner
8. "Hooray, Hooray, the Circus Is Coming to Town" (11-21-62) Burgess Meredith, Henry Jones, Edward Andrews, Richard Evans

9. "Cry a Little for Mary, Too" (11-28-62) Keir Dullea, Judith Evelyn, Edith Atwater
10. "Eat, Little Fishie, Eat" (12-5-62) Bradford Dillman, Nancy Wickwire, Barbara Stuart
11. "The Blues My Baby Gave to Me" (12-12-62) Inger Stevens, Robert Vaughn, John Zaremba, Louise Lorimer, Clark Howat
12. "Along About Late in the Afternoon" (12-26-62) Chester Morris, Franchot Tone, Edith Atwater
13. "Which Man Will Die?" (1-2-63) Harry Guardino, Carolyn Kearney, Noah Keen, Virginia Gregg, Ted Knight
14. "Where Have You Been, Lord Randall, My Son?" (1-9-63) Beatrice Straight, Scott Marlowe, Sandra Knight, Anna-Lisa, J. Edward McKinley, James Stapleton
15. "My Name Is Judith, I'm Lost, You See" (1-16-63) Jeanne Cooper, Veronica Cartwright, Joanna Barnes, Ken Lynch, Virginia Christine, Edward Asner, Gina Gillespie
16. "Where Ignorant Armies Clash by Night" (1-23-63) Keenan Wynn, Nan Martin, Linda Evans, Steven Geray
17. "Advice to the Lovelorn and Shopworn" (1-30-63) Harry Guardino, Ruth Roman, Natalie Trundy, Ann Staunton
18. "Why Am I Grown So Cold?" (2-6-63) Eleanor Parker, Dan Duryea, Lori March, Jan Peters, Arthur Peterson
19. "Like a Diamond in the Sky" (2-13-63) Julie London, Everett Sloane, Hershel Bernardi, Philip Pine
20. "Beauty Playing a Mandolin Underneath a Willow Tree" (2-20-63) Vera Miles, James Stapleton, Robert Keith, Karl Swenson, John Stephenson
21. "A Tumble from a High White Horse" (2-27-63) Telly Savalas, Walter Matthau, Frankie Avalon
22. "Five Moments Out of Time" (3-6-63) Patricia Crowley, Sylvia Sidney, Patrick O'Neal, Norman Fell
23. "The Wings of the Morning" (3-20-63) Phyllis Avery, Lynn Loring, Peter Helm, Jean Inness, Irene Hervey, Harry Townes
24. "Hang by One Hand" (3-27-63) James Franciscus, Anne Francis, Leslie Denison, Ed Faulkner, Tom Simcox
25. "Something Crazy's Going On in the Back Room" (4-3-63) Tuesday Weld, Angela Lansbury, Martin Balsam, Don Grady, Roy Thinnes
26. "Everybody Knows You've Left Me" (4-10-63) Dina Merrill, Charles Drake, Ed Nelson
27. "Try to Keep Alive Until Next Tuesday" (4-17-63) Robert Walker Jr., James Gregory, Frances Reid, John Beal, Bill Bixby, Jena Engstrom
28. "I Feel Like a Rutabaga" (4-24-63) Eddie Albert, Joan Tompkins, James Callahan, Dick Gautier
29. "A Medicine Man in This Day and Age?" (5-1-63) Don Gordon, Joey Russo, Virginia Gregg, Mario Alcaide, David Renard
30. "The Man Who Came Home Late" (5-8-63) Cliff Robertson, Joanne Linville, Robert Middleton, Katie Sweet
31. "Pressure Breakdown" (5-15-63) Michael Parks, Olive

Deering, Carroll O'Connor, Brenda Scott, Linden Chiles
32. "The Middle Child Gets All the Aches" (5-22-63) Michael Tolan, Sandra Church, Peggy Rea, Irene Martin, Jesslyn Fax, Arlene Burns

Second Season

33. "Cold Hands, Warm Heart" (10-2-63) Lola Albright, Kevin McCarthy, Preston Foster, Anne Seymour
34. "The Silence of Good Men" (10-9-63) Robert Vaughn, Charles Bickford, Veronica Cartwright, Robert F. Simon
35. "Fear Begins at Forty" (10-16-63) Ann Harding, Robert Lansing, Jacqueline Scott, William Sargent
36. "And Man Created Vanity" (10-23-63) Diahann Carroll, Robert Wagner, Shirley Knight, Michael Constantine
37. "Oh, You Shouldn't Have Done It" (10-30-63) James Coburn, Lois Nettleton, Mary La Roche, Richard Webb
38. "The Bronze Locust" (11-6-63) Elizabeth Montgomery, Robert Loggia
39. "What Did She Mean by Good Luck?" (11-13-63) Kathryn Hays, Beverly Garland, Paul Burke
40. "This Wonderful Mad Man Calls Me a Beauty" (11-20-63) Richard Kiley
41. "Four Feet in the Morning" [Part II of 'Dr. Kildare" episode of 11/21/63] (11-27-63) Tony Dow, Andrew Duggan, Ruth Roman, Marta Kristen, Phyllis Avery, Richard Chamberlain, Raymond Massey
42. "The Bride Wore Pink" (12-4-63) Irene Dailey, Katherine Crawford, Jean Stapleton
43. "There Should Be an Outfit Called Families Anonymous!" (12-11-63) Eileen Heckart, Hershel Bernardi, Sheree North, Frank Aletter
44. "La Belle Indifference" (12-18-63) Katherine Crawford, James MacArthur, Leonard Nimoy
45. "Is Mr. Martin Coming Back?" (12-25-63) Bert Lahr, Ronny Howard, Marion Ross
46. "My Door Is Locked and Bolted" (1-1-64) Piper Laurie, Gale Page
47. "Sunday Father" (1-8-64) Red Buttons, Jaye P. Morgan, Billy Mumy, Richard Bull
48. "How Do I Say 'I Love You'?" (1-15-64) Celeste Holm, Diana Millay, Shelley Fabares, Lee Kinsolving
49. "You're So Smart, Why Can't You Be Good?" (1-22-64) Fay Wray, Fabian, Noreen Corcoran, Philip Ober
50. "Who Chopped Down the Cherry Tree?" (1-29-64) Robert Ryan
51. "Cannibal Plants, They Eat You Alive" (2-5-64) Lloyd Bridges, Beau Bridges, Christine White
52. "The Only Remaining Copy Is in the British Museum" (2-12-64) Roddy McDowall, Alexander Scourby, Anne Helm
53. "87 Different Kinds of Love" (2-19-64) Diana Dors, Jenny Maxwell, Joseph Campanella
54. "The Secret in the Stone" (2-26-64) Rip Torn, Elinor

Donahue, Nellie Burt
55. "A Full Moon Every Night" (3-4-64) Diana Hyland, Elsa Lanchester
56. "Who Is to Say How the Battle Is to Be Fought?" (3-11-64) Brock Peters, Barbara McNair
57. "The Prodigy" (3-18-64) Howard Duff, Robert Lansing, Michel Petit, Alfred Ryder, Phyllis Hill
58. "Does My Mother Have to Know?" [Part I] (3-25-64) Kim Stanley, Kim Darby, Audrey Meadows, Philip Abbott, Robert Emhardt, Joan Tompkins
59. "Does My Mother Have to Know?" [Part II] (4-1-64) as above
60. "A Pattern of Sundays" (4-8-64) Paul Burke, Lois Smith, Bethel Leslie
61. "To Love Is to Live" (4-15-64) Jeanette Nolan, Dean Stockwell, Marlyn Mason, Kent Smith
62. "The Color of Sunset" (4-22-64) Edmond O'Brien, John Marley, Leonard Nimoy, Martine Bartlett


THE WIDE COUNTRY

This continuing tale of the vicissitudes of two rodeo cowboy brothers (Earl Holliman as the older and wiser Mitch Guthrie; Andrew Prine as the younger Andy) in the contemporary West achieved some fine performances from guest stars nicely suited to their roles. Laura Devon was the lady whose "candle burns at both ends" while dying of leukemia in the thirteenth episode. Margaret and Paul Schneider's "The Bravest Man in the World," with Ray Danton, resurrected what was allegedly the "life story of adventurer Warren Price." Character actor Slim Pickens, in the recurring role of Slim Walker, himself authored the story for the episode "Speckle Bird" in which his daughter appeared. And so as to keep both the setting and the action as contemporary as possible, that always interesting staple--the juvenile gang--was the subject of the episode "Our Ernie Kills People," by Mark Rodgers.

The Regulars: Mitch Guthrie, Earl Holliman; Andy Guthrie, Andrew Prine; Slim Walker, Slim Pickens (recurring role).

The Episodes:

1. "The Royce Bennett Story" (9-20-62) Steve Forrest, Jacqueline Scott, Billy Mumy, Sandy Kenyon, Lennie Geer
2. "A Guy for Clementine" (9-27-62) Joyce Bulifant, Noah Beery Jr.
3. "Journey Down a Dusty Road" (10-4-62) Wallace Ford, Nellie Burt
4. "Who Killed Eddie Gannon?" (10-11-62) Ed Nelson, Russell Johnson, Charles Aidman
5. "What Are Friends For?" (10-18-62) Jay Novello, James Westerfield, Hal Baylor

6. "Straightjacket for an Indian" (10-25-62) Claude Akins, Howard McNear
7. "Our Ernie Kills People" (11-1-62) Irene Hervey, Richard Jordan, Don Collier, John Litel
8. "A Devil in the Chute" (11-8-62) Michael Ansara, Coleen Gray, Donald Losby
9. "The Girl in the Sunshine Smile" (11-15-62) Anne Helm, Ray Walston, Peter Leeds
10. "Tears on a Painted Face" (11-29-62) Dan Duryea, Charles Robinson, Carole Wells
11. "The Bravest Man in the World" (12-6-62) Ray Danton, Ford Rainey, Peggy McCay, Yvonne Craig
12. "Good Old Uncle Walt" (12-13-62) Edgar Buchanan, Walter Burke
13. "My Candle Burns at Both Ends" (12-20-62) Laura Devon, Roy Roberts, David McMahon
14. "Memory of a Filly" (1-3-63) Ronnie Haran, Richard Hale
15. "Step Over the Sky" (1-10-63) Victor Jory, Diane Ladd, Robert Brubaker
16. "A Cry from the Mountain" (1-17-63) Jacques Aubuchon, James Caan, Tony Ray
17. "Don't Cry for Johnny Devlin" (1-24-63) James McMullan, R. G. Armstrong
18. "Speckle Bird" (1-31-63) Forrest Tucker, Chris Robinson, Maggie Lou
19. "The Man Who Ran Away" (2-7-63) John Doucette, Mala Powers, Jay Lanin
20. "Whose Hand at My Throat?" (2-14-63) Eduard Franz, Erika Peters, John Qualen
21. "The Judas Goat" (2-21-63) Eddie Albert, Kent Smith, Christine White, Bert Freed
22. "To Cindy, with Love" (2-28-63) Patty Duke
23. "The Quest of Jacob Blaufus" (3-7-63) Peter Whitney, David Macklin, Marjorie Reynolds
24. "Farewell to Margarita" (3-21-63) Barbara Luna, Vito Scotti, Frank Puglia
25. "The Girl from Nob Hill" (3-28-63) Kathryn Hays, Olive Sturgess
26. "Yanqui, Go Home!" (4-4-63)
27. "The Lucky Punch" (4-18-63) Bruce Yarnell, Audrey Dalton
28. "The Care and Handling of Tigers" (4-25-63) Anthony George, Teddy Eccles, Barbara Mansell

## THE NURSES (THE DOCTORS AND THE NURSES)

Executive producer Herbert Brodkin's and producer Arthur Lewis' superbly composed dramas on the sociology of the hospital, with special focus on two nurses--a veteran (Shirl Conway as Liz Thorpe) and a novice (Zina Bethune as Gail Lucas). The last season came to be called "The Doctors and the Nurses" in relation to the two new doctor protagonists--Dr. Alex Tazinski (Michael Tolan) and Dr. Ted Steffen (Joseph Campanella).

Subjects explored included the possibility of voodoo (in the episode "Two Black Candles") and the possibility of mercy killing (in "A Question of Mercy"), drug addiction (in Robert Schlitt's "An Unweeded Garden"), the callous nurse (Beatrice Straight's role in "The Lady Made of Stone") and the aged, incorrigible nurse (Cathleen Nesbitt's role in "The Third Generation").

Ruby Dee was excellent as the Harlem-raised nurse who attempts to divorce her past but finally comes to terms with what she has become in "Express Stop from Lenox Avenue," by Adrian Spies and directed by Stuart Rosenberg. Ron Nicholas' highly credible teleplay "The Prisoner" beckons an examination of capital punishment. Other writers for the series included Alvin Boretz ("They Are as Lions"), George Bellak ("You Could Die Laughing") and John Vlahos ("Night Shift"). Meaningful episode titles derived from such literary sources as Hilaire Belloc's For a Sundial ("Loss and Possession, death and life are one/There falls no shadow wher there shines no sun"; ergo, the teleplay "No Shadow Where There Is No Sun") and Edmund Spenser's Muiopotomos; or, The Fate of the Butterflie ("To spend, to give, to want, to be undone"; ergo, the teleplay "To Spend, to Give, to Want").

The Regulars: Liz Thorpe, Shirl Conway; Gail Lucas, Zina Bethune; Dr. Felix Reisner, Fred J. Stewart (first season only); Dr. Henden, John Beal (first season only); Miss Ayres, Hilda Simms; Dr. Kiley, Edward Binns (second season); Dr. Lowry, Stephen Brooks (second season); Dr. Alex Tazinski, Michael Tolan (last season); Dr. Ted Steffen, Joseph Campanella (last season).

The Episodes:

1. "Night Shift" (9-27-62) Viveca Lindfors, Ruth McDevitt, Joey Heatherton, Arthur Hill
2. "The Fly Shadow" (10-11-62) Colleen Dewhurst, Joanne Linville, Joseph Campanella, Martin Rudy
3. "The Barbara Bowers Story" (10-18-62) Elizabeth Ashley, Jean Stapleton
4. "Dr. Lillian" (10-25-62) Virginia Gilmore, Lonny Chapman
5. "A Private Room" (11-1-62) Barry Morse, Edward Binns, Sorrell Booke
6. "The Prisoner" (11-8-62) George Grizzard, Simon Oakland, Louis Gossett
7. "A Strange and Distant Place" (11-15-62) Zia Mohyeddin, Rosemary Murphy, Fredd Wayne
8. "Two Black Candles" (11-22-62) Dana Elcar
9. "The Lady Made of Stone" (11-29-62) Beatrice Straight, Michael Strong, Thomas Carlin, Ludi Claire
10. "Frieda" (12-6-62) Vivian Nathan, Ann Shoemaker, Peg Murray, Olympia Dukakis, Leon Stevens
11. "The Walls Came Tumbling Down" (12-20-62) Beverly Garland, Betty Field, Frank Overton, Joseph Campanella
12. "Image of Angela" (12-27-62) Angela D'Ambrosia, Jerry

Dodge, Paul Stevens
13. "A Difference of Years" (1-3-63) William Shatner, Sarah Marshall
14. "Root of Violence" (1-10-63) Susan Kohner, Joey Trent, Jose Perez
15. "Many a Sullivan" (1-17-63) Edward Binns, Frank McHugh, Kathleen Maguire, Alan Alda, Philip Bosco
16. "Night Sounds" (1-24-63) Donald Davis, Noah Keen, Patricia Benoit
17. "The Third Generation" (2-7-63) Cathleen Nesbitt
18. "The Life" (2-14-63) Joan Hackett, Edgar Stehli, David J.
19. "Circle of Choice" (2-21-63)
20. "The Perfect Nurse" (2-28-63) Patrick O'Neal, Madeleine Sherwood
21. "The Thunder of Ernie Bass" (3-7-63) Philip Carey
22. "The Saturday Evening of Time" (3-14-63) Peggy Wood, David Opatoshu
23. "A Question of Mercy" (3-21-63) William Shatner, Madlyn Rhue, J. D. Cannon
24. "Party Girl" (3-28-63) Inger Stevens, Inga Swenson, James Broderick
25. "A Dark World" (4-11-63) Martha Scott, Mary Fickett
26. "You Could Die Laughing" (4-18-63) Keenan Wynn, Alan Bunce, Conrad Janis
27. "Choice Among Wrongs" (5-2-63) Edward Binns, Stephen Brooks, Lauri Peters
28. "Express Stop from Lenox Avenue" (5-9-63) Ruby Dee, Claudia McNeil, Carl Lee, Neva Patterson, George Voskovec, Joe Mantell
29. "Bitter Pill" (5-23-63) Scott Marlowe, Jena Engstrom, David J. Stewart, Molly McCarthy
30. "Field of Battle" (5-30-63) Diane Baker, James Daly, Simon Oakland, Jerry Orbach, William Daniels
31. "They Are as Lions" (6-6-63) Kim Hunter, J. D. Cannon, Russell Collins

Second Season

32. "No Score" (9-26-63) Don Gordon, Susan Oliver, Michael Strong
33. "Show Just Cause Why You Should Weep" (10-3-63) Judson Laire, Zachary Scott, Ford Rainey
34. "Escape Route" (10-10-63) Viveca Lindfors, Barry Morse
35. "The Gift" (10-17-63) Lee Grant, Robert Webber, Anne Meacham, Edward Asner
36. "Strike" (10-24-63) Norma Crane, Clifton James, Judson Laire, Kathleen Maguire
37. "Horns of Plenty" (10-31-63) Mary Tahmin, Sybil White, Mark Richmond
38. "The Helping Hand" (11-7-63) Michael Tolan, Sada Thompson, Joe De Santis
39. "Ordeal" (11-14-63) Brandon de Wilde, Larry Gates
40. "The Guilt of Molly Kane" (11-21-63) Lois Nettleton

41. "The Unwanted" (11-28-63) Vivian Nathan, Vincent Gardenia, Ellen Holly
42. "Disaster Call" (12-5-63) Howard Da Silva, Tim O'Connor, John McGovern
43. "To Spend, to Give, to Want" (12-12-63) Lee Grant, Dana Elcar
44. "The Witch of the East Wing" (12-19-63) Elaine Stritch, Tom Bosley, Martin Sheen
45. "Rally Round, My Comrades" (12-26-63) Joey Heatherton, Audrey Christie, Julie Hirsh
46. "The Seeing Heart" (1-2-64) Fritz Weaver, Paul Mace, Sam Gray
47. "Credo" (1-9-64) Bradford Dillman, Mercedes McCambridge, John McGovern, Joseph Campanella
48. "The Rainbow Ride" (1-16-64) Geraldine Brooks, Philip Bosco, Joseph Campanella
49. "The Intern Syndrome" (1-23-64) Sandra Church, Dana Elcar
50. "Is There Room for Edward?" (1-30-64) Michael Tolan
51. "The Courage to Be" (2-6-64) James Edwards, Philip Vandervort
52. "Nurse Is a Feminine Noun" (2-13-64) Margaret Barker, Harold J. Stone, Judson Laire
53. "Imperfect Prodigy" (2-20-64) Michael Tolan, Diana Sands, Paul McGrath
54. "For the Mice and Rabbits" (2-27-64) Geraldine Page, Margaret Barker
55. "Climb a Broken Ladder" (3-12-64) George Segal, Kathryn Hays
56. "The Forever Child" (3-19-64) Richard Kiley, Theodore Bikel, Augusta Dabney
57. "A Kind of Loving" (4-2-64) Diane Lynn, William Prince, Arlene Golonka
58. "The Leopard Killer" (4-9-64) William Marshall, Jackie Price
59. "Gismo on the EEG" (4-16-64) June Harding, Joe Silver
60. "The Human Transition" (4-23-64) Virginia Gilmore, James Daly, Davey Davison
61. "To All My Friends on Shore" (5-7-64) Sylvia Sidney, Will Kuluva
62. "White on White" (5-14-64) Cedric Hardwicke, Polly Rowles, Kevin McCarthy
63. "A Postcard from Yucatan" (5-21-64) Polly Rowles, Arch Johnson, Charles Aidman
64. "The Bystanders" (5-28-64) Russell Collins, Joseph Campanella, Vincent Gardenia
65. "Where Park Avenue Runs into Vreeland" (6-11-64) Jan Sterling
66. "The Warrior" (6-18-64) Leslie Nielsen, Ivan Dixon
67. "The Love of a Smart Operator" (6-25-64) Paul Burke, Barbara Barrie

Third Season [now as THE DOCTORS AND THE NURSES]

68. "Once Bitten" (9-22-64)  Paul McGrath, Claudette Nevins
69. "The Suspect" [Part I] (9-29-64)  Shepperd Strudwick, Jessica Walter, Bert Freed, Martin Sheen
70. "The Suspect" [Part II] (10-6-64)  as above
71. "The Respect of One for Another" (10-13-64)  Ralph Meeker, Austin Willis
72. "No Shadow Where There Is No Sun" (10-20-64)  Merrie Spaeth, Jeff Corey, Michael Strong
73. "Hildie" (10-27-64)  Barbara Feldon, Darren McGavin, Frank Mahoney
74. "The Outpost" (11-10-64)  Jack Albertson, Ralph Dunn, Rudy Bond
75. "The Family Resemblance" (11-17-64)  Brock Peters, Diana Sands, Ossie Davis
76. "Time for You and Time for Me" (11-24-64)  Polly Rowles, Ruth Ford, Henry Lacose
77. "So Some Girls Play the Cello" (12-1-64)  Barbara Harris, Cedric Hardwicke, Robert Drivas
78. "Rites of Spring" (12-8-64)  Peter Helm, Tom Bosley, Michael Walker Jr., Brooke Bundy
79. "Next Stop, Valhalla" (12-15-64)  Donald Davis, Edward Hunter
80. "The Skill in These Hands" (12-22-64)  Robert Loggia, Ellen Holly
81. "A Messenger to Everyone" (12-29-64)  Lois Nettleton, Carol Rossen, Ben Hamner
82. "Last Rites for a Rag Doll" (1-5-65)  Deborah Steinberg
83. "The Patient Nurse" (1-12-65)  Polly Rowles
84. "A Couple of Dozen Tiny Pills" (1-19-65)  Lee Grant, Ruth White, Diana Muldaur, Al Freeman Jr.
85. "A Question of Murder" (1-26-65)  Ethel Griffies, J. D. Cannon
86. "Night of the Witch" (2-2-65)  Eileen Heckart, Neva Patterson, Louise Latham
87. "Sixteen Hours to Chicago" (2-9-65)  Kathleen Widdoes, Simon Oakland
88. "Act of Violence" [Part II on "For the People" episode of 2/28/65] (2-23-65)  Jeffrey Rowland, William Shatner, Howard Da Silva, Joan Lorring, Leora Dana, Nehemiah Persoff, Jessica Walter, Lonny Chapman
89. "A Dangerous Silence" (3-2-65)  Gary Merrill, Joanna Pettet, Philip Bosco
90. "Where There's Smoke" (3-9-65)  Harold J. Stone, James Olson, Richard O'Neill, Estelle Parsons
91. "The Politician" (3-16-65)  George Grizzard, Joe De Santis, Ramon Bieri
92. "The April Thaw of Dr. Mai" (3-20-65)  Diana Hyland, Carolan Daniels, Betty Walker
93. "Threshold" (4-6-65)  Irene Dailey, Arthur Sussex, George Tyne
94. "A39846" (4-20-65)  Jean Pierre Aumont, Louise Sorel,

Kermit Murdock, Thomas Carlin, Ted van Griethuysen, Frank Campanella
95. "The Witnesses" (4-27-65) Hershel Bernardi, Billy Dee Williams, Dan Travanty, Joe Silver
96. "The Heroine" (5-4-65) Brenda Vaccaro, Dustin Hoffman
97. "An Unweeded Garden" (5-11-65) Geoffrey Horne, Collin Wilcox, Dana Elcar, Louise Larabee, Carl Low

THE GALLANT MEN

Cathartic drama of the 36th Infantry Division's progress through Italy during World War II as told by war correspondent Conley Wright (Robert McQueeney) and Captain Jim Benedict (William Reynolds).

The Regulars: Captain Jim Benedict, William Reynolds; Conley Wright, Robert McQueeney; McKenna, Richard X. Slattery; D'Angelo, Eddie Fontaine; Gibson, Roger Davis; Kimbro, Robert Ridgely; Private Saunders, Sandy Kevin; Captain Jergens, Robert Fortier (recurring role); Lucavich, Roland LaStarza; Hanson, Robert Gothie.

The Episodes:

1. "The Gallant Men" (10-5-62) William Windom, Sharon Hugueny
2. "Retreat to Concord" (10-12-62) Peter Breck, Ighigenie Castiglioni
3. "And Cain Cried Out" (10-19-62) Robert Conrad
4. "The Ninety-Eight Cent Man" (10-26-62) Rudy Solari, Chana Eden, Frank De Kova
5. "One Moderately Peaceful Sunday" (11-2-62) John Dehner, Don O'Kelly, Rudy Donlan
6. "Lesson for a Lover" (11-9-62) Marianna Hill, John Van Dreelen
7. "And the End of Evil Things" (11-16-62) Stephen Lander, Buck Kartalian
8. "Some Tears Fall Dry" (11-23-62) Gail Kobe
9. "Fury in a Quiet Village" (11-30-62) Lisa Seagram, Malachi Throne
10. "Signals for an End Run" (12-7-62) Mala Powers, Rodoph Acosta, Eduardo Ciannelli
11. "Robertino" (12-14-62) Peter Soli, Renzo Cesana
12. "Advance and Be Recognized" (12-29-62) Terry Becker, Pamela Gary
13. "To Hold Up a Mirror" (1-5-63) Karl Held, Paul Carr, Patricia Woodell
14. "Boast Not of Tomorrow" (1-12-63) Laura Devon, Ray Montgomery, Genevieve Griffin
15. "The Dogs of War" (1-19-63) Dianne Foster, Dean Stockwel
16. "The Bridge" (1-26-63) Peter Brown, Ernest Sarracino

17. "The Leathernecks" (2-2-63) Philip Carey, Van Williams
18. "Next of Kin" (2-9-63) Stanley Adams, Angela Dorian
19. "Operation Secret" [unsold pilot film for projected fall series] (2-16-63) Ray Danton, Earl Hammond, Albert Paulsen
20. "The Warrior" (2-23-63) James Doohan, Adam Williams, James Best
21. "One Puka Puka" (3-2-63) Poncie Ponce, Frank Atienza
22. "Ol' Buddy" (3-9-63) Anthony Becket, Kevin Hagen
23. "A Taste of Peace" (3-16-63) Julie Adams, Glenn Cannon, DeForest Kelley
24. "The Crucible" (3-23-63) Ed Nelson, Suzi Carnell
25. "Tommy" (3-30-63) David Frankham, Dorothy Provine
26. "A Place to Die" (6-1-63) Michael Parks, Angela Dorian


## THE DAKOTAS

The corruption is pervasive in this offbeat western of celebrated gunmen and their nemeses.

The Regulars: United States Marshal Frank Rogan, Larry Ward;
J. D. Smith, Jack Elam; Del Stark, Chad Everett; Vance
Porter, Michael Green.

The Episodes:

1. "Return to Drydock" (1-7-63) Edward Binns, Richard Hale
2. "Red Sky Over Bismarck" (1-14-63) Andrew Duggan, Constance Ford, Chris Robinson
3. "Mutiny at Fort Mercy" (1-21-63) George Macready
4. "Thunder in Pleasant Valley" (2-4-63) Gregory Walcott
5. "Crisis at High Banjo" (2-11-63) Karen Sharpe
6. "Requiem at Dancer's Hill" (2-18-63) Dennis Hopper, Dick
Foran
7. "Fargo" (2-25-63) David Brian, Richard Jaeckel
8. "Incident at Rapid City" (3-4-63) Bert Freed, Maggie Pierce
9. "Justice at Eagle's Nest" (3-11-63) Everett Sloane
10. "Walk Through the Badlands" (3-18-63) Ed Nelson, Strother
Martin
11. "Trial at Grand Forks" (3-25-63) Werner Klemperer
12. "Reformation at Big Nose Butte" (4-1-63) Telly Savalas,
DeForest Kelley
13. "One Day in Vermillion" (4-8-63) Carlos Rivas, Alan Baxter
14. "Terror at Heart River" (4-15-63) Royal Dano, Coleen Gray
15. "The Chooser of the Slain" (4-22-63) Claude Akins, Beverly
Garland, Richard Loo
16. "Feud at Snake River" (4-29-63) Harry Townes, James
Westerfield
17. "Sanctuary at Crystal Springs" (5-6-63) James Anderson,
Les Tremayne
18. "A Nice Girl from Goliah" (5-13-63) Audrey Dalton, Frank
De Kova, John Carlyle

1963-1964 SEASON

## THE LIEUTENANT

Interesting Americana: an Annapolis graduate's (Gary Lockwood in the role of Lt. Bill Rice) adjustment to the ways of Camp Pendleton Marine Base at peacetime--the series' rigorous deuteragonist being Rice's Captain, Raymond Rambridge (Robert Vaughn).

The Regulars: Second Lieutenant Bill Rice, Gary Lockwood; Captain Raymond Rambridge, Robert Vaughn; Lily, Carmen Phillips; Lieutenant Samwell ("Sampan") Panosian, Steve Franken; Hiland, John Anderson; Harris, Don Penny; Kagey, John Milford.

The Episodes:

1. "A Million Miles from Clary" (9-14-63) Bill Bixby, Russell Thorson, John Doucette
2. "Cool of the Evening" (9-21-63) Kathryn Hays, Norman Fell Jack Albertson, Paul Mantee
3. "The Proud and the Angry" (9-28-63) Rip Torn, Tim Connolly
4. "The Two-Star Giant" (10-5-63) Neville Brand, Hal Gould, Richard Anderson, Linda Evans
5. "A Very Private Affair" (10-12-63) James Gregory, Stuart Margolin
6. "To Take Up Serpents" (10-19-63) John Alderman, Gregory "Pappy" Boyington
7. "A Touching of Hands" (10-26-63) Barbara Bain, David White, Ina Balin, June Vincent
8. "Captain Thomson" (11-2-63) Ken Tobey, Paul Burke, Jay Sheffield
9. "Instant Wedding" (11-9-63) Jeremy Slate, Martin West, Marlyn Mason
10. "A Troubled Image" (11-16-63) Pilar Seurat
11. "Fall from a White Horse" (11-30-63) Andrew Prine, Katharine Ross
12. "Alert" (12-14-63) Ted Bessell, Sharon Farrell, Steven Mailo, Charles McGraw, Chris Connelly
13. "The Art of Discipline" (12-21-63) John Considine, Anne Helm
14. "The Alien" (12-28-63) Frank Maxwell, Danny Nagai,

Madlyn Rhue
15. "O'Rourke" (1-4-64) Eddie Albert, Wayne Heffley, Robert Diamond
16. "Gone the Sun" (1-18-64) John Beal, Joan Tompkins, John Anderson, Ray Teal, Sherry Jackson, Strother Martin
17. "Between Music and Laughter" (1-25-64) Patricia Crowley
18. "Interlude" (2-1-64) Conrad Nagel, Joanna Moore, Arch Johnson
19. "Capp's Lady" (2-8-64) Nita Talbot, James Gregory
20. "Green Water, Green Flag" (2-15-64) Jan Marlen, Nancy Rennick
21. "To Set It Right" (2-22-64) John Marshall, Woody Strode, Dennis Hopper
22. "In the Highest Tradition" (2-29-64) Andrew Duggan, Leonard Nimoy, Martine Bartlett
23. "Tour of Duty" (3-7-64) Ricardo Montalban, Kelly Thorrisen, Louis Nye
24. "Lament for a Dead Goldbrick" (3-14-64) Joseph Campanella, Robert Duvall, John Zaremba
25. "Man with an Edge" (3-21-64) Chad Everett, Joan O'Brien
26. "Operation: Actress" (3-28-64) Leora Dana, Leslie Parrish
27. "Mother Enemy" (4-4-64) Neva Patterson, Walter Koenig
28. "The War Called Peace" (4-11-64) Lloyd Bochner, Denver Pyle
29. "To Kill a Man" (4-18-64) James Shigeta

## THE TRAVELS OF JAIMIE McPHEETERS

The odyssey of a young boy (Kurt Russell as Jaimie McPheeters) and his father (Dan O'Herlihy as Dr. Sardius McPheeters) on a wagon train to California was the subject of this well-received adaptation of the Pulitzer Prize novel by Robert Lewis Taylor.

The Regulars: Jaimie McPheeters, Kurt Russell; Jenny, Donna Anderson; "Doc" Sardius McPheeters, Dan O'Herlihy; Coe, Hedley Mattingly; Buck Coulter, Michael Whitney; The Kissel Kids, The Osmond Brothers; Mat Kissel, Mark Allen; Mrs. Kissel, Meg Wyllie; John Murrel, James Westerfield; Murdock, Charles Bronson (as of 12-15-63).

1. "The Day of Leaving" (9-15-63) Sandy Kenyon
2. "The Day of the First Trail" (9-22-63) John Chandler
3. "The Day of the First Suitor" (9-29-63) Warren Oates, Albert Salmi, Karl Swenson
4. "The Day of the Golden Fleece" (10-6-63) James Whitmore, Andrew Duggan
5. "The Day of the Last Bugle" (10-13-63) Charles Robinson
6. "The Day of the Skinners" (10-20-63) Diana Millay, Pete Whitney
7. "The Day of the Taboo Man" (10-27-63) Frank Silvera, Michael Keep

8. "The Day of the Giants" (11-3-63) Dean Harens, Don Mego-
    wan
9. "The Day of the Long Night" (11-10-63) George Kennedy,
    Collin Wilcox
10. "The Day of the Killer" (11-17-63)
11. "The Day of the Flying Dutchman" (12-1-63) Lloyd Corrigan,
    Norma Vaden
12. "The Day of the Homeless" (12-8-63) Slim Pickens, John
    Williams, Antoinette Bower
13. "The Day of the Misfits" (12-15-63) Mariette Hartley
14. "The Day of the Pawnees" [Part I] (12-22-63) Howard Caine,
    Kathy Garver, Ed Ames, Hank Worden
15. "The Day of the Pawnees" [Part II] (12-29-63) as above
16. "The Day of the Toll Takers" (1-5-64) Leif Erickson, Mary
    Anderson
17. "The Day of the Wizard" (1-12-64) Burgess Meredith, Joan
    Tompkins
18. "The Day of the Search" (1-19-64) David McCallum, Keenan
    Wynn, Charles McGraw, Karl Swenson
19. [unknown title] (1-26-64)
20. "The Day of the Tin Trumpet" (2-2-64) Wallace Ford, Arch
    Johnson, Antoinette Bower
21. "The Day of the Lame Duck" (2-9-64) Joe Mantell, Ruta
    Lee
22. "The Day of the Picnic" (2-16-64) Robert Driscoll, Paul
    Fix
23. "The Day of the 12 Candles" (2-23-64) Joan Freeman, Paul
    Carr
24. "The Day of the Pretenders" (3-1-64) Michael Petit, Steve
    Geray
25. "The Day of the Dark Deeds" (3-8-64) Barbara Nichols,
    Harold J. Stone
26. "The Day of the Reckoning" (3-15-64) Susan Oliver, John
    Fiedler

## ARREST AND TRIAL

This ninety-minute compound of a criminal's arrest (by Ben
Gazzara as Sergeant Nick Anderson) and subsequent defense in trial
(by Chuck Connors as defending attorney John Egan) remains a cur-
iosity for its sometimes titillating handling of relative guilt and innocence. So it is that Roddy McDowall, for example, is cast as a
modern day Raskolnikov; McDowall's sense of guilt over murder
his own undoing in the episode "Journey into Darkness."

The Regulars: Sergeant Nick Anderson, Ben Gazzara; D.A. John
    Egan, Chuck Connors; Miller, John Larch; Kirby, Roger
    Perry; Bone, Noah Keen; Harris, Don Galloway; Jake,
    Joe Higgins; Janet, Jo Anne Miya.

The Episodes:

1. "Call It a Lifetime" (9-15-63) Tony Franciosa, Ruta Lee
2. "Isn't It a Lovely View?" (9-22-63) Vera Miles, Barbara
   Nichols, Howard Duff, Henry Beckman
3. "Tears from a Silver Dipper" (9-29-63) Mickey Callan,
   Madlyn Rhue, Chris Robinson, Russ Conway, Harold J.
   Stone
4. "A Shield Is for Hiding Behind" (10-6-63) James MacArthur,
   Barry Sullivan, Marianne Stewart
5. "My Name Is Martin Burnham" (10-13-63) Nina Foch,
   James Whitmore, Kenneth Tobey, Richard Eyer
6. "A Flame in the Dark" (10-20-63) Broderick Crawford,
   Barry Gordon
7. "Whose Little Girl Are You?" (10-27-63) Joseph Schildkraut,
   Paul Comi, Leif Erickson, Joan Freeman
8. "The Witnesses" (11-3-63) Anne Francis, Robert Webber,
   Doug Lambert
9. "Inquest into a Bleeding Heart" (11-10-63) Richard Basehart, Kent Smith, Julie Adams
10. "The Quality of Justice" (11-17-63) Robert Duvall, Jack
    Klugman
11. "We May Be Better Strangers" (12-1-63) Michael Parks,
    Martin Sheen, Carole Wells, Everett Sloane
12. "Journey into Darkness" (12-8-63) Roddy McDowall, Anja-
    nette Comer, Martine Bartlett
13. "Some Weeks Are All Mondays" (12-15-63) Kim Hunter,
    Joey Heatherton
14. "Run, Little Man, Run" (12-22-63) Shirley Knight, John
    McIntire
15. "Funny Man with a Monkey" (1-5-64) Mickey Rooney,
    Rachel Ames, Bert Freed, Ronald Winters
16. "Signals of an Ancient Flame" (1-12-64) Martin Balsam,
    Katherine Ross, Diane Brewster
17. "Onward and Upward" (1-19-64) Richard Carlson, Diana
    Millay, William Shatner, Sharon Farrell
18. "An Echo of Consciences" (1-26-64) Shelley Fabares, Hugh
    Marlowe, Neville Brand
19. "Somewhat Lower than Angels" (2-2-64) Steve Forrest,
    Sandy Dennis
20. "People in Glass Houses" (2-9-64) Dennis Hopper, Henry
    Silva, Katherine Crawford
21. "The Best There Is" (2-16-64) Arthur O'Connell, Ken Lynch,
    Alejandro Rey, Adam Roarke
22. "A Roll of the Dice" (2-23-64) Nick Adams, Kamala Devi,
    Joyce Bulifant, Virginia Gregg
23. "The Black Flower" (3-1-64) Pat Crowley, Dewey Martin,
    Andrew Duggan, Ray Danton
24. "A Circle of Strangers" (3-8-64) Peter Fonda, Joanna
    Barnes, George Voskovec, Janet Margolin
25. "Modus Operandi" (3-15-64) Dorothy Malone, Anna Sten,
    Charles Aidman
26. "Tigers Are for Jungles" (3-22-64) Richard Conte, Marlo

Thomas, Diane McBain
27. "The Revenge of the Worm" (3-29-64) Telly Savalas, Joan Tabor, Michael Dunn, Lee Patterson
28. "He Ran for His Life" (4-5-64) George Segal, Kathryn Hays, Ed Nelson, Zachary Scott
29. "Those Which Love Has Made" (4-12-64) MacDonald Carey, Mala Powers, Chris Robinson
30. "Birds of a Feather" (4-19-64) Jim Backus, Victoria Shaw, Cesare Danova


THE OUTER LIMITS

This science fiction anthology series boasted scripts by such exceptional writers as Harlan Ellison ("Soldier" and with Seeleg Lester, "Demon with a Glass Hand"), Joseph Stefano ("Don't Open Till Doomsday," "The Bellero Shield," and with Bill S. Balinger, "The Mice"), Stephen Lord ("Specimen: Unknown" and with Milton Krims, "Keeper of the Purple Twilight") and Robert Towne ("The Chameleon"). It also boasted novel use of the camera by Kenneth Peach and Conrad Hall, exciting use of film editing by Tony Di-Marco and others, and what is perhaps the finest musical score composed for television: the eerie, futuristic composition of Dominic Frontiere and Harry Lubin.

Some teleplays had all the poetic beauty of a Ray Bradbury novel, like Harlan Ellison's "Demon with a Glass Hand," in which a Gilgamesh survivor of the space age discovers he owes his resourcefulness to the fact that he is no more than an automaton, destined to save mankind. Another episode, "The Bellero Shield," saw Sally Kellerman as the opportunistic wife of scientist Martin Landau; her ambition finally resulting in her becoming permanently entrapped in an alien force shield. Against potential annihilation by an alien plant form in "Specimen: Unknown," the earth itself demonstrated its regenerative capacity with the falling of rain, with which the plants were destroyed. The Pandora's Box that was opened by Professor Jonathan Meredith (Patrick O'Neal) in Seeleg Lester's "Wolf 359," in which the accelerated evolution of a distant planet was not yet to be borne by human eyes, illustrated this series' preoccupation with the philosophical rather than the purely scientific. Indeed, precisely because this series emphasized philosophy is the reason for its unique, sustained appeal, more than a decade after it left the network.

More attentive viewers of this series might have noted the abundant allusions in the scenarios. Who really were "The Invisibles" of the episode bearing that name? That episode, which concludes on the pious note that the "invisibles" know no territorial bounds, has implications for a post-World War II "anti-subversive" America. And what was the relationship between John Hoyt's curious character "Mr. Balfour," a perpetual visitor to Miriam Hopkins' Blanche DuBois-type "Mrs. Kry" in "Don't Open Till Doomsday"?

Not all teleplays were praiseworthy, however. "The Hundred Days of the Dragon," by Allen Balter and Robert Mint, was purely out of the Cold War with its theme of a sinister, Oriental power (as typified by Richard Loo) seeking to impersonate presidential candidate William Lyons Selby (played by Sidney Blackmer), who is all but assured of the White House. The foreign agents only half succeed, and American virtues ultimately triumph. Unfortunately for several guest stars, the series was more a writer's and technician's craft, so the acting talents of Gloria Grahame were wasted in an otherwise interesting episode about a house frozen in time in "The Guests"; likewise Gladys Cooper's role as a medium in "The Borderland" emerged ineffective.

Perhaps we owe the series' best creative efforts to its producer and sometimes writer ("The Galaxy Being" and "Production and Decay of Strange Particles") Leslie Stevens. It is more likely, though, that this effort was a collective one--and one which produced a series of a caliber for science fiction never again equaled in television.

The Episodes:

1. "The Galaxy Being" (9-16-63) Cliff Robertson, Lee Philips, Jacqueline Scott, Burt Metcalfe
2. "The Hundred Days of the Dragon" (9-23-63) Sidney Blackmer, Richard Loo, Nancy Rennick, Philip Pine
3. "The Man with the Power" (9-30-63) Donald Pleasence, Fred Beir, Priscilla Morrill, John Marley, Edward Platt, Paul Lambert
4. "The Architects of Fear" (10-7-63) Robert Culp, Leonard Stone
5. "The Sixth Finger" (10-14-63) David McCallum, Jill Haworth, Edward Mulhare, Robert Doyle
6. "The Man Who Never Was Born" (10-28-63) Martin Landau, Shirley Knight, Karl Held
7. "O.B.I.T." (11-4-63) Peter Breck, Jeff Corey, Harry Townes
8. "The Human Factor" (11-11-63) Harry Guardino, Sally Kellerman, Gary Merrill, Ivan Dixon, John Newton, Joe De Santis
9. "Corpus Earthling" (11-18-63) Robert Culp, Barry Atwater
10. "Nightmare" (12-2-63) Ed Nelson, Martin Sheen, James Shigeta, John Anderson, Edward Asner
11. "It Crawled Out of the Woodwork" (12-9-63) Scott Marlowe, Michael Forest, Barbara Luna, Kent Smith
12. "The Borderland" (12-16-63) Nina Foch, Gladys Cooper, Mark Richman
13. "Tourist Attraction" (12-23-63) Ralph Meeker, Henry Silva, Janet Blair, Jerry Douglas, Jay Novello
14. "The Zanti Misfits" (12-30-63) Michael Tolan, Bruce Dern, Robert F. Simon
15. "The Mice" (1-6-64) Henry Silva, Diana Sands, Ron Foster
16. "Controlled Experiment" (1-13-64) Carroll O'Connor, Barry

Morse, Grace Lee Whitney
17. "Don't Open Till Doomsday" (1-20-64) Miriam Hopkins, Buck Taylor, Melinda Plowman, John Hoyt, Russell Collins
18. "ZZZZ" (1-27-64) Philip Abbott, Marsha Hunt
19. "The Invisibles" (2-3-64) George Macready, Tony Mordente, Richard Dawson, Don Gordon
20. "The Bollero Shield" (2-10-64) Martin Landau, Sally Kellerman, Chita Rivera, John Hoyt
21. "The Children of Spider County" (2-17-64) Kent Smith, Lee Kinsolving, John Milford, Bennye Gatteys
22. "Specimen: Unknown" (2-24-64) Stephen McNally, Russell Johnson, Arthur Batanides, Peter Baldwin, Gail Kobe, John Kellogg, Walt Davis, Richard Jaeckel
23. "Second Chance" (3-2-64) Simon Oakland, Don Gordon, Janet De Gore, Yale Summers
24. "Moonstone" (3-9-64) Alex Nicol, Ruth Roman, Tim O'Connor, Hari Rhodes, Curt Conway
25. "The Mutant" (3-16-64) Warren Oates, Betsy Jones-Moreland, Walter Burke
26. "The Guests" (3-23-64) Geoffrey Horne, Gloria Grahame, Luana Anders, Nellie Burt, Vaughn Taylor
27. "Fun and Games" (3-30-64) Nick Adams, Nancy Malone, Ray Kellogg, Robert Johnson, Bill Hart, Harvey Gardner, Read Morgan
28. "The Special One" (4-6-64) Macdonald Carey, Richard Ney, Flip Mark, Marion Ross, Edward C. Platt
29. "A Feasibility Study" (4-13-64) Sam Wanamaker, David Opatoshu, Phyllis Love, Joyce Van Patten
30. "Production and Decay of Strange Particles" (4-20-64) George Macready, Signe Hasso, Leonard Nimoy, Rudy Solari
31. "The Chameleon" (4-27-64) Robert Duvall, Howard Caine
32. "The Forms of Things Unknown" (5-4-64) Sir Cedric Hardwicke, Vera Miles, Barbara Rush, David McCallum, Scott Marlowe

## Second Season

33. "Soldier" (9-19-64) Michael Ansara, Lloyd Nolan, Tim O'Connor, Catherine McLeod
34. "Cold Hands, Warm Heart" (9-26-64) William Shatner, Geraldine Brooks, Lloyd Gough, Malachi Throne, Dean Harens
35. "Behold, Eck!" (10-3-64) Peter Lind Hayes, Joan Freeman, Parley Baer, Douglas Henderson
36. "Expanding Human" (10-10-64) Skip Homeier, Keith Andes, James Doohan, Vaughn Taylor
37. "Demon with a Glass Hand" (10-17-64) Robert Culp, Arline Martel, Abraham Sofaer, Steve Harris, Rex Holman
38. "Cry of Silence" (10-24-64) Eddie Albert, June Havoc, Arthur Hunnicutt
39. "The Invisible Enemy" (10-31-64) Adam West, Rudy Solari,

Joe Maross, Chris Alcaide, Ted Knight
40. "Wolf 359" (11-7-64) Patrick O'Neal, Sara Shane, Peter Haskell, Ben Wright, Dabney Coleman
41. "I, Robot" (11-14-64) Howard Da Silva, Leonard Nimoy, Read Morgan, Ford Rainey, Marianna Hill
42. "The Inheritors" [Part I] (11-21-64) Robert Duvall, James Shigeta, Ivan Dixon, Steve Ihnat, Donald Harron, Dee Pollock, James Frawley
43. "The Inheritors" [Part II] (11-28-64) as above
44. "Keeper of the Purple Twilight" (12-5-64) Robert Webber, Warren Stevens, Gail Kobe, Curt Conway, Edward C. Platt
45. "The Duplicate Man" (12-19-64) Ron Randell, Constance Towers, Steven Geray, Mike Lane
46. "Counterweight" (12-26-64) Michael Constantine, Jacqueline Scott, Sandy Kenyon, Larry Ward
47. "The Brain of Colonel Barham" (1-2-65) Anthony Eisley, Grant Williams, Elizabeth Perry, Douglas Kennedy
48. "The Premonition" (1-9-65) Dewey Martin, Mary Murphy, Emma Tyson, William Bramley
49. "The Probe" (1-16-65) Peggy Ann Garner, Mark Richman, Ron Hayes, William Stevens

## THE BREAKING POINT

This psychiatrists/clientele entry from the producers of "Ben Casey" (the episode of September 9, 1963, was the pilot film) is as vibrant a series of case studies as the titles' literary inspirations suggest: A. A. Milne's Four Friends in When We Were Very Young for the episode "And James Was a Very Small Snail," Ralph Hodgson's Reason for the episode "Confounding Her Astronomers."

The Regulars: Dr. McKinley ('Dr. Mac'') Thompson, Paul Richards; Dr. William Raymer, Eduard Franz.

The Episodes:

1. "Solo for B-Flat Clarinet" [Part II; Part I on "Ben Casey" episode of 9/9/63] (9-16-63) Scott Marlowe, Sheree North, Oscar Homolka
2. "Last Summer We Didn't Go Away" (9-23-63) Anthony Franciosa, Edward Asner, Brenda Scott
3. "Fire and Ice" (9-30-63) Kevin McCarthy, Janice Rule, Irene Tedrow
4. "Bird and Snake" (10-7-63) Marisa Pavan, Robert Redford, Jack Weston
5. "There Are the Hip and There Are the Square" (10-14-63) John Cassavetes, Carol Lawrence, J. Pat O'Malley, Virginia Gregg
6. "The Bull Roarer" (10-21-63) Ralph Meeker, Lou Antonio, Mariette Hartley, Carmen Phillips
7. "Crack in an Image" (10-28-63) Kim Hunter, Mark Richman,

Paul Stewart
8. "A Pelican in the Wilderness" (11-4-63) Martin Balsam,
Akim Tamiroff, Barbara Turner, Virginia Capers
9. "And James Was a Very Small Snail" (11-11-63) Marsha
Hunt, Harold J. Stone, Martine Bartlett
10. "Whatsoever Things I Hear" (11-18-63) Shelley Berman
11. "Who Is Mimi--What Is She?" (12-2-63) Ruth Roman, Sandra
Kerr, Vivian Nathan
12. "Millions of Faces" (12-9-63) Rip Torn, Jan Sterling
13. "The Gnu, Now Almost Extinct" (12-16-63) Lillian Gish,
Walter Pidgeon, Vito Scotti, Sara Haden
14. "Heart of Marble, Body of Stone" (12-23-63) Burgess Meredith, Gena Rowlands, John Milford
15. "Don't Cry, Baby, Don't Cry" (12-30-63) Sheree North,
Juanita Moore, Kathleen Catter, Robert Ellenstein
16. "A Little Anger Is a Good Thing" (1-6-64) Rosemary De-
Camp, Arthur O'Connell, Dean Harens, Amanda Ames
17. "And If Thy Hand Offend Thee" (1-13-64) James Daly, Nobu
McCarthy, Richard Webb, Irene Tsu
18. "Better Than a Dead Lion" (1-20-64) Robert Ryan, Bettye
Ackerman, John Larkin
19. "A Land More Cruel" (1-27-64) Eleanor Parker
20. "No Squares in My Family Circle" (2-10-64) Jack Warden,
Mariette Hartley, Johnny Seven
21. "So Many Pretty Girls, So Little Time" (2-17-64) Cliff
Robertson, Mary Murphy, Alan Napier
22. "A Child of the Center Ring" (2-24-64) Jack Oakie, Susan
Strasberg, James Callahan, Cesare Danova
23. "Tides of Darkness" (3-2-64) Edmond O'Brien, Lori Martin,
Edward Platt
24. "Shadows of a Starless Night" (3-9-64) Bradford Dillman,
Russell Collins, Dianne Foster, Dan Tobin
25. "The Summer House" (3-16-64) Piper Laurie, Robert Loggia, Phyllis Love
26. "Glass Flowers Never Drop Petals" (3-23-64) James Caan,
Jessica Tandy, James Gregory, Peter Helm
27. "Never Trouble Trouble Till Trouble Troubles You" (3-30-
64) Diana Sands, Terry Carter, Frederick O'Neal, Rex
Ingram
28. "Confounding Her Astronomers" (4-6-64) Kathy Nolan,
Richard Devon, Peter Leeds, Virginia Gregg, Jennifer
Gillespie
29. "I, the Dancer" (4-20-64) Joey Heatherton, Michael Callan,
Lili Valenty
30. "My Hands Are Clean" (4-27-64) Telly Savalas, Henry Silva
Marian Seldes


EAST SIDE, WEST SIDE

David Susskind's brilliant study of a Manhattan private wel-
fare agency (performances by the best there is: George C. Scott

as social worker Neil Brock; Elizabeth Wilson as supervisor
Frieda Rechlinger; Cicely Tyson as secretary Jane Foster) graphi-
cally but unpretentiously raised a sword to the urban indifference.
Among the abject was Carol Rossen who, as the prostitute and
loyal mother of "The Sinner," won critical acclaim.

The Regulars: Neil Brock, George C. Scott; Frieda Hechlinger,
     Elizabeth Wilson; Jane Foster, Cicely Tyson.

The Episodes:

1.  "The Sinner" (9-23-63) Carol Rossen, Augusta Ciolli
2.  "Age of Consent" (9-30-63) Robert Drivas, Penny Fuller,
    Carroll O'Connor
3.  "You Can't Beat the System" (10-7-63) Martin Sheen,
    Joseph Turkel, Janet Margolin
4.  "Something for the Girls" (10-14-63) Diana Van Der Vlis,
    Philip Vandervort
5.  "I Before E" (10-21-63) Howard Da Silva, William Daniels
6.  "No Wings at All" (10-28-63) Lou Frizzell, Virginia Kaye,
    Theodore Bikel
7.  "Who Do You Kill?" (11-4-63) James Earl Jones, Diana
    Sands, Maxwell Glanville
8.  "Go Fight City Hall" (11-11-63) Clifton James, Henry
    Sharp, David Carradine
9.  "Not Bad for Openers" (11-18-63) Lee Grant, Norman Fell
10. "No Hiding Place" (12-2-63) Ruby Dee, Joseph Campanella,
    Constance Ford, Lois Nettleton
11. "Where's Harry?" (12-9-63) Norma Crane, James Edwards,
    Simon Oakland
12. "My Child on Monday Morning" (12-16-63) James Noble,
    Renee Dudley, Marian Seldes
13. "Creeps Live Here" (12-23-63) Ruth Donnelly, John Ran-
    dolph, Patricia Collinge
14. "The Five Ninety-Eight Dress" (1-13-64) Tim O'Connor,
    Kathlene Maguire
15. "The Beatnik and the Politician" (1-20-64) Robert Middleton,
    John Beal, Alan Arkin
16. "One Drink at a Time" (1-27-64) J. D. Cannon, Maureen
    Stapleton
17. "It's War, Man" (2-10-64) Alberto Castagna, Torin Thatcher
18. "Don't Grow Old" (2-17-64) Joe De Santis, James Patterson
19. "The Street" (2-24-64) Barbara Feldon, Candace Culkin,
    Louise Troy, Linden Chiles
20. "If Your Grandmother Had Wheels" (3-2-64) Alex Viespi,
    Shimon Ruskin, Vincent Gardenia
21. "The Passion of the Nickel Player" (3-9-64) Paul Mace,
    Linden Chiles, Margaret Tompson
22. "Take Sides with the Sun" (3-16-64) Jessica Walter, John
    McMartin, Linden Chiles
23. "The Name of the Game" (3-23-64) Barry Morse, Chester
    Morris, Dan Travanty
24. "Nothing but the Half Truth" (3-30-64) John Baragrey,

Colleen Dewhurst, David Susskind
25. "The Givers" (4-13-64) Linden Chiles
26. "Here Today" (4-27-64) Walter Abel, Will Geer, Michael Dunn, Linden Chiles


MR. NOVAK

The sociology of the schoolroom--the exemplary English teacher, John Novak (James Franciscus) and the discerning traditionalist principal (Dean Jagger as Albert Vane; subsequently Burgess Meredith as Martin Woodridge) at Jefferson High. Poignant, alternately quietly probing, teleplays by, among many others, Betty Ulius ("Little Girl Lost"), John D. F. Black ("The People Doll: You Wind It Up and It Makes Mistakes") and Mel Goldberg ("Let's Dig a Little Grammar").

The Regulars: John Novak, James Franciscus; Albert Vane, Dean Jagger (to episode of 2/23/65); Jerry Allen, Stephen Franken; Jean Pagano, Jeanne Bal; Marilyn Scott, Marian Collier; Mrs. Vreeland, Anne Seymour; Butler, Vince Howard; Peeples, Stephen Roberts; Miss Dorsey, Marjorie Corley; Martin Woodridge, Burgess Meredith (with episode of 2/23/65).

The Episodes:

1. "First Year, First Day" (9-24-63) Lee Kinsolving, Edward Asner
2. "To Lodge and Dislodge" (10-1-63) Kim Darby, Tony Dow, David Kent
3. "I Don't Even Live Here" (10-8-63) Hershel Bernardi, Shelley Fabares
4. "X Is the Unknown Factor" (10-15-63) David Macklin, Broo Bundy
5. "A Single Isolated Incident" (10-22-63) Gloria Calomee, Tig Andrews, Joe Mantell
6. "The Risk" (10-29-63) Alexander Scourby, Sherry Jackson, Lurene Tuttle
7. "Hello, Miss Phipps!" (11-5-63) Lillian Gish, David White, Arch Johnson
8. "To Break a Camel's Back" (11-12-63) Joey Heatherton, Royal Dano, J. Edward McKinley
9. "A Feeling for Friday" (11-19-63) Peter Breck, Diane Bak
10. "Pay the Two Dollars" (11-26-63) Macdonald Carey, Marti Landau, Beau Bridges, Tom Lowell
11. "Love in the Wrong Season" (12-3-63) Patricia Crowley, June Vincent, Tommy Kirk
12. "A Boy Without a Country" (12-10-63) Walter Koenig, Jeanne Cooper, James Chandler
13. "A Thousand Voices" (12-17-63) Frankie Avalon, Robert Simon, Bill Bloom

14. "My Name Is Not Legion" (12-24-63) Shelley Fabares
15. "He Who Can Does" (12-31-63) Edward Mulhare, Vicki Albright
16. "The Song of Songs" (1-7-64) Edward Andrews, Brooke Bundy
17. "The Exile" (1-14-64) Richard Evans, Les Tremayne, Nicky Blair
18. "Sparrow on the Wire" (1-21-64) Mike Kellin, Beau Bridges, Kathy Garver
19. "The Private Life of Douglas Morgan Jr." (1-28-64) Peter Helm
20. "The Death of a Teacher" (2-4-64) Harry Townes, Tony Dow
21. "I'm on the Outside" (2-11-64) Teno Pollick
22. "Chin Up, Mr. Novak" (2-18-64) Hermione Baddeley, Don Grady
23. "Fear Is a Handful of Dust" (2-25-64) CeCe Whitney, Brenda Scott, Tony Dow
24. "How Does Your Garden Grow?" (3-3-64) Barbara Bain, Pat Morrow
25. "The Tower" (3-10-64) Heather Angel, Gilbert Green
26. "One Way to Say Goodbye" (3-17-64) Kathryn Hays, Tom Nardini
27. "Day in the Year" (3-24-64) Richard Eyer, Malachi Throne
28. "Moment Without Armor" (3-31-64) Mike Walker, Robert Sampson
29. "Fare Thee Well" (4-7-64) Noreen Corcoran, Kevin McCarthy
30. "The Senior Prom" (4-14-64) Marta Kristen

Second Season

31. "Moonlighting" (9-22-64) Bill Zuckert, Mabel Albertson, Bert Freed, Joe De Santis
32. "With a Hammer in His Hand, Lord, Lord!" (9-29-64) Simon Oakland, Arthur Franz, Tim McIntire, Walter Koenig
33. "Visions of Sugar Plums" (10-6-64) Eddie Albert, Adrienne Hayes, Beverly Washburn, Robert Diamond
34. "Little Girl Lost" (10-20-64) Davey Davison, Buck Taylor, Arthur Franz
35. "One Monday Afternoon" (10-27-64) Brooke Bundy, Claude Akins
36. "Let's Dig a Little Grammar" (11-10-64) Tommy Sands, Johnny Crawford, Harvey Lembeck, Judith Morton
37. "The People Doll: You Wind It Up and It Makes Mistakes" (11-17-64) Burt Brinckerhoff, Malachi Throne, Bonnie Beecher
38. "Boy Under Glass" (11-24-64) Frank Silvera, Wayne Grice, Arch Johnson, Juanita Moore
39. "Born of Kings and Angels" (12-1-64) Peter Helm, Lynn Loring, Ford Rainey, Ken Lynch
40. "A as in Anxiety" (12-8-64) June Harding, Robert Cornthwaite, Norma Connolly, Richard Carlyle

41. "Johnny Ride the Pony--One, Two, Three" (12-15-64) Tony
    Dow, Stephen Carlson, Robert Logan, Denver Pyle
42. "Beyond a Reasonable Doubt" (12-22-64) Susan Tyrell, Bob
    Random, Jack Chaplin
43. "Love Among the Grownups" (12-29-64) Geraldine Brooks,
    Alexander Scourby, Karl Swenson, Lane Bradbury
44. "From the Brow of Zeus" (1-5-65) Michel Petit, Joyce
    Van Patten, Rick Sorenson, Frank Maxwell
45. "An Elephant Is Like a Tree" (1-12-65) Tony Bill, Celeste
    Holm, Edward Asner, Zalman King
46. "Enter a Strange Animal" (1-19-65) Martin Landau, Nehe-
    miah Persoff, David Macklin
47. "Beat the Plowshare: Edge the Sword" (1-26-65) Harold J.
    Stone, Jimmy Hawkins, Lyle Bettger, Tom Nardini, Mark
    Slade
48. "Faculty Follies" [Part I] (2-2-65) Burgess Meredith, Cloris
    Leachman, David Sheiner, Andre Phillipe, Larry Thor
49. "Faculty Follies" [Part II] (2-9-65) as above
50. "The Silent Dissuaders" (2-16-65) Claudine Longet, Kim
    Darby, Frances Reid, Buck Taylor
51. "Mountains to Climb" (2-23-65) Howard Duff, Milton Selzer
    Malachi Throne
52. "May Day, May Day..." (3-2-65) Donald Harron, Whit Bis-
    sell, Candace Howard, Malachi Throne
53. "Where Is There to Go, Billie, But Up?" (3-9-65) Lois
    Nettleton, Jean Inness, Paul Mantee, Alison Mills
54. "The Tender Twigs" (3-16-65) Harry Townes, Robert Culp,
    Peter Hel, Tony Dow, Johnny Crawford
55. "Honor--and All That" (3-23-65) Beau Bridges, Michael J.
    Pollard, Stephen Mines, Buck Taylor
56. "The Student Who Never Was" (3-30-65) Robert Walker Jr.
    Patricia Morrow, Bonnie Beecher, Bob Random
57. "There's a Penguin in My Garden" (4-6-65) Vera Miles,
    Al Freeman Jr., Pat Harrington, Walter Brooke, Bob
    Random
58. "The Firebrand" (4-13-65) Walter Koenig, Julie Sommars
59. "And Then I Wrote..." (4-20-65) Tommy Sands, Mike Kel-
    lin, Louise Latham, Norman Fell
60. "Once a Clown" (4-27-65) Don Grady, June Lockhart, Tom
    Drake

## THE GREATEST SHOW ON EARTH

Cecil B. DeMille's 1952 film of the Ringling Brothers and
Barnum & Bailey Circus was the inspiration for this, with Jack
Palance certainly a proper choice to play the dreaded circus manager Johnny Slate. Circus themes included a one-legged lion tamer
in search of a job (Harry Guardino's role in "Lion on Fire"), an
aging veterinarian (William Demarest) whose expertise is questioned
in "Rosetta," and the cloak-and-dagger tale "This Train Don't Stop
Till It Gets There," performed by an all-star cast.

The Regulars: Johnny Slate, Jack Palance; Otto King, Stuart Erwin.

The Episodes:

1. "Lion on Fire" (9-17-63) Harry Guardino, Joan Freeman, Alfred Ryder
2. "Silent Love, Secret Love" (9-24-63) Tuesday Weld, Ruth Roman, Robert Webber, Russ Tamblyn
3. "No Middle Ground for Harry Kyle" (10-1-63) Jose Ferrer, Martha Scott, Joey Walsh
4. "Don't Look Down, Don't Look Back" (10-8-63) Gilbert Roland, Brenda Vaccaro, Bradford Dillman
5. "Garve" (10-15-63) Hugh O'Brian, Harold J. Stone, Peggy McCay
6. "The Loser" (10-22-63) Sal Mineo, Eddie Albert
7. "Uncaged" (10-29-63) Fabian, James Coburn, Zeme North
8. "The Circus Never Came to Town" (11-5-63) Cliff Robertson, Frank Sutton, David Winters
9. "An Echo of Faded Velvet" (11-12-63) Anthony Franciosa, Felicia Farr, John Astin, John Baer
10. "The Hanging Man" (11-19-63) Ricardo Montalban, Michael Parks, Fay Spain
11. "Leaves in the Wind" (11-26-63) Nina Foch, Paul Hartman, Marlyn Mason, Paul Comi
12. "The Wrecker" (12-3-63) Dean Stockwell, Dennis Hopper, Luana Anders, Karl Swenson
13. "Lady in Limbo" (12-10-63) Lucille Ball, Roger C. Carmel, Billy Mumy, Irene Tedrow, Robert F. Simon, Dabbs Greer
14. "A Black Dress for Gina" (12-17-63) Geraldine Brooks, Steve Harris, Michael Constantine
15. "Where the Wire Ends" (1-7-64) Dorothy Malone, Alejandro Rey, John Dehner
16. "Corsicans Don't Cry" (1-14-64) Steven Hill, Billy Gray, Patricia Breslin
17. "Big Man from Nairobi" (1-21-64) Cornel Wilde, Ellen McRae, Billy Curtis, William Sargent
18. "The Show Must Go On--to Orange City" (1-28-64) Martha Hyer, Ruby Keeler
19. "A Place to Belong" (2-11-64) Louis Jourdan, Jeremy Slate, Leslie Wales
20. "Man in a Hole" (2-18-64) Jack Lord, Phyllis Avery, Russell Johnson, Arte Johnson
21. "Clancy" (2-25-64) Edmond O'Brien, Maggie McNamara, Marta Kristen, Larry Storch
22. "The Last of the Strongmen" (3-3-64) Red Buttons, Marianna Hill, Bruce Dern
23. "The Night the Monkey Died" (3-10-64) Yvonne De Carlo, Martin Landau, Barbara Bain
24. "Of Blood, Sawdust, and a Bucket of Tears" (3-17-64) Arthur O'Connell, Julie Newmar, Henry Beckman
25. "Rosetta" (3-24-64) Dwayne Hickman, Annette Funicello, Cecil Kellaway, William Demarest
26. "The Glorious Days of Used to Be" (3-31-64) Betty Hutton,

Don Ameche
27. "Love the Giver" (4-7-64) James Whitmore, Brandon de Wilde, Susan Silo
28. "This Train Don't Stop Till It Gets There" (4-14-64) Andrew Duggan, Spring Byington, Rory Calhoun, Agnes Moorehead, J. Pat O'Malley, Sheree North, Sally Kellerman, Deborah Walley
29. "There Are No Problems, Only Opportunities" (4-21-64) Barry Nelson, Joanna Moore, Edgar Bergen
30. "You're All Right, Ivy" (4-28-64) Joan Blondell, Buster Keaton, Joe E. Brown, Lynn Loring, Ted Bessell

## THE RICHARD BOONE SHOW

This fine series with its own repertory company of seasoned professionals is much distinguished by the name of the late playwright Clifford Odets, who served as editor-in-chief. Odets himself authored the episode "Big Mitch," which served as a good vehicle in capturing the brooding quality of series star Richard Boone this time cast as a father who cannot cope with his daughter's impending marriage. Anton Chekhov's The Boor served as the basis for the episode "The Hooligan," with Boone as a rancher threatened with foreclosure. Whatever the theme, even one as overdone as unwed motherhood in 'Don't Call Me Dirty Names" with June Harding, the Odets presence was felt and so well worth watching.

Repertory Company: Richard Boone, Robert Blake, Lloyd Bochner, Suzanne Cupito, Laura Devon, June Harding, Bethel Leslie Harry Morgan, Jeanette Nolan, Ford Rainey, Warren Stevens, Guy Stockwell.

The Episodes:

1. "Statement of Fact" (9-24-63)
2. "All the Comforts of Home" (10-1-63)
3. "Wall to Wall War" (10-8-63)
4. "Where Do You Hide an Egg?" (10-15-63)
5. "The Stranger" (10-22-63)
6. "Sorofino's Treasure" (10-29-63)
7. "Vote No on No. 11!" (11-5-63)
8. "The Fling" (11-12-63)
9. "Captain Al Sanchez" (11-26-63)
10. "Don't Call Me Dirty Names" (12-3-63)
11. "Big Mitch" (12-10-63)
12. "Which Are the Nuts?, Which Are the Bolts?" (12-17-63)
13. "Where's the Million Dollars?" (12-31-63)
14. "The Mafia Man" (1-7-64)
15. "The Hooligan" (1-14-64)
16. "Welcome Home, Dan" (1-21-64)
17. "First Sermon" (1-28-64)
18. 'Death Before Dishonor" (2-11-64)

19. "A Tough Man to Kill" (2-18-64)
20. "Occupational Hazard" (2-25-64)
21. "The Arena" [Part I] (3-10-64)
22. "The Arena" [Part II] (3-17-64)
23. "All the Blood of Yesterday" (3-24-64)
24. "A Need of Valor" (3-31-64)

THE FUGITIVE

Quinn Martin's modern retelling of Les Miserables (and doubtless with an assist from the Sam Sheppard murder case) recounted the adventures of Dr. Richard Kimble (David Janssen) who, accused of murdering his wife (he claimed the guilty was a "one-armed man"), perpetually ran from Police Lieutenant Philip Gerard (Barry Morse). We endured 118 hairbreadth escapes with Dr. Kimble only to discover, in George Eckstein's and Michael Zagor's concluding two-part "The Judgement," not without a sinful sense of cathartic pleasure, that our hero was guilty after all.

The Regulars: Richard Kimble, David Janssen; Lt. Philip Gerard, Barry Morse; Johnson, Bill Raisch.

The Episodes:

1. "Fear in a Desert City" (9-17-63) Brian Keith, Vera Miles, Dabbs Greer, Harry Townes
2. "The Witch" (9-24-63) Elisha Cook, Pat Crowley, Madeleine Sherwood
3. "The Other Side of the Mountain" (10-1-63) Sandy Dennis, Frank Sutton
4. "Never Wave Goodbye" [Part I] (10-8-63) Robert Duvall, Susan Oliver, Lee Philips
5. "Never Wave Goodbye" [Part II] (10-15-63) as above
6. "Decision in the Ring" (10-22-63) Ruby Dee, Hari Rhodes, James Dunn, James Edwards
7. "Smoke Screen" (10-29-63) Beverly Garland, Peter Helm, Alejandro Rey
8. "See Hollywood and Die" (11-5-63) Brenda Vaccaro, J. Pat O'Malley, Lou Antonio, Chris Robinson
9. "Ticket to Alaska" (11-12-63) Geraldine Brooks, David White, Tim O'Connor, John Larkin
10. "Fatso" (11-19-63) Glenda Farrell, Jack Weston
11. "Nightmare at North Oak" (11-26-63) Nancy Wickwire, Frank Overton, Ian Wolfe, Sue Randall
12. "The Glass Tightrope" (12-3-63) Leslie Nielsen, Edward Binns, Diana Van Der Vlis
13. "Terror at High Point" (12-17-63) Jack Klugman, Elizabeth Allen
14. "The Girl from Little Egypt" (12-24-63) Pamela Tiffin, Ed Nelson, Diane Brewster
15. "Home Is the Hunted" (1-7-64) Andrew Prine, Billy Mumy,

Jacqueline Scott
16. "The Garden House" (1-14-64) Robert Webber, Pippa Scott, Peggy McCay
17. "Come Watch Me Die" (1-21-64) Bruce Dern, Robert Doyle, John Anderson
18. 'Where the Action Is" (1-28-64) Telly Savalas
19. "Search in a Windy City" (2-4-64) Pat Hingle, Nan Martin
20. "Bloodline" (2-11-64) Nancy Malone, George Voskovec
21. "Rat in a Corner" (2-18-64) Warren Oates, Malachi Throne
22. "Angels Travel on Lonely Roads" [Part I] (2-25-64) Eileen Heckart, Albert Salmi, Ruta Lee, Rodolfo Hoyos
23. "Angels Travel on Lonely Roads" [Part II] (3-3-64) as above
24. "Flight from the Final Demon" (3-10-64) Carroll O'Connor, Ed Nelson
25. "Taps for a Dead War" (3-17-64) Lee Grant, Tim O'Connor
26. "Somebody to Remember" (3-24-64) Gilbert Roland, Madlyn Rhue
27. 'Never Stop Running" (3-31-64) Claude Akins, Joanna Moore
28. "The Homecoming" (4-7-64) Richard Carlson, Gloria Grahame, Shirley Knight
29. 'Storm Center" (4-14-64) Bethel Leslie, Dennis Patrick
30. "The End Game" (4-21-64) Joseph Campanella, John McGiver, Martine Bartlett, John Fiedler

Second Season

31. "Man in a Chariot" (9-15-64) Ed Begley, Robert Drivas
32. 'World's End" (9-22-64) Carmen Matthews, Suzanne Pleshette, Henry Beckman, Woodrow Parfrey
33. "Man on a String" (9-29-64) Lois Nettleton, Patricia Smith, Russell Collins, John Larch, Malcolm Atterbury
34. 'When the Bough Breaks" (10-6-64) June Vincent, Royal Dano, Jud Taylor, Diana Hyland
35. "Nemesis" (10-13-64) John Doucette, Kurt Russell, Slim Pickens
36. "Tiger Left, Tiger Right" (10-20-64) Leslie Nielsen, Carol Rossen, Jeanne Bal, David Sheiner
37. "Tug of War" (10-27-64) Arthur O'Connell, Don Gordon, Harry Townes, Katie Sweet
38. 'Dark Corner" (11-10-64) Tuesday Weld, Elizabeth Macrae, Paul Carr, Crahan Denton
39. "Escape into Black" (11-17-64) Betty Garrett, Tom Troupe, Ivan Dixon, Bernard Kates, Herb Vigran, Donald Barry
40. "The Cage" (11-24-64) Joe De Santis, Brenda Scott, Tim O'Connor, Richard Evans, John Kellogg
41. "Cry Uncle" (12-1-64) Ronny Howard, Brett Somers, Edward Binns, Steve Ihnat
42. 'Detour on a Road Going Nowhere" (12-8-64) Elizabeth Allen, Walter Brooke, Phyllis Thaxter, Lee Bowman
43. "The Iron Maiden" (12-15-64) Stephen McNally, Nan Martin, Richard Anderson, Christine White
44. 'Devil's Carnival" (12-22-64) Warren Oates, Phillip Abbott, Strother Martin

45. "Ballad for a Ghost" (12-29-64) Janis Paige, Mark Richman, Paul Fix, Anne Helm
46. "Brass Ring" (1-5-65) Angie Dickinson, John Ericson, Robert Duvall, Karl Swenson
47. "The End Is but the Beginning" (1-12-65) Barbara Barrie, Andrew Duggan
48. "Nicest Fella You'd Ever Want to Meet" (1-19-65) Pat Hingle, Dabney Coleman, Dabbs Greer, Bert Mustin
49. "Fun and Games and Party Favors" (1-26-65) Katherine Crawford, Mark Goddard
50. "Scapegoat" (2-2-65) Dianne Foster, John Anderson, Whit Bissell
51. "Corner of Hell" (2-9-65) Bruce Dern, Sharon Farrell, R. G. Armstrong
52. "Moon Child" (2-16-65) June Harding, Murray Hamilton, David Sheiner, Virginia Christine
53. "The Survivors" (3-2-65) Louise Sorel, Lloyd Gough, Ruth White
54. "Everybody Gets Hit in the Mouth Sometime" (3-9-65) Geraldine Brooks, Jack Klugman, G. B. Atwater, Michael Constantine
55. "May God Have Mercy" (3-16-65) Telly Savalas, Carol Rossen, Norman Fell, Jud Taylor
56. "Masquerade" (3-23-65) Norma Crane, John Milford, Edward Asner
57. "Runner in the Dark" (3-30-65) Ed Begley, Diana Van Der Vlis, Richard Anderson, Vaughn Taylor
58. "A. P. B." (4-6-65) Shirley Knight, Paul Richards, Lou Antonio
59. "The Old Man Picked a Lemon" (4-13-65) Celeste Holm, Ben Piazza
60. "Last Second of a Big Dream" (4-20-65) Steve Forrest, Milton Selzer, Lawrence Naismith

Third Season

61. "Wings of an Angel" (9-14-65) Greg Morris, Ned Glass, Val Avery, Harold Gould, Lin McCarthy, Lane Bradford, Sue Randall, Ted Gehrig
62. "Middle of a Heat Wave" (9-21-65) J. D. Cannon, Sarah Marshall, John Lasell, Carol Rossen, James Doohan
63. "Crack in a Crystal Ball" (9-28-65) Larry Blyden, Joanna Moore, J. Pat O'Malley, Nellie Burt, Frank Maxwell, Walter Brooke
64. "Trial by Fire" (10-5-65) Tommy Rettig, Charles Aidman, Marion Ross, Frank Aletter, Jacqueline Scott, Booth Colman
65. "Conspiracy of Silence" (10-12-65) Donald Harron, Malachi Throne, Robert Cornthwaite, Mort Mills
66. "Three Cheers for Little Boy Blue" (10-19-65) Richard Anderson, Edward Asner, Fay Spain, Milton Selzer, Woodrow Parfrey, Vaughn Taylor
67. "All the Scared Rabbits" (10-26-65) Suzanne Pleshette,

Nancy Rennick, R. G. Armstrong, Liam Sullivan
68. "An Apple a Day" (11-2-65) Arthur O'Connell, Kim Darby, Sheree North
69. "Landscaping with Running Figures" [Part I] (11-16-65) Jud Taylor, Hershel Bernardi, Barbara Rush, Arthur Franz
70. "Landscaping with Running Figures" [Part II] (11-23-65) as above
71. "Set Fire to a Straw Man" (11-30-65) Joseph Campanella, Edward Binns, Clint Howard, Diana Hyland
72. "Stranger in the Mirror" (12-7-65) William Shatner, Julie Sommars, Norman Fell, Tony Face, Paul Bryar, Jeff Burton
73. "The Good Guys and the Bad Guys" (12-14-65) Earl Holliman
74. "End of the Line" (12-21-65) Andrew Prine, Barbara Dana
75. "When the Wind Blows" (12-28-65) Georgeann Johnson, Larry Ward
76. "Not with a Whimper" (1-4-66) Laurence Naismith, Lee Meriwether, Audrey Christie, Jimmy Stiles, Jack Dodson
77. "Wife Killer" (1-11-66) Kevin McCarthy, Janice Rule
78. "This'll Kill You" (1-18-66) Nita Talbot, Mickey Rooney
79. "Echo of a Nightmare" (1-25-66) Shirley Knight, Ford Rainey
80. "Stroke of Genius" (2-1-66) Beau Bridges, Telly Savalas
81. "Shadow of the Swan" (2-8-66) Joanna Pettet, Andrew Duggan
82. "Running Scared" (2-22-66) Jacqueline Scott, James Daly
83. "The Chinese Sunset" (3-1-66) Laura Devon, Paul Richards
84. "Ill Wind" (3-8-66) John McIntire, Tim McIntire, Jeanette Nolan
85. "With Strings Attached" (3-15-66) Donald Pleasence, Rex Thompson
86. "The White Knight" (3-22-66) Steven Hill, Jessica Walter, Nancy Wickwire, James Callahan
87. "The 2130" (3-29-66) Melvyn Douglas, Jason Wingreen
88. "A Taste of Tomorrow" (4-12-66) Fritz Weaver, Brenda Scott, Michael Constantine, Dabbs Greer
89. "In a Plain Paper Wrapper" (4-19-66) Lois Nettleton, Pat Cardi, Kurt Russell
90. "Coralee" (4-26-66) Antoinette Bower, Murray Hamilton

Fourth Season

91. "The Last Oasis" (9-13-66) Hope Lange, Mark Richman, Arch Johnson, John McLiam
92. "Death Is the Door Prize" (9-20-66) Howard Da Silva, June Vincent, Lois Nettleton, Ossie Davis
93. "A Clean and Quiet Town" (9-27-66) Eduardo Ciannelli, Carol Rossen, Michael Strong, Ed Deemer
94. "The Sharp Edge of Chivalry" (10-4-66) Madlyn Rhue, Rosemary Murphy, Robert Drivas, Eduard Franz
95. "Ten Thousand Pieces of Silver" (10-11-66) Joe Maross, Lin McCarthy
96. "Joshua's Kingdom" (10-18-66) Kim Darby, Harry Townes,

Tom Skerritt, Walter Burke, Vaughn Taylor

97. "Second Light" (10-25-66) Tim Considine, Ned Glass, Bill Sargent, Ted Knight

98. "Wine Is a Traitor" (11-1-66) Roy Thinnes, James Gregory, Pilar Seurat, Dabbs Greer, Carlos Romero

99. "Approach with Care" (11-15-66) Michael Conrad, Dabney Coleman, Collin Wilcox, Denny Miller

100. "Nobody Loses All the Time" (11-22-66) Barbara Baxley, Don Dubbins, Joanna Moore

101. "Right in the Middle of the Season" (11-29-66) Dean Jagger, James Callahan

102. "The Devil's Disciples" (12-6-66) Bruce Dern, Diana Hyland, Lou Antonio, Hal Lynch, Frank Marth, Robert Sorrells

103. "The Blessings of Liberty" (12-20-66) Tony Musante, Julie Sommars, Noam Pitlik, Ludwig Donath

104. "The Evil Men Do" (12-27-66) Elizabeth Allen, James Daly

105. "Run the Man Down" (1-3-67) Georgeann Johnson, James Broderick, Edward Asner, Val Avery, Sam Melville, Robert Doyle

106. "The Other Side of the Coin" (1-10-67) Joseph Campanella, Parley Baer, John Larch, Beau Bridges

107. "The One That Got Away" (1-17-67) Charles Bronson, Charles Drake, Frank Maxwell, Anne Francis

108. "Concrete Evidence" (1-24-67) Jack Warden, Celeste Holm, Harold Gould

109. "The Breaking of the Habit" (1-31-67) Eileen Heckart, Linden Chiles

110. "There Goes the Ball Game" (2-7-67) Martin Balsam, Lynda Day, Susan Seaforth, Vincent Gardenia

111. "The Ivy Maze" (2-21-67) Geraldine Brooks, William Windom, Lori Scott

112. "Goodbye My Love" (2-28-67) Patricia Smith, Jack Lord, Marlyn Mason

113. "Passage to Helena" (3-7-67) James Farentino, Percy Rodriguez

114. "The Savage Street" (3-14-67) David Macklin, Michael Ansara, Gilbert Roland, Tom Nardini

115. "Death Is a Very Small Killer" (3-21-67) Arthur Hill, Carol Lawrence, Carlos Romero

116. "Dossier on a Diplomat" (3-28-67) Ivan Dixon, Lloyd Gough, Diana Sands, Diana Hyland

117. "Walls of Night" (4-4-67) Barbara Wells, Sheree North, Janice Rule, Steve Ihnat, Tige Andrews

118. "The Shattered Silence" (4-11-67) Laurence Naismith, Paul Mantee, Antoinette Bower

119. "The Judgement" [Part I] (8-22-67) Diane Baker, Michael Constantine, Joseph Campanella, J. D. Cannon, Richard Anderson, Louise Latham, Diane Brewster, Jacqueline Scott

120. "The Judgement" [Part II] (8-29-67) as above

ESPIONAGE

High quality intrigue, minus the satire of the James Bond television genre which followed.

The Episodes:

1. "A Covenant with Death" (10-2-63) Bradford Dillman, Don Barisenko
2. "The Weakling" (10-9-63) John Gregson, Dennis Hopper, Patricia Neal
3. "The Incurable One" (10-16-63) Steven Hill, Ingrid Thulin
4. "The Gentle Spies" (10-23-63) Barry Foster, Angela Douglas, Michael Hordern
5. "He Rises on Sunday and We on Monday" (10-30-63) Patrick Troughton, Billie Whitelaw
6. "To the Very End" (11-6-63) James Fox, Michael Anderson Jr., David Buck, Clifford Evans
7. "The Dragon Slayer" (11-13-63) Lee Montague, Patrick Cargill, Thorley Walters
8. "The Whistling Shrimp" (11-20-63) Arthur Kennedy, Earl Hyman, Nancy Wickwire, Larry Gates
9. "The Light of a Friendly Star" (12-4-63) Ronald Morley, Carl Schelt
10. "Festival of Pawns" (12-11-63) George Grizzard, Diane Cilento
11. "A Camel to Ride" (12-18-63) Bill Travers, Marne Maitland
12. "Never Turn Your Back on a Friend" (1-1-64) Pamela Brown, Donald Madden, George Voskovec
13. "Medal for a Turned Coat" (1-15-64) Fritz Weaver, Nigel Stock
14. "The Final Decision" (1-22-64) Martin Balsam, Ann Lynn
15. "Do You Remember Leo Winters?" (1-29-64) George A. Cooper, Peter Madden, Cyril Luckham, Rhoda Lewis
16. "We, the Hunted" (2-5-64) Joseph Campanella, Madlyn Rhue
17. "The Frantick Rebel" (2-12-64) Stanley Baxter, Jill Bennett, Roger Livesey
18. "Castles in Spain" (2-19-64) Chester Morris, Ronald Culver
19. "Snow on Mount Kama" (2-26-64) Bernard Lee, Maureen Connell
20. "Once a Spy" (3-4-64) William Lucas, Earl Cameron, Millicent Martin
21. "The Liberators" (3-11-64) Robert Webber, Michael Tolan, Donald Pleasence
22. "Some Other Kind of World" (3-18-64) Ron Randell, Tom Stern, Dora Reisser
23. "A Free Agent" (3-25-64) Stan Phillips, Norman Foster, Anthony Quayle
24. "A Tiny Drop of Poison" (5-20-64) Jim Backus, William Smithers

CHANNING (a.k.a. THE YOUNG AND THE BOLD)

    Satisfying journey through an idealized Academe; an appro-
priate grace note to its contemporary high school drama, "Mr.
Novak." It would do well to compare "Channing College"'s pro-
fessoriate (Jason Evers as attractive English professor Joseph
Howe in the limelight), students and sagacious Dean (Henry Jones
as Fred Baker) with their real-life counterparts in an era of vigi-
lance and discontent on campuses some years later.

The Regulars: Joseph Howe, Jason Evers; Dean Fred Baker,
    Henry Jones.

The Episodes:

1.  "Message from the Tin Room" (9-18-63) John Cassavetes,
    Robert Ellenstein, Katherine Crawford
2.  "Exercise in a Shark Tank" (9-25-63) Leslie Nielsen,
    Marion Ross, Noreen Corcoran
3.  "An Obelisk for Benny" (10-2-63) Peter Fonda, Michael
    Parks
4.  "No Wild Games for Sophie" (10-9-63) Michael Constantine,
    Barbara Harris
5.  "Dragon in the Den" (10-23-63) Maggie Pierce, Denver Pyle,
    William Shatner, Gene Raymond
6.  "The Potato Bash World" (10-30-63) Suzanne Pleshette,
    Jeanne Cooper
7.  "Collision Course" (11-6-63) Nancy Olsen, Forrest Tucker
8.  "A Patron Saint for the Cargo Cult" (11-13-63) George Se-
    gal, Greg Morris, Norma Crane
9.  "Beyond His Reach" (11-27-63)
10. "A Doll's House With Pompons and Trophies" (12-4-63) Rip
    Torn, Leslie Parrish
11. "A Window on the War" (12-11-63) Wendell Corey, Don
    Gordon, Jacqueline Scott
12. "The Last Testament of Buddy Crown" (12-18-63) Russ
    Tamblyn, David Wayne, Mariette Hartley
13. "A Hall Full of Strangers" (12-25-63) Bob Crane, Donald
    Davis, George Voskovec
14. "Memory of a Firing Squad" (1-1-64) Frank Silvera, Ivan
    Dixon, Nico Minardos
15. "A Rich, Famous, Glamorous Folk Singer Like Me" (1-8-64)
    Joan Hackett, Lew Ayres, Marsha Hunt
16. "Swing for the Moon" (1-15-64) Ralph Meeker, Dawn Wells,
    Charles Robinson, Fay Spain
17. "Another Kind of Music" (1-22-64) Michael Parks, Hari
    Rhodes
18. "Ou Sont les Neiges..." (2-12-64) Leo G. Carroll, Rafer
    Johnson
19. "The Face in the Sun" (2-19-64) Leela Naidu, Joe Adams
20. "A Claim to Immortality" (2-26-64) Leora Dana, Telly Sa-
    valas, Larry Gates
21. "Freedom Is a Lovesome Thing, God Wot!" (3-4-64) Agnes

Moorehead, James Earl Jones
22. "The Trouble with Girls" (3-11-64) Keir Dullea, Mark Goddard, Joey Heatherton
23. "Wave Goodbye to Our Fair-Haired Boy" (3-18-64) Robert Lansing, Peggy McCay
24. "A Bang and a Whimper" (3-25-64) Susan Kohner, Robert Stephens
25. "My Son, the All American" (4-8-64) James Caan, Terry Becker, Yvonne Craig


TEMPLE HOUSTON

Mundane western focusing on a journeying lawyer (Jeffrey Hunter as Temple Houston) and his clientele.

The Regulars: Temple Houston, Jeffrey Hunter; George Taggart, Jack Elam.

The Episodes:

1. "The Twisted Rope" (9-19-63) Victor Jory, Collin Wilcox
2. "Find Angel Chavez" (9-26-63) Herbert Rudley, Rafael Campos
3. "Letter of the Law" (10-3-63) Brenda Scott, Victor French
4. "Toll the Bell Slowly" (10-17-63) Susan Kohner, Noah Beery, Everett Sloane, Royal Dano
5. "The Third Bullet" (10-24-63) Frank Sutton, Anne Helm, Hampton Fancher
6. "Gallows in Galilee" (10-31-63) Robert Lansing, Ralph Reed, Jacqueline Scott, Dabbs Greer, Elisha Cook
7. "The Siege at Thayer's Bluff" (11-7-63) William Reynolds, E. J. André, Robert Bray, Russell Thorson
8. "Jubilee" (11-14-63) Peter Whitney, Virginia Gregg, Morgan Woodward
9. "Thunder Gap" (11-21-63)
10. [unknown title] (11-28-63) Philip Ober, Russ Conway, Audrey Dalton, Ron Hayes
11. "Seventy Times Seven" (12-5-63) Susanne Cramer, Steve Ihnat, Karl Swenson
12. "Fracas at Kowa Flats" (12-12-63) Kathie Browne, Barry Kelly
13. "Enough Rope" (12-19-63) John Dehner, John Harmon, Ruta Lee
14. "The Dark Madonna" (12-26-63) Constance Ford, Don Collier
15. "The Guardian" (1-2-64) Robert Emhardt, Julie Parrish
16. "Thy Name Is Woman" (1-9-64) Charles Lane, Mary Wickes, Patricia Blair
17. "The Law and Big Annie" (1-16-64) Norman Alden, Mary Wickes, Carol Byron
18. "Sam's Boy" (1-23-64) Douglas Fowley, Kenneth Tobey, William Fawcett

19. "Tend Rounds for Bab" (1-30-64) Anne Francis
20. "The Case for William Gotch" (2-6-64) Ray Danton,
    Richard Jaeckal, Mary Wickes, James Best, Denver Pyle
21. "A Slight Case of Larceny" (2-13-64) Vito Scotti, Charles
    Watts
22. [unknown title] (2-27-64) Abraham Sofaer, Larry Ward,
    Vaughn Taylor
23. "The Gun That Swept the West" (3-5-64) Michael Pate,
    John Dehner
24. "Do Unto Others, Then Gallop" (3-19-64) Adams Williams,
    Grace Lee Whitney
25. "The Boston Terrier" (3-26-64) Robert Conrad, Parley
    Baer, Connie Stevens, Walter Sande
26. [unknown title] (4-2-64) Paula Raymond, John Baer,
    Richard X. Slattery

## KRAFT SUSPENSE THEATRE

Having capitalized on the suspense element, these original
teleplays were frequently successful in drawing interesting characterizations of various neurotic types from several big name stars.
Ed Waters' and Paul Tuckahoe's teleplay for Robert Altman's story
of "The Hunt" had Mickey Rooney playing against type as a sadistic
sheriff who pursues innocent town visitor James Caan with a pack
of vicious dogs. And while the denouement in this case was quite
predictable--Caan escapes, of course, and returns with the proper
authority to oust Rooney from his office--nonetheless the drama
explored the insanity of blind acceptance of those in power, the
lunacy of the "law and order" thesis carried to the extreme.
Berne and David Giler's "Leviathan Five" seriously examined the
question of who, if anyone, has the right to kill. A group of scientists are trapped in a room, apparently without escape and in
which oxygen is insufficient to support them all. In time, they
reason, they will surely all die--unless one member of the team
chooses to sacrifice his life so that the others can survive.
Whereupon they choose lots, go into separate chambers, and a gun
is indeed fired, killing one of them. The remainder of the teleplay is devoted to the courtroom trial of the remaining scientists
for the murder of their late partner. How could they be certain
there was insufficient air to breathe? How did they reckon the
possible escape routes were exhausted, all of them futile? How
was it determined that lots should be chosen? Which, if any of
us, has the right to play the Leviathan in a case of this kind and
decide how a man will die? With crystal clarity the prosecutor
raises these moral questions--in scenes skillfully directed by William P. McGivern--until such time as it is learned that one scientist (Andrew Duggan) indeed did murder his colleague.

"The Machine That Played God," by Robert Guy Barrows
from a story by Judith Guy Barrows, referred to the validity of
the lie detector test, of the circumstances in which it can fail, of

the reasons for its inadmissibility as evidence in a court of law. Roddy McDowall was excellent as a man caught in the dredges of dipsomania in "The Wine-Dark Sea" by Dean Hargrove from a story by Howard Browne. Jo Van Fleet was also very good as the insane protagonist of "The World I Want," by Halsted Welles--an episode of the series in which Sal Mineo was triumphant as the mute who saves a life. Yet there were teleplays with the most absurd of premises. "Four into Zero," by Don Brinkley, had its principals (Jack Kelly, Robert Conrad, Joe Mantell) involved with counterfeiting and theft on a train. After escaping some fantastic situations, the thieves decide that they don't really need the money after all. The Panama of the 1850s of John McGreevey's "Jungle of Fear" relegates the intricacies of the political situation in favor of sentimentality and melodrama.

For the series, Johnny Williams composed an appropriately suspenseful musical theme, while cinematographer Lionel Lindon benefited many dramas with his use of the camera.

The Episodes:

1. "The Case Against Paul Ryker" [Part I; this two-part drama was released as a feature film, Sergeant Ryker in 1968. The 1966 series "Court Martial" was based on this teleplay] (10-10-63) Bradford Dillman, Lee Marvin, Peter Graves, Vera Miles, Lloyd Nolan, Norman Fell, Murray Hamilton, Charles Aidman

2. "The Case Against Paul Ryker" [Part II] (10-17-63) as above

3. "The End of the World, Baby" (10-24-63) Peter Lorre, Gig Young, Nina Foch, Katherine Crawford

4. "A Hero for Our Times" (10-31-63) Lloyd Bridges, Sandra Church, Geraldine Brooks, John Ireland, Dabbs Greer

5. "Are There Any More Out There Like You?" (11-7-63) Robert Ryan, Katherine Ross, Sharon Farrell, Phyllis Avery, Adam Roarke

6. "One Step Down" (11-14-63) Leslie Nielsen, Ida Lupino, Don Collier, Gena Rowlands, Jack Weston, Philip Pine

7. "The Machine That Played God" (12-5-63) Anne Francis, Gary Merrill, Josephine Hutchinson

8. "The Long, Lost Life of Edward Smalley" (12-12-63) James Whitmore, Richard Crenna, Ron Hayes, Arch Johnson, Philip Abbott

9. "The Hunt" (12-19-63) Mickey Rooney, James Caan, Bruce Dern

10. "The Name of the Game" (12-26-63) Jack Kelly, Pat Hingle, Nancy Kovack, Barry Atwater, Steve Ihnat

11. "The Deep End" (1-2-64) Aldo Ray, Ellen McRae, Clu Gulager, Tina Louise

12. "A Truce to Terror" (1-9-64) John Gavin, Michael Ansara, Lyle Bettger, Steve Forrest, Frank Silvera

13. "Who Is Jennifer?" (1-16-64) Gloria Swanson, David Brian, Dan Duryea, Brenda Scott

14. "Leviathan Five" (1-30-64) Arthur Kennedy, Andrew Duggan,

Harold J. Stone, Robert Webber, Frank Overton, Judson Laire

15. "My Enemy, This Town" (2-6-64) Philip Carey, Scott Marlowe, Diane McBain, Barbara Nichols

16. "The Action of the Tiger" (2-20-64) Peter Brown, Telly Savalas, Ulla Jacobsson, Stephen McNally

17. 'Doesn't Anyone Know Who I Am?" (2-27-64) Kathryn Grant Crosby, Martha Hyer, Cornel Wilde

18. "The Threatening Eye" (3-12-64) Jack Klugman, Pat O'Brien, Coleen Gray, Annie Farge, Phyllis Thaxter

19. "A Cause of Anger" (3-19-64) Brian Keith, Nancy Malone, Audrey Totter, Anthony Caruso

20. "Knight's Gambit" (3-26-64) Roger Smith, Eleanor Parker, Chester Morris, Murray Matheson, H. M. Wynant

21. "Once Upon a Savage Night" (4-2-64) Charles McGraw, Philip Abbott, Ted Knight

22. "Portrait of an Unknown Man" (4-16-64) Clint Walker, Jay C. Flippen, Mala Powers, Robert Duvall

23. "Their Own Executioners" (4-23-64) Dean Stockwell, Hershel Bernardi, Lilia Skala

24. "The Sweet Taste of Vengeance" (4-30-64) John Forsythe, Diana Hyland, Robert Ellenstein

25. "Charlie, He Couldn't Kill a Fly" (5-7-64) Richard Kiley, Keenan Wynn, Beverly Garland, Michael Burns

26. "The Watchman" (5-14-64) Telly Savalas, Victoria Shaw, Jack Warden, Lawrence Dobkin

27. "The Robrioz Ring" (5-28-64) Julie Harris, Robert Loggia, Julie Adams, Virginia Gregg

28. "A Cruel and Unusual Night" (6-4-64) Scott Marlowe, Ronald Reagan, Anne Helm

## Second Season

29. "The World I Want" (10-1-64) Jo Van Fleet, Sal Mineo, Albert Dekker, Leonard Nimoy, Patricia Hyland

30. 'Operation Grief" (10-8-64) Robert Goulet, Linden Chiles, Claudine Longet, Claude Akins, Peter Helm

31. "A Lion Amongst Men" (10-22-64) James Whitmore, Tommy Sands, Ron Hayes, Arch Johnson

32. "That He Should Weep for Her" (11-5-64) Milton Berle, Carol Lawrence, Alejandro Rey

33. "The Kamchatka Incident" (11-12-64) John Forsythe, Leslie Parrish, Roger Perry, Malachi Throne, Frank Maxwell

34. "The Jack Is High" (11-19-64) Pat O'Brien, Edd Byrnes, Henry Jones, Larry Storch

35. "Graffiti" (11-26-64) Louis Jourdan, Robert Ellenstein, Philippe Forquet

36. 'One Tiger to a Hill" (12-3-64) James Gregory, Barry Nelson, Diane McBain, Peter Brown, Warren Stevens

37. "Threepersons" (12-10-64) John Gavin, Ralph Meeker, Linda Lawson, Vincent Gardenia

38. "The Gun" (12-24-64) Eddie Albert, Dina Merrill, Isabel Jewell, Peter Lazer

39. "The Wine-Dark Sea" (12-31-64) Roddy McDowall, Myrna
    Fahey, John Larkin, David Sheiner, Robert Ball
40. "In Darkness, Waiting" [Part I] (1-14-65) Barbara Rush,
    Hugh O'Brian, Neil Hamilton, Harry Townes
41. "In Darkness, Waiting" [Part II] (1-21-65) as above
42. "That Time in Havana" (2-11-65) Dana Wynter, Victor Jory,
    Steve Forrest, Frank Silvera
43. "Four into Zero" (2-18-65) Jack Kelly, Martha Hyer,
    Robert Conrad, Joe Mantell, Jesse White
44. "Streetcar, Do You Read Me?" (2-25-65) Richard Long,
    Martin Milner, Jack Ging, Nancy Malone
45. "The Last Clear Chance" (3-11-65) Glenn Corbett, Bruce
    Bennett, Barry Sullivan, Suzanne Cramer, Ben Wright
46. "Won't It Ever Be Morning?" (3-18-65) John Cassavetes,
    Gena Rowlands, Carl Benton Reid, Jack Klugman, Than
    Wyenn
47. "Nobody Will Ever Know" (3-25-65) Pippa Scott, Tom Tryon
    Myrna Fahey, David Lewis
48. "The Green Felt Jungle" (4-1-65) Leslie Nielsen, Macdonald
    Carey, Richard Conte, Larry Pennell
49. "Rapture at Two-Forty" (4-15-65) Ben Gazzara, Michael
    Rennie, Antoinette Bower, Marcel Hillaire
50. "Jungle of Fear" (4-22-65) Ann Blyth, Robert Fuller,
    Robert Loggia, Richard Anderson, Warren Stevens, Tony
    Davis, Suzanne Cramer, Charles Briggs, Harold Sakata
51. "Kill No More" (4-29-65) Lew Ayres, Robert Webber, Julie
    Adams, Leonard Nimoy, Robert F. Simon
52. "The Long Ravine" (5-6-65) Jack Lord, Andrew Prine,
    Lisabeth Hush, Broderick Crawford
53. "The Easter Breach" (5-13-65) Richard Beymer, Katherine
    Crawford, Karen Verne, Ilka Windish
54. "The Safe House" (5-20-65) Dane Clark, Francis Lederer,
    Steven Hill, Albert Paulsen
55. "Twixt the Cup and the Lip" (6-3-65) Ethel Merman, Larry
    Blyden, Jean Hale, Joan Blackman, Charles McGraw, Lan
    Bradford, John Hoyt, Lee Patterson
56. "The Trains of Silence" (6-10-65) Jeffrey Hunter, Tippi
    Hedren, Lloyd Bochner
57. "Kill Me on July 20th" (6-17-65) Jack Kelly, Kathryn Hays
58. "The Rise and Fall of Eddie Carew" (6-24-65) Dean Jones,
    Sheilah Wells
59. "Connery's Hands" (7-1-65) Gary Lockwood, Don Gordon,
    Sally Kellerman

# THE GREAT ADVENTURE

Another of producer John Houseman's gifts to American television, this being an anthology series of American history narra-
tives.

Narrators: Van Heflin (first 13 episodes); Russell Johnson (last 13 episodes).

The Episodes:

1. "The Hunley" (9-27-63) James MacArthur, Jackie Cooper, Wayne Rogers, Gene Evans
2. "The Death of Sitting Bull" [Part I] (10-4-63) Ricardo Montalban, James Dunn, Noah Beery, Lloyd Nolan, Anthony Caruso, Joseph Cotton
3. "Massacre at Wounded Knee" [Part II] (10-11-63) as above
4. "Six Wagons to the Sea" (10-18-63) Lee Marvin, Gene Lyons, Richard X. Slattery, Walter Koenig
5. "The Story of Nathan Hale" (10-25-63) Jeremy Slate, John Anderson, Nancy Malone, Torin Thatcher
6. "Go Down, Moses" (11-1-63) Ruby Dee, Brock Peters, Ethel Waters, Ossie Davis
7. "The Great Diamond Mountain" (11-8-63) Barry Sullivan, Dick Foran, John McGiver, Philip Abbott
8. "The Treasure Train of Jefferson Davis" (11-15-63) Michael Rennie, Tim O'Connor, Harry Townes, Carl Benton Reid
9. "The Outlaw and the Nun" (12-6-63) Leif Erickson, Joan Hackett, Marion Ross, Andrew Prine
10. "The Man Who Stole New York City" (12-13-63) James Daly, Carroll O'Connor, Edward Andrews
11. "A Boy at War" (12-20-63) Richard Eyer, Flip Mark, Bernard Fox, Jean Engstrom
12. "Wild Bill Hickcok--The Legend and the Man" (1-3-64) Lloyd Bridges, Sheree North, Tom Reese, Ed Knight
13. "The Colonel from Connecticut" (1-10-64) Richard Kiley, Walter Brooke, Wallace Ford, Maggie McNamara, Whit Bissell, Woodrow Parfrey
14. "Teeth of the Lion" (1-17-64) Earl Holliman, Collin Wilcox, Julie Sommers
15. "Rodger Young" (1-24-64) James MacArthur, George Kennedy, Geoffrey Horne, Ted Bessell, H. M. Wynant
16. "The Testing of Sam Houston" (1-31-64) Kent Smith, Robert Culp, Victor Jory, Mario Alcaide
17. "The Special Courage of Captain Pratt" (2-14-64) Paul Burke, Antoinette Bower, Ivan Dixon
18. "The Night Raiders" (2-21-64) Jack Klugman, Torin Thatcher
19. "Plague" (2-28-64) Robert Cummings, John Dehner, Jacqueline Scott, Ronny Howard
20. "The Pathfinder" (3-6-64) Carroll O'Connor, Rip Torn, Joe De Santis, Robert F. Simon
21. "The President Vanishes" (3-13-64) Leif Erickson, Barry Sullivan, George Macready, Skip Homeier, Harry Townes
22. "The Henry Bergh Story" (3-20-64) Brian Keith, Frank Aletter, Bernie Hamilton, Marion Ross, June Dayton
23. "Kentucky's Bloody Ground" [Part I] (4-3-64) Peter Graves, Peggy McCay, Andrew Duggan, Arthur Hunnicutt, David McCallum
24. "The Siege of Boonesborough" [Part II] (4-10-64) as above

25. "Escape" (4-17-64) Fritz Weaver, Jack Warden, Sorrell
    Booke, Michael Constantine
26. "The Pirate and the Patriot" (5-1-64) Ricardo Montalban,
    Frank Silvera, Kent Smith, John McGiver, Paul Picerni,
    Jean Lafitte


BURKE'S LAW

Frank D. Gilroy's fable of a millionaire police captain
(Gene Barry as Amos Burke) and the assorted eccentrics he encounters as he investigates a murder. Star-studded episodes first
reveal the murder (but never the murderer), then, in a blend of
comedy and drama, the suspects are individually questioned by
Burke and his fellow detectives Sergeant Lester Hart (Regis Toomey
and Tim Tillson (Gary Conway). The privilege of identifying the
guilty party is solely the Captain's.

Writers, such as Richard Levinson and William Link ("Who
Killed Mother Goose?") and Gwen Bagni and Paul Dubov ("Who
Killed Nobody Somehow?"), could not surmount the disadvantage of
an inflexible lead character. A predictable dialogue permeates the
teleplays. There is some good photography by Chas E. Burke and
George E. Diskant.

The Regulars: Captain Amos Burke, Gene Barry; Detective Tim
        Tillson, Gary Conway; Detective Sergeant Lester Hart,
        Regis Toomey; Henry, Leon Lontoc; Sergeant Ames, Eileen
        O'Neill.

The Episodes:

1. "Who Killed Holly Howard?" (9-20-63) Fred Clark, Rod
    Cameron, Bruce Cabot, Stephen McNally, Sir Cedric Hard
    wicke, Suzy Parker, Elizabeth Allen
2. "Who Killed Mr. X?" (9-27-63) Elizabeth Montgomery, Ann
    Harding, Dina Merrill, Charles Ruggles, Jim Backus
3. "Who Killed Cable Roberts?" (10-4-63) Zsa Zsa Gabor,
    Paul Lynde, Charlene Holt, Mary Astor, Keenan Wynn,
    John Saxon, Lizabeth Scott
4. "Who Killed Harris Crown?" (10-11-63) Lola Albright,
    Barbara Eden, Gene Nelson, Joan Blondell, Eva Gabor,
    Ruth Roman, Juliet Prowse
5. "Who Killed Julian Buck?" (10-18-63) Ed Begley, Terry-
    Thomas, Keenan Wynn, Michael Fox, Rita Moreno, Karl
    Boehm, Corinne Calvet
6. "Who Killed Alex Debbs?" (10-25-63) Sammy Davis Jr.,
    Arlene Dahl, Burgess Meredith, John Ireland, Jan Ster-
    ling, Suzy Parker, Diana Dors
7. "Who Killed Sweet Betsy?" (11-1-63) Carolyn Jones (in a
    four-part role), Gladys Cooper, Richard Carlson, John
    Ericson, Michael Wilding

8. "Who Killed Billy Joe?" (11-8-63) Kelly Gordon, Elaine
   Stewart; in cameos: Ida Lupino, Howard Duff, Nick
   Adams, Tina Louise, Cesar Romero, Tom Tully, Laraine
   Day, Phil Harris
9. "Who Killed Wade Walker?" (11-15-63) Rhonda Fleming,
   Frankie Laine, Michael Fox, Dana Wynter, Jay C. Flippen,
   Martha Hyer, Anne Francis
10. "Who Killed the Kind Doctor?" (11-29-63) Joan Caulfield,
   Elaine Devry, Philip Reed, Dewey Martin, Susan Oliver,
   Celeste Holm
11. "Who Killed Purity Mather?" (12-6-63) Telly Savalas,
   Charles Ruggles, Wally Cox, Janet Blair, Gloria Swanson
12. "Who Killed Cynthia Royal?" (12-13-63) Frankie Avalon,
   Macdonald Carey, Una Merkel, Marilyn Maxwell, Kathy
   Nolan
13. "Who Killed Eleanor Davis?" (12-20-63) Nick Adams, Elsa
   Lanchester, Edward Everett Horton, Debra Paget, Terry
   Moore, Arthur Hunnicutt, Jane Darwell
14. "Who Killed Beau Sparrow?" (12-27-63) June Allyson,
   Yvonne De Carlo, Agnes Moorehead, Dan Tobin, Ken Mur-
   ray
15. "Who Killed Jason Shaw?" (1-3-64) Burgess Meredith, Joyce
   Jameson, Tammy Grimes, Keenan Wynn, Oscar Homolka,
   Marlyn Mason
16. "Who Killed Snooky Martinelli?" (1-10-64) Janice Rule,
   Hoagy Carmichael, Broderick Crawford, Carl Reiner,
   Arlene Dahl, Cesar Romero
17. "Who Killed What's His Name?" (1-17-64) Edgar Bergen,
   Andy Devine, Reginald Gardiner, Elizabeth Allen, Dick
   Clark, Gena Rowlands
18. "Who Killed Madison Cooper?" (1-24-64) Jeanne Crain,
   Kevin McCarthy, Marty Ingels, Carolyn Jones, Dorothy
   Lamour, Terry-Thomas, David White
19. "Who Killed April?" (1-31-64) Eddie Bracken, Martha Hyer
20. "Who Killed Carrie Cornell?" (2-14-64) Michael Ansara,
   Joanie Sommers, Jim Backus, Diana Lynn, Fernando
   Lamas, William Shatner
1. "Who Killed His Royal Highness?" (2-21-64) Elizabeth Mont-
   gomery, Bert Parks, Gale Storm, Telly Savalas, Mickey
   Rooney, Linda Darnell, Michael Ansara
2. [unknown title] (2-28-64) Luciana Paluzzi, Glynis Johns,
   Marie Wilson, John Ericson, Don Taylor, Hershel Bernardi
3. [unknown title] (3-6-64) Felicia Farr, Chill Wills, Ed Wynn,
   Broderick Crawford
4. "Who Killed Andy Zygmunt?" (3-13-64) Ann Blyth, Tab
   Hunter, Deborah Walley, Macdonald Carey, Aldo Ray,
   Jack Weston
5. "Who Killed the Paper Dragon?" (3-20-64) Howard Duff,
   Dan Duryea, Miyoshi Umeki, James Shigeta, Barbara Eden
6. "Who Killed Molly?" (3-27-64) Jayne Mansfield, Hoagy Carmichael, Nanette Fabray, Arthur O'Connell, Jay C. Flippen
7. "Who Killed Who IV?" (4-3-64) Lola Albright, Steve Cochran,

Reginald Gardiner, Fess Parker, Patsy Kelly, Nancy Kovack

28. "Who Killed Annie Foran?" (4-10-64) John Cassavetes, Don
Ameche, Gena Rowlands, Wendell Corey, Jackie Coogan,
Sterling Holloway

29. "Who Killed My Girl?" (4-17-64) Stephen McNally, Gene
Raymond, Jane Greer, Richard Carlson, Ruta Lee, Don
Taylor

30. "Who Killed the Eleventh Best Dressed Woman in the World?"
(4-24-64) Jeanne Crain, Joanne Dru, Hazel Court, Martha
Hyer, Susan Strasberg, Josephine Hutchinson

31. "Who Killed Don Pablo?" (5-1-64) John Cassavetes, Patricia Medina, Agnes Moorehead, Cesar Romero, Forrest
Tucker, Cecil Kellaway

32. "Who Killed Half of the Glory Eagle?" (5-8-64) Joan Blondell, Nina Foch, Anne Helm, Betty Hutton, Buster Keaton,
Giselle MacKenzie

Second Season

33. "Who Killed the Surf Board?" (9-16-64) Macdonald Carey,
Sharon Farrell, Dorothy Lamour, Dewey Martin, Theodore
Bikel

34. "Who Killed Vaudeville?" (9-23-64) Gene Nelson, Shary
Marshall, Eddie Foy Jr., Gloria Swanson, Paul Dubov,
Jim Backus, Gypsy Rose Lee, Phil Harris

35. "Who Killed Cassandra Cass?" (9-30-64) Louis Nye, Nancy
Kovack, Nehemiah Persoff, Shelley Berman, Lola Albright,
Elsa Lanchester

36. "Who Killed the Horne of Plenty?" (10-7-64) David Wayne,
Vera Miles, John Saxon, Terry Moore, Edward Platt,
Richard Devon

37. "Who Killed Everybody?" (10-14-64) Arlene Dahl, Margaret
Leighton, June Havoc, Susan Silo, Norman Leavitt, Alan
Mowbray, Corinne Calvet

38. "Who Killed Mr. Cartwheel?" (10-21-64) Fred Clark, Nick
Adams, Diane McBain, Patsy Kelly, Ed Begley, Sheldon
Leonard

39. "Who Killed Cornelius Gilbert?" (10-28-64) Barbara Eden,
Alvy Moore, Martha Hyer, Dane Clark, Nanette Fabray,
Edgar Bergen

40. "Who Killed Lenore Wingfield?" (11-4-64) Dean Stockwell,
Anne Helm, Ida Lupino, Charles Ruggles, Victor Jory,
Dub Taylor

41. "Who Killed the Richest Man in the World?" (11-11-64)
George Hamilton, Pilar Seurat, Karen Sharpe, Diana Lynn
Ricardo Montalban, Tom Smothers, Dick Smothers

42. "Who Killed the Tall One in the Middle?" (11-25-64) Juliet
Prowse, Diane McBain, Eduardo Ciannelli, Steve Cochran,
Hal March

43. "Who Killed Merlin the Great?" (12-2-64) Nick Adams, Jill
St. John, Paul Lynde, Charles Ruggles, Joan Huntington,
Janet Blair

44. "Who Killed 711?" (12-9-64) Burgess Meredith, Hans Conried, Rhonda Fleming, Dan Duryea, Broderick Crawford,
Lisa Seagram
45. "Who Killed Supersleuth?" (12-16-64) Zsa Zsa Gabor,
Francine York, J. Carrol Naish, Carl Reiner, Thomas
Gomez
46. "Who Killed the Swinger on a Hook?" (12-23-64) Bek Nelson,
Leif Erickson, Gil Stuart, Dick Clark, Gloria DeHaven,
Janis Paige
47. "Who Killed Davidian Jones?" (12-30-64) Lisa Seagram,
Sheree North, Ruta Lee, Cesar Romero, Broderick Craw-
ford, Dennis Day, Reginal Gardiner, Peter Bourne
48. "Who Killed the Strangler?" (1-6-65) Frankie Avalon,
Robert Middleton, Annette Funicello, Jeanne Crain, Una
Merkel
49. "Who Killed Mother Goose?" (1-13-65) Alvy Moore, Madge
Blake, Suzanne Cupito, Lola Albright, Ann Blyth, Jan
Murray, Walter Pidgeon, George Hamilton
50. "Who Killed the Toy Soldier?" (1-20-65) Chill Wills, Abbe
Lane, Louis Nye, Joan Caulfield, Richard Hale, Martha
Hyer
51. "Who Killed Rosie Sunset?" (1-27-65) Francine York,
Michael Fox, Lisa Seagram, Hans Conried, Russ Tamblyn,
Dennis Day, Eddie Albert
52. "Who Killed Wimbledon Hastings?" (2-3-65) Nick Adams,
Edgar Bergen, Gale Storm, Debra Paget, Marie Wilson,
Vic Dana
53. "Who Killed the Fat Cat?" (2-10-65) Michael Fox, Mac-
donald Carey, Billy De Wolfe, Diana Hyland, Martha Raye,
Don Rickles
54. "Who Killed the Man on the White Horse?" (2-17-65) Vir-
ginia Mayo, Fernando Lamas, Nancy Kovack, Telly Savalas,
Robert Middleton, Barbara Eden
55. "Who Killed the 13th Clown?" (2-24-65) Corinne Calvet,
Joan Caulfield, Betty Hutton, Terry-Thomas, Jack Weston
56. "Who Killed Mr. Colby in Ladies' Lingerie?" (3-3-65) Joan
Bennett, Edd Byrnes, Arlene Dahl, Paul Lynde, Bert
Parks, Jonathan Hole, Chris Noel, Michael Fox
57. "Who Killed the Rest?" (3-17-65) Cesar Romero, Steve
Cochran, Eartha Kitt, Theodore Bikel, Janice Rule, Lisa
Gaye
58. "Who Killed Cop Robin?" (3-24-65) Hal March, James Whit-
more, Susan Strasberg, Herbie Faye, Ricardo Montalban,
Terry Moore
59. "Who Killed Nobody Somehow?" (3-31-65) Kevin McCarthy,
Lola Albright, Rory Calhoun, Tom Ewell, Diane McBain,
Steve Brodie
60. "Who Killed Hamlet?" (4-7-65) John Cassavetes, Eddie Foy
Jr., Edward Everett Horton, Agnes Moorehead, Basil
Rathbone, Susan Bay
61. "Who Killed the Rabbit's Husband?" (4-14-65) Gloria Grahame, Sal Mineo, Paul Richards, Una Merkel, John Ireland, Francine York, Lou Krugman

62. "Who Killed the Jackpot?" [This episode introduces Anne Francis and John Ericson in their "Honey West" roles] (4-21-65) Anne Francis, John Ericson, Jan Sterling, Steve Forrest, Louis Hayward, Nancy Gates
63. "Who Killed the Grand Piano?" (4-28-65) Ed Begley, John Cassavetes, Martha Hyer, Marilyn Maxwell, Nehemiah Persoff, Hugh Hefner
64. "Who Killed the Card?" (5-5-65) Les Crane, Wally Cox, Jill Haworth, Eddie Bracken, Hazel Court


THE BOB HOPE CHRYSLER THEATRE

　　　　Varying between extremes of excellence and disaster, this anthology series had writers of the calibre of Rod Serling ("A Killing at Sundial," "Slow Fade to Black," and "Exit from a Plane in Flight"), Edward Anhalt ("A Time for Killing"), Budd Schulberg ("The Meal Ticket"), Elick Moll ("A Clash of Cymbals") and William Inge ("Out on the Outskirts of Town"). One telecast, "Seven Miles of Bad Road," had Jeffrey Hunter the lead player in a familiar theme of an itinerant whose presence in a small town ferments the passions of the residents (Eleanor Parker and Neville Brand among them). A potboiler, surely, but one with its lid firmly in place.

The Episodes:

1. "A Killing at Sundial" (10-4-63) Angie Dickinson, Melvyn Douglas, Stuart Whitman, Robert Emhardt
2. "Something About Lee Wiley" (10-11-63) Piper Laurie, Claude Rains, Steven Hill, Alfred Ryder
3. "Seven Miles of Bad Road" (10-18-63) Jeffrey Hunter, James Anderson, Eleanor Parker, Neville Brand, Bernie Hamilton
4. "Four Kings" (11-1-63) Peter Falk, Susan Strasberg, Paul Lukas, John Van Dreelen, Vito Scotti, Simon Oakland, Robert Strauss, Than Wyenn
5. "One Day in the Life of Ivan Denisovich" (11-8-63) Jason Robards Jr., Hurd Hatfield, Albert Paulsen, Harold J. Stone
6. Special: "The House Next Door" (11-15-63) Kathryn Crosby Bob Hope, Harold J. Stone, Jill St. John, Jesse White
7. "The Fifth Passenger" (11-29-63) Mel Ferrer, Dana Wynter Eric Berry, Alan Napier, Jacques Aubuchon
8. "The Candidate" (12-6-63) Milton Berle, Ruth Roman, Dina Merrill, Hope Holiday, Robert Webber
9. "It's Mental Work" (12-20-63) Harry Guardino, Lee J. Cobb, Gena Rowlands, Archie Moore
10. "Corridor 400" (12-27-63) Theodore Bikel, Suzanne Pleshett Joseph Campanella, Frank Overton, Andrew Duggan
11. "War of Nerves" (1-3-64) Louis Jourdan, Stephen Boyd, Emile Genest, Monique Le Marie

12. "Runaway" (1-10-64) Joey Heatherton, Hugh O'Brian, Keenan Wynn, Berkely Harris
13. "The Seven Little Foys" (1-24-64) Mickey Rooney, Osmond Brothers, George Tobias, Eddie Foy Jr., Elaine Edwards, Naomi Stevens, narrated by Bob Hope
14. "Two Is the Number" (1-31-64) Shelley Winters, Martin Balsam
15. "A Wind of Hurricane Force" (2-7-64) Dana Andrews, Marisa Pavan, Joe De Santis, Tony Musante
16. "Wake Up, Darling" (2-21-64) Janet Blair, Roddy McDowall, Barry Nelson, Ann B. Davis, Joyce Jameson
17. "The Meal Ticket" (2-28-64) Cliff Robertson, Janice Rule, Broderick Crawford, Chris Robinson
18. "The Square Peg" (3-6-64) Robert Cummings, Joanna Moore, Burgess Meredith, Allyn Joslyn, Stanley Adams
19. "White Snow, Red Ice" (3-13-64) Jack Kelly, Senta Berger, Walter Matthau, Grace Lee Whitney
20. Comedy Special: "Her School for Bachelors" (3-20-64) Bob Hope, Eva Marie Saint
21. "Slow Fade to Black" (3-27-64) Rod Steiger, Robert Culp, James Dunn, Sally Kellerman
22. "A Case of Armed Robbery" (4-3-64) Anthony Franciosa, Pat O'Brien, Bethel Leslie, Russell Collins
23. Comedy Special: "Time for Elizabeth" (4-24-64) Groucho Marx, Eden Marx, Roland Winters, Kathryn Eames
24. "A Game with Glass Pieces" (5-1-64) George Peppard, Marvin Kaplan, Madlyn Rhue, Darren McGavin, Don Gordon
25. "The Command" (5-22-64) Robert Stack, Andrew Duggan, Robert Walker, Milton Selzer, Edward Binns
26. "The Sojourner" (5-29-64) Efrem Zimbalist Jr., Vera Miles, Howard Duff
27. "Echo of Evil" (6-5-64) Joan Hackett, Barry Sullivan, Jane Wyatt, John Saxon, Nehemiah Persoff

## Second Season

28. Musical: "Think Pretty" (10-2-64) Fred Astaire, Reta Shaw, Louis Nye, Barrie Chase, Jean Hersholt, Roger Perry
29. "Murder in the First" (10-9-64) Janet Leigh, Bobby Darin, Lloyd Bochner, Eduard Franz
30. "Have Girls, Will Travel" (10-16-64) Rod Cameron, Rhonda Fleming, Jill St. John, Aldo Ray, Marilyn Maxwell
31. "The Turncoat" (10-23-64) George Hamilton, Rodolfo Acosta, Margaret O'Brien, Jack Weston, Carroll O'Connor
32. "The Timothy Heist" (10-30-64) Art Carney, Spring Byington, Reginald Denny, Ted Cassidy
33. "Out on the Outskirts of Town" (11-6-64) Anne Bancroft, Jack Warden, Fay Bainter, Lane Bradford, Paul Fix
34. "Parties to the Crime" (11-27-64) Robert Strauss, Jeffrey Hunter, Sally Kellerman, Darren McGavin, Nancy Kovack
35. "Mr. Biddle's Crime Wave" (12-4-64) Roddy McDowall, Pat Crowley, Shari Lewis, Willard Waterman, Lloyd Nolan
36. "The Shattered Glass" (12-11-64) Shirley Jones, William

Shatner, Dan O'Herlihy

37. "A Clash of Cymbals" (12-25-64) Jack Klugman, Louis Jourdan, Laura Devon
38. "Double Jeopardy" (1-8-65) Zsa Zsa Gabor, Lauren Bacall, Jack Kelly, Tom Poston, Jean Hale, Nobu McCarthy, Diane McBain, Lee Meriwether
39. "Exit from a Plane in Flight" (1-22-65) Hugh O'Brian, Lloyd Bridges, Constance Townes, Sorrell Booke
40. "The Loving Cup" (1-29-65) Patrick O'Neal, Polly Bergen, Lee Marvin, Peter Adams
41. "The Fliers" (2-5-65) John Cassavetes, Chester Morris, Carol Lynley, Alfred Ryder
42. "Cops and Robbers" (2-19-65) Bert Lahr, Claude Rains, Ken Murray, Eduardo Ciannelli, Cyril Delevanti, Billy De Wolfe, John Qualen
43. "Terror Island" (2-26-65) Ginger Rogers, Carol Lawrence, Donnelly Rhodes, Katherine Ross
44. "The War and Eric Kurtz" (3-5-65) Jack Ging, Lloyd Bochner, Warren Oates, Martin Milner
45. "In Any Language" (3-12-65) John Forsythe, Nanette Fabray, Ricardo Montalban, Ed Hashim
46. "Perilous Times" (3-19-65) Peter Falk, Diane Baker, Arlene Dahl
47. "Memorandum for a Spy" [Part I] (4-2-65) Robert Stack, Victor Buono, Felicia Farr, Michael Constantine, George Macready, Albert Paulsen, John Van Dreelen
48. "Memorandum for a Spy" [Part II] (4-9-65) as above
49. "A Time for Killing" (4-30-65) Michael Parks, George C. Scott, Freddie Johnson, Peter Duryea

Third Season

50. "The Game" (9-15-65) Cliff Robertson, Maurice Evans, Dina Merrill, Nehemiah Persoff, Cyril Delevanti, Renzo Cesana, Ivan Triesault, Aleta Rotell
51. "The Crime" (9-22-65) Pat O'Brien, Sheree North, Jack Lord, Dana Wynter, Oliver McGowan, Karen Steele
52. "March from Camp Tyler" (10-6-65) Peter Lawford, Bethel Leslie, Broderick Crawford, Dan Tobin, Ben Johnson, Charles McGraw
53. "Kicks" (10-13-65) Mickey Rooney, Melodie Johnson, Jack Weston, Don Gordon, Harold J. Stone
54. "Back to Back" (10-27-65) Shelley Winters, Jack Hawkins, Grayson Hall, Warren Stevens, Phyllis Love
55. "Mr. Governess" (11-10-65) Tom Tryon, Carol Lawrence, Jacques Bergerac, Robert Clary, Fred Clark, Suzie Kay, Alice Backes, Marc Winters, Michael Blake
56. Comedy Special: "Russian Roulette" (11-17-65) Bob Hope, Jill St. John
57. "The Highest Fall of All" (12-1-65) Stuart Whitman, Joan Hackett, Gary Merrill, Terry Moore, Robert Q. Lewis, Steve Ihnat
58. "The Admiral" (12-29-65) Robert Young, Robert Reed

59. "The Enemy on the Beach" (1-5-66) Robert Wagner, Sally
    Ann Howes, Torin Thatcher, James Donald
60. "After the Lion, Jackals" (1-26-66) Eduardo Ciannelli,
    Stanley Baker, Suzanne Pleshette, John Saxon
61. "When Hell Froze" (2-2-66) Jane Wyman, Martin Milner,
    Steve Carlson, Leslie Nielsen
62. "A Small Rebellion" (2-9-66) George Maharis, Simone Signo-
    ret, Sam Levene
63. "Wind Fever" (3-2-66) Leo G. Carroll, William Shatner,
    Pippa Scott, John Cassavetes, Wilfrid Hyde-White
64. "Guilty or Not Guilty" (3-9-66) Robert Ryan, Richard Bey-
    mer, Pippa Scott, Leif Erickson, Robert Duvall, Dina
    Hyland, Leslie Nielsen
65. "Brilliant Benjamin Boggs" (3-30-66) Broderick Crawford,
    Donald O'Connor, Susan Silo, Emily Banks, Jean Hale,
    Eddie Mayehoff
66. "The Sister and the Savage" (4-6-66) Connie Francis, James
    Farentino, Steve Carlson, Anne Seymour
67. "The Faceless Man" (5-4-66) Charles Drake, Shirley Knight,
    Jack Lord, Jack Weston
68. "Holloway's Daughters" (5-11-66) Robert Young, David
    Wayne, Meg Wyllie, Brooke Bundy, Barbara Hershey
69. "One Embezzlement and Two Margaritas" (5-18-66) Michael
    Rennie, Antoinette Bower, Jocelyn Lane, Jack Kelly
70. "Runaway Bay" (5-25-66) Robert Wagner, Carol Lynley,
    Lola Albright, Sean Garrison
71. "Shipwrecked" (6-8-66) Hope Lange, Jason Robards Jr.
72. "In Pursuit of Excellence" (6-22-66) Glenn Corbett, Ed
    Begley, Joanne Medley, John Williams

Fourth Season

73. "Nightmare" (9-14-66) Julie Harris, Thomas Gomez, Farley
    Granger, Joan Huntington
74. "Time of Flight" (9-21-66) Jack Kelly, Jack Klugman,
    Juliet Mills, Woodrow Parfrey, Jeanette Nolan
75. Comedy Special: "And Baby Makes Five" (10-5-66) Angie
    Dickinson, Cliff Robertson, Walter Abel, Nina Foch
76. "Crazier Than Cotton" (10-12-66) Kevin McCarthy, Jean
    Simmons, Bradford Dillman, Charles Aidman, Georgia
    Simmons
77. Comedy Special: "Murder at N.B.C." (10-19-66) Red But-
    tons, Johnny Carson, Milton Berle, Don Adams
78. "Massacre at Fort Phil Kearney" (10-26-66) Richard Egan,
    Robert Fuller, Robert Pipe, Peter Duryea, Phyllis Avery,
    Carroll O'Connor
79. "Dear Deductible" (11-9-66) Peter Falk, Janet Leigh, Nor-
    man Fell, Christopher Cary
80. Comedy Special: "Fantastic Stomach" (11-16-66) Bing Cros-
    by, Jackie Gleason
81. "The Blue-Eyed Horse" (11-23-66) Ernest Borgnine, Paul
    Lynde, Joan Blondell, Joyce Jameson
82. "The Fatal Mistake" (11-30-66) Roddy McDowall, Arthur

Hill, Marge Redmond, Alice Rawlings
83. "Storm Crossing" (12-7-66) Barbara Rush, James Daly, Julie Sommars, Jack Lord, Mort Mills, Peter Mamakos
84. "The Eighth Day" (12-21-66) George Maharis, Barbara Barrie, Andrew Duggan, Michael Tolan
85. "Free of Charge" (12-28-66) John Cassavetes, Diane Baker, Johnny Seven, Suzy Parker, Ben Gazzara
86. "Code Name: Heraclitus" (1-4-67) Stanley Baker, Leslie Nielsen, Sheree North, Jack Weston, Ricardo Montalban, Malachi Throne, Signe Hasso
87. "A Time to Love" (1-11-67) Ralph Bellamy, Claire Bloom, Maximilian Schell, Nina Foch, Barry Russo, George Neise
88. "The Lady Is My Wife" (2-1-67) Alex Cord, Jean Simmons, Bradford Dillman
89. "Blind Man's Bluff" (2-8-67) Bob Cummings, Farley Granger, Laurence Naismith, Susan Clark, Brenda Dillon, Michael Rennie
90. "A Song Called Revenge" (3-1-67) Sal Mineo, Edd Byrnes, Jack Weston, June Harding, Herb Edelman, Peggy Lipton
91. "The Reason Nobody Hardly Ever Seen a Fat Outlaw in the Old West Is As Follows:" (3-8-67) Arthur Godfrey, Don Knotts, Percy Helton
92. "Verdict for Terror" (3-29-67) Cliff Robertson, Jo Van Fleet, Michael Constantine, Bettye Ackerman, Michael Sarrazin
93. "Dead Wrong" (4-5-67) Patrick O'Neal, Tony Bill, Lynn Loring, Donnelly Rhodes
94. "Don't Wait for Tomorrow" (4-19-67) Telly Savalas, Rossano Brazzi, Juliet Mills, Donnelly Rhodes, Will Kuluva
95. "Wipeout" (4-26-67) Shelley Winters, Tom Tryon, Les Crane, Don Stroud, Fabian, Marcel Hillaire
96. "To Sleep, Perchance to Scream" (5-10-67) Ricardo Montalban, Pat Hingle, Lola Albright, Joanne Dru, Paul Hartman, Henry Beckman
97. "Deadlock" (5-17-67) Jack Kelly, Lee Grant, Percy Rodriguez, Tige Andrews, Brooke Bundy, Dorothy Rice

DESTRY

John Gavin is a peregrinating avenger in this western, a bleak adaptation of the 1932 and 1954 motion pictures derived from Max Brand's Destry Rides Again.

The Regulars: Destry, John Gavin.

The Episodes:

1. "The Solid Gold Girl" (2-14-64) Neville Brand, Tammy Grimes, Broderick Crawford, Claude Akins
2. "Destry Had a Little Lamb" (2-21-64) Fess Parker, David White, Lee Van Cleef

3.  "Law and Order Day" (2-28-64) Una Merkel, Elisha Cook
4.  "Stormy Is a Lady" (3-6-64) Janet Blair, John Hoyt, Robert Cornthwaite, Charles Macaulay
5.  "The Nicest Girl in Gomorrah" (3-13-64) Albert Salmi, Patricia Barry, Marie Windsor, John McGiver
6.  "Big Deal at Little River" (3-20-64) Katherine Crawford, Richard Devon
7.  "Go Away, Little Sheba" (3-27-64) Joyce Bulifant, James Best
8.  "Deputy for a Day" (4-3-64) John Abbott, J. Pat O'Malley, Charles Ruggles
9.  "Ride to Rio Verde" (4-10-64) Lawrence Dobkin, Charles McGraw
10. "Blood Brother-in-Law" (4-17-64) Shary Marshall, Ron Hayes, Paul Newlan
11. "Red Brady's Kid" (4-24-64) Charles Drake, Roger Mobley, John Milford
12. "The Infernal Triangle" (5-1-64) John Astin, Marlyn Mason
13. "One Hundred Bibles" (5-8-64) Susan Oliver, Torin Thatcher


SUSPENSE

The Regulars: Sebastian Cabot, host.

The Episodes:

1.  "I, Mike Kenny" (3-25-64) Arthur Kennedy, Martin Balsam
2.  "I, Christopher Bell" (4-1-64) Charles Bickford
3.  "I, Bradford Charles" (4-8-64) Andrew Prine, Norman Fell, Victor Jory
4.  "I, Buck Larsen" (4-15-64) Vic Morrow, James Whitmore
5.  "The Savage" (4-22-64) Neville Brand, Corey Allen
6.  "I, Donald Roberts" (4-29-64) Harry Townes, James Daly
7.  "I, Dan Krolik" (5-6-64) Pat Crawford, James Ambandos
8.  "The Hunter" (5-20-64) Gary Merrill, Chester Morris
9.  "I, Lloyd Denson" (5-27-64) Ralph Meeker
10. "The Leader" (6-3-64) Basil Rathbone
11. "Brother Lathrop" (6-10-64) Skip Homeier, Edward Binns
12. "The Waiting House" [repeat of episode of 3/23/56 of "Schlitz Playhouse of the Stars"] (6-24-64) Phyllis Kirk

## MR. BROADWAY

His "Peter Gunn" image yet firmly ingrained, Craig Stevens ventured again into series television as Mike Bell, a press agent in palpitating Manhattan--certainly a fitting locale for scenarist Garson Kanin, who created the series.

The Regulars: Mike Bell, Craig Stevens; Hank McClure, Horace MacMahon; Toki, Lani Miyazaki.

The Episodes:

1. "Keep an Eye on Emily" (9-26-64) Tuesday Weld, Steve Cochran
2. "Try to Find a Spy" (10-10-64) Barbara Feldon, Jack Gilford, Simon Oakland, Paul McGrath
3. "Between the Rats and the Finks" (10-17-64) Larry Hagman, Dyan Cannon, Larry Gates, Norman Alden
4. "Nightingale for Sale" (10-24-64) Liza Minelli, Eduardo Ciannelli
5. "The He-She Chemistry" (10-31-64) Tammy Grimes, Jack Cassidy, William Hickey
6. "Don't Mention My Name in Sheboygan" (11-7-64) Sandy Dennis, Robert Webber, Chester Morris, Joan Bennett
7. "Maggie, Queen of the Jungle" (11-21-64) Nina Foch, Liliane Montevecchi, Alvin Epstein, Andre Plamondon
8. "Smelling Like a Rose" (11-28-64) Art Carney, Val Avery, Rosemary Forsyth, Peter de Vise
9. "Bad Little Rich Girl" (12-5-64) Larry Pennell, Diana Van Der Vlis, Shepperd Strudwick
10. "Sticks and Stones May Break My Bones" (12-12-64) Lola Albright, Philip Abbott, Louis Edmonds, Nancy Cushman
11. "Something to Sing About" (12-19-64) Lauren Bacall, Martin Balsam, Paul Larsen, Richard Schaal
12. "Pay Now, Die Later" (12-26-64) David Wayne, John Ireland, Marianna Hill

PROFILES IN COURAGE

Very good historical dramas, the inspiration being, of course, the late President John Kennedy's Pulitzer prize winner of the same title (Kennedy adapted his chapter on Edmund G. Ross, with James Whitmore in the title role, for the "Kraft Theatre" episode of May 16, 1956; Ross' celebrated anti-impeachment vote for Andrew Johnson was again enacted in the nineteenth episode). Among the champions: Janice Rule as Prudence Crandall, who fought against school segregation; Wendy Hiller as Anne Hutchinson, who rebelled against religious intolerance in Puritan New England; David McCallum as the founding father John Adams.

The Episodes:

1. "The Oscar W. Underwood Story" (11-8-64) Sidney Blackmer, Victor Jory
2. "The Mary S. McDowell Story" (11-15-64) Rosemary Harris, Albert Salmi, Audrey Christie, Woodrow Parfrey
3. "Thomas Hart Benton" (11-29-64) Brian Keith, Carl Benton Reid, Meg Wyllie, Russell Collins
4. "Richard T. Ely" (12-6-64) Dan O'Herlihy, Edward Asner, Karl Swenson, Ford Rainey, Leonard Nimoy, Marsha Hunt
5. "Sam Houston" (12-13-64) J. D. Cannon, Warren Stevens, Peggy McCay, Slim Pickens, Noah Keen, John Hoyt
6. "Governor John M. Slaton" (12-20-64) Walter Matthau, Whit Bissell, Michael Constantine, Alan Baxter, Betsy Jones-Moreland, Frank Marth
7. "John Adams" (12-27-64) David McCallum, Torin Thatcher, Andrew Prine, Gene Lyons, Paul Comi, Russell Collins, Phyllis Love, Jeff Cooper
8. "Robert A. Taft" (1-3-65) Lee Tracy, David Opatoshu, Lou Frizzell, Sue Randall, Loring Smith, Louise Lorimer
9. "Anne Hutchinson" (1-10-65) Wendy Hiller, Donald Harron, Michael Pate, Neil Hamilton, Rhys Williams
10. "General Alexander William Doniphan" (1-17-65) Peter Lawford, Robert Emhardt, Michael Constantine, Simon Oakland, James Callahan, Tim O'Connor
11. "John Peter Altgeld" (1-24-65) Burgess Meredith, John Kerr, Howard St. John, Milton Selzer, John Cassavetes
12. "Frederick Douglass" (1-31-65) Frederick O'Neal, Robert Hooks, Harry Townes, Alfred Ryder
13. "Daniel Webster" (2-7-65) Martin Gabel, Martine Bartlett, Robert F. Simon, Sandy Kenyon, Carl Benton Reid
14. "Woodrow Wilson" (2-14-65) Whit Bissell, John Hoyt, Philip Ober
15. "Prudence Crandall" (2-21-65) Janice Rule, John Ericson, Ken Lynch, King Donovan, Gloria Calomee
16. "Andrew Johnson" (2-28-65) Walter Matthau, Alfred Ryder, Conlan Carter, Paul Fix, John Abbott
17. "Hamilton Fish" (3-7-65) Henry Jones, Mark Richman, Robert Emhardt, Frank Silvera, Edward Asner
18. "Charles Evans Hughes" (3-14-65) Kent Smith, Harry Bellaver,

Strother Martin, Kevin Hagen
19. "Edmund G. Ross" (3-21-65) Bradford Dillman, Simon Oakland, Cyril Delevanti, Barry Morse, Hershel Bernardi, James Westerfield
20. "George W. Norris" (3-28-65) Tom Bosley, Torin Thatcher, George Mitchell, Peter Whitney, Herbert Voland
21. "Grover Cleveland" (4-4-65) Carroll O'Connor, Barbara Feldon, George Macready, Paul Lambert
22. "John Quincy Adams" (4-11-65) Douglas Campbell, Nancy Wickwire, Laurence Naismith, Parley Baer
23. "John Marshall" (4-18-65) Gary Merrill, Booth Colman, Murray Matheson, Christopher Dark
24. "Judge Ben B. Lindsey" (4-25-65) George Grizzard, David Brian, Edith Atwater, John Crawford
25. "George Mason" (5-2-65) Laurence Naismith, Arthur Franz, John Colicos
26. "Thomas Corwin" (5-9-65) George Rose, John Colicos, Lester Rawlins, H. M. Wynant

# THE ROGUES

This initially acclaimed series about a international family of con men has not endured well the passing of time, possibly because much of the praise was intended for the teaming of a quintet of professionals (Gig Young as the American Tony Fleming, Charles Boyer as the French Marcel St. Clair; Gladys Cooper, David Niven and Robert Coote as Britishers Margaret St. Clair, Alec Fleming, and Timmy St. Clair, respectively).

Today, when so many big-name film stars have ventured into television, the pretentiousness of the teleplays is all the more obvious. The framing of wealthy villains (Darren McGavin in Charles Hoffman's "The Diamond-Studded Pie," Telly Savalas in Stephen Kandel's "Viva Diaz!") always a success; all the family members emerging unscathed--these elements are not made palatable by the charm of the principals alone. One episode, Warren Duff's "Mr. White's Christmas," does seem to have aged well, however, probably because it was meant as a holiday fable. John McGiver was properly cast as the scrooge-turned-philanthropist for this teleplay directed by Don Taylor.

The Regulars: Tony Fleming, Gig Young; Alec Fleming, David Niven; Marcel St. Clair, Charles Boyer; Margaret St. Clair, Gladys Cooper; Timmy St. Clair, Robert Coote.

The Episodes:

1. "The Personal Touch" (9-13-64) Walter Matthau, Dina Merrill, Alfred Ryder, John Dehner, Dabbs Greer, Marcel Hillaire
2. "The Day They Gave Diamonds Away" (9-20-64) James

Gregory, Nancy Berg
3. "The Stefanini Dowry" (9-27-64) Susan Strasberg, Fritz Weaver, David Sheiner, Michael Constantine
4. "Viva Diaz!" (10-4-64) Telly Savalas, Danielle de Metz, Sandra Giles, George Savalas
5. "House of Cards" (10-11-64) Jessica Walter, Patric Knowles, John Williams, John Orchard, Gil Stuart
6. "Death of a Fleming" (10-25-64) Peter Whitney, Quinn O'Hara, Alvy Moore, Susan Cramer
7. "The Project Man" (11-1-64) Robert Middleton, Marlyn Mason, Ray Teal, Parley Baer
8. "Two of a Kind" (11-8-64) Ida Lupino, Patricia Medina, George Hamilton, Brooke Hayward
9. "Take Me to Paris" (11-15-64) Gia Scala, Alexander Scourby, Vincent Gardenia, Emile Genest
10. "Fringe Benefits" (11-22-64) Suzy Parker, John Williams, Jackie Russell, Simon Scott, James Doohan
11. "Plavonia, Hail and Farewell" (11-29-64) Oscar Homolka, Leon Askin, Barbara Bouchet
12. "The Boston Money Party" (12-6-64) J. D. Cannon, Diana Van Der Vlis, Woodrow Parfrey, Russell Arms
13. "The Computer Goes West" (12-13-64) Malachi Throne, Suzanne Cramer, George Kennedy, Marcel Hillaire
14. "Hugger-Mugger by the Sea" (12-20-64) Ricardo Montalban, Kamala Devi, Marie Windsor, Raquel Welch
15. "The Real Russian Caviar" (12-27-64) Elsa Martinelli, Peter Brocco, Robert Ellenstein, Chuck Hicks
16. "Money Is for Burning" (1-3-65) Susan Oliver, Lloyd Gough, Alan Napier, Ben Wright
17. "Gambit by the Golden Gate" (1-10-65) Broderick Crawford, Michael Walker, Jean Hale, Milton Selzer, Jacqueline Beer, Steven Geray
18. "Bless You, G. Carter Huntington" (1-17-65) Howard Duff, Sally Kellerman, Edgar Stehli, Eileen O'Neill
19. "The Golden Ocean" (1-24-65) Eddie Albert, Pippa Scott, Harry Millard, Ray Fulner
20. "The Diamond-Studded Pie" (1-31-65) Darren McGavin, Dianne Foster, Don Marshall
21. "Bow to a Master" (2-7-65) Zachary Scott, Laura Devon, James Griffith, Christopher Dark
22. "Run for the Money" (2-14-65) Helmut Dantine, Diana Hyland
23. "The Laughing Lady of Luxor" (2-21-65) Gia Scala, Nico Minardos, Louise Latham, Everett Sloane, John Orchard
24. "The Bartered MacBride" (2-28-65) Simon Oakland, Joanna Moore, Howard Freeman
25. "The Pigeons of Paris" (3-7-65) Jill St. John, John Williams, Gerald Mohr, Marcel Hillaire
26. "Our Man in Marawat" (3-14-65) Dana Wynter, Christopher Dark, Philip Ahn
27. "Wherefore Art Thou, Harold?" (3-21-65) Robert Webber, Barbara Eden, Estelle Winwood, Robert Phillips
28. "Grave Doubts" (3-28-65) Jocelyn Lane, Jonathan Harris,

Otto H. Harris
29. "Mr. White's Christmas" (4-4-65) Jill Haworth, John Mc-
Giver, Larry Hagman, Hedley Mattingly
30. "A Daring Step Backward" (4-18-65) Dina Merrill, George
Sanders, Larry Hagman, Camilla Sparv


SLATTERY'S PEOPLE

James Moser's engrossing study of the workings of a state
legislature and its heroic minority leader, James Slattery (Richard
Crenna) who was periodically in the midst of major controversy.
Moser's own "Question: What Is Truth?" finds Slattery in a lively
debate with a veteran fellow representative (James Whitmore as
Harry Sanborn) who has been charged with unethical conduct. Shel
don Stark's "How Impregnable Is a Magic Tower?" dramatizes the
building of the Watts Towers, with a fictional equivalent of Simon
Rodia. Pat Fiedler's "The Unborn" gravely questioned therapeutic
abortion. Reminiscent of the heydey of un-American activities
committees was "Color Him Red" with John McIntire in the role of
an alleged communist sympathizer. Other writers for the series
included Preston Wood ("The Hero" and "A Sitting Duck Named
Slattery"), Dean Riesner ("Question: Remember the Dark Sins of
Youth?") and David Karp ("The Last Commuter"). Regulars included Alejandro Rey as Slattery's aide Mike Valera, the represen
ative's secretary (Francine York as Wendy Wendkoski) and girl
friend (Kathie Browne as Liz Andrews).

The Regulars: James Slattery, Richard Crenna; Bert Metcaff, Tol
Avery; B. J. Clawson, Maxine Stuart (first season); Johnn
Ramos, Paul Geary (first season); Frank Radcliffe, Edwar
Asner (first season); Mike Valera, Alejandro Rey (second
season); Liz Andrews, Kathie Browne (second season);
Wendy Wendkoski, Francine York (second season).

The Episodes:

1. "Question: What Is Truth?" (9-21-64) James Whitmore,
Elizabeth Allen, Leora Dana, Malachi Throne
2. "Question: Why the Lonely ... Why the Misbegotten?" (9-
28-64) Tommy Sands, Torin Thatcher, Paul Lambert
3. "Question: Remember the Dark Sins of Youth?" (10-5-64)
Arthur Hill, Michael Constantine, Arthur Crenna, Joan
Blackman, Steve Ihnat
4. "Question: What Ever Happened to Ezra?" (10-12-64)
Richard Kiley, Ed Wynn, David White, Hilda Browner
5. "Question: What Are You Doing Out There, Waldo?" (10-19-
64) Sally Kellerman, Joe Maross, Paul Fix
6. "Question: What Became of the White Tortilla?" (10-26-64)
Ricardo Montalban, Miriam Colon, Milton Selzer, Lane
Bradford
7. "Question: Where Vanished the Tragic Piper?" (11-2-64)

Larry Gates, Lee Grant, Burt Brinckerhoff, Davey Davison

8. "Question: Is Laura the Name of the Game?" (11-9-64) Jack Warden, James Griffith, Joyce Meadows

9. "Question: What's a Genius Worth This Week?" (11-16-64) Paul Burke, Arch Johnson, Nancy Berg

10. "Question: What Is Honor ... What Is Death?" (11-23-64) Barry Sullivan, Jeanette Nolan, Philip Abbott, Len Wayland

11. "Question: Do the Ignorant Sleep in Pure White Beds?" (11-30-64) Lori Martin, Charles Aidman, Andrew Duggan, Peggy McCay, Allan Hunt

12. "Question: Which One Has the Privilege?" (12-7-64) Edward Binns, Phyllis Coates, DeForest Kelley

13. "Question: How Long Is the Shadow of a Man?" (1-1-65) Vera Miles, Gene Lyons, Lloyd Gough, Walter Brooke

14. "Question: What Is a Requiem for a Loser?" (1-8-65) Martin Milner, Warren Oates, Carl Benton Reid

15. "Question: What Did You Do All Day, Mr. Slattery?" (1-15-65) Eduardo Ciannelli, Carroll O'Connor, Charles Drake, Arthur Franz, Whit Bissell, Denver Pyle, Sally Brophy, Russ Conway

16. "Question: How Do You Fall in Love with a Town?" (1-22-65) James Dunn, Lee Tracy, L. Q. Jones, Julie Sommars, R. G. Armstrong

17. "Question: Does Nero Still at Ringside Sit?" (2-5-65) Robert Blake, Gene Evans, Madlyn Rhue, Richard Anderson, Val Avery, John Lupton

18. "Question: How Do You Catch a Cool Bird of Paradise?" (2-12-65) Raymond St. Jacques, Simon Oakland, Susan Bay, June Dayton, Frank Maxwell

19. "Question: When Do We Hang the Good Samaritan?" (2-19-65) Barbara Eden, Claude Akins, Larry Ward, William Hansen

20. "Question: Is Democracy Too Expensive?" (2-26-65) Ed Begley, John Larch, Rosemary Murphy, Stephen Brooks

21. "Question: Did He Who Made the Lamb Make Thee?" (3-5-65) Janice Rule, Alfred Ryder, Ken Lynch, James Patterson

22. "Question: Who You Taking to the Main Event, Eddie?" (3-12-65) Zohra Lampert, Percy Rodriguez, Cicely Tyson, Tige Andrews, Warren Stevens

23. "Question: What's New in Timbuctoo?" (3-19-65) Pat O'Brien, Jean Wickwire, David McLean, John Lasell

24. "Question: Bill Bailey, Why Did You Come Home?" (4-2-65) Fred Clark, Forrest Tucker, Louise Troy, Kathleen Freeman

25. "Question: What Time Is the Next Bandwagon?" (4-9-65) Murray Hamilton, Dianne Foster, Ford Rainey, Joan Tompkins

26. "Question: What's a Swan Song for a Sparrow?" (4-16-65) Al Freeman Jr., Elsa Lanchester, Sorrell Booke, Russell Collins

Second Season

27. "A Sitting Duck Named Slattery" (9-17-65) Carroll O'Connor
    Robert F. Simon, Howard Caine, Laurence Haddon, Wil-
    liam Bramley, Charlie Briggs, Hal Baylor, Paul Potash,
    Larry Anthony
28. "He Who Has Ears, Let Him Bug Somebody Else" (9-24-65)
    Allan Melvin, William Hansen, J. P. Burns, David Fresc
29. "How Impregnable Is a Magic Tower?" (10-1-65) Eduardo
    Ciannelli, Pilar Seurat, Judson Pratt, Manuel Padilla,
    Paul Mantee, Paul Sorensen
30. "The Unborn" (10-8-65) Joyce Van Patten, Fred J. Scollay,
    John Randolph, Trevor Bardette
31. "Rally 'Round Your Own Flag, Mister" (10-15-65) Lloyd
    Nolan, Warren Oates, Clifton James, Tom Peters, Dan
    Frazer
32. "What Can You Do with a Wounded Tiger?" (10-22-65) Ossi
    Davis, Pat Cardi, Lonny Chapman, Robert Nichols
33. "The Hero" (11-5-65) Earl Holliman, Larry Blyden, Lloyd
    Gough
34. "Of Damon, Pythias and Sleeping Dogs" (11-12-65) Robert
    Lansing, Michael Walker, Tisha Sterling, Juanita Moore,
    Stacy Harris
35. "The Last Commuter" (11-19-65) Lew Ayres, Joan Blondell
    Robert Q. Lewis, David Sheiner, Jack Collins
36. "Color Him Red" (11-26-65) John McIntire, Martha Scott,
    Gene Lyons, Ben Aliza, Angela Dorian

## VOYAGE TO THE BOTTOM OF THE SEA

This Irwin Allen venture into science fiction, the first in a
succession (i.e. "Lost in Space," "The Time Tunnel" and "The
Land of the Giants") initially proceeded with enough trepidation of
Communist Russia so as to produce some moralizing--and amusing
--teleplays. In Robert Hamner's "The Human Computer," Commander Lee Crane is left the sole participant on a mission to test
the effectiveness of a computer which has taken over the function-
ing of the Seaview (the principal set piece for the series was an
"atomic submarine of the future" by this name). After a time
Crane realizes that there is a saboteur aboard and, after a merry
chase through ship compartments and corridors, he thwarts the
plans, of course, of this "enemy agent." In another episode, the
Seaview's Admiral Harriman Nelson (Richard Basehart) finds himself cast adrift with his ideological antithesis (Edward Asner). A
verbal exchange of the opposite virtues ensues and the conclusion
of "The Exile" has the Admiral triumphant--along with his Wester
virtues. Periodically "the enemy" resurfaced, as in "The Traitor
by William Welch and Al Gail and starring George Sanders. Yet
the first season was not without its share of the purely fantastic.
Richard Landau's "The Indestructible Man," about a robot run
amuck, set the tone for the later season episodes, which had

completely departed from the seriousness (whatever the pretension) of their predecessors. An assortment of the better-known Hollywood character actors and special effects were all that distinguished such last season episodes as Charles Bennett's "The Deadly Dolls" with Vincent Price, Arthur Weiss' "Fires of Death" with Victor Jory, and William Welch's "Cave of the Dead" with Warren Stevens.

Of far greater significance for the popular success of the series was the technical know-how of Hollywood professionals Jack Martin Smith and Stan Jolley, the art directors, cinematographers Winton Hoch, Sam Leavitt and Carl Guthrie and musicians Morton Stevens and Lennie Hayton. Pulp fiction capitalized on the success of "Voyage" with a series of Gold Key comics begun in 1965.

The Regulars: Admiral Harriman Nelson, Richard Basehart; Commander Lee Crane, David Hedison; Lieutenant Commander Chip Morton, Bob Dowdell; Chief Petty Officer Curley Jones, Henry Kulky (first season only); Chief Francis Sharkey, Terry Becker (last three seasons); Dr. Gamma, Theodore Marcuse (first season episodes only); Kowalski, Del Monroe; Sparks, Arch Whiting; Patterson, Paul Trinka; Riley, Allan Hunt; Doc, Richard Bull.

The Episodes:

1. "Eleven Days to Zero" (9-14-64) Eddie Albert, Mark Slade, John Zaremba, Booth Colman
2. "The City Beneath the Sea" (9-21-64) Hurd Hatfield, Linda Cristal, John Alderson
3. "The Fear Makers" (9-28-64) Edgar Bergen, Lloyd Bochner
4. "The Midst of Silence" (10-5-64) Rita Gam, Alejandro Rey, Mike Kellin, Edward Colmans
5. "The Price of Doom" (10-12-64) Jill Ireland, David Opatoshu, John Milford, Steve Ihnat
6. "The Sky Is Falling" (10-19-64) Charles McGraw
7. "Turn Back the Clock" (10-26-64) Nick Adams, Yvonne Craig, Les Tremayne
8. "The Village of Guilt" (11-2-64) Anna-Lisa, Richard Carlson, Frank Richards, Steve Geray
9. "Hot Line" (11-9-64) Michael Ansara, Everett Sloane, Ford Rainey, Robert Carson
10. "Submarine Sunk Here" (11-16-64) Carl Reindel, Eddie Ryder, Wright King
11. "The Magnus Beam" (11-23-64) Mario Alcaide, Malachi Throne, Jacques Aubuchon
12. "No Way Out" (11-30-64) Than Wyenn, Danielle de Metz, Jan Merlin, Oscar Beregi
13. "The Blizzard Makers" (12-7-64) Werner Klemperer, Milton Selzer, Kenneth McDonald
14. "The Ghost of Moby Dick" (12-14-64) June Lockhart, Edward Binns, Bob Beekman
15. "Long Live the King" (12-21-64) Carroll O'Connor, Michel

Petit, Michael Pate
16. "Hail to the Chief" (12-28-64) Viveca Lindfors, John Hoyt
17. "The Last Battle" (1-4-65) John Van Dreelen, Joe De Santis, Rudy Solari, Ben Wright
18. "Mutiny" (1-11-65) Harold J. Stone, Steve Harris
19. "Doomsday" (1-18-65) Donald Harron, Ford Rainey, Paul Carr
20. "The Invaders" (1-25-65) Robert Duvall
21. "Indestructible Man" (2-1-65) Michael Constantine
22. "The Buccaneer" (2-8-65) Barry Atwater, Emile Genest
23. "The Human Computer" (2-15-65) Harry Millard, Simon Scott, Ted De Corsia
24. "The Saboteur" (2-22-65) Warren Stevens, Bert Freed
25. "Cradle of the Deep" (3-1-65) John Anderson, Paul Carr, Howard Wendell
26. "The Amphibians" (3-8-65) Skip Homeier, Curt Conway, Frank Graham, Zale Parry
27. "The Exile" (3-15-65) Edward Asner, David Sheiner, Harry Davis
28. "The Creature" (3-22-65) Leslie Nielsen, Robert Lipton
29. "The Enemies" (3-29-65) Henry Silva, Malachi Throne
30. "The Secret of the Loch" (4-5-65) Torin Thatcher, Hedley Mattingly, George Mitchell
31. "The Condemned" (4-12-65) Arthur Franz, J. D. Cannon, John Goddard, Alvy Moore
32. "The Traitor" (4-19-65) George Sanders, Michael Pate

Second Season

33. "Jonah and the Whale" (9-19-65) Gia Scala
34. "Time Bomb" (9-26-65) Ina Balin, Susan Flannery, Richard Loo, John Zaremba
35. "... And Five of Us Are Left" (10-3-65) Kent Taylor, James Anderson, Robert Doyle, Philip Pine
36. "The Cyborg" (10-10-65) Victor Buono, Brooke Bundy
37. "Escape from Venice" (10-17-65) Renzo Cesana, Vincent Gardenia
38. "The Left-Handed Man" (10-24-65) Regis Toomey, Cyril Delevanti, Charles Dierkop
39. "The Deadliest Game" (10-31-65) Lloyd Bochner, Robert F. Simon, Audrey Dalton, Robert Cornthwaite
40. "Leviathan" (11-7-65) Liam Sullivan, Karen Steele
41. "The Peacemaker" (11-14-65) John Cassavetes, Whit Bissell, Irene Tsu
42. "The Silent Saboteurs" (11-21-65) Pilar Seurat, George Takei, Bert Freed
43. "The 'X' Factor" (12-5-65) John McGiver, Jan Merlin
44. "The Machines Strike Back" (12-12-65) Roger C. Carmel
45. "Monster from Outer Space" (12-19-65) Lee Delano, Wayne Heffley
46. "Terror on Dinosaur Island" (12-26-65) Paul Carr
47. "The Hunters" (1-2-66) Michael Ansara, Patrick Wayne
48. "Deadly Creature Below" (1-9-66) Nehemiah Persoff, Paul Comi

49. "The Phantom Strikes" (1-16-66) Alfred Ryder
50. "The Sky's on Fire" (1-23-66) Robert H. Harris, Frank
   Marth
51. "Graveyard of Fear" (1-30-66) Robert Loggia, Marian Moses
52. "The Shape of Doom" (2-6-66) Kevin Hagen
53. "Dead Man's Doubloons" (2-13-66) Albert Salmi, Robert
   Brubaker
54. "The Death Ship" (2-20-66) Lew Gallo, David Sheiner, June
   Vincent, Elizabeth Parry
55. "The Monster's Web" (2-27-66) Mark Richman, Barry Coe
56. "The Manfish" (3-6-66) Gary Merrill, John Dehner
57. "The Mechanical Man" (3-13-66) Arthur O'Connell, James
   Darren
58. "The Return of the Phantom" (3-20-66) Alfred Ryder, Vitina
   Marcus

## Third Season

59. "The Monster from the Inferno" (9-18-66) Arthur Hill
60. "Werewolf" (9-25-66) Charles Aidman, Douglas Bank
61. "The Day the World Ended" (10-2-66) Skip Homeier
62. "Night of Terror" (10-9-66) Henry Jones, Jerry Catron
63. "The Terrible Toys" (10-16-66) Paul Fix, Francis X. Bushman
64. "Day of Evil" (10-23-66) regulars only
65. "Deadly Waters" (10-30-66) Don Gordon, Lew Gallo
66. "Thing from Inner Space" (11-6-66) Hugh Marlowe
67. "The Death Watch" (11-13-66) regulars only
68. "Deadly Invasion" (11-20-66) Warren Stevens
69. "Haunted Submarine" (11-27-66) regulars only
70. "The Plant Man" (12-4-66) William Smithers
71. "The Lost Bomb" (12-11-66) John Lupton, Gerald Mohr
72. "The Brand of the Beast" (12-18-66) regulars only
73. "The Creature" (1-1-67) Lyle Bettger
74. "Death from the Past" (1-8-67) John Van Dreelen, Jan Merlin
75. "The Heat Monster" (1-15-67) Alfred Ryder, Don Knight
76. "The Fossil Men" (1-22-67) Brendon Dillon, Jerry Catron
77. "The Mermaid" (1-29-67) Diane Webber
78. "The Mummy" (2-5-67) regulars only
79. "The Shadowman" (2-12-67) Jerry Catron, Tyler McVey
80. "No Escape from Death" (2-19-67) regulars only
81. "Doomsday Island" (2-26-67) regulars only
82. "The Wax Men" (3-5-67) Michael Dunn
83. "The Deadly Cloud" (3-12-67) Robert Carson, Bill Baldwin
84. "Destroy Seaview" (3-19-67) regulars only

## Fourth Season

85. "Fires of Death" (9-17-67) Victor Jory
86. "The Deadly Dolls" (9-24-67) Vincent Price
87. "Cave of the Dead" (10-8-67) Warren Stevens
88. "Journey with Fear" (10-15-67) Gene Dynarski, Jim Gosa

89.  "Sealed Orders" (10-22-67) regulars only
90.  "Man of Many Faces" (10-29-67) Jock Gaynor
91.  "Fatal Cargo" (11-5-67) Woodrow Parfrey
92.  "Time Lock" (11-12-67) John Crawford
93.  "Rescue" (11-19-67) Don Dubbins
94.  "Terror" (11-26-67) regulars only
95.  "A Time to Die" (12-3-67) Henry Jones
96.  "Blow Up" (12-10-67) regulars only
97.  "Deadly Amphibians" (12-17-67) Don Matheson
98.  "The Return of Blackbeard" (12-31-67) Malachi Throne
99.  "The Terrible Leprechaun" (1-7-68) Walter Burke
100.  "The Lobster Man" (1-21-68) Victor Lundin
101.  "Nightmare" (1-28-68) Paul Mantee
102.  "The Abominable Snowman" (2-4-68) regulars only
103.  "Secret of the Deep" (2-11-68) Mark Richman
104.  "Man-Beast" (2-18-68) Lawrence Montaigne
105.  "Savage Jungle" (2-25-68) Perry Lopez
106.  "Flaming Ice" (3-3-68) Michael Pate
107.  "Attack" (3-10-68) Skip Homeier
108.  "Edge of Doom" (3-17-68) regulars only
109.  "The Death Clock" (3-24-68) Chris Robinson
110.  "No Way Back" (3-31-68) Henry Jones, Barry Atwater, William Beckley

## WORLD WAR I

John Sharnik and Isaac Kleinerman produced this excellent documentary on the Great War, with a musical score by Morton Gould.

The Regulars: Robert Ryan, narrator.

The Episodes:

1.  "The Summer of Sarajevo" (9-22-64)
2.  "The Clash of the Generals" (9-29-64)
3.  "The Doomed Dynasties" (10-6-64)
4.  "Atrocity 1914" (10-13-64)
5.  "They Sank the Lusitania" (10-27-64)
6.  "Verdun the Inferno" (11-10-64)
7.  "The Battle of Jutland" (11-17-64)
8.  "The Trenches" (11-24-64)
9.  "D-Day at Gallipoli" (12-1-64)
10.  "America the Neutral" (12-8-64)
11.  "Wilson and the War" (12-20-64)
12.  "Revolution in Red" (12-27-64)
13.  "Behind the German Lines" (1-3-65)
14.  "Year of Lost Illusions" (1-10-65)
15.  "Over There" (1-17-65)
16.  "Over Here" (1-24-65)
17.  "Daredevils and Dogfights" (1-31-65)

18.  "The Agony of Caporetto"  (2-14-65)
19.  "Tipperary and All That Jazz"  (2-21-65)
20.  "The Promised Lands"  (2-28-65)
21.  "The Tide Turns"  (3-7-65)
22.  "The Battle of the Argonne"  (3-14-65)
23.  "The Day the Guns Stopped Firing"  (3-28-65)
24.  "Wilson and Peace"  (4-4-65)
25.  "The Allies in Russia"  (4-11-65)
26.  "Heritage of War"  (4-18-65)


THE MAN FROM U.N.C.L.E.

The Kennedy era extolled the virtues of the erudite class; it no less celebrated the vitality of youth. The Cold War was yet an obsession with the American masses in the early 1960s: what then if one could capture both the obsession and the vitality into a single art form? The cinema's James Bond cycle did just that, with 1962's Dr. No, 1963's From Russia with Love, and what many regard as the finest in the sequence, 1964's Goldfinger. But television in 1964 had yet no counterpart, and that is why, one supposes, producer Norman Felton and writer Sam Rolfe conceived of "The Man from U.N.C.L.E." "U.N.C.L.E.," as any devotee of this series well knew, stood for "United Network Command for Law and Enforcement," a pseudonymous title and--one hopes--organization which was nevertheless cited in the credits with the statement "We wish to thank the United Network Command for Law and Enforcement, without whose co-operation this program would not have been possible."

Several factors explain the enormous success of this series, which spawned numerous imitators, with the television audience: the period was ripe for the Bond genre, as earlier explained; the appeal of its youthful protagonists--Napoleon Solo (Robert Vaughn) and Illya Kuryakin (David McCallum)--which cut across the generations; a wonderful collaboration of photography (Fred Koenekamp), editing (Henry Berman and John D. Dunning), art direction (George W. Davies and Merrill Pye), sound (Franklin Milton) and music (Morton Stevens and Walter Sharf with a jazz theme by Jerry Goldsmith), writing and direction. Yet another factor was the construction of exotic, sadistic villains who week after week devised elaborate schemes to infiltrate and destroy U.N.C.L.E. and/or its agents, while frequently working for U.N.C.L.E. nemesis T.H.R.U.S.H. T.H.R.U.S.H., as writer John Brosnan noted in his James Bond in the Cinema, stood for "The Technological Hierarchy for the Removal of Undesirables and the Subjugation of Humanity."

Actors and actresses had a field day with their evil incarnate roles, while fulfilling their character's own (and perhaps the television audience's) sadistic impulses. Thus agent Solo was variously racked (by George Sanders in "The Gazebo in the Maze

Affair"), flogged (by Robert Culp in "The Shark Affair"), drugged
(by Carroll O'Connor in "The Green Opal Affair") and nearly
broiled (in the pilot "The Vulcan Affair")--all in the first season!
Jeanne Cooper made a wickedly authoritarian "schoolmarm" named
Mother Fear in "The Children's Day Affair"; octogenarian Estelle
Winwood was something of the same in "The Her Master's Voice
Affair." George Sanders was typically sauve and heinous as
Squire G. Emory Partridge, who monopolizes control of an entire
village in Dean Hargrove's and Antony Ellis' "The Gazebo in the
Maze Affair," and as Partridge again in "The Yukon Affair."
Anne Francis, who was the distaff side of the spy genre a season
later with "Honey West," was a beautiful nemesis in the character
Gervaise Ravel in two first season episodes: "The Quadripartite
Affair" and "The Giuoco Piano Affair"; in both cases U. N. C. L. E.
agents engaged the help of Marion Raven, who was played by co-
star McCallum's then real-life spouse, Jill Ireland. Both Jack
Palance and Janet Leigh brought a stylized madness to their characters in the two-part episode "The Concrete Overcoat Affair."

The finely satirical nature of several first season episodes,
in which the craftiest of pretensions were mixed with dramatic
turns, was later supplanted by pure fantasy in subsequent seasons.
And so we were asked to believe in vampires (Martin Landau in
"The Bat Cave Affair"), voodoo (in Boris Ingster's "The Very Important Zombie Affair" with Claude Akins), a lady tarzan (Vitina
Marcus in "The My Friend, the Gorilla Affair"), a medieval bout
with the lance in an imaginary modern day kingdom in "The Round
Table Affair" with Reginald Gardiner and Valora Noland--other
themes equally absurd.

Yet "The Man from U. N. C. L. E. ," in its pristine episodes,
so skillfully made use of its highly imaginative techniques that its
heavy social impact seemed destined. The conception of allowing
the "ordinary" citizen to fulfill his pipe dream of attaining a global
pre-eminence by being swept up in the whirlwind of U. N. C. L. E.
and T. H. R. U. S. H. rivalry was particularly inspired. What matter
if we never learned whose side, exactly, Ricardo Montalban was on
in Robert Towne's "The Dove Affair" so long as schoolteacher June
Lockhart would have a hand in the outcome? If the housewife who
has her grocery shopping interrupted and finds herself with agent
Solo running from cheetahs is a reluctant participant in the goings-
on of Robert E. Thompson's "The Green Opal Affair," still we nod,
as she sighs a relief when it is all over, that she would surely do
it again. If we watched dubiously as Sue Ane Langdon and Herbert
Anderson, a couple on board Robert Culp's contemporary pirate
ship, never seemed to understand what their captain was really
after in Alvin Sapinsley's "The Shark Affair," yet we knew, even
as they descend onto lifeboats from the sinking ship (and its captain going down with it), that this would be the adventure of their
lifetime. In each episode the action quite literally flowed, divided
into four "acts" to skirt the commercial problem which had up to
that time broken the continuity of too many dramas.

"U. N. C. L. E. , " then, was a series of carefully planned plot devices designed to achieve maximum intensity out of the television medium, where escapism meant everything. In that goal--with its pristine episodes anyway--it succeeded, so much so that its significance for mid-1960s America cannot be overemphasized. One could think of the series as something of a watershed in television programming--the point between the end of the live dramas and the decline of the medium as a result of contract writing replete with plot variations on familiar themes. Yet the satirical approach to the Cold War, which was U. N. C. L. E. 's central theme, apparently never quite caught on with the greater part of its following. When an interest group campaign against "sex and violence" on television led to the creation of a "family viewing hour" on the networks in 1975, "The Man from U. N. C. L. E. " came under attack and practically disappeared from syndication, where it had once been a blue chip property. The fantasy element was mistaken for truth; the abundant police shows which replaced the genre which the series initiated were far more violent and considerably less palatable. Even bearing in mind the revelations of our C. I. A. and F. B. I. misconduct abroad and domestically with the political scandals of the 1970s, it is still difficult to conceive of an "enemy agent" literally sneezing herself to death with an explosive handkerchief as Patricia Medina did in "The Foxes and Hounds Affair. "

In 1965, Ace books began a series of paperbacks based on the series, though the stories were too mature for what was acceptable on television at the time. And Gold Key comics served to further popularize the series with children and young adolescents with their "U. N. C. L. E. " books beginning 1965. Some literature worth consulting would be the aforementioned John Brosnan's James Bond in the Cinema (Cranbury, N. J. : A. S. Barnes & Co. , 1972), and three reviews: Scot Leavitt's "A Show that Wouldn't Say Uncle, " in Life, 11 June 1965, p. 22; "The Man Inside the Man from U. N. C. L. E. , " in Time, 29 January 1965, p. 68; the exhilarating piece by Peter Bogdanovich for TV Guide, October 24-30, 1964, pp. 10-13.

The Regulars: Napoleon Solo, Robert Vaughn; Illya Kuryakin, David McCallum; Alexander Waverly, Leo G. Carroll; Del Floria, Mario Siletti.

The Episodes:

1. "The Vulcan Affair" [this was released as a feature film titled To Trap a Spy] (9-22-64) Patricia Crowley, Fritz Weaver, William Marshall, Ivan Dixon, Victoria Shaw, Rupert Crosse, Eric Berry
2. "The Iowa Scuba Affair" (9-29-64) Katherine Crawford, Slim Pickens, Shirley O'Hara, Margarita Cordova
3. "The Quadripartite Affair" (10-6-64) Jill Ireland, Anne Francis, Richard Anderson, Roger C. Carmel, John Van Dreelen, Robert Carricart
4. "The Shark Affair" (10-13-64) Robert Culp, Sue Ane Langdon,

Herbert Anderson, James Doohan, Hedley Mattingly, Rockne Tarkington

5. "The Deadly Games Affair" (10-20-64) Alexander Scourby, Janine Gray, Burt Brinckerhoff, Brooke Bundy, Ben Wright

6. "The Green Opal Affair" (10-27-64) Carroll O'Connor, Joan O'Brien

7. "The Giuoco Piano Affair" (11-10-64) Jill Ireland, Anne Francis, John Van Dreelen, James Frawley, Gorden Gilbert

8. "The Double Affair" [this was released as the feature film The Spy with My Face] (11-17-64) Senta Berger, Sharon Farrell, Michael Evans, Donald Harron

9. "The Project Strigas Affair" (11-24-64) William Shatner, Leonard Nimoy, Peggy Ann Garner, Susan Kraner, Werner Klemperer, Woodrow Parfrey

10. "The Finny Foot Affair" (12-1-64) Kurt Russell, Leonard Strong, Jay Simms

11. "The Neptune Affair" (12-8-64) Marta Kristen, Henry Jones, Jeremy Slate

12. "The Dove Affair" (12-15-64) Ricardo Montalban, June Lockhart, Emile Genest, Henry Lascol

13. "The King of Knaves Affair" (12-22-64) Paul Stevens, Diana Millay, Arlene Martel, Jan Merlin

14. "The Terbuf Affair" (12-29-64) Madlyn Rhue, Albert Paulsen, Alan Caillou, Jacques Aubuchon, Michael Forest

15. "The Deadly Decoy Affair" [episode with new opening sequence and special introduction by Vaughn] (1-11-65) Joanna Moore, Ralph Taeger, Irene Tedrow, Berry Kroeger

16. "The Fiddlesticks Affair" (1-18-65) Dan O'Herlihy, Marlyn Mason, Ken Murray

17. "The Yellow Scarf Affair" (1-25-65) Linden Chiles, Kamala Devi, Neile Adams, Murray Matheson, Vito Scotti, David Sheiner

18. "The Mad, Mad, Tea Party Affair" (2-1-65) Zohra Lampert, Richard Haydn, Peter Haskell, Lee Meriwether, Dean Harens

19. "The Secret Scepter Affair" (2-8-65) Gene Raymond, Lili Darvas, Ziva Rodann, Paul Lukather

20. "The Bow-Wow Affair" (2-15-65) Susan Oliver, Pat Harrington, Antoinette Bower

21. "The Four Steps Affair" (2-22-65) Luciana Paluzzi, Michel Petit, Malachi Throne, Susan Seaforth

22. "The See-Paris-and-Die Affair" (3-1-65) Kathryn Hays, Gerald Mohr, Lloyd Bochner, Alfred Ryder, Kevin Hagen, Marcel Hillaire

23. "The Brain Killer Affair" (3-8-65) Elsa Lanchester, Yvonne Craig, Abraham Sofaer, David Hurst, Henry Beckman, Nancy Kovack

24. "The Hong Kong Shilling Affair" (3-15-65) Glenn Corbett, Gavin MacLeod, Karen Sharpe, Richard O'Brien

25. "The Never-Never Affair" (3-22-65) Barbara Feldon, Cesar Romero, John Stephenson

26. "The Love Affair" (3-29-65) Eddie Albert, Robert H. Harris,

Maggie Pierce, Tracey Roberts
27. "The Gazebo in the Maze Affair" (4-5-65) George Sanders, Jeanette Nolan, John Alderson, John Orchard
28. "The Girls of Nazarone Affair" (4-12-65) Kipp Hamilton, Danica d'Hondt, Marion Moses
29. "The Odd Man Affair" (4-19-65) Martin Balsam, Barbara Shelley, Ronald Long, Hedley Mattingly

Second Season

30. "The Alexander the Greater Affair" [Part I; this was released as the film One Spy Too Many] (9-19-65) Rip Torn, Dorothy Provine, David Opatoshu, David Sheiner, Leon Lontoc, Donna Michelle
31. "The Alexander the Greater Affair" [Part II] (9-26-65) as above
32. "The Ultimate Computer Affair" (10-1-65) Judy Carne, Charles Ruggles, Roger C. Carmel, Susan Wedell, Judith Loomis
33. "The Foxes and Hounds Affair" (10-8-65) Patricia Medina, Vincent Price, Julie Sommars, Adam Roarke
34. "The Discotheque Affair" (10-15-65) Harvey Lembeck, Ray Danton, Evelyn Ward, Judi West
35. "The Re-Collectors Affair" (10-22-65) George Macready, Jocelyn Lane, Jacqueline Beer, Theodore Marcuse
36. "The Arabian Affair" (10-29-65) Phyllis Newman, Michael Ansara, Jerome Thor, Robert Ellenstein, Irene Tedrow
37. "The Tigers Are Coming Affair" (11-5-65) Jill Ireland, Lee Bergere, Jose De Vega, Florence Marley
38. "The Deadly Toys Affair" (11-12-65) Diane McBain, Angela Lansbury, Jay North, John Hoyt
39. "The Cherry Blossom Affair" (11-19-65) France Nuyen, Woodrow Parfrey
40. "The Virtue Affair" (12-3-65) Ronald Long, Mala Powers, Frank Marth, Marcel Hillaire
41. "The Children's Day Affair" (12-10-65) Jeanne Cooper, Warren Stevens, Eduardo Ciannelli, Susan Silo
42. "The Adriatic Express Affair" (12-17-65) Jesse Royce Landis, Juliette Mills
43. "The Yukon Affair" (12-24-65) George Sanders, Tianne Gabrielle, Marion Thompson, Bernie Gozier
44. "The Very Important Zombie Affair" (12-31-65) Claude Akins, Linda Gaye Scott
45. "The Dippy Blonde Affair" (1-7-66) Joyce Jameson, Robert Strauss
46. "The Deadly Goddess Affair" (1-14-66) Victor Buono, Brioni Farrell, Michael Strong, Steven Geray
47. "The Birds and the Bees Affair" (1-21-66) John McGiver, John Abbott, Vincent Beck, Anna Capri
48. "The Waverly Ring Affair" (1-28-66) Larry Blyden, Elizabeth Allen
49. "The Bridge of Lions Affair" [Part I] (2-4-66) Maurice Evans, Vera Miles, Bernard Fox, Ann Elder

50.  "The Bridge of Lions Affair" [Part II] (2-11-66) as above
51.  "The Foreign Legion Affair" (2-18-66) Howard Da Silva,
     Danielle de Metz, Rupert Crosse, Michael Pate
52.  "The Moonglow Affair" (2-25-66) Kevin McCarthy, Mary
     Ann Mobley, Norman Fell, Mary Carver
53.  "The Nowhere Affair" (3-4-66) Diana Hyland, David Sheiner,
     J. Pat O'Malley, Lou Jacobi
54.  "The King of Diamonds Affair" (3-11-66) Ricardo Montalban,
     Nancy Kovack
55.  "The Project Deephole Affair" (3-18-66) Jack Weston, Bar-
     bara Bouchet
56.  "The Round Table Affair" (3-25-66) Valora Noland, Reginald
     Gardiner, Bruce Gordon, Don Francks
57.  "The Bat Cave Affair" (4-1-66) Martin Landau, Joan Free-
     man, Whit Bissell
58.  "The Minus 'X' Affair" (4-8-66) Eve Arden, Sharon Farrell,
     Theodore Marcuse
59.  "The Indian Affairs Affair" (4-15-66) Richard Loo, Angela
     Dorian, Joe Mantell, Ted De Corsia

Third Season

60.  "The Her Master's Voice Affair" (9-16-66) Estelle Winwood,
     Joseph Ruskin, Marianne Osborne, Victoria Young
61.  "The Do-It-Yourself Dreadful Affair" (9-23-66) Jeannine
     Riley, Pamela Curran, Barry Atwater, Woodrow Parfrey
62.  "The Galatea Affair" (9-30-66) Joan Collins, Noel Harrison,
     Carl Esmond, Michael St. Clair
63.  "The Super Colossal Affair" (10-7-66) Shelley Berman, J.
     Carrol Naish, Carol Wayne
64.  "The Monks of St. Thomas Affair" (10-14-66) Celeste Yar-
     nell, David J. Stewart, John Wengraf, Horst Ebersberg,
     Henry Calvin
65.  "The Pop Art Affair" (10-21-66) Robert H. Harris, Sabrina
     Schaff, Sherry Alberoni, Nellie Burt
66.  "The Thor Affair" (10-28-66) Harry Davis, Bernard Fox,
     Linda Foster, Ken Renard, Arthur Batanides
67.  "The Candidate's Wife Affair" (11-4-66) Diana Hyland,
     Richard Anderson, Larry D. Mann, Anna-Lisa, Than Wyenn
68.  "The Come with Me to the Casbah Affair" (11-11-66) Abbe
     Lane, Danielle de Metz, Jacques Aubuchon, Pat Harrington
69.  "The Off-Broadway Affair" (11-18-66) Shari Lewis, Joan
     Huntington, Leon Askin, Charles Dierkop
70.  "The Concrete Overcoat Affair" [Part I] (11-25-66) Jack
     Palance, Janet Leigh, Joan Blondell, Eduardo Ciannelli,
     Allen Jenkins, Jack LaRue, Will Kuluva, Peggy Santon
71.  "The Concrete Overcoat Affair" [Part II] (12-2-66) as above
72.  "The Abominable Snowman Affair" (12-9-66) Anne Jeffreys,
     David Sheiner, Pilar Seurat, Stewart Hsich
73.  "The My Friend, the Gorilla Affair" (12-16-66) Percy
     Rodriguez, Joyce Jillson, Vitina Marcus, Alan Mowbray,
     George Barrows, Arthur Malet
74.  "The Jingle Bells Affair" (12-23-66) Akim Tamiroff, Ellen

Willard, Leon Belasco, Leonid Kinskey
75. "The Flying Saucer Affair" (12-30-66) Nancy Sinatra, Paul Lambert, Whitney Blake
76. "The Suburbia Affair" (1-6-67) Victor Borge, Beth Brickell, Reta Shaw, Richard Erdman
77. "The Deadly Smorgasbord Affair" (1-13-67) Robert Emhardt, Pamela Curran, Lynn Loring, Peter Brocco, Horst Ebersberg
78. "The Yo-Ho-Ho and a Bottle of Rum Affair" (1-20-67) Dan O'Herlihy, Kevin Hagen, Eddie Quillan, Peggy Taylor
79. "The Napoleon's Tomb Affair" (1-27-67) Kurt Kasznar, Ted Cassidy, Mercedes Moliner, Joseph Sirola
80. "The It's All Greek to Me Affair" (2-3-67) Harold J. Stone, Linda Marsh, George Keymas, Ted Roter
81. "The Hula Doll Affair" (2-17-67) Jan Murray, Patsy Kelly, Pat Harrington, Grace Gaynor
82. "The Pieces of Fate Affair" (2-24-67) Grayson Hall, Theodore Marcuse, Sharon Farrell, Charles Seel
83. "The Matterhorn Affair" (3-3-67) Bill Dana, Norman Chase, Vito Scotti, Oscar Beregi
84. "The Hot Number Affair" (3-10-67) Sonny and Cher Bono, George Tobias, Ned Glass, Joe Mantell
85. "The When in Rome Affair" (3-17-67) Julie Sommars, Cesare Danova, Kathleen Freeman, Than Wyenn
86. "The Apple-a-Day Affair" (3-24-67) Robert Emhardt, Jeannine Riley, Gil Lamb, Harry Swoger
87. "The Five Daughters Affair" [Part I] (3-31-67) Telly Savalas, Joan Crawford, Terry-Thomas, Herbert Lom, Jill Ireland, Curt Jurgens, Kim Darby, Diane McBain, Danielle de Metz
88. "The Five Daughters Affair" [Part II] (4-7-67) as above
89. "The Cap and Gown Affair" (4-14-67) Henry Jones, Tom Palmer, Larry Mann, Carole Shelyne, Melanie Alexander

## Fourth Season

90. "The Summit-5 Affair" (9-11-67) Albert Dekker, Lloyd Bochner, Don Chastain, Suzanne Cramer
91. "The Test Tube Killer Affair" (9-18-67) Christopher Jones, Paul Lukas, Lynn Loring, Lyn Peters, John Nealson, Martin Kosleck, Milton Parsons, D'Urville Martin
92. "The 'J' for Judas Affair" (9-25-67) Broderick Crawford, Chad Everett, Delphi Lawrence, Kevin Hagen, Claude Woolman
93. "The Prince of Darkness Affair" [Part I] (10-2-67) Bradford Dillman, Carol Lynley, Lola Albright, John Dehner, Julie London, John Carradine
94. "The Prince of Darkness Affair" [Part II] (10-9-67) as above
95. "The Master's Touch Affair" (10-16-67) Jack Lord, Nehemiah Persoff, Leslie Parrish
96. "The THRUSH Roulette Affair" (10-23-67) Michael Rennie, Charles Drake, Nobu McCarthy
97. "The Deadly Quest Affair" (10-30-67) Darren McGavin, Marlyn Mason, Timothy Carey, Peter Bourne, Bob Braiver

98. "The Fiery Angel Affair" (11-6-67) Joe Sirola, Perry Lopez, Rodolfo Hoyos, Madlyn Rhue, Victor Lundin
99. "The Survival School Affair" (11-20-67) Richard Beymer, Chris Robinson, Charles McGraw, Susan Odin, Ray Girardin
100. "The Gurnius Affair" (11-27-67) George Macready, Judy Carne, Will Kuluva, Joseph Ruskin, Frank Arno
101. "The Man from THRUSH Affair" (12-4-67) Barbara Luna, Robert Wolders, John Larch, Mario Alcaide
102. "The Maze Affair" (12-18-67) Anna Capri, Lawrence Montaigne, William Marshall, Barry Cahill, Charles Mayer, Ralph Moody
103. "The Deep Six Affair" (12-25-67) Alfred Ryder, Diana Van Der Vlis, Peter Bromilow, Dale Ishimoto
104. "The Seven Wonders of the World Affair" [Part I] (1-8-68) Eleanor Parker, Barry Sullivan, Mark Richman, Leslie Nielsen, Hugh Marlowe, Tony Bill, Dan O'Herlihy, Ruth Warrick, Albert Paulsen, Edgar Stehli, David Hurst, Richard Bull, Amy Thomson, Inger Stratton, Annella Bassett, Arthur Hanson
105. "The Seven Wonders of the World Affair" [Part II] (1-15-68) as above


DANIEL BOONE

Its back to historicity, this series made much of the legendary frontiersman. The name Boone is herein synonymous with words of action ("Boone what a doer," "Dream comer-truer") and of ego ("Daniel Boone was a man; yes, a big man")--curious Americana, it was certain to amass a large crowd of viewers. Fess Parker, well remembered as Walt Disney's Davy Crockett, was the hero; Patricia Blair as Boone's wife Rebecca; Darby Hinton as son Israel; Veronica Cartwright as daughter Jemina; Ed Ames as Indian friend Mingo.

The Regulars: Daniel Boone, Fess Parker; Rebecca Boone, Patricia Blair; Israel Boone, Darby Hinton; Jemima Boone, Veronica Cartwright; Cincinnatus, Dallas McKennon; Mingo, Ed Ames (first four seasons); Yadkin, Albert Salmi (first season only); Jericho Jones, Robert Logan (from episode of 9/23/65 to 4/28/66); Gideon, Don Pedro Colley (fifth season only); Josh Clements, Jimmy Dean (last two seasons); Gabe Cooper, Roosevelt Grier (last season only).

The Episodes:

1. "Ken-Tuck-E" (9-24-64) Robert Simon, Arch Johnson, Stephen Courtleigh, George Lindsey
2. "Tekaurtha McLeod" (10-1-64) Lynn Loring, Chris Alcaide, Edna Skinner
3. "My Brother's Keeper" (10-8-64) Ford Rainey, Peter Coe

4. "The Family Fluellen" (10-15-64) Bethel Leslie, Harold J. Stone, Donald Losley
5. "The Choosing" (10-29-64) David Brian, Richard Devon, Larry Chance
6. "Lac Duquesne" (11-5-64) Emile Genest, James Griffith
7. "The Sound of Wings" (11-12-64) Michael Rennie, Michael Pate, Frank de Kova
8. "A Short Walk to Salem" (11-19-64) James Waterfield, Charles Briggs
9. "The Sisters O'Hannrahan" (12-3-64) Fay Spain, Nina Shipman, Don Megowan
10. "Pompey" (12-10-64) Brock Peters, Peter Whitney
11. "Mountain of the Dead" (12-17-64) Leslie Nielsen, Ed Peck
12. "Not in Our Stars" (12-31-64) Walter Pidgeon, John Veryan
13. "The Hostages" (1-7-65) Madlyn Rhue, Ellen Corby, Rhodes Reason
14. "The Returning" (1-14-65) Pat Hingle, George Lewis
15. "The Prophet" (1-21-65) John Russell, Kevin Hagen, Patricia Huston
16. "The First Stone" (1-28-65) Geraldine Brooks, Kurt Russell, Gene Evans
17. "A Place of 1000 Spirits" (2-4-65) Macdonald Carey, Claude Akins
18. "The Sound of Fear" (2-11-65) Dan Duryea, Peter Duryea, Jack Elam, Jacques Aubuchon
19. "The Price of Friendship" (2-18-65) Lloyd Nolan, Kurt Russell, Myrna Fahey
20. "The Quietists" (2-25-65) Alexander Scourby, Mary Jayne Saunders
21. "The Devil's Four" (3-4-65) Bruce Cabot, James Best, Sean McClory, Whit Bissell
22. "The Reunion" (3-11-65) John McIntire, Marvin Brody
23. "The Ben Franklin Encounter" (3-18-65) Edward Mulhare, Laurie Main, Anna Lee
24. "Four-Leaf Clover" (3-25-65) George Gobel, Frank de Kova
25. "Cain's Birthday" [Part I] (4-1-65) Cesare Danova, Ted De Corsia, Connie Gilchrist
26. "Cain's Birthday" [Part II] (4-8-65) as above
27. "Daughter of the Devil" (4-15-65) Pilar Seurat, Frank Silvera, Mario Alcaide
28. "Doll of Sorrow" (4-22-65) Edward Binns, Chris Williams
29. "The Courtship of Jericho Jones" (4-29-65) Robert Logan, Anne Helm

## Second Season

30. "Empire of the Lost" (9-16-65) Edward Mulhare
31. [unknown title] (9-23-65) Laurie Main, Peter Mamakos, James Griffith
32. [unknown title] (9-30-65) Henry Silva, Simon Oakland
33. "My Name Is Rawls" (10-7-65) Rafer Johnson, Michael Conrad, Lawrence Montaigne
34. [unknown title] (10-14-65) Cyril Delevanti, Val Avery

35. "The Trek" (10-21-65) Ted White, Aldo Ray, John Lupton
36. "The Aaron Burr Story" (10-28-65) Leif Erickson, Michael
    St. Clair
37. "Cry of Gold" (11-4-65) Sarah Marshall, Maxwell Reed,
    Kenneth MacDonald, William O'Connell
38. "The Peace Tree" (11-11-65) Liam Redmond, Larry Doma-
    sin, Peter Oliphant, Nestor Paiva, Harold Goodwin, Ted
    White, Abel Fernandez
39. "The Thanksgiving Story" (11-25-65) John McIntire, Ted
    White, Abraham Sofaer, Rodolfo Acosta
40. "A Rope for Mingo" (12-2-65) Peter Coe, George Kennedy,
    Gloria Manon
41. "The First Beau" (12-9-65) Fabian Forte, Sam Jaffe, Myron
    Healey
42. "Perilous Journey" (12-16-65) Steve Ihnat, Alan Napier
43. "The Christmas Story" (12-23-65) Alizia Gur
44. "The Tamarack Massacre Affair" (12-30-65) Dina Merrill,
    Robert Lansing
45. "Gabriel" (1-6-66) Cesar Romero, Carlos Romero, Jacque-
    line Beer
46. "Seminole Territory" (1-13-66) Leonard Nimoy, Diana Ladd,
    Channing Pollack
47. "The Deserter" (1-20-66) Slim Pickens, Dick Sargent
48. "Crisis by Fire" (1-27-66) Rhodes Reason, George Sanders,
    Jeanne Cooper
49. "The Gun" (2-3-66) Robert Middleton, Milton Selzer
50. "The Prisoners" (2-10-66) Warren Stevens, Chris Alcaide
51. "The Fifth Man" (2-17-66) Cameron Mitchell, John Hoyt
52. "Gun-Barrel Highway" (2-24-66) John Kellogg, Arthur Space
53. "The Search" (3-3-66) Nita Talbot, Michael Ansara
54. "Fifty Rifles" (3-10-66) Henry Wilcoxon, William Mims
55. [unknown title] (3-17-66) Lloyd Bochner, Jack Lambert
56. "The Accused" (3-24-66) Jerome Thor, Joanna Moore, Ken
    Scott, E. J. Andre, Vaughn Taylor, L. E. "Buck" Young
57. "Cibola" (3-31-66) Royal Dano, Alejandro Rey
58. "The High Cumberland" [Part I] (4-14-66) Jacqueline Evans,
    Armando Silvestre
59. "The High Cumberland" [Part II] (4-21-66) as above

Third Season

60. "Dan'l Boone Shot a B'ar" (9-15-66) Dick Foran, Slim
    Pickens
61. "The Allegiances" (9-22-66) Paul Fix, Michael Pate
62. "Goliath" (9-29-66) Woody Strode, Jack Oakie, Ed Peck,
    Jerome Cowen
63. "Grizzly" (10-6-66) Rodolfo Acosta, Jeff York
64. "First in War, First in Peace" (10-13-66) Michael Rennie,
    Lane Bradford, John Hoyt
65. "Run a Crooked Mile" (10-20-66) Arthur Hunnicutt, Peter
    Graves, Myron Healey
66. "The Matchmaker" (10-27-66) Laurie Main, Brenda Benet,
    Peter Mamakos

67. [unknown title]  (11-3-66)  Raymond St. Jacques, Alan Baxter, Virginia Capers
68. "The Loser's Race"  (11-10-66)  Cameron Mitchell, Richard Devon
69. "The Enchanted Gun"  (11-17-66)  Michael Ansara, Robert Wilke
70. "Requiem for Craw Green"  (12-1-66)  John Crawford, Jeffrey Hunter, Sabrina Scharf, Malcolm Atterbury
71. "The Lost Colony"  (12-8-66)  Kathryn Walsh, Buck Taylor, John McLiam, Joseph Hoover
72. "River Passage"  (12-15-66)  Leif Erickson, Jim Davis, Robert Brubaker
73. "When a King Is a Pawn"  (12-22-66)  Cesare Danova, George Wallace, Morgan Mason, Lilyan Chauvan
74. "The Symbol"  (12-29-66)  Ricardo Montalban, Jeff Morrow, David Peel, Carole Cook, Jon Locke, Mike Ragan
75. "The Williamsburg Cannon" [Part I]  (1-12-67)  Keith Andes, Warren Stevens, Arch Johnson, Jack Lambert, Richard X. Slattery, Booth Colman, Michael Blodgett, George Backman
76. "The Williamsburg Cannon" [Part II]  (1-19-67)  as above
77. "The Wolf Man"  (1-26-67)  R. G. Armstrong, Ken Tobey, Don Haggerty
78. "The Jasser Ledbedder Story"  (2-2-67)  Sidney Blackmer, Corey Fischer
79. "When I Became a Man, I Put Away Childish Things"  (2-9-67)  Richard Sargent, Mala Powers
80. "The Long Way Home"  (2-16-67)  William Marshall, Lawrence Montaigne
81. "The Young Ones"  (2-23-67)  Claire Wilcox, Kurt Russell, Jeanne Cooper, Bob Anderson, Frankie Kabott
82. 'Delo Jones"  (3-2-67)  Jimmy Dean, Lyle Bettger, John Orchard
83. "The Necklace"  (3-9-67)  Philip Carey
84. "Fort West Point"  (3-23-67)  Kent Smith, Bill Fletcher, Alan Caillou, Hampton Fancher
85. "Bitter Mission"  (3-30-67)  Simon Oakland, Cesar Romero, Barry Kroeger, Mark Bailey
86. "Take the Southbound Stage"  (4-6-67)  Torin Thatcher, Arnold Moss, Henry Darrow, Paul Brinegar
87. "The Fallow Land"  (4-13-67)  John Ireland, Michael Forest, Steven Darrell, John Lodge

## Fourth Season

88. "The Ballad of Sidewinder and Cherokee"  (9-14-67)  Vito Scotti, Victor Buono, Forrest Tucker
89. "The Ordeal of Israel Boone"  (9-21-67)  Jim Davis, Teddy Eccles, Billy Corcoran, Rory O'Brien
90. "The Renegade"  (9-28-67)  Mark Richman, Gregory Walcott, Ric Natoli, Phyllis Avery
91. "Tanner"  (10-5-67)  Neville Brand, John Pickard, James Dobson
92. "Beaumarchais"  (10-12-67)  Robert Wolders, Maurice Evans,

Louise Sorel
93. "The King's Shilling" (10-19-67) Barbara Hershey, John Orchard, Mort Mills, Peter Bromilow, Jeff Pomerantz, Robie Porter
94. "The Inheritance" (10-26-67) regulars only
95. "The Traitor" (11-2-67) Kelly Thordsen, Patrick O'Moore, Lyn Peters, Joe Jenckes
96. "The Value of a King" (11-9-67) James Gregory, Ken Gampu, Dort Clark
97. "The Desperate Raid" (11-16-67) Jacques Bergerac, Hampton Fancher, William Mims
98. "The Spanish Horse" (11-23-67) Michael Burns, Robert Emhardt, Bill Williams, Henry Jones, Russ McCubbin, Jimmy Murphy
99. "Chief Mingo" (12-7-67) John Larch
100. "The Secret Code" (12-14-67) David Opatoshu, Lloyd Bochner, Edward Mulhare
101. "A Matter of Blood" (12-28-67) William Smith, Andrienne Hayes, Harry Bellaver, Mme. Spivy
102. "The Scrimshaw Ivory Chart" (1-4-68) Ted Cassidy, James Westerfield, Jim Backus
103. "The Imposter" (1-18-68) Jimmy Dean, Lloyd Bochner, Harold Gould
104. "The Witness" (1-25-68) John Carradine, Virginia Gregg, Sheldon Collins, Jon Walmsley
105. "The Flaming Rocks" (2-1-68) Jimmy Dean, Dorothy Green, R. G. Armstrong, Michael Witney
106. "Then Who Will They Hang from the Yardarm if Willy Gets Away?" (2-8-68) Wilfrid Hyde-White, Martin Horsey
107. "Fort New Madrid" (2-15-68) Gary Conway, Theo Marcuse, Ken Swofford
108. "Heroes Welcome" (2-22-68) Charles Drake, Sarah Marshall, Robert Wilke
109. "Orlando, the Prophet" (2-29-68) Hans Conried, Anthony Alda
110. "The Far Side of Fury" (3-7-68) Don Pedro Colley, Med Flory, Johnny Cardos, Ezekial Williams
111. "Nightmare" (3-14-68) Hans Wedemeyer
112. "Thirty Pieces of Silver" (3-28-68) Herbert Anderson, Warren Kemmerling, Andrew Prine, Virginia Christine
113. "Faith's Way" (4-4-68) Julie Harris, Jeff Morrow, Claude Woolman

Fifth Season

114. "Be Thankful for the Fickleness of Women" (9-19-68) Sean McClory, Brooke Bundy, James Davidson
115. "The Blackbirder" (10-3-68) Timothy Carey, Jim McMullan
116. "The Dandy" (10-10-68) Sheldon Allman, David Watson, Johnny Cardos
117. "The Fleeing Nuns" (10-24-68) Kathleen Freeman, Brioni Farrell, Maurice Marsac, Marcel Hillaire, Jim McMulla
118. "The Plague That Came to Ford's Run" (10-31-68) Charle

Drake, Gail Kobe, Ted White, Kevin Hagen, Richard
Devon, Pete Logan
119. "The Bait" (11-7-68) Skip Ward, Kelly Thordsen, Lois
Nettleton
120. "Big, Black and Out There" (11-14-68) Yaphet Kotto
121. "Flag of Truce" (11-21-68) William Smith, Mort Mills,
Mark Miranda, H. M. Wynant
122. "The Valley of the Sun" (11-28-68) Mariette Hartley, Severn Darden
123. "The Patriot" (12-5-68) Ford Rainey, Tom Lowell, Teddy
Eccles
124. "The Return of Sidewinder" (12-12-68) Forrest Tucker,
Rex Holman
125. "Minnow for a Shark" (1-2-69) Henry Jones, Ivor Barry,
George Keymas, Jack Bannon, Morry Ogden
126. "To Slay a Giant" (1-9-69) Don Pedro Colley, Torin
Thatcher
127. "A Tall Tale of Prater Beasely" (1-16-69) Lyle Bettger,
Jeff Donnell, Burl Ives, Rory Stevens
128. "Copperhead Izzy" (1-30-69) Vincent Price, Elena Verdugo,
J. Pat O'Malley
129. "Three Score and Ten" (2-6-69) Burgess Meredith, Paul
Fix
130. "Jonah" (2-13-69) Yaphet Kotto, Michael Lane
131. "Bickford's Bridge" (2-20-69) Simon Oakland, Kurt Russell
132. "A Touch of Charity" (2-27-69) Shelley Fabares, John
Davidson
133. "For Want of a Hero" (3-6-69) Richard Anderson, Arch
Johnson
134. "Love and Equity" (3-13-69) Victor French, Burl Ives,
Med Flory
135. "The Allies" (3-27-69) Dick Foran, Ronne Troup
36. "A Man Before His Time" (4-3-69) Ronny Howard, Warren
Vanders
137. "For a Few Rifles" (4-10-69) Michael Dante, Ted De Corsia
38. "Sweet Molly Malone" (4-17-69) Barbara Bel Geddes, Jack
Kruschen
39. "A Pinch of Salt" (5-1-69) Joan Hackett, Donna Baccala

## ixth Season

40. "A Very Small Rifle" (9-18-69) Roger Miller, Eddie Little
Sky, Johnny Jensen, Armando Silvestre, Kevin Hagen
41. "The Road to Freedom" (10-2-69) Floyd Patterson, George
Spell, Warren Vanders, Jim Davison
42. "Benvenuto ... Who?" (10-9-69) Marj Dusay, Leon Askin
43. "The Man" (10-16-69) George Backman, Gene Evans
44. "The Printing Press" (10-23-69) Fredd Wayne, Peter
Bromilow
45. "The Traitor" (10-30-69) Jill Ireland, Ed Flanders
46. "The Grand Alliance" (11-13-69) Cesar Romero, Armando
Silvestre

147. "Target Boone" (11-20-69) Will Geer, Kurt Russell, Ron Soble
148. "A Bearskin for Jamie Blue" (11-27-69) Christopher Connelly
149. "The Cache" (12-4-69) James Doohan, Alex Carras, Vaughn Taylor, John Kellogg
150. "The Terrible Tarbots" (12-11-69) Strother Martin, Anthony Costello, Zalman King
151. "Hannah Comes Home" (12-25-69) Teddy Eccles
152. "An Angel Cried" (1-8-70) Mariette Hartley, Carlos Rivas
153. "Perilous Passage" (1-15-70) Gloria Graham, John Davidson, Liam Sullivan
154. [unknown title] (1-22-70) Gail Kobe, Laurie Main, Ian Ireland
155. "Mamma Cooper" (2-5-70) Ethel Waters, Tyler McVey
156. "Before the Tall Man" (2-12-70) Marianna Hill, Burr De Benning
157. "Run for the Money" (2-19-70) Jack Albertson, Peter Mamakos
158. "A Matter of Vengeance" (2-26-70) Linda Marsh, David McLean
159. "The Landlords" (3-5-70) Lloyd Bochner, Victor French
160. "Readin', Ritin', and Revolt" (3-12-70) Tony Davis, William O'Connell
161. "Noblesse Oblige" (3-26-70) Philip Proctor, Virginia Christine, Murray MacLeod, David Watson, Elizabeth Bauer
162. "The Homecoming" (4-9-70) David Opatoshu
163. "Bringing Up Josh" (4-16-70) Ty Wilson, Jodie Foster
164. "How to Become a Goddess" (4-30-70) Paul Mantee, Ruth Warrick
165. "Israel and Love" (5-7-70) Tim O'Connor, Robin Mattson

TWELVE O'CLOCK HIGH

Frequently as mournful as a dirge (ponder the plight, for one, of the former actor whom the War leaves disfigured in "The Albatross"), this was based on the superior 1949 film of the Sy Bartlett and Berne Lay Jr. novel of members of the 8th Air Force stationed in England. As Brigadier General Frank Savage, Robert Lansing could castigate with the intensity of his film predecessor, Gregory Peck.

The Regulars: Brig. Gen. Frank Savage, Robert Lansing (first season only); Col. Joe Gallagher, Paul Burke (last two seasons); Maj. Gen. Wiley Crowe, John Larkin; Maj. Gen. Harvey Stovall, Frank Overton; Maj. Joe Cobb, Lew Gallo; Maj. 'Doc" Kaiser, Barney Phillips; T/Sgt. Sandy Komansky, Chris Robinson; Brig. Gen. Ed Britt, Andrew Duggan; Fowler, Robert Dornan (last season only).

The Episodes:

1. "Golden Boy Had Nine Black Sheep" (9-18-64) Paul Burke
2. "Follow the Leader" (9-25-64) Andrew Prine
3. "The Men and the Boys" (10-2-64) Lou Antonio, Glenn Corbett
4. "The Sound of Distant Thunder" (10-16-64) Jill Haworth, Peter Fonda, John Alderman
5. "The Climate of Doubt" (10-23-64) Viveca Lindfors, Bernard Fox, Carl Benton Reid
6. "Pressure Point" (10-30-64) Larry Gates, Robert Doyle, Paul Newlan
7. "Decision" (11-6-64) John Van Dreelen, Tim O'Connor
8. "The Hours Before Dawn" (11-13-64) Glynis Johns, Fritz Weaver
9. "Appointment at Liége" (11-20-64) Gary Lockwood, Nancy Kovack
10. "Interlude" (11-27-64) Dana Wynter, Ken Berry, Rhys Williams
11. "Here's to Courageous Cowards" (12-4-64) Dabney Coleman, Brandon DeWilde, Noreen Corcoran, Gerald O'Loughlin
12. "Soldiers Sometimes Kill" (12-11-64) John Williams, Victoria Shaw, Murray Matheson
13. "The Suspected" (12-18-64) Michael Callan, Edward Binns, Antoinette Bower
14. "An Act of War" (12-25-64) Michael Davis, John Kerr, Jay Novello, Emile Genest
15. "Those Who Are About to Die" (1-1-65) Sally Kellerman, Glenn Corbett, Tom Skerritt, Dee Pollock, Robert Yuro, Ken Lynch
16. "In Search of My Enemy" (1-8-65) Steve Forrest, Barbara Shelley, Roy Thinnes, Hazel Court, John Milford
17. "The Albatross" (1-15-65) Robert Drivas, Janine Gray, Martin West
18. "The Lorelei" (1-22-65) Rip Torn, Bruce Dern, Diana Van Der Vlis
19. "Faith, Hope, and Sergeant Aronson" (1-29-65) Sorrell Booke, Phyllis Love, Antoinette Bower
20. "To Heinie, with Love" (2-5-65) Keir Dullea, Jill Haworth, Paul Newlan, Stewart Moss
21. "The Clash" (2-12-65) Albert Paulsen, Burt Metcalfe
22. "The Ticket" (2-26-65) Earl Holliman, Elen Willard, Jud Taylor
23. "The Trap" (3-5-65) Hermione Baddeley, John Leyton, David Frankham
24. "End of the Line" (3-12-65) Paul Burke, Barbara Feldon, Sarah Marshall
25. "The Threat" (3-19-65) Stanja Lowe, Harold Gould, Laurence Naismith
26. "Mutiny at 10,000 Feet" (3-26-65) Larry Blyden, John Kerr, Robert Brown
27. "The Mission" (4-2-65) Burt Brinckerhoff, Bruce Dern, Rudy Solari

28. "The Cry of Fallen Birds" (4-9-65) Dana Wynter, Lloyd
     Bochner, John Zaremba
29. "V for Vendetta" (4-16-65) Gary Lockwood, Lin McCarthy
30. "P.O.W." [Part I] (4-23-65) Alf Kjellin, James Farentino,
     Peter Haskell, Donald Harron, John Van Dreelen
31. "P.O.W." [Part II] (4-30-65) as above
32. "The Hero" (5-7-65) James Whitmore, John Zaremba

Second Season

33. "The Loneliest Place in the World" (9-13-65) Robert Col-
     bert, Claudine Longet, Paul Carr, William Arvin, Jack
     Raine, Leo Gordon
34. "Rx for a Sick Bird" (9-20-65) Gia Scala, Tige Andrews,
     J. D. Cannon, James Brolin, Don Quine, Paul Comi
35. "Then Came the Mighty Hunter" (9-27-65) Beau Bridges,
     Tom Skerritt, Ted Bessell, Carol Booth, Willard Sage
36. "The Idolater" (10-4-65) Gary Lockwood, Lee Meriwether
37. "Big Brother" (10-11-65) Julie Adams, Jack Lord, Robert
     Colbert, Bernard Fox
38. "The Hot Shot" (10-18-65) Jill Ireland, Warren Oates, Jill
     Haworth, Walter Brooke
39. "Show Me a Hero, I'll Show You a Bum" (10-25-65) Lloyd
     Bochner, Lois Nettleton, Burt Reynolds, Anne Whitfield
40. "Runaway in the Dark" (11-1-65) Jill Haworth, Albert Paul-
     sen, Jack Weston, Pat Cardi
41. "I Am the Enemy" (11-8-65) William Shatner, Elen Willard,
     Peter Marko, Walter Gregg, Claude Johnson
42. "Grant Me No Favor" (11-15-65) Barry Sullivan, Frank
     Aletter, Jacqueline Russell
43. "Storm at Twilight" (11-22-65) Ted Knight, William Cort,
     James Devine
44. "We're Not Coming Back" (11-29-65) Ina Balin, George
     Voskovec, Gunnar Hellstrom, John Hoyt, Michael Forest
45. "The Jones Boys" (12-6-65) Bruce Dern, Andrew Prine,
     John Ward, Burt Reynolds, Susan Seaforth, Mark Richman,
     Logan Field
46. "Between the Lines" (12-13-65) Donald Harron, Larry Gates
47. "Target 802" (12-27-65) Lisa Pera, Lou Antonio
48. "Falling Star" (1-3-66) James Daly, Barbara Shelley, David
     Macklin, Paul Comi
49. "The Slaughter Pen" (1-10-66) Michael Rennie, Harry
     Guardino
50. "The Underground" (1-17-66) Robert Walker Jr., Claudine
     Longet, Whit Bissell
51. "Which Way the Wind Blows" (1-24-66) Dina Merrill,
     Robert Yuro
52. "The Outsider" (1-31-66) James MacArthur, Lee Meriwether
53. "Back to the Drawing Board" (2-7-66) Alf Kjellin, Burgess
     Meredith, Robert Doyle
54. "Twenty-Fifth Mission" (2-14-66) Bradford Dillman, Don
     Galloway
55. "The Survivor" (2-21-66) Jill Ireland, Don Quine, Don Gord

56. "Angel Babe" (2-28-66) Roddy McDowall, Frank Aletter
57. "Decoy" (3-7-66) Michael Callan, Steve Harris
58. "The Hollow Man" (3-14-66) Robert Drivas, Paul Carr
59. "Cross-Hairs on Death" (3-21-66) James Franciscus, Roger Perry
60. "Day of Reckoning" (3-28-66) Charles Aidman, John Van Dreelen
61. "Siren Voices" (4-4-66) Edward Mulhare, Victoria Shaw

Third Season

62. "Gauntlet of Fire" (9-9-66) William Windom, Tim McIntire, Linden Chiles, Ron Foster
63. "Massacre" (9-16-66) Kevin McCarthy, Michael Constantine, Kathleen Widdoes, Paul Comi, John Zaremba, Lt. Gen. Archie Old (portrays himself)
64. "Face of a Shadow" (9-23-66) Jack Lord, Phillip Pine, Luciana Paluzzi
65. "Fortress Weisbaden" (9-30-66) Christiane Schmidtmer, Bernard Fox, Lloyd Bochner
66. "A Distant Cry" (10-7-66) Robert Blake, Roy Thinnes, Wayne Rogers, Susan Seaforth
67. "Practice to Deceive" (10-14-66) Diana Hyland, Eduard Franz, John Van Dreelen
68. "The All-American" (10-28-66) Robert Doyle, Susan Brown, Norman Fell, Matt Healswit
69. "The Pariah" (11-4-66) Albert Salmi, Robert Walker Jr.
70. "Fighter Pilot" (11-11-66) Marlyn Mason, Stephen Young, Don Gordon
71. "To Seek and Destroy" (11-18-66) Richard Anderson, David Frankham
72. "Burden of Guilt" (12-2-66) James Broderick, John Ward, Richard Anderson, Wesley Addy
73. "The Ace" (12-9-66) James Whitmore, Joe Maross
74. "Six Feet Under" (12-16-66) Rudy Solari, Martin Milner, Richard Anderson
75. "Duel at Mont Sainte Marie" (12-23-66) Joseph Campanella, Lilia Skala, Edward Mulhare
76. "Graveyard" (12-30-66) Don Marshall, Ossie Davis, Jon Voight, Joe Maross
77. "A Long Time Dead" (1-6-67) Peter Graves, Anne Helm, Tom Skerritt
78. "The Hunters and the Hunted" (1-12-67) Ralph Bellamy, Michael Witney, Anna Capri

THE REPORTER

Playwright Jerome Weidman conceived this not well received study of a New York roving reporter and columnist (Harry Guardino as Danny Taylor) and his hard-nosed editor (Gary Merrill as Lou Sheldon). The initial teleplay of a juvenile gang rape was composed by Hal Lee and Tom Gries; other episodes were authored by George Bellak ("How Much for a Prince?") and Weidman himself ("Rope's End"). Other regulars were George O'Hanlon as cabdriver Artie Burns and Remo Pisani as bartender Ike Dawson.

The Regulars: Danny Taylor, Harry Guardino; Lou Sheldon, Gary Merrill; Artie Burns, George O'Hanlon; Ike Dawson, Remo Pisani.

The Episodes:

1. "Extension Seven" (9-25-64)
2. "Hideout" (10-2-64) Richard Conte, Anne Francis, Kurt Kasznar, Earl Wilson (as himself)
3. "How Much for a Prince?" (10-9-64) Jack Lord, Nick Adams, Herb Edelman; Frank Gifford in a cameo role
4. "Rope's End" (10-16-64) Millie Perkins, Renee Taylor, Nan Martin, William Hickey, James Luisi
5. [unknown title] (10-30-64) William Shatner, Gene Raymond
6. "The Man Behind the Badge" (11-6-64) Franchot Tone, Constance Bennett, Dyan Cannon, Dan Fraser
7. "Super-Star" (11-20-64) Janice Rule, Efrem Zimbalist Jr., Zohra Lampert, James Farentino
8. "Murder by Scandal" (11-27-64) Larry Blyden
9. "A Time to Be Silent" (12-4-64) Eddie Albert, Sidney Blackmer, Claude Rains, Lee Philips, Mildred Dunnock, Pippa Scott, Michael Conrad
10. "The Lost Lady Blues" (12-11-64) Barry Sullivan, Elizabeth Allen, Roy Thinnes
11. "Vote for Murder" (12-18-64) Arthur Hill, Myrna Fahey, Simon Oakland, Edward Asner

BRANDED

"What do you do when you're branded?"/You fight for your name"--the musical refrain which essentially explained the premise in this weekly parable of trust and mistrust, courage and cowardice (as the producers saw it). The avenger was Captain Jason McCord (Chuck Connors) who was ceremoniously dismissed in disgrace when believed a deserter at the Battle of Bitter Creek.

The Regulars: Jason McCord, Chuck Connors.

The Episodes:

1. "Survival" (1-24-65) Alex Cord
2. "The Vindicators" (1-31-65) June Lockhart, Claude Akins, John Litel, Harry Carey Jr., Johnny Jensen
3. "The Test" (2-7-65) Jason Evers, Joe De Santis, Michael Keep, Jay Silverheels
4. [unknown title] (2-14-65) Jeanne Cooper, Brad Weston,

Russ Conway
5. "The Bounty" (2-21-65) Pat Conway, Gene Evans, Michael Ansara, Julie Reding
6. "Leap Upon Mountains..." (2-28-65) John Ireland, John Leslie
7. "Coward Step Aside" (3-7-65) Richard Arlen, Johnny Crawford
8. "The Mission" [Part I] (3-14-65) John Carradine, Kamala Devi, Macdonald Carey, Peter Breck, H. M. Wynant, Rochelle Hudson
9. "The Mission" [Part II] (3-21-65) as above
10. "The Mission" [Part III] (3-28-65) as above
11. "The First Kill" (4-4-65) Chad Everett, James Dunn, John Pickard
12. "Very Few Heroes" (4-11-65) Tom Drake, Kathryn Hays
13. "One Way Out" (4-18-65) John Dehner, Paul Brent, Jim Davis, Eddie Little Sky, X Brands, Iron Eyes Cody
14. "That the Brave Endure" (4-25-65) Marie Windsor, Tommy Sands, Willard Sage
15. "A Taste of Poison" (5-2-65) Carol Rossen, Walter Burke, Stuart Margolin
16. "Price of a Name" (5-23-65) Marilyn Maxwell, Keith Andes, Don Megowan

Second Season

17. "Judge Not" (9-12-65) Tom Drake, Warren Oates, Kathleen Crowley, Willard Sage, Harry Harvey Sr., Clint Sharp
18. "Now Join the Human Race" (9-19-65) Burt Reynolds, Noah Beery, James Anderson, Ann Morell
19. "Mightier than the Sword" (9-26-65) Lola Albright, Kevin Hagen, Michael Lane, Maureen Arthur
20. "I Killed Jason McCord" (10-3-65) Bruce Bennett, Karen Steele, Larry Pennell
21. "The Bar Sinister" (10-10-65) Stephen McNally, Michel Petit, Marian Seldes
22. "Seward's Folly" (10-17-65) Coleen Gray, Ian Wolfe, J. Pat O'Malley
23. "Salute the Soldier Briefly" (10-24-65) Michael Rennie, Jim Davis, John Pickard, Claude Hall
24. "The Richest Man in Boot Hill" (10-31-65) Lee Van Cleef, J. Pat O'Malley
25. "Fill No Glass for Me" [Part I] (11-7-65) Greg Morris, Michael Keep, Harry T. Lauter, Duncan McLeod, Henry Brandon
26. "Fill No Glass for Me" [Part II] (11-14-65) as above
27. "The Greatest Coward on Earth" (11-21-65) Pat O'Brien, Dick Clark, James Chandler, Pamela Curran
28. "$10,000 for Durango" (11-28-65) Martha Hyer, John Agar, Gregg Palmer, Lloyd Bochner
29. "Romany Roundup" [Part I] (12-5-65) Nico Minardos, Gary Merrill, Anna Capri, Joan Huntington, Don Collier, Alan Batter

30. "Romany Roundup" [Part II] (12-12-65) as above
31. "A Proud Town" (12-19-65)
32. "The Golden Fleece" (1-2-66) Harry Townes, Bing Russell, William Phipps
33. "The Wolfers" (1-9-66) Zeme North, Bruce Dern, Morgan Woodward
34. "This Stage of Fools" (1-16-66) Martin Landau, Rex Ingram
35. "A Destiny Which Made Us Brothers" (1-23-66) James MacArthur, William Bryan
36. "McCord's Way" (1-30-66) Mona Freeman, Ben Johnson
37. "Nice Day for a Hanging" (2-6-66) John Anderson, Whitney Blake, Beau Bridges
38. "Barbed Wire" (2-13-66) Rod Cameron, Sherry Jackson, Leif Erickson
39. "Yellow for Courage" (2-20-66) Patricia Medina, Michael Forest
40. "Call to Glory" [Part I] (2-27-66) David Brian, Robert Lansing, Michael Pate, Lee Van Cleef, Kathie Browne, H. M. Wynant, Felix Locher
41. "Call to Glory" [Part II] (3-6-66) as above
42. "Call to Glory" [Part III] (3-13-66) as above
43. "The Ghost of Murrieta" (3-20-66) Dolores Del Rio, Jose De Vega, Rafael Campos, Linda Dangcil
44. "The Assassins" [Part I] (3-27-66) Peter Graves, John Carradine, Kamala Devi
45. "The Assassins" [Part II] (4-3-66) as above
46. "Headed for Doomsday" (4-10-66) Burgess Meredith, Robert Q. Lewis
47. "Cowards Die Many Times" (4-17-66) Lola Albright, John Ireland, Bill Catching
48. "Kellie" (4-24-66) Suzanne Cupito

FOR THE PEOPLE

Once again the disenfranchised have their causes wonderfully championed (the former convict whose testimony is doubted in David Karp's "A Competent Witness"; a wrongly accused vagrant of Dave and Andy Lewis' "... guilt shall not escape nor innocence suffer ...") in this excellent Herbert Brodkin successor to his classic "The Defenders."

The Regulars: Assistant District Attorney David Koster, William Shatner; Phyllis Koster, Jessica Walter; Celese, Howard Da Silva; Malloy, Lonny Chapman.

The Episodes:

1. "... to prosecute all crimes ..." (1-31-65) Allan Bunce, Patrick McVey, Gerald O'Loughlin
2. "... guilt shall not escape nor innocence suffer ..." (2-14-65) Paul Hartman, Tom Carlin, Ruth White

3. "The Influence of Fear" (2-21-65) Philip Bosco, Jamie Sanchez, Diana Douglas
4. "Act of Violence" [Part II of 2/23/65 episode of "The Nurses"] (2-28-65) Joan Lorring, Leora Dana, Joseph Campanella, Nehemiah Persoff
5. "Between Candor and Shame" (3-7-65) Lloyd Gough, Phil Leeds, Neva Patterson, John C. Backer
6. "... the killing of one human being ..." (3-14-65) Peggy Wood, Martin Sheen, Robert Drivas, Larry Haines, Philip Bosco
7. "Dangerous to the Public Peace and Safety" (3-21-65) Tony Bill, Lesley Ann Warren, David Doyle
8. "Secure Any Special Privilege or Advantage" (3-28-65) Carol Rossen, Dick Shawn
9. "The Right to Kill" (4-4-65) Gary Merrill, Polly Rowles, Al Freeman Jr., Horace MacMahon
10. "With Intent to Influence" (4-11-65) John Beal, Lee Grant, John Randolph, Larry Gates
11. "Seized, Confined and Detained" (4-25-65) Lloyd Bochner, Don Francks, Logan Ramsey, John Henry Faulk
12. "Any Benevolent Purpose" (5-2-65) James Whitmore, William Daniels, Eduard Franz
13. "A Competent Witness" (5-9-65) Ned Glass, Lou Antonio, Larry Haines, Arny Freeman

SECRET AGENT

Patrick McGoohan returned as security agent John Drake (introduced with the 1961 entry 'Danger Man") in this acclaimed, subtle espionage tale.

The Regulars: John Drake, Patrick McGoohan.

The Episodes:

1. "The Battle of the Cameras" (4-3-65) Dawn Addams, Niall MacGinnis
2. "A Room in the Basement" (4-10-65) Jane Merrow, William Lucas, Mark Digman
3. "Fair Exchange" (4-17-65) Lelia Goldoni, James Maxwell, George Mikell
4. "Fysh on the Hook" (4-24-65) Dawn Addams, Peter Bowles
5. "No Marks for Servility" (5-1-65) Howard Marion Crawford, Mervyn Johns, Francesa Annis
6. "Yesterday's Enemies" (5-15-65) Peter Copley, Maureen Connell
7. "The Professionals" (5-22-65) Alex Scott, Nadja Regin
8. "A Date with Doris" (5-29-65) Jane Merrow, Ronald Radd, James Maxwell
9. "The Mirror's New" (6-5-65) Donald Houston, Mary Yeomans
10. "Colony Three" (6-12-65) Katherine Woodville

11. "It's Up to the Lady" (6-19-65) Sylvia Sidney, Robert Urquhart
12. "Whatever Happened to George Foster?" (6-26-65) Bernard Lee, Adrienne Corri, Jill Melford
13. "The Galloping Major" (7-3-65) William Marshall, Errol John
14. "The Colonel's Daughter" (7-10-65) Michael Trubshawe, Zia Moyheddin
15. "That's Two of Us Sorry" (7-17-65) Frances Annis, Finlay Currie, Nigel Green
16. "Such Men Are Dangerous" (7-24-65) Lee Montague, John Cairney, Georgina Ward
17. "A Man to Be Trusted" (7-31-65) Harvey Ashby, Patricia Donahue
18. "The Affair at Castelevara" (8-7-65) Eric Pohlmann, Harold Goldblatt
19. "Don't Nail Him Yet" (8-14-65) John Fraser, Sheila Allen
20. "The Ubiquitous Mr. Lovegrove" (8-21-65) Eric Barker, Adrienne Corri
21. "Have a Glass of Wine" (8-28-65) Ann Lynn, Warren Mitchell
22. "You're Not in Any Trouble, Are You?" (9-4-65) Susan Hampshire, André Van Gyseghem
23. "Sting in the Tail" (9-11-65) Darren Nesbitt, Ronald Radd

Second Season

24. "The Black Book" (12-4-65) Georginna Ward, Griffith Jones, Jack Gwillim, Patricia Haines
25. "English Lady Takes Lodgers" (12-11-65) Gabriella Licudi
26. "Loyalty Always Pays" (12-18-65) Johnny Sekka, Errol John
27. "Are You Going to Be More Permanent?" (12-25-65) Susan Hampshire, Maxwell Shaw
28. "Parallel Lines Sometimes Meet" (1-1-66) Moira Redmond, Errol John, Earl Cameron, Clifton James
29. "A Very Dangerous Game" (1-8-66) Yvonne Furneaux, Peter Arne, Poulet Tu
30. "The Mercenaries" (1-15-66) Patricia Donahue, John Slater
31. "The Outcast" (1-22-66) Bernard Breslaw, Patricia Haines
32. "Judgment Day" (1-29-66) Alexandra Stewart, John Woodrine
33. "To Our Good Friend" (2-5-66) Donald Houston, Ann Bell
34. "Say It with Flowers" (2-12-66) Ian Hendry
35. "The Man on the Beach" (2-19-66) Barbara Steele, Glyn Houston
36. "The Man Who Wouldn't Talk" (2-26-66) Jane Merrow, Norman Rodway
37. "Someone Is Liable to Get Hurt" (3-5-66)
38. "Dangerous Secret" (3-12-66) Elizabeth Shepherd, Lydon Brook
39. "I Can Only Offer You Sherry" (3-19-66) Wendy Craig, Anthony Newlands, Bernard Archard, Ben Ari
40. "The Hunting Party" (3-26-66) Moira Lister, Denholm Elliot
41. "Two Birds with One Bullet" (4-2-66) Geoffrey Keen, Lelia

Goldoni
42. "I Am Afraid You Have the Wrong Number" (4-9-66) Paul
Eddington, Jeanne Moody
43. "The Man with the Foot" (4-16-66) Bernard Lee, Robert
Urquhart
44. "The Paper Chase" (4-23-66) Joan Greenwood, Kenneth J.
Warren
45. "The Not-So-Jolly Roger" (4-30-66) Edwin Richfield, Lisa
Daniely

TRIALS OF O'BRIEN

At long last--the earthy attorney--as conceived by Richard Alan Simmons, with Peter Falk wonderful as the divorced protagonist, his mannerisms (years before "Columbo") believable. Superlative scripts by veteran television writers George Ballak ("The Trouble with Archie"), David Ellis ("No Justice for the Judge") and Don M. Mankiewicz ("The 10-Foot, Six-Inch Pole").

The Regulars: Daniel J. O'Brien, Peter Falk; Katie O'Brien, Joanna Barnes; Miss G, Elaine Stritch; Margaret, Ilka Chase; Great McGonigle, David Burns; Garrison, Dolph Sweet.

The Episodes:

1. "Over Defense Is Out" (9-18-65) Murray Hamilton, Kathy Cody, Vincent Gardenia, Ned Glass
2. "Bargain Day on the Street of Regret" (9-25-65) Robert Blake, Hershel Bernardi, Tony Musante, Albert Dekker, Charles Dierkop, Judi West
3. "Notes on a Spanish Prisoner" (10-2-65) Buddy Hackett, Martyn Green, Mary Tahmin
4. "Never Bet on Anything that Talks" (10-9-65) Phil Foster, Marian Hailey, Kenneth Mars
5. "What Can Go Wrong?" (10-16-65) Roger Moore, Michael Constantine
6. "Good-bye and Keep Cool" (10-23-65) Cloris Leachman, Marian Hailey, Robert Loggia
7. "A Gaggle of Girls" (10-30-65) Reni Santoni, Tammy Grimes, Jennifer West, David Doyle
8. "The Trouble with Archie" (11-6-65) Theodore Bikel, Lou Jacobi, Alice Ghostley, Simon Oakland
9. "How Do You Get to Carnegie Hall?" (11-13-65) Kurt Kasznar, Zohra Lampert, Dana Elcar, Norman Fell, Frank Langella
10. "Charlie Has All the Luck" (11-20-65) Jack Albertson, Martin Sheen, Tony Roberts, Philip Bosco, Judi West, Joe Smith
11. "Picture Me a Murder" (11-27-65) Alan Alda, Harold J. Stone, Joanna Pettet, Jessica Walter, John Randolph
12. "Dead End on Flugel Street" (12-3-65) Milton Berle, Rita

Moreno, Ann Corio, Hal March
13. "No Justice for the Judge" (12-10-65) Burgess Meredith
14. "Leave It to Me" (12-17-65) Angela Lansbury
15. "Alarums and Excursions" (1-7-66) John McGiver, Estelle Parsons, Marc Connelly
16. "The 10-Foot, Six-Inch Pole" (1-14-66) Faye Dunaway, Murray Hamilton, Albert Paulsen, Will Geer
17. "A Horse Called Destiny" (1-21-66) Barbara Barrie, J. D. Cannon, Jack Ging
18. "The Blue Steel Suite" (1-28-66) Pat Hingle, Warren Finnerty, Tony Musante, Al Freeman Jr.
19. "The Partridge Papers" (2-4-66) Paul Massie, Sheila MacRae
20. "The Greatest Game" [Part I] (3-4-66) Nehemiah Persoff, Britt Ekland, David Carradine, George Coulouris
21. "The Greatest Game" [Part II] (3-11-66) as above
22. "The Only Game in Town" (3-18-66) Gene Hackman, Brock Peters, Alejandro Rey, Will Geer, Robert Walker Jr.


THE LONER

Unusual western (its theme a welcome relief) of an Appomattox veteran (Lloyd Bridges as William Colton) who embarks on a philosophical odyssey of personal fulfillment once obsessed with the ravages of war. A Rod Serling conception, several of the episodes bear his artistic stamp.

The Regulars: William Colton, Lloyd Bridges.

The Episodes:

1. "An Echo of Bugles" (9-18-65) Tony Bill, Whit Bissell, John Hoyt
2. "The Vespers" (9-25-65) Jack Lord, Joan Freeman, Ron Soble
3. "The Lonely Calico Queen" (10-2-65) Jeanne Cooper, Edward Faulkner, Tracy Morgan
4. "The Kingdom of McComb" (10-9-65) Leslie Nielsen, Tom Lowell, Ken Drake, Ed Peck
5. "One of the Wounded" (10-16-65) Anne Baxter, Lane Bradford, Paul Richards
6. "The Flight of the Arctic Tern" (10-23-65) Janine Gray, Tom Stern, Larry Ward
7. "Widow on the Evening Stage" (10-30-65) Katherine Ross, Tom Stern
8. "The House Rules at Mrs. Wayne's" (11-6-65) Nancy Gates
9. "The Sheriff of Fetterman's Crossing" (11-13-65) Allan Sherman, Harold Peary, Dub Taylor, Robin Hughes
10. "The Homecoming of Lemuel Stove" (11-20-65) Brock Peters, Russ Conway, Don Keefer, John Pickard
11. "Westward the Shoemaker" (11-27-65) David Opatoshu,

Warren Stevens
12.  "The Oath" (12-4-65) Barry Sullivan
13.  "Escort for a Dead Man" (12-11-65) Sheree North
14.  "Hunt the Man Down" (12-18-65) Burgess Meredith, Tom Tully
15.  "The Ordeal of Bud Windom" (12-25-65) Sonny Tufts
16.  "To the West of Eden" (1-1-66) Ina Balin, Zalman King
17.  "Mantrap" (1-8-66) Bethel Leslie, Pat Conway
18.  "A Little Stroll to the End of the Line" (1-15-66) Dan Duryea, Robert Emhardt
19.  "The Trial in Paradise" (1-22-66) Robert Lansing, Edward Binns
20.  "A Question of Guilt" (1-29-66) James Gregory, Jean Hale
21.  "The Mourners for Johnny Sharp" [Part I] (2-5-66) Beau Bridges, James Whitmore, Pat Hingle
22.  "The Mourners for Johnny Sharp" [Part II] (2-12-66) as above
23.  "Incident in the Middle of Nowhere" (2-19-66) Mark Richman, Beverly Garland
24.  "Pick Me Another Time to Die" (2-26-66) Martin Brooks, Ed Peck, Lewis Charles
25.  "The Burden of the Badge" (3-5-66) Victor Jory, Lonnie Chapman
26.  "To Hang a Dead Man" (3-12-66) Bruce Dern, Howard Da Silva

THE F.B.I.

By the grace of J. Edgar Hoover--weekly dramas drawn from its files, with rather posh use of the camera (William W. Spencer) and an indefatigable agent hero (Efrem Zimbalist Jr. as Lew Erskine). The series--suggesting more than coincidence--ceased filming just about the time the agency itself was having its ethics scrutinized.

The Regulars: Inspector Lewis Erskine, Efrem Zimbalist Jr.; Barbara Erskine, Lynn Loring (first season episodes); Assistant Director Arthur Ward, Philip Abbott; Jim Rhode Stephen Brooks (first two seasons); Tom Colby, William Reynolds (third through eighth seasons); Chris Daniels, Shelly Novack (last season).

The Episodes:

1.  "The Monster" (9-19-65) Jeffrey Hunter, Dina Merrill, Estelle Winwood, Julie Parrish
2.  "Image in a Cracked Mirror" (9-26-65) Jack Klugman, Brett Somers, Ed Peck, Pat Cardi
3.  "A Mouthful of Dust" (10-3-65) Alejandro Rey, Robert Blake, R. G. Armstrong, Noam Pitlik
4.  "Slow March Up a Steep Hill" (10-10-65) Peter Deuel,

Harold Gould, Dabney Coleman, Lee Meriwether
5. "The Insolents" (10-17-65)  Eileen Heckart, Susan Seaforth, Ben Wright, Joan Marshall, James Ward
6. "To Free My Enemy" (10-24-65)  Jill Haworth, James Gregory, Katherine Bard, Billy Halop
7. "The Problem of the Honorable Wife" (10-31-65)  Mark Richman, Jason Evers, Miiko Taka, Donald Harron
8. "Courage of a Conviction" (11-7-65)  Susan Oliver, Barry Russo, Edward Andrews
9. "The Exiles" (11-14-65)  Marisa Pavan, Carlos Montalban, Lin McCarthy, Perry Lopez, John Zaremba
10. "The Giant Killer" (11-21-65)  Robert Duvall, David Sheiner, Patricia Smith, Lee Meriwether, William Zuckert, Robert Brubaker
11. "All the Streets Are Silent" (11-28-65)  James Farentino, Burt Reynolds, Pilar Seurat, Norman Fell, Joe Maross
12. "An Elephant Is Like a Rope" (12-5-65)  Beau Bridges, Wright King, Larry Gates, Ted Knight
13. "How to Murder an Iron Horse" (12-12-65)  David Macklin, Claude Akins
14. "Pound of Flesh" (12-19-65)  Leslie Nielsen, Bruce Dern
15. "The Hijackers" (12-26-65)  John McIntire, Arthur O'Connell
16. "The Forests of the Night" (1-2-66)  John Anderson, Michael Burns, Robert Colbert, Ellen Corby, Ian Wolfe, Val Avery, Med Florey, Ruth Packard
17. "The Chameleon" (1-9-66)  James Daly, Margaret Leighton, Lloyd Gough
18. "The Sacrifice" (1-16-66)  Ed Begley, Nancy Wickwire, Albert Paulsen
19. "Special Delivery" (1-23-66)  Earl Holliman, Barbara Luna, Donald May
20. "Quantico" (1-30-66)  Michael Callan, Robert Walker Jr.
21. "The Spy Master" (2-6-66)  Kevin McCarthy, Patrick O'Neal, Keye Luke
22. "The Baby Sitter" (2-13-66)  Colleen Dewhurst, Geoffrey Horne, Collin Wilcox
23. "Flight to Harbin" (2-27-66)  Arthur Hill, Milton Selzer, Jason Evers, Jessica Walter
24. "The Man Who Went Crazy by Mistake" (3-6-66)  J. D. Cannon, Anthony Eisley, Simon Scott
25. "The Divided Man" (3-20-66)  Bradford Dillman, Jacqueline Scott, Dabbs Greer, Douglas Henderson, William Sargent
26. "The Defector" [Part I] (3-27-66)  Paul Lukas, Dana Wynter, John Van Dreelen, George Voskovec, Carl Benton Reid
27. "The Defector" [Part II] (4-3-66)  as above
28. "The Tormentors" (4-10-66)  Lew Ayres, Wayne Rogers, Edward Asner
29. "The Animal" (4-17-66)  Charles Bronson, Tim McIntire
30. "The Plunderers" (4-24-66)  Ralph Meeker, Albert Salmi, Don Quine
31. "The Bomb That Walked Like a Man" (5-1-66)  Robert Drivas, Andrew Duggan

Second Season

32. "The Price of Death" (9-18-66) Robert Blake, Scott Mar-
    lowe, Milton Selzer, John Larch, David Macklin, Barry
    Russo
33. "The Escape" (10-2-66) Roy Thinnes, Marlyn Mason, Steve
    Ihnat, Paul Comi
34. "The Assassin" (10-9-66) William Windom, Dean Jagger,
    Ted Knight, Tom Skerritt
35. "The Cave-In" (10-16-66) John McIntire, Buck Taylor, Tim
    McIntire, John McLiam
36. "The Scourge" (10-23-66) Robert Duvall, Lin McCarthy,
    Will Kuluva, David Sheiner, Mary La Roche
37. "The Plague Merchant" (10-30-66) Arthur Hill, Peggy
    McCay, Michael Strong, Eduard Franz
38. "Ordeal" (11-6-66) Gerald S. O'Loughlin, Jacqueline Scott,
    George Wallace, Paul Bryar
39. "Collision Course" (11-13-66) Jack Lord, Malcolm Atter-
    bury, Pilar Seurat, Richard Anderson
40. "Vendetta" (11-20-66) John Van Dreelen, David Opatoshu,
    Alfred Ryder, Lois Nettleton
41. "Anatomy of a Prison Break" (11-27-66) Joseph Campanella,
    Carol Rossen, James Broderick
42. "The Contaminator" (12-4-66) Linden Chiles, Sarah Mar-
    shall, William Sargent, William Stephens
43. "The Camel's Nose" (12-11-66) Diane Baker, Murray Hami-
    ton, Fritz Weaver
44. "List for a Firing Squad" (12-18-66) Charles Korvin, Suzan
    Pleshette, Oscar Beregi, Anthony Eisley
45. "The Death Wind" (12-25-66) Ralph Bellamy, Elizabeth
    Allen, Mark Richman
46. "The Raid" (1-1-67) Nita Talbot, Ralph Meeker, John Mil-
    ford, Rudy Solari, Ken Lynch
47. "Passage into Fear" (1-8-67) Collin Wilcox, James Calla-
    han, Ford Rainey, Virginia Christine
48. "The Courier" (1-15-67) Gene Hackman, Ruth Roman,
    Phyllis Love, Dean Harens, Harold Gould, Cherylene Lee
49. "A Question of Guilt" (1-22-67) Andrew Duggan, Larry
    Gates, Don Dubbins, Paul Mantee
50. "The Gray Passenger" (1-29-67) Barbara Luna, Alejandro
    Rey, Henry Wilcoxon
51. "The Conspirators" (2-5-67) Michael Rennie, Julie Sommar
    Phyllis Thaxter, Arthur Franz, Dabney Coleman
52. "Rope of Gold" (2-12-67) Peter Graves, Louis Jourdan,
    William Smithers, Jessica Walter, Joanne Linville
53. "Hostage" (2-19-67) Edward Mulhare, Paul Lukas, Delphi
    Lawrence, Diana Hyland
54. "Sky on Fire" (2-26-67) Bradford Dillman, Lynda Day,
    Davey Davison
55. "Flight Plan" (3-5-67) J. D. Cannon, Antoinette Bower
56. "The Executioners" [Part I] (3-12-67) Robert Drivas, Susan
    Strasberg, Celeste Holm, Telly Savalas, Robert Duvall,
    Walter Pidgeon

7. "The Executioners" [Part II] (3-19-67) as above
8. "The Satellite" (4-2-67) Tim O'Connor, Karen Black, Tim McIntire, Ellen Corby, Paul Comi, Tom Lowell
9. "Force of Nature" (4-9-67) James Franciscus, Anne Helm, Tige Andrews, Vaughn Taylor
0. "The Extortionist" (4-16-67) Wayne Rogers, Barbara Luna, Carlos Montalban, Ned Romero, Rodolfo Hoyos

Third Season

1. "Gold Card" (9-17-67) James Daly, Joanna Moore, Larry Gates, Vic Perrin
2. "Counter-Stroke" (10-1-67) Kevin McCarthy, William Smithers, Skip Ward, Jessica Walter
3. "Flood Verdict" (10-8-67) Kent Smith, Pilar Seurat, R. G. Armstrong, Mario Alcaide, Norma Crane, Ken Lynch, Robert Doyle
4. "Traitor" (10-15-67) Andrew Duggan, Phyllis Thaxter, Richard Anderson, Delphi Lawrence
5. "By Force and Violence" [Part I] (10-22-67) William Windom, Arthur Hill, Phyllis Love, David Macklin, Louise Latham, Don Gordon, Dabbs Greer
6. "By Force and Violence" [Part II] (10-29-67) as above
7. "A Sleeper Wakes" (11-5-67) John Kerr, Dana Wynter, Eduard Franz, John Van Dreelen, Viveca Lindfors, Virginia Smith
8. "Overload" (11-12-67) Diana Hyland, Scott Marlowe, Harry Bellaver, Martha Scott, John Considine
9. "Line of Fire" (11-26-67) Lynda Day, Henry Silva, Dean Harens, Lyn Edgington, Carlos Romero, George Keymas, Jan Shepard
0. "Blueprint for Betrayal" (12-3-67) Alf Kjellin, Antoinette Bower, Maria Palmer, Donald Davis
1. "False Witness" (12-10-67) Carol Lynley, Peter Deuel, Victor French, Forrest Compton, Jay Lanin, Parley Baer, Kelly Thordsen, Paul Lukather, Dean Harens
2. "The Legend of John Rim" (12-31-67) Tom Skerritt, Wayne Rogers, Katherine Justice, Royal Dano, Ford Rainey, Ralph Moody
3. "The Dynasty" (1-7-68) Martin Sheen, Edward Asner, Russell Johnson, John Kerr, Jim McMullan
4. "The Daughter" (1-14-68) Michael Rennie, Harold Gould, Julie Sommars, Phyllis Hill, Charles Bateman
5. "Act of Violence" (1-21-68) Burt Reynolds, Diana Muldaur, Michael Strong, Frank Aletter, Johnny Seven
6. "Crisis Ground" (1-28-68) Robert Drivas, Simon Scott, Robert Hogan, Arch Johnson
7. "Ring of Steel" (2-4-68) Michael Callan, Tom Bosley, Brooke Bundy, Michael Tolan
8. "The Homecoming" (2-11-68) David Opatoshu, John Kerr, Richard Kiley, Bettye Ackerman, Victoria Shaw
9. "The Phone Call" (2-18-68) John Ericson, Sarah Marshall, Laraine Stephens, Roy Poole

80. "Region of Peril" (2-25-68) Anne Baxter, Mark Roberts,
    Arthur Franz, Hal Lynch, Steve Ihnat
81. "Southwind" (3-3-68) Bradford Dillman, John Vernon, Mako
    Mario Alcaide
82. "The Messenger" (3-17-68) Robert Walker Jr., Robert
    Doyle, Patricia Harty, Anthony Eisley
83. "The Ninth Man" (3-24-68) Burr DeBenning, Murray Hamil
    ton, Milton Selzer, Anne Helm, Wayne Rogers, Rodolfo Hoy
84. "The Mechanized Accomplice" (3-31-68) Andrew Prine,
    Bobby Sherman, Lynn Bari, Will Kuluva, Jason Wingreen
85. "The Predators" (4-7-68) Mark Richman, Linden Chiles,
    Nico Minardos, Diana Van Der Vlis, Richard X. Slattery
86. "The Tunnel" (4-21-68) Scott Marlowe, Joanna Moore, Ed-
    ward Binns, Paul Mantee, Charles Aidman
87. "The Mercenary" (4-28-68) Richard Anderson, Fritz Weav-
    er, Suzanne Pleshette, Norman Fell, Celeste Yarnell,
    Peter Brocco, Barry Atwater, Lew Brown

Fourth Season

88. "Wind It Up and It Betrays You" (9-22-68) Louis Jourdan,
    Michael Tolan, Kaz Garas, Nancy Kovack, Lawrence
    Dane, George Neise, Lyn Edgington, James Sikking
89. "Out of Control" (9-29-68) James Franciscus, Simon Scott
    Armando Silvestre
90. "The Quarry" (10-6-68) Dean Stockwell, Suzanne Pleshette
    John Milford, Roy Poole, Noam Pitlik, Richard Devon,
    Lou Frizzell
91. "The Runaways" (10-13-68) J. D. Cannon, Ronny Howard,
    Dabbs Greer, Jan Shepard
92. "Death of a Fixer" (10-20-68) Joseph Campanella, Dan
    Travanty, Jessica Walter, Brooke Bundy
93. "The Enemies" (11-3-68) Jeffrey Hunter, Al Freeman Jr., Ri
    chard Anderson, Cicely Tyson, Dean Harens, Curt Lowens
94. "The Nightmare" (11-10-68) William Windom, Bruce Dern,
    Lee Meriwether, Patricia Smith
95. "Breakthrough" (11-17-68) Mark Richman, Dorothy Provine
    Grant Williams, Edward Andrews
96. "The Harvest" (11-24-68) Diane Baker, Robert Duvall,
    Larry Gates, Burt Brinckerhoff
97. "The Intermediary" (12-1-68) Maurice Evans, Burr De Be
    ning, Michael Strong, Monte Markham
98. "The Butcher" (12-8-68) Ralph Bellamy, Harold Gould, A
    Helm, Charles Korvin
99. "The Flaw" (12-15-68) Barry Morse, Victoria Shaw, Donald
    Harron
100. "The Hero" (12-22-68) Chad Everett, Lynda Day, Patrick
    Wayne, Paul Lukather
101. "Eye of the Storm" (1-5-69) Billy Dee Williams, Denise
    Nicholas, Moses Gunn
102. "The Fraud" (1-12-69) Hal Holbrook, Nan Martin, William
    Smithers
103. "A Life in the Balance" (1-19-69) James Caan, Jennifer

West, Julie Sommars, Murray Hamilton, Quentin Dean
104. "Caesar's Wife" (1-26-69) Michael Rennie, Claudine Longet, Russell Johnson
105. "The Patriot" (2-2-69) Ned Romero, Gilbert Roland, Thomas Gomez, James Callahan, Marianna Hill
106. "The Maze" (2-9-69) Simon Oakland, Ina Balin, Steve Ihnat, Joan Van Ark
107. "Attorney" (2-16-69) Arthur Hill, Linden Chiles, Tim O'Connor
108. "The Catalyst" (2-23-69) Alejandro Rey, Norman Fell, Pilar Seurat
109. "Conspiracy of Silence" (3-2-69) Kent Smith, Kevin McCarthy, James Daly, Gene Tierney
110. "The Young Warriors" (3-9-69) Scott Marlowe, Lin McCarthy, Anthony Caruso, Barbara Luna
111. "The Cober List" (3-23-69) Harold J. Stone, Rudy Solari, Don Gordon, Fred Beir, Alfred Ryder
112. "Moment of Truth" (3-30-69) Richard Carlson, Marlyn Mason, Michael Witney, Gary Vinson, Dean Harens

Fifth Season

113. "Target of Interest" (9-14-69) Linden Chiles, Diane Baker, Eduard Franz, Melissa Murphy
114. "Nightmare Road" (9-21-69) Burr DeBenning, Davey Davison, Robert Duvall
115. "Swindler" (9-28-69) Vera Miles, Peter Donat, William Schallert
116. "Boomerang" (10-5-69) Carl Betz, Brooke Bundy, Jeff Bridges
117. "Silent Partners" (10-12-69) Cicely Tyson, Robert Hooks, Walter Burke, Robert Yuro, Wesley Addy
118. "Gamble with Death" (10-19-69) Michael Callan, Laraine Day, Simon Scott, Anne Helm
119. "Flight" (10-26-69) Michael Witney, Charlotte Stewart, Brenda Benet
120. "The Challenger" (11-2-69) Fritz Weaver, Richard Anderson, Joanne Linville
121. "Blood Tie" (11-9-69) Julie Adams, Scott Marlowe, Michael Tolan, Donna Baccala
122. "The Sanctuary" (11-16-69) Billy Dee Williams, Lola Falana, Booker Bradshaw
123. "The Scapegoat" (11-23-69) Brenda Vaccaro, Arthur Franz, Michael Burns
124. "The Inside Man" (11-30-69) Lloyd Bochner, Lawrence Dane, Oscar Beregi, Janis Hansen
125. "The Prey" (12-7-69) Mildred Dunnock, Steve Ihnat, Joanna Barnes, Bettye Ackerman
126. "Journey into Night" (12-14-69) John Vernon, Anthony Eisley, Dabbs Greer, Michael Kearney
127. "The Doll Courier" (12-21-69) Viveca Lindfors, William Smithers, Josephine Hutchinson, Penny Fuller
128. "Tug-of-War" (12-28-69) Barry Nelson, Don Gordon, Michele Carey, Frank Campanella

129. "The Fatal Imposter" (1-4-70) Gerald S. O'Loughlin, Norma Crane, David Cassidy, Mary Fickett
130. "Conspiracy of Corruption" (1-11-70) James Olson, Katherine Justice, J. D. Cannon
131. "The Diamond Millstone" (1-18-70) Jack Klugman, Pilar Seurat, Dan Travanty, Murray Matheson
132. "Deadly Reunion" (1-25-70) Alf Kjellin, Dana Wynter, Sandra Smith, Chris Robinson, John Van Dreelen
133. [unknown title] (2-1-70) David Opatoshu, Phyllis Love
134. "Summer Terror" (2-8-70) Lin McCarthy, Pamela McMyler Joe Don Baker
135. "Return to Power" (2-15-70) Mark Richman, Christopher George, Lynda Day, Anthony Caruso
136. "The Dollar" (2-22-70) Nina Foch, Edward Binns, Paul Mantee, Vincent Beck
137. "Deadfall" (3-1-70) Zohra Lampert, Robert Drivas, Anne Francis, Paul Picerni, Wayne Rogers
138. "The Quest" (3-8-70) Earl Holliman, Larry Gates, Morgan Sterne, Richard O'Brien

Sixth Season

139. "The Condemned" (9-20-70) Martin Sheen, Royal Dano, Tim McIntire, Joan Van Ark
140. "The Traitor" (9-27-70) Bradford Dillman, Wayne Rogers, William Sargent, Antoinette Bower
141. "Escape to Terror" (10-4-70) Harry Guardino, James Olson, Marge Redmond, Linda Marsh
142. "The Architect" (10-11-70) Monte Markham, Billy Dee Williams, Dabbs Greer, Arthur Franz
143. "The Savage Wilderness" (10-18-70) Don Stroud, Ellen Corby, Darleen Carr, David Macklin
144. "Time Bomb" (10-25-70) Wayne Maunder, Diana Ewing, Geoffrey Deuel, Mark Jenkins
145. "The Innocents" (11-1-70) Lois Nettleton, Larry Blyden, Joan Hotchkis
146. "The Deadly Pact" (11-8-70) Ivan Dixon, Hari Rhodes, Robert Loggia, James McEachin, Booker Bradshaw
147. "The Impersonator" (11-22-70) Phyllis Kirk, Stuart Whitman, Mariette Hartley, Kent Smith, Marj Dusay
148. "Antennae of Death" (11-29-70) William Shatner, Bettye Ackerman, Astrid Warner, Felice Orlandi, Victor Campo
149. "The Target" (12-6-70) Eric Braeden, Karin Dor, David Frankham, Jerry Douglas
150. "The Witness" (12-13-70) Roger Perry, Murray Hamilton, Flora Plumb, June Dayton, Don Grady
151. "Incident in the Desert" (12-20-70) Richard Evans, Charles Robinson, Steve Ihnat, Dabney Coleman
152. "The Inheritors" (12-27-70) Suzanne Pleshette, Ray Danton Gene Raymond, Lawrence Linville
153. "The Unknown Victim" (1-3-71) Fabian Forte, Tom Skerrit Lynne Marta, John Lasell, Woodrow Parfrey, Norma Connolly

154. "The Stalking Horse" (1-10-71)  Steve Forrest, Diana Hyland, Lawrence Pressman, Harold Gould
155. "Center of Peril" (1-17-71)  Vic Morrow, Gary Collins, Susan Howard, Robert Cornthwaite
156. "Eye of the Needle" (1-24-71)  Richard Kiley, Michael Baseleon, Robert Yuro, Coleen Gray
157. "The Fatal Connection" (1-31-71)  Barbara Billingsley, Scott Marlowe, Andrew Duggan, Gary Crosby
158. "The Replacement" (2-7-71)  Charles Korvin, Phyllis Thaxter, Sorrell Booke, Peter Brandon
159. "Death Watch" (2-14-71)  Glenn Corbett, Richard Jaeckel, Frank Hotchkiss, Solomon Sturges, Diane Keaton, Angel Tompkins
160. "Downfall" (2-21-71)  Carl Betz, Michael Burns, Anne Archer
161. "The Hitchhiker" (2-28-71)  Michael Douglas, Donna Mills, Richard Kelton
162. "Turnabout" (3-7-71)  Warren Oates, Joyce Van Patten, Ahna Capri, Berry Kroeger
163. "The Natural" (3-14-71)  Peter Mark Richman, Anthony Costello, Victor Holchak, Walter Burke
164. "Three Way Split" (3-21-71)  Lex Barker, Albert Salmi

Seventh Season

165. "Death on Sunday" (9-12-71)  Frank Converse, Linda Marsh, Andrew Prine
166. "Recurring Nightmare" (9-19-71)  Belinda Montgomery, Ralph Meeker, Tim McIntire, Barbara Billingsley
167. "The Last Job" (9-26-71)  David Canary, John McIntire, Guy Stockwell, Jess Walton, Jeanette Nolan
168. "The Deadly Gift" (10-3-71)  Fritz Weaver, Dana Wynter, Joan Van Ark, John Lasell
169. "Dynasty of Hate" (10-10-71)  Earl Holliman, Bryan Montgomery, Henry Silva, Dabbs Greer
170. "The Mastermind" [Part I] (10-17-71)  Bradford Dillman, Steve Ihnat, Scott Marlowe, Clu Gulager, Jennifer Billingsley
171. "The Mastermind" [Part II] (10-24-71)  as above
172. "The Watch Dog" (10-31-71)  Stuart Whitman, Sharon Acker, Joan Delaney, Charles Robinson
173. "The Game of Terror" (11-7-71)  Alex Nicol, Richard Thomas, Gary Tigerman, Jerry Houser
174. "End of a Hero" (11-21-71)  Ed Nelson, Lee Meriwether, Kaz Garas, Joseph Hindy
175. "Superstition Rock" (11-28-71)  Wayne Rogers, Lou Antonio, Dana Elcar, Michael Baseleon
176. "The Minerva Tapes" (12-5-71)  Louis Jourdan, David Birney, Donald Harron
177. "Bitter Harbor" (12-12-71)  Cameron Mitchell, Joseph Wiseman
178. "The Recruiter" (12-19-71)  Arthur Franz, Jessica Walter, Monte Markham

179. "The Buyer" (1-2-72) Tim O'Connor, Stefanie Powers, David Hedison
180. "A Second Life" (1-9-72) Martin Sheen
181. "The Break-Up" (1-16-72) Donna Mills, Jerry Ayres
182. "Judas Goat" (1-23-72) John Davidson, Linden Chiles, Katherine Justice
183. "The Hunters" (1-30-72) Hurd Hatfield, Richard Kiley, George Voskovec, Robert Mandan, Nan Martin
184. "Arrangement with Terror" (2-6-72) Diana Hyland, Robert Loggia, Roger Perry, Reni Santoni
185. "The Set-Up" (2-13-72) Burr DeBenning, Sian Barbara Allen, Jessica Tandy, Robert Pine, Gerald S. O'Loughlin
186. "The Test" (2-20-72) John Colicos, Robert Foxworth, Harold Gould, Jay Novello, Barbara Babcock
187. "The Corruptor" (2-27-72) Robert Drivas, Rick Kelman, Pamela Shoop
188. "The Deadly Species" (3-5-72) Penny Fuller, Tom Skerritt, Milt Kamen, James Hampton
189. "Dark Journey" (3-12-72) Claude Akins, William Schallert, Lindsay Wagner
190. "Escape to Nowhere" (3-19-72) Diana Muldaur, John Vernon, Lee Harcourt Montgomery, Joseph Perry, Gene Lyons

Eighth Season

191. "The Runner" (9-17-72) David Soul, Belinda Montgomery, Jim Davis, Robert Urich, Arch Whiting, John Yates
192. "Edge of Desperation" (9-24-72) Michael Tolan, Jacqueline Scott, Anthony Costello, Karen Carlson
193. "The Fatal Showdown" (10-1-72) Joseph Campanella, Wayne Maunder, Marlyn Mason, Karl Held
194. "The Franklin Papers" (10-8-72) Dina Merrill, Richard Anderson, Dan Travanty, Jennifer Salt
195. "The Gopher" (10-15-72) Peter Mark Richman, Reni Santoni, Jonathan Lippe, Arlene Golonka
196. "End of a Nightmare" (10-22-72) Dean Stockwell, Darleen Carr, Regis Toomey
197. "The Engineer" (10-29-72) Ed Nelson, Michael Strong, Andrew Parks, Robert Yuro
198. "A Game of Chess" (11-5-72) Patrick O'Neal, George Nader, David Frankham, Alfred Ryder, Russ Conway, Lew Palter
199. "The Wizard" (11-12-72) Ross Martin, Norman Alden, Larry Golden, Marj Dusay
200. "The Loner" (11-19-72) Billy Green Bush, Lane Bradbury, John Anderson
201. "Canyon of No Return" (11-26-72) Frank Converse, Albert Salmi, Henry Darrow, Louise Sorel, Jack Ging, Mark Allen
202. "Holiday with Terror" (12-3-72) Patricia Mattick, June Dayton, Christopher Stone, Jeff Donnell, Lynne Marta, Mark Miller

203. "The Jug-Marker" (12-10-72) William Windom, Tom Troupe, Ben Frank, Victor Holchaki
204. "The Outcast" (12-17-72) Michael Callan, Katherine Justice, John Larch, Richard Evans, Val Avery
205. "Dark Christmas" (12-24-72) Don Gordon, Eugene Peterson, Sondra Locke, John Lupton
206. "The Rap Taker" (1-7-73) Scott Marlowe, Stephen McNally, Robert Drivas, Brooke Bundy, Milt Kamen, Carol Vogel
207. "A Gathering of Sharks" (1-14-73) David Hedison, Jessica Walter, Jill Haworth, Quinn Redeker, Joe di Reda
208. "The Disinherited" (1-21-73) Martin Sheen, Heidi Vaughn, Dan Tobin, John McLiam
209. "Desperate Journey" (1-28-73) Vic Morrow, Burr DeBenning, Sandra Smith
210. "The Double Play" (2-4-73) Stuart Whitman, Robert Foxworth, Tim McIntire, Mariette Hartley, Biff Elliott
211. "The Wedding Gift" (2-11-73) Penny Fuller, Dewey Martin, John Ericson
212. "The Detonator" (2-25-73) Richard Jordan, Tim O'Connor, Roger Perry, Meredith MacRae
213. "Sweet Evil" (3-4-73) Andrew Prine, Melissa Murphy, Jo Ann Harris, Michael Baseleon, Robert H. Harris, Dabbs Greer
214. "Memory of a Legend" (3-11-73) Pat Hingle, Geoffrey Deuel, Lawrence Dane, Brett Somers
215. "Night of the Long Knives" (3-25-73) Tim O'Connor, Meredith MacRae, Roger Perry, Richard Jordan, Alex Cord, Edward Haynes
216. "The Loper Gambit" (4-1-73) Robert F. Lyons, Leslie Charleston, Larry Gates, Tom Lowell

Ninth Season

217. "The Big Job" (9-16-73) Mark Gordon, Richard Anderson, Paul Fix, Charles Knox Robinson, Marj Dusay
218. "The Confession" (9-30-73) Nancy Wilson, Hal Linden, Lorraine Gary, Lynne Moody
219. "Break-In" (10-7-73) Jackie Cooper, Don Stroud, Nancy Malone, Kevin Coughlin, Lou Frizzell
220. "The Payoff" (10-14-73) Earl Holliman, Jacqueline Scott, Paul Richards, Gene Dynarski, Joseph Wiseman
221. "The Exchange" (10-21-73) Ron Randell, Scott Marlowe, Antoinette Bower, Jesse Vint
222. "Town of Terror" (10-28-73) Mario Roccuzzo
223. "Fatal Reunion" (11-4-73) Ed Nelson, Hari Rhodes, Susan Oliver, Alfred Ryder, Michael Bell, Dana Elcar
224. "Rules of the Game" (11-18-73) John Marley
225. "Fool's Gold" (11-25-73) Leslie Nielsen, Lou Antonio
226. "The Killing Truth" (12-9-73) Lloyd Nolan, Tim O'Connor
227. "The Bought Jury" (12-16-73) Frank De Kova, Joel Fabiani, Frank Campanella, Mark Allen
228. "Ransom" (12-30-73) Anne Francis, Zalman King, Jo Ann Harris, Michael Conrad

229. "A Piece of the Action" (1-6-74) Charles Cioffi, Anthony Eisley, Joan Hotchkis, Kelly Thordsen
230. "Selkirk's War" (1-27-74) Peter Haskell, Richard Jaeckel, Roger Robinson, Lawrence Dobkin
231. "The Betrayal" (2-3-74) James Olson, Michael Tolan
232. "The Animal" (2-17-74) Gary Lockwood, Peter Mark Richman, Meg Foster, Roger Perry, Del Monroe
233. "The $2,000,000. Hit" (2-24-74) Henry Silva, Sharon Farrell
234. "Diamond Run" (3-10-74) Laurence Luckinbill, Eric Braeden, Elizabeth Ashley
235. "Deadly Ambition" (3-17-74) Harvey Keitel, Vincent Beck, Claudia Jennings, Robert Hooks, Don Gordon
236. "The Lost Man" (3-24-74) Robert Foxworth, Don Porter
237. "Vendetta" (4-7-74) John Vernon, Joan Van Ark
238. "Survival" (4-28-74) Jon Cypher, John Lupton, Gary Clarke, Julie Gregg, Dabney Coleman


THE WACKIEST SHIP IN THE ARMY

World War II comedy-satire of a Pacific schooner under the auspices of Major Simon Butcher (Jack Warden) and Lieutenant "Rip" Riddle (Gary Collins).

The Regulars: Major Simon Butcher, Jack Warden; Lt. (j.g.) Richard "Rip" Riddle, Gary Collins; General Cross, Bill Zuckert; Chief Miller, Mike Kellin; Admiral Beckett, Charles Irving; Nagurski, Rudy Solari; Tyler, Don Penny; Hollis, Mark Slade; Trivers, Fred Smoot.

The Episodes:

1. "Shakedown" (9-19-65) Karen Steele, Jack Soo, James Hong
2. "The Sisters" (9-26-65) Diana Hyland, Patricia Dunne, Antoinette Bower, Irene Tsu
3. [unknown title] (10-3-65) Michael Ansara, George Takei
4. "The Day the Crew Paced the Deck" (10-10-65) Ford Rainey, June Dayton
5. "The Colonel and the Geisha" (10-17-65) Nobu McCarthy, David Chow
6. "Bottoms Up" (10-24-65) Bill Glover, Anne Sargent
7. "The Stowaway" (10-31-65) Ruta Lee
8. "Boomer McKye" (11-7-65) Chips Rafferty, Leon Lontoc, Hedley Mattingly, Joe Higgins, Maurice Dallimore, Clive Wayne
9. "Vive La Kiwi" (11-14-65) Hans Gudegast, André Phillippe, Milton Selzer
10. "The Lady and the Luluai" (11-21-65) Harry Morgan, Hazel Court, Rupert Crosse, Peter Brooks
11. "A Shade of Kaiser Bill" (11-28-65) Barbara Shelley, Oscar Beregi, Greg Mullavey, Grant Woods

12. "... and Tyler Too" (12-5-65)  Jack Collins, Jack Dodson, Herbert Voland, Steven Bell
13. "Last Path to Garcia" (12-12-65)  Barbara Luna, Keye Luke
14. "I'm Dreaming of a White Isthmus" (12-18-65)  Diana Hyland, Antoinette Bower
15. "The Lamb Who Hunted Wolves" [Part I] (1-2-66)  John Anderson, Gail Kobe, Joseph Turkel, Richard Loo, James Hong, Butch Cavell
16. "The Lamb Who Hunted Wolves" [Part II] (1-9-66)  as above
17. "What Is Honor--a Word" (1-16-66)  Robert Loggia
18. "Hail the Chief" (1-30-66)  Leon Lontoc
19. "Liberty Was a Lady" (2-6-66)  Jill Ireland, Lou Antonio
20. "My Father's Keeper" (2-13-66)  George Takei, Henry Bellaver
21. "Brother Love" (2-20-66)  Barbara Shelley, Antoinette Bower
22. "And Two If by Sea" (2-27-66)  Lloyd Bochner
23. "The Ghost of Lord Nelson--San" (3-6-66)  Nancy Kovack
24. [unknown title] (3-13-66)  John Holland
25. "Girl in the Polka-Dot Swimsuit" (3-20-66)  Sharon Farrell, Aki Aleong, Tad Horino, George Zalma, Kenneth Chung
26. "Chinese Checkers" (3-27-66)  Ellen Madison, William Bramley
27. "My Island" (4-3-66)  Stefan Schnabel
28. "Fun Has More Blondes" (4-10-66)  Felice Orlandi, Leonard Strong
29. "Routine Assignment" (4-17-66)  Raymond St. Jacques, Vito Scotti


THE LEGEND OF JESSE JAMES

Strongly reminiscent of the 1957 motion picture The True Story of Jesse James (wherein Jesse was seen as a devoted, if sadly confused, avenger) is this moody study of the rebellious (but not necessarily murderous) James Brothers.

The Regulars: Jesse James, Christopher Jones; Frank James, Allen Case; Mrs. James, Ann Doran; Marshall Sam Corbett, Robert J. Wilke.

The Episodes:

1. "Three Men from Now" (9-13-65)  Jack Elam, Virginia Gregg, Robert McQueeney
2. "The Dead Man's Hand" (9-20-65)  Lloyd Bochner, Buck Taylor, Susan Lee Albert
3. "Put Me in Touch with Jesse" (9-27-65)  Michael Anderson Jr., Tom Fedden, John Milford, Tim McIntire
4. "The Pursuers" (10-11-65)  Eddie Firestone, Willard Sage, Ayllene Gibbons, Dennis Cross
5. "The Raiders" (10-18-65)  Peter Whitney, Warren Vanders
6. "Vendetta" (10-25-65)  Gene Evans, John Milford, James

Anderson, Lyle Talbot
7. "The Quest" (11-1-65) John Cassavetes, Marie Windsor
8. "The Judas Boot" (11-8-65) Zalman King, Richard Reeves
9. "Jail Break" (11-15-65) Royal Dano, Don Haggerty
10. "One Too Many Mornings" (11-22-65) Douglas Kennedy, Edith Atwater
11. "Manhunt" (11-29-65) Woodrow Parfrey, Zeme North, John Marley, Robert Phillips
12. "The Celebrity" (12-6-65) Jan Merlin, Merrie Spaeth
13. "The Man Who Was" (12-13-65) Robert F. Simon
14. "The Widow Fay" (12-20-65) Ann Sothern, Stanley Adams
15. "The Man Who Killed Jesse" (12-27-65) Alvy Moore, Tom Tully, Del Monroe
16. "The Empty Town" (1-3-66) Nehemiah Persoff
17. "Reunion" (1-10-66) Susan Strasberg, Gary Lockwood, Christopher Dark
18. "The Colt" (1-17-66) Claude Akins, Kurt Russell
19. "A Real Rough Town" (1-24-66) Paul Hartman, Gregg Palmer, Emile Meyer, Thomas Carney
20. "Return to Lawrence" (1-31-66) George Kennedy, Jean Hale
21. "The Cave" (2-7-66) Richard Chambers, Robert Yuro, Peter Helm
22. "South Wind" (2-14-66) Warren Stevens, Dennis Hopper, Whitney Blake, John Milford, J. Pat O'Malley
23. "The Lonely Place" (2-21-66) Albert Salmi, Sally Kellerman
24. [unknown title] (2-28-66) Liam Sullivan, Hank Patterson
25. "The Chase" (3-7-66) Charles Bronson
26. "Things Just Don't Happen" (3-14-66) Victor Jory, Vaughn Taylor, Regis Toomey, Kevin O'Neil
27. "As Far as the Sea" (3-21-66) John Carradine, John Milford
28. "1863" (3-28-66) John Howard, Rex Holman
29. "The Last Stand of Captain Hammel" (4-4-66) Joseph Wiseman, Richard Cutting
30. "The Hunted and the Hunters" (4-11-66) Glenn Corbett, John Anderson
31. "Dark Side of the Moon" (4-18-66) Robert Doyle, Kevin Tate
32. "A Field of Wild Flowers" (4-25-66) Jeffrey Hunter, Michael Burns, Harold J. Stone
33. "Wanted: Dead and Only" (5-2-66) Slim Pickens, Kelly Thordsen
34. "A Burying for Rosey" (5-9-66) Kevin McCarthy, Mariette Hartley


A MAN CALLED SHENANDOAH

That tragic figure of American folklore, commemorated lyrically as "doomed to wander", was now also an amnesiac in search of his lost identity in the years after the Civil War.

The Regulars: Shenandoah, Robert Horton.

The Episodes:

1.  "The Onslaught" (9-13-65) Beverly Garland, Noah Keen, Richard Devon, Robert Foulk, Steve Gravers
2.  "Survival" (9-20-65) Jeanne Cooper, John Davis Chandler, Dennis Patrick, John Anderson
3.  "The Fort" (9-27-65) Edward Binns, Warren Oates, Milton Selzer
4.  "The Caller" (10-11-65) Cloris Leachman, David Sheiner, Kent Smith
5.  "The Debt" (10-18-65) Charles McGraw, Paul Carr, Whit Bissell
6.  "Obion--1866" (10-25-65) Claude Akins, James Griffith
7.  "The Verdict" (11-1-65) Edward Asner, Bruce Dern, Harry Townes, Bill Zuckert
8.  "Town on Fire" (11-8-65) Elinor Donahue, Don McGowan, Henry Jones, Simon Scott
9.  "Incident at Dry Creek" (11-15-65) Leif Erickson, Michael Burns, Nina Shipman, Kelly Thordsen
10. "The Locket" (11-22-65) Martin Landau, Trevor Bardette, Mort Mills, Chris Alcaide
11. "The Reward" (11-29-65) Kevin Hagen, Hank Patterson, Karen Steele, Lloyd Bochner
12. "Special Talent for Killing" (12-6-65) Madlyn Rhue, George Kennedy, James Frawley
13. "The Siege" (12-13-65) Charles Aidman, Malcolm Atterbury, Hal Baylor
14. "The Bell" (12-20-65) Nehemiah Persoff
15. "The Young Outlaw" (12-27-65) John Dehner
16. "The Accused" (1-3-66) Albert Salmi, Fay Spain
17. "Run, Killer, Run" (1-10-66) Sally Kellerman, Leonard Nimoy
18. "Rope's End" (1-17-66) Michael Ansara, Susan Oliver
19. "The Lost Diablo" (1-24-66) Robert Loggia, James Gregory
20. "A Long Way Home" (1-31-66) Geraldine Brooks, Lyle Bettger
21. "End of a Legend" (2-7-66) Gail Kobe, Karl Swenson, J. D. Cannon
22. "Run and Hide" (2-14-66) Andrew Duggan, Lynn Loring
23. "The Riley Brand" (2-21-66) Joanna Pettet, Warren Stevens
24. "Muted Fifes, Muffled Drums" (2-28-66) Norman Fell, Anne Helm
25. "Plunder" (3-7-66) Pat Hingle, Paul Fix
26. "Marlee" (3-14-66) John Ireland, Nina Foch
27. "The Death of Matthew Eldridge" (3-21-66) Douglas V. Fowley, Louise Latham, Woodrow Parfrey, Gergory Walcott, Byron Morrow
28. "Aces and Kings" (3-28-66) Antoinette Bower, Bert Freed, Steve Brodie, Strother Martin
29. "The Imposter" (4-4-66) Jay C. Flippen, Juliet Mills
30. "An Unfamiliar Tune" (4-11-66) Diana Hyland, Harold J. Stone
31. "The Clown" (4-18-66) Frank Gorshin, Arthur O'Connell

32. "Requiem for the Second" (5-2-66) Martin Milner, Ross Elliott
33. "Care of General Delivery" (5-9-66) Jeanette Nolan, John McIntire
34. "Macauley's Cure" (5-16-66) Gary Merrill, Eduard Franz


RUN FOR YOUR LIFE

  Roy Huggins' study of the globe-trotting adventures of Paul Bryan (Ben Gazzara), given but two years to live (but he lived longer, didn't he?) left unanswered the question of how a dying man would have the means, much less the energy (boundless, to be certain) to be a globe-trotter in the first place. Composers for the series included Frank Fenton and John Thomas James (the pilot "The Cold, Cold, War of Paul Bryan"), Luther Davis ("The Girl Next Door Is a Spy" and the two-part "Cry Hard, Cry Fast"), Alvin Sargent ("In Search of April") and Tom Allen ("Strangers at the Door").

The Regulars: Paul Bryan, Ben Gazzara.

The Episodes:

1. "The Cold, Cold, War of Paul Bryan" (9-13-65) Katherine Ross, Robert Loggia, Stephen McNally, Celeste Holm, Jacques Bergerac, Hans Gudegast, Jacqueline Beer
2. "The Girl Next Door Is a Spy" (9-20-65) Macdonald Carey, Diana Hyland, Robert Knapp, Britt Semand
3. "Someone Who Makes Me Feel Beautiful" (9-27-65) Fernando Lamas, Alex Montoya, Tippi Hedren, Henry Beckman
4. "Never Pick Up a Stranger" (10-11-65) Barry Sullivan, Brenda Scott, Paul Newlan, Vaughn Taylor, Gregg Palmer, Russell Thorson
5. "How to Sell Your Soul for Fun and Profit" (10-18-65) Telly Savalas, Gia Scala, Hans Gudegast, Jeremy Slate
6. "Our Man in Limbo" (10-25-65) Macdonald Carey, Janine Gray
7. "Where Mystery Begins" (11-1-65) Dana Wynter, Keith Andes, Cyril Delevanti, Ian Wolfe, Walter Brooke, Booth Colman
8. "The Savage Season" (11-8-65) Jill Haworth, Henry Silva, Harold J. Stone, Gene Evans, Leslie Perkins, Lyle Talbot, Quinn O'Hara, Leslie Summers
9. "This Town for Sale" (11-15-65) James Whitmore, Mary Ann Mobley, R. G. Armstrong, Paul Fix
10. "A Girl Named Sorrow" (11-22-65) David Opatoshu, Ina Balm, William Bayett, Charles Wagenheim
11. "The Voice of Gina Milan" (11-29-65) Susan Strasberg, Linda Watkins, Renzo Cesana, Vinton Hayworth
12. "The Time of the Sharks" (12-6-65) Howard Keel, Melodie Johnson, Dolores Dorn-Heft, Tony Bill, Bernie Hamilton

13. "Make the Angels Weep" (12-13-65) Carol Lawrence, Anne Seymour, Mario Alcalde
14. "Strangers at the Door" (1-3-66) Robert Drivas, Lynn Carey, George Chandler
15. "The Carnival Ends at Midnight" (1-20-66) Peter Lawford, Anne Helm
16. "Rapture at Two-Forty" [repeat of "Kraft Suspense Theatre" episode of 4/15/65] (1-17-66)
17. "The Rediscovery of Charlotte Hyde" (1-24-66) Gena Rowlands, Fernando Lamas, Emile Genest
18. "The Night of the Terror" (1-31-66) Sharon Farrell, Donnelly Rhodes
19. "Keep My Share of the World" (2-7-66) Rossano Brazzi, Jeremy Slate, Louise Troy
20. "In Search of April" (2-14-66) Carol Lynley, George Furth, Don Galloway, William Lundigan, Don Rickles, K. T. Stevens, Larry D. Mann, Gail Bonney, Robert Wolders, Robert Easton
21. "Hoodlums on Wheels" (2-21-66) John Barrymore Jr., Marsha Hunt
22. "Who's Watching the Fleshpot?" (3-7-66) Bobby Darin, Eve Arden, Jeff Corey, Davey Davison
23. "Sequestro!" [Part I] (3-14-66) Sal Mineo, Harry Guardino, Marianna Hill, David Mauro
24. "Sequestro!" [Part II] (3-21-66) as above
25. "Don't Count on Tomorrow" (3-28-66) Roddy McDowall, Michael Constantine
26. "The Cruel Fountain" (4-4-66) Kathryn Hays, Murray Hamilton, Jan Sterling, Robert Pine, Tom Stern, Jeff Scott, Johnny Aladdin, Amentha Dymally, Kai Hernandez
27. "Night Train from Chicago" (4-11-66) Brock Peters, Louise Sorel
28. "The Last Safari" (4-25-66) Leslie Nielsen, Lesley Ann Warren
29. "The Savage Machines" (5-2-66) Edward Mulhare, Sally Ann Howes, Jeremy Slate
30. "The Sadness of a Happy Time" (5-16-66) Claudine Longet, Stephen McNally, Lili Valenty, Don Diamond, Michael Stanwood

Second Season

31. "The Day Time Stopped" (9-12-66) Carol Lawrence, Paul Lukas, John Ireland, John Kerr, Sheree North, Anne Helm, Robert Strauss
32. "I Am the Late Diana Hays" (9-19-66) Diana Hyland, Jack Palance, Anthony Eisley
33. "The Borders of Barbarism" (9-26-66) Stephen McNally, Alf Kjellin, Joan Collins, Reginald Owen
34. "The Committee for the 25th" (10-3-66) Wendell Corey, Edward Asner, Brooke Bundy, Peter Brocco
35. "The Dark Beyond the Door" (10-10-66) Peter Graves, Michael Dunn, Delphi Lawrence

36. "The Sex Object" (10-17-66) Sharon Farrell, Fernando Lamas, Joan Hackett, Pepé Hern
37. "The Grotenberg Mask" (10-24-66) Elizabeth Ashley, Skip Homeier, Tom Simcox, Henry Beckman, Pat Randall
38. "Edge of the Volcano" (10-31-66) Alejandro Rey, John Dehner, Katherine Crawford
39. "The Treasure Seekers" (11-14-66) Collin Wilcox, Bruce Dern, Jack Albertson, Anne Helm, Rosemary Murphy
40. "The Man Who Had No Enemies" (11-21-66) Kurt Kasznar, Nancy Malone, Joanna Moore, Victoria Shaw
41. "A Game of Violence" (11-28-66) Ossie Davis, Sugar Ray Robinson, Carol Lawrence, Tige Andrews
42. "Hang Down Your Head and Laugh" (12-5-66) Kim Darby, Jacqueline Scott, Larry Ward, Fabian Dean, Marvin Brody
43. "Tears from a Glass Eye" (12-12-66) Donnelly Rhodes, Mary Ann Mobley, Gerald O'Loughlin, Bill Glover, Otis Young
44. "Time-and-a-Half on Christmas Eve" (12-19-66) Ernest Borgnine, Charles McGraw, Melanie Alexander
45. "The Shock of Recognition" (12-26-66) Farley Granger, Marlyn Mason, Frank Silvera, Gavin MacLeod, José Ramon Tirado, Walter Mathews, Eric Mason
46. "Flight from Tirana" [Part I] (1-9-67) Ossie Davis, Sam Wanamaker, George Voskovec, Will Kuluva, Nicholas Colasanto, Gloria Edwards
47. "A Rage for Justice" [Part II] (1-16-67) as above
48. "The List of Alice McKenna" (1-23-67) Geraldine Brooks, William Windom, Cloris Leachman, Malcolm Atterbury, Mario Alcalde
49. "The Face of the Antagonist" (1-30-67) Aldo Ray, Henry Beckman, Richard Anderson
50. "Baby, the World's on Fire" (2-6-67) Jack Kelly, Suzanne Pleshette, Hans Lee
51. "Rendezvous in Tokyo" (2-13-67) Martin Milner, Joan Blackman, Ron Foster, Mickey Shaughnessy
52. "The Calculus of Chaos" (2-20-67) Inger Stratton, John Van Dreelen, Pat Harrington Jr.
53. "The Assassin" (2-27-67) Arthur Hill, Joan Shawlee, Harold Gould, Andrew Duggan
54. "The Carpella Affair" (3-6-67) Helmut Dantine
55. "A Very Small Injustice" (3-13-67) Slim Pickens, Burr DeBenning
56. "East of the Equator" (3-20-67) Dina Merrill, Rudy Solari, Alan Bergmann
57. "A Choice of Evils" (4-3-67) John Forsythe, Barbara Stanek, Coleen Gray, Wesley Lau
58. "Tell It to the Dead" (4-10-67) Karen Black, Linden Chiles Michele Carey
59. "Better World Next Time" (4-17-67) Martin Milner, Leonar Stone, Michael Pataki
60. "The Word Would Be Goodbye" (4-24-67) Claudine Longet, Albert Paulsen, Emile Genest, Ted Roter

## Third Season

61. "Who's Che Guevara?" (9-13-67) Rita Moreno, Alex Montoya, Nico Minardos, Victor Mullan
62. "The Inhuman Predicament" (9-20-67) Fernando Lamas, Vera Miles, Kurt Kasznar, Katherine Justice
63. "Three Passengers for the Lusitania" (9-27-67) Cliff Potter, Murray MacLeod
64. "The Frozen Image" (10-4-67) Mel Tormé, Michael Cole, Sandra Smith
65. "Trip to the Far Side" (10-11-67) Ralph Bellamy, Geoffrey Horne, Marianna Hill, Bruce Dern, Don Knight
66. "The Company of Scoundrels" [sequel to episode of 10/3/66] (10-18-67) Pat Hingle, Ford Rainey, Robert Yuro, Lou Frizzell, Dean Harens
67. "At the End of the Rainbow, There's Another Rainbow" (10-25-67) Anne Helm, Bruce Dern, Jeff Corey, Fabian Dean
68. "Down with Willy Hatch" (11-1-67) Don Rickles, Robert Donner, Clarke Gordon
69. "The Naked Half-Truth" (11-8-67) Fernando Lamas, Leticia Roman, Joe De Santis, Edward Andrews, Frank Puglia
70. "Tell It Like It Is" (11-15-67) Franchot Tone, Joan Huntington, James Daly
71. "Cry Hard, Cry Fast" [Part I] (11-22-67) James Farentino, Charles Aidman, Jack Albertson, Robyn Millan, Susan Clark, Diana Muldaur, Joan Van Ark
72. "Cry Hard, Cry Fast" [Part II] (11-29-67) as above
73. "The Mustafa Embrace" (12-6-67) Katherine Crawford, Stanley Waxman, William Sargent, Edmund Hashim
74. "It Could Only Happen in Rome" (12-20-67) Tisha Sterling, Robert Brown, Renzo Cesana, Sal Ponti
75. "Fly by Night" (12-27-67) Felicia Farr, Andrew Duggan, Jason Evers, Don Stroud, Bruce Glover
76. "A Dangerous Proposal" (1-3-68) Albert Dekker, Judy Carne, Carlos Romero, Mark Lenard, Marino Masé
77. "One Bad Turn" (1-10-68) Warren Oates, Bert Freed, Anne Helm, Walter Brooke, Strother Martin, Jon Lormer
78. "The Rape of Lucrece" (1-17-68) Julie Harris, Audrey Totter, Donald Foster, Vincent Van Lynn
79. "The Killing Scene" (1-31-68) Robert Duvall, Will Geer, Tom Skerritt, Dana Elcar, Walter Brooke
80. "Saro-Jane, You Never Whispered Again" (2-7-68) Barbara Hershey, Frank Marth, Austin Willis, Robert F. Simon, James Oliver
81. "The Dead on Furlough" (2-21-68) Ina Balin, Hans Gudegast, Ronald Feinberg, Nate Esformes
82. "Beware My Love" (2-28-68) Anna-Lisa, John Van Dreelen, Michael Evans, Grant Woods
83. "Carol" (3-6-68) Kim Darby, Ron Russell, Jana Taylor
84. "Life Among the Man-Eaters" (3-13-68) Anne Baxter, Jacques Bergerac, Peter Donat, Philip Chapin
85. "The Exchange" (3-27-68) Janice Rule, Stephen McNally, David Hurst, Lee Bergere, John Bryant

LOST IN SPACE

Irwin Allen's children's series of the outer space wander-
ings of an American "Swiss Family Robinson" (the Robinsons, in
this case, being Guy Williams as the astrophysicist father John;
June Lockhart as his biochemist wife Maureen; Marta Kristen and
Angela Cartwright as their daughters Judy and Penny; Billy Mumy
as son Will) is best when its fantasy flows freely, not imperiled
by didactic parental interjections.

In the first season, when the Robinsons and their fellow
travelers, young geologist Don West (Mark Goddard) and "reluctant
stowaway" Dr. Zachary Smith (who sabotaged the family's initial
mission to alpha Centauri), are confined to a single planet, the ac
tion can be particularly cumbersome.  It is then that scenarist
Jackson Gillis tactfully imbues plot with the unvitiated imagination
of the child.  Gillis' invisible but audible "My Friend, Mr. Nobody," which Penny has discovered in a grotto, explores without
pretense a child's need for rapport.  And Gillis' "The Magic Mirror" takes Penny "through the looking glass" into a realm where
vanity is meaningfully augmented.  In both these episodes, mood
is enhanced by the soft musical refrains of composers Johnny Williams and Lionel Newman.

In many other episodes, dialogue is unfortunately both predictable and wooden.  Love conquers "over the greatest forces in
the universe" in Barney Slater's "Follow the Leader," in which
Professor Robinson is possessed by a vindictive alien.  William
Welch's "Lost Civilization" is a tired version of the "Sleeping
Beauty" theme.  And although veteran character actor Jonathan
Harris gave the series a certain distinction, his "Zachary Smith"
idiosyncrasies--hypochondriacal and egocentric that he is--are
labored.

Where scenarists may fail in Irwin Allen series, technicia
sometimes succeed--for which reason the names Jack Martin Smit
Carl MacCauley, Robert Kinoshita (art directors) and Winton Hoch
Frank Carson (photographers) merit our attention.

The Regulars:  Professor John Robinson, Guy Williams; Maureen
         Robinson, June Lockhart; Major Donald West, Mark God-
         dard; Judy Robinson, Marta Kristen; Penny Robinson,
         Angela Cartwright; Will Robinson, Billy Mumy; Dr. Zach
         ary Smith, Jonathan Harris; the robot, Bob May.

The Episodes:

1.  "The Reluctant Stowaway"  (9-15-65)  regulars only
2.  "The Derelict"  (9-22-65)  Don Forbes
3.  "Island in the Sky"  (9-29-65)  regulars only
4.  "There Were Giants in the Earth"  (10-6-65)  regulars only
5.  "The Hungry Sea"  (10-13-65)  regulars only
6.  "Welcome, Stranger"  (10-20-65)  Warren Oates

7.  "My Friend, Mr. Nobody" (10-27-65) regulars only
8.  "Invaders from the Fifth Dimension" (11-3-65) regulars only
9.  "The Oasis" (11-10-65) regulars only
10. "The Sky Is Falling" (11-17-65) Don Matheson, Francoise Ruggieri, Eddie Rosson
11. "Wish Upon a Star" (11-24-65) regulars only
12. "The Raft" (12-1-65) regulars only
13. "One of Our Dogs Is Missing" (12-8-65) regulars only
14. "Attack of the Monster Plants" (12-15-65) regulars only
15. "Return from Outer Space" (12-29-65) Reta Shaw
16. "The Keeper" [Part I] (1-12-66) Michael Rennie
17. "The Keeper" [Part II] (1-19-66) as above
18. "The Sky Pirate" (1-26-66) Albert Salmi
19. "Ghost in Space" (2-2-66) regulars only
20. "The War of the Robots" (2-9-66) regulars only
21. "The Magic Mirror" (2-16-66) Michael J. Pollard
22. "The Challenge" (3-2-66) Kurt Russell, Michael Ansara
23. "The Space Trader" (3-9-66) Torin Thatcher
24. "His Majesty Smith" (3-16-66) Liam Sullivan, Kevin Hagen
25. "The Space Croppers" (3-30-66) Mercedes McCambridge, Sherry Jackson, Dawson Palmer
26. "All That Glitters" (4-6-66) Werner Klemperer
27. "Lost Civilization" (4-13-66) Royal Dano, Kim Karath
28. "A Change of Space" (4-20-66) Frank Graham
29. "Follow the Leader" (4-27-66) regulars only

Second Season

0.  "Blast Off into Space" (9-14-66) Strother Martin
1.  "Wild Adventure" (9-21-66) Vitina Marcus
2.  "The Ghost Planet" (9-28-66) regulars only
3.  "Forbidden World" (10-5-66) Wally Cox
4.  "Space Circus" (10-12-66) James Westerfield, Michael Green, Melinda Fee
5.  "The Prisoners of Space" (10-19-66) regulars only
6.  "The Android Machine" (10-26-66) Dee Hartford, Tiger Joe Marsh, Fritz Feld
7.  "The Deadly Games of Gamma Six" (11-2-66) Mike Kellin, Peter Brocco
8.  "The Thief from Outer Space" (11-9-66) Malachi Throne, Ted Cassidy, Maxine Gates
9.  "The Curse of Cousin Smith" (11-16-66) Henry Jones
10. "West to Mars" (11-30-66) Allan Melvin, Ken Mayer, Mickey Manners
11. "A Visit to Hades" (12-7-66) Gerald Mohr
12. "Wreck of the Robot" (12-14-66) regulars only
13. "The Dream Monster" (12-21-66) John Abbott, Dawson Palmer
14. "The Golden Man" (12-28-66) Dennis Patrick, Ronald Gans, Bill Troy
15. "The Girl from the Green Dimension" (1-4-67) Vitina Marcus, Harry Raybould
16. "The Questing Beast" (1-11-67) Hans Conried, Jeff County

47. "The Toymaker" (1-25-67) Walter Burke, Fritz Feld
48. "Mutiny in Space" (2-1-67) Ronald Long
49. "The Space Vikings" (2-8-67) Sheila Mathews, Bern Hoffman
50. "Rocket to Earth" (2-15-67) Al Lewis
51. "The Cave of the Wizards" (2-22-67) regulars only
52. "Treasure of the Lost Planet" (3-1-67) Albert Salmi, Jim Boles, Craig Duncan
53. "Revolt of the Androids" (3-8-67) Leonard Stone, Gary Tigerman
54. "The Colonists" (3-15-67) Francine York
55. "Trip through the Robot" (3-22-67) regulars only
56. "The Phantom Family" (3-29-67) Alan Hewitt
57. "The Mechanical Men" (4-5-67) regulars only
58. "The Astral Traveler" (4-12-67) Sean McClory
59. "The Galaxy Gift" (4-26-67) John Carradine

Third Season

60. "The Condemned of Space" (9-6-67) Marcel Hillaire
61. "Visit to a Hostile Planet" (9-13-67) Robert Foulk, Pitt Herbert
62. "Kidnapped in Space" (9-20-67) Grant Sullivan, Carol Williams
63. "Hunter's Moon" (9-27-67) Vincent Beck
64. "The Space Primevals" (10-4-67) Arthur Batanides
65. "Space Destructors" (10-11-67) Tommy Farrell
66. "The Haunted Lighthouse" (10-18-67) Woodrow Parfrey, Lou Wagner
67. "Flight into the Future" (10-25-67) regulars only
68. "Collision of the Planets" (11-8-67) Dan Travanty
69. "Space Creature" (11-15-67) regulars only
70. "The Deadliest of the Species" (11-22-67) Sue England, Lyl Waggoner
71. "A Day at the Zoo" (11-29-67) Leonard Stone, Gary Tigerman
72. "Two Weeks in Space" (12-13-67) Fritz Feld, Edy Williams Eric Matthews, Richard Krisher
73. "Castles in Space" (12-20-67) Alberto Monte, Corinna Tsopei
74. "The Antimatter Man" (12-27-67) regulars only
75. "Target: Earth" (1-3-68) James Gosa
76. "Princess of Space" (1-10-68) Robert Foulk, Arte Johnson, Sheila Mathews
77. "Time Merchant" (1-17-68) John Crawford
78. "The Promised Planet" (1-24-68) Gil Rogers
79. "Fugitives in Space" (1-31-68) Michael Conrad, Tol Avery
80. "Space Beauty" (2-14-68) Leonard Stone, Dee Hartford
81. "The Flaming Planet" (2-21-68) Abraham Sofaer
82. "The Great Vegetable Rebellion" (2-28-68) Stanley Adams, James Millhollin
83. "Junkyard in Space" (3-6-68) Marcel Hillaire

THE BIG VALLEY

A well-written and opulently photographed (by Wilfred M. Cline) western of a wealthy matriarch (Barbara Stanwyck as Mrs. Victoria Barkley) and her family living in the San Joaquin Valley of the 1870s. The Barkley siblings were Attorney Jarrod (Richard Long); Nick (Peter Breck), in charge of the family spread; Eugene (Charles Briles), a college student; Audra (Linda Evans), and Heath (Lee Majors), illegitimately sired by Victoria's late husband Tom. The best of the episodes were those with the offbeat themes. Bradford Dillman triumphed as the deranged doctor out to avenge the death of his father in "A Noose Is Waiting." Robert Walker Jr. was a particularly pathetic derelict in "My Son, My Son." Adam West was a murdering misogynist obsessed with "adultery" in the episode "In Silent Battle."

In other episodes, Jeanne Cooper was excellent as the impoverished would-be extortionist who attempts to conceal the facts regarding Heath's birthright in "Boots with My Father's Name." Arthur O'Connell was in fine form as Jubal Tanner, who dies defending his rights to a property of sentimental value in the fifth teleplay. And James Whitmore, always a fascinating actor to watch, was superb in four episodes: as the ruthless bounty hunter of "The Death Merchant," as the surreptitious politician of "Target," as the reckless marshal of "Shadow of a Giant," and as the licentious sheriff of "Night in a Small Town." A great actress-- Colleen Dewhurst--was supreme as the outlaw and matriarch (yet not entirely the antithesis of Victoria) of "A Day of Terror."

Composers of teleplays included Christopher Knopf ("Palms of Glory"), Bernard McEveety ("A Time to Kill"), Peter Packer ("By Force and Violence"), Gilbert Ralston ("Day of the Comet"), Robert Goodwin ("Joshua Watson"), Margaret Armen ("Night of the Wolf" and "Alias Nellie Handley") and Oliver Crawford ("Earthquake" which was directed by actor Paul Henreid). George Dunning composed the musical theme.

The Regulars: Victoria Barkley, Barbara Stanwyck; Jarrod Barkley, Richard Long; Nick Barkley, Peter Breck; Heath Barkley, Lee Majors; Audra Barkley, Linda Evans; Eugene Barkley, Charles Briles; Silas, Napoleon Whiting; Sheriff Madden, Douglas Kennedy; Sheriff, Mort Mills (first season episodes).

The Episodes:

1. "Palms of Glory" (9-15-65) Malachi Throne, Vincent Gardenia, Len Wayland, Dennis Cross, Dallas McKennon
2. "Forty Rifles" (9-22-65) Andrew Duggan, John Milford, Calvin Brown
3. "Boots with My Father's Name" (9-29-65) Jeanne Cooper, Beah Richards, John Anderson, Richard Devon, John Harmon

4. "Young Marauders" (10-6-65) Sean Garrison, Buck Taylor, Virginia Christine, Kevin Hagen, James Patterson
5. "The Odyssey of Jubal Tanner" (10-13-65) Arthur O'Connell, Jason Evers, Harlan Warde
6. "Heritage" (10-20-65) Anne Helm, Sherwood Price, Ford Rainey, Richard Hale
7. "Winner Lose All" (10-27-65) Katherine Ross, Henry Wilcoxon, Karl Swenson, Naomi Stevens
8. "My Son, My Son" (11-3-65) Robert Walker Jr., R. G. Armstrong, Katherine Bard
9. "Earthquake" (11-10-65) Charles Bronson, Alizia Gur, Wesley Lau, Audrey Dalton, Robert B. Williams, William Fawcett, John Craven
10. "The Murdered Party" (11-17-65) Warren Oates, Larry D. Mann, Paul Fix, Fred Holliday, Paul Potash, Walter Woolf King
11. "The Way to Kill a Killer" (11-24-65) Martin Landau, Rodolfo Acosta, Pepe Hern, Arthur Space
12. "Night of the Wolf" (12-1-65) Ronny Howard, Nancy Olson, Yuki Shimoda, Ted Gehring, Chubby Johnson
13. "The Guilt of Matt Bentell" (12-8-65) John Anderson, Anthony Zerbe, Martine Bartlett, Morgan Woodward
14. "The Brawlers" (12-15-65) Claude Akins, Eleanor Audley, J. Pat O'Malley
15. "Judgment in Heaven" (12-22-65) Lynn Loring, R. J. Porter, Nicolas Surovy
16. "Invaders" (12-29-65) John Anderson, Yvonne Craig
17. "By Fires Unseen" (1-5-66) Diane Baker, Frank Scannell, King Johnson
18. "A Time to Kill" (1-19-66) William Shatner, Frank Marth, George Kennedy, Robert Cornthwaite
19. "Teacher of Outlaws" (1-26-66) Harold J. Stone, Steve Ihnat, Tim Carey
20. "Under a Dark Sea" (2-9-66) Bruce Dern, Albert Salmi
21. "Barbary Red" (2-16-66) Jill St. John, George Kennedy, Donna Michelle, John Hoyt
22. "The Death Merchant" (2-23-66) James Whitmore, Royal Dano
23. "The Fallen Hawk" (3-2-66) Marlyn Mason, Peter Haskell, Paul Comi, Dennis Cross
24. "Hazard" (3-9-66) Robert Yuro, Lew Gallo, Bert Freed, Audrey Dalton
25. "Into the Widow's Web" (3-23-66) Kathleen Nolan, David Sheiner, Ken Lynch, Joe Higgins, King Donovan
26. "By Force and Violence" (3.30-66) Bruce Dern, L. Q. Jones
27. "The River Monarch" (4-6-66) Chips Rafferty, Katherine Justice, John Rayner, Curt Conway, J. P. Burns, Sam Jarvis
28. "The Midas Man" (4-13-66) Tom Tryon, Richard O'Brien
29. "Tunnel of Gold" (4-20-66) Warren Stevens, Jeanne Cooper, Malachi Throne, Paul Trinka
30. "Last Train to the Fair" (4-27-66) Richard Anderson, Karl Swenson

Second Season

31. "Lost Treasure" (9-12-66) Bruce Dern, Buddy Hackett, John Milford
32. "Legend of a General" [Part I] (9-19-66) Nehemiah Persoff, Rudy Solari, Paul Comi, Angela Dorian, Michael Davis, John Hoyt, Carlos Romero
33. "Legend of a General" [Part II] (9-26-66) as above
34. "Caesar's Wife" (10-3-66) Dianne Foster, Tim O'Kelly, Bert Freed, Bern Hoffman
35. "Pursuit" (10-10-66) James Gregory, Malachi Throne
36. "The Martyr" (10-17-66) Joseph Campanella, Nico Minardos, Clyde Ventura, Philip Bourneuf
37. "Target" (10-31-66) Julie Adams, James Whitmore, Sherwood Price, Strother Martin
38. "The Velvet Trap" (11-7-66) Laura Devon, Fred Beir, Kelly Thordsen
39. "The Man from Nowhere" (11-14-66) Sheree North, Anne Seymour, Gregory Walcott, Duane Chase
40. "The Great Safe Robbery" (11-21-66) Warren Oates, Christopher Cary, Kelton Garwood, Lee Krieger, Bill Quinn, Joe Higgins
41. "Iron Box" (11-28-66) David Sheiner, Paul Picerni, Yaphet Kotto, Frank Marth, Walter Burke
42. "Last Stage to Salt Flats" (12-5-66) Lamont Johnson, Norma Crane, Rex Holman, Dennis Cross, Kevin Hagen, Steven Mines
43. "A Day of Terror" (12-12-66) Colleen Dewhurst, Ross Hagen, Ken Swofford, Michael Burns
44. "Hide the Children" (12-19-66) Stephen McNally, Louise Sorel, Royal Dano, Celia Lovsky
45. "Day of the Comet" (12-26-66) Bradford Dillman, Douglas Kennedy, Chuck Bail, Ken Drake, Roberto Contreras
46. "Wagonload of Dreams" (1-2-67) Tige Andrews, Dennis Safren, Karl Swenson, William Mims
47. "Image of Yesterday" (1-9-67) Dan O'Herlihy, Vincent Gardenia, Don Chastain, Sam Melville
48. "Boy into Man" (1-16-67) Richard Dreyfuss, Diane Ladd, J. Pat O'Malley
49. "Down Shadow Street" (1-23-67) Robert Middleton, Dan Ferrone
50. "The Stallion" (1-30-67) Paul Fix, Brooke Bundy, Virginia Gregg
51. "The Haunted Wheel" (2-6-67) Andrew Duggan, George Kennedy, Robert Ellenstein, Roger Davis, Joyce Jameson
52. "Price of Victory" (2-13-67) Larry Pennell, Sandra Smith, Hal Baylor, Lee Krieger
53. "Brother Love" (2-20-67) Robert Goulet, Strother Martin, Gavin MacLeod
54. "Court Martial" (3-6-67) Henry Jones, L. Q. Jones, Alan Bergmann, Paul Comi
55. "Plunder at Hawk's Grove" (3-13-67) Cloris Leachman, Dennis Hopper, Frank McGrath, Lonny Chapman

56. "Turn of a Card" (3-20-67) Joseph Campanella, Don Chastain, Joe Higgins, Marayat Andriane
57. "Showdown in Limbo" (3-27-67) Tom Lowell, Arch Johnson, L. Q. Jones, John Carter
58. "The Lady from Mesa" (4-3-67) Lee Grant, Frank Marth, E. J. André, Regan Wilson, Robert Cornthwaite
59. "Cage of Eagles" (4-24-67) Pernell Roberts, Harold Gould, John Pickard, Bing Russell

Third Season

60. "Joaquin" (9-11-67) Fabrizio Mioni, Robert Carricart, Margarita Cordova
61. "Ambush" (9-18-67) James Gregory, L. Q. Jones, Toian Matchinga, Rex Holman, Ruben Moreno, Robert Karnes
62. "A Flock of Trouble" (9-25-67) Milton Berle, Robert Fuller, Eileen Baral
63. "The Time After Midnight" (10-2-67) Lloyd Bochner, Shep Menken, Ed Bakey, Carol Booth
64. "Night in a Small Town" (10-9-67) Susan Strasberg, James Whitmore, Doug Lambert, Kevin Hagen
65. "Ladykiller" (10-16-67) Marlyn Mason, Royal Dano, Anthony James, Roy Jenson, James Boles, Chris Alcaide, Clyde Howdy, Jason Johnson
66. "Guilty" (10-30-67) Norman Alden, Robert Nichols, Joyce Ebert, Harlan Warde, Frankie Kabott
67. "The Disappearance" (11-6-67) Lew Ayres, Richard Anderson, John Milford, Walter Burke, Owen Bush, Gail Bonney
68. "A Noose Is Waiting" (11-13-67) Bradford Dillman, Ellen Corby, Martin Ashe, Lillian Adams, I. Stanford Jolley
69. "Explosion!" [Part I] (11-20-67) Judy Carne, Stuart Erwin, Leticia Roman, Arlene Golonka, Carl Esmond, Eddie Firestone, Harry Swoger, Paul Sorensen, Edward Colmans
70. "Explosion!" [Part II] (11-27-67) as above
71. "Four Days to Furnace Hill" (12-4-67) Fritz Weaver, Bruce Dern, Rafael Campos, Don Chastain, Jull Reding
72. "Night of the Executioners" (12-11-67) David Sheiner, Dennis Hopper, Peter Whitney, Dabbs Greer
73. "Journey into Violence" (12-18-67) Quentin Dean, Richard Peabody, Charles Tyner
74. "The Buffalo Man" (12-25-67) Albert Salmi, Lonny Chapman, Yaphet Kotto, Andreas Teuber
75. "The Good Thieves" (1-1-68) Russell Johnson, Charles Grodin, Flip Mark
76. "Days of Wrath" (1-8-68) Michael Strong, Sandra Smith, Kevin Hagen, Peter Hobbs
77. "Miranda" (1-15-68) Barbara Luna, Don Randolph, Sherwood Price
78. "Shadow of a Giant" (1-29-68) James Whitmore, Richard Evans, Walter Brooke, Stuart Randall, Ed Bakey, Rayford Barnes
79. "Fall of a Hero" (2-5-68) Richard Anderson, Dennis Patrick, L. Q. Jones, Dub Taylor

80. "The Emperor of Rice" (2-12-68) Julie Adams, Keye Luke, Harry Townes, Kam Tong
81. "Rimfire" [unsold pilot episode for projected fall series] (2-19-68) Van Williams, Mako, Lisa Lu, John Daniels, Robert Middleton
82. "Bounty on a Barkley" (2-26-68) Leslie Parrish, Peter Haskell, Mike Wagner, John J. Fox, Earl Nickel
83. "The Devil's Masquerade" (3-4-68) John Doucette, Ray Danton, Anne Helm
84. "Run of the Savage" (3-11-68) Michael Burns, Grace Lee Whitney, Harry Swoger, Willard Sage, Carolyn Conwell
85. "The Challenge" (3-18-68) James Gregory, Harold Gould

## Fourth Season

86. "In Silent Battle" (9-23-68) Adam West, Don Knight
87. "They Called Her Delilah" (9-30-68) Julie London, Paul Lambert, Robert Nichols
88. "Presumed Dead" (10-7-68) Lew Ayres, Gavin MacLeod, Richard O'Brien, Warren Vanders
89. "Run of the Cat" (10-21-68) Pernell Roberts, Lisa Lu, Janis Hansen, John Milford, Jon Lormer
90. "Deathtown" (10-28-68) Jason Evers, Antoinette Bower, Michael Dante, Frank Marth, Kathie Browne
91. "The Jonah" (11-11-68) Marty Allen, Wayne Rogers
92. "Hell Hath No Fury" (11-18-68) Carol Lynley, Don Dubbins, Conlan Carter, Steve Franken
93. "The Long Ride" (11-25-68) Richard Anderson, Paul Peterson
94. "The Profit and the Lost" (12-2-68) Robert Loggia, Bert Freed
95. "A Stranger Everywhere" (12-9-68) Julie Harris, Richard Devon, Dennis Patrick
96. "The Prize" (12-16-68) Bruce Dern, Peter Haskell, Ondine Vaughn, Noah Keen
97. "Hunter's Moon" (12-30-68) Lawrence Dobkin, Susan O'Connell, Bruce Glover, John Crawford
98. "Top of the Stairs" (1-6-69) Ron Harper, Jean Inness, Paul Fix, Robert Ellenstein, Walter Sande, Byron Morrow
99. "Joshua Watson" (1-20-69) Lou Rawls, Royal Dano, Greg Mullavey, Robert Sampson, Michael Bell, Mark Tapscott, Marvin J. Downey
100. "The Secret" (1-27-69) Simon Oakland, Nancy Malone, Kelly Corcoran
101. "The Twenty-five Graves of Midas" (2-3-69) Anne Baxter, Linda Marsh, Arch Johnson, Kevin Hagen, Gary Beban
102. "Lightfoot" (2-17-69) Joe Don Baker, Amy Thomson, Harry Lauter, Walter Coy
103. "Alias Nellie Handley" (2-24-69) Susan Oliver, Richard Anderson, Gavin MacLeod
104. "The Royal Road" (3-3-69) Kathy Garver, Sajid Kahn, Harold Gould

105. "A Passage of Saints" (3-10-69) Fritz Weaver, Donna Bac-
        cala, Olive Dunbar, Paul Lambert
106. "The Battle of Mineral Springs" (3-24-69) Jack Albertson,
        Dennis Patrick, Conlan Carter
107. "The Other Face of Justice" (3-31-69) John Crawford,
        James Gregory
108. "Town of No Exit" (4-7-69) Leslie Nielsen, John Carra-
        dine, Lorri Scott, Diana Ewing
109. "Danger Road" (4-21-69) Maurice Evans, Anthony James,
        Logan Ramsey
110. "Flight from San Miguel" (4-28-69) Gerald Mohr, Pat
        Delany, H. M. Wynant, Nate Esformes
111. "Point and Counterpoint" (5-19-69) Clifford David, Walter
        Burke, Russell Thorsen

I SPY

    A well-paced sort of travelogue with the central figures be-
ing a white tennis player (Robert Culp as Kelly Robinson) and his
black attendant and confidant (Bill Cosby as Alexander Scott)--both
of them government agents--enmeshed in global intrigue, this
series was also a properly restrained commentary on the necessity
for breaking racial barriers. What kept this series a level above
the usual Cold War humdrums and endless stereotypes were the
witty tête-à-têtes between the heroes. This attribute was particularly effective in the episode "Home to Judgment," by Robert Culp
and directed by Richard C. Saraphian, about the agents' temporary
hideaway at an Idaho farm owned by Kelly's aunt (Una Merkel) and
uncle (Will Geer). Even the normal extemporizing fails to quell
the genuine fear the agents have for their steadily advancing nemeses. Michael Zagor's "A Room with a Rack," in which Kelly un-
dergoes the torture of fifteenth-century Spain, explores the serious
theme of the frailties of the human condition. Love interest for
either of the agents invariably condescended to chase sequences
and gunplay in such episodes as "Shana" by Robert Lewin and directed by Christian Nyby and "Tatia" also by Robert Lewin and directed by David Friedkin. At times the love interest grew maudlin as in "Affair in T'Sien Cha" with Vera Miles and directed by
the series' executive producer, Sheldon Leonard, who also appeared
in several episodes. There were also several more comical episodes, such as "Chrysanthemum" by Edward J. Lakso and directed
by David Friedkin, and "Father Abraham" by Stephen Kandal and
directed by Tony Leader. And yet violence could erupt unrelieved,
as it did in "So Coldly Sweet."

    Whether the locale was Rome, Greece, Hong Kong or Mar-
rakech, Fouad Said's very inventive photography was a player in
itself. Earl Hagen composed the musical theme.

The Regulars: Kelly Robinson, Robert Culp; Alexander Scott, Bill
        Cosby.

The Episodes:

1. "So Long, Patrick Henry" (9-15-65) Ivan Dixon, Cicely Tyson, Richard Loo, Rickey Der, Tiger Joe Marsh, John Lassell
2. "A Cup of Kindness" (9-22-65) David Friedkin, Irene Tsu, Lee Kolina
3. "Carry Me Back to Old Tsing-Tao" (9-29-65) Philip Ahn, Pilar Seurat, Michael Conrad, David Sheiner
4. "Chrysanthemum" (10-6-65) Marcel Hillaire, John Hoyt
5. "Dragon's Teeth" (10-13-65) Joanne Linville, Kam Tong, Walter Burke, Laya Rahi, Mike Faulkner, Gilbert Ralston
6. "The Loser" (10-20-65) Eartha Kitt, Albert Paulsen
7. "Danny Was a Million Laughs" (10-27-65) Martin Landau, Jeanette Nolan, Keye Luke, Linda Ho
8. "The Time of the Knife" (11-3-65) Warren Stevens, Madlyn Rhue, John Van Dreelen, Jay Novello
9. "No Exchange on Damaged Merchandise" (11-10-65) Sue Randall, Kurt Kreuger, Mako, Byron Morrow, H. T. Tsiang, Jo-Anne Miya, Martin Priest
10. "Tatia" (11-17-65) Laura Devon, Richard Garland, John Rayner
11. "Weight of the World" (12-1-65) Albert Salmi, Rex Ingram, Marlyn Mason, Jeanne Arnold, Yuki Shimoda
12. "Three Hours on a Sunday Night" (12-8-65) Julie London, James Shigeta, Sheldon Leonard, Arthur Shields, Simon Scott
13. "Tigers of Heaven" (12-15-65) Hiroshi Nakajima, Miiko Taka, Teru Shimada, Grant Sullivan, Maureen Arthur, George Matsui, David Friedkin
14. "Affair in T'Sien Cha" (12-29-65) Vera Miles, Roger C. Carmel, John Orchard
15. "Tiger" (1-5-66) Lew Ayres, France Nuyen, Robert Brubaker, Allen Yung
16. "The Barter" (1-12-66) Roger C. Carmel, John Abbott
17. "Always Say Goodbye" (1-26-66) France Nuyen, Kent Smith, Jerry Fujikawa
18. "Court of the Lion" (2-2-66) Godfrey Cambridge, Ed Parker
19. "Turkish Delight" (2-9-66) Victor Buono, Diana Sands
20. "Bet Me a Dollar" (2-16-66) Pepito Hector Galindo, Danielle de Metz, Lou Krugman
21. "Return to Glory" (2-23-66) Victor Jory, Dolores Del Rio, Antoinette Bower
22. "The Conquest of Maude Murdock" (3-2-66) Jeanette Nolan, Philip Bourneuf
23. "A Day Called 4 Jaguar" (3-9-66) Rory Calhoun, George Montgomery, Kamala Devi
24. "Crusade to Limbo" (3-23-66) Howard Duff, Frank Silvera, Antoinette Bower, Gene Lyons
25. "My Mother, the Spy" (3-30-66) Sally Kellerman, Alejandro Rey, Theodore Marcuse
26. "There Was a Little Girl" (4-6-66) Mary Jane Saunders, Jose De Vega

27. "It's All Done with Mirrors" (4-13-66) Carroll O'Connor, Fay Spain, Richard Bull
28. "One Thousand Fine" (4-27-66) Susan Oliver, Dane Clark, Stacy Harris, Alex Montoya

Second Season

29. "So Coldly Sweet" (9-14-66) Diana Hyland, Michael Conrad, Charles Korvin, Larry Thor
30. "Lori" (9-21-66) Billy Gray, Nancy Wilson, Greg Morris, Frank Maxwell, Malachi Throne
31. "Sophia" (9-28-66) Rafaella Carra, Enzo Cerusico, Caterina Boratto
32. "Vendetta" (10-5-66) Victor Francen, Oswaldo Ruggieri, Massimo Serato, Patrizia Valturri, Fausto Tozzi
33. "A Gift from Alexander" (10-12-66) Anna Karina, Michael Constantine, Jay Novello, Alan Oppenheimer
34. "Trial by Treehouse" (10-19-66) Michael J. Pollard, Cicely Tyson, Raymond St. Jacques, Marge Redmond
35. "Sparrowhawk" (10-26-65) Clive Clerk, Walter Koenig, Michael Constantine, Andrea Darvi
36. "Will the Real Good Guys Please Stand Up?" (11-2-66) Lee Philips, Hari Rhodes, Anna Capri, Henry Wilcoxon
37. "Bridge of Spys" (11-9-66) Barbara Steele, Carlo Croccolo
38. "One of Our Bombs Is Missing" (11-16-66) Dewey Martin, David Mauro, David Bond
39. "To Florence with Love" [Part I] (11-23-66) Joey Heatherton, Gabriele Ferzetti, Eleanor Sommers
40. "To Florence with Love" [Part II] (11-30-66) as above
41. "Lisa" (12-7-66) Linda Marsh, Jack Kruschen, James Best, Steve Harris, Reta Shaw, Adam Williams
42. "Little Boy Lost" (12-14-66) Ronny Howard, Sarah Marshall, Richard Anderson, Oscar Beregi
43. "Father Abraham" (12-21-66) Tony Bill, David Sheiner, Jill Donahue, Austin Willis
44. "Rome ... Take Away Three" (12-28-66) Nehemiah Persoff, Alf Kjellin, Ulla Stromstedt, Elisha Cook, Sam Reese, David Mauro, Valerie Starrett, Lisa Donzell
45. [unknown title] (1-4-67) Leslie Uggams, David Opatoshu, Ronald Feinberg
46. "Child Out of Time" (1-11-67) Nina Foch, Eileen Baral, Paul Lambert, Charles MacCaulay
47. "The Trouble with Temple" (1-25-67) Carol Wayne, Jack Cassidy, Kurt Kasznar
48. "The War Lord" (2-1-67) Jean Marsh, Cecil Parker, Patrick Barr, Carl Rapp
49. "A Rome with a Rack" (2-8-67) Salome Jens, Keith Andes, Cyril Delevanti, Jean Del Val, José Pepe Nieto
50. "Mainly on the Plains" (2-22-67) Boris Karloff, Carl Schell
51. "Get Thee to a Nunnery" (3-1-67) Peter Lawford, Lilia Skala, Vincent Gardenia
52. "Blackout" (3-8-67) Zohra Lampert, Lawrence Dane
53. "Magic Mirror" (3-15-67) Virginia Grey, Ricardo Montalban,

France Nuyen
54. "Night Train to Madrid" (3-22-67) Barbara McNair, Don
    Rickles, Michael Strong, Marianna Hill
55. "Casanova from Canarsie" (3-29-67) Wally Cox, Leticia
    Roman, Will Kuluva, Sandy Kenyon, Thordis Brandt, Joan
    Marshall
56. "Cops and Robbers" (4-12-67) Jim Brown, Beah Richards

Third Season

57. "Let's Kill Karlovassi" (9-11-67) Walter Slezak, Ruth Ro-
    man, Peter Wyngarde
58. "The Beautiful Children" (9-18-67) Harold J. Stone, Eduardo
    Ciannelli, Paris Alexander, John Aniston, Anna Brazzou
59. "Laya" (9-25-67) Janet MacLachlan, Michael Rennie, Keith
    Andes, Marino Masé
60. "The Medarra Block" (10-2-67) Jack Kruschen, Arthur
    Batanides, Joe Bernard, Norman Fell
61. "Philotimo" (10-9-67) Harold J. Stone, John Megna, Arthur
    Batanides, Eleanor Sommers, Barney Phillips
62. "The Honorable Assassins" (10-16-67) Nehemiah Persoff,
    Dorothy Lamour, Edgar Stehli, Sivi Aberg
63. "Now You See Her, Now You Don't" (10-23-67) Barbara
    Mullen, Keith Andes, Gregoire Aslan
64. "Red Sash of Courage" (10-30-67) Louise Sorel, John Qua-
    len, Roger C. Carmel, Andrea Teuber, Charles Horvath
65. "The Seventh Captain" (11-13-67) Harold J. Stone, Nick
    Dennis, George Economu, Robert Patten, Jack Stany
66. "Apollo" (11-20-67) Pippa Scott, Nancy Kovacs, Ron Rich,
    Charlene Jones
67. "Oedipus at Colonus" (11-27-67) Maurice Evans, Delia Boc-
    cardo, Ken Tobey
68. "The Lotus Eater" (12-11-67) Vivian Ventura, Michael
    Evans, Sheldon Leonard
69. "An American Empress" (12-25-67) France Nuyen, Philip
    Ahn, Benson Fong
70. "Home to Judgment" (1-8-68) Will Geer, Una Merkel,
    Robert Donner, Bob Sampson, Walter Coy
71. "Anyplace I Hang Myself Is Home" (1-15-68) Henry Silva,
    Mary Murphy, Denny Miller, Ken Tobey
72. "Tag, You're It" (1-22-68) John Smith, Paul Mantee, Peter
    Duryea, Norman Burton, Richard Webb, Rosemary Eliot,
    Roy Jenson, Leigh French, Roger Bowen, Ron Burke
73. "A Few Miles West of Nowhere" (1-29-68) Andrew Duggan,
    Diahn Williams, Richard Kiel, Ken Swofford, Leonard
    Stone
74. "This Guy Smith" (2-5-68) Richard Denning, Diana Muldaur,
    John Lupton, Ken Tobey
75. "Turnabout for Traitors" (2-19-68) Peter Donat, Jose
    Chavez, Rodolfo Hoyos, Ross Elliott, Regina Torne
76. "Happy Birthday ... Everybody" (2-26-68) Gene Hackman,
    Jim Backus, Tony Fraser
77. "Shana" (3-4-68) Gloria Foster, Albert Dekker, Wolf

Rubinski
78. "The Name of the Game" (3-11-68) Lloyd Nolan, Ken Tobey, Barbara Angely, Joge Russek
79. "Suitable for Framing" (3-25-68) Dan Tobin, John Fiedler, James Best, Francisco Cordova
80. "The Spy Business" (4-1-68) Dane Clark, Paul Richards, William Mims, George Voskovec
81. "Carmelita Is One of Us" (4-8-68) Marie Gomez, Nate Esformes, Paul Bertova
82. "Pinwheel" (4-15-68) Arlene Golonka, Victor Sen Yung, Marino Masé


AMOS BURKE, SECRET AGENT

Michael Dunn's brutally memorable performance as the sadistic "Mr. Sin" of the seventh teleplay is the hallmark of this espionage entry, with Gene Barry's Burke's Law character Amos Burke divested of his police captain credentials.

The Regulars: Amos Burke, Gene Barry; The Man, Carl Benton Reid.

The Episodes:

1. "Balance of Terror" (9-15-65) Susanne Cramer, Will Kuluva Michele Carey, Gerald Mohr, Peter Mamakos, Theo Marcuse, Arthur Batanides, Lawrence Montaigne
2. "Operation Long Shadow" (9-22-65) Rosemary De Camp, Barry Kroeger, Antoinette Bower, Dan Tobin
3. "Steam Heat" (9-29-65) Nehemiah Persoff, Kipp Hamilton, James Best, Joan Huntington, Jack Lambert, Jane Wald
4. "Password to Death" (10-6-65) Janette Scott, Joseph Ruskin, Michael Pate, Bill Glover
5. "The Man with the Power" (10-13-65) Thomas Gomez, Steven Geray, John Abbott, Fred Beir
6. "Nightmare in the Sun" (10-20-65) Barbara Luna, Edward Asner, Nico Minardos, Elisha Cook, Alex Montoya
7. "The Prisoners of Mr. Sin" (10-27-65) Michael Dunn, Robert Cornthwaite, J. Pat O'Malley, France Nuyen
8. "Peace, It's a Gasser" (11-3-65) Henry Jones, Brooke Bundy, Ruta Lee, Paul Carr
9. "The Weapon" (11-10-65) Dyan Cannon, David Sheiner, Bernard Fox, Elisa Ingram, Norman Alden, Whit Bissell
10. "Deadlier than the Male" (11-17-65) Julie Adams, Arnold Moss, Richard Loo, Lisa Gaye
11. "Whatever Happened to Adriana, and Why Won't She Stay Dead?" (12-1-65) Albert Paulsen, Jocelyn Lane, Richard Angerola, Rodolfo Hoyos
12. "The Man's Men" (12-8-65) Nancy Gates, Louis Quinn, Whit Bissell, Norman Alden, Vaughn Taylor, Bartlett Robinson

13.  "Or No Tomorrow" (12-15-65)  Abbe Lane
14.  "A Little Gift from Cairo" (12-22-65)  Jeanette Nolan
15.  "A Very Important Russian Is Missing" (12-29-65)  Phyllis
     Newman, Nina Shipman, Farley Baer
16.  "Terror in a Tiny Town" [Part I] (1-5-66)  Kevin McCarthy,
     Lynn Loring, Robert Middleton, Joan Huntington
17.  "Terror in a Tiny Town" [Part II] (1-12-66)  as above


## LAREDO

Western satire of Texas Rangers (Neville Brand as Reese
Bennett; Peter Brown as Chad Cooper; William Smith as Joe Riley),
commandeered by one Parmalee (Philip Carey).

The Regulars:  Reese Bennett, Neville Brand; Chad Cooper, Peter
     Brown; Joe Riley, William Smith; Parmalee, Philip Carey;
     Erik, Robert Wolders.

The Episodes:

1.   "Lazyfoot, Where Are You?" (9-16-65)  Burgess Meredith,
     Beverly Garland, Mario Alcaide, Harry Hickox, Leo Gor-
     don, Bern Hoffman, Dorothy Dells, Ernest Anderson
2.   "I See by Your Outfit" (9-23-65)  James Farentino, Vito
     Scotti, John Marley, James Doohan, Carlos Romero
3.   "Yahoo" (9-30-65)  Martin Milner, Cliff Osmond, Dub Tay-
     lor, Shelly Morrison
4.   "Rendezvous at Arillo" (10-7-65)  Julie Harris, Donnelly
     Rhodes, Bruce Dern, Woodrow Parfrey, Lane Bradford,
     Don Stewart
5.   "Three's Company" (10-14-65)  David Brian, Myrna Fahey,
     James Seay
6.   "Anybody Here Seen Billy?" (10-21-65)  Mickey Finn, Joan
     Staley, Robert Hoy
7.   "A Question of Discipline" (10-28-65)  Barbara Nichols,
     Marlyn Mason, Barbara Werle
8.   "The Golden Trail" (11-4-65)  Jeanette Nolan, Jim Davis,
     Arthur Hunnicutt, Tom Reese
9.   "A Matter of Policy" (11-11-65)  Robert F. Simon, Charles
     Gray, Mickey Finn, Jon Locke, Mike Ragen, I. Stanford
     Jolley, Gil Perkins
10.  "Which Way Did They Go?" (11-18-65)  Eve Arden, Rex
     Holman, Lyle Talbott, Myron Healey
11.  "Jinx" (12-2-65)  Albert Salmi, Shelley Morrison, Richard
     Devon, John Abbott
12.  "The Land Grabbers" (12-9-65)  Fred Clark, Audrey Dalton,
     Alan Napier, Bart Burns, Keith Jones, Dennis McCarthy
13.  "Pride of the Rangers" (12-16-65)  George Kennedy, George
     Shaughnessy
14.  "The Heroes of San Gill" (12-23-65)  Lonny Chapman
15.  "A Medal for Reese" (12-30-65)  Stacy Harris, Emile Genest

16. "Calico Kid" (1-6-66) George Chandler, Mimsy Farmer, Wesley Lau, Harry Hickox
17. "Above the Law" (1-13-66) Jack Lord, Lola Albright, John Kellogg
18. "That's Noway, Thataway" (1-20-66) Peter Graves, Arch Johnson, Marlyn Mason
19. "Limit of the Law Larkin" (1-27-66) Claude Akins, John Hoyt
20. "Meanwhile, Back at the Reservation" (2-10-66) Kurt Russell, Robert Yuro
21. "The Treasure of San Diablo" (2-17-66) Claude Akins, Jan Arvan
22. "No Bugles, One Drum" (2-24-66) Shelley Morrison, Richard Devon, Michael Conrad
23. "Miracle at Massacre Mission" (3-3-66) Barbara Rush, Tina Holland
24. "It's the End of the Road, Stanley" (3-10-66) Fernando Lamas, Jeanette Nolan
25. "A Very Small Assignment" (3-17-66) Richard Hadyn, Ken Lynch
26. "Quarter Past Eleven" (3-24-66) Lee Van Cleef, Stanley Adams, Roy Roberts
27. "The Deadliest Kid in the West" (3-31-66) Jack Kelly, Gin Gillespie
28. "Sound of Terror" (4-7-66) John Carradine, DeForest Kell Tiger Joe Marsh, Tom Simcox, Virginia Christine, Laraine Stephens
29. "The Would-Be Gentleman of Laredo" (4-14-66) Joe De Santis, Donnelly Rhodes, Madlyn Rhue
30. "A Taste of Money" (4-28-66) Charles Ruggles, Noah Bee

Second Season

31. "The Legend of Midas Mantee" (9-16-66) Rex Holman, Cli Osmond
32. "The Dance of the Laughing Death" (9-23-66) Abraham Sof aer, Myron Healey
33. "A Double Shot of Nepenthe" (9-30-66) Will Kuluva, Warre Kemmerling
34. "Coup de Grace" (10-7-66) Barbara Luna, Arnold Moss, John Hoyt
35. "The Land Slickers" (10-14-66) Gene Raymond, Anna Cap Leo Gordon, Alan de Witt
36. "Finnegan" (10-21-66) Malachi Throne, Ken Lynch, Mort Mills, John Harmon, Stuart Anderson, K. L. Smith
37. "Any Way the Wind Blows" (10-28-66) Melodie Johnson, Michael Evans, Tiger Joe Marsh
38. "The Sweet Gang" (11-4-66) Ellen Corby, Kathie Browne, Robert Beecher, Lennie Weinrib
39. "One Too Many Voices" (11-18-66) Whitney Blake, Jim Goodwin
40. "Road to San Remo" (11-25-66) Claire Wilcox, Dabbs Gre
41. "The Last of the Caesars--Absolutely" (12-2-66) Jack

Weston, E. J. André, Sig Haig, Joan Huntington
42. "A Prince of a Ranger" (12-9-66) Mimsy Farmer, Lisabeth
Hush, Ivor Barry
43. "Oh Careless Love" (12-23-66) Thomas Gomez, Ken Scott
44. "Leave It to Dixie" (12-20-66) Donald Barry, Peter Dunhill,
Clint Howard, Barbara Werle
45. "The Seventh Day" (1-6-67) Alfred Ryder, Wesley Lau,
William Bramley
46. "Scourge of San Rosa" (1-20-67) Robert Yuro, Kathleen
Freeman
47. "The Short, Happy Fatherhood of Reese Bennett" (1-27-67)
Rick Natoli, Michael Green
48. "The Bitter Yen of General Ti" (2-3-67) Henry Silva,
Philip Ahn, Larry Montaigne, Irene Tsu
49. "The Other Cheek" (2-10-67) Barbara Anderson, Robert F.
Simon, Malcolm Atterbury, Edward Faulkner
50. "Enemies and Brothers" (2-17-67) Jack Kelly, Mary Murphy,
Barbara Werle
51. "Hey Diddle Diddle" (2-24-67) Marilyn Erskine, Jacques
Aubuchon, Claude Akins, Carl Ballentine, Michael Forest,
Michael Keep
52. "The Small Chance Ghost" (3-3-67) Jeanne Cooper, Edward
Binns, Ted Cassidy
53. "A Question of Guilt" (3-10-67) Patsy Kelly
54. "Like One of the Family" (3-24-67) Jeanette Nolan, Parley
Baer, Don Beddoe
55. "Walk Softly" (3-31-67) Joe Flynn, Claude Akins, George
Furth
56. "Split the Difference" (4-7-67) Shelley Morrison, Monica
Lewis, Gerald Mohr, Myron Healey

## THE LONG, HOT SUMMER

That splendrous and eternal summer of the Varner clan
(pansophic, pater familias Will; his comely daughter Clara; brooding son Jody) and their sultry compatriots at Frenchman's Bend--
all cathartically affected by the presence of drifter Ben Quick (believed a "barn-burner")--was the subject of this apocryphal William
Faulkner tale. Far better was the Irving Ravetch and Harriet
Frank Jr. screenplay for the 1958 motion picture The Long Hot
Summer which was ostensibly derived from the Faulkner 1940 novel
The Hamlet and 1939 short story The Barn Burning.

The cast, however, performed admirably; guest stars in
roles as flamboyant as the teleplay titles.

The Regulars: Will Varner, Edmond O'Brien (to episode of 12/30/
65); Varner thereafter played by Dan O'Herlihy; Ben Quick,
Roy Thinnes; Clara Varner, Nancy Malone; Jody Varner,
Paul Geary (Tom Lowell substituted for Geary with episode
of 3/9/66); Minnie, Ruth Roman; Duane Galloway, John

Kerr; Eula, Lana Wood; Sheriff Harve Anders, Paul Bryar
Lucas Taney, Warren Kemmerling; Bo Chamberlain, Harol
Gould; Sam Ruddabaw, William Mims; Shad Taney, Mike
Zaslow; Mitch Taney, Brian Cutler; Agnes, Josie Lloyd;
Dr. Clark, Jason Wingreen; Andrew, Charles Lampkin;
Dr. Talicott, Jimmy Hayes.

The Episodes:

1. "The Homecoming" (9-16-65) regulars
2. "A Time for Living" (9-23-65) Tisha Sterling
3. "A Stranger to the House" (9-30-65) Tisha Sterling, Zalmar
   King, Wayne Rogers
4. "The Twisted Image" [Part I] (10-7-65) Ford Rainey, Karer
   Steele
5. "The Twisted Image" [Part II] (10-14-65) as above
6. "Home Is a Nameless Place" (10-21-65) Jill Haworth, Dan
   Ferrone
7. "No Hiding Place" (10-28-65) Ray Stricklyn
8. "Run, Hero, Run" (11-4-65) Gary Conway, Logan Field
9. "The Desperate Innocent" (11-11-65) Richard Kiley, Brenda
   Scott, George Selk, Ed Peck, Gerry Lock
10. "Bitter Harvest" (11-18-65) Julie Adams, Stewart Moss,
    Richard Reeves, Mason Curry
11. "Hunter to the Wind" (12-2-65) Barry Sullivan
12. "Nor Hell a Fury ... " (12-9-65) Joanne Dru, Warren
    Stevens, Whit Bissell
13. "Return of the Quicks" (12-16-65) Dan Duryea
14. "Track the Man Down" (12-30-65) Royal Dano
15. "Face of Fear" (1-6-66) Celeste Holm, Tony Benson, Jean
    Willes
16. "Evil Angel" (1-13-66) Geraldine Page, Joanne Roos
17. "A Day of Thunder" (1-19-66) Gary Lockwood
18. "The Warning" (1-26-66) John Alderman, Bobby Pickett,
    Rick Murray, David Carlile, Bob Alden
19. "The Intruders" (2-2-66) John Cassavetes, Dolores Sutton,
    Jan Merlin
20. "From This Day Forward" (2-9-66) Gena Rowlands
21. "A Time to Die" (2-16-66) Ralph Meeker, Wayne Rogers
22. "Reunion--Italian Style" (2-23-66) Collin Wilcox
23. "Blaze of Glory" (3-2-66) Uta Hagen
24. "Crisis" (3-9-66) regulars
25. "Carlotta, Come Home" (3-30-66) Nina Foch, Steven
    Franken
26. "Man with Two Faces" (4-13-66) Ricardo Montalban, Jame
    Brolin

THE WILD, WILD, WEST

With the Cold War surveillance techniques made popular by
1964's "The Man from U. N. C. L. E. " and with the sustained

popularity of (although increasingly less so) the western genre, "The Wild, Wild, West" attempted to merge the idioms by placing its secret service protagonist, Major James T. West (Robert Conrad) in the post-Civil War days of Ulysses S. Grant. The difficulty with this premise was that the surveillance techniques utilized in the teleplays could not have been conceived of for years.

The principal creative significance of this series rests in its construction of offbeat villains, who served as a perfect foil for the resourceful youthful protagonist. In their maleficent glory, madness became stylish; a sophistication to be intensely studied, if not--let the puritans gasp--emulated. Veteran Hollywood character actors went about their craft with a precision that could only have come from an adoration of inspired typecasting.

Agnes Moorehead was her vitriolic finest in the role of Emma Valentine, the deadly matchmaker of "The Night of the Vicious Valentine"--for which Moorehead won an Emmy. The continental Ricardo Montalban was likewise perfectly suited to the role of a madman who had learned to travel through the fourth dimension in Henry Sharp's "The Night of the Lord of the Limbo." Victor Buono romped through the role of the magician Count Manzeppi in Charles Bennett's "The Night of the Eccentrics" and again in Henry Sharp's "The Night of the Feathered Fury." Jo Van Fleet was the dictatorial chairman of a steadily diminishing board of directors in Louis Vittes' "The Night of the Tycoons." Hurd Hatfield triumphed in John Kneubuhl's interesting piece on déjà vu, "The Night of the Man-Eating House." Ed Begley was the vindictive judge in Shimon Wincelberg's "The Night of the Infernal Machine." Nehemiah Persoff was the scheming "victim" of a prison stockade in Max Hodge's "The Night of the Underground Terror."

One fascinating episode, Ken Kolb's "The Night of the Burning Diamond," involved a brilliant Midas-type character (in this case Morgan Midas), who had discovered a way in which a diamond elixir could make one travel faster than could be detected by the human eye. The role was played, with considerable finesse, by actor Robert Drivas. Irving J. Moore directed the teleplay.

Perhaps the most macabre character was that played by the brilliant actor Michael Dunn--Dr. Miguelito Loveless, whose genius ran the gamut from creating a mechanical man in John Kneubuhl's "The Night of the Green Terror" to literally living in the period conveyed by paintings in John Kneubuhl's "The Night of the Surreal McCoy." Loveless ostensibly owed his villainy to the "curse" of his midget size. While he of course could never thwart his opposition, he was nonetheless once pronounced dead and resurrected in Henry Sharp's "The Night Dr. Loveless Died."

The technical skill is particularly obvious in this series-- Alan J. Jaggs' and Grant K. Smith's film editing, Ted Voigtlander's photography, Richard Markowitz's music, and Albert Heschong's excellent art direction.

The Regulars: Major James T. West, Robert Conrad; Artemus Gordon, Ross Martin; Tennyson, Charles Davis (first season only); Jeremy Pike, Charles Aidman (last season episodes only).

The Episodes:

1. "The Night of the Inferno" (9-17-65) Suzanne Pleshette, Victor Buono, Nehemiah Persoff, James Gregory, Bebe Louie, Walter Woolf King, Chet Stratton, Alberto Morin
2. "The Night of the Deadly Bed" (9-24-65) Barbara Luna, J. D. Cannon, Bob Herron, Danica d'Hondt
3. "The Night the Wizard Shook the Earth" (10-1-65) Michael Dunn, Leslie Parrish, William Mims, Richard Kiel
4. "The Night of the Sudden Death" (10-8-65) Robert Loggia, Sandy Kenyon, Antoinette Bower, Julie Payne
5. "The Night of the Casual Killer" (10-15-65) John Dehner, Ruta Lee, Bill Williams, Mort Mills, Len Lesser
6. "The Night of a Thousand Eyes" (10-22-65) Jeff Corey, Diane McBain, Linda Ho, Victor French, Donald O'Kelly
7. "The Night of the Glowing Corpse" (10-29-65) Kipp Hamilton, Philip Pine, Oscar Beregi
8. "The Night of the Dancing Death" (11-5-65) Mark Richman, Ilze Taurins, Arthur Batanides, Francoise Ruggieri, Booth Colman, Leslie Brander
9. "The Night of the Double-Edged Knife" (11-12-65) Leslie Nielsen, John Drew Barrymore, Katherine Ross, Elisha Cook, Harry Townes, Vaughn Taylor, Tyler McVey, Ed Peck, Susan Silo, Lew Brown, Harry Lauter, Arthur Space, Robert B. Williams, Robert Nash, Julia Montoya
10. "The Night the Terror Stalked the Town" (11-19-65) Michael Dunn
11. "The Night of the Red-Eyed Madman" (11-26-65) Martin Landau, Joan Huntington, Shary Marshall, Gregg Martell, Marianna Case, Nelson Olmsted
12. "The Night of the Human Trigger" (12-3-65) Burgess Meredith, Kathie Browne, Gregg Palmer, Hank Patterson
13. "The Night of the Torture Chamber" (12-10-65) Alfred Ryder, Henry Beckman, Sigrid Valdis, H. M. Wynant, Nadia Sanders, Viviane Ventura, Mike Abelar
14. "The Night of the Howling Light" (12-17-65) Sam Wanamaker, Ralph Moody, Linda Marsh, E. J. Andre, Don Kennedy
15. "The Night of the Fatal Trap" (12-24-65) Ron Randell, Charles Davis, Joseph Ruskin, Don Briggs
16. "The Night of the Steel Assassin" (1-7-66) John Dehner, Sue Ane Langdon, Allen Jaffe, Arthur Malet, Sara Taft, Roy Engel
17. "The Night the Dragon Screamed" (1-14-66) Philip Ahn, Richard Loo, Ben Wright, Pilar Seurat
18. "The Night of the Grand Emir" (1-28-66) Robert Middleton, Yvonne Craig, Don Francks, Richard Jaeckel
19. "The Night of the Flaming Ghost" (2-4-66) John Doucette, Lynn Loring, Karen Sharpe

0. "The Night of the Whirring Death" (2-18-66) Michael Dunn, Barbara Nichols, Pamela Austin, Jesse White, Richard Kiel
1. "The Night of the Puppeteer" (2-25-66) Lloyd Bochner, John Hoyt
2. "The Night of the Bars of Hell" (3-4-66) Arthur O'Connell, Elisha Cook, Indus Arthur, Milton Parsons
3. "The Night of the Two-Legged Buffalo" (3-11-66) Nick Adams, Dana Wynter, Robert Emhardt, Paul Comi
4. "The Night of the Druid's Blood" (3-25-66) Don Rickles, Ann Elder, Sam Wade, Rhys Williams, Simon Scott, Bartlett Robinson
5. "The Night of the Freebooters" (4-1-66) Keenan Wynn, André Philippe
6. "The Night of the Burning Diamond" (4-8-66) Robert Drivas, Christine Schmidtmer, Dan Tobin, Vito Carbonara, Calvin Brown, Whitey Hughes
7. "The Night of the Murderous Spring" (4-15-66) Michael Dunn, Janie Jackson
8. "The Night of the Sudden Plague" (4-22-66) Theodore Marcuse, Nobu McCarthy, H. M. Wynant, Elliott Reid

## Second Season

9. "The Night of the Eccentrics" (9-16-66) Victor Buono, Richard Pryor, Anthony Eisley, Paul Wallace
0. "The Night of the Golden Cobra" (9-23-66) Boris Karloff, Michael York, Audrey Dalton, Jose De Vega
1. "The Night of the Raven" (9-30-66) Michael Dunn, Phyllis Newman, Sandy Josel, Phoebe Dorin
2. "The Night of the Big Blast" (10-7-66) Patsy Kelly, Ida Lupino, Mala Powers, Robert Miller Driscall
3. "The Night of the Returning Dead" (10-14-66) Peter Lawford, Sammy Davis Jr., Ken Lynch, Hazel Court, Alan Baxter
4. "The Night of the Flying Pie Plate" (10-21-66) William Windom, Leslie Parrish, Ford Rainey, Woodrow Chambliss
5. "The Night of the Poisonous Posey" (10-28-66) Delphi Lawrence, Percy Rodriguez, Hal Lynch, André Phillipe, H. M. Wynant, George Keymas
6. "The Night of the Bottomless Pit" (11-4-66) Theodore Marcuse, Tom Drake, Joan Huntington, Mabel Albertson
7. "The Night of the Watery Death" (11-11-66) John Van Dreelen, John Ashley, Jocelyn Lane
. "The Night of the Green Terror" (11-18-66) Michael Dunn, Paul Fix, Anthony Caruso
. "The Night of the Ready-Made Corpse" (11-25-66) Carroll O'Connor, Alan Bergmann, Karen Sharpe
. "The Night of the Man-Eating House" (12-2-66) Hurd Hatfield, William Talman

41. "The Night of the Skulls" (12-16-66) Donald Woods, Lisa
    Gaye, Douglas Henderson
42. "The Night of the Infernal Machine" (12-23-66) Ed Begley,
    Elaine Dunn, Will Kuluva, Vito Scotti
43. "The Night of the Lord of the Limbo" (12-30-66) Ricardo
    Montalban, Dianne Foster, Felice Orlandi
44. "The Night of the Tottering Tontine" (1-6-67) Robert Em-
    hardt, Harry Townes, Henry Darrow, Michael Road, Lisa
    Perá, Arthur Space, William Wintersole
45. "The Night of the Feathered Fury" (1-13-67) Victor Buono,
    Perry Lopez, Michelle Carey, George Murdock
46. "The Night of the Gypsy Peril" (1-20-67) Mark Slade, Ruta
    Lee, Arthur Batanides
47. "The Night of the Tartar" (2-3-67) John Astin, Malachi
    Throne, Susan Odin
48. "The Night of the Vicious Valentine" (2-10-67) Agnes Moore-
    head, Sherry Jackson, Diane McBain, Henry Beckman
49. "The Night of the Brain" (2-17-67) Edward Andrews, Brioni
    Farrell, Allen Jaffe
50. "The Night of the Deadly Bubble" (2-24-67) Alfred Ryder,
    Judy Lang, Lou Krugman
51. "The Night of the Surreal McCoy" (3-3-67) Michael Dunn,
    John Doucette
52. "The Night of the Colonel's Ghost" (3-10-67) Kathie Browne
    Lee Bergere, Alan Hewitt, Walker Edmiston, Roy Engel,
    Arthur Hunnicutt
53. "The Night of the Deadly Blossom" (3-17-67) Nehemiah Per
    soff, Miko Taka
54. "The Night of the Cadre" (3-24-67) Richard Jaeckel, Don
    Gordon, Sheilah Wells, Vince Howard
55. "The Night of the Wolf" (3-31-67) Joseph Campanella, John
    Marley, Lorri Scott, Jonathan Lippe
56. "The Night of the Bogus Bandits" (4-7-67) Michael Dunn,
    Patsy Kelly, Marianna Hill, Grace Gaynor

Third Season

57. "The Night of the Bubbling Death" (9-8-67) Madlyn Rhue,
    Harold Gould, William Schallert, Timmy Brown
58. "The Night of the Firebrand" (9-15-67) Pernell Roberts,
    Lana Wood, Paul Lambert
59. "The Night of the Assassin" (9-22-67) Robert Loggia, Dona
    Woods, Conlan Carter, Nina Roman, Ramon Novarro
60. "The Night Dr. Loveless Died" (9-29-67) Michael Dunn,
    Susan Oliver, Robert Ellenstein, Anthony Caruso
61. "The Night of the Jack O'Diamonds" (10-6-67) Frank Silver
    Mario Alcalde, James Alamanzar, David Renard
62. "The Night of the Samurai" (10-13-67) Irene Tsu, Paul
    Stevens, Thayer David, Khigh Dhiegh
63. "The Night of the Hangman" (10-20-67) Martin Brooks,
    Anna Capri, Sarah Marshall, Dean Stanton, Paul Fix
64. "The Night of Montezuma's Hordes" (10-27-67) Ray Walstor
    Jack Elam, Edmund Hashim, Roland La Starza, Hal Jon

Norman, Carla Borelli

65. "The Night of the Circus of Death" (11-3-67) Joan Huntington, Arlene Martel, Phil Bruns
66. "The Night of the Falcon" (11-10-67) Robert Duvall, Kurt Kreuger, Lisa Gaye
67. "The Night of the Cut-throats" (11-17-67) Jackie Coogan, Bradford Dillman, Beverly Garland, Walter Burke
68. "The Night of the Legion of Death" (11-24-67) Kent Smith, Donnelly Rhodes, Karen Jensen, Toian Matchinga
69. "The Night of the Turncoat" (12-1-67) John McGiver, Marj Dusay, Douglas Henderson, Bebe Louie
70. "The Night of the Iron Fist" (12-8-67) Mark Lenard, Ford Rainey, Lisa Pera, Bill Fletcher
71. "The Night of the Running Death" (12-15-67) Jason Evers, T. C. Jones, Karen Arthur, Maggie Thrett
72. "The Night of the Arrow" (12-29-67) Jeannine Riley, Robert Phillips, Robert Wilke, Frank Marth
73. "The Night of the Headless Woman" (1-5-68) Richard Anderson, Theodore Marcuse, Dawn Wells, John McLiam
74. "The Night of the Vipers" (1-12-68) Nick Adams, Sandra Smith, Donald Davis
75. "The Night of the Underground Terror" (1-19-68) Nehemiah Persoff, Jeff Corey, Douglas Henderson
76. "The Night of the Death Masks" (1-26-68) Milton Selzer, Patty McCormack, Judy McConnell, Louis Quinn
77. "The Night of the Undead" (2-2-68) Hurd Hatfield, Joan Delaney, Priscilla Morrill, John Zaremba
78. "The Night of the Amnesiac" (2-9-68) Sharon Farrell, Edward Asner, Kevin Hagen
79. "The Night of the Simian Terror" (2-16-68) John Abbott, Dabbs Greer, Felice Orlandi, Grace Gaynor
80. "The Night of the Death-Maker" (2-23-68) Wendell Corey, Angel Tompkins, J. Pat O'Malley, Arthur Batanides, Roy Engel

## Fourth Season

81. "The Night of the Big Blackmail" (9-27-68) Harvey Korman, Wilhelm Von Homburg, Roy Engel, Ron Rich
82. "The Night of the Doomsday Formula" (10-4-68) Kevin McCarthy, E. J. Andre, Melinda Plowman
83. "The Night of the Juggernaut" (10-11-68) Floyd Patterson, Simon Scott, Gloria Calomee
84. "The Night of the Sedgewick Curse" (10-18-68) Jay Robinson, Sharon Acker, Maria Lennard, Richard Hale
85. "The Night of the Gruesome Games" (10-25-68) William Schallert, Sherry Jackson, Robert Ellenstein
86. "The Night of the Krakan" (11-1-68) Jason Evers, Anthony Caruso, Ted Knight, Marj Dusay
87. "The Night of the Fugitives" (11-8-68) Simon Oakland, Charles McGraw, J. S. Johnson, Susan Hart, Mickey Hargitay
88. "The Night of the Egyptian Queen" (11-15-68) Tom Troupe,

Sorrell Booke, William Marshall, Penny Gaston, Walter
Brooke

89. "The Night of the Fire and Brimstone" (11-22-68) Charles
Macaulay, Robert Phillips, Dabbs Greer, John Crawford,
Leslie Charleson

90. "The Night of the Camera" (11-29-68) Pat Paulsen, Barry
Atwater, Lou Procopio

91. "The Night of the Avaricious Actuary" (12-6-68) Harold
Gould, Emily Banks, Ross Elliott, Jenny Maxwell

92. "The Night of Miguelito's Revenge" (12-13-68) Michael
Dunn, Susan Seaforth, Douglas Henderson, Arthur Batanides, Jim Shane, Don Pedro Colley, Percy Helton, Byron Morrow, Walter Coy, Linda Chandler, Peter Bruni,
Johnny S. Luer

93. "The Night of the Pelican" (12-27-68) Khigh Dhiegh, Vincent Beck, Francine York

94. "The Night of the Spanish Curse" (1-3-69) Thayer David,
Toian Matchinga, Richard Angarola

95. "The Night of the Winged Terror" [Part I] (1-17-69) Wil-
liam Schallert, Jackie Coogan, Bernard Fox, Christopher
Cary, Michele Carey, John Harding, Robert Ellenstein,
Roy Engel

96. "The Night of the Winged Terror" [Part II] (1-24-69) as
above

97. "The Night of the Sabatini Death" (2-7-69) Jill Townsend,
Jim Backus, Bethel Leslie, Alan Hale, Tom Geas, Donald Barry

98. "The Night of the Janus" (2-14-69) Jack Carter, Anthony
Eisley, Jackie DeShannon, Arthur Malet, Gail Billings

99. "The Night of the Pistoleros" (2-21-69) Edward Binns,
Robert Pine, Henry Wilcoxon, Perry Lopez, Richard
O'Brien

100. "The Night of the Diva" (3-7-69) Patrice Munsel

101. "The Night of the Bleak Island" (3-14-69) John Williams,
Beverly Garland, Robert H. Harris, Richard Erdman,
Jana Taylor, James Westerfield, John Van Dreelen, Gene
Tyburn

102. "The Night of the Cossacks" (3-21-69) Guy Stockwell, Nina
Foch, John Van Dreelen, Donnelly Rhodes, Jennifer Douglas, Alizia Gur

103. "The Night of the Tycoons" (3-29-69) Jo Van Fleet, Steve
Carlson, Joanie Sommers, Tol Avery

104. "The Night of the Plague" (4-4-69) Lana Wood, William
Bryant, Cliff Norton, John Hoyt, James Lanphier, Douglas Henderson, Eddie Firestone

CONVOY

Bleak World War II maritime drama of a convoy of some
200 ships replenishing supplies for the European front. Much is
made of the ambivalence of freighter Captain Ben Foster (John

Larch) toward sagacious Commander Dan Talbot (John Gavin) of the escort destroyer DD 181. Composers included Alfred Hayes ("Passage to Liverpool," and with Preston Wood, "Sink U-116!") and Theodore Apstein and Hank Searls ("The Man with the Saltwater Socks").

The Regulars: Cdr. Dan Talbot, John Gavin; Capt. Ben Foster, John Larch; Chief Officer Steve Kirkland, Linden Chiles.

The Episodes:

1. "Passage to Liverpool" (9-17-65) Gia Scala, John McLiam, Micele Montau, James McMullan, Scott Hale, James McCallion
2. "Flight from Norway" (9-24-65) Dana Wynter, Donnelly Rhodes, Simon Scott, Paul Carr
3. "Felicia" (10-1-65) Katherine Crawford, Liam Sullivan, Antoinette Bower
4. "The Many Colors of Courage" (10-8-65) Jack Palance, Barbara Rush, Dennis Hopper, Jeannine Riley
5. "Lady on the Rock" (10-15-65) Eleanor Parker, Sean McClory, James Doohan, Peter Mamakos, John Marley
6. "The Duel" (10-22-65) Edward Mulhare, Frank Marth, Milton Selzer, Kingston Trio
7. [unknown title] (10-29-65) Nehemiah Persoff, Diana Hyland
8. "Admiral Do-Right" (11-5-65) Andrew Prine, Seymour Cassel, Ed Peck, Paul Genge
9. "Sink U-116!" (11-12-65) Leslie Nielsen
10. "The Heart of an Enemy" (11-19-65) Diane Baker, John Leyton, Sandy Kenyon, Horst Ebersberg
11. "No More Souvenirs" (11-26-65) Jan Shepard, Harold Gould
12. "The Assassin" (12-3-65) Jeremy Slate, Carl Esmond, Marisa Collier, Bart Burns
13. "The Man with the Saltwater Socks" (12-10-65) Don Galloway

## HONEY WEST

Anne Francis won an Emmy nomination for her role as the distaff side of the video secret agent "Honey West"--proficient, of course, in the martial arts; accompanied by an always admiring, if less resourceful, adventurer Sam Bolt (John Ericson).

The Regulars: Honey West, Anne Francis; Sam Bolt, John Ericson; Aunt Meg, Irene Hervey.

The Episodes:

1. "The Swingin' Mrs. Jones" (9-17-65) Ray Danton, Winnie Coffin, Marvin Brody, Louise Arthur
2. "The Owl and the Eye" (9-24-65) Richard Loo, Hershel

Bernardi, Lloyd Bochner, William Bramley

3. "The Abominable Snowman" (10-1-65) Henry Jones, Barry Kelly

4. "A Matter of Wife and Death" (10-8-65) Dianne Foster, Michael Fox, James Best, Henry Beckman

5. "Live a Little ... Kill a Little" (10-15-65) Warren Stevens, Herb Edelman, Mary Murphy

6. "Whatever Lola Wants ... " (10-22-65) Audrey Christie, Johnny Haymer

7. "The Princess and the Paupers" (10-29-65) Michael J. Pollard, Philip Ober, Bobby Sherman

8. "In the Bag" (11-5-65) Everett Sloane, Robert Carricart, Maureen McCormick, Len Lesser

9. "The Flame and the Pussycat" (11-12-65) Liam Sullivan, Ken Lynch, Sean McClory

10. "A Neat Little Package" (11-19-65) J. Pat O'Malley, Arthur Batanides

11. "A Stitch in Crime" (11-26-65) Laurie Main, Charlene Holt, James Sikking

12. "A Million Bucks in Anybody's Language" (12-3-65) Steve Ihnat, Ken Lynch

13. "The Great Lady" (12-10-65) Kevin McCarthy, Cesare Danova

14. "Invitation to Limbo" (12-17-65) Louise Troy, Peter Leeds, Wayne Rogers, Stacy Harris, Dan Frazier

15. "Rockabye the Hard Way" (12-24-65) Vincent Beck, Paul Sorenson

16. "A Nice Little Till to Tap" (12-31-65) Anthony Eisley, Howard McNear

17. "How Brillig, O Beamish Boy?" (1-7-66) John McGiver, Norman Alden

18. "King of the Mountain" (1-14-66) David Opatoshu, Dennis Patrick

19. "It's Earlier Than You Think" (1-21-66) James Griffith, Ken Lynch

20. "The Perfect Un-Crime" (1-28-66) David Brian, John Harmon

21. "Like Visions and Omens ... and All That Jazz" (2-4-66) Nehemiah Persoff, June Vincent

22. "Don't Look Now, but Isn't That Me?" (2-11-66) Alan Reed, Louis Quinn

23. "Come to Me, My Litigation Baby" (2-18-66) Ellen Corby, James Brown

24. "Slay, Gypsy, Slay" (2-25-66) Michael Pate, Byron Morrow

25. "The Fun-Fun Killer" (3-4-66) Marvin Kaplan, John Hoyt, Woodrow Parfrey

26. "Pop Goes the Easel" (3-11-66) George Furth, Larry D. Mann, Robert Strauss

27. "Little Green Robin Hood" (3-18-66) Edd Byrnes, Severn Darden

28. "Just the Bear Facts, Ma'am" (3-25-66) Richard Carlyle, Frank Wilcox

29. "There's a Long, Long Fuse A-Burning" (4-1-66) Dick

Clark, Paul Dubov
30. "An Eerie, Airy Thing" (4-8-66) Lisa Seagram, Ken Lynch, Alan Williams


MR. ROBERTS

The cynicism of the Thomas Heggen book and of the Heggen/ Joshua Logan play has given way to total comedy in this television adaptation. A major reason, of course, would be that in this case Lieutenant Roberts (Roger Smith), mentor to the crew of the cargo ship Reluctant but anathema to the ship's neurotic Captain Morton (Richard X. Slattery), does not die.

The Regulars: Mr. Roberts, Roger Smith; Captain Morton, Richard X. Slattery; Ensign Pulver, Steve Harmon; Doc, George Ives; Mannion, Ronald Starr.

The Episodes:

1. "Bookser's Honeymoon" (9-17-65) Timothy Rooney, Roland Winters, Charla Doherty, William Cort, Randy Kirby
2. "Liberty" (9-24-65) Henry Gibson, John McCook
3. "Physician, Heal Thyself" (10-1-65) Henry Gibson, Danny Walton
4. "The Conspiracy" (10-8-65) Albert Morin, Tsu Kobayashi, Danny Nagai
5. "Old Rustysides" (10-15-65) Woodrow Parfrey, Lou Wills
6. "Lover, Come Forward" (10-22-65) Dennis Robertson, Lisa Gaye
7. "The Captain's Party" (10-29-65) Gladys Holland, Danny Walton
8. "Happy Birthday to Who?" (11-5-65) regulars only
9. "Love at 78 RPM" (11-12-65) Richard Sinatra, Ray Reese, Dennis Robertson, John McCook
10. "Don't Look Now ... but Isn't That the War?" (11-19-65) Stanley Clements
11. "Which Way Did the War Go?" (11-26-65) George Takei, Gene Boland
12. "Getting There Is Half the Fun" (12-3-65) George Takei, James Stacy
13. "Dear Mom" (12-10-65) regulars only
14. "Reluctant Mutiny" (12-17-65) Richard Sinatra
15. "Rock-a-Bye Reluctant" (12-24-65) Naomi Stevens, Ratna Assan
16. "Carry Me Back to Cocoa Island" (12-31-65) Henry Gibson
17. "The Replacement" (1-7-66) Shelley Berman, Robert Ives
18. "Black and Blue Market" (1-14-66) Joan Freeman, Tiger Joe Marsh
19. "The World's Greatest Lover" (1-21-66) Linda Gaye Scott
20. "Eight in Every Port" (1-28-66) Alan Mowbray
21. "The Super Chief" (2-4-66) Jack Carter

22. "Doctor's Dilemma" (2-11-66) Patrice Wymore
23. "The Reluctant Draggin'" (2-18-66) Edd Byrnes
24. " "&$?" the Torpedoes" (2-25-66) Yvonne Craig
25. "A Turn for the Nurse" (3-4-66) Gayle Hunnicutt, Barbara Stuart
26. "Son of Eight in Every Port" (3-11-66) Alan Mowbray, Keely Smith
27. "Unwelcome Aboard" (3-18-66) Barrie Chase
28. "Undercover Cook" (3-25-66) Wally Cox, Tom Brown, Soon Taik Oh, Robert Ito
29. "In Love and War" (4-1-66) Mamie Van Doren, Walter Matthews
30. "Captain, My Captain" (4-8-66) Barbara Werle, Kam Tong


BATMAN

"Batman" cannot be called drama; its irreverence for its own material--a refreshing "self-satire"--and its social impact merits its inclusion here. Marvelous characterizations: Burgess Meredith a waddling "Penguin"; Victor Buono a reincarnated Pharaoh; Shelley Winters in a take-off on Ma Barker; Estelle Winwood a college educated witch; Cesar Romero a heavily powdered "Joker," Malachi Throne a faceless villain announced in the credits with a "?"; both Eartha Kitt and Julie Newmar as the purring "Catwoman" and--among many others--Pierre Salinger as an underhanded defense attorney in the fifty-ninth teleplay. All ran amuck in Gotham City with its lovingly stereotyped police force.

The Regulars: Bruce Wayne/Batman, Adam West; Dick Grayson/ Robin, Burt Ward; Aunt Harriet, Madge Blake; Commissioner Gordon, Neil Hamilton; Officer O'Hara, Stafford Repp; Alfred, Alan Napier; Barbara Gordon/Batgirl, Yvonne Craig (last season only).

The Episodes:

1. a) "Hey Diddle Riddle" (1-12-66) Frank Gorshin, Jill St. John
   b) "Smack in the Middle" (1-13-66) as above
2. a) "Fine Feathered Finks" (1-19-66) Burgess Meredith
   b) "The Penguin's a Jinx" (1-20-66) as above
3. a) "Instant Freeze" (1-26-66) George Saunders, Shelby Grant, Robert Hogan
   b) "Rats Like Cheese" (1-27-66) as above
4. a) "The Joker Is Wild" (2-2-66) Cesar Romero, David Lewi
   b) "Batman Gets Riled" (2-3-66) as above
5. a) "Inescapable Doom Trap" (2-9-66) Anne Baxter, Barbara Helere, Jack Kruschen
   b) "Zelda Takes the Rap" (2-10-66) as above
6. a) "A Riddle a Day Keeps the Riddler Away" (2-16-66) Frank Gorshin, Reginald Denny

b) "When the Rat's Away, the Mice Will Play" (2-17-66) as above

7.  a) "The Thirteenth Hat" (2-23-66) David Wayne, Diane McBain, Monique Lemaire, Gil Perkins
    b) "Batman Stands Pat" (2-24-66) as above

8.  a) "The Joker Goes to School" (3-2-66) Cesar Romero
    b) "He Meets His Match--the Grisly Ghoul" (3-3-66) as above

9.  a) "True or Falseface" (3-9-66) Malachi Throne, Myrna Fahey, Brenda Howard, John Launer
    b) "Super Rat Race" (3-10-66) as above

10. a) "The Purr-fect Crime" (3-16-66) Julie Newmar, Jock Mahoney
    b) "Better Luck Next Time" (3-17-66) as above

11. a) "The Penguin Goes Straight" (3-23-66) Burgess Meredith, Al Checco, Kathleen Crowley, Harvey Lembeck
    b) "Not Yet, He Ain't" (3-24-66) as above

12. a) "Ring of Wax" (3-30-66) Frank Gorshin
    b) ""Give 'Em the Axe" (3-31-66) as above

13. a) "The Joker Trumps an Ace" (4-6-66) Cesar Romero, Angela Green, Norm Alden, Dan Seymour, Owen Bush, Jane Wald
    b) "Batman Sets the Pace" (4-7-66) as above

14. a) "The Curse of Tut" (4-13-66) Victor Buono, Ziva Rodann, Don Barry, Emanuel Thomas, Frank Christi
    b) "The Pharaoh's in a Rut" (4-14-66) as above

15. a) "The Bookworm Turns" (4-20-66) Roddy McDowall, Jan Peters, Francine York, John Crawford
    b) "While Gotham City Burns" (4-21-66) as above

16. a) "Death in Slow Motion" (4-27-66) Frank Gorshin, Theo Marcuse, Francis X. Bushman, Sherry Jackson, Burt Brandon
    b) "The Riddler's False Notion" (4-28-66) as above

17. a) "Five Finny Fiends" (5-4-66) Burgess Meredith, Victor Lunden, Julie Gregg, Louie Elias, Dal Jenkins
    b) "Batman Makes the Scenes" (5-5-66) as above

## Second Season

18. a) "Shoot a Crooked Arrow" (9-7-66) Art Carney, Dick Clark, Robert Cornthwaite, Barbara Nichols
    b) "Walk the Straight and Narrow" (9-8-66) as above

19. a) "Hot Off the Griddle" (9-14-66) James Brolin, Jack Kelly, Julie Newmar, David Fresco
    b) "The Cat and the Fiddle" (9-15-66) as above

20. a) "The Minstrel's Shakedown" (9-21-66) Van Johnson
    b) "Barbecued Batman" (9-22-66) as above

21. a) "The Spell of Tut" (9-28-66) Victor Buono
    b) "Tut's Case Is Shut" (9-29-66) as above

22. a) "The Greatest Mother of Them All" (10-5-66) Shelley Winters, David Lewis, Tisha Sterling
    b) "Ma Parker" (10-6-66) as above

23. a) "The Clock King's Crazy Crimes" (10-12-66) Walter

Slezak, Eileen O'Neil
b) "The Clock King Gets Crowned" (10-13-66) as above
24. a) "An Egg Grows in Gotham" (10-19-66) Vincent Price,
Steve Dunne, Edward Everett Horton
b) "The Yegg Foes in Gotham" (10-20-66) as above
25. a) "The Devil's Fingers" (10-26-66) Liberace, Marilyn
Hanold, Sivi Aberg, Edy Williams
b) "The Dead Ringers" (10-27-66) as above
26. a) "Hizzonner the Penguin" (11-2-66) Burgess Meredith,
Woodrow Parfrey
b) "Dizzonner the Penguin" (11-3-66) as above
27. a) "Green Ice" (11-9-66) Otto Preminger, Byron Keith,
Marie Windsor, Dee Hartford, Nicky Blair
b) "Deep Freeze" (11-10-66) as above
28. a) "Impractical Joker" (11-16-66) Cesar Romero, Kathy
Kersh, Larry Anthony
b) "The Joker's Provokers" (11-17-66) as above
29. a) "Marsha, Queen of Diamonds" (11-23-66) Estelle Winwood,
Woody Strode, Carolyn Jones
b) "Marsha's Scheme with Diamonds" (11-24-66) as above
30. a) "Come Back, Shame" (11-30-66) Cliff Robertson, Joan
Staley, Jack Carter
b) "It's the Way You Play the Game" (12-1-66) as above
31. a) "The Penguin's Nest" (12-7-66) Burgess Meredith, Vito
Scotti, Grace Gaynor, Lane Bradford
b) "The Bird's Last Jest" (12-8-66) as above
32. a) "The Cat's Meow" (12-14-66) Julie Newmar, Sharyn
Winters, Tom Castronova, Joe Flynn, Chad Stuart and
Jeremy Clyde as themselves
b) "The Bat's Kow Tow" (12-15-66) as above
33. a) "The Puzzler Is Coming" (12-21-66) Maurice Evans, Paul
Smith, Barbara Stuart
b) "The Duo Is Slumming" (12-22-66) as above
34. a) "The Sandman Cometh" (12-28-66) Michael Rennie, Julie
Newmar, Spring Byington, Pat Becker, Jeanie Moore,
Tony Ballen, Richard Peel
b) "The Catwoman Goeth" (12-29-66) as above
35. a) "The Contaminated Crowl" (1-4-67) David Wayne, Jean
Hale, Barbara Morrison
b) "The Mad Hatter Runs Afoul" (1-5-67) as above
36. a) "The Zodiak Crimes" (1-11-67) Cesar Romero, Terry
Moore, Burgess Meredith, Hal Baylor, Joe Di Reda, Dick
Crockett, Charles Fredericks, Charles Picerni
b) "The Joker's Hard Times" (1-12-67) as above
c) "The Penguin Declines" (1-18-67) as above
37. a) "That Darn Catwoman" (1-19-67) Julie Newmar, Lesley
Gore, Allen Jenkins, J. Pat O'Malley
b) "Scat, Darn Catwoman" (1-25-67) as above
38. a) "Penguin Is a Girl's Best Friend" (1-26-67) Carolyn
Jones, Burgess Meredith, Estelle Winwood
b) "Penguin Sets a Trend" (2-1-67) as above
c) "Penguin's Disastrous End" (2-2-67) as above
39. a) "Batman's Anniversary" (2-8-67) John Astin, Deanna Lund

Ken Scott

    b) "A Riddling Controversy" (2-9-67) as above

40. a) "The Joker's Last Laugh" (2-15-67) Cesar Romero, Phyllis Douglas, Lawrence Montaigne
    b) "The Joker's Epitaph" (2-16-67) as above

41. a) "Catwoman Goes to College" (2-22-67) Julie Newmar, Whitney Blake, Jacques Bergerac, Paul Mantee
    b) "Batman Displays His Knowledge" (2-23-67) as above

42. a) "A Piece of the Action" (3-1-67) Roger C. Carmel, Bruce Lee, Van Williams, Alex Rocco, Diane McBain
    b) "Batman's Satisfaction" (3-2-67) as above

43. a) "King Tut's Coup" (3-8-67) Victor Buono, Lloyd Haynes, Lee Meriwether, Tol Avery, Tim O'Kelly, James O'Hara, Grace Lee Whitney
    b) "Batman's Waterloo" (3-9-67) as above

44. a) "The Black Widow Strikes Again" (3-15-67) Tallulah Bankhead, Meg Wylie, Donald Barry, Michael Lane
    b) "Caught in the Spider's Den" (3-16-67) as above

45. a) "Pop Goes the Joker" (3-22-67) Cesar Romero, Diane Ivarson, Reginald Gardiner, Jan Arvan
    b) "Flop Goes the Joker" (3-23-67) as above

46. a) "Ice Spy" (3-29-67) Elisha Cook, Eli Wallach, Leslie Parrish, H. M. Wynant
    b) "The Duo Defy" (3-30-67) as above

## Third Season

47. "Enter Batgirl, Exit Penguin" (9-14-67) Burgess Meredith, Anne Baxter, Vincent Price

48. "Ring Around the Riddler" (9-21-67) Frank Gorshin, Joan Collins, Peggy Ann Garner

49. "The Wail of the Siren" (9-28-67) Joan Collins

50. a) "The Sport of Penguins" (10-5-67) Burgess Meredith, Ethel Merman, Horace McMahon
    b) "A Horse of Another Color" (10-12-67) as above

51. "The Unkindest Tut of All" (10-19-67) Victor Buono, Patti Gilbert, Cathleen Cordell, James Gammon

52. "Louie, the Lilac" (10-26-67) Milton Berle, Lisa Seagram

53. a) "The Ogg and I" (11-2-67) Vincent Price, Anne Baxter
    b) "How to Hatch a Dinosaur" (11-9-67) as above

54. "Surf's Up! Joker's Under" (11-16-67) Cesar Romero

55. a) "The Londinium Larcenies" (11-23-67) Rudy Vallee, Glynis Johns, Lyn Peters, Lyn Lawrence, Monty Landis, Harvey Jason, Stacy Maxwell, Aleta Rotell, Maurice Dallimore, Larry Anthony
    b) "The Foggiest Notion" (11-30-67) as above
    c) "The Bloody Tower" (12-7-67) as above

56. "Catwoman's Dressed to Kill" (12-14-67) Eartha Kitt, Rudi Gernreich

57. "The Ogg Couple" (12-21-67) Vincent Price, Eartha Kitt, Anne Baxter, Cesar Romero

58. "The Funny Feline Felonies" (12-28-67) Cesar Romero, Eartha Kitt, Dick Kallman

59. "The Joke's on Catwoman" (1-4-68) Eartha Kitt, Cesar Romero, Pierre Salinger
60. "Louie's Lethal Lilac Time" (1-11-68) Milton Berle, Percy Helton, Nobu McCarthy, John Dennis, Ronal Knight
61. "Nora Clavicle and the Ladies' Crime Club" (1-18-68) Barbara Rush
62. "Penguin's Clean Sweep" (1-25-68) Burgess Meredith, Monique Van Vooren
63. a) "The Great Escape" (2-1-68) Cliff Robertson, Dina Merrill, Hermione Baddeley
    b) "The Great Train Robbery" (2-8-68) as above
64. "I'll Be Mummy's Uncle" (2-22-68) Victor Buono
65. "The Joker's Flying Saucer" (2-29-68) Cesar Romero, Corrine Calvert
66. "The Entrancing Dr. Cassandra" (3-7-68) Ida Lupino, Howard Duff, David Lewis
67. "Minerva, Mayhem, and Millionaires" (3-14-68) Zsa Zsa Gabor

BLUE LIGHT

Conventional World War II espionage tale with Robert Goule the double agent protagonist.

The Regulars: David March, Robert Goulet; Suzanne Duchard, Christine Carere.

The Episodes:

1. "The Last Man" (1-12-66) John Van Dreelen, Donald Harro Werner Peters, Oscar Beregi, Christine Schmidtmer
2. "Target--David March" (1-19-66) Edward Binns, Alan Cuthbertson
3. "The Fortress Below" [Part I] (1-26-66) John Van Dreelen, Eva Pflug, Peter Capell, Horst Frank
4. "The Weapon Within" [Part II] (2-2-66) as above
5. "Traitor's Blood" (2-9-66) David Macklin, Henry Beckman, Lyle Bettger
6. "Agent of the East" (2-16-66) Jan Malmsjo, Dick Davalos, James Mitchell
7. "Sacrifice!" (2-23-66) Larry Pennell, John Ragin, Barry Ford
8. "The Secret War" (3-2-66) Kevin Hagen, Gail Kobe
9. "Invasion by the Stars" (3-9-66) Francis Lederer
10. "The Return of the Elm" (3-23-66) Malachi Throne, Werne Peters, Lawrence Montaigne
11. "Jet Trail" (4-6-66) Philippe Nicaud, Lamont Johnson, Tony Lo Bianco, E. J. André
12. "How to Kill a Toy Soldier" (4-13-66) Walter Altzmann, Todd Martin, Michael Shea
13. "The Deserters" (4-20-66) George Backman, James Davids

Stuart Margolin, Ken Lynch
14. "The Other Fuehrer" (4-27-66) David Sheiner, Paul Carr, Jack Colvin
15. "The Key to the Code" (5-4-66) Hans Gudegast, Vincent Van Lynn, Arthur Batanides
16. "Field of Dishonor" (5-11-66) Steve Ihnat, James Frawley, Harry Basch
17. "The Friendly Enemy" (5-18-66) Mark Richman, Robert Doyle, Richard Carlyle


THE BARON

Undistinguished British-produced espionage tale of a government agent and--a convenient cover--art dealer.

The Regulars: John Mannering, Steve Forrest; Templeton Greene, Colin Gordon; David, Paul Ferris; Cordelia, Sue Lloyd.

The Episodes:

1. "Diplomatic Immunity" (1-20-66) Dora Reisser, Michael Wolf
2. "Red Horse, Red Rider" (1-27-66) Jane Marrow, John Bennett
3. "Epitaph for a Hero" (2-3-66) Paul Maxwell, Patricia Haines
4. "Samurai Sword" (2-10-66) Lee Montague, Jeanne Roland
5. "Something for a Rainy Day" (2-17-66) Michael Gwynn, Patrick Allen
6. "Portrait of Louisa" (2-24-66) Moira Redmond, Terence Alexander
7. "Enemy of the State" (3-3-66) Anton Diffring, Michael Wolf
8. "There's Something Close Behind You" (3-17-66) Richard Wyler, Jerome Willis
9. "The Persuaders" (3-24-66) James Villiers, Georgina Ward
10. "And Suddenly You're Dead" (3-31-66) Kay Walsh, Alan MacNaughtan
11. "Run Wild, Run Wide" (4-14-66) Sylvia Syms, Patrick Bedford
12. "A Memory of Evil" (4-21-66) Ann Bell, Robert Hardy
13. "Masquerade" [Part I] (4-28-66) Bernard Lee, Yvonne Furneaux
14. "The Killing" [Part II] (5-5-66) as above


THE AVENGERS

A stylish British import, this addition to the secret agent genre is distinguished by some fine underplaying by Patrick Macnee as the wealthy John Steed and Diana Rigg as his attractive companion skilled in the martial arts, Mrs. Emma Peel. For so many American counterparts in the genre, it is the emphasis on the weapon--the shooting to kill--that is the labefaction. Agents Steed and Peel, however, frequently supplanted the pistol with the hand and the cane.

In the episode "The Joker" all the finer elements were under control. That familiar set piece--the "haunted house"--to which Mrs. Peel is called, serves as a showcase for both the talents of Miss Rigg and the series' superb technical crew. In a veritable maze of dimly lighted corridors, alone and trapped, the normally indefatigable agent ultimately shows the signs of strain. It is not the conventional devices she cannot surmount (nor we, the audience, anticipating them); it is that persistent German musical refrain, a room suddenly filled with red roses and just as suddenly free of them, a whispering of "Emma" in and out of seemingly nowhere. She confronts her tormentor--because he allows her to--while the camera pans across a full portrait of Mrs. Peel gradually being snipped into fragments by a man seated at the far end of a long dinner table with formal setting. The man's face is not yet revealed to us as he explains, in a disturbing lisp, that Mrs. Peel had been responsible for his downfall. This might have been a cliché were it not for the intricacies with which he executed his final meeting with the lady agent. Mrs. Peel is rescued, of course, by her compatriot Steed, the man who equals but never exceeds her own resourcefulness. Indeed, it is a tribute to the series that the talented Mrs. Peel, fiercely courageous yet wholly feminine, surely struck a minor victory for the women's liberation movement without in the series saying of it so much as a word. Whatever the episode, however fantastic the theme (voodoo in Philip Levene's "Small Game for Big Hunters," ghost hunting in the episode "The Living Dead"), Steed necessarily complemented Emma Peel and Emma Peel John Steed. This continued until one day, in the episode "The Forget-Me-Knot," Mrs. Peel's long lost husband was found and the duo could function together no longer. The final scene has Mrs. Peel calling Steed "John" for the first time and Steed for the first time reciprocating with "Emma." Descending the stairway to the front door Mrs. Peel meets her replacement, Tara King (the victim of a reference to "ta-ra-ra-boom de-ay"), explaining that he (Steed) "likes his tea stirred counterclockwise," and so departed. And with Diana Rigg's departure so too, the style of the series. Linda Thorson's Tara King could not amass even a fraction of the cult of her predecessor; even as no one else could. Miss Rigg eventually attempted the situation comedy with 1973's "Diana"--a program unfortunately short-lived.

A Berkley Medallion series of paperbacks followed through with the series' popularity in the later 1960s.

The Regulars: John Steed, Patrick Macnee; Mrs. Emma Peel, Diana Rigg; Tara King, Linda Thorson (with episode of 3/20/68); Mother, Patrick Newell (with episode of 9/30/68).

The Episodes:

1.  "Cybernauts" (3-28-66) Michael Gough, John Hollis
2.  "Small Game for Big Hunters" (4-4-66) James Villiers,
    Liam Redmond, Bill Fraser, A. J. Brown, Peter Burton,
    Esther Anderson, Tom Gill
3.  'Death at Bargain Prices" (4-11-66) Andre Morell, T. P.
    McKenna, Allan Cuthbertson, George Sellway, Harvey
    Ashby, John Cater, Ronnie Stevens, Diane Clare, Peter
    Howell
4.  "The Hour That Never Was" (4-24-66) Gerald Harper, Dud-
    ley Foster, Roger Booth, Fred Haggerty, Daniel Moynihan,
    Dave Morrell
5.  "Castle De'Ath" (5-2-66) Gordon Jackson, Robert Urquhart,
    Jack Lambert
6.  "Two's a Crowd" (5-9-66) Warren Mitchell, Alec Mango,
    Maria Machado, Wolfe Morris, Julian Glover
7.  "The House That Jack Built" (5-16-66) Michael Goodliffe,
    Griffith Davies, Michael Wynne, Keith Pyott
8.  "The Girl from Auntie" (6-6-66) Liz Fraser, Alfred Burke,
    Bernard Cribbins, David Bauer, Mary Merrall, Ray Mar-
    tine, Sylvia Coleridge
9.  "How to Succeed at Murder" (6-13-66) Sarah Lawson, Ange-
    la Browne, Anne Cunningham, Artre Morris, Jerome Willis
10. "A Sense of History" (6-20-66) Nigel Stock, John Ringham,
    Patrick Mower
11. "Room with a View" (6-27-66) Paul Whitsun-Jones, Peter
    Jeffrey, Richard Bebb, Philip Latham, Peter Arne, Peter
    Madden, Jeanne Roland
12. "The Danger Makers" (7-4-66) Nigel Davenport, Douglas
    Wilmer, Fobia Drake, Moray Watson, Richard Coleman,
    Adrian Ropes
13. "The Master Minds" (7-11-66) Laurene Hardy, Patricia
    Haines, Georgina Ward, Manning Wilson, John Wentworth
14. 'Dial a Deadly Number" (7-21-66) Clifford Evans, Jan Hol-
    den, Anthony Newlands, John Carson, Peter Bowles
15. 'What the Butler Saw" (7-28-66) Thorley Walters, Denis
    Quilley, Kynaston Reeves, Howard Marion Crawford, Ewan
    Hooper
16. "The Gravediggers" (8-4-66) Ronald Fraser, Paul Masale,
    Caroline Blakiston
17. "Too Many Christmas Trees" (8-11-66) Mervyn Johns, Ed-
    win Richfield, Jeanette Sterke, Alex Scott, Barry Warren,
    Robert James
18. "The Thirteenth Hole" (8-18-66) Patrick Allen, Hugh Man-
    ning, Peter Jones, Victor Maddern, Francis Matthews,
    Donal Hewlett, Norman Wynne, Richard Marner
19. "Man Eater of Surrey Green" (8-25-66) Derek Farr, Athene
    Seyler, Gillian Lewis, William Job, Edwin Finn, Harry
    Schacklock, Ross Hutchinson, David Hutchenson, David
    Oliver, Johy Blanchard
20. "The Town of No Return" (9-1-66) Alan MacNaughton,
    Patrick Newell, Terrance Alexander, Jeremy Burnham

## Second Season

21. "From Venus with Love" (1-20-67) Barbara Shelley, Philip
    Locke, Paul Gillard, Jon Pertwee, Jeremy Lloyd, Derek
    Newark
22. "Fear Merchants" (1-27-67) Patrick Cargill, Brian Wilde,
    Annette Corell, Garfield Morgan
23. "The See-Through Man" (2-3-67) Moira Lester, Warren
    Mitchell, Ray Kinnear, Jonathan Elsom
24. "The Winged Avenger" (2-17-67) Nigel Green, Jack MacGow-
    ran, Neil Hallett, Colin Jeavons, Roy Patrick
25. "The Living Dead" (3-3-67) Julian Glover, Pamela Ann
    Davy, Howard Marion Crawford, Jack Woolgar, Jack Wat-
    son, Edward Underdown, John Cater, Alister Williamson
26. "The Bird Who Knew Too Much" (3-10-67) Ron Moody,
    Kenneth Cope, Ilona Rodgers, Michael Cales, John Wood
27. "The Hidden Tiger" (3-17-67) Ronnie Barker, Lyndon Brook,
    Gabrielle Drake, John Phillips, Michael Forrest, Stanley
    Meadows, Jack Givillam, Brian Haines, John Moore
28. "The Correct Way to Kill" (3-24-67) Anna Quayle, Michael
    Gough, Philip Madoc, Terence Alexander, Peter Barkworth
29. "Never, Never Say Die" (3-31-67) Christopher Lee, Jeremy
    Young, Patricia English, David Kernan, Christopher Ben-
    jamin
30. "Epic" (4-14-67) Peter Wyngarde, Isa Miranda, Kenneth
    Warren
31. "The Superlative Seven" (4-21-67) Charlotte Rampling, Brian
    Blessed, James Maxwell, Hugh Manning, Leon Greene,
    Gary Hope, Donald Sutherland, John Hollis, Margaret Neale
32. "A Funny Thing Happened on the Way to the Station" (4-28-
    67) Drewe Henley, Isla Blair, Tim Barrett, John Laurie,
    Richard Caldicat
33. "Something Nasty in the Nursery" (5-5-67) Dudley Foster,
    Yootha Jayce, Paul Eddington, Paul Hardwick, Patrick
    Newell
34. "The Joker" (5-12-67) Peter Jeffrey, Ally Nesbitt
35. "Who's Who?" (5-19-67) Freddie Jones, Patricia Haines,
    Campbell Singer, Peter Reynolds, Arnold Diamond

## Third Season

36. "Mission--Highly Improbable" (1-10-68) Kevin Stoney,
    Francis Matthews, Noel Howlett, Ronald Radd, Jane Mer-
    row, Stefan Gryff
37. "The Positive-Negative Man" (1-17-68) Ray McAnally,
    Michael Latimer, Caroline Blakiston
38. "You Have Just Been Murdered" (1-24-68) Barrie Ingham,
    Robert Flemyng, Leslie French
39. "Death's Door" (1-31-68) Clifford Evans, Allan Cuthbert-
    son, William Lucas, Marne Maitland, Terry Yorke
40. "Murdersville" (2-7-68) Colin Blakely, John Ronane, Ronald
    Hines, John Sharp
41. "The Return of the Cybernauts" (2-21-68) Peter Cushing,

Frederick Jaegar, Terry Richards

42. "The Fifty Thousand Pound Breakfast" (2-28-68) Cecil Parker, Yolande Turner, David Langton, Pauline Delaney, Annexe Wills, Eric Woolfe, Cardrew Robinson

43. "Dead Man's Treasure" (3-13-68) Norman Bowler, Valerie Van Ost, Edwin Richfield, Neil McCarthy, Arthur Love, Ivor Dean

44. "The Forget-Me-Knot" (3-20-68) Patrick Kavanaugh, Jeremy Burnham, Jeremy Young, Alan Lake

45. "The Invasion of the Earthmen" (3-27-68) William Lucas, Christian Roberts, Lucy Fleming, Christopher Chittel

46. "The Curious Case of the Countless Clues" (4-3-68) Anthony Bate, Kenneth Cope, Peter Jones, Edward De Stouza, George A. Cooper, Tracy Reed, Tony Selby

47. "Split" (4-10-68) Maurice Good, Nigel Davenport, Julian Glover, Christopher Benjamin, Bernard Archard

48. "Get-A-Way" (4-24-68) Andrew Kier, Peter Bowles, William Wilde, Peter Bayliss

49. "Have Guns--Will Haggle" (5-1-68) Johnny Sekka, Nicola Pagett, Jonathan Burn, Roy Stewart

50. "Look, Stop Me If You've Heard This One, but There Were These Two Fellers" (5-8-68) Jimmy Jewel, Julian Chagrin, John Cleese, Bernard Cribbins, William Kendall

51. "Escape in Time" (7-17-68) Peter Bowles, Geoffrey Balydon, Imogen Hassell, Judy Parfitt

## Fourth Season

2. "Game" (9-23-68) Peter Jeffrey, Garfield Morgan, Anthony Newlands, Alex Scott, Aubrey Richards

3. "The Super Secret Cypher Snatch" (9-30-68) John Carlisle, Ivor Dean, Nicholas Smith, Allan Cuthbertson, Donald Gee, Angela Scoular

4. "You'll Catch Your Death" (10-7-68) Roland Culver, Fulton McKay, Sylvia Kay, Charles Lloyd Pach

5. "Noon--Doomsday" (10-28-68) Ray Brooks, T. P. McKenna, Peter Bromilow, David Glover, Anthony Ainley

6. "Legacy of Death" (11-4-68) Stratford Johns, Tutte Lemkow, Ferdy Mayne, Ronald Lacey

7. "They Keep Killing Steed" (11-11-68) Ian Ogilvy, Ray McAnally, Norman Jones

8. "Wish You Were Here" (11-18-68) Liam Redmond, Robert Urquhart, Dudley Foster, Derek Newark, Gary Watson

9. "False Witness" (11-25-68) Rhonda Parker

10. "All Done with Mirrors" (12-2-68) Dinsdale Landen, Joanna Jones, Peter Copley, Michael Trubshawe

11. "Whoever Shot Poor George Oblique Stroke XR40?" (12-9-68) Clifford Evans, Dennis Price, Anthony Nicholis, Frank Windsor, Judy Parfitt

12. "The Rotters" (12-16-68) Jerome Willis, Gerald Sim, Frank Middlemass, Eric Barker, John Nettleton, Charles Morgan

13. "Killer" (12-30-68) William Franklyn, Charles Houston,

Harry Towb
64. "My Wildest Dream" (1-6-69) Peter Vaughan, Edward Fox, Derek Godfrey, Susan Travers
65. "The Interrogators" (1-20-69) Christopher Lee, David Smuner, Glynn Edwards, Neil Stacy, Eric Chung, Vincent Wong
66. "The Morning After" (1-27-69) Penelope Horner, Joss Ackland
67. "Love All" (2-3-69) Robert Harris, Veronica Strong, Terence Alexander, Brian Oulton, Patsy Rowlands
68. "Take Me to Your Leader" (2-10-69) Michael Hawkins, Patrick Barr, Michael Robbins
69. "Fog" (2-17-69) Guy Wolfe
70. "Stay Tuned" (2-24-69) Gary Bond
71. "Who Was that Man I Saw You With?" (3-3-69) Alan Browning, Alan Wheatley
72. "Pandora" (3-10-69) Julian Glover, James Cossins, Anthony Roye
73. "Homicide and Old Lace" (3-17-69) Gerald Harper, Keith Baxter
74. "Thingumajig" (3-24-69) Jeremy Lloyd, Ian Cuthbertson, John Horsley, Hugh Manning
75. "Requiem" (3-31-69) Angela Douglas, John Cairney, John Paul, Harvey Ashby, Denis Shaw
76. "Take-Over" (4-14-69) Tom Adams, Elizabeth Sellars, Hilary Pritchard, Michael Gwynn
77. "Bizarre" (4-21-69) Roy Kinnear, Sally Nesbitt, James Kerry, George Innes, Fulton Mackay

## COURT MARTIAL

The pilot film for this World War II drama of attorneys in the Judge Advocate's office and their clientele was the initial two-part teleplay (telecast October 10, 1963 and October 17, 1963) for the "Kraft Suspense Theatre." That generally satisfying mystery-drama had Lee Marvin in the role of Sergeant Ryker, who is accused of conspiring with the enemy. Found guilty of treason, his case is taken up by a prosecutor (Bradford Dillman) who is successful in attaining a stay of execution. Sudsy moments follow (as, for example, when Ryker's wife--Vera Miles' role--has a fling with his counsel) and there is much grumbling by the higher-ups who are convinced of Ryker's guilt. But the razzle-dazzle courtroom conclusion establishes Ryker's innocence when it is revealed that one of those higher-ups (Murray Hamilton) had unwittingly divulged government secrets during a drunken evening with a girlfriend (an enemy agent). In the film, Peter Graves portrayed Dillman's courtroom adversary. Both Dillman and Graves returned as the officer attorneys of this twenty segment British produced series which follows.

The Regulars: Captain David Young, Bradford Dillman; Major

Frank Whitaker, Peter Graves; Sergeant MacCaskey, Kenneth J. Warren; Wendy, Diene Claire.

The Episodes:

1. "Silence Is the Enemy" (4-8-66) Joan Hackett, Fred Sadoff, Henry Gilbert, Wendy Gifford
2. "Taps for the Sergeant" (4-15-66) Lee Montague, Jeremy Young, Frederick Jaeger, Moira Redmond, George Roubicek
3. "The House Where He Lived" (4-29-66) Sal Mineo, Anthony Quayle, Kathleen Breck, Frank Woolf, Peter Halliday, Joe Cuby
4. "Let No Man Speak" (5-6-66) Michael Hodern, John Carson, Terence Knapp, Judi Dench, Michael Culver, Stephen Brooke
5. "Savior of Vladik" (5-13-66) Michael Gough, Leslie Sands, Guy Deghy, Bill Mitchell, Sonia Fox, Shay Gorman
6. "All Roads Lead to Callaghan" (5-20-66) Darren McGavin, Warren Mitchell, Michael Goodliffe, Maria Landi, Cec Linder, Terence Edmond
7. "The Logistics of Survival" (5-27-66) Nadia Gray, Anna Turner, Kate O'Mara, Alan Tilvern, Barry Lowe, John Lee
8. "Judge Them Gently" (6-3-66) Joan Hackett
9. "La Belle France" (6-10-66) Diane Cilento, Oliver Reed, Dermot Walsh, Francis Napier, Phil Brown, Cec Linder
10. "All Is a Dream to Me" (6-17-66) Hans Verner, Gwen Watford, John McLaren, Richard Wyler, Donald Sutherland
11. "Without Spear or Sword" (6-24-66) Dennis Hopper, Susan Hampshire, William Mervyn, Frances De Wolff
12. "Retreat from Life" (7-1-66) Lelia Goldoni, Don Borisenko, Derek Sydney, Mark Lester, David Bauer
13. "How Ethical Can You Be?" (7-8-66) John Bonney, Reginald Marsh, Elizabeth Shepard, Martin Boddey, Alan Browning, John Morris
14. "Let Slip the Dogs of War" (7-15-66) Dennis Price, Zena Marshall, Karen Stepanek, Bruno Barnabe, Ferdy Mayne
15. "Where There Was No Echo" (7-22-66) Cameron Mitchell, Jeremy Wilkin, Alan Tilvern, George Roubicek
16. "The Bitter Wind" (7-29-66) Moira Lister, Andrew Keir, James Caffrey, Brian Rawlinson
17. "The Liberators" (8-12-66) Lee Montague, Rosemary Leach, David Lander, Paul Whitsun-Jones, Roger Delgado, Walter Sparrow
18. "Redress of Wrongs" (8-19-66) William Sylvester, Gary Cockrell, Roland Brand, Patrick Cargill, Katherine Schofield
19. "Achilles' Heel" (8-26-66) Neil McCallum, Geoffrey Keen, Ewen Solon, Martin Benson, Pauline Munro
20. "Flight of a Tiger" (9-2-66) John Doucette, Bernard Lee, Robert Hutton

PREVIEW TONIGHT

The Episodes:

1. "Pursue and Destroy" (8-14-66) Jessica Walter, Van Williams, David Thorpe, Paul Comi, Dame Edith Evans, Ward Wood, Henry Wilcoxon, Dee Pollack, Thad Williams
2. "Somewhere in Italy ... Company B!" (8-21-66) John Van Dreelen, Renzo Cesana, Robert Reed, Harold J. Stone, Richard Evans, Barbara Shelley, Tim O'Kelley, Jack Colvin, Vassili Lambrinos, Frank Puglia
3. "The Cliff Dwellers" (8-28-66) Hal Holbrook, Carol Rossen, Bert Convy, Beverlee McKinsey, Lee Allen, James Beck, Robert Hooks, Terence Logan
4. "Roaring Camp" (9-4-66) Jim McMullan, Bibi Osterwald, Katherine Justice, Ian Hendry, Richard Bradford
5. "Great Bible Adventures: Seven Rich Years ... and Seven Lean" (9-11-66) Hugh O'Brian, Joseph Wiseman, Eduardo Ciannelli, Torin Thatcher, Katherine Ross, John Abbott, Paul Mantee, Anthony Caruso

SHANE

George Stevens' 1953 classic underwent this bleak television adaptation about a hero, Shane (Alan Ladd's best-remembered role), helping terrorized (by Jack Palance as gunfighter Wilson) Wyoming homesteaders.

The Regulars: Shane, David Carradine; Marian Starett, Jill Ireland; Joey Starett, Christopher Shea; Tom Starett, Tom Tully; Grafton, Sam Gilman; Rufe Ryker, Bert Freed.

The Episodes:

1. "The Distant Bell" (9-10-66) Diane Ladd, Larry Mann, Owen Bush, Karl Lukas
2. "The Hant" (9-17-66) John Qualen, Carl Reindel
3. "The Wild Geese" (9-24-66) Bill Smithers, Don Gordon
4. "An Echo of Anger" (10-1-66) Warren Oates, Cliff Osmond
5. "The Bitter, the Lonely" (10-8-66) Steve Ihnat, Ned Romero
6. "Killer in the Valley" (10-15-66) Joseph Campanella, Paul Grant, George Keymes, Robert Hoy
7. "Day of the Hawk" (10-22-66) James Whitmore, Jason Wingreen, Gregory Walcott, Dee Pollack, Ned Romero
8. [unknown title] (10-29-66) Robert Brown, Owen Bush, Larry Mann
9. "Poor Tom's A-Cold" (11-5-66) Robert Duvall, Phyllis Love, Claire Wilcox
10. "High Road in Viator" (11-12-66) X Brands, Anne Morrell
11. "The Day the Wolf Laughed" (11-19-66) Skip Homeier, J. D. Cannon
12. "The Silent Gift" (11-26-66) Jack Ging, J. Pat O'Malley, Claude Hall
13. [unknown title] (12-3-66) Joanne Linville, Bill Fletcher
14. "The Big Fifty" (12-10-66) Wayne Rogers, Larry Mann, Owen Bush
15. "The Great Invasion" [Part I] (12-17-66) Bradford Dillman, Constance Ford, Archie Moore, Ross Hagen, Frank Marth, Larry Mann, Hal Lynch, Larry Thor, Charles Grodin, E. J. Andre
16. "The Great Invasion" [Part II] (12-24-66) as above
17. "A Man'd Be Proud" (12-31-66) Owen Bush, Larry Mann

MISSION: IMPOSSIBLE

     Bruce Geller's adult comic strip of an "Impossible Mission Force" consisting of a veritable circus troup (impersonator Rollin Hand, his female counterpart Cinnamon Carter, technical expert Bernard Collier and strongman Willy) under the direction of government agent Dan Briggs (Steven Hill; subsequently replaced by Peter Graves as Jim Phelps) has the artifice lie in the film editing. It is, however, for the most part an offensive Cold War tale with the "IMF" team in callous disregard (and frequently in unrepressed delight) of the heinous fate awaiting "the enemy" they have successfully thwarted. Arty (and imitated) set pieces included a tape recording of instructions that would "self destruct in ten seconds" and an "IMF" portfolio, the contents of which were regularly splashed (by agent Phelps) over a café table at the outset of the teleplays. Martin Landau quit the Rollin Hand role and his wife Barbara Bain the Cinnamon Carter role in 1969, after some well-publicized quarreling with management. Replacements, in roles very similar to their predecessors, were Leonard Nimoy (as "Paris") for Landau; Lee Meriwether (as "Tracey"), Lesley Ann Warren (as "Dana"), Lynda Day George (as "Casey") and Barbara Anderson (as "Mimi") for Miss Bain.

The Regulars: Dan Briggs, Steven Hill (first season only); Jim Phelps, Peter Graves (from second season); Cinnamon Carter, Barbara Bain (first three seasons); Rollin Hand, Martin Landau (first three seasons); Bernard Collier, Greg Morris; Willy, Peter Lupus; Paris, Leonard Nimoy (fourth and fifth seasons); Tracey, Lee Meriwether (fourth season episodes); Dana, Lesley Ann Warren (fifth season); Casey, Lynda Day George (sixth and seventh seasons); Mimi, Barbara Anderson (seventh season); Doug, Sam Elliott (with episode of 10/17/70).

The Episodes (simple plot "capsules" are provided for the most part in lieu of titles):

1. Mission: retrieve nuclear warheads (9-17-66) Wally Cox, Harry Davis, Patricia Campbell
2. "The Butcher of the Balkans" (9-24-66) Leonard Stone, Albert Paulsen
3. Mission: secure the safety of a United States city threatened by an enemy agent (10-1-66) Fritz Weaver, Allen Joseph
4. Mission: rescue a Balkan libertarian [Part I] (10-8-66) Monte Markham, Mary Ann Mobley, Cyril Delevanti, Joseph Ruskin
5. Mission: rescue a Balkan libertarian [Part II] (10-15-66) as above
6. "Odds on Evil" (10-22-66) Nehemiah Persoff, Nico Minardos, Lawrence Montaigne
7. Mission: sustain free elections in a foreign nation (10-28-66) Percy Rodriguez, Mark Lenard, Jonathan Kidd
8. Mission: grapple with a racketeer (11-5-66) William

Smithers, Joe Mantell, Lin McCarthy
9. Mission: retrieve a recording of a chemical warfare project (11-12-66) Richard Devon, Warren Vanders, Michael Shea, Curt Lowens
10. Mission: prevent the spread of a plague virus (11-19-66) George Takei, Arthur Hill, Barry Russo
11. Mission: prevent a woman's divulging information to the Communists (11-26-66) Martine Bartlett, Donald Davis, Beatrice Straight
12. Mission: extradite a narcotics czar (12-3-66) Lloyd Bridges, Ken Bernard, Gary Lasdun, Kathleen O'Malley
13. Mission: rehabilitate a jeopardous agent (12-10-66) Barbara Luna, Barry Atwater, Abraham Sofaer
14. Mission: avert the murder of an expatriate (12-17-66) Albert Dekker, Hans Gudegast, Joe Sirola
15. Mission: stop the creation of a Fourth Reich (1-7-67) Donald Harron, John Crawford, Lee Bergere
16. Mission: free a scientist and fellow agent from behind the Iron Curtain (1-14-67) Joseph Campanella, Mala Powers, John Colicos
17. Mission: frame a crime czar (1-21-67) Simon Oakland, Arthur Batanides, Joe De Santis
18. Mission: come to the aid of Briggs, on trial for espionage behind the Iron Curtain (1-28-67) Carroll O'Connor, David Opatoshu, Michael Strong, Gail Kobe
19. Mission: retrieve stolen diamonds in an African nation (2-4-67) John Van Dreelen, Woodrow Parfrey, Harry Davis, Peter Bourne
20. Mission: prevent a Nazi revival in the United States (2-11-67) Gunnar Hellstrom, Gene Roth
21. Mission: thwart the director of a penal colony (2-18-67) Ricardo Montalban, Emile Genest, Warren Kemmerling
22. Mission: foil an extremist Cold War ploy (2-25-67) Kent Smith, David Sheiner, Pat Hingle
23. Mission: thwart a communist film producer (3-4-67) J. D. Cannon
24. Mission: prevent a Middle East nation from going to war (3-11-67) Nehemiah Persoff, Nico Minardos, Vincent Van Lynn
25. Mission: expose a European traitor (3-18-67) William Windom, William Schallert, Noah Keen, Richard Bull
26. Mission: prevent the dishonor of a United States envoy (3-25-67) James Daly, Sorrell Booke, Vic Perrin
27. Mission: rescue an agent in the guise of a drug addict (4-1-67) Francis Lederer, Kurt Kreuger, Jacques Denbeaux
28. Mission: recover stolen information from a defector (4-15-67) Eartha Kitt, Lonny Chapman, Malachi Throne, Frank Marth
29. Mission: work alongside NATO in a South American mission (4-22-67) Barry Sullivan, Richard Anderson, Milton Selzer, Paul Mantee

Second Season

30. "The Widow" (9-10-67) William Windom, Joe Maross
31. Mission: sustain the economic survival of a Latin American nation (9-17-67) Dan O'Herlihy, Mark Lenard, Michael Pate
32. Mission: rescue two kidnapped scientists (9-24-67) Albert Paulsen, Lawrence Dane, John McLiam
33. Mission: infiltrate an East Berlin bank (10-1-67) James Daly, Pierre Jalbert, Gene Dynarski
34. "The Slave" [Part I] (10-8-67) Joseph Ruskin, Antoinette Bower, Warren Stevens, Percy Rodriguez, Steve Franken, David Mauro
35. "The Slave" [Part II] (10-15-67) as above
36. Mission: suppress a potential Communist take-over of a European nation (10-22-67) Pernell Roberts, Michael Strong, Robert Karnes
37. Mission: thwart an African imperialist (10-29-67) Brock Peters, Michael Shillo
38. Mission: recover a neutral nation's sacred seal (11-5-67) Darren McGavin, Mort Mills
39. Mission: quash a charity racket (11-12-67) Fritz Weaver, Hazel Court, J. P. Burns
40. Mission: thwart a syndicate effort to exhaust the U.S. gold reserve [Part I] (11-19-67) Paul Stevens, Vincent Gardenia, Nick Colasanto, Stu Nisbet, Robert Phillips, Eduardo Ciannelli, Paul Lambert
41. Mission: thwart a syndicate effort to exhaust the U.S. gold reserve [Part II] (11-26-67) as above
42. "The Astrologer" (12-3-67) Steve Ihnat, David Hurst, Don Hanmer, Bob Tiedemann, Ed McCready, Barbara Bishop
43. Mission: prevent the coming to power of a neo-Hitler (12-10-67) Wilfrid Hyde-White, Hans Gudegast, Richard Morrison, Gregory Mullavey
44. Mission: prevent the spread of a pneumonic plague (12-17-67) Anthony Zerbe
45. Mission: thwart a victimizing bank director (12-31-67) James Daly
46. Mission: assure the safety of NATO missile-defense plans (1-7-68) Joseph Campanella, Kate Woodville, Karl Swenson, George Sperdakos
47. Mission: prevent the theft of gold bullion (1-14-68) Don Francks, William Wintersole
48. Mission: prevent the theft of an emerald by a communist agent (1-21-68) William Smithers, Michael Strong, Claude Woolman, Francisco Ortego, Jacques Denbeaux
49. Mission: clear a man framed for the murder of an expatriate (1-28-68) Peter Donat, Will Kuluva, Marianna Hill
50. Mission: prevent the flow of counterfeit drugs (2-4-68) Edmond O'Brien, Noah Keen, Frank Campanella
51. Mission: prevent the murder of a communist defector (2-18-68) Will Geer, Eddie Ryder

52. Mission: quash a ring of assassins (2-25-68) Gerald S. O'Loughlin, Roy Jenson
53. Mission: attempt a museum countertheft (3-3-68) Alf Kjellin, Scott Hale, Charles Radilac, Peggy Rae, Mills Watson
54. Mission: rescue a Latin American resister (3-10-68) Michael Tolan, Joseph Bernard, Paul Winfield
55. Mission: penetrate an Iron Curtain laboratory (3-17-68) Bradford Dillman, Emile Genest

## Third Season

56. Mission: prevent a democratic nation's military overthrow (9-19-68) Charles Aidman, Rudy Solari, Torin Thatcher
57. "The Contenders" [Part I] (10-6-68) Ron Randell, John Dehner, Sugar Ray Robinson, Ron Rich, Robert Phillips, Angus Duncan
58. "The Contenders" [Part II] (10-13-68) as above
59. Mission: discredit an African colonel (10-27-68) Pernell Roberts, Skip Homeier, Victor Tayback, Bo Svenson
60. "The Execution" (11-10-68) Luke Askew, Vincent Gardenia, Val Avery, Byron Keith
61. Mission: free an incarcerated cardinal (11-17-68) Theodore Bikel, Paul Stevens, Barbara Babcock
62. Mission: set up an "eternal youth" ploy (11-24-68) Ruth Roman
63. Mission: deceive enemy agents as to the value of stolen documents (12-1-68) Fernando Lamas, Lee Grant, Alfred Ryder, Sid Haig
64. Mission: prevent the overthrow of a pro-Western premier (12-8-68) John Colicos, Michael Tolan, John McLiam, Barry Atwater
65. Mission: prevent the resurgence of a deposed dictator (12-15-68) Albert Paulsen, Warren Stevens, Nate Esformes
66. "The Freeze" (12-22-68) Donnelly Rhodes, John Zaremba
67. Mission: rescue a kidnapped Cinnamon (1-5-69) John Vernon, Will Kuluva, Robert Ellenstein
68. Mission: deceive an enemy agent (1-12-69) Steve Ihnat, Jason Evers, Edward Asner, Vic Perrin
69. Mission: prevent a pestilence (1-19-69) David Hurst, Richard Bull, Noah Keen
70. Mission: thwart a gambling syndicate (1-26-69) James Patterson, Robert Yuro, Art Lewis
71. Mission: liberate a freedom leader (2-2-69) Lloyd Bochner, Larry Linville, Richard Garland, Lou Robb
72. "Doomsday" (2-16-69) Philip Ahn, Alf Kjellin, Arthur Batanides, Khigh Dhiegh, Wesley Lau
73. Mission: keep the "cover" of an American agent. (2-23-69) Martin Sheen, Anthony Zerbe
74. Mission: free a kidnapped nuclear scientist [Part I] (3-2-69) David Sheiner, Milton Selzer, George Fisher, George Sperdakos, Lee Meriwether
75. Mission: free a kidnapped nuclear scientist [Part II] (3-9-69) as above

76. Mission: secure the safety of a government building (3-23-69) Titos Vandis, Mark Lenard, Sandor Szabo
77. Mission: rescue an incarcerated Phelps (3-30-69) Joan Collins, Logan Ramsey
78. Mission: thwart a Latin American despot (4-6-69) Nehemiah Persoff, Rodolfo Acosta
79. Mission: thwart an enemy takeover of a police force (4-13-69) Fritz Weaver, Martin E. Brooks, Kevin Hagen
80. Mission: uncover an enemy secret (4-20-69) Gunnar Hellstrom, Erik Holland, Henry Silva

Fourth Season

81. Mission: thwart an attempted enemy invasion (9-28-69) Alexandra Hay, Nate Esformes, Michael Constantine
82. Mission: prevent the resurgence of a dictator (10-5-69) Don Francks, Karl Swenson, Torin Thatcher
83. Mission: prevent the release of a manipulatory drug [Part I] (10-12-69) Dina Merrill, Brooke Bundy, H. M. Wynant, David Sheiner, Alfred Ryder
84. Mission: prevent the release of a manipulatory drug [Part II (10-19-69) as above
85. "Fool's Gold" (10-26-69) David Opatoshu, Nehemiah Persoff, Sally Ann Howes
86. Mission: free a libertarian (11-2-69) Lawrence Dane, Arthur Batanides, Sid Haig, Rodolfo Hoyos
87. Mission: recover a stolen formula (11-9-69) Anne Helm, Jason Evers, James Patterson
88. Mission: thwart a Nazi war criminal (11-16-69) Stephen McNally, Ramon Bieri
89. [unknown title] (11-23-69) Malachi Throne
90. Mission: quash an extortion plan (11-30-69) Donnelly Rhodes, Paul Stewart, William Bryant
91. Mission: rescue an imprisoned freedom leader (12-7-69) Michele Carey, Joseph Ruskin, Lloyd Battista
92. Mission: deactivate an explosive (12-14-69) Barbara Luna, Bert Freed, Morgan Sterne
93. Mission: recover a nuclear compound (12-21-69) Steve Ihnat, Anthony Zerbe, Julie Gregg
94. "The Falcon" [Part I] (1-4-70) Diane Baker, Noel Harrison, John Vernon, Logan Ramsey
95. "The Falcon" [Part II] (1-11-70) as above
96. "The Falcon" [Part III] (1-18-70) as above
97. [unknown title] (1-25-70) Fernando Lamas, Jock Gaynor, Percy Rodriguez
98. Mission: avert a kidnap scheme (2-1-70) Rudy Solari, Barry Atwater, Mark Richman, Barry Williams, Margarit Cordova
99. Mission: thwart a dictator (2-8-70) Luther Adler, Antoinet Bower
100. Mission: free a libertarian from a well-guarded prison (2-15-70) Michael Tolan, David Opatoshu, Arlene Martel, Joe De Santis

101. Mission: quash an extortion scheme (2-22-70) Jane Merrow, John Williams, Don Knight
102. Mission: prevent an assassination (3-1-70) Booth Colman, Jessica Walter, Albert Paulsen
103. Mission: retain democratic rule in a foreign nation (3-8-70) Felice Orlandi, Don Eitner, Carl Betz
104. Mission: clear Barney, accused of murder (3-15-70) Cicely Tyson, Pernell Roberts, Leon Askin
105. Mission: thwart a mystic and despot (3-22-70) Nan Martin, Arthur Franz, Alan Bergmann, Sid Haig

Fifth Season

106. Mission: thwart a hired assassin (9-19-70) Robert Conrad, Davis Roberts
107. "Flip Side" (9-26-70) Sal Mineo, Robert Alda
108. "The Innocent" (10-3-70) Christopher Connelly, Robert Ellenstein
109. Mission: investigate a chain of murders (10-10-70) Jacqueline Scott, Joe Maross, Loretta Swit, Fred Beir, Patricia Smith, Larry Linville
110. "The Flight" (10-17-70) John Colicos, Lloyd Battista, John Almanzar
111. Mission: prevent Phelps' assassination (10-24-70) Jill Haworth, Mark Richman, Wesley Lau, Bruce Glover
112. Mission: clear an American executive accused of murder (10-31-70) Khigh Dhiegh, James Shigeta, Benson Fong, Lisa Lu, Helen Funai
113. "Decoy" (11-7-70) Julie Gregg, Michael Strong, Paul Stevens
114. Mission: recover a secret weapon (11-14-70) Anthony Zerbe, Lisa Pera, Ronald Feinberg
115. "Hunted" (11-21-70) Ta-Tanisha, Ivor Barry, John Anderson
116. Mission: liberate a freedom fighter (11-28-70) Mark Lenard, Jonathan Lippe, Robert Purvey
17. Mission: thwart a narcotics racket (12-12-70) Albert Paulsen, Nico Minardos, Albert Carrier, Victoria Vetri, Nick Georgiade
18. Mission: rescue a kidnapped Paris (12-19-70) Joe De Santis, Lou Antonio, Lee Duncan
19. Mission: thwart a surreptitious political maneuver (1-2-71) Lloyd Bochner, Ken Swofford, Richard K. Elton, Todd Martin
20. Mission: find the killer of Barney's brother (1-9-71) Hari Rhodes, Abbey Lincoln, William Wintersole, Kelly Thordsen
21. Mission: thwart an enemy spy (1-16-71) David Sheiner, John Pickard, John Beck
22. "The Field" (1-23-71) Barry Atwater, H. M. Wynant, Patricia Bloch
23. "Blast" (1-30-71) Henry Darrow, Kevin Hagen
24. Mission: prevent a weapons buildup (2-6-71) John Vernon,

Will Kuluva, Ramon Bieri, Sam Irwin, Johnny Bench (cameo)

125. Mission: free an African libertarian (2-20-71) Lawrence Dobkin, Rex Holman, Robert DoQui

126. Mission: prevent the release of a nerve gas (2-27-71) Andrew Duggan, Marion Ross, William Ross

127. Mission: expose an enemy secret (3-6-71) Antoinette Bower, Alfred Ryder, Frank Marth, Arthur Batanides

128. Mission: prevent a weapons sale (3-13-71) George Sanders, Jo Morrow, Jan Merlin, Ken Drake

Sixth Season

129. Mission: exonerate a fellow agent (9-18-71) Jason Evers Tom Bosley, Peter Brown

130. "Encore" (9-25-71) William Shatner, Michael Baseleon, Paul Mantee

131. Mission: abort a syndicate maneuver (10-2-71) Victor French, Felice Orlandi

132. Mission: thwart a crazed doctor's brainwashing of renegades (10-9-71) Leonard Frey, Donald Moffat, Bill Fletcher, Dennis Cross

133. Mission: quash syndicate influence on a waterfront (10-16-71) Christopher Stone, Robert Mandan, Gerald S. O'Loughlin, Lonny Chapman

134. Mission: terminate a narcotics control (10-23-71) Joe D. Baker, Billy Dee Williams, Ronald Feinberg

135. "Encounter" (10-30-71) Lawrence Dane, Elizabeth Ashley Val Avery, William Smith

136. Mission: recover a hoard of stolen jewels (11-6-71) Fri Weaver, Jeremy Slate, Robert Yuro, Desmond Wilson

137. Mission: retrieve stolen secrets (11-13-71) Kevin McCa thy, Ted Gehring, Scott Walker

138. Mission: quash syndicate control of a recording industry (11-20-71) William Windom, Ed Flanders, Vince Howa Alex Rocco

139. Mission: prevent syndicate control of state elections (11-27-71) Steve Forrest, Richard Bull

140. Mission: abort the release of a lethal gas (12-4-71) Christopher George, Rafer Johnson, Tyne Daly, Paul Stevens

141. "Run for the Money" (12-11-71) Richard Jaeckel

142. "The Connection" (12-18-71) Anthony Zerbe, Joe Maross Bruce Watson, Jeff Morris

143. "The Bride" (1-1-72) James Gregory, Charles Dierkop, Brad Dexter, Woodrow Parfrey

144. Mission: confirm the guilt of a syndicate killer (1-8-72) Bradford Dillman, Robert Ellenstein, Arthur Batanides

145. [unknown title] (1-15-72) Joan Hackett, Lawrence Luckin bill, George Voskovec

146. "Committed" (1-22-72) Susan Howard, Bert Freed, Alan Bergmann

147. Mission: quash a syndicate influence (1-29-72) Georg

Stanford Brown, Robert Colbert, Glenn R. Wilder
148.  Mission: rescue a kidnapped Willy (2-12-72) Irene Tsu, Norman Alden, Lou Antonio, Paul Kosto
149.  Mission: incriminate a syndicate boss (2-19-72) Jack Cassidy, Eddie Ryder, Richard Devon
150.  Mission: quash an extortion racket (2-26-72) Bert Convy, Tom Tully, Sharon Acker, Jon Cypher

## Seventh Season

151.  Mission: quash a gambling syndicate (9-16-72) Robert Conrad, Carl Betz, Robert Mandan
152.  Mission: recover stolen plutonium (9-23-72) Vic Morrow, David White, Don Diamond, Mort Mills, Ivor Barry
153.  Mission: abort a syndicate scheme (9-30-72) Robert Webber, Lana Wood, Van Williams
154.  Mission: rescue an incarcerated fellow agent (10-7-72) Robert Goulet, Dewey Martin, Pippa Scott, William Boyett
155.  Mission: prevent the spread of a lethal disease (10-14-72) Peter Haskell, Ray Walston
156.  Mission: quash a narcotics racket (10-21-72) Milton Selzer, William Shatner, Stephen McNally
157.  Mission: quash an elaborate extortion operation (10-28-72) Peter Mark Richman, Dennis Cross, H. M. Wynant, Robert Middleton
158.  Mission: quash syndicate control of a motion picture studio (11-4-72) David Brian, John Vernon, William Smith
159.  Mission: free and incriminate an imprisoned hood (11-11-72) Dane Clark, Tony Young, Robert Reed
160.  Mission: deactivate a nuclear bomb (11-18-72) Madlyn Rhue, Murray Hamilton
161.  Mission: rescue a kidnapped Phelps (12-2-72) Charles Drake, Geoffrey Lewis, Jack Ging, John Ireland
162.  Mission: quash a ring of assassins (12-9-72) Peter Breck, Marlyn Mason, Arthur Franz, Alex Cord
163.  Mission: abort an extortion scheme (12-22-72) Roddy McDowall, Val Avery, Richard Devon, John Larch
164.  Mission: extradite a criminal (1-5-73) Kim Hunter, Robert Hogan, Bob Hoy, Alex Rocco
165.  Mission: protect the wife of a syndicate chief (1-12-73) Laraine Stephens, Walter Barnes, Robert Feinberg, Richard Reed
166.  Mission: determine a fellow agent's allegiance (1-19-73) Gary Lockwood, Jason Evers, Elizabeth Ashley, Richard Van Vleet
167.  Mission: set up a "fountain of youth" ploy to capture a syndicate chief (1-26-73) George Maharis, Cameron Mitchell, Luke Askew, Carlos Rivas
168.  Mission: quash syndicate control of boxing matches (2-9-73) William Windom, Geoffrey Deuel, Joe Maross, Jennifer Shaw
169.  Mission: quash a narcotics operation (2-16-73) Jenny

Sullivan, Claude Akins, Ron Soble, Charles Bateman
170. Mission: abort a terrorist scheme (2-23-73) Dean Stockwell, Scott Brady, Frank Maxwell, Jack Donner, Leon Lontoc
171. Mission: recover stolen art treasures (3-2-73) Ed Nelson, Michael Ansara, Barry Atwater, Frank Farmer
172. Mission: quash a band of jewel thieves (3-30-73) Barbara McNair, Pernell Roberts, Jack Bernardi, Charles McGraw

## THE IRON HORSE

Somniferous western of railroad construction workers of the 1870s.

The Regulars: Ben Calhoun, Dale Robertson; Nils Torvald, Roger Torrey; Dave Tarrant, Gary Collins; Barnabas Rogers, Bob Random.

The Episodes:

1. "Joy Unconfined" (9-12-66) Diana Hyland, David Sheiner, Steve Ihnat
2. "The Dynamite Drive" (9-19-66) Malachi Throne, Tom Reese
3. "High Devil" (9-26-66) Louise Sorel, James Best, Rex Holman
4. "Right of Way Through Paradise" (10-3-66) Sean McClory, Hoyt Axton, E. J. André
5. "Pride at the Bottom of the Barrel" (10-10-66) Rod Cameron, Victor Jory, Nina Shipman, Gene Evans
6. "Broken Gun" (10-17-66) Leigh Chapman, Robert Lyons, Strother Martin, Philip Ober
7. "Cougar Man" (10-24-66) Henry Darrow, Richard Hale, Morgan Woodward, Rodolfo Acosta
8. "War Cloud" (10-31-66) Stephen McNally, Milton Selzer, John Pickard, Abel Fernandez
9. "No Wedding Bells for Tony" (11-7-66) David Brian, Jeff Morrow, Virginia Field, Susan Browning
10. "The Man from New Chicago" (11-14-66) Madlyn Rhue, John Milford, James Anderson, Duane Gray
11. "Explosion at Waycrossing" (11-21-66) Burr De Benning, Tol Avery, Michael T. Mikler, Mort Mills, Toian Matchinga
12. "Through Ticket to Gunsight" (11-28-66) Sandra Smith, John Pickard, K. T. Stevens
13. "Town Full of Fear" (12-5-66) William Windom, Richard Evans, Antoinette Bower, Dennis Cross
14. "Big Deal" (12-12-66) Hazel Court, Michael Ansara, Woodrow Parfrey, Pat Conway
15. "A Dozen Ways to Kill a Man" (12-19-66) Sheree North,

Skip Homeier, Ford Rainey, Royal Dano

16. "Hellcat" (12-26-66) Arlene Martel, Vincent Beck, Harry Landers

17. "Welcome for the General" (1-2-67) Royal Dano, Lisabeth Hush, James Griffith, David Macklin

18. "The Pembrooke Blood" (1-9-67) Bert Freed, Sharon Farrell, Tim McIntire, Martine Asne

19. "Volcano Wagon" (1-16-67) Land Bradbury, Dean Harens

20. "The Bridge at Forty-Mile" (1-23-67) Elena Verdugo, Douglas Kennedy, Richard X. Slattery, Katherine Justice

21. "Shadow Run" (1-30-67) Mary Ann Mobley, Richard Devon, Frank Marth, Renny McEvoy

22. "Banner with a Strange Device" (2-6-67) Jeff York, Brenda Benet, Anthony Zerbe, Dean Pollack

23. "Appointment with an Epitaph" (2-13-67) Gloria Graham, John Ireland, Susan Howard, Lew Gallo, Bill Bixby, Robert Emhardt

24. "The Red Tornado" (2-20-67) Michael Rennie, Tony Davis, Jock Gaynor, Anne Karen

25. "Decision at Sundown" (2-27-67) Joan Huntington, Russ Tamblyn, Gus Trikonis, Victor French

26. "The Passenger" (3-6-67) Mark Richman, Linda Cristal, Alejandro Rey

27. "The Execution" (3-13-67) Julie Gregg, Noam Pitlik, Michael Whitney, Paul Brinegar

28. "Death by Triangulation" (3-20-67) Gigi Perreau, Monte Markham, George Murdock, Christopher Dark

29. "The Golden Web" (3-27-67) Gerald Mohr, David Sheiner, Patricia Barry

30. "Sister Death" (4-3-67) Barbara Stuart, Mark Lenard, Bridget Hanley, Rita D'Amico

## Second Season

1. "Diablo" (9-16-67) Strother Martin, Lloyd Gough, Ellen McRae

2. "Consignment, Betsy the Boiler" (9-23-67) Michael Constantine, Linda Marsh, Warren Vanders, Paul Lambert

3. "Gallows for Bill Pardew" (9-30-67) Tom Heaton, Jeff Corey, David Lewis, John Marley, Bill Zuckert, Ellen McRae

4. "Five Days to Washtiba" (10-7-67) John Anderson, Lane Bradford, Louise Troy, Richard Hale

5. [unknown title] (10-14-67) Steve Ihnat, Peter Haskell, Ken Lynch, Ellen Madison

6. "Grapes of Grass Valley" (10-21-67) Lonny Chapman, Emile Genest, Laurie Main, Marie Gomez

7. "Leopards Try, but Leopards Can't" (10-28-67) Gene Hackman, Sam Melville, Roy Barcroft

8. "The Return of Hode Avery" (11-4-67) Warren Oates, Susan Howard

9. "Four Guns to Scalplock" (11-11-67) Warren Stevens, Joan Hotchkiss

40. "Steel Chain to a Music Box" (11-18-67) Harold J. Stone, Paul Peterson, Anna Capri, Tom Baker, Ken Mayer, Anna Wainwright
41. "Six Hours to Sky High" (11-25-67) Gavin MacLeod, Joe Maross, Fay Spain, Sherwood Price, Rex Holman, Bryan O'Byrne
42. "T Is for Traitor" (12-2-67) Peter Whitney, Kenneth Tobey, Woodrow Parfrey
43. "Dealer's Choice" (12-9-67) Jack Kelly, Douglas V. Fowley, Lee Meriwether, Duane Grey, Bill Quinn
44. "Wild Track" (12-16-67) Joanna Moore, Whit Bissell, Alan Hewitt
45. "Death Has Two Faces" (12-23-67) Joyce Van Patten, John Abbott, Dabney Coleman, Norm Alden, William Bramley
46. "The Prisoners" (12-30-67) Edward Asner, Karen Black
47. "Dry Run to Glory" (1-6-68) J. D. Cannon, Leslie Parrish, Dennis Cooney

THE RAT PATROL

A World War II drama of American and British North African desert commandos persevering through 58 raids on the enemy (typified here by Hans Gudegast as the Nazi Capt. Hans Dietrich).

The Regulars: Sgt. Sam Troy, Christopher George; Mark Hitchcock, Larry Casey; Sgt. Jack Moffitt, Gary Redmond; Pvt. Tully Pettigrew, Justin Tarr; Capt. Hans Dietrich, Hans Gudegast.

The Episodes:

1. "The Chase of Fire Raid" (9-12-66) Larry Ward, Janine Gray
2. "The Life Against Death Raid" (9-19-66) Albert Paulsen, Edward Asner
3. "The Wildwest Raid of All" (9-26-66) Wolfgang Preiss, Ric Hutton
4. "The Kill or Be Killed Raid" (10-3-66) Milton Selzer
5. "The Chain of Death Raid" (10-10-66) Frank Silvera, Manfred Lating
6. "The Do or Die Raid" (10-17-66) Warren Stevens
7. "The Blind Man's Bluff Raid" (10-24-66) Salome Jens, James Philbrook
8. "The Fatal Chase Raid" (10-31-66) Gavin MacLeod, John Clark
9. "The Blow Sky High Raid" (11-7-66) Hamilton Camp
10. "The Moment of Truce Raid" (11-14-66) Marc Lawrence
11. "The Deadly Double Raid" (11-21-66) John Doucette, Rober Palmer
12. "The Gun Runner Raid" (11-28-66) Steve Franken, Fay Spain

13. "The Lighthouse Raid" (12-5-66) Emile Genest, Eric Chapman, Monique Lemaire
14. "The Daredevil Rescue Raid" (12-12-66) Norman Woodland
15. "The Last Harbor Raid" [Part I] (12-19-66) Claudine Longet, Stanley Adams, Harry Landers, Will Kuluva, John Anderson
16. "The Last Harbor Raid" [Part II] (12-26-66) as above
17. "The Last Harbor Raid" [Part III] (1-2-67) as above
18. "The This One That Got Away Raid" (1-9-67) Jack Colvin, Alan Bergmann, Charles Maxwell, Walter Friedel
19. "The Two for One Raid" (1-16-67) Mark Devries, Karl Swenson
20. "The Last Chance Raid" (1-23-67) Michael Evans
21. "The B Negative Raid" (1-30-67) Fabian Forte
22. "The Exhibit 'A' Raid" (2-6-67) Robert F. Simon, Robert Knapp
23. "The Holy War Raid" (2-13-67) Abraham Sofaer
24. "The Two Against Time Raid" (2-20-67) regulars only
25. "The Wild Goose Raid" (2-27-67) Martin Milner
26. "The Bring 'Em Back Alive Raid" (3-13-67) William Schallert
27. "The Take Me to Your Leader Raid" (3-20-67) Richard Mulligan, Vincent Gardenia
28. "The Double or Nothing Raid" (3-27-67) Ben Wright, Barry Ford, Morgan Jones, Michael Vandever
29. "The Hour Glass Raid" (4-3-67) Austin Willis, Carol Booth
30. "Mask-A-Raid" (4-10-67) Than Wyenn, Rick Traeger
31. "The Fire and Brimstone Raid" (4-24-67) Robert Kelljan, Michael Pate
32. "The Delilah Raid" (5-1-67) Lisabeth Hush, Wesley Addy

## Second Season

33. "The Truce at Aburah Raid" (9-11-67) Joseph Turkel
34. "The David and Goliath Raid" (9-18-67) Manfred Lating
35. "The Trial by Fire Raid" (9-25-67) Milton Selzer, Gabe Garnet
36. "The Darers Go First Raid" (10-2-67) regulars only
37. "The Love Thine Enemy Raid" (10-9-67) Susanne Cramer
38. "The Darkest Raid" (10-16-67) Alfred Ryder
39. "The Death Do Us Part Raid" (10-30-67) Pippa Scott, Barry Robins
40. "The Do-Re-Mi Raid" (11-6-67) Jack Jones, Harvey Jason
41. "The Kingdom Come Raid" (11-13-67) Matt Clark
42. "The Hide-and-Go-Seek Raid" (11-20-67) Mark Anthony
43. "The Violent Truce Raid" (11-27-67) regulars only
44. "The Life-for-a-Life Raid" (12-4-67) Kamala Devi, Paul Stevens
45. "The Fifth Wheel Raid" (12-11-67) Michael Tolan, Ben Wright
46. "The Two If by Sea Raid" (12-18-67) Than Wyenn, Michael Vandever, Walter Brooke
47. "The Street Urchin Raid" (12-25-67) Rica Diallina, Gerald

Michenaud
48. "The Pipeline to Disaster Raid" (1-1-68) John Anderson
49. "The Boomerang Raid" (1-8-68) Dick Sargent
50. "The Fatal Reunion Raid" (1-15-68) Louise Sorel, Gilbert Green
51. "The Decoy Raid" (1-22-68) Richard Davalos, Doreen Mc-Lean, Jay Novello, Socrates Ballis, Nick Kopp
52. "The Touch-and-Go Raid" (2-5-68) regulars only
53. "The Field of Death Raid" (2-12-68) Albert Paulsen, Nikos George
54. "The Double Jeopardy Raid" (2-19-68) Clive Clerk, Todd Martin, Danielle Roter
55. "The Hickory, Dickory Dock Raid" (2-26-68) David Gross, Gary Lasdun
56. "The Tug-of-War Raid" (3-4-68) Brioni Farrell, Michael Shillo
57. "The Never-Say-Die Raid" (3-11-68) Fabrizio Mioni, Frank Marth
58. "The Kill at Koorlea Raid" (3-18-68) William C. Watson, Phil Bruns

## THE FELONY SQUAD

The Regulars: Sgt. Sam Stone, Howard Duff; Det. Jim Briggs, Dennis Cole; Dan, Ben Alexander; Captain Nye, Frank Maxwell.

The Episodes:

1. "The Streets Are Paved with Quicksand" (9-12-66) Darren McGavin, Jean Marie
2. "A Walk to Oblivion" (9-19-66) Jason Wingreen, Charles Francisco, Larry D. Mann
3. "The Broken Badge" (9-26-66) Eileen Heckart, John Larch, Ned Glass
4. "Strikeout" (10-3-66) Kevin Hagen, Val Avery, Whit Bissell
5. "A Date with Terror" (10-10-66) Charles Aidman, Gregory Morton, Jan Shutan, Lee Delano
6. "Flame Out" (10-17-66) Pippa Scott, Tom Lowell, James Best, Alan Oppenheimer
7. "The Immaculate Killer" (10-24-66) James Patterson, Richard Karlen, Susan Flannery
8. "Death of a Dream" (10-31-66) Robert Duvall, Lloyd Hayne, Robert Doyle, Jaime Sanchez
9. "Prologue to Murder" (11-7-66) Richard Anderson, Robert Drivas
10. "Killer with a Badge" (11-14-66) Diana Hyland, Paul Carr
11. "Between Two Fires" (11-21-66) Kevin McCarthy, Richard Evans
12. "The Terror Trap" (11-28-66) Michael Conrad, Howard Caine, Stanley Ralph Ross

13. "The Killer Instinct" (12-5-66) William Smithers, Paul Kent, Roy Madden, Gail Kobe, Edward Asner
14. "Fear Below" (12-12-66) Nicolas Coster, Lynda Day, Milton Selzer, Alex Gerry
15. "A Penny Game, a Two-Bit Murder" (12-19-66) Charles Grodin, Diana Ivarson
16. "Miss Reilly's Revenge" (12-26-66) Joanna Moore, Michael Tolan, Lew Gallo
17. "A Death for a Death" (1-2-67) Ken Lynch, Ed Griffith, Vince Howard
18. "The Deadly Partner" (1-9-67) John Anderson, Gene Dynarski
19. "The Night of the Shark" [Part I] (1-16-67) James Daly, Harry Townes, Karen Steele, Len Wayland, Lawrence Montaigne, Vince Howard, John Harmon
20. "The Night of the Shark" [Part II] (1-23-67) as above
21. "The Strangler" (1-30-67) Dean Harens, Jason Evers, Kathie Browne, Norma Crane
22. "Breakout" (2-6-67) Philip Pine, Michael Pataki
23. "The Desperate Silence" (2-13-67) Virginia Field, Kent Smith, Sam Gilman, Chris Robinson
24. "Target!" (2-20-67) Will Kuluva, Steve Ihnat
25. "Echo of a Killing" (2-27-67) Gail Kobe, John Milford
26. "Live Coward, Dead Hero" (3-13-67) Lew Gallo, Lamont Johnson, Joe Di Reda
27. "A Blueprint for Dying" (3-20-67) Ricardo Montalban, Douglas Henderson
28. "The Fear Merchant" (3-27-67) Mark Richman, Robert H. Harris
29. "The Savage Streets" (4-3-67) Harold Gould, Frank Marth, Stuart Nisbet, David Renard
30. "Debt of Fear" (4-10-67) Lawrence Dobkin, Joseph Turkel

Second Season

31. "Let Him Die" (9-11-67) Philip Bourneuf, Abraham Sofaer, Lawrence Dane, Robert Brown, Barney Phillips, Jon Kowai
32. "The Counterfeit Cop" (9-18-67) Harry Townes, Paul Carr
33. "A Most Proper Killing" (9-25-67) Peter Bromilow, Don Keefer, William Beckley
34. "The 30-Gram Kill" (10-2-67) Bradford Dillman, George Furth
35. "The Death Bag" (10-9-67) Collin Wilcox, Mort Mills
36. "The Deadly Junkman" (10-16-67) Ivan Dixon, Joseph Ruskin, Nate Esformes
37. "The Pat Hand of Death" (10-30-67) Dan Tobin, Maurine Dawson, Leon Askin, Pamela Curran, Lawrence Dane
38. "Hit and Run, Run, Run" (11-6-67) Martin Milner, Mark Lenard, Jason Wingreen
39. "Time of Trial" (11-13-67) Patricia Barry, R. G. Armstrong, Len Wayland, Anna Lee
40. "Who'll Take Care of Joey?" (11-20-67) Robert Drivas, Beatrice Straight

41. "My Mommy Got Lost" (11-27-67) Antoinette Bower, Joe Don Baker, Melinda Plowman
42. "Ordeal by Terror" (12-4-67) Beau Bridges, Jack Hogan, Loretta Leversee, Peter Lazer
43. "An Arrangement with Death" [Part I] (12-11-67) David Opatoshu, Harold J. Stone, Michael Conrad, Morgan Stone, Natalie Trundy, Blaisdel Makee
44. "An Arrangement with Death" [Part II] (12-18-67) as above
45. "No Sad Songs for Charlie" (12-25-67) Simon Oakland, Philip Carey
46. "Bed of Strangers" (1-1-68) Charles Aidman, Joanne Linville, Pamela Dunlap
47. "Killing, Country Style" (1-8-68) Pat Hingle, Scott Brady, Gail Kobe, Woodrow Parfrey, Dee Carroll, Frederic Downs
48. "The Flip Side of Fear" [Part I] (1-15-68) Roddy McDowall, Lynda Day, Michael Christian
49. "The Flip Side of Fear" [Part II] (1-22-68) as above
50. "The Love Victim" (2-5-68) Michael Callan, Julie Sommars, Richard Anderson
51. "The Deadly Abductors" (2-12-68) John Larch, Larry Perkins
52. "Nightmare on a Dead-End Street" (2-19-68) Gerald S. O'Loughlin, Roger Perry, Linda Marsh, Ellen Corby, Dick Dial, Phil Terry
53. "Epitaph for a Cop" (2-26-68) Don Gordon, Tom Fielding, Rodolfo Hoyos, Carol Kane
54. "Man on Fire" (3-4-68) John Fiedler, Alan Hewitt, Don Briggs
55. "Image of Evil" (3-11-68) Kevin McCarthy, Karen Huston, James Wainwright, Paul Piscerni
56. "The Human Target" (3-18-68) Russell Johnson, Ron Soble, Lelia Goldoni

Third Season

57. "A Fashion for Dying" (9-27-68) Ricardo Montalban, Joan Van Ark
58. "Jury of One" (10-4-68) John Vernon, David Macklin
59. "Underground Nightmare" (10-11-68) Andrew Prine, Julie Sommars, Amy Thomson
60. "Deadly Innocents" (10-18-68) Glenda Farrell, Brooke Bundy, Donald Woods
61. "Dark Memory" (10-25-68) Katherine Crawford, Jason Evers, Paul Mantee
62. "Kiss Me, Kill You" (11-1-68) Heather Young, Jeremy Clyde, Ross Elliott
63. "The Nowhere Man" [Part I] (11-8-68) Rupert Crosse, Robert Doqui, Larry D. Mann, Cleavon Little, Gloria Camolee
64. "The Nowhere Man" [Part II] (11-15-68) as above
65. "Matched for Murder" (11-22-68) Melinda Plowman, Tom Skerritt, Louise Troy

66. "The Fatal Hours" (11-29-68) Neva Patterson, Alfred Ryder
67. "The Hostage" (12-13-68) Nobu McCarthy, Skip Homeier, Teru Shimada, Jerry Summers, Marie Schroeder, Johnny Jacobs
68. "The Distant Shore" (12-20-68) Diana Muldaur, James Best, Judy Norton, Richard Bakalyan
69. "The Last Man in the World" (1-3-69) Richard Dreyfuss, Lana Wood, Lawrence Dane
70. "Conspiracy of Power" [Part I] (1-10-69) Gail Kobe, Marj Dusay, Fritz Weaver, Richard Anderson
71. "Conspiracy of Power" [Part II] (1-17-69) as above
72. "Blind Terror" (1-24-69)
73. "The Law and Order Blues" [Part I of a two-part episode concluded on "Judd for the Defense" 1/31/69] (1-31-69) Brock Peters, Carl Betz, Stephen Young, Morgan Sterne, Larry McCormick

## THE ROAD WEST

The immortal trek west again, endured by--the name should tell you much--the Pride family in the 1850s. Barry Sullivan was a suitable patriarch.

The Regulars: Ben Pride, Barry Sullivan; Tim Pride, Andrew Prine; Midge Pride, Brenda Scott; Grandpa Pride, Charles Seel; Kip Pride, Kelly Corcoran; Elizabeth Reynolds, Kathryn Hays; Chance Reynolds, Glenn Corbett.

The Episodes:

1. "This Savage Land" [Part I] (9-12-66) George C. Scott, Rex Holman, John Drew Barrymore, Roy Roberts
2. "This Savage Land" [Part II] (9-19-66) as above
3. "The Gunfighter" (9-26-66) James Daly, James Gammon
4. "The Lean Years" (10-3-66) Charles Aidman, Willard Sage
5. "This Dry and Thirsty Land" (10-10-66) Anthony Caruso, Jess Pearson
6. "Long Journey to Leavenworth" (10-17-66) Geoffrey Horne, Robert F. Simon, E. J. Andre, Don Dubbins
7. "Ashes and Tallow and One True Love" (10-24-66) Robert Walker Jr., Kelly Thordsen, Adam Roarke, Deanna Lund
8. "Piece of Tin" (10-31-66) Wendell Corey, William Smithers, John McLiam, Hampton Fancher
9. "Lone Woman" (11-7-66) Lonny Chapman, George Wallace
10. "Shaman" (11-14-66) Elisha Cook, Henry Wilcoxon, David Astor, Anne Meacham
11. "To Light a Candle" (11-28-66) Katherine Ross, Mike Constantine
12. "Pariah" (12-5-66) Barbara Anderson, Tom Drake, Donnelly Rhodes, John Mitchum, Phyllis Hill, Stuart Nisbet
13. "Have You Seen the Aurora Borealis?" (12-12-66) Dan

O'Herlihy, Jackie Russell
14. "Power of Fear" (12-26-66) John Dehner, Joseph Campa-
    nella, Barbara Werle
15. "Reap the Whirlwind" (1-9-67) James Farentino, Lauri
    Peters, Richard X. Slattery, John Lodge
16. "Beyond the Hill" (1-16-67) Victor Jory, Gena Rowlands
17. "The Predators" (1-23-67) Tony Bill, John Marshall, Lane
    Bradford, Willard Sage
18. "A Mighty Hunter Before the Lord" (1-30-67) Lloyd Nolan,
    Strother Martin
19. "No Sanctuary" (2-6-67) Jan Shepard, Keenan Wynn
20. "The Insider" (2-13-67) Jason Evers, Collin Wilcox, Ross
    Hagen, Rex Holman, Myron Healey, Tyler McVey
21. "Road to Glory" (2-20-67) John Anderson, Emile Genest,
    Bonnie Beecher
22. "Fair Ladies of France" (2-27-67) Signe Hasso, Kim Darby
23. "Never Chase a Rainbow" (3-6-67) Kevin McCarthy, Jack
    Carter, Barbara Anderson
24. "Eleven Miles to Eden" (3-13-67) Jan Sterling, Michael
    Burns, Tisha Sterling
25. "Charade of Justice" (3-27-67) Kurt Russell, Jay C. Flip-
    pen, Melodie Johnson, Tom Tryon
26. "The Eighty-Seven Dollar Bride" (4-3-67) Gavin MacLeod,
    Cloris Leachman, Lou Antonio, William Bramley
27. "A War for the Gravediggers" (4-10-67) Michael Ansara,
    Joe De Santis
28. "The Agreement" (4-24-67) James Gammon, Barbara Werle,
    Dan Frazer, Jason Wingreen
29. "Elizabeth's Odyssey" (5-1-67) Albert Salmi, Dabbs Greer

## THE GIRL FROM U. N. C. L. E.

Successor, of course, to "The Man from U. N. C. L. E. " (the
episode of February 25, 1966 with Mary Ann Mobley in the lead
role was the pilot for "The Girl from U. N. C. L. E. "), this series
is distinguished only for its assorted eccentrics joyously played
by many guest stars. Principal players Stefanie Powers as April
Dancer (a favorite pastime of producers of the series evidently
was the creation of catchy character names; ergo, "April Dancer"
the female counterpart to "Napoleon Solo") and Noel Harrison as
Mark Slate barely had time to display any acting skill, so subordi-
nate were they to the dominating idiosyncrasies of their nemeses.
Raymond Massey was wonderful as B. Elzie Bubb (the catchy name
again) in a Faustian romp titled "The Faustus Affair. " Monty
Landis was Genghis Gomez VIII, a sadistic self-appointed island
monarch with a bizarre preference for the playing of "Three Blind
Mice" (once atop April Dancer's head) in "The Paradise Lost Affair. "

Boris Karloff satirized his own film image with a role as
Mother Muffin who directed a school for assassins in "The Mother

Muffin Affair. " This last episode also starred Robert Vaughn in his "U. N. C. L. E. " Napoleon Solo role (agents Dancer, Solo, Illya Kuryakin and Slate at times appeared in each other's series, with chief man Alexander Waverly--Leo G. Carroll's role--appearing consistently in both series).

Berne and David Giler's "The Low Blue C Affair" had Hermione Gingold and Broderick Crawford as cousins with competing interests in attaining the throne of a dukedom. But the most fantastic of all the episodes was "The Carpathian Killer Affair, " in which April Dancer is nearly burned in a giant toaster until she is saved by a bouncing ball which has made its way through hotel hallways and down several flights of stairs when at long last it depresses the lever that ejects her to safety! A case may be made that "The Girl from U. N. C. L. E. " was short-lived because from the outset it had none of the understated satire of its parent series in its first year. By the year 1967, when "The Man from U. N. C. L. E. " had also been canceled, the American television audience had become so saturated with the dizzying fantasy of the Bond genre that it had welcomed a rest. What replaced it was a reversion to the stale car-chasing sequences of policeman or detective-as-hero programming, where television has smouldered since.

The Regulars: April Dancer, Stefanie Powers; Mark Slate, Noel Harrison; Alexander Waverly, Leo G. Carroll.

The Episodes:

1. "The Dog-Gone Affair" (9-13-66) Kurt Kasznar, Marcel Hillaire, Luciana Paluzzi, Jan Arvin
2. "The Prisoner of Zalamar Affair" (9-20-66) Michael Ansara, Brenda Benet, Abraham Sofaer, John Gabriel
3. "The Mother Muffin Affair" (9-27-66) Boris Karloff, Robert Vaughn, Bruce Gordon, Bernard Fox
4. "The Mata Hari Affair" (10-4-66) Edward Mulhare, Jocelyn Lane, David Hurst, Christopher Carey
5. "The Montori Device Affair" (10-11-66) John Carradine, Edward Andrews, Ted Cassidy, Lisa Loring, Dee Hartford
6. "The Horns-of-the-Dilemma Affair" (10-18-66) Fernando Lamas, Alejandro Rey, Peter Mamakos, Sandra Sullivan
7. "The Danish Blue Affair" (10-25-66) Dom De Luise, Lloyd Bochner, Virginia Gregg, William Bramley
8. "The Garden of Evil Affair" (11-1-66) Arnold Ross, Oscar Beregi, Anna-Lisa, Lisa Seagram, Than Wyenn
9. "The Atlantis Affair" (11-15-66) Sidney Blackmer, Denny Miller, Claude Woolman, Khigh Dhiegh, Carlos Rivero, Kenneth Parker, Joan Connors
10. "The Paradise Lost Affair" (11-22-66) Monty Landis, Chips Rafferty, Raymond St. Jacques, Mokihana, Harry Swoger
11. "The Lethal Eagle Affair" (11-29-66) Cesare Danova, Margaret Leighton, Michael Wilding
12. "The Romany Lie Affair" (12-6-66) Gladys Cooper, Lloyd

Bochner, Audrey Dalton, Cal Bolder
13. "The Little John Doe Affair" (12-13-66)  Pernell Roberts,
Wally Cox, Robert Carricart
14. "The Jewels of Ubango Affair" (12-20-66)  Leslie Uggams,
Brock Peters, John Qualen, Barry Kelly, Alan Caillou,
Rupert Crosse
15. "The Faustus Affair" (12-27-66)  Raymond Massey, Tom
Bosley, Carol Wayne, Dick Crockett, Guy Way, Milton
Parsons, Kelton Garwood
16. "The U. F. O. Affair" (1-3-67)  Joan Blondell, Fernando
Lamas, Anthony Caruso, Janet MacLachlan
17. "The Moulin Ruse Affair" (1-17-67)  Yvonne De Carlo, Shel-
ley Berman, Barry Robins, Ellen Corby, Thordis Brandt,
Burt Mustin, Tura Santana
18. "The Catacomb and Dogma Affair" (1-24-67)  Eduardo Ciannelli, Danielle de Metz, Fabrizio Mioni, Gerald Mohr,
Peter Marcus
19. "The Drublegratz Affair" (1-31-67)  Patricia Barry, Vito
Scotti, Jill Townsend, Christopher Held
20. "The Fountain of Youth Affair" (2-7-67)  Gene Raymond,
Gena Rowlands, Philip Ahn, Donnelly Rhodes
21. "The Carpathian Killer Affair" (2-14-67)  Ann Sothern, Jack
Cassidy, Joyce Jameson, Stan Freberg
22. "The Furnace Flats Affair" (2-21-67)  Peggy Lee, Ruth Roman, Susan Browning, Herb Edelman
23. "The Low Blue C Affair" (2-28-67)  Broderick Crawford,
Hermione Gingold, Stanley Clements, Leonid Kinskey
24. "The Petit Prix Affair" (3-7-67)  Nanette Fabray, Marcel
Hillaire, Steve Harmon, Michael Shillo
25. "The Phi Beta Killer Affair" (3-14-67)  Lynn Bari, Victor
Buono, Barbara Nichols
26. "The Double-O-Nothing Affair" (3-21-67)  Edward Asner,
Sorrell Booke, Don Chastain
27. "The Samurai Affair" (3-28-67)  Signe Hasso, Michael J.
Pollard, James McCallion, Richard Roat
28. "The High and Deadly Affair" (4-4-67)  Julie Adams, David
Brian, Grayson Hall, Murray Matheson, Eileen Baral,
Barry Cahill
29. "The Kooky Spook Affair" (4-11-67)  Estelle Winwood, Arthur
Malet, Edward Ashley, John Orchard


THE MONROES

A familiar theme of the struggle for sustenance of orphaned
children (the Monroe siblings "Big Twin," "Little Twin," and Amy
under the guidance of eldest brother Clayt and eldest sister Kathy)
in 1870s Wyoming.

The Regulars: Clayt Monroe, Michael Anderson Jr.; Kathy Monroe, Barbara Hershey; Big Twin, Keith Shultz; Little Twin,
Kevin Shultz; Amy Monroe, Tammy Locke; Major Mapoy,

Liam Sullivan; Jim, Ron Soble.

The Episodes:

1. "The Intruders" (9-7-66) John Doucette, Ben Johnson, Jim Westmoreland
2. "Night of the Wolf" (9-14-66) James Gammon, Richard Bakalyan
3. "Ride with Terror" (9-21-66) Jeanne Cooper, James Stacy, Claude Akins, Peter Leeds
4. "The Forest Devil" (9-28-66) Warren Oates, Ralph Moody
5. "Wild Dog of the Tetons" (10-5-66) Albert Salmi
6. "Incident at Hanging Tree" (10-12-66) Robert Middleton, James Brolin
7. "Ordeal by Hope" (10-19-66) Edward Faulkner, John Bryant, Jack Williams
8. "Hunter" (10-26-66) James Whitmore, Roy Jenson, Rex Holman, Sean McClory
9. "War Arrow" (11-2-66) Anne Navarro, Morgan Woodward, Dub Taylor
10. "The Friendly Enemy" (11-9-66) Harry Townes
11. "Court Martial" (11-16-66) Robert Fuller, John McLiam
12. "Silent Night, Deadly Night" (11-23-66) Robert Middleton, James Brolin, Tim O'Kelly, Ray Teal, Hampton Fancher, Lisa Jak
13. "Lost in the Wilderness" (11-30-66) Noah Beery, George C. Fisher
14. "Gold Fever" (12-14-66) Dan Duryea, Alan Baxter, Hank Brandt, Hardie Albright
15. "Range War" (12-21-66) Robert Middleton, James Brolin
16. "Pawnee Warrior" (12-28-66) Alejandro Rey
17. "Mark of Death" (1-4-67) Robert Middleton, James Brolin, Mario Alcaide
18. "To Break a Colt" (1-11-67) Buck Taylor, Fredd Wayne, Elisha Cook Jr.
19. "Race for the Rainbow" (1-18-67) James Wilder, Buck Taylor, Lisa Jak
20. "Gun Bound" (1-25-67) Nick Adams, John Dehner, Michael Green
21. "Killer Cougar" (2-1-67) Robert Walker Jr., Robert J. Wilke
22. "Wild Bull" (2-15-67) Jeffrey Hunter
23. "Trapped" (2-22-67) regulars only
24. "Manhunt" (3-1-67) Robert Lansing, Billie Hayes
25. "Teach the Tigers to Purr" (3-8-67) Ronny Howard, Clint Howard
26. "Ghosts of Paradox" (3-15-67) Michael Dunn, Richard Kiel, Anna Capri, Jack Bailey

THE MAN WHO NEVER WAS

     Impossible espionage drama of an American agent (Robert Lansing as Peter Murphy) who impersonates a jet-setter (who has died; not to the knowledge of "the enemy"). Dana Wynter is the compliant jet-setter's widow who muddles through the façade (not surprisingly).

The Regulars: Peter Murphy/Mark Wainwright, Robert Lansing; Eva Wainwright, Dana Wynter; Roger Wainwright, Alex Davion; Jack Forbes, Murray Hamilton.

The Episodes:

1. [unknown title] (9-7-66) regulars only
2. "The Last of Peter Murphy" (9-14-66) Helmut Schneider, Ernst Konstantin
3. "Search for a Bent Twig" (9-21-66) John Van Dreelen, Annette Carell
4. [unknown title] (9-28-66) Beba Loncar, Carlo Rizzo
5. "The Escape" (10-5-66) Peter Capel, Barbara Stanek
6. "Death in Vienna" (10-12-66) Lisa Daniely, Christopher Ball
7. "A Little Ignorance" (10-19-66) Yvonne Furneaux, Alex D'Arcy
8. [unknown title] (10-26-66) William Berger, Gabriele Tinti
9. "The Big Fish" (11-2-66) George Pravda, Barry Letts
10. "Pay Now, Pray Later" (11-9-66) Emily McLauglin, Paul Stewart
11. "Game of Death" (11-16-66) John Ireland, Rosemary Dexter
12. "If This Be Treason" (11-23-66) Frank Maxwell, Martin Benson
13. "To Kill an Albatross" (11-30-66) Aldo Sandrell, Hunt Powers
14. "Things Dead and Done" (12-7-66) Diana King, Derek Frances, Alan Cuthberton
15. "The Perfect Game" (12-14-66) Gertan Klauber, John Paul
16. "In Memory of Davos" (12-21-66) Joe De Santis, Elizabeth Wallace
17. "Drop by Drop" (12-28-66) Eric Pohlmann, Ralph Neville, Andre Monreal, Derek Ball
18. "I Take This Woman" (1-4-67) William Dexter

ABC STAGE '67

The Episodes:

1. "The Love Song of Barney Kempinski" [original comedy by Murray Schisgal] (9-14-66) Alan Arkin, Sir John Gielgud, Alan King, Lee Grant, Arlene Golonka
2. "Dare I Weep, Dare I Mourn" [by Stanley Mam from John Le

Carre story] (9-21-66) James Mason, Jill Bennett, Hugh
Griffith
3.   "The Kennedy Wit" [documentary produced by Jack Paar,
host] (10-5-66) David Francis Powers, guest
4.   "Olympus 7-0000" [musical by Richard Adler and Jerome
Chodorov] (10-12-66) Donald O'Connor, Phyllis Newman,
Larry Blyden, Fred Clark, Eddie Foy Jr., Lou Jacobi,
New York Jets
5.   "The Confession" (10-19-66) Arthur Kennedy, Dana Elcar,
Kathreen Houghton, Hugh Franklin, Brandon De Wilde
6.   "The Canterville Ghost" [musical by Jerry Bock and Sheldon
Harnick from Oscar Wilde story] (11-2-66) Michael Red-
grave, Douglas Fairbanks Jr., Natalie Shafer, Peter
Noone, Tippy Walker
7.   "The People Trap" (11-9-66) Estelle Winwood, Vera Miles,
Connie Stevens, Stuart Whitman, Jackie Robinson, Pearl
Bailey, Mercedes McCambridge, Lew Ayres, Lee Grant
8.   "Evening Primrose" [musical by Stephen Soundheim] (11-16-
66) Anthony Perkins, Larry Gates, Charmian Carr,
Dorothy Stickney
9.   "Noon Wine" [by Katherine Anne Porter; directed by Sam
Peckinpah] (11-23-66) Jason Robards Jr., Theodore
Bikel, Olivia de Havilland, Peter Robbins, Per Oscarsson,
Robert Emhardt
10.  "The Life and Legend of Marilyn Monroe" [narrated by John
Huston] (11-30-66)
11.  "On the Flip Side" [spoof of teen music madness] (12-7-66)
Rick Nelson, Joanie Sommers, The Celestials
12.  "The Brave Rifles" [documentary written, directed, and produced by Laurence E. Mascott; narrated by Arthur Ken-
nedy] (12-14-66)
13.  "A Christmas Memory" [by Truman Capote, who narrated]
(12-21-66) Geraldine Page, Donnie Melvin
14.  "The Trap of Solid Gold" (1-4-67) Conrad Nagel, John
Baragrey, James Broderick, Dustin Hoffman, Cliff Robertson, Dina Merrill
15.  "Sex in the Sixties" [narrated by Joseph Julian] (1-12-67)
16.  "General Eisenhower on 'The Military Churchill'" [interview
by Alistair Cooke] (1-26-67)
17.  "David Frost's Night Out in London" (2-2-67) Albert Fin-
ney, Sir Laurence Olivier, Peter Sellers
18.  "The Light Fantastic, or How to Tell Your Past, Present,
and Maybe Your Future Through Social Dancing" [by Marc
Breaux and Tom Hatcher on American dance] (2-9-67)
Lauren Bacall, John Forsythe
19.  "C'est La Vie" [musical revue by Jean Christopher Averty]
(2-23-67) Maurice Chevalier, Diahann Carroll
20.  "Rodgers and Hart TODAY" [songs performed in contemporary style] (3-2-67) Petula Clark, The Supremes, Bobby
Darin, Count Basie, The Doodletown Pipers, The Mamas
and the Papas
21.  "Trilogy: The American Boy" [three short films hosted by
Robert Young] a) "Skatedater"; b) "River Boy";

c) "Reflections" (3-9-67)

22. "I'm Getting Married" [musical by Betty Comden, Adolph
Green, and Jule Styne] (3-16-67) Anne Bancroft, Dick
Shawn
23. "A Time for Laughter" [revue of Negro humor in the United
States] (4-6-67) Harry Belafonte, Sidney Poitier,
Diahann Carroll
24. "The Wide Open Door" (4-20-67) Tony Randall, Honor
Blackman, Bernard Fox, Reginald Gardiner
25. "The Human Voice" [by Jean Cocteau; adapted by Clive Exton
directed by Ted Kotcheff; produced by David Susskind and
Lars Schmidt] (5-4-67) Ingrid Bergman


JERICHO

Norman Felton produced this often seen espionage tale of a
crackerjack team of international Nazi fighters.

The Regulars: Nicholas Gage, John Leyton; Sheppard, Don Franck
André, Marino Masé.

The Episodes:

1. "Dutch and Go" (9-15-66) Tom Bosley, John Qualen, Susan
Cramer
2. "A Jug of Wine, a Loaf of Bread--and POW!" (9-22-66)
William Wintersole, Lisa James, Albert Paulsen, John
Wengraf
3. "Upbeat and Underground" (9-29-66) Nehemiah Persoff, Gia
Scala, Jacqueline Beer
4. "Have Traitor, Will Travel" (10-6-66) Albert Salmi, Danie
De Metz, Lee Bergere, Rex Holman
5. "Panic in the Piazza" (10-13-66) John Van Dreelen, Marianna Hill
6. "The Big Brass Contraband" (10-20-66) Gunnar Hellstrom,
Emile Genest, Patric Knowles
7. "Wall to Wall Kaput" (10-27-66) John Dehner, Tige Andrew
Whit Bissell
8. "Eric the Redhead" (11-3-66) Jay North, James Doohan,
Barry Atwater, Lew Gallo
9. "Two for the Road" [Part I] (11-10-66) Jan Merlin, Vic
Damone, Titos Vandis, Mark Richman, Antoinette Bower,
Eduardo Ciannelli
10. "Two for the Road" [Part II] (11-17-66) as above
11. [unknown title] (12-1-66) Michael Rennie, Barbara Anderso
John Orchard, Peter Church
12. "Long Journey Across a Short Street" (12-8-66) Mala
Powers, Mark Lenard, Virginia Christine, Frank Marth,
Malachi Throne, Ted De Corsia
13. [unknown title] (12-15-66) William Smithers, Anthony Benson, Phyllis Hill, Walter Koenig, Ian Wolfe, Fred Bier

14.  [unknown title]  (12-29-66)  John Drew Barrymore, Milton
         Selzer, Patricia Huston, Christopher Cary, Alan Caillou
15.  [unknown title]  (1-5-67)  Robert Cornthwaite, Paul Comi,
         Hans Gudegast, Marilyn Devin, Lenny Weinrub, Paul Sav-
         ior
16.  [unknown title]  (1-19-67)  Lawrence Dane, Johnny Seven,
         Donna Baccala, Billy Barly


STAR TREK

        This series has amassed what is most surely the most siz-
able cult in the history of American television.  Its membership is
reputedly diverse ideologically and generationally.  One immediately
considers the show's apparent vision--of a universe of disparate
cultures and life styles finding a method of peaceful co-existence
(and so a cliché)--as holding the key to its appeal.  But such a
premise, and others, are best left to the thinking of the "Trek-
kies," as the cultists call themselves.  For purposes of this dis-
cussion, the relative merit (and in many cases an absence of
merit) of each episode as drama is of importance.  With this in
mind, "Star Trek" is reduced to being much ado about very little
or nothing.

        Scenarios were interwoven around the various nuances or
idiosyncracies of principals James T. Kirk (William Shatner), a
captain of the starship Enterprise, his first officer Spock (a "Vulcan" played complete with pointed ears by Leonard Nimoy), ship
medical doctor Leonard McCoy (DeForest Kelley), engineering officer "Scotty" (James Doohan), and communications officer Uhura
(Nichelle Nichols).  In one of the series' better episodes, Harlan
Ellison's "The City on the Edge of Forever," Joan Collins was
cast as humanitarian Edith Keeler, whose impending death is interrupted by an anachronistic Dr. McCoy, thus disturbing the proper
evolution of history.  In an effort to rectify things, Kirk and
Spock are sent back through time.  Kirk inevitably falls in love
with Keeler, not knowing her to be the source of the problem.
The episode concludes with both Kirk and McCoy restrained from
interfering with the fatal auto accident Keeler must have.

        Several episodes were essentially variations on familiar
themes.  In D. C. Fontana's and Gene Roddenberry's "Charlie 'X',"
Robert Walker Jr. was a youth unable to come to terms with his
special powers; Captain Kirk offering the predictable heavy doses
of paternalistic advice.  Perfect serenity proved an anathema to
Kirk as a taste of Utopia did to Candide's crew in the episode
"This Side of Paradise," by D. C. Fontana and Nathan Butler.
The way to fight the seemingly omnipotent "Squire of Gothos" of
Paul Scheider's teleplay was through his megalomania--an often
utilized theme.  The punishment assigned to the egotistical Harry
Mudd (Roger C. Carmel) on a planet of mechanical twins in Stephen
Kandel's "I, Mudd," was to forbear the presence of more than one

nagging wife. Kandel's script was typical of several silly ones, of which the popular "Trouble with Tribbles" (in which an all-too-prolific species of "cuddly" animals wreak havoc on the Enterprise) by David Gerrold, was another.

An interesting episode on racial prejudice was Oliver Crawford's "Let That Be Your Last Battlefield" with a half white and half black Frank Gorshin. Margaret Armen handled well a more mature theme on the nature of hero worship with her "The Paradise Syndrome." But there were also a number of pretentious episodes, such as the resurrection of Nazi Germany in "Pattern of Force" by John Meredyth Lucas or the re-creation of Roman gladiatorial combat in "Bread and Circuses" by Gene Roddenberry, Gene L. Coon and John Kneubuhl.

Gene Roddenberry's creation gave the science fiction buff his desired abundance of technological terminology. Whatever its failings as drama (many of the series' writers have done far better work previously), one could revel in the futuristic sets and skillful use of special effects. Some technicians worth mentioning, among several others, would be photographer Jerry Finnermann, art director Walter M. Jeffries, and the composer of the series' score, Alexander Courage.

A wealth of literature has come forth as a result of the series' great popularity. The most indispensable reference for the devotee, "Trekkie" or not, would be the Star Trek Concordance (Los Angeles: Mathom House Publications, 1969), compiled by Dorothy Jones and edited by Bjo Trimble. Two books are also of great value: The Making of Star Trek (New York: Ballantine Books, 1968) by Gene Roddenberry and Stephen E. Whitfield, and The World of Star Trek (New York: Ballantine Books, 1973) by David Gerrold.

The Regulars: Captain James T. Kirk, William Shatner; Commander Spock, Leonard Nimoy; Leonard McCoy, M.D., DeForest Kelley; Lieutenant Commander James Montgomery Scott, James Doohan; Lieutenant Uhura, Nichelle Nichols; Lieutenant Sulu, George Takei; Ensign Pavel Checkov, Walter Koenig; Nurse Christine Chapel, Majel Barrett; Yeoman Janis Rand, Grace Lee Whitney (first season episodes only).

The Episodes:

1. "The Man Trap" (9-8-66) Jeanne Bal, Alfred Ryder
2. "Charlie X" (9-15-66) Robert Walker Jr., Abraham Sofaer Patricia McNulty
3. "Where No Man Has Gone Before" (9-22-66) Sally Kellerman, Paul Carr, Gary Lockwood, Paul Fix
4. "The Naked Time" (9-29-66) Bruce Hyde, Stewart Moss
5. "The Enemy Within" (10-6-66) Jim Goodwin
6. "Mudd's Women" (10-13-66) Roger C. Carmel, Karen Steel

Maggie Thrett
7. "What Are Little Girls Made Of?" (10-20-66) Sherry Jackson, Ted Cassidy, Michael Strong
8. "Miri" (10-27-66) Kim Darby, John Megna, Michael J. Pollard, Keith Taylor
9. "Dagger of the Mind" (11-3-66) James Gregory, Morgan Woodward, Marianna Hill, Ed McCready
10. "The Corbomite Maneuver" (11-10-66) Clint Howard, Anthony Call
11. "The Menagerie" [Part I] (11-17-66) Jeffrey Hunter, Susan Oliver, Malachi Throne, Meg Wyllie
12. "The Menagerie" [Part II] (11-24-66) as above
13. "The Conscience of the King" (12-8-66) Barbara Anderson, Arnold Moss, Bruce Hyde
14. "Balance of Terror" (12-15-66) Mark Lenard, Paul Comi, Lawrence Montaigne, Stephen Mines, Garry Walberg
15. "Shore Leave" (12-29-66) Emily Banks, Oliver McGowan, Perry Lopez, Bruce Mars, Shirley Bonne, Barbara Baldavin, Marcia Brown
16. "The Galileo Seven" (1-5-67) Don Marshall, John Crawford, Peter Marko, Phyllis Douglas
17. "The Squire of Gothos" (1-12-67) William Campbell, Richard Carlyle, Michael Barrier, Venita Wolf
18. "Arena" (1-19-67) Carole Shelyne, Grant Woods, Tom Troupe, Jerry Ayres
19. "Tomorrow Is Yesterday" (1-26-67) Roger Perry, Hal Lynch
20. "Court Martial" (2-2-67) Percy Rodriguez, Elisha Cook, Joan Marshall, Richard Webb
21. "The Return of the Archons" (2-9-67) Torin Thatcher, Harry Townes, Charles Macauley, Sid Haig
22. "Space Seed" (2-16-67) Ricardo Montalban, Madlyn Rhue
23. "A Taste of Armageddon" (2-23-67) David Opatoshu, Gene Lyons, David Ross, Robert Sampson
24. "This Side of Paradise" (3-2-67) Jill Ireland, Frank Overton
25. "The Devil in the Dark" (3-9-67) Ken Lynch, Barry Russo, Brad Weston, Biff Elliot
26. "Errand of Mercy" (3-23-67) John Abbott, John Colicos, Peter Brocco, Victor Lundin
27. "The Alternative Factor" (3-30-67) Robert Brown, Janet MacLachlan, Arch Whiting, Richard Derr
28. "The City on the Edge of Forever" (4-6-67) Joan Collins, David Ross, John Harmon, Hal Baylor
29. "Operation--Annihilate!" (4-13-67) Craig Hundley

## Second Season

30. "Amok Time" (9-15-67) Celia Lovsky
31. "Who Mourns for Adonais?" (9-22-67) Leslie Parrish, Michael Forest
32. "The Changeling" (9-29-67) regulars only
33. "Mirror, Mirror" (10-6-67) Barbara Luna, Vic Perrin
34. "The Apple" (10-13-67) Keith Andes, Celeste Yarnall
35. "The Doomsday Machine" (10-20-67) William Windom

36. "Cats-Paw" (10-27-67) Antoinette Bower, Theodore Marcuse, Michael Barrier, John Winston, Jimmy Jones
37. "I, Mudd" (11-3-67) Roger C. Carmel, Rhae and Alyce Andrece, Maureen and Colleen Thornton, Tamara and Starr Wilson, Tom and Ted Le Garde
38. "Metamorphosis" (11-10-67) Glenn Corbett, Elinor Donahue
39. "Journey to Babel" (11-17-67) Jane Wyatt, Mark Lenard, William O'Connell
40. "Friday's Child" (12-1-67) Julie Newmar, Tige Andrews, Michael Dante
41. "The Deadly Years" (12-8-67) Charles Drake, Beverly Washburn, Sarah Marshall, Felix Locher, Carolyn Nelson, Laura Wood
42. "Obsession" (12-15-67) Stephen Brooks
43. "Wolf in the Fold" (12-22-67) John Fiedler
44. "The Trouble with Tribbles" (12-29-67) William Schallert, William Campbell, Stanley Adams, Whit Bissell, Michael Pataki
45. "The Gamesters of Triskelion" (1-5-68) Joseph Ruskin, Angelique Pettyjohn
46. "A Piece of the Action" (1-12-68) Anthony Caruso, Victor Tayback, Lee Delano
47. "The Immunity Syndrome" (1-19-68) regulars only
48. "A Private Little War" (2-2-68) Nancy Kovack, Michael Whitney
49. "Return to Tomorrow" (2-9-68) Diana Muldaur
50. "Patterns of Force" (2-16-68) David Brian, Skip Homeier
51. "By Any Other Name" (2-23-68) Warren Stevens, Barbara Bouchet, Stewart Moss
52. "The Omega Glory" (3-1-68) Morgan Woodward, Joey Jenson
53. "The Ultimate Computer" (3-8-68) William Marshall, Barry Russo, Sean Morgan
54. "Bread and Circuses" (3-15-68) William Smithers, Ian Wolfe
55. "Assignment: Earth" [unsold pilot film for projected fall series] (3-29-68) Robert Lansing, Terri Garr, Don Keefer, Lincoln Demyan, Morgan Jones

Third Season

56. "Spock's Brain" (9-20-68) Marj Dusay, James Daris, Sheila Leighton
57. "The Enterprise Incident" (9-27-68) Joanne Linville
58. "The Paradise Syndrome" (10-4-68) Rudy Solari, Sabrina Scharf
59. "And the Children Shall Lead" (10-11-68) Att. Melvin Belli, Craig Hundley, James Wellman
60. "Is There In Truth No Beauty?" (10-18-68) Diana Muldaur, David Frankham
61. "Spectre of the Gun" (10-25-68) Ron Soble, Rex Holman, Bonnie Beecher, Sam Gilman, Charles Maxwell
62. "Day of the Dove" (11-1-68) Michael Ansara, Susan Howard

63. "For the World Is Hollow and I Have Touched the Sky" (11-8-68) Kate Woodville
64. "The Tholian Web" (11-15-68) regulars only
65. "Plato's Stepchildren" (11-22-68) Michael Dunn, Liam Sullivan, Barbara Babcock
66. "Wink of an Eye" (11-29-68) Jason Evers, Kathie Browne
67. "The Empath" (12-6-68) Kathryn Hays, Willard Sage, Alan Bergmann
68. "Elaan of Troyius" (12-20-68) France Nuyen
69. "Whom Gods Destroy" (1-3-69) Steve Ihnat, Yvonne Craig
70. "Let That Be Your Last Battlefield" (1-10-69) Frank Gorshin, Lou Antonio
71. "The Mark of Gideon" (1-17-69) Sharon Acker, David Hurst
72. "That Which Survives" (1-24-69) Lee Meriwether
73. "The Lights of Zetar" (1-31-69) Jan Shutan
74. "Requiem for Methuselah" (2-14-69) James Daly, Louise Sorel, Anise Seed, Leroy Harvey
75. "The Way to Eden" (2-21-69) Skip Homeier, Charles Napier, Mary-Linda Rapelye
76. "The Cloud Minders" (2-28-69) Jeff Corey
77. "The Savage Curtain" (3-7-69) Lee Bergere
78. "All Our Yesterdays" (3-14-69) Mariette Hartley, Ian Wolfe
79. "Turnabout Intruder" (3-28-69) Sandra Smith

# HAWK

A hard-hitting study of an American Indian police detective; the embellishment for the series being his authentic nocturnal New York associates.

The Regulars: John Hawk, Burt Reynolds; Sam Crown, John Marley; Carter, Wayne Grice; Asst. District Attorney, Leon Janney.

The Episodes:

1. "Do Not Mutilate or Spindle" (9-8-66) Gene Hackman, Kathleen Maguire, Fredd Wayne, Elaine Nadeau
2. "The Longleat Chronicles" (9-15-66) Diane Baker, John Karlen
3. "Thanks for the Honeymoon" (9-22-66) Geraldine Brooks, Reni Santori, William Prince, Dana Elcar
4. "Game with a Dead End" (9-29-66) Bert Convy, Lynda Day, Phillip Bosco
5. "Death Comes Full Circle" (10-6-66) Bradford Dillman, Martin Sheen, Marian Winters, Ann Wedgeworth
6. "The Theory of the Innocent Bystander" (10-13-66) Robert Duvall, Carol Rossen, Murray Hamilton, Stanley Beck
7. "The Man Who Owned Everyone" (10-20-66) Diana Muldaur, Lonny Chapman, Edward Binns, Patrick McVey
8. "How Close Can You Get?" (10-27-66) Irene Dailey, Peter

Donat, Jose Perez
9. "The Living End of Sister Baby" (11-3-66)  King Donovan, Patricia Roe, Ben Piazza, Jill Townsend, Paula Wayne
10. "The Shivering Pigeon" (11-10-66)  Lou Antonio, Carlos Montalban, Bernard Kates, Robert Burr
11. "Ulysses and the Republic" (11-17-66)  Henry Jones, Ann Williams, Horace McMahon
12. "Legacy for a Lousy Future" (11-24-66)  Vincent Gardenia
13. "H Is for a Dirty Letter" (12-1-66)  Frank Converse, Jennifer West, Stephen Elliott, Tony Lo Bianco, Val Biscogeco
14. "Some Devil Whispered in His Ear" (12-8-66)  Larry Haines, Richard Jordan, Ellen Madison, Joe Bova
15. "The Hands of Corlin Claybrooke" (12-15-66)  George Voskovec, Tom Hunter, Jane Rose
16. "Wall of Silence" (12-22-66)  Kim Hunter, Scott Glenn, Emily Prager, Beverlee McKinsey
17. "Blind Man's Bluff" (12-29-66)  James Best, Philip Bruns

## THE GREEN HORNET

The Regulars:  Britt Reid/Green Hornet, Van Williams; Kato, Bruce Lee; Casey, Wende Wagner; D.A. Scanlon, Walter Brooke; Mike Axford, Lloyd Gough.

The Episodes:

1. "The Silent Gun" (9-9-66)  Henry Evans, Lloyd Bochner, Charles Francisco
2. "Give 'Em Enough Rope" (9-16-66)  Diana Hyland, Mort Mills
3. "Programmed for Death" (9-23-66)  Signe Hasso, Richard Cutting
4. "Crime Wave" (9-20-66)  Peter Haskell, Sheilah Wells, Ron Burke
5. "The Frog Is a Deadly Weapon" (10-7-66)  Victor Jory
6. "Eat, Drink, and Be Dead" (10-14-66)  Jason Evers, Harry Lauter, Eddie Ness
7. "Beautiful Dreamer" [Part I] (10-21-66)  Geoffrey Horne, Pamela Curran, Victoria George, Barbara Gates, Maurice Manson
8. "Beautiful Dreamer" [Part II] (10-28-66)  as above
9. "The Ray Is for Killing" (11-11-66)  Grant Woods, Robert McQueeney, Biel Baldwin, Mike Mahoney
10. "The Praying Mantis" (11-18-66)  Mako, Allen Jung, Tom Drake
11. "The Hunters and the Hunted" (11-25-66)  Robert Strauss, Charles Bateman, Douglas Evans
12. "Deadline for Death" (12-2-66)  James Best, Lynda Day
13. "The Secret of Sally Bell" (12-9-66)  Walter Kemmerling, Beth Brickell, Dave Perna, Greg Benedict
14. "Freeway to Death" (12-16-66)  Jeffrey Hunter, David Fresc

15. "May the Best Man Lose" (12-23-66) Linden Chiles, Robert Hoy, Harold Gould
16. "The Firefly" (1-6-67) Ralph Meeker, Raymond St. Jacques, Paul Carr, John Baer
17. "Corpse of the Year" [Part I] (1-13-67) Joanne Dru, Cesare Danova, Tom Simcox, Celia Kaye
18. "Corpse of the Year" [Part II] (1-20-67) as above
19. "Ace in the Hole" (2-3-67) Richard Anderson, Tony Epper, Richard X. Slattery, Bill Couch
20. "Bad Bet on a 459-Silent" (2-10-67) Bert Freed, Brian Avery
21. "Trouble for Prince Charming" (2-17-67) Alberto Morin, Susan Flannery, James Lanphier
22. "Alias 'The Scarf'" (2-24-67) John Carradine, Ian Wolfe, Patricia Barry, Paul Gleason
23. "Hornet, Save Thyself" (3-3-67) Michael Strong, Marvin Brody
24. "Invasion from Outer Space" [Part I] (3-10-67) Linda Gaye Scott, Larry Mann, Christopher Dark, Arthur Batanides
25. "Invasion from Outer Space" [Part II] (3-17-67) as above

TARZAN

This adaptation of the Edgar Rice Burroughs' classic (Ron Ely a very youthful Tarzan) diminishes from the underlying romance of the original. Tarzan is obviously anachronistic with the upbeat missionaries (The Supremes, no less) of "The Convert" and with the flower children of the two-part "Mountains of the Moon."

The Regulars: Tarzan, Ron Ely; Jai, Manuel Padilla Jr.; Jason Flood, Alan Caillou; Rao, Rockne Tarkington; Tall Boy, Stewart Rafill.

The Episodes:

1. "Eyes of the Lion" (9-8-66) Ned Romero, Laurie Sibbald
2. "The Ultimate Weapon" (9-16-66) Jock Mahoney, Andrew Prine, Sheilah Wells, Laurence Haddon
3. "Leopard on the Loose" (9-23-66) Russ Tamblyn, Ken Scott
4. "A Life for a Life" (9-30-66) Jon Alver, John Levingston
5. "The Prisoner" (10-7-66) Robert J. Wilke, Charles Maxwell
6. "The Three Faces of Death" (10-14-66) Woody Strode, Ena Hartman
7. "The Prodigal Puma" (10-21-66) Gigi Perreau, Rafer Johnson
8. "The Deadly Silence" [Part I] (10-28-66) Jock Mahoney, Nichelle Nichols, Woody Strode, Jose Chavez, Robert Doqui, Gregorio Acosta
9. "The Deadly Silence" [Part II] (11-4-66) as above
10. "The Figurehead" (11-11-66) Ronald Long, Ricky Cordell, Anthony Caruso

11. "Village of Fire" (11-18-66) Nobu McCarthy, Chuck Wood
12. "Day of the Golden Lion" (12-2-66) Suzy Parker, George Murdock, Curt Lowens, Chuck Wood
13. "Pearls of Tanga" (12-9-66) Carlos Rivas, John Kelly, Pearla Walter
14. "The End of the River" (12-16-66) Michael Whitney, George Murdock, Jill Donahue, Robert Wilke
15. "The Ultimate Duel" (12-23-66) Don Megowan, Henry Silva, Booker Bradshaw, Gail Kobe
16. "The Fire People" (12-30-66) Morris Erby, Mel Lettman, Francisco Reyguera
17. [unknown title] (1-6-67) Lloyd Bochner, Pippa Scott, Harry Lauter
18. "The Day the Earth Trembled" (1-13-67) Susan Oliver, John Anderson, Jacques Aubuchon
19. "Cap'n Jai" (1-20-67) Chips Rafferty, Gregg Palmer, Russ McCubbin
20. "A Pride of Assassins" (1-27-67) Gene Evans, Michael Whitney, Victor French, Jill Donahue
21. "The Golden Runaway" (2-3-67) Gia Scala, Sean McClory, Stacy Harris
22. "Basil of the Bulge" (2-10-67) Maurice Evans, Warren Stevens, Bernie Hamilton, Howard Morton, Lewis Martin, Dillard Hayeson
23. "Mask of Rona" (2-17-67) Nancy Malone, Leslie Parrish, Martin Gabel, Woody Strode
24. "To Steal the Rising Sun" (2-24-67) Ron Glenn Sr., James Earl Jones, John Van Dreelen, Victoria Shaw
25. "Jungle Dragnet" (3-3-67) Victoria Meyerink, Simon Oakland, William Marshall, Pedro Galvin, Virgil Richardson
26. "The Perils of Charity Jones" [Part I] (3-10-67) Julie Harris, Woody Strode, Edward Binns, Bernie Hamilton
27. "The Perils of Charity Jones" [Part II] (3-17-67) as above
28. "The Circus" (3-24-67) Chips Rafferty, Sally Kellerman, Jack Elam, Leo Gordon
29. "The Ultimatum" (3-31-67) Ruth Roman, Ralph Meeker, Jeff Burton, William Gunn, Henry Corden
30. "Algie B for Brave" (4-7-67) Maurice Evans, Arthur Franz, Todd Garrett, Robert Brubaker, Lewis Martin
31. "Man Killer" (4-14-67) Tammy Grimes, Jeremy Slate, James Gregory, Lloyd Haynes

Second Season

32. "Tiger, Tiger" (9-15-67) James Whitmore, Anne Jeffreys, Oscar Beregi, Michael Pate
33. "Voice of the Elephant" (9-22-67) Murray Matheson, Percy Rodriguez, John Doucette
34. "Thief Catcher" (9-29-67) Don Mitchell, George Kennedy, Yaphet Kotto, John Haymer
35. "The Blue Stone of Heaven" [Part I] (10-6-67) Sam Jaffe, Lloyd Haynes, Ulla Stromstedt, William Marshall, Jason Evers, Harry Lauter

36. "The Blue Stone of Heaven" [Part II] (10-13-67) as above
37. "Maguma Curse" (10-20-67) Barbara Luna, Simon Oakland, Ken Renard, Sydney Charles McCoy
38. "The Fanatics" (10-27-67) Diana Hyland, William Smithers, Donald Marshall, George Murdock, Chuck Wood
39. "Last of the Supermen" (11-3-67) Antoinette Bower, Alf Kjellin, Brock Peters, Michael Burns
40. "Hotel Hurricane" (11-10-67) Michael Tolan, Bert Freed, Donnelly Rhodes, Jean Hale
41. "The Pride of a Lioness" (11-17-67) Helen Hayes, James MacArthur, Geoffrey Holder
42. "Mountains of the Moon" [Part I] (11-24-67) Ethel Merman, Perry Lopez, Harry Lauter, Strother Martin, Harry Townes, William Marshall
43. "Mountains of the Moon" [Part II] (12-1-67) as above
44. "Jai's Amnesia" (12-15-67) John Dehner, John Alderson, Hal Baylor
45. "Creeping Giants" (12-29-67) Raymond St. Jacques, Will Kuluva, Robert Wilke
46. "The Professional" (1-5-68) Pat Conway, Karl Swenson, Clarence Williams
47. "The Convert" (1-12-68) Diana Ross and the Supremes, Malachi Throne, James Earl Jones
48. "King of the Dwsari" (1-26-68) Robert Loggia, Morgan Woodward, Judy Pace, Ernie Terrell
49. "A Gun for Jai" (2-2-68) Peter Whitney, Geoffrey Holder, Ed Bakey
50. "Trek to Terror" (2-9-68) Michael Ansara, John Pickard, Booker T. Bradshaw
51. "End of a Challenge" (2-16-68) Chill Wills, Henry Jones, Woody Strode, Pepe Brown
52. "Jungle Ransom" (2-23-68) Fernando Lamas, Ted Cassidy, Jack Hogan, Barbara Bouchet
53. "Four O'Clock Army" [Part I] (3-1-68) Maurice Evans, Julie Harris, Bruce Gordon, Bernie Hamilton
54. "Four O'Clock Army" [Part II] (3-8-68) as above
55. "Rendezvous for Revenge" (3-15-68) John Vernon, Laraine Stephens, Booth Colman, Don Knight
56. "Alex the Great" (3-22-68) Neville Brand, Michael Dunn, Read Morgan, Diane Williams, Jim Shayne, Dick Crockett
57. "Trina" (4-5-68) Stacey Maxwell, Nehemiah Persoff, Barbara Hancock, Susan Howard

THE TIME TUNNEL

   This juvenile series, if one has accepted its basic premise --two government scientists finding themselves "lost among the infinite corridors of time"--is frequently historically inaccurate. In the episode "Revenge of the Gods," for example, about the Homeric Trojan War, the gods and goddesses are referred to with Roman names. The war in the South Pacific of Bob and Wanda Duncan's

"Kill Two by Two" has taken on the peculiar turn of a personal vendetta by a crazed American-educated Japanese soldier--with time-travelers Tony Newman (James Darren) and Doug Phillips (Robert Colbert) as his targets. Dr. Ann MacGregor's (the Lee Meriwether role) skepticism of Biblical text in "The Walls of Jericho" was no impediment to the conclusion of Ellis St. Joseph's script, which allowed for the walls to "come tumbling down" anyway. Better suited was the series to the pure fiction of the distant future, such as in Bob and Wanda Duncan's (they wrote several of the episodes) "Visitors from Beyond the Stars."

But of course it is the technical credits which matter most in Irwin Allen series, so Winton Hoch's cinematography, Jack Martin Smith's and Roger E. Maus' art direction and Johnny Williams' musical theme deserve mentioning.

The Regulars: Tony Newman, James Darren; Doug Phillips, Robert Colbert; Dr. Ann MacGregor, Lee Meriwether; General Heywood Kirk, Whit Bissell; Dr. Raymond Swain, John Zaremba; Sergeant Jiggs, Wesley Lau.

The Episodes:

1. "Rendezvous with Yesterday" (9-9-66) Michael Rennie, Gary Merrill, Susan Hampshire, Don Knight
2. "One Way to the Moon" (9-16-66) Warren Stevens, James Callahan, Larry Ward, Ben Cooper, Ross Elliott
3. "End of the World" (9-23-66) Paul Fix, James Westerfield, Paul Carr, Gregory Morton
4. "The Day the Sky Fell In" (9-30-66) Linden Chiles, Susan Flannery, Sam Groom, Lew Gallo
5. "The Last Patrol" (10-7-66) Carroll O'Connor, John Napier, Michael Pate
6. "Crack of Doom" (10-14-66) Torin Thatcher, Ellen McRae
7. "Revenge of the Gods" (10-21-66) John Doucette, Joseph Ruskin, Paul Carr, Dee Hartford, Tony Brand, Abraham Sofaer
8. "Massacre" (10-28-66) Joe Maross, George Mitchell, Christopher Dark, Paul Comi, Perry Lopez
9. "Devil's Island" (11-11-66) Marcel Hillaire, Theodore Marcuse, Oscar Beregi
10. "Reign of Terror" (11-18-66) David Opatoshu, Monique Lemaire
11. "Secret Weapon" (11-25-66) Michael Ansara, Nehemiah Persoff
12. "The Death Trap" (12-2-66) Scott Marlowe, R. G. Armstrong, Ford Rainey, Tom Skerritt
13. "The Alamo" (12-9-66) Rhodes Reason, John Lupton, Jim Davis, Rodolfo Hoyos, Elizabeth Rogers
14. "Night of the Long Knives" (12-16-66) Malachi Throne, David Watson, Perry Lopez, Peter Brocco, Brendan Dillon
15. "Invasion" (12-23-66) Lyle Bettger, John Wengraf, Robert Carricart, Joey Tata

16. "Revenge of Robin Hood" (12-30-66) John Crawford, John Orchard, Donald Harron
17. "Kill Two by Two" (1-6-67) Philip Ahn, Mako, Kam Tong, Brent Davis
18. "Visitors from Beyond the Stars" (1-13-67) Jan Merlin, Fred Beir, Ross Elliott, Byron Foulger, Gary Haynes
19. "The Ghost of Nero" (1-20-67) Eduardo Ciannelli, Gunnar Hellstrom, John Hoyt
20. "The Walls of Jericho" (1-27-67) Myrna Fahey, Arnold Moss, Rhodes Reason, Lisa Gaye, Abraham Sofaer
21. "Idol of Death" (2-3-67) Anthony Caruso, Lawrence Montaigne, Teno Pollick
22. "Billy the Kid" (2-10-67) Robert Walker Jr., John Crawford, Allen Case, Harry Lauter
23. "Pirates of Deadman's Island" (2-17-67) Victor Jory, Regis Toomey, James Anderson
24. "Chase Through Time" (2-24-67) Robert Duvall, Lew Gallo
25. "The Death Merchant" (3-3-67) Malachi Throne, Kevin Hagen, John Crawford
26. "The Attack of the Barbarians" (3-10-67) John Saxon
27. "Merlin the Magician" (3-17-67) Christopher Carey, James McMullan, Vincent Bek, Lisa Jak
28. "The Kidnappers" (3-24-67) Michael Ansara, Del Monroe
29. "Raiders from Outer Space" (3-31-67) Jack Crawford, Kevin Hagen
30. "Town of Terror" (4-7-67) Mabel Albertson, Gary Haynes, Heather Young, Kelly Thordsen


T. H. E. CAT

Dubious if well photographed tale of a (supposed) cat burglar turned bodyguard whose missions call for seemingly impossible calisthenics.

The Regulars: Thomas Hewitt Edward Cat, Robert Loggia; Captain McAllister, R. G. Armstrong; Pepe, Robert Carricart.

The Episodes:

1. "To Kill a Priest" (9-16-66) Jason Evers, Sorrell Booke
2. "Sandman" (9-23-66) Lee Bergere, Signe Hasso, Dennis Patrick
3. "Payment Overdue" (10-7-66) Laura Devon, Donald Barry
4. "Little Arnie from Long Ago" (10-14-66) James Whitmore, Jack Gilford
5. "None to Weep, None to Mourn" (10-21-66) Diana Muldaur, Cyril Delevanti, Jaime Sanchez
6. "Moment of Truth" (10-28-66) Mark Richman, Linda Cristal
7. "Brotherhood" (11-4-66) Albert Salmi, Michael Constantine, Ted Knight, Sandy Brown
8. "Crossing at Destino Bay" (11-18-66) Robert Duvall,

Susanne Cramer, Robert H. Harris
9. "To Bell T. H. E. Cat" (11-25-66) Shary Marshall, Henry Darrow
10. "Curtains for Miss Winslow" (12-2-66) Lloyd Bochner, Virginia Field, Sam Melville
11. "King of Limpets" (12-9-66) John Dehner, Indus Arthur, Rafael Campos, Stefan Arngrim
12. "The System" (12-16-66) Joseph Wiseman, Lynda Day
13. "The Canary Who Lost His Voice" (12-23-66) James Dunn, Theo Marcuse
14. "The Ring of Anasis" (12-30-66) William Daniels, Ross Hagen, Michele Carey
15. "Queen of Diamonds, Knave of Hearts" (1-6-67) Cesar Romero, Liliane Montevecchi
16. "A Hot Place to Die" (1-13-67) Joe Maross, Karen Steele, Richard Anderson
17. "A Slight Family Trait" (1-20-67) John Colicos, Carol Booth
18. "If Once You Fall" (2-3-67) Pippa Scott, Louise Hadley, Robert Emhardt, H. M. Wynant, Lindon Tanner, William Wintersole
19. "Design for Death" (2-10-67) Patricia Cutts, Henry Darrow, Joanna Moore
20. "Matter over Mind" (2-17-67) Sally Kellerman, Steve Franken, Robert H. Harris
21. "Blood-Red Night" (2-24-67) Cathleen Nesbitt, John Hoyt, Antoinette Bower, Donald Barry
22. "Ninety Per Cent Blues" (3-3-67) Warren Stevens, Gene Roland, Carol Cole
23. "The Long Chase" (3-10-67) Robert Duvall
24. "Twenty-One and Out" (3-24-67) Susan Oliver, John Marley, Robert Sampson
25. "Lisa" (3-31-67) Diana Van Der Vlis, Victor Buono

## THE INVADERS

Fascinating Quinn Martin entry--not of course as rigidly adhering to the "documentary tone" of The Untouchables--but a compelling tale of an architect (Roy Thinnes as David Vincent) "out to convince a disbelieving world that 'the invaders' have landed." It is particularly effective in drawing a thin line between who are the aliens and who are not (the aliens are in human form). It is also --what with its underlying theme of basic mistrust--reminiscent of the McCarthy witch-hunt era, when apparent loyalty was an intractable alternative to blacklisting.

Superb photography and art direction (windswept, thinly populated towns, with a special attention to climate) do much to enhance the sense of forboding.

The Regulars: David Vincent, Roy Thinnes; Edgar Scoville, Kent

Smith (with episode of 12/5/67).

The Episodes:

1.  "Beachhead" (1-10-67) Diane Baker, James Daly, J. D.
    Cannon, Ellen Corby, John Milford
2.  "The Experiment" (1-17-67) Roddy McDowall, Laurence
    Naismith, Harold Gould, Dabbs Greer
3.  "The Mutation" (1-24-67) Suzanne Pleshette, Edward An-
    drews
4.  "The Leeches" (1-31-67) Arthur Hill, Mark Richman, Diana
    Van Der Vlis, Robert H. Harris, Peter Brocco, Theo
    Marcuse
5.  "Genesis" (2-7-67) John Larch, Carol Rossen, Frank Over-
    ton, Tim McIntire, William Sargent, Louise Latham
6.  "Vikor" (2-14-67) Jack Lord, Alfred Ryder, Diana Hyland
7.  "Nightmare" (2-21-67) Robert Emhardt, Kathleen Widdoes,
    Jeanette Nolan, James Callahan
8.  "Doomsday Minus One" (2-28-67) William Windom, Andrew
    Duggan, Wesley Addy
9.  "Quantity Unknown" (3-7-67) Susan Strasberg, James Whit-
    more, William Talman
10. "The Innocent" (3-14-67) Michael Rennie, William Smithers,
    Patricia Smith, Dabney Coleman
11. "The Ivy Curtain" (3-21-67) Susan Oliver, Jack Warden,
    Murray Matheson, David Sheiner
12. "The Betrayed" (3-28-67) Ed Begley, Laura Devon, Nancy
    Wickwire, Norman Fell
13. "The Storm" (4-4-67) Barbara Luna, Simon Scott, Joseph
    Campanella, Dean Harens, Carlos Romero, Paul Comi
14. "Panic" (4-11-67) Robert Walker, Jr., Lynn Loring, R. G.
    Armstrong
15. "Moonshot" (4-18-67) John Ericson, Peter Graves, Kent
    Smith, Anthony Eisley, Joanne Linville, John Lupton,
    Strother Martin
16. "Wall of Crystal" (5-2-67) Burgess Meredith, Linden Chiles,
    Julie Sommars, Edward Asner
17. "The Condemned" (5-9-67) Ralph Bellamy, Murray Hamil-
    ton, Marlyn Mason

Second Season

18. "Condition: Red" (9-5-67) Antoinette Bower, Jason Evers
19. "The Saucer" (9-12-67) Anne Francis, Charles Drake, Dab-
    ney Coleman
20. "Watchers" (9-19-67) Shirley Knight, Kevin McCarthy
21. "Valley of the Shadow" (9-26-67) Nan Martin, Harry
    Townes, Roy Hayes, Joe Maross
22. "The Enemy" (10-3-67) Barbara Barrie, Richard Anderson
23. "The Trial" (10-10-67) Lynda Day, Harold Gould, Don Gor-
    don
24. "The Spores" (10-17-67) Gene Hackman, Mark Miller,
    Patricia Smith, Wayne Rogers, John Randolph, James

Gammon
25. "Dark Outpost" (10-24-67) Andrew Prine, Dawn Wells, Tim McIntire, Tom Lowell, William Sargent
26. "The Summit Meeting" [Part I] (10-31-67) Eduard Franz, Diana Hyland, Michael Rennie, William Windom
27. "The Summit Meeting" [Part II] (11-7-67) as above
28. "The Prophet" (11-14-67) Zina Bethune, Pat Hingle
29. "Labyrinth" (11-21-67) Ed Begley, Sally Kellerman, James Callahan, Virginia Christine, Ed Peck, Martin Blaine
30. "The Captive" (11-28-67) Dana Wynter, Fritz Weaver, Don Dubbins, Lawrence Dane, Douglas Henderson, Jock Gaynor, Tom Palmer
31. "The Believers" (12-5-67) Carol Lynley, Anthony Eisley, Donald Davis, Rhys Williams, Than Wyenn, Maura Mc-Giveney
32. "The Ransom" (12-12-67) Laurence Naismith, Alfred Ryder, Karen Black
33. "Task Force" (12-26-67) Linden Chiles, Nancy Kovack, John Lassell
34. "The Possessed" (1-2-68) Michael Tolan, Michael Constantine
35. "Counterattack" (1-9-68) Lin McCarthy, Donald Davis, Anna Capri
36. "The Pit" (1-16-68) Joanne Linville, Charles Aidman, Donald Harron
37. "The Organization" (1-30-68) J. D. Cannon, Chris Robinson, Larry Gates, Roy Poole
38. "The Peacemaker" (2-6-68) James Daly, Phyllis Thaxter, Alfred Ryder, Lin McCarthy
39. "The Vise" (2-20-68) Raymond St. Jacques, Roscoe Lee Browne, Janet MacLachlan
40. "The Miracle" (2-27-68) Barbara Hershey
41. "The Life Seekers" (3-5-68) Barry Morse, Diana Muldaur, R. G. Armstrong, Arthur Franz, Stephen Brooks, Paul Comi, Morgan Jones, Herb Armstrong, Barry Cahill, Scott Graham
42. "The Pursued" (3-12-68) Suzanne Pleshette, Will Geer, Rudolfo Acosta, Gene Lyons
43. "Inquisition" (3-26-68) Susan Oliver, Mark Richman, John Milford

THE SAINT

The Regulars: Simon Templar, Roger Moore; Inspector, Ivor Dean.

The Episodes:

1. "The Death Game" (5-21-67) Angela Douglas, John Steiner, Bernard Horsfall, Alan MacNaughton
2. "The Angel's Eye" (5-28-67) Jane Merrow, Cyril Shaps,

Anthony Nichols, Donald Pickering, Liam Redmond
3. "The Fast Woman" (6-4-67) Jan Holden, Kate O'Mara, John Hollis, John Carson
4. "To Kill a Saint" (6-11-67) Annette Andre, Derek Bond, Peter Dyneley, Francis Matthews
5. "Little Girl Lost" (6-18-67) June Ritchie, Noel Purcell, Edward Burnham, Maurice Good
6. [unknown title] (6-25-67) Fiona Lewis, William Gaunt, Imogen Hassell, Marne Maitland
7. "The Man Who Likes Lions" (7-2-67) Suzanne Lloyd, Jeremy Young, Michael Forrest, Peter Wyngarde
8. "Escape Route" (7-9-67) Wanda Ventham, Jean Marsh, John Gregson, Donald Sutherland
9. "Locate and Destroy" (7-16-67) John Barrie, Julia Arnell, Francesca Annis, Maurice Kaufmann
10. "The Counterfeit Countess" (7-23-67) Kate O'Mara, Derek Newark, Alexandra Bastedo, Philip Madoc
11. "The Art Collectors" (7-30-67) Ann Bell, Geoffrey Bayldon, Peter Bowles, James Maxwell
12. "Queen's Ransom" (8-6-67) Dawn Addams, George Pastell, Nora Nicholson, Catherine Feller, Stanley Meadows, Nevele Becker
13. "The Russian Prisoner" (8-13-67) Yootha Joyce, Penelope Horner

## Second Season

14. "Invitation to Danger" (2-17-68) Shirley Eaton, Robert Hutton
15. "A Double in Diamonds" (2-24-68) Cecil Parker, Anton Rodgers
16. "The Best Laid Schemes" (3-2-68) Gabrielle Drake, Sylvia Syms
17. "The Power Artist" (3-9-68) Pauline Munro, Ivor Dean
18. "When Spring Is Sprung" (3-16-68) Toby Robins, Allan Cuthbertson
19. "The Gadic Collection" (3-23-68) Georgia Brown, Peter Wyngarde
20. "The Gadget Lovers" (3-30-68) Mary Peach, Campbell Singer
21. "The Better Mousetrap" (4-6-68) Alexandria Stewart, Leon Janney
22. "The House on Dragon's Rock" (4-13-68) Annette Andre, Anthony Bate
23. "The Persistent Patriots" (4-27-68) Edward Woodward

## Third Season

24. "Legacy for the Saint" (4-18-69)
25. "The Double Take" (4-25-69) Gregorie Aslan, Kate O'Mara, Denise Buckley
26. "The Man Who Gambled with Life" (5-2-69)
27. "Simon and Delilah" (5-9-69) Suzanne Lloyd, Lois Maxwell

28. "Portrait of Brenda" (5-16-69) Anne De Vigier, Petra
    Davies, Anna Carteret, Marne Maitland
29. "The Helpful Pirate" (5-23-69) Paul Maxwell, George Prav-
    da, Erika Remberg, Redmond Phillips
30. "The Paper Chase" (5-30-69) Ronald Hines, Niall MacGinnis
    Penelope Horner, Gordon Gostelow
31. "Interlude in Venice" (6-6-69)
32. "The Reluctant Revolution" (6-13-69) Jennie Linden, Barry
    Morse, Peter Iling, Gerald Heinz


CORONET BLUE

Compelling study of an amnesiac's search for his identity,
admirably performed by Frank Converse as the searching protagonist.

The Regulars: Michael Alden, Frank Converse; Brother Anthony,
    Brian Bedford; Max, Joe Silver.

The Episodes:

1. "A Time to Be Born" (5-29-67) Chester Morris, Donald
   Woods
2. "The Assassins" (6-12-67) Signe Hasso, Janet Margolin
3. "The Rebel" (6-19-67) Richard Kiley, Candice Bergen,
   Jon Voight
4. "A Dozen Demons" (7-3-67) Lynda Day, John Beal, House
   Jameson, Donald Moffatt
5. [unknown title] (7-10-67) Hal Holbrook, Mitchell Ryan,
   Phyllis Thaxter, Mark Hulswit, Michael Walker
6. "Man Running" (7-17-67) Denholm Elliott, Juliet Mills,
   Bramwell Fletcher, Alan Ansara, Carlos Montalban
7. "A Charade for Murder" (7-24-67) Jack Cassidy, Brenda
   Vaccaro, Bernice Massi
8. "Saturday" (7-31-67) Doug Chapin, Neva Patterson, Miles
   Chapin, Arthur Sussex, Charles Randall, Mark Kearney
9. "The Presence of Evil" (8-7-67) Joseph Wiseman, Viveca
   Lindfors, Judi West, Carol Crist, Leonard Elliot, Susel
   Tair
10. "Six Months to Mars" (8-14-67) Alan Alda, Patrick O'Neal
    Billy Dee Williams, Jock Gaynor, Barbara Blake, Ed
    Wagner
11. "The Flip Side of Timmy Devon" (9-4-67) Murray the K,
    Dick Clark, Peter Duchin


AFRICA

Breathtaking panorama of the Dark Continent--dark, it
would appear, not much longer.

Narrator: Gregory Peck

Telecast 9-10-67 on ABC-TV, 7:00-11:00.

Part I: "Africa's Animals"; "A Window on the Past" [with Louis S. B. Leakey]; "Africa's Dawn of Civilization" [Ethiopia]; "The Birth of a Nation" [transference of power from England to Bechuanaland, creating nation of Botswana]

Part II: "Tribalism, the Internal Conflict"; "Scourge of the Continent" [health hazards]; "Hope of the Continent" [focus on education]; "Ambition Humbled--Ghana and Nkrumah" [with Howard K. Smith, African leaders]

Part III: "The Universality of Sports"; "Africa's Lively Arts" [Miriam Makeba]; "Slavery"; "Kenya"; "The Congo"

Part IV: "The Overseas Provinces"; "A Controversy of Colonialism"; Summary by Howard K. Smith; concluding remarks by Gregory Peck.

MAYA

Stunning India location photography uplifts this familiar tale of estranged youths (Jay North as the American Terry Bowen; Sajid Khan the Indian Raji) pursued by assorted reprobates and aided by the consummate animal of the jungle, the elephant Maya. The story was told as a 1966 feature film with the aforementioned regulars and Clint Walker.

The Regulars: Terry Bowen, Jay North; Raji, Sajid Khan.

The Episodes:

1. "Blood of the Tiger" (9-16-67)  Jai Raj
2. "The Allapur Conspiracy" (9-23-67)  Iftikhar Ahmed, Askah Deep, Zul Vellani, Faryal
3. "Tiger Boy" (10-7-67)  Shahid
4. "The Caper of the Golden Roe" (10-14-67)  Jagdev, Iftikhar Ahmed
5. "Twilight of Empire" (10-21-67)  Ivor Barry, Fred Beir
6. "Will the Real Prince Please Get Lost?" (10-28-67)  Zul Vellani, Manmohan Krishna
7. "The Demon of Kalanemi" (11-4-67)  M. A. Lateef, Neelum
8. "The Khandur Uprising" (11-18-67)  Oliver McGowan, S. P. Sinha, Chanda Joglekar, Satyadev Dubey
9. "A Bus for Ramabad" (11-25-67)  Mubarak Merchant, I. S. Johar
10. "The Root of Evil" (12-2-67)  Prem Nath, Bimal Raj
11. "Deadly Passage" (12-9-67)  Nehemiah Persoff, Gajanan Jagirdar
12. "Natira" (12-23-67)  Salome Aaron, I. S. Johar, Jai Raj
13. "Mirrcan's Magic Circus" (1-6-68)  David Opatoshu, Tun Tun, Milton Chang, Om Shivpuri, Z. A. Baig
14. "The Son of Gammu Ghat" (1-13-68)  Sachin Sharad, Mahes Desai, Manhar Desai
15. "The Treasure Temple" (1-20-68)  Michael Pate, Jai Raj, Bimal Raj, Karan Dewan
16. "The Ransom of Raji" (1-27-68)  Manmohan Krishna, Rakes Pande
17. "The Witness" (2-3-68)  Surindernath, Mort Mills, S. P. Sinha

18. "The Legend of Whitney Markham" (2-10-68) E. J. Andre, Mort Mills


## MANNIX

Joe Mannix progressed from a regularly ordered about (by Joseph Campanella as Wickersham in the first season) law enforcer, unto private investigator. Gail Fisher made a lasting impression as the beautiful and discerning secretary.

The Regulars: Joe Mannix, Mike Connors; Peggy, Gail Fisher; Wickersham, Joe Campanella (first season only); Sgt. Tobias, Robert Reed (with episode of 9/27/69 to episode of 3/8/72); Lt. Malcolm, Ward Wood (with episode of 9/17/72).

The Episodes:

1. "My Name Is Mannix" (9-16-67) Lloyd Nolan, John Colicos, Kim Hunter, Bob Garrett, Buzz Henry, K. L. Smith, Barbara Anderson
2. [unknown title] (9-23-67) Charles Drake, Marion Moses, Elizabeth Fraser, Wende Wagner
3. [unknown title] (9-30-67) Gloria De Haven, Frank Aletter, Robert H. Harris, Leslie Perkins
4. [unknown title] (10-7-67) David Hurst, John Marley
5. [unknown title] (10-14-67) John Randolph, Phillip Pine, Amber Flower, Letitia Roman
6. [unknown title] (10-21-67) Marlyn Mason, Henry Beckman, Donnelly Rhodes, Henry Calvin
7. "Warning: Live Blueberries" (10-28-67) Tom Skerritt, Brooke Bundy, Robert Emhardt
8. "Beyond the Shadow of a Dream" (11-4-67) Robert Yuro, Ann Prentiss, Richard Mulligan, Judi Meredith
9. [unknown title] (11-18-67) Ford Rainey, Steve Ihnat, Sandra Smith, Paul Stevens
10. [unknown title] (11-25-67) Frank Campanella, Diana Muldaur, Gabriel Dell, Ross Bagdaarian, Whitney Blake, Norman Fell
11. "Catalog of Sin" (12-2-67) Fay Spain, Joe Maross, Percy Rodriguez, Jennifer Billingsly
12. [unknown title] (12-9-67) Noam Pitlik, Linden Chiles, Nita Talbot, C. D. Spradlin, Lloyd Gough, Sharon Hillyer, Dabbs Greer, John Crawford, Hampton Fancher, Madge Blake
13. [unknown title] (12-16-67) Ruta Lee, Joyce Van Patten, John Abbott, Malachi Throne
14. [unknown title] (12-30-67) Sean McClory, Julie Adams, John Anderson, Lynda Day, Dorothy Green
15. "The Falling Star" (1-6-68) Jan Sterling, Lee Bergere, Marion Seldes, Barbara Hunter, Douglas Henderson

16. "License to Kill--Limit Three People" (1-13-68) Karen Black, Peter Haskell, Wright King
17. "Deadfall" [Part I] (1-20-68) Michael Tolan, Beverly Garland, Roscoe Lee Browne, Antoinette Bower
18. "Deadfall" [Part II] (1-27-68) as above
19. "You Can Get Killed Out There" (2-3-68) Howard Da Silva, Marianna Hill, Scott Marlowe
20. [unknown title] (2-10-68) Jan Shepard, Paul Comi, Larry Storch
21. "Eight to Five, It's a Miracle" (2-17-68) Larry Perkins, Brenda Scott, William Smithers
22. "Delayed Action" (3-2-68) Louise Sorel
23. [unknown title] (3-9-68) Paul Peterson, Ted Cassidy, Michael Strong, Patti Chandler
24. "The Girl in the Frame" (3-16-68) Leslie Parrish, William Windom

Second Season

25. "The Silent Cry" (9-28-68) Laurence Naismith, Jason Evers, Audree Norton
26. [unknown title] (10-5-68) Sheree North, Lee Bergere, Gerald S. O'Loughlin
27. "Pressure Point" (10-12-68) Harold J. Stone, Paul Stewart, Pamela Dunlap
28. [unknown title] (10-19-68) Jill Ireland, Hugh Beaumont, Joe Mantell, Peter Haskell, Nick Colasanto
29. "End of the Rainbow" (10-26-68) Kathryn Hays, Jack Ging
30. "A Copy of Murder" (11-2-68) Barbara Rush, Kevin Hagen, Clifton James
31. "Edge of the Knife" (11-9-68) Fritz Weaver, Geraldine Brooks
32. [unknown title] (11-16-68) Charles Robinson, Barry Atwater, Linda Marsh
33. "The Need of a Friend" (11-23-68) Cloris Leachman, Marie Windsor, John Colicos, Barbara Babcock
34. "Night Out of Time" (12-7-68) David Brian, Wright King, Frank Campanella, Mart Hulswit
35. [unknown title] (12-14-68) Katie Woodville, Hazel Court, Michael Wilding, Frank Campanella
36. "Fear I to Fall" (12-21-68) Joanna Barnes, Marian Collier, Dana Elcar, John Considine, Richard Anderson
37. "Death Run" (1-4-69) Madlyn Rhue, John Milford, Fred Beir
38. "A Pittance of Faith" (1-11-69) David Opatoshu, E. J. Andre, Lawrence Linville
39. [unknown title] (1-18-69) Bettye Ackerman, Peter Donat, John Dehner, Slim Pickens, Patricia Barry
40. "Shadow of a Man" (1-25-69) Antoinette Bower, William Windom, Don Chastain, Lawrence Linville
41. "The Girl Who Came In with the Tide" (2-1-69) Lloyd Bochner, Robert Reed, Nancy Kovack
42. "Death in a Minor Key" (2-8-69) Anthony Zerbe, Evans

Evans, Yaphet Kotto
43. "End Game" (2-15-69) Steve Ihnat, Arch Johnson
44. "All Around the Money Tree" (2-22-69) Christopher Cary,
John Orchard, Marian MacAndrew
45. "The Odds Against Donald Jordan" (3-1-69) Susan Oliver,
James Olson, Paul Winfield, Nan Martin
46. "Last Rites for Miss Emma" (3-8-69) Robert Hooks, Ron
Randall, Dabbs Greer, Rhys Williams
47. "The Solid Gold Web" (3-22-69) Sally Kellerman, Robert
Ellenstein, Whit Bissell, John Randolph
48. "Merry-Go-Round for Murder" (4-5-69) Warren Stevens,
Ruth McDevitt, Sue Ane Langdon
49. [unknown title] (4-12-69) Pilar Seurat, Gail Kobe

## Third Season

50. [unknown title] (9-27-69) Georg Stanford Brown, Geoffrey
Deuel
51. [unknown title] (10-4-69) John Beck, Virginia Gregg, Victor
Jory, Jason Evers
52. "Return to Summer Grove" (10-11-69) Vera Miles, Larry
Pennell, Victor Jory
53. "The Playground" (10-18-69) Robert Conrad, Ben Cooper,
Leslie Parrish
54. [unknown title] (10-25-69) Tom Troupe, Scott McKay, Lee
Meriwether
55. "A Penny for the Peepshow" (11-1-69) Edd Byrnes, Sabrina
Scharf
56. "A Sleep in the Deep" (11-8-69) Skip Homeier, Paul Stewart, Milton Selzer
57. [unknown title] (11-22-69)
58. "The Nowhere Victim" (11-29-69) Richard Bull, Marc
Lawrence, Corinne Camacho
59. "The Sound of Darkness" (12-6-69) Joby Baker, James Edwards, Gilbert Green, Peter Brocco
60. "Who Killed Me?" (12-13-69) Paul Richards, Susan Howard,
Yvonne Craig
61. "Missing: Sun and Sky" (12-20-69) Gene Raymond, Alex
Dreier, Anita Louise
62. "Tooth of the Serpent" (12-27-69) Bert Freed, Harrison
Page, Lynn Hamilton, Percy Rodriguez
63. "Medal for a Hero" (1-3-70) Frank Marth, Bobby Troup,
Terry Carter, Jack Ging
64. "Walk with a Dead Man" (1-10-70) Mark Richman, Dane
Clark, Parley Baer, Marian McCargo
65. [unknown title] (1-17-70) Dewey Martin, Jan Merlin, Scott
Brady
66. "Blind Mirror" (1-24-70) Linda Marsh, Diane McBain,
Robert Lansing
67. [unknown title] (1-31-70) Don Knight, Karen Steele, Peter
Whitney
68. "Who Is Sylvia?" (2-7-70) Robert Collier, Jessica Walter,
Lawrence Linville

69. "Only One Death to a Customer" (2-14-70) Loretta Swit, Garr Walbert
70. "Fly, Little One" (2-21-70) Woodrow Parfrey, Julie Gregg, Lawrence Dane
71. "The Search for Darrell Andrews" (2-28-70) Van Williams, Dana Elcar, Harry Townes
72. "Murder Revisited" (3-7-70) Arlene Martel, Don De Fore
73. "War of Nerves" (3-14-70) Hugh Beaumont, Mort Mills, Paul Picerni
74. "Once Upon a Saturday" (3-21-70) Bethel Leslie, Carlos Rivas, Michael Conrad, Pamela Kingsley, Barbara Rhoades

Fourth Season

75. "A Ticket to the Eclipse" (9-19-70) Darren McGavin, Paul Mantee, Dane Clark, Mark Stewart
76. "One for the Lady" (9-26-70) Jo Van Fleet
77. "Time out of Mind" (10-3-70) Brock Peters, Kim Hamilton, Juanita Moore
78. "Figures in a Landscape" (10-10-70) Victor French, Loretta Swit
79. "The Mouse That Died" (10-17-70) Patricia Smith, Richard Bull, Hugh Beaumont, Douglas Henderson
80. "The Lost Art of Dying" (10-24-70) Alex Dreier, Julie Parrish, Ramon Bieri, Val Avery
81. "The Other Game in Town" (10-31-70) Martine Beswick, Rich Little, Leslie Parrish, Don Dubbins, Alan Bergmann
82. "The World Between" (11-7-70) Hari Rhodes, Ford Rainey, Jerry Douglas
83. [unknown title] (11-14-70) Pat Quinn, Barry Atwater, Paul Carr
84. "To Cage a Sea Gull" (11-21-70) Norman Alden, Ben Cooper, Michael Vandever, Ward Wood
85. "Bang, Bang, You're Dead" (11-28-70) Patti Cohoon, Larry Linville, Loretta Leversee
86. "Déjà Vu" (12-12-70) Brenda Scott, Kim Hunter, Paul Stewart, Morgan Sterne
87. "Duet for Three" (12-19-70) Katherine Justice, Robert Colbert, Gloria Graham, John Considine
88. "Round Trip to Nowhere" (1-2-71) Tim O'Connor, Kevin Hagen, Susan Howard, Jerry Douglas, Larry Pennell, Stuart Nisbet
89. "What Happened to Sunday?" (1-9-71) Kate Woodville, Fred Beir, J. Pat O'Malley, Francine York, Milton Selzer
90. "The Judas Touch" (1-16-71) Robert Lansing, Ruth Roman, James Wainwright, Brenda Benet
91. "With Intent to Kill" (1-23-71) Joan Hotchkis, Dane Clark, Lee Stanley
92. "The Crime That Wasn't" (1-30-71) Dewey Martin, Vincent Beck, Rosemary De Camp, Robert Hogan, Jacqueline Susann
93. "A Gathering of Ghosts" (2-6-71) Diana Muldaur, Jason Evers, Robert Webber, Marj Dusay, Charles Aidman

94. "A Day Filled with Shadows" (2-13-71) John Colicos, Sam Chew Jr., Tiffany Bolling, Fred Krone, Charles Picerni
95. "Voice in the Dark" (2-20-71) Carol Lynley, Paul Picerni, Jim Antonio, Paul Bertoya
96. "The Color of Murder" (2-27-71) John McLiam, John Lupton, Diane Keaton, Virginia Gregg
97. "Shadow Play" (3-6-71) Jan Murray, John Vernon, Julie Gregg, Paul Mantee
98. "Overkill" (3-13-71) Jeff Corey, Lawrence Dane, Marc Lawrence, Jay Robinson

## Fifth Season

99. "Dark So Early, Dark So Long" (9-15-71) Rosemary Forsyth, Guy Stockwell, Sam Melville, Alan Calliou
100. "Cold Trail" (9-22-71) Heidi Vaughn, Gregory Morton, George Voskovec, Patricia Medina
101. "A Step in Time" (9-29-71) Dean Stockwell, Shelley Fabares, Hildy Brooks
102. [unknown title] (10-6-71) Perry Lopez, Victor Jory, Anthony Caruso
103. "Woman in the Shadows" (10-13-71) Ina Balin, Eric Braeden, John Considine
104. "Days Beyond Recall" (10-20-71) Robert Foxworth, Elizabeth Allen, Vic Morrow
105. [unknown title] (10-27-71) Charlotte Stewart, Jonathan Lippe, Val Avery, Woodrow Parfrey, Jason Wingreen, J. Pat O'Malley
106. "The Glass Trap" (11-3-71) Robert Foxworth, H. M. Wynant
107. "A Choice of Evils" (11-10-71) Stephen McNally, Georg Stanford Brown, Robert Colbert
108. "A Button for General D" (11-17-71) David Sheiner, Ross Hagen, Joanna Pettet, Irene Tedrow
109. "The Man Outside" (11-24-71) Coleen Gray, Andrew Duggan, Kathie Browne, Tom Drake
110. "Murder Times Three" (12-1-71) Pippa Scott, Dan Travanty, Joe Maross, Gene Evans
111. "Catspaw" (12-8-71) Armando Silvestre, Peter Donat, Vincent Beck
112. [unknown title] (12-15-71) Tina Chen, James Douglas
113. [unknown title] (12-29-71) Milton Berle, Jesse White, Mary Nancy Burnett
114. [unknown title] (1-5-72) Melodie Johnson, Nita Talbot, William Mims, Paul Stevens
115. [unknown title] (1-12-72) Madlyn Rhue, Jack Ging
116. "Moving Target" (1-19-72) Charles Aidman, Jessica Walter
117. "Cry Pigeon" (1-26-72) Barry Sullivan, Tony Young, John Colicos, Richard Devon, Corinne Camacho, Joseph Hindy
118. [unknown title] (2-9-72) Ed Flanders, Jeanne Cooper, Mary Wilcox, Robert Colbert
119. [unknown title] (2-16-72) Lou Rawls, Jack Ging, Ta-Tanisha

120. [unknown title] (2-23-72) Julie Parrish, Steve Ihnat, Joan Hotchkis, Fred Beir, J. Pat O'Malley
121. [unknown title] (3-1-72) Lane Bradbury, John Vernon, Rex Holman, Paul Fix
122. "Death in the Fifth Gear" (3-8-72) Mariette Hartley, Elsa Lanchester, Jason Evers, Eddie Ryder

Sixth Season

123. [unknown title] (9-17-72) Eddie Egan, John McLiam, Rip Torn, Jimmy Putnam, Maggie Johnson
124. [unknown title] (9-24-72) Anthony Zerbe, Joe Maross, Geoffrey Lewis, Fay Spain
125. "The Crimson Halo" (10-1-72) Joe Campanella, Robert Burr, Fionnuala Flanagan, Burgess Meredith
126. [unknown title] (10-8-72) Don McGovern, Jon Cypher, Anjanette Comer, John Lasell
127. "Portrait of a Hero" (10-15-72) John Milford, William Bryant, Dabney Coleman, Lee Stanley
128. [unknown title] (10-22-72) John Colicos, Nancy Mehta, Robert Mandan
129. [unknown title] (10-29-72) Ford Rainey, Ben Piazza, Martin Sheen, John Vernon
130. [unknown title] (11-5-72) Tom Stewart, Stanley Kamel, Frank Marth
131. [unknown title] (11-12-72) Belinda J. Montgomery, Christopher Connelly, Del Monroe, Harold Gould
132. [unknown title] (11-19-72) Sean Garrison, Joe De Santis, Jeanette Nolan, Linda Marsh, Paul Mantee, Henry Beckman
133. "A Puzzle for One" (11-26-72) Adam West, Nehemiah Persoff, Jack Ging, Carol Wayne, Charles Picerni, Don Hanmer
134. [unknown title] (12-3-72) Michele Marsh, Peter Hooten, Paul Jenkins, Harry Townes
135. "See No Evil" (12-10-72) Sandy Champion, Norman Alden, Felton Perry, Royce Wallace
136. [unknown title] (12-17-72) Christine Belford, Christina Sinatra, Murray Matheson, Cesare Danova
137. [unknown title] (12-24-72) Adam Williams, Meg Foster, Paul Stevens, Marta Kristen, Alan Bergmann, Jack Ging
138. "The Man Who Wasn't There" (1-7-73) Clu Gulager, Robert Reed, Robert Middleton, Ken Lynch
139. "The Sound of Murder" (1-14-73) Elsa Lanchester, Dana Elcar, Ruth McDevitt, Jack Knight, Abe Vigoda, Mel Novak
140. [unknown title] (1-21-73) Joyce Van Patten, Paul Carr, Leonard Stone, Oscar Beregi, Virginia Capers, James A. Watson Jr.
141. [unknown title] (1-28-73) Jason Evers, Victoria Racimo, Jane Merrow, Eddie Ryder
142. [unknown title] (2-4-73) Susan Strasberg, Tina Louise, Fred Sadoff, Woodrow Parfrey, John Considine, Walter Brooke

143. [unknown title] (2-18-73) William Shatner, Noam Pitlik, Susan Flannery, Yvonne Craig, Karen Carlson, Milton Selzer
144. [unknown title] (2-25-73) David Wayne, Jonathan Lippe, Lloyd Bochner, Peggy Rea, Barbara Babcock, Byron Mabe, Maurice Marsac
145. [unknown title] (3-4-73) Fritz Weaver, Marion Ross, Anne Archer, John Randolph, Joe E. Tata
146. [unknown title] (3-11-73) Jessica Walter, John Gavin, Richard Bradford

## Seventh Season

147. "The Girl in the Polka Dot Dress" (9-16-73) Alfred Ryder, Joan Van Ark, Robert Brown, Paul Lukather
148. "A Way to Dusty Death" (9-23-73) Howard Duff, Donna Bacalla, Janis Paige, George Skaff, June Whitley Taylor, George Murdock, Tony Geary
149. "Climb a Deadly Mountain" (9-30-73) Greg Morris, Robert Donner, Guy Raymond, Claudia Bryar, Ted Hartley, Robert Ruth
150. "Little Girl Lost" (10-7-73) Pernell Roberts, Dawn Lyn, Julie Adams, Sam Elliott, Beverly Garland, Dean Harens, Rosemary De Camp, Barry Atwater, H. M. Wynant
151. "The Gang's All Here" (10-14-73) Thomas Leopold, Paul Carr, Eddie Firestone, Stephen Hudis, Nadyne Turney
152. "Desert Run" (10-21-73) John Doucette, Ford Rainey, Jeanette Nolan, Bill Vint, Charles Dierkop, Ken Tobey, Pamela McMyler, Mark Lenard
153. "Silent Target" (10-28-73)
154. [unknown title] (11-4-73) Peter Haskell, Alan Gibbs, Tiffany Bolling, Michael Conrad, Read Morgan, Peggy Walton, Joe E. Tata
155. [unknown title] (11-11-73) Nancy Mehta, Paul Stevens, Liam Sullivan, Janice Lynde, Laraine Stephens, Stacy Keach Sr.
156. "Search in the Dark" (11-25-73) Victor Buono, Eddie Ryder, Bethel Leslie
157. "The Deadly Madonna" (12-2-73) Anne Baxter
158. "Cry Danger" (12-9-73)
159. "All the Dead Were Strangers" (12-16-73) Julie Gregg, Anthony Zerbe, Donald Moffat, Paul Jenkins, Woodrow Parfrey
160. "A Matter of the Heart" [Part I] (1-6-74) Cesare Danova, John Colicos, Ina Balin, Alan Bergmann, Paul Mantee, Rita Gam
161. "Race Against Time" [Part II] (1-13-74) as above
162. "The Dark Hours" (1-20-74) Elizabeth Ashley, William Devane, Paul Shenar, Victor French
163. "A World Full of Darkness" (1-27-74) Michael McGuire, Jack Ging, Michael Baseleon, Paul Lambert
164. "Walk a Double Line" (2-10-74) Davey Davison, Hildy

Brooks, John Bennett Perry, Val Avery
165. "The Girl from Nowhere" (2-17-74) Robert Yuro, Lucille
Benson, Rosemary Forsyth, Lew Brown
166. "Rage to Kill" (2-24-74)
167. "Mask for a Charade" (3-3-74) Dennis Patrick, Claude
Akins, Marj Dusay, Dennis Redfield
168. "A Question of Murder" (3-10-74) H. B. Barnum III, Mae
Mercer, Charles Picerni, Pat Renella
169. "Trap for a Pigeon" (3-24-74)
170. "The Ragged Edge" (3-31-74)

Eighth Season

171. "Game Plan" (9-29-74) James Olson, Jane Actman, Rue
McClanahan, Lee Paul, Norman Alden, Jay Hammer
172. "A Fine Day for Dying" (10-6-74) Pamela Franklin, Alan
Fudge, James Naughton, Jim Boles, Walter Brooke,
Marc Lawrence
173. "Walk on the Blind Side" (10-13-74) Lincoln Kilpatrick,
Kim Hamilton, Leonard Stone, Eddie Firestone, Alex
Henteloff
174. "The Green Men" (10-20-74) Scott Marlowe, Elisha Cook,
Russell Johnson, Anne Lee, Frank Cristi, Chuck Daniel
175. "Death Has No Face" (10-27-74) Lynn Carlin, Warren
Vanders, Tom Stern, Ron Thompson, Diane Shalet, Paul
Sorensen
176. "A Small Favor for an Old Friend" (11-10-74) Val Avery,
Ben Hammer
177. "Enter Tami Okada" (11-17-74)
178. "Picture of a Shadow" (11-24-74) Rosemary Forsyth, Jay
Robinson, Michael Bell, Frank Ramirez, Eddie Ryder
179. "Desert Sun" (12-1-74)
180. "The Survivor Who Wasn't" (12-15-74) Paul Burke, Carol
Lawrence, Philip Pine, John Milford
181. "A Choice of Victims" (12-22-74) Rona Barrett, Gail
Kobe, Vincent Baggetta, Jack Ging, Karen Jensen
182. "A Word Called Courage" (1-5-75) Anthony Zerbe, Brenda
Benet
183. [unknown title] (1-12-75) Madlyn Rhue, Joseph Hindy
184. "Chance Meeting" (1-19-75) Felton Perry, Geoffrey Deuel,
Lurene Tuttle, Mark Stewart
185. "Edge of the Web" (2-2-75)
186. [unknown title] (2-9-75)
187. "The Empty Tower" (2-16-75)
188. "Quartet for Blunt Instrument" (2-23-75)
189. "Bird of Prey" [Part I] (3-2-75) Richard Evans, Robert
Loggia, Dimitra Arliss, Jay Novello, Alexander Scourby,
Andrea Marcovicci
190. "Bird of Prey" [Part II] (3-9-75) as above
191. [unknown title] (3-23-75) Barbara Rush, Erica Hagen,
Dennis Patrick, George Ives, Carmen Zapata, David
Mauro
192. "Search for a Dead Man" (4-6-75) John Hillerman, Paul

Mantee, Robert Symonds, Mary Wilcox
193. "Hardball" (4-13-75)


## THE HIGH CHAPARRAL

Like his "Bonanza" before it, David Dortort's "The High Chaparral," set in the Arizona of the 1870s, is a blend of drama, comedy and at times even fantasy. An example of the last of these would be the episode "Tornado Frances," in which a prim advocate of Prohibition (Kathryn Hays) is, by way of love (and liqueur!), proselytized to engage in the simpler pursuits. Composers of teleplays included Richard Carr ("Best Man for the Job"), Michael Fessier (the comedy "The Champion of the Western World"), and Walter Black (the suspense drama "The Long Shadow" and the comedy "The Reluctant Deputy"). Principal characters were "High Chaparral" ranch owner "Big John" Cannon (Leif Erickson), his pleasure-seeking brother Buck (Cameron Mitchell), Cannon's son Blue (Mark Slade) and second wife Victoria (Linda Cristal) whom he married to appease rival rancher Victoria's father Don Sebastian Montoya (Frank Silvera). Manolito Montoya (Henry Darrow), Don Sebastian's son, also worked at "The High Chaparral." John Cannon's first wife, Anna Lee (Joan Caulfield), was killed in the two-hour pilot episode.

The Regulars: "Big John" Cannon, Leif Erickson; Victoria, Linda
Cristal; Blue ("Blue Boy") Cannon, Mark Slade; Buck Cannon, Cameron Mitchell; Manolito Montoya, Henry Darrow; Don Sebastian Montoya, Frank Silvera; Sam, Don Collier; Pedro, Roberto Contreras; Vaquero, Rodolfo Acosta; Reno, Ted Markland; Joe, Bob Hay.

The Episodes:

1. "The High Chaparral" [two hour pilot film] (9-10-67) Joan
   Caulfield
2. [unknown title] (9-17-67) Patrick Horgan
3. "Best Man for the Job" (9-24-67) Warren Stevens, Ron
   Hagerthy, Lane Bradford
4. "A Quiet Day in Tucson" (10-1-67) Marie Gomez, Richard
   Devon, Vaughn Taylor
5. "Young Blood" (10-8-67) Alex Montoya
6. "Shadows on the Land" (10-15-67) Kevin Hagen, Jan Arvan,
   Ronald Trujillo, John Pickard
7. "The Fillibusteros" (10-22-67) Dan O'Herlihy, Beverly
   Hills
8. "The Doctor from Dodge" (10-29-67) Jack Kelly, Richard
   Angarola
9. "Sudden Country" (11-5-67) John Kerr, Jan Shepard
10. "A Hanging Offense" (11-12-67) Denver Pyle, Alan Berg-
    mann, Ken Drake
11. "The Pride of Revenge" (11-19-67) Ralph Meeker, Geraldine

Brooks
12. "The Widow from Red Rock" (11-26-67) Patricia Barry,
Carlos Romero
13. "Mark of the Turtle" (12-10-67) Robert Lansing, Anthony
Caruso
14. "The Terrorist" (12-17-67) Henry Silva, Pilar Seurat, Ned
Romero
15. "The Firing Wall" (12-31-67) Fernando Lamas, Barbara
Luna
16. "The Assassins" (1-7-68) X Brands, James Almanzar
17. "Survival" (1-14-68) Robert Phillips
18. "Gold Is Where You Leave It" (1-21-68) Leo Gordon, Dean
Stanton, Shelby Grant, Ted Gehring, Eddie Little Sky,
William Tannen
19. "The Kinsman" (1-28-68) Jack Lord, William C. Watson,
Rayford Barnes
20. "The Champion of the Western World" (2-4-68) Charles
Aidman, Walter Brooke, Charles N. Gray, Maria Gomez
21. "Ride the Savage Land" (2-11-68) Mary Jo Kennedy, George
Keymas, Claire Wilcox
22. "Bad Day for a Thirst" (2-18-68) Jose De Vega, Dennis
Safren, Adam Williams
23. "Tiger by the Tail" (2-25-68) Ricardo Montalban, Noah
Keen, Daniel Ades
24. "The Peacemaker" (3-3-68) Victor Jory, Barbara Hershey,
Paul Fix
25. "The Hair Hunter" (3-10-68) Richard Evans, James Gregory,
Kelly Thordsen
26. "A Joyful Noise" (3-24-68) Ramon Novarro, Laurie Mock,
Robert Yuro
27. "Threshold of Courage" (3-31-68) Pat Hingle, Ron Hayes,
Rex Holman, Charles Maxwell

Second Season

28. "The Stallion" (9-20-68) Clive Clerk, Michael Keep
29. "Ten Little Indians" (9-27-68) Armando Islas
30. "Follow Your Heart" (10-4-68) Ed Begley, Miriam Colon,
Abraham Sofaer, Jeff Pomerantz
31. "Tornado Frances" (10-11-68) Kathryn Hays, Charles Robinson
32. "The Covey" (10-18-68) Anthony Caruso, Kelly Thordsen,
Sara Vardi
33. "The Promised Land" (10-25-68) Joe Maross, Alex Montoya
34. "Ebenezer" (11-1-68) John McGiver, Leonard Stone
35. "North to Tucson" (11-8-68) Kevin McCarthy, Jack Elam
36. "The Deceivers" (11-15-68) Robert Loggia, Bonnie Bedelia
37. "The Buffalo Soldiers" (11-22-68) Yaphet Kotto, Morgan
Woodward, Charles H. Gray, Robert DoQui, Charles Maxwell
38. "For What We Are About to Receive" (11-29-68) Christopher
Cary, Marie Gomez

39. "A Way of Justice" (12-13-68) Anthony Carbone, Frank De Kova, Denny Miller, Mills Watson, Kathleen Freeman, Joaquin Martinez
40. "Our Lady of Guadalupe" (12-20-68) Ricardo Montalban, Jan Shepard, Bill Fletcher, Mike de Anda, Norbert Schiller
41. "Sea of Enemies" (1-3-69) Paul Winfield, John Pickard
42. "Shadow of the Wind" (1-10-69) Luke Askew, Fabrizio Mioni
43. "No Irish Need Apply" (1-17-69) John Vernon, Eddie Firestone, Robert Cornthwaite, Charles Tyner, Ed Peck, Garry Walberg
44. "The Last Hundred Miles" (1-24-69) Robert Clary, Tom Tully
45. "The Glory Soldiers" (1-31-69) Elizabeth Allen, Anthony Caruso, Sean McClory, Heidi Vaughn
46. "Feather of an Eagle" (2-7-69) Quentin Dean, Frank Ramirez, Alicia Bond
47. "Once, on a Day in Spring" (2-14-69) Kathleen Crowley
48. "Stinky Flanagan" (2-21-69) Frank Gorshin, Richard X. Slattery
49. "Surtee" (2-28-69) John Dehner, Christopher Dark
50. "A Fella Named Kilory" (3-7-69) Bert Freed, Roy Hayes
51. "No Bugles, No Women" (3-14-69) Bethel Leslie, William Sylvester, Pamelyn Ferdin, George Walcott
52. "The Lion Sleeps" (3-28-69) Brenda Benet, Jorge Russek, Rico Alaniz
53. "For the Love of Carlos" (4-4-69) Michael Ansara, Armando Islas, Fernando Pereira, Pamelyn Ferdin

Third Season

54. "Time of Your Life" (9-19-69) James Mitchum, Tammy August, Ted Gehring
55. "A Time to Laugh, a Time to Cry" (9-26-69) Victor Campos, Donna Baccala, Julio Medina
56. "The Brothers Cannon" (10-3-69) regulars
57. "A Piece of Land" (10-10-69) Lou Frizzell, John Zaremba, Miguel Landa
58. "Bad Day for Bad Men" (10-17-69) Marianna Hill, Malachi Throne, Robert Yuro
59. "To Stand for Something More" (10-24-69) Don Diamond, Gino Conforti
60. "Trail to Nevermore" (10-31-69) Milton Selzer, Bo Svenson, Rayford Barnes
61. "Apache Trust" (11-7-69) Chief Dan George, Ronald Feinberg, Evans Thornton
62. "Lady Fair" (11-14-69) Joanna Moore, Dub Taylor, Joseph Ruskin
63. "The Lost Ones" (11-21-69) Richard Lapp, Christopher Dark
64. "The Legacy" (11-28-69) Pamela Dunlap
65. "Alliance" (12-12-69) Robert Viharo, Donald Buka
66. "The Little Thieves" (12-26-69) Jo Ann Harris, William Sylvester, Heather Menzies, William Vint

67. "The Long Shadow" (1-2-70) Gregory Sierra, Richard Anderson
68. "The Journal of Death" (1-9-70) John Colicos, Morgan Woodward
69. "Friends and Partners" (1-16-70) Howard Caine, Charles Dierkop
70. "Jelks" (1-23-70) Mitchell Ryan
71. "The Guns of Johnny Rondo" (2-6-70) Steve Forrest, Kurt Russell
72. "Mi Casa, Su Casa" (2-20-70) Lew Palter
73. "The Lieutenant" (2-27-70) Robert Pine, Donald Moffat, Renne Jarrett
74. "The Reluctant Deputy" (3-6-70) Charles Durning, Robert Donner
75. "New Hostess in Town" (3-20-70) Jim Davis, Ed Bakey, Mills Watson
76. "Too Many Chiefs" (3-27-70) Noah Beery, Sandy Rosenthal
77. "Auld Lang Syne" (4-10-70) Gregory Walcott, Jonathan Lippe
78. "Generation" (4-17-70) Aspa Nakopoulou
79. "No Trouble at All" (5-1-70) William C. Watson, Tony Russell, Felice Orlandi

Fourth Season

80. "An Anger Greater Than Mine" (9-18-70) Alejandro Rey, Nate Esformes
81. "Spokes" (9-25-70) William Conrad, Vincent Van Patten, E. J. Andre
82. "Only the Bad Come to Sonora" (10-2-70) Bruce Dern, Margarita Cordova
83. "Wind" (10-9-70) Scott Brady, Tyler McVey, R. G. Armstrong
84. "A Matter of Survival" (10-16-70) Barry Sullivan
85. "It Takes a Smart Man" (10-23-70) Richard Bradford, Garry Walberg
86. "A Good Sound Profit" (10-30-70) Harold Gould, Joe De Santis, Edward Colmans
87. "Too Late the Epitaph" (11-6-70) Monte Markham, Mayf Nutter
88. "The Forge of Hate" (11-13-70) Robert Loggia, Michael Baseleon, Ted De Corsia, Alan Caillou
89. "Fiesta" (11-20-70) Nehemiah Persoff, Miguel Alejandro, Rodolfo Hoyos
90. "A Matter of Vengeance" (11-27-70) Barry Sullivan
91. "Pale Warrior" (12-11-70) Frank Webb
92. "The Badge" (12-18-70) Morgan Woodward, Jonathan Lippe, Alan Oppenheimer
93. "The New Lion of Sonora" [two hour episode] (2-19-71) Gilbert Roland, Albert Paulsen
94. "Sangre" (2-26-71) Pat Renella, Kaz Garas
95. "The Hostage" (3-5-71) Edmond O'Brien
96. "A Man to Match the Land" (3-12-71) Albert Salmi, Michael Keep, Jennifer Rhodes, Allen Dexter

COWBOY IN AFRICA

Tepid rodeo adventure yarn with Chuck Connors as the rider Jim Sinclair in charge of rounding up African wildlife for breeding purposes.

The Regulars: Jim Sinclair, Chuck Connors; John Henry, Tom Nardini; Commander Hayes, Ronald Howard; Samson, Gerald B. Edwards.

The Episodes:

1. "The New World" (9-11-67) Antoinette Bower, Frank Marth
2. "Kifaru! Kifaru!" (9-18-67) Joanna Moore, Peter Bromilow, Dodie Marshall, Mel Scott
3. "Incident at Derati Wells" (9-25-67) Yaphet Kotto, Rupert Crosse
4. "What's an Elephant Mother to Do?" (10-2-67) Lynda Day, Torin Thatcher, Paul Winfield
5. "Search for Survival" (10-9-67) Anne Baxter, Izack Fields
6. "Stone Age Safari" (10-16-67) James McEachin, Emily Banks, Anthony Ghazio Sr., Wacira Gethaiga, Chips Robinson
7. "The Adopted One" (10-23-67) William Mims, Lisa Perá
8. "Fang and Claw" (10-30-67) James Gregory, Louis Gossett, Arthur Adams
9. "The Time of the Predator" (11-6-67) Ken Gampu, Chester Washington
10. "Lake Sinclair" (11-13-67) Gloria Calomee, Rockne Tarkington
11. "Tomorrow on the Wind" (11-20-67) Cicely Tyson, Richard Elkins
12. "Little Boy Lost" (11-27-67) Todd Martin, Stan Duke, Charles Lampkin, Kenneth Lupper, Tony White, Kyle Johnson
13. "The Man Who Has Everything" (12-4-67) Edward Mulhare, James Wainwright, Hagan Beggs
14. "To Build a Beginning" (12-11-67) Kamala Devi, Kay Kuter, Don Megowan
15. "The Hesitant Hero" (12-18-67) Brooke Bundy, Richard Eastham
16. "African Rodeo" [Part I] (1-15-68) Jan Murray, Alejandro Rey, Michael Conrad, Ronald Feinberg, Michael Jackson, Tom Kelly, Bob Morgan, Albert Popwell
17. "African Rodeo" [Part II] (1-22-68) as above
18. "First to Capture" (1-29-68) James Whitmore, Rex Holman, Alex Dreier, Michael Burns
19. "The Red Hand of Michael O'Neill" (2-5-68) Timothy Carey, Bonnie Beecher
20. "The Quiet Death" (2-19-68) Lou Gossett, Len Birman, Bob DoQui
21. "A Man of Value" (2-26-68) Patrick Horgan, James Edwards, John Alderson

22. "Search and Destroy" (3-4-68) Cliff Osmond, Jeff Burton, Jason Wingreen, Don Drysdale
23. "Work of Art" (3-18-68) Madlyn Rhue
24. "John Henry's Eden" (3-18-68) Harvey Jason, William Tannen
25. "The Lions" (3-25-68) Antoinette Bower, Royal Dano, Guy Edwards
26. "The Kasubi Death" (4-1-68) Michael Ansara, Rex Ingram, Sue England

## GARRISON'S GORILLAS

Reminiscent of the Robert Aldrich film The Dirty Dozen is this tale of lawless rogues transformed into Nazi fighters and commandeered by Lieutenant Craig Garrison (Ron Harper).

The Regulars: Lieutenant Craig Garrison, Ron Harper; "Actor", Cesare Danova; "Casino", Rudy Solari; "Chief", Brendon Boone; "Goniff", Christopher Cary.

The Episodes:

1. "The Big Con" (9-5-67) Telly Savalas, Gilbert Roland
2. "Breakout" (9-12-67) John Van Dreelen, Larry Thor
3. "The Grab" (9-19-67) Jeff Corey
4. "Banker's Hours" (9-26-67) Jack Klugman
5. "Forty-eight Hours to Live" (10-3-67) Malachi Throne, Frank Marth, Celia Lovsky
6. "The Great Theft" (10-10-67) Robin Hughes, Maurice Marsac
7. "The Deadly Masquerade" (10-17-67) Will Geer, Michael Conrad
8. "Now I Lay Me Down to Die" (10-24-67) Glenn Corbett, Curt Lowens
9. "Operation Hellfire" (10-31-67) Barry Sullivan
10. "Thieves Holiday" (11-7-67) Frank Gorshin, Jacques Aubuchon
11. "Twenty Gallons to Kill" (11-14-67) John Saxon, Fabian Dean, Eduardo Ciannelli
12. "Friendly Enemies" (11-21-67) Harold Gould, Curt Lowens, Pat Renella, John Lodge, Eddie Ness, Paul Busch, Hagen Smith
13. "Black Market" (11-28-67) Roger Perry, Gavin MacLeod, Fabrizio Mioni, John Carter, Jamie Farr, Mike Farrell, Rita Rogers, Aladdin
14. "The Great Crime Wave" (12-5-67) Ray Walston, Henry Beckman, Oscar Beregi
15. "The Magnificent Forger" (12-19-67) Larry Storch, William Campbell, Carl Schell
16. "The Expendables" (12-26-67) Kevin McCarthy, George Perina

17. "War Games" (1-2-68) Skip Homeier, Jack Hogan
18. "Run from Death" (1-9-68) Julie Harris, Marcel Hillaire, Patrick Michenaud, Timothy Scott
19. "The Death Sentence" (1-16-68) Joe Maross, Fred Beir, William Stevens
20. "The Big Lie" (1-23-68) Philip Pine, Robert Cornthwaite, Rudolph Anders, Alice Reinheart, George Perina, Heinz Brinkman
21. "Ride of Terror" (1-30-68) Claude Akins, Maurice Marsac
22. "War and Crime" [Part I] (2-13-68) Faith Domergue, Richard Kiley, William Bryant
23. "The Plot to Kill" [Part II] (2-20-68) as above
24. "The Frame-Up" (2-27-68) Gena Rowlands, Jan Merlin, H. M. Wynant
25. "The War Diamonds" (3-5-68) Hans Gudegast, Michael Forest, Ted Knight, Sheldon Allman, Maurice Marsac, Henry Brandt
26. "Time Bomb" (3-12-68) Peter Haskell, Ron Soble

## N. Y. P. D.

Daniel Melnick's truly adult study of the workings of the New York City Police Department, boasting excellent location photography. Themes explored by some top-notch veteran television writers included homosexual extortion (in Albert Ruben's "Shakedown"), a character study of the criminal veteran (in George Bellak's "Old Gangsters Never Die"), and the unorthodox pursuits of an unrelenting newscaster (in Ian McLellan's "Murder for Infinity").

The Regulars: Lt. Mike Haines, Jack Warden; Det. Johnny Corso, Frank Converse; Det. Jeff Ward, Robert Hooks.

The Episodes:

1. "Shakedown" (9-5-67) James Broderick, Dana Elcar, Conrad Bain
2. "Fingerman" (9-12-67) Joel Fabiani, Nat Frey
3. "The Screaming Woman" (9-19-67) Verna Bloom, Meg Myles, Patricia Collinge, William Devane
4. "Fast Gun" (9-26-67) Gregory Reese, Tom Rosqui
5. "Walking Target" (10-3-67) Graham Jarvis, Tresa Hughes, Jess Osuna, Flora Elkins
6. "Money Man" (10-10-67) Vincent Gardenia, Charles Grodin, Ralph Dunn, John Ryan
7. "Old Gangsters Never Die" (10-17-67) Howard Da Silva, Victor Arnold, Jason Gero, Jack Knight, Tom Rosqui, Ted Beniades, Andrew Duncan, Charles Durning
8. "To Catch a Hero" (10-31-67) Robert Forster, Sylvia Miles
9. "Murder for Infinity" (11-7-67) John Karlen, Ralph Waite, Sam Waterston
10. "The Pink Gumdrop" (11-14-67) Jane Elliot, Robert Gentry

11. "The Witness" (11-21-67) Donald Davis, Rudy Bond, Nicholas Coster, James Coco, Denise Nicholas
12. "The Boy Witness" (11-28-67) Steven Oliva, Mitch Ryan
13. "Joshua Fit the Battle of Fulton Street" (12-5-67) Dane Clark, Fred J. Scollay, Martin Wolfson
14. "The Bomber" (12-12-67) Dixie Marquis, Jon Voight, Denise Nicholas
15. "Wire Finish" (12-19-67) Robert Salvio, Alan Manson
16. "Cruise to Oblivion" (12-26-67) Hugh Franklin, James Hall Leslie Charleson, Ellen Weston
17. "The Patriots" (1-2-68) Dino Fanio, Albert Paulsen, Titos Vandis
18. "Red Headed Pigeon" (1-16-68) Pat McAneny
19. "Which Side Are You On?" (1-30-68) Beverly Todd, Maxwell Glanville
20. "Cry Brute" (2-6-68) Tony Lo Bianco, Roy Schneider, Phil Bruns, Dan Frazer, Clarice Blackburn
21. "Last Port of Call" (2-13-68) Louis Zorich, Janis Young, Alice Spivak, David Manning
22. "Macho" (2-20-68) Jaimie Sanchez
23. "Stones" (2-27-68) Tony Lo Bianco, Jennifer West, Don Scardino
24. "The Private Eye Puzzle" (3-5-68) Murray Hamilton, Donna McKechnie, Joe Ponazecki, Ted Beniades
25. "Nothing Is Real But the Dead" [Part I] (3-12-68) Ossie Davis, Fritz Weaver, Connie Scott, Marcia Jean Kurtz, Mary Fickett, Jim Forat, Richard Castellano, Ted Beniades, Don Billet, Walker Daniels, Bob Fass
26. "Nothing Is Real But the Dead" [Part II] (3-19-68) as above

Second Season

27. "Naked in the Streets" (10-1-68) Susan Trustman, Larry Luckinbill, Cliff Gorman, Oliver Clark, Eugene Wood
28. "Encounter on a Rooftop" (10-8-68) Paul Falzone, Denise Nicholas
29. "Day Tripper" (10-15-68) C. C. Courtney, Tom Rosqui, Blythe Danner
30. "What's a Nice Girl Like You ... " (10-29-68) Philip Bosco Paul Collins, Shellie Feldman, Pamela Kingsley, Nancy Marchand
31. "Deadly Circle of Violence" (11-12-68) Jill Clayburgh, Graham Brown, Al Pacino, William Jay
32. "The Case of the Shady Lady" (11-19-68) Robert Alda, Gretchen Corbett, Ted Beniades, Harvey Keitel
33. "The Golden Fleece" (11-26-68) John Harkins, Ted Beniades
34. "The Peep Freak" (12-3-68) Martin Sheen, Janice Young
35. "Walk the Long Pier" (12-10-68) Hugh Franklin, John Ryan, Dolph Sweet, C. K. Alexander
36. "The Witch of 116th Street" (12-17-68) Carlos Montalban, Joel Castro, Gonzalo Madurga, Rene Enriques
37. "L Is for Love and Larceny" (12-24-68) Ralph Waite, Jo-Anna Miles

38. "The Love Hustle" (12-31-68) Terry Kiser, Val Avery, Lara Parker, Brenda Smiley
39. "The Body in a Trunk" (1-7-69) House Jameson
40. "The Night Watch" (1-21-69) James Tolkan, Jane Alexander
41. "Three-Fifty-Two" (1-28-69) Andy Robinson, Denise Nicholas, Fred Forrest, Ted Beniades
42. "The Attacker" (2-4-69) William Hickey, Richard Castellano, Mariclare Costello, William Macy
43. "Candy Man" [Part I] (2-11-69) James Earl Jones, Jeff Chandler, Fred Dennis, Seth Allen, Tom Aldredge, Rudy Bond, Matthew Cowles, Bette Henritze
44. "Candy Man" [Part II] (2-18-69) as above
45. "Who's Got the Bundle?" (2-25-69) James Coco, M. Emmett Walsh
46. "The Face on the Dart Board" (3-4-69) Frank Campanella, Matt Clark, Janet Ward
47. "Boys' Night Out" (3-11-69) Robert Drivas, Victor Arnold, Fred J. Scollay
48. "Everybody Loved Him" (3-18-69) Leora Dana, Walter McGinn, Jack Somack, Ted Van Grietthuysen
49. "No Day Trippers Need Apply" (3-25-69) John Randolph, Barry Morse, Leonard Frey

## CUSTER

At times taut (but one might question the account of the history) study of the legendary recalcitrant cavalry officer with Wayne Maunder as the sultry principal.

The Regulars: Lt. Col. George Armstrong Custer, Wayne Maunder; California Joe Milner, Slim Pickens; Sgt. James Bustard, Peter Palmer; Capt. Myles Keogh, Grant Woods; Crazy Horse, Michael Dante; Terry, Robert F. Simon; Rio, Hick Hill.

The Episodes:

1. [unknown title] (9-6-67) Mary Ann Mobley, Alex Davion
2. "Accused" (9-13-67) Chris Robinson, James Daly
3. "Glory Rider" (9-20-67) Ralph Meeker
4. "To the Death" (9-27-67) Larry Pennell, Art Lund
5. "Massacre" (10-4-67) Philip Carey, Arthur Franz, Jan Arvan
6. "War Lance and Saber" (10-11-67) James Craig, Bob Beck, R. G. Armstrong
7. "Suspicion" (10-18-67) Robert Loggia, Pierre Jalbert, Paul Peterson
8. "Breakout" (11-1-67) Ray Walston, Gene Evans, Burr de Benning, Kathleen Nolan
9. [unknown title] (11-8-67) Lloyd Bochner, Darren McGavin, Bill Gray, Charles Dierkop

10. "Under Fire" (11-15-67) William Windom, John Nealson
11. "Death Hunt" (11-22-67) Patricia Harty, William Smith, Barbara Hale
12. "Blazing Arrows" (11-29-67) Rory Calhoun, Adam Williams, Stacy Harris, Rod Redwing, Hal Lynch
13. "Dangerous Prey" (12-6-67) Albert Salmi, Robert Doyle, Donnelly Rhodes
14. "Spirit Woman" (12-13-67) Agnes Moorehead, James Whitmore, Read Morgan, Chick Casey, Eugene Martin, Christopher Milo
15. "The Gauntlet" (12-20-67) Edward Mulhare, Barbara Rush, Dennis Patrick
16. "The Raiders" (12-27-67) Yvonne DeCarlo, Peter Adams, Jeff Scott


DUNDEE AND THE CULHANE

The presence of a stylish actor--John Mills as Dundee--alone makes worth viewing this western of a pair of traveling lawyers.

The Regulars: Dundee, John Mills; Culhane, Sean Garrison.

The Episodes:

1. "The Turn the Other Cheek Brief" (9-6-67) Warren Oates, Mark Allyson, John Drew Barrymore, Michael Constantine
2. [unknown title] (9-13-67) Donnelly Rhodes, Frank Silvera, Benson Fong
3. [unknown title] (9-27-67) Roy Poole, Walter Gregg, Eddie Firestone, Matt Clark
4. "The Dead Man's Brief" (10-4-67) David Canary, John McIntire, Sally Kellerman, Douglas V. Fowley
5. [unknown title] (10-18-67) Simon Oakland, Evi Marandi, Julie Sommars, Tige Andrews, Dabney Coleman
6. [unknown title] (10-25-67) Ralph Meeker, Michael Burns, Michael Pataki, Ingrid Pitt
7. [unknown title] (11-1-67) Louise Troy, Ed Bakey, Carroll O'Connor
8. "The 3:10 to a Lynching Brief" (11-8-67) George Coulouris, Dub Taylor, Larry Perkins, Lonny Chapman
9. [unknown title] (11-15-67) John Anderson, James Dunn, Clyde Ventura
10. [unknown title] (11-22-67) William Windom, Mitch Vogel
11. "The Widow's Weeds Brief" (11-29-67) Dana Wynter, Fred J. Scollay, William Campbell
12. [unknown title] (12-13-67) Steve Ihnat, June Harding, Sam Melville

CIMARRON STRIP

A sprawling, frequently tedious ninety-minute western in which Stuart Whitman is unfortunately cast as Jim Crown, the marshal who presides over an incredible space of Oklahoma territory in the 1880s. Efforts at filling vacuity included the macabre theme of an unseen killer in the eleventh episode to the creation of a particularly unsavory character for guest star Richard Boone in William Wood's "The Roarer." Harlan Ellison composed the suspected Jack the Ripper-type mystery "Knife in the Darkness." In addition to actor Whitman, regulars were Percy Herbert as Deputy MacGregor, Randy Boone as newspaper reporter Francis Wilde, Jill Townsend as inn proprietress Dulcey Coopersmith, and Karl Swenson as Doc Kihlgren.

The Regulars: Marshall Jim Crown, Stuart Whitman; Deputy MacGregor, Percy Herbert; Francis Wilde, Randy Boone; Dulcey Coopersmith, Jill Townsend; Dr. ("Doc") Kihlgren, Karl Swenson.

The Episodes:

1. "Journey to a Hanging" (9-7-67) John Saxon, Henry Silva, Michael Strong, Shug Fisher
2. [unknown title] (9-14-67) Beau Bridges, Darren McGavin, Barbara Luna
3. "Broken Wing" (9-21-67) Pat Hingle, Steve Forrest, Arch Johnson, Larry Gates, Tim O'Kelly
4. "The Battleground" (9-28-67) Telly Savalas, Warren Oates, R. G. Armstrong, Andrew Duggan, Robert Wilke
5. "The Hunted" (10-5-67) David Carradine, Steve Ihnat, James Gregory, Arthur Batanides
6. [unknown title] (10-12-67) Michael J. Pollard, Gene Evans, Henry Wilcoxon, Richard X. Slattery
7. [unknown title] (10-19-67) Peter Kastner, John Anderson, Fred Colby, Robert B. Williams, James Almanzar, Meg Wyllie, Glen Vernon
8. "The Roarer" (11-2-67) Richard Boone, Andrew Duggan, Ed Flanders, Robert Duvall, Morgan Woodward, Steven Beck, Lindsay Workman
9. "The Search" (11-9-67) Joseph Cotten, Martha Scott, Zalman King, Jonathan Lippe, Jim Davis, L. Q. Jones
10. "Till the End of the Night" (11-16-67) Suzanne Pleshette, Clifton James, Victor French, Dean Stanton
11. [unknown title] (11-30-67) Leslie Nielsen, Royal Dano, Simon Oakland, Gail Kobe, Lola Albright, Paul Carr
12. [unknown title] (12-7-67) Warren Oates, William C. Watson, Hal Smith, Richard Bakalyan
13. [unknown title] (12-14-67) Albert Salmi, Morgan Woodward, Denver Pyle, Tom Reese, Robert Wilke
14. [unknown title] (12-21-67) J. D. Cannon, Lyle Bettger, Larry Pennell, Marj Dusay, Anthony James
15. "The Judgment" (1-4-68) James Stacy, Burr DeBenning,

        Don Keefer, Leonard Stone, Kip Whitman, John Orchard, Charles Dierkop, Solomon Sturges, James Chandler

16.  "The Assassin" (1-11-68) Robert Lansing, Slim Pickens, Bob Random, Russell Thorsen, Lew Brown, William Bramley

17.  [unknown title] (1-18-68) Tuesday Weld, Bernie Hamilton, Robert Phillips, Morgan Woodward

18.  "Knife in the Darkness" (1-25-68) Jennifer Billingsley, David Canary, Jeanne Cooper, Philip Carey, Tom Skerritt, Patrick Horgan, George Murdock

19.  "Sound of a Drum" (2-1-68) Steve Forrest, Gerald S. O'Loughlin, Lloyd Gough

20.  [unknown title] (2-8-68) Mariette Hartley, Donnelly Rhodes, Eddie Hodges, Jack Elam, Timothy Carey, Richard O'Brien

21.  "The Blue Moon Train" (2-15-68) Broderick Crawford, Donald Barry, Kevin Hagen, Robert Foulk

22.  "Without Honor" (2-29-68) Chester Morris, Andrew Duggan, Jon Voight, Paul Mantee

23.  "The Greeners" (3-7-68) Mark Lenard, David Brian, Dub Taylor, Peter Jason, Dan Ferrone, Donna Baccala

## IRONSIDE

     Raymond Burr, still acting very much like "Perry Mason," is now a wheelchair handicapped but undeterred San Francisco Chief of Detectives, Robert Ironside. He is assisted by Detective Sergeant Ed Brown (Don Galloway), Policewoman Eve Whitfield (Barbara Anderson) and Policewoman Fran Belding (Elizabeth Baur, with the fifth season) and protégé Mark Sanger (Don Mitchell); the series itself is assisted by Quincy Jones' musical score.

The Regulars: Chief Robert Ironside, Raymond Burr; Det. Sgt. Ed Brown, Don Galloway; Mark Sanger, Don Mitchell; Commissioner, Gene Lyons; Policewoman Eve Whitfield, Barbara Anderson (through fourth season); Policewoman Fran Belding, Elizabeth Baur (with fifth season); Lt. Carl Reese, Johnny Seven.

The Episodes:

1.  "Message from Beyond" (9-14-67) Madlyn Rhue, Gene Evans, Kathleen Freeman, James Gregory, Kent McCord, George Chandler

2.  "The Leaf in the Forest" (9-21-67) John Larch, Edward Andrews, Barbara Barrie

3.  "Dead Man's Tale" (9-28-67) Jack Lord, Suzanne Cramer, Simon Scott, Stuart Nisbet, Byron Morrow, Ben Wright

4.  "Eat, Drink, and Be Buried" (10-5-67) Lee Grant, Farley Granger, Quincy Jones, John Lodge, Richard Anderson

5.  "The Taker" (10-12-67) Robert Alda, Jan Shepard, Mark

Richman, William Schallert
6. "An Inside Job" (10-19-67) Don Stroud, John Saxon, John Alvin, Norman Fell, Eileen Wesson, Harry Hickox
7. "Tagged for Murder" (10-26-67) Jack Kelly, Gene Nelson, Antoinette Bower
8. "Backfire" (11-2-67) Ivan Dixon, Ena Hartman, Don Marshall, Maidie Norman, Peter Mamakos
9. "Light at the End of the Journey" (11-9-67) Bill Fletcher, Robert Reed, Katherine Crawford
10. "The Monster of Comus Towers" (11-16-67) Warren Stevens, Kevin Hagen, David Hartman, Michael Forest, Joan Huntington
11. "The Man Who Believed" (11-23-67) Guy Stockwell, George Furth, Barbara Rhodes, Cliff Potter, Arthur Adams, Michael Constantine, Marcia Strassman
12. "A Very Cool Hot Car" (11-30-67) Bernie Hamilton, Peter Helm, Jay C. Flippen, K. L. Smith, Arch Johnson, Pamela Dunlap
13. "The Past Is Prologue" (12-7-67) Victor Jory, Jill Donahue, Jean Inness, Harrison Ford
14. "Girl in the Night" (12-21-67) Donnelly Rhodes, Steve Carlson, Susan St. James
15. "The Fourteenth Runner" (12-28-67) Edward Asner, Steve Ihnat, John Van Dreelen
16. "Force of Arms" (1-4-68) Gene Raymond, Linden Chiles, Diane Brewster, Frank Gerstle, Harold J. Stone
17. "Memory of an Ice Cream Stick" (1-11-68) Ena Hartman, Mel Scott, Jim Creech, Francine York, Jack Kruschen, Jackie Russell
18. "To Kill a Cop" (1-25-68) Pernell Roberts, Ruta Lee
19. "The Lonely Hostage" (2-1-68) Robert Lansing, Kathie Browne, William Fawcett
20. "The Challenge" (2-8-68) Sue Ane Langdon, Tom Simcox, Coleen Gray, Nick Colasanto
21. "All in a Day's Work" (2-15-68) Jeanette Nolan
22. "Something for Nothing" (2-22-68) James Farentino, Vincent Gardenia, Susan St. James
23. "Barbara Who" (2-29-68) Vera Miles, Philip Carey
24. "Perfect Crime" (3-7-68) Peter Deuel, Brenda Scott, Ron Russell
25. "Officer Bobby" (3-14-68) Nancy Malone, Paul Carr, Jeanne Cooper
26. "Trip to Hashbury" (3-21-68) William Windom, Monica Lewis, Cliff Osmond, Stacy Maxwell, David Macklin, Judy Brown
27. "Due Process of Law" (3-28-68) David Carradine, Parley Baer, Dwayne Hickman, Burr De Benning
28. "Return of the Hero" (4-4-68) Gary Collins, Ron Hayes, Gavin MacLeod, Ned Romero

## Second Season

29. "Shell Game" (9-19-68) Sorrell Booke, Charles Aidman

30. "Split Second to an Epitaph" [two-hour episode] (9-26-68)
    Lilia Scala, Andrew Prine, Joseph Cotten, Don Stroud,
    Troy Donahue, Margaret O'Brien
31. "The Sacrifice" (10-3-68) Philip Pine, Robert Alda, Elena
    Verdugo, Rafael Campos, Ricardo Montalban
32. "Robert Phillips vs. the Man" (10-10-68) Paul Winfield,
    Jack Hogan
33. "Desperate Encounter" (10-24-68) Gene Raymond, Ron
    Hayes, Tom Simcox
34. "I, the People" (10-31-68) Julie Adams, Milton Berle, Jack
    Cassidy, Dane Clark, Patricia Barry
35. "Price Tag--Death" (11-7-68) Ralph Meeker, Clu Gulager
36. "An Obvious Case of Guilt" (11-14-68) Anne Baxter, War-
    ren Stevens
37. "Reprise" (11-21-68) Nancy Wickwire, Stuart Rice, Irene
    Hervey, Eddie Firestone
38. "The Macabre Mr. Micawber" (11-28-68) Burgess Meredith
39. "Side Pocket" (12-5-68) Michael Christian, Jack Albertson,
    Carl Reindel
40. "Sergeant Mike" (12-12-68) Bill Bixby, John Dehner,
    Robert Cornthwaite
41. "In Search of an Artist" (1-2-69) Broderick Crawford
42. "Up, Down, and Even" (1-9-69) Susan O'Connell, Richard
    Anderson, Alfred Ryder
43. "Why the Tuesday Afternoon Bridge Club Met on Thursday"
    (1-23-69) Jessie Royce Landis, Arthur O'Connell, Gail
    Kobe
44. "Rundown on a Bum Rap" (1-30-69) Janet MacLachlan,
    James Gregory, Clifton James
45. "The Prophecy" (2-6-69) Martha Scott, Paul Stewart, Wil-
    liam Bramley
46. "A World of Jackals" (2-13-69) William Smithers, Ena
    Hartman, Lynn Borden
47. "And Be My Love" (2-20-69) Chad Everett
48. "Moonlight Means Money" (2-27-69) Linden Chiles, John
    Marley, Skip Homeier, Murray MacLeod
49. "A Drug on the Market" (3-6-69) Ray Danton, Victoria Shaw
    Betsy Jones-Moreland
50. "Puzzlelock" (3-13-69) Simon Oakland, Dennis Cooney
51. "The Tormentor" (3-27-69) Mary Ann Mobley, Gary Collins
52. "A Matter of Love and Death" (4-3-69) Susan Howard,
    Pamela McMyler, Bettye Ackerman
53. "Not with a Whimper, but a Bang" (4-10-69) Edward Asner,
    John Zaremba, Gerald S. O'Loughlin

Third Season

54. "Alias Mr. Braithwaite" (9-18-69) Joseph Campanella, Beah
    Richards
55. "Good-by to Yesterday" [two-hour episode] (9-25-69) Philip
    Carey, Dane Clark, Vera Miles, Slim Pickins, Cloris
    Leachman
56. "Poole's Paradise" (10-2-69) Steve Forrest, Clu Gulager,

William Smith, Louise Latham
57. "Eye of the Hurricane" (10-9-69) Dana Elcar, Virginia Gregg, Jackie Coogan Jr.
58. "A Bullet for Mark" (10-16-69) Robert Alda, Donald Barry
59. "Love My Enemy" (10-23-69) Philip Ahn, Jeffrey Lynn, James Shigeta, Khigh Dhiegh
60. "Seeing Is Believing" (10-30-69) Audrey Totter, Norman Fell, Robert Ellenstein, Beatrice Kay
61. "The Machismo Bag" (11-13-69) Vito Scotti, A Martinez, Mort Mills
62. "Programmed for Danger" (11-20-69) Anne Baxter, Roger Perry
63. "Five Miles High" (11-27-69) Norma Crane, Frank Aletter, Milton Selzer
64. "L'Chayim" (12-4-69) David Opatoshu, Shelly Novack, Hal Frederick
65. "Beyond a Shadow" (12-11-69) Dana Wynter, Mort Sahl, Simon Scott, James McCallion, Harold Ayer, Russ Conway
66. "Stolen on Demand" (12-25-69) David Cassidy, Marion Brash, Pamela McMyler, Alan Oppenheimer
67. "Dora" (1-8-70) Ann Doran, Hank Brandt, Barbara Rhodes
68. "Beware the Wiles of the Stranger" (1-22-70) John Ericson, Tina Louise
69. "Eden Is the Place We Leave" (1-29-70) John Marley, Jill Townsend, Patrick Adiarte
70. "The Wrong Time, the Wrong Place" (2-5-70) Frank Maxwell, George Petrie, Tiffany Bolling
71. "Return to Fiji" (2-12-70) Bernard Fox, Alan Napier, Larry D. Mann
72. "Ransom" (2-10-70) John Saxon, Fritz Weaver, Carla Borelli
73. "One Hour to Kill" (2-26-70) Robert Lipton, Henry Corden
74. "Warrior's Return" (3-5-70) Stephen McNally, DeForest Kelly, Ned Romero
75. "Little Jerry Jessup" (3-12-70) William Shatner, Mitch Vogel, Michael Bell, Nancy Malone
76. "Good Will Tour" (3-26-70) Bradford Dillman, Wesley Addy
77. "Little Dog, Gone" (4-2-70) Leo G. Carroll, Martin West, Marsha Hunt
78. "Tom Dayton Is Loose Among Us" (4-9-70) Bill Bixby, William Bramley, Amzie Strickland, William Smithers, Ross Elliott

Fourth Season

79. "A Killing Will Occur" (9-17-70) Dane Clark, Barry Brown
80. "No Game for Amateurs" (9-24-70) Martin Sheen, Tony Brande, Pamela McMyler, Lew Brown, Michael Greer, Carl Reindel, Michael Christian
81. "The Happy Dreams of Hollow Men" (10-1-70) Joseph Campanella, Lloyd Battista, Harry Lauter, Warren Hammack, Bruce Kirby
82. "The People Against Judge McIntire" (10-8-70) James Daly,

George Murdock, Mala Powers, Tyne Daly
83. "Noel's Gonna Fly" (10-15-70) Tim Considine, Richard Basehart
84. "The Lonely Way to Go" (10-22-70) Carl Betz, Denny Miller
85. "Check, Mate: And Murder" [Part I] (10-29-70) Hermione Gingold, Karin Dor, Emile Genest, Alain Patrick, Alan Bergmann
86. "Check, Mate: And Murder" [Part II] (11-5-70) as above
87. "Too Many Victims" (11-12-70) Forrest Tucker, Kathy Lloyd, Lincoln Kilpatrick, Paul Carr, Andrew Rubin, Eddie Ryder, Alex Kravett
88. "The Man on the Inside" (11-19-70) Roger Perry, Simon Scott, Gerald S. O'Loughlin
89. "Backfire" (12-3-70) Kay Peters, Robert F. Lyons, James Wainwright
90. "The Laying on of Hands" (12-10-70) Phyllis Love, Paul Fix, David Burton
91. "This Could Blow Your Mind" (12-17-70) Jerry Douglas, John Lupton, George Grizzard, Bradford Dillman
92. "Blackout" (12-31-70) Jack Albertson, Bill Quinn, Roman Gabriel, Sandy Kenyon, Myron Healey
93. "The Quincunx" (1-7-71) David Carradine, Than Wyenn, Michael Blodgett, Paul Bryan, Carla Borelli, Bob Hastings, Mabel Albertson
94. "From Hruska with Love" (1-21-71) Diana Hyland, Ron Soble, Robert Contreras
95. "The Target" (1-28-71) Earl Holliman, Luana Anders, Vincent Van Patten, Joe Mantell
96. "A Killing at the Track" (2-4-71) Joel Gray, Karl Swenson, Ron Ely, Dana Elcar
97. "Escape" (2-11-71) Scott Glenn, Cal Bellini, Nico Minardos, Robert Ellenstein, Nate Esformes
98. "Love, Peace, Brotherhood, and Murder" (2-18-71) Angel Tompkins, Sally Struthers, Ella Edwards
99. "The Riddle in Room Six" (2-25-71) Andrew Duggan, Marsha Hunt, Paul Stevens, Joe Maross
100. "The Summer Soldier" (3-4-71) Theodore Bikel, Linda Marsh, Andrew Rubin, Walter Koenig
101. "The Accident" (3-11-71) Juanita Moore, Anna Capri, Edward Binns, Jay Novello, Charles Drake, Chelsea Brown
102. "Lesson in Terror" (3-18-71) Simon Oakland, Brad David, David Soul, Heather North, Christina Crawford
103. "Grandmother's House" (4-1-71) Burr De Benning, Jessie Royce Landis, Nevada Spencer
104. "Walls Are Waiting" (4-15-71) William Shatner, Roger C. Carmel, Michael Larrain, Patricia Mattick

Fifth Season

105. "Contract: Kill Ironside" (9-21-71) Marion Ross, James Olson
106. "The Professionals" (9-28-71) James Drury, Michael

Lerner, Michael Baseleon

107. "The Gambling Game" (10-5-71) Madlyn Rhue, Bobby Darin, Van Williams
108. "Ring of Prayer" (10-12-71) Paul Stewart, Ray Walston, Barbara Rush
109. "In the Line of Duty" (10-19-71) Ned Romero, Vera Miles, Brandon De Wilde
110. "Joss Sticks and Wedding Bells" (10-26-71) Miko Mayama, Soon Taik-Oh, Dana Elcar
111. "Murder Impromptu" (11-2-71) Barbara Hale, Anne Archer, Roddy McDowall, Joe Foreman
112. "Dean Fran" (11-9-71) Christine Belford, Victor Holchak
113. "The Good Samaritan" (11-23-71) Michael Callan, Robert Pratt, Diana Muldaur, Warren Stevens
114. "License to Kill" (12-2-71) Jackie Coogan, Roger Perry, David Carradine, Richard Anderson
115. "Class of '57" (12-16-71) Marlyn Mason, Gary Crosby, Charles Robinson
116. "No Motive for Murder" (12-23-71) James Shigeta, David Carradine
117. "But When She Was Bad" (12-30-71) Suzanne Pleshette, Dane Clark
118. "Unreasonable Facsimile" (1-6-72) Burgess Meredith, Frank Aletter, Bernie Kopell, Myron Healey, Susan Seaforth, Susan Stafford, Russell Thorson
119. "Find a Victim" (1-13-72) Pat Hingle
120. "And Then There Was One" (1-20-72) Percy Rodriguez, Scott Hylands
121. "Death by the Numbers" (1-27-72) Marilyn Erskine, Burr De Benning
122. "Bubble, Bubble, Toil and Murder" (2-3-72) Jodie Foster, Rod Serling, John Schucks, Lee Paul
123. "Achilles' Heel" (2-17-72) Kerwin Matthews, Rick Lenz, William Windom, James Douglas
124. "His Fiddlers Three" (3-2-72) Tim Matheson, Kathy Lloyd, Paul Koslo, Rick Kelman, Collin Wilcox-Horne
125. "A Man Named Arno" (3-9-72) Anne Francis, Aldine King, Nico Minardos

## Sixth Season

126. "Five Days in the Death of Sergeant Brown" [Part I; concluded 9/19/72 with episode of "The Bold Ones"] (9-14-72) E. G. Marshall, David Hartman, Vic Morrow, Christina Hart
127. "The Savage Sentry" (9-21-72) Anthony Zerbe, Bo Svenson, Gilbert Green, Dana Elcar
128. "Programmed for Panic" (9-28-72) James Gregory, John Ragin, Russell Johnson, Ed Begley Jr.
129. "Down Two Roads" (10-12-72) Felton Perry, Eugene Roche, David Spielberg
130. "Camera ... Action ... Murder!" (10-26-72) Joe Don Baker, Anthony Caruso, Elliott Street, Dennis Patrick

131. "Riddle Me Death" (11-2-72) Sian Barbara Allen, Ernest
     Karada, William Devane, William Bryant
132. "Nightmare Trip" (11-9-72) Don Stroud, Rudy Solari, Jack
     Ging, Bill Williams
133. "Hey Buddy, Can You Spare a Life?" (11-16-72) Geraldine
     Brooks, Kerwin Matthews, Cameron Mitchell, Roger
     Perry
134. "The Countdown" (11-23-72) Jackie Cooper, Richard Jaeck-
     el, Cameron Mitchell
135. "The Deadly Gamesmen" (11-30-72) Noel Harrison, Scott
     Marlowe, Nichele Nichols
136. "Who'll Cry for My Baby?" (12-7-72) Tisha Sterling, John
     Quade, Titos Vandis
137. "Cold, Hard Cash" (12-14-72) Jack Kelly, Barbara Rush,
     Kaz Garas, Kay Lenz, Richard Anderson
138. "Shadow Soldiers" (12-21-72) Lloyd Bochner, Ivor Berry,
     Michael Bell, Donald Moffat, Hedley Mattingley
139. "Ollinger's Last Case" (1-4-73) Kenny Mars, Loretta Swit,
     Warren Kemmerling, Albert Salmi, Mills Watson, Wil-
     liam Bramley
140. "A Special Person" (1-11-73) Barry Sullivan, Sandy Baron,
     Robert Viharo, Melendy Britt
141. "The Caller" (1-25-73) L. Q. Jones, Paul Lambert, Dab-
     ney Coleman, Barry Livingston
142. "Love Me in December" (2-1-73) Madlyn Rhue, Cathy
     Cannon, Steve Forrest
143. "The Ghost of the Dancing Doll" (2-15-73) Christopher
     Connelly, Warner Anderson, Abner Biberman
144. "All About Andrea" (2-22-73) Myrna Loy, Neva Patterson,
     Jacqueline Scott
145. "Another Shell Game" (3-1-73) Dan O'Herlihy
146. "All Honorable Men" (3-8-73) William Daniels, Fred Beir,
     Leonard Stone, Sandra Smith
147. "The Best Laid Plans" (3-15-73) Don Stroud, Rafael Camp-
     os, Frank Marth, Whit Bissell
148. "A Game of Showdown" (3-22-73) Robert Webber, Scott
     Brady, Don Hanmer, Mary Murphy

Seventh Season

149. "Confessions from a Lady of the Night" (9-13-73) Dorothy
     Malone, Lynn Carlin, William Schallert, Tom Drake,
     Jeanne Cooper
150. "Murder by One" (9-20-73) Mary Ure, Michael Baseleon,
     Herb Edelman, Clu Gulager, Robert Van Decar
151. "In the Forests of the Night" (9-27-73) Dana Wynter, Lyle
     Bettger, Frank Aletter, Mae Mercer, Peter Von Zerneck
152. "Fragile Is the House of Cards" (10-4-73) James Olson,
     Lorraine Gary, Sandra De Bruin, Noah Keen
153. "The Armageddon Gang" (10-11-73) Hildy Brooks, Harold
     Gould, Joseph Campanella, Ted Hartley, Tom Stewart,
     Laurence Haddon, Ramon Bieri, Dennis Cross
154. "House of Terror" (10-25-73) Sharon Glass, Dennis Rucker

Russell Wiggins, Aldine King, Dabbs Greer, Lenore
Kasdorf, William Durkin
155. "The Helping Hand" (11-1-73) Cameron Mitchell
156. "Downhill All the Way" (11-8-73) William Smith, David
Doyle, Roger Perry, William Devane, Kim Darby, David
Wayne, Lee H. Montgomery
157. "Mind for Murder" (11-15-73) Ross Martin, Louise Sorel,
John Doucette, Burr De Benning
158. "The Hidden Man" (11-29-73) Cliff Potts
159. "The Double-Edged Corner" (12-6-73) Albert Salmi, Nancy
Malone
160. "The Last Payment" (12-20-73) Roger Robinson, Felton
Perry, Scatman Crothers, Fred Beir, Albert Popwell,
Dave Turner, Clarice Taylor, Dick Williams
161. "For the Love of God" (1-3-74)
162. "Two Hundred Large" (1-10-74) Paul Burke, Michael Bell,
Woodrow Parfrey, Kres Mersky
163. "Once More for Joey" (1-17-74) Pamela Bellwood, Roger
Davis, Geoffrey Deuel, Judy Carne, Kip Niven, Richard
B. Shull, Bert Holland, Paul Hampton
164. "Terror on Grant Avenue" (1-31-74) Irene Tsu, Benson
Fong, Frank Michael Liu, Mako, George Chiang, Dalton
Leong
165. "Class of '40" (2-7-74) Anne Francis, Jackie Cooper, Leif
Erickson
166. "A Taste of Ashes" (2-14-74) Kim Hunter, Gretchen Corbett, Whit Bissell, James Keach, Scott Hylands, Anne
Seymour, James McCallion
167. "A Death in Academe" (2-21-74) Michael Parks, Mike Kellin, Mary Layne, Malachi Throne, Jennifer Leak, Doug
Jacoby, Naomi Stevens, Monica Lewis
168. "Close to the Heart" (2-28-74) Elizabeth Ashley
169. "Come Eleven, Come Twelve" (3-7-74) Andy Robinson,
Paul Kent, Bill Zuckert, Paul Comi, Michael Strong,
George Murdock, David Huddleston
170. "Riddle at 24,000" (3-14-74) Desi Arnaz Sr.
171. "Amy Prentiss: AKA The Chief" [two-hour episode] (5-23-
74) Jessica Walter

Eighth Season

172. "Raise the Devil" [Part I] (9-12-74) Sian Barbara Allen,
Bill Bixby, Carolyn Jones, Michael Anderson, Dane
Clark, Paul Richards
173. "Raise the Devil" [Part II] (9-19-74) as above
174. "What's New with Mark?" (9-26-74) Ned Glass, Frank
Gorshin, Cameron Mitchell, Ken Tobey, Jason Wingreen,
Penny Santon
175. "Trial of Terror" (10-3-74) Joan Van Ark, Pamela Hensley, Harold J. Stone, Tom Troupe, Ted Gehring, Larry
Watson
176. "Cross Doublecross" (10-10-74) Gary Lockwood
177. "Set-Up: Danger!" (10-24-74) Barry Sullivan, Rudy Solari,

Gary Crosby, John Vernon, Pat Renella, Byron Mabe, Michael Richardson

178. "The Lost Cotillion" (10-31-74) Kim Hunter, Cesar Romero, Dana Andrews, Jess Walton, Frank Maxwell, Alan Napier, Virginia Gregg, Meg Wyllie

179. "Run Scared" (11-7-74) Ed Nelson, Kathleen Quinlan, Ron Thompson, Michael Bell, Bettye Ackerman, Philip Pine, John Lupton

180. "Act of Vengeance" (11-14-74) Paul Burke

181. "Far Side of the Fence" (11-21-74) Peter Mark Richman, Shelley Fabares, Jim Hutton

182. "The Over-the-Hill Blues" (12-5-74) Leslie Nielsen, Beth Brickwell, Beverly Garland

183. "Speak No Evil" (12-12-74) Christopher Connelly, Lonny Chapman, Jean Allison, Jack Bender, Mary Murphy, John McLiam, Lee Delano

184. "Fall of an Angel" (12-19-74) Judy Pace, William Elliott, Henry Beckman, Val Bisoglio, Jarrod Johnson, Casey Kasern, Richard X. Slattery

185. "The Visiting Fireman" (12-26-74) John Williams, Joseph George, Larry Blake, Keith McConnell, Hedley Mattingley

186. "The Return of Eleanor Rogers" (1-2-75) Joseph Campanella, Ina Balin

187. "The Faded Image" (1-16-75) Richard Anderson, Gary Frank, Donald Barry, Julie Gregg


OFF TO SEE THE WIZARD

This was a network title for a mélange of feature films, nature documentaries and one original musical ("Who's Afraid of Mother Goose?" with choreography by Peter Gennaro). Animated "Wizard of Oz" characters introduced each segment.

The Episodes:

1. "Clarence the Cross-Eyed Lion" [1965 film; Part I] (9-8-67) Marshall Thompson, Richard Haydn, Cheryl Miller, Maurice Marsac, Betsy Drake, Alan Caillou

2. "Clarence the Cross-Eyed Lion" [Part II] (9-15-67) as above

3. "Rhino!" [1964 film] (9-22-67) Robert Culp, Shirley Eaton, Harry Guardino

4. "The Adventures of Huckleberry Finn" [1960 film; Part I] (9-29-67) Eddie Hodges, Archie Moore, Tony Randall, Neville Brand, Patty McCormack, Andy Devine, John Carradine, Finley Currie, Parley Baer, Josephine Hutchinson, Mickey Shaughnessy, Sherry Jackson, Stanley Holloway, Buster Keaton, Judy Canova, Dean Stanton

5. "The Adventures of Huckleberry Finn" [Part II] (10-6-67) as above

6. "Who's Afraid of Mother Goose?" [original family musical]

(10-13-67)  Maureen O'Hara, Peter Gennaro, Nancy Sinatra, Frankie Avalon, Fred Clark, Margaret Hamilton

7.  "Lili" [1952 film; Part I]  (10-20-67)  Leslie Caron, Mel Ferrer, Kurt Kasznar, Jean-Pierre Aumont, Amanda Blake, Zsa Zsa Gabor

8.  "Lili" [Part II]  (10-27-67)  as above

9.  "Untamed World" [documentary narrated by Andrew Duggan]  (11-3-67)

10.  "Island of the Lost" [1967 film; Part I]  (11-10-67)  Richard Greene, Luke Halpin, Mark Hulswit

11.  "Island of the Lost" [Part II]  (11-17-67)  as above

12.  "The Hellcats" [1964 film]  (11-24-67)  George Hamilton, Warren Berlinger, Nehemiah Persoff, John Craig, Barbara Eden

13.  "Flipper" [1963 film; Part I]  (12-1-67)  Chuck Connors, Luke Halpin, Kathleen Maguire, Connie Scott

14.  "Flipper" [Part II]  (12-8-67)  as above

15.  "Gypsy Colt" [1956 film]  (12-15-67)  Ward Bond, Frances Dee, Lee Van Cleef, Donna Corcoran, Larry Keating

16.  "Zebra in the Kitchen" [1965 film; Part I]  (12-22-67)  Jay North, Joyce Meadows, Jim Davis, Martin Milner, Andy Devine

17.  "Zebra in the Kitchen" [Part II]  (12-29-67)  as above

18.  "Mike and the Mermaid" [1964 unsold television pilot film]  (1-5-68)  Kevin Brodie, Jeri Lynne Fraser, Med Flory, Rachel Ames, Dan Tompkins

19.  "Captain Sinbad" [1963 film; Part I]  (1-12-68)  Guy Williams, Heidi Bruhl, Abraham Sofaer, Bernie Hamilton, Rolf Wanka, Pedro Armendariz

20.  "Captain Sinbad" [Part II]  (1-19-68)  as above

21.  "Alexander the Great" [1964 unsold television pilot film]  (1-26-68)  William Shatner, John Cassavetes, Joseph Cotten, Simon Oakland, Ziva Rodann, Cliff Osmond

22.  "Cinderella's Glass Slipper" [1955 film; Part I]  (2-2-68)  Leslie Caron, Michael Wilding, Keenan Wynn, Amanda Blake, Elsa Lanchester, Estelle Winwood

23.  "Cinderella's Glass Slipper" [Part II]  (2-9-68)  as above

24.  "Wild World" [documentary narrated by Hal Holbrook]  (2-16-68)

25.  "Tarzan, the Ape Man" [1959 film]  (2-23-68)  Denny Miller, Joanna Barnes, Cesare Danova, Robert Douglas


HONDO

Sluggish western of a cavalry scout; predictable situations.

The Regulars:  Hondo Lane, Ralph Taeger; Angie Dow, Kathie Browne; Buffalo Baker, Noah Beery; Captain Richards, Gary Clarke; Vittoro, Michael Pate.

The Episodes:

1.  "Hondo and the Eagle Claw"  (9-8-67)  Robert Taylor, John

Smith, Gary Merrill, Randy Boone
2. "The War Cry" (9-15-67) Michael Rennie, Robert Taylor, Randy Boone
3. "Hondo and the Singing Wire" (9-22-67) Perry Lopez, Pat Conway, Donald Woods
4. "The Superstition Massacre" (9-29-67) Robert Reed, Nancy Malone
5. "The Savage" (10-6-67) Nico Minardos, Charles McGraw
6. [unknown title] (10-13-67) Farley Granger, Nick Adams
7. "Hondo and the Hawks" (10-20-67) John Carroll, Lawrence Montaigne
8. "Hondo and the Mad Dog" (10-27-67) James MacArthur, Royal Dano, James Beck, Ben Wright, William Benedict, Michael Harris
9. "Hondo and the Judas" (11-3-67) John Agar, John Carradine, Ricky Nelson, Forrest Tucker
10. "Hondo and the Commancheros" (11-10-67) Fernando Lamas
11. "Hondo and the Sudden Town" (11-17-67) Gene Raymond, Rod Cameron, Leonard Stone, Tom Reese, Glenn Langan
12. "The Ghost of Ed Dow" (11-24-67) David Brian, Chris Alcaide, Ted Jordan, June Dayton
13. "Hondo and the Death Drive" (12-1-67) Alan Hale, L. Q. Jones, J. Pat O'Malley, Terry Wilson, Reed Hadley
14. "Hondo and the Hanging Town" (12-8-67) Dan O'Herlihy, Gary Crosby, Morgan Woodward, Denver Pyle
15. "The Gladiators" (12-15-67) Claude Akins, Richard Hale, Barton MacLane
16. "The Apache Trail" (12-22-67) Nick Adams, Barry Nelson
17. "The Rebel Hat" (12-29-67) Jack Elam, Rafael Campos, Rudy Battaglia, Linda Dangcil, Eugene Iglesias, John Inrisano


THE GUNS OF WILL SONNETT

So much dwelling on a tired theme: the family of James Sonnett (Jason Evers in a recurring role)--son Jeff (Dack Rambo) father Will (Walter Brennan)--search for their wanted refugee relation. Periodic interjections of great wisdom for grandson Jeff by Brennan as Will.

The Regulars: Will Sonnett, Walter Brennan; Jeff Sonnett, Dack Rambo; James Sonnett, Jason Evers (recurring guest star).

The Episodes:

1. [unknown title] (9-8-67) Claude Akins, Paul Fix, J. Pat O'Malley, Perry Cook, Rex Holman
2. "A Bell for Jeff Sonnett" (9-15-67) Charles Grodin, Ford Rainey
3. "A Grave for James Sonnett" (9-22-67) Jay Novello, Don

Diamond
4.  "The Natural Way" (9-29-67) Wendell Corey, Myron Healey, Bartlett Robinson, Hal Baylor, Charla Doherty, Jack Catron
5.  "Of Lasting Summers and Jim Sonnett" (10-6-67) Peter Whitney, Paul Richards, James Anderson
6.  "Message at Noon" (10-13-67) Jason Evers, Strother Martin, Lonny Chapman, Sam Melville
7.  "A Son for a Son" (10-20-67) Royal Dano, Virginia Gregg, Jack Elam
8.  "Meeting at Devil's Fork" (10-27-67) James Best, Dean Stanton, Bill Foster, Claudia Bryar, Arthur Peterson, Tom Reese, Janice Yarbrough
9.  "First Love" (11-3-67) Cherie Latimer, James Westmoreland, Harry Harvey Sr., Hank Patterson
10. "The Favor" (11-10-67) Stephen McNally, Tom Tully
11. "Ride the Man Down" (11-17-67) Kevin McCarthy, Vaughn Taylor, Charlie Brooks
12. "The Turkey Shoot" (11-24-67) R. G. Armstrong, Paul Sorensen, David Macklin
13. "And a Killing Rode into Town" (12-1-67) Cloris Leachman
14. "Find a Sonnett, Kill a Sonnett" (12-8-67) J. D. Cannon, Dennis Hopper, Rex Holman, Robert Karnes, Jim Boles
15. "Sunday in Paradise" (12-15-67) Joan Blondell
16. "The Secret of Hangtown Mine" (12-22-67) Jean Willes, Sam Gilman, Norman Alden
17. "The Hero" (12-29-67) Robert Wilke, Patricia Barry
18. "What's in a Name?" (1-5-68) Edward Andrews, Ross Hagen, Bo Hopkins, Harry Swoger
19. "End of the Rope" (1-12-68) Jason Evers, Richard Devon, Don Haggerty
20. "And He Shall Lead the Children" (1-19-68) Ann Doran, Bert Freed, Soloman Sturges
21. "Look for the Hound Dog" (1-26-68) William Schallert, Laurie Main, Robert Donner, John Alderson, Dub Taylor
22. "Stopover in a Troubled Town" (2-2-68) Anna Capri, Karl Swenson
23. "Alone" (2-9-68) Jason Evers
24. "The Sins of the Father" (2-23-68) Torin Thatcher, Annette Andre
25. "The Warriors" (3-1-68) Richard Webb, Denver Pyle, Anthony Caruso, Jim Davis
26. "A Fool and His Money" (3-8-68) Paul Brinegar, Heather Angel

## Second Season

27. "Reunion" (9-27-68) Jason Evers, Tim O'Kelly
28. "The Trap" (10-4-68) Royal Dano, Robert Doqui, Arthur Malet, Walter Burke
29. "Chapter and Verse" (10-11-68) Henry Jones, Rex Holman
30. "Pariah" (10-18-68) Ellen Corby, Paul Fix, Harry Lauter
31. "Joby" (11-1-68) Jason Evers, Strother Martin

32. "The Straw Man" (11-8-68) Madlyn Rhue, Walter Burke
33. "A Difference of Opinion" (11-15-68) Lonny Chapman, Myron Healey, James Wainwright
34. "Home Free" (11-22-68) Malcolm Atterbury, Richard Evans, Hal Baylor, Victoria Thompson
35. "Guilt" (11-29-68) Bo Hopkins, Robert Donner
36. "Meeting in a Small Town" (12-6-68) Jason Evers, Ford Rainey, Robert J. Wilke
37. "The Fearless Man" (12-13-68) Paul Richards, William Smith
38. "Where There's Hope" (12-20-68) Cindy Eilbacher, Jean Howell
39. "Join the Army" (1-3-69) Robert Pine, Tom Tully, Parley Baer
40. "Time Is the Rider" (1-10-69) James Griffith, Rayford Barnes, Douglas V. Fowley
41. "Robber's Roost" (1-17-69) James Best, Jess Walton
42. "Trail's End" (1-31-69) Ruta Lee, Morgan Woodward
43. "A Town in Terror" [Part I] (2-7-69) Jason Evers, Sean McClory, Harry Lauter, Mort Mills
44. "A Town in Terror" [Part II] (2-14-69) as above
45. "Jim Sonnett's Lady" (2-21-69) Jason Evers, Norma Crane
46. "The Trial" (2-28-69) Jason Evers
47. "One Angry Juror" (3-7-69) John Milford, Judson Pratt
48. [unknown title] (3-14-69) Jacqueline Scott, Don Dubbins, Teddy Eccles
49. "The Man Who Killed James Sonnett" (3-21-69) Jay Novello

JUDD, FOR THE DEFENSE

No matter that the procedural humdrum of the actual process is gone; Paul Monash's courtroom drama stages its theatrics well, making for an at times strikingly packaged social commentary. So one can tolerate a stereotypic protagonist--brash and brilliant millionaire Attorney Clinton Judd (Carl Betz)--when the clientele includes a mute couple pleading to adopt a child in "To Love and Stand Mute" (which concludes with the court saying no), and an unemployed, alienated victim to no more than middle age (Kevin McCarthy's role in "You Remember Joe Maddox").

Two superbly performed occult dramas were the episodes "To Kill a Madman" and "Thou Shalt Not Suffer a Witch to Live"; in the former, Carmen Matthews was cast as a psychic whose vision of "sac-a-main" (French for purse) helps uncover a psychotic in the latter, Betty Field starred as a self-professed witch who "hexes" (convincingly, it turns out) a young couple's forthcoming baby.

The Regulars: Att. Clinton Judd, Carl Betz; Att. Ben Caldwell, Stephen Young.

The Episodes:

1. "Tempest in a Texas Town" (9-8-67)  Christopher Jones, Pat Hingle, Jim Henaghan, Patti Peterson, James Anderson
2. "The Deep End" (9-15-67)  Beverly Garland, Leslie Nielsen
3. "The Other Face of the Law" (9-22-67)  Robert Viharo, Edward Asner, Jeff Corey, John Doucette, Joyce Taylor
4. "A Civil Case of Murder" (9-29-67)  Dan Travanty, Scott Brady, Brooke Bundy, John Dehner, Clint Howard, Ford Rainey, Virginia Christine, Alan Hewitt, Noam Pitlik, Alice Nunn
5. "Shadow of a Killer" (10-6-67)  Quentin Dean, Joe Don Baker, Harold Gould, Vincent Gardenia, Charles McGraw
6. "Conspiracy" (10-13-67)  James Daly, Kim Darby, Kevin McCarthy
7. "The Confessional" (10-20-67)  Chill Wills, Burr De Benning, Lurene Tuttle, Marilyn Devin, Richard Anderson, Hal Baylor
8. "Death from a Flower Girl" (11-3-67)  Gene Raymond
9. "Citizen Ritter" (11-20-67)  Murray Hamilton, Norma Crane, Paula Wayne
10. "The Money Farm" (11-17-67)  Martha Hyer, James Whitmore
11. "To Kill a Madman" (11-24-67)  Len Birman, William Schallert, Carmen Matthews, Natalie Trundy, Jason Wingreen
12. "Commitment" (12-1-67)  Brock Peters, William Windom, David Sheiner
13. "To Love and Stand Mute" (12-8-67)  Tom Troupe, Loretta Leversee, Ruta Lee, Edith Atwater, Shiela Larken, Jenny Maxwell, William Sargent, Roy Engel, Barbara Babcock, Clark Howat
14. "The Living Victim" (12-15-67)  Robert Alda, John Larch, Joan Hackett, William Wintersole, Don Hanmer, Sam Gilman, Dean Harens, Robert Ball
15. "Firebrand" (12-22-67)  Rodolfo Joyos, Mark Lenard
16. "Everybody Loved Harlan but His Wife" (12-29-67)  Vera Miles, Claude Akins, Charles Gray, Noah Keen
17. "Fall of the Skylark--The Trial" [Part I] (1-5-68)  Bradford Dillman, Diana Hyland, Lee Bowman, Malachi Throne, Barry Morse, John Kellogg, Joe Mantell, June Dayton
18. "Fall of the Skylark--The Appeal" [Part II] (1-12-68)  as above
19. "No Law Against Murder" (1-19-68)  Earl Holliman, Jason Evers, Mariette Hartley, Frank Maxwell, Jacqueline Mayo, James Dobson, Bo Hopkins, John Ward
20. "The Grand Old Man" (1-26-68)  Christopher Connelly, Albert Dekker, Joe Maross, Alfred Ryder, Lin McCarthy
21. "What You Can Do With Money" (2-2-68)  Albert Salmi, Janice Rule
22. "Kingdom of the Blind" (2-9-68)  Ida Lupino, Tim O'Connor, Patricia Barry, Jane Elliot, Lawrence Dobkin
23. "The Devil's Surrogate" (2-23-68)  James Franciscus

24. "Square House" (3-1-68) Robert Duvall, Simon Oakland, Hugh Marlowe
25. "The Worst of Both Worlds" (3-15-68) Luke Halpin, Frank Marth, Pippa Scott, Malcolm Atterbury, John Randolph
26. "You Remember Joe Maddox" (3-22-68) Kevin McCarthy, Coleen Gray, Simon Scott, Ray Stricklyn, Patricia Hyland, Roy Engel, Martin West, Parley Baer

Second Season

27. "In a Puff of Smoke" (9-27-68) Katherine Houghton, Robert Forster, Jack Ging, Zalman King
28. "Transplant" (10-4-68) John Vernon, Lloyd Bochner, Julie Sommars, Richard Bull, Gilbert Green
29. "The Ends of Justice" (10-11-68) Georg Stanford Brown, Bernie Hamilton, Paul Lambert, Tom Palmer
30. "The Name of the Game Is Acquittal" (10-18-68) Patricia Crowley, Clarke Gordon, Virginia Gregg, Don Hanmer
31. "The Sound of the Plastic Axe" (10-25-68) Robert F. Lyons, Norman Fell, Peter Haskell, Dennis Olivieri
32. "The Death Farm" (11-1-68) Wright King, Bonnie Bedelia, Arch Johnson, James Gregory, Woodrow Parfrey
33. "Weep the Hunter Home" (11-8-68) Richard Dreyfuss, Peter Jason, Dana Elcar, Priscilla Morrill, Harold Gould
34. "The Gates of Cerberus" (11-15-68) Sam Wanamaker, Lee Grant, Phil Bruns, Martin E. Brooks, Christine Burke
35. "My Client, the Fool" (11-22-68) Arthur Hill, Donna Baccala, Jacques Aubuchon, Jim Davis
36. "Punishments, Cruel and Unusual" (12-6-68) James Daly, Jessica Tandy, David Sheiner, Charles McGraw, Cloris Leachman
37. "Thou Shalt Not Suffer a Witch to Live" (12-13-68) Linden Chiles, Betty Field, Patricia Smith, John Lasell, John Ward
38. "A Swim with Sharks" (12-20-68) Gerald S. O'Loughlin, Simon Oakland, Pamela Dunlap
39. "The Crystal Maze" (1-3-69) Margaret Leighton, Brian Bedford, Penny Fuller, Carrie Snodgrass, Dabbs Greer
40. "Borderline Girl" (1-10-69) Brooke Bundy, Jay C. Flippen, Geraldine Brooks, Michael Larrain, Sandy Kenyon
41. "Epitaph on a Computer Card" (1-17-69) William Daniels, Peter Donat, Jacqueline Scott, Don Porter
42. "The Poisoned Tree" (1-24-69) Nancy Wickwire, Melissa Murphy, Michael Strong, Lonny Chapman, Dennis Patrick
43. "The Law and Order Blues" [Part II of "Felony Squad" episode of 1/31/69] (1-31-69) Brock Peters, Larry McCormick, George Ives, Howard Duff, Dennis Cole
44. "Between the Dark and the Daylight" (2-7-69) Clive Clerk, Ronny Howard, Harry Townes, Louise Latham, Kevin Coughlin, Ford Rainey, William Sargent, Lane Bradbury
45. "The Holy Ground: The Killing" [Part I] (2-14-69) Richard Kiley, Joanne Linville, Edward Binns, John Dehner, Walter Brooke

46. "The Holy Ground: The Killers" [Part II] (2-21-69) as
   above
47. "An Elephant in a Cigar Box" (2-28-69) Paul Henreid, Joanna Barnes, Hanna Landy, Charles Bodin
48. "The View from the Ivy Tower" (3-7-69) Al Freeman Jr.,
   Dennis Weaver
49. "Runaway" (3-14-69) Jacqueline Scott, Susan Anspach, Jeff
   Pomeranz, James Broderick, Frank Maxwell
50. "Visitation" (3-21-69) Jack McMartin, Joanna Moore, Gavin
   MacLeod, Elizabeth MacRae

IT TAKES A THIEF

This dubious espionage entry (the pilot composed by Leslie
Stevens and Roland Kibbee) involved a habitual thief (Robert Wagner
as Alexander Mundy) who bargained his way out of a prison cell by
offering to steal for the SIA (represented here by Malachi Throne
as Noah Bain). It was Senta Berger who gave the finest of the
guest performances as Mundy's love interest (and a counterspy) in
producer Glen A. Larsen's "Flowers from Alexander." The series
theme was intended as no more than farce, kleptomania being
charming (else why cast a Hollywood symbol of sophistication--
Fred Astaire--as Mundy's thieving father and mentor, Alister?)
but revelations of bizarre practices by intelligence agencies left it
not charming at all.

The Regulars: Alexander Mundy, Robert Wagner; Noah Bain, Malachi Throne (first two seasons); Alister Mundy, Fred Astaire (last season episodes only).

The Episodes:

1. "A Thief Is a Thief Is a Thief" [ninety-minute pilot episode
   also known as "The Magnificent Thief"] (1-9-68) John
   Saxon, Kurt Kasznar, Doug McClure, James Drury, Leslie
   Nielsen, Joe Louis, Wally Cox, Senta Berger, Susan St.
   James, Raymond Burr
2. "It Takes One to Know One" (1-16-68) Susan St. James,
   Alfred Ryder, Mark Richman
3. "When Boy Meets Girl" (1-30-68) Suzy Parker
4. "A Very Warm Reception" (2-6-68) Simon Oakland, Katherine
   Crawford
5. "One Illegal Angel" (2-13-68) Fernando Lamas
6. "Totally by Design" (2-20-68) Tina Louise
7. "When Thieves Fall In" (2-27-68) Susan St. James
8. "A Spot of Trouble" (3-5-68) William Campbell, Katherine
   Crawford
9. "When Good Friends Get Together" (3-12-68) Rosemary
   Forsyth, James Shigeta, John Forsythe
10. "Birds of a Feather" (3-19-68) Taina Elg, Charles Macaulay,
   Tisha Sterling, Mark Lenard, Strother Martin

11. "To Steal a Battleship" (3-26-68) Bill Bixby
12. "Turnabout" (4-2-68) Ida Lupino
13. "The Radomir Miniature" (4-9-68) Ina Balin, Than Wyenn
14. "Locked in the Cradle of the Keep" (4-16-68) Ina Balin
15. "A Matter of Royal Larceny" (4-23-68) Henry Wilcoxon, Lynda Day
16. "The Lay of the Land" (4-30-68) Hermione Gingold, Sheila Larken, Stuart Margolin

Second Season

17. "One Night on Soledad" (9-24-68) Thomas Gomez, Nancy Kovack, Madlyn Rhue
18. "A Sour Note" (10-1-68) Suzanne Pleshette, Bruce Gordon, Harvey Lembeck
19. "The Bill Is in Committee" (10-8-68) Yvonne Craig
20. "The Thingumabob Heist" (10-15-68) Ricardo Montalban, Sharon Acker, Bill Russell
21. "Get Me to the Revolution on Time" (10-22-68) Ivan Dixon, Morgan Woodward
22. "The Packager" (10-29-68) Alex Dreier, William Smithers, Lee Meredith
23. "Hands Across the Border" [Part I] (11-12-68) Frank De Kova, Joseph Cotten, Johy Hoyt, Pamela Austin, Georg Stanford Brown
24. "Hands Across the Border" [Part II] (11-19-68) as above
25. "A Case of Red Turnips" (11-26-68) Noel Harrison
26. "The Galloping Skin Game" (12-3-68) Ricardo Montalban, James McEachin
27. "Glass Riddle" (12-17-68) Jason Evers, Marion Marshall, Linda Lawson
28. "To Catch a Roaring Lion" (12-31-68) Brock Peters, Denis Nicholas
29. "Guess Who's Coming to Rio?" (1-7-69) Michael Ansara, Dana Wynter, Alejandro Rey, John Russell
30. "The Artist Is for Framing" (1-21-69) Paul Henreid, Gia Scala
31. "The Naked Billionaire" (1-28-60) Sally Kellerman, Mark Richman, Richard Carlson
32. "A Matter of Grey Matter" [Part I] (2-4-69) Joey Heatherton, Paul Lukas
33. "A Matter of Grey Matter" [Part II] (2-11-69) as above
34. "Cat's Paw" (2-18-69) Fernando Lamas
35. "Boom at the Top" (2-25-69) Carol Lynley, Barry Sullivan, Roddy McDowall
36. "The Funeral Is on Mundy" (3-11-69) Julie Newmar
37. "The Baranoff Time Table" (3-18-69) Jessica Walter, Ray Danton
38. "Rock-Bye, Bye" (3-25-69) Edmond O'Brien, Jerome Thor, Melodie Johnson, Gavin MacLeod
39. "The Family" (4-1-69) Geraldine Brooks, Carla Borelli, Cyril Delevanti
40. "38-23-36" (4-8-69) Nancy Kovack

41. "The Great Chess Gambit" (4-15-69) Nehemiah Persoff, Ben Cooper
42. "Mad in Japan" (4-22-69) Alex Dreier, Sharon Acker, Nobu McCarthy

Third Season

43. "Saturday Night in Venice" (9-25-69) Delia Boccardo
44. "Who'll Bid Two Million Dollars?" (10-2-69) Peter Sellers, Edward Binns, Jacques Herlen
45. "The Beautiful People" (10-9-69) John Van Dreelen, Terrie Garr, Sandrine Weiss
46. "The Great Casino Caper" (10-16-69) Edward Binns, Francesco Mule, Adolfo Celli
47. "Flowers from Alexander" (10-23-69) Senta Berger, Nigel Patrick
48. "The Blue, Blue Danube" (10-30-69) Liliane Montevecchi, John Russell
49. "The Three Virgins of Rome" (11-6-69) Victor Buono, Edmund Purdom, Karin Dor
50. "Payoff in the Piazza" (11-13-69) John Russell, Susan St. James, Richard Loo, Rudy Solari, David Opatoshu
51. "The King of Thieves" (11-20-69) Lex Barker, Edward Binns, Martha Hyer, Lionel Stander
52. "A Friend in Deed" (11-27-69) Henry Silva, Thomas Gomez, John Russell, Frankie Avalon
53. "The Second Time Around" (12-4-69) Edward Binns, Adolfo Celli, Alice Ghostley
54. "The Cold Who Came in from the Spy" (12-11-69) Francis Lederer, Elsa Lanchester
55. "To Lure a Man" (12-18-69) Joseph Cotten, Christina Sinatra, Wilfrid Hyde-White
56. "The Scorpio Drop" (12-25-69) Gale Sondergaard, Brenda Benet, Eduard Franz
57. "Nice Girls Marry Stock Brokers" (1-15-70) Paul Stewart, Michele Carey, Geoffrey Holder
58. "The Steal-Driving Man" (1-19-70) Fernando Lamas, Mario Andretti, Dick Smothers
59. "Touch of Magic" (1-26-70) Bette Davis
60. "Fortune City" (2-2-70) Broderick Crawford
61. "Situation Red" (2-9-70) Barry Sullivan, Earl Holliman
62. "Sing a Song of Murder" (2-23-70) Joseph Cotten, Beah Richards, Marilyn McCoo
63. "The Suzie Simone Caper" (3-2-70) Jane Morgan, Susan St. James
64. "An Evening with Alister Mundy" (3-9-70) Edward Binns
65. "Beyond a Treasonable Doubt" (3-16-70) Joseph Cotten, Cesar Romero
66. "Project X" (3-23-70) Wally Cox, Christina Sinatra, Lloyd Bochner, Keye Luke, John Colicos

MAN IN A SUITCASE

In terms of plot, this series operated at the crest of the Cold War fever (and so anachronistically; most of the "U.N.C.L.E." genre had come and gone). Treason is the charge against protagonist McGill (Richard Bradford), our embodiment of Cold War spirit. Ostracized, he tirelessly searches for the Intelligence man who can exonerate him. The fine line between truth and illusion was the gist of such dramas as "Three Blinks of the Eyes," about a bizarre murder case, "Web with Four Spiders" about a curious blackmail scheme, and the thriller "Who's Mad Now?."

The Regulars: McGill, Richard Bradford.

The Episodes:

1. "Man from the Dead" (5-3-68) John Barrie, Angela Browne, Stuart Damon
2. "Brainwash" (5-10-68) Colin Blakely, Howard Marion Crawford, Suzan Farmer
3. "Day of Execution" (5-17-68) Rosemary Nichols, Donald Sutherland
4. "Burden of Proof" (5-24-68) John Gregson, Nicola Pagett
5. "The Whisper" (5-31-68) Patrick Allen, Colin Blakely
6. "No Friend of Mine" (6-14-68) Clive Morton, Errol John, Allan Cuthbertson
7. "Why They Killed Nolan" (6-21-68) Sam Kydd, Ursula Howells
8. "Web with Four Spiders" (7-5-68) Ray McAnally, Jacqueline Ellis, Simon Oates
9. "The Bridge" (7-12-68) Rodney Bewes, Jane Merrow, Bill Owen, Anthony Nicholls
10. "Essay in Evil" (7-19-68) Donald Houston, Peter Vaughan
11. "All That Glitters" (7-26-68) Michael Goodliffe, Barbara Shelley, Duncan Lamont
12. "Which Way Did He Go?" (8-2-68) Donald Sutherland, Jennifer Jayne, Hugh McDermott
13. "Who's Mad Now?" (8-9-68) Robert Hutton, Audine Leith
14. "Three Blinks of the Eyes" (8-16-68) Faith Brook, Dora Reisser, Drewe Henley
15. "Variation on a Million Bucks" [Part I] (8-23-68) Anton Rogers, Yoko Tani, Guy Hamilton
16. "Variation on a Million Bucks" [Part II] (8-30-68) as above

THE PRISONER

Actor Patrick McGoohan's controversial enigma in which an intelligence man is banished (for no explained reason) to a "village" of nameless and manipulated inhabitants. As the incarcerated "Number 6" McGoohan is in fine form, but the series itself, a blend of Freud and Kafka and an abundance of literary and historical allusions, emerges more ostentatious than meaningful.

The Regulars: "Number 6", Patrick McGoohan; the butler, Angelo Muscat.

The Episodes:

1. "The Arrival" (6-1-68) Guy Doleman, Virginia Maskell, Paul Eddington, Stephanie Randall
2. "Chimes of Big Ben" (6-8-68) Nadia Gray, Leo McKern, Finlay Currie, Richard Wattis
3. "A, B & C" (6-22-68) Katherine Kath, Sheila Allen, Peter Bowles
4. "Free for All" (6-29-68) Eric Portman, Rachel Herbert, George Benson, Harold Berens, John Cazabon
5. "Schizoid Man" (7-6-68) Jane Merrow, Anton Roger
6. "The General" (7-13-68) Colin Gordon, John Castle, Peter Howell, Betty McDowall
7. "Many Happy Returns" (7-20-68) Georgia Cookson, Donald Sinden, Patrick Cargill
8. "Dance of the Dead" (7-27-68) Marry Morris, Duncan Macrae, Norma West, Alan White, Denise Huckley
9. "Do Not Forsake Me" (8-3-68) Zena Walker, Clifford Evans, Nigel Stock, Hugo Schuster
10. "It's Your Funeral" (8-10-68) Derrin Nesbitt, Mark Eden, Annette Andre, Martin Miller, Mark Burns, Andre Van Gyseghem
11. "Checkmate" (8-17-68) Rosalie Crutchley, Ronald Radd, George Coulouris, Peter Wyngarde, Patricia Jessell
12. "A Change of Mind" (8-24-68) Angela Browne, John Sharpe, George Pravda, Kathleen Breck, Peter Swanick
13. "Hammer into Anvil" (8-31-68) Patrick Cargill, Basil Hoskins, Victor Maddern, Norman Space
14. "The Girl Who Was Death" (9-7-68) Justine Lord, Kenneth Griffith, Michael Brennan
15. "Once Upon a Time" (9-14-68) Leo McKern
16. "Fallout" (9-21-68) Leo McKern, Kenneth Griffin, Alexis Kanner

## THE CHAMPIONS

A blending of the supernatural and Cold War espionage, this British entry had its principals the beneficiaries of extrasensory powers and great physical prowess. Craig Stirling (Stuart Damon), Sharron Macready (Alexandra Bastedo) and Richard Barrett (William Gaunt) endure incredibly freezing temperatures (in "Operation Deep-Freeze"), surmount the forces of witchcraft (in "The Night People") and, on one occasion anyway (in "The Dark Island"), very possibly prevent World War III--all of this performed by relegating the fists in favor of telepathy. In the meantime, Tremayne, their organization ("Nemesis") head, displays the expected sense of amazement and perplexity.

The Regulars: Craig Stirling, Stuart Damon; Sharron Macready, Alexandra Bastedo; Richard Barrett, William Gaunt; Tremayne, Anthony Nicholls.

The Episodes:

1. "To Trap a Rat" (6-10-68) Guy Rolfe, Edina Ronay, Michael Standing, Kate O'Mara, Toke Townley
2. "The Dark Island" (6-17-68) Vladek Sheybal, Alan Gifford
3. "The Invisible Man" (6-24-68) Peter Wyngarde
4. "Get Me Out of Here" (7-1-68) Frances Cuka, Ronald Radd, Philip Madoc
5. "The Gilded Cage" (7-8-68) John Carson, Jennie Linden, Clinton Greyn
6. "The Mission" (7-15-68) Dermot Kelly, Anthony Bate
7. "Operation Deep-Freeze" (7-29-68) Patrick Wymark, Robert Urquhart
8. "Happening" (8-12-68) Michael Gough, Jack MacGowan, Grant Taylor
9. "The Night People" (8-19-68) Terence Alexander, Adrienne Cori, David Lodge, Anne Sharp
10. "The Silent Enemy" (9-9-68) Paul Maxwell, James Maxwell, Warren Stanhope, Marne Maitland

LAND OF THE GIANTS

      Irwin Allen's last science fiction series of the 1960s con-
cerns a 1983 plane crash on a "land of giants." The situations
these "little people" survivors encounter are obvious. In Gilbert
Ralston's and William Welch's "Ghost Town" our heroes have become the playthings of an unruly "giant" child. In Peter Packer's
"The Flight Plan" they are deceived by a fellow "little person"
who, not surprisingly, has been conspiring with the giants. At
least Howard Schwartz could be particularly (albeit necessarily)
innovative with his use of the camera; the same being true for
Jack Martin Smith and Roger E. Maus with their art direction.
John Williams composed the musical theme.

The Regulars: Captain Steve Burton, Gary Conway; Dan Erickson
        (co-pilot), Don Marshall; Betty Hamilton (stewardess),
        Heather Young; passengers, Mark (Don Matheson); Valerie
        (Deanna Lund); Fitzhugh (Kurt Kasznar); Barry (Stefan
        Arngrim).

The Episodes:

1. "The Crash" (9-22-68) Anne Dore, Don Watters
2. "Ghost Town" (9-29-68) Amber Flower
3. "Framed" (10-6-68) Paul Carr
4. "Underground" (10-20-68) John Abbott
5. "Terror-Go-Round" (11-3-68) Joseph Ruskin, Arthur Batanides
6. "The Flight Plan" (11-10-68) Linden Chiles
7. "Manhunt" (11-17-68) John Napier
8. "The Trap" (11-24-68) Morgan Jones
9. "The Creed" (12-1-68) Paul Fix, Henry Corden
10. "Double Cross" (12-8-68) Willard Sage, Lane Bradford
11. "The Wierd World" (12-22-68) Don Gazzaniga
12. "The Golden Cage" (12-29-68) Celeste Yarnell, Douglas
      Bank
13. "The Lost Ones" (1-5-69) Zalman King, Tommy Webb
14. "Brainwash" (1-12-69) Warren Stevens, Robert Dowdell,
      Leonard Stone
15. "The Bounty Hunter" (1-19-69) Paul Sorensen, Kimberly
      Beck
16. "On a Clear Night You Can See Earth" (1-26-69) Michael

Ansara
17. "Deadly Lodestone" (2-2-69) Paul Fix, Kevin Hagen
18. "The Night of the Thrombeldinbar" (2-16-69) Alfred Ryder, Jay Novello
19. "Seven Little Indians" (2-23-69) Kevin Hagen, Cliff Osmond
20. "Target: Earth" (3-2-69) Arthur Franz, Dee Hartford, Peter Mamakos
21. "Genius at Work" (3-9-69) Jacques Aubuchon, Ronny Howard
22. "Return of Inidu" (3-16-69) Jack Albertson, Peter Haskell
23. "Rescue" (3-23-69) Lee Meriwether, Dan Collier, Tom Reese
24. "Sabotage" (3-30-69) Robert Colbert, John Marley, Parley Baer
25. "Shell Game" (4-13-69) Larry Ward, Jan Shepard, Gary Dubin, Tol Avery
26. "The Chase" (4-20-69) Robert F. Lyons, Timothy Scott, Patrick Sullivan Burke

Second Season

27. "The Mechanical Man" (9-21-69) Broderick Crawford, Stuart Margolin
28. "Six Hours to Live" (9-28-69) Richard Anderson, Anne Seymour
29. "The Inside Rail" (10-5-69) Ben Blue, Arch Johnson
30. "Deadly Pawn" (10-12-69) Alex Dreier, John Zaremba
31. "The Unsuspected" (10-19-69) Leonard Stone
32. "Giants and All That Jazz" (10-26-69) Sugar Ray Robinson, Mike Mazurki
33. "Collector's Item" (11-2-69) Guy Stockwell, Robert H. Harris
34. "Every Dog Needs a Boy" (11-9-69) Michael Anderson Jr., Tom Nardini
35. "Chamber of Fear" (11-16-69) Cliff Osmond, Christopher Cary, Joan Freeman
36. "Comeback" (11-23-69) John Carradine, Jesse White, Olan Soule
37. "The Clones" (11-30-69) William Schallert, Sandra Giles
38. "A Place Called Earth" (12-7-69) Warren Stevens, Rex Holman, Jerry Douglas, Jerry Quarry
39. "Land of the Lost" (12-14-69) Nehemiah Persoff, Clint Ritchie
40. "Home Sweet Home" (12-21-69) Mort Mills, June Dayton, John Milford
41. "Our Man O'Reilly" (12-28-69) Alan Hale, Alan Bergmann
42. "Nightmare" (1-4-70) Yale Summers, Torin Thatcher
43. "Pay the Piper" (1-11-70) Peter Leeds
44. "The Secret City of Limbo" (1-18-70) Malachi Throne, Joseph Ruskin
45. "Panic" (1-25-70) Jack Albertson, Mark Richman, Diane McBain
46. "The Deadly Dart" (2-1-70) John Dehner, Madlyn Rhue
47. "Doomsday" (2-15-70) Francine York, Kevin Hagen, Charles

Dierkop
48. "A Small War" (2-22-70) Sean Kelly, Charles Drake
49. "The Marionettes" (3-1-70) Frank Ferguson, Victoria Vetri
50. "Wild Journey" (3-8-70) Bruce Dern, Sheila Mathews, Yvonne Craig
51. "Graveyard of Fools" (3-22-70) Albert Salmi, John Crawford

## THE OUTCASTS

Interesting, poignant and (for its time) novel post-Civil War western about an unsteady but necessary companionship between two bounty hunters--a former slave owner (Don Murray as Earl Corey) and a former slave (Otis Young as Jemal David). Its theme has subsequently undergone a comical variation with the James Garner/ Lou Gossett film Skin Game.

The Regulars: Earl Corey, Don Murray; Jemal David, Otis Young.

The Episodes:

1. [unknown title] (9-23-68) Slim Pickens, Burr De Benning, Gino Conforti, Warren Finnerty
2. "A Ride to Vengeance" (9-30-68) Charles McGraw, Diana Muldaur, Ken Lynch, Erik Holland, Frank Marth
3. "Three Ways to Die" (10-7-68) James Gregory
4. "The Understanding" (10-14-68) William Mims, Nico Minardos
5. "Take Your Lover in the Ring" (10-28-68) Gloria Foster, John Dehner, Virginia Gregg, Walter Coy
6. "The Heroes" (11-11-68) Royal Dano, Michael Margotta, James Westerfield
7. "My Name Is Jemal" (11-18-68) James Edwards, Arthur Franz, John Marley, Charles Dierkop, James Michelle, Walter Brooke, Roy Jenson
8. "The Night Riders" (11-25-68) Steve Ihnat, Larry Gates, Isabelle Cooley, Joan Hotchkis, Jeff Pomerantz
9. "The Heady Wine" (12-2-68) William C. Watson, Kay Reynolds, Logan Ramsey, Lou Frizzell, Jan Burrell
10. "The Man from Bennington" (12-16-68) Fritz Weaver, Michael Conrad, Kenneth Tobey, Hayden Rorke
11. "The Bounty Children" (12-23-68) Michael Burns, Charles Aidman, Dan Tobin, Linda Sue Risk
12. "They Shall Rise Up" (1-6-69) William Bramley, Sean McClory, Mort Mills, Frank Ramirez
13. "Alligator King" (1-20-69) Paul Mantee, William Wintersole, John Lawrence, Jerry Daniels, John War Eagle
14. "The Candidates" (1-27-69) Susan Howard, Grant Williams, Madeleine Sherwood, Art Metrano, Edward Faulkner, Bill Walker
15. "The Glory Wagon" (2-3-69) Jack Elam, Ezekial Williams, Bing Russell

16. "Act of Faith" (2-10-69) Brock Peters, Robert F. Simon, Karl Swenson, Ron Soble
17. "The Thin Edge" (2-17-69) Ida Lupino, Paul Fix, Harry Carey Jr., George Clifton, Ross Hagen
18. "Gideon" (2-24-69) Roscoe Lee Brown
19. "And Then There Was One" (3-3-69) Harvey Jason, Alejandro Rey, Arthur Hunnicutt
20. "Hung for a Lamb" (3-10-69) Tammy Grimes, Mike Road, Kevin Hagen, John Zaremba, Ed Peck
21. "A Time of Darkness" (3-24-69) A Martinez
22. "The Town That Wouldn't" (3-31-69) Ruth Roman, Pippa Scott, Tom Palmer, Robert F. Lyons, Hilarie Thompson, Leo Gordon, John Dennis, Michael Michaelian, Dennis Cross
23. "The Stalking Devil" (4-7-69) William Windom, Rodolfo Acosta, Robert Phillips
24. "Give Me Tomorrow" (4-21-69) Nancy Malone, Dick Sargent
25. "The Long Ride" (4-28-69) William Bassett
26. "How Tall Is Blood?" (5-5-69) Phil Bruns, H. M. Wynant, Lilyan Chauvin, Parley Baer, Rex Holman

THE MOD SQUAD

Aaron Spelling produced this study of three young rebels (Michael Cole as Pete Cochran, Peggy Lipton as Julie Barnes and Clarence Williams III as Linc Hayes) who find it within themselves to go with the system (some would call it apostasy, and in this series did) long enough to serve Los Angeles Police Captain Adam Greer (Tige Andrews). Three dynamic guest performances were those by Richard Dreyfuss and Lee Grant in "Mother of Sorrow," a painful teleplay of neglect and the vendetta which follows it; Jo Van Fleet, resplendent, as usual, as the much maligned teacher who champions the cause of sex education in schools in " 'A' Is for Annie."

The Regulars: Pete Cochran, Michael Cole; Lincoln Hayes, Clarence Williams III; Julie Barnes, Peggy Lipton; Captain Adam Greer, Tige Andrews.

The Episodes:

1. "The Teeth of the Barracuda" (9-24-68) Brooke Bundy, Fred Beir, Lonny Chapman, Noam Pitlik, Addison Powell
2. "Bad Man on Campus" (10-1-68) Clive Clerk, Norman Alden, Judy Pace, Booke Bradshaw, J. Pat O'Malley
3. "My, What a Pretty Bus" (10-8-68) Henry Jones
4. "When Smitty Comes Marching Home" (10-22-68) Lou Gossett, Valerie Allen, Edward Faulkner
5. "You Can't Tell the Players Without a Programmer" (10-29-68) Linda Marsh, Mark Goddard, Julie Adams, Byron Foulger, Jerry Harper

6. "A Time to Love--a Time to Cry" (11-12-68) Robert Lansing, Jerry Ayres, Harry Townes, Rex Reason
7. "Find Tara Chapman!" (11-19-68) Yvonne Craig, Della Reese, Gene Nelson, John Van Dreelen
8. "The Price of Terror" (11-26-68) Gail Kobe, James Best, Richard Bakalayan
9. "A Quiet Weekend in the Country" (12-3-68) James Gregory, Anna Capri, Dub Taylor, Joe Higgins, Clyde Ventura, Hal Baylor
10. "Love" (12-10-68) Diana Ewing, Arthur Franz, Nina Foch, Dee Pollock, Robert Yuro, Louise Lane, Isabell Sanford, Norman Stevens, Corey Fischer
11. "Twinkle, Twinkle, Little Starlet" (12-17-68) Richard Evans, Joan Van Ark, William Smithers, Alan Oppenheimer, Virginia Gregg, Norman Grabowski
12. "The Guru" (12-31-68) Jane Elliot, Adam Roarke, Max Julien, Dabney Coleman
13. "The Sunday Drivers" (1-7-69) Paul Carr, Woodrow Parfrey, Quentin Dean, Chick Chandler
14. "Hello Mother, My Name Is Julie" (1-14-69) Nan Martin, Leonard Stone, William Windom, Joseph Mell
15. "Flight Five Doesn't Answer" (1-21-69) Marvin Kaplan, Larry Casey, Whit Bissell, Will Kuluva, Murray MacLeod, Russ Conway
16. "Shell Game" (1-29-69) Michael Margotta, Jeff Pomerantz, John Carter, William Wintersole
17. "Fear Is the Bucking Horse" (2-4-69) Monte Markham, Ed Begley, Ross Elliott, Nina Shipman
18. "A Hint of Darkness, a Hint of Light" (2-11-69) Gloria Foster, John Milford, Lou Krugman, Virginia Gregg
19. "The Uptight Town" (2-18-69) Jason Evers, Cliff Osmond, Lou Gossett, Donna Baccala
20. "A Reign of Guns" (2-25-69) J. D. Cannon, Sean Garrison, Glen Wilder
21. "A Run for the Money" (3-11-69) Tom Bosley, Chuck Roberson, Leslie Ann Warren, Bob Hoy, Lee Duncan, Ed McNamara
22. "Child of Sorrow, Child of Light" (3-18-69) Ida Lupino, Dan Travanty, Heidi Vaughn, William Zuckert
23. "Keep the Faith, Baby" (3-25-69) Sammy Davis Jr., Ron Hayes, Robert Duvall, William Schallert
24. "Captain Greer, Call Surgery" (4-1-69) Kim Hamilton, Sheilah Wells, Edward Andrews, David Opatoshu
25. "Peace Now--Arly Blau" (4-8-69) Christopher Connelly, Kevin Hagen, Hal Lynch, Ross Elliott, Noah Keen
26. "A Seat by the Window" (4-15-69) Julie Gregg, Bob Hopkins, Tom Heaton, Wayne McLaren, John Beck, Tiffany Bolling, Ellen Moss, Bill Quinn

Second Season

27. "The Girl in Chair Nine" (9-23-69) Cesare Danova, Sylvia Hayes, Robert E. Cannon, John Stephenson

28. "My Name Is Manolette" (9-30-69) Fabian Gregory, Rex
    Holman, Bruce Watson, Paul Sorensen, Alma Beltran
29. "An Eye for an Eye" (10-7-69) Nancy Gates, William
    Vaughn, Arthur Batanides, Francis De Sales
30. "Ride the Man Down" (10-14-69) Brenda Scott, Lynn Bolden
    Richard Anderson
31. "To Linc--With Love" (10-21-69) Janet MacLachlin, Allan
    Melvin, Mia Fullmore, Fred Pinkard
32. "Lisa" (11-4-69) Carolyn Jones, Troy Melton, Arthur Franz
    Joseph Ruskin, Barney Phillips, Herbie Faye
33. "Confrontation!" (11-11-69) Simon Oakland, Sid McCoy,
    Robert F. Simon, B. J. Mason, Ta Ta Nisha, Maurice
    Warfield, Jorge Moreno
34. "Willie Poor Boy" (11-18-69) Don Travanty, Joe Don Baker
    Stanley Adams, Wesley Lau, Arthur Peterson
35. "The Death of Wild Bill Hannachek" (11-25-69) Murray
    MacLeod, Tyne Daly, Tim O'Kelly, Sheb Wooley, James
    Griffith, Bob Swan, Will Mackenzie
36. "A Place to Run, a Heart to Hide In" (12-2-69) Don Defore
    Paul Lukather, Tom Tully, Chris Stone, Geoffrey Deuel,
    Mike McGreevy, Ben Archibek
37. "The Healer" (12-9-69) Paul Richards, Doreen Land, Dway
    Hickman
38. "In This Corner--Sol Albert" (12-16-69) Marvin Kaplan,
    Noam Pitlik, Loretta Leversee, Vince Howard, Steve
    Franken, Sheldon Collins, Austin Stoker
39. "Never Give the Fuzz an Even Break" (12-23-69) Maurice
    Evans, Frank Wilcox, Louise Fitch, William Smith, Amaz
    Strickland, Harriet E. MacGibbons
40. "The Debt" (12-30-69) Nehemiah Persoff, Peter Brown, Ja
    Novello, Solomon Sturges, Ross Elliott, Marj Dusay
41. "Sweet Child of Terror" (1-6-70) Martine Bartlett, Robert
    Salvio, Dennis Patrick, Marjorie Bennett, Yolanda Gon-
    zalez
42. "The King of Empty Cups" (1-20-70) Noel Harrison, Simon
    Scott, Renne Jarrett
43. "A Town Called Sincere" (1-27-70) Ford Rainey, Tom Ster
    J. Kenneth Campbell, Lisa Gaye
44. "The Exile" (2-3-70) Nico Minardos, Ben Aliza
45. "Survival House" (2-10-70) Sammy Davis Jr., John Roper,
    William Smithers, Billy Daniels, Mira Waders, Martin
    Braddock, Isabelle Cooley
46. "Mother of Sorrow" (2-17-70) Richard Dreyfuss, Lee Grant
    Harry Basch, Sherry Miles
47. "The Deadly Sin" (2-24-70) Lynn Loring, Bert Freed, Don
    Dubbins
48. "A Time for Remembering" (3-3-70) Gary Vinson
49. "Return to Darkness, Return to Light" (3-17-70) Gloria
    Foster, Ivan Dixon, Karl Swenson
50. "Call Back Yesterday" (3-24-70) Edmon Ryan, Anita Louis
    Margot Kidder, James Farley, Mark Goddard, Morgan
    Sterne
51. "Should Auld Acquaintance Be Forgot!" (3-31-70) Frank

Converse, Edward Asner, Paul Stewart
52. "The Loser" (4-7-70) Diana Muldaur, David Cassidy, Frank Aletter, Charles Aidman

## Third Season

53. "Long Road Home" (9-22-70) Anjanette Comer, Lou Antonio, Bruce Watson
54. "See the Eagles Dying" (9-29-70) Lane Bradbury, Paul Carr, Judd Lawrence, James Nusser, Ross Elliott
55. "Who Are the Keepers, Who Are the Inmates?" (10-6-70) Richard Kiley, Harry Basch, Booth Colman, Jerry Summers, Meg Foster, Richard Shello
56. " 'A' Is for Annie" (10-13-70) Jo Van Fleet, Ron Hayes, Edmund Gilbert, Hank Jones, Jewel Blanch, Cindy Eilbacher
57. "The Song of Willie" (10-20-70) Sammy Davis Jr. , Jed Allen, Lola Falana, Lawrence Cook, Norman Alden
58. "Search and Destroy" (10-27-70) Michael Baseleon, Brad David, Steve Ihnat, Bill Zuckert, Kathy Lloyd, Bruce Glover, Gareth McClain, Wayne Storm
59. "Just Ring the Bell Once" (11-3-70) Lawrence Dane, Brian Dewey, Millie Lawrence, Linda Meiklejohn
60. "Welcome to the Human Race, Levi Frazee!" (11-10-70) Cal Bellini, Bo Svenson, Robert Foulk, Veleka Gray, Edgar Buchanan
61. "A Far Away Place So Near" (11-17-70) Ben Murphy, Mike Margotta, Pilar Seurat, Tom Nardini, Bo Hopkins
62. "A Time of Hyacinths" (12-1-70) Charles McGraw, Cynthia Hull, Warren Stevens, Vincent Price
63. "The Judas Trap" (12-8-70) Don Porter, Barry Brown, Marj Dusay, Richard Webb, Sid McCoy
64. "Fever" (12-15-70) Robert Viharo, Brooke Bundy, Frank Maxwell, David Mutch
65. "Is There Anyone Left in Santa Paula?" (12-29-70) Fernando Lamas, Bert Santos, Victor Millan, Amparo Pilar, Ricardo Romanos
66. "A Short Course in War" (1-5-71) Bob Balaban, Jack Bender, Mike Warren, Paul Lent, Josephine Hutchinson
67. "Kicks Incorporated" (1-12-71) Jack Cassidy, Barbara Rush, Diane McBain, Cal Wilson, Richard Kim Milford
68. "A Bummer for R. J. " (1-19-71) Carl Betz, Annette O'Toole
69. "The Hot, Hot Car" (1-26-71) Greg Mullavey, Arthur Franz, Robert Donner, John Gruber, Lloyd Battista, Frank Farmer
70. "Suffer, Little Children" (2-9-71) Kaz Garas, Sheldon Allman, Jill Choder, Jenny Sullivan
71. "Is That Justice? No, It's Law" (2-16-71) Nehemiah Persoff, Burr De Benning
72. "A Double for Danger" (2-23-71) Michael Ansara, Ray Walston, Ron Soble, Ben Frank
73. "Welcome to Our City" (3-2-71) Virginia Gregg, John Carter, Billy Bowles, Allan Garfield, Edward Faulkner
74. "The Comeback" (3-9-71) Sugar Ray Robinson, Hilly Hicks,

Rod McCary, Rocky Graziano, Ernie Indian Red Lopez
75. "We Spy" (3-16-71) Rene Auberjonois, Jay Novello, William Smith, Joanna Phillips
76. "The Price of Love" (3-23-71) Paul Richards, Barry Atwater, Clint Howard

Fourth Season

77. The Sentinels" (9-14-71) Scott Marlowe, Hal England, Lynne Marta, Stephen Hudis
78. "Cricket" (9-21-71) Lee Harcourt Montgomery, Susan Howard, Victor Holchak, Andrea Cagan, Paul Kent
79. "Home Is the Streets" (9-28-71) Cameron Mitchell, Buddy Lester, Brooke Bundy, Flora Plumb
80. "Survival" (10-5-71) John Rubinstein, Karen Huston, Elliott Street
81. "Color of Laughter, Color of Tears" (10-12-71) Michael Baseleon, Anne Archer, Dan Ferron, Charles Briggs, Edward Asner
82. "The Medicine Men" (10-19-71) Robert Foxworth, Lou Antonio, Burr De Benning, Billy Dee Williams
83. "The Sands of Anger" (10-26-71) Shelly Novack, Arthur Franz, Stewart Bradley, Tony Dow, Steve Carlson, Walter Edmiston, Betty Ann Rees
84. "The Poisoned Mind" (11-2-71) Jack Collins, Murray MacLeod, Laraine Stephens
85. "Exit the Closer" (11-9-71) Larry Blyden, Austin Willis, Sandy Kenyon, Ross Elliott, Ruta Lee, Gloria Mason, William Long Jr.
86. "Whatever Happened to Linc Hayes?" (11-16-71) Lance Taylor Sr., Lee De Broux
87. "And a Little Child Shall Bleed Them" (11-23-71) Milton Berle, Keenan Wynn, Juen Dayton, Henry Jones, Eddie Ryder
88. "The Loser" (11-30-71) Martin Sheen, Harold Gould, William Smith
89. "Death of a Nobody" (12-7-71) Brock Peters, Perry Lopez, Martin E. Brooks, Meg Foster
90. "Feet of Clay" (12-14-71) Desi Arnaz Jr., Kevin Dobson, Robert Donner, Wayne Storm, Gary Dubin, Alan Oppenheimer
91. "I Am My Brother's Keeper" (1-4-72) Guy Stockwell, Linda Marsh, John Kerr, Brooke Mills, Jack Ging
92. "Deal with the Devil" (1-11-72) Leslie Nielsen, Vikki Carr
93. "Kill Gently, Sweet Jessie" (1-18-72) Al Freeman Jr., Mort Mills, Glynn Turman, Leslie Uggams
94. "Shockwave" (1-25-72) Michael Anderson Jr., Lynn Loring, Elliott Montgomery
95. "No More Oak Leaves for Ernie Holland" (2-1-72) Cal Bellini, Henry Darrow, Robert Pine
96. "The Cave" (2-8-72) Karl Swenson, Patricia George
97. "The Wild Weekend" (2-15-72) Brenda Scott, Stephen Young, Dennis Patrick, Nicholas Cortland

98. "The Tangled Web" (2-22-72) Bobby Sherman, Frank Marth, Norman Alden, Judy Strangis
99. "Outside Position" (2-29-72) John Calvin, Simon Scott, Woodrow Parfrey
100. "Big George" (3-7-72) Andy Griffith, Sharon Acker, Buddy Pantsari, Stanley Kamel, Michael-James Wixted

Fifth Season

101. "The Connection" (9-14-72) Stefanie Powers, Barbara McNair, Edward Asner, Bradford Dillman, Robert Reed, Cesar Romero, Cleavon Little, Richard Pryor, Claudia McNeil, Gene Washington
102. "The Thunder Makers" (9-21-72) Bobby Sherman, John Lasell, Joe Hooker, Paul Carr, Frank Ramirez, John McLiam
103. "Yesterday's Ashes" (9-28-72) Jo Ann Harris, Robert Pine, Nino Candido, Ivor Francis
104. "A Gift for Jenny" (10-5-72) Paul Richards, Del Monroe, Bo Svenson, Gwenn Mitchell, Victoria George, Ralph James, Charlen Polite, Booker Bradshaw, Norman Bartold
105. "Taps, Play It Louder" (10-12-71) Peter Hooten, Michele Nicholas, Ann Doran, Robert F. Simon, Patricia McAnery
106. "Eyes of the Beholder" (10-19-72) Beverly Garland, Janet Margolin, Richard Rust
107. "Good Times Are Just Memories" (10-26-72) Leif Erickson, Tyne Daly, Sam Elliott, Tony Geary
108. "Corbey" (11-2-72) Nehemiah Persoff, Jane Byron, Russell Arms, Simon Scott, Nick Georgiade, Mitchell Silberman
109. "Can You Hear Me Out There?" (11-9-72) Lou Gossett, Tina Andrews, Cal Bellini, Larry D. Mann, Ed Call, Kim Hamilton
110. "Another Final Game" (11-16-72) Clu Gulager, Zara Cully, Woodrow Parfrey, Beverlee McKinsey
111. "Crime Club" (11-23-72) Mark Slade, Robert Lipton, Pamela Shoop, Hilly Hicks, Joe Renteria
112. "The Twain" (11-30-72) Fritz Weaver, Edward Bell, Charles Seel, Vic Tayback, Victoria Recimo, Allan Arbus, John Haymer
113. "Belinda--End of Little Miss Bubble Gum" (12-7-72) Ruth Roman, Cathy Burns, Dane Clark, John Karlen, Robert Balaban, Len Lesser, Anthony Jones
114. "Kristie" (12-14-72) Michael Anderson Jr., Robert Patten, Jed Allen, Jean Hall, Debbie Lytton, William Bassett
115. "Sanctuary" (12-21-72) Glenn Corbett, Victor Buono, John Launer, Hal England
116. "Run, Lincoln, Run" (1-4-73) James A. Watson Jr., Emily Yaney, Justin Smith, Nick Lewis, Stefan Gierasch, Elliott Street, June Dayton, Taylor Lacher
117. "Don't Kill My Child" (1-18-73) Nina Foch, Marlyn Mason, Murray MacLeod, Ty Wilson
18. "Death in High Places" (1-25-73) Fernando Lamas, Jim

           Backus, Bing Russell, Anna Capri, Carmen Zapata, Pris-
           cilla Garcia
119.   "Put Out the Welcome Mat for Death"   (2-1-73)   Howard Duff
           Martha Scott, Kristina Holland
120.   "Scion of Death"   (2-8-73)   Don Porter, Julie Adams, Larry
           Golden, Ross Elliott, Dennis Dugan, Mitzi Hoag
121.   "The Night Holds Terror"   (2-15-73)   Brooke Bundy, Ben
           Piazza, Richard Dreyfuss, Libby Alexander
122.   "Cry Uncle"   (2-22-73)   Theodore Bikel, Mills Watson,
           Gino Conforti, Dena Dietrich, Geoffrey Lewis, Bryn
           Morgan, Kathleen Freeman
123.   "And Once for My Baby"   (3-1-73)   Ed Nelson, Linda Marsh,
           Rex Holman, John Kerr, Robert Phillips, Lee McCain,
           Cal Bartlett


THE OUTSIDER

       Roy Huggins once again ventured into the private detective
genre.   The hero of this one is David Ross (Darren McGavin).

The Regulars: David Ross, Darren McGavin.

The Episodes:

   1.   "For Members Only ..."   (9-18-68)   Warren Stevens, Kathie
           Browne, Timothy Carey
   2.   "What Flowers Daisies Are"   (9-25-68)   Farley Granger
   3.   "Along Came a Spider"   (10-2-68)   Marsha Hunt, Claude
           Akins
   4.   "Wide Place in the Road"   (10-9-68)   Louise Latham, Verne
           Breckenridge
   5.   "As Cold as Ashes"   (10-16-68)   Keye Luke, Don Knight,
           Kate Woodville
   6.   "A Time to Run"   (10-30-68)   Don Stroud, Brenda Scott
   7.   "Love Is Under L"   (11-6-68)   Robert H. Harris, Simon Oak-
           land, Will Koopman
   8.   "The Twenty Thousand Dollar Carrot"   (11-13-68)   Pat Har-
           rington, Sandra Smith
   9.   "One Long-Stemmed American Beauty"   (11-20-68)   Marie
           Windsor, Betty Field, Julie Adams
  10.   "I Can't Hear You Scream"   (11-27-68)   James Edwards,
           Juanita Moore, Ena Hartman
  11.   "Tell It Like It Was ... and You're Dead"   (12-4-68)   Jacki
           Coogan, Marilyn Maxwell, Ted Knight, Whitney Blake
  12.   "The Land of the Fox"   (12-18-68)   Susan Oliver, Russell
           Thorson, Kent McCord
  13.   "There Was a Little Girl"   (12-25-68)   Joan Blondell
  14.   "The Girl from Missouri"   (1-8-69)   Rick Jason, Mariette
           Hartley, Jaye P. Morgan
  15.   "The Secret of Mareno Bay"   (1-15-69)   Walter Brooke,
           Estelle Winwood, Larry Linville, Pippa Scott, Grace Lee

Whitney
16. "The Old School Tie" (1-22-69) Aldo Ray
17. "A Bowl of Cherrie" (1-29-69) Scott Marlowe
18. "Behind God's Back" (2-5-69) Thomas Gomez, Virginia
    Mayo, Anna Capri
19. "Take the Key and Lock Him Up" (2-12-69) Roger Perry,
    Bert Freed
20. "The Flip Side" (2-26-69) Carrie Snodgrass, Nicol William-
    son
21. "Handle with Care" (3-5-69) Paul Stewart
22. "All the Social Graces" (3-12-69) Geraldine Brooks
23. "A Lot of Muscle" (3-26-69) James Gregory, Susan O'Con-
    nell
24. "Periwinkle Blue" (4-2-69) Lois Nettleton
25. "Service for One" (4-9-69) Henry Jones, William Windom
26. "Through a Stained-Glass Window" (4-16-69) Walter Burke,
    Arch Johnson, Ruth McDevitt


HAWAII FIVE-O

Moody law enforcement drama of a phenomenally successful
investigative unit with dynamic Steve McGarrett (Jack Lord) at the
helm. Its frequent journeys into violence are a perfect discordant
against the Hawaiian paradise. Some superior recurring performances: Nehemiah Persoff as a mafia chieftain; Luther Adler,
Harold Gould and Robert Drivas as father, son and grandson Vashon whose criminal reign is the study of the three-part "V for
Vashon."

The Regulars: Steve McGarrett, Jack Lord; Danny Williams,
    James MacArthur; Chin Ho, Kam Fong; Kono, Zulu (to
    episode of 3/7/72); Jenny, Peggy Sherman; Ben, Al Har-
    rington (with episode of 9/12/72); Duke, Herman Wede-
    meyer (with episode of 9/12/72); Governor, Richard Den-
    ning; Doc, Al Eben.

The Episodes:

1. "Full Fathom Five" (9-26-68) Kevin McCarthy, Louise Troy,
   Patricia Smith, Arlene McQuade
2. "One Day We Shall Be Strangers in Our Own Land" (10-3-
   68) Simon Oakland, Jeanne Bates, Paul Kent, Anne Barton
3. [unknown title] (10-10-68) Harold J. Stone, Sal Mineo,
   Sam Melville, Cliff Eblen, Bobby George
4. "Samurai" (10-17-68) Ricardo Montalban, Morgan White,
   Karen Norris, Caroline Barrett
5. [unknown title] (11-7-68) John Larch, Vivi Janiss
6. "The 24 Karat Kill" (11-14-68) Kaz Garas, Paul Richards,
   Marj Dusay, Richard Loo
7. "The Ways of Love" (11-21-68) James Patterson, Josie

Over, Don Knight, Robert Harker
8. [unknown title] (12-5-68) Tommy Sands, Sandra Smith, Robert Random
9. [unknown title] (12-12-68) Johnny Crawford, Anne Helm, Jonathan Lippe, Will Kuluva
10. "Deathwatch" (12-25-68) Nehemiah Persoff, Maura McGiveney, James Shigeta, Kent Bowman
11. [unknown title] (1-1-69) Denny Miller, Ron Feinberg, Robert M. Luck, Marla Kyo
12. "King of the Hill" (1-8-69) Yaphet Kotto, Richard Bull, Jeff Corey, Lawrence Temple, L. Q. Jones
13. "Up Tight" (1-15-69) Ed Flanders, Brenda Scott, John McLiam, James Bertino
14. [unknown title] (1-22-69) Jackie Coogan, Soon Taik-Oh, David Opatoshu, Nancy Kovack
15. "The Box" (1-29-69) Gerald S. O'Loughlin, Gavin McLeod, Robert Doyle, R. G. Armstrong, Victor Sen Yung
16. [unknown title] (2-5-69) Farley Granger, Paul Collins, Jeanette Nolan
17. "Golden Boy in Black Trunks" (2-12-69) Frank De Kova, Mark Richman, Jesse White, Morgan White, Jean Hale, Charles Lampkin, Hal Baylor
18. [unknown title; Part I] (2-19-69) Joanne Linville, John Carter, David Sheiner, Bill Zuckert, Nancy Malone, William Schallert, Bartlett Robinson, Beah Richards
19. [unknown title; Part II] (2-26-69) as above
20. "Not That Much Difference" (3-5-69) Ann Prentiss, Lee Paul, Stewart Moss
21. [unknown title] (3-12-69) Antoinette Bower, Gerald S. O'Loughlin, Than Wyenn, Robert Errecarte
22. [unknown title] (3-19-69) John Marley

Second Season

23. "A Thousand Pardons, You're Dead" (9-24-69) Barbara Luna, James Hong, Harry Guardino, Barbara Nichols
24. "To Hell with Babe Ruth" (10-1-69) Mark Lenard, Sheila Larkin, Will Kuluva
25. [unknown title] (10-8-69) Will Geer, Khigh Dhiegh, Sabrina Scharf
26. "Just Lucky, I Guess" (10-15-69) Albert Paulsen, Herb Vigran, John Randolph, Anne Helm
27. "Savage Sunday" (10-22-69) Henry Silva, Tom Nardini, Julie Gregg
28. "A Bullet for McGarrett" (10-29-69) Eric Braeden, Khigh Dhiegh, Sheila Larkin, Marian McAndrews
29. "Sweet Terror" (11-5-69) Philip Ahn, Theodore Bikel, Soon Taik-Oh
30. "The King Kamehameha Blues" (11-12-69) Brandon De Wilde, Jennifer Leak, Vince Eder
31. [unknown title] (11-19-69) Marj Dusay, Dick Brady
32. "All the King's Horses" (11-26-69) Lyle Bettger
33. [unknown title] (12-3-69) Frank Silvera, Titos Vandis, Joe

De Santis, Cynthia Hull
34. "The Devil and Mr. Frog" (12-10-69) Frank Marth, Geoffrey Thorpe, William Zuckert, Laurie Main
35. "The Joker's Wild, Man, Wild ... " (12-17-69) Kaz Garas, Beverly McKinsey, Eddie Firestone, Lani Kai
36. [unknown title] (12-24-69) William Windom, Philip Pine, Jackie Coogan, Don Mundell
37. "Blind Tiger" (12-31-69) Peggy Ryan, Marion Ross, Robert Edwards, Bob Gleason
38. "Bored, She Hung Herself" (1-7-70) Don Quine, William Smithers, Pamela Murphy
39. "Run, Johnny, Run" (1-14-70) Jack Ging, Marcia Browne, Christopher Walkin
40. "Killer Bee" (1-21-70) Jeff Pomerantz, David Arkin
41. "The One with the Gun" (1-28-70) Arthur Franz, John Colicos, Julie Gregg, Jack Soo
42. "Cry Lie!" (2-4-70) Martin Sheen, George Petrie, Evelyn Carlson
43. "Most Likely to Murder" (2-11-70) Tom Skerritt, Sam Melville, Jennifer Billingsley
44. [unknown title] (2-18-70) Charles Aidman, Pilar Seurat, Ronald Long, Fred Beir
45. [unknown title; Part I] (2-25-70) Ed Flanders, Loretta Swit, Karl Swenson, Dana Elcar, Joseph Sirola
46. [unknown title; Part II] (3-4-70) as above
47. "Kiss the Queen Good-Bye" (3-11-70) Joanne Linville, Christopher Cary

## Third Season

48. "And a Time to Die ... " (9-16-70) Gerald S. O'Loughlin, Khigh Dhiegh, Donald Moffatt
49. "Trouble in Mind" (9-23-70) Nancy Wilson, Mort Stevens, Harry Guardino, Milton Selzer
50. "The Second Bullet" (9-30-70) John Marley, Eric Braeden, Charlene Polite
51. "Time and Memories" (10-7-70) Diana Muldaur, Martin Sheen, Edward Andrews, Kathy Cannon
52. "The Guarnerius Caper" (10-14-70) Ed Flanders, Albert Paulsen, Anthony James
53. "Forces of Waves" (10-28-70) Dewey Martin, James Daris, John Vernon, Linda Marsh
54. "The Reunion" (11-4-70) Simon Oakland, Joe Maross, Barry Atwater, Teru Shimada
55. "The Late John Louisiana" (11-11-70) Don Stroud, Al Harrington, Marianne McAndrew, Alfred Ryder
56. "The Last Eden" (11-18-70) Ray Danton, Paul Stevens, Robert M. Luck
57. "Over 50? Steal" (11-25-70) Hume Cronyn, John Hunt
58. "Beautiful Screamer" (12-2-70) Lloyd Bochner, Anne Archer, Laraine Stephens, Valerie Holmes
59. "The Payoff" (12-9-70) Warren Vanders, Madlyn Rhue, Albert Salmi, Joyce Van Patten

60. [unknown title] (12-16-70) Monte Markham
61. "Paniolo" (12-30-70) Frank Silvera, Royal Dano, Marilyn Chris
62. "Ten Thousand Diamonds and a Heart" (1-6-71) Tim O'Connor, Paul Stewart, Logan Ramsey
63. "The Ransom" (1-20-71) Andrew Duggan, Lloyd Gough, Ron Hayes, Peter Bonerz
64. "F.O.B. Honolulu" [Part I] (1-27-71) Khigh Dhiegh, John McMartin, Monte Landis, Joseph Sirola, Sabrina Scharf, Roger C. Carmel
65. "F.O.B. Honolulu" [Part II] (2-3-71) as above
66. "The Gunrunner" (2-10-71) Paul Burke, George Murdock, Marian McCargo, Arthur Batanides
67. "Dear Enemy" (2-17-71) Vera Miles, Gary Collins, Dub Taylor, John Lupton
68. "The Bomber and Mrs. Moroney" (2-24-71) Mark Jenkins, Hope Summers, Roland Maauaro
69. "The Grandstand Play" [Part I] (3-3-71) Elliott Street, Josie Over, Pernell Roberts, Barry Atwater, Don Chastain
70. "The Grandstand Play" [Part II] (3-10-71) as above

Fourth Season

71. "Highest Castle, Deepest Grave" (9-14-71) Herbert Lom, Jeff Corey, France Nuyen, Wilfred Keale
72. [unknown title] (9-21-71) Henry Darrow, Ron Feinberg, Beth Brickell
73. "3000 Crooked Miles to Honolulu" (10-5-71) Buddy Ebsen, David Canary, Judi Meredith
74. "Two Doves and Mr. Heron" (10-12-71) Vic Morrow, John Ritter
75. "... And I Want Some Candy and a Gun That Shoots" (10-19-71) Michael Burns, Jeanne Cooper
76. [unknown title] (10-26-71) Barney Phillips, James Hong, Marion Ross, Michael Strong, Ward Benson, Don Chastain
77. "For a Million, Why Not?" (11-2-71) Robert Fields, Sam Melville, Jack Kruschen, Leigh Christian
78. [unknown title] (11-9-71) Jackie Cooper, Lou Antonio, Loretta Leversee
79. "Rest in Peace, Somebody" (11-16-71) Norman Alden, Clarence Aina
80. "A Matter of Mutual Concern" (11-23-71) David Opatoshu, Mari Marno
81. "Nine, Ten, You're Dead" (11-30-71) Moses Gunn, Albert Paulsen, Robert Costa, Frank Webb, Mama Luna, Henry Porter
82. "Wednesday, Ladies Free" (12-14-71) Monte Markham, Soon Taik-Oh, Sheilah Wells, Marie Windsor
83. "Odd Man In" (12-28-71) Hume Cronyn
84. "Bait Once, Bait Twice" (1-4-72) Loretta Swit, James Olson, Malachi Throne
85. "The Ninety-Second War" [Part I] (1-11-72) Donald Pleasence, Dana Wynter
86. "The Ninety-Second War" [Part II] (1-18-72) as above
87. [unknown title] (1-25-72) Lee Paul, Murray MacLeod

88. "While You're at It, Bring in the Moon" (2-1-72) Barry Sullivan, Fred Ball, Ed Flanders, H. M. Wynant, Milton Selzer, Steve Merrick
89. [unknown title] (2-8-72) Ray Danton, Jason Evers, Jay Robinson
90. "Good Night, Baby--Time to Die" (2-15-72) Beth Brickett, William Watson
91. "Didn't We Meet at a Murder?" (2-22-72) Joanna Barnes, Bill Edwards, Simon Oakland
92. "Follow the White Brick Road" (2-29-72) David Birney, Mark Jenkins, David Doyle, Moki Palacio
93. "R&R&R" (3-7-72) Alan Vint, James Davidson, Richard Le Pore

Fifth Season

94. [unknown title] (9-12-72) Michael Ansara, Glenn Cannon, George Chakiris, Lorraine Stevens
95. "Death Wish on Tantalus Mountain" (9-19-72) Ricardo Montalban, Wendell Martin, Diana Muldaur, Michael Margotta
96. "You Don't Have to Kill to Get Rich--But It Helps" (9-26-72) William Shatner, Ric Marlow, Bill Edwards, Wisa D'Orso
97. [unknown title] (10-3-72) John Rubinstein, Louise Latham, James Simpson, Dennis Redfield
98. [unknown title] (10-10-72) Khigh Dhiegh, Soon Taik-Oh, Daniel Kamekona, Bob Nelson
99. "Fools Die Twice" (10-17-72) Clu Gulager, Michael Conrad, Anita Alberts, Sam Edwards
100. [unknown title] (10-24-72) Linden Chiles, Lou Frizzell, Mary Frann, Dirk Benedict
101. "Journey Out of Limbo" (10-31-72) Philip Ahn, Keenan Wynn, Lorna Ho, Sam Peters
102. "V for Vashon: The Son" [Part I] (11-14-72) Robert Drivas, Harold Gould, Luther Adler, John Beatty, John Stalker, Wisa D'Orso
103. "V for Vashon: The Father" [Part II] (11-21-72) as above
104. "V for Vashon: The Patriarch" [Part III] (11-28-72) as above
105. [unknown title] (12-5-72) Manie Tupou, Cris Callow, Patrick Adiarte, Henry Bal
106. "I'm a Family Crook--Don't Shoot" (12-19-72) Andy Griffith, Bob Basso, Joyce Van Patten, Kimberly Louis, Bryan Da Silva, Seth Sakai
107. "The Child Stealers" (1-2-73) Richard Hatch, Meg Foster, Richard Anderson, Jack Hogan
108. [unknown title] (1-9-73) Richard Collier, Patty Duke, Carol Lawrence, Larry Kert, Lane Bradford, Glenn Cannon
109. "The Listener" (1-16-73) Robert Foxworth, Linda Ryan, Greg Mullavey, Radames Pera
110. [unknown title] (1-23-73) Monte Markham, Sandra Smith, Madlyn Rhue, Douglas Kennedy, Richard Brady, Lawrence Montaigne

111. "The Odd Lot Caper" (1-30-73) Richard Basehart, Ron
       Hayes, William Bigelow, John Farias, Jack Hogan, Daws
       Dawson
112. "Will the Real Mr. Winkler Please Die?" (2-6-73) Nehe-
       miah Persoff, Sally Thompson, Malachi Throne, Mark
       Lenard
113. [unknown title] (2-13-73) Nina Foch, Tisha Sterling, Ron
       Feinberg, Jackie Coogan, Brook Graham, Josie Over
114. [unknown title] (2-20-73) Milton Selzer, Leonard Stone,
       Douglas Kennedy, Seth Sakai, Mitch Mitchell, Carol Kai
115. [unknown title] (2-27-73) Irene Tsu, Simon Oakland, Erik
       Estrada, Bob Turnbull
116. "The Diamond That Nobody Stole" (3-6-73) Eric Braeden,
       Melvin Cobb, Beulah Qui, Frank Trott
117. [unknown title] (3-13-73) Edward Binns, Glenn Cannon,
       Paul Camen, Arthur Malet, Susan Berger, Douglas Ken-
       nedy

Sixth Season

118. "Hookman" (9-11-73) Jay J. Armes
119. "Draw Me a Killer" (9-18-73) Audrey Totter, Jean Tar-
       rant, Elliott Street, Susan Foster, Nora Marlowe, George
       Kennedy
120. "Charter for Death" (9-25-73) Nehemiah Persoff, Bert
       Convy, Jeannine Brown, Norman Dupont
121. "One Big Happy Family" (10-2-73) Slim Pickens, Robyn
       Millan, Barbara Baxley, Ric Marlow, Bo Hopkins,
       Lynette Kim
122. "The Sunday Torch" (10-9-73) Michael Anderson Jr., Lyle
       Bettger, Tom Simcox, Jo Pruden
123. "Murder Is a Taxing Affair" (10-16-73) Don Porter, Sally
       Kirkland, Jenny Sullivan, Jack Dodson
124. "Tricks Are No Treats" (10-23-73) Glynn Turman, Wilfred
       Keale, Gregory Sierra, Ron Glass, Pat Morita, Seth
       Sakai
125. "Why Wait 'Till Uncle Kevin Dies?" (10-30-73) Lawrence
       Pressman
126. "Flash of Color, Flash of Death" (11-6-73) Don Knight,
       George Herman, Lynne Kimoto, Al Avalon
127. "A Bullet for Diablo" (11-13-73) A Martinez, Richard
       Yniguez, Edith Diaz, Richard Angarola
128. "The Finishing Touch" (11-20-73) George Voskovec, Lynn
       Carlin, Glenn Cannon, Linda Ryan, Seth Sakai, Kent
       Bowman
129. "Anybody Can Build a Bomb" (11-27-73) Lew Ayres
130. "Try to Die on Time" (12-4-73) Jack Carter
131. "The $100,000. Nickle" (12-11-73) Victor Buono
132. "The Flip Side Is Death" (12-18-73) Peter Haskell, Don
       Stroud, Robert Harker, Larry Goeas, Gerald Waialae,
       Frank Liu
133. "The Banzai Pipeline" (1-1-74)
134. "One Born Every Minute" (1-8-74) Ed Flanders, Lynette

Mettey, Michael Strong, John Stalker, Doug Mossman, Tommy Fujiwara
135. "Secret Witness" (1-15-74) Cindy Williams, Mark Lenard, Mark Jenkins, Ted Scott, Mark Gordon, Samuel Peters
136. "Death with Father" (1-22-74) Andrew Duggan, Kwan Hi Lim, Peter Strauss, Janice Wu, Richard Rivera, Seth Sakai
137. "Murder with a Golden Touch" (1-29-74) Peter Donat, James Davidson, James J. Sloyan, John Mamo, John Orchard, Peter Carew
138. "Nightmare in Blue" (2-5-74) John Beck, Katherine Justice, Elissa Dulce, Alan Fudge
139. "Mother's Deadly Helper" (2-12-74) Anthony Zerbe, Casey Kasem, Glenn Cannon, Frank Cady, Ted Scott, Richard Villard
140. "Killer at Sea" (2-19-74) John Byner, William Devane, Peter Leeds, Keene Curtis, Gail Strickland, Kent Bowman
141. "30,000 Rooms and I Have the Key" (2-26-74) David Wayne

Seventh Season

142. "The Young Assassins" (9-10-74) Scott Marlowe, Larry Wilcox, Will Seltzer
143. "Hawaiian Nightmare" (9-17-74) James Olson, Sheree North, Felice Orlandi, Seth Sakai
144. "I'll Kill 'Em Again" (9-24-74) Dan Goldman, Ivor Francis, Lei Kayahara, Linda Ryan
145. "Steal Now, Pay Later" (10-1-74) Ray Danton, Joseph Geremia, Jacques Aubuchon, Casey Kasem
146. "Bomb, Bomb, Who's Got the Bomb?" (10-8-74) William Windom, Linda Ryan, Melody Patterson, Marc Singer
147. "Right Grave, Wrong Body" (10-15-74) Charles Cioffi, Josie Over, William Watson, Carole Kai
148. "We Hang Our Own" (10-22-74) Leslie Nielsen, Elissa Dulce, Jerry Waialae, Perry King
149. "The Two-Faced Corpse" (10-29-74) Jessica Walter, Alan Fudge, Abe Vigoda, Sam Elliott
150. "How to Steal a Masterpiece" (11-12-74) Luther Adler
151. "A Gun for McGarrett" (11-26-74) Carol White, Jim Demarest, Douglas Mossman, Ivor Barry
152. "Welcome to Our Branch Office" (12-3-74)
153. "Presenting in the Center Ring--Murder" (12-10-74) Khigh Dhiegh, Bill Edwards, Richard Yniguez, James Hong, Corey Rand, Shawn Sherman
154. "Hara-Kiri ... Murder" (12-31-74) Ossie Davis
155. "Bones of Contention" (1-7-75) Vic Tayback, Keene Curtis, Bill Edwards, Glenn Cannon
156. "Computer Killer" (1-14-75)
157. "A Woman's Work Is with a Gun" (1-21-75) Patricia Hindy, Dale Morse, Patricia Wynand, Eugene Roche
158. "Small Witness, Large Crime" (1-28-75) France Nuyen, Joshua Farin, Elizabeth Smith, John Kerry
159. "Ring of Life" (2-4-75) Don Knight, William Prince,

> Penelope Windust, Harvey Jason
160. "A Study in Rage" (2-11-75)
161. "And the Horse Jumped Over the Moon" (2-18-75)
162. "Hit Gun for Sale" (2-25-75) Nehemiah Persoff, Sal Mineo, Tommy Sands, Darcy Cook, Seth Sakai, Les Freed
163. "The Hostage" (3-11-75) Dane Clark, Scott Brady, Linda Purl, Jack Denton
164. "Diary of a Gun" (3-18-75)
165. "6,000 Deadly Tickets" (3-25-75) Jack Hogan, Jack Kossly, Bill Edwards, Kwan Hi Lim

[Continuing]


## JOURNEY TO THE UNKNOWN

"Matakitis Is Coming," with Vera Miles as a woman who finds herself alone and quite literally incarcerated in a library after doing research on a dead madman, and "The Last Visitor" in which Patty Duke is stalked by a landlady who assumes the identity of her late husband, were two of the best shockers in this British anthology.

The Episodes:

1. "Eve" (9-26-68) Carol Lynley, Michael Gough, Hermione Baddeley, Dennis Waterman
2. "The New People" (10-3-68) Robert Reed, Jennifer Hilary, Patrick Allen, Milo O'Shea, Adrienne Corri
3. "Jane Brown's Body" (10-10-68) Julie Harris, Stefanie Powers, Alan MacNaughton, Sarah Lawson, David Burk
4. "Miss Belle" (10-24-68) George Maharis, Barbara Jefford, Kim Burfield, Adrienne Posta
5. "Do Me a Favor and Kill Me" (11-7-68) Joseph Cotten, Kenneth Haigh, Joyce Blair, Judy Parfitt
6. "Somewhere in a Crowd" (11-14-68) David Hedison, Ann Bell, Jane Asher
7. "The Paper Dolls" (11-21-68) Michael Tolan, Nanette Newman, Barnaby Shaw, Roderick Shaw
8. "Matakitis Is Coming" (11-28-68) Vera Miles, Leon Lissek
9. "The Beckoning Fair One" (12-12-68) Robert Lansing, John Fraser, Gabrielle Drake
10. "One on a Desert Island" (12-19-68) Brandon de Wilde, Suzanna Leigh
11. "Girl of My Dreams" (12-26-68) Michael Callan, Zena Walker
12. "The Last Visitor" (1-2-69) Patty Duke, Kay Walsh
13. "Poor Butterfly" (1-9-69) Chad Everett
14. "Stranger in the Family" (1-16-69) Janice Rule, Arthur Corlan, Maurice Kaufmann
15. "The Killing Bottle" (1-23-69) Roddy McDowall, Ingrid Brett, Barry Evans, William Malrowe

16. "The Madison Equation" (1-30-69) Barbara Bel Geddes, Jack Hedley, Alan Cuthbertson


THE NAME OF THE GAME

Playwright Leslie Stevens, who has authored many an outstanding teleplay, did us wrong by way of this prosaic study of Howard Publications' country-skipping higher ups: the magazine's premier Glenn Howard (Gene Barry), senior editor Dan Farrell (Robert Stack) of Crime Magazine, investigative reporter for People Magazine Jeff Dillon (Anthony Franciosa)--their assistants Joe Sample, Andy Hill, Ross Craig and Peggy Maxwell (Susan St. James). The all-star guest casts only served to further bury the already banal dialogue.

The Regulars: Glenn Howard, Gene Barry; Dan Farrell, Robert Stack; Jeff Dillan, Anthony Franciosa; Peggy Maxwell, Susan St. James; Joe Sample, Ben Murphy; Andy Hill, Cliff Potter; Ross Craig, Mark Miller. Robert Culp is featured as reporter Paul Tyler in two episodes; Peter Falk is featured as reporter Lewis Corbett in one episode; Robert Wagner is featured as reporter Dave Corey in one episode.

The Episodes:

1. "The Fear of High Places" [Anthony Franciosa] (9-20-68) John Payne, Zsa Zsa Gabor, Jeanne Crain, Herb Jeffries, Robert Webber, Claudine Longet
2. "Witness" [Robert Stack] (9-27-68) Ruth Roman, Joan Hackett, Joseph Campanella, Victor Jory, Jack Carter, Murray MacLeod
3. "The Taker" [Gene Barry] (10-4-68) Burl Ives, Bradford Dillman, Laraine Day, Lois Nettleton, Estelle Winwood
4. "Collector's Edition" [Anthony Franciosa] (10-11-68) John Saxon, Senta Berger, Nina Foch, Paul Lucas, Robert Loggia, Hagan Beggs, Francine York, Don Gordon, Noah Keen
5. "Nightmare" [Robert Stack] (10-18-68) Martin Balsam, John Agar, Cloris Leachman, Troy Donahue, Larry Storch, Josephine Hutchinson, Laraine Stephens, Steve Ihnat
6. "Incident in Berlin" [Gene Barry] (10-25-68) Dane Clark, Anne Francis, Geraldine Brooks, Kevin McCarthy, John Van Dreelen
7. "Shine On, Shine On, Jesse Gil" [Anthony Franciosa] (11-1-68) Darren McGavin, Juliet Prowse, Gypsy Rose Lee, Gary Collins, Simon Scott, Kathie Browne
8. "Lola in Lipstick" [Gene Barry] (11-8-68) Ed Begley, Louis Jourdan, Dana Wynter, Cesare Danova, William Windom, Harvey Lembeck, Kathie Browne, Carla Borelli, Benito Prezia
9. "The Protector" [Gene Barry] (11-15-68) Ralph Meeker,

Robert Young, Anne Baxter, Stephen McNally, Jeff Morrow, Mercer Harris

10. "The Ordeal" [Robert Stack] (11-22-68) Jessica Walter, David Opatoshu, Lloyd Bochner, Farley Granger, Martha Hyer, Sean Garrison

11. "The White Birch" [Gene Barry] (11-29-68) Boris Karloff, Peter Deuel, Roddy McDowall, Susan Oliver, Richard Jaeckel, Lilia Skala, Jean-Pierre Aumont, Bethel Leslie

12. "High on a Rainbow" [Robert Stack] (12-6-68) June Allyson, Scott Brady, Van Johnson, Broderick Crawford, Kevin Coughlin, Veronica Cartwright, Arch Johnson, Ed Peck, Amy Fields, Charles Brewer, Dennis Olivieri

13. "The Black Answer" [Anthony Franciosa] (12-13-68) Ivan Dixon, Abbey Lincoln, Herb Jeffries, Raymond St. Jacques, D'Urville Martin, Albert Popwell, Mona Kelsch, James McEachin, Otis Greene, Elven Havard

14. "Pineapple Rose" [Gene Barry] (12-20-68) Susan Strasberg, Don Stroud, Nancy Ames, Mel Torme, Andrew Prine, Mark Richman, Sidney Blackmer, Dean Stanton, Richard Van Vleet, James Oliver, Tom Stewart, Joan Shawlee, Judy Jordan

15. "The Revolutionary" [Gene Barry] (12-27-68) Harry Guardino Simon Oakland, Vera Miles, Albert Paulsen, Nehemiah Persoff, Corbett Monica, Elana Eden, Sharon Harvey

16. "Swingers Only" [Robert Stack] (1-10-69) Jack Klugman, Ann Blyth, Robert Lansing, Paul Stewart, Clu Gulager, Anna Capri, Nancy Kovack

17. "The Inquiry" [Gene Barry] (1-17-69) Barry Sullivan, Gia Scala, Jack Kelly, Ray Danton, Fritz Weaver, Gene Evans, Edward Asner

18. "The Incomparable Connie Walker" [Anthony Franciosa] (1-24-69) Ivan Dixon, Dina Merrill, Bernie Hamilton, Jay C. Flippen, Larry D. Mann, Mel Scott, Shirley O'Hara, Georgia Carr

19. "Love-in at Ground Zero" [Gene Barry] (1-31-69) Keenan Wynn, Henry Jones, Jan Sterling, Tisha Sterling, Jackie DeShannon, Jordan Christopher, Bo Svenson

20. "The Suntan Mob" [Robert Stack] (2-7-69) Suzanne Pleshette, Donald Sutherland, Paul Winfield, Wilfrid Hyde-White, Robert F. Lyons

21. "Keep the Doctor Away" [Anthony Franciosa] (2-14-69) Robert Goulet, Carol Lawrence, Vera Miles, David Brian, Harold J. Stone

22. "The Bobby Currier Story" [Robert Stack] (2-21-69) Julie Harris, Brandon de Wilde, Anne Baxter, Tisha Sterling, Steve Forrest

23. "A Wrath of Angels" [Robert Stack] (2-28-69) Ricardo Montalban, John Kerr, Burr De Benning, Edward Andrews, Mort Mills, Anne Helm, Felice Orlandi

24. "The Third Choice" [Gene Barry] (3-7-69) Ossie Davis, Shirley Jones, Roscoe Lee Browne, Janet MacLachlan, John Marley, Frank Marth, Albert Popwell

25. "Breakout to a Fast Buck" [Robert Stack] (3-14-69) Barry

Nelson, Arthur O'Connell, Shelly Novack, Bert Freed, Phillip Pine

26. "An Agent for the Plaintiff" (3-21-69) Honor Blackman, Maurice Evans, Brian Bedford, Anthony Caruso, Murray Matheson, Richard Peel

Second Season

27. "Lady on the Rocks" [Gene Barry] (9-19-69) Janice Rule, Laurence Naismith, Nigel Davenport, James Robertson Justice, Peter Davies
28. "A Hard Case of the Blues" [Robert Stack] (9-26-69) Sal Mineo, Russ Tamblyn, Percy Rodriguez, Norman Fell, Sharon Farrell, Michael Anderson Jr.
29. "Blind Man's Bluff" [Anthony Franciosa] (10-3-69) Broderick Crawford, Jack Klugman, Denny Miller, Michelle Carey
30. "The Emissary" [Gene Barry] (10-10-69) Charles Boyer, Craig Stevens, Natasha Parry, Ivan Tchenko
31. "Chains of Command" [Robert Stack] (10-17-69) Dorothy Lamour, Pernell Roberts, Jay C. Flippen, Sidney Blackmer, Steve Ihnat
32. "Goodbye, Harry" [Gene Barry] (10-24-69) Darren McGavin, James Whitmore, Dane Clark, Jan Sterling, Marsha Hunt, Strother Martin, Michael Larrain
33. "Give Till It Hurts" [Robert Stack] (10-31-69) Diane Baker, Larry Storch, Dennis Weaver, Phyllis Kirk
34. "The Perfect Image" [Gene Barry] (11-7-69) Hal Holbrook, Ida Lupino, Diana Hyland, Joanna Barnes, Charles Drake, Clu Gulager, Stephen McNally, Edward Andrews
35. "The Prisoner Within" [Anthony Franciosa] (11-14-69) Steve Forrest, Ron Hayes, Richard Van Vleet
36. "The Civilized Men" [Robert Stack] (11-28-69) Jack Kelly, Rod Cameron, Jill St. John, Kaz Garas
37. "High Card" [Gene Barry] (12-5-69) Barry Sullivan, Gene Raymond, Paul Stewart, John Colicos, Martine Beswick
38. "The Power" [Robert Stack] (12-12-69) William Conrad, John Ireland, Broderick Crawford, Barbara Werle, Gene Raymond, Steve Sandor
39. "Laurie Marie" [Anthony Franciosa] (12-19-69) Mark Richman, Antoinette Bower, John Kerr, Carla Borelli, Edward G. Robinson Jr.
40. "The Tradition" [Gene Barry] (1-2-70) Ina Balin, Nico Minardos
41. "The Brass Ring" [Robert Stack] (1-9-70) Celeste Holm, Van Johnson, Jack Carter, Lazaro Perez, Tim O'Connor
42. "Island of Gold and Precious Stones" [Anthony Franciosa] (1-16-70) Henry Jones, Rudy Vallee, Lee Meriwether, Yvonne DeCarlo, Estelle Winwood, Hazel Court, Edward Everett Horton, Michael Walker
43. "The Takeover" [Gene Barry] (1-23-70) Gloria Grahame, Warren Stevens, Anne Baxter, Michael Ansara, David Opatoshu, H. M. Wynant, David Sheiner
44. "The Garden" [Robert Stack] (1-30-70) Richard Kiley, Anne

Francis, Michael Ansara, Brenda Scott, Burt Brinckerhoff
Madeleine Sherwood
45. "Tarot" [Gene Barry] (2-13-70) William Shatner, Lee Grant
Jose Ferrer, Luther Adler, David Carradine, Bethel
Leslie
46. "The King of Denmark" [Anthony Franciosa] (2-20-70)
Joseph Cotten, Noel Harrison, Margaret Leighton
47. "The Skin Game" [Robert Stack] (2-27-70) Suzanne Pleshette
Hari Rhodes, Rossano Brazzi, Charles Drake
48. "Man of the People" [Gene Barry] (3-6-70) Fernando Lamas
Robert Alda, Patricia Medina, Jackie Coogan, Vera Miles
James Gregory, Gene Evans
49. "Echo of a Nightmare" [Robert Stack] (3-20-70) Ricardo
Montalban, Tom Drake, Arthur Hill, Andrew Prine, Hoagy
Carmichael, Michael Callan
50. "Jenny Wilde Is Drowning" [Anthony Franciosa] (3-27-70)
Pamela Franklin, Frank Gorshin, Gavin MacLeod
51. "One of the Girls in Research" [Gene Barry] (4-3-70) Bren
Vaccaro, Stephen McNally, Judi West, Will Geer, Sheree
North, Rose Craig
52. "The Other Kind of a Spy" [Anthony Franciosa] (4-10-70)
Joseph Campanella, Leslie Nielsen, Ed Begley, Jeanette
Nolan, Edward Andrews, Robert Lipton

Third Season

53. "So Long, Baby, and Amen" [Robert Stack] (9-18-70) Julie
Harris, Sal Mineo, James Gregory, Harold J. Stone,
Laurie Prange
54. "A Love to Remember" [Gene Barry] (9-25-70) Lee Grant,
Ray Milland, J. D. Cannon, Tom Bosley, Joanna Moore,
Charles McGraw, Jacqueline de Wit, Darlene Conley
55. "Cynthia Is Alive and Living in Avalon" [Robert Culp] (10-2-
70) Barbara Feldon, Mickey Rooney, Tom Skerritt
56. "The Battle at Gannon's Bridge" [Robert Stack] (10-9-70)
Darren McGavin, Keenan Wynn, Joan Blondell, Percy
Rodriguez, Jan Murray, Jaime Sanchez
57. "The Enemy Before Us" [Anthony Franciosa] (10-16-70)
Katina Paxinou, Richard Conte, Orson Welles, Martin
Balsam, Lazaro Perez, Renee Tetro
58. "The Time Is Now" [Gene Barry] (10-23-70) Yaphet Kotto,
Jack Klugman, Dana Andrews, David Brian, William Win-
dom, Georg Stanford Brown, Roscoe Lee Browne, Max
Julien, Chelsea Brown, Marlene Warfield
59. "The War Merchants" [Robert Stack] (10-30-70) Robert Wag
ner, Scott Brady, Rosemary Forsyth, Frank Aletter, Pau
Sorensen, Art Lund
60. "Little Bear Died Running" [Robert Culp] (11-6-70) Dean
Jagger, Steve Forrest, Edgar Buchanan, Simon Oakland,
Slim Pickens, Sheila Sullivan, Robert Cornthwaite
61. "All the Old Familiar Faces" [Gene Barry] (11-13-70) Anne
Baxter, Stephen McNally, Lois Nettleton, Burgess Meredith, Michael Constantine, Frank Maxwell, Jonathan Lippe

Lucille Meredith
62. "I Love You, Billy Baker" [Part I; Anthony Franciosa]   (11-20-70)   Sammy Davis Jr., Janet MacLachlan, Carla Borelli, Bernie Hamilton; appearances by Joey Bishop, Dionne Warwick, Ray Charles, Xavier Cugat, Tony Martin, Jack Carter, Ike and Tina Turner, Norm Crosby, Mickey Manners
63. "I Love You, Billy Baker" [Part II; Franciosa]   (11-27-70)   as above
64. "Why I Blew Up Dakota" [Robert Stack]   (12-4-70)   Roddy McDowall, Clu Gulager, Jose Ferrer, Carolyn Jones, Paul Stewart
65. "Aquarius Descending" [Gene Barry]   (12-11-70)   Arthur Hill, Brenda Scott, Michael Callan, Hermione Gingold, William Smithers
66. "The Glory Shouter" [Robert Stack]   (12-18-70)   Howard Duff, William Shatner, Dina Merrill, Edward Binns, Jackie Coogan, Joe Flynn, William Smithers
67. "A Sister from Napoli" [Peter Falk]   (1-8-71)   Geraldine Page, David Wayne, Shepperd Strudwick, Angel Tompkins, Tom Ewell, Robert Emhardt, Kurt Kasznar, Sy Kramer, Bill Lucking
68. "Los Angeles 2017" [Gene Barry]   (1-15-71)   Barry Sullivan, Edmond O'Brien, Sharon Farrell, Paul Stewart, Regis J. Cordic, Louise Latham, Severn Darden
69. "The Man Who Killed a Ghost" [Robert Wagner]   (1-29-71)   Janet Leigh, Kim Stanley, David Hartman, Lex Barker, Lurene Tuttle, Alfred Ryder, William Bryant, Jack Soo, Teddy Eccles, Donald Barry
70. "Seek and Destroy" [Robert Stack]   (2-5-71)   Leif Erickson, Kathy Nolan, Susan Oliver, Tom Bosley, John McGiver, John Vernon, Forrest Tucker
71. "A Capitol Affair" [Gene Barry]   (2-12-71)   Monte Markham, Suzanne Pleshette, Larry Hagman, Leon Ames, Mercedes McCambridge
72. "The Savage Eye" [Robert Stack]   (2-19-71)   Peter Deuel, Jim Hutton, Marianna Hill
73. "Appointment in Palermo" [Gene Barry]   (2-26-71)   Harry Guardino, Brenda Vaccaro, Gabriel Dell, John Marley, Joe De Santis
74. "Beware of the Watchdog" [Robert Stack]   (3-5-71)   Richard Kiley, Diana Muldaur, Nancy Olson, Pernell Roberts, Ed Flanders
75. "The Broken Puzzle" [Gene Barry]   (3-12-71)   Chuck Connors, Patricia Crowley, Charles Aidman, Alex Dreier
76. "The Showdown" [Gene Barry]   (3-19-71)   Warren Oates, Albert Salmi, Jessica Walter, Jack Albertson, Ron Turbeville, Jack Garner

MY FRIEND TONY

The Regulars: John Woodruff, James Whitmore; Tony, Enzo Cerusico.

The Episodes:

1. "Corey Doesn't Live Here Anymore" (1-5-69) Brooke Bundy Mark Richman, Corey Allen, Sherwood Price, Mark Roberts, Robert Emhardt, Ford Rainey
2. "Death Comes in Small Packages" (1-12-69) Larry Pennell, Kenneth Washington, Paul Stewart, Kirk Kirksey, Richard Anderson
3. "Voices" (1-19-69) Julie Adams, Leslie Parrish, Lloyd Bochner
4. "Let George Do It" (1-26-69) William Daniels, Richard Anderson, Dee Hartford, Val Avery, Larry Pennell, Anna Haggan
5. "The Lost Hours" (2-2-69) Eduard Franz, Don Dubbins, Grant Williams, Lana Wood, Willi Koopman, Marcia Rodd
6. "The Hazing" (2-16-69) Steve Franken, Tom Fielding
7. "Encounter" (2-23-69) Geraldine Brooks, Barry Russo, Marianna Hill, Skip Homeier
8. "Dead Reckoning" (3-9-69) Cecil Kellaway, Frances Bavier
9. "Wedding Cake Blues" (3-23-69) Rose Marie, Cesare Danova
10. "The Twenty Mile Jog" (4-13-69) Pat O'Brien, Dwayne Hickman, Ben Carruthers
11. "Molly" (5-18-69) Molly Picon, Sue Taylor
12. [unknown title] (5-25-69) Diane Varsi, Sheree North, Richard Anderson, Ned Glass
13. "Casino" (6-1-69) Janet MacLachlan, Hal Frederick, Bill Fletcher, George Sperdakos, Carol Booth
14. "Kidnap" (6-8-69) Will Geer, Fay Spain, John McLiam, Larry Perkins, Susan Michaels
15. "The Shortest Courtship" (6-15-69) William Windom, Karen Valentine
16. "Welcome Home, Jerry Stanley" (6-22-69) Monte Markham, Denny Miller

THE BOLD ONES

This excellent series examined, on alternating weeks, contemporary medicine, the law profession, law enforcement and government.

One of the most extraordinary episodes of the segment "The
Law Enforcers" (with Leslie Nielsen as Deputy Police Chief Danforth and Hari Rhodes as District Attorney Washburn)--indeed of
the entire series--was Adrian Spies' "If I Should Wake Before I
Die," inspired by the Caryl Chessman case. Robert Drivas was
brilliant as Martin Sitomer, the Death Row convict purportedly guilty of a rape-murder. Sitomer himself is a brilliant actor in the
episode, finally successful at attaining a retrial; casting his elaborate spell on the ever-pursuing media. Yet under Daryl Duke's
artful direction, the teleplay becomes a merciless exhortation
against execution. In the superbly paced courtroom denouement,
Sitomer (still vivid be our memories of this incarcerated youth who
could not long endure the camera light of his assailing reporters)
argues his own case before the jury. Evidence has been gathered
which confirms his guilt. In a last desperate effort to triumph
and live, he calls to the witness stand the man (Edmond O'Brien in
the role of Warden Millbank) who has vociferously opposed his going to die. Asks Sitomer: "How can I convince them?" And
Millbank, now himself the wiser, tells Sitomer to relent; an admis-
sion that will sustain the belief that rehabilitation has been fully
achieved. The episode concludes, leaving us uncertain of the ominous question on which it began; but the crash of a cell door, the
memory of those prison corridors, is indelibly disturbing.

The most prestigious episode of the Emmy-award winning
segment "The Senator" would surely be David W. Rintels' "A Con-
inual Roar of Musketry," basing its theme of campus unrest much
in the manner of the student shootings at Kent State and Jackson
State Universities in the spring of 1970. The drama finds Senator
Hays Stowe (Hal Holbrook) heading a special investigating committee
which is seeking to determine culpability for the shootings of two
campus demonstrators by National Guardsmen in Stowe's home
state. Town Mayor (John Marley), University Chancellor (Laurence
Luckinbill), Governor (John Randolph), members of the National
Guard and other administrative officials give conflicting testimonies

before the committee. But student witnesses refuse to testify, convinced of the committee's establishment bias. One student leader (Robert Pratt) is particularly vehement in his opposition. A personal visit to his apartment by Senator Stowe proves futile, although Stowe does convince the student leader's girlfriend (Pamela McMyler) to give testimony.

To this point Rintels and director Robert Day have done an admirable job of establishing opposing viewpoints: the guilt-ridden officer of the Guard who swears he would not return to active duty on the campus if ordered to do so; the member of the guard, certain of his "Americanism," who has no memory of the names of the students he has shot and killed; the reckless Governor and Mayor, neither of whom can understand the need for the protest; the courageous student leader who unflinchingly evicts his girlfriend when she has informed--altogether these form an arena of consciences. Yet the teleplay becomes maudlin when Stowe's fellow committeeman, in a heated dispute on the question of who to blame, nearly throws a paperweight at his rival, tearfully comprehending his action's significance. And so the committee recommends the Guard and administrative officers be formally questioned and if guilty prosecuted. But the committee recommendation expectedly fails to single out the blame, for despite Rintels' noble teleplay, it goes no farther than television in 1970 (the year of the Kent and Jackson State shootings) would allow.

For "The Doctors" segment (with E. G. Marshall as Dr. David Craig, John Saxon as Dr. Ted Stuart and David Hartman as Dr. Paul Hunter, all of the Craig Institute), Ron Bishop, for one, composed an absorbing teleplay on a child hemophiliac with "The Velvet Prison." Other topics explored included an embryo transplant (in "A Substitute Womb"), impotence (in "A Standard for Manhood"), and a moving polemic by terminal patients over a dignified way to die in "An Absence of Loneliness."

"The Lawyers" consisted of a firm with senior partner Walter Nichols (Burl Ives) and brothers Brian (Joseph Campanella) and Neil (James Farentino) Darrell. Among the several excellent dramas in this segment were William D. Gordon's murder mystery "The Strange Secret of Yermo Hill" (in which former California governor Edmund G. Brown appeared) and an indictment of the pace of the contemporary legal process (dramatized by a shocking climax) with "Justice Is a Sometime Thing."

The Regulars: The Doctors: Dr. Benjamin Craig, E. G. Marshall; Dr. Ted Stuart, John Saxon (through the third season); Dr. Paul Hunter, David Hartman; Intern Martin Cohen, Robert Walden (with episode of 10/10/72). The Lawyers: Att. Walter Nichols, Burl Ives; Att. Brian Darrell, Joseph Campanella; Att. Neil Darrell, James Farentino. The Law Enforcers (also known as "The Protectors"): Deputy Police Chief Danforth, Leslie Nielsen; District Attorney Washburn, Hari Rhodes. The Senator: Senator Hays Stowe

Hal Holbrook; Mrs. Stowe, Sharon Acker; Norma Stowe, Cindy Eilbacher; Jordan Boyle (assistant to Senator Stowe), Michael Tolan.

The Episodes:

1.  The Doctors: "To Save a Life" (9-14-69) Pat Hingle, Gene Raymond, Rick Kelman, Virginia Gregg, Linda Dangcil, Jason Bernard
2.  The Lawyers: "A Game of Chance" (9-21-69) Steve Ihnat, John Milford
3.  The Law Enforcers: "A Case of Good Whiskey at Christmas Time" (9-28-69) Edward Andrews, Charles Drake, Lorraine Gray, Amy Thompson, Michael Bell, Frank Maxwell, Bart Carpenelli
4.  The Doctors: "What's the Price of a Pair of Eyes?" (10-5-69) Tisha Sterling, Jason Evers, Chris Hansen, Berkeley Harris
5.  The Lawyers: "The People Against Ortega" (10-12-69) John Randolph, Robert Webber, Frank Ramirez
6.  The Doctors: "Rebellion of the Body" (10-19-69) Eileen Baral, William Smithers
7.  The Law Enforcers: "If I Should Wake Before I Die" (10-26-69) Robert Drivas, Edmond O'Brien, Gene Evans, Milton Selzer
8.  The Lawyers: "The Crowd Pleaser" (11-2-69) Mel Tormé, Juanita Hall, Georg Stanford Brown, Dana Elcar
9.  The Doctors: "Man Without a Heart" (11-9-69) Howard Duff, Joanna Cameron, John Zaremba, Paul Bryar, Henry Hunter, Dan Kemp, Richard Simmons
10. The Lawyers: "Rockford Riddle" (11-16-69) Claudine Longet, Charles Aidman, Leslie Persins, George Murdock
11. The Doctors: "A Small Step for Man" (11-23-69) Terry Carter, Yale Summers, Gloria Calomee, Ted Hartley, Hal England, Savannah Bentley
12. The Lawyers: "Shriek of Silence" (11-30-69) Craig Stevens, George Murdock, Morgan Sterne, Richard Van Vleet
13. The Doctors: "Crisis" (12-7-69) Bradford Dillman, Jeffrey Lynn, Sue Lyon, Tom Helmore, Morgan Jones
14. The Law Enforcers: "Draw a Straight Man" (12-14-69) Michael Bell, Janine Gray
15. The Doctors: "And Those Unborn" (12-21-69) Stephen McNally, Lois Nettleton, Tim Weldon
16. The Lawyers: "Trial of a Mafioso" (1-4-70) Richard Conte, Joe De Santis, Linda Marsh, Frank Campanella
17. The Law Enforcers: "The Carrier" (1-11-70) Louise Sorel, Barbara Babcock
18. The Doctors: "If I Can't Sing, I'll Listen" (1-18-70) Josephine Hutchinson, Susan Albert
19. The Lawyers: "Point of Honor" (1-25-70) Veronica Cartwright, Roger Davis, Paul Stevens
20. The Law Enforcers: "A Thing Not of God" (2-1-70) John Rubinstein, James Broderick

21. The Doctors: "This Day's Child" (2-8-70) Sheila Larken, Bethel Leslie
22. The Lawyers: "The Shattered Image" (2-15-70) Will Geer, Audrey Totter, Ford Rainey, Karen Huston
23. The Doctors: "Dark Is the Rainbow, Loud Is the Silence" (3-1-70) Jack Klugman, Kate Woodville
24. The Law Enforcers: "Memo from the Class of '76" (3-8-70) Billy Gray, Norma Crane

Second Season

25. The Senator: "To Taste of Death but Once" (9-13-70) Gerald S. O'Loughlin, Michael Bell, James Wainwright
26. The Doctors: "This Will Really Kill You" (9-20-70) Tisha Sterling, Michael Anderson Jr., Richard X. Slattery, Darby Hinton, Rodolfo Hoyos, Ann Prentiss, George Murdock
27. The Lawyers: "The Verdict" (9-27-70) Stephen McNally, John Kerr, Will Geer, Florence St. Peter, Mary Gregory
28. The Senator: "The Day the Lion Died" (10-4-70) Will Geer, Ann Doran, Frank Maxwell
29. The Doctors: "Killer on the Loose" (10-11-70) Robert Hooks, Della Reese, Georg Stanford Brown, Julie Adams, Keith Andes, Eric Laneuville
30. The Lawyers: "Panther in a Cage" (10-18-70) Georg Stanford Brown, Charles Lampkin, Gloria Calomee, John McLiam, Val Avery, Gerald Hiken, Frank Campanella
31. The Doctors: "Giants Never Kneel" (10-25-70) Arthur Hill, Carol Lynley, DeForest Kelley, Roger Perry, Kevin Hagen
32. The Senator: "Power Play" (11-1-70) Burgess Meredith, Anna Lee, Michael C. Gwynne, Holly Near
33. The Lawyers: "Trial of a Pfc." (11-8-70) Peter Deuel, Jane Elliot, Jared Martin, Walter Brooke
34. The Doctors: "First--No Harm to the Patient" (11-15-70) Richard Dreyfuss, Dolores Mann, James Broderick
35. The Senator: "A Continual Roar of Musketry" [Part I] (11-22-70) John Randolph, Edward Binns, Laurence Luckinbill, Paul Stewart, Bernie Hamilton, Robert Pratt, Pamela McMyler, John Marley, Noam Pitlik, Randolph Mantooth
36. The Senator: "A Continual Roar of Musketry" [Part II] (11-29-70) as above
37. The Lawyers: "The People Against Dr. Chapman" (12-6-70) Monte Markham, Ramon Bieri
38. The Doctors: "In Dreams They Run" [directed by Jerry Lewis] (12-13-70) Joanne Linville, Jason Karpf, Lincoln Kilpatrick, Arch Johnson, Ella Edwards
39. The Lawyers: "The Loneliness Racket" (12-20-70) Marj Dusay, Patricia Donahue, Phyllis Love, Diane Shalet
40. The Doctors: "A Matter of Priorities" (1-3-71) Pernell Roberts, Kim Hunter, Harold J. Stone, Mark Miranda, Linda Dangcil, Katherine Crawford, Carmen Zapata, Christine Avila, Gary Morgan

41. The Lawyers: "The Search for Leslie Grey" (1-10-71)
    Charles Aidman, Rodolfo Hoyos, Leo Gordon
42. The Senator: "Someday They'll Elect a President" (1-17-71)
    John Randolph, Murray Hamilton, Kermit Murdock
43. The Doctors: "An Absence of Loneliness" (1-24-71) Edward
    Binns, Julie Adams, Kathryn Hays, Coleen Gray, Brad
    David, Philip Pine, Ann Doran, Mae Mercer, Kasey
    Rogers
44. The Lawyers: "The Hyland Confession" (1-31-71) Tisha
    Sterling, Steven Darden
45. The Senator: "George Washington Is a Liar" (2-7-71) Reni
    Santoni, Louise Sorel, Malcolm Atterbury, Robert Donner,
    George Mitchell
46. The Doctors: "Tender Predator" (2-14-71) Karen Valentine,
    Stephen Young, Katherine Crawford, Melissa Hart
47. The Lawyers: "The Price of Justice" (2-21-71) Cal Bellini,
    Lee Delano, Julie Gregg
48. The Senator: "A Single Blow of the Sword" (2-28-71) Logan
    Ramsey, David Sheiner

## Third Season

49. The Doctors: "Broken Melody" (9-19-71) Jennifer, Joyce
    Van Patten
50. The Lawyers: "The Invasion of Kevin Ireland" (9-26-71)
    Darren McGavin, Kathie Browne, Dana Elcar, Todd Mar-
    tin, John Ragin, Clarke Gordon, Martin Ashe
51. The Doctors: "The Angry Man" (10-3-71) Zooey Hall, Dina
    Merrill
52. The Lawyers: "The Strange Secret of Yermo Hill" (10-17-
    71) Randolph Mantooth, Mills Watson, John Milford,
    David Spielberg; former California governor Edmund
    Brown played a judge
53. The Doctors: "One Lonely Step" (10-24-71) Patricia Crow-
    ley, Lou Gossett, Kirk Calloway
54. The Lawyers: "Hall of Justice" (10-31-71) Richard Van
    Vleet, Ramon Bieri
55. The Doctors: "Close Up" (11-7-71) Joan Van Ark, Peggy
    Feury, Stan Schneider
56. The Lawyers: "In Defense of Ellen McKay" (11-14-71)
    Susan Clark, David Spielberg
57. The Doctors: "The Convicts" (11-21-71) Don Stroud, Val
    Avery, Loretta Swit, Wally Taylor, Rafael Lopez, June
    Dayton, Kathryn Kelly Wiget
58. The Lawyers: "By Reason of Insanity" (11-28-71) Charles
    Aidman, Tim Matheson, Nina Shipman, Todd Martin, Ann
    Summers, Walter Brooke, John Milford, Charles Davis
59. The Doctors: "The Glass Cage" (12-5-71) Dick Shawn,
    Brock Peters, Lynn Carlin, Pat Hingle, Frank Campanella,
    John Carter, Marcy Lafferty
60. The Lawyers: "Justice Is a Sometime Thing" (12-12-71)
    A Martinez, Richard Jordan, Edith Diaz
61. The Doctors: "Dagger in the Mind" (12-19-71) Robert

Sterling, Collin Wilcox-Horne, Jeffrey Pomerantz, Mary Layne

62. The Lawyers: "The Letter of the Law" (12-26-71) James Olson, Will Geer, Gale Sondergaard, Milton Selzer, Michael Conrad, Carol Wayne, Carla Borelli, Michael Griswold, Joseph DeAngelo

63. The Doctors: "Moment of Crisis" (1-2-72) Lloyd Bochner, Edward Andrews, Christopher West, Athena Lorde, Joaquin Martinez, Jim Boles, Wonderful Smith, William Elliott

64. The Lawyers: "The Long Morning After" [Part I] (1-9-72) Pat Hingle, Anne Helm, Pamela McMyler, Roger Davis, John Milford, Robert Corff

65. The Lawyers: "The Long Morning After" [Part II] (1-16-72) as above

66. The Doctors: "Short Flight to a Distant Star" (1-23-72) Cameron Mitchell

67. The Lawyers: "In Sudden Darkness" (1-30-72) Carol Lawrence, Sian Barbara Allen, David Spielberg, Tim O'Connor, Frank Aletter, John Milford, Barry Higgins

68. The Doctors: "A Threatened Species" (2-6-72) Norma Crane, Clu Gulager

69. The Lawyers: "Lisa, I Hardly Knew You" (2-13-72) Tiffany Bolling, Ellen Burstyn, Michael Bell, Douglas Watson, John Milford, Peter Hobbs, Ivor Francis, Moss Mabry

70. The Doctors: "Discovery at Fourteen" [unsold pilot film for projected series] (3-5-72) Jane Wyman, Mike Farrell, Ronny Howard, Lynnette Mettey

Fourth Season

71. The Doctors: "Five Days in the Death of Sgt. Brown" [Part II of "Ironside" episode of 9/14/72] (9-19-72) Vic Morrow, Christina Hart, Raymond Burr, Don Galloway, Elizabeth Baur

72. The Doctors: "Is This Operation Necessary?" (9-26-72) Richard Basehart, Dorothy Malone

73. The Doctors: "A Nation of Human Pincushions" (10-3-72) Jack Albertson, Lloyd Nolan, Carl Reiner, Jeff Corey

74. The Doctors: "Time Bomb in the Chest" (10-10-72) Joanne Linville, John Vernon, Johnny Lee

75. The Doctors: "A Standard for Manhood" (10-17-72) Frank Converse, Shirley Knight Hopkins

76. The Doctors: "A Substitute Womb" (10-24-72) Carl Betz, Stefanie Powers, Sheila Larken

77. The Doctors: "A Very Strange Triangle" (10-31-72) Donna Mills, Hildy Brooks

78. The Doctors: "A Quality of Fear" (11-14-72) Marlyn Mason, Herb Edelman

79. The Doctors: "An Inalienable Right to Die" (11-28-72) Susan Clark, Robert Foxworth, James Douglas

80. The Doctors: "A Purge of Madness" (12-5-72) Milton Berle, Ross Martin

81.  The Doctors: "Endtheme" (12-12-72) Clu Gulager, Don
     Johnson, Lane Bradbury, Michael Baseleon, David Roy,
     Susan Damante, Gene Tyburn, Lyvonne Walder
82.  The Doctors: "The Velvet Prison" (12-19-72) Diana Mul-
     daur, Charles Cioffi, Gene Andrusco
83.  The Doctors: "Terminal Career" (1-2-73) Ida Lupino,
     Susan Howard, Michael Constantine, Jill Haney, Stack
     Pierce, Lloyd King, Abigail Shelton, Gail Bonney, Patrick
     Culliton, Patricia Sides
84.  The Doctors: "A Tightrope to Tomorrow" (1-9-73) William
     Shatner, Alfred Ryder, Burr DeBenning
85.  The Doctors: "The Night Crawler" (1-16-73) Henry Dar-
     row, Jess Walton

## THE FORSYTE SAGA

One could never exhaust Galsworthy, but the Nobel Laure-
ate's chronicles were beautifully adapted in this immensely popular
BBC entry.

The Cast: Jo Forsyte, Kenneth More; Soames Forsyte, Eric
     Porter; Winifred Forsyte, Margaret Tyzack; Fleur Forsyte,
     Susan Hampshire; Irene Forsyte, Nyree Dawn Porter;
     Michael Mont, Nicholas Pennell; Old Jolyon, Joseph O'Con-
     or; Helene, Lana Morris; Jon, Martin Jarvis; Aunt Ann,
     Fay Compton; Frances, Ursula Howells; Mrs. Heron, Jen-
     ny Laird; Lomax, Campbell Singer; June, June Barry;
     Bosinney, John Bennett; Jolly, Michael York; James, John
     Welsh; Monty, Terence Alexander; Annette, Dallia Penn;
     Val, Jonathan Burn.

The Episodes [telecast via PBS Sundays, 9:00-10:00]:

1.   "A Family Festival" [I] (10-5-69)
2.   "A Family Scandal" [II] (10-12-69)
3.   "The Pursuit of Happiness" [III] (10-19-69)
4.   "Dinner at Swithins" [IV] (10-26-69)
5.   "A Man of Property" [V] (11-2-69)
6.   "Decisions" [VI] (11-9-69)
7.   "Into the Dark" [VII] (11-16-69)
8.   "Indian Summer of a Forsyte" [VIII] (11-23-69)
9.   "In Chancery" [IX] (11-30-69)
10.  "The Challenge" [X] (12-7-69)
11.  "In the Web" [XI] (12-14-69)
12.  "Birth of a Forsyte" [XII] (12-21-69)
13.  "Encounter" [XIII] (12-28-69)
14.  "Conflict" [XIV] (1-4-70)
15.  "To Let" [XV] (1-11-70)
16.  "A Family Wedding" [XVI] (1-18-70)
17.  "The White Monkey" [XVII] (1-25-70)
18.  "The Afternoon of a Dryad" [XVIII] (2-1-70)

19. "No Retreat" [XIX]  (2-8-70)
20. "A Silent Wooing" [XX]  (2-15-70)
21. "Action for Libel" [XXI]  (2-22-70)
22. "The Silver Spoon" [XXII]  (3-1-70)
23. "Strike" [XXIII]  (3-8-70)
24. "Afternoon at Ascot" [XXIV]  (3-15-70)
25. "Portrait of Fleur" [XXV]  (3-22-70)
26. "Swan Song" [XXVI]  (3-29-70)

THE NEW PEOPLE

   Television's attempt at coping with Vietnam War era American youth rebelliousness produced, for one, this absurd entry in
which a planewrecked group of exchange students wrestle with their
disparate convictions in order to survive their isolated island prison. Not even a playwright of the calibre of Rod Serling, who composed the initial teleplay, could bring stature to a premise like that.

The Regulars: Susan, Tiffany Bolling; Bob Lee, Zooey Hall; Wash-
    ington, David Moses; George, Peter Ratray; Stanley, Den-
    nis Olivieri; Ginny, Jill Jaress.

The Episodes:

1. [unknown title]  (9-22-69)  Richard Kiley, Parley Baer, Lee
    Jay Lambert
2. "Panic in the Sands"  (9-29-69)  Richard Dreyfuss
3. "The Tin God"  (10-6-69)  Donna Baccala
4. "Murderer"  (10-13-69)  Carl Reindel
5. "Comes the Revolution, Use the Girls' Shower"  (10-20-69)
    Susan Batson
6. "Lifeline"  (10-27-69)  Brenda Scott, Clive Clerk
7. "Marriage, Bomano Style"  (11-3-69)  Robert Cannon, Kate
    Heflin
8. "Is This Any Way to Run an Island?"  (11-10-69)  Richard
    Anthony, Clive Clerk, Tim O'Kelly, Elizabeth Berger
9. "The Dark Side of the Island"  (11-17-69)  Dan Ferrone,
    Melissa Murphy, Lee Stanley, Dan Hardstack
10. "A Bride in Basic Black--The Courtship" [Part I]  (11-24-69)
    Jim McMullan
11. "A Bride in Basic Black--The Surrender" [Part II]  (12-1-69)
    as above
12. "The Pied Piper of Pot"  (12-8-69)  Richard Evans
13. "Speed Kills"  (12-15-69)  Robert Drivas
14. "The Guns of Bomano"  (12-22-69)  Aron Kincaid, Solomon
    Sturges
15. "The Prisoner of Bomano"  (12-29-69)  Billy Dee Williams,
    Judy Pace
16. "The Siege of Fern's Castle"  (1-5-70)  Dennis Redfield
17. "On the Horizon"  (1-12-70)  Tyne Daly, Benjamin Archibek

THE SURVIVORS

Harold Robbins' expectedly short-lived examination of (what else?) the jet set, featuring Lana Turner (who else?) as the troubled daughter Tracy of wealthy banker Baylor Carlyle (Ralph Bellamy). Other characters include George Hamilton as Tracy's playboy brother Duncan, Kevin McCarthy as Tracy's defalcating husband Philip Hastings and Tracy's illegitimate son Jeffrey Hastings (Jan-Michael Vincent).

The Regulars: Duncan Carlyle, George Hamilton; Tracy Carlyle, Lana Turner; Jeffrey Hastings, Jan-Michael Vincent; Baylor Carlyle, Ralph Bellamy; Philip Hastings, Kevin McCarthy; Jonathan Carlyle, Louis Hayward; Belle, Diana Muldaur; Jean Vale, Louise Sorel; Riakos, Rossano Brazzi; Miguel Santerra, Robert Viharo; Sam Thomas, Burr DeBenning; Zack, Zalman King; Max, Schell Rasten; Mike, David Cassidy; Stafford, Foster Brooks; Mendes, Gregory Morton; Priest, Claudio Miranda; Senator Jennings, Clu Gulager; Marguerita, Donna Baccala; Sheila, Kathy Cannon; Eleanor, Natalie Schafer; Tom, Robert Lipton; Art, Hal Frederick.

The Episodes [indicated by chapter numbers]:

1. "Chapter One" (9-29-69)
2. "Chapter Two" (10-6-69)
3. "Chapter Three" (10-13-69)
4. "Chapter Four" (10-20-69)
5. "Chapter Five" (10-27-69)
6. "Chapter Six" (11-10-69)
7. "Chapter Seven" (11-17-69)
8. "Chapter Eight" (11-24-69)
9. "Chapter Nine" (12-1-69)
10. "Chapter Ten" (12-8-69)
11. "Chapter Eleven" (12-15-69)
12. "Chapter Twelve" (12-22-69)
13. "Chapter Thirteen" (12-29-69)
14. "Chapter Fourteen" (1-5-70)
15. "Chapter Fifteen" (1-12-70)


MARCUS WELBY, M.D.

Producer David Victor's valentine to the medical profession casts Robert Young (whose "Father Knows Best" Jim Anderson lingers in the memory of millions) as the widower general practitioner Dr. Marcus Welby who dispenses his paternal wisdom to his fellow resident, young and ardent (of course) Dr. Steven Kiley (James Brolin). Predictably, this being a protagonist "image" series, there are for the most part grandly sentimental teleplays. Jane Wyatt, for years the television spouse of Young's "Jim

Anderson," appeared in Ian Chevron's episode "Designs." Barry Brown was cast as Dr. Kiley's (so as to keep the situations close to home) ailing younger brother Mike, featured in the twenty-ninth episode.

In "Four-Plus Hot" the bitter controversy over American involvement in Vietnam is reduced to a debate between ideal representatives of either philosophical side who just happen to be old friends. A truce is attained when it is learned that the conscientious objector (Ben Murphy) has contracted a terminal illness--so gaining the sympathy of the war veteran (Scott Newman--actor Paul's son) at last.

Ruth Roman, at least, was fascinating as the faith healer with nonetheless superb medical credentials in "Diagnosis: Fear."

A flurry of protest greeted the televising of "The Outrage," about a boy's homosexual assault.

The Regulars: Dr. Marcus Welby, Robert Young; Dr. Steven Kiley, James Brolin; Nurse Consuelo Lopez, Elena Verdugo.

The Episodes:

1. "Hello, Goodbye, Hello" (9-23-69) Susan Clark, Michael Barbara, Catherine McLoud, Gary Dubin
2. "The Foal" (9-30-69) Lynn Carlin, Steve Ihnat, Brian Dewey
3. "Don't Ignore the Miracles" (10-7-69) Julie Adams, William Sylvester, Dorothy Green, Amy Thomson
4. "Silken Threads and Silver Hooks" (10-14-69) Barbara Rush, Alexander Scourby, Peter Brandon
5. "All Flags Flying" (10-21-69) Henry Wilcoxon, Butch Patrick, Ruta Lee
6. "Echo of a Baby's Laugh" (10-28-69) Belinda Montgomery, Richard Thomas, Nora Marlowe
7. "The White Cane" (11-4-69) Carrie Snodgrass, Cliff Potter, Lawrence Linville, Dee Carroll
8. "The Vrahnas Demon" (11-11-69) Frank Silvera, Linda Marsh, Michael Hardstark, Tony Patino
9. "Madonna with Knapsack and Flute" (11-18-69) Anne Baxter, Darleen Carr, Michael Larrain
10. "Homecoming" (11-25-69) Robert Lipton, Nehemiah Persoff
11. "Let Ernest Come Over" (12-9-69) Percy Rodriguez, James Doohan, Georgia Carr
12. "The Chemistry of Hope" (12-16-69) Bradford Dillman, Nancy Malone, Heather Menzies, Barry Williams
13. "Neither Punch nor Judy" (12-23-69) Earl Holliman, Peter Hooten, Ronne Troup
14. "Diagnosis: Fear" (12-30-69) Ruth Roman, Tom Drake, John Findlater
15. "The Soft Phrase of Peace" (1-6-70) Richard Van Vleet, Melvin Stuart, Bob Gullaume
16. "Fun and Games and Michael Ambrose" (1-13-70) David

Cassidy, John McMartin
17. "The Legacy" (1-27-70) Dolores Del Rio, Janet Blair, John Roper
18. "Dance to No Music" (2-3-70) Joseph Campanella, Celia Lovsky, Joan Darling
19. "Go Get 'Em, Tiger!" (2-10-70) Jack Albertson, Barry Brown, Jeanne Bates, William Smithers
20. "Nobody Wants a Fat Jockey" (2-17-70) Michael Burns, Strother Martin, Arch Johnson, Rafael Campos
21. "The Other Side of the Chart" (2-24-70) Don Stroud, Elizabeth Hubbard, Joanna Cameron
22. "The Merely Syndrome" (3-3-70) Skye Aubrey, Vera Miles
23. "Sea of Security" (3-10-70) John Ericson, Katherine Crawford, Ben Cooper
24. "The Daredevil Gesture" (3-17-70) Marsha Hunt, Frank Webb
25. "Enid" (3-24-70) Flora Plumb, Ezekial Williams, Robert McQueeney
26. "The Rebel Doctor" (4-14-70) Kaz Garas, Virginia Grey, Harry Townes

Second Season

27. "A Very Special Sailfish" (9-22-70) Lee Purcell, Cloris Leachman, William Schallert, David Carson
28. "The Worth of a Man" (9-29-70) Gary Merrill, Kaz Garas, Beth Brickell, Carle Bensen
29. "Warn the World About Mike" (10-6-70) Barry Brown, Rhoda Williams
30. "Epidemic" (10-13-70) Michele Lee, Hope Summers, Jeanette Nolan, Marlene Clark
31. "To Get Through the Night" (10-20-70) Larry Hagman, Barbara Anderson, Anthony Eisley
32. "Daisy in the Shadows" (10-27-70) Suzanne Pleshette, David Hartman, Michael Barbara, Carmen Zapata
33. "The Labyrinth" (11-10-70) Ricardo Montalban, Jan Shepard
34. "The Girl from Rainbow Beach" (11-17-70) Sheila James, Tiffany Bolling, Don Galloway
35. "Aura of a New Tomorrow" (11-24-70) Charles Drake, Shelby Grant, John Considine, Hilly Hicks
36. "Sounding Brass" (12-1-70) Michael Larrain, Pamela McMyler
37. "To Carry the Sun in a Golden Cup" (12-8-70) Bill Williams, Jo Ann Pflug, Mariette Hartley
38. "All the Golden Dandelions" (12-15-70) Richard Thomas, Belinda Montgomery, Denis Graham
39. "Brave on a Mountain Top" (12-22-70) James Farentino, Judy Blair
40. "Another Buckle for Wesley Hill" (1-5-71) Glenn Corbett, Chill Wills, John Smith, Elaine Devry
41. "False Spring" (1-19-71) Robert Lansing, Dana Wynter
42. "A Passing of Torches" (1-26-71) Peter Deuel, Steve Franken, Walter Pidgeon

43. "A Woman's Place" (2-2-71) Rachel Roberts, Keye Luke,
     Dana Elcar, Lee Montgomery
44. "A Spanish Saying I Made Up" (2-16-71) Joseph Campanella,
     Richard Yniguez, Barbara Sigel
45. "Cynthia" (2-23-71) Diana Hyland, Robert Lipton, John Van
     Dreelen, William Lundigan
46. "Don't Kid a Kidder" (3-2-71) Kay Medford, Robert Pratt,
     Kathy Lloyd
47. "Elegy for a Mad Dog" (3-9-71) Christina Crawford, Brad
     David, Johnny Seven, Margarita Cordova
48. "The Contract" (3-16-71) Geraldine Brooks, Pat Harrington,
     Monica Lewis, Mabel Albertson
49. "The Windfall" (3-23-71) Alexis Smith, Craig Stevens,
     Laurie Prange
50. "The House of Alquist" (3-30-71) Jessica Walter, Don Chas-
     tain, Alexander Scourby

Third Season

51. "The Tender Comrade" (9-14-71) Diana Muldaur, Pernell
     Roberts, Clint Howard, Dawn Lyn
52. "A Portrait of Debbie" (9-21-71) George Grizzard, Patricia
     Crowley, Pamelyn Ferdin
53. "In My Father's House" (9-28-71) Kathryn Hays, Barry
     Brown, Alan Hale
54. "I Can Hardly Tell You Apart" (10-5-71) Sally Field, Rus-
     sell Johnson
55. "This Is Max" (10-12-71) Tom Helmore, Vincent Van Pat-
     ten, Brian Tochi
56. "Men Who Care" [Part I; concluded with episode of 10/21/71
     of "Owen Marshall, Counselor at Law"] (10-19-71) Ed
     Nelson, Rick Ely, Belinda Montgomery, Arthur Hill
57. "Ask Me Again Tomorrow" (10-26-71) Sharon Acker, Wil-
     liam Windom, Dorothy Green
58. "Don't Phase Me Out" (11-2-71) Joseph Campanella, Jacque-
     line Scott
59. "Echo from Another World" (11-9-71) Ted Bessell, Dorothy
     Lamour, Laraine Stephens
60. "The Best Is Yet to Be" (11-16-71) Betty Bronson, Ruth
     Hussey, Patric Knowles, Robert Clarke
61. "A Yellow Bird" (11-23-71) Skye Aubrey, Christopher Stone,
     Brian Dewey
62. "They Grow Up" (11-30-71) Fred Holliday, Sian Barbara
     Allen, Michael Blodgett
63. "Of Magic Shadow Shapes" (12-7-71) Barry Sullivan, Robert
     Pratt, Doris Singleton
64. "Cross-Match" (12-14-71) Mike Warren, Johnny Whitaker
65. "The Basic Moment" [Part I] (1-4-72) Michele Lee, Chris-
     tine Belford, Richard Van Vleet, Berkeley Harris
66. "The Basic Moment" [Part II] (1-11-72) as above
67. "All the Pretty People" (1-25-72) Nico Minardos, Lindsay
     Wagner
68. "I'm Really Trying" (2-1-72) Gary Collins, Sean Kelly,

Virginia Gregg, Elaine Devry
69. "Is It So Soon That I Am Done For--I Wonder What I Was Begun For?" (2-8-72) Michael Callan, Sallie Schockley, Charles Seel, Tiger Williams
70. "Just a Little Courage" (2-15-72) David McCallum, Leslie Charlson, Barry Higgins
71. "Don't Talk About Darkness!" (2-22-72) Barbara Rush, Neville Brand, Don Keefer
72. "Once There Was a Bantu Prince" (2-29-72) Juanita Moore, Chelsea Brown, Felton Perry, Mary Gregory
73. "A Taste of Salt" (3-7-72) Anne Jackson, Nancy DeCarl, Charles Aidman
74. "Solomon's Choice" (3-14-72) Jack Kelly, John Lupton, Lee Purcell, Randolph Mantooth, Brett Hadley

Fourth Season

75. "A Fragile Possession" (9-12-72) Beverly Garland, Joanna Cameron, Kathy Lloyd, Mark Travis
76. "Love Is When They Say They Need You" (9-19-72) Bruce Davidson, Mike Farrell, Peggy McCay
77. "We'll Walk Out of Here Together" (9-26-72) Jordan Rhodes, Sian Barbara Allen, Dana Elcar
78. "In Sickness and in Health" (10-3-72) Heidi Vaughn, Kaz Garas, Eric Braeden, Cathy-Lee Crosby
79. "House of Mirrors" (10-10-72) Patrick O'Neal, Steve Sherman, Brenda Vaccaro, Robert F. Simon
80. "He Could Sell Iceboxes to Eskimos" (10-17-72) Jack Haley, Agnes Moorehead, Sharon Farrell
81. "The Wednesday Game" (10-24-72) Katherine Justice, Russell G. Wiggins
82. "Don and Denise" (10-31-72) Lindsay Wagner, Rick Lenz, Dana Elcar
83. "Please Don't Send Flowers" (11-14-72) Lawrence Pressman, Susan Clark
84. "With a Shout, Not a Whimper" (11-21-72) Leif Erickson, Joel Fabiani, Martin Brooks
85. "Jason Be Nimble, Jason Be Quick" (11-28-72) James Stacy, Linda Marsh, Lee Montgomery, Lois Hall
86. "Unto the Next Generation" (12-5-72) Jess Walton, Harvey Fisher, Shelley Morrison, Alan Oppenheimer
87. "Heartbeat for Yesterday" (12-12-72) William Shatner, Robert Rhodes, Chief Dan George, Cal Bellini
88. "Dinner of Herbs" (12-19-72) Margaret O'Brien, Anthony Eisley, Vincent Van Lynn, Marjorie Arnold, Richard Derr
89. "A More Exciting Case" (1-2-73) Jessica Walter, James Callahan, Charles Drake, Robert Walker Jr.
90. "A Necessary End" (1-9-73) Anne Baxter, Murray Matheson, Tom Drake, Susan Howard
91. "Who Are You, Arthur Kolinski?" (1-16-73) Nehemiah Persoff, Peter Mark Richman, Michael Rupert
92. "Gemini Descending" (1-23-73) James Coco, Aneta Corseaut
93. "The Problem with Charlie!" (1-30-73) Don Stroud, Elaine

Giftos, Jackie Coogan
94. "Catch Ring That Isn't There" (2-6-73) Gloria DeHaven, Jan-Michael Vincent, Norman Fell, Lane Bradford
95. "The Working Heart" (2-13-73) Joanna Barnes, Donnelly Rhodes, Kristina Holland, Frank Sinatra Jr., Whit Bissell
96. "The Other Martin Loring" (2-20-73) Mark Miller, Sharon Acker, Martha Scott, Scott Jacoby
97. "The Day After Forever" (2-27-73) Pernell Roberts, Sally Ann Howes, Lyle Waggoner, Maureen McCormick
98. "The Tortoise Dance" (3-6-73) Darrel Larson, Janet Blair Richard Bradford, Darlene Carr, Anthony Eldridge

Fifth Season

99. "The Panic Path" (9-11-73) Paul Burke, Vera Miles, Laurette Spang, Ansom Williams, Brooke Mills
100. "A Joyful Song" (9-18-73) Fionnuala Flanagan, Peter Kastner, Randames Pera, Greg Mullavey
101. "For Services Rendered" (9-25-73) Tige Andrews, Kim Hunter, Ray Oliver, Dan Tobin, Ross Elliott
102. "Blood Kin" (10-2-73) Sonny Bono, Lawrence Pressman, Suzanne Charney, Deanna Denee Martin
103. "The Light at the Threshold" (10-9-73) Audrey Landers, Carol Lawrence, Rodney Allen Rippy, Ryan MacDonald
104. "A Question of Fault" (10-16-73) Barbara Luna, Lou Frizzell, Armand Alzamora, Claudio Martinez
105. "Friends in High Places" (10-23-73) Frank Langella, Jack Kruschen, Viola Harris
106. "The Endless Moment" (10-30-73) Stefanie Powers
107. "The Tall Tree" (11-6-73) Tony Musante, Susan Howard, Pamelyn Ferdin, Sharon Gless
108. "The Circles of Shame" (11-20-73) Leslie Charleson, Barbara Baxley, Colby Chester
109. "Nguyen" (11-27-73) Robert Hooks, Joan Pringle
110. "A Cry in the Night" (12-11-73) Dina Merrill, Claude Akins
111. "Death Is Only a Side Effect" (12-18-73) Joanna Barnes, Lynne Marta, Alan Bergmann, Robert Urich
112. "The Comeback" (1-1-74) Penny Fuller, Ed Flanders
113. "A Full Life" (1-8-74) Richard Basehart, Phyllis Thaxter, Murray MacLeod, Milton Selzer, Jack Hogan
114. "No Charity for the MacAllisters" (1-15-74) Pamela McMyler, Tom Lester, R. G. Armstrong, Edd Byrnes, Stacy Keach Sr.
115. "Each Day a Miracle" (1-22-74) Ronne Troup, Andy Robinson, Clark Howat, Maidie Norman
116. "Fear of Silence" (1-29-74) Christopher Connelly, Gretchen Corbett, Robert Ellenstein
117. "Angela's Nightmare" (2-5-74) Mary MacDonald, James Olson
118. "The Mugging" (2-12-74) Lorraine Gary, Jim Hutton, Craig Hundley, John Lupton

119. "The Latch-Key Child" (2-19-74) Marcia Strassman, Tracie Savage, Brad Savage, Lois January
120. "Out of Control" (2-26-74) George Maharis, Barbara Anderson
121. "I've Promised You a Father" [Part I; concluded with episode of 3/9/74 of "Owen Marshall, Counselor at Law"] (3-5-74) Kim Darby, Lynda Day George, Arthur Hill
122. "Designs" (3-12-74) Jane Wyatt, Mel Ferrer

Sixth Season

123. "The Brittle Warrior" (9-10-74) Forrest Tucker, Peggy McCay, Patty McCormack, Alan Fudge
124. "The Faith of Childish Things" (9-17-74) Kristoffer Tabori, Barbara Hale, Sian Barbara Allen, Jacques Aubuchon
125. "Last Flight to Babylon" (9-24-74) Cliff DeYoung, Greg Mullavey, Christine Belford, June Lockhart, Jim Backus, Jeff Donnell
126. "To Father a Child" (10-1-74) Diane Baker, Ron Ely, Paul Lambert, S. John Launer
127. "The Outrage" (10-8-74) Sean Kelly, Gretchen Corbett, Patrick Wayne, Edward Power, Edward Winter
128. "The Fatal Challenge" (10-15-74) Jess Walton, Joe Kapp, Ketty Lester, Anna Navarro
129. "A Fevered Angel" (10-22-74) Robert Drivas, Donna Mills, Eric Braeden, Quinn Redeker
130. "Feedback" (10-29-74) Herbert Jefferson Jr., Leslie Uggams, Peter Brandon, Norman Alden, Henry Beckman
131. "No Gods in Sight" (11-12-74) Carl Betz
132. "Hell Is Upstairs" (11-19-74) Shirley Knight
133. "The Last Rip-off" (11-26-74) Richard Basehart, Anne Schedeen, Jerry Fogel, Kasey Rogers, Irene Tedrow, Virginia Gregg
134. "Child of Silence" (12-3-74) Lois Nettleton, Dawn Lyn
135. "The 266 Days" (12-10-74) Gena Rowlands, Jed Allen, Stewart Moss, Aldine King
136. "The Resident" (12-17-74) Cliff Potts, Helen Verbit, Wallace Rooney, Mel Stewart
137. "Dark Fury" [Part I] (1-7-75) Lindsay Wagner, Dack Rambo, Diana Hyland
138. "Dark Fury" [Part II] (1-14-75) as above
139. "Public Streets" (1-21-75) Mark Miller, Logan Ramsey, Juliet Mills, Kathryn Reynolds
140. "The Time Bomb" (1-28-75) Lucie Arnaz, Joan Hotchkis, Gavan O'Herlihy, Victor Millan
141. "Four-Plus Hot" (2-4-75) Ben Murphy, Scott Newman
142. "Jake's Okay" (2-11-75) Belinda J. Montgomery, Scott Jacoby
143. "Save the Last Dance for Me" (2-18-75) Pamela Hensley, Elaine Giftos
144. "Unindicted Wife" (2-25-75) Patty Duke Astin, John Astin
145. "Dark Corridors" (3-4-75) Joanne Dru, Robin Mattson, Rosemary DeCamp, Douglas V. Fowley

146. "Loser in a Dead Heat" (3-11-75) Larry Hagman

[Continuing]


MEDICAL CENTER

The Regulars: Dr. Joe Gannon, Chad Everett; Dr. Paul Lochner, James Daly; Nurse Chambers, Jayne Meadows; Dr. Bartlett, Corinne Camacho; Nurse Wilcox, Audrey Totter (recurring guest role).

The Episodes:

1. "The Last 10 Yards" (9-24-69) Cicely Tyson, Edward Asner, O. J. Simpson, Randames Pera, Lincoln Kilpatrick, Dana Elcar
2. "Victim" (10-1-69) Dyan Cannon, Robert Lansing, Don Clarke, David Frank
3. "Emergency in Ward E" (10-8-69) Joseph Buloff, Robert Pine, Gerald S. O'Loughlin, Simon Scott
4. "A Life Is Waiting" (10-15-69) Barbara Rush, John McMartin
5. "The Battle of Lily Wu" (10-22-69) France Nuyen, Harold J. Stone
6. "The Crooked Circle" (10-29-69) Tim Considine, Nan Martin, Richard Webb, Charlotte Stewart
7. "Thousands and Thousands of Miles" (11-12-69) Brooke Bundy, Michael Brandon, Carolyn Conwell, Peter Donat
8. "The Sharpest Edge" (11-19-69) John Marley, John Ericson, Lynn Carlin
9. "Jeopardy" (11-26-69) Michael Burns
10. "The Fallen Image" (12-3-69) Viveca Lindfors, Paul Stevens, Linden Chiles, Walter Pidgeon
11. "The Loner" (12-10-69) Farley Granger, Lee Grant, James Shigeta
12. "24 Hours" (12-17-69) Belinda Montgomery, Ned Glass, Tom Fielding, Bettye Ackerman
13. "The Adversaries" (12-31-69) Inga Swenson, Patricia Quinn, Christopher Stone
14. "The Deceived" (1-7-70) Pat Hingle, Carrie Snodgrass, Inga Swenson
15. "Moment of Decision" (1-14-70) Percy Rodriguez, Tyne Daly, Robert Gentry
16. "Runaway" (1-21-70) Richard Thomas, Pam Peter, James Shigeta, Simon Oakland
17. "Fright and Flight" (2-4-70) Steve Ihnat, Heidi Vaughn, Martine Bartlett
18. "A Duel with Doom" (2-11-70) Bruce Davison, June Taylor, Martin Sheen
19. "A Matter of Tomorrow" (2-25-70) Mercedes McCambridge, Cliff Potts
20. "Care Is No Cure" (3-4-70) Walter Matthews, Shelby Grant

Stephen Brooks
21.  "The Professional"  (3-11-70)  Slim Pickens, Jo Ann Harris,
     Forrest Tucker
22.  "The Combatants"  (3-18-70)  William Shatner, Renne Jarrett
23.  "The V.D. Story"  (3-25-70)  Carl Betz, James Shigeta
24.  "His Brother's Keeper"  (4-1-70)  Tim O'Connor, Ben Mur-
     phy, David Cassidy
25.  "The Rebel in White"  (4-8-70)  Georg Stanford Brown, David
     Opatoshu, Will Geer, Paula Kelly
26.  "Between Dark and Daylight"  (4-15-70)  Sharon Farrell,
     Rudy Solari, Tom Skerritt, Walter Koenig

Second Season

27.  "Brink of Doom"  (9-16-70)  Elizabeth Ashley, George Grizzard
28.  "Undercurrent"  (9-23-70)  Paul Burke, Andrew Duggan,
     Salome Jens
29.  "Junkie"  (9-30-70)  Heidi Vaughn, Michael Anderson Jr.,
     Murray Hamilton, Phyllis Thaxter
30.  "Assailant"  (10-7-70)  Gary Lockwood, Bradford Dillman
31.  "The Clash"  (10-14-70)  Vera Miles, Charles Aidman, Patri-
     cia Stich
32.  "Ghetto Clinic"  (10-21-70)  William Devane, Robert F. Lyons
33.  "Scream of Silence"  (10-28-70)  Lois Nettleton, Jason Evers,
     Fred Holliday
34.  "Death Grip"  (11-4-70)  Steve Forrest, Laurie Prange, Hugh
     Beaumont
35.  "Witch Hunt"  (11-11-70)  Dana Wynter, Joan Delaney, Dick
     Kallman, John Abbott, Jeff Donnell
36.  "Deadly Encounter"  (11-18-70)  Barry Sullivan, Diane Baker
37.  "Trial by Terror"  (11-25-70)  Frank Converse, George Cha-
     kiris, C. Elliott Montgomery
38.  "Accused"  (12-2-70)  Belinda Montgomery, James Olson,
     Jonathan Brooks
39.  "Crisis"  (12-9-70)  Roddy McDowall, Keenan Wynn, Mark
     Jenkins
40.  "Man at Bay"  (12-16-70)  Gary Lockwood, Stefanie Powers
41.  "The Savage Image"  (12-30-70)  Geoffrey Deuel, Rudy Solari,
     Dan Travanty, Eduard Franz
42.  "Woman in Question"  (1-6-71)  Dennis Cole, Brenda Scott,
     Nancy Priddy
43.  "Web of Darkness"  (1-13-71)  Jessica Walter, Roger Davis,
     Janet Margolin, Alfred Ryder
44.  "Danger Point"  (1-27-71)  Joanne Linville, Frank Aletter,
     Paul Picerni, James A. Watson Jr., Don Dubbins
45.  "Secret Heritage"  (2-3-71)  Pamela Franklin, Kim Stanley,
     Karl Swenson, Inga Swenson
46.  "Edge of Violence"  (2-10-71)  Jack Carter, Joan Van Ark,
     Liam Sullivan
47.  "Countdown"  (2-17-71)  Peter Strauss, Brooke Bundy, Wil-
     liam Lundigan
48.  "Perfection of Vices"  (2-24-71)  Dina Merrill, Charlotte
     Stewart

49. "The Man in Hiding" (3-3-71) Richard Kiley, Gena Rowlands, Georg Stanford Brown
50. "Crossroads" (3-10-71) Pat Hingle, Jan Sterling, Lynne Marta, Robert Pine

Third Season

51. "Blood Line" (9-15-71) William Windom, Carol Lawrence, Percy Rodriguez
52. "The Corrupted" (9-22-71) Steve Lawrence, Pippa Scott, David Opatoshu
53. "The Imposter" (9-29-71) Kim Hunter, Forrest Tucker, Joy Bang
54. "Double Jeopardy" (10-6-71) Stefanie Powers, Paul Stevens, Scott Marlowe, Jack Kruschen
55. [unknown title] (10-13-71) Pamela Payton-Wright, Roger Davis
56. "Circle of Power" (10-20-71) Barry Sullivan, Jessica Walter, Michael Burns
57. "The Shattered Man" (10-27-71) Bradford Dillman, Collin Wilcox-Horne, David Wayne
58. "The Albatross" (11-3-71) Michael Douglas, Anne Helm, John Ericson, Pamela McMyler
59. [unknown title] (11-10-71) Paul Stewart, Jo Van Fleet, Jess Walton, Michael Larrain
60. "Suspected" (11-17-71) Earl Holliman, Diana Hyland, Louise Latham
61. "The Loser" (11-24-71) Susan Strasberg, Greg Mullavey, Tom Ligon
62. "The Pawn" (12-1-71) George Maharis, Fred Holliday, Louise Sorel
63. "Conspiracy" (12-8-71) Leslie Nielsen, Suzanne Pleshette, Lee Harcourt Montgomery
64. "The Nowhere Child" (12-15-71) Diana Sands
65. "Shock!" [Part I] (12-29-71) Glenn Corbett, Vera Miles, Sheree North, Robert F. Lyons
66. "Shock!" [Part II] (1-5-72) as above
67. "Fatal Decision" (1-19-72) Fritz Weaver, Wendell Burton, Claudine Auger
68. "Terror" (1-26-72) Larry Blyden, Kathy Lloyd, Anthony Caruso
69. [unknown title] (2-2-72) Michael Callan, Jeanette Nolan, Marianne McAndrew
70. "The Choice" (2-9-72) Monte Markham, Tyne Daly, Clu Gulager
71. [unknown title] (2-16-72) Michael Tolan, Jo Ann Harris, Peter Brown, Lincoln Kilpatrick
72. [unknown title] (2-23-72) Jack Ging, Barbara Rush, Craig Stevens, Dick Van Patten
73. [unknown title] (3-1-72) Howard Duff, Ida Lupino, Meg Foster, James Shigeta
74. [unknown title] (3-8-72) Chris Robinson, Tisha Sterling, Martin E. Brooks, Shelly Novack

Fourth Season

75. [unknown title] (9-20-72) James Stacy, Mike Masters, Nancy
    Walker, Ivan Bonar, Pamela Payton-Wright
76. [unknown title] (9-27-72) Lola Albright, Karl Held, Sarah
    Marshall, Sean Kelly, Stephen Hudis
77. [unknown title] (10-4-72) Estelle Parsons, Tim O'Connor,
    Kristoffer Tabori, Martin Braddock
78. "The Torn Man" (10-11-72) Harry Guardino, Marcia Rodd,
    Robert H. Harris
79. "Betrayed" (10-18-72) Geraldine Page, Joyce Van Patten,
    Martin E. Brooks, Charles Aidman
80. "Doctor and Mr. Harper" (10-25-72) Paul Burke, Diana
    Muldaur, Darlene Carr, Peter Kastner
81. [unknown title] (11-1-72) Peter Haskell, Fred Beir, George
    Tobias, Lee Purcell
82. [unknown title] (11-8-72) George Chakiris, Gilbert Roland,
    Carmen Zapata, Priscilla Garcia
83. "The Outcast" (11-15-72) Ken Howard, Kay Medford, Dick
    Kallman, Louise Sorel
84. "No Sanctuary" (11-22-72) Shelby Grant, Simon Oakland,
    John Lupton, Tammi Bula, Mary McCarthy
85. [unknown title] (11-29-72) Joe Knapp, William Devane, Rus-
    sell Wiggins, Leslie Charleson
86. "Visions of Doom" (12-6-72) Susan Oliver, Lynn Carlin,
    William Windom, Kate Murtaugh
87. "A Game for One Player" (12-13-72) Jessica Walter, Norm
    Alden, Robert Foxworth, Patricia Harty
88. [unknown title] (12-20-72) Bill Bixby, Joanna Miles, Dianne
    Hull, Ed Hall
89. "No Way Out" (12-27-72) Lois Nettleton, Will Geer, Nico
    Minardos, Scott Jacoby
90. [unknown title] (1-3-73) Brenda Scott, Shelly Novack, Bettye
    Ackerman, John Ward, Charlotte Stewart, Aldine King
91. [unknown title] (1-10-73) Ruth Buzzi, Sheila Larken, Tom
    Bosley, John Karlen
92. [unknown title] (1-17-73) Dean Jagger, Lynne Marta, Jeanette
    Nolan, John Ritter
93. [unknown title] (1-24-73) Jason Wingreen, Ed Hall, Barbara
    Feldon, Larry Hagman
94. [unknown title] (1-31-73) Marlyn Mason, Adam Roarke,
    Audrey Totter, Brandon Cruz
95. "No Margin for Error" (2-7-73) Celeste Holm, Wesley
    Addy, Jack Kruschen, Shelley Morrison
96. [unknown title] (2-14-73) Barbara Rush, Earl Holliman, Vin-
    cent Van Patten
97. [unknown title] (2-21-73) Stefanie Powers, Gary Merrill,
    Michael Parks
98. [unknown title] (2-28-73) Dana Wynter, Jim Backus, Elayne
    Heilveil

## Fifth Season

99. "The Guilty" (9-10-73) Julie Harris, Lara Parker, Steve Forrest, John Lupton, Stephen Brooks, Belinda Montgomery
100. "Time of Darkness" (9-17-73) Jo Van Fleet, Lonny Chapman, Pamela Franklin, Claude Akins
101. "Broken Image" (9-24-73) William Windom, Amanda McBroom, Laraine Day
102. "Impasse" (10-1-73) Lois Nettleton, Nick Nolte, Tim Matheson, Jamie Smith Jackson
103. "Clash of Shadows" (10-8-73) Diane Baker, Andrew Duggan, Martin Sheen, Audrey Totter, Rae Allen
104. "The Casualty" (10-22-73) Barbara Anderson, Joseph Campanella, Michael Morgan, Stephen Coit
105. "Stranger in Two Worlds" (10-29-73) Joan Blondell, Lynne Marta, Gary Lockwood
106. "Child of Violence" (11-12-73) Gena Rowlands, Louise Fletcher, Lee H. Montgomery
107. "Woman for Hire" (11-19-73) Jessica Walter
108. "A Life at Stake" (11-26-73) Bradford Dillman, Stefanie Powers
109. "Nightmare" (12-3-73)
110. "Deadly Game" (12-10-73) Kay Medford, Tyne Daly, Bruce Kirby, Anne Loos
111. "Web of Intrigue" (1-7-74) Michael Brandon, Damu King, Celeste Holm, Meg Foster
112. "Trial by Knife" (1-14-74) Rosemary Murphy, Judy Pace, Felton Perry, Harv Selsby
113. "Choice of Evils" (1-21-74) Paul Burke, Barbara Rush, Jill Clayburgh, William Campbell
114. "No Escape" (1-28-74) Cameron Mitchell, Lola Albright, Ayn Ruymen, Eddie Garrett, Barney Phillips
115. "Dark Warning" (2-11-74) Ed Nelson, Joanna Miles, David Hedison
116. "Girl from Bedlam" (2-18-74) Joanna Pettet, Leonard Frey, Andre Phillipe, Murray Hamilton
117. "Spectre" (2-25-74) Dean Jones
118. "The Enemies" (3-4-74) Carol Lawrence, Anne Meara
119. "The Conspirators" (3-11-74) John David Carson, Kay Len, Joey Aresco, Barbara Colby
120. "The World's a Balloon" (3-25-74) Dom De Luise
121. "Hexed" (4-1-74) Will Geer, Louise Sorel, Peter Haskell
122. "Appointment with Danger" (4-15-74) Nancy Kelly, Leif Erickson

## Sixth Season

123. "Adults Only" (9-9-74) Joan Van Ark, Tony Young, Monte Markham, Gale Sondergaard
124. "Demi-God" (9-16-74) Marjoe Gortner, Ed Hall, Meredith Baxter, John Marley, Jacqueline Scott
125. "The Faces of Peril" (9-23-74) John Randolph, Eric Serve

Andrea Marcovicci, Ron Castro, Robert Walden
126. "Three-Cornered Cage" (9-30-74) Dennis Cole, Diane
Baker, Diana Hyland, Kate Murtaugh, Barney Phillips
127. "The Shattered Mask" (10-7-74) Cameron Mitchell, Deborah
Winters
128. "May God Have Mercy" (10-21-74) Tim O'Connor, Rita
Moreno, Vic Tayback, Greg Leydig
129. "The Prisoners" (10-28-74) Shelby Grant, Frank Maxwell,
James Wainwright
130. "The Bribe" (11-4-74) Vera Miles, Peter Coffield, Pamela
Franklin, Harv Selsby, Brick Huston
131. "Tainted Lady" (11-11-74) Lloyd Bochner
132. "Heel of the Tyrant" (11-18-74)
133. "Three on a Tightrope" (11-25-74) Kristina Holland, Richard Hatch, Len Lesser, Allyn Ann McLerie
134. "Midwife" (12-2-74) Brooke Bundy
135. "Kiss and Kill" (12-9-74) Belinda J. Montgomery, David
Soul, Kim Hunter, Delores Sutton, Paul Carr, George
Tobias, Caroline Kido
136. "Saturday's Child" (12-16-74) Kathy Lloyd, Michael Tolan,
Rose Gregorio, Paula Kelly, John Travolta
137. "The Hostile Heart" (12-30-74) Rodney Allen Rippy, Lois
Nettleton, Janet MacLachlan, Thalmus Rasulala, Peter
Haskell
138. "No Way Home" (1-6-75) Cyd Charisse, Joseph Campanella
139. "Captives" (1-13-75)
140. "Crown of Thorns" (2-3-75) Suzy Kendall
141. "The Invisible Wife" (2-10-75) Beverly Garland, Ed Nelson,
Penny Fuller, Lew Horn
142. "If Mine Eye Offends Me" (2-24-75) David Birney, Donna
Mills
143. "Survivors" (3-3-75) Peter Strauss, George Tobias, Darleen Carr, Richard Lawson, Mimi Maynard, Robert Douglas
144. "Aftershock" (3-10-75) Louise Sorel, Burr DeBenning
145. "Half a Life" (3-17-75) Ken Barry, Sheree North, Cesare
Danova

[Continuing]


... THEN CAME BRONSON

Television's answer to Dennis Hopper's cult film Easy Rider
casts Michael Parks as the motorcycle nomad Jim Bronson.

The Regulars: Jim Bronson, Michael Parks.

The Episodes:

1. "The Runner" (9-17-69) Jack Klugman, Mark Lester, Penny
Marshall, Karen Huston, Arlene Kaier, Stephen Vinovich

2. "The Old Motorcycle Fiasco" (9-24-69) Keenan Wynn, Martine Bartlett
3. "A Famine Where Abundance Grows" (10-1-69) Carol Rossen, Charlotte Stewart, Paul Gleason
4. "The Circle of Time" (10-8-69) Elsa Lanchester, Woodrow Chambliss
5. "Where Will the Trumpets Be?" (10-15-69) Fernando Lamas, Jessica Walter, Lane Bradbury
6. "Amid Splinters of the Thunderbolt" (10-22-69) Zohra Lampert, Bruce Dern, James Doohan
7. "The 3:13 Arrives at Noon" (10-29-69) Gloria Grahame, Larry Gates, Royal Dano, John Hubbard, Garry Walberg, Bob Steele
8. "Old Tigers Never Die--They Just Run Away" (11-5-69) Gabe Dell, Diane Ladd, Will Geer, Iron Eyes Cody
9. "Your Love Is Like a Demolition Derby in My Heart" (11-19-69) Tim McIntire, David Huddleston, Flora Plumb, Alan Vint
10. "Two Percent of Nothing" (11-23-69) Patricia Quinn
11. "All the World and God" (12-3-69) Lois Nettleton, Rex Holman, Josephine Hutchinson, Lynn Hamilton, Charles Seel
12. "A Long Trip to Yesterday" (12-10-69) Robert Hooks, Lee Duncan, Florence St. Peter, Slim Gaillard
13. "The Spitball Kid" (12-17-69) Kurt Russell, Don Drysdale, David Sheiner, Stefanie Mann
14. "Against a Cold Blank Wall" (12-24-69) Robert Loggia, Pilar Seurat, Manuel Padilla
15. "Sybil" (12-31-69) Renne Jarrett, Joseph Raymond, Marjorie Eaton, Michael Lipton
16. "A Pickin' an' a Singin'" (1-14-70) Michael Burns, Skip Homeier, Jana Taylor
17. "The Gleam of the Eagle Mind" (1-21-70) Jan Shepard, John Dehner, Jay Novello, Richard Webb
18. "That Undiscovered Country" (1-28-70) Bebe Kelly, Mark Jenkins, Heidi Vaughn, Rance Howard
19. "Lucky Day" (2-4-70) Lynne Marta, Barry Brown
20. "Mating Dance for Tender Grass" (2-11-70) Buffy Sainte-Marie, Eddie Little Sky
21. "The Mountain" (2-18-70) James Whitmore, Melendy Britt
22. "Still Waters" (2-25-70) John Colicos, Veronica Cartwright, Jean Allison
23. "The Forest Primeval" (3-4-70) Lee DeBroux, Gary Clarke
24. "The Ninety-Nine Mile Circle" (3-11-70) David Burns, Gwynne Gilford, Paula Victor, Barbara Dodd
25. "The Mary R" (3-25-70) Gerald S. O'Loughlin, Bob Random, Beverly Garland
26. "What's an Ark Without Centaurs?" (4-1-70) Anjanette Comer, Morgan Woodward

# BRACKEN'S WORLD

Television, years a stigma in the cinema, retaliated with this eviscerating journey through a chthonian Hollywood. "Bracken's World," so named for "Century Studios" executive John Bracken (Leslie Nielsen) is a veritable deluge of stereotypes--of struggling ingénues, acerbic directors, tragic veterans of the grind--all designed to make the evisceration the more painful.

The Regulars: Kevin Grant (producer and director), Peter Haskell; Sylvia Caldwell (secretary to John Bracken), Eleanor Parker (to episode of 1/9/70); Ann (secretary to Bracken), Bettye Ackerman (with episode of 1/16/70); Tom Huston (actor), Stephen Oliver (first season only); Davey Evans (actor), Dennis Cole (first season only); Mrs. Kevin Grant, Madlyn Rhue (first season only); Rachel Holt (actress), Karen Jensen; Diane Waring (actress), Laraine Stephens; Paulette Douglas (actress), Linda Harrison; John Bracken, Leslie Nielsen (with second season).

The Episodes:

1. "Fade-In" (9-19-69) Omar Sharif, Tony Curtis, Raquel Welch
2. "Panic" (9-26-69) Scott Brady, Edward G. Robinson
3. "King David" (10-3-69) Zsa Zsa Gabor, Jay C. Flippen, Carolyn Jones
4. "Don't You Cry for Susannah" (10-10-69) Ray Milland, Diana Ewing, Vernon Weddle
5. "Options" (10-17-69) Robert Colbert, Warren Berlinger, Debbie Reynolds
6. "Closed Set" (10-24-69) John Van Dreelen, Yvonne Wilder, Philip Pine
7. "The Sweet Smell of Failure" (10-31-69) Ricardo Montalban, Paul Picerni
8. "The Stunt" (11-7-69) Gary Collins, Bobby Riha
9. "All the Beautiful Young Girls" (11-14-69) Arthur Hill, Luke Halpin, Diana Dye, Ed Bach, Kevin Hagen
10. "A Package Deal" (11-28-69) Shelley Fabares
11. "It's the Power Structure, Baby" (12-5-69) Debbie Reynolds
12. "Move in for a Close-up" (12-12-69) Peter Donat, Marie Windsor
13. "Stop Date" (12-19-69) Dane Clark, Cliff Robertson, Marie Windsor, Richard Anderson
14. "The Chase Sequence" (12-26-69) Marlyn Mason, Clint Ritchie
15. "Focus on a Gun" (1-2-70) Dennis Patrick, Joe Don Baker, George Murdock
16. "The Money Men" (1-9-70) Carl Betz, Jan Sterling, Liam Sullivan, Sue England
17. "Meanwhile, Back at the Studio" (1-16-70) James Hampton, Michael Baseleon
18. "A Perfect Piece of Casting" (1-30-70) Broderick Crawford, Monte Markham, Warren Berlinger

19. [unknown title] (2-6-70) Andy Devine, Stephen McNally, Lee Majors, Warren Berlinger
20. "Whatever Happened to Happy Endings?" (2-13-70) Lee Grant, Flora Plumb, Jack Riley
21. "Fallen, Fallen, Is Babylon" (2-20-70) Richard Thomas, Dabbs Greer, Margo Sappington
22. "Papa Never Spanked Me" (2-27-70) Martin Sheen, Jack Albertson
23. "A Beginning, a Middle, and an End" (3-6-70) Joseph Campanella, Virginia Wing
24. "Diffusion" (3-13-70) Anne Baxter, Don Knight, Zooey Hall, Fred Sadoff
25. "Day for Night" (3-20-70) James Gregory
26. "One, Two, Three ... Cry" (3-27-70) Barry Sullivan, Jo Ann Pflug, Susan Cabot, William Mims

Second Season

27. "Love It or Leave It, Change It or Lose It" (9-18-70) Forrest Tucker, Tony Bill, Burr DeBenning, Freeman King
28. "Murder--Off Camera" (9-25-70) Stuart Whitman, Ellen Corby
29. "Jenny, Who Bombs Buildings" (10-2-70) Sally Field, Rick Gates
30. "Together Again--For the Last Time" (10-9-70) Janice Rule, Charles Drake, Jeff Donnell, John Archer
31. "A Preview in Samarkand" (10-16-70) William Schallert, Suzanne Charny, Stanley Clements, Ed Peck
32. "The Mary Tree" (10-23-70) Edward G. Robinson, Diana Hyland
33. "Hey, Gringo--Hey, Pocho" (10-30-70) Ricardo Montalban, John Randolph
34. "A Team of One-Legged Acrobats" (11-6-70) Tom Skerritt, Kim Hunter
35. "The Anonymous Star" (11-13-70) Janet Leigh, Ida Lupino, Marie Windsor
36. "Infinity" (10-20-70) Darren McGavin, Ann Givin, Ned Glass, Sean Kelly
37. "The Nude Scene" (11-27-70) Lois Nettleton, Craig Stevens, Steve Ihnat
38. "A Score Without Strings" (12-4-70) Jim McMullan
39. "Will Freddy's Real Father Please Stand Up?" (12-11-70) Rupert Crosse, George Spell, Warren Berlinger, Diana Sands
40. "The Country Boy" (12-18-70) Tim Matheson
41. "Miss Isabel Blue" (12-25-70) Sally Ann Howes, Armando Silvestre, David Astor, Virginia Capers

PARIS 7000

George Hamilton, fresh out of the disaster of "The Survivors," was seen again on television, this time as a man offering assistance to troubled Americans in Paris while working out of a United States Consulate.

The Regulars: Jack Brennan, George Hamilton; Jules Maurois, Jacques Aubuchon.

The Episodes:

1. "Beyond Reproach" (1-22-70) E. G. Marshall, Anne Baxter, Robert Ellenstein, Pamela McMyler
2. "No Place to Hide" (1-29-70) Nina Foch, Joseph Campanella, John Rayner, Gene Raymond
3. "Call Me Lee" (2-5-70) Barbara Anderson, Will Kuluva, Brenda Benet, Perry Lopez, Fabrizio Mioni
4. "Journey to Nowhere" (2-12-70) Diane Baker, Steve Ihnat, John Van Dreelen, H. M. Wynant
5. "To Cage a Lion" (2-19-70) Leif Erickson
6. "Ordeal" (2-26-70) Wilfrid Hyde-White, Greg Mullavey, John Orchard, Peter Bromilow
7. "The Shattered Idol" (3-5-70) Carol Lawrence, William Shatner, Roger Perry
8. "Elegy for Edward Shelby" (3-12-70) Elizabeth Allen, Warren Stevens, Belinda Montgomery
9. "The Last Grand Tour" (3-19-70) Jack Albertson, Martha Scott, Herbert Rudley
10. "Call Me Ellen" [sequel to episode of 2/5/70] (3-26-70) Barbara Anderson, Paul Henreid

1970-1971 SEASON

## THE MOST DEADLY GAME

Impossible situations are not the only failings of this mystery series, the principals being criminologists Jonathan Croft (George Maharis), Vanessa Smith (Yvette Mimieux) and Mr. Arcane (Ralph Bellamy).

The Regulars: Jonathan Croft, George Maharis; Vanessa Smith, Yvette Mimieux; Mr. Arcane, Ralph Bellamy.

The Episodes:

1. "Little David" (10-10-70) Roger Davis, Marj Dusay, Louise Troy, Christine Schmidtmer, Bob Random
2. "Witches' Sabbath" (10-17-70) Jill Haworth, Barry Atwater, Michael Baseleon, Richard Mulligan
3. "Gabrielle" (10-24-70) Vince Howard, Diana Ewing, Quinn Redeker, Robert Viharo
4. "Breakdown" (10-31-70) Jessica Walter, Tom Bosley, Greg Mullavey, Sandy Kenyon
5. "Who Killed Kindness?" (11-7-70) Carol Lynley, Paul Richards, Sheree North, Andrew Prine, Robert J. Wilke
6. "Photo Finish" (11-14-70) Marlyn Mason, Stephen Young, Craig Littler
7. "War Games" (11-28-70) Pat Harrington, Barbara Luna, Peter Brown, Billy Dee Williams
8. "Nightbirds" (12-12-70) Jeff Bridges
9. "Model for Murder" (12-19-70) Barbara Hale, Frank Converse, Douglas Hume, William Smith
10. "The Classic Burial Position" (1-2-71) Skye Aubrey, Anjanette Comer, Hugh Beaumont, Woodrow Parfrey, Carl Reindel
11. "The Lady from Praha" (1-9-71) Bert Convy, May Britt, Brenda Benet, Hank Brandt
12. "I, Said the Sparrow" (1-16-71) Wilfrid Hyde-White, Mildred Natwick, John Fiedler, Joan Huntington, Dick Cavett

## THE YOUNG REBELS

Just why it should have been that this short-lived tale of

youthful American 1776 revolutionaries was--despite the liberties
with historical record--charming, it would be difficult to say.    Perhaps the reason lay in the fact that our "Yankee Doodle Society,"
as the revolutionaries called themselves, were--now an affirmation
of how liberty was in fact attained--youthful.

The Regulars:  Jeremy Larkin, Rick Ely; Isak Poole, Lou Gossett;
          Henry Abington, Alex Henteloff; Elizabeth Coates, Hilarie
          Thompson; General Lafayette, Philippe Forquet.

The Episodes:

  1.    "Father and I Went Down to Camp"   (9-20-70)  Frank Con-
          verse, Will Geer
  2.    "The Ring of Freedom"   (9-27-70)  Will Geer, Lawrence
          Linville
  3.    "The Blood of an Englishman"   (10-4-70)  John Colicos
  4.    "To Hang a Hero"   (10-11-70)  Brandon de Wilde
  5.    "Fort Hope"   (10-18-70)  Byron Webster, Willard Sage
  6.    "Suicide Squad"   (10-25-70)  Steve Ihnat, Paul Carr
  7.    "Alias Ben Todd"   (11-1-70)  Lee Purcell, Michael Evans,
          Patrick Horgan
  8.    "The Hostages"   (11-8-70)  Eric Braeden, Eric Christmas
  9.    "The Age of Independence"   (11-15-70)  Will Geer, David Soul
 10.    "Stalemate"   (11-22-70)  Harvey Jason, Terence Stammell,
          John Orchard
 11.    "Valley of the Guns"   (11-29-70)  Ron Randell, Monte Mark-
          ham
 12.    "Dangerous Ally"   (12-6-70)  Richard Kelton
 13.    "The Infiltrator"   (12-20-70)  Stephen Young, Elizabeth Baur,
          Peter Church, Bernard Fox
 14.    "Unbroken Chains"   (12-27-70)  Paul Winfield
 15.    "To Kill a Traitor"   (1-3-71)  Ben Wright, Gary Lockwood


THE YOUNG LAWYERS

          Very well meaning, if at times sentimental, account of the
cases tried by law students Aaron Silverman (Zalman King), Pat
Walters (Judy Pace) and (in later episodes) Chris Blake (Philip
Clark) under the discerning eyes of veteran attorney David Barrett
(Lee J. Cobb) in a "Neighborhood Law Office" in Boston.    The
underprivileged clientele included a drug addict (Susan Strasberg's
role in "The Whimper of Whipped Dogs") and an intern accused of
malpractice (Frank Converse's role in "Is There a Good Samaritan
in the House?").

The Regulars:  Att. David Barrett, Lee J. Cobb; Aaron Silverman,
          Zalman King; Pat Walters, Judy Pace; Chris Blake, Philip
          Clark (with episode of 2/3/71).

The Episodes:

1. "Is There a Good Samaritan in the House?" (9-21-70) Frank
   Converse, David Sheiner, Gordon Pinsent, Walter Brooke,
   Ann Summers
2. "A Simple Thing Called Justice" (9-28-70) John Larch, Eric
   Laneuville, Paul Winfield, Betsy Jones-Moreland, Arthur
   Space
3. "The Two Dollar Thing" (10-5-70) Peter Strauss, Joan De-
   laney, Ellen Weston, Virginia Vincent, Russ Conway, Joy
   Bang
4. "The Alienation Kick" (10-12-70) Kim Hunter, Douglas
   Henderson, Mary Layne, Ford Rainey, Gwynne Gilford
5. "Where's Aaron?" (10-19-70) Philip Kenneally, Brian Cutler,
   Richard Eastham, Jonathan Lippe
6. "We May Be Better Strangers" (10-26-70) Tim O'Connor,
   John Rubinstein, Marsha Hunt, Sam Melville, David Carson,
   Douglas Henderson
7. "The Glass Prison" (11-2-70) Peter Deuel, Barbara Luna,
   Lonny Chapman, Harry Townes
8. "The Russell Incident" (11-9-70) Jim McMullan, Ellen Moss,
   Gerald S. O'Loughlin, Lee Bergere, Geoffrey Lewis, Paul
   Bertoya
9. "At the Edge of the Night" (11-16-70) Robert F. Lyons, Ben
   Hammer, Angela Clarke, Willard Sage
10. "Are You Running with Me, Jimmy?" (11-23-70) Martin
    Sheen, Paul Fix, Sherry Lynn Diamant, Don Hanmer, John
    Lupton
11. "A Busload of Bishops" (11-30-70) Simon Oakland, John
    McLiam, Antoinette Bower, Oscar De Gruy Jr., Paula
    Kelly
12. "The Legacy of Miles Turner" (12-7-70) Tim McIntire,
    David Sheiner, Peter Donat, Charlotte Stewart, Peter Ja-
    son
13. "Remember Chris Gately?" (12-14-70) Flora Plumb, Arch
    Johnson, Whit Bissell, Lawrence Linville, Carl Reindel
14. "MacGillicuddy Always Was a Pain in the Neck" (12-21-70)
    Edmond O'Brien, Dabbs Greer, Carmen Argenziano, Alan
    Vint
15. "False Witness" (1-4-71) Robert Webber, John Kerr, Bren-
    da Scott, Devra Korwin
16. "Legal Maneuver" (1-20-71) Eli Wallach, Peter Mark Rich-
    man, Ford Rainey, Lynn Loring
17. "The Outspoken Silence" (2-3-71) Pat Hingle, Kelly Jean
    Peters, Scott Glenn, Doreen Lang, Douglas Henderson
18. "The Victims" (2-10-71) Martha Hyer, Heidi Vaughn,
    Michael Strong, Gary Tigerman
19. "The Bradbury War" (2-17-71) Janet Margolin, John Beck,
    Russell Johnson
20. "And the Walls Came Tumbling Down" (2-24-71) Nan Martin,
    Julie Adams, Ray Danton, Kathy Cannon, D'Urville Martin
21. "Down at the House of Truth, Visiting" (3-3-71) Richard
    Dreyfuss, Tom Drake, Paul Stewart, Paul Stevens, Lane

Bradbury, Jon Lormer
22. "The Whimper of Whipped Dogs" (3-10-71) Susan Strasberg, Allen Garfield, June Dayton
23. "Conrad and the Taxi Squad" (3-17-71) Kristoffer Tabori, Steve Ihnat, Elizabeth Allen, Gwynne Gilford
24. "I've Got a Problem" (3-24-71) Gary Lockwood, Warren Anderson, Fred Wayne


THE SILENT FORCE

Corruption itself was body and soul--else what to do with all the banalities?--of this nominal tale of a team of government workers whose objective is the lawless higher-ups.

The Regulars: Ward Fuller, Ed Nelson; Jason Hart, Percy Rodriguez; Amelia Cole, Lynda Day.

The Episodes:

1. "Prosecutor" (9-21-70) Lloyd Bochner, Mark Tapacott, Eddie Firestone
2. "The Hero" (9-28-70) James A. Watson Jr., Murray Matheson, Martin E. Brooks, Diane Summerfield
3. "A Deadly Game of Love" (10-5-70) Mark Richman, Joan Van Ark
4. "The Shopping List" (10-12-70) Dane Clark, Kevin Hagen
5. "The Judge" (10-19-70) John Dehner, DeForest Kelley, Paul Carr
6. "Wax Jungle" (10-26-70) Linda Marsh, Robert Yuro, Jared Martin, Regis Philbin, Dick Patterson, John Armond, Billy Shannon
7. "Horse in a White Collar" (11-9-70) Bert Convy, Mala Powers, Anthony Eisley, Natalie Trundy
8. "A Cry in Concrete" (11-16-70) Jeanne Cooper, Michael Conrad, Duncan McLeod
9. "In by Nine, Out by Five" (11-23-70) Tom Bosley, Paul Lambert, Paul Harris, Aspa Nakapoulou, Del Monroe, Carmen Zapata
10. "Take as Directed for Death" (11-30-70) Steve Ihnat, Michael Bell, Arthur Batanides
11. "The Courier" (12-7-70) Edward G. Robinson
12. "A Family Tradition" (12-14-70) Stewart Moss, Anthony Caruso, Roy Jenson
13. "The Octopus" (12-21-70) Austin Willis, Albert Paulsen
14. "The Banker" [Part I] (1-4-71) John Vernon, Paul Stewart, Robert Pine, Carla Borelli
15. "The Banker" [Part II] (1-11-71) as above

## THE STOREFRONT LAWYERS

Another youth oriented series of the 1970-71 season, this one deals with gifted young attorneys who, good samaritans all of them, offer free legal services to those who might otherwise go without them.

The Regulars: David, Robert Foxworth; Deborah, Sheila Larken; Gabe, David Arkin; Roberto, A Martinez; Att. Devlin McNeil, Gerald S. O'Loughlin (with episode of 2/3/71).

The Episodes:

1. "A Man's Castle" (9-16-70) Dean Jagger, Barry Morse, Carmen Mathews, Edward Andrews, Gerald S. O'Loughlin
2. "The Law Can't Touch Him" (9-23-70) James McMullan, Melinda Dillon, William Quinn
3. "Murph Collins vs. Tomorrow" (9-30-70) James Stacy, Harrison Page, Lonny Chapman, Mariclaire Costello, Ramon Bieri, Joan Shawlee
4. "The Electric Kid" (10-7-70) Leon Ames, Dana Elcar, Joyce Van Patten, J. Pat O'Malley, William Sargent
5. "The Emancipation of Bessie Gray" (10-14-70) Paul Stewar Claudia McNeil, Paula Myers, Rupert Crosse
6. "Survivors Will Be Prosecuted" (10-21-70) William Conrad Murray Hamilton, Edith Diaz, Emilio Delgado
7. [unknown title] (10-28-70) Sharon Farrell, Lou Antonio, N Glass, Maidie Norman
8. "Where Are You At?" (11-4-70) Tony Roberts, Kenneth Tobey, Bill Zuckert, Joaquin Martinez
9. "Shadows of Doubt" (11-11-70) Anne Archer, Lloyd Gough, Jonathan Lippe, William Quinn, Charles H. Gray
10. [unknown title] (11-18-70) Lloyd Bochner, Kurt Russell, Patricia Smith, David Doyle
11. "The Pastures of Hell" (11-25-70) Steve Ihnat, James McEachin, Gerald S. O'Loughlin, Tony Martinez, Harry Hickox
12. "Where Were We, Waldo?" (12-9-70) Anthony Zerbe, Jacqueline Scott, Paula Victor
13. "First ... We Get Rid of the Principal" (1-13-71) Sheldon Collins, Carmen Zapata, Nancy Burnett, Val de Vargas

[Hereafter titled MEN AT LAW]

14. "The Climate of Doubt" (2-3-71) Rich Kalman, Logan Ram sey, Dan Travanty
15. "Marathon" (2-10-71) Jack Cassidy, Sue Lyon, Nina Foch, Glynn Turman, Greg Mullavey
16. "The Dark World of Harry Anders" (2-17-71) Harry Guardino, Jeanne Cooper, Lane Bradbury, John McLiam
17. "Hostage" (2-24-71) John Rubinstein, Meg Foster, Felice Orlandi, Ford Rainey, John Ragin
18. "The Truth, the Whole Truth--and Anything Else That Works

|      | (3-3-71) David Wayne, Cloris Leachman, Jean Hale |
|------|---|
| 19.  | "Let the Dier Beware" (3-17-71) Jessica Walter, William Windom, Pippa Scott, Larry Linville, Paul Fix |
| 20.  | "The View from the Top" (3-24-71) Steve Forrest, Ramon Bieri, Kay Medford, Wayne Rogers, Marilyn Maxwell, Noah Keen |
| 21.  | "Yesterday Is but a Dream" (3-31-71) Lee Grant, John Vernon, Ivor Francis, Garry Walberg, Ford Rainey |
| 22.  | "This Money Kills Dreams" (4-7-71) Tom Skerritt, Katherine Justice, Fritz Weaver |
| 23.  | "One American" (4-14-71) William Shatner, Jan-Michael Vincent, Ron Hayes, Brenda Dickson |

FOUR-IN-ONE

This network composite of four six-segment series twice succeeded and twice failed. The successes were Rod Serling's "Night Gallery" (chronicled separately in this volume) and producer Norman Felton's eloquent successor to his 1962 "The Eleventh Hour" with "The Psychiatrist." Even if the psychiatrist in this case were less than credible (Roy Thinnes as Dr. James Whitman, for whom NBC, following the year's vogue to "go youthful," felt compelled to provide a "mod" image), the patient's disturbances movingly unfolded in such high-voltage dramas as Jack Morse's "Such Civil War in My Love and Hate" (Brenda Vaccaro a depressed divorcee) and Steven Spielberg's "Par for the Course" (terminally ill golfer Clu Gulager).

"San Francisco International" is in reference to an airport and features Lloyd Bridges as airport manager James Conrad and Clu Gulager as security chief Hatten. Its failings were in its obsession with Cold War, pacifism versus militarism philosophy (ergo, a confused pro-disarmament scientist threatens the airport with a poisonous gas in William McGivern's "Emergency Alert"; a hostile reception awaits a United States general in William Read Woodfield's and Robert Sabaroff's "We Once Came Home to Parades").

The fourth segment was the ludicrous "McCloud" law and order entry. Its premise was that the simple virtues can and should triumph in a sinful megalopolis. Dennis Weaver was cast as the New Mexico Deputy Marshal transferred to New York City.

The Regulars: "McCloud": Deputy Marshal Sam McCloud, Dennis Weaver; Chief of Detectives Peter Clifford, J. D. Cannon; Sergeant Broadhurst, Terry Carter; "Night Gallery": Rod Serling, host; "San Francisco International": James Conrad, Lloyd Bridges; Hatten, Clu Gulager; June (secretary to Conrad), Barbara Werle; Suzie, Barbara Sigel; "The Psychiatrist": Dr. James Whitman, Roy Thinnes; Dr. Bernard Altman, Luther Adler.

The Episodes ["McCloud" continued with the "NBC Wednesday Mystery Movie" beginning September 22, 1971; subsequently with the "NBC Sunday Mystery Movie" beginning October 1 1972]:

1. McCloud: "Who Says You Can't Make Friends in New York City?" (9-16-70) Diana Muldaur, Carl Betz, Marj Dusay
2. McCloud: "Horse Stealing on Fifth Avenue" (9-23-70) Lorraine Gary, Leo Gordon, Angus Duncan, Diana Muldaur, Howard Curtis
3. McCloud: "The Concrete Corral" (9-30-70) Joanna Moore, Albert Salmi, Burr DeBenning
4. McCloud: "The Stage Is All the World" (10-7-70) Christina Sinatra, Murray Matheson, Richard Dawson, Albert Popwell, Richard Van Vleet
5. McCloud: "Walk in the Dark" (10-14-70) Nina Foch, Susan Saint James, Ann Prentiss, Stewart Bradley, Ken Scott, Mary Gregory
6. McCloud: "Our Man in Paris" (10-21-70) Susan Strasberg, Alfred Ryder, Ken Scott, John Van Dreelen, Marcel Hillaire
7. San Francisco International: "Emergency Alert" (10-28-70) James Olson, William Sylvester, Richard X. Slattery, Russ Conway, Richard McMurray, Sallie Shockley
8. San Francisco International: "We Once Came Home to Parades" (11-4-70) Robert Webber, Tim Matheson, Mills Watson, Edward Faulkner
9. San Francisco International: "Hostage" (11-11-70) Henry Silva, Scott Brady, Robert Viharo, Robert Karnes
10. San Francisco International: "Crisis" (11-18-70) Charles Aidman, Dane Clark, Russell Johnson, Russ Conway, Peter Whitney
11. San Francisco International: "Supersonic Transport" (11-25-70) Lew Ayres, Tim O'Connor, John Kellogg, David Lew Philip Pine
12. San Francisco International: "The High Cost of Nightmares" (12-2-70) Albert Salmi, Lorraine Gary, Severn Darden
13-18. ["Night Gallery" premiered December 16, 1970; the six consecutive episodes continuing through January 20, 1971]
19. The Psychiatrist: "In Death's Other Kingdom" (2-3-71) Melendy Britt, Peter Brocco, Jonathan Daly
20. The Psychiatrist: "The Private World of Martin Dalton" (2-10-71) Jim Hutton, Kate Woodville, Stephen Hudis
21. The Psychiatrist: "Such Civil War in My Love and Hate" (2-17-71) Brenda Vaccaro, Jeff Corey, Paul Carr
22. The Psychiatrist: "The Longer Trail" (2-24-71) Reni Santoni, Jill Haworth, Jay Silverheels
23. The Psychiatrist: "Ex-Sgt. Randell File, U.S.A." (3-3-71) John Rubinstein, Kiel Martin, Jonathan Brooks
24. The Psychiatrist: "Par for the Course" (3-10-71) Clu Gulager, Joan Darling, Michael C. Gwynne, Carl Reindel, David Astor, Bruce Glover

NIGHT GALLERY

The late playwright Rod Serling composed several of the dramas in this anthology series, for which he served as host. Serling departed from the supernatural teleplays that constituted the greater part of the series with his serious examination of the derision that accompanies the quiet resignation to a necessarily slower-paced middle age in "They're Tearing Down Tim Riley's Bar" with William Windom perfect as the protagonist. Serling's "Lindemann's Catch" is about a sea captain in love with a mermaid and what happens when he tries to give her human legs (she acquires the legs, but at the price of also acquiring an amphibian head). And Serling's "The Boy Who Predicted Earthquakes" sadly recounts the tale of a boy seer who has envisioned the end of the world.

In other episodes, Agnes Moorehead, Rachel Roberts, Grayson Hall and Louis Hayward were sterling in a story of a murdered sister's retribution from beyond the grave in Rod Serling's "Certain Shadows on the Wall," while déjà vu was the theme of Serling's "The House," an adaptation of an André Maurois story, and of "The Tune in Dan's Cafe." The inimitable Orson Welles narrated an excellent rendition of the classic Conrad Aiken short story Silent Snow, Secret Snow. "Cool Air," from the H. P. Lovecraft story, about a resurrected dead man who must exist in a world of ice and cold, is both tragic and frightening. "A Question of Fear" gives the familiar horror story--an evening in a haunted house--an interesting variation. Fritz Weaver as the house owner, who has heretofore been unsuccessful in scaring his overnight visitor Leslie Nielsen, tells his inhabitant that he has unknowingly been poisoned and will soon transform into a hideous crawling worm-like creature (a total lie, of course, which nonetheless succeeds in making the visitor kill himself). Alvin Sapinsley's "Pickman's Model" is a well-acted (Bradford Dillman and Louise Sorel in the lead roles) drama of a painter whose grotesque creature images are quite real. And "Fright Night" was a good satire of the Halloween legend.

Yet there were some deliberately absurd teleplays such as the several vignettes by series producer Jack Laird ("Quoth the Raven," "How to Cure the Common Vampire," and "Professor Peabody's Last Lecture"), Richard Matheson's "Big Surprise," and Gene Kearney's "The Witches' Feast." But whatever the drama, Lionel Lindon's photography dipped, so it seemed, both setting and characters in the most vibrant of hues, and was masterful.

The Episodes:

1. a) "The Dead Man" (12-16-70) Carl Betz, Jeff Corey, Michael Blodgett, Louise Sorel; b) "The Housekeeper" Larry Hagman, Suzy Parker, Jeanette Nolan
2. a) "Room with a View" (12-23-70) Joseph Wiseman, Angel Tompkins; b) "The Little Black Bag" Burgess Meredith, Chill Wills, George Furth; c) "The Nature of the Enemy"

Joseph Campanella
3. a) "The House" (12-30-70) Joanna Pettet, Paul Richards, Steve Franken; b) "Certain Shadows on the Wall" Agnes Moorehead, Rachel Roberts, Louis Hayward, Grayson Hall
4. a) "Make Me Laugh" (1-6-71) Godfrey Cambridge, Jackie Vernon, Al Lewis, Tom Bosley; b) "Clean Kills and Other Trophies" Raymond Massey, Tom Troupe, Barry Brown
5. a) "Pamela's Voice" (1-13-71) Phyllis Diller, John Astin; b) "Lone Survivor" Torin Thatcher, John Colicos; c) "The Doll" Shani Wallis, Henry Silva, John Williams
6. a) "The Last Laurel" (1-20-71) Jack Cassidy; b) "They're Tearing Down Tim Riley's Bar" William Windom, Diane Baker, Bert Convy

## Second Season

7. a) "The Boy Who Predicted Earthquakes" (9-15-71) Clint Howard, Michael Constantine; b) "Miss Lovecraft Sent Me" Joseph Campanella, Sue Lyon; c) "The Hand of Borgus Weems" Ray Milland, George Maharis; d) "The Phantom of What Opera?" Leslie Nielsen, Mary Ann Beck
8. a) "A Death in the Family" (9-22-71) E. G. Marshall, Desi Arnaz Jr.; b) "The Merciful" Imogene Cocoa; c) "The Class of '99" Vincent Price, Brandon De Wilde; d) "The Witches' Feast" Agnes Moorehead, Ruth Buzzi
9. a) "Since Aunt Ada Came to Stay" (9-29-71) James Farentino, Jeanette Nolan, Michelle Lee; b) "With Apologies to Mr. Hyde" Adam West, Jack Laird; c) "The Flip Side of Satan" Arte Johnson
10. a) "A Fear of Spiders" (10-6-71) Patrick O'Neal, Kim Stanley; b) "Junior" Wally Cox; c) "Marmalade Wine" Robert Morse, Rudy Vallee; d) "The Academy" Pat Boone, Leif Erickson
11. a) "The Phantom Farmhouse" (10-20-71) David McCallum, Linda Marsh; b) "Silent Snow, Secret Snow" Radames Pera [narrated by Orson Welles]
12. a) "A Question of Fear" (10-27-71) Leslie Nielsen, Fritz Weaver; b) "The Devil Is Not Mocked" Helmut Dantine, Francis Lederer
13. a) "Midnight Never Ends" (11-3-71) Susan Strasberg, Robert F. Lyons; b) "Brenda" Laurie Prange, Glenn Corbett
14. a) "The Diary" (11-10-71) Patty Duke, Virginia Mayo; b) "A Matter of Semantics" Cesar Romero, E. J. Peaker; c) "The Big Surprise" John Carradine; d) "Professor Peabody's Last Lecture" Carl Reiner
15. a) "House--With Ghost" (11-17-71) Bob Crane, Jo Anne Worley; b) "A Midnight Visit to the Neighborhood Blood Bank" Victor Buono; c) "Dr. Stringfellow's Rejuvenator" Forrest Tucker; d) "Hell's Bells" John Astin
16. a) "The Dark Boy" (11-24-71) Elizabeth Hartman, Gale Sondergaard; b) "Keep in Touch--We'll Think of Something" Alex Cord, Joanna Pettet
17. a) "Pickman's Model" (12-1-71) Bradford Dillman, Louise

Sorel; b) "The Dear Departed" Steve Lawrence, Harvey
Lembeck, Maureen Arthur; c) "An Act of Chivalry" Rod
Stein, Dierdre Hudson

18. a) "Cool Air" (12-8-71) Barbara Rush, Henry Darrow; b)
"Camera Obscura" Ross Martin, Rene Auberjonois; c)
"Quoth the Raven" Marty Allen

19. a) "The Messiah on Mott Street" (12-15-71) Tony Roberts,
Edward G. Robinson, Rosemary De Camp; b) "The Painted
Mirror" Zsa Zsa Gabor, Arthur O'Connell

20. a) "The Different Ones" (12-29-71) Dana Andrews, Jon
Korkes; b) "Tell David ... " Sandra Dee, Jared Martin;
c) "Logoda's Heads" Patrick Macnee, Denise Nicholas,
Brock Peters, Tim Matheson

21. a) "Green Fingers" (1-5-72) Elsa Lanchester, Cameron
Mitchell; b) "The Funeral" Werner Klemperer, Joe Flynn;
c) "The Tune in Dan's Cafe" Pernell Roberts, Susan Oliver

22. a) "Lindemann's Catch" (1-12-72) Stuart Whitman, Anabel
Garth; b) "A Feast of Blood" Sandra Locke, Norman
Lloyd; c) "The Late Mr. Peddington" Kim Hunter, Harry
Morgan

23. a) "The Miracle at Camefeo" (1-19-72) Harry Guardino,
Julie Adams, Ray Danton; b) "The Ghost of Sorworth Place"
Richard Kiley

24. a) "The Waiting Room" (1-26-72) Steve Forrest, Buddy Ebsen, Albert Salmi, Gilbert Roland; b) "Last Rites for a
Dead Druid" Bill Bixby, Carol Lynley, Donna Douglas

25. a) "Deliveries in the Rear" (2-9-72) Kent Smith, Cornel
Wilde, Rosemary Forsyth; b) "Stop Killing Me" Geraldine
Page, James Gregory; c) "Dead Weight" Bobby Darin,
Jack Albertson

26. a) "I'll Never Leave You--Ever" (2-16-72) Royal Dano,
John Saxon, Lois Nettleton; b) "There Aren't Any More
MacBanes" Joel Grey, Howard Duff

27. a) "You Can't Get Help Like That Anymore" (2-23-72) Brod-
erick Crawford, Cloris Leachman, Henry Jones; b) "The
Sins of the Fathers" Geraldine Page, Richard Thomas,
Michael Dunn

28. a) "The Caterpillar" (3-1-72) Laurence Harvey, Joanna
Pettet, Don Knight; b) "Little Girl Lost" William Windom,
Ed Nelson

## Third Season

29. "The Return of the Sorcerer" (9-24-72) Vincent Price, Bill
Bixby

30. "The Girl with the Hungry Eyes" (10-1-72) James Farentino, Joanna Pettet, John Astin

31. "Fright Night" (10-15-72) Stuart Whitman, Barbara Anderson, Ellen Corby

32. "Rare Objects" (10-22-72) Raymond Massey, Mickey Rooney

33. "Spectre in Tap Shoes" (10-29-72) Dane Clark, Sandra Dee,
Christopher Connelly

34. "The Ring with the Red Velvet Ropes" (11-5-72) Chuck Connors, Gary Lockwood, Joan Van Ark
35. "You Can Come Up Now, Mrs. Millikan" (11-12-72) Harriet Hilliard, Ozzie Nelson, Roger Davis
36. "The Other Way Out" (11-19-72) Ross Martin, Burl Ives
37. "Finnegan's Flight" (12-3-72) Burgess Meredith, Barry Sullivan, Cameron Mitchell
38. "She'll Be Company for You" (12-24-72) Leonard Nimoy, Kathryn Hays, Jack Oakie, Lorraine Gray
39. "Something in the Woodwork" (1-14-73) Geraldine Page, Leif Erickson, John McMurtry
40. "Death on a Barge" (3-4-73) Lesley Ann Warren, Robert Pratt
41. "The Doll of Death" (5-20-73) Susan Strasberg, Alejandro Rey, Murray Matheson
42. a) "Hatred Unto Death" (5-27-73) Steve Forrest, Dina Merrill, Fernando Lamas; b) "How to Cure the Common Vampire" Richard Deacon, Johnny Brown

DAN AUGUST

At times repulsive for its law and order stance (indicative, perhaps, of the popular obsession of the period) this Quinn Martin series focuses on the heroics of an uncompromising police detective (played--as the writers must have intended him to be played-- stiffly by Burt Reynolds as Dan August). One pretentious telecast had Richard Basehart as a university professor advocating student dissidence; the professor, we were to believe, an inciting anti-hero. After a lengthy polemic between representative of system (August) and of dissidence (Basehart), the conclusion finds August successful in tracking down a killer (a student, it turns out).

The Regulars: Det. Dan August, Burt Reynolds; Sergeant Charles Wilentz, Norman Fell; Chief George Untermeyer, Richard Anderson; Sergeant Joe Rivera, Ned Romero; Katy Grant, Ena Hartman.

The Episodes:

1. "Murder by Proxy" (9-23-70) Anne Francis, Diana Muldaur, Burr De Benning, Milton Selzer, Ford Rainey, Roger Perry
2. "The Murder of a Small Town" (9-30-70) Anne Navarro, Ricardo Montalban, John Marley, Cal Bellini
3. "Love Is a Nickel Bag" (10-7-70) Brad David, Annette O'Toole, June Dayton
4. "The King Is Dead" (10-14-70) Dabney Coleman, Jane Elliot, Janice Rule, Fred Beir
5. "In the Eyes of God" (10-21-70) Bradford Dillman, James Best, Donna Mills, Thomas Gomez
6. "The Color of Fury" (10-28-70) Nehemiah Persoff, Richard

O'Brien, Raymond St. Jacques, Ray Danton
7. "Invitation to Murder" (11-4-70) Tim O'Connor, Michael Strong, Kaz Garas, Alexandra Hay
8. "The Union Forever" (11-11-70) Vic Morrow, Frank Campanella, Linda Marsh, Joe De Santis, Joan Van Ark, Paul Bryan, Andrew Prine
9. "Epitaph for a Swinger" (11-18-70) Julie Adams, Brooke Bundy, John Milford, William Mims, Robert Hogan, Norman Alden, Marcy Brown, Gordon Pinsent, Sharon Kierkins
10. "When the Shouting Dies" (11-25-70) Vera Miles, Mike Henry, Victor French, Gerold Michael Atkins
11. "The Soldier" (12-2-70) Michael Ontkean, Jack Ging, Hal Lynch, Lynn Marta, Peter De Anda
12. "Quadrangle for Death" (12-16-70) Richard Basehart, Lizabeth Hush, Robert Lipton
13. "Passing Fair" (12-30-70) Michael Tolan, Cliff Gorman, Beth Brickell, Lee Philips
14. "The Titan" (1-6-71) Barry Sullivan, Robert Fuller, Sherry Lansing, Nancy Malone, Joan Huntington
15. "Death Chain" (1-21-71) Gerald S. O'Loughlin, Chris Robinson, Jan-Michael Vincent
16. "Dead Witness to a Killing" (1-28-71) Laurence Luckinbill, Barney Phillips, John Lasell, Martin Sheen, Monte Markham, Milton Kamen, Charles Bateman
17. "The Law" (2-4-71) Walter Pidgeon, Lee Meriwether, Larry Hagman
18. "The Worst Crime" (2-11-71) Ellen Corby, Tom Troupe, Sal Mineo, Fernando Lamas
19. "Circle of Lies" (2-18-71) Christopher Connelly, Jason Evers, Geraldine Brooks, Barbara Press
20. "Trackdown" (2-25-71) Karl Swenson, Julie Mannix
21. "Bullet for a Hero" (3-4-71) Tina Chen, Lou Antonio, Meg Foster, Peter White
22. "The Manufactured Man" (3-11-71) Peter Brown, David Soul, Mickey Rooney, Keith Andes, Barney Phillips, Harrison Ford, Billy Dee Williams
23. "The Meal Ticket" (3-18-71) Dane Clark, Art Aragon, Don Stroud, William Smith, Karin Wolfe, Simon Oakland
24. "Days of Rage" (3-25-71) Diana Hyland, Victor Holchak, Pamela McMyler, Alf Kjellin
25. "Prognosis, Homicide" (4-1-71) Fritz Weaver, Susan Oliver, Ken Scott, Jerry Ayres, Ahna Capri, Dean Harens, Mark Roberts, Sheilah Wells, John Lasell
26. "The Assassin" (4-8-71) Carolyn Jones, Joan Hackett, Charles MacCauley, Gary Collins, John Beck, Hal Baylor, Bill Erwin, H. M. Wynant, Sidney Clute, Lillian Bronson

## MATT LINCOLN

Excellent performances from featured guest stars (Patty

Duke as the unwed mother groping over the question of keeping her baby in the initial episode; Martin Sheen as the depressed but trigger happy "Charlie" of the second film) hallmark these stories of those who seek the help of a community psychiatric clinic run by Dr. Matt Lincoln (Vince Edwards).

The Regulars: Dr. Matt Lincoln, Vince Edwards; assistants to Dr. Lincoln, Ann (June Harding); Tag (Chelsea Brown); Kevin (Michael Larrain); Jimmy (Felton Perry).

The Episodes:

1. "Sheila" (9-24-70) Patty Duke, Sam Chew, Christina Crawford, Jed Allen
2. "Charles" (10-1-70) Martin Sheen, Herb Edelman, Simon Scott
3. "Nina" (10-8-70) Belinda Montgomery, Jack Cassidy, Jeanne Ball, Michael Bow
4. "Steve" (10-15-70) John Vernon, Barry Brown, Brenda Scott
5. "Jilly" (10-22-70) Barbara Feldon, Jeffrey Linn, Tom Simcox, Clarke Gordon
6. "Nick" (10-29-70) Peter Deuel, Joan Van Ark, Marc Hannibal
7. "Lori" (11-5-70) Mary Layne, Andrew Prine, Kathy Cannon, Priscilla Pointer
8. "Doc" (11-12-70) David Wayne, Beatrice Straight, Penny Santon, Pamela McMyler
9. "Angie" (11-19-70) Linda Morand, Dean Jagger, Philippe Forquet, Dan Tobin, Reta Shaw, Randolph Mantooth
10. "Yumiko" (12-3-70) Miko Mayama, Jeff Pomerantz, John Zaremba, Milton Selzer
11. "Billy" (12-10-70) Darren McGavin, Charles McGraw, Jean Allison, George Spell
12. "Lia" (12-17-70) Katherine Crawford, Dean Jagger, Dan Tobin, Frank Maxwell, John Scott Lee, Reta Shaw
13. "Adam" (12-24-70) Johnny Scott Lee, Dean Jagger, Natalie Schafer, Katherine Crawford, Reta Shaw
14. "Jimmy" (12-31-70) Guy Stockwell, Wesley Addy, Arch Johnson, Patricia Smith, Julie Gregg, Bill Vint
15. "Karen" (1-7-71) Hilarie Thompson, Tim Matheson, Sid McCoy, Logan Ramsey
16. "Christopher" (1-14-71) John Rubinstein, Christine Belford, Dan Tobin

THE IMMORTAL

A superhuman (Christopher George as Ben Richards) whose blood composition has granted him eternal youth is relentlessly pursued by bloodthirsty (literally) power-hungry agents who realize what samples of the substance can mean. Mercifully, both Richards and his pursuers left their tired series premise in mid-season

The Regulars: Ben Richards, Christopher George; Maitland, David
Brian; Fletcher, Don Knight.

The Episodes:

1. "Sylvia" (9-24-70) Carol Lynley, Glenn Corbett, Sherry
   Jackson
2. "White Elephants Don't Grow on Trees" (10-1-70) Ross
   Martin, Mitch Vogel
3. "Reflections on a Lost Tomorrow" (10-8-70) Jack Albertson,
   Rosemary Forsyth
4. "Legacy" (10-15-70) Mario Alcaide, Susan Howard
5. "The Rainbow Butcher" (10-22-70) Vic Morrow, Collin
   Wilcox-Horne, Jerry Ayres, Byron Mabe
6. "Man on a Punched Card" (10-29-70) Lynda Day, Lee Patterson
7. "White Horse, Steel Horse" (11-5-70) John Dehner, Warner
   Anderson, Stephen Oliver
8. "Queen's Gambit" (11-12-70) Lee Meriwether, Nico Minardos, Karl Swenson, Dom Tattoli
9. "By Gift of Chance" (11-19-70) Michael Conrad
10. "Dead Man, Dead Man" (12-3-70) Henry Beckman, Joan
    Hotchkis, Byron Keith
11. "Paradise Bay" (12-10-70) Tisha Sterling, Howard Duff,
    Scott Brady, Aron Kincaid
12. "To the Gods Alone" (12-31-70) Barry Sullivan, Bruce Dern
13. "Sanctuary" (1-7-71) Sal Mineo, Paul Picerni, Donald Barry,
    Iron Eyes Cody, Fred Lerner, Allen Gibbs
14. "Brother's Keeper" (1-14-71) Michael Strong, Marj Dusay

## THE INTERNS

Surprisingly interesting, considering the frequency of its
theme (it reminds one of Wilton Schiller's 1964 film The New Interns, although it is not that well composed) series of the interns
and their clientele at "New North Hospital." The most unusual
(and finest) guest performance was that delivered by Lois Nettleton
as the woman with two opposing personalities in "Metamorphosis."

Broderick Crawford made a properly irascible intern supervisor, Dr. Peter Goldstone.

The Regulars: Dr. Peter Goldstone, Broderick Crawford; Dr.
   Gregory Pettit, Stephen Brooks; Dr. "Pooch" Hardin,
   Christopher Stone; Dr. Lydia Thorpe, Sandra Smith; Dr.
   Cal Barrin, Hal Frederick; Dr. Sam Marsh, Mike Farrell;
   Mrs. (Bobbe) Marsh, Elaine Giftos; Dr. Jacoby, Skip
   Homeier.

The Episodes:

1. "The Quality of Mercy" (9-18-70) Bert Convy, Diane Baker,

Torin Thatcher, Michael McClanatham
2. "Death Wish" (9-25-70) Jana Taylor, Barbara Press, Dabbs
   Greer, Mary Patton
3. "Some Things Don't Change" (10-2-70) Skye Aubrey, Pat
   Harrington, Christopher Connelly, Henry Beckman, Shelley
   Morrison
4. [unknown title] (10-9-70) Albert Salmi, William DeVane,
   Brooke Bundy, Peggy McCay
5. "Eyes of the Beholder" (10-16-70) Milt Kamen, Phyllis Love,
   Med Foster
6. [unknown title] (10-23-70) Bridget Hanley, Ned Glass, George
   Grizzard
7. "The Price of Life" (10-30-70) Peter Deuel, Gene Raymond,
   Susan O'Connell, Paul Hampton, Bill Hayes
8. "The Oath" (11-6-70) Mills Watson, Malachi Throne
9. "Act of God" (11-20-70) Charles Aidman, Jane Elliot, Lane
   Bradbury, Roger Garrett
10. "Mondays Can Be Fatal" (11-27-70) Ron Rifkin, Sabrina
    Scharf, Frank Marth, Pamela Shoop
11. "The Fever" (12-4-70) Viveca Lindfors, Eduard Franz,
    Randames Pera, John Lupton
12. [unknown title] (12-11-70) Warner Anderson, Kaz Garas,
    Mitzi Hoag, Robert Sampson
13. [unknown title] (12-18-70) Eric Laneuville, John Randolph
14. [unknown title] (1-1-71) Robert Lansing, Melendy Britt,
    George Morgan
15. "The Secret" (1-22-71) Martin Sheen, Joan Hotchkis, Joe
    Maross, Fred Beir, Lonny Chapman
16. [unknown title] (1-29-71) Signe Hasso, Warren Kemmerling,
    Charlotte Stewart, Ron O'Neal
17. "Metamorphosis" (2-5-71) Lois Nettleton
18. "The Challenger" (2-12-71) Frank Gorshin, Sheree North,
    Edward Faulkner, Robert F. Simon
19. "The Casualty" (2-19-71) Diana Hyland, Pat Harrington,
    Ron O'Neal, John Davidson
20. "The Guardian" (3-5-71) Lew Ayres, Shelley Fabares, Peter
    Haskell
21. "The Manly Art" (3-12-71) Janet MacLachlan, Ron O'Neal,
    Jackie Coogan
22. [unknown title] (3-19-71) Pat Carroll, Janet Margolin, James
    Luisi, Harold J. Stone
23. "The Choice" (3-26-71) Isabel Sanford, Dan Travanty, Hal
    Lynch

MASTERPIECE THEATRE

The Regulars: Alistair Cooke, host.

"The First Churchills"
        The Cast: John Churchill, John Neville; Sarah Churchill,
        Susan Hampshire; York, John Westbrook; Charles II,

James Villiers; Princess Mary, Lisa Daniely; William, Alan Rowe; Mrs. Jennings, Daphne Hearl; Shaftesbury, Frederick Peisley; Sidney Godolphin, John Standing; Titus Oates, Nicholas Smith; Laurence Hyde, John Ringham; Becket, John Tordoff; Margaret Godolphin, Holly Wilson.

The Episodes:
1. "The Chaste Nymph" [I] (1-10-71)
2. "Bridals" [II] (1-17-71)
3. "Plot Counter-plot" [III] (1-24-71)
4. "The Lion and the Unicorn" [IV] (1-31-71)
5. "Rebellion" [V] (2-7-71)
6. "The Protestant Wind" [VI] (2-14-71)
7. "Trial of Strength" [VII] (2-21-71)
8. "The Queen Commands" [VIII] (2-28-71)
9. "Reconciliation" [IX] (3-7-71)
10. "A Famous Victory" [X] (3-14-71)
11. "Breaking the Circle" [XI] (3-21-71)
12. "Not Without Honor" [XII] (3-28-71)

"The Spoils of Poynton"
The Cast: Mrs. Gereth, Pauline Jameson; Owen Gereth, Ian Ogilvy; Mona Brigstock, Diane Fletcher; Mrs. Brigstock, June Ellis; Fleda Vetch, Gemma Jones.

The Episodes:
1. "Pride of Possession" [I] (4-4-71)
2. "Sharp Practice" [II] (4-11-71)
3. "Trial of Strength" [III] (4-18-71)
4. "Retribution" [IV] (4-25-71)

"The Possessed"
The Cast: Nikolay Stavrogin, Keith Bell; Mme. Stavrogin, Rosalie Crutchley; Verkhovensky, Joseph O'Connor; Dasha, Anne Stallybrass; Shatov, James Caffrey.

The Episodes:
1. Chapter I (5-2-71)
2. Chapter II (5-9-71)
3. Chapter III (5-16-71)
4. Chapter IV (5-23-71)
5. Chapter V (5-30-71)
6. Chapter VI (6-6-71)

"Père Goriot"
The Cast: Père Goriot, Michael Goodliffe; Eugene de Rastignac, David Dundas; Vautrin, Andrew Keir; Victorine, Anna Cropper; Anastasie, Angela Browne; Delphine, June Ritchie; Mme. de Beauseant, Moira Redmond.

The Episodes:
1. Chapter I (6-13-71)
2. Chapter II (6-20-71)
3. Chapter III (6-27-71)
4. Chapter IV (7-4-71)

## Second Season

"Jude the Obscure"
> The Cast: Jude, Robert Powell; Arabella Donn, Alex
> Marshall; Sue Bridehead, Feona Walker; Aunt Drusilla,
> Daphne Heard; Richard Philloston, John Franklyn Robbins;
> Mrs. Edith, Gwen Nelson; Landlady, Sheila Fay; Little
> Jude, Gary Rich.

The Episodes:
1. "At Marygreen" [I]   (10-3-71)
2. "To Christminster" [II]   (10-10-71)
3. "To Melchester" [III]   (10-17-71)
4. "To Shaston" [IV]   (10-24-71)
5. "To Aldbrickham" [V]   (10-31-71)
6. "Christminster Again" [VI]   (11-7-71)

"The Gambler"
> The Cast:  Grandmamma, Dame Edith Evans; Alexei,
> Maurice Roeves; Astley, Corin Redgrave; Polina, Georgina
> Ward; The General, John Phillips; Marquis de Grieux,
> Philip Madoc.

The Episodes:
1. Chapter I   (11-14-71)
2. Chapter II   (11-21-71)

"Resurrection"
> The Cast:  Dimitri, Alan Doble; Maslova, Bridget Turner;
> Agrafena, Eithne Dunne; Sophia, Constance Lorne; Court
> President, Clifford Parrish; Prosecutor, David Webb; De-
> fense Counsel, Ian Mullins.

The Episodes:
1. "Dimitri"   (11-28-71)
2. "Maslova"   (12-5-71)
3. "Temptation"   (12-12-71)
4. [unknown title]   (12-19-71)

"Cold Comfort Farm" [special two-hour episode]   (12-26-71)
> The Cast:  Flora, Sarah Badel; Amos, Alastair Sim;
> Judith, Rosalie Crutchley; Aunt Ada, Fay Compton; Seth,
> Peter Egan; Elfine, Sharon Gurney; Reuben, Brian Blessed;
> Rennett, Sheila Grant; Adam, Billy Russell; Miriam, Char-
> lotte Howard.

"The Six Wives of Henry VIII" [repeat of episodes telecast via
> CBS-TV 8/1/71 to 9/5/71]   (1-2-72 through 2-6-72)

"Elizabeth R"
> The Cast:  Elizabeth, Glenda Jackson; King Philip, Peter
> Jeffrey; Walsingham, Stephen Murray; Sir Francis Drake,
> John Woodvine; Burghley, Ronald Hines; Earl of Essex,
> Robin Ellis.

The Episodes:
1. "The Lion's Cub" [I]   (2-13-72)

2.  "The Marriage Game" [II]  (2-20-72)
3.  "Shadow in the Sun" [III]  (2-27-72)
4.  "Horrible Conspiracies" [IV]  (3-5-72)
5.  "The Enterprise of England" [V]  (3-12-72)
6.  "Sweet England's Pride" [VI]  (3-19-72)

"The Last of the Mohicans"
> The Cast: Heyward, Tim Goodman; Magua, Philip Madoc; Cora, Patricia Maynard; Alice, Joanna David; Colonel Munro, Andrew Crawford; General Webb, Noel Coleman; David, David Leland; Hawkeye, Kenneth Ives; Uncas, Richard Warwick.

The Episodes:
1.  Chapter I  (3-26-72)
2.  Chapter II  (4-2-72)
3.  Chapter III  (4-9-72)
4.  Chapter IV  (4-16-72)
5.  Chapter V  (4-23-72)
6.  Chapter VI  (4-30-72)
7.  Chapter VII  (5-7-72)
8.  Chapter VIII  (5-14-72)

## Third Season

"Vanity Fair"
> The Cast: Becky Sharp, Susan Hampshire; Amelia, Marilyn Taylerson; Rawden, Dyson Lovell; Jos, John Moffatt; Dobbin, Bryan Marshall; Lord Steyne, Robert Flemyng; Pitt Crowley, Michael Rothwell; George, Frank Berry; Wendhem, Tom Criddle; Mrs. Sedley, Barbara Leake; Mr. Sedley, Noel Howlett; Mr. Osborne, Richard Caldicot; Count, Michael Mulcaster.

The Episodes:
1.  Chapter I  (10-1-72)
2.  Chapter II  (10-8-72)
3.  Chapter III  (10-15-72)
4.  Chapter IV  (10-22-72)
5.  Chapter V  (10-29-72)

"Cousin Bette"
> The Cast: Bette Fischer, Margaret Tyzack; Steinbock, Colin Baker; Hector, Thorley Walters; Johann Fischer, Robert Spraight; Adeline, Ursula Howells; Hortense, Harriet Harper; Valerie, Helen Mirren; General Hulot, Edmond Knight; Monte, Edward De Souza; Marneffe, Oscar Quitak.

The Episodes:
1.  Chapter I  (11-5-72)
2.  Chapter II  (11-12-72)
3.  Chapter III  (11-19-72)
4.  Chapter IV  (11-26-72)
5.  Chapter V  (12-3-72)

"The Moonstone"
> The Cast: Rachel, Vivien Heilbron; Franklin Blake, Robin Ellis; Godfrey Abelwhite, Martin Jarvis; Lady Verinder, Kathleen Bryon; Rosanna Spearman, Anna Cropper; Penelope, Maureen Morris; Gabriel Betteredge, Basil Dignam; Bruff, Peter Sellis; Dr. Candy, Philip Ray; Murthwaite, Brian Badcol; Sergeant Cuff, John Welsh; Systemus Luker, Brian Murphy; Tomlinson, Roy Macready.

The Episodes:
1. Chapter I   (12-10-72)
2. Chapter II  (12-17-72)
3. Chapter III (12-24-72)
4. Chapter IV  (12-31-72)
5. Chapter V   (1-7-73)

"Tom Brown's Schooldays"
> The Cast: Tom, Anthony Murphy; Ned, Simon Turner; Squire Brown, John Paul; Sir Richard Flashman, Gerald Flood; Brooke, Barry Stokes; Gerald Flashman, Richard Morant; Dr. Arnold, Iain Cuthbertson; Diggs, David Hampshire; Denning, Sean Bury; Darcy, Christopher Guard; Cuthbertson, Mark Rodgers; Sir Reginald Harcourt, Lindsay Campbell; Cully, Dan Meadan; Rosy, Valerie Holliman.

The Episodes:
1. Chapter I   (1-14-73)
2. Chapter II  (1-21-73)
3. Chapter III (1-28-73)
4. Chapter IV  (2-4-73)
5. Chapter V   (2-11-73)

"Point Counter Point"
> The Cast: Frank Illidge, David Graham; Philip Quarles, Lyndon Brook; Sidney Quarles, John Wentworth; Phil, Matthew Jacobs; Elinor Quarles, Patricia English; Everard Webley, Edward Judd; Walter Bidlake, Tristram Jellinek; John Bidlake, Max Adrian.

The Episodes:
1. Chapter I   (2-18-73)
2. Chapter II  (2-25-73)
3. Chapter III (3-4-73)
4. Chapter IV  (3-11-73
5. Chapter V   (3-18-73)

"The Golden Bowl"
> The Cast: Adam Verver, Barry Morse; Maggie Verver, Jill Townsend; Prince Amerigo, Daniel Massey; Charlotte Stant, Gayle Hunnicutt; Bob Assingham, Cyril Cusack; Fanny Assingham, Kathleen Byron.

The Episodes:
1. Chapter I   (3-25-73)
2. Chapter II  (4-1-73)
3. Chapter III (4-8-73)
4. Chapter IV  (4-15-73)

5. Chapter V (4-22-73)
6. Chapter VI (4-29-73)

## Fourth Season

"Clouds of Witness"

The Cast: Lord Peter Wimsey, Ian Carmichael; Bunter, Glyn Houston; Lady Mary, Rachel Herbert; Parker, Mark Eden; Duke of Denver, David Langton; Cathcart, Anthony Ainley; Duchess of Denver, Georgina Cookson; Grimethorpe, George Coulouris; Rachel, Petronella Ford; Mrs. Grimethrope, Judith Arthy.

The Episodes:
1. Chapter I (10-7-73)
2. Chapter II (10-14-73)
3. Chapter III (10-21-73)
4. Chapter IV (10-28-73)
5. Chapter V (11-4-73)

"The Man Who Was Hunting Himself"

The Cast: David Foster, Donald Burton; Caroline Foster, Carol Austin; Captain Mason, David Savile; Martin, Conrad Phillips; Planner, Garfield Morgan; Doctor, Brian Wilde; Chairman, Norman Ettlinger.

The Episodes:
1. Chapter I (11-11-73)
2. Chapter II (11-18-73)
3. Chapter III (11-25-73)

"The Unpleasantness at the Bellona Club"

The Cast: Lord Peter Wimsey, Ian Carmichael; Ann, Anna Cropper; Robert, Terrence Alexander; George, John Quentin; Penbarthy, Donald Pickering.

The Episodes:
1. Chapter I (12-2-73)
2. Chapter II (12-9-73)
3. Chapter III (12-16-73)
4. Chapter IV (12-23-73)

"The Little Farm" (12-30-73)

The Cast: Tom, Bryan Marshall; Edna, Barbara Ewing; Jack, Michael Elphick.

"Upstairs, Downstairs"

The Cast: Rose, Jean Marsh; Sarah, Pauline Collins; Hudson, Gordon Jackson; Mrs. Bridges, Angela Baddeley; Emily, Evin Crowley; Alfred, George Innes; Lady Marjorie, Rachel Gurney; Alice, Susan Porrett; James, Simon Williams; Elizabeth, Nicola Pagett; Henrietta, Jenifer Armitage; Lawrence, Ian Ogilvy; Lord Richard Bellamy, David Langton.

The Episodes:
1. Chapter I (1-6-74)

2. Chapter II   (1-13-74)
3. Chapter III   (1-20-74)
4. Chapter IV   (1-27-74)
5. Chapter V   (2-3-74)
6. Chapter VI   (2-10-74)
7. Chapter VII   (2-17-74)
8. Chapter VIII   (2-24-74)
9. Chapter IX   (3-3-74)
10. Chapter X   (3-10-74)
11. Chapter XI   (3-17-74)
12. Chapter XII   (3-24-74)
13. Chapter XIII   (3-31-74)

Fifth Season

"Murder Must Advertise"
        The Cast: Lord Peter Wimsey, Ian Carmichael; Parker,
        Mark Eden; Pamela, Gwen Taylor; Ingleby, John Hallam;
        Willis, Christopher Timothy; Miss Meteyard, Fiona Walk-
        er; Pym, Peter Pratt; Lady Mary, Rachel Herbert.
The Episodes:
1. Chapter I   (10-6-74)
2. Chapter II   (10-13-74)
3. Chapter III   (10-20-74)
4. Chapter IV   (10-27-74)

"Upstairs, Downstairs"
        The Cast: Rose, Jean Marsh; Hudson, Gordon Jackson;
        Hazel, Meg Wynn Owen; Richard Bellamy, David Langton;
        James Bellamy, Simon Williams; Lady Marjorie, Rachel
        Gurney; Mrs. Bridges, Angela Baddeley; Lili, Angela
        Browne; Kurt, Sandor Eles; Gwyneth, Janet Lees Price.
The Episodes:
1. Chapter I   (11-3-74)
2. Chapter II   (11-10-74)
3. Chapter III   (11-17-74)
4. Chapter IV   (11-24-74)
5. Chapter V   (12-1-74)
6. Chapter VI   (12-8-74)
7. Chapter VII   (12-15-74)
8. Chapter VIII   (12-22-74)
9. Chapter IX   (12-29-74)
10. Chapter X   (1-5-75)
11. Chapter XI   (1-12-75)
12. Chapter XII   (1-19-75)
13. Chapter XIII (1-26-75)

"Country Matters"
The Episodes:
1. "The Higgler" [I]   (2-2-75)
2. "The Black Dog" [II]   (2-9-75)
3. "Watercress Girl" [III]   (2-16-75)
4. "The Mill" [IV]   (2-23-75)

"Vienna, 1900: Games with Love and Death"
The Cast: Boria, Lynn Redgrave; Emil, Sandor Eles; Dr. Graesler, Robert Stephens; Anna, Jacqueline Pearce; Rupius, Lyndon Brook; Klingemann, Sydney Tafler; Richard, Peter Settelen; Hugo, Christopher Guard; Fritz, Richard Morant; Baroness, Adrienne Corri; Herr Welponer, Bernard Lee.

The Episodes:
1. "Mother and Son" [I]  (3-2-75)
2. "The Man of Honour" [II]  (3-9-75)
3. "A Confirmed Bachelor" [III]  (3-16-75)
4. "A Confirmed Bachelor" [IV]  (3-23-75)
5. "The Gift of Life" [V]  (3-30-75)
6. "The Spring Sonata" [VI]  (4-6-75)

"The Nine Tailors"
The Cast: Lord Peter Wimsey, Ian Carmichael; Bunter, Glyn Houston; Rector, Donald Eccles; Mrs. Tebbut, Maryann Turner; Mary, Elizabeth Proud; Jim Thoday, David Jackson; Ezra, Dan Meadan; Dr. Baines, Bill Gavin; Hillary, Gail Harrison.

The Episodes:
1. Chapter I  (4-13-75)
2. Chapter II  (4-20-75)
3. Chapter III  (4-27-75)
4. Chapter IV  (5-4-75)

[Continuing]

## THE STRANGE REPORT

All that distinguishes this British mystery entry is the presence of Anthony Quayle as criminologist Adam Strange.

The Regulars: Adam Strange, Anthony Quayle; "Ham" Gynt (assistant to Strange), Kaz Garas; Evelyn, Anneke Wills.

The Episodes:

1. "Skeleton--Let Sleeping Heroes Lie" (1-8-71) Eric Portman, Tom Adams, Edward Cast, Hugh Burden
2. "Hostage--If You Won't Learn, Die" (1-15-71) Eric Young, Kenneth Haigh, Peter Craze, Robert Lee, Gerald Sim
3. "Hands--A Matter of Witchcraft" (1-22-71) Cecilia Darby, Keith Barron, Renee Asherson, Helen Lindsay
4. "Grenade--What Price Change?" (1-29-71) Anthony Corlan, Bernard Lee, Jeremy Bulloch
5. "Cult--Murder Shrieks Out" (2-5-71) Pamela Franklin, Ray McAnally
6. "Revenge--When a Man Hates" (2-12-71) Julian Glover, Rosemary Leach, John Thaw, Wade Barker, James Cossins, Llewellyn Rees

7.  "Heart--No Choice for the Donor" (2-26-71) Robert Hardy, Barbara Murray
8.  "Sniper--When Is Your Cousin Not?" (3-5-71) Michael Turner, Vladek Sheybal
9.  "Epidemic--A Most Curious Crime" (3-12-71) Zienia Merton, Peter Vaughn, Shivendra Sinha
10. "Shrapnel--Wish in the Dream" (3-19-71) Leo Genn, Sylvia Syms, Gerald Flood
11. "X-Ray--Who Weeps for the Doctor?" (3-26-71) Trisha Mortimer, Ann Firbank
12. "Swindle--Square Root of Evil" (4-2-71) John Carlisle, Pauline Yates
13. "Lonelyhearts--Who Killed Dan Cupid?" (4-9-71) Geraldine Moffatt, Donald Douglas
14. "Cover Girl--Last Year's Model" (4-16-71) Lisa Daniely, Elaine Taylor, Richard Vanstone
15. "Kidnap--Whose Pretty Girl Are You?" (5-7-71) Sally Geeson, David Bauer, Ian Ogilvy, Richard O'Sullivan
16. "Racist--A Most Dangerous Proposal" (5-14-71) Guy Doleman, Jane Morrow, Karl Held

THE SIX WIVES OF HENRY VIII

This much acclaimed BBC entry offers a wonderful performance by Keith Michell as the bellicose King Henry but an even greater one by Dorothy Tutin as Anne Boleyn. Brilliant teleplays were composed by, among others, Nick McCarty ("Anne Boleyn"), Jean Morris ("Anne of Cleves") and John Prebble ("Catherine Parr").

The Cast: King Henry VIII, Keith Michell; Catherine of Aragon, Annette Crosbie; Anne Boleyn, Dorothy Tutin; Anne of Cleves, Elvi Hale; Catherine Howard, Angela Pleasence; Catherine Parr, Rosalie Crutchley; Wolsey, John Baskcomb; Maria, Margaret Ford; Norfolk, Patrick Troughton; Chapuys, Edward Atienza; Cardinal Campeggio, Ronald Adam; Princess Mary, Verina Greenlaw; Dona Elvira, Sally Travers; Lady Rochford, Sheila Burrell; Thomas Culpepper, Ralph Bates; Francis Dereham, Simon Prebble; Dowager Duchess of Norfolk, Catherine Lacey; Archbishop Cranmer, Bernard Hepton; Mark Smeaton, Michael Osborn; Cromwell, Wolfe Morris; Holbein, James Mellor; Robert Barnes, Robert James; Lord Hertford, Daniel Moynihan; Bishop Gardiner, Basil Dignam; Thomas Seymour, John Ronane; Thomas Wriothesley, Patrick Godfrey; Princess Mary, Alison Frazer.

The Episodes [subsequently telecast as part of PBS' "Masterpiece Theatre" from 1/2/72 through 2/6/72]:

1.  "Catherine of Aragon" (8-1-71) CBS
2.  "Anne Boleyn" (8-8-71) CBS

3.  "Jane Seymour"  (8-15-71)  CBS
4.  "Anne of Cleves"  (8-22-71)  CBS
5.  "Catherine Howard"  (8-29-71)  CBS
6.  "Catherine Parr"  (9-5-71)  CBS

1971-1972 SEASON

THE PERSUADERS

It was "hands across the border" with this international espionage tale of a British Lord (Roger Moore as Brett Sinclair) and
a homespun but wealthy American (Tony Curtis as Danny Wilde)
who pursue la dolce vita by acting as "crime busters" when the
urge arises.

The Regulars: Danny Wilde, Tony Curtis; Brett Sinclair, Roger
Moore; Judge Fulton, Laurence Naismith.

The Episodes:

1.  "Overture" (9-18-71) Richard Lester, Michael Godfrey
2.  "Powerswitch" (9-25-71) Anette Andre, John Phillips
3.  "Take Seven" (10-2-71) Sinead Cusack, Christian Roberts
4.  "The Man in the Middle" (10-9-71) Terry-Thomas, Suzy
    Kendall
5.  "Chain of Events" (10-16-71) Suzanna Leigh, Peter Vaughan
6.  "The Old, the New, and the Deadly" (10-23-71) Patrick
    Troughton, Anna Gael
7.  "The Time and the Place" (10-30-71) Ian Hendry, Anna Palk
8.  "Greensleeves" (11-13-71) Andrew Keir, Rosemary Nichols
9.  "Someone Like Me" (11-27-71) Jeremy Burnham, Joanne
    Dainton
10. "A Home of One's Own" (12-4-71) John Ronane, Leon Green
11. "Morning After" (12-11-71) Catherine Schell, Tony Bonner
12. "Someone Waiting" (12-18-71) Penelope Horner, Maxwell
    Shaw
13. "The Ozerov Inheritance" (1-1-72) Gladys Cooper, Gary
    Raymond
14. "A Death in the Family" (1-12-72) Diane Cilento, Denholm
    Elliott
15. "Anyone Can Play" (1-19-72) Dudley Foster, Cyd Hayman
16. "The Gold Napoleon" (1-26-72) Susan George, Harold Gold-
    blatt
17. "The Long Goodbye" (2-2-72) Leo Genn, Nicola Pagett
18. "To the Death, Baby" (2-9-72) Jenny Linden, Terence Mor-
    gan
19. "Five Miles to Midnight" (2-16-72) John Collins, Robert
    Hutton

20. "Nuisance Value" (2-23-72) Vivian Ventura, Ralph Bates
21. "Element of Risk" (3-1-72) Peter Bowles, William Marlowe
22. "Angie, Angie" (3-8-72) Larry Storch, John Alderson


SARGE

Offbeat law and order yarn of a parish priest and detective; George Kennedy is fine in the lead role.

The Regulars: Sarge Cavanaugh, George Kennedy; Barney Verick, Ramon Bieri; Valerie, Sallie Shockley; Kenji, Harold Sakata.

The Episodes:
1. "A Terminal Case of Vengeance" (9-21-71) Jack Albertson, Mike Farrell, James Wainwright
2. [unknown title] (9-28-71) Martin Sheen, Joe De Santis, Corrine Camacho, Irene Tsu, Roy Jenson
3. "Psst! Wanna Buy a Dirty Picture?" (10-5-71) Vincent Gardenia, Warren Stevens, Tom Bosley, Janis Paige
4. [unknown title] (10-12-71) Pippa Scott, Sheila Larken, Bill Fletcher
5. "A Push Over the Edge" (10-26-71) Vic Morrow, Marion Ross
6. "John Michael O'Flaherty Presents the Eleven O'Clock War" (11-2-71) Jack Cassidy, Julie Gregg, Dana Elcar
7. "Silent Target" (11-9-71) Leslie Nielsen, Joseph Perry, Allison McKay
8. "Quicksilver" (11-16-71) Carol Lawrence, Michael Baseleon, Gerald S. O'Loughlin
9. "A Bad Case of Monogamy" (11-23-71) Monte Markham, David Sheiner, Arlene Golonka
10. "The Combatants" (11-30-71) Morgan Woodward, Lindsay Wagner, Don Johnson
11. "A Company of Victims" (12-7-71)
12. "A Party to the Crime" (12-28-71) Lou Frizzell, Leo Hartbeck, Robert Lyons
13. "An Accident Waiting to Happen" (1-4-72) Robert Sampson, Susan Oliver
14. "Napoleon Never Wanted to Be a Cop" (1-11-72) Michael Burns


CANNON

Quinn Martin produced--to the plaudits of thousands--this celebration of the cases of an obese private detective, Frank Cannon (William Conrad).

The Regulars: Frank Cannon, William Conrad.

The Episodes:

1. "Salinas Jackpot" (9-14-71) Tom Skerritt, Sharon Acker, Vincent Van Patten, Charles Bateman, John Perak
2. "Death Chain" (9-21-71) William Windom, Don Gordon, Sorrell Booke
3. "Call Unicorn" (9-28-71) Wayne Rogers, Joe Maross, Patricia Smith
4. "Country Blues" (10-5-71) Clu Gulager, Diane Darsi, Joan Van Ark
5. "Scream of Silence" (10-12-71) Tim O'Connor, Jason Evers, Rodolfo Hoyos, Gregg Palmer, Whit Bissell, Radames Pera, Jean Allison, Charles Dierkop
6. "Fool's Gold" (10-19-71) Andrew Duggan, Ron Harper, Mitchell Ryan
7. "Girl in the Electric Coffin" (10-26-71) Kim Hunter, Andrew Prine, Lynne Marta, Signe Hasso
8. [unknown title] (11-9-71) Brooke Bundy, Bernard Hughes, James Wainwright, John McLiam
9. "A Lonely Place to Die" (11-16-71) Harold Gould, Carol Rossen, R. G. Armstrong
10. "The Pockets in the Shroud" (11-23-71) Arthur O'Connor, Linda Marsh, Roy Schneider
11. [unknown title] (11-30-71) Dack Rambo, Don Chastain, Lou Antonio, Robert Doyle, Richard Anderson, Gary Boyle
12. [unknown title] (12-7-71) Ed Nelson, Simon Scott, Marian McAndrew
13. "The Nowhere Man" (12-14-71) Fritz Weaver, Robert Webber, Richard O'Brien, Lynn Carlin, Hal England
14. [unknown title] (12-28-71) Cesare Danova, Barbara Luna, Victor Millan, Peter Mamakos, Joaquin Martinez, John Fiedler
15. [unknown title] (1-4-72) Martin Sheen, Dan Travanty, Collin Wilcox-Horne
16. [unknown title] (1-11-72) Tab Hunter, Alejandro Rey, Judson Pratt, Victoria Racimo
17. "Blood on the Vine" (1-18-72) Theodore Bikel, Hal Baylor, Katherine Justice, Christopher Connelly, Murray MacLeod, Ivor Francis
18. "To Kill a Guinea Pig" (2-1-72) Arthur Franz, Vera Miles, Michael Strong, John Zaremba, Robert Madden, Stephen Hudis
19. [unknown title] (2-8-72) Keenan Wynn, John Lasell, Jacqueline Scott, James Olson
20. "A Deadly Quiet Town" (2-15-72) Rick Weaver, Ann Lockhart, John Rubinstein, John Larch, Keith Andes, Russell Thorson, Dianne Hull, Louise Latham, Allyn Ann McLerie
21. "A Flight of Hawks" (2-22-72) Percy Rodriguez, Martin Sheen, Joyce Van Patten, Gerald S. O'Loughlin
22. [unknown title] (2-29-72) Larry Blyden, Anthony Zerbe, Richard Carlson, Sheilah Wells
23. [unknown title] (3-7-72) Bradford Dillman, Dana Elcar, Carmen Matthews, David Birney

24. [unknown title] (3-14-72) Burr De Benning, Julie Gregg, Mitchell Ryan, Frank Marth, Lloyd Gough, Lin McCarthy

## Second Season

25. [unknown title] (9-13-72) Michael Tolan, James Luisi, Larry Linville, Marj Dusay, Severn Darden
26. [unknown title] (9-20-72) Richard Hatch, Ken Lynch, Leslie Charleson, Ken Scott, Tom Pittman, Nora Marlowe
27. [unknown title] (9-27-72) Scott Hylands, Irene Tsu, Lloyd Bochner, James Oliver, Mickey Dolenz, Jim Watkins
28. [unknown title] (10-4-72) Jessica Walter, Jeff Davis, Robert Webber, Don Hanmer, Biff Elliott, Booth Colman
29. [unknown title] (10-11-72) Belinda Montgomery, Sheree North, Patrick O'Neal, Mike Farrell, Frank Maxwell, Charles Bateman, Curt Conway
30. "The Predators" (10-18-72) Phyllis Thaxter, Pamela Franklin, Robert Pine, David Sheiner
31. [unknown title] (10-25-72) James A. Watson Jr., Rosemary Murphy, Dana Elcar, Victor Campos, Sandy Kenyon, Lawrence Cook
32. [unknown title] (11-1-72) Stephanie Powers, George Maharis, Martin Braddock, Robert Mandan
33. [unknown title] (11-15-72) Warren Kemmerling, Clu Gulager, Julie Adams, Murray MacLeod
34. [unknown title] (11-22-72) Lois Nettleton, Bert Freed, Simon Scott, Richard Eastham, Jared Martin, Scott Walker
35. [unknown title] (11-29-72) Lynette Mettey, Alex Rocco, William Daniels, Wesley Lau, Linden Chiles, Louise Troy
36. [unknown title] (12-13-72) Katherine Justice, Billy Green Bush, Carl Betz, Hal England, Andrew Duggan, Neva Patterson
37. [unknown title] (12-20-72) Tom Skerritt, John Marley, Michael Glaser, Corinne Camacho
38. [unknown title] (1-3-73) John Vernon, Fritz Weaver, Charlotte Stewart, Greg Mullavey, Peggy Walton, Kelly Thordsen
39. [unknown title] (1-10-73) David Hedison, Barbara Babcock, Arlene Golonka, Michael Whiting
40. [unknown title] (1-17-73) Sondra Locke, Tim O'Connor, Malachi Throne, David Soul
41. [unknown title] (1-31-73) Susan Oliver, Keith Andes, Gordon Pinsent, Richard Carlson, Charles Bateman
42. [unknown title] (2-7-73) Dick Van Patten, Mary Frann, Jason Evers, Don Chastain, Noam Pitlik, Charles Bateman
43. [unknown title] (2-14-73) Scott Marlowe, John Larch, Christine Belford, Michael Pataki, Ramon Bieri, Stewart Moss, Arch Whiting
44. "The Prisoners" (2-21-73) Geraldine Brooks, John David Carson, Shelley Duvall, Julie Cobb, Richard Angarola, Harold Gould, James McCallion
45. [unknown title] (2-28-73) Barry Nelson, Robert Donner, Jim Davis, Lou Frizzell, Eldon Quick

46.  "Catch Me If You Can" (3-7-73) Anthony Zerbe, Dana Wynter, William Sargent, Jack Riley
47.  "Press Pass to the Slammer" (3-14-73) Marlyn Mason, Lane Bradford, Stuart Margolin, Oscar Beregi, Ron Hayes, Geoffrey Horne, Hank Brandt, John Zaremba
48.  [unknown title] (3-21-73) Lynne Marta, Beverly Garland, John Anderson, David Macklin

Third Season

49.  "He Who Digs a Grave" (9-12-73) Anne Baxter, David Janssen, Barry Sullivan, Lee Purcell, Martine Bartlett, Royal Dano, Tim O'Connor, Virginia Gregg, Murray Hamilton, R. G. Armstrong, Dennis Rucker
50.  "Memo from a Dead Man" (9-19-73) Martin Sheen, Robert Webber, Sheila Larken, Regis Cordic, Dennis Redfield, Lee Paul, John Carter, James Oliver
51.  "Hounds of Hell" (9-26-73) Geoffrey Deuel, Ford Rainey, Joel Fabiani, Bill Zuckert, James McMullan
52.  "Target in the Mirror" (10-3-73) Claude Akins, Frank Marth, Julie Gregg, Gil Peterson, Paul Carr, Alex Rocco
53.  "Murder by Proxy" (10-10-73) Linden Chiles, Anne Francis, Ross Hagen, Marj Dusay, Charles Bateman, James Nolan
54.  "Night Flight to Murder" (10-17-73) John Vernon, David Hedison, Jamie Smith Jackson, Norman Alden, Robert Patten, Barney Phillips, Jay Varella
55.  "Come Watch Me Die" (10-24-73) Michael Tolan, Don Stroud, Ahna Capri, Will Kuluva, Gene Dynarski, John Larch, Meg Foster, Gene Peterson
56.  "The Perfect Alibi" (10-31-73) Tom Troupe, William Watson, Whit Bissell, L. Q. Jones, Richard Anderson
57.  "Dead Lady's Tears" (11-7-73) Peter White, Charles Haid, Dabney Coleman, Paul Camen, Amanda McBroom, Don Hanmer, John Considine
58.  "The Limping Man" (11-14-73) Anthony Zerbe, Jason Evers, Richard O'Brien, Ben Wright, Barbara Stuart, Vic Tayback, Charles Macaulay
59.  "Trial by Terror" (11-21-73) Kelly Miles, Simon Scott
60.  "Murder by the Numbers" (11-28-73) Dina Merrill, Jane Merrow, Burr De Benning, Glenn Corbett, Ben Wright, Quinn Redecker, Nora Marlowe, Oscar Beregi
61.  "Valley of the Damned" (12-5-73) Leslie Nielsen
62.  "A Well Remembered Terror" (12-12-73) Robert Goulet
63.  "Arena of Fear" (12-19-73) John Marley, Pat Renella, Nick Nolte, James McCallion, Jess Walton, John Ward, Reta Shaw, Alan Dexter
64.  "Photo Finish" (1-2-74) Jack Cassidy, Herb Edelman, Lenore Kasdorf, Ben Marino, Hal Williams, Sandy Kenyon
65.  "Duel in the Desert" (1-16-74) James Wainwright, Joan Van Ark, Paul Brinegar, Denver Pyle, Les Lannom, David Lewis, Mavis Neal
66.  "Where's Jennifer?" (1-23-74) Pamela Franklin, Ann Doran, Christopher Stone, Bill Quinn, Michael Rupert, Russ Conwa

67. "Blood Money" (2-6-74) Peter Haskell, Diana Muldaur
68. "Death of a Hunter" (2-13-74) Sharon Acker, Edward Mulhare, Jill Jaress, Lee De Broux, Herbert Jefferson Jr.
69. "The Cure That Kills" (2-20-74) Peter Strauss, Herman Poppe, Andrew Parks, Norman Foster, Ramon Bieri, Susannah Darrow, Richard X. Slattery
70. "Bobby Loved Me" (2-27-74) Collin Wilcox-Horne, Pippa Scott
71. "Endangered Species" (3-6-74) Andrew Duggan
72. "Triangle of Terror" (3-13-74) Dana Wynter, Lloyd Bochner, Thalmus Rasulala, Don Knight, Ta-Tanisha, David Frankham
73. "The Stalker" (3-20-74)

Fourth Season

74. "Kelly's Song" (9-11-74) Stefanie Powers, Fred Beir, James Sloyan, Steve Mitchell, Frank Marth, Janice Haiden
75. "The Hit Man" (9-18-74) Richard Kiley, Ray Danton, Christopher Connelly, Michael Bell, Val Avery, Richard O'Brien, Than Wyenn
76. "Voice from the Grave" (9-25-74) Robert Webber, Ford Rainey, Jason Evers, Dennis Patrick, Michael Baseleon, Madlyn Rhue, Patricia Stich, Richard Bakalyan
77. "Lady in Red" (10-2-74) Steve Forrest, David Soul, Robert Emhardt, Larry Ward, Laraine Stephens, Lawrence Montaigne
78. "The Deadly Trail" (10-16-74) Kevin McCarthy, Ronne Troup, William Smithers, Bill Quinn, Katherine Cannon, John Milford, Whitney Blake
79. "The Exchange" (10-23-74) Robert Loggia, Edward Binns, Russell Thorson, Ray Vitte, George McCallister, Suzann Arnold, Abel Franco
80. "The Avenger" (10-30-74) Dane Clark, Robert Walker, Greg Mullavey, Kay Lenz, Diana Douglas, Henry Beckman
81. "A Killing in the Family" (11-6-74) Peter Strauss, Simon Scott, Robert Mandan, Carl Franklin, Paul Koslo, Joseph Perry, Jane Kean, Lauren Gilbert
82. "Flashpoint" (11-13-74) Kristoffer Tabori, Ruth Roman
83. "The Men Who Couldn't Forget" (11-20-74) Leslie Nielsen, Alf Kjellin, Alfred Ryder, James Keach, Joan Van Ark
84. "The Sounds of Silence" (12-4-74)
85. "The Prisoner" (12-11-74) Steven Keats, Peter Haskell, Paul Jenkins, Tim Herbert, Ed Power, Edmund Gilbert
86. "Daddy's Little Girl" (12-18-74) Kitty Winn, Leif Erickson, Frank Christi, Ed Bakey, Vincent Baggetta, Conrad Janis, Adam Williams
87. "The Conspirators" (1-1-75) Tom Skerritt, Hilly Hicks
88. "Coffin Corner" (1-15-75) Gary Lockwood, Karl Swenson, Patty McCormack, James McMullan, Joe E. Tata, Corinne Michaels, Richard Evans, Austin Willis
89. "Perfect Fit for a Frame" (1-22-75) Kathleen Cody, Mitchell Ryan, Ralph Meeker, Robert Donner, Robert Gentry,

Jay Varella
90. "Killer on the Hill" (1-29-75) Michael Tolan, Brooke Bundy, Milton Selzer, Ellen Weston, Lawrence Pressman, George DiCenzo, Ken Lynch
91. "Missing at FL307" (2-5-75) Leslie Charleson, Andrew Prine, Vince Howard, Estelle Winwood, David White, Charles Dierkop, William Prince, Robert Quarry
92. "The Set Up" (2-12-75)
93. "The Investigator" (2-26-75) Cameron Mitchell, Marianne McAndrew, Hari Rhodes, Kelly Peters, Morgan Paull, Keith Andes
94. "Lady on the Run" (3-5-75) Barbara Rush, Vic Mohica, Russell Johnson, Jean Hale, Barbara Luna, Barry Atwater
95. "Vengeance" (3-12-75) Monte Markham
96. "Tomorrow Ends at Noon" (3-19-75)
97. "Search and Destroy" (4-2-75) Dana Wynter


NBC WEDNESDAY MYSTERY MOVIE

In addition to the previously discussed (in conjunction with "Four in One") "McCloud," this NBC law and order feature film package brought superstar status to actor Peter Falk, a fine dramatic performer, now seeming to wallow in the mannerisms of "Columbo." "Columbo," as conceived by Richard Levinson and William Link, is a hunched, slow-paced police lieutenant whose suppliant manner conceals a clockwork thinking process when persistently questioning murder suspects. The series--and "Columbo" --operates on the premise that there is no perfect crime; that the killer exposes himself. Granted some rather ingeniously thought-out "crimes," the series is a worship of its protagonist and a familiar, if stylish, rendering of the "we always get our man" theme. "McMillan and Wife" is strictly a Rock Hudson vehicle; he is the pluperfect San Francisco police commissioner whose flighty wife Sally (Susan St. James) provides (along with Nancy Walker as the housemaid Mildred) the comic relief. "Cool Million" finds James Farentino a super-suave private eye who purportedly only works for a million dollars. "Banacek" is a George Peppard vehicle, he being an insurance investigator confronted with the grandest of enigmas. "Madigan" is a generally absorbing (and so against the vogue here) drama of a maverick New York detective; his deductions are within reason--a character of this earth. Two brilliant veteran actresses--Helen Hayes and Mildred Natwick --condescended to play the mystery loving siblings whose homespun style of crime detection amazes the pros. "Tenafly," a black private detective played by James McEachin, won acclaim for its lack of pretension. Finally, "Faraday and Company" refers to a father and son detective team (Dan Dailey and James Naughton); the far-fetched premise has father Faraday a quarter-century veteran of the prison cell--and unjustly so.

The Regulars: "McCloud": Deputy Marshal Sam McCloud, Dennis

Weaver; Chief Peter Clifford, J. D. Cannon; Sergeant
Broadhurst, Terry Carter; "Columbo": Lieutenant Colum-
bo, Peter Falk; "McMillan and Wife": Commissioner
Stuart McMillan, Rock Hudson; Sally McMillan, Susan St.
James; Mildred, Nancy Walker; Sergeant Enright, John
Schuck; "Banacek": Thomas Banacek, George Peppard;
Carlie, Christine Belford; Felix, Murray Matheson; Jay,
Ralph Manza; "Madigan": Detective Sergeant Madigan,
Richard Widmark; "Cool Million": Jefferson Keyes, James
Farentino; "Faraday and Company": Detective Frank Fara-
day, Dan Dailey; Steve Faraday, James Naughton; Lou,
Geraldine Brooks; Holly, Sharon Glass; "Tenafly": Harry
Tenafly, James McEachin; Ruth, Lillian Lehman; Lorrie,
Rosanna Huffman; Lieutenant Church, David Huddleston;
Herb, Paul Jackson; "The Snoop Sisters": Ernesta, Helen
Hayes; Gwen, Mildred Natwick; Barney, Lou Antonio; Os-
trowski, Bert Convy.

The Episodes:

1. Columbo: "Murder by the Book" (9-15-71) Martin Milner,
   Jack Cassidy, Rosemary Forsyth, Barbara Colby
2. McCloud: "Encounter with Aries" (9-22-71) Sebastian Cabot
3. McMillan and Wife: "Murder by the Barrel" (9-29-71) Kenneth Mars, William Traylor
4. Columbo: "Death Lends a Hand" (10-6-71) Robert Culp,
   Ray Milland, Patricia Crowley
5. McMillan and Wife: "The Easy Sunday Murder Case" (10-20-
   71) June Havoc, Wally Cox, Linda Watkins, Shepperd
   Strudwick, Read Morgan, Yale Summers
6. Columbo: "Dead Weight" (10-27-71) Eddie Albert, Suzanne
   Pleshette
7. McCloud: "Top of the World, Ma?" (11-3-71) Joan Blondell,
   Bo Svenson, Stefanie Powers
8. McMillan and Wife: "Husbands, Wives, and Killers" (11-10-
   71) Cesare Danova, Ed Flanders
9. Columbo: "Suitable for Framing" (11-17-71) Kim Hunter,
   Don Ameche, Ross Martin, Curt Conway, Rosanna Huffman, Joan Shawlee, Vic Tayback, Barney Phillips
10. McCloud: "Somebody's Out to Get Jennie" (11-24-71) Julie
    Sommars, Gabriel Dell, Barry Sullivan, Cameron Mitchell,
    Priscilla Pointer
11. McMilland and Wife: "Death Is a Seven Point Favorite" (12-
    8-71) Don Stroud, Andrew Duggan
12. Columbo: "Lady in Waiting" (12-15-71) Susan Clark, Leslie
    Nielsen, Jessie Royce Landis, Richard Anderson
13. McCloud: "The Disposal Man" (12-29-71) Patrick O'Neal,
    James Olson, Arthur O'Connell, Jack Carter, Nita Talbot,
    Diana Muldaur, Jean Allison, James McEachin, Murray
    Matheson
14. McMillan and Wife: "The Face of Murder" (1-5-72) Claude
    Akins, Edward Andrews, Hazel Court, Clifford David,
    Richard Deacon, Jon Cypher

15. McCloud: "A Little Plot, a Tranquil Valley" (1-12-72)
16. Columbo: "Short Fuse" (1-19-72) Roddy McDowall, Ida Lupino, William Windom, Anne Francis, James Gregory
17. "Cutter" [special mystery film] (1-26-72) Peter DeAnda, Barbara Rush, Cameron Mitchell, Gabriel Dell, Archie Moore, Robert Webber
18. McCloud: "The Fifth Man in a String Quartet" (2-2-72) Richard Haydn, Alex Henteloff, Avery Schreiber, Joseph Wiseman, Gary Collins, Shelley Fabares, Lilia Skala, Neville Brand, Rick Weaver
19. Columbo: "Blueprint for Murder" (2-9-72) Forrest Tucker, Janis Paige
20. McMillan and Wife: " 'Til Death Do Us Part" (2-16-72) Lawrence Pressman, Samantha Jones, Linda Watkins
21. McCloud: "Give My Regrets to Broadway" (2-23-72) Milton Berle, Barbara Rush

Second Season

22. Banacek: "Let's Hear It for a Living Legend" (9-13-72) Stefanie Powers, Marlyn Mason, Robert Webber, John Brodie, Deacon Jones, Ben Davidson, Tom Mack
23. Madigan: "The Manhattan Beat" (9-20-72) Ronny Cox, Tony Lo Bianco, James J. Sloyan, Jennifer Harmon
24. Banacek: "Project Phoenix" (9-27-72) William Windom, Bert Convy, Percy Rodriguez
25. Madigan: "The Midtown Beat" (10-4-72) Charles Durning, Cab Calloway, Nathan George, Dennis Hines, Robert Moore, Marlene Warfield, Madge Sinclair, Tim Pelt
26. Banacek: "No Sign of the Cross" (10-11-72) Broderick Crawford, Victor Jory, Peter Donat, Louise Sorel, Ned Romero, Gordon Pinsent
27. Cool Million: "Hunt for a Lonely Girl" (10-25-72) Ray Milland, Kim Darby
28. Banacek: "A Million the Hard Way" (11-1-72) Don Porter
29. Madigan: "The London Beat" (11-8-72)
30. Banacek: "To Steal a King" (11-15-72) Kevin McCarthy, Janis Paige, Brenda Vaccaro, Pernell Roberts, Roger C. Carmel, Logan Ramsey, Tod Andrews, David Spielberg
31. Cool Million: "Assault on Gavaloni" (11-22-72) Pamela Franklin, Ilka Chase, Nehemiah Persoff, Wilfrid Hyde-White, Joanna Barnes, John Abbott, Mills Watson
32. Cool Million: "The Abduction of Baynard Barnes" (12-6-72) Barry Sullivan
33. McMillan and Wife: "Terror Times Two" (12-13-72) Andrew Duggan
34. Cool Million: "The Million Dollar Misunderstanding" (12-20-72)
35. Madigan: "The Lisbon Beat" (1-3-73) Damien Thomas, Peter Vaughn, Weston Gavin, Tom Adams
36. Banacek: "Ten Thousand Dollars a Page" (1-10-73) David Wayne, Stella Stevens
37. Banacek: "The Greatest Collection of Them All" (1-24-73)
38. Madigan: "The Naples Beat" (1-31-73) Rosanno Brazzi,

Raf Vallone, Arnolda Foa, Franco Giornelli
39. Banacek: "The Two Million Clams of Cap'n Jack" (2-7-73)
Jessica Walter
40. "Poor Devil" [comedy special] (2-14-73) Sammy Davis Jr.,
Jack Klugman, Gino Conforti, Adam West, Christopher
Lee, Madlyn Rhue, Emily Yancy
41. "The Norliss Tapes" [special mystery film] (2-21-73) Roy
Thinnes, Claude Akins, Angie Dickinson, Nick Dimitri,
Hurd Hatfield, Michele Carey, Don Porter, Vonetta McGee,
Bob Schott
42. Madigan: "The Park Avenue Beat" (2-28-73) Rae Allen,
John Larch, Charles Cioffi, David Spielberg, Val Avery,
Sally Gracie
43. "Mr. Inside/Mr. Outside" [special mystery film] (3-14-73)
Hal Linden, Tony Lo Bianco

Third Season

44. Faraday and Company: "Say Hello to a Dead Man" (9-26-73)
Howard Duff, Ruth Roman, Craig Stevens, David Wayne,
Percy Rodriguez, Liam Dunn
45. Banacek: "No Stone Unturned" (10-3-73) Gary Lockwood,
Don Stroud, Larry Pennell, Scott Brady, Linden Chiles,
Joe Maross
46. Tenafly: "Joyride to Nowhere" (10-10-73) Tom Bosley,
Ross Martin, Pat O'Brien, Ellen Corby, Tina Andrews,
Michael Bell, Larry Storch
47. Faraday and Company: "A Wheelbarrow Full of Trouble" (10-24-
73) Edd Byrnes, Andrew Duggan, Joe Flynn, Holly Irving
48. Tenafly: "The Cash and Carry Caper" (10-31-73) William
Windom, Luciana Paluzzi, Jessica Walter, Don Porter,
Del Monroe
49. Banacek: "If Max Is So Smart, Why Doesn't He Tell Us
Where He Is?" (11-7-73) Anne Baxter, Paul Richards,
Jim Davis, John Zaremba, Richard Jordan, Alan Fudge,
Sabrina Scharf
50. Banacek: "The Three Million Dollar Piracy" (11-21-73)
Linden Chiles, Don Knight, Titos Vandis, Dick Gautier,
Arlene Martell
51. Tenafly: "The Window That Wasn't" (12-5-73) Robert Web-
ber, Ruby Dee
52. Faraday and Company: "Fire and Ice" (12-12-73) Roger
Davis, Jack Kelly, Pat Harrington
53. The Snoop Sisters: "Corpse and Robbers" (12-19-73) Sam
Jaffe, Geraldine Page, Neva Patterson, Kaz Garas, Pene-
lope Gillet, Liam Dunn
54. Tenafly: "Man Running" (1-2-74) Sal Mineo, Bob Crane,
Joseph Campanella, Henry Beckman, John Doucette,
Dolores Dorn, Barry Miller
55. Faraday and Company: "A Matter of Magic" (1-9-74) Ralph
Meeker, Don Keefer, J. Pat O'Malley, Charles Cioffi,
Carmen Zapata, Leigh Chapman, Jeanne Bates

[Hereafter NBC TUESDAY MYSTERY MOVIE]

56. Banacek: "The Vanishing Chalice" (1-15-74) John Saxon, Cesar Romero, Sue Ane Langdon, Eric Braeden, George Murdock, Robert Wolders
57. Banacek: "Horse of a Slightly Different Color" (1-22-74) Anne Francis, Tim O'Connor, Lane Bradbury, Ramon Bieri, Linden Chiles, John Crawford, Harry Carey Jr.
58. The Snoop Sisters: "Fear Is a Free Throw" (1-29-74) Bernie Casey, Walter Pidgeon, Maurice Evans, Steve Allen, Bo Svenson, Warren Vanders, Gloria Hendry
59. Banacek: "Rocket to Oblivion" (2-12-74) Linda Evans, Don Gordon, Andrew Prine, Tom Drake, Philip Carey, Dick Van Patten
60. Banacek: "Fly Me--If You Can Find Me" (2-19-74) Jack Kelly, Sterling Hayden, Virginia Principal, Don Hanmer, Paul Cavonis
61. The Snoop Sisters: "The Devil Made Me Do It" (3-5-74) George Maharis, Alice Cooper
62. Banacek: "Now You See Me ... Now You Don't" (3-12-74)
63. The Snoop Sisters: "Black Day for Bluebeard" (3-19-74) Vincent Price, Tammy Grimes


THE MAN AND THE CITY

If anyone could salvage respectability in the mire (the common attitude, after all) of big city politics it is Anthony Quinn, who performed admirably as Thomas Jefferson Alcala, the mayor of a New Mexico megalopolis in this sadly short-lived series.

The Regulars: Mayor Thomas Jefferson Alcala, Anthony Quinn; Andy Hays (assistant to Alcala), Mike Farrell; Marian Crane (secretary to Alcala), Mala Powers.

The Episodes:

1. "Hands of Love" (9-15-71) June Lockhart, Audree Norton, Lou Fant, Carmen Zapata, Lee Harcourt Montgomery, Walter Brooke
2. "A Hundred Black Pages" (9-22-71) Janice Rule, William Schallert, William Wintersole
3. "I Should Have Let Him Die" (9-29-71) Christopher Connelly, Fay Spain, Henry Jones, Severn Darden
4. "A Very Special Gift" (10-6-71) Ed Nelson, Sheila Sullivan, Laurie Prange
5. "Reprisal" (10-13-71) Simon Oakland, Charles McGraw, Michael Bell, Jean Allison
6. "Disaster on Turner Street" (10-20-71) Broderick Crawford, Dack Rambo, William Schallert
7. "The Handwriting on the Door" (10-27-71) Henry Darrow, Lynne Marta, Ken Lynch

8. "Running Scared" (11-3-71) Angie Dickinson, Charles Drake, Ken Lynch
9. "The Deadly Fountain" (11-10-71) William Windom, John Van Dreelen, Diana Ewing, Patricia Barry
10. "Run for Daylight" (11-17-71) Robert Hooks, Larry Wilcox, Kim Hamilton
11. "The Cross-Country Man" (12-1-71) Royal Dano, Robert Foxworth, Laraine Stephens, Ken Lynch
12. "Pipe Me a Loving Tune" (12-8-71) David McCallum, Burgess Meredith, William Schallert
13. "The Girls in Truck Seven" (12-15-71)
14. "Jennifer" (12-29-71) Lois Nettleton, Jack Albertson, Patricia Wynand, Sam Melville
15. "Diagnosis: Corruption" (1-5-72) Charles Aidman, Carolyn Conwell, Clark Howat, Dan Travanty, Skip Ward, Norma Connolly

## LONGSTREET

Scenarist Stirling Silliphant's trite (we've seen it in comic strips) if well intended detective series centers around a blind but so specially gifted insurance investigator, Mike Longstreet (James Franciscus).

The Regulars: Mike Longstreet, James Franciscus; Duke Paige, Peter Mark Richman; Nikki, Marlyn Mason.

The Episodes:

1. "The Way of the Intercepting Fist" (9-16-71) Bruce Lee, Lou Gossett, John Milford, Del Monroe
2. "A World of Perfect Complicity" (9-23-71) James Broderick, Douglas Henderson, Josephine Hutchinson
3. "One in the Reality Column" (9-30-71) Murray MacLeod, Tyne Daly, Victor French
4. "So, Who's Fred Hornbeck?" (10-7-71) Victor Jory, Martha Scott, Michael Ontkean
5. "Elegy in Brass" (10-14-71) Brock Peters, Janet MacLachlan, Robert DoQui, Berry Kroeger
6. "Spell Legacy Like Death" (10-21-71) Barry Nelson
7. "The Shape of Nightmares" (10-28-71) Dana Elcar, Paul Koslo, William Smith, Scott Walker
8. "The Girl with a Broom" (11-4-71) Shelley Fabares, Nan Martin, Michael Bell, Melendy Britt, Stacy Keach Sr.
9. "Wednesday's Child" (11-11-71) Tim McIntire, Gene Evans, Lee Harcourt Montgomery, Paul Fix, Marion Ross, Virginia Vincent
10. "I See, Said the Blind Man" (11-18-71) Bert Freed, George Murdock, John Lupton
11. "This Little Piggy Went to the Marquette" (12-2-71) Barry Sullivan, Madlyn Rhue, Michael Strong

12. "There Was a Crooked Man" (12-9-71) Murray Hamilton,
    Pippa Scott, Danielle de Metz
13. "The Old Team Spirit" (12-16-71) Leif Erickson, John Eric-
    son
14. "The Long Way Home" (12-30-71) Susan Oliver, John Mc-
    Liam, Skip Homeier, Rosemary DeCamp, David Huddleston
15. "Let the Memories Be Happy Ones" (1-6-72) Rosemary
    Forsyth, Lonny Chapman, Karl Swenson
16. "Survival Times Two" (1-13-72) Neville Brand, Jan Shepard
17. "Eye of the Storm" (1-20-72) Claude Akins
18. "Please Leave the Wreck for Others to Enjoy" (1-27-72)
    John McIntire, Wendell Burton
19. "Anatomy of a Mayday" (2-3-72) Arch Johnson, Harold J.
    Stone, Kathie Browne, Stephen McNally
20. "Sad Songs and Other Conversations" (2-10-72) Brooke
    Bundy, John Colicos, Jeanne Cooper, Richard Anderson,
    Dennis Olivieri, Frank Maxwell
21. "Field of Honor" (2-17-72) Robert Horton, Bernie Casey,
    Tol Avery, Robert Mandan
22. "Through Shattering Glass" (2-24-72) Peggy McCay, Stacy
    Harris, Lee Meriwether
23. "The Sound of Money Talking" (3-2-72) Peter Haskell, Luke
    Askew, Walter Burke, Vic Tayback

OWEN MARSHALL, COUNSELOR AT LAW

The legal process is yet distorted here, but David Victor's
veteran lawyer Owen Marshall (Arthur Hill) is less syrupy than his
medical doctor counterpart, Marcus Welby (who appeared in two of
the episodes). One of the most provocative of the teleplays,
"Words of Summer," sensitively dealt with an accusation of lesbian
assault. A fine supporting continuing performance came from Reni
Santoni as Attorney Danny Paterno. Other regulars were Lee Majors as Attorney Jess Brandon, Joan Darling as secretary Frieda
Krause, and Christine Matchett as Owen's daughter Melissa.

The Regulars: Att. Owen Marshall, Arthur Hill; Att. Jess Bran-
        don, Lee Majors; Frieda Krause, Joan Darling; Melissa
        Marshall, Christine Matchett; Danny Paterno, Reni Santoni
        (with episode of 10/3/73); Ted, David Soul (last season
        episodes only).

The Episodes:

1. "Legacy of Fear" (9-16-71) Glenn Corbett, Dane Clark, Pat
    Harrington, Richard Eastham, Darby Hinton, Rosemarie
    Bowe
2. "A Lonely Stretch of Beach" (9-23-71) Michael Tolan, Lor-
    raine Gary
3. "Eulogy for a Wide Receiver" (9-30-71) Stephen Young
4. "The Forest and the Trees" (10-7-71) Janet Margolin, John

Fink, Charles Robinson, Richard O'Brien
5. "Make No Mistake" (10-14-71) Ross Martin, Christine Belford
6. "Men Who Care" [Part II of "Marcus Welby, M.D." episode
of 10/19/71] (10-21-71) Ed Nelson, Robert Young, Belinda Montgomery, Russell Johnson, Frank Marth, Lindsay
Workman, James Brolin
7. "Shadow of a Name" (10-28-71) Barry Sullivan
8. "Eighteen Years Next April" (11-4-71) Alejandro Rey, Nancy
Malone
9. "Nothing Personal" (11-11-71) Tom Troupe, Kathryn Hays,
Gary Collins, Jim Antonio, Felton Perry, Judyann Elder,
William Wintersole
0. "The Baby Sitter" (11-18-71) Gary Grimes, Gerald S.
O'Loughlin
1. "Burden of Proof" (12-2-71) Lawrence Pressman, Shelley
Fabares, Paul Stevens, Joey Forman
2. "Until Proven Innocent" (12-9-71) Dana Wynter, Lindsay
Wagner, Henry Beckman, Randolph Mantooth
3. "Voice from a Nightmare" (12-16-71) Will Geer, William
Schallert, Kip Niven, Skip Homeier, Leonard Stone, Hildy
Brooks, Ben Hammer, Robert Patten
4. "The Triangle" (12-30-71) Stephen Brooks, Donna Mills,
Michael Larrain
5. "Warlock at Mach 3" (1-6-72) George Nader, Patricia Crowley, Nicolas A. Beauvy, Robert Hogan
6. "Eight Cents Worth of Protection" (1-13-72) Vic Morrow,
Dick Sargent, Pat Harrington, Jane Actman
7. "Run, Carol, Run" (1-20-72) Lane Bradbury, Keenan Wynn,
Jeanne Crain
8. "Victim in Shadows" (1-27-72) Rick Nelson, Stefanie Powers
9. "Shine a Light on Me" (2-3-72) James Brolin
0. "The Color of Respect" (2-10-72) Susan Strasberg, Tim
O'Connor, Sorrell Booke, Pippa Scott, Wright King, Edward Andrews, Richard Deacon
1. "Smiles from Yesterday" (2-17-72) Peggy Lee, Hoagy Carmichael
2. "A Question of Degree" (2-24-72) Lloyd Nolan, Pat Hingle
3. "Murder in the Abstract" (3-2-72) Karen Valentine, Fritz
Weaver

## Second Season

4. "Words of Summer" (9-14-72) Barbara Rush, Craig Stevens,
Meredith Baxter, Denise Nickerson, Russell Johnson,
Kristina Holland
5. "Lines from an Angry Book" (9-21-72) Julie Sommars,
Andrew Duggan, Pat Harrington
6. "Libel Is a Dirty Word" (9-28-72) John Davidson, Louise
Sorel
7. "Hour of Judgment" (10-5-72) Paul Burke, Lew Ayres,
Percy Rodriguez, Pat Harrington, Mike Farrell, Kaz
Garas

28. "Journey Through Limbo" (10-12-72) Michael Brandon, Pa
    Harrington, Norma Crane, Sheila Larken, Russell Johnsc
29. "The Trouble with Ralph" (10-19-72) Pernell Roberts, Joe
    Fabiani, Paul Carr, Arlene Golonka, Steve Franken,
    Joseph Perry
30. "Five Will Get You Six" (10-26-72) Sam Jaffe, William
    Shatner
31. "Who Saw Him Die?" (11-2-72) Ed Nelson, Neva Patterso
32. "Love Child" (11-9-72) Patty Duke, David Soul, Leif Erick
    son
33. "Charlie Gave Me Your Number" (11-16-72) Diana Muldau
    Edward Andrews, Rory Calhoun
34. "The First Day of Your Life" (11-30-72) Wayne Newton,
    Melissa Murphy, Madeleine Sherwood, Jewel Blanch, Joh
    Zaremba, Walter Brooke
35. "Starting Over Again" (12-7-72) James Stacy, Tab Hunter,
    Frank Campanella
36. "A Piece of God" (12-14-72) Barry Nelson, Jacqueline Scc
    Pat Harrington
37. "Sigh No More, Lady" (12-21-72) Joan Hotchkis, Glenn
    Corbett
38. "An Often and Familiar Ghost" (1-4-73) Louis Gossett,
    Gabrial Keel
39. "Sometimes Tough Is Good" (1-17-73) Beverly Garland, G
    Stockwell
40. "Seed of Doubt" (1-24-73) Martin Sheen
41. "Requiem for Young Lovers" (1-31-73) John David Carson
    Laura Owens, Gloria DeHaven, Celia Lovsky, Russell
    Johnson
42. "Why Is a Crooked Letter" (2-7-73) Tim Matheson
43. "They've Got to Blame Somebody" (2-14-73) Don Stroud,
    Leslie Charleson, Robert Reed, Robert Hogan, Lorraine
    Gary, Norman Alden
44. "Some People in a Park" (2-21-73) Brooke Bundy, Roger
    Davis, Collin Wilcox-Horne, Pat Harrington, John Fink,
    Charles Drake, Bill Quinn
45. "Final Semester" (3-7-73) Diana Hyland, William Smithers
46. "A Girl Named Tham" (3-14-73) Robert Ulrich

Third Season

47. "A Lesson in Loving" (9-12-73) Diana Muldaur, Kristoffer
    Tabori, Nina Foch, Howard Platt, Tom Falk, Ayn Ruym
    Kaz Garas, Byron Morrow, Diana Douglas
48. "Once a Lion" (9-19-73) Jason Evers, Milton Selzer, Ral
    Bellamy, Neva Patterson, Russell Johnson, Titos Vandis
49. "The Pool House" (9-26-73) Mark Hamill, Nan Martin,
    Sheree North, Arthur Franz, Pat Harrington, Lisa Eil-
    bacher
50. "Sweet Harvest" (10-3-73) Inga Swenson, Dack Rambo, An
    drew Duggan, Scott Hylands, Carmen Zapata
51. "N Is for Nightmare" (10-17-73) Eric Braeden, Vera Mile
    Richard Lenz, Jack Bender, Dean Harens, Pat Harringto

2. "The Camerons Are a Special Clan" (10-24-73) John Denver, John Larch, Teresa Wright, Brooke Bundy, Mike Farrell, Pat Harrington, Micky Dolenz, Stephen Coit, Kristina Holland
3. "Poor Children of Eve" (10-31-73) Cliff Potts, Bridget Hanley, Pat Harrington
4. "The Sin of Susan Gentry" (11-17-73) Martha Scott, Elayne Heilveil, Kermit Murdock, Fred Beir, June Dayton
5. "Child of Wednesday" (11-28-73) Pat Boone, Nancy Malone
6. "Snatches of a Crazy Song" (12-5-73) Madlyn Rhue, Mariette Hartley
7. "The Prowler" (12-12-73) Donna Mills, Lawrence Pressman
8. "The Second Victim" (12-19-73) Lee McCain, Todd Susman, Richard Ely, Sada Thompson, Paul Comi, Laurette Spang, Mala Powers, Angela Clarke
9. "Etude for a Kidnapper" (1-2-74) James G. Richardson, Dick Sargent, Bethel Leslie, Marshall Thompson, Pat Harrington, Lara Parker
10. "House of Friends" (1-19-74) David Hartman, Joyce Van Patten, Kathleen Quinlan, Barbara Baxley, Paul Shenar
11. "The Attacker" (1-26-74) Clu Gulager, Dana Wynter, Pat Harrington, Richard Loo, Morgan Jones, Byron Morrow
12. "A Foreigner Among Us" (2-2-74)
13. "A Killer with a Badge" (2-9-74) Scott Jacoby, Tim Matheson, Fred Karger, Jack Ging, Richard Anderson, Pat Smith, Pat Harrington, Ford Rainey
14. "The Sterilization of Judy Simpson" (2-16-74) Eve Arden, Dawn Smith, Claire Taylor, Bill Quinn, Victor Izay, Barbara Sammeth
15. "The Break-In" (3-2-74) Jane Wyatt, Allen Hunt
16. "I've Promised You a Father" [Part II of "Marcus Welby, M.D." episode of 3/5/74] (3-9-74) Kim Darby, Lynda Day George, Robert Young, James Brolin
17. "To Keep and Bear Arms" (3-23-74) Paul Burke, Barbara Anderson
18. "The Desertion of Keith Ryder" (3-30-74) Jane Wyman, Macdonald Carey, Randolph Mantooth
19. "The Ghost of Buzz Stevens" (4-6-74)

THE D.A.

Typically stilted dialogue (courtesy of producer Jack Webb) makes for these insipid teleplays drawn from the files of the Los Angeles County District Attorney's office.

The Regulars: District Attorney Paul Ryan, Robert Conrad; Chief Deputy H. M. Stafford, Harry Morgan; Bob Ramirez, Ned Romero; Deputy Public Defender Katy Benson, Julie Cobb; Charlotte, Sonja Dunson.

The Episodes:

1. "The People versus Drake" (9-17-71) Thomas Geas, Booth
   Colman, Ellen Corby, Pamela McMyler
2. "The People versus Swammerdam" (9-24-71) Russ Conway,
   Donald Woods
3. "The People versus Gayda" (10-8-71) John David Carson,
   Dennis Rucker
4. "The People versus Edwards" (10-15-71) Sharon Farrell,
   Lloyd Bochner
5. "The People versus Slovick" (10-22-71) Tim Matheson, Vic
   tor Izay, Ray Ballard
6. "The People versus Lindsey" (11-5-71) Jack Bailey, Dawn
   Lyn, Virginia Gregg
7. "The People versus Barrington" (11-12-71) Gene Raymond,
   David Nelson, Parley Baer
8. "The People versus Fowler" (11-26-71) Anne Whitfield,
   Victor Izay
9. "The People versus Howard" (12-3-71) Robert Pratt, Roger
   Perry, Michael Stokey, Nichele Nichols
10. "The People versus Nelson" (12-10-71) Robert Lipton, John
    Hubbard
11. "The People versus Whitehead" (12-17-71) Susan Oliver
12. "The People versus Walsh" (12-24-71) Victor Izay, William
    Schallert
13. "The People versus Boley" (1-7-72) Shelly Novack

THE SIXTH SENSE

The world of parapsychology--replete with poltergeists and witches--was the subject of this series, featuring Gary Collins as university professor Dr. Michael Rhodes. The best of the guest performances was delivered by Joan Crawford, not untypically being terrified in "Dear Joan, We Are Going to Scare You to Death," by Jonathan Stone and directed by John Newland.

The Regulars: Dr. Michael Rhodes, Gary Collins; Nancy Murphy
    (assistant to Dr. Rhodes), Catherine Ferrar.

The Episodes:

1. "I Do Not Belong to the Human World" (1-15-72) Belinda
   Montgomery, Christina Crawford, Kip Niven, James Mc-
   Mullan
2. "The Heart that Wouldn't Stay Buried" (1-22-72) Jessica
   Walter, Barry Sullivan
3. "Lady, Lady, Take My Life" (1-29-72) John Saxon, Tisha
   Sterling, Alf Kjellin, Than Wyenn, James McEachin
4. "The House That Cried Murder" (2-5-72) Carol Lynley,
   Corinne Camacho, Robert Yuro, Lawrence Linville
5. "The Man Who Died at Three and Nine" (2-12-72) Joseph

Campanella, Susan Howard, Simon Scott

6. "Death at the Top of the Stairs" (2-26-72) William Shatner, Bettye Ackerman, Anne Archer, Pam Peters, Alison McKay

7. "With This Ring, I Thee Kill" (3-4-72) Lucie Arnaz, Lee Majors, Will Geer, Stacy Harris, Richard Loo, Florence Lake

8. "Witch, Witch, Burning Bright" (3-11-72) Cloris Leachman, Mike Farrell, Tiffany Bolling

9. "Eye of the Hunted" (3-18-72) Louise Latham, Mariette Hartley, James Wainwright, Rudy Solari

10. "Echo of a Distant Scream" (4-1-72) Stefanie Powers, Jim Davis, A Martinez, Steve Forrest

11. "Whisper of Evil" (4-8-72) Frank Converse, Percy Rodriguez, Philip Pine, Coleen Gray, Paul Stewart, Carole Wells

12. "Shadow in the Well" (4-15-72) Mary Ann Mobley, Jeanette Nolan, Will Geer, Henry Silva

13. "Face of Ice" (4-22-72) Christine Belford, Bradford Dillman, George Murdock

## Second Season

14. "Two Hour Streets" (9-16-72) Jess Walton, Ed Nelson

15. "Coffin, Coffin, in the Sky" (9-23-72) Marge Redmond, Stephen McNally, Barbara Babcock

16. "Dear Joan, We Are Going to Scare You to Death" (9-30-72) Joan Crawford, David Ladd, Scott Hylands, Kelly Jean Peters

17. "Witness Within" (10-7-72) June Allyson, Michael Strong, Tippy Walker, Nan Martin

18. "With Affection, Jack the Ripper" (10-14-72) Patty Duke, Robert Foxworth, Percy Rodriguez

19. "Once Upon a Chilling" (10-28-72) Susan Strasberg, Ruth Roman, Joel Fabiani, David Huddleston

20. "Through a Flame, Darkly" (11-4-72) Sandra Dee, John Karlen, John Anderson

21. "I Did Not Mean to Slay Thee" (11-11-72) Pernell Roberts, Pamela Franklin, Michael Baseleon, Michael Witney

22. "And Scream by the Light of the Moon, the Moon" (11-25-72) Sally Shockley, Scott Glenn, Josephine Hutchinson, Michael Glaser

23. "If I Should Die Before I Wake" (12-2-72) Jane Wyman, Stefanie Powers, Michael Lane, Gene Evans

24. "Five Women Weeping" (12-9-72) Barry Sullivan, Hank Brandt, Ellen Weston, Mary Ann Mobley

25. "Gallows in the Wind" (12-16-72) Meg Foster, Gary Clarke, R. G. Armstrong, Richard Hatch, Virginia Gregg

26. "The Eyes That Would Not Die" (12-23-72) Percy Rodriguez, Rudy Solari, Tom Bosley, Lisa Moore

THE SEARCH FOR THE NILE

This fascinating series, produced jointly by the BBC and
Time-Life films, traces with a high regard for historical accuracy
Victorian England's great expeditions to find the source of the
River Nile.   Kenneth Haigh is towering as the central figure, explorer and linguist Sir Richard Burton.   Haigh's performance makes
Burton the majestic thread in a finely woven tapestry; a microcosm
for the geographical obsession of a century ago.   Excellent supporting performances are delivered by Michael Gough as the humanitarian Dr. David Livingstone; Keith Buckley as the American journalist Henry Stanley; John Quentin as Burton's rival explorer John
Hanning Speke; Ian McCulloch as Speke's aide Capt. James Grant,
and by Norman Rossington and Catherine Schell as the sportsman
Samuel Baker and his wife Florence.   James Mason was the inspired choice for narrator.   The color photography--exploring
parties reflected in shimmering streams, frenetic jungle foliage,
auburn sunsets--is breathtaking.

For those for whom the fascination lingers, Alan Moorehead's The White Nile (New York:  Harper & Row, 1960) and Moorehead's sequel The Blue Nile (New York:  Harper & Row, 1962) are
highly recommended.

The Episodes [telecast via NBC]:

1.   "The Dream of the Wanderer" [Part I]   (1-25-72)  focuses on
       Sir Richard Burton
2.   "Discovery and Betrayal" [Part II; initially telecast on the
       same evening as Part I]   (1-25-72)  Burton and Speke ex-
       plore Africa
3.   "The Secret Fountains" [Part III]   (2-1-72)  focuses on Speke
       and Grant
4.   "The Great Debate" [Part IV]   (2-15-72)  focuses on the
       Bakers
5.   "Find Livingstone" [Part V]   (2-22-72)  the search for Dr.
       Livingstone
6.   "Conquest and Death" [Part VI]   (2-29-72)  Henry Stanley
       finds the source

KUNG FU

Strictly for eastern mystics (or martial arts lovers) is this moralizing offbeat western of an eternally pursued (he killed a royal murderer) Chinese-American (David Carradine as "Caine"). Catch-phrases included Master Kan's instructions to the young Caine (there are periodic flashbacks): "When you can snatch this pebble from my hand ..."--indicating it will then be time for Caine to go it alone. Elaborate use of the camera, especially in the fight sequences.

The Regulars: Caine, David Carradine; Master Kan, Philip Ahn; Po, Keye Luke; Young Caine, Radames Pera.

The Episodes:

1. "King of the Mountain" (10-14-72) John Saxon, Lara Parker, Richard Loo, Brandon Cruz
2. "Dark Angel" (11-11-72) Robert Carradine, John Carradine, Dean Jagger
3. "Blood Brother" (1-18-73) John Anderson, Benson Fong, Robert Urich, Scott Hylands
4. "An Eye for an Eye" (1-25-73) Lane Bradbury, Harry Townes, Tim McIntire, Ross Elliott, Robert J. Wilke, L. Q. Jones, Parley Baer
5. "The Tide" (2-1-73) Andrew Duggan, Tina Chan, James Hong, Brian Tochi, Mako, Kenneth O'Brien, Robert Donner
6. "The Soul Is the Warrior" (2-8-73) Pat Hingle, Shelly Novack, John Doucette, Robert Foulk
7. "Nine Lives" (2-15-73) Geraldine Brooks, Albert Salmi, Merlin Olsen, Dana Elcar, Ross Hagen, Michael Cameron
8. "Sun and Cloud Shadow" (2-22-73) Morgan Woodward, Richard Lawrence Hatch, Soon Taik-Oh, Yuki Shimoda, Ronald Feinberg
9. "Alethea" (3-15-73) Jodie Foster, Ken Tobey, Byron Mable, William Mims, Frank Wilcox, Charles Tyner
0. "A Praying Mantis Kills" (3-22-73) Norman Alden, Wendell Burton, William Schallert, Don Knight
1. "Superstition" (4-5-73) Ford Rainey, Fred Sadoff, Roy Jenson, Woodrow Parfrey
2. "The Stone" (4-12-73) Jean Peters, Gregory Sierra, Sean

Marshall, Moses Gunn
13. "The Third Man" (4-26-73) Sheree North, Robert Hoy, John Anderson, Ed Nelson, Barbara Stuart, Fred Beir
14. "The Ancient Warrior" (5-3-73) Will Geer, Chief Dan George, Kenneth O'Brien, Denver Pyle, Victor French

Second Season

15. "The Well" (9-27-73) Hal Williams, Jim Davis, Tim McIntire
16. "The Assassin" (10-4-73) Dana Elcar, Nobu McCarthy, James Keach, William Glover
17. "The Chalice" (10-11-73) William Smith, Gilbert Roland, Charles Dierkop
18. "The Brujo" (10-25-73) Henry Darrow, Elena Bordero, Emilo Fernandez
19. "The Squaw Man" (11-1-73) Jack Elam, Elliott Street, Logan Ramsey
20. "The Spirit Helper" (11-8-73) Bo Svenson, Scott Hylands, Khigh Dhiegh, Don Johnson
21. "The Tong" (11-15-73) Diana Douglas, Richard Loo, Carey Wong
22. "The Soldier" (11-29-73) Tim Matheson, Myron Healey, John Dennis, Douglas Dirkson
23. "The Salamander" (12-6-73) David Huddleston, Ed Flanders
24. "The Hoots" (12-13-73) Anthony Zerbe, Howard Da Silva
25. "The Elixir" (12-20-73) Diana Muldaur, David Canary, Don Megowan, Matt Clark, Richard Caine
26. "The Gunman" (1-3-74) Andrew Prine, Katherine Woodville
27. "Empty Pages of a Dead Book" (1-20-74) Robert Foxworth, Slim Pickens, Nate Esformes, Bruce Carradine
28. [unknown title] (1-17-74) Howard Duff, Sorrell Booke, John Drew Barrymore, Ruth Roman, Tina Louise
29. "The Raiders" (1-24-74) Victor Sen Yung, Ron Soble, Fritz Weaver, Robert Ito, Gary Merrill, June Vincent
30. "Night of the Owls, Day of the Doves" (2-14-74) Barry Atwater, Anne Francis, Claire Nono, Arlene Farber
31. "Cross-ties" (2-21-74) Barry Sullivan, Denver Pyle, Andy Robinson, John Anderson
32. "The Passion of Chen Yi" (2-28-74) Bethel Leslie, Robert Middleton
33. "Arrogant Dragon" (3-14-74) Richard Loo
34. "The Nature of Evil" (3-21-74) Morgan Woodward, Selby Novack
35. "The Cenotaph" [Part I] (4-4-74) Nancy Kwan
36. "The Cenotaph" [Part II] (4-11-74) as above

Third Season

37. "Blood of the Dragon" (9-14-74) Patricia Neal, Eddie Albert, Edward Albert
38. "A Small Beheading" (9-21-74) William Shatner, Rosemary Forsyth, France Nuyen

39. "This Valley of Terror" (9-28-74) Sandra Locke, Howard Duff, Jan Sterling
40. "The Predators" (10-5-74) Cal Bellini, Anthony Zerbe, George DiCenzo, Robert Phillips
41. "My Brother, My Executioner" (10-12-74) Carol Lawrence, A Martinez, James Wainwright, John Vernon, Richard Kelton
42. "Cry of the Night Beast" (10-19-74) Albert Salmi, Don Stroud, Stefanie Powers, Alex Henteloff, Victor Jory
43. "The Devil's Champion" (11-1-74)
44. "The Garments of Rage" (11-8-74) James Shigeta, James Olson, James Hong, Harrison Page
45. "Besieged: Death on Cold Mountain" [Part I] (11-15-74) Barbara Seagull
46. "Besieged: Cannon at the Gate" [Part II] (11-22-74) as above
47. "The Demon God" (12-13-74) Brian Tochi, Michael Greene, Victor Sen Yung, Tad Horino
48. "The Vanishing Image" (12-20-74) Lew Ayres, Tom Nardini, Benson Fong, Jonathan Hole
49. "A Lamb to the Slaughter" (1-11-75) Barbara Luna, Alejandro Rey
50. "Forbidden Kingdom" (1-18-75) James Shigeta, Clyde Kusatsu, Adele Yoshioka, Evan C. Kim
51. "One Step to Darkness" (1-25-75) Leslie Charleson, Byron Mabe, Bruce Carradine, Lloyd Kino, David Huddleston
52. "Battle Hymn" (2-8-75)
53. "Barbary House" (2-15-75)
54. "Flight to Orion" (2-22-75)
55. "The Brothers Kain" (3-1-75) Leslie Nielsen, John Vernon, Juanita Moore, Tim McIntire, John Blyth Barrymore
56. "Full Circle" (3-8-75) Leslie Nielsen, A Martinez
57. "The Thief of Chendo" (3-29-75) James Hong
58. "The Last Raid" (4-5-75) Hal Williams, L. Q. Jones, Charles Aidman

## THE STREETS OF SAN FRANCISCO

Undistinguished Quinn Martin celebration of the exploits of two San Francisco police detectives (the talents of two fine actors-- Karl Malden and Michael Douglas--unable to surmount the banality of their dialogue). It is given to sensationalism: John Davidson was a transvestite-impersonator in "Mask of Death"; Rick Nelson was a murdering procurer in "Harem"; Brenda Vaccaro a hit-lady with whom Det. Keller was romantically involved in "The Most Deadly Species."

The Regulars: Lt. Mike Stone, Karl Malden; Det. Steve Keller, Michael Douglas; Jean Stone, Darleen Carr.

The Episodes:

1.  "The Streets of San Francisco" [two-hour pilot episode] (9-
    16-72) Robert Wagner, Kim Darby, Tom Bosley, Andrew
    Duggan, Naomi Stevens, Brad David, Edward Andrews,
    Mako, John Rubinstein, Lawrence Dobkin, Carmen Matthews
2.  "The Thirty Years Pin" (9-23-72) Edmond O'Brien, Rex
    Holman, Tim O'Connor, Leo Gordon, Eileen Heckart,
    David Opatoshu
3.  "The First Day of Forever" (9-30-72) Janice Rule, James
    Olson, Phillip Pine, Joby Baker, Lawrence Montaigne,
    Ken Lynch
4.  "Forty-Five Minutes from Home" (10-7-72) William Windom,
    Robert Hogan, Jo Ann Harris, Stephen Oliver, Paul Soren-
    sen, John Lasell, Dick Van Patten, Jacqueline Scott
5.  "Whose Little Boy Are You?" (10-14-72) James Stacy,
    Stephen Manley, Linda Marsh, Richard O'Brien, Nancy
    Wickwire
6.  "Tower Beyond Tragedy" (10-28-72) Edward Mulhare, Se-
    lette Cole, Stefanie Powers, Doris Dowling
7.  "Hall of Mirrors" (11-4-72) David Soul, Priscilla Garcia,
    A Martinez, Carmen Zapata
8.  "Timelock" (11-11-72) Peter Strauss, Bernie Casey, Elaine
    Giftos, Scott Walker
9.  "In the Midst of Strangers" (11-25-72) David Wayne, Louise
    Latham, Robert Foxworth, Ivan Bonar, David Pritchard,
    Ramon Bieri, Richard Eastham, Dennis Redfield
10. "The Takers" (12-2-72) Harold Gould, Heidi Vaughn, Bar-
    bara Baxley, Michael Lerner
11. "The Year of the Locusts" (12-9-72) Michael Ansara, John
    Roper, George Voskovec, Peggy Santon, Christopher Stone
12. "The Bullet" (12-16-72) Carl Betz, Geraldine Brooks, Pat
    Conway, Barney Phillips
13. "Bitter Wine" (12-23-72) Nehemiah Persoff, Robert F.
    Simon, Michael Glaser, Scott Marlowe, Donna Baccala,
    Michael Margotta
14. "A Trout in the Milk" (1-6-73) Roscoe Lee Brown, Carol
    Lawson, Brenda Sykes, Michael Greer
15. "Deathwatch" (1-13-73) Victor French, Mort Mills, Rodolfo
    Hoyos, Hari Rhodes, Nicholas Colasanto, Lou Krugman
16. "Act of Duty" (1-18-73) Brenda Vaccaro, Fred Sadoff,
    Michael Burns, Anne Collings
17. "The Set-Up" (1-25-73) Stuart Whitman, Jason Evers, Jack
    Albertson, John Kerr, Claudine Longet, George Wallace
18. "A Collection of Eagles" (2-1-73) Joseph Cotten, Hari
    Rhodes, John Saxon, Richard Bull, Belinda Montgomery,
    Jamie Farr
19. "A Room with a View" (2-8-73) Steve Forrest, Sandy Ken-
    yon, Shirley Knight Hopkins, Michael Strong, Richard An-
    derson
20. "Deadline" (2-15-73) Geoffrey Deuel, Thomas Kirk, Barry
    Sullivan, Greg Mullavey, Terrence O'Connor
21. "The Trail of the Serpent" (2-22-73) Tim O'Connor, Paul

Micale, Doug Chapin, Cal Bellini, Brad David, Brian Tochi, Frank Liu, Keme Young

22. "The House on Hyde Street" (3-1-73) Lew Ayres, Clint Howard, Albert Salmi, Michael Morgan, Joyce Van Patten, Jay MacIntosh
23. "Beyond Vengeance" (3-8-73) Joe Don Baker, Ken Swofford
24. "The Albatross" (3-15-73) Ed Nelson, John Kerr, Douglas V. Fowley, Kaz Garas
25. "Shattered Image" (3-22-73) Barbara Rush, Scott Hylands, Dick Sargent, Jeff Corey, Robert F. Simon, Jim Davis
26. "The Unicorn" (4-5-73) Richard Egan, John Kellogg, Jonathan Lippe, Paul Gange, Mitchell Ryan, Charles Aidman
27. "Legion of the Lost" (4-12-73) Leslie Nielsen, Tom Troupe, Karen Carlson, Ray Goman, Dean Stockwell, Vaughn Taylor

## Second Season

28. "A Wrongful Death" (9-13-73) Michael Constantine, Ina Balin, Robert F. Simon, John Kerr, Gregory Sierra, Andrew Rubin
29. "The Betrayed" (9-20-73) Martin Sheen, Johnny Silver, Collin Wilcox-Horne, Tony Haig, Joe Whipp, Lenore Kasdorf
30. "For the Love of God" (9-27-73) Leif Erickson, Jay Novello, Peter Strauss, Fred Sadoff, Marshall Thompson, James Gregory, Dave Cass, David Lewis
31. "Before I Die" (10-4-73) Leslie Nielsen, Ray Danton, Jo Ann Linville, James Wainwright, Steven Marlo, Paul Cavonis
32. "Going Home" (10-11-73) Tom Bosley, Sheree North, Arch Johnson, Paul Mantee, Milton Selzer, Brad Savage, Barry Atwater, Todd Martin
33. "The Stamp of Death" (10-18-73) Earl Holliman, Harry Davis, Jessica Walter, Robert Emhardt, Woodrow Parfrey, Byron Morrow, Byron Chung, Richard Derr, Vince Howard
34. "Harem" (10-25-73) Rick Nelson, Vince Howard, Laurette Spang, Kay Lenz
35. "No Badge for Benjy" (11-1-73) Mark Miller, William Watson, Judi Ann Elder
36. "The Twenty-Four Karat Plague" (11-8-73) Vic Morrow, Herb Edelman, Paul Jenkins, Wright King, Anthony Zerbe, Milt Kamen, Robert F. Simon, Simon Scott
37. "Shield of Honor" (11-15-73) Mariette Hartley, John Kerr, Robert Foxworth, Ed Knight, Stephen Sandor, Gary Vinson, Bing Russell, Ayr Ruymen
38. "The Victims" (11-29-73) Henry Silva, Jo Ann Harris
39. "The Runaways" (12-6-73) Jeanette Nolan
40. "Winterkill" (12-13-73) Paul Fix, Linden Chiles, Denver Pyle, John Qualen, Ruth McDevitt, Burt Mustin, Alan Bergmann, William Jordan
41. "Most Feared in the Jungle" (12-20-73) Kitty Wynn, Walter Brooke, Nan Martin, Joel Fabriani, John McLiam, Patricia Smith, Beverly Washburn

42. "Commitment" (1-3-74) Geoffrey Daniel
43. "Chapel of the Damned" (1-17-74) William Campbell, Stephen
    Oliver, Signe Hasso, Diana Douglas, Steven Marlo, Richard
    Kelton
44. "Blockade" (1-24-74) Ida Lupino, Don Stroud, Karl Swenson,
    Gloria LeRoy, Charlie Martin Smith, Patty McCormack
45. "Crossfire" (1-31-74) Pamela Franklin, Nick Nolte, Celeste
    Holm, June Dayton, Frank Steel, Kate Harper
46. "A String of Puppets" (2-7-74) Claude Akins, Lola Falana,
    Robert F. Simon, Ben Frank, Hari Rhodes, James Oliver,
    James J. Sloyan, Roger Mosley
47. "Inferno" (2-14-74) Barry Sullivan, Kaz Garas, Katherine
    Justice, Glenn Corbett, John Larch, Richard Ely, Bill
    Zuckert, Tony Haig, Anthony Carnata, David Moses
48. "The Hard Breed" (2-21-74) Jim Davis, Arell Blanton,
    Stephen Bradley, Noah Beery, Sam Elliot, Harry Carey
    Jr., Lane Bradbury, Ed Deemer
49. "Rampage" (2-28-74) Robert Hooks, Janet MacLachlan
50. "Death and the Favored Few" (3-14-74) Rosemary Murphy,
    Harold Gould

Third Season

51. "One Last Shot" (9-12-74) Leslie Nielsen, Ric Carrott,
    Robert Drivas, Jock Mahoney, Susan Strasberg, Jacqueline
    Scott
52. "The Most Deadly Species" (9-19-74) Brenda Vaccaro,
    James Luisi, Steve Sandor, Joseph Ruskin, Barry Sullivan,
    Dennis Patrick
53. "Target-Red" (9-26-74) William Sargent, Bill Bixby, Cheryl
    Miller, Andrew Duggan, Curt Lowens, Byron Morrow,
    William Bramley, Linda Marsh
54. "Mask of Death" (10-3-74) John Davidson, Anne Helm, Herb
    Edelman, Ivor Barry, John Fiedler, John Zaremba
55. "I Ain't Marchin' Anymore" (10-10-74) Michael Burns, Don
    Stroud
56. "One Chance to Live" (10-17-74) Pippa Scott, Steven Keats,
    Edward Mulhare, Herb Vigran, Joanne Linville, Paul Ca-
    vonis
57. "Jacob's Bay" (10-24-74) Brock Peters, Mitch Vogel, Dab-
    ney Coleman, Robert Walden
58. "Flags of Terror" (10-31-74) Carl Franklin, Robert Hogan,
    Richard Eastham, Elliott Street, Katherine Cannon,
    Adrienne La Russa
59. "Cry Help" (11-7-74) Mariette Hartley, Ed Barth, Clint
    Howard, David Gruner, Marge Redmond, Joseph Perry
60. "For Good or Evil" (11-14-74) Mike Evans, Berlinda Tol-
    bert, Don Pedro Colley, Herbert Jefferson Jr., Alexandra
    Hay, Hari Rhodes
61. "Bird of Prey" (11-21-74) Dennis Cole, Vivi Janiss, Chris-
    topher Stone, Kaz Garas, William Watson, Francine York,
    Martin Braddock
62. "License to Kill" (12-5-74) Murray Hamilton, Ivan Bonar,

Burr De Benning, Tommy Cook, Amy Farrell, Brendan Dillon
63. "The Twenty-Five Caliber Plague" (12-12-74) Jonathan Lippe, Todd Martin, Robert Webber, Mary Murphy, Lee H. Montgomery, Owen Bush, Davey Davison, Tony Geary
64. "Mister Nobody" (12-19-74) Sam Jaffe, Luther Adler
65. "False Witness" (1-9-75) A Martinez, Lloyd Battista
66. "Letters from the Grave" (1-16-75) Peter Strauss, William Windom
67. "Endgame" (1-23-75) Stephen Young, Paul Mantee, Tim O'Connor, Pat Conway, Richard Lawson, John Kerr
68. "Ten Dollar Murder" (1-30-75) Carol Rossen, Mark Wheeler, Michael Talbott, Jerry Douglas, Bruce Kirby, Ted Hartley
69. "The Programming of Charlie Blake" (2-6-75) William Smithers, Sharon Acker
70. "River of Fear" (2-13-75) Peter Haskell, Paul Fix, Patricia Smith, Irene Tedrow, Kim Richards, James Gammon, Stephen Manley
71. "Asylum" (2-20-75) James Olson, Belinda J. Montgomery
72. "Labyrinth" (2-27-75) Michael McGuire, Julie Adams
73. "Solitaire" (3-13-75) Tony Lo Bianco

[Continuing]


NBC SUNDAY MYSTERY MOVIE

Hours of murders, car chases, espionage and dreary dialogue--that would seem to characterize much of this NBC feature film law and order package. Of "McCloud" and "McMillan and Wife," discussed elsewhere in this volume, no more need be said. "Hec Ramsey" is the product of producer Jack Webb and features Richard Boone as a turn of the century deputy sheriff. "Amy Prentiss," introduced on "Ironside" and featuring Jessica Walter in the title role, is labored around Miss Prentiss' being a chief of detectives; one can imagine the prejudice and the situations. Richard Levinson and William Link's "Columbo" did, however, present two exceptional telecasts with two superb performances: that by Donald Pleasance as the murdering wine connoisseur of "Any Old Port in a Storm," and Patrick McGoohan's role as the ruthless director of a military academy in "By Dawn's Early Light."

The Regulars: "McCloud": Deputy Marshal Sam McCloud, Dennis Weaver; Chief Peter Clifford, J. D. Cannon; Sergeant Broadhurst, Terry Carter; "Columbo": Lieutenant Columbo, Peter Falk; "McMillan and Wife": Commissioner Stuart McMillan, Rock Hudson; Sally McMillan, Susan St. James; Mildred, Nancy Walker; Sergeant Enright, John Schuck; "Hec Ramsey": Hec Ramsey, Richard Boone; Chief Stamp, Rick Lenz; "Amy Prentiss": Detective Chief Amy Prentiss, Jessica Walter; Pena, Art Metrano.

The Episodes:

1. Columbo: "Etude in Black" (9-17-72) John Cassavetes,
   Myrna Loy, Anjanette Comer, Dawn Frame, James Mc-
   Eachin, James Olson, Blythe Danner
2. McMillan and Wife: "The Night of the Wizard" (9-24-72)
   Cameron Mitchell, Paul Richards, John Astin, Sharon
   Acker, Carole Cook
3. McCloud: "The New Mexican Connection" (10-1-72) Jackie
   Cooper, Rick Nelson, Gilbert Roland, Diana Muldaur,
   Murray Hamilton
4. Hec Ramsey: "Hec Ramsey" [two-hour premiere episode]
   (10-8-72) Harry Morgan, Sharon Acker, R. G. Armstrong,
   Robert Pratt, Ray Middleton, Dick Van Patten
5. Columbo: "The Greenhouse Jungle" (10-15-72) Ray Milland,
   Sandra Smith, Bradford Dillman, Bob Dishy
6. McMillan and Wife: "Blues for Sally M" (10-22-72) Keir
   Dullea, Don Mitchell, Edie Adams, James Atwood, Tom
   Troupe
7. Hec Ramsey: "Hangman's Wages" (10-29-72) Stella Stevens,
   Perry Lopez, Steve Forrest, Lee H. Montgomery
8. Columbo: "The Most Crucial Game" (11-5-72) Robert Culp,
   Valerie Harper, Dean Jagger, Dean Stockwell, James
   Gregory, Val Avery, Susan Howard
9. McMillan and Wife: "Cop of the Year" (11-19-72) Michael
   Ansara, John Astin, Edmond O'Brien, Paul Winchell, Kenneth Mars, Kathleen King, Martin E. Brooks, Lorraine
   Gary, Charles Nelson Reilly
10. Columbo: "Dagger of the Mind" (11-26-72) Honor Blackman,
    Bernard Fox, Richard Basehart, John Williams, Arthur
    Malet, Wilfrid Hyde-White
11. McCloud: "The Barefoot Stewardess Caper" (12-3-72) Britt
    Ekland, Jo Ann Pflug, Patrick O'Neal, Ivor Berry, Mar-
    lene Clark, Don Knight, Ginny Golden, John Williams,
    Jacques Aubuchon, Marcel Hillaire
12. Hec Ramsey: "The Green Feather Mystery" (12-17-72)
    Rory Calhoun, Marie Windsor, Lorraine Gary, Alan Hewitt,
    Morgan Woodward, Lloyd Bochner
13. McCloud: "The Park Avenue Rustlers" (12-24-72) Eddie
    Albert, Norman Fell, Brenda Vaccaro, Diana Muldaur,
    Lloyd Bochner, Roddy McDowall
14. McCloud: "Showdown at the End of the World" (1-7-73) Lee
    J. Cobb, Jaclyn Smith, Bradford Dillman, Eddie Egan,
    Arthur Batanides, Bruce Kirby
15. McMillan and Wife: "No Hearts, No Flowers" (1-14-73)
    Sheree North, Albert Salmi, Leon Askin, Dick Van Patten,
    Martin E. Brooks, Scott Brady
16. Columbo: "Requiem for a Falling Star" (1-21-73) Ross
    Martin, Mel Ferrer, Kim Hunter, Don Ameche, Anne Bax-
    ter, Frank Converse, Pippa Scott, William Bryant, Kevin
    McCarthy
17. Hec Ramsey: "The Mystery of the Yellow Rose" (1-28-73)
    Diana Muldaur, David Brian, Claude Akins, Don Stroud,

Philip Bourneuf, Ian Wolfe, Virginia Gregg, Ken Renard, Francine York, George Murdock

18. McCloud: "The Million Dollar Roundup" (2-4-73) Harry Guardino, Terri Garr, Nehemiah Persoff, Teri Turner, Jay Novello, Eric Braeden, Diana Muldaur, Robert Middleton

19. Columbo: "A Stitch in Crime" (2-11-73) Will Geer, Leonard Nimoy, Anne Francis, Nita Talbot, Jared Martin, Victor Millan

20. Hec Ramsey: "Mystery of Chalk Hill" (2-18-73) Sharon Acker, Bruce Davison, Louise Latham, Pat Hingle, John Anderson, Henry Jones, Jeanette Nolan, Lee Paul, Bernie Hamilton, Robert Fuller

21. Columbo: "The Most Dangerous Match" (3-4-73) Laurence Harvey, Lloyd Bochner, Michael Fox, Jack Kruschen, Oscar Beregi, Heidi Bruhl

22. McMillan and Wife: "The Fine Art of Staying Alive" (3-11-73) Paul Sorensen, Henry Jones, Cesare Danova, Alan Hale, Ken Jones, Felici Orlandi

23. Columbo: "Double Shock" (3-25-73) Martin Landau, Julie Newmar, Paul Stewart, Dabney Coleman, Tim O'Connor, Jeanette Nolan

24. McMillan and Wife: "Two Dollars on Trouble to Win" (4-1-73) Jackie Coogan, Lou Wagner, Rafael Campos, John Astin, Robert Donner, William Demarest, Murray Matheson

Second Season

25. Columbo: "Lovely but Lethal" (9-23-73) Vera Miles, Martin Sheen, Vincent Price, Bruce Kirby, Colby Chester, Fred Draper, Sian Barbara Allen, David Toma

26. McMillan and Wife: "Death of a Monster ... Birth of a Legend" (9-30-73) Roddy McDowall, John McLiam, Denise Bell, Jennifer Leak, Charmion King, Laurie Main, Diane Webster, Roger C. Carmel, James E. Brodhead

27. Columbo: "Any Old Port in a Storm" (10-7-73) Donald Pleasance, Dana Elcar, Julie Harris, Joyce Jillson, Gary Conway, Robert Walden, Robert Ellenstein, Reid Smith

28. McCloud: "Butch Cassidy Rides Again" (10-14-73) Linda Evans, Pat O'Brien, Stefanie Powers, Roger Davis, Lloyd Nolan, William Daniels, Buddy Lester, Carol Brooks

29. McMillan and Wife: "The Devil, You Say" (10-21-73) Keenan Wynn, Robert Hooks, Werner Klemperer, Rita Gam, Joshua Shelley, John Fiedler, Barbara Colly

30. Columbo: "Candidate for Crime" (11-4-73) Jackie Cooper, Ken Swofford, Joanne Linville, Vito Scotti, Tisha Sterling, Mario Gallo

31. McMillan and Wife: "Free Fall to Terror" (11-11-73) Dick Haymes, Barbara Feldon, James Olson, Barbara Rhodes Edward Andrews, Tom Bosley, Carole Cook, Tom Troupe, John Fiedler

32. Hec Ramsey: "A Hard Road to Vengeance" (11-25-73) Ruth

Roman, Keenan Wynn, Stuart Whitman
33. McCloud: "The Solid Gold Swingers" (12-2-73) Steve Allen, Joanna Pettet, Ross Martin, Joanna Barnes
34. Columbo: "Double Exposure" (12-16-73) Robert Culp, Louise Latham, Robert Middleton, Francis De Sales, Peter Walker, Arlene Martel, Chuck McCann, Ann Driscoll, Bobby Johnson
35. Hec Ramsey: "The Detroit Connection" (12-30-73) Kim Hunter, Richard Jordan, Luther Adler, Kelly Thordsen, Marshall Thompson, Angie Dickinson, Frank Campanella
36. McMillan and Wife: "Man Without a Face" (1-6-74) Steve Forrest, Dana Wynter, William Bryant, Nira Barab, Donna Douglas, Logan Field, Nehemiah Persoff, Stephen McNally, Vito Scotti, Gino Conforti, Ned Wertimer
37. Columbo: "Publish or Perish" (1-13-74) Jack Cassidy, John Chandler, Mariette Hartley, Alan Fudge, Mickey Spillane, Harvey Jason, Gregory Sierra, Jacques Aubuchon
38. McCloud: "Cowboy in Paradise" (1-20-74) Martha Hyer, Louise Lasser, James Gregory, Ken Lynch, Richard Denning, Don Ho, Bob Basso, Robert Luck
39. McMillan and Wife: "Reunion in Terror" (1-27-74) Buddy Hackett, Salome Jens, Michael Ansara, Carole Cook, Ned Wertimer, Barry Cahill, Bebe Kelly, Mary Betten, Rosey Grier, Milt Kogan
40. Hec Ramsey: "Dead Heat" (2-3-74) Jackie Cooper, Sheree North
41. Columbo: "Mind over Mayhem" (2-10-74) Jose Ferrer, Robert Walker, Jessica Walter, Lou Wagner, Lew Ayres, Arthur Batanides, Lee Harcourt Montgomery
42. McMillan and Wife: "Cross and Double Cross" (2-17-74) Morgan Woodward, Walt Davis, Rhonda Fleming, Carole Cook, Jackie Coogan, Richard Balin
43. McCloud: "The Colorado Cattle Caper" (2-24-74) John Denver
44. Columbo: "Swan Song" (3-3-74) Johnny Cash, Ida Lupino
45. Hec Ramsey: "Scar Tissue" (3-10-74) Kurt Russell, Chill Wills, Dick Haymes
46. McCloud: "This Must Be the Alamo" (3-24-74) Van Johnson, Jack Kelly, Laraine Stephens
47. Hec Ramsey: "Only Birds and Fools" (4-7-74) Robert Foxworth, Cliff Potts
48. Columbo: "A Friend in Deed" (5-5-74) Richard Kiley, Rosemary Murphy, Michael McGuire

Third Season

49. Columbo: "An Exercise in Fatality" (9-15-74) Robert Conrad, Phil Burns, Collin Wilcox, Jude Farese, Gretchen Corbett, Pat Harrington
50. McCloud: "The Barefoot Girls of Bleeker Street" (9-22-74) Shelley Winters, Kay Lenz, Gordon MacRae, Whit Bissell, Bill Fletcher, Robyn Millan
51. McMillan and Wife: "Downshift to Danger" (9-29-74) Van

Johnson, Alex Karras, Jim Antonio, Pamela Hensley, R. G. Armstrong, Bert Convy

52. Columbo: "Negative Reaction" (10-6-74) Dick Van Dyke, Don Gordon, Antoinette Bower

53. McCloud: "The Gang That Stole Manhattan" (10-13-74) Fernando Lamas, Toni Holt, Larry Hagman, Leslie Parrish, Marc Lawrence, Edward Binns

54. McMillan and Wife: "The Game of Survival" (10-20-74) George Maharis, Bobby Riggs, Stefanie Powers, Titos Vandis, Robert Wolders, William Windom, Rodolfo Hoyos, Andrew Duggan

55. Columbo: "By Dawn's Early Light" (10-27-74) Patrick McGoohan, Mark Wheeler, Tom Simcox, Burr De Benning, Sidney Armus, Karen Lamm

56. McCloud: "Shivaree on Delancey Street" (11-3-74) Danny Thomas, Lou Gossett, Jack Kruschen, John Quade, Cesare Danova, Jesse Willes

57. McMillan and Wife: "Buried Alive" (11-10-74) Barry Sullivan, Donna Mills, Jose Feliciano, Don Keefer, Francis De Sales, Ken Cory, Emmet Walsh, Larry Pennell

58. McCloud: "The 42nd Street Cavalry" (11-17-74) Julie Sommars, Bert Freed, Rafael Campos, Michael Parks, Peter Mark Rogers

59. McCloud: "The Concrete Jungle Caper" (11-24-74) Joseph Campanella, Angel Tompkins, Terri Garr, Brock Peters, John Marley, Sidney Clute, John Russell, James Carrol Jordan

60. Amy Prentiss: "Baptism of Fire" (12-1-74) William Shatner, Peter Haskell

61. McMillan and Wife: "Guilt by Association" (12-8-74) Susan Strasberg, David Soul, John Randolph, Paul Stevens, Felton Perry, Pat Harrington

62. Amy Prentiss: "The Desperate World of Jane Doe" (12-22-74) Cameron Mitchell, Don Murray, Andrew Prine, Michael Pataki, Joyce Van Patten, Frank Campanella, Corinne Michaels, Harvey Jason

63. McCloud: "The Man with the Golden Hat" (1-12-75) Don Ameche, Robert Webber, Philip Carey

64. McMillan and Wife: "Night Train to L.A." (1-19-75) Paul Burke, James McEachin, Linda Evans, Murray Matheson, Morgan Jones, Michael Callan, Elizabeth Lane

65. McCloud: "Lady on the Run" (1-26-75) Mariette Hartley, Clu Gulager, Pancho Cordova, George Belanger, Roger Cudney, Jorge Martinez De Hoyos

66. Amy Prentiss: "Profile in Evil" (2-2-75) Tige Andrews, Barbara Anderson

67. Columbo: "Troubled Waters" (2-9-75) Robert Vaughn, Jane Greer, Dean Stockwell, Bernard Fox, Patrick Macnee, Susan Damante

68. McMillan and Wife: "Love, Honor, and Swindle" (2-16-75) David Birney, Mildred Natwick

69. McCloud: "Sharks!" (2-23-75) Pat Hingle, Christopher George, Lynda Day George

70.   Columbo: "Playback" (3-2-75) Oskar Werner, Martha Scot
      Gena Rowlands, Trisha Noble, Patricia Barry, Robert
      Brown
71.   McCloud: "Return to the Alamo" (3-30-75) Diana Muldaur,
      Larry Storch
72.   Columbo: "A Deadly State of Mind" (4-27-75) George Ham
      ilton, Lesley Ann Warren


THE ROOKIES

      Obsessed with the rigors of police training is this routine
law and order entry of the adventures of "rookie" cops Mike Dank
(Sam Melville), Terry Webster (Georg Stanford Brown) and Willie
Gillis (Michael Ontkean)--their taskmaster being Lieutenant Ryker
(Gerald S. O'Loughlin).   Kate Jackson appears as the wife of Offi
cer Danko.

The Regulars: Officer Mike Danko, Sam Melville; Officer Terry
            Webster, Georg Stanford Brown; Jill Danko, Kate Jackson
            Lt. Ryker, Gerald S. O'Loughlin; Officer Willie Gillis,
            Michael Ontkean (to episode of 3/18/74); Officer Chris
            Owens, Bruce Fairbairn (with episode of 9/9/74).

The Episodes:

1.    "Concrete Valley, Neon Sky" (9-11-72) William Elliott,
      Hilly Hicks, Ian Sandor, Shelly Novack
2.    "Dead, Like a Lost Dream" (9-18-72) Mark Slade, William
      Mims, Dane Clark, Tom Tully
3.    "The Informant" (9-25-72) Joe Knapp, Margaret Avery, Ka
      Garas, Henry V. Brown Jr., Ian Wolfe, Jim Nolan
4.    "The Commitment" (10-2-72) Darleen Carr, Bo Svenson,
      Arlene Golonka, Dal Jenkins
5.    "Covenant with Death" (10-9-72) Lou Gossett, Terry Lumley
      John Randolph, Alan Weeks
6.    [unknown title] (10-16-72) Joe Maross, Craig Stevens, Wil
      liam Windom, Lynn Marta
7.    "The Bear That Didn't Get Up" (10-23-72) Simon Scott,
      Pamela Shoop, Warren Kemmerling
8.    "Dirge for Sunday" (10-30-72) Roddy McDowall, Lew Brow
      Tom Troupe, Vincent Gardenia
9.    "The Good Die Young" (11-13-72) Gwenn Mitchell, James
      Olson, Michael Fox, Leslie Charleson
10.   "To Taste of Terror" (11-20-72) S. John Launer, Tom
      Palmer, Andy Robinson, Lee Farr
11.   "A Deadly Velocity" (11-27-72) Burr De Benning, Don Por
      er, Belinda Montgomery, Alan Vint
12.   "A Bloody Shade of Blue" (12-11-72) Pat Stitch, Stanley
      Kamel, Brooke Bundy, Jared Martin
13.   "A Very Special Piece of Ground" (12-18-72) Earl Hollima
      Pippa Scott, Charles Gray, Paul Bryer

4. "The Rabbits on the Runway" (12-25-72) Michael Pataki, James Luisi, Charles Aidman, Susan Sennett
5. "The Tarnished Idol" (1-8-73) Lou Antonio, Norman Alden, Radames Pera
6. "Crossfire" (1-15-73) Percy Rodriguez, Eric Lanueville, Wayne Maunder, Clint Howard
7. "The Snow Job" (1-29-73) Martin Sheen, Don Dubbins, Ron Soble, Suzanne Charney
8. "Point of Impact" (2-5-73) Victor Campos, Ford Rainey, Tina Cole, Rafael Campos
9. "Three Hours to Kill" (2-12-73) Jacqueline Scott, Paul Carr, Beverly Garland, Bill Williams, William Bryant
0. "The Wheel of Death" (2-19-73) Michael Farrell, Ross Hagen, Michael-James Wixted, Bill Campbell, Ken Lynch, Corinne Camacho
1. "Tribute to a Veteran" (2-26-73) Pat Hingle, Mark Lenard, John Dewey, John Gruber, Dick Van Patten
2. "A Farewell Tree from Marly" (3-5-73) Tyne Daly, Logan Ramsey, Jean Allison, Paul Stevens, Dennis Patrick, Philip Proctor
3. "Easy Money" (3-19-73) Hilly Hicks, Teresa Graves, Lonny Chapman, Curt Conway, Jonathan Lippe

## econd Season

4. "Cauldron" (9-10-73) John Saxon, Vince Howard, Michael Baseleon
5. "Margin for Error" (9-17-73) Claude Akins, Robert Waldon, Jean Allison, Tom Falk, Charles Gray
6. "A Deadly Cage" (9-24-73) Robert Hooks, Victor French, William Watson, Ford Rainey, Thom Carney, Robert Phillips
7. "Frozen Smoke" (10-1-73) Scott Jacoby, John Travolta, Walter Brooke, Judy Farrell, Charles Shull, Sally Carter Ihnat
8. "Get Ryker!" (10-8-73) Joseph Campanella, Sid McCoy, Bill Williams, Robert Donner, Thalmus Rasulala, Gil Stuart
9. "Cry Wolf" (10-15-73) Anthony Eisley, Ken Swofford, Pat Harrington, Joan Blondell
). "Justice for Jill Danko" (10-22-73) James Olson, Joseph Bernard, Judson Pratt, Richard Bull, Willard Sage, Bill Ewing
1. "Blood Brother" (10-29-73) Glynn Turman, Herb Jefferson Jr.
2. "Code 261" (11-5-73) Tannis G. Montgomery, Mark Slade, Jan Shepard, Joe Hooker, John Dennis, Kim Hamilton
3. "Prayers Unanswered, Prayers Unheard" (11-12-73) Florida Friebus, Johnny Brown, Larry Golden, Jennifer Leak
4. 'Down Home Boy" (11-19-73) Jim Nabors
5. "Lots of Trees and a Running Stream" (12-3-73) Richard Hatch
. "Another Beginning for Ben Fuller" (12-10-73) Leif Erickson,

Ned Glass

37. "Sound of Silence" (12-17-73) Sissy Spacek, Jason Evers, Joseph Perry, Ted Eccles, Bettye Ackerman, Jared Martin

38. "Trial by Doubt" (1-7-74) Malcolm Atterbury, Hank Brandt, Scott Walker, Fionnuala Flanagan, Barry Cahill, John Chandler, Anthony Carlson

39. "The Authentic Death of Billy Stomper" (1-14-74) Esther Anderson, Sally Frei, Joe Maross, Trish Mahoney, Rex Holman, Keith Walker, Troy Melton, Steve Sandor

40. "The Late Mr. Brent" (1-28-74) Darleen Carr, Olive Sturgess, William Smithers, Matt Clark

41. "The Teacher" (2-4-74) Strother Martin, Don Johnson

42. "Eyewitness" (2-11-74) Wendell Burton, Frank Arno, Donal Barry, Lurene Tuttle, Dick Crockett, Robert Harland

43. "Something Less than a Man" (2-18-74) Dane Clark, Don Gordon, Johnny Seven, Paul Pepper, Bill Zuckert, Abe Vigoda, Suzann Arnold, Bill Williams

44. "Rolling Thunder" (2-25-74) Brad David, Andy Parks

45. "Timelock" (3-4-74) Robert Walden

46. "Death Watch" (3-18-74) Anthony Zerbe

Third Season

47. "An Ugly Way to Die" (9-9-74) Lou Antonio, Kim Hamilton Jesse Vint, Larry Pennell

48. "Keywitness" (9-23-74) Trish Stewart, Jon Cypher, Sally Carter Ihnat, Jared Martin

49. "Legacy of Death" (9-30-74) Jeremy Slate, Alex Rocco, James Keach, Robin Strasser, Michael Christian, Christian Jutner

50. "Death at 6 A.M." (10-7-74) Bo Hopkins, Christina Hart, John Zaremba, Kenneth Tobey, Charlie Martin Smith

51. "Walk a Tightrope" (10-21-74) Kristoffer Tabori, Francis De Sales, James Carrol Jordan, Robert Harland, Mary Jackson, Arthur Hansen

52. "Judgment" (10-28-74) Stefanie Powers, Nancy Bell, Elliott Street, Joseph Perry, Eduard Franz, Robert Harland

53. "Johnny Lost His Gun" (11-4-74) Fred Williamson, Emily Yancy, Gerald Hiken, David White, Anthony Carbone, Robert Ellenstein

54. "Prelude to Vengeance" (11-11-74) Ronne Troup, Andy Robinson, Penny Santon, Titos Vandis, Gerrit Graham, Bernard Barrows

55. "Vendetta" (11-18-74) Laurence Luckinbill

56. "The Old Neighborhood" (11-25-74) Katherine Helmond, Bill Katt, Stephen Keats, Ned Glass, Lance Taylor, Arthur Franz

57. "A Test of Courage" (12-2-74) David Soul, David Canary, Laurie Burton, Vic Mehick, David Huddleston

58. "The Assassin" (12-9-74) Darleen Carr, Eric Braeden, Frank Baxter, Frank Lugo

59. "Blue Christmas" (12-16-74) Elinor Donahue, Lou Krugman

Kamme Hartling, Ruth McDevitt, Charles Lampkin, Barbara Nichols
60. "Take Over" (12-30-74) Vic Tayback, Ray Walston, Harold J. Stone, Vince Baggetta, Barbara Baxley
61. "The Hunting Ground" (1-20-75) William Shatner, Anthony James, Linda Foster, Richard O'Brien, Michael Lembeck, Stack Pierce
62. "Solomon's Dilemma" (1-27-75) Shelley Fabares, John Ragin, Kathy Lloyd, Peter Coffield, Edward Andrews, Bettye Ackerman
63. "Angel" (2-3-75) Susan Dey, Dack Rambo
64. "The Shield" (2-10-75) Jonathan Lippe, Ralph Meeker
65. "S. W. A. T. " [pilot for series "S. W. A. T. "] (2-17-75) Steve Forrest, Leslie Nielsen
66. "A Deadly Image" (2-24-75) Jane Actman, Richard Hatch
67. "Cliffy" (3-3-75) Mark Slade, Lonny Chapman, Glynnis O'Connor, Tyne Daly, Alan Fudge, Norman Alden
68. "Nightmare" (3-17-75)

# SEARCH

But for the presence of superlative character actor Burgess Meredith, one would not have noticed the passing of this espionage tale of agents Lockwood (Hugh O'Brian), Grover (Doug McClure) and Bianco (Anthony Franciosa) rather reluctantly ordered about by boss Cameron (Meredith) and his computerized gadgetry.

The Regulars: Lockwood, Hugh O'Brian; C. R. Grover, Doug McClure; Nick Bianco, Tony Franciosa; Cameron, Burgess Meredith; Gloria Harding, Angel Tompkins; Dr. Barnett, Ford Rainey; Kuroda, Byron Chung; Miss James, Pamela Jones; Harris, Tom Hallick; Griffith, Albert Popwell; Carlos, Ron Castro; Keach, Ginny Golden.

The Episodes:

1. "The Murrow Disappearance" [Hugh O'Brian] (9-13-72) Maurice Evans, David White, Capucine, Lawrence Cook
2. "One of Our Probes Is Missing" [Tony Franciosa] (9-20-72) Stefanie Powers, Larry Linville, Milton Selzer, Jacqueline Hyde
3. "Short Circuit" [Doug McClure] (9-27-72) Jeff Corey, Mary Ann Mobley, Nate Esformes
4. "Moonrock" [Hugh O'Brian] (10-4-72) Jo Ann Pflug, George Pan, William Wintersole, Ann Prentiss
5. "Live Men Tell Tales" [Tony Franciosa] (10-11-72) Louise Sorel, Martin Koslek, Leslie Charleson
6. "Operation Iceman" [Tony Franciosa] (10-25-72) Edward Mulhare, Mary Frann, Edward Bell
7. [unknown title] (11-1-72) Alan Bergman, Ina Balin, Robert Boon, Malachi Throne

8. "In Search of Midas" [Doug McClure] (11-8-72) Barbara Feldon, Logan Ramsey
9. "The Adonis File" [Hugh O'Brian] (11-15-72) Bill Bixby, Victoria George, Brenda Benet
10. "Flight to Nowhere" [Tony Franciosa] (11-22-72) Linda Cristal, Don Dubbins, Warren Vanders, Joanna Cameron, William Patterson
11. "The Bullet" [Hugh O'Brian] (12-20-72) Hurd Hatfield, Kurt Kasznar, Michael Bow, Bill Fletcher
12. "Let Us Prey" [Tony Franciosa] (1-3-73) Diana Hyland, Victor Millan, Albert Paulsen, Walter Friedel, Mike DeAnda
13. "A Honeymoon to Kill" [Doug McClure] (1-10-73) George Coulouris, Luciana Paluzzi, Rudy Solari, Gerry Clarke, Antoinette Bower
14. "The Twenty-Four Carat Hit" [Tony Franciosa] (1-24-73) Lane Bradford, Wally Cox, Nehemiah Persoff, Dane Clark, Michael Conrad, William Smith
15. "Numbered for Death" [Doug McClure] (1-31-73) Luther Adler, Lauri Peters, Peter Mark Richman, Bert Convy
16. "Countdown to Panic" [Hugh O'Brian] (2-7-73) Ed Nelson, Howard Duff, Anne Francis, Jack Ging, Robert Webber, Frank Down
17. "The Clayton Lewis Document" [Tony Franciosa] (2-14-73) Rhonda Fleming, Anna Capri, Don Gordon, Craig Stevens, Anthony James, Julie Adams
18. "Goddess of Destruction" [Doug McClure] (2-21-73) Anjanette Comer, Than Wyenn, Alfred Ryder, Jose De Vega, Reggie Nalder, John Vernon
19. "The Mattson Papers" [Tony Franciosa] (2-28-73) Nancy Wilson, Tim O'Connor, Cameron Mitchell, John Kerr, Don Pedro Colley, Terry Carter, Ivor Francis, Ella Edwards
20. "Moment of Madness" [Doug McClure] (3-14-73) Patrick O'Neal, Keith Andes, Brooke Bundy, James Sikking
21. "Ends of the Earth" [Tony Franciosa] (3-21-73) Diana Muldaur, Milt Kamen, Sebastian Cabot, Jay Robinson, Simon Scott, William Bassett
22. "Suffer My Child" [Hugh O'Brian] (3-28-73) Mel Ferrer, Paul Mantee, Dianne Hull, Dabney Coleman
23. "The Packagers" [Doug McClure] (4-11-73) Michael Pataki, Titos Vandis, John Holland, Xenia Gratsos

THE WALTONS

Earl Hamner's sentimental tale of a Depression era family (replete with picturesque Blue Ridge Mountains) has its mawkish moments but the suitability of performers to their characters and the feeling for atmosphere and period resurrects it. Particularly effective are those episodes emphasizing the urban versus rural life style: "The Shivaree," in which a bewildered city-bred

bridegroom is abducted to take part in a country ritual; the social-
ite who is imbued with a sense of the past after returning to Walton's Mountain in "The Spoilers." A quintet of strong performances
by Ralph Waite and Michael Learned as the father and mother of
seven; Richard Thomas their eldest son John-Boy; Will Geer and
Ellen Corby as the grandparents.

The Regulars: John-Boy Walton, Richard Thomas; John Walton,
Ralph Waite; Olivia Walton, Michael Learned; Grandpa
Walton, Will Geer; Grandma Walton, Ellen Corby; Jim-
Bob Walton, David S. Harper; Elizabeth Walton, Kami
Cotler; Mary Ellen Walton, Judy Norton; Jason Walton,
Jon Walmsley; Ben Walton, Eric Scott; Erin Walton, Mary
Elizabeth McDonough; Sheriff Bridges, John Crawford;
Emily Baldwin, Mary Jackson; Mamie Baldwin, Helen
Kleeb; Ike, Joe Conley.

The Episodes:

1. [unknown title] (9-14-72) Charlotte Stewart, Erica Hunton,
Richard Kelton
2. [unknown title] (9-21-72) Billy Barty, Gino Conforti, Barbara Davis, John Harper
3. [unknown title] (9-28-72) Leonard Stone
4. [unknown title] (10-5-72) Tom Peters, Theodore Wilson,
James Nusser
5. [unknown title] (10-12-72) George Tobias
6. [unknown title] (10-19-72) Iggie Wolfington, Jack Collins
7. [unknown title] (10-26-72) John Ritter, Collin Wilcox-Horne
8. [unknown title] (11-2-72) Michael Rupert
9. [unknown title] (11-9-72) Noah Keen, Ellen Geer, Radames
Pera
10. [unknown title] (11-16-72) Jim Antonio
11. [unknown title] (11-30-72) David Huddleston
12. [unknown title] (12-7-72) Warren Vanders, Ken Wolger, Jay
MacIntosh, Robert Donner
13. [unknown title] (12-14-72) Denver Pyle, Adele Clair
14. "The Minstrel" (12-21-72) Peter Hooten, Marie Earle
15. [unknown title] (1-4-73) Pippa Scott, Dorothy Neumann
16. "The Fire" (1-11-73) Laurie Prange, Richard Bradford,
Mariclare Costello
17. [unknown title] (1-18-73) Sian Barbara Allen, Byron Morrow, Diane Shalet, Gordon Rigsby
18. [unknown title] (1-25-73) Eduard Franz, Donna Hansen, John
Ritter
19. [unknown title] (2-1-73) Gregory Sierra, Victor Argo, William Bramley, Barry Miller, Karen Kondan, Celia Lovsky
20. [unknown title] (2-8-73) George Tobias, Robert Donner,
Randall Carver, Jenny Sullivan, Shirley O'Hara
21. [unknown title] (2-22-73) Lynn Hamilton, Royce Wallace,
Mariclare Costello
22. [unknown title] (3-1-73) Ned Beatty, Ivy Jones, Lou Frizzell
23. [unknown title] (3-8-73) Sissy Spacek, Nicholas Hammond

## Second Season

24. "The Journey" (9-13-73)  Linda Watkins, Tammi Bula, Victor Izay
25. "The Odyssey" (9-20-73)  Sissy Spacek, Allyn Ann McLerie, Frances Williams
26. "The Separation" (9-27-73)  Ed Call, John Fox
27. "The Theft" (10-4-73)  Diane Webster, Vern Rowe, Dennis Dugan, Janit Baldwin
28. "The Roots" (10-11-73)  Lynn Hamilton, Erin Blunt, Hal Williams
29. "The Chicken Thief" (10-18-73)  Robert Donner, Meg Wyllie, Richard O'Brien
30. "The Prize" (10-25-73)  Peter Donat, Dana Elcar, Louise Lorimer
31. "The Braggart" (11-1-73)  Michael McGreevey
32. "The Fawn" (11-8-73)  Charles Tyner, Matt Clark, Jimmy Davilla, Jim Gammon
33. "The Thanksgiving Story" [two-hour episode] (11-15-73)  Sian Barbara Allen, Mariclare Costello, Diane Shalet, Nadine Turney, Victor Izay, Rance Howard
34. [unknown title] (11-22-73)  Catherine Burns
35. "The Bequest" (11-29-73)
36. "The Air-Mail Men" (12-13-73)  Michael Glaser, Julie Cobb
37. "The Triangle" (12-20-73)  Mariclare Costello, John Ritter, Nora Marlowe
38. "The Awakening" (1-3-74)  James Carroll Jordan, David Doremus
39. "The Honeymoon" (1-10-74)  Tammi Bula, Greg Mabrey
40. "The Heritage" (1-17-74)  Nora Marlowe, Noah Beery, Norman Andrews
41. "The Gift" (1-24-74)  Ron Howard, Pat Quinn, Ken Swofford, Rance Howard
42. "The Cradle" (1-31-74)  Victor Izay, Nora Marlowe
43. "The Fulfillment" (2-7-74)
44. "The Ghost Story" (2-14-74)  Kristopher Marquis, Jim Gammon, Wilford Brimley
45. "The Graduation" (2-21-74)  Tammi Bula
46. "The Five Foot Shelf" (3-7-74)
47. "The Car" (3-14-74)

## Third Season

48. "The Conflict" (9-12-74)  Beulah Bondi, Richard Hatch, Morgan Woodward, Paul Fix
49. "The First Day" (9-19-74)  Lawrence Dobkin, Devon Ericson
50. "The Thoroughbred" (9-26-74)  Brendan Burns, Kathleen Quinlan
51. "The Runaway" (10-3-74)  Herbert Nelson, Ann Noland, Geoffrey Lewis
52. "The Romance" (10-10-74)  David Selby, Biff Warren, Roger Price, Iris Korn
53. "The Ring" (10-17-74)  Kathleen Cody, Ted Eccles

54. "The System" (10-24-74) Richard Masur, Tom Lacy, Jacques Aubuchon
55. "The Spoilers" (10-31-74) Mark Miller, David Gruner, Barbara Cason, Linda Purl
56. "The Marathon" (11-7-74) Deidre Lenihan, Bernie Barrow, Charles Haid, Joyce Jameson, Ellen Moss
57. "The Book" (11-14-74)
58. "The Job" (11-21-74) Elaine Heilveil
59. "The Departure" (12-5-74) Joanna Moore, Panos Christi
60. "The Visitor" (12-12-74) John Beal, Madge Sinclair
61. "The Birthday" (12-19-74) Rance Howard, Brion James
62. "The Beguiled" (1-16-75)
63. "The Caretakers" (1-23-75) Ronnie Claire Edwards, Britt Leach, Nora Marlowe
64. "The Shivaree" (1-30-75) Bruce Davison, Debbie White, Robert Donner, E. J. Andre, John Ritter, James Gammon
65. "The Choice" (2-6-75)
66. [unknown title] (2-13-75) Ronnie Claire Edwards
67. "The Song" (2-20-75)
68. "The Woman" (2-27-75)
69. "The Venture" (3-6-75) M. Emmet Walsh, John Carter, Rance Howard, Claudia Bryar

[Continuing]


THE MEN

Yet another law and order entry, this one accorded the significance of being international in scope. The government agents were Jake Webster (Robert Conrad) of United States Intelligence, research worker Glenn Garth Gregory (Laurence Luckinbill), Lt. Frank Dain (James Wainwright) of the California Missing Persons Bureau.

The Regulars: "Jigsaw": Frank Dain, James Wainwright; Sergeant Gustafson, Pernell Roberts; "Delphi Bureau": Glenn Garth, Laurence Luckinbill; Sybil Van Loween, Anne Jeffreys; "Assignment: Vienna": Jake Webster, Robert Conrad; Major Codwell, Charles Cioffi; Inspector Hoffman, Anton Diffring.

The Episodes:

1. Assignment: Vienna: "Last Target" (9-28-72) Eduard Franz, Leslie Nielsen, Belinda J. Montgomery
2. Delphi Bureau: "The Deadly Errand Project" (10-5-72) Martha Scott, Harry Townes, Tina Chen
3. Jigsaw: "Hard Time" (10-12-72) Catherine Burns, Jim Davis, James Carrol Jordan, Reid Smith, Tom Reese
4. Assignment: Vienna: "Hot Potato" (10-19-72) John Ireland, Skye Aubrey, Kathy Cannon, Don Edwards

5. Delphi Bureau: "The Man Upstairs--the Man Downstairs Project" (10-26-72) Arlene Golonka, Harold Gould, Roddy McDowall, L. Q. Jones
6. Jigsaw: "The Bradley Affair" (11-2-72) Skye Aubrey, James Gregory, Don Stroud, Maria-Elena Cordero
7. Assignment: Vienna: "Queen's Gambit" (11-9-72) Anne Francis, Joby Baker, Robert F. Simon
8. Delphi Bureau: "The White Plague Project" (11-16-72) William Schallert, William Bramley, E. J. Andre, Mariette Hartley, Len Lesser
9. Jigsaw: "To Stalk the Night" (11-30-72) James Olson, Diana Ewing, Ramon Bieri, Gregory Eaton, James McEachin, Kathleen Dabney
10. Assignment: Vienna: "Annalisa" (12-7-72) Rosemary Forsyth, Victor Buono, John Ericson, Peter Herald, Paul Mantee, Abraham Sofaer
11. Delphi Bureau: "The Top Secret Secret Project" (12-14-72) Charles Lampkin, Dana Elcar, Jennifer Leak, Kathy Lloyd, William Sargent, Michael Lerner
12. Jigsaw: "Finder's Fee" (12-21-72) Sheree North, John Lupton, Regis Toomey, Corinne Camacho
13. Assignment: Vienna: "There Was an Old Woman" (1-13-73) Susan Strasberg, Peter Wajde, Alexander Scourby, Eric Braeden, Frank Baur, Victor Brandt
14. Assignment: Vienna: "So Long, Charlie" (2-3-73) Cameron Mitchell, Veit Relin, Maria Schell, Jack Kruschen
15. Assignment: Vienna: "A Deadly Shade of Green" (2-10-73) Walter Slezak, Bob Gentry, Peter Haskell, L. Q. Jones, Gerry Crampton, Janaire Skidmore
16. Jigsaw: "Kiss the Dream Goodbye" (2-17-73) Jessica Walter, Ned Romero, Cameron Mitchell, Nico Minardos, Broderick Crawford, Jackie Coogan
17. Jigsaw: "Girl on the Run" (2-24-73) Shirley Knight Hopkins, Frank Aletter, Ben Hamner, Skye Aubrey, Brenda Scott, David Spielberg, Del Monroe
18. Jigsaw: "In Case of Emergency, Notify Clint Eastwood" (3-3-73) Christine Belford, Harry Cooper, Harry Hickox, Claire Brennan, Eileen Brennan, Michael Baseleon, Stefan Arngrim, Richard Anderson
19. Delphi Bureau: "The Terror Broker Project" (3-17-73) Dean Jagger, Lauri Peters, Arlene Martel, Robert Hogan, William Windom
20. Delphi Bureau: "The Day of Justice Project" (3-24-73) Fritz Weaver, Sandy Kenyon, Peter Hobbs, Brenda Scott, Lawrence Pressman, Andrew Prine
21. Delphi Bureau: "The Self-Destruct Project" (3-31-73) George DiCenzo, Bert Convy, Jo Ann Pflug, Ted Gehring, Shelly Novack, Willard Sage
22. Delphi Bureau: "The Face That Never Was Project" (4-7-73) Richard Anderson, Jon Lormer, Oliver Clark, Lani O'Grady, Robin Strasser, Tom McDonald

GHOST STORY

Despite the running contrivance--Sebastian Cabot the poltergeist of a swank New York hotel and host for the series--William
Castle's tales of the macabre were a welcome relief from the gush
of contemporary law and order entries. Two genuine shockers:
Rip Torn and Geraldine Page are grandly maleficent as the couple
in "Touch of Madness," and Janet Leigh is the victim of voodoo
in "Death's Head."

The Regulars: Winston Essex, host: Sebastian Cabot (first thirteen episodes).

The Episodes:

1. "The Dead We Leave Behind" (9-15-72) Jason Robards,
Stella Stevens, Jack Kelly, John McLiam, Burr Smidt,
Skip Ward
2. "The Concrete Captain" (9-22-72) Stuart Whitman, Gena
Rowlands
3. "At the Cradle Foot" (9-29-72) Elizabeth Ashley, James
Franciscus
4. "Bad Connection" (10-6-72) Karen Black, Michael Tolan,
Sandra Dee, Kaz Garas, James A. Watson Jr., Skip
Homeier, Curt Conway, Ellen Geer, Florida Friebus,
Med Flory
5. "The Summer House" (10-13-72) Carolyn Jones, Steve Forrest, William Windom
6. "Alter-Ego" (10-27-72) Helen Hayes, Geoffrey Horne
7. "Half a Death" (11-3-72) Eleanor Parker, Pamela Franklin
8. "House of Evil" (11-10-72) Melvyn Douglas, Joan Hotchkis,
Mildred Dunnock, Richard Mulligan, Jodie Foster, Alan
Fudge, Brad Savage
9. "Cry of the Cat" (11-24-72) Doug McClure, Lauri Peters,
Jackie Cooper, Mariette Hartley
10. "Elegy for a Vampire" (12-1-72) Marlyn Mason, Hal Linden
11. "Touch of Madness" (12-8-72) Geraldine Page, Rip Torn,
Lynn Loring
12. "Creatures of the Canyon" (12-15-72) Angie Dickinson, John
Ireland, Madlyn Rhue
13. "Time of Terror" (12-22-72) Patricia Neal, Craig Stevens,
Alice Ghostley

[Hereafter titled CIRCLE OF FEAR]

14. "Death's Head" (1-5-73) Janet Leigh, Rory Calhoun, Gene
Nelson, Ayn Ruymen, Doreen Lang, Joshua Bryant, Madeleine Taylor Holmes
15. "Dark Vengeance" (1-12-73) Martin Sheen, Kim Darby
16. "Earth, Air, Fire and Water" (1-19-73) Frank Converse,
Joan Blackman
17. "Doorway to Death" (1-26-73) Barry Nelson, Susan Dey
18. "The Night of the Toad" (2-2-73) Shirley Knight Hopkins,

Jon Cypher, Kathryn Hays, Neva Patterson, Bridget Hanley, James Luisi, John Ventantonio, Paul Carr
19. "The Graveyard Shift" (2-16-73) Patty Duke Astin, John Astin, Joe Renteria, William Castle, Douglas Henderson, David Barry, Paul Picerni
20. "Spare Parts" (2-23-73) Susan Oliver, Rick Lenz, Christopher Connelly, Meg Foster, Alex Rocco, Don Knight, Barbara Stuart, Lee Kroeger, Larry J. Blake
21. "The Ghost of Potter's Field" (3-23-73) Tab Hunter [in dual role], Louise Sorel
22. "The Phantom of Herald Square" (3-30-73) Victor Jory, David Soul, Sheila Larken

BANYON

The feel for the period and the presence of Joan Blondell-- as well as the refreshing respite against the police infatuation so prevalent at the time--gave reason to watch this tale of a 1930s private investigator (Robert Forster as Miles Banyon).

The Regulars: Miles Banyon, Robert Forster; Peggy Revere, Joan Blondell; Pete McNeil, Richard Jaeckel; Abby, Julie Gregg.

The Episodes:

1. "The Decent Thing to Do" (9-15-72) Marlyn Mason, Peter White, Frank Aletter, William Traylor, Collin Wilcox-Horne, Vincent Van Lynn
2. "The Old College Try" (9-22-72) Darrell Larson, Bob Diamond, Shelly Novack, Jessica Walter, Tim O'Connor, Michael DeLano
3. "The Graveyard Vote" (9-29-72) Pat O'Brien, Diana Hyland, Larry Gates, Tom Bosley
4. "Completely Out of Print" (10-6-72) Fritz Weaver, Phillip Pine, John Sylvester White, Rosemary Murphy
5. "Meal Ticket" (10-13-72) Gabriel Dell, Sharon Farrell, James McCallion, Bo Svenson
6. "The Clay Clarinet" (10-27-72) John Saxon, Jack Sheldon, Fred Sadoff, E. J. Peaker
7. "Dead End" (11-3-72) Jack Cassidy, Morgan Sterne, Diana Muldaur, Billy Green Bush
8. "Time to Kill" (11-10-72) Jo Ann Pflug, Fred Beir, Dick Van Patten, Barbara Babcock
9. "Think of Me Kindly" (11-17-72) Gerald Hiken, Norma Crane, Anna Capri, Dabney Coleman
10. "A Date with Death" (11-24-72) Alan Garfield, Anita Alberts, Eileen Heckart, Meredith MacRae
11. "Sally Overman Is Missing" (12-1-72) Joann Harris, Robert Webber, Curt Conway, Karen Carlson
12. "The Lady Killer" (12-8-72) Kristina Holland, Elaine Giftos, Mary Jackson, Paul Sorensen, Don Chastain, Arch Johnson

13. "The Murder Game" (12-15-72) Skye Aubrey, Leon Hamilton, Kaz Garas, Gregory Sierra
14. "Just Once" (12-22-72) Janice Rule, Murray Matheson, Dennis Redfield, Ed Flanders, Jennifer Shaw, Meg Wyllie
15. "Time Lapse" (1-12-73) Donna Mills, John Williams, John Fiedler, Anne Seymour, Charles McGraw, Joan Crosby, Estelle Winwood, Ken Lynch

BARNABY JONES

The Regulars: Barnaby Jones, Buddy Ebsen; Betty Jones, Lee Meriwether.

The Episodes:

1. [unknown title] (1-28-73) William Conrad, Erica Hagen, Bradford Dillman, Robert Hogan, Robert Patten, Keith Charles
2. "To Catch a Dead Man" (2-4-73) William Shatner, Janice Rule, Victoria Shaw, Darleen Carr
3. [unknown title] (2-25-73) Gary Lockwood, Jeff Donnell, Conlan Carter, Vince Howard, Lynn Hamilton, Corinne Camacho
4. "The Murdering Class" (3-4-73) Andy Parks, Geraldine Brooks, Jerry Houser, Booth Colman, David Moses, Henry Brandt
5. "Perchance to Kill" (3-11-73) Eric Braeden, Sharon Acker, Nancy Wickwire, Ross Elliott, Richard Hatch, Frank Maxwell, Barbara Stuart, Jamie Smith Jackson
6. [unknown title] (3-18-73) Lloyd Bochner, Ted Gehring, Nico Minardos, Michael Blodgett, Christine Belford, Richard N. Sterling
7. "Murder in the Doll's House" (3-25-73) Anne Francis, Whit Bissell, Jack Cassidy, Richard Derr, Estelle Winwood, Philip Pine
8. [unknown title] (4-1-73) Arlene Golonka, Heidi Vaughn, Jackie Coogan, Paul Lambert, Paul Sorensen, Judi Strangis, Dan Tobin, Jonathan Lippe
9. "See Some Evil ... Do Some Evil" (4-8-73) Marlyn Mason, Reni Santoni, Roddy McDowall, Don Dubbins, Vince Howard, Patricia Donahue
.0. "Murder-Go-Round" (4-15-73) Claude Akins, Geoffrey Lewis, Neva Patterson, James Luisi, Lou Frizzell, Dabbs Greer
.1. [unknown title] (4-22-73) Bill Bixby, William Lanteau, Louise Troy, Vince Howard, Jill Jaress, Nora Marlowe
.2. "Murder at Malibu" (4-29-73) Barry Sullivan, Meg Foster, Carol Ohmart, Byron Morrow, Alex Henteloff, Mark Thomas, Brendan Dillon, Don Ross
.3. [unknown title] (5-6-73) Peter Haskell, Gary Owens, Marie Windsor, Bert Freed, Robert H. Harris, Susanne Hildur

Second Season

14.  "Blind Terror" (9-16-73) Belinda J. Montgomery, Christo-
     pher Stone, Patricia Smith, Peggy McCay, Richard Bull,
     Robert Doyle, Dabney Coleman, Stephen Coit
15.  "Death Leap" (9-23-73) Tim O'Connor, Brooke Bundy, Ben
     Frank, Jonathan Lippe, Reta Shaw, Edward Colmans, Ra-
     mon Bieri, J. Duke Russo, Susan Howard, James McCal-
     lion
16.  "Echo of a Murder" (9-30-73) Wayne Rogers, Dan Travanty
     Stefanie Powers, Bill Quinn, Helen Kleeb, Ross Elliott,
     Bill Erwin, Irene Tedrow, Sandy Kenyon, John Ragin
17.  "Day of the Viper" (10-7-73) Andrew Prine, Arch Johnson,
     Vincent Van Patten, Katherine Justice, Read Morgan, For
     Rainey
18.  "Trial for Death" (10-14-73) Clu Gulager, Anne Collings,
     Eddie Firestone, Margot Kidder, G. J. Mitchell, Karl
     Swenson, Mark Roberts, Len Wayland
19.  "Catch Me If You Can" (10-21-73) James Olson, Frank
     Maxwell, Charles Knox Robinson, Claudia Bryar, Eddie
     Ryder, Mary-Robin Redd, Peter Mamakos, Mary Jackson
20.  "Divorce--Murder's Style" (10-28-73) Glenn Corbett, Lynn
     Marta, Nina Foch
21.  "The Deadly Prize" (11-4-73) George Maharis, Albert Salr
     James Luisi, Madlyn Rhue, Alfred Ryder, Noam Pitlik,
     Val Avery, Hank Brandt
22.  "Stand-In for Death" (11-11-73) Carl Betz, Lynda Day
     George, Stephens Brooks, Barra Grant, Arch Whiting,
     Shirley O'Hara
23.  "The Black Art of Dying" (11-25-73)
24.  "The Killing Defense" (12-2-73) Leslie Nielsen
25.  "Fatal Flight" (12-9-73) Richard Anderson, Jerry Ayres,
     Pippa Scott, Murray Hamilton
26.  "Secret of the Dunes" (12-16-73) Patrick O'Neal, Don Por
     er, Frank Marth, Robert Hogan, John Carter, Thom Car
     ney, Laraine Stephens, Philip Pine
27.  "Venus As in Fly Trap" (1-6-74) Ed Nelson, Jessica Wal-
     ter, Robert F. Simon, Jack Ging, Olive Dunbar, Carol
     Lawson, Bettye Ackerman, Don McGovern
28.  "The Deadly Jinx" (1-13-74) Meredith Baxter, Ida Lupino,
     Christopher Connelly, Jim Gammon, Richard O'Brien,
     Mark Miller, Jerry Summers, Richard Evans
29.  [unknown title] (1-20-74) Gary Lockwood, Penny Fuller,
     John Lasell, Frank Christi, John Carter, Milton Selzer,
     Herb Armstrong, Val Avery, June Dayton, Dean Harens
30.  "Programmed for Killing" (1-27-74) Don Stroud, Donna
     Bacalla, Michael Burns, Don Keefer, Ginny Golden, Lou
     Frizzell, Felice Orlandi, John Kerr
31.  "Gold Record for Murder" (2-10-74) Marjoe Gortner, Jasc
     Evers, Meg Foster, Michael Zaslow, Jill Jaress, Lenor
     Kasdorf, Doreen Lang, Arthur Franz
32.  "Friends Till Death" (2-17-74) Susan Oliver, Ross Martin
     Scott Marlowe, Fred Sadoff, Gail Strickland, Tom Geas,

Peter Brocco, John Carter
33. "Rendezvous with Terror" (2-24-74) Gilbert Roland, Cal Bellini, Carlos Romero, Joe Santos
34. "Dark Legacy" (3-3-74) David Wayne, Eileen Heckart
35. "Woman in the Shadows" (3-10-74) Susan Clark, John Vernon
36. "Image in a Cracked Mirror" (3-24-74) Bradford Dillman
37. "Foul Play" (3-31-74) Victor Holchak, John Carter, Reni Santoni, Andrew Duggan, Don Megowan, George DiCenzo

Third Season

38. "A Gathering of Thieves" (9-10-74) Robert Foxworth, Tyne Daly, Laraine Stephens, Richard Evans
39. "Dead Man's Run" (9-17-74) Jessica Walter, Richard Bull, Lawrence Pressman, Peter Mark Richman, William Schallert, Ross Elliott
40. "The Challenge" (9-24-74) Patrick O'Neal, Hank Brandt, Joan Van Ark, Charles Aidman, Robert Patten, Cheryl Miller, William Sargent, Stuart Nisbet
41. "Conspiracy of Terror" (10-1-74) Fritz Weaver, Don Dubbins, Eugene Patterson, Anne Helm, Harris Yulin, Maria Adams
42. "Odd Man Loses" (10-8-74) Christopher Stone, Robert Hogan, Jo Ann Harris, Dick Van Patten
43. "Forfeit by Death" (10-15-74) Sheree North, Mark Jenkins, Steve Sandor, Lynne Marta, Ann Strickland, Val Avery, Jerry Douglas, John Van Dreelen
44. "Blueprint for a Caper" (10-29-74) Gary Lockwood, Joby Baker, Meg Foster, Anthony Carbone, Phillip Pine, Oscar Beregi
45. "Mystery Cycle" (11-12-74) Mariette Hartley, Bill Baldwin, James Luisi, Claudette Nevins
46. "Dark Homecoming" (11-19-74) Julie Sommars, Jerry Ayres, Andrew Prine, Jim McMullan, Linda Kelsy, John McLiam
47. "Time to Kill" (11-26-74) Laurence Luckinbill, Ellen Weston, Than Wyenn, Maurice Marsac, Kaz Garas, Val Avery, Kent Smith
48. "Death on Deposit" (12-3-74) Lois Nettleton, Ed Flanders
49. "Web of Deceit" (12-10-74) Don Porter, Joel Fabiani, Jane Morrow, Peggy McCay
50. "The Last Contract" (12-31-74) Darleen Carr
51. "Trap Play" (1-7-75) Nick Nolte, Marc Singer, Sheila Larken, Simon Scott
52. "Murder Once Removed" (1-21-75) Pamela Franklin, Bill Quinn, Phyllis Thaxter, Ed Power, Kristina Holland, Richard Eastham, Tom Pittman, Robert Pine
53. "Counterfall" (2-4-75) Mitchell Ryan, Jacqueline Scott, James Callahan, Robert Mandan
54. "Dangerous Summer" (2-11-75) John Rubinstein, Hilly Hicks, Katherine Cannon, Joan Hotchkis
55. "Image of Evil" (2-18-75) Tom Skerritt, Dennis Cole, Sharon Spelman, Audra Lindley
56. "Fantasy of Fear" (2-25-75) Shirley Knight Hopkins

57. "Doomed Alibi" (3-11-75) Monte Markham
58. "The Deadlier Species" (3-18-75) Bradford Dillman, Patricia Smith, Mariclare Costello, Walter Brooke
59. "Poisoned Pigeon" (3-25-75) Penny Fuller, Michael Callan, Jonathan Lippe, Jack Riley, Wayne Tippet, Phyllis Hill, Alex Henteloff, Ken Scott
60. "Jeopardy for Two" (4-1-75) Eric Braeden, John Anderson, Bernard Fox, Karen Carlson
61. "Bond of Fear" (4-15-75) Sharon Acker, Arlene Golonka, Ben Piazza, Roger Perry

[Continuing]

1973-1974 SEASON

THE SIX MILLION DOLLAR MAN

      Comic strip of a severly injured astronaut transformed into
bionic superman for Uncle Sam; it has, as of this writing,
pawned its share of equally juvenile imitators.

The Regulars: Col. Steve Austin, Lee Majors; Oscar Goldman,
      Richard Anderson; Dr. Wells, Alan Oppenheimer.

The Episodes:

1.  "Wine, Women and War" [ninety minute film]  (10-20-73)
     Earl Holliman, David McCallum, Britt Ekland, Eric Brae-
     den, Michele Carey, Lee Bergere, Simon Scott, Cathe-
     rine Ferrar
2.  "The Solid Gold Kidnapping" [ninety minute film]  (11-17-73)
     John Vernon, Elizabeth Allen, Maurice Evans
3.  "Population Zero" [first in hour series]  (1-18-74)  Penny
     Fuller, Don Porter, Walter Brooke, Stuart Nisbet, Paul
     Fix, Paul Carr, Virginia Gregg
4.  "Survival of the Fittest"  (1-25-74)  William Smith, James
     McEachin, Christine Belford, Randall Carver, Laurette
     Spang, Jo Anne Worley
5.  "Operation Firefly"  (2-1-74)  Pamela Franklin, Simon Scott,
     Erik Holland, Jack Hogan, Joseph Ruskin, Joe Kapp
6.  "Day of the Robot"  (2-8-74)  John Saxon, Henry Jones
7.  "Little Orphan Airplane"  (2-22-74)  Greg Morris, Scoey
     Mitchlll, Marge Redmond, Susan Powell
8.  "Doomsday and Counting"  (3-1-74)  Gary Collins
9.  "Eyewitness to Murder"  (3-8-74)  Gary Lockwood, William
     Schallert
10.  "The Rescue of Athena One"  (3-15-74)  Farrah Fawcett-Ma-
     jors, Jules Bergman
11.  "Dr. Wells Is Missing"  (3-29-74)  John Van Dreelen,
     Michael Dante
12.  "The Last of the Fourth of Julys"  (4-5-74)  Steve Forrest
13.  "Burning Bright"  (4-12-74)  William Shatner, Quinn Redeker,
     Warren Kemmerling, Rodolfo Hoyos
14.  "The Coward"  (4-19-74)  George Montgomery, France Nuyen,
     George Takei
15.  "Run, Steve, Run"  (4-26-74)  Noah Beery, Henry Jones

Second Season

16. "Nuclear Alert" (9-13-74) Carol Lawrence, Fred Beir, Felice Orlandi, George Gaynes
17. "The Pioneers" (9-20-74) Joan Darling, Mike Farrell, Vince Howard, Robert F. Simon
18. "Pilot Error" (9-27-74) Pat Hingle, Alfred Ryder, Stephen Nathan, Suzanne Zenor
19. "The Pal-Mir Escort" (10-4-74) Anne Revere, Leo Fuchs, Nate Esformes, Denny Miller
20. "The Seven Million Dollar Man" (11-1-74) Monte Markham, Joan Van Ark, Maggie Sullivan, Marshall Reed
21. "Straight on 'Til Morning" (11-8-74) Meg Foster, Christopher Mears, Cliff Osmond, Donald Billett
22. "The Midas Touch" (11-15-74) Farley Granger, Noam Pitlik, Richard D. Hurst, Kate McKeown
23. "The Deadly Replay" (11-22-74) Clifton James, Jack Ging
24. "Act of Piracy" (11-29-74) Stephen McNally, Carlos Romero, Lenore Kasdorf, Hagan Beggs
25. "The Peeping Blonde" (12-20-74) Farrah Fawcett-Majors, Roger Perry, Hari Rhodes, W. T. Zacha
26. "Cross Country Kidnap" (1-10-75) Donna Mills, Tab Hunter
27. "Lost Love" (1-17-75) Linda Marsh, Jeff Corey, Wesley Lau, Joseph Ruskin, Than Wyenn
28. "Return of the Robot Maker" (1-26-75) Henry Jones, Troy Melton, Ben Hammer, Iris Edwards
29. "Taneha" (2-2-75) Jess Walton, Bill Fletcher, James Griffith, Paul Brinegar
30. "Look Alike" (2-23-75) George Foreman, Robert DoQui, Jack Colvin, Robert Salvio
31. "E.S.P. Spy" (3-2-75) Robbie Lee, Philip Bruns, Dick Van Patten, Bert Kramer
32. "The Bionic Woman" [Part I] (3-16-75) Lindsay Wagner, Malachi Throne, Martha Scott, Ford Rainey, Paul Carr
33. "The Bionic Woman" [Part II] (3-23-75) as above
34. "Stranger in Broken Fork" (3-30-75) Sharon Farrell, Robert Donner, Arthur Franz, Bill Henry, Troy Melton
35. "Outrage in Balinderry" (4-20-75) Martine Beswick, Gavan O'Herlihy, Richard Erdman, David Frankham, Alan Caillou, Richard O'Brien
36. "Steve Austin, Fugitive" (4-27-75) Gary Lockwood, Jennifer Darling

[Continuing]

GRIFF

The Regulars: Wayde "Griff" Griffin, Lorne Greene; Mike Murdoch, Ben Murphy; Captain Barney Marcus, Vic Tayback; Gracie Newcombe, Patricia Stich.

The Episodes:

1. "The Framing of Billy the Kid" (9-29-73) Robert Webber, Susan Howard, Norman Alden, Nick Nolte, Philip Thomas, William Jordan
2. "Death by Prescription" (10-6-73) Barbara Feldon, Mark Miller, Linda Marsh, Jared Martin, Paul Kent, Warren Stevens, Monte Landis, Richard Stahl
3. "All the Lonely People" (10-13-73) Patricia Crowley, Lawrence Pressman, Jess Walton, Dabney Coleman, Herbert Rudley, Barbara Rhoades, Gino Conforti, Leigh Christian
4. "Don't Call Us, We'll Call You" (10-20-73) Joan Darling, Kaz Garas, Martin E. Brooks, Ben Piazza, Jeanne Bates, Walker Edmiston
5. "Prey" (10-27-73) Sal Mineo, Albert Paulsen
6. "The Last Ballad" (11-10-73) William Windom, Kim Hunter, Charles Robinson, Corrine Camacho, Joanne Frank, Sam Edwards
7. "Countdown to Terror" (11-17-73) Ricardo Montalban
8. "Elephant in a Cage" (11-24-73) Harold J. Stone, Robert Sampson
9. "Her Name Was Nancy" (12-8-73) Christopher Connelly, Hildy Brooks
10. "Hammerlock" (12-15-73) Norman Fell, Katherine Glass, Robert Yuro, Frank Christi, Maidie Norman, Eddie Firestone
11. "Isolate and Destroy" (12-22-73) Inga Swenson, Steven Keats, Robert Donner, Scatman Crothers
12. "Fugitive from Fear" (1-5-74) James McEachin, Janet MacLachlan, Eric Woods, George Murdock, Jim Antonia, Lew Palter, Bill Zuckert, Susan Barrister


THE WORLD AT WAR

Sir Laurence Olivier narrated this deeply moving and expertly pieced together documentary on the events leading up to, during, and as a result of the Second World War.

The Episodes [telecast via PBS Sundays 7:00-8:00]:

1. "Germany: 1933-1939" [I] (9-23-73)
2. "Distant War: 1939-1940" [II] (9-30-73)
3. "France Falls: May-June 1940" [III] (10-7-73)
4. "Alone: May 1940-May 1941" [IV] (10-14-73)
5. "Barbarossa: June-December 1941" [V] (10-21-73)
6. "Banzai!: December 1941-February 1942" [VI] (10-28-73)
7. "On Our Way" [VII] (11-4-73)
8. "Desert: 1940-1943" [VIII] (11-11-73)
9. "Stalingrad" [IX] (11-18-73)
10. "Wolf Pack: September 1939-May 1943" [X] (11-25-73)
11. "Red Star" [XI] (12-2-73)

12. "Whirlwind" [XII] (12-9-73)
13. "Tough Old Gut" [XIII] (12-16-73)
14. "It's a Lovely Day Tomorrow" [XIV] (12-23-73)
15. "Home Fires: 1940-1944" [XV] (12-30-73)
16. "Inside the Reich" [XVI] (1-6-74)
17. "Morning" [XVII] (1-13-74)
18. "... and Not Cry Out" [XVIII] (1-20-74)
19. "Pincers" [XIX] (1-27-74)
20. "Genocide" [XX] (2-3-74)
21. "Nemesis" [XXI] (2-10-74)
22. "Japan" [XXII] (2-17-74)
23. "Pacific" [XXIII] (2-24-74)
24. "The Bomb" [XXIV] (3-3-74)
25. "Reckoning-Aftermath" [XXV] (3-10-74)
26. "Remember?" [XXVI] (3-17-74)


THE EVIL TOUCH

At times unsettling (Ray Walston a ruthless carnival owner whose performers plan a bizarre vengeance; Mildred Natwick an ultimately terrified murderer's accomplice) British-produced horror tales.

The Regulars: Anthony Quayle, host.

The Episodes [telecast in New York Sundays, 10:30-11:00]:

1. "The Lake" (9-16-73) Robert Lansing, Anne Haddy, Lanna Bowden
2. "Heart to Heart" (9-23-73) Mildred Natwick
3. "Dr. McDermitt's New Patients" (9-30-73) Kim Hunter
4. "The Obituary" (10-7-73) Leslie Nielsen
5. "Happy New Year, Aunt Carrie" (10-14-73) Julie Harris
6. "A Game of Hearts" (10-21-73) Darren McGavin
7. "Seeing Is Believing" (10-28-73) Robert Lansing
8. "The Upper Hand" (11-4-73) Julie Harris
9. "Murder's for the Birds" (11-11-73) Vic Morrow
10. "Marci" (11-18-73) Susan Strasberg
11. "George" (11-25-73) Darren McGavin
12. "Scared to Death" (12-2-73) Mildred Natwick
13. "The Homecoming" (12-9-73) Harry Guardino
14. "Dear Beloved Monster" (12-16-73) Ray Walston
15. "Campaign 2" (1-13-74) James Daly
16. "Faulkner's Choice" (1-20-74) Noel Harrison
17. "The Trial" (2-3-74) Ray Walston
18. "The Fans" (2-10-74) Vic Morrow
19. "Kadaitcha Country" (2-24-74) Leif Erickson
20. "Gornak's Prison" (3-3-74) Darren McGavin
21. "The Voyage" (3-10-74) Leslie Nielsen
22. "Death by Dreaming" (3-24-74) Carol Lynley

THE NEW PERRY MASON

Erle Stanley Gardner's attorney was never particularly ebullient; certainly not on the video. Now, however, he is more intense than he has ever been; his fierce mien too easy to be put off by, even with regard to the jurors who are supposedly dazzled.

The Regulars: Perry Mason, Monte Markham; Della Street, Sharon Acker; Hamilton Burger, Harry Guardino; Paul Drake, Albert Stratton; Lieutenant Tragg, Dane Clark; Gertie, Brett Somers.

The Episodes:

1. "The Case of the Horoscope Homicide" (9-16-73) Fionnuala Flanagan, Peter Mark Richman, Ruth Hussey, Sorrell Booke, Robert Mandan, Harvey Fisher, Victor Millan, Wayne Heffley
2. "The Case of the Prodigal Prophet" (9-23-73) Beverly Garland
3. "The Case of the Ominous Oath" (9-30-73) Joanna Barnes, Simon Oakland, Tim McIntire, Paul Carr, Kathleen Gackle, Jed Allen, Leonard Stone, Doreen Lang, Quinn Redeker
4. "The Case of the Wistful Widower" (10-7-73) Bruce Kirby, Donnelly Rhodes, Jacqueline Scott, Dennis Patrick, Arthur Franz, Jordan Rhodes, Loretta Leversee, Walter Brooke
5. "The Case of the Telltale Trunk" (10-14-73) Richard Anderson, Mary Ann Mobley, Keenan Wynn, Mary-Robin Redd, Stewart Moss, John Lasell, James Hong, Vaughn Taylor
6. "The Case of the Deadly Deeds" (10-21-73) Will Hutchins, Don Porter, Tiffany Bolling, David Huddleston, Jodie Foster, Ellen Geer, Andrea King, Joy Jenson
7. "The Case of the Murdered Murderer" (10-28-73) Roger Davis, Sharon Farrell
8. "The Case of the Furious Father" (11-11-73) George Murdock, Pat Harrington, Edward Winter, Donna Baccala, Michael Lerner, Regis J. Cordic
9. "The Case of the Cagey Cager" (11-25-73) Bill Overton, Paul Richards, Ross Elliott, Sabrina Scharf, Richard Collier, Woodrow Parfrey, Byron Morrow, Kenneth Tobey
10. "The Case of the Jailed Justice" (12-2-73) Andrew Duggan, Clu Gulager
11. "The Case of the Spurious Spouse" (12-9-73) Carl Betz, Irene Tsu
12. "The Case of the Frenzied Feminist" (12-16-73) Linda Marsh, David Hedison, Carolyn Jones, Lloyd Bochner, Gino Conforti, Keith Rogers, Felice Orlandi, Martin Blaine
13. "The Case of the Perilous Pen" (12-30-73) Robert F. Lyons, William Watson
14. "The Case of the Tortured Titan" (1-13-74) Elaine Giftos, Arthur O'Connell, Bethel Leslie, Michael Evans, Ron Glass, John Howard

15. "The Case of the Violent Valley" (1-20-74) Denver Pyle,
    Katherine Justice, Andy Robinson, Lee McCain, David Hay-
    ward, William Jordan, Vic Campos, Eddie Firestone,
    Kevin Hagen, John Milford, Paul Fix


THE MAGICIAN

Predictable mystery yarn of a magician (Bill Bixby as Anthony Blake) who dabbles in detective work between (and by the use
of) legerdemain.

The Regulars: Anthony Blake, Bill Bixby; Max Pomeroy, Keene
    Curtis; Dennis, Todd Crespi; Jerry, Jim Watkins; Domi-
    nick, Joseph Sirola (with episode of 1/14/74).

The Episodes:

1. "The Manhunter" (10-2-73) Marlyn Mason, Stephen McNally,
   Vincent Beck, Scott Walker, Mort Thompson, Lenore
   Stevens, Jerry Quarry, Robert Nash
2. "The Vanishing Lady" (10-9-73) Amanda McBroom, Peter
   Brown, John Karlen, Ramon Bieri, Lilyan Chauvin, Patti
   Elder
3. "Illusion in Terror" (10-23-73) Brenda Benet, Cameron
   Mitchell, Macdonald Carey, Tom Geas, John Pickard,
   Bill Zuckert
4. "Lightning on a Dry Day" (10-30-73) Mark Hamill, Neville
   Brand
5. [unknown title] (11-6-73) Jack Kruschen, Susan Oliver, Roy
   Jenson, Walter Brooke, Joe Pronto, Barry Brooks
6. "Men on Fire" (11-20-73) Carl Betz, Brad David, Lloyd
   Bochner
7. "Lady in a Trap" (11-27-73) Kristina Holland, William Jordan
8. "The Man Who Lost Himself" (12-11-73) Joe Flynn, George
   Murdock
9. "Nightmare in Steel" (12-18-73) Robyn Millan, Leif Erickson, Christopher Stone, Frank Christi
10. "Shattered Image" (1-8-74) Joseph Campanella, Tommy
    Madden, Tara Talboy, Wesley Lau, Bob Hoy, Edmund
    Gilbert, Leslie Parrish
11. "The Illusion of the Curious Counterfeit" [Part I] (1-14-74)
    Carol Lynley, Lloyd Nolan, John Colicos, Dean Harens,
    Joe Maross, L. Q. Jones
12. "The Illusion of the Curious Counterfeit" [Part II] (1-21-74)
    as above
13. "The Stainless Steel Lady" (1-28-74) Nina Foch, Anthony
    Zerbe, Beth Brickell, Edward Winter, Mark Lenard, Ian
    Wolfe, Penny Santon
14. "The Illusion of the Queen's Gambit" (2-4-74)
15. "The Illusion of Black Gold" (2-11-74) Lynda Day George,

Eric Braeden, Milton Selzer, Curt Lowens, Normann Burton, Abraham Sofaer
16. "The Illusion of the Lost Dragon" (2-18-74) France Nuyen, Joseph Wiseman, Philip Ahn, Soon-Taik Oh, Pat Li, Nobu McCarthy
17. "The Illusion of the Deadly Conglomerate" (2-25-74) Jack Ging
18. "The Illusion of the Fatal Arrow" (3-4-74) Jeremy Slate, Tim Matheson, Pamela Franklin
19. "The Illusion of the Lethal Playthings" (3-18-74) Louis Hayward
20. "The Illusion of the Cat's Eye" (3-25-74) John Dehner, Don Gordon
21. "The Illusion of Evil Spikes" (4-15-74) Jessica Walter, Lew Ayres

CHASE

The Regulars: Captain Chase Reddick, Mitchell Ryan; Det. Sgt. MacCaray, Wayne Maunder; Hamilton, Reid Smith; Baker, Michael Richardson; Sing, Brian Fong.

The Episodes:

1. "The Wooden Horse Caper" (9-11-73) Michael Baseleon, Lou Wagner, Albert Reed, Susan Damonte
2. "Gang War" (9-18-73) Tom Bosley, Edward Bach, Albert Reed, John Mark Robinson, Wesley Lau, J. H. Lawrence
3. "Foul-Up" (9-25-73) George DiCenzo, Tom Falk, Jean Allison, Tim O'Connor, Laurette Spang, William Bryant, Aldine King, Fred Dale
4. "The Winning Ticket Is a Loser" (10-2-73) Garry Walberg, Robert Braiver, Charles Dierkop, Elizabeth St. Clair
5. "One for You, Two for Me" (10-9-73) Alan Oppenheimer, Ed Bakey, Clint Ritchie, Greg Walcott, Woodrow Parfrey, Albert Reed
6. "The Scene Stealers" (10-23-73) Jed Allen, Eddie Ryder, Harry Davis, Timothy Blake
7. "Six for Five" (10-30-73) Victor Perrin, Robert Corff
8. "The Dealer-Wheelers" (11-6-73) Roy Jenson, Howard Platt, Abigail Shelton, Albert Reed, Gary Clarke, Del Monroe
9. "The Dice Rolled Dead" (11-20-73) Craig Stevens
10. "The Garbage Man" (11-27-73) Elaine Giftos, Morgan Woodward
11. "A Bit of Class" (12-11-73) Cesar Romero
12. "Sizzling Stones" (12-18-73) Ray Ballard, Charlie Martin Smith, Albert Reed, Steve Kanaly
13. "Right to an Attorney" (1-8-74) Andy Robinson, Warren Stevens, Les Lannon, Dolores Quinton, Virginia Gregg, Olan Soule
14. "Joe Don Ducks" (1-16-74) Harold Gould, Roger Perry,

William Sargent, Linda Marsh, Maurice Marsac, John Dennis

15. "$35. Will Fly You to the Moon" (1-23-74) Elliott Street, Pat Harrington, Mel Torme, Sherry Jackson, Larry Manetti, Eric Server
16. "The Game Ball" (1-30-74) Henry Brown, Ji-tu Cumbuka, Ramon Bieri, Jack Hogan
17. "Vacation for a President" (2-6-74) Henry Darrow
18. "Hot Beef" (2-13-74) Dana Elcar, Ronald Feinberg, Will Hutchins, Paul Carr
19. "Out of Gas?" (2-20-74) Don Porter, Dabbs Greer, Lou Frizzell, Jack Kelly
20. "Remote Control" (2-27-74) Robert Reed, Michael Lerner
21. "Eighty Six Proof TNT" (3-20-74) James McEachin, Murray Hamilton

## HAWKINS

The Regulars: Billy Jim Hawkins, James Stewart; R. J. Hawkins, Strother Martin; Jeremiah Stocker, Mayf Nutter.

The Episodes:

1. "Murder in Movieland" (10-2-73) Sheree North, Cameron Mitchell, William Smithers, Kenneth Mars, Maggie Wellman, Thaao Penghlis
2. "Die, Darling, Die" (10-23-73) Julie Harris, Diana Douglas, Murray Hamilton, Henry Jones, Sam Elliott, Melissa Newman, Judson Morgan
3. "Death and the Maiden" [repeat of the series' pilot film] (11-6-73) Bonnie Bedelia, Kate Reid, Robert Webber, David Huddleston, Dana Elcar, Antoinette Bower
4. "A Life for a Life" (11-13-73) William Windom, John Ventantonio, James Hampton, Noam Pitlik, Tyne Daly, Jeanne Cooper, Joe Maross, Curt Conway
5. "Blood Feud" (12-4-73) Lew Ayres, Jeanette Nolan
6. "Murder in the Slave Trade" (1-22-74) Ellen Weston, Peter Mark Richman, James Luisi, Joseph Hindy, Dick Gautier, Warren Kemmerling, Robert Sampson, Stephen McNally, Clark Howat, Stacy Keach Sr.
7. "Murder on the Thirteenth Floor" (2-5-74) Teresa Wright, Jeff Corey
8. "Candidate for Murder" (3-5-74) Paul Burke, Pernell Roberts, Diana Hyland, Andrew Prine, John Ericson, Mark Gordon

## SHAFT

The Regulars: John Shaft, Richard Roundtree; Lieutenant Ross,

Ed Barth.

The Episodes:

1. "The Executioners" (10-9-73) Robert Culp, Richard Jaeckel, Dean Jagger, Kaz Garas, Judie Stein, Richard Lawson, Noah Keen
2. "The Killing" (10-30-73) Ja'net DuBois, Leonard Frey
3. "Hit-Run" (11-20-73) Tony Curtis, Howard Duff
4. "The Kidnapping" (12-11-73) Paul Burke, Karen Carlson
5. "Cop Killer" (1-1-74) Darren McGavin, George Maharis
6. "The Capricorn Murders" (1-29-74) David Hedison, Cathy Lee Crosby, Arthur O'Connell, Don Knight, Robert Phillips, Thelma Pelish
7. "The Murder Machine" (2-19-74) Clu Gulager, Fionnuala Flanagan, Judie Stein, Joe Warfield, Mills Watson, Sheldon Allman

POLICE STORY

Joseph Wambaugh enlightened millions by way of his exposé of the rigors of police activity; shattering, at long last, the blood and guts superman myth of the cop on the beat. Superb guest performances; eloquent scripts.

The Episodes:

1. "Dangerous Games" (10-2-73) James Farentino, Elizabeth Ashley, Fred Williamson, Michael Strong, Charles Dierkop, Janet Margolin, Chelsea Brown, Eric Server
2. "Requiem for an Informer" (10-9-73) Tony Lo Bianco, Marjoe Gortner, Don Meredith, Michael Ansara, Sharon Farrell, John Larch
3. "The Ten Year Honeymoon" (10-23-73) Claude Akins, Paul Burke, Verna Bloom, Michael Baseleon, Anthony James, Vic Tayback
4. "Violent Homecoming" (10-30-73) Pedro Armendariz Jr., Sean Garrison
5. "The Ho Chi Minh Trail" (11-6-73) George Maharis, Clifton Davis, Herb Edelman, Raymond St. Jacques, Aldine King, Bernie Hamilton, Donald Woods, Antonio Fargas, Ken Lynch, Alan Weeks
6. "Collision Course" (11-20-73) Hugh O'Brian, Sue Ane Langdon
7. "Death on Credit" (11-27-73) John Saxon, David Canary, Rory Calhoun, Howard Duff, Tina Louise
8. "The Big Walk" (12-4-73) Don Murray, Dorothy Provine
9. "Man on a Rack" (12-11-73) Martin Balsam, Kim Hunter
10. "Line of Fire" (12-18-73) Cameron Mitchell, Jan-Michael Vincent, Alex Cord, Edmund Gilbert, Brooke Bundy, Paul Carr, Robert Viharo, Russell Thorson, Otis Greene,

Henry Brown
11. "Chain of Command" (1-8-74) Stuart Whitman, Edmond
    O'Brien, Patty McCormack, Rockne Tarkington, Burr De-
    Benning, Anthony Carbone, Charles McGraw, Sally Ihnat
12. "Countdown" [Part I] (1-15-74) Vic Morrow, Tige Andrews,
    Joe Santos, Laraine Stephens, John Randolph, Tony Caru-
    so, Ray Danton, Michael Callan, Scott Brady, Paul Stevens,
    Christine Schmidtmer, Taylor Lacher, Mel Scott, Anjanette
    Comer, Frank Castellano
13. "Countdown" [Part II] (1-22-74) as above
14. [unknown title] (1-29-74) Christopher George, Glenn Corbett,
    Albert Paulsen, John Ericson, Ken Swofford, Abby Dalton,
    Scott Brady, Brandon Cruz
15. "The Ripper" (2-12-74) Darren McGavin, Michael Cole,
    Kathie Browne, Peter Mark Richman, Donnelly Rhodes,
    Leslie Parrish, Barry Atwater, Pat Carroll, Sheila Larken,
    John Fiedler, Lloyd Gough, Ray Young, Cynthia Hull
16. "Country Boy" (2-19-74) Kurt Russell, Clu Gulager, Jason
    Evers, Gary Collins, Jeremy Slate, Gail Strickland, Mi-
    chele Nichols, Bobbi Jordan
17. "The Hunters" (2-26-74) Tony Lo Bianco, Don Meredith,
    Jackie Cooper
18. "The Wyatt Earp Syndrome" (3-5-74) Cliff Gorman, Kim
    Darby, Smokey Robinson, Harry Guardino, Scott Brady,
    Mel Ferrer, Arthur Franz, Michael Baseleon
19. "Fingerprint" (3-12-74) Earl Holliman, Mary Ann Mobley,
    Tim Matheson, Nita Talbot
20. "Chief" (3-19-74) John Forsythe, Michael Ansara, Barbara
    Rush
21. "The Gamble" (3-26-74) Angie Dickinson, Joseph Campanella

Second Season

22. "A Dangerous Age" (9-10-74) Edward Asner, Scott Brady,
    David Huffman, Albert Salmi, Janis Paige, Tom Drake,
    Ken Swofford, Richard Drout Miller
23. "Requiem for C. Z. Smith" (9-17-74) James Farentino,
    Harry Guardino, Tina Louise, Hari Rhodes, Bruce Davi-
    son, Janet Margolin, Tim O'Connor, Marsha Hunt, Felice
    Orlandi, James Daris
24. "Robbery: 48 Hours" (9-24-74) Jackie Cooper, Joe Santos,
    Shelly Novack, Burr DeBenning, Philip Pine, Glenn Corbett,
    Jeremy Slate, Noam Pitlik
25. "Fathers and Sons" (10-1-74) Tony Musante, Kaz Garas,
    Ramon Bieri, Richard Jaeckel, Harold Gould, Elaine Joyce,
    Jay Varela, Peter Coe, Titos Vandis
26. "A World Full of Hurt" (10-8-74) Paul Burke, Nancy Wilson
27. "Glamour Boy" (10-29-74) Larry Hagman, Tony Lo Bianco,
    Don Meredith, Joanna Pettet, David Doyle, Bettye Acker-
    man, Michael Callan, Rod Cameron, Barry Atwater, Ken-
    neth Tobey
28. "Across the Line" (11-12-74) James Wainwright, Chuck
    Connors, Linda Cristal, Alejandro Rey, Val de Vargas,

Frank De Kova, Charles McGraw, Scott Brady, Lloyd Gough, Alex Colon

29. "Wolf" (11-19-74) Lloyd Bridges
30. "Love, Mabel" (11-26-74) William Shatner, Michael Learned, Dean Stockwell, Raymond St. Jacques, Peter Brown, Larry Storch, John Russell, Aldo Ray, Royal Dano, R. G. Armstrong
31. "Explosion" (12-3-74) Tony Lo Bianco, Don Meredith
32. "Capt. Hook" (12-17-74) David Birney, Richard Egan, Dennis Cole, Kim Darby, Barry Atwater, Timothy Blake, Philip Pine, Amanda McBroom
33. "Incident in the Kill Zone" (1-7-75) James Farentino, Jan-Michael Vincent, Lyle Bettger, Cliff Osmond, Robert Sampson, Joseph Wambaugh (cameo)
34. "Headhunter" (1-14-75) Don Murray, Howard Duff, Michael Anderson Jr., Shani Wallis, Joan Leslie, Madlyn Rhue, Scott Brady, Bill Elliott
35. "Year of the Dragon" [Part I] (1-21-75) Robert Culp, Wayne Maunder, Jo Anna Linn, Laraine Stephens, Edward Binns, Godfrey Cambridge, Joseph Garagiola, Benson Fong, Jack Soo, Ken Swofford
36. "Year of the Dragon" [Part II] (1-28-75) as above
37. "To Steal a Million" (2-4-75) Pernell Roberts, Christopher Stone, Alex Cord, Barbara Anderson, Robert Brown, Henry Beckman, Pat Harrington, John Van Dreelen, Anne Jeffreys, Jack Donner
38. "Sniper" (2-11-75) Tony Lo Bianco, Glenn Corbett, Patty Duke Astin
39. "The Execution" (2-18-75) Christopher George, Scoey Mitchlll, John Ericson, Sharon Farrell, Jonelle Allen, Edward Andrews, Philip Carey, Don Marshall
40. "The Man in the Shadows" (2-25-75) Robert Forster, Patricia Crowley, Richard Yniguez, Barbara Luna, John Ireland, Joby Baker, Michael Callan, Ben Hammer
41. "War Games" (3-4-75) Marjoe Gortner, Michael Parks, Neville Brand, Murray Hamilton, Robert Alda, Brooke Bundy, Mills Watson, Mel Scott
42. "The Witness" (3-11-75) Michael Cole, Don Meredith, James McEachin, James Gregory, Elaine Joyce, Jackie Coogan, Noam Pitlik, Richard Erdman, John Kerr

[Continuing]


GREAT MYSTERIES

The inimitable Orson Welles was suitably chosen to introduce each of the classic (e.g. O. Henry's Compliments of the Season and W. W. Jacobs' The Monkey's Paw) and modern mysteries in this syndicated package filmed in England.

The Regulars: Orson Welles, host.

The Episodes [shown in New York City via channel 2, Wednesdays 7:30-8:00]:

1. "A Terribly Strange Bed" (9-12-73) Edward Albert
2. "The Ingenious Reporter" (9-19-73) David Birney
3. "Farewell to the Faulkners" (9-26-73) Keith Baxter, Jane Baxter
4. "The Inspiration of Mr. Budd" (10-3-73) Hugh Griffith, Donald Donnelly
5. "Money to Burn" (10-10-73) Victor Buono
6. "Battle of Wits" (10-17-73) Ian Bannen, Brewster Mason
7. "The Dinner Party" (10-24-73) Joan Collins, Anthony Sharp, Anton Rodgers
8. "The Monkey's Paw" (10-31-73) Cyril Cusack
9. "For Sale--Silence" (11-7-73) Jack Cassidy
10. "Unseen Alibi" (11-14-73) Dean Stockwell
11. "La Grande Breteche" (11-21-73) Susannah York, Peter Cushing
12. "Death of an Old-Fashioned Girl" (11-28-73) Carol Lynley
13. "Captain Rogers" (12-12-73) Donald Pleasance
14. "Compliments of the Season" (12-19-73)
15. "Come into My Parlor" (12-26-73) Anne Jackson
16. "In the Confessional" (1-9-74) Jose Ferrer, Milo O'Shea, Philip Davis
17. "Ice Storm" (1-30-74)
18. "Power of Fear" (2-6-74) Don Murray, Shirley Knight
19. "The Furnished Room" (2-13-74) Clarence Williams III
20. "Under Suspicion" (2-20-74) Janice Rule
21. "Where There's a Will" (3-6-74) Richard Johnson, Hannah Gordon
22. "The Trial for Murder" (3-13-74)
23. "An Affair of Horror" (3-27-74) Harry Andrews
24. "Point of Law" (4-3-74) Alec McCowan
25. "Leather Funnel" (4-17-74)

DOC ELLIOT

The Regulars: Dr. Benjamin R. Elliot, James Franciscus; Eldred McCoy, Bo Hopkins; Mags Brimble, Neva Patterson; Barney Weeks, Noah Beery.

The Episodes:

1. "... And All Ye Need to Know" (10-10-73) Meredith Baxter, Mills Watson, Lou Massad, William Mims, Woodrow Chambliss
2. "A Man of Importance" (11-3-73) Will Geer, Leif Garrett, Willard Sage, Victor Campos, Russell Thorson
3. "The Touch of God" (1-23-74) Tyne Daly, Ford Rainey, Royal Dano, Jessica Myerson, Tom Waters
4. "No Place to Go" (1-30-74) John David Carson, Kathleen

Cody, Maggie Malooly, R. L. Armstrong
5. "A Small Hand of Friendship" (2-6-74) Beverly Garland, Clint Howard
6. "The Runner" (2-13-74) Sam Bottoms, Morgan Woodward, Harry Carey Jr.
7. "The Carrier" (2-20-74) Lonnie Chapman, Jeanne Cooper, John Lupton, Heather North
8. "A Time to Live" (2-27-74)
9. "A Time to Grow" (3-6-74) Brandon Cruz, Susan Brown
10. "The Gold Mine" (3-13-74) Heidi Vaughn, Merle Haggard, Edith Atwater
11. "Survival" (3-27-74) John Ericson, Christine Belford
12. "Things That Might Have Been" (4-3-74) Lane Bradbury, Tim O'Connor, Joan Blackman, Stuart Nesbit
13. "The Brothers" (4-10-74)
14. "The Pharmacist" (5-1-74) Paul Fix, Mitch Vogel, Jordan Rhodes, John Karlen

# LOVE STORY

The Episodes:

1. "Love Came Laughing" (10-3-73) Michael Brandon, Bonnie Bedelia, Eileen Heckart, Gary Walberg, Donald Woods, Michael Lerner
2. "All My Tomorrows" (10-10-73) Robert Foxworth, Susan Anspach, Anne Baxter, Barnard Hughes, Bill Quinn, John Sebastion
3. "The Roller Coaster Stops Here" (10-24-73) Don Murray, Barbara Seagull, Louise Lasser, Joan Tompkins, Tony Becker, Shane Thompson, Tom Scott
4. "The Cardboard House" (10-31-73) Vic Morrow, Samantha Eggar
5. "Mirabelle's Summer" (11-7-73) Pamela Franklin, David Huffman, Martin Sheen, Nancy Olson, David Doyle, Phyllis Thaxter, Marcia Strassman
6. "The Soft, Kind Brush" (11-21-73) James Farentino, Trish Van Devere
7. "Beginner's Luck" (11-28-73) Janet Leigh, Jan Smithers, Kurt Russell
8. "When the Girls Came Out to Play" (12-5-73) Frank Langella, Victoria Principal, Valerie Perrine
9. "Joie" (12-12-73) Kim Darby, John David Carson, Sada Thompson
10. "The Youngest Lovers" (12-19-73) Diane Baker, Larry Hagman, Jodie Foster, Michael-James Wixted, Susan Oliver, Kevin McCarthy
11. "A Glow of Dying Embers" (12-26-73) Clifton Davis, Greg Morris, Janet MacLachlan, Ed Bernard, Tina Andrews, Charles Lampkin, Maidie Norman
12. "Time for Love" (1-2-74) Dean Jagger, Kay Lenz, Bruce

Davison, Joan Pringle, Robert Mandan, Dennis Olivieri, Chuck Daniel

## KOJAK

Initiating with Abby Mann's superlative teleplay "The Marcus Nelson Murders" most of these episodes of an uncompromising Greek-American New York police lieutenant fall far short of it. Nonetheless, Telly Savalas is excellent in the title role of Theo Kojak and there are at least two brilliant guest performances: Ruth Gordon as the psychic of "I Want to Report a Dream," and Zohra Lampert an Emmy award winner for her role as a con artist in "Queen of the Gypsies."

The Regulars: Lt. Theo Kojak, Telly Savalas; Sgt. Bobby Crocker, Kevin Dobson; Cpt. Frank McNeil, Dan Frazer; Stavros, Demosthenes (George Savalas); Saperstein, Mark Russell; Rizzo, Vince Conti; Agajanian, Darrell Zwerling; Prince, Borah Silver; Gomez, Victor Campos; Commissioner, Bart Burns.

The Episodes:

1. "Siege of Terror" (10-24-73) Harvey Keitel, James J. Sloyan, William Hansen, Jude Farese, John Garwood
2. "Web of Death" (10-31-73) Hector Elizondo, Barbara Rhoades
3. "One for the Morgue" (11-7-73) Roger Robinson, Art Metrano, Anthony Charnota, Arnold Williams
4. "Knockover" (11-14-73) Joseph Hindy, Paul Savior, Alex Rocco, Lynnette Mettey
5. "The Girl in the River" (11-21-73) James Keach, Mark Gordon
6. "Requiem for a Cop" (11-28-73) James Luisi, Bruce Kirby
7. "The Corrupter" (12-5-73) Lola Albright, Robert Webber
8. "Dark Sunday" (12-12-73) Richard Jordan, Larry Block
9. "Conspiracy of Fear" (12-19-73) Larry Kert, Michael McGuire, Nicholas Colasanto, Gretchen Corbett, Michael Keep, William Prince
10. "Cop in a Cage" (1-2-74) John P. Ryan, Penny Santon, Nick Dennis, Janice Heiden, Edward Ansara, Sally Kirkland
11. "Marker for a Dead Bookie" (1-16-74) Roger Robinson, Val Avery, Henry Brown, Edith Diaz, Lorraine Gary, Don Calfa
12. "Last Rites for a Dead Priest" (1-23-74) Jackie Cooper, Paul Cavonis, Stanley Kamel, Vincent Martorano
13. "Death Is Not a Passing Grade" (1-30-74) James Woods, Jack Murdock, Mariclare Costello, Pamela Hensley
14. "Die Before They Wake" (2-6-74) Tina Louise
15. "Deliver Us Some Evil" (2-13-74) John Ritter, Fred Sadoff,

Ruth McDevitt, Nora Marlowe, Gary Walberg, Karen Lamm
16. "Eighteen Hours of Fear" (2-20-74) Jack Colvin, Lynne
    Marta, Chuck McCann, Abe Vigoda, Barbara Brownell,
    Eddie Fontaine
17. "Before the Devil Knows" (2-27-74) Henry Darrow
18. "Dead on His Feet" (3-6-74) Harry Guardino, Joanne Lin-
    ville, Malachi Throne
19. "Down a Long and Lonely River" (3-20-74) Sian Barbara
    Allen
20. "Mojo" (3-27-74) Dennis Patrick, Ed Lauter
21. "Therapy in Dynamite" (4-10-74) Steven Keats, Elizabeth
    Allen, Dabney Coleman, Jane Elliott, Philip Bruns, Joan
    Pringle
22. "The Only Way Out" (5-8-74) Lee H. Montgomery, Joshua
    Bryant

Second Season

23. "The Chinatown Murders" [special two-hour film] (9-15-74)
    Michael Constantine, Leonardo Cimino, Robert Ito, Sheree
    North, Tige Andrews, Shirlee Kong
24. "Hush Now, or You'll Die!" (9-22-74) Kathleen Quinlan,
    Todd Susman, Mike Kellin, Grayson Hall, Carmen Zapata,
    Brendon Burns
25. "A Very Deadly Game" (9-29-74) Art Lund, Burr DeBen-
    ning, Alex Colon, Roger Robinson
26. "Wall Street Gunslinger" (10-6-74) Alan Feinstein, Bernard
    Barrow, Zitto Kazann, Ann Coleman
27. "Slay Ride" (10-13-74) Julie Gregg, Stephen McHattie, Paul
    Benedict, Francine York, Don Hanmer, Melendy Britt
28. "Nursemaid" (10-20-74) Kay Medford, Eugene Troobnick,
    Frank Christi, Allan Miller, Lynnette Mettey, Don McGovern
29. "You Can't Tell a Hurt Man How to Holler" (10-27-74) Harrison
    Page, Roger E. Mosley, Roger Robinson, Margaret Avery
30. "The Best Judge Money Can Buy" (11-3-74) John Randolph,
    Walter McGinn, Melissa Murphy, Abe Vigoda, Dorothy
    Tristan, John Aniston
31. "A Souvenir from Atlantic City" (11-10-74) Jaime Sanchez,
    Daniel J. Travanti
32. "A Killing in the Second House" (11-17-74) Martin Balsam,
    Dimitra Arliss, John Lehne, Nedra Deen
33. "The Best War in Town" (11-24-74) Mark Shera, David
    Doyle, Normann Burton
34. "Cross Your Heart and Hope to Die" (12-1-74) Andrea
    Marcovicci, Lenny Baker, Lenka Peterson, Angela Clarke
35. "The Betrayal" (12-15-74) Paul Anka, Richard Romanus,
    Roger Robinson, Paul Picerni
36. "Loser Takes All" (12-22-74) Leslie Nielsen, Ja'net DuBois,
    Antonio Fargas, Quinn Redeker
37. "Close Cover Before Killing" (1-5-75) Alex Rocco, David
    Ackroyd, Nate Esformes, Nira Barab, Richard X. Slattery
38. "Acts of Desperate Men" (1-12-75) Eugene Roche, Bruce
    Kirby Jr., Elaine Joyce, Thayer David, Nick Dennis

39. "Queen of the Gypsies" (1-19-75) Zohra Lampert, Lane
    Smith, Peter Mamakos, Donald Billet, Robert Emhardt,
    Charles Picerni
40. "Night of the Piraeus" (1-26-75) Norman Lloyd, Ivor Fran-
    cis, Paul Shenar, Robert Viharo, Elizabeth McRae, Gale
    Garnett, Thaao Penghlis, Buddy Lester
41. "Elegy in an Asphalt Graveyard" (2-2-75) Stephen Elliott,
    Roger Robinson, John Glover, Walter Brooke, Priscilla
    Pointer, Terence Locke
42. "The Good Luck Bomber" (2-9-75) Jack Ging, Richard
    Bradford, Ellen Madison, Bonnie Bartlett, Nick Dennis,
    Archie Hahn
43. "Unwanted Partners" (2-16-75) James Sutorius, Michael
    Delano, Brad Dexter, Carole Demas
44. "Two-Four-Six for Two Hundred" (2-23-75) Robert Loggia,
    Dick O'Neill, Rose Marie
45. "The Trade-Off" (3-2-75) Mark Stevens, Michael C. Gwynne,
    Jean Le Bouvier, Liam Dunn
46. "I Want to Report a Dream" (3-9-75) Ruth Gordon, Andy
    Robinson, Cynthia Harris, Tracy Reed

[Continuing]


TOMA

    Remarkably taut police drama commemorating the maverick
style of a real-life New York detective, David Toma (who guest
starred in many of the teleplays). Gripping performances by Tony
Musante in the title role, Susan Strasberg as wife Patty and Simon
Oakland as Inspector Spooner. It is particularly effective in its
evocation of seedy underworld hideaways and of a permeating evil
ready to express itself in both derelict and noblesse alike. Composers included Lonne Elder III ("Blockhouse Breakdown") and Musante himself (along with wife Jane) for the episode "Rock-a-Bye"
and the ninth telecast.

The Regulars: Detective David Toma, Tony Musante; Patty Toma,
        Susan Strasberg; Inspector Spooner, Simon Oakland; Jimmy
        Toma, Sean Manning; Donna Toma, Michelle Livingston.

The Episodes:

1. "The Oberon Contract" (10-4-73) Martin Sheen, Joe Santos,
   Tiffany Bolling, Wyman Pendleton, Philip M. Thomas,
   Kenneth Sansom, Caesar Cordova, Dennis McCarthy
2. "Ambush on 7th Avenue" (10-11-73) Geoffrey Deuel, Roy
   Jenson, Victor Arnold, Claire Brennen
3. "Crime Without Victim" (10-18-73) Brett Halsey, Madeleine
   Sherwood, Alex Dreier, Scott Jacoby, Tony de Costa,
   David Toma
4. "Stakeout" (10-25-73) Skye Aubrey, Jared Martin, Don

Gordon, Oscar DeBruy Jr., David Toma
5. "The Cain Connection" (11-1-73) Michael Tolan, Judi Meredith, Frank Campanella, Peter Brocco, Eddie Firestone,
Frank Christie
6. "Blockhouse Breakdown" (11-8-73) Jan-Michael Vincent,
Rudy Solari, Joan Pringle, Barry Cahill, Betsy Jones-
Moreland
7. "Frame-Up" (11-15-73) Joe De Santis, Richard Davalos,
Linda Marsh, Nicholas Colasanto, John Chandler, Sharon
Gless
8. "The Bambara Bust" (12-6-73) Kathleen Widdoes
9. "50" (1-18-74) Steven Keats, Laurie Ferrone, Louise Troy,
Barbara Rhoades, Leigh Christian, Richard Eastham, Wil-
liam Bryant, David Toma
10. "Rock-a-Bye" (1-25-74) Frederick Rule, Charles Johnson,
Philip M. Thomas, Mary Layne, Nora Heflin, Laurie
Ferrone
11. "Stillwater--492" [Part I] (2-1-74) William Daniels, Michael
Baseleon, Hilly Hicks, James G. Richardson, Bruce
Kirby Sr., Michael Richardson, David Toma
12. "A Time and a Place Unknown" [Part II] (2-15-74) as above
13. "A Funeral for Max Fabian" (2-22-74) Albert Salmi, Roy
Poole, Melvin Stewart, Peter Brocco, Timothy Carey,
George Burrafato
14. "The Big Dealers" (3-1-74) Jack Bender, Gianni Russo
15. "The Contract on Alex Cordeen" (3-8-74) Frank De Kova,
Harold J. Stone
16. "Joey the Weep" (3-22-74) Jack Kelly, Art Metrano
17. "The Friends of Danny Beecher" (3-29-74) Kristoffer Tabori, Ralph Meeker
18. "The Madam" (4-12-74) Ina Balin, Suzanne Charney
19. "Pound of Flesh" (4-19-74) Ray Danton, Hildy Brooks
20. "The Street" (5-3-74) Percy Rodriguez, Michael Glaser,
Henry Brown, Don Pedro Colley, Scatman Crothers, Abe
Vigoda, Philip M. Thomas, Tom Castronova
21. "The Accused" (5-10-74) Claude Akins


APPLE'S WAY

Earl Hamner's contemporary successor to "The Waltons"
concerns a disgruntled architect (Ronny Cox as George Apple) who
makes the rural transition with his wife Barbara (Lee McCain) and
four children. Again, the simple virtues are celebrated: George
climbs up a tree in the initial episode to protest its intended destruction (he climbs down when his action has an adverse effect on
the children). Hefty doses of homespun moralizing throughout.

The Regulars: George Apple, Ronny Cox; Barbara Apple, Lee
McCain; Paul Apple, Vincent Van Patten; Cathy Apple,
Patti Cohoon; Patricia Apple, Franny Michel; Steven Apple,
Eric Olson; Grandpa, Malcolm Atterbury (with episode of

3/10/74).

The Episodes:

1. "The Tree" (2-10-74) Steve Benedict, Leonard Stone, Richard Bull, Lucille Benson
2. "The Musician" (2-17-74) Mitch Vogel, Patsy Garrett, Richard Bradford, Sally Kemp
3. "The Zoo" (2-24-74)
4. "The Teacher" (3-3-74)
5. "The Miller" (3-10-74) featuring Malcolm Atterbury
6. "The Coach" (3-24-74) Gene Raymond
7. "The Witness" (3-31-74)
8. "The Temptation" (4-7-74) Abby Dalton, Heather Totter, Peter Mark Richman, Al Rude
9. "The Land" (4-14-74)
10. "The Applicant" (4-21-74) Sierra Bandit, Jerry Dexter, Eduard Franz, Bobbi Jordan
11. "The Pen Pal" (4-28-74) Tracy Tannen, Karl Swenson, John Lupton, Olan Soule, Jacques Aubuchon
12. "The Accident" (5-5-74) Andy Stevens, Morgan Upton, Percy Rodriguez, Virginia Gregg
13. "The Fair" (5-12-74)
14. "The Lamb" (5-19-74) Van Williams, Leif Gerrett, Millie Perkins, Norman Andrews

Second Season

15. "The Storm" (9-15-74) regulars only
16. "The Circus" (9-22-74) Mary Frann, Parley Baer, Neva Patterson, Alan Fudge
17. "The Friend" (9-29-74) Jordan Gerler, Lew Brown
18. "The Returning" (10-6-74) John David Carson, James Gavin
19. "First Love" (10-13-74) Farrah Fawcett-Majors, Lisa Eilbacher
20. "The Engagement" (10-20-74) Linda Watkins, Jack Manning Shirley Mitchell, Lew Brown
21. "The Candy Drive" (10-27-74) Alan Fudge, Marie Denn
22. "The Winning Season" (11-10-74)
23. "The Flag" (11-17-74)
24. "The Real Thanksgiving" (11-24-74) John Lupton
25. "Apprentice" (12-1-74)
26. "The Outsider" (12-15-74) Gerald Hiken, Mark Wheeler, Robert Palmer, Norman Alden
27. "The Still Life" (12-22-74) Hal Dawson, Frank De Kova, Charles Seel, Victor Killian
28. "The Outing" (1-5-75)
29. "The Price" (1-12-75)

THE NEW LAND

Undoubtedly the Jan Troell superior films ("The Emigrants" and "The New Land") were inspiration for these beautifully photographed teleplays of Swedish immigrants in America.

The Regulars: Christian Larsen, Scott Thomas; Anna Larsen, Bonnie Bedelia; Bo Larsen, Kurt Russell; Tuliff Larsen, Todd Lookinland; Anneliese Larsen, Debbie Lytton; Molly, Gwen Arner; Lundstrom, Donald Moffat; Murdock, Lou Frizzell; Rhodie, Stephanie Steele.

The Episodes:

1. "The Word Is: Persistence" (9-14-74) James Olson, Mike Farrell, Sally Carter Ihnat
2. "The Word Is: Growth" (9-21-74) Ed Lauter, Ellen Geer, June Dayton
3. "The Word Is: Acceptance" (9-28-74) regulars only
4. "The Word Is: Mortal" (10-5-74) Salome Jens, Don Dubbins, Lin McCarthy, Robert Emhardt, Maxine Stuart
5. "The Word Is: Alternative" (10-12-74) Belinda Montgomery, Paul Sorenson, Keith Atkinson
6. "The Word Is: Celebration" (10-19-74) Wendell Wellman, Tenaya Torres, Charles Wagenheim


NAKIA

The Regulars: Deputy Sheriff Nakia Parker, Robert Forster; Sheriff Sam Jericho, Arthur Kennedy; Irene, Gloria DeHaven; Half Cub, John Tenorio Jr.; Hubbell, Taylor Lacher; Elliot, Ben Zeller.

The Episodes:

1. "The Non-Person" (9-21-74) A Martinez, Elizabeth Chauvet, Edward Bell, Victor Jory, Sandra Smith
2. "The Quarry" (9-28-74) Burr DeBenning, Beth Brickell, Gale Sondergaard, Crawford MacCallum, Ray Greenway,

Claudia Baca, Robert Vigil
3. "The Sand Trap" (10-5-74) Jan Clayton, Jo Ann Harris,
    Mariana Hill, Richard Kelton, David Huddleston, Robert
    Ginty
4. "The Hostage" (10-12-74) Kay Lenz, David Huffman, Jeanne
    Stein, Emmett S. Robbins, Michael C. Eiland
5. "No Place to Hide" (10-19-74) Gabe Dell, Ray Danton, Gwen
    Van Dam, Marc Singer
6. "A Beginning in the Wilderness" (10-26-74) Greg Mabrey,
    Joanne Linville, Cameron Mitchell, Robert Urich
7. "The Driver" (11-2-74) Geoffrey Deuel, Tim O'Connor,
    Todd Armstrong, Robert Doyle, Victoria Racimo, Harry
    Basch, Peter Prouse
8. "The Moving Target" (11-9-74) Marjoe Gortner
9. "The Dream" (11-23-74) Michael Ansara, Richard Hatch,
    Kent Lane, Betty Ann Carr, Judson Morgan
10. "Roots of Anger" (11-30-74)
11. [unknown title] (12-7-74) Charles Aidman, Pat Carroll,
    Farley Granger, Jared Martin, Susan Richardson, Kipp
    Whitman
12. "Pete" (12-21-74) Johnny Doran, George Maharis, Shirley
    Knight, Carmen Zapata
13. "The Fire Dancer" (12-28-74) Anthony Caruso, Victor Jory

## BORN FREE

African location photography is all that distinguishes this ineffective adaptation of the George and Joy Adamson story and film.

The Regulars: George Adamson, Gary Collins; Joy Adamson,
    Diana Muldaur; Makedda, Hal Frederick; Joe Kanini,
    Joseph de Graft; Nuru, Peter Lukoye.

The Episodes:

1. [unknown title] (9-9-74) Peter Lawford, Erastus Kague, Seth
    Adagala
2. "Elephant Trouble" (9-16-74) Hari Rhodes, James Vickery,
    Janet Young, Bartholomew Sketch
3. "A Matter of Survival" (9-23-74) Susan Dey, Barry Gaymer
4. "Death of a Hunter" (9-30-74) Dan O'Herlihy, Alex Okoth,
    Dick Agudah, Salami Coker, William Alot
5. "Africa's Child" (10-7-74) Dawn Lyn, John DeVilliers,
    Ngigi Gitau, Isaac Munyua, Lydia Kubo
6. "The Massai Rebels" (10-14-74) Glenn Corbett, Ewart J.
    Walters, James Falkland, Cy Grant, David Mulwa
7. "The Flying Doctor of Kenya" (10-28-74) Juliet Mills,
    Freddie Achieng, Tommy Eytle, Lucita Lijertwood, Mar-
    lene Docherty, Dr. Michael Woods, Rosemary Jommo,
    Nelson Kajuna
8. "The Trespassers" (11-4-74) Alex Cord, Louis Mahoney,

Johnny Angaya, Sam Karanji, Paul Makua, James Gatau
9. "The Man Eaters of Merti" (11-11-74) James Vickery, Gordon Heath
10. "Elsa's Odyssey" (11-18-74) Mary Ann Mobley, Dawn Lyn
11. "The White Rhino" (11-25-74) John DeVilliers, Dawn Lyn, George Sewell, Deji Young, John Anderson, Quentin Seacombe
12. "The Raiders" (12-9-74) Francis Njugana, Dane Clark, David Kiranji, Abdulla Sonado, Angus Simpson, Hussein Kareithi
13. "The Devil Leopard" (12-30-74) Barbara Parkins

## SONS AND DAUGHTERS

The fifties were never more maudlin (but in Hollywood were they ever maudlin?) than as they appeared in this extreme dramatic answer to ABC's popular comedy (and fantasy) "Happy Days." It seems that Anita Cramer is worried about a sordid reputation over her relationship with steady Jeff Reed, her mother who has left her father, and Jeff's interceding mother. We've seen the situation countless times before.

The Regulars: Jeff Reed, Gary Frank; Anita Cramer, Glynnis O'Connor; Lucille, Jay W. MacIntosh; Walter, John S. Ragin; Danny, Michael Morgan; Ruth, Jan Shutan; Stash, Scott Colomby; Moose, Barry Livingston; Charlie, Lionel Johnston; Evie, Debralee Scott; Mary Anne, Laura Siegel; Cody, Christopher Nelson.

The Episodes:

1. "The Locket" (9-11-74) Jane Lambert
2. "Anita's Reputation" (9-18-74) Priscilla Pointer, Paula Victor, Jean Allison, Mary Ann Gibson
3. "The Runner" (9-25-74) James Callahan, Howard Platt, Michael O'Keefe
4. "Lucille's Problem" (10-2-74) regulars only
5. "The Accident" (10-9-74) Jerome Guardino, William Traylor, Don Keefer
6. "The Rejection" (10-16-74) Philip Bruns, Joyce Jameson, Garry Walberg, Millie Slavin, Richard Doran, Meegan King, Paul Hinckley
7. "The Pregnancy" (10-23-74) Linda Purl, Fred Sadoff, Susan Brown, Jay Hammer, Jana Bellan
8. "The Invitation" (10-30-74) regulars only
9. "The Tryst" (11-6-74) regulars only

## THE LITTLE HOUSE ON THE PRAIRIE

Super-saccharin adaptation of the "Big House" books of Laura Ingalls Wilder (we are overdue for a re-evaluation of these classics), several of the episodes composed and directed by series star Michael Landon in the role of Charles Ingalls. As clear as crystal good and bad characters (nasty Nellie and nasty Willie Oleson, prompted by their nastier mother, incessantly taunt poor little Laura). A fine performance, however, by Forrest Tucker as the competitive hero in his twilight years of the teleplay "Founder's Day."

The Regulars: Charles Ingalls, Michael Landon; Caroline Ingalls, Karen Grassle; Laura Ingalls, Melissa Gilbert; Mary Ingalls, Melissa Sue Anderson; Carrie Ingalls, Sidney Green Bush/Lindsey Green Bush; Mr. Oleson, Richard Bull; Mrs. Oleson, Katherine MacGregor; Nellie Oleson, Alison Arngrim; Willie Oleson, Jonathan Gilbert; Dr. Baker, Kevin Hagen; Miss Beadle, Charlotte Stewart; Mr. Edwards, Victor French (recurring guest role).

The Episodes:

1. "A Harvest of Friends" (9-11-74) Ramon Bieri
2. "Country Girls" (9-18-74) Robert Hoffman
3. "The 100 Mile Walk" (9-25-74) Don Knight, Bill Zuckert, Richard Hurst, Celia Kaye
4. "Mr. Edwards' Homecoming" (10-2-74) Victor French, Robert Swann, Bonnie Bartlett
5. "The Love of Johnny Johnson" (10-9-74) Mitch Vogel
6. "If I Should Wake Before I Die" (10-23-74) Josephine Hutchinson, Ruth McDevitt, Henry Olek, Betty Lynn
7. "Town Party, Country Party" (10-30-74) Kim Richards, Jan Merlin
8. "Ma's Holiday" (11-6-74) Victor French, Olive Dunbar, Bonnie Bartlett, Norma Connelly
9. "School Mom" (11-13-74) Dirk Blocker
10. "The Raccoon" (11-20-74) Tracie Savage
11. "The Voice of Tinker Jones" (12-4-74) Chuck McCann
12. "The Award" (12-11-74) Eddie Rayden, Ruth Foster
13. "The Lord Is My Shepherd" [two-hour episode] (12-18-74) Ernest Borgnine, Bill Cort, Dabbs Greer, Victor French
14. "Christmas at Plum Creek" (12-25-74) regulars only
15. "Family Quarrel" (1-15-75) Dabbs Greer
16. "Doctor's Lady" (1-22-75) Anne Archer, Steve Kunze, Bea Morris, Douglas Dirkson
17. "Plague" (1-29-75) Victor French, Helen Clark, Bradley Greene, Matt Clark
18. "The Circus Man" (2-5-75) Red Buttons
19. "Child in Pain" (2-12-75) Harris Yulin, Johnny Lee
20. "Money Crop" (2-19-75) Julie Cobb
21. "Survival" (2-26-75) Jack Ging, Robert Tessier, Carl Pitti
22. "To See the World" (3-5-75) Mitch Vogel, Victor French,

James Griffith, Bob Hoy
23.  "Founder's Day" (5-7-75)  Forrest Tucker, Ann Doran

[Continuing]


GET CHRISTIE LOVE!

Lost in the deluge of law and order entries of the season was this ridiculous series built entirely around the character of a black nonconformist police woman--Teresa Graves as Christie Love.

The Regulars: Christie Love, Teresa Graves; Lt. Matthew Reardon, Charles Cioffi; Belmont, Dennis Rucker; Caruso, Andy Romano; Captain Ryan, Jack Kelly (joined in mid-season); Sgt. Pete Gallagher, Michael Pataki (joined in mid-season).

The Episodes:

1.  "Market for Murder" (9-11-74)  Peter Mark Richman, Howard Caine, Tom Atkins, Ken Kercheval, Anne Schedeen
2.  "Deadly Betrayal" (9-18-74)  Tom Skerritt, Harold Oblong, John Sebastian, Melissa Greene, Jason Ronard, Tom Bower, Larry Ward
3.  "Emperor of Death Street" (9-25-74)  Calvin Lockhart, Russell Wiggins, Stanley Kamel, Ji-tu Cumbuka, June Christopher, Kenneth O'Brien
4.  "Pawn Ticket for Murder" (10-2-74)  Scott Brady, Sig Haig, Ken Tobey, Dick O'Neill, Quinn Redeker
5.  "Death on Delivery" (10-9-74)  Stephen McNally, Alex Rocco, Allan Miller, Robert B. Lang, Robert Phillips, Linda Nesbitt
6.  "For the Family Honor" (10-23-74)  Robert Alda, Titos Vandis, Vincent Baggetta, Michael Keep, William Sylvester, Scott Peters
7.  "Highway to Murder" (10-30-74)  Clu Gulager, John Quade, Migdia Valera, Donna J. Anderson, Rudy Ramos, Jack Ryland, Pat Corley, Douglas Dirkson, Patch McKenzie
8.  "Fatal Damage" (11-6-74)  Jared Martin, Max Gale, Robert Yuro, Richard Rust, Richard Lawson, Claire Brennen
9.  "Downbeat for a Dead Man" (11-13-74)  Tim O'Connor, Louise Clark, Philip R. Allen, Frank Sinatra Jr.
10.  "Bullet from the Grave" (11-20-74)  Eric Braeden, Kevin Hagen, Anne Lockhart, Amy Robinson
11.  "Deadly Justice" (12-4-74)  Michael Cole
12.  "The Longest Fall" (12-11-74)  Michael J. Pollard, Linda Scruggs, James Wainwright, Roger Robinson, Scott Peters
13.  "The Deadly Sport" (1-8-75)  Brenda Scott, James Louis Watkins, Alexander Courtney, Tony Young, Doris Dowling, Eric C. Laneuville
14.  "Too Many Games in Town" (1-15-75)  Erin Blunt, Otis E. Young, Warren Stevens, Scott Peters
15.  "Our Lady in London" (1-29-75)  John Astin, Steven Keats,

Wilfrid Hyde-White, Dick Burch, Paul Napier, Eric Christmas

16. "Murder on High C" (2-5-75) Frank Gorshin, Sally Kemp,
    Heidi Bruhi, Barbara Collentine, Maurice Marsac, Maurice
    Sherbanee
17. "My Son, the Murderer" (2-12-75) E. J. Peaker, Michael
    Parks
18. "The Big Rematch" (2-19-75) Karen Machon, Kenneth Tobey,
    Phillip Pine, Rick Jason, Fred Holliday, James G. Richardson
19. "From Paris with Love" (3-5-75) Frank Gorshin, Sally
    Kemp, Heidi Bruhl, Maurice Marsac
20. [unknown title] (3-12-75) Don Galloway, Jaclyn Ellen Smith,
    Marjorie Wallace, Mel Gallagher
21. "A Few Excess People" (3-26-75) Phil Silvers, Rose Marie,
    Robert Donner, Val Bisoglio, Bob Random, Troy Melton,
    Herbert Jefferson Jr.
22. "I'm Your New Neighbor" (4-4-75) Ed Nelson, Roger C.
    Carmel, Karen Klein


LUCAS TANNER

David Victor's sentimental study of a Missouri high school
English teacher (David Hartman as Lucas Tanner) who, by virtue
of charm (and with an assist by the fact that he is a former professional baseball star) is hero to both disgruntled student roman-
tics and impetuous athletes. Much tired moralizing.

The Regulars: Lucas Tanner, David Hartman; Mrs. Margaret
    Blumenthal, Rosemary Murphy; Jaytee, Alan Abelew;
    Glendon, Robbie Rist; Cindy, Trish Soodik; Hamilton, John
    Randolph; Terry, Kimberly Beck; Wally, Michael Dwight
    Smith.

The Episodes:

1. "A Matter of Love" (9-11-74) Lee Purcell, Bruce Kimmel,
   Bettye Ackerman, Julie Adams
2. "Instant Replay" (9-18-74) Marlyn Mason, Melissa Greene,
   Jeanne Bates, Ron Kolman
3. "Thirteen Going on Twenty" (10-2-74) Pamela Hensley,
   Linda Purl, Alfred Lutter, Carol Lawson
4. "Winners and Losers" (10-9-74) Andrew Parks, Dirk
   Blocker, Richard Jaeckel, Lonny Chapman
5. "Three Letter Word" (10-23-74) Kathleen Quinlan, Michael
   Baseleon, Nancy Malone, Jim Bradford
6. "By the Numbers" (11-6-74) Janet Margolin, Alan Fudge,
   Chris Beaumont, Bettye Ackerman
7. "Echoes" (11-13-74) June Dayton, John Doucette, Dimitra
   Arliss, Kasey Rogers
8. "Look the Other Way" (11-20-74) Dirk Blocker, Ayn Ruymen, Lynn Carlin, Ned Stewart, Jack Kelly, Michael
   Conrad

9. "Cheers" (12-4-74) Sam Bottoms, Pat Hingle, Louise La-
    tham, Michael Fox, Ben Cooper, Lloyd Battista
10. "Merry Gentleman" (12-25-74) Barry Sullivan, Paul Napier,
    Anne Schedeen
11. "Bonus Baby" (1-8-75)
12. "Pay the Man the Two Dollars" (1-15-75) Larry Hagman
13. "Those Who Cannot, Teach" (1-22-75) Hershel Bernardi,
    Charlie Martin Smith, Marge Redmond, Sharon Gless
14. "What's Wrong with Bobbie?" (1-29-75) Greg Morris, Ty
    Henderson, Ta-Tanisha, Tom Middleton
15. "Collision" (2-5-75)
16. "Why Not a Happy Ending?" (2-12-75) Diane Baker, Barry
    Livingston
17. "Shattered" (2-19-75) William Windom, Samantha Eggar
18. "The Noise of a Quiet Weekend" (2-26-75) Jaye P. Morgan,
    Norman Fell, Betty White, Michael Lerner, Barbara
    Rhoades
19. [unknown title] (3-12-75) Tyne Daly, Milton Selzer, Patti
    Cohoon, Christopher Stafford Nelson
20. "A Touch of Bribery" (4-3-75)
21. "One to One" (4-9-75) Jose Feliciano, Mitch Vogel, Andrew
    Duggan, Claire Brennen, Jason Wingreen

## PETROCELLI

Razzle-dazzle distortion of the legal system, our hero being
a cocky Ivy League educated attorney who makes the Southwest--
from which now pour assorted felons--his domain. Tony Petrocelli
(Barry Newman) solves in meticulous and flamboyant fashion his
every murder case; this despite the fact that as defense counsel he
is obligated to do far less.

The Regulars: Anthony Petrocelli, Barry Newman; Maggie Petrocelli, Susan Howard; Pete Ritter, Albert Salmi.

The Episodes:

1. "The Golden Cage" (9-11-74) Rosemary Forsyth, William
    Windom, Joseph Campanella, Morgan Woodward
2. "Music to Die By" (9-18-74) Rick Nelson, David Doyle,
    Jeremy Slate, David Huddleston, Britt Leach, Henry Ken-
    drick
3. "By Reason of Madness" (9-25-74) Lynda Day George, John
    Vernon, Loretta Swit, James McEachin, Rory Calhoun,
    Riley Hill
4. "Edge of Evil" (10-2-74) William Shatner, Susan Oliver,
    Lynn Carlin, Dana Elcar, Morgan Paull, Glenn Corbett
5. "A Life for a Life" (10-9-74) Geoffrey Deuel, Sharon Far-
    rell, John Anderson, Henry Jones, Felice Orlandi, Walter
    Brooke
6. "Death in High Places" (10-23-74) Belinda J. Montgomery,

Harold Gould, Cameron Mitchell, Barney Phillips, Gregory Sierra, Joe Mantell, Dick Alexander, Richard Elman

7. "Double Negative" (10-30-74) Michael Burns, Fritz Weaver, Lisa Farringer, David Huddleston, Gene Tyburn, Ron Foster

8. "Mirror, Mirror on the Wall" (11-6-74) Stephanie Powers, Harold Gould, William Bramley, Erica Hagen, Kurt Grayson, Arnold Jeffers

9. "An Act of Love" (11-13-74) John David Carson, John Marley, Simon Scott, Claudette Nivens, Alan Oppenheimer, Angela Clarke, Christina Hart, Kenneth Dobbs

10. "A Very Lonely Lady" (11-27-74) Russell Wiggins, Lou Gossett, Arlene Martell, Jack Ging, John Milford, Lucille Benson

11. "Counterplay" (12-4-74)

12. "A Convenant with Evil" (12-18-74) Charlie Martin Smith, Paul Carr, Dean Harens, David Huddleston, Julie Cobb, Arthur Malet

13. "The Sleep of Reason" (1-15-75) Christopher Connelly, Logan Ramsey, Pamela Franklin, David Huddleston, Albert Stratton, Francine York, Lowell Gleason, Alberta R. Eacret

14. "A Fallen Idol" (1-22-75) Lou Gossett, Don Stroud, Susan Strasberg, Richard Ward, George Petrie, Ben Hammer, Don Starr, Paul C. Thomas

15. "Once Upon a Victim" (1-29-75) John Dehner, Renne Jarrett, Della Reese, Jonathan Lippe, Alan Fudge, Barbara Rhoades, Jack Collins, Fred Ashley

16. "The Kidnapping" (2-5-75) Kim Darby

17. "A Lonely Victim" (2-19-75) Anjanette Comer, Madlyn Rhue, David Huddleston, Simon Scott, Donald Dubbins, Fred Beir, Mark Goddard, Arnold Jeffers

18. "The Outsiders" (2-26-75) Mitch Vogel, Lucille Benson, Mark Hamill, Marion Ross, David Huddleston, William Bramley

19. "Vengeance in White" (3-5-75) Michael Anderson Jr., Brenda Scott, Elinor Donahue, Michael Bell, Ken Swofford, Francesca Jarvis, Gene Earle, David Huddleston

20. [unknown title] (3-12-75) Strother Martin, Shug Fisher, Paul Brinegar, Eddie Firestone

21. "Death in Small Doses" (3-27-75) Stephen Elliott, Robert Mandan, Michael Baseleon, Paul Shenar, George O'Hanlon Jr., Elizabeth MacRae

22. "A Night of Terror" (4-2-75) Lois Nettleton

[Continuing]


THE MANHUNTER

But a faint whisper of "The Untouchables"--lackluster Quinn Martin tale of a 1930s crimefighter.

The Regulars: Dave Barrett, Ken Howard; Elizabeth Barrett, Hilary Thompson; James Barrett, Ford Rainey.

The Episodes:

1. "The Ma Gentry Gang" (9-11-74) Ida Lupino, Tim O'Connor, Sam Elliott, Don Stroud, Beverly Washburn, Don Howard, Davey Davison
2. "The Man Who Thought He Was Dillinger" (9-18-74) Ray Danton, David Hedison, Mitchell Ryan, Alexandra Hay, Jerry Summers, Robert Emhardt, Don Keefer, Shirley O'Hara
3. "The Baby-Faced Killers" (9-25-74) Michael Burns, Denver Pyle, Lynne Marta, Paul Koslo, Darrell Fetty, Joan Tompkins, Laurence Haddon, Bob Hastings
4. "Death on the Run" (10-2-74) Harry Guardino, William Schallert, Bo Hopkins, William Watson, Robert Hogan, Kelly Thordsen
5. "Trackdown" (10-9-74) Chris Robinson, Neva Patterson, R. G. Armstrong, Katherine Justice, Roy Applegate, Mary Jackson, Herman Poppe, Bucklind Beery
6. "Terror from the Skies" (10-16-74) Glenn Corbett, Billy Green Bush, Linda Marsh, Regis J. Cordic, Harry Lauter, Don Dubbins, Larry Ward, Tony Epper
7. "The Doomsday Gang" (10-23-74) Monte Markham, Jason Evers, Marj Dusay, Dana Elcar, Russell Thorson, Robert Doyle, Ramon Bieri, Jack Donner
8. "The Deadly Brothers" (10-30-74) Peter Haskell, Robert Webber, Joan Van Ark, Jerry Douglas, Robert Pine, James Luisi, Arlene Golonka, Adrian Ricard
9. "The Truck Murders" (11-6-74) Celeste Holm, Fred Sadoff, Patty McCormack, Charles Knox Robinson, Sorrell Booke, Liam Sullivan, Claudia Jennings, Jim Boles
10. "Jacknife" (11-13-74) Leslie Nielsen, Andrew Duggan
11. "The Carnival Story" (11-20-74) Robert Foxworth, Anne Helm
12. "The Lodester Ambush" (12-4-74) William Smithers, Burr DeBenning, Dabbs Greer, Charles Tyner, Martine Bartlett, Mark Hamill, William Campbell, Suzanne Charny, Anthony Charnota, Eunice Christopher
13. "A. W. O. L. to Kill" (12-11-74) Geoffrey Deuel, Stephen Elliott, Dabney Coleman, Alan Fudge, James Hampton, Frank Maxwell, Kurt Grayson, Adrienne La Russa, Devon Ericson, Robert Hogan
14. "Flight to Nowhere" (12-18-74) Stephen Brooks, Tom Skerritt, Christine Belford, Norman Alden, John Zaremba, David Walker, Jim Andronica, Walker Edmiston, Casey Connors
15. "Web of Fear" (1-1-75) Shirley Knight
16. "Day of Execution" (1-15-75) Bradford Dillman, Bill McKinney
17. "Man in a Cage" (1-22-75) Michael Constantine, Greg Morris, John Durren, James Keach, Jack Dodson, Dal

Jenkins, Stuart Nisbet, Daxson Thomas, Abigail Shelton, Jim Bohan

18. "The Seventh Man" (1-29-75) Darleen Carr, Edward Binns, Frank Marth, Murray Matheson, Kaz Garas, George D. Wallace, Barbara Rhoades, Charles Briscoe, Barbara Collentine, Dale Tarter
19. "The Wrong Man" (2-5-75) James Sloyan, Laurie Prange
20. "The Death Watch" (2-19-75) Susan Oliver, Colin Wilcox-Horne
21. "To Kill a Tiger" (2-26-75) Kevin McCarthy, Jo Ann Harris
22. "Trial by Terror" (3-5-75) Woody Strode, Claudia Bryar, Conrad Janis, Allen Jaffe, John Fiedler, Parley Baer, Betty Bresler, Robert Hogan

MOVIN' ON

The "citizens band radio" vogue did much to popularize this lethargic tale of a pair of truckers (Frank Converse the eastern-educated law school graduate; Claude Akins the road veteran--the old contrast, yet uninspired).

The Regulars: Sonny Pruett, Claude Akins; Will Chandler, Frank Converse.

The Episodes:

1. "The Time of His Life" (9-12-74) Michael J. Pollard, Elisha Cook, Karen Jensen, Charles Macaulay
2. "Roadblock" (9-19-74) Mackenzie Phillips, Richard Jaeckel, Rick Coleman, Kevin Hagen
3. "Grit" (9-26-74) James Olson, Mary-Lynn Bolger, Bernard Leopold, Pamela Payton-Wright
4. "Lifetime" (10-3-74) Lois Nettleton, Clint Howard, John Qualen
5. "The Trick Is to Stay Alive" (10-10-74) Aldo Ray, Marilyn Hassett, Robert Sorrells, James Keach
6. "Cowhands" (10-24-74) Glenn Corbett, Tina Louise, A Martinez, Edward Faulkner
7. "The Good Life" (11-7-74) George Maharis, Gary Merrill, Lynn Redding, Laraine Stephens
8. "Games" (11-14-74) Michael Parks
9. "Hoots" (11-21-74)
10. "Good for Laughs" (11-28-74) Frank Gorshin, Skip Homeier, Jonathan Lippe
11. "High Rollers" (12-5-74) Christina Raines, Robert F. Lyons, John Barone, Scott Brady
12. "Goin' Home" [Part I] (12-12-74) Sheree North, John Vernon, Jamie Smith Jackson, Will Hutchins, Woodrow Parfrey
13. "Goin' Home" [Part II] (12-19-74) as above
14. "Antiques" (12-26-74) Jeanette Nolan, Gene Earle, Don Knight, Jerry Houser

15. "Explosion" (1-2-75)
16. "Landslide" (1-16-75) Cameron Mitchell
17. "Fraud" (1-30-75) Barry Sullivan, Richard Bull, Roosevelt Grier, Jenny Sullivan
18. "Ammo" (2-6-75) Gloria De Haven
19. "Tattoos" (2-13-75) James Callahan, Lynette Mettey
20. "Ransom" (2-20-75) Ralph Meeker, Karen Carlson, Madilyn Clark, Patricia Smith
21. "The Price of Loving" (4-2-75) Anne Francis, Frank Campanella, Kelly Jean Peters, Christopher Crew
22. "Wedding Bells" (4-9-75) Janet Leigh, Debralee Scott, Bill Catching, Ray Goman


# HARRY O

Above average law and order entry of a San Diego police detective forced into retirement (officially that is; he of course stays active) by reason of an injured back. The best recurring performance was delivered by Henry Darrow as Lieutenant Manny Quinlan, who is murdered (by Sal Mineo) in the teleplay "Elegy for a Cop. "

The Regulars: Harry Orwell, David Janssen; Lt. Manny Quinlan, Henry Darrow (to episode of 2/27/75); Lt. Trench, Anthony Zerbe (with episode of 3/13/75); Sgt. Frank Cole, Tom Atkins; Sue, Farrah Fawcett-Majors (recurring guest role).

The Episodes:

1. "Gertrude" (9-12-74) Julie Sommars, Fred Sadoff, Michael McGuire, Clay Tanner, Mel Stewart, Les Lannom
2. "The Admiral's Lady" (9-19-74) Leif Erickson, Sharon Acker, John McMartin, Charles Held, Ellen Weston, David Moses, Sally Carter Ihnat
3. "Guardian at the Gates" (9-26-74) Barry Sullivan, Linda Evans, Anne Archer, Richard Helton
4. "Mortal Sin" (10-3-74) Laurence Luckinbill, Walter McGinn, Carol Rossen, Charles Drake, Barry Cahill, John Doucette, Mary Murphy, Phillip Pine
5. "Coinage at the Realm" (10-10-74) Joan Darling, David Moses, Kenneth Mars, David Dukes, Dawn Lyn, Florence Stanley
6. [unknown title] (10-17-74) George Spell, Ty Henderson, Margaret Avery, David Moody, James McEachin, Hal Williams
7. "Shadows at Noon" (10-24-74) Guy Stockwell, Diana Ewing, Michael Strong, Bob Hayes, Marla Adams, Jack Mullavey
8. "Ballinger's Choice" (10-31-74) Juliet Mills, Jim McIntire, Paul Burke, Ken Johnson, John McLiam, Lisa Gerritsen
9. "Second Sight" (11-7-74) Stefanie Powers, Mitzi Hoag, Michael Baseleon, Anne Seymour, Henry Oliver
10. "Material Witness" (11-14-74) Barbara Anderson, James

Olson, Mike Farrell
11. "Forty Reasons to Kill" [Part I] (12-5-74) Joanna Pettet, Craig Stevens, Broderick Crawford, Hillary Thompson, Eric Christmas, Kevin Hagen, Ned Romero, Bret Quinn
12. "Forty Reasons to Kill" [Part II] (12-12-74) as above
13. "Accounts Balanced" (12-26-74) Robert Reed, Gerrit Graham, Linda Marsh, John Crawford
14. "Eyewitness" (1-2-75) James McEachin, Rosalind Cash
15. "The Last Heir" (1-9-75)
16. "For the Love of Money" (1-16-75) Mariclare Costello, Sharon Farrell, Joe Silver
17. "Confetti People" (1-23-75) Diana Hyland, Marsha Hunt, Harvey Jason, Scott Hylands, John Rubinstein, Scott McKa
18. "Sound of Trumpets" (1-30-75) Jim Backus, Cab Calloway, Julius Harris, Henry Cordon, Ron Soble, Brenda Sykes
19. "Silent Kill" (2-6-75) James Wainwright, Kathy Lloyd
20. "Double Jeopardy" (2-13-75)
21. "Lester" (2-20-75) Jamie Smith Jackson, Richard Schaal
22. "Elegy for a Cop" (2-27-75) Sal Mineo, Carmen Zapata, Margaret Avery, Kathy Lloyd, Clay Tanner, Mel Stewart, Julio Medina, Jennifer Lee
23. "Street Games" (3-13-75) Claudette Nevins, John McMurtry, Kitty Lester, Maureen McCormick, Philip Sterling Jr., Leslie Dalton

[Continuing]


## PLANET OF THE APES

Incredible adaptation of the Pierre Boule novel and cycle of films of astronauts who crash land and discover that evolution has reversed itself--the apes are literate and have enslaved the human In one episode, our astronauts Virdon (Ron Harper) and Burke (James Naughton) are forced to compete in a chariot race to the amusement of cheering apes in an arena (all reminiscent of Ben Hur). Indeed, with each of the thirteen episodes one had the feeling of having seen it all before. Roddy McDowall repeated his film role as the compassionate ape friend of the astronauts, Galen Mark Lenard was the bellicose ape Urko and Booth Colman was the ape sage Zalus.

The Regulars: Alan Virdon, Ron Harper; Pete Burke, James Naughton; Galen, Roddy McDowall; Zalus, Booth Colman; Urko, Mark Lenard.

The Episodes:

1. "Escape from Tomorrow" (9-13-74) Royal Dano, Jerome Thor, Bobby Porter, Biff Elliot, Woodrow Parfrey, William Beckley
2. "The Gladiators" (9-20-74) John Hoyt, Marc Singer, Willia

Smith, Pat Renella, Eddie Fontaine
3. "The Trap" (9-27-74) Norman Alden, John Milford, Eldon
   Burke, Ron Stein, Cindy Eilbacher, Wallace Earl, Mickey
   Leclair
4. "The Good Seeds" (10-4-74) Jacqueline Scott, Geoffrey Deuel,
   Lonny Chapman, Bobby Porter, Eileen Dietz Elber, Dennis
   Cross
5. "The Legacy" (10-11-74) Zina Bethune, Jackie Earle Haley,
   Robert Phillips, Wayne Foster, Jon Lormer
6. "Tomorrow's Tide" (10-18-74) Roscoe Lee Browne, Jay
   Robinson, Jim Storm, Kathleen Bracken, John McLiam,
   Frank Orsatti, Tom McDonough
7. [unknown title] (10-25-74) Jacqueline Scott, Martin Brooks,
   Jamie Smith Jackson, Michael Strong, Ron Stein, Peter
   Ireland
8. "The Deception" (11-1-74) Jane Actman, John Milford,
   Baynes Barron, Pat Renella, Eldon Burke, Tom McDonough,
   Ron Stein, Hal Baylor
9. "The Horse Race" (11-8-74) John Hoyt, Morgan Woodward,
   Meegan King, Richard Devon, Wesley Fuller
10. "The Interrogation" (11-15-74) Beverly Garland
11. "The Tyrant" (11-22-74) Percy Rodriguez, Tom Troupe
12. "The Cure" (11-29-74) David Sheiner, Sondra Locke, Eldon
    Burke, Ron Soble
13. "Up Above the World So High" (12-20-74) Joanna Barnes,
    Frank Aletter, Martin Brooks, Glenn Wilder, William
    Beckley, Ron Stein

## THE ROCKFORD FILES

Trite private detective yarn (of which it can be positively
said that the cop-as-hero vanishes; he's now a meddling and at
times incompetent boor) with James Garner the protagonist Jim
Rockford, Noah Beery his father "Rocky." Garner's series have
been parodies ("Maverick" and "Nichols") not aspiring to the pretentious levels of their many contemporaries. There is no reason
to watch this car screecher; it is, however, intended as parody.

The Regulars: Jim Rockford, James Garner; Rocky (Jim Rockford
         Sr.), Noah Beery; Sgt. Dennis Becker, Joe Santos; Beth,
         Gretchen Corbett.

The Episodes:

1. "The Kickoff Case" (9-13-74) Julie Sommars, Roger Davis,
   Abe Vigoda, James Woods
2. "The Dark and Bloody Ground" (9-20-74) Nancy Malone,
   Linden Chiles, Walter Brooke, Patricia Smith
3. "The Countess" (9-27-74) Susan Strasberg, Dick Gautier,
   Harold J. Stone, Art Lund
4. "Exit Prentiss Carr" (10-4-74) Corinne Michaels, Warren

Kemmerling, Mills Watson, Stephen McNally
5. "Tall Woman in Red Wagon" (10-11-74) Sian Barbara Allen, Angus Duncan, John Crawford, George DiCenzo
6. "This Case Is Closed" (10-18-74) Joseph Cotten, Sharon Gless, James McEachin, Del Monroe, Eddie Fontaine, Fred Sadoff
7. "The Big Ripoff" (10-25-74) Jill Clayburgh, Nedra Deen, Fred Beir, Kelly Thordsen, Norman Burton, Warren Vanders
8. "Find Me If You Can" (11-1-74) Joan Van Ark, Jean Allison, Michael Glaser, James Lydon
9. "In Pursuit of Carol Thorne" (11-8-74) Lynette Mettey, Irene Tedrow, Jim Antonio, Bill Fletcher
10. "The Dexter Crisis" (11-15-74) Tim O'Connor, Lee Purcell, Linda Kelsey, Burke Byrnes, Ron Soble, Joyce Jameson
11. "Caledonia, It's Worth a Fortune" (12-6-74)
12. "Profit and Loss" [Part I] (12-20-74) Ned Beatty, Michael Lerner, Sharon Spellman, John Carter, Val Bisoglio, Paul Jenkins
13. "Profit and Loss" [Part II] (12-27-74) as above
14. "Aura Lee, Farewell" (1-3-75) Lindsay Wagner
15. "Sleight of Hand" (1-17-75)
16. "Counter Gambit" (1-24-75) Eddie Fontaine, Mary Frann, Eric Server, M. Emmet Walsh, Stuart Margolin, Ford Rainey, Burr De Benning
17. "Claire" (1-31-75) Linda Evans, Jackie Cooper, Lane Smith, Douglas V. Fowley
18. "Say Goodbye to Jennifer" (2-7-75) Pamela Hensley, Thayer David, Hector Elizonde, Regis Cordic
19. "Charlie Harris at Large" (2-14-75) Tony Musante, Diana Muldaur
20. "The Four Pound Brick" (2-21-75) Edith Atwater, Jess Walton, Paul Carr, Stuart Margolin, William Watson, Tom Atkins
21. "Just by Accident" (2-28-75) David Spielberg, Neva Patterson, Fred Sadoff, E. J. Peaker, Steven Keats, Oliver Clark
22. "Roundabout" (3-7-75) Virginia Gregg, Ron Rilkin, Mills Watson, Jesse Welles, George Wyner, Joe E. Tata

[Continuing]


POLICE WOMAN

David Gerber's unlikely successor to his superb "Police Story," with Angie Dickinson and Earl Holliman as the principals (sadly so, both have done far better elsewhere). The series' most controversial episode was a tale of lesbianism and murder-- "Flowers of Evil."

The Regulars: Sergeant Pepper Anderson, Angie Dickinson; Lieutenant Bill Crowley, Earl Holliman; Detective Joe Styles, Ed Bernard; Detective Pete Royster, Charles Dierkop.

The Episodes:

1. "The End Game" (9-13-74) Paul Burke, Jonelle Allen, Deirdre Lenihan, Scott Walker, Bill Williams, Susanne Benton, Skip Homeier, James Murtaugh
2. "The Beautiful Die Young" (9-20-74) William Windom, Kathleen Quinlan, Karen Lamm, Val Bisoglio, Harvey Jason, Jeane Byron, Antonio Fargas
3. "Warning: All Wives ... " (9-27-74) Don Stroud, Marsha Scott, Elinor Donahue, Joyce Bulifant, William Katt, Val Bisoglio, Joan Darling, Robert F. Simon, Kirk Scott, Joan Tompkins
4. "Seven-Eleven" (10-4-74) Larry Hagman, John Larch, Chuck McCann, Karen Carlson, Albert Popwell, Jeanie Bell
5. "Anatomy of Two Rapes" (10-11-74) Rhonda Fleming, Angel Tompkins, Philip Carey, Hal Williams, Pat Morita, Damon Douglas, Joshua Shelley, Donald "Red" Barry, Eddie Firestone
6. "It's Only a Game" (10-25-74) Dane Clark, Patrick Wayne, Philip Thomas, Hector Elias, Peter Gonzales, Dan Ades, Mwako Cumbuka
7. "Fish, the Police Woman" (11-1-74) Conny Van Dyke, Marian Mercer, Morgan Woodward, Lester Rawlins, Sarina C. Grant, Ray Young, Marged Wakeley
8. "Flowers of Evil" (11-8-74) Laraine Stephens, Lynn Loring, Fay Spain, Meg Wyllie, Florence Lake, Elizabeth Kerr, Ann Morrison, Dick Balduzzi, Garry Walberg, Ysabel MacCloskey
9. "The Stalking of Joey Marr" (11-22-74) Monte Markham
10. "Requiem for Bored Wives" (11-29-74) Bob Crane, E. J. Peaker, W. L. LeGault, Della Reese, Jane Merrow, Theodore Wilson, Betty Anne Rees, Melendy Britt
11. "Smack" (12-6-74) William Shatner, Smokey Robinson
12. "The Child Buyers" (12-13-74) John Vernon, Sharon Farrell, Cliff Emmich, Doug Fowley, Arlene Golonka, Judy Lewis, Harry Bartell
13. "Shoefly" (12-20-74) Ed Nelson, Audrey Dalton, David White, Rory Calhoun, Murray MacLeod, Tony Young, Annette O'Toole, Robyn Hilton, Kandi Keith, Philip Pine, John Finnegan
14. "Target Black" (1-3-75) Ruby Dee, Warren Stevens, Pervis Atkins, Mary Alice, Terrence Locke, Alan Weeks, Eddie Ryder, Jason Wingreen, Karen Morley, Borah Silver
15. "Sidewinder" (1-17-75) Glenn Corbett, John P. Ryan
16. "Blast" (1-24-75) Robert Vaughn, Laraine Stephens, George Murdock, Joyce Jillson, Ned Romero, George Marshall, Robert Emhardt
17. "No Place to Hide" (1-31-75) David Selby, Stephen Young, Katherine Justice, Tom Rosqui, Spence Wil Dee, Lindsay Workman, Jim Malinda
18. "Nothing Left to Lose" (2-14-75) Patty Duke Astin, John Astin, Kathy Lloyd, Verne Rowe, Lee Paul, Patricia Barry, Dorothy Shay, Naomi Stevens, Victor Sen Yung,

Bruce Gordon
19. "The Company" (2-21-75) Paula Kelly, Shelley Berman, Rick Jason, Kaz Garas, Johnny Seven, Frank De Kova, Victor Holchak, Timothy Blake, Cedric Hardman, Jack Ryland, Jack Sheldon, John Crawford
20. "Ice" (2-28-75) Michael Parks
21. "Bloody Nose" (3-7-75) David Birney, Joyce Jameson, Joan Goodfellow, Eddie Egan, Jack Soo
22. "The Loner" (3-14-75) Don Meredith

[Continuing]


THE NIGHT STALKER

Surprisingly, this fantasy of a Chicago reporter who weekly unearths a monster ("The Doppleganger" incinerates its victims; "The Rakshasa" is an anti-Semitic killer) was a rousing success. The reason, as many were apt to point out, was that Darren McGavin at last came into his own as the rebellious, occult investigator hero. Fine continuing performances were delivered by Simon Oakland as the irascible editor Tony Vincenzo, Ruth McDevitt the eccentric social columnist, Jack Grinnage the fine arts reviewer.

The Regulars: Carl Kolchak, Darren McGavin; Anthony Vincenzo, Simon Oakland; Monique, Carol Ann Susi; Emily Cowles, Ruth McDevitt; Ron Updyke, Jack Grinnage.

The Episodes:

1. "Jack the Ripper" (9-13-74) Beatrice Colon
2. "Zombie" (9-20-74) Joseph Sirola, Earl Faison, Charles Aidman, John Fiedler, Antonio Fargas, Pauline Myers
3. "U.F.O." (9-27-74) James Gregory, Mary Wickes, Dick Van Patten, Tony Rizzo
4. "Vampire" (10-4-74) Kathleen Nolan, William Daniels, Suzanne Charny, John Doucette, Milt Kamen, Anne Whitfield
5. "Werewolf" (11-1-74) Eric Braeden, Nita Talbot, Lewis Charles, Henry Jones, Dick Gautier, Jackie Russell, Barry Cahill
6. "The Doppleganger" (11-8-74) Fred Beir, Philip Carey, Madlyn Rhue, David Doyle, Alice Backes
7. "The Devil's Platform" (11-15-74) Andrew Prine
8. "Bad Medicine" (11-29-74) Alice Ghostley, Victor Jory, Ramon Bieri, Richard Kiel, Marvin Kaplan
9. "The Spanish Moss Murderer" (12-6-74) Keenan Wynn, Severn Darden, Virginia Gregg, Randy Boone, Johnny Silver, Ned Glass, Richard Kiel, Maurice Marsac
10. "Matchemonedo" (12-13-74) William Smith, Michael Strong, John Alvin, Elaine Giftos, Michael Fox, Tom Drake, Robert Yuro
11. "The Rakshasa" (12-20-74) Phil Silvers, Benny Rubin,

Abraham Sofaer, Herb Vigran, Naomi Stevens, Shelly Novack, Eric Server

12. "Mr. R. I. N. G. " (1-20-75) Julie Adams, Bert Freed
13. "Primal Scream" (1-17-75) John Marley, Pat Harrington,
Lindsay Workman, Katharine Woodville, Jamie Farr,
Jeanie Bell, Barbara Rhoades, Byron Morrow, Vince How-
ard, Regis J. Cordic
14. "The Trevi Collection" (1-24-75) Nina Foch, Lara Parker,
Marvin Miller, Peter Leeds, Priscilla Morrill, Douglas V.
Fowley, Dick Bakalyan, Henry Slate
15. "Chopper" (1-31-75) Sharon Farrell, Jim Backus, Larry
Linville, Art Metrano, Frank Aletter, Jay Robinson,
Steven Franken
16. "Demon in Lace" (2-7-75) Andrew Prine, Keenan Wynn,
Carolyn Jones, Jackie Vernon, Kritina Holland, Carmen
Zapata, Maria Grimm, Benjamin Masters, Milton Parsons
17. "Legacy of Terror" (2-14-75) Ramon Bieri, Pippa Scott,
Erik Estrada, Sondra Currie, Carlos Romero, Victor
Campos, Sorrell Booke, Udana Power, Cal Bartlett, Er-
nesto Macias
18. "The Knightly Murders" (3-7-75) John Dehner, Hans Con-
ried, Lieux Dressier, Shug Fisher, Robert Emhardt, Don
Carter, Lucille Benson, Bryon O'Byrne, Sidney Clute
19. "The Youth Killer" (3-14-75) Demosthenes, Dwayne Hickman, Kathleen Freeman
20. "Sentry" (3-28-75) Kathie Browne, Albert Paulsen, Tom
Bosley, Frank Campanella, Frank Marth, Cliff Norton,
Margaret Avery, John Hoyt


THE ASCENT OF MAN

The late Dr. Jacob Bronowski's intellectual feast for public
television, this was a series of scientific dissertations as incredibly
complex as the hidden significance of a floor mosaic to a moving
re-enactment of the Galileo trial and a numbing indictment of scientific irresponsibility in the creation of an Auschwitz.

The Regulars: Anthony Hopkins, host.

The Episodes (telecast via PBS Tuesdays 8:30-9:30):

1. "Lower than the Angels" [I] (1-7-75) beginnings
2. "The Harvest of the Seasons" [II] (1-14-75) beginnings of
architecture
3. "The Grain in the Stone" [III] (1-21-75) use of tools
4. "The Hidden Structure" [IV] (1-28-75) beginning of chemistry
5. "The Music of the Spheres" [V] (2-4-75) mathematics
6. "The Starry Messenger" [VI] (2-11-75) trial of Galileo
7. "The Majestic Clockwork" [VII] (2-18-75) Newton and Einstein
8. "The Drive for Power" [VIII] (2-25-75) Industrial Revolution

9. "The Ladder of Creation" [IX] (3-4-75) Darwin and Wallace
10. "World Within World" [X] (3-11-75) atomic energy
11. "Knowledge or Certainty" [XI] (3-18-75) scientific knowledge and responsibility
12. "Generation Upon Generation" [XII] (3-25-75) Gregor Mendel
13. "The Long Childhood" [XIII] (4-1-75) a personal evaluation of twentieth century man

## BARETTA

Robert Blake is excellent as the unorthodox New York cop in this slick study of the 53rd precinct. The best of these early episodes--"Keep Your Eye on the Sparrow"--is a melancholy tale of a retarded modern day "Robin Hood." Other continuing performers are Tom Ewell as the owner and manager of the King Edward Hotel, where Baretta resides; Michael D. Roberts as the black pimp and police informant "Rooster" and Dana Elcar as the irritable Lieutenant Schiller. Roger Rosenblatt's New Republic (8 November 1975) piece on this series should be consulted.

The Regulars: Det. Tony Baretta, Robert Blake; Billy, Tom Ewell; Rooster, Michael D. Roberts; Lt. Shiller, Dana Elcar.

The Episodes:

1. "He'll Never See Daylight Again" (1-17-75) Madlyn Rhue, Andrew Prine, Timothy Carey, Lew Brown, Joseph Mascolo, George Loros
2. "The Five and a Half Pound Junkie" (1-24-75) Gerrit Graham, Ayn Ruymen, Mario Roccuzzo, Victor Argo, James L. Watkins, Sarah Cunningham
3. [unknown title] (1-31-75) Ann Coleman, Brock Peters, Ed Lauter, Severn Darden, Carole Cook, Bill McKinney
4. "If You Can't Pay the Price" (2-7-75) John Marley, Jan Merlin, Roy Jenson, Val Bisoglio, Bert Santos
5. "Half a Million Dollar Baby" (2-14-75) Ann Prentiss
6. "Ragtime Billy Peaches" (2-28-75) Richard A. Dysart, Meg Foster
7. "The Copelli Oath" (3-7-75) John Friedrich, Marie Lillo, George DiCenzo, Kathy Beller, Joe Stefano, Richard Cox
8. "Walk Like You Talk" (3-14-75) Michael Parks, Lee de Broux
9. "The Mansion" (4-2-75) Allyn Ann McLerie, Eddie Fontaine, John Durren, John Sylvester White, George Loros, Frank Christi, Sondra Blake
10. "Keep Your Eye on the Sparrow" (4-9-75) Burt Young, Gene Krischer, Shepherd Sanders, Jerry Hausner
11. "The Secret of Terry Lake" (4-16-75) Margot Kidder, Norman Cole, Nicholas Colasanto, M. Emmet Walsh, Joe Santos, Rickey Johnson

12. "This Ain't My Bag" (4-30-75) Michael Murphy, Keene Curtis, Maggie Sullivan, Cranville Van Dusen

[Continuing]


ARCHER

Phenomenally short-lived (even considering its time) private detective series with Brian Keith as the hero of Ross MacDonald's mysteries, Lew Archer.

The Regulars: Lew Archer, Brian Keith; Lieutenant Brighton, John P. Ryan.

The Episodes:

1. "The Turkish Connection" (1-30-75) Marjoe Gortner, Jan Clayton, Dori Brenner, Zitta Kozann, Barney Phillips, Richard Kelton
2. "The Arsonist" (2-6-75)
3. "The Body Beautiful" (2-13-75) Kim Darby, Archie Moore, Neva Patterson
4. "Shades of Blue" (2-20-75)
5. "The Vanished Man" (3-6-75) Anne Francis, Walter Scott, Clifford David, Don Porter, Karen Carlson, Victoria Young
6. "Blood Money" (3-13-75) Dane Clark


CARIBE

Not the balmy locale of the Caribbean could salvage this Quinn Martin law-and-order entry, with Stacy Keach (a brilliant Shakespearean actor, from whom one expected no condescension to the banalities of series television) a member of a police force (Carl Franklin his colleague; Robert Mandan their chief). A single episode has Keach managing to avert a rocket headed for the White House while simultaneously being placed before a firing squad.

The Regulars: Ben Logan, Stacy Keach; Mark Walters, Carl Franklin; Rawlings, Robert Mandan.

The Episodes:

1. "The Plastic Connection" (2-17-75) Jack Ging, Paul Jenkins, Julie Adams, Ellen Weston, Ray Danton, Harvey Jason
2. "Vanished" (2-24-75) Joanna Pettet, Jason Evers
3. "The Survivor" (3-3-75) George Grizzard, Peter Mark Richman, John Orchard, Lynne Marta, Bernard Ivey, William Joyce
4. "The Mercenary" (3-10-75) Rudy Solari, Marlyn Mason
5. "Lady Killer" (3-17-75) Monte Markham, Linda Marsh,

Judy Pace, James Callahan, East Carlo, Jim Davis
6. "Flowers of Death" (3-24-75) Glenn Corbett, Darlene Carr, Ja'net Du Bois, Will Kuluva, James McMullan, David McLean
7. "Murder in Paradise" (3-31-75) Robert Leslie, Peter Haskell
8. "School for Killers" (4-7-75) Stuart Whitman, Robert Yuro, Claudia Jennings, Eugene Peterson, Hal Williams, Luke Halpin
9. "One Second to Doom" (4-14-75) Joanna Miles, Larry Gates, Charles Drake, Keith Andes, James Olson, Benson Carroll
10. "The Patriots" (4-21-75) Maurice Evans, Edward Binns, Patrick Macnee, Alan Calliou, Lisa Eilbacher, Christopher Cary
11. "Counterfeit Killer" (4-28-75) Diana Muldaur, Robert Loggia, Oscar Beregi, Dabney Coleman, Don Moody, Claire Brennen
12. "The Assassin" (5-5-75) Paul Stewart, Harris Yulin, Tisha Sterling, Lou Gossett, Melinda Fee, Charles Robinson
13. "Assault on the Calavera" (5-12-75) Chris Robinson, Simon Scott, Fay Wray, Robert Emhardt, Sheila Larken, Richard O'Brien

THE LAW

The best lawyer series in television history began as a harrowing journey through the legal process with a telefeature (telecast October 22, 1974) in which a public defender (Judd Hirsch as Murray Stone) pleads the case of an accused murderer. So much human emptiness in the hurricane: the plea bargaining, the humiliating ritual preceding incarceration, vituperative lawyer has-beens, the attorney-celebrity who callously accepts but brutally sensationalizes his consummate case; in the backdrop, the defendant waiting out his time for nought. As the recalcitrant Stone, Hirsch performs with a mercurial intensity. Hirsch's grand match, both in the telefeature and in terms of performance, is Barbara Baxley as a sadistic lady judge. As for the concluding credits of the teleplays-- no background music plays; all that is heard is conversation or the courtroom commotion against which so many travesties have been sadly played.

The Regulars: Atty. Murray Stone, Judd Hirsch; Van Lorn, Alex Nicol; Michael, Fiona Guinness.

The Episodes:

1. "Complaint Amended" (3-19-75) Annazette Chase, Howard Platt, Dori Brenner, Michael Bell, George Gaynes, Alex Hentelhoff
2. "Prior Consent" (3-26-75) Tyne Daly, Michael McGuire, Robert Hogan, Dick O'Neill, George Wyner, Carol Lawson,

Ben Piazza, Ben Hammer, Grayland R. Gleason, M. Emmet Walsh
3. "Special Circumstances" (4-16-75) Nicholas Colasanto, Jim Antonio, Eugene Roche

SPECIAL PROGRAMMING

This section contains programming appearing
through a season or seasons on irregular days
and times.


THE NATIONAL GEOGRAPHIC SOCIETY SPECIALS

The Society has graced television for eleven years by way
of its documentaries, showing a consummate use of the camera in
capturing a subtle, alternately thrilling form of drama in nature,
science and in history.

The Episodes:

First Season

1. "Americans on Everest" [narrated by Orson Welles] (9-10-
   65 CBS)
2. "Miss Goodall and the Wild Chimpanzees" [narrated by Orson
   Welles] (12-22-65 CBS)
3. "The Voyage of the Brigantine Yankee" [narrated by Orson
   Welles] (2-11-66 CBS)
4. "The World of Jacques-Yves Cousteau" [narrated by Orson
   Welles] (4-28-66 CBS)

Second Season

5. "Dr. Leakey and the Dawn of Man" [narrated by Alexander
   Scourby] (11-5-66 CBS)
6. "The Hidden World" [narrated by Alexander Scourby] (12-13-
   66 CBS)
7. "Alaska!" [narrated by Alexander Scourby] (2-7-67 CBS)
8. "Yankee Sails Across Europe" [narrated by Alexander Scourby]
   (4-8-67 CBS)

Third Season

9. "Grizzly!" [narrated by Alexander Scourby] (11-1-67 CBS)
10. "Winged World" [narrated by Alexander Scourby] (12-11-67
    CBS)

11. "Amazon" [narrated by Alexander Scourby]  (2-20-68 CBS)
12. "The Lonely Dorymen: Portugal's Men of the Sea" [narrated by Alexander Scourby]  (4-16-68 CBS)

## Fourth Season

13. "America's Wonderlands: The National Parks" [narrated by Alexander Scourby]  (10-23-68 CBS)
14. "Reptiles and Amphibians" [narrated by Joseph Campanella]  (12-3-68 CBS)
15. "Australia: The Timeless Land" [narrated by Alexander Scourby]  (2-18-69 CBS)
16. "Polynesian Adventure" [narrated by Alexander Scourby]  (4-15-69 CBS)

## Fifth Season

17. "The Mystery of Animal Behavior" [narrated by Joseph Campanella]  (10-14-69 CBS)
18. "Siberia: The Endless Horizon" [narrated by Joseph Campanella]  (12-2-69 CBS)
19. "Wild River" [narrated by Joseph Campanella]  (2-10-70 CBS)
20. "Holland Against the Sea" [narrated by Joseph Campanella]  (4-12-70 CBS)

## Sixth Season

21. "Zoos of the World" [narrated by Joseph Campanella]  (10-13-70 CBS)
22. "Ethiopia: The Hidden Empire" [narrated by Joseph Campanella]  (12-2-70 CBS)
23. "The Great Mojave Desert" [narrated by Joseph Campanella]  (2-13-71 CBS)
24. "Journey to the High Arctic" [narrated by Joseph Campanella]  (4-13-71 CBS)

## Seventh Season

25. "Monkeys, Apes, and Man" [narrated by Leslie Nielsen]  (10-12-71 CBS)
26. "The Last Tribes of the Mindanao" [narrated by Leslie Nielsen]  (1-12-72 CBS)
27. "Man of the Serengeti" [narrated by Leslie Nielsen]  (2-22-72 CBS)
28. "The Last Vikings" [narrated by Leslie Nielsen]  (3-27-72 CBS)

## Eighth Season

29. "Strange Creatures of the Night" [narrated by Leslie Nielsen]  (1-17-73 CBS)
30. "The Violent Earth" [narrated by Leslie Nielsen]  (2-15-73 CBS)

31. "The Haunted West" [narrated by Leslie Nielsen] (4-12-73 CBS)

## Ninth Season

32. "Wind Raiders of the Sahara" [narrated by Leslie Nielsen] (9-6-73 ABC)
33. "Journey to the Outer Limits" [narrated by Leslie Nielsen] (1-10-74 ABC)
34. "The Big Cats" [narrated by Leslie Nielsen] (3-15-74 ABC)
35. "The Bushmen of the Kalahari" [narrated by Leslie Nielsen] (5-17-74 ABC)

## Tenth Season

36. "The Incredible Machine" [narrated by E. G. Marshall] (10-28-75 PBS)
37. "This Britain: Heritage of the Sea" (12-9-75 PBS)
38. "The Search for the Great Apes" [narrated by Richard Kiley] (1-13-76 PBS)
39. "The Animals Nobody Loved" [narrated by Hal Holbrook] (2-10-76 PBS)

## Eleventh Season

40. "Treasure!" [narrated by Alexander Scourby] (12-7-76 PBS)
41. "Voyage of the Hokule'a" [narrated by E. G. Marshall] (1-18-77 PBS)


## THE HALLMARK HALL OF FAME

The Episodes [chronicled from the fifth season]:

1. "The Corn Is Green" [by Emlyn Williams] (1-8-56 Sunday 4:00-5:30 NBC) Carmen Mathews, Melville Cooper, Eva Le Gallienne, Joan Lorring, John Kerr
2. "The Good Fairy" [adapted by Jean Kerr from Ferenc Molnar's comedy] (2-5-56 Sunday 4:00-5:30 NBC) Julie Harris, Walter Slezak, Roddy McDowall, Cyril Ritchard
3. "The Taming of the Shrew" (3-18-56 Sunday 4:00-5:30 NBC) Maurice Evans, Diane Cilento, Lilli Palmer, Philip Bourneuf
4. "The Cradle Song" [adapted by James Costigan from the drama by Gregorio Martinez Sierra and his wife Maria] (5-6-56 Sunday 4:00-5:30 NBC) Judith Anderson, Evelyn Varden, Siobhan McKenna, Barry Jones, Deidre Owen, Anthony Franciosa

## Sixth Season

5. "Born Yesterday" (10-28-56 Sunday 7:30-9:00 NBC) Paul Douglas, Mary Martin, Arthur Hill
6. "Man and Superman" (11-25-56 Sunday 9:00-10-30 NBC)

[George Bernard Shaw's comedy; directed by George Schaefer]
Maurice Evans, Joan Greenwood, Walter Greaza

7. "The Little Foxes" [adapted by Robert Hartung from the Lillian Hellman play] (12-16-56 Sunday 7:30-9:00 NBC) Greer Garson, Franchot Tone, Sidney Blackmer, E. G. Marshall, Eileen Heckart

8. "The Lark" [adapted by James Costigan from the Lillian Hellman version of the Jean Anouilh play] (2-10-57 Sunday 9:00-10:30 NBC) Julie Harris, Boris Karloff, Basil Rathbone, Denholm Elliott, Eli Wallach, Jack Warden

9. "There Shall Be No Night" [adapted by Morton Wishengrad from the Robert E. Sherwood play] (3-17-57 Sunday 7:30-9:00 NBC) Charles Boyer, Katherine Cornell, Ray Walston, Theodore Bikel, Phyllis Love

10. "The Yeoman of the Guard" [adaptation of the Gilbert and Sullivan play] (4-10-57 Wednesday 8:30-10:00 NBC) Alfred Drake, Celeste Holm, Bill Hayes, Barbara Cook

Seventh Season

11. "The Green Pastures" [adapted by Marc Connelly from his play] (10-17-57) William Warfield, Eddie Anderson, Frederick O'Neal, Earle Hyman, Terry Carter

12. "On Borrowed Time" (11-17-57 Sunday 5:30-7:00 NBC) Beulah Bondi, Claude Rains, Ed Wynn, Dennis Kohler

13. "Twelfth Night" (12-15-57 Sunday 6:30-8:00 NBC) Maurice Evans, Rosemary Harris, Howard Morris, Max Adrian

14. "Hans Brinker or the Silver Skates" (2-9-58 Sunday 6:30-8:00 NBC) Tab Hunter, Peggy King, Basil Rathbone, Dick Button, Carmen Matthews, Jarmila Novotina

15. "Little Moon of Alban" [by James Costigan] (3-24-58 Monday 9:30-11:00 NBC) Julie Harris, George Peppard, Christopher Plummer, Barry Jones, Frank Conroy

16. "Dial M for Murder" [by Frederick Knott] (4-25-58 Fri. 8:30-10:00 NBC) Maurice Evans, John Williams, Rosemary Harris

Eighth Season

17. "Johnny Belinda" [adapted by Theodore Apstein from the Elmer Harris play] (10-13-58 Monday 9:30-11:00 NBC) Julie Harris, Christopher Plummer, Victor Jory

18. "Kiss Me, Kate" (11-20-58 Thurs. NBC) Alfred Drake, Patricia Morison, Julie Wilson, Jack Klugman, Bill Hayes

19. "Berkeley Square" [adapted by Theodore Apstein from the John L. Balderston play] (2-5-59 Thursday 9:30-11:00 NBC) John Kerr, Jeannie Carson, Edna Best, Janet Munro, Mildred Trares, Norah Howard, John Colicos, Jerome Kitty, Winston Ross, Frances Reid, Sheila Coonan

20. "The Green Pastures" [restaged; by Marc Connelly] (3-23-59 Monday 9:30-11:00 NBC) William Warfield, Eddie Anderson, Earle Hyman, Frederick O'Neal, Terry Carter, Butterfly McQueen, Estelle Hemsley, Sheila Guyse, Muriel Rahn, Avon Long, William Dillard, Dots Johnson, Mantan

Moreland
21. "Ah, Wilderness!" [by Robert Hartung from the Eugene
O'Neill comedy] (4-28-59 Tuesday 9:30-11:00 NBC) Helen
Hayes, Lloyd Nolan, Burgess Meredith, Betty Field, Lee
Kinsolving, Dolores Sutton, Abigail Kellogg, Nicholas Pry-
or, Roy Poole, Norman Feld

Ninth Season

22. "Winterset" [adapted by Robert Hartung from the Maxwell
Anderson play] (10-26-59 Monday 9:30-11:00 NBC) Don
Murray, Piper Laurie, George C. Scott, Charles Bick-
ford, Martin Balsam, George Mathews, Anatol Winogra-
doff
23. "A Doll's House" [adapted by James Costigan from the Henrik
Ibsen drama] (11-15-59 Sunday 7:30-9:00 NBC) Julie
Harris, Christopher Plummer, Eileen Heckart, Jason Robards Jr., Hume Cronyn
24. "The Hallmark Christmas Festival" (12-13-59 Sunday 5:30-
6:30 NBC) Act I. "The Borrowed Christmas" [by Ludwig
Bemelman] Walter Slezak, Jules Munshin; Act II. "The
Ice Princess" [skating fantasy with Dick Button]; Act III.
"The Obernkirchen Children's Choir; Act IV. "The Story
of the Nativity" ["painted on light" by Andre Girard; with
the voice of Judith Anderson]
25. "The Tempest" [adapted by John Edward Friend from the
Shakespeare play] (2-3-60 Wednesday 7:30-9:00 NBC)
Maurice Evans, Richard Burton, Tom Poston, Liam Redmond, Ronald Radd, William H. Bassett, Geoffrey Lumb,
William Le Massena, Paul Ballantyne, Chris Gampel
26. "The Cradle Song" [restaged; adapted by James Costigan from
the drama by Gregorio Martinez Sierra and his wife Maria]
(4-10-60 Sunday 6:30-8:00 NBC) Helen Hayes, Judith Anderson, Siobhan McKenna, Charles Bickford, Geoffrey
Horne, Kathy Willard, Joanna Roos, Mildred Trares,
Deidre Owen, Zohra Lampert, Katharine Raht, Val Avery,
Kate Harrington
27. "Captain Brassbound's Conversion" [adapted by Theodore Ap-
stein from the George Bernard Shaw comedy] (5-2-60
Monday 9:30-11:00 NBC) Greer Garson, Christopher Plum-
mer, Loring Smith, Felix Aylmer, Liam Redmond, George
Rose, Henry Brandon, Howard Caine, Robert Carricart,
Harry Ellerbe, Chris Gampel, Patrick Westwood, Douglas
Henderson, Robert Redford, William Lanteau

Tenth Season

28. "Shangri-La" [musical adaptation of the James Hilton novel,
with music by Harry Warren and book by Jerome Lawrence and Robert E. Lee] (10-24-60 Monday 9:30-11:00
NBC) Claude Rains, Alice Ghostley, Richard Basehart,
Marisa Pavan, Gene Nelson, Helen Gallagher, John Abbott, James Valentine

29. "Macbeth" [restaged] (11-20-60 Sunday 6:00-8:00 NBC)
    Maurice Evans, Judith Anderson, Michael Hordern, Ian
    Bennen, Felix Aylmer, Malcolm Keen, George Rose, Megs
    Jenkins, Jeremy Brett, William Hutt, Valerie Taylor,
    April Olrich, Anita Sharp-Bolster, Charles Carson, Trader
    Faulkner
30. "Golden Child" [original Christmas folk opera from the Crea-
    tive Workshop of the University of Iowa, with music by
    Philip Bezanson and libretto by Paul Engle] (12-16-60
    Friday 8:30-10:00 NBC) Patricia Neway, Brenda Lewis,
    Jerome Hines, Stephen Douglass, Judy Sanford, Enrico
    DiGiuseppe, David Lloyd, Chester Ludgin, Patricia Brooks,
    John Wheeler
31. "Time Remembered" [adapted by Theodore Apstein from the
    Patricia Moyes' version of the Jean Anouilh comedy]
    (2-7-61 Tuesday 7:30-9:00 NBC) Christopher Plummer,
    Edith Evans, Janet Munro, Barry Jones, Paul Hartman,
    Sig Arno, Rex O'Malley, George Ebeling, Iggie Wolfington,
    Sibyl Bowan
32. "Give Us Barabbas!" [by Henry Denker] (3-24-61 Sunday
    6:30-8:00 NBC) James Daly, Kim Hunter, Dennis King,
    Robert Carroll, Leonardo Cimino, Ludwig Donath, Keir
    Dullea, Muni Seroff, John Gerstad, Kermit Murdock,
    Allen Nourse, Eric Sinclair, John Straub, Richard Thomas,
    Theodore Tenley, Toni Darney
33. "The Joke and the Valley" [by Jerry C. McNeely] (5-5-61
    Friday 8:30-10:00 NBC) Dean Stockwell, Thomas Mitchell,
    Keenan Wynn, Russell Collins, Logan Ramsey, Mildred
    Trares, Frank Tweddell, Daniel F. Keyes, June Prud-
    'homme, Walter Neal, Leora Thatcher

## Eleventh Season

34. "Macbeth" [repeat of episode of 11/20/60] (10-20-61 Friday
    8:30-10:30 NBC)
35. "Victoria Regina" [adapted by Robert Hartung from the play
    by Laurence Housman] (11-30-61 Thursday 9:30-11:00
    NBC) Julie Harris, James Donald, Basil Rathbone, Felix
    Aylmer, Pamela Brown, Isabel Jeans, Barry Jones, Inga
    Swenson, Olga Fabian, George Turner, Sorrell Booke,
    Louis Edmonds, Geoffrey Lumb, Francis Compton
36. "Arsenic and Old Lace" (2-5-62 Monday 9:30-11:00 NBC)
    Tony Randall, Mildred Natwick, Dorothy Stickney, Boris
    Karloff, George Voskovec, Tom Bosley

## Twelfth Season

37. "Teahouse of the August Moon" [adapted by Robert Hartung
    from the play by George Patrick] (10-26-62 Friday 8:30-
    10:00 NBC) John Forsythe, David Wayne, Miyoshi Umeki,
    Paul Ford, William Le Massena, Fred Kareman, Osceola
    Archer
38. "Cyrano de Bergerac" [adapted by Robert Hartung from the

Brian Hooker translation of the Edmond Rostand drama]
(12-6-62 Thursday 9:30-11:00 NBC) Christopher Plummer,
Hope Lange, Donald Harron, George Rose, John Colicos,
William Hutt

39. "Pygmalion" [adapted by Robert Hartung from the George
Bernard Shaw play] (2-6-63 Wednesday 7:30-9:00 NBC)
Julie Harris, James Donald, Gladys Cooper, John Wil-
liams, George Rose, Dorothy Sands, John D. Irving

40. "The Invincible Mr. Disraeli" [by James Lee] (4-4-63
Thursday 8:30-10:00 NBC) Trevor Howard, Greer Garson,
Eric Berry, Denholm Elliott, Hurd Hatfield, Geoffrey Keen,
Kate Reid, Frederick Worlock, Joan White

Thirteenth Season

41. "The Tempest" [repeat of episode of 2/3/60] (10-20-63
Sunday 6:00-7:30 NBC)

42. "The Patriots" [by Sidney Kingsley] (11-15-63 Friday 9:30-
11:00 NBC) Charleton Heston, John Fraser, Peggy Ann
Garner, Howard St. John

43. "A Cry of Angels" [by Sherman Yellen] (12-15-63 Sunday
4:00-5:00 NBC) Walter Slezak, Maureen O'Hara, Hurd
Hatfield, Hermione Gingold

44. "Abe Lincoln in Illinois" (2-5-64 Wednesday 7:30-9:00 NBC)
Jason Robards Jr., Kate Reid, James Broderick

45. "Little Moon of Alban" [restaged; by James Costigan] (3-18-
64 Wednesday 7:30-9:00 NBC) Dirk Bogarde, Julie Harris,
Stephen Brooks, Liam Redmond, Ruth White, Alan Webb

Fourteenth Season

46. "The Fantasticks" [adapted by Robert Hartung from the musi-
cal by Tom Jones and Harvey L. Schmidt] (10-18-64
Sunday 10:00-11:00 NBC) John Davidson, Susan Watson,
Ricardo Montalban, Bert Lahr, Stanley Holloway

47. "The Other World of Winston Churchill" [documentary, narrated by Paul Scofield] (11-30-64 Monday 10:00-11:00 NBC)

48. "The Magnificent Yankee" [adapted by Robert Hartung from
the Emmet Lavery biography] (1-28-65 Thursday 9:30-
11:00 NBC) Alfred Lunt, Lynn Fontanne, Eduard Franz,
Robert Emhardt, James Daly, Brenda Forbes, Walter
Moulder, Ion Berger, Dennis Cooney, Lee Goodman, William Griffis, Nan McFarland, Donald Symington

49. "The Holy Terror" [by James Lee] (4-7-65 Wednesday 7:30-
9:00 NBC) Julie Harris

Fifteenth Season

50. "Eagle in a Cage" [by George Ross] (10-20-65 Wednesday
7:30-9:00 NBC) Trevor Howard, James Daly, Pamela
Franklin

51. "Inherit the Wind" [by Jerome Lawrence and Robert E. Lee]
(11-18-65 Thursday 9:30-11:00 NBC) Melvyn Douglas,

Ed Begley, Diane Baker, Murray Hamilton

52. "Lamp at Midnight" [adapted by Robert Hartung from the play by Barrie Stavis] (4-27-66 Wednesday 7:30-9:00) Melvyn Douglas, David Wayne, Michael Hordern, Hurd Hatfield, George Voskovec, Kim Hunter, Thayer David, Gaylord Cavallaro, Richard Woods, House Jameson, Ted van Griethuysen

## Sixteenth Season

53. "Barefoot in Athens" [adapted by Robert Hartung from the play by Maxwell Anderson] (11-11-66 Friday 9:30-11:00 NBC) Geraldine Page, Peter Ustinov, Salome Jens, Anthony Quayle, Eric Berry

54. "Blithe Spirit" [Noel Coward's play] (12-7-66 Wednesday 7:30-9:00 NBC) Dirk Bogarde, Rosemary Harris, Rachel Roberts, Ruth Gordon

55. "Anastasia" [adapted by John Edward Friend from the stage play by Guy Bolton] (3-17-67 Friday 9:30-11:00 NBC) Lynn Fontanne, Julie Harris, Charles D. Gray, Paul Roebling

56. "Soldier in Love" [by Jerome Ross] (4-26-67 Wednesday 7:30-9:00 NBC) Jean Simmons, Keith Michell, Basil Rathbone, Claire Bloom

## Seventeenth Season

57. "A Bell for Adano" [adapted by Roger O. Hirson from the John Hersey novel] (11-11-67 Saturday 7:30-9:00 NBC) John Forsythe, Murray Hamilton, Kathleen Widdoes, Peter Brandon, Robert Ellenstein, Tom Skerritt

58. "St. Joan" [adapted by Robert Hartung from the George Bernard Shaw drama] (12-4-67 Monday 9:00-11:00 NBC) Genevieve Bujold, Roddy McDowall, Maurice Evans, James Donald, James Daly, Theodore Bikel, Raymond Massey, David Birney, Leo Genn, George Rose

59. "Elizabeth the Queen" [adapted by John Edward Friend from the Maxwell Anderson play] (1-31-68 Wednesday 7:30-9:00 NBC) Judith Anderson, Charlton Heston, Alan Webb, Michael Allinson, Harry Townes, Anne Rogers

60. "The Admirable Crichton" [adapted by Robert Hartung from the James M. Barrie satire] (5-2-68 Thursday 8:30-10:00 NBC) Bill Travers, Virginia McKenna, Laurence Naismith, Janet Munro, Richard Easton, Pamela Brown

## Eighteenth Season

61. "A Punt, a Pass, and a Prayer" (11-20-68 Wednesday 7:30-9:00 NBC) Hugh O'Brian, Shelly Novack, Don DeFore, Betsy Palmer, Ralph Meeker, Nancy Dussault, Bert Freed

62. "Pinocchio" [adapted by Ernest Kinoy from the Carlo Collodi story; songs by Walter Marks] (12-8-68 Sunday 7:00-8:30) Burl Ives, Peter Noone, Anita Gillette, Mort Marshall,

Charlotte Rae, Pierre Epstein
63. "Teacher, Teacher" [by Allan E. Sloane] (2-5-69 Wednesday
7:30-9:00 NBC) David McCallum, Ossie Davis, George
Grizzard, Billy Schulman, Anthony Jones
64. "Give Us Barabbas!" [by Henry Denker; repeat of episode of
3/24/61] (3-28-69 Friday 8:30-10:00 NBC)

Nineteenth Season

65. "The File on Devlin" [adapted by Michael Dyne and Edward
Essex from the novel by Catherine Gaskin] (11-21-69
Friday 8:30-10:00 NBC) David McCallum, Judith Anderson,
Elizabeth Ashley, Helmut Dantine
66. "The Littlest Angel" [musical adaptation of the Charles Taze-
well story; songs by Lan O'Kun] (12-6-69 Saturday 7:30-
9:00 NBC) Johnnie Whitaker, Fred Gwynne, Cab Calloway,
Tony Randall, John McGiver, Connie Stevens, James Coco,
George Rose
67. "A Storm in Summer" [by Rod Serling] (2-6-70 Friday 8:30-
10:00 NBC) Peter Ustinov, N'Gai Dixon, Peter Bonerz,
Marlyn Mason, Penny Santon, Frances Robinson
68. "Neither Are We Enemies" [by Henry Denker] (3-13-70 Friday 8:30-10:00 NBC) Van Heflin, Kristoffer Tabori, J. D.
Cannon, Ed Begley, Kate Reid, Leonard Frey

Twentieth Season

69. "Hamlet" [adapted by John Barton from the Shakespeare play]
(11-17-70 Tuesday 9:00-11:00 NBC) Richard Chamberlain,
Margaret Leighton, John Gielgud, Michael Redgrave,
Richard Johnson, Claran Maddon, Martin Shaw, Nicholas
Jones
70. "The Price" [adapted by Arthur Miller from his own play]
(2-3-71 Wednesday 7:30-9:00 NBC) George C. Scott,
Colleen Dewhurst, David Burns, Barry Sullivan
71. "Gideon" [adapted by Robert Hartung from the play by Paddy
Chayefsky] (3-26-71 Friday 8:30-10:00 NBC) Peter Usti-
nov, Jose Ferrer, Arnold Moss, Little Egypt, Eric
Christmas, Booth Colman, Harry Davis

Twenty-first Season

72. "The Snow Goose" [by Paul Gallico from his novella] (11-15-
71 Monday 8:00-9:00 NBC) Richard Harris, Jenny Agutter,
Graham Crowden, Ludmilla Nova, Freda Bamford, Noel
Johnson, William Marlowe
73. "All the Way Home" [by Tad Mosel] (12-1-71 Wednesday
8:30-10:00 NBC) Joanne Woodward, Richard Kiley, Pat
Hingle, Eileen Heckart, James Woods, Shane Nickerson,
Betty Garde, Barney Hughes
74. "The Littlest Angel" [repeat of episode of 12/6/69] (12-12-
71 Sunday 7:30-9:00 NBC)
75. "Love! Love! Love!" [variety program with Robert Wagner,

Mac Davis, Helen Reddy and the singing group Bread] (2-8-72 Tuesday 7:30-8:30 NBC)

76. "Harvey" [the Mary Chase play] (3-22-72 Wednesday 8:30-10:00 NBC) James Stewart, Helen Hayes, John McGiver, Marian Halley, Richard Mulligan, Jesse White, Arlene Francis, Madeline Kahn, Martin Gabel, Fred Gwynne, Dorothy Blackburn

## Twenty-second Season

77. "The Hands of Cormac Joyce" (11-17-72 Friday 8:30-10:00 NBC) Stephen Boyd, Colleen Dewhurst, Dominick Guard, Cyril Cusack, Deryck Barnes, Lynette Floyd
78. "The Man Who Came to Dinner" [adapted by Bill Persky and Sam Denoff from the play by Moss Hart and George S. Kaufman] (11-29-72 Wednesday 8:30-10:00 NBC) Orson Welles, Lee Remick, Joan Collins, Peter Haskell, Edward Andrews, Don Knotts, Mary Wickes, Michael Gough, Marty Feldman, Marcella Markham, Anita Sharp
79. "The Small Miracle [by Paul Gallico] (4-11-74 Wed. 8:30-10:00 NBC) Vittorio de Sica, Raf Vallone

## Twenty-third Season

80. "Lisa, Bright and Dark" (11-28-73 Wednesday 8:30-10:00 NBC) John Forsythe, Anne Baxter, Kay Lenz
81. "The Country Girl" [Clifford Odets play] (2-5-74 Wednesday 8:30-10:00 NBC) Jason Robards, Shirley Knight Hopkins, George Grizzard
82. "Crown Matrimonial" [by Royce Ryton] (4-3-74 Wednesday 8:30-10:00 NBC) Greer Garson, Peter Barkworth

## Twenty-fourth Season

83. "Brief Encounter" [Noel Coward play] (11-12-74 Tuesday 8:30-10:00 NBC) Sophia Loren, Richard Burton
84. "The Gathering Storm" [from Winston Churchill memoirs] (11-29-74 Friday 8:30-10:00 NBC) Richard Burton, Virginia McKenna, Ian Bannen, Robert Hardy, Ian Ogilvy, Clive Francis
85. "All Creatures Great and Small" [adapted by Hugh Whitemore from the James Herriot novel] (2-4-75 Tuesday 8:30-10:00 NBC) Simon Ward, Anthony Hopkins, Lisa Harrow, Brian Stirner, John Collin, Burt Palmer

[Continuing]

# THEATRE '62

This series of specials commemorated the film legacy of producer and scenarist David O. Selznick.

The Episodes [via CBS television]:

1. "The Spiral Staircase" (10-4-61) Elizabeth Montgomery,
   Lillian Gish, Gig Young, Edie Adams, Eddie Albert
2. "Intermezzo" (11-19-61) Jean Pierre Aumont, Ingrid Thulin,
   Teresa Wright
3. "Notorious" (12-10-61) Joseph Cotten, Barbara Rush,
   George Grizzard, Cathleen Nesbitt
4. "The Farmer's Daughter" (1-14-62) Lee Remick, Peter
   Lawford, Charles Bickford, Murray Hamilton, Jerome
   Cowan, Cornelia Otis Skinner
5. "Spellbound" (2-11-62) Hugh O'Brian, Maureen O'Hara
6. "The Paradine Case" (3-11-62) Viveca Lindfors, Richard
   Basehart, Boris Karloff
7. "Rebecca" (4-8-62) James Mason, Joan Hackett, Nina Foch,
   Lloyd Bochner

## THE DUPONT SHOW OF THE MONTH

### First Season

1. "Crescendo" [an American musical panorama, featuring Rex
   Harrison; produced by Paul Gregory] (9-29-57 Sunday
   9:00-10:30 CBS) Julie Andrews, Diahann Carroll, Louis
   Armstrong, Benny Goodman, Lizzie Miles, Stanley Hollo-
   way, Eddie Arnold, Peggy Lee, Mahalia Jackson, Stubby
   Kaye, Sonny James, Turk Murphy, Dinah Washington
2. "The Prince and the Pauper" [adapted by Leslie Slote from
   the Mark Twain classic] (10-28-57 Monday 9:30-11:00
   CBS) Rex Thompson, Johnny Washbrook, Rosemary Harris, Sir Cedric Hardwicke, Christopher Plummer, Hurd
   Hatfield, John Carradine
3. "Beyond This Place" [adapted by Vance Bourjaily from the
   Archibald Joseph Cronin murder mystery] (11-25-57
   Monday 9:30-11:00 CBS) Farley Granger, Peggy Ann Garner, Shelley Winters
4. "Junior Miss" [a new version of the 1941 Broadway play derived from Sally Benson's stories, with songs by Burton
   Lane and lyrics by Dorothy Fields] (12-20-57 Friday
   7:30-9:00 CBS) Carol Lynley, Don Ameche, Joan Bennett,
   David Wayne, Diana Lynn, Paul Ford
5. "The Bridge of San Luis Rey" [adapted by Ludi Claire from
   the Thornton Wilder novel] (1-21-58 Tuesday 9:30-11:00
   CBS) Judith Anderson, Rita Gam, Hume Cronyn, Viveca
   Lindfors, Kurt Kasznar, Eva La Gallienne, Steven Hill,
   Theodore Bikel, Peter Cookson
6. "Aladdin" [a musical version with music and lyrics by Cole
   Porter; book by S. J. Perelman; choreography by Rod
   Alexander; music direction by Robert Emmett Dolan; cos-
   tumes by Irene Sharaff] (2-21-58 Friday 7:30-9:00 CBS)
   Cyril Ritchard, Sal Mineo, Basil Rathbone, Geoffrey

Holder, Una Merkel, Howard Morris, Anna Maria Alberghetti

7. "A Tale of Two Cities" [adapted by Michael Dyne from the Charles Dickens classic; directed by Robert Mulligan] (3-27-58 Thursday 9:30-11:00 CBS)  Eric Portman, James Donald, Gracie Fields, Agnes Moorehead, Denholm Elliott, Fritz Weaver, Walter Fitzgerald, Rosemary Harris, Alfred Ryder, George C. Scott

8. "The Red Mill" [adapted by Robert Alan Arthur from the Victor Herbert operetta]  (4-19-58 Saturday 7:30-9:00 CBS) Shirley Jones, Donald O'Connor, Harpo Marx, Evelyn Rudie, Mike Nichols and Elaine May

9. "Wuthering Heights" [adapted by James Costigan from the Emily Brontë classic]  (5-9-58 Friday 9:30-11:00 CBS) Richard Burton, Yvonne Furneaux, Angela Thornton, John Colicos, Cathleen Nesbitt, Denholm Elliott, Barry Jones

10. "The Member of the Wedding" [adapted by Jacqueline Babbin and Audrey Gellen from the Carson McCullers play; directed by Robert Mulligan; produced by David Susskind] (6-12-58 Thursday 9:30-11:00 CBS)  Collin Wilcox, Dennis Kohler, Claudia McNeil

## Second Season

11. "Harvey" [adapted by Jacqueline Babbin and Audrey Gellen from the play by Mary Ellen Chase]  (9-22-58 Monday 9:30-11:00 CBS)  Art Carney, Marion Lorne, Elizabeth Montgomery, Loring Smith, Charlotte Rae, Fred Gwynne, Jack Weston, Ruth White, Larry Blyden

12. "The Count of Monte Cristo" [adapted by Sumner Locke Elliott from the Alexander Dumas classic; directed by Sidney Lumet; produced by David Susskind]  (10-28-58 Tuesday 7:30-9:00 CBS)  Colleen Dewhurst, Michael Ebert, Hurd Hatfield, Torin Thatcher, Ina Balin, Elizabeth Sellars, John Colicos, Max Adrian, Douglas Campbell, George Voskovec

13. "The Winslow Boy" [adapted by Sumner Locke Elliott from the play by Terrence Rattigan]  (11-13-58 Thursday 9:30-11:00 CBS)  Rex Thompson, Noel Williams, Siobhan McKenna, Florence Eldridge, Denholm Elliott, Fredric March

14. "The Hasty Heart" [John Patrick's 1945 play]  (12-18-58 Thursday 9:30-11:00 CBS)  Don Murray, Fred Gwynne

15. "What Every Woman Knows" [adapted by Jacqueline Babbin and Audrey Gellen from the James M. Barrie comedy classic; directed by Robert Mulligan]  (1-28-59 Wednesday 9:30-11:00 CBS)  Siobhan McKenna, Martita Hunt, James Donald, Diana Van Der Vlis, Liam Redmond, Cyril Cusack, John Williams

16. "Hamlet" [Old Vic version of the Shakespeare play]  (2-24-59 Tuesday 7:30-9:00 CBS)  John Neville, Oscar Neville, Fredric March, John Humphrey

17. "The Human Comedy" [adapted by S. Lee Pogostin from the William Saroyan play]  (3-28-59 Saturday 9:30-11:00 CBS)

Jo Van Fleet, Russell Collins, Michael J. Pollard, David
Francis, Thomas Chalmers, R. G. Armstrong; Burgess
Meredith narrated.

18. "The Browning Version" [adapted by Jacqueline Babbin and
Audrey Gellen from the play by Terrence Rattigan] (4-23-
59 Thursday 8:00-9:30 CBS) Sir John Gielgud, Margaret
Leighton, Robert Stephens, Cecil Parker

19. "Billy Budd" [adapted by Jacqueline Babbin and Audrey Gellen
from the Herman Melville classic] (5-25-59 Thursday
9:30-11:00 CBS) Don Murray, Roddy McDowall, Alfred
Ryder, James Donald

## Third Season

20. "Body and Soul" [adapted by Eliot Asinoff from the 1947 film
scenario by Abraham L. Polonsky; Jack Demsey was
technical advisor] (9-28-59 Monday 8:30-10:00 CBS) Ben
Gazzara, Franchot Tone, Neville Brand, Ellen Madison,
Martin Balsam

21. "The Fallen Idol" [by Graham Greene] (10-14-59 Wednesday
8:30-10:00 CBS) Jack Hawkins, Jessica Tandy, Dina
Merrill, Jacques Hirshler, Myra Carter

22. "I, Don Quixote" [adapted by Dale Wasserman from the Cer-
vantes classic; the basis for the 1965 Broadway musical
"Man of La Mancha"] (11-9-59 Monday 9:30-11:00 CBS)
Lee J. Cobb, Eli Wallach, Peter Donat, Hurd Hatfield

23. "Oliver Twist" [adapted by Michael Dyne from the Charles
Dickens classic] (12-4-59 Friday 7:30-9:00 CBS) Frederick Clark, Robert Morley, Inga Swenson, Eric Portman, John
McGiver, Nancy Wickwire, Richard Harris, Michael Hordern

24. "Arrowsmith" [adapted by Phil Reisman Jr. from the novel
by Sinclair Lewis] (1-17-60 Sunday 9:30-11:00 CBS) Farley Granger, Diane Baker, Oscar Homolka, Francis
Lederer, Robert Emhardt

25. "Ethan Frome" [adapted by Jacqueline Babbin and Audrey
Gellen from the novel by Edith Wharton] (2-18-60 Thurs-
day 9:30-11:00 CBS) Julie Harris, Clarice Blackburn,
Sterling Hayden

26. "Treasure Island" [adapted by Michael Dyne from the Robert
Louis Stevenson classic] (3-5-60 Saturday 7:30-9:00 CBS)
Hugh Griffith, Richard O'Sullivan; narrated by Boris Kar-
loff

27. "Years Ago" [adapted by Jacqueline Babbin and Audrey Gellen
from the autobiographical play by Ruth Gordon; directed
by Alex Segal] (4-21-60 Thursday 8:00-9:30 CBS) Robert
Preston, Sandra Church, Peggy Conklin

## Fourth Season

28. "Men in White" [by Sidney Kingsley] (9-30-60 Friday 8:30-
10:00 CBS) Lee J. Cobb, Richard Basehart, Lois Smith,
Dina Merrill

29. "Heaven Can Wait" [adapted by Jacqueline Babbin and Audrey
     Gellen from the play by Harry Segall] (11-16-60 Wednes-
     day 9:30-11:00 CBS) Anthony Franciosa, Robert Morley,
     Joey Bishop, Elizabeth Ashley, Frank McHugh, Wally Cox,
     Diana Van Der Vlis
30. "The Prisoner of Zenda" [adapted by Sumner Locke Elliott
     from the novel by Anthony Hope] (1-18-61 Wednesday
     8:30-10:00 CBS) Christopher Plummer, Farley Granger,
     Inger Stevens, John Williams, Nancy Wickwire
31. "The Lincoln Murder Case" [adapted by Dale Wasserman from
     Theodore Roscoe's "The Web of Conspiracy"] (2-18-61
     Saturday 9:30-11:00 CBS) Luther Adler, Andrew Prine,
     House Jameson, Alexander Scourby, Roger Evan Boxill
32. "The Night of the Storm" [by Horton Foote] (3-21-61 Tuesday
     9:30-11:00 CBS) Julie Harris, Fritz Weaver, Marc Con-
     nelly, E. G. Marshall, Mildred Dunnock

# INDEX OF SERIES TITLES